your Bovée?

Balanced Presentation of Fundamentals

ISBN: 0-13-141965-X

Excellence in Business Communication Custom One-Color Option

The Core

W9-COY-527

$40.00!
for the core nine chapters
- Net price to bookstore

Optional Chapters

$5.00!
each additional chapter
- Net price to bookstore

Contact your local PH Rep for more information on the custom/core option.

Excellence in Business Communication

SIXTH EDITION

Excellence in Business Communication

SIXTH EDITION

JOHN V. THILL
Chief Executive Officer
Communications Specialists of America

COURTLAND L. BOVÉE
Professor of Business Communication
C. Allen Paul Distinguished Chair
Grossmont College

PEARSON
Prentice
Hall

Upper Saddle River, New Jersey 07458

Library of Congress Cataloging-in-Publication Data

Thill, John V.
   Excellence in business communication / John V. Thill, Courtland L. Bovée.—6th ed.
      p. cm.
   Supplemented by a companion website. Various other multimedia instructional
   materials are available to supplement the text.
   ISBN 0-13-141965-X
   1. Business communications—United States—Case studies. I. Thill, John V. II.
Title.

HF5718.2.U6T45 2005
658.4'5–dc22   2003070740

Senior Acquisition Editor: David Parker
Project Manager: Ashley Keim
Editorial Assistant: Melissa Yu
Media Project Manager: Jessica Sabloff
Executive Marketing Manager: Shannon Moore
Marketing Assistant: Patrick Danzuso
Senior Managing Editor (Production): Judy Leale
Production Editor: Cindy Durand
Production Assistant: Joseph DeProspero
Permissions Researcher: Justin Somma
Production Manager: Arnold Vila
Design Manager: Maria Lange
Art Director: Blair Brown
Interior Design: Blair Brown
Cover Design: Blair Brown
Cover Illustration / Photo: Ryan McVay/Getty Images—Photodisc; Jules Frazier/Getty Images—Photodisc; C Squared Studios/
Getty Images—Photodisc Green
Illustrator (Interior): ElectraGraphics
Photo Researcher: Melinda Alexander
Manager, Print Production: Christy Mahon
Formatter: Suzanne Duda
Composition / Full Service Project Management: Lynn Steines, Carlisle Communications
Printer / Binder: Quebecor

Credits and acknowledgments borrowed from other sources and reproduced, with permission, in this textbook appear on page AC-1.

Microsoft® and Windows® are registered trademarks of the Microsoft Corporation in the U.S.A. and other countries. Screen shots and icons
reprinted with permission from the Microsoft Corporation. This book is not sponsored or endorsed by or affiliated with the Microsoft Corporation.

Pearson Education Ltd.   Pearson Education Australia PTY, Limited
Pearson Education Singapore, Pte. Ltd.   Pearson Education North Asia Ltd.
Pearson Education, Canada, Ltd.   Pearson Educación de Mexico, S.A. de C.V.
Pearson Education–Japan   Pearson Education Malaysia, Pte. Ltd.

10 9 8 7 6 5 4
ISBN 0-13-141965-X

Contents in Brief

Contents

Preface

Learn How We Blend Text and Technology to Create a Total Teaching and Learning Solution

Excellence in Business Communication is a compelling model of today's most effective instructional techniques. Students can experience business communication firsthand through a variety of highly involving simulations, activities, and real-world examples that no other textbook matches.

This textbook offers an extraordinary number of devices to simplify teaching, promote active learning, stimulate critical thinking, and develop career skills. That's why it's the most effective teaching and learning tool you'll find for a business communication course. As you'll see on the pages that follow, this text makes classes livelier, more relevant, and more enjoyable.

NEW TECHNOLOGY IN THIS EDITION

Integrated Approach to Technology. Students are introduced to the pervasive role of communication technology in a special four-page photo essay in Chapter 1, "Powerful Tools for Communicating Effectively." Colorful photos and informative text illustrate e-mail, instant messaging, wireless networks,

Powerful Tools for Communicating Effectively

The tools of business communication evolve with every new generation of digital technology. Selecting the right tool for each situation can enhance your business communication in many ways. In today's flexible office settings, communication technology helps people keep in touch and stay productive. When co-workers in different cities need to collaborate, they can meet and share ideas without costly travel. Manufacturers use communication technology to keep track of parts, orders, and shipments—and to keep customers well-informed. Those same customers can also communicate with companies in many ways at any time of day or night.

Flexible Workstations
Many professionals have abandoned desktop PCs for laptops they can carry home, on travel, and to meetings. Back at their desks, a docking station transforms the laptop into a full-featured PC with network connection. Workers without permanent desks sometimes share PCs that automatically reconfigure themselves to access each user's e-mail and files.

Wireless Networks
Laptop PCs with wireless access cards let workers stay connected to the network from practically anywhere within the office—any desk, any conference room. This technology offers high-speed Internet access within range of a wireless access point.

Follow-me Phone Service
To be reachable without juggling multiple forwarding numbers, some people have follow-me phone service. Callers use one number to reach the person anywhere—at the office, a remote site, a home office. The system automatically forwards calls to a list of preprogrammed numbers and transfers unanswered calls to voice mail.

Redefining the Office
Technology makes it easier for people to stay connected with co-workers and retrieve needed information. Some maintain that connection without having a permanent office, a desktop PC, or even a big filing cabinet. For example, Sun Microsystems lets staff members choose to work either at the main office or at remote offices called "drop-in centers." Many Sun facilities have specially equipped "iWork" areas that can quickly reconfigure phone and computer connections to meet individual requirements.

Electronic Presentations
Combining a color projector with a laptop or personal digital assistant (PDA) running the right software lets people give informative business presentations that are enhanced with sound, animation, and even website hyperlinks. Having everything in electronic form also makes it easy to customize a presentation or to make last-minute changes.

Intranets
Businesses use Internet technologies to create an intranet, a private computer network that simplifies information sharing within the company. Intranets can handle company e-mail, instant messaging (IM), websites, and even Internet phone connections. To ensure the security of company communication and information, intranets are shielded from the public Internet.

Wall Displays
Teams commonly solve problems by brainstorming at a whiteboard. Wall displays take this concept one step further, letting participants transmit words and diagrams to distant colleagues via the corporate intranet. Users can even share the virtual pen to make changes and additions from more than one location.

Web-based Meetings
Workers can actively participate in web-based meetings by logging on from a desktop PC, laptop, or cell phone. Websites such as WebEx help users integrate voice, text, and video, and let them share applications such as Microsoft PowerPoint and Microsoft Word in a single browser window.

Internet Videophone
Person-to-person video calling has long been possible through popular instant messaging programs. Internet videophone services do even more, letting multiple users participate in a videoconference without the expense and complexity of a full-fledged videoconferencing system. Some services are flexible enough to include telecommuters who have broadband Internet connections.

Collaborating
Working in teams is essential in almost every business. Teamwork can become complicated, however, when team members work in different parts of the company, in different time zones, or even for different companies. Technology helps bridge the distance by making it possible to brainstorm, attend virtual meetings, and share files from widely separated locations. Communication technology also helps companies save money on costly business travel without losing most of the benefits of face-to-face collaboration.

Shared Workspace
Online workspaces such as eRoom and Groove make it easy for far-flung team members to access shared files anywhere, any time. Accessible through a browser, the workspace contains a collection of folders and has built-in intelligence to control which team members can read, edit, and save specific files.

COMMUNICATING IN THE OFFICE   **COMMUNICATING REMOTELY**

Videoconferencing and Telepresence
Less costly than travel, videoconferencing provides many of the same benefits as an in-person meeting. Advanced systems include telepresence and robot surrogates, which use computers to "place" participants in the room virtually, letting them see and hear everyone while being seen and heard themselves. Such realistic interaction makes meetings more productive.

web-based meetings, videoconferencing and telepresence, intranets, extranets, Internet videophones, flexible workstations, electronic wall displays, electronic presentations, corporate blogs, and online workspaces. This overview helps students quickly grasp how technology is helping businesspeople communicate effectively.

"Document Makeovers." In each chapter of the book, an assignment overview directs students to the OneKey website, where interactive exercises help them apply chapter concepts to an actual business document. "Document Makeovers" offer students an appealing opportunity to refine and reinforce their writing skills in a dynamic multimedia environment.

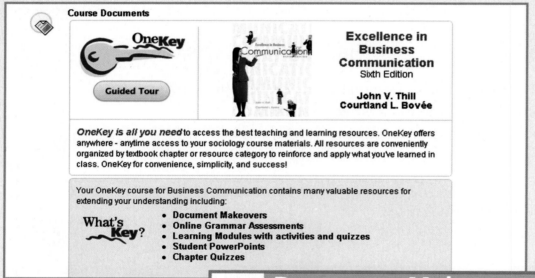

Course Documents

OneKey

Guided Tour

Excellence in Business Communication
Sixth Edition

John V. Thill
Courtland L. Bovée

OneKey is all you need to access the best teaching and learning resources. OneKey offers anywhere - anytime access to your sociology course materials. All resources are conveniently organized by textbook chapter or resource category to reinforce and apply what you've learned in class. OneKey for convenience, simplicity, and success!

Your OneKey course for Business Communication contains many valuable resources for extending your understanding including:

What's Key?

- Document Makeovers
- Online Grammar Assessments
- Learning Modules with activities and quizzes
- Student PowerPoints
- Chapter Quizzes

Document Makeover

IMPROVE THIS MEMO

To practice correcting drafts of actual documents, visit **www.prenhall.com/onekey** on the web. Click "Document Makeovers," then click Chapter 1. You will find a memo that contains problems and errors relating to what you've learned in this chapter about overcoming communication barriers in business messages. Use the Final Draft decision tool to create an improved version of this memo. Check the memo for an audience-centered approach, ethical communication, communicating efficiently, and facilitating feedback.

"Peak Performance Grammar and Mechanics." In each chapter, students are directed to the OneKey website to improve their skills with mechanics and specific parts of speech by using the "Peak Performance Grammar and Mechanics" module. Students can take the pretest to determine whether they have any weak areas; then they can review those areas in the module's refresher course. Students can also take a follow-up test. For an extra challenge or advanced practice, students can take the advanced test.

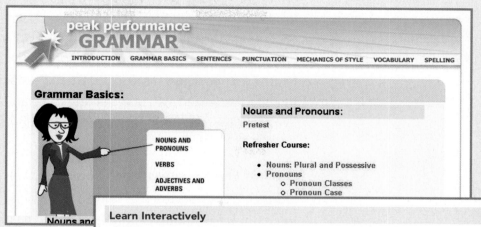

Learn Interactively

INTERACTIVE STUDY GUIDE

Visit the Companion Website at www.prenhall.com/thill. For Chapter 2, take advantage of the interactive "Study Guide" to test your chapter knowledge. Get instant feedback on whether you need additional studying. Read the "Current Events" articles to get the latest on chapter topics, and complete the exercises as specified by your instructor.

This site's "Study Hall" helps you succeed in this course. "Talk in the Hall" lets you leave messages and meet new friends online. If you have a question, you can "Ask the Tutor." And to get a better grade in this course, you can find more help at "Writing Skills," "Study Skills," and "Study Tips."

PEAK PERFORMANCE GRAMMAR AND MECHANICS

To improve your skill with pronouns, use the "Peak Performance Grammar and Mechanics" module on the web. Visit www.prenhall.com/thill, click "Peak Performance Grammar and Mechanics," then click "Nouns and Pronouns." Take the Pretest to determine whether you have any weak areas. Then review those areas in the Refresher Course. Take the Follow-Up Test to check your grasp of pronouns. For an extra challenge or advanced practice, take the Advanced Test. Finally, for additional reinforcement, go to the "Improve Your Grammar, Mechanics, and Usage" section that follows, and complete those exercises.

NEW CONTENT IN THIS EDITION

"Improve Your Grammar, Mechanics, and Usage" exercises. To give students additional practice in and reinforcement of English skills, each chapter includes one set of 10 exercises. These exercises help students identify specific areas of weakness so that they can overcome them by studying the "Handbook of Grammar, Mechanics, and Usage," which appears near the end of the book. Students are directed to the text's website for additional exercises that they can complete online using the "Handbook of Grammar, Mechanics, and Usage Practice Sessions."

Improve Your Grammar, Mechanics, and Usage

The following exercises help you improve your knowledge of and power over English grammar, mechanics, and usage. Turn to the "Handbook of Grammar, Mechanics, and Usage" at the end of this textbook and review all of Section 1.2 (Pronouns). Then look at the following 10 items. Underline the preferred choice within each set of parentheses. (Answers to these exercises appear on page AK-3.)

1. The sales staff is preparing guidelines for (*their, its*) clients.
2. Few of the sales representatives turn in (*their, its*) reports on time.
3. The board of directors has chosen (*their, its*) officers.
4. Gomez and Archer have told (*his, their*) clients about the new program.
5. Each manager plans to expand (*his, their, his or her*) sphere of control next year.
6. Has everyone supplied (*his, their, his or her*) Social Security number?
7. After giving every employee (*his, their, a*) raise, George told (*them, they, all*) about the increased work load.
8. Bob and Tim have opposite ideas about how to achieve company goals. (*Who, Whom*) do you think will win the debate?
9. City Securities has just announced (*who, whom*) it will hire as CEO.
10. Either of the new products would readily find (*their, its*) niche in the marketplace.

For additional exercises focusing on pronouns, go to www.prenhall.com/thill and select "Handbook of Grammar, Mechanics, and Usage Practice Sessions."

Increased Coverage of Listening and Teams. To help students strengthen their communication skills, material on listening and working in teams effectively has been expanded and updated to include the latest information. Improved coverage provides students with the foundation they'll need to gain a competitive edge in today's workplace.

Increased Coverage of Business Etiquette. To obtain employment and succeed on the job, students need to understand and practice workplace etiquette in areas such as personal appearance, face-to-face interactions (smiles, handshakes, introductions, and dinner meetings), and telephone interactions (receiving calls, making calls, and using voice mail). New material on business etiquette covers all these topics and more.

Business Communication Video Library. Entirely new, professionally produced videos cover topics such as ethics, technology, globalization, and intercultural communication. Each video features real-world examples and is designed to effect a deeper understanding of the concepts and issues covered in the text. Video cases and teaching guides, located at www.prenhall.com/thill, are introduced with a synopsis, and exercises ask students to react to the videos by responding to questions, making decisions, and taking the initiative to solve real business communication problems. Titles in the video library:

- *Technology and the Tools of Communication*, 2003, 5.13 minutes

- *Communicating Effectively in the Global Workplace*, 2003, 11.12 minutes

- *Ethical Communication*, 2003, 11.40 minutes

- *Impact of Culture on Business*, 2004, 18.26 minutes

- *Global Business and Ethics*, 2004, 12.07 minutes

- *Teamwork and the WNBA's Connecticut Sun*, 2005, 12.05 minutes

- *Second City: Communication, Innovation, & Creativity*, 2005, 11.13 minutes

Chapter-Framing "On-the-Job" Vignettes and Simulations. Each chapter opens with a vignette that describes communication in an actual company, and each chapter closes with a simulation that provides situational problems for students to solve. Both "On the Job" features vividly demonstrate the link between chapter contents and life on the job, while offering students an opportunity for real-world decision making.

Emphasis on Process and Product. To help students write business messages quickly, easily, and effectively, chapters are organized into a series of three easy-to-follow steps (planning, writing, and completing business messages). A "Three-Step Writing Process" graphic not only illustrates the general process but is also applied to specific examples throughout the book.

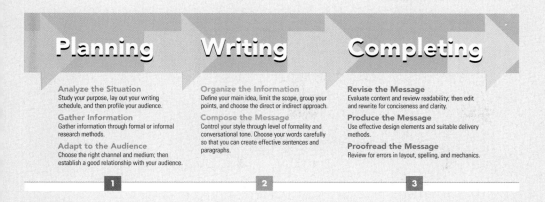

Planning — **Writing** — **Completing**

Analyze the Situation
Study your purpose, lay out your writing schedule, and then profile your audience.

Gather Information
Gather information through formal or informal research methods.

Adapt to the Audience
Choose the right channel and medium; then establish a good relationship with your audience.

Organize the Information
Define your main idea, limit the scope, group your points, and choose the direct or indirect approach.

Compose the Message
Control your style through level of formality and conversational tone. Choose your words carefully so that you can create effective sentences and paragraphs.

Revise the Message
Evaluate content and review readability; then edit and rewrite for conciseness and clarity.

Produce the Message
Use effective design elements and suitable delivery methods.

Proofread the Message
Review for errors in layout, spelling, and mechanics.

1   2   3

Checklists. Useful during the course and even years after completion, checklists help students organize their thinking when they begin a project, make decisions as they write, and check their own work. Operating as reminders rather than "recipes," these checklists provide useful guidelines without limiting creativity.

Special Feature Sidebars. Boxed and strategically placed within each chapter, special-feature sidebars extend the chapter material and center on four well-integrated themes: **Promoting Workplace Ethics**, **Achieving Intercultural Communication**, **Sharpening Your Career Skills**, and **Using the Power of Technology**. The boxes provide students with additional opportunities to analyze business communication principles and practices.

Sample Documents with Annotated Comments. Students can examine numerous sample documents, many collected by the authors in their consulting work at well-known companies. Some documents are accompanied by a three-step-writing-process graphic, and all documents include marginal annotations to help students understand how to apply the principles being discussed.

"Documents for Analysis." Students have the opportunity to critique and revise a wide selection of documents, including letters, memos, e-mail, graphic aids, and résumés. Hands-on experience in analyzing and improving sample documents helps students revise their own business messages, and extends the experience students gain working with the Document Makeover feature in OneKey.

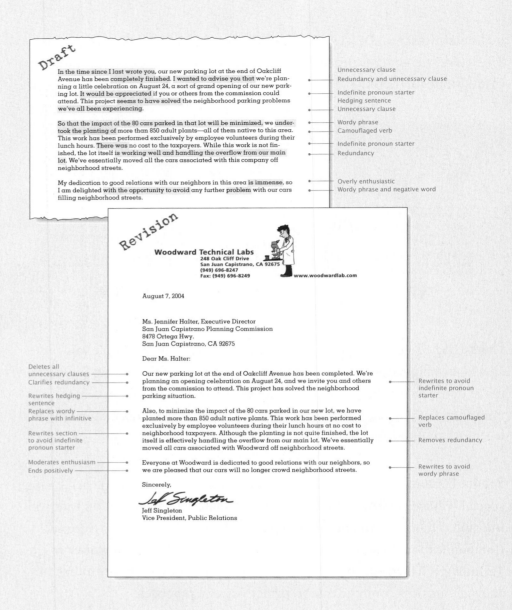

Exercises and Cases. Hundreds of exercises challenge students with practical assignments like those they will most often face at work. Each exercise is labeled by type (such as "Team," "Ethical Choices," "Self-Assessment," or "Internet") to make it easier for instructors to assign specific types of homework activities. Exercises appear in each chapter of the book. Real-world cases are based on actual organizations and appear in Chapters 7–9, 11–12, and 14–15. All exercises and cases have suggested answers in the instructor's manual.

INSTRUCTOR'S SUPPLEMENTS

- Instructor's Resource Manual

- Test Item File

- Electronic Test Generator

- Color Acetate Transparency Program

- PowerPoint Presentation—Basic and Enhanced Versions

- Video Series

- Instructor Resource Center on CD and online includes all supplements and is available for downloading

- Authors' E-Mail Hotline for Faculty (hotline@leadingtexts.com)

- Course Management: WebCt, Blackboard, and Course Compass—all available in OneKey

STUDENT'S SUPPLEMENTS

- **Study Guide**

- **Companion Website** for students includes a student version of the PowerPoint package, an online Study Guide, the English-Spanish Audio Glossary of Business Terms, the Handbook of Grammar, Mechanics, and Usage Practice Sessions, and the Business Communication Study Hall—which allows students to brush up on several aspects of business communication— grammar, writing skills, critical thinking, report, résumé, and PowerPoint development.

- **OneKey Learning Modules** Each chapter is divided in approximately four sections. Each section has a pretest of five questions, a summary for review, an online learning activity, and a post test of 10 questions. Also included in the OneKey website are a grammar assessment tool and document makeovers which allow students to practice their revision skills.

REVIEWERS

We especially want to thank the reviewers of this new, sixth edition. Their detailed and perceptive comments resulted in excellent refinements. These reviewers include Cynthia Drexel, Western State College; J. Thomas Dukes, University of Akron; Karen Eickhoff, University of Tennessee; Joyce Hicks, Valparaiso University; Mark Hilton, Lyndon State College; Sandie Idziak, University of Texas; Jennifer Loney, Portland State University; Melinda McCannon, Gordon College; Bronna McNeely, Midwestern State University; William McPherson, Indiana University of Pennsylvania; Russ Meade, Tidewater Community College; Joe Newman, Faulkner University; Barbara Oates, Texas A&M University; Salvatore Safina, University of Wisconsin; Andrea Smith-Hunter, Siena College; Carol Smith White, Georgia State University; Karen Sneary, Northwestern Oklahoma State University; Terisa Tennison, Florida International University; Robert von der Osten, Ferris State University; Karl V. Winton, Marshall University.

Thanks to the many individuals whose valuable suggestions and constructive comments contributed to the success of this book. The authors are deeply grateful to Anita S. Bednar, Central State University; Donna Cox, Monroe Community College; Sauny Dills, California Polytechnic State University–San Luis Obispo; Charlene A. Gierkey, Northwestern Michigan College; Sue Granger, Jacksonville State University; Bradley S. Hayden, Western Michigan University; Michael Hignite, Southwest Missouri State; Cynthia Hofacker, University of Wisconsin–Eau Claire; Louise C. Holcomb, Gainesville College; Larry Honl, University of Wisconsin–Eau Claire; Kenneth Hunsaker, Utah State University; Robert O. Joy, Central Michigan University; Paul Killorin, Portland Community College; Al Lucero, East Tennessee State University; Rachel Mather, Adelphi University; Betty Mealor, Abraham Baldwin College; Mary Miller, Ashland University; Richard Profozich, Prince George's Community College; Brian Railsback, Western Carolina University; John Rehfuss, California State University–Sacramento; Joan C. Roderick, Southwest Texas State University; Jean Anna Sellers, Fort Hays State University; Carla L. Sloan, Liberty University; Michael Thompson, Brigham Young University; Betsy Vardaman, Baylor University; Billy Walters, Troy State University; George Walters, Emporia State University; F. Stanford Wayne, Southwest Missouri State; Robert Wheatley, Troy State University; Rosemary B. Wilson, Washtenaw Community College; Beverly C. Wise, SUNY–Morrisville; Janet Adams, Minnesota State University–Mankato; Gus Amaya, Florida International University; Ruthann Dirks, Emporia State University; Mary DuBoise, DeVry Institute of Technology–Dallas; Lindsay S. English, Ursuline College; Mike Flores, Wichita State University; Paula R. Kaiser, University of North Carolina–Greensboro; Linda M. LaDuc, University of Massachusetts–Amherst; Linda McAdams, Westark Community College; Jeanne Stannard, Johnson County Community College; John L. Waltman, Eastern Michigan University; Aline Wolff, New York University; Bonnie Yarbrough, University of North Carolina–Greensboro.

REVIEWERS OF "DOCUMENT MAKEOVER" FEATURE

Lisa Barley, Eastern Michigan University; Marcia Bordman, Gallaudet University; Jean Bush-Bacelis, Eastern Michigan University; Bobbye Davis, Southern Louisiana University; Cynthia Drexel, Western State College; Kenneth Gibbs, Worcester State College; Ellen Leathers, Bradley University; Diana McKowen, Indiana University; Bobbie Nicholson, Mars Hill College; Andrew Smith, Holyoke Community College; Jay Stubblefield, North Carolina Wesleyan College; Dawn Wallace, South Eastern Louisiana University.

Personal Acknowledgments

Excellence in Business Communication, Sixth Edition, is the product of the concerted efforts of a number of people. A heartfelt thanks to our many friends, acquaintances, and business associates who provided materials or agreed to be interviewed so that we could bring the real world into the classroom.

Our thanks to Terry Anderson, whose outstanding communication skills, breadth of knowledge, and organizational ability assured this project's clarity and completeness.

We are grateful to Jackie Estrada for her remarkable talents and special skills; to George Dovel for his dedication and expertise; to Lianne Downey for her unique insights and valuable contributions; to Gail Olson for her astute attention to details and exceptional abilities; and to Joe Glidden for his research efforts.

We also appreciate the notable talents and distinguished contributions of Deborah Valentine, Emory University; Anne Bliss, University of Colorado–Boulder; Carolyn A. Embree, University of Akron; Carla L. Sloan, Liberty University; Doris A. Van Horn Christopher, California State University–Los Angeles; and Susan S. Rehwaldt, Southern Illinois University.

We also feel it is important to acknowledge and thank the Association for Business Communication, an organization whose meetings and publications provide a valuable forum for the exchange of ideas and for professional growth.

Thanks to the many individuals whose valuable suggestions and constructive comments contributed to the success of this book. The authors are deeply grateful to Anita S. Bednar, Central State University; Donna Cox, Monroe Community College; Sauny Dills, California Polytechnic State University–San Luis Obispo; Charlene A. Gierkey, Northwestern Michigan College; Sue Granger, Jacksonville State University; Bradley S. Hayden, Western Michigan University; Michael Hignite, Southwest Missouri State; Cynthia Hofacker, University of Wisconsin–Eau Claire; Louise C. Holcomb, Gainesville College; Larry Honl, University of Wisconsin–Eau Claire; Kenneth Hunsaker, Utah State University; Robert O. Joy, Central Michigan University; Paul Killorin, Portland Community College; Al Lucero, East Tennessee State University; Rachel Mather, Adelphi University; Betty Mealor, Abraham Baldwin College; Mary Miller, Ashland University; Richard Profozich, Prince George's Community College; Brian Railsback, Western Carolina University; John Rehfuss, California State University–Sacramento; Joan C. Roderick, Southwest Texas State University; Jean Anna Sellers, Fort Hays State University; Carla L. Sloan, Liberty University; Michael Thompson, Brigham Young University; Betsy Vardaman, Baylor University; Billy Walters, Troy State University; George Walters, Emporia State University; F. Stanford Wayne, Southwest Missouri State; Robert Wheatley, Troy State University;

Rosemary B. Wilson, Washtenaw Community College; and Beverly C. Wise, SUNY–Morrisville.

The supplements package for *Excellence in Business Communication* has benefited from the able contributions of several individuals. We would like to express our thanks to them for creating the finest set of instructional supplements in the field. The supplement authors include William Wardrope, Southwest Texas State University, who wrote the study guide; Myles Hassell of New Orleans, who created the PowerPoint package; and Jay Stubblefield, North Carolina Wesleyan College, who wrote the test bank.

We want to extend our warmest appreciation to the devoted professionals at Prentice Hall. They include Jerome Grant, president; Jeff Shelstad, vice-president and editorial director; David Parker, acquisition editor; Shannon Moore, executive marketing manager; Ashley Keim, assistant editor, Melissa Yu, editorial assistant; all of Prentice Hall Business Publishing, and the outstanding Prentice Hall sales representatives. Finally, we thank Judy Leale, senior managing editor of production, and Cindy Durand, production editor, for their dedication; and we are grateful to Lynn Steines, project manager at Carlisle Communications; Melinda Alexander, photo researcher; and Blair Brown, art director, for their superb work.

John V. Thill
Courtland L. Bovée

Part I
Understanding the Foundations of Business Communication

Chapter 1

Achieving Success Through Effective Business Communication

Learning Objectives

AFTER STUDYING THIS CHAPTER, YOU WILL BE ABLE TO

1 Explain what effective communication is and highlight five characteristics of effective business messages

2 Discuss three developments in the workplace that are intensifying the need to communicate effectively

3 Describe how organizations share information internally and externally

4 List eight ways the Internet facilitates business communication

5 Define the six phases of the communication process

6 Identify and briefly discuss five types of communication barriers

7 Discuss four guidelines for overcoming communication barriers

8 Explain the attributes of ethical communication, and differentiate between an ethical dilemma and an ethical lapse

On the Job:

COMMUNICATING AT GE INDUSTRIAL SYSTEMS

BRINGING GOOD THINGS TO LIFE WITH FREE-FLOWING INFORMATION

How do you keep a company competitive when it employs 40,000 employees in 96 major facilities worldwide? How do you make sure that everyone gets up-to-date information in time to make the right decisions? Lloyd G. Trotter can tell you. He is president and chief executive officer of GE Industrial Systems, one of the 11 major businesses in the General Electric Company. Headquartered in Plainville, Connecticut, Trotter's company produces electrical and electronic products that control, distribute, protect, and monitor electrical power for industry, commercial buildings, and homes. With so many employees all over the world, GE Industrial Systems must communicate successfully to compete and survive.

Trotter has built GE Industrial Systems into a heavyweight division, posting annual revenues of around $6 billion, and he plans to double the size of the business in the next three years. Effective communication is an important factor in his success. He makes sure that every employee can exchange information with every other inside the company, from entry-level receptionists and maintenance workers to top-level managers. He also ensures that GE employees can communicate effectively with numerous people outside the company, such as customers, suppliers, investors, and public communities, just to name a few. Trotter emphasizes audience focus and stresses policies such as "giving customers what they want, when they want it, and in the mix or varieties they need." He actively encourages managers, hourly employees, and customers to "rub elbows" and work together to solve problems.

GE Industrial Systems benefits from the open communication culture established at the corporate level—which focuses on sharing, and putting into action, the best ideas and practices from across the company and around the world. For example, at lit-

Since Thomas Edison founded the General Electric Company in 1882, GE Industrial Systems has been known for technical innovation. The company focuses on fulfilling customer needs, pursuing new markets, and maintaining its leadership position. To accomplish these goals, it promotes effective communication with its employees, its customers, its stakeholders, and the community.

erally thousands of "Work-Out" town meetings, the views and ideas of every employee, from every function, in every business, are solicited and turned into action—usually on the spot. Because people see the value that is attached to their input, their ideas flow in torrents.

Trotter keeps GE Industrial Systems competitive by keeping his people up to date on communication technology. This technology helps employees handle the vast amount of information available today without getting bogged down. Technology also helps employees communicate effectively with people who may be located within the same building or halfway around the world, who may or may not speak English, and who may have different cultural views of the best way to conduct business.

Trotter encourages his people to work in teams, using technology whenever possible. For example, GE Industrial Systems was the first of the GE businesses to use real-time collaboration tools to interact with customers and suppliers. These software tools make e-mail seem slow; they improve information sharing and tear down geographic and cultural barriers. They allow employees to create shared web workspaces, use instant messaging and real-time conferencing, manage documents electronically, and even use the web for training.

To help employees face today's challenges, Trotter also does what he can to increase diversity in the company and in business worldwide. For example, he started a group called the African-American Forum, where employees get together every three months to talk about their careers and who controls them. "You control your own career," says Trotter. "You say, 'My most valuable asset is myself,' and then you focus on caring for and feeding that asset."[1]

www.ge.com

3

COMMUNICATION, BUSINESS, AND YOU

As Lloyd Trotter suggests, your career success depends largely on you. One of the best ways to care for your most valuable asset is to improve your ability to communicate effectively. **Communication** is the process of sending and receiving messages. However, communication is *effective* only when the message is understood and when it stimulates action or encourages a receiver to think in new ways.

Effective communication helps you and your organization succeed.

When you communicate effectively, you increase productivity, both yours and your organization's (see Figure 1–1). Only through effective communication can you anticipate problems, make decisions, coordinate work flow, supervise others, develop relationships, and promote products and services. Effective communication helps you shape the impressions you and your company make on colleagues, employees, supervisors, investors, and customers, and it helps you perceive and respond to the needs of these **stakeholders** (the various groups you interact with).[2]

Conversely, ineffective communication can interfere with sound business solutions and can often make problems worse.[3] Without effective communication, people misunderstand each other and misinterpret information. Ideas misfire or fail to gain attention, and people and companies flounder.

Characteristics of Effective Business Messages

Business communication differs from communication in other settings.

Effective business messages have a number of common characteristics. As you study the communication examples in this book, see how they[4]

- **Provide practical information.** Business messages usually describe how to do something, explain why a procedure was changed, highlight the cause of a problem or a possible solution, discuss the status of a project, or explain why a new piece of equipment should be purchased.

- **Give facts rather than impressions.** Effective business messages use concrete language and specific details. Their information is clear, convincing, accurate, and ethical because they present hard evidence (not just opinion) and present all sides of an argument before committing to a conclusion.

FIGURE 1–1
The Benefits of Effective Communication

- **Clarify and condense information.** Business messages frequently use tables, charts, photos, or diagrams to clarify or condense information, to explain a process, or to emphasize important information.

- **State precise responsibilities.** Effective business messages are directed to a specific audience. They clearly state what is expected of, or what can be done for, that particular audience.

- **Persuade others and offer recommendations.** Business messages frequently persuade employers, customers, or clients to adopt a plan of action or to purchase a product or service. Persuasive messages are effective when they show just how an idea, a product, or a service will benefit readers specifically.

Keep these five characteristics in mind as you review Figure 1–2. Although the draft for this message *appears* to be well constructed, the revised version is more effective, as explained in the document's margins. In this course you will learn how to create the effective messages that are crucial for meeting the communication challenges facing businesses today.

Communication Challenges in Today's Workplace

Good communication skills have always been important in business. They are even more important in today's changing environment, which brings communication challenges such as advances in technology, globalization and workforce diversity, and increased emphasis on team-based organizations.

Advances in Technology   The Internet, e-mail, voice mail, faxes, pagers, and other wireless devices have revolutionized the way people communicate. Such technological advances not only bring new and better tools to the workplace but also increase the speed, frequency, and reach of communication. People from opposite ends of the world can work together seamlessly, 24 hours a day. Moreover, advances in technology make it possible for more and more people to work away from the office—in cars, airports, hotels, and at home.

> The use of technology showcases your communication skills and intensifies the need to communicate effectively.

This increased use of new technology requires employees to communicate more effectively and efficiently. (See the photo essay on "Powerful Tools for Communicating Efficiently" on page 8.) Technology showcases your communication skills—your writing skills are revealed in every e-mail message, and your verbal skills are revealed in audio and video teleconferences.[5] Furthermore, *intranets* (private corporate networks based on Internet technology), and *extranets* (the extension of private networks to certain outsiders such as suppliers) facilitate communication among employees, managers, customers, suppliers, and investors. More businesses are installing such networks and are increasingly engaging in **electronic commerce (e-commerce)**, the buying and selling of goods and services over the Internet.

At Staples, managers must communicate clearly with the employees they supervise, regardless of differences in age, gender, culture, or ethnic background.

Globalization and Workforce Diversity   Businesses today are crossing national boundaries to compete on a global scale. Over 2 million North Americans now work for multinational employers, and the number of foreign companies that have built plants in the United States is increasing.[6] In addition to this expanding

> The increases in international business dealings and in the diversity of the workforce create communication challenges.

FIGURE 1–2
Effective Communication by Memo

Draft

FROM: Tom Ristoff   **SUBJECT:** Company website

I have found three website designers who can help us improve our company website. As you know, there are many problems with our website. We have received numerous complaints from customers concerning the length of time it takes for our website to load. Customers also complain about overuse of banner advertising, it fails to provide adequate company and product information, difficulty in navigating the site, registration forms take too long to fill out, and out-of-date articles posted on the website.

On Tuesday, July 14, I met with Josh Allen, the owner of WebDezine, a marketing firm that specializes in developing, designing, updating, and managing websites. Josh showed me several samples of his company's work. His current client list and letters of reference are impressive. Josh has several recommendations for improving our website.

On Wednesday, July 15, I met with Steven Sanchez, manager of Your Web Design, and Betsy Delany, owner of Delany Websites. Both companies perform the same type of work as WebDezine. Both have an impressive list of clients and good credentials. However, I did not think Delany's Web ideas were as innovative as the other two companies.

I have invited all three companies to make a presentation to management at a special meeting scheduled on Wednesday, July 22 at 9:00 a.m. Each company will make a short presentation showing us specific samples of their work, outline suggestions for our company website, and discuss their fees and timeline. At that meeting, they will also address any questions and concerns you may have.

I strongly suggest you attend this meeting so that we can select the best candidate and get the revision project underway. Minimally, it will take a designer at least three months to complete this project. The longer we delay in the selection process, the longer it will take us to develop a website that matches our competitors'.

Please let me know if you will be able to attend.

Annotations (right):
- Fails to capture reader's interest with a specific subject
- Wastes reader's time with impractical information that managers already know about
- Complicates sentence structure by ignoring parallelism, thus making a simple list difficult to read
- Takes too long to get to the point by including irrelevant information
- Gives impressions rather than fact, making the message less effective
- Does not clarify whether the meeting is scheduled for 9:00 A.M. or whether the presentation begins at 9:00 A.M.
- Buries the main idea at the end of the message (Why not state this in the beginning?)
- Fails to state when managers should respond or how

Revision

BRAXTON & TEAGUE CONSULTING

MEMO

TO: All Department Managers   **DATE:** July 17, 2004

FROM: Tom Ristoff   **SUBJECT:** Meeting with prospective website developers

I have identified three prospective website developers to help us improve our company website. Each candidate will deliver a short presentation at a special meeting on Wednesday, July 22. The meeting will begin at 9:00 a.m., and the presentations will begin immediately.

I encourage you to attend so that we can expedite our revision project. The project will take *at least three months* to complete. This estimate does not include the time it will take to negotiate a contract with the developer.

All three candidates specialize in designing, developing, and managing websites. The candidates include the following:

• Josh Allen, owner of WebDezine (Del Mar, CA), specializes in developing, designing, updating, and managing websites. He's been designing web pages for eight years. His current client list, letters of reference, and sample sites are impressive, and he has several exciting recommendations for improving our website.

• Steven Sanchez, manager of Your Web Design (Orange, CA), specializes in developing and updating website designs. His company has been designing websites for five years and has an impressive list of clients. However, his company does not manage websites on a continuing basis.

• Betsy Delany, owner of Delany Websites (Laguna Beach, CA), develops, designs, updates, and manages websites. Her credentials are excellent, but her list of clients is short since she's been in business for less than a year.

I have reviewed samples from all three candidates, and you'll have an opportunity to see them and learn more about each company at the meeting. In addition, each candidate will present recommendations for improving our website, a projected timeline, and estimated costs.

Please check your calendar and let me know by e-mail before Monday, July 20, whether you'll be able to attend this meeting. If you can't attend and have specific questions or concerns that you would like addressed, please send them along in your response.

Annotations (left):
- Provides important information up front without wasting time on preliminaries
- Uses concise language, ample white space, and bullets to make this document easier to skim
- Withholds early impressions and sticks to the facts

Annotations (right):
- Lets readers know the purpose of the memo by using a descriptive subject line
- Persuades managers to attend, using italics to emphasize urgency
- Uses body of memo to provide managers with practical information about each candidate
- Clearly states what is expected of the audience

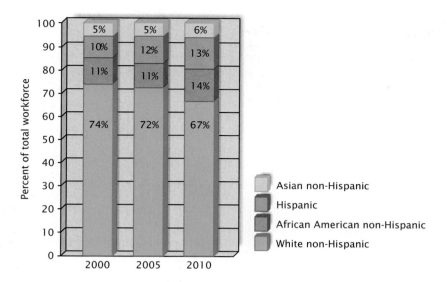

FIGURE 1–3
Ethnic Composition of the
U.S. Workforce

globalization, a growing percentage of the U.S. workforce is made up of people with diverse cultural and ethnic backgrounds, a trend that will continue in the years ahead. In the United States, for example, ethnic minorities are entering the workforce in record numbers (see Figure 1–3).

Increased globalization and workforce diversity mean that employees must understand the laws, customs, and business practices of many countries and be able to communicate with people who speak other languages. Look at 3Com's sprawling modem factory in Chicago. The plant employs 1,200 people, the vast majority of whom are immigrants. Urban Asians with multiple college degrees work alongside people who have recently arrived from Central American villages. Serbs work with Bosnian Muslims and with Iraqis, Peruvians, and South Africans. The employees speak more than 20 different languages, including Tagalog, Gujarati, and Chinese. English of varying degrees ties them together.[7]

Today's employees must communicate with people who speak English as a second language.

Chapter 3 discusses intercultural communication in detail, and special boxes throughout this text explore cultural issues that you will likely encounter in the global workplace.

Team-Based Organizations The command-and-control style of traditional management structures is ineffective in today's fast-paced, e-commerce environment.[8] Successful companies like GE Industrial Systems no longer limit decisions to a few managers at the top of a formal hierarchy. Instead, organizations use teams and collaborative work groups to make the fast decisions required to succeed in a global and competitive marketplace. Although working in teams has many advantages, it also offers many challenges, since team members often come from different departments, perform different functions, and come from diverse cultural backgrounds. Chapter 2 discusses teams in detail. One requirement for succeeding in teams is a basic understanding of how communication works in organizational settings.

Earth and Environmental Services in San Francisco encourages its employees to work collaboratively so that they can benefit from the knowledge of other team members.

When working in teams, you should be able to clarify, confirm, give feedback, explore ideas, and credit others.

Powerful Tools for Communicating Effectively

The tools of business communication evolve with every new generation of digital technology. Selecting the right tool for each situation can enhance your business communication in many ways. In today's flexible office settings, communication technology helps people keep in touch and stay productive. When co-workers in different cities need to collaborate, they can meet and share ideas without costly travel. Manufacturers use communication technology to keep track of parts, orders, and shipments—and to keep customers well-informed. Those same customers can also communicate with companies in many ways at any time of day or night.

Flexible Workstations

Many professionals have abandoned desktop PCs for laptops they can carry home, on travel, and to meetings. Back at their desks, a docking station transforms the laptop into a full-featured PC with network connection. Workers without permanent desks sometimes share PCs that automatically reconfigure themselves to access each user's e-mail and files.

Wireless Networks

Laptop PCs with wireless access cards let workers stay connected to the network from practically anywhere within the office—any desk, any conference room. This technology offers high-speed Internet access within range of a wireless access point.

Redefining the Office

Technology makes it easier for people to stay connected with co-workers and retrieve needed information. Some maintain that connection without having a permanent office, a desktop PC, or even a big filing cabinet. For example, Sun Microsystems lets staff members choose to work either at the main office or at remote offices called "drop-in centers." Many Sun facilities have specially equipped "iWork" areas that can quickly reconfigure phone and computer connections to meet individual requirements.

Electronic Presentations

Combining a color projector with a laptop or personal digital assistant (PDA) running the right software lets people give informative business presentations that are enhanced with sound, animation, and even website hyperlinks. Having everything in electronic form also makes it easy to customize a presentation or to make last-minute changes.

Follow-me Phone Service

To be reachable without juggling multiple forwarding numbers, some people have follow-me phone service. Callers use one number to reach the person anywhere—at the office, a remote site, a home office. The system automatically forwards calls to a list of preprogrammed numbers and transfers unanswered calls to voice mail.

Intranets

Businesses use Internet technologies to create an intranet, a private computer network that simplifies information sharing within the company. Intranets can handle company e-mail, instant messaging (IM), websites, and even Internet phone connections. To ensure the security of company communication and information, intranets are shielded from the public Internet.

COMMUNICATING IN THE OFFICE

Wall Displays

Teams commonly solve problems by brainstorming at a whiteboard. Wall displays take this concept one step further, letting participants transmit words and diagrams to distant colleagues via the corporate intranet. Users can even share the virtual pen to make changes and additions from more than one location.

Web-based Meetings

Workers can actively participate in web-based meetings by logging on from a desktop PC, laptop, or cell phone. Websites such as WebEx help users integrate voice, text, and video, and let them share applications such as Microsoft PowerPoint and Microsoft Word in a single browser window.

Collaborating

Working in teams is essential in almost every business. Teamwork can become complicated, however, when team members work in different parts of the company, in different time zones, or even for different companies. Technology helps bridge the distance by making it possible to brainstorm, attend virtual meetings, and share files from widely separated locations. Communication technology also helps companies save money on costly business travel without losing most of the benefits of face-to-face collaboration.

Internet Videophone

Person-to-person video calling has long been possible through popular instant messaging programs. Internet videophone services do even more, letting multiple users participate in a videoconference without the expense and complexity of a full-fledged videoconferencing system. Some services are flexible enough to include telecommuters who have broadband Internet connections.

Shared Workspace

Online workspaces such as eRoom and Groove make it easy for far-flung team members to access shared files anywhere, any time. Accessible through a browser, the workspace contains a collection of folders and has built-in intelligence to control which team members can read, edit, and save specific files.

COMMUNICATING REMOTELY

Videoconferencing and Telepresence

Less costly than travel, videoconferencing provides many of the same benefits as an in-person meeting. Advanced systems include telepresence and robot surrogates, which use computers to "place" participants in the room virtually, letting them see and hear everyone while being seen and heard themselves. Such realistic interaction makes meetings more productive.

Warehouse RFID

In an effort to reduce the costs and delays associated with manual inventory reports, Wal-Mart asked its top suppliers to put radio-frequency identification (RFID) tags on all their shipping cases and pallets by 2005. These tags automatically provide information that was previously collected by hand via barcode scanners.

Extranet

Extranets are secure, private computer networks that use Internet technology to share business information with suppliers, vendors, partners, and customers. Think of an extranet as an extension of the company intranet that is available to people outside the organization by invitation only.

Wireless Warehouse

Communication technology is a key source of competitive advantage for shipping companies such as FedEx and UPS. Hand-worn scanners use wireless links to help warehouse personnel access instant information that lets them process more packages in less time at transit hubs. Currently, 300 package loaders at four UPS hub facilities are testing the new wireless application called UPScan. A pager-size cordless scanner worn on the loader's hand captures data from a package bar code and transmits the data via Bluetooth® wireless technology to a Symbol Technologies wireless terminal worn on the loader's waist.

Sharing the Latest Information

Companies use a variety of communication technologies to create products and services and deliver them to customers. The ability to easily access and share the latest information improves the flow and timing of supplies, lowers operating costs, and boosts financial performance. Easy information access also helps companies respond to customer needs by providing them timely, accurate information and service and by delivering the right products to them at the right time.

Package Tracking

Senders and receivers often want frequent updates when packages are in transit. Handheld devices such as the FedEx PowerPad enhance customer service by letting delivery personnel instantly upload package data to the FedEx network. The wireless PowerPad also aids drivers by automatically receiving weather advisories.

COMMUNICATING ABOUT PRODUCTS AND SERVICES

Supply Chain Management

Advanced software applications let suppliers, manufacturers, and retailers share information—even when they have incompatible computer systems. Improved information flow increases report accuracy and helps each company in the supply chain manage stock levels.

Over-the-shoulder Support

For online shoppers who need instant help, many retail websites make it easy to connect with a live sales rep via phone or instant messaging. The rep can provide quick answers to questions and, with permission, can even control a shopper's browser to help locate particular items.

Help Lines

Some people prefer the personal touch of contact by phone. Moreover, some companies assign preferred customers special ID numbers that let them jump to the front of the calling queue. Many companies are addressing the needs of foreign-language speakers by connecting them with external service providers who offer multilingual support.

Corporate Blogs

Web-based journals let companies offer advice, answer questions, and promote the benefits of their products and services. Elements of a successful blog include frequent updates and the participation of knowledgeable contributors. Adding a subtle mix of useful commentary and marketing messages helps get customers to read or listen to them.

Interacting

Maintaining an open dialog with customers is a great way to gain a better understanding of their likes and dislikes. Today's communication technologies make it easier for customers to interact with a company whenever, wherever, and however they wish. A well-coordinated approach to phone, web, and in-store communication helps a company build stronger relationships with its existing customers, which increases the chances of doing more business with each one.

Retail RFID

Customers can't buy what they can't find, and manual reporting is often too slow for fast-paced retailing. To keep enough goods on the shelves, some retailers use RFID tags to monitor products on display. Clerks use wireless readers to scan tagged products and report stock data to a computerized inventory system that responds with an up-to-the-minute restocking order.

COMMUNICATING WITH CUSTOMERS

In-store Kiosks

Staples is among the retailers that let shoppers buy from the web while they're still in the store. Web-connected kiosks were originally used to let shoppers custom-configure their PCs, but the kiosks also give customers access to roughly 8,000 in-store items as well as to the 50,000 products available online.

COMMUNICATION IN ORGANIZATIONAL SETTINGS

To succeed, organizations must share information with people both inside and outside the company.

When you join a company, you become a link in its information chain. Whether you're a top manager or an entry-level employee, you have information that others need, and others have information that is crucial to you. Whether your organization is large, small, or virtual, sharing information among its parts and with the outside world is the glue that binds it together.

Communicating Internally

You are a contact point in both the external and internal communication networks.

Internal communication refers to the exchange of information and ideas within an organization. As an employee, you are in a position to observe things that your supervisors and co-workers cannot see: a customer's first reaction to a product display, a supplier's brief hesitation before agreeing to a delivery date, an odd whirring noise in a piece of equipment, or a slowdown in the flow of customers. Managers and co-workers need these little gems of information in order to do their jobs. If you don't pass it along, nobody will—because nobody else knows.

Much of this information can be exchanged internally by phone, fax, interoffice memo, company intranet, or e-mail—as it is for example, at Carnival Corporation, the world's largest multiple-night cruise company. Lauren Eastman, assistant director of sales, used e-mail to request capacity information from the company's operations manager, Brad Lymans (see Figure 1–4).

Internal communication helps employees do their jobs, develop a clear sense of the organization's mission, and identify and react quickly to potential problems. To maintain a healthy flow of information within the organization, effective communicators use both formal and informal channels.

FIGURE 1–4
Effective Internal Communication by E-Mail

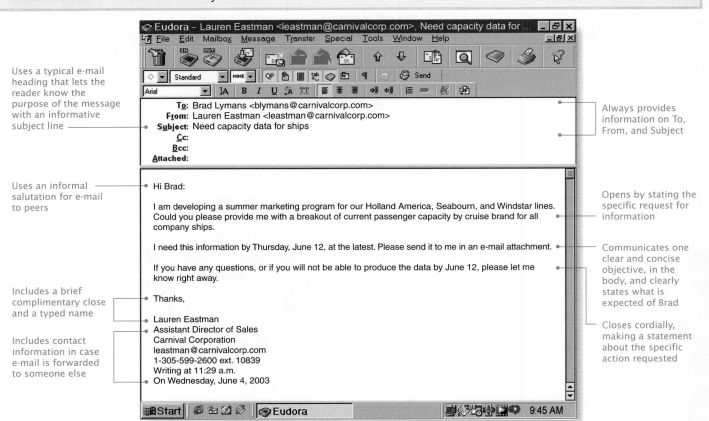

Uses a typical e-mail heading that lets the reader know the purpose of the message with an informative subject line

Always provides information on To, From, and Subject

Uses an informal salutation for e-mail to peers

Opens by stating the specific request for information

Communicates one clear and concise objective, in the body, and clearly states what is expected of Brad

Includes a brief complimentary close and a typed name

Closes cordially, making a statement about the specific action requested

Includes contact information in case e-mail is forwarded to someone else

Formal Communication Network   The **formal communication network** is typically shown as an organization chart like the one in Figure 1–5. Such charts summarize the lines of authority; each box represents a link in the chain of command, and each line represents a formal channel for the transmission of official messages. Information may travel down, up, and across an organization's formal hierarchy.

The formal flow of information follows the official chain of command.

- **Downward flow.** Organizational decisions are usually made at the top and then flow down to the people who will carry them out. Most of what filters downward is geared toward helping employees do their jobs. From top to bottom, each person must understand each message, apply it, and pass it along.

Information flows down, up, and across the formal hierarchy.

- **Upward flow.** To solve problems and make intelligent decisions, managers must learn what's going on in the organization. Because they can't be everywhere at once, executives depend on lower-level employees to furnish them with accurate, timely reports on problems, emerging trends, opportunities for improvement, grievances, and performance.

- **Horizontal flow.** Communication also flows from one department to another, either laterally or diagonally. This horizontal communication helps employees share information and coordinate tasks, and it is especially useful for solving complex and difficult problems.[9]

Formal organization charts illustrate how information is *supposed* to flow. However, such charts may not be accurate models for every business. Moreover, in actual practice, lines and boxes on a piece of paper cannot prevent people from talking with one another.

Informal Communication Network   Every organization has an **informal communication network**—a *grapevine*—that supplements official channels. As people go about their work, they have casual conversations with their friends in the office. They joke and share and discuss many things: their apartments, their families, restaurants, movies, sports, and other people in the company. Although many of these conversations deal with personal matters, about 80 percent of the information that travels along the grapevine pertains to business, and 75 to 95 percent of it is accurate.[10]

The informal communication network carries information along the organization's unofficial lines of activity and power.

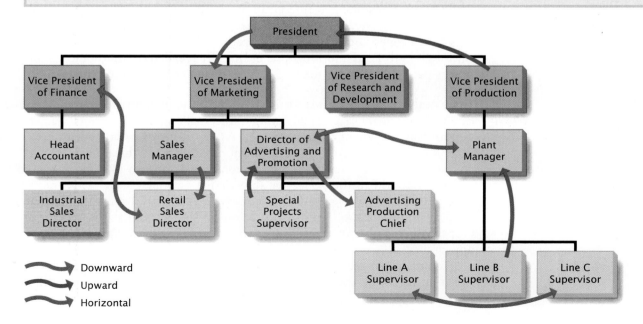

FIGURE 1–5
Formal Communication Network

The grapevine is an important source of information in most organizations.

Some executives are wary of the informal communication network, possibly because it threatens their power to control the flow of information. However, savvy managers tap into the grapevine, using it to spread and receive informal messages.[11] Since it is virtually impossible to eliminate the grapevine, sophisticated companies minimize its importance by making certain that the official word gets out.

Communicating Externally

The external communication network links the organization with the outside world of customers, suppliers, competitors, and investors.

Just as internal communication carries information up, down, and across the organization, **external communication** carries it into and out of the organization. Companies constantly exchange messages with customers, vendors, distributors, competitors, investors, journalists, and community representatives. Sometimes this external communication is carefully orchestrated—especially during a crisis. At other times it occurs informally as part of routine business operations.

Companies use external communication to create a favorable impression.

Formal External Communication   Whether by letter, website, phone, fax, Internet, or videotape, good communication is the first step in making a favorable impression on outsiders. As Lloyd Trotter can attest, carefully constructed letters, reports, memos, oral presentations, and websites convey an important message about the quality of your organization (see Figure 1–6). Messages such as statements to the press, letters to investors, advertisements, price increase announcements, and litigation updates require special care because of their delicate nature. Therefore, such documents are often drafted by a marketing or public relations team—a group of individuals whose sole job is to create and manage the flow of formal messages to outsiders.

The way a company handles a crisis can have a profound effect on the organization's subsequent performance.

The public relations team is also responsible for helping management plan for and respond to crises—a broad range of possibilities that can include environmental accidents, sabotage situations, strikes, massive product failure, major litigation, or even an abrupt change in management. To minimize the impact of any crisis, expert communicators advise managers to communicate honestly, openly, and often (see Table 1–1 on page 16).[12] If handled improperly, a crisis can destroy a company's reputation, drain its financial strength, erode employee morale, and result in negative publicity.

Ford and Bridgestone/Firestone were criticized for not taking appropriate action when reports started surfacing about the faulty tires manufactured by Bridgestone/Firestone and fitted on Ford Explorer sport utility vehicles. When the vehicles were driven at high speed, the treads separated from the tires, causing the cars to roll over and leading to the serious injury—even death—of passengers. Although both Ford and Firestone eventually recalled 6.5 million tires, both companies paid the price for making serious mistakes in handling the crisis.[13]

Every employee informally accumulates facts and impressions that contribute to the organization's collective understanding of the outside world.

Informal External Communication   Although companies usually communicate with outsiders in a formal manner, informal contacts with outsiders are important for learning about customer needs. As a member of an organization, you are an important informal conduit for communicating with the outside world. In the course of your daily activities, you unconsciously absorb bits and pieces of information that add to the collective knowledge of your company. Moreover, every time you speak for or about your company, you send a message. Outsiders may form an impression of your organization on the basis of the subtle, unconscious clues you transmit through your tone of voice, facial expression, and general appearance.

Top managers rely heavily on informal contacts with outsiders to gather information that might be useful to their companies. Much of their networking involves

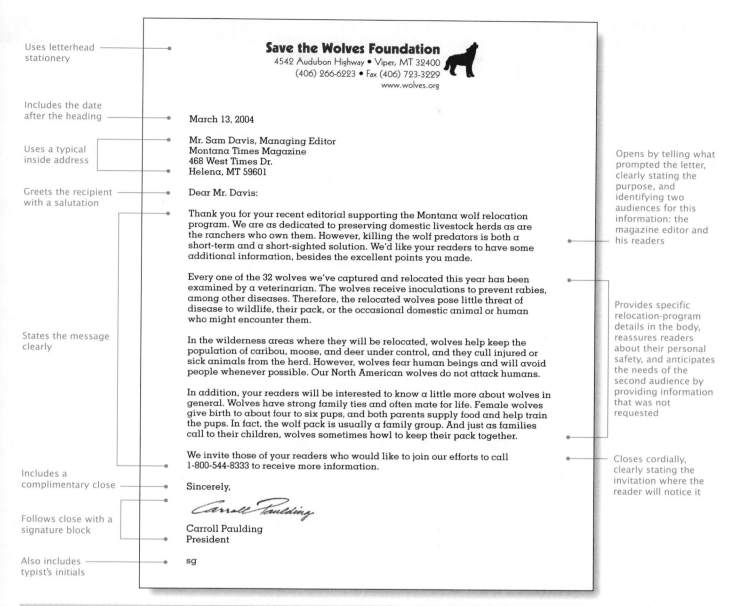

Uses letterhead stationery

Includes the date after the heading

Uses a typical inside address

Greets the recipient with a salutation

States the message clearly

Includes a complimentary close

Follows close with a signature block

Also includes typist's initials

Opens by telling what prompted the letter, clearly stating the purpose, and identifying two audiences for this information: the magazine editor and his readers

Provides specific relocation-program details in the body, reassures readers about their personal safety, and anticipates the needs of the second audience by providing information that was not requested

Closes cordially, clearly stating the invitation where the reader will notice it

Save the Wolves Foundation
4542 Audubon Highway • Viper, MT 32400
(406) 266-6223 • Fax (406) 723-3229
www.wolves.org

March 13, 2004

Mr. Sam Davis, Managing Editor
Montana Times Magazine
468 West Times Dr.
Helena, MT 59601

Dear Mr. Davis:

Thank you for your recent editorial supporting the Montana wolf relocation program. We are as dedicated to preserving domestic livestock herds as are the ranchers who own them. However, killing the wolf predators is both a short-term and a short-sighted solution. We'd like your readers to have some additional information, besides the excellent points you made.

Every one of the 32 wolves we've captured and relocated this year has been examined by a veterinarian. The wolves receive inoculations to prevent rabies, among other diseases. Therefore, the relocated wolves pose little threat of disease to wildlife, their pack, or the occasional domestic animal or human who might encounter them.

In the wilderness areas where they will be relocated, wolves help keep the population of caribou, moose, and deer under control, and they cull injured or sick animals from the herd. However, wolves fear human beings and will avoid people whenever possible. Our North American wolves do not attack humans.

In addition, your readers will be interested to know a little more about wolves in general. Wolves have strong family ties and often mate for life. Female wolves give birth to about four to six pups, and both parents supply food and help train the pups. In fact, the wolf pack is usually a family group. And just as families call to their children, wolves sometimes howl to keep their pack together.

We invite those of your readers who would like to join our efforts to call 1-800-544-8333 to receive more information.

Sincerely,

Carroll Paulding

Carroll Paulding
President

sg

FIGURE 1–6
Effective External Communication by Letter

interaction with fellow executives. However, plenty of high-level managers recognize the value of keeping in touch with "the real world" by creating opportunities to talk with and get feedback from customers and frontline employees. This sort of feedback is one important reason the Internet is becoming so popular with companies around the world.

Communicating Through the Internet

The challenges of communicating effectively with people inside and outside the organization are magnified as more businesses communicate through the Internet. When entering the business world, you'll be expected to know how to use the Internet for effective workplace communication.

Table 1–1   WHAT TO DO IN A CRISIS

When a Crisis Hits:

Do	Don't
Do prepare for trouble ahead of time by identifying potential problems, appointing and training a response team, and preparing and testing a crisis management plan.	Don't blame anyone for anything.
	Don't speculate in public.
	Don't refuse to answer questions.
Do get top management involved as soon as the crisis hits.	Don't release information that will violate anyone's right to privacy.
Do set up a news center for company representatives and the media, equipped with phones, computers, and other electronic tools for preparing news releases.	Don't use the crisis to pitch products or services.
	Don't play favorites with media representatives.
• Issue at least two news updates a day, and have trained personnel to respond to questions around the clock.	
• Provide complete information packets to the media as soon as possible.	
• Prevent conflicting statements and provide continuity by appointing a single person, trained in advance, to speak for the company.	
• Tell receptionists to direct all calls to the news center.	
Do tell the whole story—openly, completely, and honestly. If you are at fault, apologize.	
Do demonstrate the company's concern by your statements and your actions.	

How Businesses Use the Internet

The Internet is greatly influencing business interactions, both inside and outside organizations.

Businesses are using the Internet to make closer connections with organizations and customers all over the planet. The Internet is changing the way customers, suppliers, companies, and other stakeholders interact. It's also changing the way companies operate internally, by allowing speedy, convenient exchanges of ideas and information—anytime, anywhere, across thousands of miles or across the street. Companies use the Internet to

- Share text, photos, slides, videos, and other data within the organization
- Permit employees to **telecommute**, or work away from a conventional office, whether at home, on the road, or across the country[14]
- Recruit employees cost-effectively
- Locate information from external sources
- Find new business partners and attract new customers
- Locate and buy parts and materials from domestic and international suppliers
- Promote and sell goods and services to customers in any location

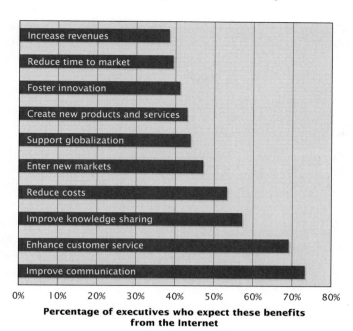

FIGURE 1–7
Expected Internet Benefits

Percentage of executives who expect these benefits
from the Internet

- Provide customers with service, technical support, and product information
- Collaborate with local, national, and international business partners
- Inform investors, industry analysts, and government regulators about business developments

Executives expect a number of benefits from the Internet, the most important of which is to improve communication (see Figure 1–7). So exactly how does the Internet help?

How the Internet Facilitates Communication

The Internet offers businesses a wide variety of choices for online communication, all of which provide convenience, speed, and the ability to communicate across time zones:

The Internet increases the convenience, speed, and reach of business communication.

- **E-mail.** Electronic mail (e-mail) enables users to create, send, and read written messages entirely on computer, as Chapter 4 points out. An e-mail document may be a simple text message, or it might include complex files or programs.

- **Discussion mailing lists.** Also known as *listservs*, **discussion mailing lists** are discussion groups to which you subscribe by sending a message to the list's e-mail address. From then on, copies of all messages posted by any other subscriber are delivered to you via e-mail.

- **Newsgroups.** Consisting of posted messages and responses on a particular subject, a **Usenet newsgroup** posts messages on its website, which you must visit and access by using a news reader program. Messages posted to a newsgroup can be viewed by anyone.

- **Instant messaging and chat.** Many companies encourage the use of instant messaging and chat for work purposes, as Chapter 4 explains. Within a few years, more than 200 million employees will be using instant messaging for job-related communication.[15]

- **Videoconferencing.** As Chapter 2 points out, more businesses are using online videoconferencing to replace face-to-face meetings with colleagues, customers, and suppliers.

- **Telnet.** This Internet application program lets you communicate with other computers on a remote network, even if your computer is not a permanent part of that network. For instance, you would use **Telnet** to access your county library's electronic card catalog from your home computer.

- **Internet telephony.** Internet users can converse vocally over the web using **Internet telephony.** Much less expensive than calling over standard phone lines, Internet telephony can also be more efficient, allowing an organization to accommodate more users on a single line at once.[16]

- **File transfers.** An Internet service known as **file transfer protocol (FTP)** enables you to **download** files (transfer data from a server to your computer) and **upload** files (transfer data from your computer to another system).[17] FTP also allows you to attach formatted documents to your e-mail messages and download formatted files.[18] Using the Internet and software, people can exchange files directly (from user to user) without going through a central server.

The Internet helps you communicate inside and outside the organizational setting. However, whether you're communicating through the Internet, in a letter, on the phone, or face to face, you will do so more effectively if you understand the process of communication. The following section gives you a basic overview of what happens during communication.

THE COMMUNICATION PROCESS

The communication process consists of six phases linking sender and receiver.

Communication doesn't occur haphazardly in organizations. Nor does it happen all at once. It is more than a single act. Communication is a dynamic, transactional (two-way) process that can be broken into six phases (see Figure 1–8):

1. **The sender has an idea.** You conceive an idea and want to share it.

2. **The sender encodes the idea.** When you put your idea into a message that your receiver will understand, you are **encoding** it. You decide on the message's

FIGURE 1–8
The Successful
Communication Process

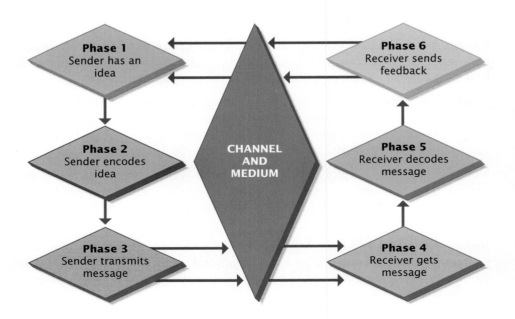

form (word, facial expression, gesture), length, organization, tone, and style—all of which depend on your idea, your audience, and your personal style or mood.

3. **The sender transmits the message.** To physically transmit your message to your receiver, you select a **communication channel** (spoken or written) and a **medium** (telephone, letter, memo, e-mail, report, face-to-face exchange). This choice depends on your message, your audience's location, your need for speed, and the formality required.

4. **The receiver gets the message.** For communication to occur, your receiver must first get the message. If you send a letter, your receiver has to read it before understanding it. If you're giving a speech, your listeners have to be able to hear you, and they have to be paying attention.

5. **The receiver decodes the message.** Your receiver must **decode** (absorb and understand) your message. The decoded message must then be stored in the receiver's mind. If all goes well, the receiver interprets your message correctly, assigning the same meaning to your words as you intended.

6. **The receiver sends feedback.** After decoding your message, the receiver may respond in some way and signal that response to you. This **feedback** enables you to evaluate the effectiveness of your message: If your audience doesn't understand what you mean, you can tell by the response and refine your message.

As Figure 1–8 illustrates, the communication process is repeated until both parties have finished expressing themselves.[19] Moreover, effective business communicators try not to cram too much information into one message. Instead, they limit the content of a message to a specific subject and use this back-and-forth exchange to provide additional information or details in subsequent messages.

However, Figure 1–8 does not illustrate how complicated the communication process actually is. Both sender and receiver may be trying to communicate at the same time, or their cultures or backgrounds may be so different that they won't understand one another without some allowance for these differences. Also, the receiver may not always respond to the message, so the sender may need to evaluate whether to send the message again. In fact, the communication process can fail in any number of ways.

> The actual process of communication is much more complicated than the model.

COMMUNICATION BARRIERS

Communication is successful only when the receiver understands the message intended by the sender. Any step in the communication process can be blocked by some sort of interference, or *noise*. Such noise can be caused by a variety of **communication barriers,** including perceptual and language differences, restrictive environments, distractions, deceptive communication tactics, and information overload.

> Communication barriers block the communication process.

Perceptual and Language Differences

The world constantly bombards us with sights, sounds, scents, and so on. Our minds organize this stream of sensation into a mental map that represents our **perception** of reality. Even when two people have experienced the same event, their mental images of that event will not be identical. Because your perceptions are unique, the ideas you want to express differ from other people's, and you may have difficulty being understood. As a sender, you choose the details that seem important to you. As a receiver, you try to fit new details into your existing pattern; however, if a detail doesn't quite

> Perception is people's individual interpretation of the sensory world around them.

fit, you are inclined to distort the information rather than rearrange your pattern—a process known as **selective perception.**

Similarly, language is an arbitrary code that depends on shared definitions. However, there's a limit to how completely any two people can share the same meaning for a given word. Take the simple word *cookie*, for example. You might think of oatmeal, chocolate chip, and sugar. However, others might think of *cookie* in its computer context—that is, a text file stored on a visitor's computer to identify each time the user visits a website.

The more experiences you share with another person, the more likely you are to share perception and thus share meaning. Both perception and language are heavily influenced by culture, which is discussed in detail in Chapter 3.

The more experiences people share, the more likely they will understand each other.

Restrictive Environments

The communication climate suffers when information is distorted, fragmented, or blocked by an authoritarian style of management.

Every link in the communication chain is open to error. By the time a message travels all the way up or down the chain, it may bear little resemblance to the original idea. Moreover, if a company's formal communication network limits the flow of information in any direction (upward, downward, or horizontal), communication becomes fragmented. Lower-level employees may obtain only enough information to perform their own isolated tasks, leaving only the people at the very top of the organization to see "the big picture."

When managers use a directive and authoritarian leadership style, information moves down the chain of command, but not up. In a recent poll of 638 employees, 90 percent said they had good ideas on how their companies could run more successfully. Yet more than 50 percent said they were prevented from communicating these thoughts because of a lack of management interest and a lack of effective means for sharing their ideas.[20]

Deceptive Tactics

Using deceptive tactics to manipulate receivers blocks communication and ultimately leads to failure.

Since language itself is made up of words that carry values, you need only say things a certain way to influence how others perceive your message, to shape expectations and behaviors.[21] Given such power, your responsibility to communicate honestly and honorably is a grave one. No organization can create illegal or unethical messages and still be credible or successful in the long run. Still, some business communicators try to manipulate their receivers by using deceptive tactics.

For example, deceptive communicators may exaggerate benefits, quote inaccurate statistics, or hide negative information behind an optimistic attitude. They may state opinions as facts, leave out crucial information, or portray graphic data unfairly. Unscrupulous communicators may seek personal gain by making others look better or worse than they are. And they may allow personal preferences to influence their own perception and the perception of others.

Distractions

Your audience members are more likely to receive your message accurately if they are not distracted by physical or emotional distractions or by information overload or round-the-clock accessibility.

Business messages can be interrupted or distorted by uncountable types of distractions, including physical distractions, emotional distractions, information overload, and round-the-clock accessibility:

- **Physical distractions.** Bad connections, poor acoustics, or illegible copy may seem trivial, but they can block an otherwise effective message. Your receiver might be distracted by an uncomfortable chair, poor lighting, health problems, or some other irritating condition.

- **Emotional distractions.** When you are upset, hostile, or fearful, you have a hard time shaping a message objectively. If your receivers are emotional, they may ignore or distort your message. It's practically impossible to avoid all communication in which emotions are involved, but try to remember that emotional messages have a greater potential for misunderstanding.

- **Information overload.** Every day, the number of documents on the Internet increases by 7.5 million. On top of that, people receive more and more messages by e-mail, overnight service, fax, voice mail, website, regular mail, pager, and cell phone.[22] On a typical day, the average office worker sends and receives over 200 messages.[23] The sheer number of messages can be distracting, making it difficult to discriminate between useful and useless information.

- **Round-the-clock accessibility.** Technology's demand for instant answers means that professionals find themselves constantly tied to work.[24] They make business calls on cell phones as they commute. They check pagers and voice mail at business meetings, at home, and at the grocery store. They plug into their company's intranet in the evening. And even on vacation, some find it easier to check e-mail daily and quickly respond than to return to work and tackle over 1,000 e-mail messages.[25]

GUIDELINES FOR OVERCOMING COMMUNICATION BARRIERS

Effective communicators work hard at perfecting the messages they deliver. When they make mistakes, they learn from them. If a memo they've written doesn't get the response they had hoped for, they change their approach the next time. If a meeting they're running gets out of control or proves unproductive, they do things differently at the next one. If they find that they have to explain themselves over and over again, they reevaluate their choice of words and rework their messages.

To be effective, business messages must constantly be perfected.

The coming chapters present real-life examples of both good and bad communication and explain what's good or bad about them. After a while you'll notice that four themes keep surfacing: (1) adopting an audience-centered approach, (2) fostering an open communication climate, (3) committing to ethical communication, and (4) creating efficient messages. Guidelines based on these themes will help you overcome barriers and improve your communication.

Guideline 1: Adopt an Audience-Centered Approach

Adopting an **audience-centered approach** means focusing on and caring about your audience—making every effort to get your message across in a way that is meaningful to receivers. As Lloyd Trotter knows, you need to learn as much as possible about the biases, education, age, status, and style of your audience to create an effective message. When you address strangers, try to find out more about them; if that's impossible, try to project yourself into their position by using your common sense and imagination. By writing and speaking from your audience's point of view, you can help receivers understand and accept your message.

Using an audience-centered approach means keeping your audience in mind at all times when communicating.

Guideline 2: Foster an Open Communication Climate

An organization's communication climate is a reflection of its **corporate culture:** the mixture of values, traditions, and habits that give a company its atmosphere or personality. Successful companies such as GE Industrial Systems encourage employee

The organization's communication climate affects the quantity and quality of the information exchanged.

At Amy's Ice Cream parlors, the corporate culture of "fun" leads to an open communication climate and makes it easy for all employees to speak up.

contributions by making sure that communication flows freely down, up, and across the organization chart. They encourage candor and honesty, and their employees feel free to confess their mistakes, disagree with the boss, and express their opinions. These companies create an open climate in two ways: by modifying the number of organizational levels and by facilitating feedback.

Modify the Number of Organizational Levels   To foster an open communication climate, companies today are reducing the number of levels in their organization's structure. A flat structure has fewer levels with more people reporting to each supervisor. Thus, the organi-

Adjusting organizational levels can improve the communication climate.

zation's communication chain has fewer links and is less likely to introduce distortion. Flatter organizations enable managers to share information with colleagues and employees and to include employees in decision making, goal setting, and problem solving.[26] However, designing too few formal channels and having too many people report to a single individual can block effective communication by overburdening that key individual.

Companies that encourage feedback achieve the open communication climate that allows them to respond to the ideas and needs of employees.

Facilitate Feedback   Giving your audience a chance to provide feedback is crucial to maintaining an open communication climate. What employees want the most from employers is personal feedback (even more than money).[27] Knowing how to give constructive criticism or feedback is an important communication skill, as highlighted in Table 1–2. To encourage feedback, companies use employee surveys, open-door policies, company newsletters, memos, e-mail, task forces, and even real-time two-way chat. Still, feedback isn't always easy to get. You may have to draw out the other person by asking specific questions. You can also gain useful information by encouraging your audience to express general reactions.

Table 1–2	GIVING CONSTRUCTIVE FEEDBACK

To Give Constructive Feedback

- Focus on particular behaviors. Feedback should be specific rather than general.

- Keep feedback impersonal. No matter how upset you are, keep feedback job related, and never criticize someone personally.

- Use "I" statements. Instead of saying, "You are absent from work too often," say, "I feel annoyed when you miss work so frequently."

- Keep feedback goal oriented. If you have to say something negative, make sure it's directed toward the recipient's goals. Ask yourself whom the feedback is supposed to help. If the answer is essentially you, bite your tongue.

- Make feedback well-timed. Feedback is most meaningful when there is a short interval between the recipient's behavior and feedback about that behavior.

- Ensure understanding. If feedback is to be effective, make sure the recipient understands it.

- Direct negative feedback toward behavior that is controllable by the recipient. Little value is gained by reminding a person of some shortcoming over which he or she has no control.

Guideline 3: Commit to Ethical Communication

Ethics are the principles of conduct that govern a person or a group. Unethical people say or do whatever it takes to achieve an end. Ethical people are generally trustworthy, fair, and impartial, respecting the rights of others and concerned about the impact of their actions on society. Former Supreme Court Justice Potter Stewart defined ethics as "knowing the difference between what you have a right to do and what is the right thing to do."[28]

Ethical communication includes all relevant information, is true in every sense, and is not deceptive in any way. In contrast, unethical communication can include falsehoods and misleading information or exclude important information. Some examples of unethical communication include:[29]

- **Plagiarism.** Stealing someone else's words or work and claiming it as your own

- **Selective misquoting.** Deliberately omitting damaging or unflattering comments to paint a better (but untruthful) picture of you or your company

- **Misrepresenting numbers.** Increasing or decreasing numbers, exaggerating, altering statistics, or omitting numerical data

- **Distorting visuals.** Making a product look bigger or changing the scale of graphs and charts to exaggerate or conceal differences

An ethical message is accurate and sincere. It avoids language that manipulates, discriminates, or exaggerates. When communicating ethically, you do not hide negative information behind an optimistic attitude, you don't state opinions as facts, and you portray graphic data fairly. You are honest with employers, co-workers, and clients, and you never seek personal gain by making others look better or worse than they are. You don't allow personal preferences to influence your perception or the perception of others, and you act in good faith. On the surface, such ethical practices appear fairly easy to recognize. But deciding what is ethical can be quite complex (see "Promoting Workplace Ethics: Ethical Boundaries: Where Would You Draw the Line?").

Recognize Ethical Choices   Every company has responsibilities to various groups: customers, employees, shareholders, suppliers, neighbors, the community, and the nation. But sometimes what's right for one group may be wrong for another.[30] At other times, as you attempt to satisfy the needs of one group, you may be presented with an option that seems right on the surface but somehow feels wrong. When you must choose between conflicting loyalties and weigh difficult trade-offs, you are facing a dilemma.

An **ethical dilemma** involves choosing between alternatives that aren't clear-cut (perhaps two conflicting alternatives are both ethical and valid, or perhaps the alternatives lie somewhere in the vast gray area between right and wrong). Suppose you are president of a company that's losing money. You have a duty to your shareholders to try to cut your losses and to your employees to be fair and honest. After looking at various options, you conclude that you'll have to lay off 500 people immediately. You suspect you may have to lay off another 100 people later on, but right now you need those 100 workers to finish a project. What do you tell them? If you confess that their jobs are shaky, many of them may quit just when you need them most. However, if you tell them that the future is rosy, you'll be stretching the truth.

Unlike a dilemma, an **ethical lapse** is making a clearly unethical or illegal choice. Suppose you have decided to change jobs and have discreetly landed an interview with your boss's largest competitor. You get along great with the interviewer, who is

Ethics are the principles of conduct that govern a person or a group.

Ethical communication is truthful and relevant.

Conflicting priorities and the vast gray areas between right and wrong create ethical dilemmas for an organization's communicators.

Self-interest and a lack of scruples create ethical lapses for business communicators.

PROMOTING WORKPLACE ETHICS

Ethical Boundaries: Where Would You Draw the Line?

At the very least, you owe your employer an honest day's work for an honest day's pay: your best efforts, obedience to the rules, a good attitude, respect for your employer's property, and a professional appearance. Such duties and considerations seem clear-cut, but where does your obligation to your employer end? For instance, where would you draw the line in communication situations such as the following?

- Writing your résumé so that an embarrassing two-year lapse won't be obvious

- Telling your best friend about your company's upcoming merger right after mailing the formal announcement to your shareholders

- Hinting to a co-worker (who's a close friend) that it's time to look around for something new, when you've already been told confidentially that she's scheduled to be fired at the end of the month

- Saying nothing when you witness one employee taking credit for another's successful idea

- Preserving your position by presenting yourself to supervisors as the only person capable of achieving an objective

- Buying one software package for use by three computer operators

- Making up an excuse when (for the fourth time this month) you have to pick up your child from school early and miss an important business meeting

- Calling in sick because you're taking a few days off and you want to use up some of the sick leave you've accumulated

The ethics involved in these situations may seem perfectly clear . . . until you think about them. But wherever you are, whatever the circumstances, you owe your employer your best efforts. And time and again, it will be up to you to decide whether those efforts are ethical.

CAREER APPLICATIONS

1. List ethical behaviors you would expect from your employees, and compare your list with those of your classmates.

2. As the supervisor of the records department, you must deal with several clerks who have a tendency to gossip about their co-workers. List five things you might do to resolve the situation.

---

impressed enough with you to offer you a position on the spot. Not only is the new position a step up from your current job, but the pay is double what you're getting now. You accept the job and agree to start next month. Then as you're shaking hands with the interviewer, she asks you to bring along profiles of your current company's 10 largest customers when you report for work. Do you comply with her request? How do you decide between what's ethical and what is not?

Laws provide ethical guidelines for certain types of messages.

Make Ethical Choices   One place to look for guidance is the law. Ask your boss or your company's attorney, and if saying or writing something is clearly illegal, you have no dilemma: You obey the law. However, even though legal considerations will resolve some ethical questions, you'll often have to rely on your own judgment and principles. If your intent is honest, the statement is ethical, even though it may be factually incorrect; if your intent is to mislead or manipulate the audience, the message is unethical, regardless of whether it is true. If a message does not violate civil law or company policy, you might ask yourself three questions:[31]

Asking the right questions can help you decide what is ethical.

1. **Is this message balanced?**   Does it do the most good and the least harm? Is it fair to all concerned in the short term as well as the long term? Does it promote positive win–win relationships? Did you weigh all sides before drawing a conclusion?

2. **Is it a message you can live with?**   Does it make you feel good about yourself? Does it make you proud? Would you feel good about your message if a newspaper published it? If your family knew about it?

3. **Is this message feasible?** Can it work in the real world? Have you considered your position in the company? Your company's competition? Its financial and political strength? The likely costs or risks of your message? The time available?

Motivate Ethical Choices   Some companies lay out an explicit ethical policy by using a written **code of ethics** to help employees determine what is acceptable. In addition, many managers use **ethics audits** to monitor ethical progress and to point out any weaknesses that need to be addressed. They know that being ethical is simply the right thing to do. Plus, it's contagious. Others will follow your example when they observe you being ethical and see the success you experience both in your interpersonal relationships and in your career.[32]

> Organizations can foster ethical behavior
> - By formalizing a written code of ethics
> - By using ethics audits
> - By setting a good ethical example

Guideline 4: Create Efficient Messages

Too much information is as bad as too little; it reduces the audience's ability to concentrate on the most important data. For the leanest messages, you need to determine which information is unnecessary and make necessary information easily available. Try to give information meaning, rather than just passing it on, and set priorities for dealing with the overall message flow. Successful communicators overcome information overload and other communication barriers by reducing the number of messages, minimizing distractions, and fine-tuning their business communication skills.

> Attending to relevance, meaning, and priorities will help you create lean messages.
>
> Eliminate physical distractions such as the messy appearance of a written message or poor acoustics in an oral presentation.
>
> Do your best to control emotions before they block the communication process.
>
> Organizations save time and money by sending only necessary messages.

Minimize Physical and Emotional Distractions   Although you don't have power over every eventuality, do your best to overcome physical barriers by exercising as much control as possible over the physical transmission link: If you're preparing a written document, make sure its appearance doesn't detract from your message. If you're delivering an oral presentation, choose a setting that permits the audience to see and hear you without straining. Help listeners by connecting your subject to their needs, using language that is clear and vivid, and relating your subject to familiar ideas.

When you're the audience, learn to concentrate on the message rather than on any distractions. As discussed in Chapter 2, you can overcome listening barriers by paraphrasing what you've heard. Try to view the situation through the speaker's eyes, and resist jumping to conclusions. Listen without interrupting, and clarify meaning by asking nonthreatening questions.

Overcome emotional barriers by recognizing the feelings that arise in yourself and in others as you communicate, and try to avoid causing these emotions. For example, choose neutral words to avoid arousing strong feelings unduly. Avoid placing blame and try not to react subjectively. Most important, be aware of the greater potential for misunderstanding that accompanies emotional messages.

In the creative environment of Industrial Light & Magic (ILM), visual effects supervisor Eric Brevig has firsthand knowledge of how distractions can block the effective communication of an idea. Concentrating on the message is one way to minimize distractions.

Reduce the Number of Messages   A good way to make your messages more effective is to send fewer of them. Think twice before sending one. For example, if

Document Makeover

IMPROVE THIS MEMO

To practice correcting drafts of actual documents, visit **www.prenhall.com/onekey** on the web. Click "Document Makeovers," then click Chapter 1. You will find a memo that contains problems and errors relating to what you've learned in this chapter about overcoming communication barriers in business messages. Use the Final Draft decision tool to create an improved version of this memo. Check the memo for an audience-centered approach, ethical communication, communicating efficiently, and facilitating feedback.

a written message merely adds to the information overload, it's probably better left unsent or handled some other way—such as by a quick telephone call or a face-to-face chat. Holding down the number of messages reduces the chance of information overload.

Fine-Tune Your Business Communication Skills   The key to making your business communication effective is to improve your communication skills. Many companies provide employees a variety of opportunities for training. But even though you may ultimately receive communication training on the job, don't wait. Start mastering business communication skills right now, in this course. People with good communication skills have an advantage in today's workplace.

Don't wait for communication training on the job.

Lack of experience may be the only obstacle between you and effective messages, whether written or spoken. Perhaps you have a limited vocabulary, or maybe you're uncertain about questions of grammar, punctuation, and style. Perhaps you're simply frightened by the idea of writing something or appearing before a group. People aren't "born" writers or speakers. Their skills improve the more they speak and write. Someone who has written 10 reports is usually better at it than someone who has written only two.

Practice and constructive criticism help you improve your communication skills.

One of the great advantages of taking a course in business communication is that you get to practice in an environment that provides honest and constructive criticism. For instance, this course gives you an understanding of acceptable and unacceptable techniques so that you can avoid making costly mistakes on the job. It provides the kind of communication practice that will help you get the job you want, boost your chances for a promotion, start your own business, or succeed at whatever you choose to do in the future.

In this course you'll learn how to collaborate in teams, listen well, master non-verbal communication, ensure successful meetings, and communicate across cultures and through the Internet. This book presents a three-step process for composing business messages. It gives tips for writing letters, memos, e-mail messages, reports, and oral presentations, and it provides a collection of good and bad communication examples with annotated comments to guide you in your own communication efforts. It also provides a handbook of the fundamentals of grammar, punctuation, and usage (see the "Handbook of Grammar, Mechanics, and Usage" at the end of this textbook). Finally, it explains how to write effective résumés and application letters and how to handle employment interviews.

Focus on building skills in the areas where you've been weak.

Perhaps the best place to begin strengthening your communication skills is with an honest assessment of where you stand. In the next few days, watch how you handle the communication situations that arise. Try to figure out what you're doing right and what you're doing wrong. Then, as you progress through this course in the months ahead, focus on those areas in which you need the most work.

APPLYING WHAT YOU'VE LEARNED

In this chapter, you've met GE Industrial Systems's Lloyd Trotter, and throughout the book you'll meet a cross section of real people—men and women who work for some of the most fascinating organizations around. At the beginning of this chapter, you read about communicating at GE Industrial Systems. A similar slice-of-life vignette titled "On the Job: Communicating at . . ." begins every chapter. As you read through each chapter, think about the person and the company highlighted in the vignette. Become familiar with the various concepts presented in the chapter, and imagine how they might apply to the featured scenario.

At the end of each chapter, you'll take part in an innovative simulation called "On the Job: Solving Communication Dilemmas." You'll play the role of a person working in the highlighted organization, and you'll face a situation you'd encounter there. You will be presented with several communication scenarios, each with several possible courses of action. It's up to you to recommend one course of action from each scenario as homework, as teamwork, as material for in-class discussion, or in a host of other ways. These scenarios let you explore various communication ideas and apply the concepts and techniques from the chapter.

Now you're ready for the first simulation. As you tackle each problem, think about the material you covered in this chapter and consider your own experience as a communicator. You'll probably be surprised to discover how much you already know about business communication.

On the Job:

SOLVING COMMUNICATION DILEMMAS AT GE INDUSTRIAL SYSTEMS

At GE Industrial Systems, Lloyd Trotter keeps communication flowing and makes sure that everyone receives necessary information by helping employees overcome all the potential barriers to effective communication. You are Trotter's administrative assistant, and he has put you in charge of several communication decisions—both internal and external. Use your knowledge of communication to choose the best response for each of the following situations. Be prepared to explain why your choice is best.

1. An employee from the company's commercial division has an idea for changing the production process so that it is more efficient and less expensive. She wants to send an e-mail message to her production manager, and she comes to you for advice on how to focus her message on the audience. Which of the following message openings would you recommend?

   a. "I have thought long and hard about how to make the production process more efficient."
   b. "You told us to come to you with new ideas."
   c. "Here is an idea for saving money on the production process."
   d. "A small change in the production process could save us both time and money."

2. A highly placed manager is uncomfortable with GE's "reverse-mentoring" program. In business, mentoring is nothing new: Older, experienced managers act as mentors to teach young, up-and-coming employees new skills. But GE's program is "reversed" because veteran managers must seek out young, Internet-savvy employees to help them improve their own Internet skills. In this case, the veteran wants no

part of "learning new tricks from some young pup." Trotter has participated in the program, and he believes "the key to our success is that no matter at what level we find ourselves in the organization, we can accept change." What feedback would you suggest that Trotter give this manager?

   a. "You need to think of this as a process of give and take. You have a lot to offer our younger employees, and your mentor will probably learn just as much from you as you learn from your mentor. You'll see firsthand the bright, young talent that represents the future leadership of our business."
   b. "I know that when I was first presented with the possibility of having a young employee mentor me, I found it a bit daunting. But for both of us, the program has been an excellent tool for mutual learning and growth. It's been a rewarding experience, helping me get a fast start in understanding the tool and its power."
   c. "Other GE managers meet with their employees for web lessons. They discuss the articles and books their mentors give them for homework, and they ask lots of stupid questions. But they also learn how to use the Internet effectively."
   d. "Anyone who is not open to learning—top down or bottom up—is slamming down the gate on their own career."

3. A rumor begins circulating that a major product line will be dropped and the workers in that area will be laid off. The rumor is false. What is the first action Trotter should take?

   a. Create an official statement and distribute it to top managers, with instructions for them to pass the statement on to middle managers, who will pass it on to their employees.

b. Try to plant a counter-rumor on the grapevine so that employees will get the right message the same way they got the wrong one.

c. Schedule a meeting with all employees on the affected product line. At the meeting, Trotter can explain the facts and publicly state that the rumor is false.

d. Ignore the rumor. Like all false rumors, it will eventually die out.

4. Trotter promoted a brilliant engineer who turned out to be a bad manager. Instead of setting an agenda for his team, giving them support, and then allowing them to flourish, the engineer micromanaged his employees. Trotter tried to point out that the engineer was holding his team down by asking him: "Why are so many on your staff sitting on the sidelines and waiting for you to make decisions? Why is your team unable to move ahead when you take a two-week vacation?" But the engineer has not changed his style, so Trotter must remove him from the manage-ment position. Even so, Trotter would like this brilliant engineer to stay with the company. Which of the following choices would be both ethical and good for the company?

a. The only way to be ethical is for Trotter to tell the engineer the whole truth—that he has failed as a manager but could be successful in a different role.

b. It is perfectly ethical for Trotter to reassign the engineer to another department in which he has no managerial responsibilities. Trotter is the boss and owes the engineer no explanation for the transfer.

c. The most ethical way for Trotter to resolve the situation is to find a pressing engineering problem (that requires no managerial responsibilities) and offer that challenge to the engineer.

d. To be completely above board and ethical, Trotter must fire the engineer for not fulfilling his mission. It's too bad he has to lose such a brilliant engineer, but the price of being ethical can sometimes be very high.[33]

Learning Objectives Checkup

To assess your understanding of the principles in this chapter, read each learning objective and study the accompanying exercises. For fill-in items, write the missing text in the blank provided; for multiple choice items, circle the letter of the correct answer. You can check your responses against the answer key on page AK-1.

Objective 1.1: Explain what effective communication is and highlight five characteristics of effective business messages.

1. Communication is effective when it
   a. Helps people understand each other
   b. Stimulates others to take action
   c. Encourages others to think in new ways
   d. Does all of the above

2. Effective business messages have the following characteristics:
   a. They provide practical information such as instructions, explanations, problems, solutions, and status reports.
   b. They give impressions and opinions that help make your business messages more persuasive.
   c. They include as much information as possible, and avoid visual aids in favor of textual descriptions.
   d. They put a "positive spin" on every message, and leave out anything that could be perceived as negative.

Objective 1.2: Discuss three developments in the workplace that are intensifying the need to communicate effectively.

3. Because of advances in _____, people can communicate more quickly, more frequently, and from remote locations.

4. Increased workforce diversity requires employees to focus on _____ communication so that people from different backgrounds can avoid misunderstandings.

5. Rather than the traditional command-and-control style of management, today's fast-paced organizations rely on collaborative work groups and _____.

Objective 1.3: Describe how organizations share information internally and externally.

6. Within an organization, the formal communication network may be depicted as
   a. Links joined in a long chain from top to bottom
   b. An organization chart of connected squares depicting the company's hierarchy
   c. A flow chart showing all information moving in one direction

7. Within an organization, the informal communication network is called
   a. The rumor mill
   b. Word of mouth
   c. The grapevine
   d. Hearsay

8. Communication between organizations and the outside world is
   a. More formal than internal communication, such as a news release carefully prepared by a marketing or public relations team
   b. As formal as or as informal as the situation calls for
   c. More informal than internal communication, such as talking with a customer or letting your appearance transmit an impression of your organization

Objective 1.4: List eight ways the Internet facilitates business communication.

9. Online groups that deliver posted messages to you via e-mail are called
   a. Telnet
   b. Discussion mailing lists
   c. Newsgroups
   d. Instant messaging and chat

10. When users converse vocally over the web, they are using
    a. Instant messaging and chat
    b. Telnet
    c. Internet telephony
    d. File transfer protocol

11. To replace in-person "face-to-face" meetings with online meetings, you would use
    a. Discussion mailing lists
    b. Internet telephony
    c. Videoconferencing
    d. E-mail

12. Users who wish to conduct real-time conversations over the computer would use
    a. Instant messaging and chat
    b. Telnet
    c. Internet telephony
    d. File transfer protocol

Objective 1.5: Define the six phases of the communication process.

13. The first phase of the communication process occurs when
    a. The sender transmits the message
    b. The receiver sends feedback
    c. The sender has an idea
    d. The receiver gets the message

14. The last phase of the communication process occurs when
    a. The sender transmits the message
    b. The receiver sends feedback
    c. The sender has an idea
    d. The receiver gets the message

Objective 1.6: Identify and briefly discuss five types of communication barriers.

15. The more experiences people share, the more likely they are to share meaning; however, each experience is strongly influenced by

a. Differences in perception and language
b. Restrictive structures
c. Distractions or information overload
d. Deceptive communication tactics

16. When communicators consider their own needs above those of their audience, they are likely to engage in
   a. Perceptual differences
   b. Restrictive structures
   c. Deceptive communication tactics
   d. Distractions or information overload

Objective 1.7: Discuss four guidelines for overcoming communication barriers.

17. When you encourage employee contributions, candor, and honesty, you are
    a. Adopting an audience-centered approach
    b. Fostering an open communication climate
    c. Committing to ethical communication
    d. Creating efficient messages

18. When you try to give information meaning, rather than just passing it on, you are
    a. Adopting an audience-centered approach
    b. Fostering an open communication climate
    c. Committing to ethical communication
    d. Creating efficient messages

Objective 1.8: Explain the attributes of ethical communication, and differentiate between an ethical dilemma and an ethical lapse.

19. Which of the following is *not* an attribute of ethical communication?
    a. The message is true in every sense.
    b. It avoids language that manipulates, discriminates, or exaggerates.
    c. It does not conceal negative information by misrepresenting numbers or distorting visual aids.
    d. It omits damaging or unflattering comments to paint a better picture of your company.

20. An ethical _____ involves choosing between two or more alternatives that are neither clearly ethical nor clearly unethical, whereas an ethical _____ involves choosing an alternative that is clearly unethical or illegal.

Apply Your Knowledge

1. Why do you think good communication in an organization improves employees' attitudes and performance? Explain briefly.

2. Under what circumstances might you want to limit the feedback you receive from an audience of readers or listeners? Explain briefly.

3. Would written or spoken messages be more susceptible to noise? Why?

4. As a manager, how can you impress on your employees the importance of including both negative and positive information in messages?

5. **Ethical Choices** Because of your excellent communication skills, your boss always asks you to write his reports for him. When you overhear the CEO complimenting him on his logical organization and clear writing style, he responds as if he'd written all those reports himself. What kind of ethical choice does this response represent? What can you do in this situation? Briefly explain your solution and your reasoning.

Practice Your Knowledge

DOCUMENT FOR ANALYSIS

Read the following document, then (1) analyze whether the document is effective or ineffective communication (be sure to explain why); and (2) revise the document so that it follows this chapter's guidelines.

It has come to my attention that many of you are lying on your time cards. If you come in late, you should not put 8:00 on your card. If you take a long lunch, you should not put 1:00 on your card. I will not stand for this type of cheating. I simply have no choice but to institute a time-clock system. Beginning next Monday, all employees will have to punch in and punch out whenever they come and go from the work area.

The time clock will be right by the entrance to each work area, so you have no excuse for not punching in. Anyone who is late for work or late coming back from lunch more than three times will have to answer to me. I don't care if you had to take a nap or if you girls had to shop. This is a place of business, and we do not want to be taken advantage of by slackers who are cheaters to boot.

It is too bad that a few bad apples always have to spoil things for everyone.

Exercises

For live links to all websites discussed in this chapter, visit this text's website at www.prenhall.com/thill. Just log on, select Chapter 1, and click on "Student Resources." Locate the page or the URL related to the material in the text. For the "Learning More on the Web" exercises, you'll also find navigational directions. Click on the live link to the site.

1.1 **Effective Business Communication: Understanding the Difference** Bring to class a memo that you received at work or a sales letter that you received in the mail. Comment on how well the communication
   a. Provides practical information
   b. Gives facts rather than impressions
   c. Clarifies and condenses information
   d. States precise responsibilities
   e. Persuades others and offers recommendations

1.2 **Internal Communication: Planning the Flow** For the following tasks, identify the necessary direction of communication (downward, upward, horizontal), suggest an appropriate type of communication (casual conversation, formal interview, meeting, workshop, videotape, newsletter, memo, bulletin board notice, and so on), and briefly explain your suggestion.
   a. As personnel manager, you want to announce details about this year's company picnic.
   b. As director of internal communication, you want to convince top management of the need for a company newsletter.
   c. As production manager, you want to make sure that both the sales manager and the finance manager receive your scheduling estimates.
   d. As marketing manager, you want to help employees understand the company's goals and its attitudes toward workers.

1.3 **Ethical Choices** An old college friend phoned you out of the blue to say, "Truth is, I had to call you. You'd better keep this under your hat, but when I heard my company was buying you guys out, I was dumbfounded. I had no idea that a company as large as yours could sink so fast. Your group must be in pretty bad shape over there!" Your stomach suddenly turned queasy, and you felt a chill go up your spine. You'd heard nothing about any buyout, and before you could even get your college friend off the phone, you were wondering what you should do. Of the following, choose one course of action and briefly explain your choice.
   a. Contact your CEO directly and relate what you've heard.
   b. Ask co-workers whether they've heard anything about a buyout.
   c. Discuss the phone call confidentially with your immediate supervisor.
   d. Keep quiet about the whole thing (there's nothing you can do about the situation anyway).

1.4 **Ethical Choices** In less than a page, explain why you think each of the following is or is not ethical:
   a. Deemphasizing negative test results in a report on your product idea
   b. Taking a computer home to finish a work-related assignment
   c. Telling an associate and close friend that she'd better pay more attention to her work responsibilities or management will fire her
   d. Recommending the purchase of excess equipment to use up your allocated funds before the end of the fiscal year so that your budget won't be cut next year

1.5 **The Changing Workplace: Always in Touch** Technological devices such as faxes, cellular phones, electronic mail, and voice mail are making businesspeople easily accessible at any time of day or night, at work and at home. What kind of impact might frequent intrusions have on their professional and personal lives? Please explain your answer in less than a page.

1.6 **Internet** As a manufacturer of aerospace, energy, and environmental equipment, Lockheed Martin has developed a code of ethics that it expects employees to abide by. Visit Lockheed Martin's website at www.lockheedmartin.com/about/ethics/standards/print.html, and review the six important virtues and the company's code of ethics (scroll down). In a brief paragraph, describe three specific examples of things you could do that would violate these provisions. Now scroll down and study the list of "Warning Signs" of ethics violations and take the "Quick Quiz." In another brief paragraph, describe how you could use this advice to avoid ethical problems as you write business letters, memos, and reports. Submit both paragraphs to your instructor.

1.7 Communication Process: Know Your Audience Top management has asked you to speak at an upcoming executive meeting to present your arguments for a more open communication climate. Which of the following would be most important for you to know about your audience before giving your presentation? (Briefly explain your choice.)

a. How many top managers will be attending

b. Your audience's preferred management style

c. How firmly these managers are set in their ways

1.8 Ethical Choices Your boss often uses you as a sounding board for her ideas. Now she seems to want you to act as an unofficial messenger by passing her ideas along to the staff without mentioning her involvement and informing her of what staff members say without telling them you're going to repeat their responses. What questions should you ask yourself as you consider the ethical implications of this situation? Write a short paragraph explaining the ethical choice you will make in this situation.[34]

1.9 Formal Communication: Self-Introduction Write a memo or prepare an oral presentation introducing yourself to your instructor and your class. Include such things as your background, interests, achievements, and goals. If you write a memo, keep it under one page, and use Figure 1.2 on page 6 as a model for the format. If you prepare an oral presentation, plan to speak for no more than two minutes.

1.10 Teamwork Your boss has asked your work group to research and report on corporate child-care facilities. Of course, you'll want to know who (besides your boss) will be reading your report. Working with two team members, list four or five other things you'll want

to know about the situation and about your audience before starting your research. Briefly explain why each of the items on your list is important.

1.11 Communication Process: Analyzing Miscommunication Use the six phases of the communication process to analyze a miscommunication you've recently had with a co-worker, supervisor, classmate, teacher, friend, or family member. What idea were you trying to share? How did you encode and transmit it? Did the receiver get the message? Did the receiver correctly decode the message? How do you know? Based on your analysis, identify and explain the barriers that prevented your successful communication in this instance.

1.12 Ethical Choices You've been given the critical assignment of selecting the site for your company's new plant. After months of negotiations with landowners, numerous cost calculations, and investments in ecological, social, and community impact studies, you are about to recommend building the new plant on the Lansing River site. Now, just 15 minutes before your big presentation to top management, you discover a possible mistake in your calculations: Site-purchase costs appear to be $50,000 more than you calculated, nearly 10 percent over budget. You don't have time to recheck all your figures, so you're tempted to just go ahead with your recommendation and ignore any discrepancies. You're worried that management won't approve this purchase if you can't present a clean, unqualified solution. You also know that many projects run over their original estimates, so you can probably work the extra cost into the budget later. On your way to the meeting room, you make your final decision. In a few paragraphs, explain the decision you made.

1.13 Communication Barriers: Eliminating Noise Whenever you report negative information to your boss, she never passes it along to her colleagues or supervisors, even though you think the information is important and should be shared. What barriers to communication are operating in this situation? What can you do to encourage more sharing of this kind of information?

Expand Your Knowledge

LEARNING MORE ON THE WEB

Check Out These Resources at the Business Writer's Free Library www.mapnp.org/library/commskls/cmm_writ.htm

The Business Writer's Free Library is a terrific resource for business communication material. Categories of information include basic composition skills, basic writing skills, correspondence, reference material, and general resources and advice. Log on and read about the most common errors in English, become a word detective, ask Miss Grammar, review samples of common forms of correspondence, fine-tune your interpersonal skills, join a newsgroup, and more. Follow the links and improve your effectiveness as a business communicator.

ACTIVITIES

It takes plenty of practice and hard work to become an effective communicator. Start now by logging on to the Business Writer's Free Library and expand your knowledge of the topics discussed in this chapter.

1. How do the objectives of professional writing differ from the objectives of composition and literature?

2. What is the purpose of feedback?

3. What are some basic guidelines for giving feedback?

EXPLORING THE WEB ON YOUR OWN

Review these chapter-related websites on your own to learn more about achieving communication success in the workplace.

1. Netiquette Home Page, www.albion.com/netiquette/index.html. Learn the do's and don'ts of online communication at this site, then take the Netiquette Quiz.
2. You Can Work from Anywhere, www.youcanworkfrom anywhere.com. Click on this site's Info and Tech Center and follow the links. Review the tips, tools, articles, ideas, and other helpful resources to improve your productivity as a telecommuter (a mobile or home-based worker).
3. Internet Help, www.city.grande-prairie.ab.ca/h_email.htm. Learn the ins and outs of e-mail at this comprehensive site so that your e-mail will stand out from the crowd.

Learn Interactively

INTERACTIVE STUDY GUIDE

Go to the Companion Website at www.prenhall.com/bovee. For Chapter 1, take advantage of the interactive "Study Guide" to test your knowledge of the chapter. Get instant feedback on whether you need additional studying. Also, visit this site's "Study Hall" where you'll find an abundance of valuable resources that will help you succeed in this course.

PEAK PERFORMANCE GRAMMAR AND MECHANICS

To improve your skill with nouns, use the "Peak Performance Grammar and Mechanics" module on the web. Visit www.prenhall.com/onekey, click "Peak Performance Grammar and Mechanics," then click "Nouns and Pronouns." Take the Pretest to determine whether you have any weak areas. Then review those areas in the Refresher Course. Take the Follow-Up Test to check your grasp of nouns and pronouns. For an extra challenge or advanced practice, take the Advanced Test. Finally, for additional reinforcement, go to the "Improve Your Grammar, Mechanics, and Usage" section that follows, and complete those exercises.

Improve Your Grammar, Mechanics, and Usage

The following exercises help you improve your knowledge of and power over English grammar, mechanics, and usage. Turn to the "Handbook of Grammar, Mechanics, and Usage" at the end of this textbook and review all of Section 1.1 (Nouns). Then look at the following 10 items. Underline the preferred choice within each set of parentheses. (Answers to these exercises appear on page AK-3.)

1. She remembered placing that report on her (*bosses, boss's*) desk.
2. We mustn't follow their investment advice like a lot of (*sheep, sheeps*).
3. Jones founded the company back in the early (*1990's, 1990s*).
4. Please send the (*Joneses, Jones'*) a dozen of the following: (*stopwatchs, stopwatches*), canteens, and headbands.
5. Our (*attorneys, attornies*) will talk to the group about incorporation.
6. Make sure that all (*copys, copies*) include the new addresses.
7. Ask Jennings to collect all (*employee's, employees'*) donations for the Red Cross drive.
8. Charlie now has two (*sons-in-law, son-in-laws*) to help him with his two online (*business's, businesses*).
9. Avoid using too many (*parentheses, parenthesises*) when writing your reports.
10. Follow President (*Nesses, Ness's*) rules about what constitutes a (*weeks, week's*) work.

For additional exercises focusing on nouns, go to www.prenhall.com/thill and select "Handbook of Grammar, Mechanics, and Usage Practice Sessions."

Chapter 2

Communicating in Teams and Mastering Listening, Nonverbal Communication, and Business Etiquette Skills

Learning Objectives

AFTER STUDYING THIS CHAPTER, YOU WILL BE ABLE TO

1 Highlight the advantages and disadvantages of working in teams

2 Identify the characteristics of effective teams

3 Explain how you can improve meeting productivity through preparation, leadership, and participation

4 Describe three barriers that interfere with the listening process and four guidelines for improving your listening

5 Briefly describe six categories of nonverbal communication

6 Clarify the functions of nonverbal communication

7 List three categories of business etiquette and give brief examples of each

On the Job:

COMMUNICATING AT AMERICAN EXPRESS

TAKING CHARGE OF BUSINESS THROUGH TEAMWORK

Don't leave home without it! That powerful message warns against traveling without an American Express card tucked into your pocket, and millions of customers heed that advice, making American Express the world's largest travel agency and a leading provider of global financial services. To serve all those customers, 84,000 American Express employees rely on teamwork—and they'd better not leave home without that.

The team concept permeates American Express. Just ask David House, president of American Express Worldwide Establishment Services, the division that signs up merchants to accept the American Express card. Managers in this division are leaders, not bosses. Employees are partners, not competitors. It's up to House to get every employee to contribute to and participate in the team approach—whether telecommuting from home in Los Angeles or working from company offices in London or Lisbon.

Each year, House commends outstanding team effort by awarding lavish prizes to the top 75 sales reps for their contributions. But to be recognized, people need more than an impressive sales record; they must follow House's agenda for building a winning team: (1) staying close to the customer, (2) having a commitment to excellence, (3) making a difference every day, (4) being accountable for results, and (5) sharing with peers. For example, House recognized one sales rep who focused on her team's regional sales objectives instead of her own quotas: She accompanied other reps on sales calls in her region and distributed copies of her winning presentation to every sales rep in the country.

House relies heavily on effective communication among team members and between teams and upper management. To promote communication within each team, he ensures that every employee has access to the company's highly efficient computer network. Team members conduct virtual meetings with colleagues around the world, and they take advantage of e-mail and videoconferencing to brainstorm and collaborate on projects. Several units in House's division use a buddy system that requires remote workers to chat with on-site colleagues by phone every morning, covering topics ranging from new customers to office politics. Other telecommuters report to a local or regional office several times each week, meeting with co-workers for specific purposes. Team meetings have predetermined agendas and follow regular schedules to reduce wasted meeting time while allowing team members to communicate face-to-face. From the newest recruits to top executives, House makes sure that everyone at American Express contributes to the company's success through effective teamwork.[1]

www.americanexpress.com

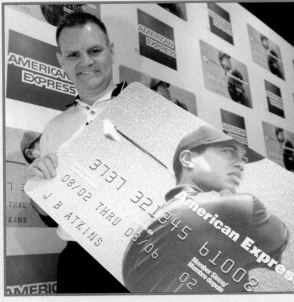

With over 58,000 employees in the United States, American Express is recognized as a top corporate employer (in leading publications such as Fortune's "100 Best Companies to Work For"). American Express helps its employees succeed in their jobs by encouraging teamwork and free-flowing communication throughout the organization. As a financial services giant and as the world's number-one travel agency, the company issues travelers checks, publishes magazines, and provides financial advisory services.

WORKING IN TEAMS

American Express's David House knows that working in teams and small groups puts everyone's communication skills to the test. A **team** is a unit of two or more people who work together to achieve a goal. Team members share a mission and the responsibility for working to achieve it.[2]

Whether the task is to write reports, give oral presentations, produce a product, solve a problem, or investigate an opportunity, team members must communicate effectively among themselves and with people outside their team. Companies look for people who can successfully interact in teams and collaborate with others. Why? For one thing, organizations working in teams experience the highest improvement in performance.[3] Also, teams encourage creativity in workers through **participative management**—involving employees in the company's decision making.

> Team members have a shared mission and are collectively responsible for their work.
>
> Companies like to hire people who work effectively in teams.

Types of Teams

Companies can create various types of teams. *Formal teams* become part of the organization's structure. *Informal teams* are not part of the formal organization but rather are formed to solve a problem, work on a specific activity, or encourage employee participation.

Problem-solving teams and **task forces** are informal teams that assemble to resolve specific issues and then disband once their goal has been accomplished. Team members often include representatives of many departments so that those who have a stake in the outcome are allowed to provide input.[4]

A **committee** usually has a long life span and can become a permanent part of the organizational structure. Committees typically deal with regularly recurring tasks. For example, a grievance committee may be formed as a permanent resource for handling employee complaints and concerns.

Virtual teams bring together geographically distant employees to interact, share information, and accomplish goals. At Texas Instruments, microchip engineers in Texas can collaborate with colleagues in India and Japan, pooling ideas, designing and debugging new chips—even though they're 8,000 miles and 12 time zones apart.[5] Virtual teams can use computer networks, teleconferencing, e-mail, video-conferencing, and web technology to build teams that are as effective as those in organizations functioning under a single roof.

Teams can play a vital role in helping an organization reach its goals, as American Express can attest. However, teams are not appropriate for every situation. When deciding whether to use teams, managers must weigh both the advantages and disadvantages of doing so.[6]

> Two popular types of informal teams are problem-solving teams and task forces.
>
> Committees are long-term teams.
>
> Virtual teams conduct their business by using advanced communication technology.

Advantages and Disadvantages of Teams

At their best, teams can be an extremely useful forum for making key decisions. The interaction of the participants and the combined intelligence of the group produce better decisions than what might have been achieved had the members worked independently. Teams improve several factors that affect decision making:[7]

> The advantages of teams outweigh the disadvantages.

- **Information and knowledge.** By pooling the resources of several individuals, teams bring more information to the decision-making process.

- **Diversity of views.** Team members bring a variety of perspectives to the decision-making process.

- **Acceptance of a solution.** Those who participate in making a decision are more likely to support it enthusiastically and encourage others to accept it.

- **Performance levels.** Team members share a sense of purpose and mutual accountability, which can fill the need to belong to a group, reduce boredom, increase feelings of dignity and self-worth, reduce stress and tension between workers, and unleash vast amounts of creativity and energy.

Regardless of such advantages, teams also have potential disadvantages. At their worst, teams are unproductive, frustrating, and a waste of everyone's time. Some may actually be counterproductive. Teams can arrive at bad decisions for several reasons:

> Bad team decisions can result from peer pressure, personal motives, noncontributing team members, and limited time or money.

- **Groupthink.** Individual members may be willing to set aside their personal opinions and go along with everyone else, simply because belonging to the team is more important to them than making the right decision. Groupthink can lead to poor decisions and ill-advised actions and can even induce people to act unethically.

- **Hidden agendas.** Private motives can affect the group's interaction. Sam might want to prove that he's more powerful than Laura; Laura might be trying to share the risk of making a decision; and Don might be looking for a chance to postpone doing "real" work. Each person's hidden agenda can detract from the team's effectiveness.

- **Free riders.** Some members don't contribute their fair share to the group's activities because they aren't being held individually accountable for their work. The free-ride attitude can lead to certain tasks going unfulfilled.

- **High cost of coordinating group activities.** Aligning schedules, arranging meetings, and coordinating individual parts of a project can eat up a lot of the team's time and money.

Group Dynamics

> Group dynamics are the interactions and processes that take place in a team.

The interactions and processes that take place in a team are called **group dynamics.** Some teams are more effective than others simply because the dynamics of the group facilitate member input and the resolution of differences. To keep things moving forward, productive teams also tend to develop rules that are conducive to business. Often these rules are unstated; they just become standard group practice, or **norms—** informal standards of conduct that members share and that guide member behavior. For example, members may have an unspoken agreement that it's okay to be 10 minutes late for meetings but not 15 minutes late, or that it's preferable to use e-mail rather than the phone to communicate with other team members.

> Each member of a group plays a role that affects the outcome of the group's activities.

Team Roles   Members of a team can play various roles, which fall into three categories (see Table 2–1). Members who assume **self-oriented roles** are motivated mainly to fulfill personal needs, so they tend to be less productive than other members. Far more likely to contribute to team goals are those members who assume **team-maintenance roles** to help everyone work well together and those members who assume **task-facilitating roles** to help solve problems or make decisions.

> Roles are often determined by status, which can vary from team to team.

To a great extent, the roles that individuals assume in a group depend on their status in that group and whether they joined the group voluntarily. Status depends on many variables, including personal attractiveness, competence in a particular field, past successes, education, age, social background, and organizational position. A person's status also varies from team to team. In most teams, as people try to establish their relative status, an undercurrent of tension can get in the way of the real work. Until roles and status have stabilized, a team may have trouble accomplishing its goals.

Decision Making in Teams   Whenever teams tackle decision-making tasks, they typically pass through five phases, regardless of what task or what type of decision is being considered:[8]

TEAM ROLES PEOPLE PLAY   **Table 2–1**

Dysfunctional	*Functional*	
Self-Oriented Roles:	**Team-Maintenance Roles:**	**Task-Facilitating Roles:**
Controlling: Dominating others by exhibiting superiority or authority	**Encouraging:** Drawing out other members by showing verbal and nonverbal support, praise, or agreement	**Initiating:** Getting the team started on a line of inquiry
Withdrawing: Retiring from the team either by becoming silent or by refusing to deal with a particular aspect of the team's work	**Harmonizing:** Reconciling differences among team members through mediation or by using humor to relieve tension	**Information giving or seeking:** Offering (or seeking) information relevant to questions facing the team
Attention seeking: Calling attention to oneself and demanding recognition from others	**Compromising:** Offering to yield on a point in the interest of reaching a mutually acceptable decision	**Coordinating:** Showing relationships among ideas, clarifying issues, summarizing what the team has done
Diverting: Focusing the team's discussion on topics of interest to the individual rather than on those relevant to the task		**Procedure setting:** Suggesting decision-making procedures that will move the team toward a goal

- **Orientation.** Team members socialize, establish their roles, and begin to define their task or purpose.

- **Conflict.** Team members begin to discuss their positions and become more assertive in establishing their roles. If members have been carefully selected to represent a variety of viewpoints and expertise, disagreements are a natural part of this phase.

- **Brainstorming.** Team members air all the options and discuss the pros and cons fully. At the end of this phase, members begin to settle on a single solution to the problem.

- **Emergence.** After all members have had an opportunity to communicate their positions and feel that they have been listened to, the team reaches a decision. Consensus is reached when the team finds a solution that is acceptable enough for all members to support (even if they have reservations).

- **Reinforcement.** Group feeling is rebuilt and the solution is summarized. Members receive their assignments for carrying out the group's decision, and they make arrangements for following up on those assignments.

Group decision making passes through five phases: orientation, conflict, brainstorming, emergence, and reinforcement.

Conflict in Teams   Conflict can arise for any number of reasons, such as competition for scarce resources, disagreement about who is responsible for a specific task, or misunderstanding or misperception of other team members. Basic differences in values, attitudes, and personalities may lead to arguments. Conflict can also arise from power struggles or because individuals or teams are pursuing different goals.[9]

Conflict is constructive if it forces important issues into the open, increases the involvement of team members, and generates creative ideas for the solution to a problem. Conflict is destructive if it diverts energy from more important issues, destroys the morale of teams or individual team members, or polarizes or divides the team.[10] For instance, if you believe that the only solution is for one party to win and

Team conflict can be constructive or destructive.

The important thing to remember about resolving conflict is that people can usually get what they want if they are willing to work together. In many cases, the resolution process is an exchange of opinions and information that gradually leads to a mutually acceptable solution.

the other party to lose (*win–lose strategy*), the outcome of the conflict will surely make someone unhappy. Unfortunately, some conflicts degenerate to the point that both parties would rather lose than see the other party win (*lose–lose strategy*).

On the other hand, if you approach conflict with the idea that both parties can satisfy their goals at least to some extent (*win–win strategy*), no one loses. The win–win strategy assumes that parties in conflict can better solve their problems by working together than by waging war. Thus, everyone involved must believe that it's possible to find a solution both parties can accept, that cooperation is better for the organization than competition, that the other party can be trusted, and that higher status doesn't entitle one party to impose a solution.

One of the first steps in finding a win–win solution is to focus on your audience and consider the other person's needs. Before you meet, try to find out what might be acceptable to the other party. Keep your eyes and ears open; ask questions that will help you understand the other person's wants. Search for mutually satisfactory solutions or compromises that result in joint gain.[11]

When you face irrational resistance, try to remain calm and detached so that you can avoid destructive confrontations and present your position in a convincing manner:

A win–win strategy is based on the idea that a solution can be found to satisfy all parties.

To avoid destructive conflict, practice empathy, directness, fair-mindedness, and patience.

- **Express understanding.** Show that you sympathize. You might say, "I can understand that this change might be difficult, and if I were in your position, I might be reluctant myself." Help the other person relax and talk about his or her anxiety so that you have a chance to offer reassurance.[12]

- **Make people aware of their resistance.** When people are noncommittal and silent, they may be tuning you out without even knowing why. Continuing with your argument is futile. Deal directly with the resistance, without being accusing. You might say, "You seem cool to this idea. Have I made some faulty assumptions?" Such questions help people face and define their resistance.[13]

- **Evaluate others' objections fairly.** When the person opens up, try to understand the basis for the resistance. Focus on what the other person is expressing, both the words and the feelings. Others' objections may raise legitimate points that you'll need to discuss, or they may reveal problems that you'll need to minimize.[14]

- **Hold your arguments until the other person is ready for them.** Getting your point across depends as much on the other person's frame of mind as it does on your arguments. You can't assume that a strong argument will speak for itself. By becoming more audience-centered, you will learn to address the other person's emotional needs first.

Characteristics of Effective Teams

Members of effective teams recognize that each individual brings valuable assets, knowledge, and skills to the effort. They are willing to exchange information, examine issues, and work through conflicts that arise. They trust each other and look toward the greater good of the team and organization instead of focusing on personal agendas, making unilateral decisions, or pulling power plays.[15] To ensure that your team is effective, follow these guidelines:[16]

✓ CHECKLIST: Developing an Effective Team

Select Team Members Wisely

✓ Involve stakeholders.
✓ Limit size to no more than 12 to 15 members.
✓ Select members with diverse views.
✓ Select creative thinkers.

Build a Sense of Fairness in Decision Making

✓ Keep everyone informed.
✓ Present all the facts.
✓ Consider all proposals.
✓ Allow members to communicate openly and honestly.
✓ Encourage debate and disagreement without fear of reprisal.
✓ Build consensus by allowing members to examine, compare, and reconcile differences.
✓ Avoid quick votes.

Stay on Track

✓ Make sure everyone understands the team's purpose.
✓ Communicate what is expected of team members.
✓ Don't deviate from the core assignment.
✓ Develop and adhere to a schedule.
✓ Develop rules and obey norms.

Manage Conflict Constructively

✓ Share leadership.
✓ Encourage equal participation.
✓ Discuss disagreements.
✓ Focus on the issues, not the people.
✓ Don't let things get out of hand.

- **Have a clear sense of purpose.** Team members clearly understand the task at hand, what is expected of them, and their role on the team.

- **Communicate openly and honestly.** The team culture encourages open and honest discussion and debate, without the threat of anger, resentment, or retribution. Because members listen to and value feedback from others, all team members participate.

- **Reach decisions by consensus.** No easy, quick votes are taken. Once all members have expressed their opinions and engaged in debate, the emerging decision is generally supported by all.

- **Think creatively.** Effective teams encourage original thinking and consider options beyond the usual.

- **Remain focused.** Team members get to the core issues of the problem and stay focused on key issues.

- **Resolve conflict effectively.** The ability to handle conflict—clashes over ideas, opinions, goals, or procedures—is a key contributing factor to a team's overall effectiveness.

Effective teams
- Understand their purpose
- Communicate openly
- Build consensus
- Think creatively
- Stay focused
- Resolve conflict

For a brief review of the characteristics that make an effective team, see the "Checklist: Developing an Effective Team." Your ability to collaborate with teammates may be tested on any number of tasks, including writing collaborative messages and running productive meetings.

WRITING COLLABORATIVE MESSAGES

Teams often jointly produce a single document or presentation known as a **collaborative message**. Team members might participate in an all-out group effort to write a company's business plan or to draft and deliver a major sales presentation. Such collaborative messages can involve a project manager, researchers, writers, typists, graphic artists, and editors. The collective energy and expertise of all these people can create something that transcends what you could do otherwise.[17] Even so, team

Collaborative messages benefit from multiple perspectives and various skills; however, team members may have to work hard to overcome differences in background and working habits.

members coming from different backgrounds will have different work habits or concerns, different writing styles, and different personality traits.

Guidelines for Composing Effective Collaborative Messages

When collaborating on messages, you must be flexible and open to the opinions of others—focus on your team's objectives instead of your own.[18] Before anyone begins to write, team members must agree on the purpose of the project and on the audience. Your team must also plan the organization, format, and style of the document—after all, the final message must look and sound as if one writer prepared it. The following guidelines will help you produce team messages that are clear, seamless, and successful:[19]

- **Select the right team members.** Choose team members who have strong interpersonal skills, understand team dynamics, and care about the project.

- **Choose a responsible leader.** Identify a group leader who will keep members informed and will intervene when necessary.

- **Promote cooperation.** Establish communication standards that motivate accuracy, openness, and trust.

- **Clarify goals.** Make sure team goals are aligned with individual expectations.

- **Elicit commitment.** Create a sense of ownership and shared responsibility for the document.

- **Clarify responsibilities.** Assign specific roles and establish clear lines of reporting.

- **Foster prompt action.** Establish a timeline and deadlines for every part of the project.

- **Ensure technological compatibility.** Have everyone use the same word-processing program to facilitate combining files.

- **Apply technology wisely.** Use electronic tools to communicate quickly and effectively with other team members.

Guidelines for Critiquing the Writing of Others

When critiquing someone else, provide specific, constructive comments.

Whether you're writing in teams or reviewing a document prepared by someone else for your signature, you will sometimes need to critique the writing of another. When you do, be sure to provide specific, constructive comments. To help the writer make meaningful changes, you need to say more than simply "This doesn't work" or "This isn't what I wanted" or "I don't see what you're trying to say."[20] When critiquing a document, concentrate on four elements:[21]

- **Are the assignment instructions clear?** Be sure to determine whether the directions given with the initial assignment were clear and complete.

- **Does the document accomplish the intended purpose?** Does it state the purpose clearly? Does the body support the purpose? Does the evidence support the conclusion? Are the arguments logical?

Document Makeover

IMPROVE THIS LETTER

To practice correcting drafts of actual documents, visit **www.prenhall.com/onekey** on the web. Click "Document Makeovers," then click Chapter 2. You will find a letter that contains problems and errors relating to what you've learned in this chapter about critiquing collaborative writing. Use the Final Draft decision tool to create an improved version of the letter. Check the message for unified writing style, clarity of purpose, a body that supports the purpose, logical arguments, and clear language.

SHARPENING YOUR CAREER SKILLS

Mastering the Art of Constructive Criticism

For anyone working on a document, project, or other assignment, taking criticism from others can often be difficult. When you must tell someone "You did it wrong" or "You need to do it again," the way you handle the criticism can destroy goodwill and cooperation, or it can build the relationship and help the person learn, improve performance, and retain self-esteem. To criticize more constructively, follow these suggestions:

- *Don't act in haste.* Never criticize in an offhand manner. Treat the situation seriously, and take the time to state the problem in detail. Explain your criticism calmly, rationally, and objectively, clarifying what is wrong and why.

- *Phrase your remarks impersonally.* Criticize the work (the report or the results of the project), not the person. Focus your remarks on performance only, and analyze it thoughtfully.

- *Preface the criticism with a kind word or a compliment.* Start with a few words of praise or admiration, pointing out what's good about the work. First the good news, then the bad.

- *Avoid an abusive tone.* Ridiculing someone, talking down to a person, or using sarcasm prevents people from accepting what you have to say.

- *Be specific.* Don't talk in generalities; say exactly what was done wrong. Then, avoid dwelling on the error or mistake; explain how to correct the work and do things right.

- *Ask for cooperation.* Don't demand cooperation. Asking makes the person feel like a team member and provides an incentive to improve.

- *Follow up.* Make sure the person is acting on your suggestions and doing things right.

If you follow these guidelines, constructive criticism can benefit you, your company, and—most important—the person whose work you're criticizing.

CAREER APPLICATIONS

1. Think back over your own experience. How did you feel when someone told you that you were doing something wrong? Did that person make the situation better or worse? Did you benefit from the criticism? Explain your answers in a brief paragraph.

2. Using the memo format from Figure 1.2, write a brief message to your assistant, explaining that he left several important facts out of a recent report. What the employee turned in is well-written and informative, but the report must be revised to include the missing facts. With a partner, trade memos and critique them. What did the writer do right? What could be improved?

- **Is the factual material correct?** A proposal to provide nationwide computer-training services for $15 million would create major problems if your intention was to provide those services for $150 million.

- **Does the document use clear language?** If you interpret a message differently from what a writer intended, the document must be revised.

Once these elements are deemed satisfactory, decide whether to request other changes. Minor changes can be made at any time in the critiquing process. However, if these four criteria have been met, don't request a major revision, unless (1) the document can truly be improved, (2) you can justify the time needed for a rewrite or revision, and (3) your request won't have a negative impact on morale.[22] Whenever you must critique someone else's writing, make your criticism constructive, as explained in "Sharpening Your Career Skills: Mastering the Art of Constructive Criticism."

Be careful about requesting major revisions that aren't really necessary.

MAKING MEETINGS PRODUCTIVE

Meetings are a prime tool for solving problems, developing ideas through giving and getting feedback, identifying opportunities, and deciding how to maximize the company's resources. As more and more companies increase their use of teams, the number of meetings you'll attend will also increase. Already, more than 25 million meetings take place worldwide every day.[23] Unfortunately, many of them are unproductive. You can improve your meetings by the way you prepare for, conduct, and participate in them.

Preparing for Meetings

The best preparation for a meeting is having a specific goal that would be best handled in a face-to-face situation.

Before you call a meeting, satisfy yourself that one is truly needed. Perhaps you could communicate more effectively in a memo or through individual conversations. If you do require the interaction of a group, you want to bring the right people together in the right place for just enough time to accomplish your goals:

- **Decide on your purpose.** *Informational meetings* involve sharing information and often coordinating action. Briefings may come from each participant or from the leader, who then answers attendees' questions. *Decision-making meetings* involve persuasion, analysis, and problem solving—often including a brainstorming session and a debate on the alternatives. Many meetings combine these two purposes.

- **Select participants.** Invite only those people whose presence is essential. For purely informational sessions where one person does most of the talking, you can include a relatively large group. But to solve a problem, develop a plan, or reach a decision, invite no more than 6 to 12 people.[24] The more participants, the more

Working with team members in different locations is less of a challenge when you bridge the distance with interactive websites such as WebEx (www.webex.com). Following the site's prompts, you simply enter the meeting date and time and send e-mail announcements to attendees. Then, at meeting time, participants log onto WebEx, enter a special code, and join the meeting.

comments and confusion, and the longer the meeting. However, be sure to include key decision makers who can contribute.

- **Choose an appropriate location.** Decide where you'll hold the meeting, and reserve the location. For work sessions, morning meetings are usually more productive than afternoon sessions. Consider the seating arrangements: Are rows of chairs suitable, or do you need a conference table? Also pay attention to room temperature, lighting, ventilation, acoustics, and refreshments. These things may seem trivial, but they can make or break a meeting.

- **Set and follow an agenda.** Meeting agendas help participants prepare by putting the meeting plan into a permanent, written form. Small, informal meetings may not require a formal agenda, but even they benefit if you prepare at least a list of matters to be discussed. Distribute the agenda to participants several days before the meeting so that they will know what to expect and can come prepared to respond to the issues.

Distribute the agenda ahead of time.

Look at the agenda in Figure 2–1. A productive agenda answers three key questions: (1) What do we need to do in this meeting to accomplish our goals? (2) What

FIGURE 2–1
Typical Meeting Agenda

AGENDA

PLANNING COMMITTEE MEETING

Monday, October 21, 2004
10:00 A.M. to 11:00 A.M.

Executive Conference Room

   I. Call to Order

  II. Roll Call

 III. Approval of Agenda

 IV. Approval of Minutes from Previous Meeting

  V. Chairperson's Report on Site Selection Progress

		Person	Proposed Time
VI.	Subcommittee Reports		
	a. New Markets	Alan	5 minutes
	b. New Products	Jennifer	5 minutes
	c. Finance	Craig	5 minutes
VII.	Old Business—Pricing Policy for New Products	Terry	10 minutes
VIII.	New Business		
	a. Carson and Canfield Data on New Product Sales	Sarah	10 minutes
	b. Restructuring of Product Territories due to New Product Introductions	Edith	10 minutes
IX.	Announcements		
X.	Adjournment		

issues will be of greatest importance to all the participants? (3) What information must be available in order to discuss these issues?[25] Agendas also include the names of the participants, the time, the place, and the order of business.

Conducting and Participating in Meetings

A meeting's success depends largely on the effectiveness of its leader. If the leader is prepared and has selected participants carefully, notes American Express's David House, the meeting will generally be productive.

Keep the Meeting on Track   Good leaders guide, mediate, probe, stimulate, and summarize, letting others thrash out their ideas. That's why leaders such as David House avoid being so domineering that they close off suggestions. Of course, they must also avoid leaning too far the other way and being so passive that they lose control of the group.

As leader, you're responsible for keeping the meeting moving along. If the discussion lags, call on those who haven't been heard. Pace the presentation and discussion so that you'll have time to complete the agenda. As time begins to run out, interrupt the discussion and summarize what has been accomplished. However, don't be too rigid. Allow enough time for all the main ideas to be heard, and give people a chance to raise related issues. If you cut off discussion too quickly or limit the subject too narrowly, no real consensus can emerge.

Don't be so rigid that you cut off discussion too quickly.

Follow Parliamentary Procedure   One way you can improve the productivity of a meeting is by using **parliamentary procedure**, a time-tested method for planning and running effective meetings. Anyone who holds regular meetings should understand the basic principles of parliamentary procedure. Used correctly, it can help groups[26]

- Transact business efficiently

- Protect individual rights

- Maintain order

- Preserve a spirit of harmony

- Accomplish team and organizational goals

Robert's Rules of Order is the most common guide to parliamentary procedure.

The most common guide to parliamentary procedure is *Robert's Rules of Order,* available in various editions and revisions. Also available are less technical guides based on *Robert's Rules.* As leader, you determine how strictly you want to adhere to parliamentary procedure. For small groups you may be quite flexible, but for larger groups you'll want to use a more formal approach.

Encourage Participation   You'll discover that some participants are too quiet and others are too talkative. To draw out the shy types, ask for their input on issues that particularly pertain to them. You might say something like "Roberto, you've done a lot of work in this area. What do you think?" For the overly talkative, simply say that time is limited and others need to be heard from. The best meetings are those in which everyone participates, so don't let one or two people dominate your meeting while others doodle on their notepads. As you move through your agenda, stop at the end of each item, summarize what you understand to be the feelings of the group, and state the important points made during the discussion.

Don't let one or two members dominate the meeting.

If you're a meeting participant, try to contribute to both the subject of the meeting and the smooth interaction of the participants. Listen and observe carefully to size up the interpersonal dynamics of the people; then adapt your behavior to help the group achieve its goals. Speak up if you have something useful to say, but don't monopolize the discussion.

Close Effectively   At the conclusion of the meeting, tie up the loose ends. Either summarize the general conclusion or list the actions to be taken. Wrapping things up ensures that all participants agree on the outcome and gives people a chance to clear up any misunderstandings. Before the meeting breaks up, briefly review who has agreed to do what by what date.

Following Up After Meetings

As soon as possible after the meeting, make sure all participants receive a copy of the minutes or notes, showing recommended actions, schedules, and responsibilities. Generally, the secretary who attends the meeting prepares a set of minutes for distribution to all attendees and other interested parties. An informal meeting may not require minutes. Instead, attendees simply make their own notes. Follow-up is then their responsibility, although the meeting leader may need to remind them to do so through an e-mail or phone call.

Meeting minutes are prepared in much the same format as a memo or letter, except for the heading, which takes this form:

Following up with minutes of the meeting allows you to remind everyone of what happened and who needs to take action.

Minutes

Planning Committee Meeting

Monday, October 21, 2002

Present: [All invited attendees who were present are listed here, generally by rank, in alphabetical order, or in some combination.]

Absent: [All invited attendees who were not present are listed here, in similar order.]

The body of the minutes follows the heading: It notes the times the meeting started and ended, all major decisions reached at the meeting, all assignments of tasks to meeting participants, and all subjects that were deferred to a later meeting. In addition, the minutes objectively summarize important discussions, noting the names of those who contributed major points. Outlines, subheadings, and lists help organize the minutes, and additional documentation (such as tables or charts submitted by meeting participants) are noted in the minutes and attached.

At the end of the minutes, the words *Submitted by* should be added, followed by a couple of blank lines for a signature and then the signer's printed (or typed) name and title (if appropriate). If the minutes have been written by one person and prepared by another, the preparer's initials should be added, just as reference initials are added to a letter or memo. Well-constructed minutes will remind everyone of what took place, provide a reference for future actions, and make meetings more productive. To review the tasks that contribute to productive meetings, see the "Checklist: Improving Meeting Productivity."

✓ CHECKLIST: Improving Meeting Productivity

Prepare Carefully

✓ Determine the meeting's objectives.
✓ Select participants.
✓ Determine the location, and reserve a room.
✓ Determine whether the lighting, ventilation, acoustics, and temperature of the room are adequate.
✓ Determine seating needs: chairs only or table and chairs.
✓ Arrange for light refreshments, if appropriate.
✓ Work out an agenda that will achieve your objectives.

Be an Effective Leader

✓ Begin and end the meeting on time.

✓ Control the meeting by following the announced agenda and a set procedure.
✓ Encourage full participation, either confronting or ignoring those who seem to be working at cross-purposes with the group.
✓ Sum up decisions, actions, and recommendations as you move through the agenda, and restate main points at the end.

Remember to Follow Up

✓ Distribute the meeting's notes or minutes on a timely basis.
✓ Take the follow-up action agreed to.

IMPROVING YOUR LISTENING SKILLS

Most people prefer oral communication to written communication.

Whether speaking with team members, supervisors, customers, suppliers, or members of the community, your success depends on effective communication—much of which is spoken, either face-to-face or over the phone. Given a choice, people would rather talk to each other than write to each other (see Figure 2–2). Talking takes less time and needs no composing, keyboarding, rewriting, duplicating, or distributing. Even more important, oral communication provides the opportunity for immediate feedback. When people communicate orally, they can ask questions and test their understanding of the message; they can share ideas and work together to solve problems.

Oral communication lacks the ability to revise a message but offers the luxury of immediate feedback.

Nonetheless, oral communication has its drawbacks. You have far less opportunity to revise your spoken words than to revise your written words. You can't cross out what you just said and start all over. Furthermore, in oral communication, you

FIGURE 2–2
Percentage of Time Spent on Various Channels

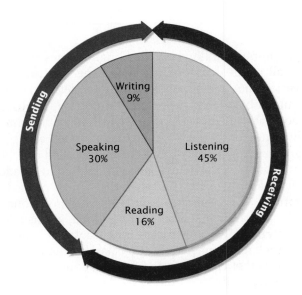

are responsible for more than simply speaking. First, learn how to listen effectively. Second, understand how to interpret the nonverbal signals and attitudes that communicate information without words. And third, recognize the etiquette that is commonly expected of businesspeople.

Look again at Figure 2–2. In addition to underscoring the importance of oral communication, it illustrates that people spend more time *receiving* information than transmitting it. Listening and reading are every bit as important as speaking and writing. Key to the quality of your work and the effectiveness of your professional efforts is your ability to listen well.[27]

By understanding the **listening process**, you begin to understand why oral messages are so often lost. Listening involves five related activities that usually occur in sequence:[28]

1. **Receiving:** Physically hearing the message and taking note of it.

2. **Interpreting:** Assigning meaning to sounds according to your own values, beliefs, ideas, expectations, roles, needs, and personal history.

3. **Remembering:** Storing a message for future reference.

4. **Evaluating:** Applying critical thinking skills to weigh the speaker's remarks.

5. **Responding:** Reacting once you've evaluated the speaker's message, either by giving appropriate feedback or by acting on the speaker's message.

> Listening involves five steps: receiving, interpreting, remembering, evaluating, and responding.

Barriers to Effective Listening

Most people aren't very good listeners. We face so many distractions that we often give speakers less than our full attention. We listen at or below a 25 percent efficiency rate, remember only about half of what's said during a 10-minute conversation, and forget half of that within 48 hours.[29] Furthermore, when questioned about material we've just heard, we are likely to get the facts mixed up. That's because although we tend to listen to words, we don't necessarily listen to the message.[30]

> Most people need to improve their listening skills.

Too many listeners assume that speakers control communication more than listeners do. But no matter how good a speaker is, you decide whether or not to listen. When you decide not to listen, you give up your responsibility in the communication process. If you tune out, become self-involved, or jump to conclusions, you have no way of knowing what you've missed.[31] Because listening requires a mix of physical and mental activities, each activity in the listening process is subject to a variety of barriers:

> Listening barriers prevent effective communication.

- **Physical distraction.** Reception is blocked by environmental noise, impaired hearing, or the speaker's style of delivery or appearance.

- **Differing viewpoints.** Interpretation is blocked by the speaker's frame of reference. Your values, ideas, and personal history may be quite different from the speaker's, so the meaning you assign to the message may differ from what the speaker intended.

- **Poor note taking.** Retention is blocked if you're too distracted to make a mental outline of the speaker's key points or if you try to take extensive notes on facts and figures rather than taking quick notes that summarize key concepts.

- **Prejudgment.** Evaluation is blocked if you can't separate fact from opinion and analyze the evidence. To function in life, people must make some assumptions. However, these assumptions are often incorrect in new situations, and yet defensive listeners view every comment as a personal attack. They distort messages by tuning out anything that doesn't conform to their preconceived ideas or by arguing before they've heard the entire message.

Whether interacting with customers or with fellow employees, people at Harley Davidson's Kansas City plant must know how to listen. Developing good listening skills helps team members overcome distractions so that they can work together successfully and respond to customers' needs.

- **Self-centeredness.** You cannot listen while you are speaking. If someone mentions a problem with conflict between team members, self-centered listeners eagerly relate their own problems with conflict. They trivialize the speaker's concerns by showing that their own difficulties are twice as great. No matter what the subject, they know more than the speaker—and they're determined to prove it.

- **Selective listening.** If you tune out uninteresting speakers or subjects that are dry or difficult, you're easily distracted and your mind wanders. You stay tuned out until you hear a word or phrase that gets your attention once more. Unfortunately, you don't remember what the speaker *actually* said; you remember what you *think* the speaker *probably* said.[32]

- **Speech/thought disparity.** One reason your mind tends to wander is that people think faster than they speak. Most people speak at about 120 to 150 words per minute. However, depending on the subject and the individual, people can process information at 500 to 800 words per minute.[33] This disparity between rate of speech and rate of thought can be used to evaluate what's being said, but some listeners let their minds wander and just tune out.

- **Inappropriate reaction.** Appropriate responses can be blocked if you react to emotional words and fail to keep an open mind. Further, if you fail to give verbal feedback (in a small group), fail to give supportive feedback (applause, laughter, even silence in a larger audience), or fail to take action based on what you've heard, you increase the chances of message distortion.

The important thing is to recognize these counterproductive tendencies as barriers and to work on overcoming them.

Guidelines for Listening Effectively

Effective listening requires a conscious effort and a willing mind. Effective listeners welcome new information and new ideas. Their listening efforts benefit the organization by strengthening relationships, enhancing productivity, alerting the organization to innovation from both internal and external sources, and helping to manage the growing diversity among employees and customers.[34] Effective listening also gives you a personal edge. It increases your impact when you speak, which enhances your performance and leads to raises, promotions, status, and power.[35]

Effective listening helps the listener, the speaker, and the organization.

Listening takes work. You can prepare to listen by reading, discussing, and thinking about a subject to establish your own point of view. Also, be sure to practice by listening to difficult or unfamiliar material that challenges your thinking.[36] In addition, you will listen more effectively by matching your listening style to the speaker's purpose, resisting physical distractions, listening actively, and providing feedback.

To listen effectively, begin by preparing to listen.

Match Listening Style to Speaker Purpose   Various listening styles can help you accommodate the speaker's purpose by adjusting the goal of the situation and the amount of interaction that occurs. To improve your skill, choose the appropriate listening style:[37]

Know which listening style works best in a given situation.

- **Content listening.** When the speaker's goal is simply to convey information, your goal is to understand and retain that message. You may ask questions, but basically information flows from the speaker to you. It doesn't matter whether you agree or disagree, approve or disapprove—only that you understand.[38] When the sales manager reports on how many of your department's products sold last month, you listen for content.

- **Critical listening.** When the speaker's goal is to present an argument, your goal is to understand but also to evaluate that argument on many levels. You need to weigh the logic of the argument, the strength of the evidence, the validity of the conclusions, any implications for you and your organization, the speaker's motives, and whether any relevant points were omitted. Your involvement is more interactive as you try to uncover the speaker's point of view and credibility.[39] When the sales manager presents sales projections for next year, you listen critically to evaluate the validity of the estimates and the implications for your department.

- **Empathic listening.** When the speaker's goal is to share feelings rather than ideas, your goal is to understand the speaker's feelings and needs—to appreciate his or her point of view, even if you don't share that perspective. Empathic listening helps the speaker vent emotions that would prevent a dispassionate approach to a subject. Avoid giving advice, and try not to judge the person's feelings.[40] When the sales manager relates the problems he had with his vehicle while on vacation, you listen empathically.

Fight Physical Distractions   Be physically prepared to listen by knowing your daily cycles of energy. Take listening breaks from time to time so that you don't enter a meeting or other situation when you're too tired to listen. You can rebuild your energy and create a new frame of mind by changing the environment or doing something physical.[41]

> Make sure you're not too tired to listen effectively.

Do whatever you can to reduce external distractions. Turn off radios, cell phones, and televisions. Move to a quiet area, or sit where you can see and hear. Learn to be aware of noises without being distracted by them. In addition, make sure the room doesn't get too cold or too hot. And not least, have pencil and paper handy so that as you think of things you need to do, you can write them down and get them off your mind.[42]

> Do what you can to control potential distractions, whether from extraneous noise or your own busy thoughts.

Listen Actively   Stay alert and focused by searching for something you can use, by finding areas of common interest. Ask yourself questions: What's in it for me? How does this relate to what I already know? What action should I take? Try to take the initiative. Actively pursue what the speaker knows, reaching for the idea being conveyed.[43]

> Listening is not a passive activity. To do it well, you need to take the initiative.

Do your best to keep an open mind. Withhold judgment until you understand the point the speaker is trying to make. Ask questions to clarify meaning, and restate ideas in your own words. But hold your arguments—learn to recognize words that affect you so strongly that you stop listening and start forming your rebuttal.[44]

Try to take meaningful notes. Jot down brief notes that are easy to interpret and easy to review. Sort the facts from the principles, the ideas from examples, and the evidence from opinion.[45]

Capitalize on the speech/thought disparity. Rather than using "bonus time" to daydream, summarize in your head what's been said. Use this time disparity to mentally restate and review the speaker's message. Determine how well points are supported, and monitor the progress of the theme.[46]

Finally, try to overlook the speaker's delivery. Evaluate and be critical of the content, not the speaker. Don't let the speaker's appearance, voice, mannerisms, or personality get in the way of the message. Take a sincere interest. Make an effort to slow your drive to "get things done" so that you can take the time to pay close attention to people and ideas.[47]

✓ CHECKLIST: Improving Your Listening Skills

Prepare to Listen

✓ Read, discuss, and think about the subject.
✓ Practice listening to difficult or unfamiliar material.

Adapt Your Style of Listening to the Speaker's Purpose

✓ Use content listening to understand and retain a message.
✓ Use critical listening to evaluate an argument on many levels.
✓ Use empathic listening to understand a speaker's feelings and needs.

Fight Physical Distractions

✓ Don't try to listen when you're too tired to do so properly.
✓ Close doors.
✓ Turn off radios, televisions, and cell phones.
✓ Move to a quiet location or closer to the speaker.
✓ Monitor room temperature.

✓ Write down competing thoughts to clear your mind for listening.

Listen Actively

✓ Listen for areas of common interest.
✓ Ask yourself what the speaker knows that you don't.
✓ Keep an open mind.
✓ Ask questions that clarify.
✓ Review the speaker's message and determine how well the main points are supported.
✓ Take meaningful notes that are brief and to the point.
✓ Look beyond the speaker's style; critique the message, not the speaker.

Provide Feedback

✓ Let the speaker know you're paying attention.
✓ Maintain eye contact.
✓ Offer appropriate facial expressions.
✓ Keep all feedback and criticism positive; don't externalize impatience or rejection.

To listen better, rely on more than just your ears; use your eyes, your body, and your mind to pay attention and give positive feedback.

Provide Feedback By behaving like an attentive listener, you will listen better. Make eye contact, lean forward, nod frequently, give feedback when appropriate, and remember people's names. Don't interrupt or demonstrate impatience. Avoid making facial grimaces, moving back or away from the speaker, or fidgeting in your chair. Don't gaze around the room or fixedly into space. Don't shuffle papers or wave to someone who enters the room. Your attentiveness will help you listen and will also stimulate the speaker.[48]

For a summary of how to listen effectively, see the "Checklist: Improving Your Listening Skills." Furthermore, don't forget that a large part of listening effectively is interpreting all the nonverbal cues that speakers and listeners send each other. These often-unconscious signals tell the careful observer a lot.

IMPROVING YOUR NONVERBAL COMMUNICATION

Nonverbal communication includes all the cues, gestures, facial expressions, spatial relationships, and attitudes that enable people to communicate without words. Nonverbal communication differs from verbal communication in terms of intent and spontaneity. You generally plan your words. When you say, "Please get back to me on that order by Friday," you have a conscious purpose; you think about the message, if only for a moment. However, when you communicate nonverbally, you sometimes do so unconsciously. You don't mean to raise an eyebrow or to blush. Those unconscious actions come naturally, and they can modify, reinforce, or distort any message you try to communicate. Similarly, you may be unaware that a person's posture or tone is affecting how you interpret what he or she is saying.[49]

Actions really do speak louder than words. However, no one behavior can be equated with any single meaning. A gesture that means one thing in one context may mean something entirely different in another context. Nonverbal communication must always be carefully evaluated with respect to the situation in which it occurs.[50]

Types of Nonverbal Communication

According to one estimate, there are more than 700,000 forms of nonverbal communication.[51] For discussion purposes, however, these forms can be grouped into the following general categories: facial expression, gesture and posture, vocal characteristics, personal appearance, touching behavior, and use of time and space.

Facial Expression   Your face is the primary site for expressing your emotions; it reveals both the type and the intensity of your feelings.[52] Your eyes are especially effective for indicating attention and interest, influencing others, regulating interaction, and establishing dominance. In fact, eye contact is so important in the United States that even when your words send a positive message, averting your gaze can lead your audience to perceive a negative one.[53] Of course, the interpretation of facial expressions, and of all nonverbal signals, varies from culture to culture (as discussed in Chapter 3). Moreover, people sometimes manipulate their expressions to simulate an emotion they do not feel or to mask their true feelings.

> The face, especially the eyes, commands particular attention as a source of nonverbal messages.

Gesture and Posture   By moving your body, you can express both specific and general messages, some voluntary and some involuntary. Many gestures—a wave of the hand, for example—have a specific and intentional meaning, such as "hello" or "good-bye." Other types of body movement are unintentional and express a more general message. Slouching, leaning forward, fidgeting, and walking briskly are all unconscious signals that reveal whether you feel confident or nervous, friendly or hostile, assertive or passive, powerful or powerless.

> Body language and tone of voice reveal a lot about a person's emotions and attitudes.

Vocal Characteristics   Like body language, your voice carries both intentional and unintentional messages. On a conscious level, you can use your voice to create various impressions. Consider the sentence "What have you been up to?" If you repeat that question four or five times, changing your tone of voice and stressing various words, you can convey quite different messages. However, your vocal characteristics also reveal many things of which you are unaware. The tone and volume of your voice, your accent and speaking pace, and all the little *um*'s and *ah*'s that creep into your speech say a lot about who you are, your relationship with the audience, and the emotions underlying your words.

Personal Appearance   People respond to others on the basis of their physical appearance. Because you see yourself as others see you, their expectations are often a self-fulfilling prophecy; that is, when people think you're capable and attractive, you feel good about yourself, and that feeling affects your behavior, which in turn affects other people's perceptions of you. Although an individual's body type and facial features impose limitations, most people are able to control their attractiveness to some degree. Grooming, clothing, accessories, "style"—all modify a person's appearance. If your goal is to make a good impression, adopt the style of the people you want to impress. (For specific tips, see "Improving your Business Etiquette" later in this chapter.)

> Physical appearance and personal style contribute to one's identity.

Touching Behavior   Touch is an important way to convey warmth, comfort, and reassurance. Perhaps because it implies intimacy, touching behavior is governed by relatively strict customs that establish who can touch whom and how in various circumstances. The accepted norms vary, depending on the gender, age, relative status,

> Touching behavior depends on many variables.

and cultural background of the persons involved. In business situations, touching suggests dominance, so a higher-status person is more likely to touch a lower-status person than the other way around. Touching has become controversial, however, because it can sometimes be interpreted as sexual harassment.

Use of Time and Space   Like touch, time and space can be used to assert authority. Some people demonstrate their importance by making other people wait; others show respect by being on time. People can also assert their status by occupying the best space. In U.S. companies, the chief executive usually has the corner office and the prettiest view. Apart from serving as a symbol of status, space can determine how comfortable people feel talking with each other. When others stand too close or too far away, we are likely to feel ill at ease. Again, attitudes toward punctuality and comfort zones vary from culture to culture (see Chapter 3).

Punctuality and comfort zones vary by culture and authority.

Functions of Nonverbal Communication

Nonverbal communication is more reliable and more efficient than verbal communication.

Nonverbal communication is efficient. You can transmit a nonverbal message without even thinking about it, and your audience can register the meaning unconsciously. At the same time, when you have a conscious purpose, you can often achieve it more economically with a gesture than with words. A wave of the hand, a wink, a pat on the back—all are streamlined expressions of thought. However, nonverbal communication usually blends with speech to carry part of the message—to augment, reinforce, and clarify that message:[54]

When combined with speech, nonverbal communication can reinforce or negate the message, substitute meaning, intensify the message, and regulate conversational give and take.

- Reinforcement occurs when nonverbal and verbal messages complement each other.

- Negation occurs when nonverbal and verbal messages contradict each other (in which case the nonverbal message is usually the more accurate indicator of meaning).

- Substitution occurs when nonverbal actions replace verbal messages.

- Intensification occurs when nonverbal actions accentuate the verbal message (such as slowing your speech to stress the importance of your statement or clutching your hair when you say, "I'm so angry I could pull my hair out").

- Regulation occurs when nonverbal cues are used to modulate conversational turn taking (using eye contact, posture, gestures, and voice to indicate we are finished speaking or who should talk next).

People believe nonverbal signals more than words.

Detecting the Truth   Good communicators recognize the value of nonverbal communication and use it to maximize the effectiveness of their messages. If a person says one thing but transmits a conflicting message nonverbally, listeners almost invariably believe the nonverbal signal.[55] Chances are, if you can read other people's nonverbal messages correctly, you can interpret their underlying attitudes and intentions and respond appropriately.

Words are relatively easy to control; body language, facial expressions, and vocal characteristics are not. In fact, most people can deceive others much more easily with words than they can with their bodies. Because nonverbal communication is so reliable, people generally have more faith in nonverbal cues than they do in verbal messages.

Certain signs can clarify whether someone is telling the truth or lying.

To tell whether someone is lying, look for the following telltale signs:[56]

- **Lengthy response time.** The longer the time between the end of a question and the start of a reply, the less likely a speaker is telling the truth.

- **Distancing.** When a speaker talks in the abstract and avoids the word *I* (perhaps saying "One believes," rather than "I believe . . . "), that person is probably not telling the truth.

- **Uneven speech.** Stuttering may indicate the speaker is trying to think through the lie, or suddenly talking quickly may indicate the speaker is attempting to make a sensitive subject appear less significant.

- **Gap filling.** A speaker who is too eager to fill in the gaps of conversation may feel that such silences signify disbelief on the part of the listener.

- **Raised pitch.** If a speaker's voice is raised unnaturally at the end of a reply (lifted as if asking a question, rather than dropping in pitch), that person may not be telling the truth.

- **Squirming.** If a speaker shifts around in his or her seat too much, that person may not be telling the truth.

- **Too much (or too little) eye contact.** Someone who is lying may not be able to look you in the eye or may overcompensate by looking you straight in the eyes too long.

- **Micro-expressions.** Someone who registers flickers of surprise, hurt, or anger may not be telling the truth.

- **Increased comfort gestures.** Self-touching (particularly around the nose and mouth) may indicate the speaker is being less than truthful.

By paying attention to these nonverbal cues, you can detect deception or affirm a speaker's honesty.

Maximizing Your Credibility   When communicating, you can increase your own credibility by paying close attention to your nonverbal cues and trying not to give out conflicting signals. Just be as honest as possible in communicating your sincerity, feelings, and emotions. In the United States, certain actions will attest to your credibility:[57]

> In addition to being honest and sincere, you can send nonverbal messages that increase your credibility.

- **Eye behavior.** Maintain direct, but not continuous, eye contact. Don't look down before responding to a question. And be careful not to exhibit shifty eyes. Don't look away from the other person, keep your eyes downcast, or blink excessively.

- **Gestures.** When using gestures to emphasize points or convey the intensity of your feelings, keep them spontaneous, unrehearsed, and relaxed. Keep your hands and elbows away from your body, and avoid hand-to-face gestures, throat clearing, fidgeting, and tugging at clothing. Try to avoid visible perspiration on your face and body. Don't lick your lips, wring your hands, tap your fingers, or smile out of context.

- **Posture.** Assume an open and relaxed posture. Walk confidently, with grace and ease. Stand straight, with both feet on the floor, and sit straight in your chair without slouching. Hold your head level, and keep your chin up. Shift your posture while communicating; lean forward and smile as you begin to answer a question. Avoid keeping your body rigid, crossing your arms and legs, or exhibiting general body tension.

- **Voice.** Strive for a conversational style, while speaking at a moderately fast rate. Use appropriate variation in pitch, rate, and volume. Avoid speaking in a monotone. Avoid sounding flat, tense, or nasal. Try not to speak at an excessive rate, and avoid frequent, lengthy pauses. Do your best to avoid *ah's* or *um's*, repeating words, interrupting or pausing mid-sentence, omitting parts of words, and stuttering.

To review what you can do to improve your nonverbal skills, see the "Checklist: Improving Nonverbal Communication Skills."

✓ CHECKLIST: Improving Nonverbal Communication Skills

Interpret Nonverbal Signals Carefully

✓ When what a person says conflicts with how that person moves, looks, or acts, believe the nonverbal signal.

✓ Learn to recognize the telltale signs that indicate a person is not telling the truth.

✓ Be aware that people may give false nonverbal cues.

✓ Remember, few gestures convey meaning in and of themselves.

✓ Consider nonverbal signals in the context of situation and culture.

Pay Close Attention to the Nonverbal Signals You Send

✓ Avoid giving conflicting signals.

✓ Try to be as honest as possible in communicating your emotions.

✓ Smile genuinely. (Faking a smile is obvious to observers.)

✓ Maintain the eye contact your audience expects.

✓ Be aware of your posture and of the gestures you use.

✓ Try to use appropriate vocal signals while minimizing unintentional messages.

✓ Imitate the appearance of the people you want to impress.

✓ Respect your audience's comfort zone.

✓ Adopt a handshake that matches your personality and intention.

✓ Be aware of varying attitudes toward time.

✓ Use touch only when appropriate.

IMPROVING YOUR BUSINESS ETIQUETTE

Knowing the conventions of behavior that are expected in the business world helps you succeed.

Etiquette is knowing how to act in a given situation—how to behave properly. Knowing how to behave and how to interact with people in business will help you appear polished, professional, and confident.[58] Such knowledge helps you put others at ease so that they are comfortable enough to do business with you.[59] Much of the business etiquette you'll need to master involves the nonverbal cues just discussed. The rest of this chapter focuses on business etiquette with regard to workplace appearance, face-to-face interactions, and telephone interactions.

Workplace Appearance

Your dress affects the way you are perceived by businesspeople.

Being properly dressed and groomed is one way of showing respect and consideration for your organization and for the people you interact with. Pay attention to the style of dress where you work, and adjust your wardrobe to match. Your wardrobe suggests certain things about you (see Table 2–2):[60]

- **The smooth and finished look.** At the very least, you want your wardrobe to say that you're calm, cool, collected, capable, and probably likable.

- **The elegant and refined look.** Additional wardrobe choices suggest that you have power and that you're both confident and efficient.

- **The crisp and starchy look.** Looking as if you are "all business" says that you won't let anyone down and that you know how to set and reach goals.

- **The up-to-the-minute, trendy look.** Bolder colors and a few trendy items say that you're energetic, open to new ideas, ready to accept change, and eager to contribute.

Even in the same organization, dress may differ from one department to another. In a more casual organization, for example, people in research and development might wear jeans and T-shirts while people in the production department might wear collared shirts tucked into their jeans and belts.[61]

CHOOSING YOUR WARDROBE | Table 2–2

1 *Smooth and Finished (Start with this)*	**2** *Elegant and Refined (To column 1, add this)*	**3** *Crisp and Starchy (To column 2, add this)*	**4** *Up-to-the-Minute Trendy (To column 3, add this)*
1. Wear well-tailored clothing that fits well.	1. Choose form-fitting clothing—not swinging or flowing fabrics, frills, or fussy trimmings.	1. Wear blouses or shirts that are or appear starched.	1. Add trendy clothing items to your wardrobe often.
2. Keep buttons, zippers, and hemlines in good repair.	2. Choose muted tones and soft colors or classics, such as the dark blue suit or the basic black dress.	2. Choose closed top-button shirts or button-down shirt collars, higher-neckline blouses, long sleeves with French cuffs and cuff links.	2. Choose bold colors (but sparingly so that you won't appear garish).
3. Keep shoes shined and in good condition.	3. Choose jewelry that hints at a heritage (a string of pearls or diamond cuff links).	3. Wear creased trousers or longer skirt hemlines.	3. Add pizzazz with trendy jewelry and hairstyles.
4. Make sure the fabrics you wear are clean, are carefully pressed, and do not wrinkle easily.		4. Wear jackets that complement an outfit and lend an air of formality to your appearance. Avoid jackets with more than two tones—one color should dominate.	
5. Choose colors that flatter your height, weight, skin tone, and style.			

Don't neglect accessories. Select jewelry that is appropriate to your working environment, and make sure handbags, wallets, briefcases, and belts are all in good repair. In fact, be careful to dispose of worn or shabby clothing promptly. Also be prompt about cleaning and pressing. Select a good dry cleaner, and have your garments cleaned as often as required to keep everything fresh.[62]

In addition to clothing, choice and care of accessories reflect on your image.

Besides your clothing, personal grooming affects your workplace appearance. Pay close attention to cleanliness. Some health problems can cause unexpected body odors; also, be aware of fragrances that linger from the products you use (such as perfumed soaps, colognes, shampoos, after-shave lotions). Shampoo your hair frequently, keep your hands and nails neatly manicured, routinely use mouthwash and deodorant, and make regular trips to the barber or hairdresser.[63] Try to follow company policy regarding hairstyle. Policies in more conservative industries such as banking and finance may dictate shoulder-length or shorter hair for women and off-the-neck styles for men. You may find more liberal policies in less conservative organizations.[64]

Personal grooming also affects the way people think of you.

To be as presentable on the job as possible, keep some personal supplies on hand both at home and at work:[65]

- Comb and brush
- Nail file and clippers
- Hand cream
- Toothbrush and toothpaste

- Makeup/shaving kit

- Nail polish/lacquer

- Hair spray

- Extra socks or hosiery

- Lint brush

- Facial tissue

- Premoistened towelettes

- Breath mints

- Safety pins

- Small sewing kit

Face-to-Face Interactions

Your interactions with other people have a sizable impact on your success in business, no matter what your industry or field. Consider, for example, such common interactions as smiling, shaking hands, making introductions, and sharing meals.

A genuine smile affects you as well as other people.

Smiling   When you smile, do so genuinely. A fake smile is obvious because the timing is off and the expression fails to involve all the facial muscles that a genuine smile would.[66] Repeated false smiling may earn you the reputation of being a phony. Plus, if you smile too long, you make others uncomfortable, because they feel that you're not focused on the present. However, certain occasions require smiling:[67]

- **When you are introduced to someone.** Smiling is courteous and suggests that you are receptive.

- **When you are feeling uncomfortable or out of place.** Smiling masks your concerns, and your confidence level will rise quickly (always be careful that your smile is not a false one).

- **When you give or receive a compliment.** Smiling punctuates your tribute when you give praise. If you're receiving praise, smiling augments the other person's position. Even if you feel embarrassed or undeserving, don't diminish the praise-giver by revealing those feelings.

- **When you applaud someone.** Smiling is the courteous, gracious thing to do.

Shaking hands correctly can get you started in business favorably.

Shaking Hands   In the United States and Canada, most business greetings include a handshake. Other cultures may have varying approaches or completely different customs. In U.S. and Canadian cultures, extend your hand to greet business associates, regardless of gender. When seated, rise from your chair if you are physically able, and lean into the handshake. Pulling away suggests that something is wrong (people may pull away because of powerful perfume, tobacco residue on breath or clothing, or body odor). Make eye contact, smile, and nod your head to indicate that the person has your full attention. Never extend your hand while turning your head to speak to someone else.[68]

Convey confidence, assurance, interest, and respect by using a firm handshake, without squeezing too hard. Use your right hand. Your hand should touch the other person's web to web, between thumb and forefinger. Thumbs should point upward as you shake hands vertically and face one another squarely. Although your handshake should be brief, it should last long enough for both persons to speak their names and a few words of greeting.[69]

Making Introductions   The whole purpose of an introduction is to give people an opportunity to establish a connection, to get to know one another. When introducing yourself to a stranger, include a short, matter-of-fact description of your role, followed by a question about your new acquaintance. When introducing two other people, weave appropriate information into the introduction to help the individuals ease into a comfortable conversation. Try suggesting a subject of mutual interest. And remember, first and last names are mandatory. The people you're introducing need to know what to call each other and how to find each other later. You might say, "Henry Johnson, I would like you to meet Meredith Tucker, our new team member. Ms. Tucker, this is Mr. Johnson, senior manager at Lynco Systems. Ms. Tucker recently toured Yellowstone on a four-day hike. Mr. Johnson just returned from sabbatical in London."[70]

> Introductions involve more than a name.

When making introductions, gender is not a factor in who is introduced to whom; for instance, you should mention the name of the older, more senior person first. Here are some examples of preferred forms of introduction:[71]

> Introduce the person of lesser status to the person of greater status.

- Introduce younger to older ("Mr. *Older Executive*, I would like you to meet Mr. *Younger Executive*.")

- Introduce company peer to a peer in another company ("Sam Locker, I'd like to introduce Kelly Martin, our head of engineering. Kelly, this is Sam from Brent & Moran.")

- Introduce junior executive to senior executive ("Ms. *Senior Executive*, I would like to introduce Mr. *Junior Executive*.")

- Introduce fellow executive to a client or customer ("Mrs. Claire Waters, I'd like you to meet Kelly Martin, our head of engineering. Kelly, this is Mrs. Waters, one of our newest clients.")

When you're introduced to someone, take note of the person's name and use it as soon as possible. Try connecting the name with something common to you—perhaps the name is the same as a school friend or a favorite movie character. Knowing and using someone's name is a compliment, and doing so will be useful if you need to contact or refer to this person in the future.[72]

Sharing Meals   Business is often conducted over a meal. In fact, more than half of all business is finalized at the dining table.[73] Knowing a bit about accepted manners will help you appear professional and polished when sharing meals with business associates.

First, save the wine until after the business is concluded. Effective communication is difficult enough with a clear head. Leave business papers either under your chair or under the table until entrée plates have been removed. The business part of the dinner doesn't usually begin until then. Also, leave your cell phone turned off and out of sight. If you absolutely need to accept an important call, explain that to people when you sit down. Then when the phone rings, excuse yourself from the table and keep your conversation private and brief.

> During business meals, leave the wine until business is finished, don't discuss business until after the entrée plates are removed, and leave your cell phone turned off and out of sight.

In meal conversations, be sure to avoid all the following:[74]

- Getting too personal

- Complaining about business colleagues

- Finishing others' sentences

- Interrupting the conversation

- Using profanity or telling inappropriate jokes

- Starting the business conversation before the conclusion of the entrée

- Wearing inappropriate clothing

- Coughing without covering your mouth

- Burping

- Yawning

- Getting out a mirror at the table

Telephone Interactions

Just as important as how you communicate face-to-face is how you communicate using the telephone and voice mail. In fact, some experts estimate that 95 percent of most companies' daily contacts come via the telephone.[75]

Use your attitude and voice to establish your professionalism over the phone.

Over the phone, your communication loses a great deal of the visual, nonverbal richness that accompanies face-to-face conversations. Even so, your attitude and tone of voice can convey your confidence and professionalism effectively, impressing others with your eagerness to help, your willingness to listen, and your ability to communicate clearly. For effective phone conversations, try to do the following:[76]

- Use frequent verbal responses that show you're listening ("Oh yes," "I see," "That's right").

- Increase your volume just slightly to convey your confidence.

- Vary your pitch and inflection.

- Speak a bit more quickly, although always clearly and slowly enough for people to understand what you're saying.

Receiving Phone Calls   When people call your place of business, they want to quickly and easily reach someone who can help them. They don't want to be passed from department to department, to be put on hold while their party finishes with someone else, or to talk with someone who lacks the knowledge or the ability to get them the information or the action they need.

If you answer the phone for someone who is unable to take the call right away, note the caller's name, phone number, and a brief but accurate message—assuring the caller that the appropriate person will get the message and return the call. Likewise, if you'll be away from your telephone for any length of time, forward your calls so that anyone calling you won't have to be transferred again and again.[77]

To be as effective as possible when receiving calls, observe the following helpful tips:[78]

- **Answer promptly and with a smile.** Answer within two or three rings, and smile so that you sound friendly and positive.

When taking orders over the phone at Padilla's Florist Shop, Rosa Salazar sounds confident and professional. She listens carefully to verify what her customer wants and when the order is needed. Then she verbally confirms everything to make sure that she and her customer agree on the specifics of the order.

- **Identify yourself.** Announce the company name, the department, and your own name in a friendly and professional manner.

- **Establish the needs of your caller.** Immediately ask, "How may I help you?" If you know the caller's name, use it. Don't interrupt with pointless questions.

- **Be positive.** If you can, answer callers' questions promptly and efficiently; if you can't help, tell them what you can do for them.

- **Take complete, accurate messages.** Confirm names, telephone and fax numbers, e-mail addresses, and dates. Always take a return number, even if the caller says it isn't necessary. And don't forget to write neatly so that your message can be deciphered.

- **Explain what you are doing.** If you absolutely must put a caller on hold briefly or transfer the call, explain what you are doing and why. If it's necessary to hunt for information or to take another call, offer to call back.

> Give callers the information or action they need, even if that simply means taking an accurate message and making sure it gets to the right person.

When you answer your cell phone in public, consider those around you. Otherwise, you send dangerous messages: (1) that people around you aren't as important as your call and (2) that you don't respect your caller's privacy. Just because you turn your back to the crowd or cover your mouth, don't assume that you're practicing acceptable etiquette. Excuse yourself and move to someplace both quiet and private.[79]

Making Phone Calls The key to making effective telephone calls is planning. Know precisely why you're calling and exactly what you need from the person you're calling. To make effective phone calls, practice the following tips:[80]

> Plan the calls you make, and make them from a quiet location.

- **Be ready before you call.** Plan how you will handle the conversation and any possible outcomes. Have at your fingertips all necessary materials: your outline of what you'll say, a pad for additional notes, relevant account numbers, electronic files, cost figures, and so on.

- **Schedule the call.** Decide ahead of time when you'll call, based on your own readiness, the time of day, and whether your contact is in a different time zone. Don't call first thing in the morning when people are answering mail or last thing at night when they're heading home.

- **Eliminate distractions.** Don't call from a place where background noise will interfere with your concentration and your ability to hear and be heard. Also, don't tap a pencil, shuffle papers, or open and close desk drawers.

- **Make a clear, comprehensive introduction.** Immediately identify the person you're calling, give your name and organization, briefly describe why you're calling, and greet the person. Always ask: "Is this a good time to talk briefly, or should I call you back?"

- **Don't take up too much time.** Speak quickly and clearly, and get right to the point of the call.

- **Maintain audience focus throughout the call.** Ask questions and give clear answers so that both of you understand the message and can decide together what action is needed.

- **Close in a friendly, positive manner.** Double-check all vital information by summarizing what you've discussed. Check to see that you both agree on any action that either party will take, and thank the other person for his or her time. If you promise to phone back, make sure you do.

Be clear and concise when leaving voice-mail messages.

Using Voice Mail Voice mail lets you send, store, and retrieve verbal messages. It is most effective for short, unambiguous messages, and it can be used to replace short memos and phone calls that need no response. Before recording your outgoing greeting for your own voice-mail system, organize your thoughts.[81] Make your message accurate and concise:[82]

- **Be brief.** Your greeting should take no longer than 30 seconds.

- **Be accurate.** Specifically state what callers should do.

- **Sound professional.** Make sure your voice is businesslike but cheerful.

- **Keep your callers in mind.** Encourage callers to leave detailed messages, and remind them to leave a phone number.

- **Make options logical and helpful.** Limit menu selections to three or four, make one of those options an easy way to reach a live operator.

- **Keep your personal greeting current.** Update your greetings to reflect your schedule and leave special announcements if you'll be away from your desk for an extended period.

- **Respond promptly.** Check your voice mail messages regularly and return all necessary calls within 24 hours.

When you leave a message on someone else's voice-mail system, think about your message in advance, and plan it carefully. Keep in mind the following tips:[83]

- **Keep the message simple.** Leave your name, number, and purpose for calling. Designate a specific time when you can be reached (or arrange a specific time to call the person back). Repeat your name and phone number at the end of the message.

- **Sound professional.** Give your message a headline so that the listener can quickly judge its priority. Avoid background noise, and before using a cell phone, consider the effect of a bad connection or service interruption.

- **Avoid personal messages.** Remember that someone else may be in the room when your message is played back.

- **Replay your message before leaving the system.** Use this option whenever available to listen to your message objectively and make sure it is clear.

- **Don't leave multiple, repetitious messages.** Rather than a series of messages with the same information, simply leave one detailed message and follow that up with a fax or an e-mail.

- **Never hide behind voice mail.** Don't use voice mail to escape unpleasant encounters, and make sure to give praise in person, not on an answering system.[84]

On the Job:

SOLVING COMMUNICATION DILEMMAS AT AMERICAN EXPRESS

At American Express, David House does everything he can to encourage all employees in his division to work together as a team. You are the Northwest regional sales manager for American Express Worldwide Establishment Services. You must not only promote the team concept but also serve as team leader on special projects that involve sales managers throughout the country. Choose the best alternatives for handling the following situations, and be prepared to explain why your choice is best.

1. Some employees of American Express Worldwide Establishment Services have been pushing the company to adopt a corporate statement of goals. In response, David House has decided to call an executive meeting. Which purpose should House focus on during the meeting?

   a. To find out about competitors' goals and determine whether they are appropriate for American Express

   b. To inform top managers of his intention to evaluate all employees on the basis of their contributions to corporate goals

   c. To decide which managers/employees should be asked to come to a meeting about corporate goals

   d. To reach an agreement about the company's primary corporate goals

2. As leader of a team of regional sales managers, you schedule a team meeting to discuss new methods of inspiring and motivating sales representatives to achieve their quarterly sales goals. During the meeting, one regional sales manager disagrees with every suggestion offered by team members, often reacting with a sneer on his face and a belligerent tone of voice. Which of the following strategies is the best way to overcome the manager's resistance?

   a. Ignore his remarks. Keep the meeting on track and avoid destructive confrontations by asking for input from other team members.

   b. Directly confront the sales manager's concerns. Point out the flaws in his arguments, and offer support for the opinions of other team members.

   c. Remain calm and try to understand his point of view. Ask him to clarify his points, and solicit his suggestions for motivating sales representatives.

   d. Politely acknowledge his opinions, then repeat the most valid suggestions offered by other team members in a convincing manner.

3. David House has asked you and four other employees to find solutions to the lack of sufficient office space for the growing number of employees in the Northwest region. As leader, you schedule team meetings on Thursday afternoons for five weeks to address the problem. After two meetings with your co-workers, you notice that everyone is making vital

contributions to the group's efforts—except Jane. During the meetings, she displays very poor listening skills. She often jumps ahead of the topic or interrupts a speaker's train of thought. At other times, she doodles on her notepad instead of taking constructive notes. And she remains silent after team members deliver lengthy reports about possible solutions to the office space problem. What can you do as team leader to help Jane improve her listening skills?

   a. Ask Jane to take extensive notes during each meeting. The process of taking detailed notes will improve her concentration and force her to listen more carefully to team members. After the meeting, she can use her notes as a reference to clarify any questions about team decisions or the nature of assignments to individual team members.

   b. Suggest that Jane mentally summarize the speaker's ideas—or verbally rephrase the ideas in her own words—during the meeting. With some practice, Jane should be able to focus on the topics under discussion and block out distracting thoughts.

   c. Schedule future team meetings for Thursday mornings instead of Thursday afternoons. After devoting most of the workday to her regular duties, Jane may be feeling tired or sluggish by the time your team meeting rolls around.

   d. Prepare a detailed, written summary of each meeting. The summary will clarify any points that Jane may have missed during the meeting and provide her with a complete reference of team decisions and assignments.

4. The manager of the Southeast region realizes his communication skills are important for several reasons: He holds primary responsibility for successful communication in the region; he needs to communicate with the sales representatives who report to him; and his style sets an example for other employees in the region. He asks you to sit in on face-to-face meetings for several days to observe his nonverbal messages. You witness four habits. Which of the following habits do you think is the most negative?

   a. He rarely comes out from behind his massive desk when meeting people; at one point, he offered a congratulatory handshake to a sales representative, and the sales rep had to lean way over his desk just to reach him.

   b. When a sales rep hands him a report and then sits down to discuss it, he alternates between making eye contact and making notes on the report.

   c. He is consistently pleasant, even if the person he is meeting is delivering bad news.

   d. He interrupts meetings to answer the phone, rather than letting an assistant get the phone; then he apologizes to visitors for the interruption.[85]

Learning Objectives Checkup

To assess your understanding of the principles in this chapter, read each learning objective and study the accompanying exercises. For fill-in items, write the missing text in the blank provided; for multiple choice items, circle the letter of the correct answer. You can check your responses against the answer key on page AK-1.

Objective 2.1: Highlight the advantages and disadvantages of working in teams.

1. Which of the following is a disadvantage of working in teams?
   a. The diversity of views that members bring to the team
   b. The pooling of information and knowledge
   c. The tendency toward groupthink
   d. A shared sense of purpose and mutual accountability
2. Which of the following is an advantage of working in teams?
   a. The hidden agendas held by some team members
   b. Reduced performance levels when compared to what the individual team members might accomplish
   c. The high cost of coordinating group activities
   d. The free-ride attitude that can be held by some team members

Objective 2.2: Identify the characteristics of effective teams.

3. Which of the following is *not* a characteristic of effective teams?
   a. They have a clear sense of purpose.
   b. They encourage original thinking.
   c. They stay focused on key issues.
   d. They reach decisions quickly and easily through democratic voting.

Objective 2.3: Explain how you can improve meeting productivity through preparation, leadership, and participation.

4. A meeting agenda
   a. Is only necessary for the most important, formal meetings
   b. Should never be veered from
   c. Should be distributed to participants several days in advance
   d. Can be substituted verbatim for meeting minutes to save duplication of effort
5. An effective meeting leader
   a. Encourages everyone to participate
   b. Dispenses with the formality of parliamentary procedure
   c. Sits back and lets the participants take charge of the discussion
   d. Does all of the above

Objective 2.4: Describe three barriers that interfere with the listening process and four guidelines for improving your listening.

6. Most people listen at or below a _____ percent efficiency rate.
   a. 10
   b. 25
   c. 50
   d. 75

7. Which of the following is *not* a common barrier to effective listening?
   a. Physical distractions, such as environmental noise
   b. Self-centeredness on the part of the listener
   c. Failure to keep an open mind
   d. Trying to listen too closely to what the speaker is saying
8. An example of "selective listening" would be
   a. Viewing everything the speaker says as a personal attack
   b. Taking notes on only the main points the speaker makes
   c. Tuning the speaker out until he or she says a word or phrase that recaptures your attention
   d. Paying attention only to the way the speaker talks rather than what the speaker is saying
9. When you use critical listening, you focus on
   a. Trying to understand and retain the information being conveyed by the speaker
   b. Evaluating the speaker's arguments
   c. Trying to understand the speaker's feelings and needs
   d. All of the above
10. A good way to improve your listening is to
    a. Try to relate the speaker's material to your own interests and look for information useful to you
    b. Put away your pen and notepad, since note-taking serves as a distraction
    c. Concentrate on the person's speech patterns and mannerisms
    d. Formulate mental arguments to counteract the speaker's statements

Objective 2.5: Briefly describe six categories of nonverbal communication.

11. Your _____ are especially effective for indicating attention and interest, influencing others, and establishing dominance.
12. Most people are able to control their physical _____ to some degree and therefore others' perceptions of what they are like.
13. In business situations, touching is used to indicate _____ of a higher-status person in relation to a lower-status person.

Objective 2.6: Clarify the functions of nonverbal communication.

14. A telltale sign that someone might be lying is when he or she
    a. Speaks in a monotone
    b. Engages in too little or too much eye contact
    c. Leaves long, uncomfortable gaps in the conversation without jumping in with something to say
    d. Uses the pronoun *I* excessively
15. You can improve your nonverbal communications by
    a. Maintaining direct, but not continuous eye contact
    b. Crossing your arms whenever you speak
    c. Speaking as quickly as possible
    d. Keeping your lips moist by licking them periodically

Objective 2.7: List three categories of business etiquette and give brief examples of each.

16. Which of the following is *not* recommended for maintaining an appropriate workplace appearance?
    a. Follow company policy regarding hairstyle.
    b. Keep a set of personal grooming supplies on hand at work.
    c. Wear clothing that is appropriate to the department you work in, as well as to your company.
    d. Express your individuality through distinctive scents, trendy clothing, and flashy accessories.
17. Which of the following would be the most appropriate way to introduce your new assistant, Cheryl Wolff, to your boss, Jason Henderson?
    a. "Cheryl, I'd like you to meet our boss, Mr. Henderson."
    b. "Ms. Wolff, I'd like you to meet Jason Henderson, head of the department."
    c. "Jason, I'd like you to meet my new assistant, Cheryl."
    d. "Mr. Henderson, I'd like you to meet my new assistant, Cheryl Wolff."
18. If you receive a cell phone call while you are in public with business associates, the most appropriate thing to do is to
    a. Lower your voice so that the others with you will find it more difficult to overhear your conversation
    b. Turn your back to the crowd and cover your mouth as you talk
    c. Excuse yourself and move away to someplace quiet and private
    d. Say, "I told you not to call me while I'm with important people," wink at the others in your party, then take the call

Apply Your Knowledge

1. How can nonverbal communication help you run a meeting? How can it help you call a meeting to order, emphasize important topics, show approval, express reservations, regulate the flow of conversation, and invite a colleague to continue with a comment?
2. Whenever your boss asks for feedback, she blasts anyone offering criticism, which causes people to agree with everything she says. You want to talk to her about it, but what should you say? List some of the points you want to make when you discuss this issue with your boss.
3. Is conflict in a team good or bad? Explain your answer.
4. You are attending a presentation in the east conference room. Unfortunately, construction on the new office wing is going on right next door, so the air conditioning is off in this room, and it's getting hot. When the speaker tried to open the windows, the noise from the neighboring construction made it impossible to hear, so she closed them again. As you fight off the heat and growing sleepiness, you know you're missing important information. What can you do?
5. **Ethical Choices** On Tuesday, you had a business dinner with Joe Amaya whose public relations company wanted to help American Express improve its image throughout the Northwest. Joe's ideas sounded promising, but the man made a negative impression on you. Although you met at an expensive restaurant, he wore no jacket or tie. He had a good, firm handshake, but his after-shave was overpowering. He spoke quietly and smiled throughout the meal, even while eating. He carried his cell phone in his shirt pocket, and each time it rang, he said, "Please excuse me," and then conducted his calls right there at the table. One call was so intense that you excused yourself and went to the restroom. Now, on Wednesday morning, you must inform Joe of your decision. Can you reject Joe's company purely on the basis of his behavior? Explain.

Practice Your Knowledge

DOCUMENT FOR ANALYSIS

A project leader has made notes about covering the following items at the quarterly budget meeting. Prepare a formal agenda by putting these items into a logical order and rewriting, where necessary, to give phrases a more consistent sound.

- Budget Committee Meeting to be held on December 12, 2003, at 9:30 A.M.
- I will call the meeting to order.
- Site director's report: A closer look at cost overruns on Greentree site.
- The group will review and approve the minutes from last quarter's meeting.
- I will ask the finance director to report on actual versus projected quarterly revenues and expenses.
- I will distribute copies of the overall divisional budget and announce the date of the next budget meeting.
- Discussion: How can we do a better job of anticipating and preventing cost overruns?
- Meeting will take place in Conference Room 3.
- What additional budget issues must be considered during this quarter?

Exercises

For live links to all websites discussed in this chapter, visit this text's website at www.prenhall.com/thill. Just log on, select Chapter 2, and click on "Student Resources." Locate the page or the URL related to the material in the text. For the "Learning More on the Web" exercises, you'll also find navigational directions. Click on the live link to the site.

2.1 **Teamwork** With a classmate, attend a local community or campus meeting where you can observe group discussion as well as voting or other group action. Take notes individually during the meeting and then work together to answer the following questions.
  a. What is your evaluation of this meeting? In your answer, consider (1) the leader's ability to articulate the meeting's goals clearly, (2) the leader's ability to engage members in a meaningful discussion, (3) the group's dynamics, and (4) the group's listening skills.
  b. How did group members make decisions? Did they vote? Did they reach decisions by consensus? Did the naysayers get an opportunity to voice their objections?
  c. How well did the individual participants listen? How could you tell?
  d. Did any participants change their expressed views or their votes during the meeting? Why might that have happened?
  e. Did you observe any of the communication barriers discussed in Chapter 1? Identify them.

  f. Compare the notes you took during the meeting with those of your classmate. What differences do you notice? How do you account for these differences?

2.2 **Team Development: Resolving Conflict** Describe a recent conflict you had with a team member at work or at school, and explain how you resolved it. Did you find a solution that was acceptable to both of you and to the team?

2.3 **Ethical Choices** During team meetings, one member constantly calls for votes before all the members have voiced their views. As the leader, you asked this member privately about his behavior. He replied that he was trying to move the team toward its goals, but you are concerned that he is really trying to take control. How can you deal with this situation without removing the member from the group?

2.4 **Internet** Log on to the *Industry Week* website (www. industryweek.com) and enter the search term "teams." Review the list of articles produced by your search, read several of the articles, and summarize two of them in an e-mail message to your instructor.

2.5 **Listening Skills: Self-Assessment** How good are your listening skills? Rate yourself on each of the following elements of good listening; then examine your ratings to identify where you are strongest and where you can improve, using the tips in this chapter.

Element of Listening	Always	Frequently	Occasionally	Never
Do you				
1. Look for areas of interest when people speak?	_____	_____	_____	_____
2. Focus on content rather than delivery?	_____	_____	_____	_____
3. Wait to respond until you understand the content?	_____	_____	_____	_____
4. Listen for ideas and themes, not isolated facts?	_____	_____	_____	_____
5. Take notes only when needed?	_____	_____	_____	_____
6. Really concentrate on what speakers are saying?	_____	_____	_____	_____
7. Stay focused even when the ideas are complex?	_____	_____	_____	_____
8. Keep an open mind despite emotionally charged language?	_____	_____	_____	_____

2.6 **Nonverbal Communication: Analyzing Body Language** Describe what the following body movements suggest when they are exhibited by someone during a conversation. How do such movements influence your interpretation of spoken words?
  a. Shifting one's body continuously while seated
  b. Twirling and playing with one's hair
  c. Sitting in a sprawled position
  d. Rolling one's eyes
  e. Extending a weak handshake

2.7 **Business Etiquette: Telephones and Voice Mail** You are interested in the hiring policies of companies in your area. You want information about how often entry positions need to be filled, what sort of qualifications are required for these positions, and what range of pay is offered. Plan your phone call. Think about what you will say (1) to reach the person who can help you, (2) to gain the information you need, (3) in a voice-mail message. Once you've planned your approach, call three companies in your area. Briefly summarize the results of these calls in a memo to your instructor.

Expand Your Knowledge

LEARNING MORE ON THE WEB

Making Meetings Work www.3m.com/meetingnetwork
    Meetings are an essential part of business, but meetings that are poorly planned or poorly managed waste everyone's time and the company's money. Fortunately, it's easy to learn from the experts how to conduct more effective meetings. Visit the 3M Meeting Network site and click on "Articles and Advice" for a wide selection of articles on planning meetings, designing activities to build teamwork, and make better presentations.

ACTIVITIES

Log on now and find appropriate articles, then answer the following questions:

1. How can you know if a meeting should be held or not?
2. How can good leaders show they trust the group's ability to perform successfully?

3. What are the advantages and disadvantages of "open space" meetings, which take place without formal agendas or facilitation?

EXPLORING THE WEB ON YOUR OWN

Review these chapter-related websites on your own to learn more about achieving communication success in the workplace.

1. CRInfo, www.crinfo.org, is a website dedicated to providing support for conflict resolution.
2. The Center for the Study of Work Teams, www.workteams.unt.edu, has many links, articles, and research reports on the subject matter of teams.
3. Symbols.com, www.symbols.com, offers a graphical search engine that explains the meaning of 2,500 graphical symbols. Find out what that unusual symbol means, or verify that the symbols you plan to use don't convey some inappropriate nonverbal meaning.

Learn Interactively

INTERACTIVE STUDY GUIDE

Go to the Companion Website at www.prenhall.com/bovee. For Chapter 2, take advantage of the interactive "Study Guide" to test your knowledge of the chapter. Get instant feedback on whether you need additional studying. Also, visit this site's "Study Hall" where you'll find an abundance of valuable resources that will help you succeed in this course.

PEAK PERFORMANCE GRAMMAR AND MECHANICS

To improve your skill with pronouns, use the "Peak Performance Grammar and Mechanics" module on the web. Visit www.prenhall.com/onekey, click "Peak Performance Grammar and Mechanics," then click "Nouns and Pronouns." Take the Pretest to determine whether you have any weak areas. Then review those areas in the Refresher Course. Take the Follow-Up Test to check your grasp of pronouns. For an extra challenge or advanced practice, take the Advanced Test. Finally, for additional reinforcement, go to the "Improve Your Grammar, Mechanics, and Usage" section that follows, and complete those exercises.

Improve Your Grammar, Mechanics, and Usage

The following exercises help you improve your knowledge of and power over English grammar, mechanics, and usage. Turn to the "Handbook of Grammar, Mechanics, and Usage" at the end of this textbook and review all of Section 1.2 (Pronouns). Then look at the following 10 items. Underline the preferred choice within each set of parentheses. (Answers to these exercises appear on page AK-3.)

1. The sales staff is preparing guidelines for (*their, its*) clients.
2. Few of the sales representatives turn in (*their, its*) reports on time.
3. The board of directors has chosen (*their, its*) officers.
4. Gomez and Archer have told (*his, their*) clients about the new program.
5. Each manager plans to expand (*his, their, his or her*) sphere of control next year.

6. Has everyone supplied (*his, their, his or her*) Social Security number?
7. After giving every employee (*his, their, a*) raise, George told (*them, they, all*) about the increased work load.
8. Bob and Tim have opposite ideas about how to achieve company goals. (*Who, Whom*) do you think will win the debate?
9. City Securities has just announced (*who, whom*) it will hire as CEO.
10. Either of the new products would readily find (*their, its*) niche in the marketplace.

For additional exercises focusing on pronouns, go to www.prenhall.com/thill and select "Handbook of Grammar, Mechanics, and Usage Practice Sessions."

Chapter 3

Communicating Interculturally

Learning Objectives

AFTER STUDYING THIS CHAPTER, YOU WILL BE ABLE TO

1 Discuss two trends contributing to the importance of intercultural business communication in the workplace

2 Define culture and subculture, and summarize how culture is learned

3 Explain the importance of recognizing cultural differences, and list four categories of cultural differences

4 Define ethnocentrism and stereotyping, then give three suggestions for overcoming these limiting mind-sets

5 Discuss four ways to improve communication with people who speak English as a second language and three ways to improve communication with people who don't speak your language at all

6 List eight recommendations for improving your intercultural writing

7 Identify nine guidelines for improving your intercultural oral communication

On the Job:

COMMUNICATING AT TARGET STORES

TAKING AIM AT CULTURAL DIVERSITY

Rafael Rodriguez is a stock clerk supervisor at the Target store in Pasadena, California. Supervising people in the fast-paced world of retailing is demanding under any circumstances, and the rich cultural mix of Rodriguez's team makes his job even more challenging. Rodriguez is Hispanic, and his manager is African American. The employees that Rodriguez supervises have cultural backgrounds as diverse as the communities served by the nearly 700 Target retail outlets across the United States. Moreover, although most of Rodriguez's employees have grown up in the United States, many others have recently immigrated and speak English as a second language.

Like so many large companies in the United States and abroad, Target employs people with broad ethnic and cultural diversity. One key to Target's success is its commitment to training employees in the subtleties of intercultural exchanges. Training sessions may stress differences in social as well as business customs to encourage understanding, communication, and cooperation.

Rodriguez's team. Navarez quickly ran into problems when he tried to start conversations with some of his female co-workers by asking questions about their hair, nose rings, and other fashion choices. When other co-workers realized he was invading personal territory without knowing it, they explained that his questions were too personal. Not long after that, a Vietnamese employee joined the team, and other team members assumed that Navarez and the new employee would feel a sense of camaraderie based on their shared culture. But Navarez explained that even though both men were Asian, their languages and cultures were very different.

Besides ensuring that his team members stock shelves efficiently, Rafael Rodriguez tries to make sure they work and communicate well with each other and with him. Because English is a second language for some team members, Rodriguez clarifies his instructions by using easily understood vocabulary, avoiding idioms, and encouraging questions. He's patient when resolving problems and misunderstandings based on cultural differences, and he follows company policy about providing plenty of opportunity for team members to learn about the cultures of their co-workers.

When Patrick Navarez immigrated to the United States from the Philippines, he was the only Asian on

Target handles diversity issues head-on. The company offers diversity training to help employees better understand each other and work together more productively. Just as important, all levels of management at Target are ethnically diverse. When Rodriguez visited corporate headquarters in Minneapolis, he met many executives who were Hispanic, Asian, and African American, confirming his belief that his ethnicity would not keep him from being promoted if he performed well on the job. For many of Rodriguez's team members, the stock clerk job is their first real exposure to cultural differences. Target motivates each employee to cooperate and to communicate across cultures to get the job done.[1]

www.target.com

UNDERSTANDING THE IMPORTANCE OF COMMUNICATING ACROSS CULTURES

Intercultural communication allows the transfer of information between people whose cultural backgrounds lead them to interpret verbal and nonverbal signals differently.

Like Target, more and more companies are facing the challenges of communicating across cultures. **Intercultural communication** is the process of sending and receiving messages between people whose cultural background leads them to interpret verbal and nonverbal signs differently. Two trends contributing to the rapidly increasing importance of intercultural communication in the workplace are market globalization and the multicultural workforce.

The Global Marketplace

Advances in technology help companies cross national borders to find customers, materials, and money, which leads to market globalization.

Market globalization is the increasing tendency of the world to act as one market. This trend is being driven by technological advances in travel and telecommunications. For instance, new communication technologies allow teams from all over the world to work on projects and share information without leaving their desks. Advanced technologies also allow manufacturers to produce their goods in other countries that offer an abundant supply of low-cost labor.[2] Natural boundaries and national borders have disappeared as more and more domestic markets open to worldwide competition and as businesses look for new growth opportunities for their goods and services.

Companies such as Target understand that to be successful in the global marketplace, they must minimize cultural and language barriers with customers. Outdoor-equipment retailer REI uses custom-designed international websites that recognize and accommodate cultural differences. Similarly, UPS has expanded its web-based tracking services so that customers in 13 European countries can check—in their

When Recreational Equipment Inc. (REI) noticed many orders were coming from Japan, the company hired native speakers to develop a site for that country that adjusts the graphics as well as the words. For example, when an item is out of stock, the site displays a graphic of someone politely bowing.

own language—to see whether packages have reached their destinations around the world. (Visit getcustoms.com/articles.html for numerous articles on doing business in various countries around the world.)

But you need not "go global" or launch a website to interact with someone who speaks another language or who thinks, acts, or transacts business differently than you do.[3] Even if your company transacts business locally, chances are you will be communicating at work with people who come from various national, religious, and ethnic backgrounds.

To be successful in the global marketplace, you must minimize cultural and language barriers.

The Multicultural Workforce

The United States is the most demographically diverse country in the world.[4] Estimates project that by 2010, minorities will account for 50 percent of the U.S. population. Hispanics will make up about 24 percent; African Americans, 14 percent; Asian Americans, 8 percent; and Native Americans, 1 percent. Moreover, half of all new U.S. workers will be immigrants (new arrivals from Africa, Asia, Canada, Europe, India, Latin America, and elsewhere).[5] Thus, today's workforce is increasingly made up of people who differ in language, race, gender, age, culture, family structure, religion, and educational background. Such **cultural diversity** is the second trend contributing to the importance of intercultural communication. It affects how business messages are conceived, planned, sent, received, and interpreted in the workplace.

Managing this changing mix of ages, faces, values, and views is becoming increasingly difficult. Supervisors like Target's Rafael Rodriguez must be able to communicate with and motivate these diverse employees while fostering cooperation and harmony among them. To communicate successfully with people around the world and within your organization, you must be sensitive to cultural differences.

A company's cultural diversity affects how its business messages are conceived, composed, delivered, received, and interpreted.

IMPROVING INTERCULTURAL SENSITIVITY

Culture is a shared system of symbols, beliefs, attitudes, values, expectations, and norms for behavior. You belong to several cultures. The most obvious is the culture you share with all the people who influenced you as you grew up in your own family, community, and country. In addition, you belong to **subcultures**, other distinct groups that exist within a major culture—including an ethnic group, probably a religious group, and perhaps a profession that has its own special language and customs. In the United States subcultures include Mexican Americans, Mormons, wrestling fans, Russian immigrants, disabled individuals, Harvard graduates, and uncountable other groups.

As you can imagine, culture strongly affects communication. Members of a culture have similar assumptions about how people should think, behave, and communicate, and they tend to act on those assumptions in much the same way. You learn culture directly and indirectly from other members of your group. As you grow up in a culture, group members teach you who you are and how best to function in that culture. Sometimes you are explicitly told which behaviors are acceptable; at other times you learn by observing which values work best in a particular group. This multiple learning format ensures that culture is passed on from person to person and from generation to generation.[6]

Putting more people of various ethnicities on the floor—and in executive positions—is commonplace for Wal-Mart, which was recently ranked by *Fortune* magazine as one of America's 50 best companies for Asian, African, and Hispanic Americans. This diverse group of Wal-Mart managers clearly understand the importance of being sensitive to others' cultures.

Needless to say, the world does not fall into neat and tidy categories. Although some places tend to be fairly homogeneous, having few subcultural groups, other places are heterogeneous, having many subcultural groups. In the United States, for example, many subcultural groups retain their own identity and integrity, adding to the complexity of the culture in general. Generalizing about values and behaviors in such heterogeneous societies is certainly difficult, but some generalization is possible.[7]

From group to group, cultures differ widely in more than just language and gestures. Cultures vary in how quickly or easily they change. They differ in their degree of complexity and in their tolerance toward outsiders. All these differences affect the level of trust and open communication that you can achieve with the people who belong to these various cultures.

To improve your ability to communicate effectively across cultures, first be able to recognize cultural differences and then make sure you can overcome your own **ethnocentrism**—your tendency to judge all other groups according to your own group's standards, behaviors, and customs. When making such comparisons, people too often decide that their own group is superior.[8]

Recognize Cultural Differences

When you write to or speak with someone from another culture, you encode your message using the assumptions of your own culture. However, members of your audience decode your message according to the assumptions of their culture, so your meaning may be misunderstood. The greater the difference between cultures, the greater the chance for misunderstanding.[9] For example, exhibitors at a trade show couldn't understand why Chinese visitors were passing by their booth without stopping. The exhibitors were wearing green hats and giving them away as promotional items. They discovered, however, that many Chinese people associate green hats with infidelity; the Chinese expression "He wears a green hat" indicates that a man's wife has been cheating on him. As soon as the exhibitors discarded the green hats and began giving out T-shirts instead, the Chinese attendees started visiting the booth.[10]

Such problems arise when people assume, wrongly, that others' attitudes and lives are like their own. As a graduate of one intercultural training program said, "I used to think it was enough to treat people the way I wanted to be treated. But [after taking the course] . . . I realized you have to treat people the way *they* want to be treated."[11] You can increase your intercultural sensitivity by recognizing and accommodating four main types of cultural differences: contextual, ethical, social, and nonverbal.

Contextual Differences   One of the ways people assign meaning to a message is according to **cultural context**, the pattern of physical cues, environmental stimuli, and implicit understanding that convey meaning between two members of the same culture. However, from culture to culture, people convey contextual meaning differently. In fact, correct social behavior and effective communication can be defined by how much a culture depends on contextual cues (see Table 3–1).

In a **high-context culture** such as South Korea or Taiwan, people rely less on verbal communication and more on the context of nonverbal actions and environmental setting to convey meaning. A Chinese speaker expects the receiver to discover the essence of a message and uses indirectness and metaphor to provide a web of meaning.[12] In high-context cultures, the rules of everyday life are rarely explicit; instead, as individuals grow up, they learn how to recognize situational cues (such as gestures and tone of voice) and how to respond as expected.[13]

In a **low-context culture** such as the United States or Germany, people rely more on verbal communication and less on circumstances and cues to convey meaning. An English speaker feels responsible for transmitting the meaning of the message and

---

To better understand culture, remember that culture is learned and that it varies in stability, complexity, and tolerance.

Ethnocentrism is the tendency to judge all other groups according to one's own group's standards, behaviors, and customs and to see other groups as inferior by comparison.

Effective intercultural communication depends on recognizing ways in which people differ.

Cultural context is the pattern of physical cues, environmental stimuli, and implicit understanding that conveys meaning between members of the same culture.

High-context cultures rely on implicit nonverbal actions and environmental setting to convey meaning, unlike low-context cultures, which rely heavily on explicit verbal communication.

Low-context cultures emphasize quick, efficient decisions on major points, leaving the details to be worked out later; however, high-context cultures encourage lengthy decision making, with concentration on every detail.

HOW CULTURAL CONTEXT AFFECTS BUSINESS COMMUNICATION

Table 3–1

In Low-Context Companies	In High-Context Companies
Executive offices are separate with controlled access.	Executive offices are shared and open to all.
Workers rely on detailed background information.	Workers do not expect or want detailed information.
Information is highly centralized and controlled.	Information is shared with everyone.
Objective data are valued over subjective relationships.	Subjective relationships are valued over objective data.
Business and social relationships are discrete.	Business and social relationships overlap.
Competence is valued as much as position and status.	Position and status are valued much more than competence.
Meetings have fixed agendas and plenty of advance notice.	Meetings are often called on short notice, and key people always accept.

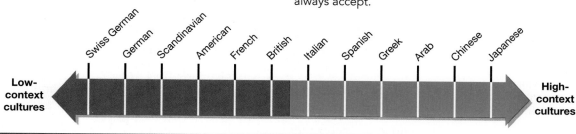

often places sentences in chronological sequence to establish a cause-and-effect pattern.[14] In a low-context culture, rules and expectations are usually spelled out through explicit statements such as "Please wait until I'm finished" or "You're welcome to browse."[15]

Contextual differences affect the way cultures approach situations such as decision making, problem solving, and negotiating:

- **Decision making.** In lower-context cultures, businesspeople try to reach decisions quickly and efficiently. They are concerned with reaching an agreement on the main points, leaving the details to be worked out later by others. However, in a higher-context culture such as Greece, executives assume that anyone who ignores the details is being evasive and untrustworthy. They believe that spending time on each little point is a mark of good faith.

- **Problem solving.** Low-context U.S. executives typically enjoy confrontation and debate, unlike high-context Japanese executives who may use a third party to avoid the unpleasant feelings that might result from open conflict. Chinese executives also try to prevent public conflict by avoiding proposal-counterproposal methods. Chinese team members cannot back down from a position without losing face, so trying to persuade them to do so will ruin the relationship.

  > Low-context cultures encourage open disagreement, whereas high-context cultures avoid confrontation and debate.

- **Negotiating.** Low-context Canadian and German negotiators tend to view negotiations as impersonal, setting their goals in economic terms and trusting the other party, at least at the outset. However, high-context Japanese negotiators prefer a more sociable negotiating atmosphere, one conducive to forging personal ties as the basis for trust. They see immediate economic gains as secondary to establishing and maintaining a long-term relationship.[16]

  > Low-context cultures view negotiations impersonally and focus on economic goals, whereas high-context cultures emphasize relationships and a sociable atmosphere when negotiating.

Legal and Ethical Differences   Cultural context also influences legal and ethical behavior. For example, because people in low-context cultures value the written word, they consider written agreements binding and tend to adhere to laws strictly.

Low-context cultures tend to value written agreements and interpret laws strictly, whereas high-context cultures value personal pledges above contracts and view laws as being more flexible.

But high-context cultures put less emphasis on the written word; they consider personal pledges more important than contracts and view laws as flexible.[17]

As you conduct business around the world, you'll find that legal systems differ from culture to culture. In the United Kingdom and the United States, someone is presumed innocent until proven guilty, a principle rooted in English common law. However, in Mexico and Turkey, someone is presumed guilty until proven innocent, a principle rooted in the Napoleonic code.[18] These distinctions can be particularly important if your firm must communicate about a legal dispute in another country.

Ethical choices can be even more complicated when communicating across cultures; for example, the bribing of officials is viewed differently from culture to culture.

As discussed in Chapter 1, making ethical choices can be difficult enough within your own culture. But what does it mean for a business to do the right thing in Thailand? Africa? Norway? What happens when a certain behavior is unethical in the United States but an accepted practice in another culture? For example, in the United States, bribing officials is illegal, but Kenyans consider paying such bribes a part of life. To get something done right, they pay *kitu kidogo* (or "something small"). In China, businesses pay *huilu*, in Russia they pay *vzyatka*, in the Middle East it's *baksheesh*, and in Mexico it's *una mordida* ("a small bite").[19] Making ethical choices across cultures can seem incredibly complicated, but doing so actually differs little from the way you choose the most ethical path in your own culture (see Chapter 1).

Keep your intercultural messages ethical by seeking common ground, withholding judgment, being honest, and respecting differences.

Keep your intercultural messages ethical by applying four basic principles:[20]

- **Actively seek mutual ground.** Both parties must be flexible and avoid insisting that an interaction take place strictly in terms of one culture or another.

- **Send and receive messages without judgment.** Both parties must recognize that values vary from culture to culture, and they must trust each other.

- **Send messages that are honest.** Both parties must see things as they are—not as they would like them to be—and must be fully aware of their personal and cultural biases.

- **Show respect for cultural differences.** Both parties must understand and acknowledge the other's needs and preserve each other's dignity.

Formal rules of etiquette are explicit and well defined, but informal rules are learned through observation and imitation.

Social Differences   In any culture, rules of social etiquette may be formal or informal. Formal rules are the specifically taught do's and don'ts of how to behave in common social situations, such as table manners at meals. When formal rules are violated, members of a culture can explain why they feel upset. In contrast, informal social rules are more difficult to identify and are usually learned by watching how people behave and then imitating that behavior. Informal rules govern how males and females are supposed to behave, when it is appropriate to use a person's first name, and so on. When informal rules are violated, members of a culture are likely to feel uncomfortable, although they may not be able to say exactly why.[21] Such informal rules are apparent in the way members value wealth, treat social roles, recognize status, define manners, and think about time.

People from the United States emphasize hard work, material success, and efficiency more than people in some other countries do.

- **Attitude toward materialism.** Although people in the United States have many different religions and values, the predominant U.S. view is that material comfort (earned by individual effort) is an important goal and that people who work hard are more admirable than those who don't. But other societies condemn such materialism, and some prize a more carefree lifestyle: Each year U.S. workers spend some 300 more hours on the job than many Germans and 60 more than their Japanese peers (see Figure 3–1).

Culture determines the roles people play in society.

- **Roles.** Culture dictates who communicates with whom, what they say, and in what way. For example, in some countries, women are not taken seriously as businesspeople. In modern western Europe, women can usually behave as they would in the United States. However, they should be more cautious in Latin America and

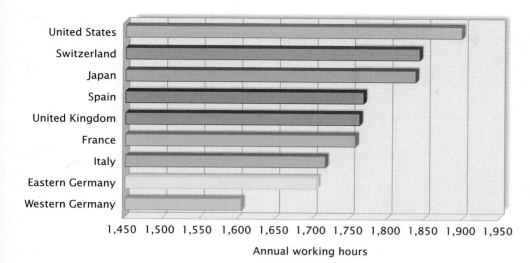

FIGURE 3–1
Working Hours Vary from
Culture to Culture

eastern Europe, and they should be extremely cautious in the Middle East and East Asia.[22]

- **Status.** Culture also dictates how people show respect and signify rank. For example, people in the United States show respect by addressing top managers as "Mr. Roberts" or "Ms. Gutierrez." However, people in China show respect by using official titles, such as "President" or "Manager."[23] Also, a U.S. executive's rank may be reflected by a large corner office, deep carpets, and expensive accessories. But high-ranking French executives sit in an open area, surrounded by lower-level employees. And in the Middle East, business is conducted in cramped and modest quarters, while fine possessions are reserved for the home.

  Respect and rank are reflected differently from culture to culture.

- **Manners.** Asking an employee "How was your weekend?" is a common way to make small talk in the United States, but the question is intrusive in cultures where business and private life are kept separate. In Arab countries taking gifts to a man's wife is impolite, but taking gifts to his children is acceptable. In Germany giving a woman a red rose is a romantic invitation. In India, if invited to visit someone's home "any time," you should make an unexpected visit without waiting for an invitation. Failure to do so would be an insult.

  The rules of polite behavior vary from country to country.

- **Time.** German and U.S. executives see time as a way to plan the business day efficiently; they focus on only one task during each scheduled period and view time as limited. However, executives from Latin America and Asia see time as more flexible. Meeting a deadline is less important than building a business relationship. So the workday is not expected to follow a rigid, preset schedule.[24]

  Although businesspeople in the United States, Germany, and some other nations see time as a way to organize the business day efficiently, other cultures see time as more flexible.

Nonverbal Differences   As discussed in Chapter 2, nonverbal communication is extremely reliable in ascertaining meaning. However, that reliability is valid only when communicators belong to the same culture. Nonverbal elements are apparent in attitudes toward personal space and in body language.

Nonverbal communication is reliable only within the same culture.

- **Concepts of personal space.** People in Canada and the United States usually stand about five feet apart during a business conversation. However, this distance is uncomfortably close for people from Germany or Japan and uncomfortably far for Arabs and Latin Americans. Thus, a Canadian manager may react negatively (without knowing exactly why) when an Arab colleague moves closer during their conversation. And the Arab colleague may react negatively (again, without knowing why) when the Canadian manager backs away.

  Culture defines the amount of personal space that people feel comfortable sharing.

The same gesture can have different meanings from culture to culture.

- **Use of body language.** Don't assume that someone from another culture who speaks your language has mastered your culture's body language. For example, people in the United States and Canada say no by shaking their heads back and forth, people in Bulgaria nod up and down, and people in Japan move their right hand. People from another culture may misread an intentional nonverbal signal, overlook the signal entirely, or assume that a meaningless gesture is significant. For example, an Egyptian might mistakenly assume that a Westerner who exposes the sole of his or her shoe is offering a grave insult.[25]

Recognition of cultural differences must be followed by the sincere attempt to accommodate those differences.

Recognizing cultural differences is only the first step in improving your intercultural communication. To achieve intercultural sensitivity, be sure to balance cultural awareness with cultural flexibility. To accommodate cultural differences without judging them, do your best to overcome the human tendency toward ethnocentrism.

Overcome Ethnocentrism

When communicating across cultures, your effectiveness depends on maintaining an open mind. Unfortunately, many people lapse into ethnocentrism. They lose sight of the possibility that their words and actions can be misunderstood, and they forget that they are likely to misinterpret the actions of others.

IBM's corporate workforce diversity staff is sensitive to cultural differences, both inside and outside the company. An important goal for staff members is to ensure effective communication among co-workers and with customers by helping fellow employees recognize and grow beyond their own ethnocentrism.

When you first begin to investigate the culture of another group, you may attempt to understand the common tendencies of that group's members by **stereotyping**—predicting individuals' behaviors or character on the basis of their membership in a particular group or class. For example, Japanese visitors often stereotype people in the United States as walking fast, being wasteful in utilizing space, speaking directly, asking too many questions in the classroom, not respecting age and status, lacking discipline, and being extravagant.[26]

Although stereotyping may be useful in the beginning, the next step is to move beyond the stereotypes to relationships with real people. Unfortunately, when ethnocentric people stereotype, they tend to do so on the basis of limited, general, or inaccurate evidence. They frequently develop biased attitudes toward the group, and they fail to move beyond that initial step.[27] So instead of talking with Abdul Karhum, unique human being, ethnocentric people are talking to "an Arab." They may believe that all Arabs are, say, hagglers, so Abdul Karhum's personal qualities cannot alter such preconceptions. His every action is forced to fit the preconceived image, even if that image is wrong.

Stereotyping is the attempt to categorize individuals by trying to predict their behavior or character on the basis of their membership in a particular group.

To overcome ethnocentrism, follow a few simple suggestions:

- **Acknowledge distinctions.** Don't ignore the differences between another person's culture and your own.

- **Avoid assumptions.** Don't assume that others will act the same way you do, that they will operate from the same assumptions, or that they will use language and symbols the same way you do.

You can overcome ethnocentrism by acknowledging distinctions, avoiding assumptions, and avoiding judgments.

- **Avoid judgments.** When people act differently, don't conclude that they are in error, that their way is invalid, or that their customs are inferior to your own.

At Target, Rafael Rodriguez has noticed that in many cases both parties in an intercultural exchange are guilty of ethnocentrism and prejudice. Little wonder, then, that misunderstandings arise when communicating across cultures.

IMPROVING COMMUNICATION ACROSS CULTURES

Once you can recognize cultural elements and overcome ethnocentrism, you're ready to focus directly on your intercultural communication skills. To communicate more effectively with people from other cultures, you need to study those cultures, overcome language barriers, and develop effective intercultural communication skills, both written and oral.

Study Other Cultures

Learning all you can about a particular culture is a good way to figure out how to send and receive intercultural messages effectively. Read books and articles about these cultures, and talk to people who have done business with members of these cultures. Concentrate on learning something about each culture's history, religion, politics, values, and customs. Find out about a country's subcultures, especially its business subculture, and any special rules or protocol. You can visit websites such as onlineedition.culturegrams.com/world/index.html to pick up quick facts about a particular country's history, people, customs, lifestyle, and more.

Learning as much as possible about another culture will enhance your ability to communicate with its members.

"In dealing with American businesspeople," says Y. A. Cho, chief operating officer of Korean Airlines, "I'm amazed at how naive most are about other cultures and the way that others do business."[28] Something as simple as a handshake differs from culture to culture. For example, in Spain a proper handshake must last five to seven strokes, and pulling away too soon may be interpreted as rejection. However, in France the preferred handshake is only a single stroke. In Arab countries, you'll insult your hosts if you turn down food, drink, or hospitality of any kind. But don't accept too quickly, either. A polite refusal (such as "I don't want to put you to any trouble") is expected before you finally accept.

People from the United States are often uninformed about the customs of other cultures.

The "Checklist: Doing Business Abroad" can help you start your investigation of another culture. However, don't expect to ever understand another culture completely. No matter how much you study German culture, for example, you'll never be a German or share the experiences of having grown up in Germany. The trick is to learn useful general information while remaining aware of and open to variations and individual differences. Then you'll be ready to communicate more effectively by following these tips:[29]

You can't expect to understand another culture as completely as someone born to that culture.

- **Assume differences until similarity is proved.** Don't assume that others are more similar to you than they actually are.

- **Take responsibility for communication.** Don't assume it's the other person's job to communicate with you.

- **Withhold judgment.** Learn to listen to the whole story and accept differences in others without judging them.

- **Show respect.** Learn how respect is communicated in various cultures (through gestures, eye contact, and so on).

- **Empathize.** Before sending a message, put yourself in the receiver's shoes. Imagine the receiver's feelings and point of view.

- **Tolerate ambiguity.** Learn to control your frustration when placed in an unfamiliar or confusing situation.

✓ CHECKLIST: Doing Business Abroad

Understand Social Customs

✓ How do people react to strangers? Are they friendly? Hostile? Reserved?

✓ How do people greet each other? Should you bow? Nod? Shake hands?

✓ How are names used during introductions?

✓ What are the attitudes toward touching people?

✓ How do people express appreciation for an invitation to lunch or dinner or to someone's home? Should you bring a gift? Send flowers? Write a thank-you note?

✓ How, when, and where are people expected to sit in social and business situations?

✓ Are any phrases, facial expressions, or hand gestures considered rude?

✓ How close do people stand when talking?

✓ How do you attract the attention of a waiter? Do you tip the waiter?

✓ When is it rude to refuse an invitation? How do you refuse politely?

✓ What are the acceptable patterns of eye contact?

✓ What gestures indicate agreement? Disagreement? Respect?

✓ What topics may or may not be discussed in a social setting? In a business setting?

✓ How is time perceived?

✓ What are the generally accepted working hours?

✓ How do people view scheduled appointments?

Learn About Clothing and Food Preferences

✓ What occasions require special clothing? What colors are associated with mourning? Love? Joy?

✓ Are some types of clothing considered taboo for one gender or the other?

✓ What are the attitudes toward human body odors? Are deodorants or perfumes used?

✓ How many times a day do people eat?

✓ How are hands or utensils used when eating?

✓ What types of places, food, and drink are appropriate for business entertainment?

✓ Where is the seat of honor at a table?

Assess Political Patterns

✓ How stable is the political situation? Does it affect businesses in and out of the country?

✓ How is political power manifested? Military power? Economic strength?

✓ What are the traditional government institutions?

✓ What channels are used for expressing official and unofficial political opinion?

✓ What information media are important? Who controls them?

✓ Is it appropriate to talk politics in social or business situations?

Understand Religious and Folk Beliefs

✓ To which religious groups do people belong?

✓ How do religious beliefs influence daily activities?

✓ Which places, objects, and events are sacred?

✓ Is there a tolerance for minority religions?

✓ How do religious holidays affect business and government activities?

✓ Does religion affect attitudes toward smoking? Drinking? Gambling?

✓ Does religion require or prohibit eating specific foods? At specific times?

✓ Which objects or actions portend good luck? Bad luck?

Learn About Economic and Business Institutions

✓ Is the society homogeneous?

✓ What minority groups are represented?

✓ What languages are spoken?

✓ Do immigration patterns influence workforce composition?

✓ What are the primary resources and principal products?

✓ What vocational/technological training is offered?

✓ What are the attitudes toward education?

✓ Are businesses generally large? Family controlled? Government controlled?

✓ Is it appropriate to do business by telephone? By fax? By e-mail?

✓ Do managers make business decisions unilaterally, or do they involve employees?

✓ How are status and seniority shown in an organization? In a business meeting?

✓ Must people socialize before conducting business?

Appraise the Nature of Ethics, Values, and Laws

✓ Is money or a gift expected in exchange for arranging business transactions?

✓ What ethical or legal issues might affect business transactions?

✓ Do people value competitiveness or cooperation?

✓ What are the attitudes toward work? Toward money?

✓ Is politeness more important than factual honesty?

✓ What qualities are admired in a business associate?

- **Look beyond the superficial.** Don't be distracted by things such as dress, appearance, or environmental discomforts.

- **Be patient and persistent.** If you want to communicate with someone from another culture, don't give up easily.

- **Recognize your own cultural biases.** Learn to identify when your assumptions are different from the other person's.

- **Be flexible.** Be prepared to change your habits and attitudes when communicating with someone from another culture.

- **Emphasize common ground.** Look for similarities to work from.

- **Send clear messages.** Make both your verbal and nonverbal signals clear and consistent.

- **Deal with the individual.** Communicate with each person as an individual, not as a stereotypical representative of another group.

- **Learn when to be direct.** Investigate each culture so that you'll know when to send your message in a straightforward manner and when to be indirect.

- **Treat your interpretation as a working hypothesis.** Once you think you understand a foreign culture, carefully assess the feedback provided by recipients of your communication to see if it confirms your hypothesis.

Such advice will help you communicate with anybody, regardless of culture, but it isn't enough. Overcoming language barriers is another good way to improve your communication across cultures.

Overcome Language Barriers

By choosing specific words to communicate, you signal that you are a member of a particular culture or subculture and that you know the code. However, the very nature of your code—your language and vocabulary—imposes its own barriers on your message. For example, the language of a lawyer differs from that of an accountant or a doctor, and the differences in their vocabularies affect their ability to recognize and express ideas.

> Language barriers can result from your choice of words and from the fact that words can be interpreted in more than one way.

Barriers also exist because words can be interpreted in more than one way. To someone from France, for example, the word *catastrophe* can be used in casual exaggeration to describe a relatively small problem. But in Germany, the word is often taken literally as an earth-shaking event. So try to choose your words with your audience in mind, whether that audience is someone who speaks English as a second language (ESL) or someone who doesn't speak your language at all.

Breaking Through ESL Barriers As the U.S. workforce becomes more culturally diverse, the number of people who speak English as a second language grows proportionately. In the United States, 18 percent of the population speaks a language other than English when at home. In California (the sixth-largest economy in the world), that number is nearly 40 percent. After English, Spanish is by far the most common spoken language, followed by French, German, Italian, and Chinese. On the web, only 32 percent of users are native English-speakers.[30] The rest of this chapter discusses ways to improve your communication in the workplace. In addition, be sure to consult the "Checklist: Communicating with a Culturally Diverse Workforce."

Of the many millions of people who use English as a second language, some are extremely fluent, while others have only an elementary command. When dealing with those less fluent in your own language, expect your audience to miss a few subtleties. Don't assume that the other person understands everything you say. Make

✓ CHECKLIST: Communicating with a Culturally Diverse Workforce

Accept Cultural Differences

✓ Study your own culture.
✓ Learn about other cultures through books, articles, videos, and other resources.
✓ Encourage employees to discuss their culture's customs.
✓ Avoid being judgmental.
✓ Create a formal forum to teach employees about the customs of all cultures represented in the firm.
✓ Train employees to see and overcome ethnocentric stereotyping.
✓ Stamp out negative labels by observing how people identify their own groups.

Improve Oral and Written Communications

✓ Define the terms people need to know on the job.
✓ Emphasize major points with repetition and recap.
✓ Use familiar words whenever possible.
✓ Be concise.
✓ Don't cover too much information at one time.
✓ Adjust your message to employees' education level.
✓ Be specific and explicit—using descriptive words, exact measurements, and examples when possible.
✓ Give the reason for asking employees to follow a certain procedure and explain what will happen if the procedure is not followed.
✓ Use written summaries and visual aids (when appropriate) to clarify your points.

✓ Demonstrate and encourage the right way to complete a task, use a tool, and so on.
✓ Reduce language barriers: Train managers in the language of their employees, train employees in the language of most customers and of most people in the company, ask bilingual employees to serve as translators, print important health and safety instructions in as many languages as necessary.

Assess How Well You've Been Understood

✓ Research the nonverbal reactions of other cultures; then be alert to facial expressions and other nonverbal signs that indicate confusion or embarrassment.
✓ Probe for comprehension.
✓ Encourage employees to ask questions in private and in writing.
✓ Observe how employees use the information you've provided, and review any misunderstood points.

Offer Feedback to Improve Communication

✓ Focus on the positive by explaining what *should* be done rather than what *shouldn't* be done.
✓ Discuss a person's behaviors and the situation, rather than making a judgment about the person.
✓ Be supportive as you offer feedback, and reassure individuals that their skills and contributions are important.

---

sure your message is not mangled by slang and idioms, local accents, vocal variations, or differing communication styles.

Slang and idioms, local accents and pronunciation, vocal variations, and communication styles can pose problems when you're speaking to people from other cultures.

Choose words that have a strong denotative meaning.

Avoid Using Slang and Idioms   Languages never translate word for word. They are **idiomatic**—constructed with phrases that mean more than the sum of their literal parts. For example, if a U.S. executive tells an Egyptian executive that a certain product "doesn't cut the mustard" or that making the monthly sales quota will be "a piece of cake," chances are that the communication will fail. When speaking to people less fluent in your language, try to choose words carefully to convey only their most specific denotative meaning. Use words that have singular rather than multiple meanings. The word *high* has 20 meanings; the word *expensive* has one.[31]

Pay Attention to Local Accents and Pronunciation   Even when people speak your language, you may have a hard time understanding their pronunciation. After transferring to Toyota's U.S. office, some English-speaking Japanese employees had to enroll in a special course to learn that "Jeat yet?" means "Did you eat yet?" and that "Cannahepya?" means "Can I help you?" Some nonnative English-speakers don't distinguish between the English sounds *v* and *w*, so they say *wery* for *very*. At the same time, many people from the United States are unable to pronounce the French *r* or the German *ch*.

Whether a Canadian is speaking Chinese or a Russian is speaking U.S. English, foreign accents can make communication difficult. When you have trouble understanding someone who has a heavy accent, try the following techniques:[32]

Numerous techniques can help you overcome the barriers imposed by foreign accents.

- **Listen very carefully.** As discussed in Chapter 2, people routinely listen to a speaker's words rather than the message; when they must also concentrate on how the words are pronounced, listening ability becomes less and less efficient.

- **Expect to understand.** If you expect the communication to fail, you'll unintentionally set up barriers before the speaker even begins. By expecting to understand, you increase the chances that you will.

- **Create a relaxed atmosphere.** Don't rush. When people are relaxed, their speech slows and their accents become less pronounced. Try speaking more slowly than usual yourself to signal that you're not being judgmental about the person's accent.

- **Listen to the entire message.** Words that may be misunderstood in their individual sense are often clarified when placed in the context of a complete message. If you are the speaker with an accent, stop periodically to ask whether the listener understands what you're saying.

- **Rephrase questions.** By phrasing questions differently, you allow a nonnative speaker to respond using different words, some of which may be easier for you to understand.

- **Invite the nonnative speaker to write the message on paper.** This request would be appropriate for those who are more comfortable expressing ideas in writing than orally, but it may not be the right strategy for everyone.

Avoiding slang and idioms is a major focus for Camco executives when preparing corporate documents. With customers and employees scattered throughout Asia and the United States, Camco wants to make sure its messages are easily understood.

Be Aware of Vocal Variations People use their voices differently from culture to culture. Russian-speakers tend to use a flat, level tone, so to some U.S. listeners they sound bored or rude. Middle Easterners tend to speak more loudly than Westerners and may therefore mistakenly be considered more emotional. On the other hand, people from Japan are soft-spoken, a characteristic that implies politeness or humility to Western listeners.

Frequency of speaking also differs from culture to culture. Many Western cultures interpret silence negatively, thinking that the person lacks adequate verbal skills, that the person is incompatible, or that the person is unwilling to communicate because he or she feels awkward, embarrassed, hostile, disinterested, disapproving, or shy. However, some Asian and southern African cultures value silence over oral communication. In many of these cultures, the person who talks excessively is regarded with suspicion.[33]

Silence is regarded differently in different cultures.

Match Your Communication Style to Your Audience Try to use the communication style that your audience expects and prefers. In the United States, workers typically prefer an open and direct communication style, considering anything else to be dishonest or insincere. In Sweden, a direct approach is also valued as a sign of efficiency, but unlike discussions in the United States, heated debates and confrontations are unusual. Swedish business culture strongly favors compromise. Workers from other cultures, such as Japan or China, tend to be less direct. Finnish and German workers

Whether people expect their messages to be direct or indirect, written or oral, formal or conversational, try to match your communication style to your audience's preferences.

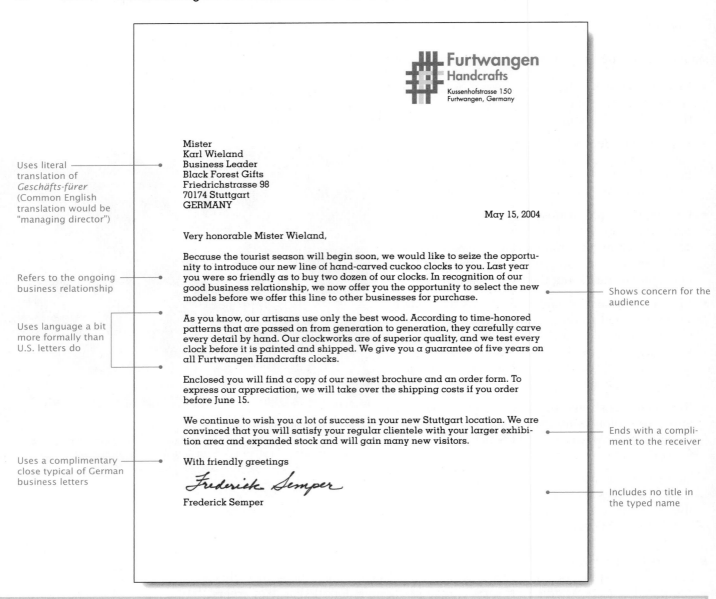

Uses literal translation of *Geschäfts-fürer* (Common English translation would be "managing director")

Refers to the ongoing business relationship

Uses language a bit more formally than U.S. letters do

Uses a complimentary close typical of German business letters

Shows concern for the audience

Ends with a compliment to the receiver

Includes no title in the typed name

FIGURE 3–2
Effective German Business Letter (Translated)

International business letters generally have a formal tone and a relatively elaborate style.

often prefer written communication instead of face-to-face interaction, so a letter recognizing employee accomplishments would be most effective in these cultures. Moreover, Italian, German, and French executives don't soften up colleagues with praise before they criticize. Doing so seems manipulative to them.[34]

In general, U.S. businesspeople need to be somewhat more formal in their international correspondence than they are when writing to people in their own country. In many cultures, writers use a more elaborate style, so your audience will expect more formal language in your letter. The letter in Figure 3–2 was written by a supplier in Germany to a nearby retailer. The tone is more formal than would be used in the United States, but the writer clearly focuses on his audience. In Germany, business letters usually open with a reference to the business relationship and close with a compliment to the recipient. Of course, if you carry formality to extremes, you'll sound unnatural.

USING THE POWER OF TECHNOLOGY

Communicating with a Global Audience on the Web

With growing global access to the World Wide Web, some U.S. corporate sites are already reporting that foreign visitors account for as much as 30 percent of their traffic and 10 percent of their commerce. Nevertheless, reaching an international audience on the web involves more than simply offering translations into the local language. Successful U.S. sites address the needs of international customers in five ways:

1. **Consider the reader's viewpoint.** Assume your audience is unfamiliar with common U.S. phrases and references. To avoid confusion, provide both U.S. units and metric equivalents for weights, measures, sizes, and temperatures. Also, use universal terms for times, dates, and geographical names. For example, consider expressing time in military format ("16:00" for 4:00 P.M.). Because Europeans read "10/04/2002" as April 10, 2002, be sure you spell out the month and year. And offer complete location descriptions, such as "Kansas City, MO, USA."

2. **Take cultural differences into account.** Since humor is rooted in cultural norms, a touch of U.S. humor may not be so funny to Asian or European readers. Don't risk offending or slighting your audience with cultural stereotypes or expressions. Avoid idioms and references that aren't universally recognized, such as "putting all your eggs in one basket" or "jumping out of the frying pan into the fire."

3. **Keep the message clear.** Use simple words and write in the active voice. Avoid complicated sentence structure to achieve a simple, straightforward tone. And don't forget to define abbreviations and acronyms.

4. **Break through language barriers with graphics.** Clarify written concepts with graphics. However, even though most graphical icons are internationally recognized, some images are more widely accepted than others. In some countries, for example, a mailbox doesn't necessarily convey the idea of sending mail. So an envelope might be a more appropriate symbol to reinforce the message "Contact us." Keep in mind that the colors you select for your graphics are equally as important. Red works well in China, where it conveys good fortune. But it's the color of death in Turkey.

5. **Consult local experts.** Work with local experts and webmasters to develop native-language keywords that will direct international customers to your site. Also seek the advice of local experts about customary phrases and references. Even terms as simple as *homepage* differ from country to country. Spanish readers refer to the "first page," or *pagina inicial*, whereas the French term is "welcome page," or *page d'accuei*.

CAREER APPLICATIONS

1. Visit the World of Sony Music Entertainment at www.sonymusic.com/world and examine Sony's sites for Argentina, France, and Germany. How does Sony "localize" each country's site?

2. Compare Sony Music's international sites to IBM's global webpages at www.ibm.com. How does Sony's approach differ from IBM's? Do both corporations successfully address the needs of a global audience? Write a two-paragraph summary that compares the international sites of both companies.

Breaking Through Foreign Language Barriers   Even though English is widely spoken in the global business marketplace, the language of business is the language of the customer, and that language isn't always English.[35] Even on the web, U.S. companies can no longer get by speaking only English (see "Using the Power of Technology: Communicating with a Global Audience on the Web"). When communicating with people who don't speak your language at all, you have three options: You can learn their language, use an intermediary or a translator, or teach them your language.

Many companies recognize that they must be able to conduct business in languages other than English.

- **Learn a foreign language.** If you're planning to live in another country or to do business there repeatedly, you might want to learn the language. The same holds true if you'll be working closely with a subculture that has its own language, such as Vietnamese Americans. Even if you're doing business in your own language, you show respect by making the effort to learn the subculture's language, or at least a few words.

If you have a long-term business relationship with people of another culture, it is helpful to learn their language.

- **Use a translator.** Experienced translators can analyze a message, understand its meaning in the cultural context, consider how to convey that meaning in another language, and use verbal and nonverbal signals to encode or decode it. For oral presentations, meet with translators ahead of time to give them a sense of what you are presenting and to discuss words or concepts that could be confusing.[36] Ensure accuracy with *back-translation:* Have one person translate a message, and then ask a different person to retranslate that message back into the original language. Compare the two versions to discover any errors or discrepancies.

- **Offer language-training programs for employees.** Many companies find it beneficial to offer language-training programs. For example, Tenneco instituted an English-language training program in New Jersey for its Spanish-speaking employees. The training concentrated on practical English for use on the job, and thanks to the classes, accidents and grievances have declined while productivity has improved.[37]

Back-translation helps ensure accuracy by allowing translators to check a second translation against the original message.

Some companies find it useful to teach English to employees for whom English is a second language.

Develop Effective Intercultural Communication Skills

Once you understand what sort of cultural differences you'll be facing, and once you discover which language barriers must be overcome, you need to decide whether using written or oral channels would be best. Then you must adapt your style and approach to make the right impression.

Whether you choose written or oral channels to communicate your message across cultures, you must adapt your style and approach.

Improve Your Writing Skills   If you understand that letter writers in other countries have other customs that you may not be used to, you can focus on the message without passing judgment on the writers. Japanese letter-writers, for example, come to the point slowly. They typically begin with a remark about the season or weather, followed by an inquiry about your health or congratulations on your success. A note of thanks for your patronage might come next. After these preliminaries, the main idea is introduced.

Be aware of various cultures' tendency to organize thoughts differently.

Familiarize yourself with the written communication preferences of your intercultural readers and adapt your approach, style, and tone to meet their expectations. To write multicultural messages as effectively as possible, follow these recommendations:[38]

- **Use plain English.** Choose short, precise words that say exactly what you mean: Use *climb* instead of *walk up*, *maintain* instead of *keep up*, and *return* instead of *bring back*.

- **Be clear.** Use specific terms and concrete examples to explain your points.

- **Address international correspondence properly.** Refer to Table 1.2 in Appendix A for an explanation of various address elements and salutations commonly used in certain foreign countries.

- **Cite numbers carefully.** Use figures (27) instead of spelling them out (twenty-seven).

- **Avoid slang and idioms.** Avoid using slang, idioms, jargon, and buzzwords. Abbreviations, acronyms (such as CAD/CAM), and unfamiliar product names may also lead to confusion.

- **Be brief.** Construct sentences that are shorter and simpler than those you might use when writing to someone fluent in your own language.

- **Use short paragraphs.** Each paragraph should stick to one topic and be no more than eight to ten lines long.

- **Use transitional elements.** Help readers follow your train of thought by using transitional words and phrases. Precede related points with expressions such as *in addition* and *first, second, third*.

Take a look at Figure 3–3 to see how an early version of an intercultural letter is improved by paying close attention to this chapter's guidelines.

Improve Your Oral Skills   If you've ever studied another language, you know it's easier to write in that language than to conduct a conversation. However, some transactions simply cannot be handled without face-to-face contact. In many countries, business relationships are based on personal relationships, and until you establish rapport, nothing happens. When speaking in English to people who speak English as a second language, you may find these guidelines helpful:

- **Try to eliminate noise.** Speak slowly. Pronounce words clearly, stop at distinct punctuation points, and make one point at a time.

- **Observe body language.** Be alert to roving eyes and glazed looks that signal a listener is lost or confused. Realize that nods and smiles don't necessarily mean understanding and that gestures and expressions mean different things in different cultures. If the other person's body language seems at odds with the message, take time to clarify the meaning.

- **Clarify your true intent with repetition and examples.** Try to be aware of unintentional meanings that may be read into your message.

- **Don't talk down to the other person.** Try not to overenunciate, and don't "blame" the listener for not understanding. Use phrases such as "Am I going too fast?" rather than "Is this too difficult for you?"

- **Use objective, accurate language.** Avoid throwing around adjectives such as *fantastic* and *fabulous*, which people from other cultures might consider unreal and overly dramatic.

- **Learn foreign phrases.** Learn common greetings and a few key phrases in the other person's native language (usually listed in travel books and in a separate section of most travel dictionaries).

- **Adapt your conversation style to the other person's.** For instance, if the other person appears to be direct and straightforward, follow suit.

- **Check frequently for comprehension.** Make one point at a time and pause to check for comprehension before moving on.

- **Clarify what will happen next.** At the end of the conversation, be sure that you and the other person agree on what has been said and decided. If appropriate, follow up by writing a letter or a memo summarizing the conversation and thanking the person for meeting with you.

In short, take advantage of the other person's presence to make sure that your message is getting across and that you understand his or her message too.

Document Makeover

IMPROVE THIS LETTER

To practice correcting drafts of actual documents, visit **www.prenhall.com/onekey** on the web. Click "Document Makeovers," then click Chapter 3. You will find a letter that contains problems and errors relating to what you've learned in this chapter about developing effective intercultural communication skills. Use the Final Draft decision tool to create an improved version of this letter. Check the message for a communication style that keeps the message brief, does not become too familiar or informal, uses transitional elements appropriately, and avoids slang, idioms, jargon, and technical language.

Face-to-face communication lets you establish a personal relationship with people from other cultures and gives you the benefit of immediate feedback.

Draft

Mr. Pierre Coll
Director of Accounting
La Cristallerie
22 Marne Blvd.
Beaune, France 21200

Dear Pierre:

I know you've had gorgeous spring weather, with sunny skies and balmy days. But here in the States, it's been a spring of another color. We've been hammered with storms, flooding, and even late snow. Travel over here has been a nightmare, which is why you'll find my expenses a bit elevated this month.

I realize that you've asked all the reps to reduce rather than increase our expenses, but there were extenuating circumstances this last month. All the bad weather we've been having has caused major bottlenecks, with flights canceled and people forced to sleep in the terminals wherever they could find a spot.

After being stuck in the Chicago airport for eighteen hours straight, I was desperate for a hot shower and some shuteye, so I decided to wait out the crunch in a hotel. I know that hotels near airports are expensive, but I struck out trying to book a cheaper room in town. The bottom line is I had to spend extra funds for a hotel at $877; meals, which came to some $175; $72 just in transportation from the terminal to the hotel, and extra phone calls totaling $38.

I appreciate your understanding these unique circumstances. I was really in a jam.

Annotations (right side of Draft):
- Fails to follow French preferences for title and address format
- Uses reader's first name, which is much too informal for most French business correspondence
- Wastes reader's time with unnecessarily dramatic and long description of weather problems
- Uses slang and idioms throughout the message, risking confusion from simple vocabulary choices (e.g., spring of another color, hammered, bottlenecks, spot, shuteye, crunch, struck out)
- Buries specific information in awkward phrasing that ignores the directness and simplicity of using lists and parallelism
- Fails to provide a total of the "extra" expenses
- Closes with a self-centered tone rather than trying to help the reader

---

Revision

La Cristallerie

Troy Halford, U.S. Sales Representative
163 Pico Boulevard
Los Angeles, CA 90032
Voice: (213) 975-8924
Fax: (213) 860-3489
halford@home.com

5 April 2004

M. Pierre Coll
Commissaire aux Comptes
La Cristallerie
22, Boulevard de la Marne
21200 Beaune
FRANCE

Dear Monsieur Coll:

Enclosed are my expense statement and receipts for March 2002. My expenses are higher than usual this month because unusual weather stranded me in Chicago for nearly five days. The airport was closed for four days, and we were forced to sleep in the terminal wherever we could find room.

After thirty-seven hours, I was able to get a hotel for the duration of the storm. I took the opportunity, even though the only accommodation was near the airport and quite expensive. The following list details the additional expenditures for March:

Three nights at the Carlton-O'Hare Hotel	$ 877
Meals over four days	175
Transportation between hotel and terminal	72
Phone calls to reschedule meetings	38
Total	$1,162

If you have any questions or need any more information about these expenses, please contact me.

Sincerely,

Troy Halford

Troy Halford
U.S. Sales Rep

Enclosures: Expense statement and receipts

Annotations (left side of Revision):
- Follows French preferences for title and address format
- Addresses the reader more formally in the salutation, as is expected in most French correspondence
- Uses clear and simple language throughout the message, avoiding any risk of confusion
- Provides a total of the "extra" expenses

Annotations (right side of Revision):
- Uses the international standard format for the date
- States the main idea directly and clearly in the opening, leaving no room for confusion about the letter's purposes
- Breaks out specific information about the extra expenses incurred during the unexpected stay in Chicago
- Closes with an offer to help the reader with any further needs

On the Job:

SOLVING COMMUNICATION DILEMMAS AT TARGET STORES

At Target, team members who communicate well are likely to receive higher evaluations. The stock clerks working with Rafael Rodriguez are learning how to succeed in a diverse workforce. Like Rodriguez, you supervise a culturally diverse team of Target stock clerks. You want to foster cooperation among your team members and encourage them to perform well. Use your skill in intercultural communication to choose the best response in each of the following situations. Be prepared to explain why your choice is best.

1. One of your Hispanic American team members, Miguel Gomez, has started making derogatory remarks about team members who are African American. Gomez is refusing to work with them and tells you that he would rather work with other team members who are Hispanic American. How do you resolve the problem?
   a. To avoid conflict, let him work with co-workers who make him most comfortable.
   b. Tell him he has to work with whomever you assign him to. If he refuses, fire him.
   c. Schedule a time for him to sit down with you and the African American team members so that all of you can discuss cultural differences.
   d. Speak with him privately about the company's goals regarding a diverse workforce, and then sign him up for the company diversity training program.

2. Amy Tam is not stocking shelves correctly: She's stacking cans too high and mixing brands in the displays. You think language may be a problem; perhaps she does not comprehend all your instructions. How do you make sure that she understands you?
   a. Write everything down in a list so that Tam can refer to it if she has questions.
   b. Have Tam repeat what you have said. If she can repeat it, she must understand it.
   c. Speak slowly and clearly, using simple terms. Pause often, repeating or writing down phrases or instructions that Tam does not seem to understand.
   d. To get and keep Tam's attention and to clarify your meaning, speak a bit more loudly and exaggerate your hand motions.

3. You have hired a new stock clerk. Vasily Pevsner has recently immigrated from Russia. He works well alone, but he resists working with other team members. How do you handle the situation?
   a. Stay uninvolved and let the situation resolve itself. Pevsner has to learn how to get along with the other team members.
   b. Tell the rest of the team to work harder at getting along with Pevsner.
   c. Tell Pevsner he must work with others or he will not progress in the company.
   d. Talk privately with Pevsner to find out why he doesn't want to work with others. Then help him understand the importance of working together as a team.

4. Your employees are breaking into ethnically based cliques. Members of ethnic groups eat together, socialize together, and chat in their native language while they work. Some other team members feel left out and alienated. How do you encourage a stronger team attitude?
   a. Ban the use of languages other than English at work.
   b. Do nothing. This is normal behavior.
   c. Have regular team meetings and encourage people to mingle and get to know each other better.
   d. Send all of your employees to diversity training classes.[39]

Learning Objectives Checkup

To assess your understanding of the principles in this chapter, read each learning objective and study the accompanying exercises. For fill-in items, write the missing text in the blank provided; for multiple choice items, circle the letter of the correct answer. You can check your responses against the answer key on page AK-1.

Objective 3.1: Discuss two trends contributing to the importance of intercultural business communication in the workplace.

1. A major trend contributing to the rising importance of intercultural business communication skills is
   a. The trade deficit between the U.S. and other countries
   b. The federal government's requirement for all businesses to be ethnically balanced
   c. Advanced technologies that are spurring the growth of the global marketplace and the dissolution of national borders
   d. All of the above

2. Estimates project that by 2010, minorities will account for _____ percent of the U.S. population.
   a. 25
   b. 35
   c. 50
   d. 65

3. By 2010, the largest minority group in the United States, making up about 24 percent of the population, will be
   a. Hispanic Americans
   b. African Americans

c. Asian Americans

d. Caucasian Americans

Objective 3.2: Define culture and subculture, and summarize how culture is learned.

4. Culture is defined as
   a. A distinct group that exists within a country
   b. A shared system of symbols, beliefs, attitudes, values, expectations, and norms for behavior
   c. The pattern of cues and stimuli that convey meaning between two or more people
   d. "High" art forms such as classical music, painting, sculpture, drama, and poetry

5. Which of the following is *not* an example of a subculture?
   a. Mormons
   b. Wrestling fans
   c. Television viewers
   d. Members of a fraternity

6. Culture is learned from
   a. Family members
   b. Explicit teaching by others in the culture
   c. Observing the behavior of others in the culture
   d. All of the above

Objective 3.3: Explain the importance of recognizing cultural differences, and list four categories of cultural differences.

7. In business, it is important to recognize cultural differences because
   a. Doing so helps reduce the chances for misunderstanding
   b. Someone from another culture may try to take advantage of your ignorance
   c. If you don't, you'll be accused of being politically incorrect
   d. Doing so helps you become more ethnocentric

8. An example of low-context cultural communication would be
   a. Someone from China using metaphors to convey meaning
   b. Someone from Greece insisting on reaching agreement on every detail of a deal
   c. Someone from Canada vigorously arguing his point of view in a problem-solving situation
   d. Someone from Japan encouraging socializing before entering into official negotiations

9. When it comes to bribing officials, this practice is
   a. Outlawed in all Middle Eastern countries
   b. Avoided by most U.S. businesses, even though it is perfectly legal under U.S. statutes
   c. Considered legal but unethical in China
   d. A natural part of doing business in African countries such as Kenya

10. If you will be visiting an Arab business executive, you
    a. Should take a gift for his wife
    b. Can expect his office to be cramped and modestly appointed
    c. Should maintain as large a physical distance as possible between the two of you
    d. Should do all of the above

Objective 3.4: Define ethnocentrism and stereotyping, then give three suggestions for overcoming these limiting mind-sets.

11. People who are ethnocentric
    a. Tend to judge all other groups according to their own group's standards, behaviors, and customs
    b. Tend to strongly support affirmative action
    c. Are usually religious fanatics
    d. Are usually the best organizers of intercultural exchanges

12. An example of stereotyping would be
    a. Expecting a basketball player to be tall
    b. Assuming that a dog owner loves all types of animals
    c. Assuming that an Italian American knows or is related to someone in the mob
    d. Expecting someone with a Ph.D. in linguistics to be good at playing Scrabble

13. One way to overcome ethnocentrism and stereotyping is to
    a. Ignore the differences between another person's culture and your own
    b. Assume that others will use language and symbols the same way you do
    c. Avoid judging others when they act differently than you would
    d. Do all of the above

Objective 3.5: Discuss four ways to improve communication with people who speak English as a second language and three ways to improve communication with people who don't speak your language at all.

14. After English, _____ is the most commonly spoken language in U.S. households.
    a. Chinese
    b. French
    c. German
    d. Spanish

15. Which of the following is *not* a guideline for talking with someone who speaks English as a second language?
    a. Use American slang and idioms to help the person feel more comfortable.
    b. Expect to understand the person, even if he or she has a heavy accent.
    c. Don't let ethnic vocal variations, such as a monotone or loudness, get in the way of understanding.
    d. Use the communication style—direct or indirect—that your audience prefers.

16. If you will be working regularly on a long-term basis with people in another country who know very little English, your best approach would be to
    a. Tell them that they need to take some English courses if they want to get along with you
    b. Hire a permanent translator to handle all your communications with the non-English-speakers
    c. Learn at least some of the language, especially the terminology related to your business
    d. Try to find a third language that everyone knows

Objective 3.6: List eight recommendations for improving your intercultural writing.

17. When writing international business letters, you should
    a. Spell out numbers rather than writing them as figures
    b. Use plain English
    c. Use long sentences and paragraphs
    d. Do all of the above

Objective 3.7: Identify nine guidelines for improving your intercultural oral communication.

18. When communicating orally to those who speak English as a second language, it is a good idea to
    a. Overenunciate
    b. Speak louder if he or she doesn't seem to understand
    c. Ignore the other person's body language
    d. Rephrase your sentences when necessary

Apply Your Knowledge

1. What are some of the intercultural differences that managers of a U.S.-based firm might encounter during a series of business meetings with a China-based company whose managers speak English fairly well?
2. What are some of the intercultural communication issues to consider when deciding whether to accept an overseas job with a firm whose headquarters are in the United States? A job in the United States with a local branch of a foreign-owned firm? Explain.
3. How do you think company managers from a country that has a relatively homogeneous culture might react when they do business with the culturally diverse staff of a company based in a less homogeneous country? Explain your answer.
4. Your company has relocated to a U.S. city where a Vietnamese subculture is strongly established. Many of your employees will be from this subculture. What can you do to improve communication between your management and the Vietnamese Americans you are currently hiring?
5. **Ethical Choices** Your office in Turkey desperately needs the supplies that have been sitting in Turkish customs for a month. Should you bribe a customs official to speed up delivery? Explain your decision.

Practice Your Knowledge

DOCUMENT FOR ANALYSIS

Your boss wants to send a brief e-mail message welcoming employees recently transferred to your department from your Hong Kong branch. They all speak English, but your boss asks you to review his message for clarity. What would you suggest your boss change in the following e-mail message—and why?

Would you consider this message to be audience centered? Why or why not?

I wanted to welcome you ASAP to our little family here in the States. It's high time we shook hands in person and not just across the sea. I'm pleased as punch about getting to know you all, and I for one will do my level best to sell you on America.

Exercises

For live links to all websites discussed in this chapter, visit this text's website at www.prenhall.com/thill. Just log on, select Chapter 3, and click on "Student Resources." Locate the page or the URL related to the material in the text. For the "Learning More on the Web" exercises, you'll also find navigational directions. Click on the live link to the site.

3.1 **Intercultural Sensitivity: Recognizing Differences** You represent a Canadian toy company that's negotiating to buy miniature truck wheels from a manufacturer in Osaka, Japan. In your first meeting, you explain that your company expects to control the design of the wheels as well as the materials that are used to make them. The manufacturer's representative looks down and says softly, "Perhaps that will be difficult." You press for agreement, and to emphasize your willingness to buy, you show the prepared contract you've brought with you. However, the manufacturer seems increasingly vague and uninterested. What cultural differences may be interfering with effective communication in this situation? Explain.

3.2 **Ethical Choices** A U.S. manager wants to export T-shirts to a West African country, but a West African official expects a special payment before allowing the shipment into his country. How can the two sides resolve their different approaches without violating U.S. rules against bribing foreign officials? On the basis of the information presented in Chapter 1, would you consider this situation an ethical dilemma or an ethical lapse? Please explain.

3.3   **Teamwork**   Working with two other students, prepare a list of 10 examples of slang (in your own language) that would probably be misinterpreted or misunderstood during a business conversation with someone from another culture. Next to each example, suggest other words you might use to convey the same message. Do the alternatives mean *exactly* the same as the original slang or idiom?

3.4   **Intercultural Communication: Studying Cultures**   Choose a specific country with which you are not familiar. Research the culture and write a brief summary of what a U.S. manager would need to know about concepts of personal space and rules of social behavior in order to conduct business successfully in that country.

3.5   **Multicultural Workforce: Bridging Differences**   Differences in gender, age, and physical abilities contribute to the diversity of today's workforce. Working with a classmate, role-play a conversation in which

   a. A woman is being interviewed for a job by a male personnel manager

   b. An older person is being interviewed for a job by a younger personnel manager

   c. A person using a wheelchair is being interviewed for a job by a person who can walk

How did differences between the applicant and the interviewer shape the communication? What can you do to improve communication in such situations?

3.6   **Intercultural Sensitivity: Understanding Attitudes**   As the director of marketing for a telecommunications firm based in Germany, you're negotiating with an official in Guangzhou, China, who's in charge of selecting a new telephone system for the city. You insist that the specifications be spelled out in detail in the contract. However, your Chinese counterpart argues that in developing a long-term business relationship, such minor details are unimportant. What can you do or say to break this intercultural deadlock and obtain the contract so that both parties are comfortable?

3.7   **Culture and Language: Understanding Differences**   Germany is a low-context culture; by comparison, France and England are high-context cultures. These three translations of the same message were posted on a lawn in Switzerland: The German sign read, "Walking on the grass is forbidden"; the English

sign read, "Please do not walk on the grass"; and the French sign read, "Those who respect their environment will avoid walking on the grass."[40] How does the language of each sign reflect the way information is conveyed in the cultural context of each nation? Write a brief (two- to three-paragraph) explanation.

3.8   **Culture and Time: Dealing with Differences**   When a company knows that a scheduled delivery time given by an overseas firm is likely to be flexible, managers may buy in larger quantities or may order more often to avoid running out of product before the next delivery. Identify three other management decisions that may be influenced by differing cultural concepts of time, and make notes for a short (two-minute) presentation to your class.

3.9   **Intercultural Communication: Using Translators**   Imagine that you're the lead negotiator for a company that's trying to buy a factory in Prague, the capital of the Czech Republic. Your parents grew up near Prague, so you understand and speak the language fairly well. However, you wonder about the advantages and disadvantages of using a translator anyway. For example, you may have more time to think if you wait for an intermediary to translate the other side's position. Decide whether to hire a translator, and then write a brief (two- or three-paragraph) explanation of your decision.

3.10   **Internet**   Some companies are experimenting with software that automatically translates business messages. To see how this works, go to the AltaVista site at www.altavista.com. Click on "translate" and enter a sentence such as "We are enclosing a purchase order for four dozen computer monitors." Select "English to Spanish" and click to complete the translation. Once you've read the Spanish version, cut and paste it into the "text for translation" box, select "Spanish to English," and click to translate. Try translating the same English sentence into German, French, or Italian and then back into English. How do the results of each translation differ? What are the implications for the use of automated translation services and back-translation? How could you use this website to sharpen your intercultural communication skills?

3.11   **Intercultural Communication: Improving Skills**   You've been assigned to host a group of Swedish college students who are visiting your college for the next two weeks. They've all studied English but this is their first trip to your area. Make a list of at least eight slang terms and idioms they are likely to hear on campus. How will you explain each phrase? When speaking with the Swedish students, what word or words might you substitute for each slang term or idiom?

Expand Your Knowledge

LEARNING MORE ON THE WEB

Improve Your Cultural Sensitivity www.executiveplanet.com

Want to improve your cultural sensitivity? Log on to ExecutivePlanet.com, where you'll find country reports, business and cultural tips, and links to interviews, profiles, articles, books, and more learning resources. Avoid culture shock by developing your ability to understand the traditions, assumptions, etiquette, and values of other cultures as well as your own. This site is your business and cultural guide to the world.

ACTIVITIES

Visit ExecutivePlanet.com and read the country reports and cultural tips. Follow the site's links to interviews, profiles, articles, books, and more. Then answer the following questions.

1. Why should you understand negotiating practices of people from a different culture?

2. Every culture has its own business protocol. What should you know about a culture's business protocol before you transact business with that culture?
3. What are some examples of cultural gift-giving taboos?

EXPLORING THE WEB ON YOUR OWN

Review these chapter-related websites on your own to learn more about intercultural communication.

1. Country Commercial Guides, at www.usatrade.gov, contains helpful information on foreign marketing practices, trade regulations, investment climate, and business travel for a number of countries.
2. Visit www.cyborlink.com/besite/hotstede.htm for many tips on conducting business around the world, including resourceful country profiles.
3. Travlang, www3.travlang.com, can help you learn a foreign language. Check out the site's translating dictionaries and learn a new word in a foreign language every day.

Learn Interactively

INTERACTIVE STUDY GUIDE

Go to the Companion Website at www.prenhall.com/bovee. For Chapter 3, take advantage of the interactive "Study Guide" to test your knowledge of the chapter. Get instant feedback on whether you need additional studying. Also, visit this site's "Study Hall" where you'll find an abundance of valuable resources that will help you succeed in this course.

PEAK PERFORMANCE GRAMMAR AND MECHANICS

To improve your skill with Verbs, use the "Peak Performance Grammar and Mechanics" module on the web. Visit www.prehnall.com/onekey, click "Peak Performance Grammar and Mechanics," then click "Verbs." Take the Pretest to determine whether you have any weak areas. Then review those areas in the Refresher Course. Take the Follow-Up Test to check your grasp of verbs. For an extra challenge or advanced practice, take the Advanced Test. Finally, for additional reinforcement, go to the "Improve Your Grammar, Mechanics, and Usage" section that follows, and complete those exercises.

Improve Your Grammar, Mechanics, and Usage

The following exercises help you improve your knowledge of and power over English grammar, mechanics, and usage. Turn to the "Handbook of Grammar, Mechanics, and Usage" at the end of this textbook and review all of Section 1.3 (Verbs). Then look at the following 10 items. Circle the letter of the preferred choice in the following groups of sentences. (Answers to these exercises appear on page AK-3.)

1. Which sentence contains a verb in the present perfect form?
   a. I became the resident expert on repairing the copy machine.
   b. I have become the resident expert on repairing the copy machine.

2. Which sentence contains a verb in the simple past form?
   a. She knows how to conduct an audit when she came to work for us.
   b. She knew how to conduct an audit when she came to work for us.
3. Which sentence contains a verb in the simple future form?
   a. Next week, call John to tell him what you will do to help him set up the seminar.
   b. Next week, call John to tell him what you will be doing to help him set up the seminar.
4. Which sentence is in the active voice?
   a. The report will be written by Leslie Cartwright.
   b. Leslie Cartwright will write the report.

5. Which sentence is in the passive voice?
   a. The transaction was never recorded by anyone.
   b. No one ever recorded the transaction.
6. Which sentence contains the correct verb form?
   a. Everyone upstairs receives mail before we do.
   b. Everyone upstairs receive mail before we do.
7. Which sentence contains the correct verb form?
   a. Neither the main office nor the branches is blameless.
   b. Neither the main office nor the branches are blameless.
8. Which sentence contains the correct verb form?
   a. C&B Sales are listed in the directory.
   b. C&B Sales is listed in the directory.
9. Which sentence contains the correct verb form?
   a. When measuring shelves, 7 inches is significant.
   b. When measuring shelves, 7 inches are significant.
10. Which sentence contains the correct verb form?
    a. About 90 percent of the employees plans to come to the company picnic.
    b. About 90 percent of the employees plan to come to the company picnic.

For additional exercises focusing on verbs, go to www.prenhall.com/thill and select "Handbook of Grammar, Mechanics, and Usage Practice Sessions."

Part II
Applying the Three-Step Writing Process

Chapter 4

Planning Business Messages

Learning Objectives

AFTER STUDYING THIS CHAPTER, YOU WILL BE ABLE TO

1 Describe the three-step writing process

2 Explain why it's important to define your purpose carefully, and list four questions that can help you test that purpose

3 Justify the importance of analyzing your audience, then list six ways of developing an audience profile

4 Identify five ways to satisfy your audience's information needs

5 List the factors to consider when choosing the most appropriate channel and medium for your message

6 Discuss six ways you can establish a good relationship with your audience

On the Job:

COMMUNICATING AT HOME DEPOT

DESIGNING A BLUEPRINT FOR SUCCESS

Whether you need a few tips on installing curtain rods or some expert guidance on kitchen remodeling, Home Depot wants to lend a helping hand. Co-founders Bernie Marcus and Arthur Blank worked hard to create a retail culture that encourages homeowners to tackle their own home improvement and repair projects without hiring contractors. And now, says CEO Robert Nardelli, "The baby boomers are moving from do-it-yourself to do-it-for-me," so the company is beginning to reorganize to better serve the needs of professional contractors. With more than 1,500 stores throughout the United States, Canada, Mexico, and Puerto Rico, Home Depot's future success centers on the company's ability to communicate effectively with employees, customers, and suppliers.

To keep operations running smoothly, Nardelli and Home Depot managers need to establish good working relationships with all three audiences. They must find out what each audience needs to know, and they must determine the right way to communicate that information. For example, before Home Depot stores can stock a new product, the company must analyze the needs of its audiences and plan appropriate messages for each one. Management must assess customer demand, educate employees about product use, and seek vendors that can deliver the right amount of merchandise in a timely manner.

Planning effective messages wasn't as difficult when Marcus and Blank opened their first four stores in Atlanta. Working in the stores each day, they personally trained every employee, helped customers find the right tools and supplies for their projects, and dealt directly with every supplier. But opening a new store every 43 hours means that Nardelli can no longer depend on oral messages to communicate with the company's various audiences. Establishing relationships with 200,000 employees, 25,000 suppliers, and millions of customers has complicated matters. Plus, adapting messages to serve the needs of

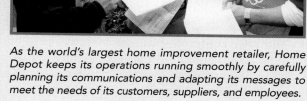

As the world's largest home improvement retailer, Home Depot keeps its operations running smoothly by carefully planning its communications and adapting its messages to meet the needs of its customers, suppliers, and employees.

each Home Depot audience requires careful planning.

For instance, the company uses a variety of media to educate their customers about various repair techniques. Management invites customers to attend small-group, in-store meetings, known as "how-to clinics," where live presenters demonstrate repair techniques and product installations. The company also distributes free product literature, installation instructions, and informational brochures throughout its stores, in addition to offering a toll-free customer service number staffed by home improvement experts and company managers who are available to answer questions and handle customer complaints immediately. Customers can also review how-to articles, either in Home Depot's magazine, *Weekend,* or on a Home Depot CD-ROM. Home Depot's television program, *House Smart,* is a regular feature on the Discovery Channel, showing viewers how to handle home improvement projects and problems.

Nardelli and Home Depot use a different communication approach with the North American suppliers, who provide 40,000 to 50,000 kinds of building materials, home improvement supplies, and lawn and garden products. Twice each year, the company sponsors weeklong vendor conferences, holding the events in large arenas throughout the country. During these conferences, managers interact in small groups to become better acquainted with new suppliers and to learn about new product offerings from current suppliers. They also make presentations to large audiences, informing suppliers about which products customers want, which ones aren't selling, and which need to be changed or dropped.

Regardless of how Home Depot communicates with customers and suppliers, the company understands that each channel and medium has its advantages and disadvantages. The important thing is to find out what the audience needs to know and then select the best way to deliver that information.[1]

www.homedepot.com

UNDERSTANDING THE THREE-STEP WRITING PROCESS

Like Home Depot's managers, you'll face a variety of communication assignments in your career, both oral and written. Some of your tasks will be routine, requiring little more than jotting down a few sentences on paper or keyboarding a brief e-mail message; others will be more complex, requiring reflection, research, and careful document preparation. Because your audience is exposed to an increasing number of business messages each day, your messages must be livelier, easier to read, more concise, and more interesting than ever before.

Of course, making your business messages interesting doesn't mean using the dramatic techniques of creative writing. Your purpose is not to dazzle your readers with your extensive knowledge or powerful vocabulary. Instead, your messages must be

To compete for attention, business messages must be purposeful, audience-centered, and concise.

- **Purposeful.** Business messages provide information, solve a problem, or request the resources necessary to accomplish a goal. Every message you prepare should have a specific purpose.

- **Audience-centered.** Business messages help audiences understand an issue, ask them to collaborate on accomplishing a goal, or persuade them to take some action. So every message you prepare must consider the audience's background, point of view, and needs.

- **Concise.** Business messages respect everyone's time by presenting information clearly and efficiently. Every message you prepare should be as short as it can be without detracting from the subject.

The goal of effective business writing is to express your ideas rather than to impress your audience. One of the best ways to do so is to follow a systematic writing process.

What Is the Three-Step Writing Process?

The specific actions you take to write business messages will vary with each situation, audience, and purpose. However, following a process of generalized steps will help you write more effective messages. As Figure 4–1 shows, this **writing process** may be viewed as comprising three simple steps: (1) planning, (2) writing, and (3) completing your business messages.[2]

The writing process has three steps.

- **Planning your message.** The first stage is to think about the fundamentals of your message. Study your purpose to make sure your reasons for communicating are clear and necessary. Schedule enough time to complete all three steps of the writing process. Analyze audience members so that you can tailor your message to their needs, and then gather the information that will inform, persuade, or motivate them. Don't forget to adapt your message: Select the best channel and medium and establish a good audience relationship. Planning messages is the focus of this chapter.

- **Writing your message.** Once you've planned your message, organize your information and begin composing your first draft. This is the stage when you commit your thoughts to words, create sentences and paragraphs, and select illustrations and details to support your main idea. Writing business messages is discussed in Chapter 5.

- **Completing your message.** After writing your first draft, step back to review the content and organization for overall style, structure, and readability. Revise and rewrite until your message comes across clearly and effectively; then edit your message for details such as grammar, punctuation, and format. Next, produce your message, putting it into the form that your audience will receive. Finally, proof the final draft for typos, spelling errors, and other mechanical problems. Completing business messages is discussed in Chapter 6.

Planning ## Writing ## Completing

Analyze the Situation
Study your purpose, lay out your writing schedule, and then profile your audience.

Gather Information
Gather information through formal or informal research methods.

Adapt to the Audience
Choose the right channel and medium; then establish a good relationship with your audience.

Organize the Information
Define your main idea, limit the scope, group your points, and choose the direct or indirect approach.

Compose the Message
Control your style through level of formality and conversational tone. Choose your words carefully so that you can create effective sentences and paragraphs.

Revise the Message
Evaluate content and review readability; then edit and rewrite for conciseness and clarity.

Produce the Message
Use effective design elements and suitable delivery methods.

Proofread the Message
Review for errors in layout, spelling, and mechanics.

1 **2** **3**

FIGURE 4–1
The Three-Step Writing Process

How Does the Three-Step Writing Process Work?

Because so many of today's business messages are composed under pressure and on a schedule that is anything but realistic, allocating your time among these three steps can be a challenge. In some cases, your audience may expect you to get your message out in record time—sometimes only minutes after speaking with a client or attending a meeting. But whether you have 30 minutes or two days, try to give yourself enough time to plan, write, and complete your message.

As a general rule, try using roughly half your time for planning—for deciding on your purpose, getting to know your audience, and immersing yourself in your subject matter. Use less than a quarter of your time for writing your document. Then use more than a quarter of your time for completing the project (so that you don't neglect important final steps such as revising and proofing).[3]

Home Depot's managers understand that there is no right or best way to write all business messages. As you work through the writing process presented in this chapter and Chapters 5 and 6, try to view it not as a list of how-to directives but as a way to understand the various tasks involved in effective business writing.[4] The three-step process will help you avoid the risky "rush in and start writing" routine.

Remember that the writing process is flexible. Effective communicators may not necessarily complete the steps in 1–2–3 order. Some jump back and forth from one step to another; some compose quickly and then revise; others revise as they go along. However, to communicate effectively, you must ultimately complete all three steps.

> When writing a business message, schedule enough time to complete all three steps.

> Effective writers complete all three steps, regardless of order.

ANALYZING THE SITUATION

When planning a business message, the first things you need to think about are your purpose, your schedule, and your audience. For a business message to be effective, its purpose and its audience must complement each other.

Define Your Purpose

Your general purpose may be to inform, to persuade, or to collaborate.

All business messages have a **general purpose**: to inform, to persuade, or to collaborate with your audience. This overall purpose determines both the amount of audience participation you need and the amount of control you have over your message. To inform your audience, you need little interaction. Audience members absorb the information and accept or reject it, but they don't contribute to message content; you control the message. To persuade your audience, you require a moderate amount of participation, and you need to retain a moderate amount of message control. Finally, to collaborate with audience members, you need maximum participation. Your control of the message is minimal because you must adjust to new input and unexpected reactions.

Business messages also have a **specific purpose**. That purpose may be straightforward (such as placing an order or communicating survey responses), or it may be more encompassing (such as convincing management to hire more part-time employees during the holiday season). To help you define the specific purpose of your message, ask yourself what you hope to accomplish with your message and what your audience should do or think after receiving your message. For instance, is your goal simply to update your audience on an event, or do you want them to take immediate action? State your specific purpose as precisely as possible, even identifying which audience members should respond.

To determine the specific purpose, think of how the audience's ideas or behavior should be affected by the message.

You must also consider whether your purpose is worth pursuing at this time. Too many business messages serve no practical purpose, and writing useless memos can destroy your credibility. So if you suspect that your ideas will have little impact, wait until you have a more practical purpose. To help you decide whether to proceed, ask yourself four questions:

Defer a message, or do not send it at all, if it isn't worth pursuing.

- **Is your purpose realistic?** If your purpose involves a radical shift in action or attitude, go slowly. Consider proposing the first step and using your message as the beginning of a learning process.

- **Is this the right time?** If an organization is undergoing changes of some sort, you may want to defer your message until things stabilize and people can concentrate on your ideas.

- **Is the right person delivering your message?** Even though you may have done all the work, achieving your objective is more important than taking the credit. You may want to play a supporting role in delivering your message if, for example, your boss's higher status could get better results.

- **Is your purpose acceptable to your organization?** If you receive an abusive letter that unfairly attacks your company, you might feel like firing back an angry reply. But your supervisors might prefer that you regain the customer's goodwill. Your response must reflect the organization's priorities.

Once you are satisfied that you have a legitimate purpose in communicating, remember to schedule your time so that you can comfortably complete all three steps in the writing process. Planning your message should take approximately half the time you have available. Now, take a closer look at your intended audience.

Develop an Audience Profile

Ask yourself some key questions about your audience:
- Who are they?
- What is their probable reaction to your message?
- How much do they already know about the subject?
- What is their relationship to you?

Who are your audience members? What are their attitudes? What do they need to know? And why should they care about your message? The answers to such questions will indicate which material you'll need to cover and how to cover it.

If you're communicating with someone you know well, perhaps your boss or a co-worker, audience analysis is relatively easy. You can predict this person's reaction

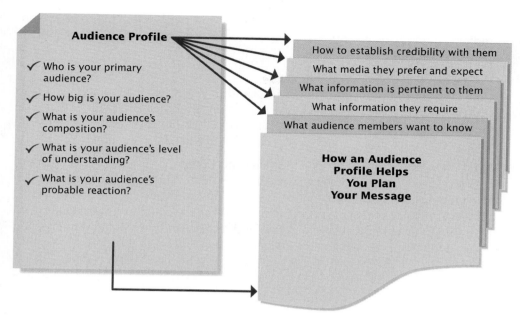

FIGURE 4–2
Audience Analysis Helps You
Plan Your Message

pretty well, without a lot of research. On the other hand, your audience could be made up of strangers—customers or suppliers you've never met, a new boss, or new employees. So just like Home Depot's Robert Nardelli, you'll have to learn about the members of your audience before you can adjust your message to their needs (see Figure 4–2).

- **Identify the primary audience.** If you can reach the decision makers or opinion molders in your audience, other audience members will fall into place. Key people often have the most organizational clout, but occasionally a person of relatively low status may have influence in one or two particular areas.

Be sure your audience profile is thorough.

- **Determine audience size.** A report for wide distribution requires a more formal style, organization, and format than one directed to three or four people in your department. Also, be sure to respond to the particular concerns of key individuals. The head of marketing would need different facts than the head of production or finance would need.

- **Determine audience composition.** Look for common denominators that tie audience members together across differences in culture, education, status, or attitude. Include evidence that touches on everyone's area of interest. To be understood across cultural barriers, consider how audience members think and learn, as well as what style they expect.[5]

- **Gauge your audience's level of understanding.** If audience members share your general background, they'll understand your material without difficulty. If not, you must educate them. But deciding how much information to include can be a challenge. As a guideline, include only enough information to accomplish your objective. Other

Nicola Shirley uses her Jamaican background and West Indian cooking talent to entice customers to eat at her restaurant or try her JaHut food products. But savory cooking is only one of her strengths. When it comes to communicating with customers, suppliers, or investors, Shirley gets results by making sure her message has a clear purpose and addresses her audience's information needs.

material is irrelevant and must be eliminated; otherwise it will overwhelm your audience and divert attention from the important points. If audience members have varying levels of understanding, gear your coverage to your primary audience (the key decision makers).

- **Consider your audience's expectations and preferences.** Will members of your audience expect complete details, or will a summary of the main points suffice? Do they want an e-mail or will they expect a formal memo? Should the memo be a brief 1- to 3-page message or a comprehensive 10- to 15-page report?

- **Estimate your audience's probable reaction.** Chapter 5 discusses how audience reaction affects message organization. If you expect a favorable response, you can state conclusions and recommendations up front and offer minimal supporting evidence. If you expect skepticism, you can introduce conclusions gradually, with more proof. By anticipating the primary audience's response to certain points, you can include evidence to address those issues.

GATHERING INFORMATION

The process of gathering information can be formal or informal.

Before you compose your message, you'll most likely need to gather some information to communicate to your audience. When writing long, formal reports, you'll conduct formal research to locate and analyze all the information relevant to your purpose and your audience. Formal techniques for finding, evaluating, and processing information are discussed in Chapter 10. Other kinds of business messages, however, require less formal information gathering.

Informal methods of gathering information will probably be sufficient for most brief business messages.

Whether you're preparing for an informational interview with your supervisor, writing an e-mail message to a close colleague, or gathering opinions for an article to appear in your organization's monthly newsletter, you can gather information to satisfy your audience's needs by using these informal methods:

- **Considering others' viewpoints.** You might put yourself in others' positions to consider what they might be thinking, feeling, or planning.

Gathering information from co-workers in conversations or informal interviews helps Levi Strauss editors determine how much detail about a project their audience expects in the company newsletter.

- **Reading reports and other company documents.** Your company's files may be a rich source of the information you need for a particular memo or e-mail message. Consider company annual reports, financial statements, news releases, memos, marketing reports, and customer surveys for helpful information.

- **Chatting with supervisors, colleagues, or customers.** Fellow workers and customers may have information you need, or they may know what your audience will be interested in. Conducting telephone or personal interviews is a convenient way to gather information.

- **Asking your audience for input.** If you're unsure of what audience members need from your message, ask them—whether through casual conversation (face-to-face or over the phone), informal surveys, or unofficial interviews.

A good message answers all audience questions. If you don't discover what audience members need to know, you're likely to serve them fruit punch and peanut butter when they're expecting champagne and caviar. The key to satisfying your audience's information needs is finding out what questions your audience has and then providing answers that are thorough, accurate, ethical, and pertinent.

Find Out Exactly What Your Audience Needs to Know

In many cases your audience's information needs are readily apparent; for example, a consumer may send you a letter asking a specific question. In other cases, your audience may not be particularly good at telling you what's needed. When your audience makes a vague request, try restating the request in more specific terms. If your boss says, "Find out everything you can about Polaroid," you might respond, "You want me to track down their market position by product line and get sales and profit figures by division for the past five years, right?" Another way to handle a vague request is to get a fix on its priority. You might ask, "Should I drop everything else and devote myself to this for the next week?" Asking a question or two forces the person to think through the request and define more precisely what is required.

By restating a vague request in more specific terms, you can get the requester to define his or her needs more precisely.

Also, try to think of information needs that your audience may not even be aware of. Suppose your company has just hired a new employee from out of town, and you've been assigned to coordinate this person's relocation. At a minimum, you would write a welcoming letter describing your company's procedures for relocating employees. With a little extra thought, however, you might include some information about the city: perhaps a guide to residential areas, a map or two, brochures about cultural activities, or information on schools and transportation facilities. In some cases, you may be able to tell your audience something they consider important but wouldn't have thought to ask. Although adding information of this sort lengthens your message, doing so creates goodwill.

Include any additional information that might be helpful, even though the requester didn't specifically ask for it.

Provide All Required Information

Once you've defined your audience's information needs, be sure you satisfy those needs completely. One good way to test the thoroughness of your message is to use the **journalistic approach**: Check to see whether your message answers *who, what, when, where, why,* and *how.* Many messages fail to pass the test—such as this letter requesting information from a large hotel:

Test the completeness of your document by making sure it answers all the important questions: who, what, when, where, why, and how.

Dear Ms. Hill:

I just got back from a great vacation in Hawaii. However, this morning I discovered that my favorite black leather shoes are missing. Since I wore them in Hawaii, I assume I left them at the Hawaii Sands Hotel. Please check the items in your "lost and found" and let me know whether you have the missing shoes.

The letter fails to tell Hill everything she needs to know. The *what* could be improved by a detailed description of the missing shoes (size, brand, distinguishable style or trim). Hill doesn't know *when* the writer stayed at the Hawaii Sands, *where* (in what room), or *how* to return the shoes. Hill will have to write or call the writer to get the missing details, and the inconvenience may be just enough to prevent her from complying with the request.

Be Sure the Information Is Accurate

There's no point in answering all your audience's questions if the answers are wrong. Your organization is legally bound by any promises you make, so be sure your company is able to follow through. Whether you're promising delivery by a given date or

Be certain that the information you provide is accurate and that the commitments you make can be kept.

agreeing to purchase an item, if you have any doubt about the organization's ability or willingness to back up your promises, check with the appropriate people *before* you make the commitment.

You can minimize mistakes by double-checking everything you write or say. If you are using outside sources, ask yourself whether they are current and reliable. If your sources are international, remember that various cultures can view accuracy differently. A German bank may insist on balancing the books to the last penny, whereas an Italian bank may be more lenient.[6] Be sure to review any mathematical or financial calculations. Check all dates and schedules, and examine your own assumptions and conclusions to be certain they are valid.

Be Sure the Information Is Ethical

Honest mistakes are certainly possible. You may sincerely believe that you have answered someone's questions correctly, and then later realize that your information was incorrect. If that happens, the most ethical course of action is to contact the person immediately and correct the error. Most people will respect you for your honesty.

Good ethics will help you determine how much detail to include in your message.

Messages can be unethical simply because information is omitted. Of course, as a business professional, you may have legal or other sound business reasons for not including every detail about every matter. So just how much detail should you include? Even though most people don't want to be buried in an avalanche of paperwork, include enough detail to avoid misleading your audience. If you're unsure about how much information your audience needs, offer as much as you believe best fits your definition of complete, then offer to provide more upon request.

Be Sure the Information Is Pertinent

Try to figure out what points will especially interest your audience; then give those points the most attention.

When deciding how to respond to your audience's information needs, remember that some points will be of greater interest and importance than others. If you're summarizing a recent conversation you had with one of your company's oldest and best customers, the emphasis you give each point of the conversation will depend on your audience's concerns. The head of engineering might be most interested in the customer's reaction to your product's new design features. The shipping manager might be most concerned about the customer's comments on recent delivery schedules. In other words, be careful to emphasize the points that will have the most impact on your audience.

If you don't know your audience, or if you're communicating with a large group of people, use your common sense to identify points of particular interest. Audience factors such as age, job, location, income, and education can give you a clue. If you were trying to sell memberships in the Book-of-the-Month Club, you would adjust your message for various types of people. Everyone would need to know the same facts about membership, but economy might be important to college students or retired people, and convenience might attract sales reps or homemakers. As Figure 4–3 shows, your main goal is to tell audience members what they need to know.

ADAPTING YOUR MESSAGE TO YOUR AUDIENCE

By now you know why you're writing, you know the audience you're writing to, and you have most of the information you need. But you're not quite ready to actually begin writing your message. First, figure out how to tailor it to your audience and your

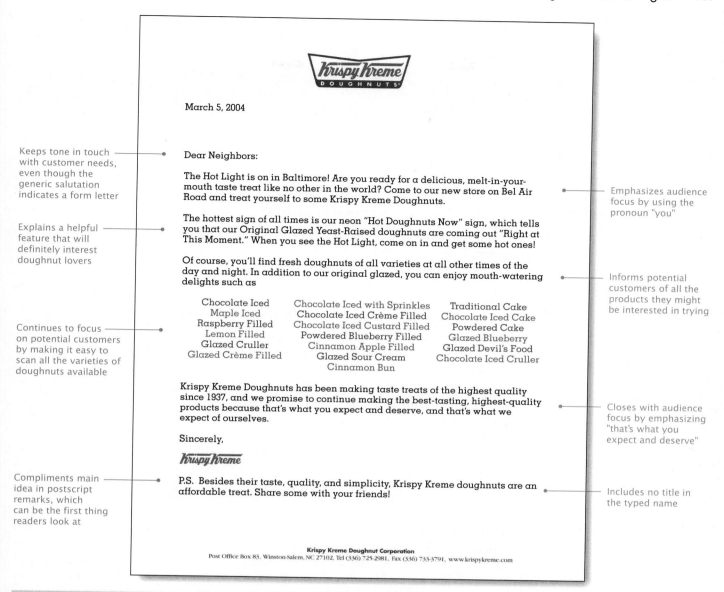

Keeps tone in touch with customer needs, even though the generic salutation indicates a form letter

Explains a helpful feature that will definitely interest doughnut lovers

Continues to focus on potential customers by making it easy to scan all the varieties of doughnuts available

Compliments main idea in postscript remarks, which can be the first thing readers look at

Emphasizes audience focus by using the pronoun "you"

Informs potential customers of all the products they might be interested in trying

Closes with audience focus by emphasizing "that's what you expect and deserve"

Includes no title in the typed name

March 5, 2004

Dear Neighbors:

The Hot Light is on in Baltimore! Are you ready for a delicious, melt-in-your-mouth taste treat like no other in the world? Come to our new store on Bel Air Road and treat yourself to some Krispy Kreme Doughnuts.

The hottest sign of all times is our neon "Hot Doughnuts Now" sign, which tells you that our Original Glazed Yeast-Raised doughnuts are coming out "Right at This Moment." When you see the Hot Light, come on in and get some hot ones!

Of course, you'll find fresh doughnuts of all varieties at all other times of the day and night. In addition to our original glazed, you can enjoy mouth-watering delights such as

Chocolate Iced	Chocolate Iced with Sprinkles	Traditional Cake
Maple Iced	Chocolate Iced Crème Filled	Chocolate Iced Cake
Raspberry Filled	Chocolate Iced Custard Filled	Powdered Cake
Lemon Filled	Powdered Blueberry Filled	Glazed Blueberry
Glazed Cruller	Cinnamon Apple Filled	Glazed Devil's Food
Glazed Crème Filled	Glazed Sour Cream	Chocolate Iced Cruller
	Cinnamon Bun	

Krispy Kreme Doughnuts has been making taste treats of the highest quality since 1937, and we promise to continue making the best-tasting, highest-quality products because that's what you expect and deserve, and that's what we expect of ourselves.

Sincerely,

Krispy Kreme

P.S. Besides their taste, quality, and simplicity, Krispy Kreme doughnuts are an affordable treat. Share some with your friends!

Krispy Kreme Doughnut Corporation
Post Office Box 83, Winston-Salem, NC 27102, Tel (336) 725-2981, Fax (336) 733-3791, www.krispykreme.com

FIGURE 4–3
Effective Audience-Centered Letter

purpose. To adapt your message, select a channel and medium appropriate to audience members, and then plan out how you'll establish a good relationship with them.

Select the Appropriate Channel and Medium

Selecting the best channel and medium for your message can make the difference between effective and ineffective communication.[7] A **communication channel** can be either oral or written. Each channel includes specific media. The oral channel includes media such as telephone conversations, face-to-face exchanges, and videotaped addresses. The written channel includes media such as letters, memos, e-mail messages, and reports. When selecting a channel and medium, you must consider how your choice will affect the style, tone, and impact of your message. To do so, you need to consider a number of important factors.

Different types of messages require different communication channels and media.

FIGURE 4–4
Media Richness

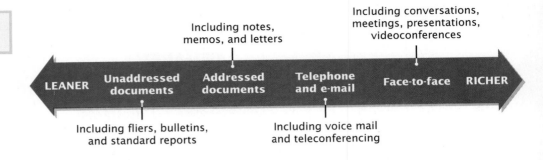

Including notes, memos, and letters

Including conversations, meetings, presentations, videoconferences

LEANER   **Unaddressed documents**   **Addressed documents**   **Telephone and e-mail**   **Face-to-face**   RICHER

Including fliers, bulletins, and standard reports

Including voice mail and teleconferencing

Factors to consider when choosing a channel and medium include the following:
- Media richness
- Formality
- Confidentiality
- Emotional commitment
- Feedback
- Urgency
- Cost
- Audience expectations

The first is **media richness**, the value of a medium in a given communication situation. Richness is determined by a medium's ability to

- Convey a message by means of more than one informational cue (visual, verbal, vocal)

- Facilitate feedback

- Establish personal focus

Face-to-face communication is the richest medium because it is personal, it provides immediate verbal and nonverbal feedback, and it conveys the emotion behind the message. But it's also one of the most restrictive media because you and your audience must be in the same place at the same time.[8] At the other end of the continuum are unaddressed documents such as fliers (see Figure 4–4). Choose the richest media for nonroutine messages intended to extend and humanize your presence throughout the organization, communicate your caring to employees, and gain employee commitment to organizational goals. Use leaner media to communicate more routine messages such as those conveying day-to-day information. Home Depot uses a rich medium (satellite video broadcasts) to educate employees and to introduce new hires to the company's culture. The company educates customers in specific home improvement skills by using a leaner medium (how-to articles in its magazine, *Weekend*).

Other factors are also important to consider when selecting channel and medium. If you want to emphasize the formality of your message, use a more formal medium, such as a memo, letter, or formal presentation. If you want to emphasize the confidentiality of your message, use voice mail rather than a fax, send a letter rather than a memo, or address the matter in a private conversation rather than during a meeting. If you want to instill an emotional commitment to corporate values, consider a visual medium (a speech, videotape, or videoconference). If you require immediate feedback, face-to-face conversation is your best choice.[9] However, if you'll need a written record, you'll probably want to write a memo or a letter.

Time is an important factor to consider when selecting a medium. If your message is urgent, you'll probably choose the phone, fax, or next-day mail. You'll also need to consider cost. For instance, you wouldn't think twice about telephoning an important customer overseas if you just discovered your company had erroneously sent the customer the wrong shipment, but you'd probably choose to fax or e-mail a routine order acknowledgment to your customer in Australia.

Finally, before choosing a channel and medium, consider what your audience expects or prefers.[10] What would you think if your college tried to deliver your diploma by fax? It would seem a bit strange, wouldn't it? You'd expect the college to hand it to you at graduation or mail it to you. In addition, various cultures tend to favor one channel over another. For example, the United States, Canada, and Germany emphasize written messages, whereas Japan emphasizes oral messages—perhaps because its high-context culture carries so much of the message in nonverbal cues and implied meaning.[11]

CHOOSING THE MOST APPROPRIATE CHANNEL AND MEDIUM   Table 4–1

Use the Written Channel When

- You need no immediate feedback
- Your message is detailed, complex, or requires careful planning
- You need a permanent, verifiable record
- Your audience is large and geographically dispersed
- You want to minimize the distortion that can occur when messages pass orally from person to person
- Immediate interaction with the audience is either unimportant or undesirable
- Your message has no emotional component

Use the Oral Channel When

- You want immediate feedback from the audience
- Your message is relatively straightforward and easy to accept
- You need no permanent record
- You can assemble your audience conveniently and economically
- You want to encourage interaction to solve a problem or reach a group decision
- You want to read the audience's body language or hear the tone of their response
- Your message has an emotional component

Use Electronic Forms When

- You need speed
- You're physically separated from your audience
- Time zones differ
- You must reach a dispersed audience personally

From media richness to audience preference—all of these factors are important to consider before choosing a channel and medium. Every medium has limitations that filter out parts of your message, and every medium influences your audience's perception of your intentions. Consider carefully and do your best to match your selection to your audience and your purpose, whether that choice is an oral or a written medium.

Before beginning to write, make sure your channel and medium match your audience and purpose.

Oral Media   Oral media traditionally include face-to-face conversations, telephone calls, speeches, presentations, and meetings (see Table 4–1). In today's fast-paced world of technological solutions, oral media also include electronic media such as voice mail, audiotape and videotape, teleconferencing and videoconferencing, closed-circuit television, and many others. Your choice between a face-to-face conversation and a telephone call would depend on audience location, message importance, and your need for the sort of nonverbal feedback that only body language can reveal.

The chief advantage of oral communication is the opportunity it provides for immediate feedback. This is the channel to use when you want the audience to ask questions and make comments or when you're trying to reach a group decision. It's also the best channel if your message has an emotional component and you want to read the audience's body language or hear the tone of their response.[12] A major drawback of many of the media in the oral channel is the reduced ability to revise your message before your audience hears it. During telephone conversations, voice mail, meetings, and so on, you can't really delete a comment once you've said it out loud. Chapter 2 discusses meetings in detail, and Chapter 13 covers speeches and presentations in depth.

In general, use an oral channel if your purpose is to collaborate with the audience.

Written Media   Written messages take many forms, both traditional and electronic. At one end are the scribbled notes people use to jog their own memories; at the other are elaborate, formal reports that rival magazines in graphic quality. Regardless of the form, written messages have one big advantage: They let you plan and control the message. However, a serious drawback to written messages is that you miss out on the immediate feedback you would receive with many oral media. A written format is appropriate when the information is complex, when a permanent record is needed for future reference, when the audience is large and geographically dispersed, and when immediate interaction with the audience is either unimportant or undesirable. The most common written media are letters, memos, e-mail messages, instant messaging reports, and proposals, but this channel also includes faxing, computer conferencing (with groupware), and websites.

Letters, Memos, and E-Mail Messages   You use memos and e-mail for the routine, day-to-day communication with people inside the organization. Such internal communication helps you do your job. It helps you and other employees develop a clear sense of the organization's mission, identify potential problems, and react quickly to ever-changing circumstances.

You use letters for communicating with outsiders. Letters not only convey a particular message but also perform an important public relations function. You may also use e-mail for external communication (1) in response to e-mail messages that you receive, (2) when the purpose of your message is informal, and (3) when your audience accepts e-mail as appropriate. External communication helps employees create a favorable impression of their company, plan for and respond to crises, and gather useful information (such as feedback from customers and other stakeholders).

Most letters, memos, and e-mail messages are relatively brief, generally less than two pages (often less than a page for e-mail). Letters are the most formal of the three. Memos are less formal, and e-mail messages are the least formal. For in-depth format information, see Appendix A: Format and Layout of Business Documents. But to distinguish between these three types of written documents, keep the following format differences in mind:

- **Letters.** Most letters appear on letterhead stationery (which includes a company's name and contact information). After the letterhead comes the date, followed by the inside address and the salutation (*Dear Mr. or Ms. Name*). Next is the message (often several paragraphs and sometimes running to a second page). After the message come the complimentary close (*Sincerely* or *Cordially*) and the signature block (space for the signature, followed by the sender's printed name and title).

- **Memos.** Less formal than letters, memos begin with a title (*Memo, Memorandum,* or *Interoffice Correspondence*) and use a *To, From, Date,* and *Subject* heading (for readers who have time only to skim messages). Memos have no salutation, discuss only one topic, use a conversational tone, and have no complimentary close or signature. Because of their open construction and delivery by interoffice mail or e-mail, they are less private than letters. However, to document all correspondence on a particular in-house issue, printed memos provide paper trails that e-mail messages do not.

- **E-mail messages.** Like memos, e-mail messages have a heading. Particulars depend on the software you use, but most programs include *To, From,* and *Subject* information, at minimum. Heading information is brief (the *To* and *From* lines sometimes show no names or titles, just e-mail addresses), and often includes information about copies and attachments. The software automatically inserts the date. After the salutation (optional but highly recommended) comes the message, followed by the complimentary close and the typed name of the sender. Contact information is sometimes included after the sender's name.

Chapters 7–9 discuss letters, memos, and e-mail messages in detail.

Reports and Proposals   Reports and proposals are factual, objective documents that communicate information about some aspect of the business. They may be distributed to insiders or outsiders, depending on their purpose and subject. They come in many formats, including preprinted forms, electronic forms, letters, memos, and manuscripts. They can run from a few to several hundred pages, and they are generally more formal in tone than a typical business letter, memo, or e-mail. Chapters 10–12 discuss reports and proposals in detail.

Reports are generally longer and more formal than letters and memos, and they have more components.

When to Choose Electronic Media

The availability of electronic media increases your communication options in both oral and written channels. The trick is to use the tool that does the best overall job in each situation. Choose an electronic medium when you need speed, when you're physically separated from your audience, when time zones differ, when you must reach a dispersed audience personally, and when you're unconcerned about confidentiality. Although no hard rules dictate which tool to use in each case, here are a few pointers that will help you determine when to select electronic over more traditional forms:[13]

In general, use electronic forms of oral and written communication for speed, to reach a widely dispersed audience personally, to overcome time zone barriers, and when confidentiality is not a concern.

- **Voice mail** can be used to replace short memos and phone calls that need no response. It is most effective for short, unambiguous messages. It solves time zone difficulties and reduces a substantial amount of interoffice paperwork.[14] Voice mail is a powerful tool when you need to communicate your emotion or tone. It is especially useful for goodwill and other positive messages.

- **Teleconferencing** is an efficient alternative to a face-to-face meeting. Best for informational meetings, it is less effective for decision-making meetings and ineffective for negotiation. Teleconferencing discourages the "secondary" conversations that occur during meetings of more than four or five people. Although participants are better able to focus on a topic without such secondary conversations, they are prevented from sharing valuable information.

- **Videotape** is often effective for getting a motivational message out to a large number of people. By communicating nonverbal cues, it can strengthen the sender's image of sincerity and trustworthiness; however, it offers no opportunity for immediate feedback.

- **Computer conferencing** allows users to meet and collaborate in real time while viewing and sharing documents electronically. It offers democracy because more attention is focused on ideas than on who communicates them. But overemphasizing a message (to the neglect of the person communicating it) can threaten corporate culture, which needs a richer medium.

- **Faxing** can be used to overcome time zone barriers when a hard copy is required. It has all the characteristics of a written message, except that (1) it may lack the privacy of a letter, and (2) the message may appear less crisp—even less professional—depending on the quality of the copies output from the receiving machine.

- **E-mail** offers speed, low cost, increased access to other employees, portability, and convenience (not just overcoming time zone problems but carrying a message to many receivers at once). It's best for communicating brief, noncomplex information that is time sensitive, but its effectiveness depends on user skill (see Figure 4–5). Because the turnaround time can be quite fast, e-mail tends to be more conversational than traditional paper-based media.

- **Instant messaging (IM)** allows people to carry on real-time, one-on-one, and small-group text conversations. More versatile than a phone call and quicker than e-mail, IM is becoming a valuable business tool. You can send your boss a text message that is immediately displayed on her or his computer screen, and you can have your response within seconds. Similarly, co-workers in branch offices can use IM to

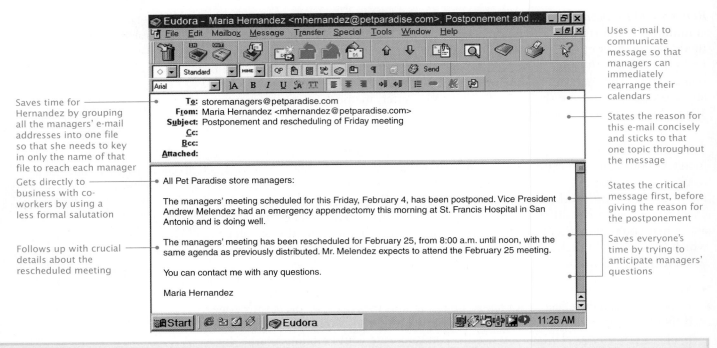

Saves time for Hernandez by grouping all the managers' e-mail addresses into one file so that she needs to key in only the name of that file to reach each manager

Gets directly to business with co-workers by using a less formal salutation

Follows up with crucial details about the rescheduled meeting

Uses e-mail to communicate message so that managers can immediately rearrange their calendars

States the reason for this e-mail concisely and sticks to that one topic throughout the message

States the critical message first, before giving the reason for the postponement

Saves everyone's time by trying to anticipate managers' questions

FIGURE 4–5
Effective E-Mail Message Conveying Time-Sensitive Material

exchange documents or hold a virtual meeting online in a private chat area. Because messages generated via instant messaging aren't recorded or saved, they don't clog the company's network system; however, they don't create a permanent record either.[15]

- **Websites** offer interactive communication through hyperlinks, allowing readers to absorb information nonsequentially; that is, readers take what they need and skip everything else. A website can tailor the same information for numerous readers by breaking up the information into linked pages. Writing for the web can be a specialized skill, as briefly discussed at the end of this chapter.

Electronic forms also have disadvantages:
- Tactless remarks causing tension
- Overuse leading to information overload
- Lack of privacy
- Reduced productivity

Even though electronic messages offer innumerable advantages, they aren't problem-free. Consider e-mail, for example. People sometimes include things in e-mail messages that they wouldn't dream of saying in person or typing in a document. So although e-mail's new openness can help companies get input from a wider variety of people, it can also create tension and interpersonal conflict. Furthermore, because e-mail is so cheap and easy to send, people tend to overuse it, distributing messages more widely than necessary and contributing to the hundreds of junk-mail messages that some executives receive every day. Overusing e-mail can also overload company networks, resulting in lost messages or even system crashes.

Another drawback is lack of privacy. Some people negate their own privacy by being careless about screening their electronic distribution lists and sending information to receivers who shouldn't have it or don't need it. Of course, even if your message goes only where you originally intended, any recipient can easily forward it to someone else. In addition, e-mail and voice mail can legally be monitored by employers, and both can be subpoenaed for court cases (see "Using the Power of Technology: Caution! E-Mail Can Bite").

Finally, employee productivity is constantly interrupted by instant messaging, e-mail, voice mail, conference calls, and faxes. Employees can also diminish their productivity by surfing the web and visiting non-business-related websites during working hours. In one report, 31 percent of the businesses surveyed cited financial losses from reduced employee productivity as a result of Internet misuse alone.[16]

USING THE POWER OF TECHNOLOGY

Caution! E-Mail Can Bite

Gone are the days when memos were dictated, typed, revised, retyped, photocopied, and circulated by interoffice "snail" mail. Today, e-mail messages are created, sent, received, and forwarded in the blink of an eye and at the stroke of a key. Despite its benefits, this quick, efficient method of communication can cause a great deal of trouble for companies.

One of the greatest features—and dangers—of e-mail is that people tend to treat it far more informally than they do other forms of business communication. They think of e-mail as casual conversation and routinely make unguarded comments. Moreover, they are led to believe that "deleting" e-mail destroys it permanently. But that's a dangerous misunderstanding of technology.

Even after you delete an e-mail message, it can still exist on the system's hard drive and backup storage devices at both the sender's and the recipient's locations. Deleting files only signals the computer that the space required to store the message is no longer needed. The space is so marked, but the data that occupy it continue to exist until the computer overwrites the space with new data. Thus, deleted messages are recoverable—even though data recovery is an involved and expensive process—and they can be used as court evidence against you.

Embarrassing e-mail has played a big role in corporate battles. In the high-profile court battle between the U.S. Justice Department and Microsoft, for instance, e-mail emerged as the star witness. Other cases using e-mail as evidence include claims of sexual harassment, discrimination, employee productivity, information leaks, and more.

So how can companies guard against potential e-mail embarrassment and resulting litigation? Besides restricting the use of e-mail by employees, monitoring employees' e-mail, developing company e-mail policies, and reprimanding or terminating offenders, they can train employees to treat e-mail as any other form of written communication. Perhaps one of the best ways to ensure that employees' messages won't come back to haunt the company is to teach employees that e-mail messages are at least as permanent as, if not more so than, letters and memos.

CAREER APPLICATIONS

1. Why do most people treat e-mail so casually? Explain in an e-mail message to your instructor.

2. What kinds of things should a company address in an e-mail policy? List and explain at least three items.

Still, the advantages of electronic media often outweigh the drawbacks, so businesses are selecting electronic forms over traditional ones more and more often (see the "Checklist: Observing E-Mail Etiquette").

Establish a Good Relationship with Your Audience

Effective communicators do more than convey information. They make sure that they establish a good relationship with their audience. The first step is to think about who you are and who your audience is. Are you friends with common interests, or are you total strangers? Are you equal in status, experience, and education, or are you clearly unequal? Your answers to these questions will help you give the right impression in your message.

An important aspect of establishing a good relationship with your audience is to avoid trying to be someone you're not. People can spot falseness very quickly, so just be yourself and be sincere. Home Depot's managers will tell you that, as in any undertaking, a good relationship is based on respect and courtesy.

To establish a good relationship, be yourself.

Some ways to establish good relationships in your business messages are to make use of the "you" attitude, emphasize the positive, establish your credibility, be polite, use bias-free language, and project the company's image.

Use the "You" Attitude   You are already becoming familiar with the audience-centered approach, trying to see a subject through your audience's eyes. Now you want to project this approach in your messages by adopting a **"you" attitude**—that is, by speaking and writing in terms of your audience's wishes, interests, hopes, and

The "you" attitude is best implemented by expressing your message in terms of the audience's interests and needs.

✓ CHECKLIST: Observing E-Mail Etiquette

Plan Your E-Mail Carefully

- ✓ Limit your purpose to sharing information such as goals, schedules, research, and company news—don't deliver tragic news or discipline via e-mail.
- ✓ Avoid personal messages at work.
- ✓ Follow the chain of command—don't abuse the convenience of e-mail by sending unnecessary messages straight to the top.
- ✓ Work offline to conserve network resources and cut the costs of Internet connect charges.

Respect Your Readers

- ✓ Send only necessary messages.
- ✓ Know who your audience is, who actually needs to hear what you have to say.
- ✓ Double-check addressees to include everyone necessary and no one else.
- ✓ Know your audience's culture before you begin composing.
- ✓ Use 24-hour military time in international e-mail (18:00 rather than 6:00 P.M.), and indicate the appropriate time zone.

- ✓ Respect your audience's schedule by making your e-mail worth reading and not sending jokes, chain letters, or derogatory comments.
- ✓ Don't send negative, insensitive, insulting, or critical e-mail: If you're upset about something or angry with someone, compose yourself before composing your e-mail.
- ✓ Don't use the *high priority* feature, unless your message is truly urgent.

Don't Let Incoming Mail Run Your Life

- ✓ Check your e-mail frequently, but don't become constantly distracted by overchecking it.
- ✓ Avoid checking e-mail while on vacation—everyone needs a little time away from the office now and again.
- ✓ Use appropriate filters to screen out unimportant or less-than-critical messages.
- ✓ Read e-mail in a last-in, first-out order; otherwise, you may respond to issues that have been resolved in later messages. The last e-mail may summarize all previous issues.

preferences. When you talk about the other person, you're talking about what most interests him or her.

Too many business messages have an "I" or "we" attitude, which make the writer sound selfish. The message loses the audience's interest by telling what the sender wants and then expecting the audience to go along with that desire. On the simplest level, you can adopt the "you" attitude by replacing terms that refer to yourself and your company with terms that refer to your audience. In other words, use *you* and *yours* instead of *I, me, mine, we, us,* and *ours:*

Instead of This	Use This
To help us process this order, we must ask for another copy of the requisition.	So that your order can be filled promptly, please send another copy of the requisition.
We are pleased to announce our new flight schedule from Atlanta to New York, which is any hour on the hour.	Now you can take a plane from Atlanta to New York any hour on the hour.
We offer the printer cartridges in three colors: black, blue, and green.	Select your printer cartridge from three colors: black, blue, and green.

Using *you* and *yours* requires finesse. If you overdo it, you're likely to create some rather awkward sentences, and you run the risk of sounding manipulative or insincere.[17] The "you" attitude is an extension of the audience-centered approach. In fact, the best way to implement it is to sincerely think about your audience.

The "you" attitude is more than replacing pronouns.

Far from simply replacing one pronoun with another, the "you" attitude is a matter of genuine empathy. You can use *you* 25 times in a single page and still ignore your audience's true concerns. Your sincere concern for your audience is what counts, not the pronoun. If you're talking to a retailer, try to think like a retailer; if you're writing to a dissatisfied customer, imagine how you would feel at the other end of the transaction.

In fact, on some occasions you'll do better to avoid using *you*. For instance, using *you* in a way that sounds dictatorial is impolite. Or, when someone makes a mistake, you may want to minimize ill will by pointing out the error impersonally. You might say, "We have a problem," instead of "You caused a problem."

Instead of This	Use This
You should never use that type of paper in the copy machine.	That type of paper doesn't work very well in the copy machine.
You must correct all five copies by noon.	All five copies must be corrected by noon.

As you practice using the "you" attitude, be sure to consider the attitudes and policies of your organization and those of other cultures. In some cultures, it is improper to single out one person's achievements because the whole team is responsible for the outcome; thus, using the pronouns *we* or *our* would be more appropriate. Similarly, some companies have a tradition of avoiding references to *you* and *I* in their memos and formal reports. If you work for a company that expects a formal, impersonal style, confine your use of personal pronouns to informal letters and memos.

Emphasize the Positive   Another way of establishing a good relationship with your audience is to emphasize the positive side of your message.[18] Focus on the silver lining, not on the cloud. Stress what is or will be instead of what isn't or won't be. Most information, even bad news, has some redeeming feature. If you can make your audience aware of that feature, your message will be more acceptable.

Jenny J. Ming, president of Old Navy, oversees everything from store operations to marketing and advertising. Her passion for fashion has helped drive the company's record growth. So has her ability to communicate effectively with others. Ming recognizes that people's needs change as quickly as the latest fashion trend. So when communicating with others, she takes extra care to focus on her audience's changing needs.

Avoid using you *and* yours *when doing so*
- *Makes you sound dictatorial*
- *Makes someone else feel guilty*
- *Goes against your organization's style*

Instead of This	Use This
It is impossible to repair your vacuum cleaner today.	Your vacuum cleaner will be ready by Tuesday.
We apologize for inconveniencing you during our remodeling.	The renovations now under way will help us serve you better.
We never exchange damaged goods.	We are happy to exchange merchandise that is returned to us in good condition.

Explain what you have done, what you can do, and what you will do— not what you haven't done, can't do, or won't do.

In addition, when you're criticizing or correcting, don't hammer on the other person's mistakes. Avoid referring to failures, problems, or shortcomings. Focus instead on what the person can do to improve:

When you are offering criticism or advice, focus on what the person can do to improve.

Instead of This	Use This
The problem with this department is a failure to control costs.	The performance of this department can be improved by tightening cost controls.
You filled out the order form wrong.	So that your order can be processed, please check your color preferences on the enclosed card.

Show your audience how they will benefit from complying with your message.

If you're trying to persuade audience members to buy a product, pay a bill, or perform a service for you, emphasize what's in it for them. Don't focus on why *you* want them to do something. An individual who sees the possibility for personal benefit is more likely to respond positively to your appeal.

Instead of This	Use This
Please buy this book so that I can make my sales quota.	The plot of this novel will keep you in suspense to the last page.
We need your contribution to the Boys and Girls Club.	You can help a child make friends and build self-confidence through your donation to the Boys and Girls Club.

Avoid words with negative connotations; use meaningful euphemisms without hiding the facts.

In general, try to state your message without using words that might hurt or offend your audience. Substitute *euphemisms* (mild terms) for those that have unpleasant connotations. You can be honest without being harsh. Gentle language won't change the facts, but it will make them more acceptable:

Instead of This	Use This
cheap merchandise	bargain prices
toilet paper	bathroom tissue
used cars	resale cars
high-calorie food	high-energy food
elderly	senior citizen
pimples and zits	complexion problems

On the other hand, don't carry euphemisms to extremes. If you're too subtle, people won't know what you're talking about. "Derecruiting" workers to the "mobility pool" instead of telling them that they have six weeks to find another job isn't really very helpful. When using euphemisms, you walk a fine line between softening the blow and hiding the facts. It would be unethical to speak to your community about "relocating refuse" when you're really talking about your plans for disposing of toxic waste. Such an attempt to hide the facts would probably backfire, damaging your business image and reputation. In the end, people respond better to an honest message delivered with integrity than they do to sugar-coated double-talk.

People are more likely to react positively to your message when they have confidence in you.

Establish Your Credibility If you're unknown to your audience members, you'll have to earn their confidence before you can win them to your point of view. Their belief in your competence and integrity is important. You want people to trust that your word is dependable and that you know what you're doing.

Credibility (or your believability) is based on how reliable you are and how much trust you evoke in others. If you're communicating with a familiar group, your credibility has already been established, so you can get right down to business. Of course, even in this case some audience members may have preconceptions about you and may have trouble separating your arguments from your personality or your field. If they think of you as, say, a "numbers person," they may question your competence in other areas. Or, what if audience members are complete strangers? Or worse, what if they start off with doubts about you? In a new or hostile situation, devote the initial portion of your message to gaining credibility, and try the following techniques:

In a new or hostile situation, you need to work at gaining credibility.

- **Call attention to what you have in common with your audience.** For example, when communicating with someone who shares your professional background, point out your connection: "As a fellow engineer [lawyer, doctor, teacher, etc.], I'm sure you can appreciate this situation." Also, try using technical or professional terms that identify you as a peer.

- **Explain your credentials.** Being careful not to sound pompous, mention one or two aspects of your background. Your title or the name of your organization might be enough to impress your audience with your abilities.

- **Mention the name of someone your audience trusts or views as an authority.** You could begin a letter with "Professor Goldberg suggested that I contact you," or you could quote a recognized authority on your subject, even if you don't know the authority personally. The fact that your ideas are shared by a credible source adds prestige to your message.

- **Provide ample evidence.** Back up your arguments, especially any material outside your usual area of expertise. Make sure your evidence can be confirmed through observation, research, experimentation, or measurement. If audience members recognize that you have the facts, they'll respect you.

On the other hand, if audience members find your evidence insufficient or lacking, your credibility will vanish. For example, avoid exaggerated claims. They are unethical and do more harm than good. A mail-order catalog promised: "You'll be absolutely amazed at the remarkable blooms on this healthy plant." Terms such as *amazing, incredible, extraordinary, sensational,* and *revolutionary* exceed the limits of believability, unless they're supported with some sort of proof.

You also risk losing credibility if you seem to be currying favor with insincere compliments. Refrain from empty flattery. Support any compliments with specific points:

You risk losing your credibility if you
- Exaggerate claims
- Pay insincere compliments
- Lack confidence

Instead of This	Use This
My deepest heartfelt thanks for the excellent job you did. It's hard these days to find workers like you. You are just fantastic! I can't stress enough how happy you have made us with your outstanding performance.	Thanks for the great job you did filling in for Gladys at the convention with just an hour's notice. Despite the difficult circumstances, you managed to attract several new orders with your demonstration of the new line of coffeemakers. Your dedication and sales ability are truly appreciated.

Another threat to credibility is too much modesty and not enough confidence. You express a lack of confidence when you use words such as *if, hope,* and *trust.* Try not to undermine your credibility with vague sentiments:

Instead of This	Use This
We hope this recommendation will be helpful.	We're glad to make this recommendation.
If you'd like to order, mail us the reply card.	To order, mail the reply card.
We trust that you'll extend your service contract.	By extending your service contract, you can continue to enjoy top-notch performance from your equipment.

If you lack faith in yourself, you're likely to communicate an uncertain attitude that undermines your credibility. The key to being believable is to believe in yourself. If you are convinced that your message is sound, you can state your case with authority so that your audience has no doubts.

Be Polite   Being polite is another good way to earn your audience's respect. By being courteous to members of your audience, you show consideration for their needs and feelings. Express yourself with kindness and tact.

You will undoubtedly be frustrated and exasperated by other people many times in your career. When that happens, you'll be tempted to say what you think in blunt terms. But venting your emotions rarely improves the situation and can jeopardize your audience's goodwill. Instead, be gentle when expressing yourself:

Although you may be tempted now and then to be brutally frank, try to express the facts in a kind and thoughtful manner.

Instead of This	Use This
You really fouled things up with that last computer run.	Let's go over what went wrong with the last computer run so that the next run goes smoothly.
You've been sitting on my order for two weeks, and we need it now!	We are eager to receive our order. When can we expect delivery?

Use extra tact when writing and when communicating with higher-ups and outsiders.

Of course, some situations require more diplomacy than others. If you know your audience well, you can get away with being less formal. However, when you are communicating with people who outrank you or with people outside your organization, an added measure of courtesy is usually needed.

In general, written communication requires more tact than oral communication. When you're speaking, your words are softened by your tone of voice and facial expression. Plus, you can adjust your approach according to the feedback you get. But written communication is stark and self-contained. If you hurt a person's feelings in writing, you can't soothe them right away. In fact, you may not even know that you have hurt the other person, because the lack of feedback prevents you from seeing your audience's reaction.

Keep these points in mind as you compare the two letters in Figure 4–6. Because of a death in the family, a restaurant owner closed his doors for three days over Labor Day weekend. Unfortunately, someone left the freezer door ajar, which burned out the motor and spoiled all the food stored there. The total cost to replace the motor and food was over $2,000. The restaurant owner requested that Eppler Appliances cover these costs, but Eppler had to refuse. Note how the revised version is more diplomatic.

Another simple but effective courtesy is to be prompt in your correspondence. If possible, answer your mail within two or three days. If you need more time to prepare a reply, call or write a brief note to say that you're working on an answer. Most people are willing to wait if they know how long the wait will be. What annoys them is the suspense.

By showing consideration in your messages, you can help readers focus on what you're saying. "Courtesy is an important part of our high standards," says Elizabeth Tanis (center), manager of consumer affairs at Sara Lee Bakery. "We want everyone to understand about the high quality and high standards at Sara Lee—that's how we made our good name, and that's how we're going to keep it."

Use Bias-Free Language   Most of us think of ourselves as being sensitive, unbiased, ethical, and fair. But being fair and objective isn't enough; to establish a good relationship with your audience, you must also *appear* to be fair.[19] **Bias-free language** avoids unethical, embarrassing blunders in language related to gender, race, ethnicity, age, and disability. Good communicators make every effort to guard against biased language of any type (see Table 4–2 on page 114).

FIGURE 4–6
Poor and Improved Versions of an Audience-Centered Letter

Dear Mr. Carpaccio:

Draft

Subject: Burned-out motor

We have received your request for reimbursement. Although your Crown Freezer is under warranty for two more months, you can't honestly expect us to be liable for the cost of a new motor and of your spoiled food when the problem clearly resulted from your own negligence. These freezers were not designed to operate at full capacity with the door ajar for any length of time, let alone for three days over Labor Day weekend in some of the hottest weather we've had in a decade.

Crown products were designed to endure everyday use in a typical commercial kitchen. They are constructed of top-quality materials, insulated with non-CFC in-place polyurethane foam, and are "performance rated" using environmentally safe refrigerants. Your top-mounted freezer model includes casters, heavy-duty lift-off hinges, durable locking stainless steel doors, and exterior dial thermometer.

However, we would like to offer to pay for the repairman's service call, in the spirit of good customer relations. I'm sorry, but that's the best we can do for you at this time.

Sincerely,

- Lacks sufficient information
- Omits specific date of warranty expiration
- Emphasizes negative aspects and places blame on the reader by using the pronoun "you" incorrectly
- Lacks any "you" attitude, focusing on what is important to Eppler rather than on what is important to the reader
- Includes irrelevant, overly technical information
- Shows bias by assuming the repairs were handled by a man
- Fails to emphasize the positive, undercutting the offer being made and ending on an extremely negative note

EPPLER APPLIANCES
7142 Conrad Avenue, Lima, OH 45801
Voice: (419) 768-1927   Fax: (419) 768-1928

Revision

September 9, 2004

Mr. Joseph Carpaccio
Carpaccio's Ristoranti
847 Broadway
Lima, OH 45806

Dear Mr. Carpaccio:

Subject: Burned-out freezer motor, Invoice # 3770 46 010122

Thank you for your letter about your freezer repairs. Your Crown Freezer is under limited warranty until November 15, and to help you defray a portion of your unforeseen costs, we would like to pay the standard $45 for the service call. The check is enclosed.

You received a copy of your warranty with your freezer, and I've enclosed another copy for your convenience. As you can see, Crown Freezers are designed to endure everyday use in a typical commercial kitchen. Their top-quality materials and performance rating guarantee that they will perform effectively and efficiently under normal operating conditions, which must exclude running for extended periods of time with the door open.

With only two months left on your limited warranty, you might consider purchasing an extended manufacturer's warranty. The basic warranty covers parts and labor for five years for only $75. Plus, you can purchase additional business insurance for just $135 more per year, which covers parts, labor, and damages—regardless of the cause. The enclosed brochure gives all the details, or visit our website at www.eppler.com.

Sincerely,

Kjiersten Lejunhud

Kjiersten Lejunhud
Customer Relations

Enclosures (3)

- Provides enough information to identify the warranty, the customer, etc.
- Includes specific date the warranty expires
- Avoids bias by not mentioning the repair person as either male or female
- Uses the "you" attitude to explain the warranty without blaming the reader
- Emphasizes the positive, with helpful information, and ends on a friendly note

- Uses the pronoun "you" correctly and emphasizes the positive by implying the refusal to pay for a new motor and any spoiled food
- Includes relevant information in language that is easy for the reader to understand
- Provides detailed information about what the reader might do to avoid such costs in the future

Table 4–2   OVERCOMING BIAS IN LANGUAGE

Examples	Unacceptable	Preferable
Gender Bias		
Using words containing "man"	Man-made	Artificial, synthetic, manufactured, constructed
	Businessman	Executive, business manager, businessperson
	Salesman	Sales representative, salesperson, clerk, sales agent
	Foreman	Supervisor
Using female-gender words	Authoress, actress, stewardess	Author, actor, cabin attendant
Using special designations	Woman doctor, male nurse	Doctor, nurse
Using "he" to refer to "everyone"	The average worker . . . he	The average worker . . . he or she
Identifying roles with gender	The typical executive spends four hours of his day in meetings.	Most executives spend four hours a day in meetings.
	the nurse/teacher . . . she	nurses/teachers . . . they
Identifying women by marital status	Phill Donahue and Marlo Phill Donahue and Ms. Thomas	Phill Donahue and Marlo Thomas Mr. Donahue and Ms. Thomas
Racial/Ethnic Bias		
Assigning stereotypes	My black assistant speaks more articulately than I do.	My assistant speaks more articulately than I do.
	Jim Wong is an unusually tall Asian.	Jim Wong is tall.
Identifying people by race or ethnicity	Mario M. Cuomo, Italian American politician and ex-governor of New York	Mario M. Cuomo, politician and ex-governor of New York
Age Bias		
Including age when irrelevant	Mary Kirazy, 58, has just joined our trust department.	Mary Kirazy has just joined our trust department.
Disability Bias		
Putting the disability before the person	Crippled workers face many barriers on the job.	Workers with physical disabilities face many barriers on the job.
	An epileptic, Tracy has no trouble doing her job.	Tracy's epilepsy has no effect on her job performance.

Replace words that inaccurately exclude women or men.

- **Gender bias.** Avoid sexist language by using the same label for everyone (don't call a woman *chairperson* and then call a man *chairman*). Reword sentences to use *they* or to use no pronoun at all. Vary traditional patterns by sometimes putting women first (*women and men, she and he, her and his*). Note that the preferred title for women in business is *Ms.*, unless the individual has some other title (such as *Dr.*) or asks to be addressed as *Miss* or *Mrs.*

Eliminate references that reinforce racial or ethnic stereotypes.

- **Racial and ethnic bias** Avoid language suggesting that members of a racial or an ethnic group have stereotypical characteristics. The best solution is to avoid identifying people by race or ethnic origin unless such a label is relevant.

Avoid references to an individual's age or physical limitations.

- **Age bias** As with gender, race, and ethnic background, mention the age of a person only when it is relevant. When referring to older people, avoid such stereotyped adjectives as *spry* and *frail*.

Always refer to people first and their disabilities second.

- **Disability bias** No painless label exists for people with a physical, mental, sensory, or emotional impairment. Avoid mentioning a disability unless it is pertinent.

However, if you must refer to someone's disability, avoid terms such as *handicapped, crippled,* or *retarded.* Put the person first and the disability second.[20] Present the whole person, not just the disability, by referring to the limitation in an unobtrusive manner.

Project the Company's Image   Even though establishing a good relationship with the audience is your main goal, give some thought to projecting the right image for your company. When you communicate with outsiders, on even the most routine matter, you serve as the spokesperson for your organization. The impression you make can enhance or damage the reputation of your entire company. Thus, your own views and personality must be subordinated, at least to some extent, to the interests and style of your company.

> Subordinate your own style to that of the company.

Say you've just taken a job with a trendy, young retail organization called Rappers. One of your first assignments is to write a letter canceling additional orders for clothing items that haven't been selling well. Here's your first draft:

Dear Ms. Bataglia:

Please cancel our purchase order 092397AA for the amount of $12,349. Our contract with your organization specifies that we have a 30-day cancellation clause, which we wish to invoke. If any shipments went out before you received this notification, they will be returned; however, we will remunerate freight charges as specified in the contract.

I am told we have ordered from you since our inception in 1993. Your previous service to us has been quite satisfactory; however, recent sales of the "Colored Denim" line have been less than forecast. We realize that our cancellation may have a negative impact, and we pledge to more accurately predict our needs in the future.

We maintain positive alliances with all our vendors and look forward to doing further business with you. Please keep us informed of new products as they appear.

After reading the draft, you realize that its formal tone may leave a feeling of ill will. Moreover, it certainly doesn't reflect the corporate culture of your new employer. You try again.

Dear Ms. Bataglia:

We appreciate the relationship we've had with you since 1993. Your shipments have always arrived on time and in good order.

However, our recent store reports show a decline in sales for your "Colored Denim" line. Therefore, we're canceling our purchase order 092397AA for $12,349. If you'll let us know the amounts, we'll pay the shipping charges on anything that has already gone out.

We're making a lot of changes at Rappers, but one thing remains the same—the positive relationship we have with vendors such as you. Please keep us informed of your new lines as they appear. We look forward to doing business with you in the future.

Document Makeover

IMPROVE THIS LETTER

To practice correcting drafts of actual documents, visit **www.prenhall.com/onekey** on the web. Click "Document Makeovers," then click Chapter 4. You will find a letter that contains problems and errors relating to what you've learned in this chapter about establishing a good relationship with your audience. Use the Final Draft decision tool to create an improved version of this letter. Check the message for the "you" attitude, positive language, politeness, bias-free language, and phrases that establish credibility.

✓ CHECKLIST: Planning Business Messages

Analyze the Situation

✓ Determine whether the purpose of your message is to inform, persuade, or collaborate.

✓ Identify the specific behavior you hope to induce in the audience.

✓ Make sure that your purpose is worthwhile and realistic.

✓ Make sure that the time is right for your purpose.

✓ Make sure the right person is delivering your message.

✓ Make sure your purpose is acceptable to your organization.

✓ Identify the primary audience.

✓ Determine the size of your audience.

✓ Determine the composition of your audience.

✓ Determine your audience's level of understanding.

✓ Estimate your audience's probable reaction to your message.

Gather Information

✓ Decide whether to use formal or informal techniques for gathering information.

✓ Find out what your audience needs to know.

✓ Provide all required information, and make sure it's accurate, ethical, and pertinent.

Adapt Your Message to Your Audience

✓ Select a channel and medium for your message by matching media richness to your audience and purpose.

✓ Select the right medium for your message by considering factors such as urgency, formality, complexity, confidentiality, emotional content, cost, audience expectation, and your need for a permanent record.

✓ Consider the problems as well as the advantages of the media you select.

✓ Establish a good audience relationship with a "you" attitude, positive language, credibility, a polite tone, bias-free language, and a good impression of your company.

This version reflects the more relaxed image of your new company. You can save yourself a great deal of time and frustration if you master your company's style early in your career.

The planning step helps you get ready to write business messages. The "Checklist: Planning Business Messages" is a reminder of the tasks and choices you address during this stage of the writing process.

On the Job:

SOLVING COMMUNICATION DILEMMAS AT HOME DEPOT

At Home Depot, Robert Nardelli emphasizes the importance of carefully planning messages to all audiences: employees, customers, and suppliers. You have recently joined Home Depot's community relations department in the company's Atlanta headquarters (known as the Store Support Center). Two of your main functions are (1) helping store managers and other company executives plan effective business messages for a variety of audiences, and (2) responding to press inquiries about Home Depot. Choose the best alternatives for handling the following situations, and be prepared to explain why your choice is best.

1. You have received a phone call from Ann Mason, a reporter for a small Idaho newspaper. She is planning to write an article about Home Depot's recent decision to open a store in her community, a small town in a rural area of Idaho. Mason has asked you for information about the economic impact of Home Depot stores in other small communities across the nation. When responding to Mason's request, what should the purpose of your letter be?

a. The general purpose is to inform. The specific purpose is to provide Mason with a brief summary of the evolution of Home Depot over the past 20 years.

b. The general purpose is to persuade. The specific purpose is to convince Mason that Home Depot creates hundreds of jobs within a community and that small, existing merchants should not feel threatened by the arrival of the home improvement giant in rural Idaho.

  c. The general purpose is to collaborate. The specific purpose is to work with Mason to develop an article that examines the history of Home Depot's entry into new markets.

  d. The general purpose is to respond. The specific purpose is to convey details requested by a journalist.

2. Assume that your purpose is to convince Mason of Home Depot's abilities to create new jobs and increase economic activity in small communities. Is your purpose worth pursuing at this time?

  a. Yes. The purpose is realistic, the timing is right, you are the right person to send the message, and the purpose is acceptable to the organization.

  b. Not completely. Realistically, many readers of Mason's newspaper may dread the arrival of Home Depot in their small community, fearing that the giant retailer may force small retailers out of business.

  c. The purpose is fine, but you are not the right person to send this message. Home Depot's chief executive officer should respond.

  d. The timing is right for this message. Stress Home Depot's involvement in small communities, citing contributions to social causes in other rural areas. Show how Home Depot cares about customers on a personal basis.

3. When planning your reply to Mason, what assumptions can you make about your audience?

  a. The audience includes not only Ann Mason but also the readers of the community's newspaper. Given their bias for a simple, rural lifestyle, the readers will probably be hostile to big business in general and to Home Depot in particular. They probably know little about large retail operations. Furthermore, they probably mistrust you because you are a Home Depot employee.

  b. Ann Mason will probably be the only person who reads the letter directly. She is the primary audience; the readers of her article are the secondary audience. Mason will be happy to hear from Home Depot and will read the information with an open mind. However, she may not know a great deal about Home Depot. Although she is a stranger to you, she trusts your credibility as a Home Depot spokesperson.

  c. Ann Mason is probably the sole and primary audience for the letter. The fact that she is writing an article about Home Depot suggests that she already knows a great deal about the company and likes the idea of Home Depot's entry into her community. In all likelihood, she will respond positively to your reply and will trust your credibility as a Home Depot representative.

  d. Ann Mason may be an industrial spy working for a rival home improvement center. She will show your reply to people who work for your competitor; they will analyze the information and use it to improve their market share of the home improvement industry.

4. A lightbulb manufacturer is unable to keep up with consumer demand for light bulbs in Home Depot stores. Customers and store managers are complaining about the shortage of light bulbs on the shelves. Home Depot's merchandising manager decides that the manufacturer must correct the supply problem within 30 days or Home Depot will have to find another, more reliable supplier that can meet the high demand. The merchandising manager asks you to suggest the best method of communicating this message to the lightbulb manufacturer. Which communication medium would you recommend?

  a. Call the manufacturer on the phone to discuss the problem; then follow up with a letter that summarizes the conversation.

  b. Call the manufacturer on the phone to discuss the issue, and inform the company of Home Depot's course of action if the problem cannot be corrected within 30 days.

  c. Send a fax asking for correction of the problem within 30 days, explaining the consequences of noncompliance.

  d. Send a form letter that states the consequences of failing to meet Home Depot's demand for products.[21]

Learning Objectives Checkup

To assess your understanding of the principles in this chapter, read each learning objective and study the accompanying exercises. For fill-in items, write the missing text in the blank provided; for multiple choice items, circle the letter of the correct answer. You can check your responses against the answer key on page AK-1

Objective 4.1: Describe the three-step writing process.

1. The first step of the three-step writing process is

  a. Writing the first draft

  b. Organizing your information

  c. Planning your message

  d. Preparing an outline

2. When using the three-step writing process, keep in mind that you should
   a. Allot roughly half your time to the planning stage
   b. Complete the steps in the order and as outlined in this chapter
   c. View it as a list of "how-to" directives
   d. Do all of the above

Objective 4.2: Explain why it's important to define your purpose carefully, and list four questions that can help you test that purpose.

3. If you were to write a letter to a manufacturer complaining about a defective product and asking for a refund, your general purpose would be
   a. To inform
   b. To persuade
   c. To collaborate
   d. To entertain

4. Which of the following is *not* a question to ask when considering whether to pursue your purpose?
   a. Is the purpose realistic?
   b. Is the right person delivering the message?
   c. Is the purpose acceptable to your organization?
   d. Have I chosen the right medium for delivering the message?

Objective 4.3: Justify the importance of analyzing your audience, then list six ways of developing an audience profile.

5. When developing an audience profile, it is important to identify the _____ audience.
   a. Primary
   b. Total
   c. Marginal
   d. Popular

6. If audience members will vary in the amount of information they already know about your topic, your best approach is to
   a. Provide as much extra information as possible to make sure everyone gets every detail
   b. Provide just the basic information; if your audience needs to know more, they can find out for themselves
   c. Gear your coverage to your primary audience and provide the information most relevant to them
   d. Include lots of graphics

Objective 4.4: Identify five ways to satisfy your audience's information needs.

7. Which of the following is *not* an informal way to gather information that will satisfy your audience's needs?
   a. Read material in your company's files, such as reports and news releases.
   b. Conduct an Internet search of material relevant to your topic.
   c. Chat with supervisors, fellow workers, or customers.
   d. Mentally put yourself in the audience's shoes and consider what they might be thinking, feeling, or planning.

8. To make sure you have provided all the necessary information, use the journalistic approach, which is to
   a. Interview your audience about its needs
   b. Check the accuracy of your information
   c. Check whether your message answers who, what, when, where, why, and how
   d. Make sure your information is ethical

9. If you realize you have given your audience incorrect information, the most ethical action would be to
   a. Say nothing and hope no one notices
   b. Wait until someone points out the error, then acknowledge the mistake
   c. Announce to the world that you have made a mistake and apologize to anyone who may have been affected
   d. Contact the audience immediately and correct the error

Objective 4.5: List the factors to consider when choosing the most appropriate channel and medium for your message.

10. The "richest" communication medium for dealing with a co-worker would be
    a. A face-to-face meeting
    b. A personal letter
    c. An e-mail message
    d. An interoffice memo

11. If you needed to get an urgent confidential message to a colleague in Hong Kong, your best choice of communication medium would be
    a. A fax
    b. An airmail letter
    c. An e-mail
    d. A voice mail

Objective 4.6: Discuss six ways you can establish a good relationship with your audience.

12. Which of the following sentences best exemplifies the "you" attitude?
    a. You made a mistake in the order you sent me.
    b. Although the plaid shirt you ordered is currently out of stock, a new shipment is due next week, and you can expect to receive your shirt in 10 to 14 days.
    c. I know I promised you the report by Tuesday, but you won't get it until Friday.
    d. If you had packed the items correctly, they wouldn't have been damaged in shipping.

13. An employee made a major spelling mistake in an important brochure, and now the brochures must be corrected and reprinted. Your message to the employee should focus on
    a. How much money the mistake has cost the company
    b. What a poor speller the employee is
    c. How the employee had better "shape up" or else
    d. What the employee can do to prevent such mistakes in the future

14. When trying to establish credibility with your audience, it is important to
    a. Use as much flattery as possible to "butter up" your audience
    b. Provide as much evidence as possible, from reputable sources, to back up your arguments
    c. Be as modest as possible to keep from seeming boastful
    d. Inflate your reputation as much as possible so the audience will take you seriously

15. You need some promised sales data from a colleague for a report that's due tomorrow, but she hasn't responded to your e-mails over the past week. Which of the following would be the most effective message to leave?
    a. "Hey, Jean, it's Lee. Can you get me those sales figures by 4 o'clock? I know you're busy, but I'll owe you one! Please call me back at extension 445."
    b. "Hey, Jean, where the heck are you? Don't you ever read your e-mail? I really have to have those sales figures today. It's now or never!"
    c. "Jean. It's Lee. I'm under the gun here for that report and you're not doing me any favors by waiting until the last minute with those sales figures. I need 'em now!"
    d. "Jean. It's Lee. Please call me back as soon as you get this. It's very important that I talk to you."

16. Your company has hired Leo Martinez, a paraplegic veteran, to work in your department. In a memo to other members of the department, what is the best way to introduce him?
    a. "Please welcome our new man, Leo Martinez, who will be wheeling his way onboard tomorrow."
    b. "We have a new Mexican American joining the staff tomorrow, Leo Martinez. Please try not to call attention to his handicap."
    c. "Joining us tomorrow will be new staffer Leo Martinez. Leo, a Gulf War veteran who uses a wheelchair, comes to us after five years in the marketing department at Dutton's."
    d. "Tomorrow, be sure to say *Hola!* to Leo Martinez, our new disabled employee."

Apply Your Knowledge

1. Some writers argue that planning a message wastes time because they inevitably change their plans as they go along. How would you respond to this argument? Briefly explain.
2. As a member of the public relations department, what medium would you recommend using to inform the local community that your toxic-waste cleanup program has been successful? Why?
3. When composing business messages, how can you be yourself and project your company's image at the same time?
4. Considering how fast and easy it is, should e-mail replace meetings and other face-to-face communication in your company? Why or why not?
5. **Ethical Choices** The company president has asked you to draft a memo to the board of directors informing them that sales in the newly acquired line of gourmet fruit jams have far exceeded anyone's expectations. As purchasing director, you happen to know that sales of moderately priced jams have declined substantially (many customers have switched to the more expensive jams). You were not directed to add that tidbit of information. What should you do?

Practice Your Knowledge

DOCUMENT FOR ANALYSIS

Read the following document; then (1) analyze the strengths and weaknesses of each sentence and (2) revise the document so that it follows this chapter's guidelines.

I am a new publisher with some really great books to sell. I saw your announcement in Publishers Weekly *about the bookseller's show you're having this summer, and I think it's a great idea. Count me in, folks! I would like to get some space to show my books. I thought it would be a neat thing if I could do some airbrushing on T-shirts live to help promote my hot new title,* T-Shirt Art. *Before I got into publishing, I was an airbrush artist,*

and I could demonstrate my techniques. I've done hundreds of advertising illustrations and have been a sign painter all my life, so I'll also be promoting my other book, hot off the presses, How to Make Money in the Sign Painting Business.

I will be starting my PR campaign about May 2003 with ads in PW and some art trade papers, so my books should be well known by the time the show comes around in August. In case you would like to use my appearance there as part of your publicity, I have enclosed a biography and photo of myself.

P.S. Please let me know what it costs for booth space as soon as possible so that I can figure out whether I can afford to attend. Being a new publisher is mighty expensive!

Exercises

For live links to all websites discussed in this chapter, visit this text's website at www.prenhall.com/thill. Just log on, select Chapter 4, and click on "Student Resources." Locate the page or the URL related to the material in the text. For the "Learning More on the Web" exercises, you'll also find navigational directions. Click on the live link to the site.

4.1   **Message Planning Skills: Self-Assessment** How good are you at planning business messages? Use the following chart to rate yourself on each of the following elements of planning an audience-centered business message. Then examine your ratings to identify where you are strongest and where you can improve, using the tips in this chapter.

Element of Planning	Always	Frequently	Occasionally	Never
Do you				
1. Start by defining your purpose?	_____	_____	_____	_____
2. Analyze your audience before writing a message?	_____	_____	_____	_____
3. Find out everything your audience needs to know?	_____	_____	_____	_____
4. Check that your information is accurate, ethical, and pertinent?	_____	_____	_____	_____
5. Consider your audience and purpose when selecting media?	_____	_____	_____	_____
6. Adopt the "you" attitude in your messages?	_____	_____	_____	_____
7. Emphasize the positive aspects of your message?	_____	_____	_____	_____
8. Establish your credibility with audiences of strangers?	_____	_____	_____	_____
9. Express yourself politely and tactfully?	_____	_____	_____	_____
10. Use bias-free language?	_____	_____	_____	_____
11. Take care to project your company's image?	_____	_____	_____	_____

4.2   **Planning Messages: General and Specific Purpose** Make a list of communication tasks you'll need to accomplish in the next week or so (for example, a job application, a letter of complaint, a speech to a class, an order for some merchandise). For each, determine a general and a specific purpose.

4.3   **Planning Messages: Specific Purpose** For each of the following communication tasks, state a specific purpose (if you have trouble, try beginning with "I want to . . . ").

   a. A report to your boss, the store manager, about the outdated items in the warehouse

   b. An e-mail message to clients about your booth at the upcoming trade show

   c. A letter to a customer who hasn't made a payment for three months

   d. A memo to employees about the office's high water bills

   e. A phone call to a supplier checking on an overdue parts shipment

   f. A report to future users of the computer program you have chosen for handling the company's mailing list

4.4.   **Planning Messages: Audience Profile** For each communication task below, write brief answers to three questions: Who is my audience? What is my audience's general attitude toward my subject? What does my audience need to know?

   a. A final-notice collection letter from an appliance manufacturer to an appliance dealer, sent 10 days before initiating legal collection procedures

   b. An unsolicited sales letter asking readers to purchase computer disks at near-wholesale prices

   c. An advertisement for peanut butter

   d. Fliers to be attached to doorknobs in the neighborhood, announcing reduced rates for chimney lining or repairs

   e. A cover letter sent along with your résumé to a potential employer

   f. A request (to the seller) for a price adjustment on a piano that incurred $150 in damage during delivery to a banquet room in the hotel you manage

4.5.   **Meeting Audience Needs: Necessary Information** Choose an electronic device (videocassette recorder, personal computer, telephone answering machine) that you know how to operate well. Write two sets of instructions for operating the device: one set for a reader who has never used that type of machine and one set for someone who is generally familiar with that type of machine but has never operated the specific model. Briefly explain how your two audiences affect your instructions.

4.6.   **Adapting Messages: Media and Purpose** List five messages you have received lately, such as direct-mail promotions, letters, e-mail messages, phone solicitations, and lectures. For each, determine the general and the specific purpose; then answer the following questions: (a) Was the message well timed? (b) Did the sender choose an appropriate medium for the message? (c) Did the appropriate person deliver the message? (d) Was the sender's purpose realistic?

4.7.   **Adapting Messages: Media Selection** Barbara Marquardt is in charge of public relations for a cruise line that operates out of Miami. She is shocked to read a letter in a local newspaper from a disgruntled passenger, complaining about the service and entertainment on a recent cruise. Marquardt will have to respond to these publicized criticisms in some way. What audiences will she need to consider in her response? What medium should she choose? If the letter had been published in a travel publication widely read by travel agents and cruise travelers, how might her course of action differ?

4.8. Teamwork Your team has been studying a new method for testing the durability of your company's electric hand tools. Now the team needs to prepare three separate reports on the findings: first, a report for the administrator who will decide whether to purchase the equipment needed for this new testing method; second, a report for the company's engineers who design and develop the hand tools; and third, a report for the trainers who will be showing workers how to use the new equipment. To determine the audience's needs for each of these reports, the team has listed the following questions: (1) Who are the readers? (2) Why will they read my report? (3) Do they need introductory or background material? (4) Do they need definitions of terms? (5) What level or type of language is needed? (6) What level of detail is needed? (7) What result does my report aim for? Working with two other students, answer the questions for each of these audiences:

a. The administrator

b. The engineers

c. The trainers

4.9. Internet More companies are reaching out to audiences through their websites. Go to the PepsiCo website at www.pepsico.com and follow the link to the latest annual report. Then locate and read the chairman's letter. Who is the audience for this message? What is the general purpose of the message? What do you think this audience needs to know from the chairman of PepsiCo? How does the chairman emphasize the positive in this letter? Summarize your answers in a brief (one-page) memo or oral presentation.

4.10. Audience Relationship: Courteous Communication Substitute a better phrase for each of the following:

a. You claim that

b. It is not our policy to

c. You neglected to

d. In which you assert

e. We are sorry you are dissatisfied

f. You failed to enclose

g. We request that you send us

h. Apparently you overlooked our terms

i. We have been very patient

j. We are at a loss to understand

4.11. Audience Relationship: The "You" Attitude Rewrite these sentences to reflect your audience's viewpoint.

a. We request that you use the order form supplied in the back of our catalog.

b. We insist that you always bring your credit card to the store.

c. We want to get rid of all our 15-inch monitors to make room in our warehouse for the 19-inch screens. Thus we are offering a 25 percent discount on all sales this week.

d. I am applying for the position of bookkeeper in your office. I feel that my grades prove that I am bright and capable, and I think I can do a good job for you.

e. As requested, we are sending the refund for $25.

4.12. Audience Relationship: Emphasize the Positive Revise these sentences to be positive rather than negative.

a. To avoid the loss of your credit rating, please remit payment within 10 days.

b. We don't make refunds on returned merchandise that is soiled.

c. Because we are temporarily out of Baby Cry dolls, we won't be able to ship your order for 10 days.

d. You failed to specify the color of the blouse that you ordered.

e. You should have realized that waterbeds will freeze in unheated houses during winter. Therefore, our guarantee does not cover the valve damage and you must pay the $9.50 valve-replacement fee (plus postage).

4.13. Audience Relationship: Emphasize the Positive Provide euphemisms for the following words and phrases:

a. Stubborn

b. Wrong

c. Stupid

d. Incompetent

e. Loudmouth

4.14. Audience Relationship: Bias-Free Language Rewrite each of the following to eliminate bias:

a. For an Indian, Maggie certainly is outgoing.

b. He needs a wheelchair, but he doesn't let his handicap affect his job performance.

c. A pilot must have the ability to stay calm under pressure, and then he must be trained to cope with any problem that arises.

d. Candidate Renata Parsons, married and the mother of a teenager, will attend the debate.

e. Senior citizen Sam Nugent is still an active salesman.

4.15. Ethical Choices Your supervisor, whom you respect, has asked you to withhold important information that you think should be included in a report you are preparing. Disobeying him could be disastrous for your relationship and your career. Obeying him could violate your personal code of ethics. What should you do? On the basis of the discussion in Chapter 1, would you consider this situation to be an ethical dilemma or an ethical lapse? Please explain.

4.16. Three-Step Process: Other Applications How can the material discussed in this chapter also apply to meetings as discussed in Chapter 2? (Hint: Review the section headings in Chapter 4 and think about making your meetings more productive.)

Expand Your Knowledge

LEARNING MORE ON THE WEB

Learn How Instant Messaging Works www.howstuffworks. com/instant-messaging.htm

No doubt the Internet has changed the way we communicate. But do you understand how all this electronic stuff works? Fret no more. Log on to Marshall Brain's How Stuff Works website and learn all about instant messaging and why the future of this form of communication is bright indeed. In fact, try using it next time you want to hold a virtual conference or collaborate on a project with teammates. You'll see why instant messaging is becoming a valuable tool in the workplace.

ACTIVITIES

Log on now to Marshall Brain's How Stuff Works website and learn all about instant messaging. Then answer these questions.
1. What are the key advantages of instant messaging?
2. What is the difference between a chat room and instant messaging?
3. Is instant messaging a secure way to communicate?

EXPLORING THE WEB ON YOUR OWN

Review these chapter-related websites on your own to learn more about achieving communication success in the workplace.
1. Learn more about the writing process, English grammar, style and usage, words, and active writing at Garbl's Writing Resources Online, www.garbl.home. attbi.com.
2. Plan your messages well, improve your organization, and learn how to write better with the sound advice and writing help at Writing Better, an electronic *Handbook for Amherst Students,* www.amherst.edu/~writing/wb_html/ wb.html.
3. Discover how e-mail works and how to improve your e-mail communications by following the steps at About Internet for Beginners—Harness E-Mail, www.learnthenet. com/english/section/email.html.

Learn Interactively

INTERACTIVE STUDY GUIDE

Go to the Companion Website at www.prenhall.com/bovee. For Chapter 4, take advantage of the interactive "Study Guide" to test your knowledge of the chapter. Get instant feedback on whether you need additional studying. Also, visit this site's "Study Hall" where you'll find an abundance of valuable resources that will help you succeed in this course.

PEAK PERFORMANCE GRAMMAR AND MECHANICS

To improve your skill with adjectives, use the "Peak Performance Grammar and Mechanics" module on the web. Visit www.prenhall.com/onekey, click "Peak Performance Grammar and Mechanics," then click "Adjectives." Take the Pretest to determine whether you have any weak areas. Then review those areas in the Refresher Course. Take the Follow-Up Test to check your grasp of adjectives. For an extra challenge or advanced practice, take the Advanced Test. Finally, for additional reinforcement, go to the "Improve Your Grammar, Mechanics, and Usage" section that follows, and complete those exercises.

Improve Your Grammar, Mechanics, and Usage

The following exercises help you improve your knowledge of and power over English grammar, mechanics, and usage. Turn to the "Handbook of Grammar, Mechanics, and Usage" at the end of this textbook and review all of Section 1.4 (Adjectives). Then look at the following 10 items. Underline the preferred

choice within each set of parentheses. (Answers to these exercises appear on page AK-3.)
1. Of the two products, this one has the (*greater, greatest*) potential.
2. The (*most perfect, perfect*) solution is d.

3. Here is the (*interesting, most interesting*) of all the ideas I have heard so far.
4. The (*hardest, harder*) part of my job is firing people.
5. A (*highly placed, highly-placed*) source revealed Dotson's (*last ditch, last-ditch*) efforts to cover up the mistake.
6. A (*top secret, top-secret*) document was taken from the president's office last night.
7. A (*30 year old, 30-year-old*) person should know better.
8. The two companies are engaged in an (*all-out no-holds-barred; all-out, no-holds-barred*) struggle for dominance.
9. A (*tiny metal; tiny, metal*) shaving is responsible for the problem.
10. You'll receive our (*usual cheerful prompt; usual, cheerful, prompt; usual cheerful, prompt*) service.

Chapter 5

Writing Business Messages

Learning Objectives

AFTER STUDYING THIS CHAPTER, YOU WILL BE ABLE TO

1 Cite four of the most common organization mistakes made by communicators

2 Explain why good organization is important to both the communicator and the audience

3 Summarize the process for organizing business messages effectively

4 Discuss three ways of achieving a businesslike tone with a style that is clear and concise

5 Briefly describe how to select words that are not only correct but also effective

6 Discuss how to use sentence style for emphasis

7 List five ways to develop a paragraph and explain how boilerplates are used

8 Explain how to capture audience attention and be more personal in e-mail messages

9 Explain how to develop a hyperlink structure, and how to modify your style and format for the web

On the Job:

COMMUNICATING AT BARNES & NOBLE

DOING MORE THAN JUST SELLING BOOKS

At Barnes & Noble (B&N), reading is big business. With more than 1,886 stores in 49 states and the District of Columbia, the company serves 7.3 million customers and sells more than $4.4 billion in books annually—which makes it the number-one bookseller in the United States. As senior vice president of corporate communications and public affairs, Mary Ellen Keating handles internal and external communications, media relations, community relations, and public affairs for the B&N corporation, the B. Dalton retail stores, Barnes&Noble.com, and Barnes & Noble College Bookstores. Keating and her team communicate effectively with a wide variety of audiences because they organize and compose their messages carefully.

For example, Keating communicates with customers and the media about B&N's Readers' Advantage program—a frequent-buyer plan that offers members 5 percent off the already discounted prices online and 10 percent off in-store purchases. In addition, B&N uses the frequent-buyer card to give members added value, such as the ability to read interviews with writers, learn about upcoming books, and sign up for special programs. In customer messages, Keating emphasizes strong organization and coherent paragraphs to focus on B&N's friendly, comfortable environment and to point out how the company provides not only the widest selection of books at the best prices but also knowledgeable booksellers who are helpful and pleasant. She conveys the ease and convenience that online customers can expect, and she emphasizes the unique experience waiting for those in-store shoppers who enjoy sipping a latte in comfortable, pleasant surroundings while browsing through section after section of new books.

When Keating communicates with authors, she chooses just the right words to convey the advantages of showcasing their work in the B&N environment. Her team is also responsible for messages that give authors advice about the publishing process, about

The people at Barnes & Noble are proud to work for the number-one bookseller in the United States. To help maintain that status, Vice President Mary Ellen Keating encourages her team to compose corporate messages that are clear, concise, and well organized.

getting the best exposure possible, and even about how to connect with the right publisher. These messages would not succeed without close attention to style and sentence construction.

For shareholders, Keating concentrates on building value. For example, her team helps explain B&N's expansion plans. The company is reviewing opportunities to open another 500 stores in the United States, each one unique and custom-built for the community. Careful organization also helps Keating explain the logic of why expanding internationally is too complicated for B&N right now—requiring the company to adapt to different publishers, languages, and distribution systems.

When reaching out to the community, Keating discusses topics such as hosting community events, providing educational activities, and running programs that put books in the hands of disadvantaged children. After the terrorist attacks of September 11, 2001, Keating's team helped B&N announce daily Storytimes for children across the nation—special events that focused on how to deal with such tragic events. The company also posted a recommended reading list for parents to help them and their children cope with the 9/11 tragedy. B&N even brought psychologists and counselors to New York Metro area stores to talk to families about their fears and concerns. In all these messages, Keating's team worked meticulously to get the tone and wording just right.

Keating is also responsible for internal messages that focus on employee needs. Her team's efforts help B&N maintain a work environment that is fair, professional, and diverse. The company helps employees flourish and grow by ensuring that its stores and offices are friendly, supportive places that run on the shared love of books and respect for others. Management wants everyone at Barnes & Noble to feel empowered to succeed, and Keating makes sure her team conveys that message.[1]

www.barnesandnobleinc.com

ORGANIZING YOUR MESSAGE

As Mary Ellen Keating knows, all business communicators face the challenge of composing messages that their audiences can easily understand. People tend not to remember isolated facts and figures, so successful communicators rely on good organization to make their messages meaningful.[2] But what exactly makes a particular organization "good"? Here's a closer look at what constitutes good organization and why it is important.

What Good Organization Means

Various cultures define good organization differently.

Although the definition of good organization varies from country to country, in the United States and Canada, it generally means creating a linear message that proceeds point by point. If you've ever received a disorganized message, you're familiar with the frustration of trying to sort through a muddle of ideas. Consider this letter from Jill Saunders, the accounting manager at General Nutrition Corporation (GNC), manufacturer of health-food products and nutritional supplements:

> General Nutrition Corporation has been doing business with ComputerTime since I was hired six years ago. Your building was smaller then, and it was located on the corner of Federal Avenue and 2nd N.W. Jared Mallory, our controller, was one of your first customers. I still remember the day. It was the biggest check I'd ever written. Of course, over the years, I've gotten used to larger purchases.
>
> Our department now has 15 employees. As accountants, we need to have our computers working so that we can do our jobs. The CD-RW drive we bought for my assistant, Suzanne, has been a problem. We've taken it in for repairs three times in three months to the authorized service center, and Suzanne is very careful with the machine and hasn't abused it. She does like playing interactive adventure games on lunch breaks. Anyway, it still doesn't work right, and she's tired of hauling it back and forth. We're all putting in longer hours because it is our busy season, and none of us has a lot of spare time.
>
> This is the first time we've returned anything to your store, and I hope you'll agree that we deserve a better deal.

Most disorganized communication suffers from problems with clarity, relevance, grouping, and completeness.

This letter displays a lack of organization that most readers find frustrating. By taking a closer look at what's wrong, you can distinguish four of the most common organization mistakes made by communicators:

- **Taking too long to get to the point.** Saunders didn't introduce her topic, the faulty CD-RW drive, until the third paragraph. Then she waited until the final paragraph to state her purpose: requesting an adjustment. *Solution:* Make the subject and purpose clear.

- **Including irrelevant material.** Does it matter that ComputerTime used to be smaller or that it was in a different location? Is it important that Saunders's department has 15 employees or that her assistant likes playing computer games during lunch? *Solution:* Include only information that is related to the subject and purpose.

- **Getting ideas mixed up.** Saunders tries to make five points: (1) Her company has money to spend, (2) it's an old customer, (3) it has purchased numerous items at ComputerTime, (4) the CD-RW drive doesn't work, and (5) Saunders wants an adjustment. However, the ideas are mixed up and located in the wrong places.

Solution: Group the ideas and present them in a logical way. For example, begin with the fact that the drive doesn't work, and group some ideas to show that the company is a valuable customer.

- **Leaving out necessary information.** ComputerTime may want to know the make, model, and price of the CD-RW drive; the date of purchase; the specific problems the machine has had; and whether the repairs were covered by the warranty. Saunders also failed to say what she wants the store to do: send her a new CD-RW drive of the same type, send her a different model, or simply refund her money. *Solution:* Include all the necessary information.

Achieving good organization can be a challenge. However, solving these common problems can help you communicate clearly. Saunders can make her letter more effective by organizing all the necessary information in a sequence that helps ComputerTime understand the message (see Figure 5–1).

Why Good Organization Is Important

Poorly organized messages can waste readers' time as they struggle to grasp your meaning. Furthermore, disorganized messages can lead to misinterpretation, which could result in poor decision making and even shattered business relationships. When you consider such costs, you begin to realize the value of clear writing and good organization.[3] Moreover, being well organized helps you compose your messages more quickly and efficiently. In business, the objective is to get work done, not to produce messages. When chief executives were asked what they would most like to improve about their own business writing, they mentioned speed of composition more often than any other factor.[4]

So before you begin to write, think about what you're going to say and how you're going to say it. Good organization helps you work better because it

- **Saves you time.** Your draft will go more quickly because you won't waste time putting ideas in the wrong places or composing material you don't need.

- **Saves you work.** You can use your organizational plan to get advance input from your audience, so you can make sure you're on the right track *before* you spend hours working on your draft.

- **Helps you delegate.** You can use your organization plan to divide large, complex writing jobs among co-workers.

In addition to helping you, good organization helps your audience by

- **Increasing reader understanding.** As Mary Ellen Keating points out, successful organization is the key to communicating effectively with audiences. By making your main point clear at the outset and stating your needs precisely, your well-organized message will satisfy your audience's need for information.

- **Making readers more receptive to your message.** Even when your message is logical, you need to select and organize your points in a diplomatic way. By softening refusals and leaving a good impression, you enhance your credibility and add authority to your messages. When ComputerTime responded to the GNC inquiry, the message was negative, but the letter was diplomatic and positive (see Figure 5–2 on page 129).

- **Saving readers time.** Well-organized messages are efficient, contain only relevant ideas, are brief, and present all the information in a logical place. Audience members receive only the information they need, and because that information is presented as accessibly and succinctly as possible, they can follow the thought pattern without a struggle.

Poor organization costs time, efficiency, and relationships.

Good organization helps you save time, work smart, and delegate.

Good organization helps your audience understand your message, accept your message, and save time.

GNC LiveWell.

September 13, 2004

Customer Service
ComputerTime
556 Seventh Ave.
Mason City, IA 50401

Dear Customer Service Representative:

GNC bought an Olympic Systems, Model PRS-2, CD-RW drive from your store on November 15, 2003, during your pre-Christmas sale, when it was marked down to $199.95. We didn't use the unit until January, because it was bought for my assistant, who unexpectedly took six weeks' leave from mid-November through December. You can imagine her frustration when she first tried using it, and it didn't work.

In January, we took the drive to the authorized service center and were assured that the problem was merely a loose connection. The service representative fixed the drive, but in April we had to have it fixed again—another loose connection. For the next three months, the drive worked reasonably well, although the response time was occasionally slow. Two months ago, the drive stopped working again. Once more, the service representative blamed a loose connection and made the repair. Although the drive is working now, it isn't working very well. The response time is still slow, and the motor seems to drag sometimes.

What is your policy on exchanging unsatisfactory merchandise? Although all the repairs have been relatively minor and have been covered by the one-year warranty, we are not satisfied with the drive. We would like to exchange it for a similar model from another manufacturer. If the new drive costs more than the old one, we will pay the difference, even though we generally look for equipment with substantial business discounts.

GNC has done business with your store for six years and until now has always been satisfied with your merchandise. We are counting on you to live up to your reputation for standing behind your products. Please let us hear from you soon.

Sincerely,

Jill Saunders

Jill Saunders
Administrative Assistant

General Nutrition Corporation, 300 Sixth Avenue, Pittsburgh, PA 15222
Tel: (412) 288-4600

Annotation labels:
- States purpose clearly
- States precisely what adjustment is being requested
- Includes all necessary information and no irrelevant facts
- Explains the situation so that the reader will understand the problem
- Presents ideas logically
- Motivates action from the reader in the close

FIGURE 5–1
Effective Letter with Improved Organization

How Good Organization Is Achieved

To organize a message, be sure to
- Define your main idea
- Limit the scope
- Group your points
- Choose the direct or indirect approach

The topic is the broad subject; the main idea makes a statement about the topic.

Understanding the *need* for good organization is half the battle. Knowing *how* to organize your messages well is the other half. When writing messages at Barnes & Noble, Mary Ellen Keating achieves good organization by defining the main idea, limiting the scope, grouping supporting points, and selecting either a direct or an indirect approach to the message sequence.

Define the Main Idea   In addition to having a general purpose and a specific purpose, all business messages can be boiled down to one main idea—one central point that sums up everything. The rest of your message supports, explains, or demonstrates this point. Your main idea is not the same as your topic. The broad subject of

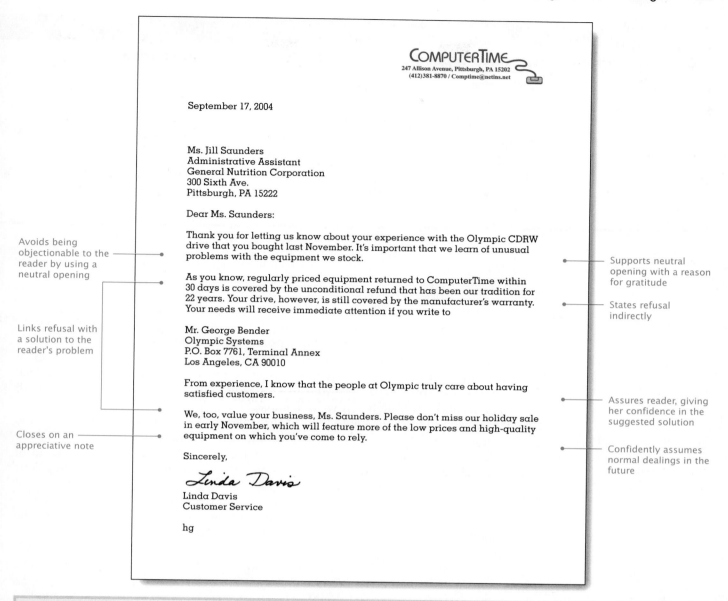

COMPUTERTIME
247 Allison Avenue, Pittsburgh, PA 15202
(412)381-8870 / Comptime@netins.net

September 17, 2004

Ms. Jill Saunders
Administrative Assistant
General Nutrition Corporation
300 Sixth Ave.
Pittsburgh, PA 15222

Dear Ms. Saunders:

Avoids being objectionable to the reader by using a neutral opening

Thank you for letting us know about your experience with the Olympic CDRW drive that you bought last November. It's important that we learn of unusual problems with the equipment we stock.

Supports neutral opening with a reason for gratitude

As you know, regularly priced equipment returned to ComputerTime within 30 days is covered by the unconditional refund that has been our tradition for 22 years. Your drive, however, is still covered by the manufacturer's warranty. Your needs will receive immediate attention if you write to

States refusal indirectly

Links refusal with a solution to the reader's problem

Mr. George Bender
Olympic Systems
P.O. Box 7761, Terminal Annex
Los Angeles, CA 90010

From experience, I know that the people at Olympic truly care about having satisfied customers.

Assures reader, giving her confidence in the suggested solution

Closes on an appreciative note

We, too, value your business, Ms. Saunders. Please don't miss our holiday sale in early November, which will feature more of the low prices and high-quality equipment on which you've come to rely.

Confidently assumes normal dealings in the future

Sincerely,

Linda Davis

Linda Davis
Customer Service

hg

FIGURE 5-2
Effective Letter Demonstrating a Diplomatic Organization Plan

your message is the **topic,** and your **main idea** makes a statement about that topic. Consider the examples in Table 5–1.

Your main idea may at times be obvious. When you're responding to a straight-forward request for information and your message has little emotional impact on your audience, your main idea may be simply, "Here is what you wanted." However, defining your main idea is more complicated when you're trying to persuade someone or when you have disappointing information to convey. In these situations, try to define a main idea that will establish a good relationship between you and your audience. For example, you may choose a main idea that highlights a common interest you share with your audience or that emphasizes a point that you and your audience can agree on.

Defining your main idea is more difficult when you're trying to persuade someone or convey disappointing information.

Longer documents and presentations unify a mass of material, so be sure to define a main idea that encompasses all the individual points you want to make. For tough assignments like these, you may want to take special measures to define your

Table 5–1   DEFINING BUSINESS MESSAGES

General Purpose	Specific Purpose	Topic	Main Idea
To inform	Teach customer service reps how to file insurance claims.	Insurance claims	Proper filing by reps saves the company time and money.
To persuade	Get top managers to approve increased spending on research and development.	Funding for research and development	Competitors spend more than we do on research and development.
To collaborate	Solicit ideas for a companywide incentive system that ties wages to profits.	Incentive pay	Tying wages to profits motivates employees and reduces compensation in tough years.

main idea. Figure 5–3 describes six techniques you can use to generate your main idea and key points.

Limit the Scope   The scope of your message (its length and detail) matches your main idea. Whether your audience expects a one-page memo or a one-hour speech, develop your main idea with major points and supporting evidence within the expected framework. Once you have a tentative statement of your main idea, test it against the length limitations that have been imposed for your message. If you lack the time and space to develop your main idea fully, or if your main idea won't fill up the time and space allotted, then redefine it.

As you adjust your message to fit the time or space available, don't change the number of major points. Regardless of how long the message will be, stick with three or four major points—five is the most your audience will remember.[5] Instead of introducing additional points, develop complex issues more fully by supporting your points with a variety of evidence.

If your message is brief (four minutes or one page), you'll have only a minute or a paragraph each for the introduction, conclusion, and major points. Because the amount of evidence you can present is limited, your main idea will have to be both easy to understand and easy to accept. However, if you're delivering a long message (say, a 60-minute presentation or a 20-page report), you can develop the major points in considerable detail. You can spend about 10 minutes or 10 paragraphs (more than three pages of double-spaced, typewritten text) on each of your key points, and you'll still have room for your introduction and conclusion.

How much information you can communicate in a given number of words depends on the nature of your subject, your audience members' familiarity with the topic, their receptivity to your conclusions, and your credibility. You'll need fewer words to present routine information to a knowledgeable audience that already knows and respects you; however, to build consensus about a complex and controversial subject, you'll need more time—especially if the audience is composed of skeptical or hostile strangers.

Structure Your Message   Once you have narrowed the scope of your message, you must provide your supporting details in the most logical and effective way. Constructing an outline of your message, as Mary Ellen Keating does, is one good way to visualize how all the points will fit together. Whether you use the outlining features provided with word-processing software or simply jot down three or four points on the back of an envelope, making a plan and sticking to it will help you cover the important details.

When you're preparing a longer, more complex message, an outline is indispensable because it helps you visualize the relationships among the various parts.

Deal with three or four major points (not more than five), regardless of message length.

A good way to visualize how all the points will fit together is to construct an outline.

Brainstorming: Generate as many possibilities as you can think of by letting your mind wander and by being completely uncensored. Then develop criteria to test your ideas against your purpose, your audience, and the facts you've gathered. Finally, eliminate ideas that fail to meet your criteria.

Random List: On a computer screen or a clean sheet of paper, list everything you can think of that pertains to your message. Once you begin your list, your thoughts will start to flow. When you've exhausted the possibilities, study the list for relationships. Sort the items into groups, as you would sort a deck of cards into suits. Look for common denominators; the connection might be geographic, sequential, spatial, chronological, or topical. Part of the list might break down into problems, cases, and solutions; another part into pros and cons. Regardless of what categories finally emerge, the sorting process will help you sift through your thoughts and decide what's important to include in your communication. Of course, the best way to decide importance is to concentrate on the points that will benefit your audience most.

FCR Worksheet: If your subject involves the solution to a problem, you might try an FCR worksheet to help you visualize the relationships among your findings (F), your conclusions (C), and your recommendations (R). For example, you might find that you're losing sales to a competitor who offers lower prices than you do (F). From this information, you might conclude that your loss of sales is due to your pricing policy (C). This conclusion would lead you to recommend a price cut (R). To make an FCR worksheet, divide a computer screen or a sheet of paper into three columns. List the major findings in the first column, then extrapolate conclusions and write them in the second column. These conclusions form the basis for the recommendations, which are listed in the third column. An analysis of the three columns should help you define the information you need to include in your communication.

Journalistic Approach: For informational messages, the journalistic approach may provide a good point of departure. Find the answers to six questions—who, what, when, where, why, and how. The answers you come up with should help you provide all the required information in your message.

Question-and-Answer Chain: Perhaps the best approach is to look at the subject of your message from your audience's point of view. Ask yourself: "What are the audience's main questions? What do audience members need to know?" Write down and examine your answers. As additional questions emerge, write down and examine those answers. Follow the chain of questions and answers until you have replied to every conceivable question that might occur to your audience. By assuming your audience's perspective, you will include the information of greatest value to your audience in your communication.

Storyteller's Tour: Turn on your tape recorder and pretend that you've just run into an old friend on the street. Give an overview of your message, focusing on your reasons for communicating, your major points, your rationale, and the implications for your audience. Listen critically to the tape; then repeat the exercise until you are able to give a smooth, two-minute summary that conveys the gist of your message. Be sure to include the key points you've defined in your communication.

FIGURE 5–3
Defining Your Main Idea

Without an outline, you may be inclined to ramble. As you're describing one point, another point may occur to you, so you describe it. One detour leads to another, and before you know it, you've forgotten the original point. With an outline to guide you, however, you can communicate in a more systematic way. Following an outline also helps you insert transitions so that your message is coherent and your audience can understand the relationships among your ideas.

You're no doubt familiar with the basic outline formats, which (1) use numbers—or letters and numbers—to identify each point and (2) indent points to show which ideas are of equal status. A good outline divides a topic into at least two parts, restricts each subdivision to one category, and ensures that each group is separate and distinct (see Figure 5–4).

Another way to visualize the structure of your message is by creating a message "organization chart" similar to the charts used to show a company's management structure (see Figure 5–5). The main idea is shown in the highest-level box and, like a top executive, establishes the big picture. The lower-level ideas, like lower-level employees, provide the details. All the ideas are logically organized into divisions of

Outlines can appear in various formats.

FIGURE 5–4
Two Common Outline Forms

ALPHANUMERIC OUTLINE

I. First Major Point
  A. First subpoint
  B. Second subpoint
    1. Evidence
    2. Evidence
      a. Detail
      b. Detail
    3. Evidence
  C. Third subpoint
II. Second Major Point
  A. First subpoint
    1. Evidence
    2. Evidence
  B. Second subpoint

DECIMAL OUTLINE

1.0 First Major Point
  1.1 First subpoint
  1.2 Second subpoint
    1.2.1 Evidence
    1.2.2 Evidence
      1.2.2.1 Detail
      1.2.2.2 Detail
    1.2.3 Evidence
  1.3 Third subpoint
2.0 Second Major Point
  2.1 First subpoint
    2.1.1 Evidence
    2.1.2 Evidence
  2.2 Second subpoint

thought, just as a company is organized into divisions and departments.[6] Using a visual chart instead of a traditional outline has many benefits. Charts help you (1) see the various levels of ideas and how the parts fit together, (2) develop new ideas, and (3) restructure your information flow.

Whether you use an outline format or an organization chart to structure your message, your message begins with the main idea, follows with major supporting points, and then illustrates these points with evidence.

Start with the Main Idea   The main idea helps you establish the goals and general strategy of the message and summarizes two things: (1) what you want your audience to do or think and (2) why they should do so. Everything in the message should either support the main idea or explain its implications.

State the Major Points   Once you've determined the main idea, identify three to five major points that support and clarify your message in more concrete terms. If you come up with more, go back and look for opportunities to combine some of your ideas. The form of your major points depends on your purpose:

Major supporting points clarify your main idea and may be grouped by physical relationship, description of a process, components of an object, historical chronology, or logical argument.

- **To inform with factual material.** Your major points might be based on something physical—something you can visualize or measure, such as activities to be performed, functional units, spatial or chronological relationships, or parts of a whole.

- **To describe a process.** The major points are almost inevitably steps in the process.

FIGURE 5–5
Organization Chart for
Organizing a Message

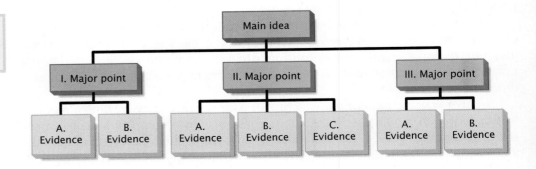

- **To describe an object.** Major points correspond to the components of the object.

- **To give a historical account.** Major points represent events in the chronological chain.

- **To persuade or collaborate.** Major points develop a line of reasoning or logical argument that proves your central message and motivates your audience to act.

Illustrate with Evidence   Specific evidence is the flesh and blood that helps your audience understand and remember the more abstract concepts you're presenting. For example, if you're advocating that your company increase its advertising budget, you can support your major point with evidence that your most successful competitors spend more on advertising than you do. You can describe how a particular competitor increased its ad budget and achieved an impressive sales gain. Then you can show that over the past five years, your firm's sales have gone up and down in relation to the amount spent on advertising.

If you're developing a long, complex message, you may need to carry the organization chart (or outline) down several levels. Remember that every level is a step along the chain from the abstract to the concrete, from the general to the specific. The lowest level contains the individual facts and figures that tie the generalizations to the observable, measurable world. The higher levels are the concepts that reveal why those facts are significant.

The more evidence you provide, the more conclusive your case will be. If your subject is complex and unfamiliar or if your audience is skeptical, you'll need a lot of facts and figures to demonstrate your points. On the other hand, if your subject is routine and the audience is positively inclined, you can be more sparing with the evidence. You want to provide enough support to be convincing but not so much that your message becomes boring or inefficient.

Keep your audience interested by varying the type of detail you use as evidence. As you draft your message, try to switch from facts and figures to narration; add a dash of description; throw in some examples or a reference to authority. And be sure to reinforce all these details with visual aids. Think of your message as a stew: a mixture of ingredients seasoned with a blend of spices. Each separate flavor adds to the richness of the whole.

> Each major point must be supported with enough specific evidence to be convincing, but not so much that it's boring.

Choose Between the Direct and Indirect Approaches

Once you've defined your ideas and outlined or diagrammed the structure of your message, you're ready to decide on the sequence you will use to present your points. When you're addressing a U.S. or Canadian audience with minimal cultural differences, you have two basic options:

- **Direct approach (deductive).** The main idea (a recommendation, conclusion, or request) comes first, followed by the evidence.

- **Indirect approach (inductive).** The evidence comes first, and the main idea comes later.

To choose between these two alternatives, you must analyze your audience's likely reaction to your purpose and message. Audience reaction will fall somewhere between eagerness to accept your message and unwillingness to accept it (see Figure 5–6). The direct approach is generally fine when audience members will be receptive—if they are eager, interested, pleased, or even neutral. But you may have better results with the indirect approach if audience members are likely to resist your message—if they are displeased, uninterested, or unwilling.

Bear in mind that each message is unique. No simple formula will solve all your communication problems. For example, audience reaction isn't the only factor to

> Use the direct approach if the audience's reaction is likely to be positive and the indirect approach if it is likely to be negative.

FIGURE 5–6
Audience Reaction Affects
Organizational Approach

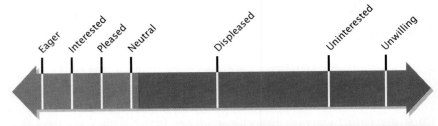

	Direct approach	Indirect approach	
Audience reaction	Eager/interested/ pleased/neutral	Displeased	Uninterested/unwilling
Message type	Routine, good news, goodwill	Bad news	Persuasive
Message opening	Start with the main idea, the request, or the good news.	Start with a neutral statement that acts as a transition to the reasons for the bad news.	Start with a statement or question that captures attention.
Message body	Provide necessary details.	Give reasons to justify a negative answer. State or imply the bad news, and make a positive suggestion.	Arouse the audience's interest in the subject. Build the audience's desire to comply.
Message close	Close with a cordial comment, a reference to the good news, or a statement about the specific action desired.	Close cordially.	Request action.

Analyze each communication situation, and choose your approach based on audience reaction, message length, and message type.

consider. True, if you're sending bad news to outsiders, an indirect approach may be best. However, if you're writing a memo to an associate, you may want to get directly to the point, even if your message is unpleasant. Also, the direct approach might be the best choice for long messages, regardless of audience attitude, because delaying the main idea could cause confusion and frustration. To summarize, your choice of a direct or an indirect approach depends on:

- **Audience reaction:** Positive, neutral, or negative
- **Message length:** Short (memos, letters, and e-mail—discussed in Part 3 of this text) or long (reports, proposals, and presentations—discussed in Part 4)
- **Message type:** (1) Routine messages; (2) bad-news messages; or (3) persuasive messages (all of which are discussed in Part 3)

Look again at Figure 5–6, which summarizes how your approach may differ depending on likely audience reaction and message type. When used with good judgment, all three message types can be powerful tools of communication.[7] In the following brief discussions, note how the opening, body, and close all play an important role in getting your message across.

Routine Messages   The most straightforward business messages are routine, good-news, and goodwill messages. If you're inquiring about products or placing an order, your audience will usually want to comply. If you're announcing a price cut, granting an adjustment, accepting an invitation, or congratulating a colleague, your audience will most likely be pleased to hear from you. If you're providing routine information as part of your regular business, your audience will probably be neutral, neither pleased nor displeased.

Routine messages benefit from the direct approach: opening with the main idea, providing details in the body, and closing cordially.

These messages get right down to business. They are easy to understand and easy to prepare because they rely on the direct approach. In the opening, state your main idea directly; you don't need a "creative" introduction. By starting off with your positive idea, you put audience members in a good frame of mind and encourage them to be receptive to whatever else you have to say. In the body of your message, provide all the necessary details. Then close cordially, emphasizing your good news or making a statement about the specific action desired. Routine messages are discussed in greater detail in Chapter 7.

Bad-News Messages   If you're turning down a job applicant, refusing credit, or denying a request for an adjustment, your audience will be disappointed. By blurting out an unpleasant message, you may think that you're just being businesslike or that your audience is too far away or too unimportant to matter. However, astute businesspeople know that every person they encounter could be a potential customer, supplier, or contributor or could influence someone who is a customer, supplier, or contributor.

Thus, successful communicators take a little extra care with their bad-news messages and often rely on the indirect approach. Your opening is neutral, acting as a transition to your reasons for the bad news. In the body, you give the reasons that justify a negative answer before actually stating or implying the bad news. Your close is always cordial.

Keep in mind that the indirect approach is neither manipulative nor unethical. The challenge lies in being honest but kind. You don't want to sacrifice ethics and mislead your audience; nor do you want to be overly blunt. To achieve a good mix of candor and kindness, focus on some aspect of the situation that makes the bad news a little easier to take. As long as you can be honest, can be reasonably brief, and can close with something fairly positive, you're likely to leave the audience feeling okay—not great, but not hostile either (which is often about all you can hope for when you must deliver negative messages). Bad-news messages are discussed further in Chapter 8.

Persuasive Messages   The indirect approach is also useful when you know that your audience will resist your message (will be uninterested in your request or unwilling to comply without extra coaxing). You might find an audience resistant to a sales letter, a collection letter, an unsolicited job application, or a request for a favor of some kind. In such cases, you have to capture people's attention before you can persuade them to do something. You have to get your audience to consider with an open mind what you have to say. So you have to make an interesting point and provide supporting facts that encourage the audience to continue paying attention.

In persuasive messages, you open by mentioning a possible benefit, referring to a problem that the recipient might have, posing a question, or citing an interesting statistic. In the body you then build interest in the subject and arouse your audience members' desire to comply. Once you have them thinking, you can introduce your main idea. Finally, you close cordially and request the desired action. Persuasive messages are discussed at greater length in Chapter 9. For a reminder of the organization tasks discussed in this chapter, see the "Checklist: Organizing Business Messages."

When Ralph Congers takes orders from phone customers, he asks for the same information that a writer would need to include in an order letter: contact information (name, address, phone, e-mail), payment information (check, credit card type and number), and item information (item description, how many, etc.). Because such orders are routine, the information is presented in a direct and straightforward manner.

If you have bad news, try to put it somewhere in the middle, cushioned by other, more positive ideas.

The indirect approach should not be used to manipulate.

Using the indirect approach gives you an opportunity to get your message across to an uninterested or skeptical audience.

Persuasive messages have their own indirect pattern.

✓ CHECKLIST: Organizing Business Messages

Recognize Good Organization

✓ Subject and purpose are clear.
✓ Information is directly related to subject and purpose.
✓ Ideas are grouped and presented logically.
✓ All necessary information is included.

Define the Main Idea and Limit the Scope

✓ Develop a global statement that sums up the central point of your message.
✓ Make your global statement audience-centered.
✓ Evaluate whether the main idea is realistic, given the imposed length limitations.

Structure the Message to Decide What you Need to Say

✓ Start with the main idea.
✓ State the major points.
✓ Illustrate with evidence.

Arrange Message Sequence According to the Audience's Probable Reaction

✓ Use the direct approach when your audience will be neutral, pleased, interested, or eager.
✓ Use the indirect approach when your audience will be displeased, uninterested, or unwilling.

COMPOSING AND SHAPING YOUR MESSAGE

Before you begin to compose your first draft, put aside your outline or organization chart for a day or two (if your schedule permits). Then review it with a fresh eye, looking for opportunities to improve the flow of ideas. Composition is easier now that you've already figured out what to say and in what order—even if you need to pause now and then to find the right word. As you go along, you may discover that you can improve on your outline. Feel free to rearrange, delete, and add ideas, as long as you don't lose sight of your purpose.

Composition is the process of drafting your message; polishing it is a later step.

As you compose, try to let your creativity flow. Don't worry about getting everything perfect at this point; that is, try not to compose and edit at the same time. Just put down your ideas as quickly as you can. You'll have time to revise and refine the material later. If you get stuck, try following some of the techniques presented in "Sharpening Your Career Skills: Beating Writer's Block: Nine Workable Ideas to Get Words Flowing."

Once you have all your thoughts and ideas jotted down, begin shaping your message. Start by paying attention to your style and tone. Select words that match the tone you want to achieve. Create the most effective sentences possible, and develop coherent paragraphs. The following sections discuss each of these elements.

Controlling Your Style and Tone

When composing your message, you can vary the style to create a tone that suits the occasion.

Style is the way you use language to achieve a certain **tone**, or overall impression. You can vary your style—your sentence structure and vocabulary—to sound forceful or objective, personal or formal, colorful or dry. The choice of tone depends on the nature of your message and your relationship with your audience. Although style can be refined during revision (see Chapter 6), you'll save time and a lot of rewriting if you develop a style that allows you to achieve the desired tone from the start.

Most business messages aim for a conversational style.

Use a Conversational Tone   The tone of your business messages may span a continuum from informal to conversational to formal. Most business messages aim for a conversational tone, using plain language that sounds businesslike without being stuffy, stiff, wordy, or full of jargon. Rather than trying to impress audiences with an extensive vocabulary, good business communicators focus on being sensible, logical, and objective; they provide supporting facts and a rationale. To achieve a con-

SHARPENING YOUR CAREER SKILLS

Beating Writer's Block: Eleven Workable Ideas to Get Words Flowing

Putting words on a page or on screen can be a real struggle. Some people get stuck so often that they develop a mental block. If you get writer's block, here are some ways to get those words flowing again:

- *Use positive self-talk.* Stop worrying about how well or easily you write, and stop thinking of writing as difficult, time-consuming, or complicated. Tell yourself that you're capable and that you can do the job. Also, recall past examples of your writing that were successful.

- *Know your purpose.* Be specific about what you want to accomplish with this particular piece of writing. Without a clear purpose, writing can indeed be impossible.

- *Visualize your audience.* Picture audience backgrounds, interests, subject knowledge, and vocabulary (including the technical jargon they use). Such visualization can help you choose an appropriate style and tone for your writing.

- *Create a productive environment.* Write in a place that's for writing only, and make that place pleasant. Set up "writing appointments." Scheduling a session from 9:30 to noon is less intimidating than an indefinite session. Also, keep your mind fresh with scheduled breaks.

- *Make an outline or a list.* Even if you don't create a formal outline, at least jot down a few notes about how your ideas fit together. As you go along, you can revise your notes, as long as you end up with a plan that gives direction and coherence.

- *Just start.* Put aside all worries, fears, distractions—anything that gives you an excuse to postpone writing. Then start putting down any thoughts you have about your topic. Don't worry about whether these ideas can actually be used; just let your mind range freely.

- *Write the middle first.* Start wherever your interest is greatest and your ideas are most developed. You can follow new directions, but note ideas to revisit later. When you finish one section, choose another without worrying about sequence. Just get your thoughts down.

- *Push obstacles aside.* If you get stuck at some point, don't worry. Move past the thought, sentence, or paragraph, and come back to it later. Prime the pump simply by writing or talking about why you're stuck: "I'm stuck because . . ." Also try brainstorming. Before you know it, you'll be writing about your topic.

- *Read a newspaper or magazine.* Try reading an article that uses a style similar to yours. Choose one you'll enjoy so that you'll read it more closely.

- *Work on nontext segments.* Work on a different part of the project, such as formatting or creating graphics or verifying facts and references.

- *When deadlines loom, don't freeze in panic.* Concentrate on the major ideas first, and save the details for later, after you have something on the page. If you keep things in perspective, you'll succeed.

CAREER APPLICATIONS

1. List the ways you procrastinate, and discuss what you can do to break these habits.

2. Analyze your own writing experiences. What negative self-talk do you use? What might you do to overcome this tendency?

---

versational tone in your messages, don't use obsolete and pompous language, intimacy, humor, or preaching and bragging.

- **Avoid obsolete and pompous language.** Business language used to be much more formal than it is today, and some out-of-date phrases still remain. Ask yourself, "Would I say this if I were talking with someone face-to-face?" Similarly, avoid using big words, trite expressions, and overly complicated sentences to impress others. Such pompous language sounds puffed up and roundabout (see Table 5–2).

- **Avoid intimacy.** Don't mention anything about anyone's personal life unless you know the individual well. Avoid phrases that imply intimacy, such as "just between you and me" and "as you and I are well aware." Be careful about sounding too folksy or chatty; such a familiar tone may be seen as an attempt to seem like an old friend when, in fact, you're not.

To achieve a warm but businesslike tone
- Don't use obsolete language
- Don't use pompous phrases
- Don't be too familiar
- Use humor only with great care
- Don't preach
- Don't brag

Table 5-2	STAYING UP TO DATE AND DOWN TO EARTH

Obsolete	Up to Date
In due course	Today, tomorrow (or a specific time)
Permit me to say that	(Permission is not necessary)
We are in receipt of	We have received
Pursuant to	(Omit)
In closing, I'd like to say	(Omit)
The undersigned	I; me
Kindly advise	Please let us know
We wish to inform you	(Just say it)
Attached please find	Enclosed is
It has come to my attention	I have just learned; or, Ms. Garza has just told me
Our Mr. Lydell	Mr. Lydell, our credit manager
Please be advised that	(Omit)

Pompous	Down to Earth
Upon procurement of additional supplies, I will initiate fulfillment of your order.	I will fill your order when I receive more supplies.
Perusal of the records indicates a substantial deficit for the preceding accounting period due to the utilization of antiquated mechanisms.	The records show a company loss last year due to the use of old equipment.

- **Avoid humor.** What seems humorous to you may be deadly serious to others. And when you're communicating across cultures, chances are slim that your audience will appreciate your humor or even realize that you're trying to be funny.[8] Also, humor changes too quickly. What's funny today may not be in a week or a month from now.

- **Avoid preaching and bragging.** Few things are more irritating than people who think that they know everything and that others know nothing. If you must tell your audience something obvious, place the information in the middle of a paragraph, where it will sound like a casual comment rather than a major revelation. Also, avoid bragging about your accomplishments or about the size or profitability of your organization (unless your audience is a part of your organization).

You can adjust the formality of your conversational tone.

Your conversational tone may become less or more formal, depending on the situation. If you're in a large organization and you're communicating with your superiors or if you're communicating with customers, your conversational tone would tend to be more formal and respectful. On the other hand, if you were sending a quick e-mail to a colleague that you've worked closely with for years, your tone would be somewhat less formal—even though it would still be conversational and businesslike.

Use Plain English   Plain English is a way of writing and arranging technical materials so that your audience can understand your meaning. Plain English is easily understood by anyone with an eighth- or ninth-grade education, so it's close to the way people normally speak. If you've ever tried to make sense of an over-written or murky passage in a legal document or credit agreement, you can understand why governments and corporations today are endorsing the plain-English movement.[9]

Plain English is already used in loan and credit card application forms, insurance policies, investment documents, and real estate contracts. Even software programmers are trying to simplify their language so that they can communicate clearly with product users who may not understand what it means to "pop out to DOS."[10]

Plain English has some limitations. It lacks the precision necessary for scientific research, intense feeling, and personal insight. Moreover, it fails to embrace all cultures and dialects equally. But even though it's intended for audiences who speak English as their primary language, plain English can also help simplify messages to audiences who speak English only as a second or even third language. For example, choosing words that have only one interpretation will surely help you communicate more clearly with your intercultural audience.[11]

Select Active or Passive Voice Appropriately   Your use of active and passive voice also affects the tone of your message. You're using **active voice** when the subject (the "actor") comes before the verb and the object of the sentence (the "acted upon") follows the verb: "John rented the office." You're using **passive voice** when the subject follows the verb and the object precedes it: "The office was rented by John." As you can see, the passive voice combines the helping verb *to be* with a form of the verb that is usually similar to the past tense. Active sentences generally sound less formal and make it easier for the reader to figure out who performed the action (see Table 5–3). In contrast, passive voice de-emphasizes the subject and implies that action was taken by something or someone.

Using active voice produces shorter, stronger sentences and makes your writing more vigorous, concise, and generally easier to understand.[12] Using passive voice

Plain English is close to spoken English and can be easily understood.

Although plain English is already being used in many areas, it isn't appropriate for every application.

Active sentences are stronger than passive ones.

CHOOSING ACTIVE OR PASSIVE VOICE		Table 5–3
Avoid Passive Voice in General	*Use Active Voice in General*	
A. The new procedure was developed by the operations team.	B. The operations team developed the new procedure.	
C. Legal problems are created by this contract.	D. This contract creates legal problems.	
E. Reception preparations have been undertaken by our PR people for the new CEO's arrival.	F. Our PR people have undertaken receptions preparations for the new CEO's arrival.	
Sometimes Avoid Active Voice	*Sometimes Use Passive Voice*	
You lost the shipment.	The shipment was lost.	
I am analyzing the production line to determine the problem.	The production line is being analyzed to determine the problem.	
We have established criteria to evaluate capital expenditures.	Criteria have been established to evaluate capital expenditures.	

produces longer sentences and, while not wrong grammatically, makes your writing cumbersome, wordy, and often unnecessarily vague.

Nevertheless, the passive voice is the right choice in some situations when you need to demonstrate the "you" attitude by shifting emphasis away from the actor:

Use passive sentences to soften bad news, to put yourself in the background, or to create an impersonal tone.

- **To be diplomatic.** When you need to point out a problem or error of some kind, passive voice seems less like an accusation.

- **To avoid attributing either credit or blame.** When you need to emphasize what's being done, passive voice leaves the actor completely out of the sentence.

- **To create an objective tone.** When you need to sound objective—in a formal report, for example—the passive voice avoids personal pronouns.

Selecting the Best Words

Correctness is the first consideration when choosing words.

Choose your words carefully.[13] First, pay close attention to correctness. If you make grammatical or usage errors, you lose credibility with your audience. Poor grammar implies that you're unaware or uninformed, and audiences put little faith in an uninformed source. Even if an audience is broad-minded enough to withhold such a judgment, grammatical errors are distracting.

If in doubt, check it out.

If you have doubts about what is correct, don't be lazy. Look up the answer, and use the proper form of expression. Check the "Handbook of Grammar, Mechanics, and Usage" at the end of this textbook, or consult any number of special reference books and resources available in libraries, in bookstores, and on the Internet. Most authorities agree on the basic conventions.

Effectiveness is the second consideration when choosing words.

Just as important as selecting the correct word is selecting the most effective word for the job at hand. Writers such as Mary Ellen Keating are careful to use functional and content words correctly and to find the words that communicate.

Functional words (conjunctions, prepositions, articles, and pronouns) express relationships among content words (nouns, verbs, adjectives, and adverbs).

Use Functional and Content Words Correctly   Words can be divided into two main categories. **Functional words** express relationships and have only one unchanging meaning in any given context. They include conjunctions, prepositions, articles, and pronouns. Your main concern with functional words is to use them correctly. **Content words** carry the meaning of a sentence and are subject to various interpretations. They include nouns, verbs, adjectives, and adverbs. In the following sentence, all the content words are underlined:

Some <u>objective observers</u> of the <u>cookie market give Nabisco</u> the <u>edge</u> in <u>quality</u>, but <u>Frito-Lay is lauded</u> for <u>superior distribution</u>.

Both functional words and content words are necessary, but your effectiveness as a communicator depends largely on your ability to choose the right content words for your message.

Content words have both a denotative (explicit, specific) meaning and a connotative (implicit, associative) meaning.

Denotation and Connotation   Content words have both a denotative and a connotative meaning. **Denotative meaning** is the literal, or dictionary, meaning. The denotation of the word *desk* is "a table used for writing." Some desks may have drawers or compartments; others may have a flat or sloping top. But the literal meaning is generally well understood.

Connotative meaning includes all the associations and feelings evoked by the word. The connotation of the word *desk* may include thoughts associated with work or study. Basically, the word *desk* has fairly neutral connotations—neither strong nor emotional.

However, some words have much stronger connotations than others. If you say that a student *failed* to pass a test, the connotative meaning suggests that the person is inferior, incompetent, below some standard of performance. Thus the connotations of the word *fail* are negative and can carry strong emotional meaning.

In business communication, avoid using terms that are high in connotative meaning. By saying that a student achieved a score of 65 percent, you communicate the facts and avoid a heavy load of negative connotations. If you use words that have relatively few possible interpretations, you are less likely to be misunderstood. Moreover, because business is about communicating in an objective, rational manner, avoid emotion-laden comments.

Business communicators avoid words with negative or multiple connotations.

Abstraction and Concreteness   An **abstract word** expresses a concept, quality, or characteristic. Abstractions are usually broad, encompassing a category of ideas. They are often intellectual, academic, or philosophical. *Love, honor, progress, tradition,* and *beauty* are abstractions.

The more abstract a word, the more it is removed from the tangible, objective world of things that can be perceived with the senses.

A **concrete word** stands for something you can touch or see. Concrete terms are anchored in the tangible, material world. *Chair, table, horse, rose, kick, kiss, red, green,* and *two* are concrete words; they are direct, clear, and exact. Because words such as *small, numerous, sizable, near, soon, good,* and *fine* are imprecise, try to replace them with terms that are more accurate. Instead of referring to a *sizable loss,* talk about a *loss of $32 million.*

You might assume that concrete words are always better than abstract words, because they are more precise, but you would sometimes be wrong. For example, try to rewrite this sentence without using the underlined abstract words:

We hold these <u>truths</u> to be <u>self-evident</u>, that all men are <u>created equal</u>, that they are <u>endowed</u> by their <u>Creator</u> with certain <u>unalienable Rights</u>, that among these are <u>Life</u>, <u>Liberty</u>, and the <u>Pursuit of Happiness</u>.

As you can see, the Declaration of Independence needs abstractions, and so do business messages. Abstractions permit us to rise above the common and tangible. They allow us to refer to concepts such as *morale, productivity, profits, quality, motivation,* and *guarantees.*

However, even though abstractions are indispensable, they can be troublesome. They tend to be fuzzy and subject to many interpretations. They also tend to be boring. It isn't always easy to get excited about ideas, especially if they're unrelated to concrete experience. The best way to minimize such problems is to blend abstract terms with concrete ones, the general with the specific. State the concept, then pin it down with details expressed in more concrete terms. Save the abstractions for ideas that cannot be expressed any other way.

In business communication, use concrete, specific terms whenever possible; use abstractions only when necessary.

Find Words that Communicate   Anyone who earns a living by crafting words is a *wordsmith*—including journalists, public relations specialists, editors, and letter and report writers. Unlike poets, novelists, or dramatists, wordsmiths don't strive for dramatic effects. Instead, they are concerned with using language to be clear, concise, and accurate. To reach their goal, they emphasize words that are strong and familiar, avoid clichés, and use jargon carefully. When you compose your business messages, do your best to think like a wordsmith (see Table 5–4):

Business communicators aim for clarity and accuracy rather than dramatic effect.

Wordsmiths choose strong words, choose familiar words, avoid clichés, and use jargon carefully.

- **Choose strong words.** Choose words that express your thoughts most clearly, specifically, and dynamically. Nouns and verbs are the most concrete, so use them as much as you can. Adjectives and adverbs have obvious roles, but use them sparingly—they often evoke subjective judgments. Verbs are especially powerful because they tell what's happening in the sentence, so make them dynamic and specific (replace *rise* or *fall* with *soar* or *plummet*).

- **Choose familiar words.** You'll communicate best with words that are familiar to your readers. However, keep in mind that words familiar to one reader might be unfamiliar to another.

Table 5–4   THINKING LIKE A WORDSMITH

Avoid Weak Phrases	*Use Strong Terms*
Wealthy businessperson	Tycoon
Business prosperity	Boom
Hard times	Slump
Avoid Unfamiliar Words	**Use Familiar Words**
Ascertain	Find out, learn
Consummate	Close, bring about
Peruse	Read, study
Circumvent	Avoid
Increment	Growth, increase
Unequivocal	Certain
Avoid Clichés	**Use Plain Language**
Scrape the bottom of the barrel	Strain shrinking resources
An uphill battle	A challenge
Writing on the wall	Prediction
Call the shots	Be in charge
Take by storm	Attack
Cost an arm and a leg	Expensive
A new ballgame	Fresh start
Worst nightmare	Strong competitor; disaster
Fall through the cracks	Be overlooked

It's fine to use jargon on the job with your peers, but when communicating with outsiders, be careful to put technical information into words that your audience can understand.

- **Avoid clichés.** Although familiar words are generally the best choice, beware of terms and phrases so common that they have become virtually meaningless. For example, instead of saying "We are hammering away at this production backup before sales drop even more," say "We are striving to relieve this production backup before sales drop even more." Because clichés are used so often, readers tend to slide right by them to whatever is coming next.

- **Use jargon carefully.** Handle technical and professional terms with care. Technical language and jargon can add precision and authority to a message, but many people won't understand it. When deciding whether to use technical jargon, let your audience's knowledge guide you. For example, when addressing a group of engineers or scientists, it's probably fine to refer to *meteorological effects on microwave propagation*; otherwise, refer to the *effects of weather on radio waves*.

Remember, good business writing is learned by imitation and practice. As you read business journals, newspapers, and even novels, make a note of the words you think are effective and keep them in a file. Then look through them before you draft your next letter or report. Try using some of these words in your document. You may be surprised how they can strengthen your writing.

Creating Effective Sentences

In English, words don't make much sense until they're combined in a sentence to express a complete thought. Thus the words *Jill, receptionist, the, smiles,* and *at* can be organized into "Jill smiles at the receptionist." Now that you've constructed the sentence, you can begin exploring the possibilities for improvement, looking at how well each word performs its particular function. Nouns and noun equivalents are the topics (or subjects) you're communicating about, and verbs and related words (or predicates) make statements about those subjects. In a complicated sentence, adjectives and adverbs modify the subject and the statement, and various connectors hold the words together.

> Every sentence contains a subject (noun or noun equivalent) and a predicate (verb and related words).

Understand the Four Types of Sentences   Sentences come in four basic varieties: simple, compound, complex, and compound-complex. A **simple sentence** has one main clause (a single subject and a single predicate), although it may be expanded by nouns and pronouns serving as objects of the action and by modifying phrases. Here's a typical example (with the subject underlined once and the predicate verb underlined twice):

> A simple sentence has one main clause.

Profits have increased in the past year.

A **compound sentence** has two main clauses that express two or more independent but related thoughts of equal importance, usually joined by *and, but,* or *or.* In effect, a compound sentence is a merger of two or more simple sentences (independent clauses) that are related. For example:

> A compound sentence has two main clauses.

Wage rates have declined by 5 percent, and employee turnover has been high.

The independent clauses in a compound sentence are always separated by a comma or by a semicolon (in which case the conjunction—*and, but, or*—is dropped).
   A **complex sentence** expresses one main thought (the independent clause) and one or more subordinate thoughts (dependent clauses) related to it, often separated by a comma. The subordinate thought, which comes first in the following sentence, could not stand alone:

> A complex sentence has one main clause and one subordinate clause.

Although you may question Gerald's conclusions, you must admit that his research is thorough.

A **compound-complex sentence** has two main clauses, at least one of which contains a subordinate clause:

> A compound-complex sentence has two main clauses and at least one dependent clause.

Profits have increased in the past year, and although you may question Gerald's conclusions, you must admit that his research is thorough.

   When constructing a sentence, choose the form that matches the relationship of the ideas you want to express. If you have two ideas of equal importance, express them as two simple sentences or as one compound sentence. However, if one of the ideas is less important than the other, place it in a dependent clause to

> Match sentence form to the relationships between your ideas.

form a complex sentence. For example, although the following compound sentence uses a conjunction to join two ideas, they aren't truly equal:

> The chemical products division is the strongest in the company, and its management techniques should be adopted by the other divisions.

By making the first thought subordinate to the second, you establish a cause-and-effect relationship. So the following complex sentence is much more effective:

> Because the chemical products division is the strongest in the company, its management techniques should be adopted by the other divisions.

Writing is more effective if it balances all four sentence types.

To make your writing as effective as possible, balance all four sentence types. If you use too many simple sentences, you won't be able to properly express the relationships among your ideas. If you use too many long, compound sentences, your writing will sound monotonous. On the other hand, an uninterrupted series of complex or compound-complex sentences is hard to follow.

Use Sentence Style to Emphasize Key Thoughts   Sentence style varies from culture to culture. German sentences are extremely complex, with lots of modifiers and appositives; Japanese and Chinese languages don't even have sentences in the same sense that Western languages do.[14] However, in English try to make your sentences grammatically correct, efficient, readable, interesting, and appropriate for your audience. In general, strive for straightforward simplicity. For most business audiences, clarity and efficiency take precedence over literary style.

Emphasize important ideas through sentence style:
- *Give important ideas more space*
- *Put them at the beginning or at the end of the sentence*
- *Make them the subject of the sentence*

In every message, some ideas are more important than others. You can emphasize these key ideas through your sentence style. One obvious technique is to give important points the most space. When you want to call attention to a thought, use extra words to describe it. Consider this sentence:

> The chairperson of the board called for a vote of the shareholders.

To emphasize the importance of the chairperson, you might describe her more fully:

> Having considerable experience in corporate takeover battles, the chairperson of the board called for a vote of the shareholders.

You can increase the emphasis even more by adding a separate, short sentence to augment the first:

> The chairperson of the board called for a vote of the shareholders. She has considerable experience in corporate takeover battles.

You can also call attention to a thought by making it the subject of the sentence. In the following example, the emphasis is on the person:

> *I* can write letters much more quickly by using a computer.

However, by changing the subject, the computer takes center stage:

> The *computer* helps me write letters much more quickly.

Another way to emphasize an idea is to place it at either the beginning or the end of a sentence:

Less Emphatic: We are cutting the *price* to stimulate demand.

More Emphatic: To stimulate demand, we are cutting the *price*.

In complex sentences, the placement of the dependent clause hinges on the relationship between the ideas expressed. If you want to emphasize the idea, put the dependent clause at the end of the sentence (the most emphatic position) or at the beginning (the second most emphatic position). If you want to downplay the idea, bury the dependent clause within the sentence:

Dependent clauses can determine emphasis.

Most Emphatic: The electronic parts are manufactured in Mexico, *which has lower wage rates than the United States.*

Emphatic: *Because wage rates are lower there*, the electronic parts are manufactured in Mexico.

Least Emphatic: Mexico, *which has lower wage rates*, was selected as the production point for the electronic parts.

Techniques like these give you a great deal of control over the way your audience interprets what you have to say.

Developing Coherent Paragraphs

A *paragraph* is a cluster of sentences all related to the same general topic. It is a unit of thought, separated from other units by skipping a line or indenting the first line. A series of paragraphs makes up an entire composition. Each paragraph is an important part of the whole, a key link in the train of thought. As you compose your message, think about the paragraphs and their relationship to one another.

Elements of the Paragraph   Paragraphs vary widely in length and form. You can communicate effectively in one short paragraph or in pages of lengthy paragraphs, depending on your purpose, your audience, and your message. The typical paragraph contains three basic elements: a topic sentence, related sentences that develop the topic, and transitional words and phrases.

Topic Sentence   Every properly constructed paragraph is *unified*; that is, it deals with a single topic. The sentence that introduces that topic is called the **topic sentence**. In business writing, the topic sentence is generally explicit and is often the first sentence in the paragraph. It gives readers a summary of the general idea that will be covered in the rest of the paragraph:

PetFoodDirect.com founder Jon Roska knows that paragraphs on the web must be short and sweet. You want to keep your paragraphs to the point. Start with an informative topic sentence so that readers can see immediately what each paragraph is about. Then follow with as few as two or three succinct sentences.

The medical products division has been troubled for many years by public relations problems. [In the rest of the paragraph, readers will learn the details of the problems.]

Relocating the plant in New York has two main disadvantages. [The disadvantages will be explained in subsequent sentences.]

To get a refund, you must supply us with some additional information. [The details of the necessary information will be described in the rest of the paragraph.]

The topic sentence
- Reveals the subject of the paragraph
- Indicates how the subject will be developed

Related Sentences   The sentences that explain the topic sentence round out the paragraph. These related sentences must all have a bearing on the general subject and must provide enough specific details to make the topic clear:

Paragraphs are developed through a series of related sentences that provide details about the topic sentence.

> The medical products division has been troubled for many years by public relations problems. Since 1997 the local newspaper has published 15 articles that portray the division in a negative light. We have been accused of everything from mistreating laboratory animals to polluting the local groundwater. Our facility has been described as a health hazard. Our scientists are referred to as "Frankensteins," and our profits are considered "obscene."

The developmental sentences are all more specific than the topic sentence. Each one provides another piece of evidence to demonstrate the general truth of the main thought. Also, each sentence is clearly related to the general idea being developed; the relation between the sentences and the idea is what gives the paragraph its unity. A paragraph is well developed when it contains enough information to make the topic sentence convincing and interesting.

Because each paragraph covers a single idea, use transitional words and phrases to show readers how paragraphs relate to each other.

Transitional Elements   In addition to being unified and well developed, effective paragraphs are *coherent;* that is, they are arranged in a logical order so that the audience can understand the train of thought. When you complete a paragraph, your readers automatically assume that you've finished with a particular idea. You achieve coherence by using transitions that show the relationship between paragraphs and among sentences within paragraphs. Transitions, words, or phrases that tie ideas together, show how one thought is related to another; they help readers understand the connections you're trying to make. You can establish transitions in various ways:

- **Use connecting words:** *and, but, or, nevertheless, however, in addition,* and so on.
- **Echo a word or phrase from a previous paragraph or sentence:** A system should be established for monitoring inventory levels. "*This system* will provide . . . "
- **Use a pronoun that refers to a noun used previously:** Ms. Arthur is the leading candidate for the president's position. "*She* has excellent qualifications."
- **Use words that are frequently paired:** The machine has a *minimum* output of . . . "Its *maximum* output is . . . "

Transitions move readers between sentences and paragraphs.

Some transitional elements serve as mood changers; that is, they alert the reader to a change in mood from the previous paragraph. Some announce a total contrast with what's gone on before, some announce a causal relationship, and some signal a change in time. They prepare your reader for the change. Here is a list of transitions frequently used to move readers smoothly between sentences and paragraphs:

Additional detail: Moreover, furthermore, in addition, besides, first, second, third, finally

Causal relationship: Therefore, because, accordingly, thus, consequently, hence, as a result, so

Comparison: Similarly, here again, likewise, in comparison, still

Contrast: Yet, conversely, whereas, nevertheless, on the other hand, however, but, nonetheless

Condition: Although, if

Illustration: For example, in particular, in this case, for instance

Time sequence: Formerly, after, when, meanwhile, sometimes

Intensification: Indeed, in fact, in any event

Summary: In brief, in short, to sum up

Repetition: That is, in other words, as I mentioned earlier

Although transitional words and phrases are useful, they're not sufficient in themselves to overcome poor organization. Your goal is first to put your ideas in a strong framework and then to use transitions to link them together even more strongly.

Consider using a transition device whenever it might help the reader understand your ideas and follow you from point to point. You can use transitions inside paragraphs to tie related points together and between paragraphs to ease the shift from one distinct thought to another. In longer reports, transitions that link major sections or chapters are often complete paragraphs that serve as mini-introductions to the next section or as summaries of the ideas presented in the section just ending. Here's an example:

> Given the nature of this product, the alternatives are limited. As the previous section indicates, we can stop making it altogether, improve it, or continue with the current model. Each of these alternatives has advantages and disadvantages, which are discussed in the following section.

Paragraph Development   Paragraphs can be developed in many ways. Your choice of technique depends on your subject, your intended audience, and your purpose. Following are five of the most common techniques:

You can develop paragraphs in five ways.

- **Illustration:** Giving examples that demonstrate the general idea
- **Comparison or contrast:** Using similarities or differences to develop the topic
- **Cause and effect:** Focusing on the reasons for something
- **Classification:** Showing how a general idea is broken into specific categories
- **Problem and solution:** Presenting a problem and then discussing the solution

In practice, you'll often combine two or more methods of development in a single paragraph. To add interest, you might begin by using illustration, shift to comparison or contrast, and then shift to problem and solution. However, before settling for the first approach that comes to mind, consider the alternatives. Think through various methods before committing yourself. If you fall into the easy habit of repeating the same old paragraph pattern time after time, your writing will be boring.

Some of the paragraphs that business communicators use in their documents are "prewritten." For example, say that you want to announce to the media that you've developed a new product or hired an executive. Such announcements—called press releases—usually end with a standard paragraph about the company and its line of business. Any standard block of text that is used in various documents without being changed is called a **boilerplate**. Using boilerplates saves time and reduces mistakes because you're not retyping the paragraph every time you use it.

A boilerplate is any standard block of text used in various documents without being changed.

For a reminder of the tasks involved in composing your messages, see the "Checklist: Composing and Shaping Business Messages."

Document Makeover

IMPROVE THIS LETTER

To practice correcting drafts of actual documents, visit **www.prenhall.com/onekey** on the web. Click "Document Makeovers," then click Chapter 5. You will find a letter that contains problems and errors relating to what you've learned in this chapter about organizing and composing business messages. Use the Final Draft decision tool to create an improved version of this letter. Check the message for the proper choice of direct or indirect approach, conversational tone, active versus passive voice, and paragraph construction.

✓ CHECKLIST Composing and Shaping Business Messages

Control Your Style and Tone

✓ Avoid obsolete and pompous language.
✓ Use the appropriate level of formality.
✓ Avoid being overly familiar.
✓ Avoid inappropriate humor.
✓ Avoid sounding preachy or bragging.
✓ Use plain English.
✓ Write mainly in the active voice, but use the passive voice to achieve specific effects.

Select the Best Words

✓ Choose words that avoid negative or multiple connotations.
✓ Choose abstract words only for ideas that cannot be expressed any other way.
✓ Blend abstract words with concrete ones, explaining the general with the specific.

✓ Rely on nouns, verbs, and specific adjectives and adverbs.
✓ Choose words that are strong and familiar while avoiding clichés and jargon.

Create Effective Sentences and Coherent Paragraphs

✓ Use simple, compound, complex, and compound-complex sentences, choosing the form that best fits the thought you want to express.
✓ Emphasize key points through sentence style, giving important points the most space.
✓ Be sure paragraphs contain a topic sentence, related sentences, and transitional elements.
✓ Choose a method of development that suits the subject: illustration, comparison or contrast, cause and effect, classification, problem and solution.

WRITING EFFECTIVE E-MAIL MESSAGES

E-mail messages need as much care and attention as other business messages.

Even though e-mail is less formal than letters and seems transitory, organization and style are just as important for these messages as for any other type of business message. In addition to the principles and techniques already discussed in this chapter, consider the following when writing e-mail messages.

Organizing Your E-Mail Messages

In your replies, include relevant parts of the original message.

If you are responding to a question or a request for information, be sure to start your e-mail by inserting the original question into your reply. You can preprogram most e-mail software packages to automatically include the sender's original message in your e-mail replies and forwards. Or you can cut and paste the message yourself. Either way, use this feature with care. Save your readers' time by editing the original message and including only enough to refresh their memory about why you are sending the e-mail and how it addresses their specific needs.

Respect your audience's limited time by keeping e-mail messages short and to the point.

Keeping your audience in mind, try to limit e-mail messages to one screen. Otherwise, include the most important information first, adding detail in descending order of importance.[15] That way you'll be sure to get your point across as early as possible, in case your reader doesn't have the time or interest to finish reading your message.

Composing Your E-Mail Messages

The level of formality in your e-mail depends on your audience and purpose.

E-mail can be as informal and casual as a conversation between old friends. But it can also emulate "snail mail" by using conventional business language, a respectful style, and a more formal format—such as a traditional greeting, formalized headings, and a formal closing and "signature."[16] As with any business communication, how formal you make your message depends on your audience and your purpose.

Before sending your e-mail message, know how to use your e-mail's address fields. When you enter more than one address in the *To:* field, you need to direct your message to all of these people. Write the message as if you're talking to everyone at once. However, if you wish to talk to only one or two people while providing copies of your message to others, then you need to handle header information differently.

In the *To:* field, insert only the address(es) of the person(s) to whom you are actually speaking. Then by entering addresses in the *Cc:* (courtesy copy) field, you can send copies of your message to additional people, and everyone who receives your e-mail will be able to see who else received a copy of it. Or by entering addresses in the *Bcc:* (blind courtesy copy) field, you can send copies of your message to additional people without other recipients knowing—a practice considered unethical by some.

Be considerate and correct when using address fields (To:, Cc:, Bcc:).

Compose your e-mail so that readers can follow it easily. Avoid lines that run off screen or wrap oddly by using the Enter key to limit lines to 80 characters (60 if e-mail will be forwarded). Also avoid styled text (boldface, italics), unless your receiver's system can read it.[17] Write short, focused, logically organized paragraphs, using the composition tips discussed throughout this chapter.

Consider your audience's ease of reading your e-mail on screen.

Some e-mail old-timers insist that spelling, grammar, capitalization, and punctuation take a back seat in cyberspace.[18] But in business communication, e-mail needs to be as clear and as easy to understand as possible. Be sure to use correct spelling and proper grammar in these messages. Also remember to create informative subject lines and to personalize your message (see Figure 5–7).

Create Informative Subject Lines   Effective e-mail subject lines grab audience attention. When e-mail recipients are deciding which messages to read first, they look at who sent each message, they check the subject line, and then they may or may not scan the first few lines. A message with a blank subject line or a general one (such as "Question" or "Read This!") will probably go unread and will perhaps be deleted.[19]

To capture your audience's attention, make your subject line informative. Do more than just describe or classify message content. You have 25 to 40 characters to build interest with key words, quotations, directions, or questions:[20]

Grab audience attention by making your subject line informative.

Ineffective Subject Line	Effective Subject Line
July sales figures	Send figures for July sales
Tomorrow's meeting	Bring consultant's report to Friday's meeting
Marketing report	Need budget for marketing report
Employee parking	Revised resurfacing schedule for parking lot
Status report	Warehouse remodeling is on schedule

If you are exchanging multiple e-mails with someone on the same topic, be sure to periodically modify the subject line of your message to reflect the revised message content. Most e-mail programs will copy the subject line when you press the Reply key. However, multiple messages with the same subject line can be confusing. In fact, newer messages may have evolved so that they now have nothing to do with the original topic. Modifying the subject line with each new response can make it easier not only for your audience but also for you to locate a message at a later date.

Change subject lines in multiple e-mails on the same topic.

Personalize Your Messages   Adding a greeting to your e-mail message makes it more personal. Naturally, whether you use a formal greeting (*Dear Professor Ingersol*) or a more casual one (*Hi Marty*) depends on your audience and your purpose. Your closing and signature also personalize your e-mail message. In most cases, select simple closings, such as *Thanks* or *Regards,* rather than traditional business closings such as *Sincerely yours.* However, you may want to use a more formal closing for international e-mail.

Use a greeting to make your e-mail more personal.

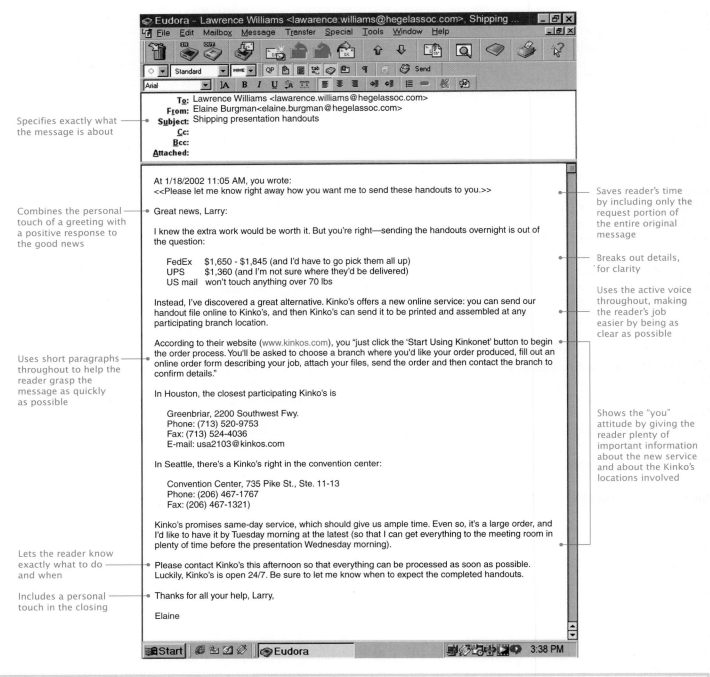

Specifies exactly what the message is about

Combines the personal touch of a greeting with a positive response to the good news

Uses short paragraphs throughout to help the reader grasp the message as quickly as possible

Lets the reader know exactly what to do and when

Includes a personal touch in the closing

Saves reader's time by including only the request portion of the entire original message

Breaks out details, for clarity

Uses the active voice throughout, making the reader's job easier by being as clear as possible

Shows the "you" attitude by giving the reader plenty of important information about the new service and about the Kinko's locations involved

FIGURE 5–7
Effective On-Screen E-Mail Message

After a simple closing, you can include a signature in several ways.

For your signature, you can simply type your name on a separate line. Or you may want to use a *signature file,* a short identifier that can include your name, company, postal address, fax number, other e-mail addresses, and sometimes even a short quotation or thought. Some business writers believe you should include only your contact information. Once you create a signature file, you can save it in your mail program and add it to e-mail messages without retyping it. You can also use a digital copy of your handwritten signature, which is becoming acceptable as legal proof in

✓ CHECKLIST: Composing E-mail with Style

Create the Right Tone

- ✓ Don't use cyberspace shorthand or offbeat acronyms such as *bcnu* ("be seeing you"), *fwiw* ("for what it's worth"), and *obo* ("or best offer").
- ✓ Avoid smileys and other gimmicks—rely on the strength of your writing to convey your message in the appropriate tone.
- ✓ Use exclamation points sparingly, if at all.

Cultivate Good Communication Skills

- ✓ Keep subject lines truthful—be careful you don't stretch the truth to grab attention.
- ✓ Limit the scope—each e-mail message should have only one purpose.
- ✓ Craft tight, meaningful messages by covering only what is necessary.
- ✓ Write short, direct messages that include all the relevant information.
- ✓ Rely on short, concise sentences to make your message easier to read on screen.
- ✓ Aim for clarity over hype—don't include thinly disguised marketing material.

Make E-Mail Easy to Read

- ✓ Use a plain typeface (Times New Roman, Courier, Arial) with a 10- to 12-point font size.
- ✓ Don't yell—avoid writing messages in all uppercase letters.
- ✓ Don't whisper—avoid writing messages in all lowercase letters.
- ✓ Use ample white space—avoid great amounts of text; separate paragraphs with a blank line.
- ✓ Use bullets and headings for clarity and ease of reading.
- ✓ Avoid double spacing.

Make Responsible, Careful Replies

- ✓ Avoid carelessly hitting the "reply to all" button.
- ✓ When you do choose to "reply to all," do so wisely.
- ✓ Keep subject lines relevant—modify them after a few rounds of replies.
- ✓ Slow down—avoid instantaneous responses and think about what you want to say.
- ✓ Reread your message to ensure it will convey exactly what you want.
- ✓ Carefully edit content, completeness, fluency, grammar, punctuation, and spelling.
- ✓ Correct misspelled proper names.

Handle Attachments Appropriately

- ✓ Ask permission to send long attachments—downloads may impose on recipients' time and could even choke their mailbox so that no other messages can be delivered.
- ✓ Use as few resources as possible by compressing attachments with WinZip or Netzip.
- ✓ In the body of your message, include a synopsis of lengthy attachments.
- ✓ Mention the attachment file name in your e-mail message so that recipients can locate it.
- ✓ Don't forget to attach your attachment.
- ✓ Send virus-free attachments (for short messages, cut and paste attachment contents directly into your e-mail message).

business transactions, especially when accompanied by a date stamp, which is automatically inserted by your mail program.

For an overview of e-mail strategies and etiquette, consult the "Checklist: Composing E-mail with Style."

WRITING EFFECTIVELY FOR THE WEB

The web is unlike any other medium you may be required to write for. People who use the web want to get information efficiently. So you need to grab their attention and make your main points immediately.[21] When writing for the web, you still follow all the guidelines discussed throughout this textbook. But you also need to address some new challenges: understanding how web audiences differ from other readers, developing a well-organized hyperlink structure, and modifying your style and format.

The web has special requirements.

Understand the Unique Needs and Expectations of Web Readers

Web readers are impatient to get the information they need.

The rapid pace of business today and the sheer amount of information available have made business readers impatient. As these readers turn to the Internet for information, they develop needs and expectations that are unique to the web environment. Reading online is

The web is physically demanding, nonlinear, interactive, and three-dimensional.

- **Cursory.** Racing to digest mountains of information, online readers hunger for instant gratification. They have hundreds of millions of pages to choose from—each page competing for attention.[22] Thus, these web readers tend to move from webpage to webpage, seeking the most appealing segments of each one in as little time as possible. This skim-and-scan style demands extreme brevity. Web writers must hook readers quickly, write concisely, and get directly to the point.

- **Difficult.** Reading speeds are about 25 percent slower on a monitor than on paper.[23] Screen settings and quality vary, but even using the best monitors, people find reading from a screen to be tiring on the eyes. Moreover, one page of written information can take up multiple screens on the web, forcing readers to scroll through a document.

- **Nonlinear and interactive.** Although most readers move through a printed document in a fairly linear path, web readers choose their own path and move about a document in any order they please. This nonlinear interactivity is possible because of **hyperlinks**—the in-text tags that let readers click on a screen element and be instantly transported to information that may be on the same webpage, on a different page in the same website, on a page in a different website, or just about anywhere on the web.

- **Three-dimensional.** The ability to jump into, out of, and all around a document gives the web its three-dimensional format. Consider the Orbitz site. Visitors may arrive from search engines, from the sites of Orbitz alliance partners (such as United, American, or Northwest Airlines), or from online newspaper articles,

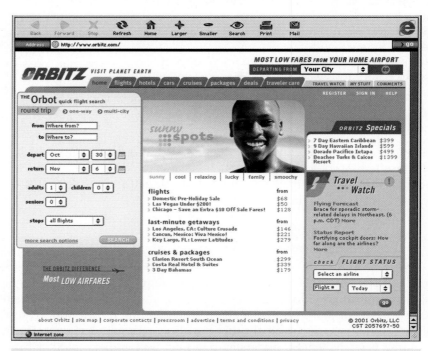

Regardless of how or why visitors arrive at the Orbitz homepage, their initial evaluation of this site determines whether they will explore further or go somewhere else.

financial sites, travel sites, and so on. Once visitors arrive (at a page that may or may not be the site's homepage), they decide whether to visit other pages on this site, return to the site later, or go elsewhere.[24]

Being able to access information from all directions is a powerful benefit for readers. But it also makes it difficult for them to judge the depth and scope of a website. Moreover, cyber content is always changing. So effective web writers help readers along by developing a hyperlink structure that is well organized.

Develop a Well-Organized Hyperlink Structure

When writing for the web, you must incorporate the effective writing skills discussed in this book, but that's not all. You must also coordinate your words with your navigational elements. Your goal is to help readers either find the information they want or bypass the information that is of no interest to them. The following tips will help you develop a well-organized hyperlink structure:

Your hyperlink structure should help readers find what they need easily.

- **Plan your navigation first.** Incorporate navigation as an integral part of your written material, not as an afterthought or an element to be left to a designer or developer.[25] Think about who your readers are and what paths they will follow to get key information.[26] Decide up front how much information you will actually write and how much your readers will access via links to other sites. This knowledge helps you avoid writing information that your readers can obtain elsewhere.

- **Let your readers be in control.** Help readers move about your document in a smooth, intuitive fashion. Be sure that each step on your navigational path makes sense and leads naturally to the next step. Also, avoid forcing readers to follow a specific path. Let them explore on their own. Consider including a search engine, a site map (an outline of your site's layout that helps readers understand the structure and depth of your site), and an index or a table of contents (placed at the top, side, or bottom margin of your webpage).

- **Write effective links.** Links can be words, graphics, phrases, or even complete sentences. You will most likely use a mixture of textual and graphical hyperlinks. If you choose to use graphical links, be careful not to overdo it. Including too many images can slow down the loading time of your webpages, and you need to accommodate those readers who conserve downloading time by turning off the graphic capabilities in their web browsers.

Modify Your Message Style and Format

Once you have established a navigational structure for your message, begin composing it in a style and format suitable for the web. Even though a good design is important for effective web messages, substantive content is what drives a site's success. One of the most common errors found on corporate websites is lackluster copy—messages written without interesting and specific details.[27]

For all the interest in graphics, the web is content-driven.

Modify Your Message for Global Audiences   Web material speaks to everyone around the globe, including people who may speak English only as a second language or not at all. Generally use a lighter, less formal tone—but without being chatty. Also, infuse as much of your organization's or your own personality into your text as possible. But be careful to avoid clever, humorous, or jargon-filled phrases that can be misunderstood by readers from other cultures.

The web is a global medium.

If many of your visitors are overseas, it may pay to have your site and material "localized" to reflect not only a region's native language but local norms, weights, measures, time, currency, and so on. Much more than simply translating your material into another language, localization makes your site and material appear as if it were originally developed in that language.

This process demands a keen understanding of your target audience so that you can adapt your style and tone, translate your text, include appropriate design elements (colors, icons, imagery), and develop a navigation system that works for your target culture. For example, local teams would know that the picture of a raised flag on a mailbox indicates mail waiting in the United States but has no meaning for many in Europe and Asia. Such teams would also understand that, in U.S. address books, names are sorted alphabetically; but in some Asian countries, names must be sorted according to the number of keystrokes.[28]

Break Your Information into Chunks   Because reading online is so difficult, you need to help web readers scan and absorb information more easily. Break text into self-contained, screen-sized chunks (or pages) that may be accessed in any order. Each chunk includes several paragraphs that are brief, are focused, and stick to a single theme.

> Carefully divide web information into chunks.

These theme-related chunks make up one webpage, but that webpage may not necessarily be viewable all at once on your computer screen (readers may have to scroll the screen to see your entire message). Breaking information into manageable chunks and then linking them to other chunks allows you to provide comprehensive coverage in a concise way. Consider these tips:

- **Make the content of each webpage independent.** Don't assume that readers approach your material in a linear order, as they might in a book. Present your message so that readers can understand the subject matter of a webpage regardless of the navigational path they followed to get there.

- **Don't force subdivisions.** Be careful not to make your readers tunnel through too many links to get the information they need. If the information can be succinctly presented in a short paragraph or on a single webpage, hyperlinks aren't necessary.

- **Reduce the length of your text.** Online text should be at least 50 percent shorter than printed text.[29] Try to limit your web articles to one computer screen. But if doing so is impossible, try not to exceed three full screens of text.

- **Handle longer documents with care.** If your written material is longer than three screens and you cannot break down your concept any further, do not randomly divide it into several webpages. Illogical interruptions in a single piece of linear material can irritate readers.[30]

- **Provide a printable version of longer documents.** Most readers prefer to print out lengthy documents and read them offline. Provide a print-ready version of your document that readers can link to. Indicate the file size so that readers can gauge how long it will take to download. Also, put your URL in the document title so that the source will print on the page.

Adopt an Inverted Pyramid Style   Make sure your online messages get right to the point and give your readers all the information they need in as little time as possible. One way to do so is to write your material using an inverted pyramid style. Journalists have long used this inverse approach—writing the main idea first and providing the details later. Then readers can stop at any time and still get the most important parts of the article.

> Using the inverted pyramid style lets your readers move on quickly without missing the most important information.

The inverted pyramid becomes even more important on the web, since users don't like to scroll and frequently read only the top portion of an article. This inverted style allows you to place your most important information above the scroll. As with newspapers, this top-level space is prime property, so use it economically. The *Wall Street Journal,* for example, reserves its front page for short summaries of articles that are discussed in detail on interior pages.

On the Job:

SOLVING COMMUNICATION DILEMMAS AT BARNES & NOBLE

At Barnes & Noble, Mary Ellen Keating is responsible for messages to customers, authors, shareholders, members of the community, booksellers, managers, and employees. As part of Keating's team, you help prepare both internal and external messages. Using the principles outlined in this chapter, handle each of the following situations to the best of your ability. Be prepared to explain your choices.

1. CEO Steve Riggio has asked your team to send an e-mail message to store managers, asking whether the Readers' Advantage program is affecting sales. Which of the following is the best subject line for this message?

   a. Readers' Advantage.
   b. Changes in recent sales.
   c. Need sales feedback on Readers' Advantage.
   d. Help us evaluate effects of the Readers' Advantage program on sales.

2. Which of the following approaches is the best organization for this message?

   a. Direct approach:
      • Introduce the main point of the message. (Please reply to the following questions about the effectiveness of the Readers' Advantage program.)
      • Give readers a reason to comply with your request. (Your feedback will help us decide whether to continue with the program, alter it, or discontinue it.)
      • Give readers a deadline for responding. (Please reply before July 15.)
   b. Indirect approach:
      • Introduce yourself. (I have recently joined Mary Ellen Keating's communication team.)
      • Explain Riggio's assignment to your readers. (Steve Riggio has asked our team to send you an e-mail message.)
      • Give readers a reason to comply with your request. (Your feedback will help us decide whether to continue the Readers' Advantage program, alter it, or discontinue it.)
      • Introduce the main point of the message. (Please reply to the following questions about the effectiveness of the Readers' Advantage program.)
      • Give readers a deadline for responding. (Please reply before July 15.)
   c. Persuasive approach:
      • Get readers thinking about the program. (Is the Readers' Advantage program working? You be the judge.)
      • Tell readers why you're writing. (We're polling all store managers for their reaction to the program. Cast your vote today.)

      • Give readers a sense of power. (Is it thumbs up or thumbs down on Readers' Advantage?)
      • Introduce the main point of the message. (Please reply to the following questions about whether the Readers' Advantage program is working.)
      • Give readers a deadline for responding. (Please reply before July 15.)

3. Which of the following best conveys the appropriate sentence structure for your e-mail message?

   a. We need to know whether you have noticed, of the specific books you've featured during the past six months, any increase in sales.
   b. During the past six months, have your featured books shown any increase in sales?
   c. Have sales of your featured books increased or decreased during the past six months?
   d. We need to know whether, of the specific books you've featured during the past six months, you have noticed any increase or decrease in the sales.

4. One of the company's buyers has drafted a letter to an author who inquired about shelf space in B&N's reference section. The self-published author is a professor of herpetology who has written a book titled *Reptiles of North America*. Keating has asked you to critique the following letter:

   > As you are undoubtedly aware, Barnes & Noble is the largest and most profitable bookselling chain in the country. Our reputation with publishers is excellent, so rest assured we deal just as fairly with individual authors.
   >
   > We are currently expanding the reference sections in some of our superstores. Accordingly, we may be able to find you a bit of shelf space for your newly self-published reference, *Reptiles of North America*.
   >
   > Of course, you'll need to send us an examination copy, so that we might determine whether your book appeals to our customers. If your book meets Barnes & Noble standards, you can expect to receive an order from us forthwith.
   >
   > Please ship your book promptly.

   a. The letter is fine the way it is—businesslike and efficient.
   b. The tone of the letter is condescending, but contents are well organized.
   c. The tone is appropriate, but the organization is poor.
   d. Both the tone and the organization need improvement.[31]

Learning Objectives Checkup

To assess your understanding of the principles in this chapter, read each learning objective and study the accompanying exercises. For fill-in items, write the missing text in the blank provided; for multiple choice items, circle the letter of the correct answer. You can check your responses against the answer key on page AK-1.

Objective 5.1: Cite four of the most common organization mistakes made by communicators.

1. Which of the following is *not* a common organizational mistake made by business communicators?
   a. Getting to the point too quickly
   b. Getting ideas mixed up
   c. Including irrelevant material
   d. Leaving out necessary information

Objective 5.2: Explain why good organization is important to both the communicator and the audience.

2. Good organization is important to you as a communicator because it
   a. Saves you time
   b. Saves you work
   c. Helps you delegate
   d. Does all of the above

3. Good organization helps your audience by
   a. Providing them with more information than they really need
   b. Dispensing with diplomacy
   c. Saving them time
   d. Doing all of the above

Objective 5.3: Summarize the process for organizing business messages effectively.

4. The first step in organizing your business messages is to
   a. Prepare an outline
   b. Define the main idea
   c. Limit the scope
   d. Choose between the direct and indirect approaches

5. Which of the following is an example of the main idea for a business message?
   a. Advertising budget
   b. To persuade the board to increase the advertising budget
   c. The current advertising budget is not comparable to the budgets of competitors and is not meeting our advertising needs
   d. All of the above are examples of main ideas.

6. If your business message will be a long one, you
   a. Can increase your number of major points up to a maximum of ten
   b. Should have one major point for each 10 minutes of a speech or each 5 pages of a report
   c. Can have more than one main idea, each with several major points
   d. Should stick to having no more than five major points

7. When you are preparing a longer, more complex message, an outline
   a. Becomes indispensable
   b. Should be replaced with an organization chart
   c. Will help you determine your main idea
   d. Should use numbers but not letters

8. When is it best to use the direct approach?
   a. When your message is nonroutine
   b. When your audience is likely to be receptive to your message
   c. Only when your message is brief
   d. When your audience is likely to resist your message

9. When writing a persuasive message, you should
   a. Leave supporting facts until the very end of the message
   b. Use the opening to catch the reader's attention
   c. Assume that your audience will be receptive to what you have to say
   d. Do all of the above

Objective 5.4: Discuss three ways of achieving a businesslike tone with a style that is clear and concise.

10. A good way to achieve a businesslike tone in your messages is to
    a. Use formal business terminology, such as "In re your letter of the 18th"
    b. Brag about your company
    c. Use a conversational style that is not intimate or chatty
    d. Use plenty of humor

11. Plain English is
    a. Never recommended when speaking with people for whom English is a second language
    b. A movement toward using "English only" in American businesses
    c. A way of writing and arranging technical materials to make them more understandable
    d. An attempt to keep writing at a fourth- or fifth-grade level

12. The passive voice
    a. Should never be used in business messages
    b. Should always be used in business messages
    c. Should be used if you want to make your messages more informal
    d. Is a good choice when you want to avoid attributing blame

Objective 5.5: Briefly describe how to select words that are not only correct but also effective.

13. Which of the following defines the connotative meaning of the word *flag*?
    a. A flag is a piece of material with a symbol of some kind sewn on it.
    b. A flag is a symbol of everything that a nation stands for.
    c. A flag is fabric on a pole used to mark a geographic spot.
    d. A flag is an object used to draw attention.

14. Which of the following is a concrete word?
    a. Little
    b. Mouse
    c. Species
    d. Kingdom

Objective 5.6: Discuss how to use sentence style for emphasis.

15. What is the most emphatic place to put a dependent clause?
    a. At the end of the sentence
    b. At the beginning of the sentence
    c. In the middle of the sentence
    d. It doesn't really matter

Objective 5.7: List five ways to develop a paragraph and explain how boilerplates are used.

16. When developing a paragraph, keep in mind
    a. That you should stick to one method of development within a single paragraph
    b. That once you use one method of development, you should use that same method for all the paragraphs in a section
    c. That your choice of technique should take into account your subject, your intended audience, and your purpose
    d. All of the above

Objective 5.8: Explain how to capture audience attention and be more personal in e-mail messages.

17. To capture attention in your e-mail messages, be sure to
    a. Make your subject line longer than you would in a memo
    b. Avoid key words, quotations, directions, and questions
    c. Make your subject line informative

d. Retain the same subject line in multiple e-mails on the same topic no matter how the content changes

18. Which of the following is *not* a good way to personalize your e-mail message?
    a. Select simple closings.
    b. Use a signature file.
    c. Add a greeting.
    d. Leave out all formal punctuation.

Objective 5.9: Describe how to develop a hyperlink structure, and tell how you modify your style and format for the web.

19. Which of the following will help you develop a well-organized hyperlink structure?
    a. Write all information completely before incorporating your navigation.
    b. Make sure each navigational step makes sense and leads naturally to the next step.
    c. Compel readers to follow the specific navigational path that you design.
    d. Use textual hyperlinks only.

20. Which of the following is *not* recommended when breaking information into theme-related chunks?
    a. Increase the length of your online text by 50 percent.
    b. Try not to force subdivisions.
    c. Provide a printable version of longer documents.
    d. Make the content of each webpage independent.

Apply Your Knowledge

1. When organizing the ideas for your business message, how can you be sure that what seems logical to you will also seem logical to your audience?

2. Would you use a direct or an indirect approach to ask employees to work overtime to meet an important deadline? Please explain.

3. Which approach would you use to let your boss know that you'll be out half a day this week to attend your father's funeral—direct or indirect? Why?

4. Select a short article from any print magazine or newspaper. Now rewrite the article in a format suitable for the web, using the techniques discussed in this chapter. Focus on writing only one webpage. Include some hyperlinks on that page and in your article, but you need not develop material for the linked page.

5. **Ethical Choices** Do you think that using an indirect approach to cushion bad news is manipulative? Discuss the ethical issues in your answer.

Practice Your Knowledge

DOCUMENT FOR ANALYSIS

A writer is working on an insurance information brochure and is having trouble grouping the ideas logically into an outline. Prepare the outline, paying attention to appropriate subordination of ideas. If necessary, rewrite phrases to give them a more consistent sound.

ACCIDENT PROTECTION INSURANCE PLAN

- Inexpensive coverage—only pennies a day
- Benefit of $100,000 for accidental death on common carrier
- Benefit of $100 a day for hospitalization as result of motor vehicle or common carrier accident
- Benefit of $20,000 for accidental death in motor vehicle accident

- Individual coverage—only $17.85 per quarter; family coverage—just $26.85 per quarter
- No physical exam or health questions
- Convenient payment—billed quarterly
- Guaranteed acceptance for all applicants
- No individual rate increases
- Free, no-obligation examination period
- Cash paid in addition to any other insurance carried
- Covers accidental death when riding as fare-paying passenger on public transportation, including buses, trains, jets, ships, trolleys, subways, or any other common carrier
- Covers accidental death in motor vehicle accidents occurring while driving or riding in or on automobile, truck, camper, motor home, or nonmotorized bicycle

Exercises

For live links to all websites discussed in this chapter, visit this text's website at www.prenhall.com/thill. Just log on and select Chapter 5, and click on "Student Resources." Locate the page or the URL related to the material in the text. For the "Learning More on the Web" exercises, you'll also find navigational directions. Click on the live link to the site.

5.1 Message Organization: Structuring Your Message Using the GNC letter on page 128 (Figure 5–1), draw an organizational chart similar to the one shown in Figure 5–5 (see page 132). Fill in the main idea, the major points, and the evidence provided in this letter. (Note: Your diagram may be smaller than the one provided in Figure 5–5.)

5.2 Message Organization: Limiting Scope Suppose you are preparing to recommend that top management install a new heating system (using the cogeneration process). The following information is in your files. Eliminate topics that aren't essential; then arrange the other topics so that your report will give top managers a clear understanding of the heating system and a balanced, concise justification for installing it.

- History of the development of the cogeneration heating process
- Scientific credentials of the developers of the process
- Risks assumed in using this process
- Your plan for installing the equipment in your building
- Stories about its successful use in comparable facilities
- Specifications of the equipment that would be installed
- Plans for disposing of the old heating equipment
- Costs of installing and running the new equipment
- Advantages and disadvantages of using the new process
- Detailed 10-year cost projections
- Estimates of the time needed to phase in the new system
- Alternative systems that management might wish to consider

5.3 Message Organization: Choosing the Approach Indicate whether the direct or the indirect approach would be best in each of the following situations; then briefly explain why. Would any of these messages be inappropriate for e-mail? Explain.

a. A letter asking when next year's automobiles will be put on sale locally

b. A letter from a recent college graduate requesting a letter of recommendation from a former instructor

c. A letter turning down a job applicant

d. An announcement that because of high air-conditioning costs, the plant temperature will be held at 78 degrees during the summer

e. A final request to settle a delinquent debt

5.4 Message Organization: Drafting Persuasive Messages If you were trying to persuade people to take the following actions, how would you organize your argument?

a. You want your boss to approve your plan for hiring two new people

b. You want to be hired for a job

c. You want to be granted a business loan

d. You want to collect a small amount from a regular customer whose account is slightly past due

e. You want to collect a large amount from a customer whose account is seriously past due

5.5 Message Composition: Controlling Style Rewrite the following letter to Mrs. Betty Crandall (1597 Church Street, Grants Pass, OR 97526) so that it conveys a helpful, personal, and interested tone:

> *We have your letter of recent date to our Ms. Dobson. Owing to the fact that you neglected to include the size of the dress you ordered, please be advised that no shipment of your order was made, but the aforementioned shipment will occur at such time as we are in receipt of the aforementioned information.*

5.6 Message Composition: Selecting Words Write a concrete phrase for each of these vague phrases:

a. Sometime this spring

b. A substantial saving

c. A large number attended

d. Increased efficiency

e. Expanded the work area

5.7 Message Composition: Selecting Words List terms that are stronger than the following:

a. Ran after

b. Seasonal ups and downs

c. Bright

d. Suddenly rises

e. Moves forward

5.8 Message Composition: Selecting Words As you rewrite these sentences, replace the clichés with fresh, personal expressions:

a. Being a jack-of-all-trades, Dave worked well in his new selling job.

b. Moving Leslie into the accounting department, where she was literally a fish out of water, was like putting a square peg into a round hole, if you get my drift.

c. I knew she was at death's door, but I thought the doctor would pull her through.

d. Movies aren't really my cup of tea; as far as I am concerned, they can't hold a candle to a good book.

e. It's a dog-eat-dog world out there in the rat race of the asphalt jungle.

5.9 **Message Composition: Selecting Words** Suggest short, simple words to replace each of the following:
   a. Inaugurate
   b. Terminate
   c. Utilize
   d. Anticipate
   e. Assistance
   f. Endeavor
   g. Ascertain
   h. Procure
   i. Consummate
   j. Advise
   k. Alteration
   l. Forwarded
   m. Fabricate
   n. Nevertheless
   o. Substantial

5.10 **Message Composition: Selecting Words** Write up-to-date versions of these phrases; write *none* if you think there is no appropriate substitute:
   a. As per your instructions
   b. Attached herewith
   c. In lieu of
   d. In reply I wish to state
   e. Please be advised that

5.11 **Message Composition: Creating Sentences** Suppose that end-of-term frustrations have produced this e-mail message to Professor Anne Brewer from a student who believes he should have received a B in his accounting class. If this message were recast into three or four clear sentences, the teacher might be more receptive to the student's argument. Rewrite the message to show how you would improve it:

I think that I was unfairly awarded a C in your accounting class this term, and I am asking you to change the grade to a B. It was a difficult term. I don't get any money from home, and I have to work mornings at the Pancake House (as a cook), so I had to rush to make your class, and those two times that I missed class were because they wouldn't let me off work because of special events at the Pancake House (unlike some other students who just take off when they choose). On the midterm examination, I originally got a 75 percent, but you said in class that there were two different ways to answer the third question and that you would change the grades of students who used the "optimal cost" method and had been counted off 6 points for doing this. I don't think that you took this into account, because I got 80 percent on the final, which is clearly a B. Anyway, whatever you decide, I just want to tell you that I really enjoyed this class, and I thank you for making accounting so interesting.

5.12 **Message Composition: Creating Sentences** Rewrite each sentence so that it is active rather than passive:
   a. The raw data are submitted to the data processing division by the sales representative each Friday.
   b. High profits are publicized by management.
   c. The policies announced in the directive were implemented by the staff.
   d. Our computers are serviced by the Santee Company.
   e. The employees were represented by Janet Hogan.

5.13 **Message Composition: Writing Paragraphs** In the following paragraph, identify the topic sentence and the related sentences (those that support the idea of the topic sentence):

Each year, McDonald's sponsors the All-American Band, made up of two high school students from each state. The band marches in Macy's Thanksgiving Day parade in New York City and the Rose Bowl Parade in Pasadena. Franchisees are urged to join their local Chamber of Commerce, United Way, American Legion, and other bastions of All-Americana. McDonald's tries hard to project an image of almost a charitable organization. Local outlets sponsor campaigns on fire prevention, bicycle safety, and litter cleanup, with advice from Hamburger Central on how to extract the most publicity from their efforts.[32]

Now add a topic sentence to this paragraph:

Your company's image includes what a person sees, hears, and experiences in relation to your firm. Every business letter you write is therefore important. The quality of the letterhead and typing, the position of the copy on the page, the format, the kind of typeface used, and the color of the typewriter ribbon—all these factors play a part in creating an impression of you and your company in the mind of the person you are writing to.[33]

5.14 **Teamwork** Working with four other students, divide the following five topics among yourselves and each of you write one paragraph on his or her selected topic. Be sure each student uses a different technique when writing his or her paragraph: One student should use the illustration technique, one the comparison or contrast technique, one a discussion of cause and effect, one the classification technique, and one a discussion of problem and solution. Then exchange paragraphs within the team and pick out the main idea and general purpose of the paragraph. Was everyone able to correctly identify the main idea and purpose? If not, suggest how the paragraph might be rewritten for clarity.
   a. Types of cameras (or dogs or automobiles) available for sale
   b. Advantages and disadvantages of eating at fast-food restaurants
   c. Finding that first full-time job
   d. Good qualities of my car (or house, or apartment, or neighborhood)
   e. How to make a dessert recipe (or barbecue a steak or make coffee)

5.15 **Internet** Visit the Securities and Exchange Commission's (SEC) plain-English website at www.sec.gov, click on "Online Publications," and review the online handbook. In one or two sentences, summarize what the SEC means by the phrase "plain English." Now read the SEC's online advice about how to invest in mutual funds. Does this document follow the SEC's plain-English guidelines? Can you suggest any improvements to organization, words, sentences, or paragraphs?

5.16 Message Organization: Transitional Elements Add transitional elements to the following sentences to improve the flow of ideas. (Note: You may need to eliminate or add some words to smooth out your sentences.)

a. Steve Case saw infinite possibilities in cyberspace. Steve Case was determined to turn his vision into reality. The techies scoffed at his strategy of building a simple Internet service for ordinary people. Case doggedly pursued his dream. He analyzed other online services. He assessed the needs of his customers. He responded to their desires for an easier way to access information over the Internet. In 1992, Steve Case named his company America Online (AOL). Critics predicted the company's demise. By the end of the century, AOL was a profitable powerhouse.

b. Facing some of the toughest competitors in the world, Harley-Davidson had to make some changes. The company introduced new products. Harley's management team set out to rebuild the company's production process. New products were coming to market and the company was turning a profit. Harley's quality standards were not on par with those of its foreign competitors. Harley's costs were still among the highest in the industry. Harley made a U-turn and restructured the company's organizational structure. Harley's efforts have paid off.

c. Whether you're indulging in a doughnut in New York or California, Krispy Kreme wants you to enjoy the same delicious taste with every bite. The company maintains consistent product quality by carefully controlling every step of the production process. Krispy Kreme tests all raw ingredients against established quality standards. Every delivery of wheat flour is sampled and measured for its moisture content and protein levels. Krispy Kreme blends the ingredients. Krispy Kreme tests the doughnut mix for quality. Krispy Kreme delivers the mix to its stores. Krispy Kreme knows that it takes more than a quality mix to produce perfect doughnuts all the time. The company supplies its stores with everything they need to produce premium doughnuts—mix, icings, fillings, equipment—you name it.

5.17 Ethical Choices More and more unhappy employees and customers are launching websites to write negative information about companies. Log on to Untied.com at www.untied.com, for example, and read what some customers and employees have to say about United Airlines. Do you think it is ethical for employees to criticize their employers in a public venue such as the web?

Expand Your Knowledge

LEARNING MORE ON THE WEB

Compose a Better Business Message owl.English.purdue.edu

At Purdue's Online Writing Lab (OWL) you'll find tools to help you improve your business messages. For advice on composing written messages, for help with grammar, and for referrals to other information sources, you'd be wise to visit this site. Purdue's OWL offers online services and an introduction to Internet search tools. You can also download a variety of handouts on writing skills. Check out the resources at the OWL homepage and learn how to write a professional business message.

ACTIVITIES

To reinforce what you've learned in this chapter about writing a business message, log on to Purdue's OWL.

1. Explain why positive wording in a message is more effective than negative wording. Why should you be concerned about the position of good news or bad news in your written message?

2. What six factors of tone should you consider when conveying your message to your audience?

3. What points should you include in the close of your business message? Why?

EXPLORING THE WEB ON YOUR OWN

Review these chapter-related websites on your own to learn more about writing business messages.

1. Write it right by paying attention to these writing tips, grammar pointers, style suggestions, and reference sources at www.webgrammar.com.

2. Looking for the perfect word? Try Word Play at www.wolinskyweb.com/word.htm, where you'll find links to more than 30 helpful sites, including Acronym Finder, Book of Clichés, Oxymorons, Rhyming Dictionary, and Word Frequency Indexer.

3. Maximize your e-mail effectiveness by visiting A Beginner's Guide to Effective E-Mail, www.webfoot.com/advice/email.top.html.

Learn Interactively

INTERACTIVE STUDY GUIDE

Go to the Companion Website at www.prenhall.com/bovee. For Chapter 5, take advantage of the interactive "Study Guide" to test your knowledge of the chapter. Get instant feedback on whether you need additional studying. Also, visit this site's "Study Hall" where you'll find an abundance of valuable resources that will help you succeed in this course.

PEAK PERFORMANCE GRAMMAR AND MECHANICS

To improve your skill with adverbs, visit this text's website at www.prenhall.com/onekey. Click "Peak Performance Grammar and Mechanics," then click "Adverbs." Take the Pretest to determine whether you have any weak areas. Review those areas in the Refresher Course, and take the Follow-Up Test to check your grasp of adverbs. For advanced practice, take the Advanced Test. Finally, for additional reinforcement, go to the "Improve Your Grammar, Mechanics, and Usage" section that follows, and complete those exercises.

Improve Your Grammar, Mechanics, and Usage

The following exercises help you improve your knowledge of and power over English grammar, mechanics, and usage. Turn to the "Handbook of Grammar, Mechanics, and Usage" at the end of this textbook and review all of Section 1.5 (Adverbs). Then look at the following 10 items. Underline the preferred choice within each set of parentheses. (Answers to these exercises appear on page AK-3.)

1. Their performance has been (*good/well*).
2. I (*sure/surely*) do not know how to help you.
3. He feels (*sick/sickly*) again today.
4. Customs dogs are chosen because they smell (*good/well*).
5. The redecorated offices look (*good/well*).
6. Which of the two programs computes (*more fast, faster*)?
7. Of the two we have in stock, this model is the (*best, better*) designed.
8. He doesn't seem to have (*any, none*).
9. That machine is scarcely (*never, ever*) used.
10. They (*can, can't*) hardly get replacement parts for this equipment (*any, no*) more.

For additional exercises focusing on adjectives and adverbs, go to www.prenhall.com/thill and select "Handbook of Grammar, Mechanics, and Usage Practice Sessions."

Chapter 6

Completing Business Messages

Learning Objectives

AFTER STUDYING THIS CHAPTER, YOU WILL BE ABLE TO

1 Discuss the main tasks involved in completing a business message

2 Explain how to evaluate the elements of your message, and indicate the order in which to evaluate them

3 Describe four writing techniques you can use to improve the readability of your messages

4 List nine tips for making your writing clear

5 List four tips for making your message more concise

6 Describe four characteristics of a successful design and explain how four specific design elements can change a document's appearance

7 Discuss the types of errors to look for when proofreading

On the Job:

COMMUNICATING AT MCDONALD'S

A LITTLE MORE POLISH ON THE GOLDEN ARCHES, PLEASE

David Giarla has been a McDonald's quality control representative for 10 years, and he still loves the smell of Egg McMuffins in the morning. On a typical day, he visits seven or eight McDonald's, samples the food, inspects the kitchen, surveys the storeroom, and chats with the manager and employees. If he likes what he eats and sees, everybody breathes a sigh of relief and goes back to flipping burgers and wiping tables. But if the food, service, or facilities are not up to snuff, Giarla might file a negative report with headquarters. And if enough negative reports pile up, McDonald's might cancel the franchisee's license.

Professionals such as David Giarla at McDonald's understand the importance of careful revision. The most successful communicators make sure their messages are the best they can be.

However, Giarla's aim is not to get people into trouble. He believes that by holding the store managers to the company's high standards, he can help them build their businesses. When he spots a problem, he always points it out and gives the manager a chance to fix it before he files a negative report. His aim is to offer criticism in a diplomatic and constructive manner, and he usually succeeds.

On a typical visit, Giarla pulls into the parking lot and checks for rubbish. The ideal McDonald's is blindingly clean from the street to the storeroom. He enters the restaurant. Are the lines moving quickly? Are the order takers smiling? You bet. A perky teenager behind the counter recognizes Giarla and asks, "Big Breakfast and a regular Diet Coke?" "Correctomundo," he replies.

He carries his tray to a table. Is it spotless? Yup. He inspects his food. Hmm. The biscuit looks a little small. He nibbles a hash brown, then heads for the kitchen. "Great hash browns," he says to the person at the deep fryer. He pauses a minute to inspect the dates stamped on the hamburger wrappers. They're fresh. So are the cucumbers, cheese, and milkshake mix.

Business is picking up, so Giarla pitches in to help make Egg McMuffins. "These are going to be terrific," he announces. He finds that helping out builds rapport. He tries to cultivate goodwill between McDonald's headquarters and the restaurant's managers and employees. He doesn't view himself as "the enemy spy." McDonald's is a team effort, and he is a coach.

When Giarla spots the restaurant manager, he mentions the small-biscuit problem. Could someone be overkneading the dough, he wonders. He recommends that the biscuit maker review the McDonald's videotape on preparing biscuits and other items.

Over the past 10 years, David Giarla has learned a great deal about the art of communication. By nature, he is a positive individual, and his communication style reflects that fact. Although his job is to spot problems, you're more likely to hear him use words such as *outstanding, terrific,* and *delicious* rather than *bad, dreadful,* or *unacceptable.* Perhaps that's why the managers and employees on his regular route always greet him with a smile.[1]

www.mcdonalds.com

MOVING BEYOND YOUR FIRST DRAFT

Once you've completed the first draft of your message, you may be tempted to breathe a sigh of relief and go on to the next project. Resist the temptation. Professional communicators like David Giarla are aware that the first draft is rarely good enough. In a first attempt, most writers don't say what they want to say—or don't say it as well as they could. You owe it to yourself and to your audience to review and refine your messages before sending them. In fact, many writing authorities suggest that you go over a document several times: one pass for content, organization, style, and tone; one for readability; and one for clarity and conciseness.

Experts recommend making multiple passes through your first draft, looking for different things each time.

You might wonder whether all this effort to fine-tune a message is worthwhile. But successful businesspeople care very much about saying precisely the right thing in precisely the right way. Their willingness to go over the same document several times shows just how important it is to communicate effectively. As Ernest Hemingway once said, "There's no such thing as writing—only rewriting." Yet, once most businesspeople have a first draft, they make one of two mistakes: They shuffle words around on the page rather than actually making improvements, or they think rewriting is too time-consuming and send the document out the moment that last period hits the page.[2]

After revising, producing, and proofreading a message, you must also check its design and mechanics.

Even after you've fine-tuned your written message, your work is not finished. Look back at the diagram of the three-step writing process (Figure 4–1 on page 95). You will see that completing your message consists of three tasks: revising, producing, and proofreading your message. Thus, to complete your business message, you must also check its design and mechanics, as well as distribute it to your audience. Start by evaluating the document as a whole before looking at details. Focusing on the big picture first is more efficient, since you won't be wasting time perfecting sections that you may eventually eliminate or change substantially.

REVISING YOUR MESSAGE

Revision takes place during and after preparation of the first draft.

Although the tendency is to separate revision from composition, revision is an activity that occurs throughout the writing process. You revise as you go along; then you revise again after you've completed the first draft. You constantly search for the best way to say something, probing for the right words, testing alternative sentences, reshaping, tightening, and juggling the existing elements. Ideally, you should let your draft age a day or two before you begin the final revision process so that you can approach the material with a fresh eye. Then read through the document quickly to evaluate its overall effectiveness before moving to finer points such as word choice, conciseness, and grammar.

Even though you want to ensure that your document is as clear and well-written as possible, be sure you stick to your schedule.

As you revise, you'll find yourself rewriting sentences, passages, and even whole sections to improve their effectiveness. Of course, you're probably also facing a deadline, so try to stick to the schedule you set during the planning stage of the project. Do your best to revise and rewrite thoroughly but also economically. With a minimal amount of rewriting, you'll end up with a stronger document. Look closely at the draft in Figure 6–1 responding to Louise Wilson's request for information about the frequent-guest program at Commerce Hotel. It has been edited using the proofreading marks shown in Appendix C. As you can see, the revised text provides the requested information in a more organized fashion, in a friendlier style, and with clearer mechanics.

Evaluating Your Content, Organization, Style, and Tone

During your first revision pass, make sure you achieve the right tone and interest level.

When you begin the revision process, you're mainly concerned with content, organization, style, and tone. To evaluate the content, ask yourself these questions:

- Is the information accurate?

- Is the information relevant to your audience?

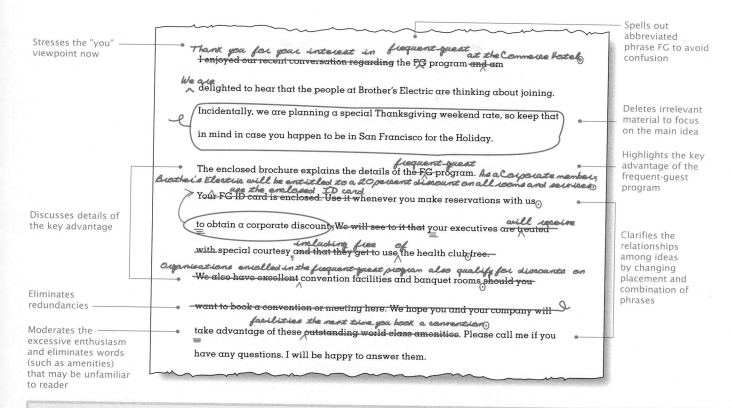

Stresses the "you" viewpoint now

Spells out abbreviated phrase FG to avoid confusion

Deletes irrelevant material to focus on the main idea

Highlights the key advantage of the frequent-guest program

Discusses details of the key advantage

Clarifies the relationships among ideas by changing placement and combination of phrases

Eliminates redundancies

Moderates the excessive enthusiasm and eliminates words (such as amenities) that may be unfamiliar to reader

FIGURE 6-1
Sample Edited Letter

- Have I provided enough information to satisfy the reader's needs?

- Is there a good balance between the general and the specific?

Once you are satisfied with the content of your message, you can review its organization. Ask yourself:

- Have I covered all the points in the most logical order?

- Do the most important ideas receive the most space, and are they placed in the most prominent positions?

- Would the message be more convincing if it were arranged in another sequence?

- Do I repeat myself?

- Are details scattered that need to be grouped together?

Finally, consider the effect that your words will actually have on readers, and ask yourself whether you have achieved the right style and tone for your audience.

In this first pass, spend a few extra moments on the beginning and ending of the message. These are the sections that have the greatest impact on the audience. Be sure that the opening of a letter or memo is relevant, interesting, and geared to the reader's probable reaction. In longer messages, check to see that the first few paragraphs establish the subject, purpose, and organization of the material. Check the ending to be sure that it summarizes the main idea and leaves the audience with a positive impression.

The beginning and end of a message have the greatest impact on readers.

Reviewing for Readability

Readability formulas gauge reading level by measuring word and sentence length.

Once you're satisfied with the content, organization, style, and tone of your message, make a second pass to check its readability. You might even apply a readability formula to gauge the difficulty of your writing. The most common readability formulas measure the length of words and sentences to give you a rough idea of how well educated your audience must be to understand your message. Figure 6–2 shows how one readability formula, the Fog Index, has been applied to an excerpt from a memo. (For more on this topic, visit www.profusion.com and enter "Fog Index" in the search box.) As the calculation shows, anyone who reads at a ninth-grade level should be able to read this passage with ease. For technical documents, you can aim for an audience that reads at a 12th- to 14th-grade level; for general business messages, your writing should be geared to readers at the 8th- to 11th-

FIGURE 6–2
The Fog Index

EXCERPT

I called Global Corporation to ask when we will receive copies of its <u>insurance</u> <u>policies</u> and <u>engineering</u> reports. Cindy Turner of Global said that they are putting the <u>documents</u> <u>together</u> and will send them by Express Mail next week. She told me that they are late because most of the <u>information</u> is in the hands of Global's <u>attorneys</u> in Boston. I asked why it was in Boston; we had <u>understood</u> that the account is serviced by the <u>carrier's</u> Dallas branch. Turner explained that the account <u>originally</u> was sold to Global's Boston <u>division</u>, so all paperwork stays there. She promised to phone us when the package is ready to ship.

1. SELECT WRITING SAMPLE
Keep the sample between 100 and 125 words long. (See excerpt.)

2. DETERMINE AVERAGE SENTENCE LENGTH
Count the number of words in each sentence. Treat independent clauses (stand-alone word groups containing subject and predicate) as separate sentences. For example, "In school we studied; we learned; we improved" counts as three sentences. Then add all word counts for each sentence to get the total word count, and divide that by the number of sentences. This excerpt has an average sentence length of 14:

$$18 + 21 + 21 + 7 + 13 + 12 + 5 + 12 = 109 \text{ words} \div 8 \text{ sentences} = 14$$

3. DETERMINE PERCENTAGE OF LONG WORDS
Count the number of long words—that is, all words that have three or more syllables (underlined in the excerpt). Omit proper nouns, combinations of short words (such as *butterfly* and *anyway*), and verbs that gain a third syllable by adding -es or -ed (as in *trepasses* and *created*). Divide the number of long words by the total number of words in the sample. The percentage of long words in this excerpt is 10 percent:

$$11 \text{ long words} \div 109 \text{ total words} = 10 \text{ percent}$$

4. DETERMINE GRADE LEVEL REQUIRED TO READ EXCERPT
Add the numbers for average sentence length and percentage of long words. Multiply the sum by 0.4, and drop the number after the decimal point. The number of years of schooling required to easily read this excerpt is 9:

14 words per sentence + 10 percent long words =
$$24 \times 0.4 = 9.6 - 0.6 = 9 \text{ (Fog Index)}$$

grade level. The Fog Index of popular business publications such as the *Wall Street Journal* and *Forbes* magazine is between 10 and 11.

Readability formulas are easy to apply; many are commonly done by computer. However, they tend to overvalue condensed prose, and they ignore some important variables that contribute to reading ease, such as sentence structure, the organization of ideas, and the appearance of the message on the page.[3] Moreover, readability indexes can't be applied to languages other than English. Counting syllables makes no sense in other languages. For example, compare the English *forklift driver* with the German *Gabelstaplerfahrer*. Also, Chinese and Japanese characters don't lend themselves to syllable counting at all.[4]

> Readability formulas have their limitations.

Of course, most business writers know that busy readers seldom read every word of a message on their first pass. Instead, they typically skim a message, reading only certain sections carefully to assess the worthiness of the document. If they determine that the document contains valuable information or requires a response, they will read it more carefully when time permits. You can adopt a number of techniques to make your message easier to skim so that readers can move through the material more quickly. Varying sentence length, using shorter paragraphs, using lists and bullets instead of narrative, and adding effective headings and subheadings ensure that your readers will notice key points, even if they do skim messages. These techniques will also make your message more appealing.

> Make messages easier to skim.

Vary the Sentence Length   Variety is the key to making your message interesting and readable. With your words and sentence structure, you create a rhythm that emphasizes important points, enlivens your writing style, and makes your information appealing to your reader. Although good business writers use short sentences most of the time, too many short sentences in a row can make your writing choppy. Conversely, if all your sentences move at the same plodding gait, you're likely to lull your reader to sleep. So to be interesting, use a variety of both short and long sentences.

> To keep readers' interest, use both long and short sentences.

Keep in mind that long sentences are usually harder to understand than short sentences because they are packed with information that must be absorbed all at once. Longer sentences are also more difficult to skim. Readers can absorb only a few words per glance. Thus, the longer your sentence, the greater the possibility that the reader who skims will not read enough words to process the full meaning.

On the other hand, long sentences are especially well suited for grouping or combining ideas, listing points, and summarizing or previewing information. Medium-length sentences (those with about 20 words) are useful for showing the relationships among ideas. Short sentences emphasize important information. Most good business writing has an average sentence length of 20 words or fewer. (For audiences abroad, varying sentence length can create translation problems for the reader, so stick to short sentences in international messages.)[5]

> Average sentence length for most good business writing is 20 words or fewer.

Keep Paragraphs Short   Most business readers are put off by large blocks of text. Unless you break up your thoughts somehow, you'll end up with a three-page paragraph that's guaranteed to intimidate even the most dedicated reader. Short paragraphs (of 100 words or fewer) are easier to read than long ones, and they make your writing look inviting. Direct-mail letters almost always use very short paragraphs because the writers know that their letters will be read more carefully that way. Even in memos, letters, and reports, you may want to emphasize an idea from time to time by isolating it in a short, forceful paragraph.

> Short paragraphs are easier to read than long ones.

As you write your message, try to use a variety of paragraph lengths, but be careful to use one-sentence paragraphs only occasionally and only for emphasis. When you want to package a big idea in short paragraphs, break the idea

One thing that Jerry Blount depends on when making a sale is contract clarity. He doesn't want his customers to feel confused about what services they're purchasing from his home security company. That's why Blount's contracts break out specific security services in bulleted lists that are easy to locate, read, and understand.

into subtopics and treat each subtopic in a separate paragraph—being careful to provide plenty of transitional elements. By breaking a large single paragraph into several shorter ones, you can make material more readable. Of course, many other approaches might be as effective. As we saw in Chapter 5, there is no "right" way to develop a paragraph.

Use Lists and Bullets for Emphasis and Clarity An effective technique for emphasizing important ideas is to set them off in a **list**—a series of words, names, phrases, or sentences. Lists can show the sequence of your ideas, visually heighten their impact, and help readers find your key points. In addition, lists provide readers with clues, simplify complex subjects, highlight the main point, break up the page visually, ease the skimming process, and give readers a breather. Consider the difference between the following two approaches to the same information:

Lists are effective tools for highlighting and simplifying material.

Narrative	**List**
Owning your own business has many advantages. One is the ease of establishment. Another advantage is the satisfaction of working for yourself. As a sole proprietor, you also have the advantage of privacy because you do not have to reveal your information or plans to anyone.	Owning your own business has three advantages: • Ease of establishment • Satisfaction of working for yourself • Privacy of information

Use bullets rather than numbers, unless item order is important.

You can separate list items with numbers, letters, or bullets (a general term for any kind of graphic element that precedes each item). For shorter lists, graphic elements aren't required. However, for longer lists, bullets are preferred over numbers, unless the sequence of items is important (when the steps in a process must be completed in a specific order, for example). In the following excerpt, the three steps need to be performed in the order indicated, and the numbers make that clear.

Before we bring the day-care issue to a vote, we must gather more information:

1. Find out how many employees would like on-site day-care facilities.
2. Determine how much space the day-care center would require.
3. Estimate the cost of converting a conference room for the on-site facility.

Use hanging indents in lists.

Lists are easier to read if the runovers are indented (aligned with the first word of the item), as the preceding example demonstrates. You can also indent the entire list. Furthermore, when using lists, make sure to introduce them clearly so that people know what they're about to read. One way to introduce lists is to make them a part of the introductory sentence.

The board of directors met to discuss the revised annual budget. To keep expenses in line with declining sales, the directors voted to

- Cut everyone's salary by 10 percent
- Close the employee cafeteria
- Reduce travel expenses

If necessary, add further discussion after the lists to complete your thought. Another way to introduce a list is to use a complete introductory sentence, followed by a colon:

The decline in profits is the result of several factors:

- Slower holiday sales
- Increased transportation and fuel costs
- Higher employee wages
- Slower inventory turnover

Regardless of the format you choose, list items should be phrased in parallel form. For example, if one list item begins with a verb, all list items should begin with a verb. If one is a noun phrase, all should be noun phrases. Parallel construction shows that the ideas are related, of similar importance, and on the same level of generality.

Construct list items in parallel form.

Avoid Nonparallel List Items	**Make List Items Parallel**
• Improve our bottom line	• Improving our bottom line
• Identification of new foreign markets for our products	• Identifying new foreign markets for our products
• Global market strategies	• Developing our global market strategies
• Issues regarding pricing and packaging size	• Resolving pricing and packaging issues

For additional discussion of parallelism, see "Editing for Clarity and Conciseness" later in this chapter.

Add Headings and Subheadings   A **heading** is a brief title that cues readers about the content of the section that follows. Headings are similar to the subject line in memos and e-mail correspondence. However, subject lines merely identify the purpose of the memo or e-mail, whereas headings also advise the reader about the material included in the paragraph.

Headings serve several important functions:

- **Organization.** Headings show your reader at a glance how the document is organized. They act as labels to group-related paragraphs and organize your material into short sections.

- **Attention.** Informative, inviting, and in some cases intriguing headings grab attention, make text easier to read, and help readers find the parts they need to read—or skip.

Use headings to grab the reader's attention and divide material into short sections.

- **Connection.** Headings and subheadings help readers see the relationship between subordinate and main ideas. They also visually indicate shifts from one idea to the next.

Informative headings are generally more helpful than descriptive ones.

Headings fall into two categories. **Descriptive headings,** such as "Cost Considerations," identify a topic but do little more. **Informative headings,** such as "A New Way to Cut Costs," communicate enough information to put your reader right into the context of your message. Informative headings guide readers to think in a certain way about the topic. They also help guide your work as a writer, especially when they are written as questions you plan to address in your document. However, informative headings are more difficult to create.

A well-written informative heading is self-contained. In other words, readers should be able to read your headings and subheadings and understand them without reading the rest of the document. For example, "Introduction" does not make sense by itself, whereas the heading "An Insight into the Need for Better Communication" makes sense by itself, catches the reader's attention, and sparks interest. Whatever category you choose, keep your headings brief, and use parallel construction as you would for an outline, a list, or a series of words.

Editing for Clarity

Clarity prevents confusion.

Once you've reviewed and revised your message for readability, make sure that your message is clear. Perhaps a sentence is so cluttered that the reader can't unravel it. Or perhaps a sentence is so poorly constructed that the reader can interpret it in several ways. If pronouns or tenses switch midsentence, the reader may lose track of who is talking or when an event took place. Perhaps sentence B is not a logical sequel to sentence A, or maybe an important word is used incorrectly.[6]

Nine techniques can help you write more clearly.

Ask yourself whether your sentences are easy to decipher. Do your paragraphs have clear topic sentences? Are the transitions between ideas obvious? Are your statements simple and direct? Remember, a clear sentence is no accident. Few sentences come out right the first time, or even the third time. See Table 6–1 for examples of the following tips:

- **Break up overly long sentences.** Don't connect too many clauses with *and*. If you find yourself stuck in a long sentence, you're probably trying to make the sentence do more than it can reasonably do, such as express two dissimilar thoughts. You can often clarify your writing style by separating one long sentence into two or more individual sentences.

- **Rewrite hedging sentences.** Sometimes you have to write *may* or *seems* to avoid stating a judgment as a fact. Nevertheless, when you have too many such hedges, you sound evasive, even though you don't mean to.[7]

- **Impose parallelism.** When you have two or more similar (parallel) ideas to express, use the same grammatical pattern for each related idea—parallel construction. Repeating the pattern makes your message more readable: It tells readers that the ideas are comparable, and it adds rhythm. Parallelism can be achieved by repeating the pattern in words, phrases, clauses, or entire sentences (see Table 6–2 on page 172).

- **Correct dangling modifiers.** Sometimes a modifier is not just an adjective or an adverb but an entire phrase modifying a noun or a verb. Be careful not to leave this type of modifier dangling with no connection to the subject of the sentence. The first unacceptable example under "Dangling Modifiers" in Table 6–1 implies that the red sports car has both an office and the legs to walk there. The second example shows one frequent cause of dangling modifiers: passive construction.

Even when you sell silly stuff, you want readers to understand your messages without difficulty. That's why clear messages are important to Steve and Sally Colby. From their website at OfftheDeepEnd.com, the Colbys sell items that run the gamut from tacky to cheesy—including flamingo lawn statues and plastic cockroaches. Their business is innovative, but their communication is clear.

Examples	Unacceptable	Preferable
OVERLY LONG SENTENCES Taking compound sentences too far	The magazine will be published January 1, and I'd better meet the deadline if I want my article included.	The magazine will be published January 1. I'd better meet the deadline if I want my article included.
HEDGING SENTENCES Overqualifying sentences	I believe that Mr. Johnson's employment record seems to show that he may be capable of handling the position.	Mr. Johnson's employment record shows that he is capable of handling the position.
UNPARALLEL SENTENCES Using dissimilar construction for similar ideas	Miss Simms had been drenched with rain, bombarded with telephone calls, and her boss shouted at her.	Miss Sims had been drenched with rain, bombarded with telephone calls, and shouted at by her boss.
	Ms. Reynolds dictated the letter, and next she signed it and left the office.	Ms. Reynolds dictated the letter, signed it, and left the office.
	To waste time and missing deadlines are bad habits.	Wasting time and missing deadlines are bad habits.
	Interviews are a matter of acting confident and to stay relaxed.	Interviews are a matter of acting confident and staying relaxed.
DANGLING MODIFIERS Placing modifiers close to the wrong nouns and verbs	Walking to the office, a red sports car passed her.	A red sports car passed her while she was walking to the office.
	Working as fast as possible, the budget was soon ready.	Working as fast as possible, the committee soon had the budget ready.
	After a 3-week slump, we increased sales.	After a 3-week slump, sales increased.
LONG NOUN SEQUENCES Stringing too many nouns together	The window sash installation company will give us an estimate on Friday.	The company that installs window sashes will give us an estimate on Friday.
CAMOUFLAGED VERBS Changing verbs and nouns into adjectives	The manager undertook implementation of the rules.	The manager implemented the rules.
	Verification of the shipments occurs weekly.	Shipments are verified weekly.
Changing verbs into nouns	Reach a conclusion about Make a discovery of Give consideration to	Conclude Discover Consider
SENTENCE STRUCTURE Separating subject and predicate	A 10 percent decline in market share, which resulted from quality problems and an aggressive sales campaign by Armitage, the market leader in the Northeast, was the major problem in 2001.	The major problem in 2001 was a 10 percent loss of market share, which resulted from both quality problems and an aggressive sales campaign by Armitage, the market leader in the Northeast.
Separating adjectives, adverbs, or prepositional phrases from the words they modify	Our antique desk is suitable for busy executives with thick legs and large drawers.	With its thick legs and large drawers, our antique desk is suitable for busy executives.
AWKWARD REFERENCES	The Law Office and the Accounting Office distribute computer supplies for legal secretaries and beginning accountants, respectively.	The Law Office distributes computer supplies for legal secretaries; the Accounting Office distributes those for beginning accountants.
TOO MUCH ENTHUSIASM	We are extremely pleased to offer you a position on our staff of exceptionally skilled and highly educated employees. The work offers extraordinary challenges and a very large salary.	We are pleased to offer you a position on our staff of skilled and well-educated employees. The work offers challenges and an attractive salary.

Table 6–2   ACHIEVING PARALLELISM

Method	Example
Parallel words:	The letter was approved by Clausen, Whittaker, Merlin, and Carlucci.
Parallel phrases:	We have beaten the competition in supermarkets, in department stores, and in specialty stores.
Parallel clauses:	I'd like to discuss the issue after Vicki gives her presentation but before Marvin shows his slides.
Parallel sentences:	In 2000 we exported 30 percent of our production. In 2001 we exported 50 percent.

When Starbucks Coffee Company Chairman and CEO Howard Schultz announced that Starbucks would expand beyond the coffee business, his message got the attention of customers and analysts alike. But Schultz has more than one message. He's launched a program to support literacy in children, and he's written a book (*Pour Your Heart Into It*) about the motivation for his ambition. In interviews, Schultz's excitement shows through, but in writing, he moderates his enthusiasm. He knows that using too many adjectives and adverbs spoils good writing, so he uses just a few to intensify the meaning.

Conciseness means efficiency.

Four techniques can help you write more concisely.

- **Reword long noun sequences.** When nouns are strung together as modifiers, the resulting sentence is hard to read. You can clarify the sentence by putting some of the nouns in a modifying phrase. Although you add a few more words, your audience won't have to work as hard to understand the sentence.

- **Replace camouflaged verbs.** Watch for word endings such as *-ion, -tion, -ing, -ment, -ant, -ent, -ence, -ance*, and *-ency*. Most of them change verbs into nouns and adjectives. Also, try not to transform verbs into nouns by writing phrases such as "we performed an analysis of" rather than "we analyzed." Prune and enliven your messages by using verbs instead of noun phrases.

- **Clarify sentence structure.** Keep the subject and predicate of a sentence as close together as possible. When subject and predicate are far apart, readers have to read the sentence twice to figure out who did what. Similarly, adjectives, adverbs, and prepositional phrases usually make the most sense when they're placed as close as possible to the words they modify.

- **Clarify awkward references.** To save words, business writers sometimes use expressions such as *the above-mentioned, as mentioned above, the afore-mentioned, the former, the latter*, and *respectively*. These words cause readers to jump from point to point, which hinders effective communication. Use specific references, even if you must add a few more words.

- **Moderate your enthusiasm.** An occasional adjective or adverb intensifies and emphasizes your meaning, but too many such modifiers can ruin your writing.

Editing for Conciseness

Most first drafts can be cut by 50 percent.[8] By reorganizing your content, improving the readability of your document, and correcting your sentence structure for clarity, you will have already eliminated most of the excess. Now it's time to examine every word you put on paper.

When you edit for conciseness, you eliminate every word that serves no function, replace every long word that could be a short word, and remove every adverb that adds nothing to the meaning already carried in the verb. To test the value of each word, try removing phrases or words that don't appear to be essential. If the meaning doesn't change, leave them out. For instance, *very* can be a useful word to achieve emphasis, but more often it's clutter. There's no need to call someone "very methodical." The person is either methodical or not. See Table 6–3 for examples of the following tips:

- **Delete unnecessary words and phrases.** Avoid words (such as *very* and *rather*) that may act as qualifiers but add nothing new to a sentence.[9] Avoid combinations

Examples	Unacceptable	Preferable
UNNECESSARY WORDS AND PHRASES		
Using unnecessary qualifiers	Very, extremely, totally, completely, really, quite, rather, somewhat	
Using wordy phrases	For the sum of	For
	In the event that	If
	On the occasion of	On
	Prior to the start of	Before
	Have the capability of	Can
	At this point in time	Now
	Due to the fact that	Because
	In view of the fact that	Because
	Until such time as	When
	With reference to	About
Using too many relative pronouns	Cars that are sold after January will not have a six-month warranty.	Cars sold after January will not have a six-month warranty.
	Employees who are driving to work should park in the underground garage.	Employees driving to work should park in the underground garage.
Using too few relative pronouns	The project manager told the engineers last week the specifications were changed.	The project manager told the engineers last week that the specifications were changed.
		The project manager told the engineers that last week the specifications were changed.
LONG WORDS AND PHRASES		
Using overly long words	During the preceding year, the company accelerated productive operations.	Last year the company sped up operations.
	The action was predicated on the assumption that the company was operating at a financial deficit.	The action was based on the belief that the company was losing money.
Using wordy phrases rather than infinitives	If you want success as a writer, you must work hard.	To be a successful writer, you must work hard.
	He went to the library for the purpose of studying.	He went to the library to study.
REDUNDANCIES		
Repeating meanings	Absolutely complete	Complete
	Basic fundamentals	Fundamentals
	Follows after	Follows
	Reduce down	Reduce
	Free and clear	Free
	Refer back	Refer
	Repeat again	Repeat
	Collect together	Collect
	Future plans	Plans
	Return back	Return
	Important essentials	Essentials
	Midway between	Between
	End result	Result
	Actual truth	Truth
	Final outcome	Outcome
	Uniquely unusual	Unique
Using double modifiers	Modern up-to-date equipment	Modern equipment
IT IS/THERE ARE STARTERS		
Starting sentences with *it* or *there*	It would be appreciated if you would sign the lease today.	Please sign the lease today.
	There are five employees in this division who were late to work today.	Five employees in this division were late to work today.

✓ CHECKLIST: Revising Business Messages

Evaluate Content, Organization, Style, and Tone

- ✓ Review your draft, and compare it against the original plan for your message.
- ✓ Check that all necessary points appear in logical order.
- ✓ Make sure your message is organized according to the audience's probable reaction.
- ✓ Verify that you present enough support to make the main idea convincing and interesting.
- ✓ Eliminate unnecessary material, and add useful material.
- ✓ Be sure the beginning and ending are effective.
- ✓ Make sure you've achieved the right tone.

Review for Readability

- ✓ Check vocabulary and sentence structure for readability.
- ✓ Consider using a readability index.
- ✓ Use a mix of short and long sentences.
- ✓ Keep paragraphs short.
- ✓ Use bulleted and numbered lists to set off key points.
- ✓ Use headings and subheadings to guide readers.

Edit for Clarity

- ✓ Break up overly long sentences.
- ✓ Rewrite hedging sentences.
- ✓ Impose parallelism.

- ✓ Correct dangling modifiers.
- ✓ Reword long noun sequences.
- ✓ Replace camouflaged verbs.
- ✓ Clarify sentence structure.
- ✓ Clarify awkward references.
- ✓ Moderate your enthusiasm.

Edit for Conciseness

- ✓ Delete unnecessary words and phrases.
- ✓ Shorten long words and phrases.
- ✓ Eliminate redundancies.
- ✓ Recast "It is/There are" starters.

Use Technology for Efficient Revisions

- ✓ Don't rely too heavily on any technology to do your work for you.
- ✓ Use word processors to help you add, delete, and move text.
- ✓ Use revision marks to help you track proposed editing changes.
- ✓ Use spell checkers to help you weed out misspellings, without relying too heavily on them.
- ✓ Use an electronic thesaurus to find a stronger or more specific word quickly.
- ✓ Use grammar checkers to help you discover potential grammar, usage, and mechanical problems, without relying too heavily on them.

of words that have more efficient, one-word equivalents. Also, avoid the clutter of too many or poorly placed relative pronouns (*who, that, which*). Even articles can be excessive (mostly too many *the's*). However, well-placed relative pronouns and articles prevent confusion.

- **Shorten long words and phrases.** Short words are generally more vivid and easier to read than long ones are. The idea is to use short, simple words, *not* simple concepts.[10] Plus, by using infinitives in place of some phrases, you not only shorten your sentences but also make them clearer.

- **Eliminate redundancies.** In some word combinations, the words tend to say the same thing. For instance, "visible to the eye" is redundant because *visible* is enough; nothing can be visible to the ear.

- **Recast "It is/There are" starters.** If you start a sentence with an indefinite pronoun (an expletive) such as *it* or *there*, odds are that the sentence could be shorter.

As you rewrite, concentrate on how each word contributes to an effective sentence and how that sentence develops a coherent paragraph. As David Giarla cautions, be sure to consider the effect your words will actually have on readers (not just the effect you *plan* for them to have). Look for opportunities to make the material more interesting through the use of strong, lively words and phrases (as discussed in Chapter 5). For a reminder of the tasks involved in revision, see the "Checklist: Revising Business Messages."

Using Technology to Revise Your Message

When it's time to revise and polish your message, your word processor can help you add, delete, and move text with functions such as *cut and paste* (moving a block of text from one section to another) and *search and replace* (tracking down words or phrases and changing them). Be careful when using the "replace all" option. For example, finding *power* and replacing all occurrences with *strength* would also change the word *powerful* to *strengthful.*

Programs such as Microsoft Word can track proposed editing changes and provide a history of a document's revisions. The revisions appear in different colors until you accept or reject them. In addition, revision marks can help you attach electronic notes and keep track of editing changes made by team members—especially helpful when writing collaborative messages (see Figure 6–3).

Spell checkers compare your document with an electronic dictionary, highlight unrecognized words, and suggest correct spelling. Spell checkers are a wonderful way to weed major typos out of your documents, but they can't do the whole job for you. For example, if you use *their* when you mean to use *there*, your spell checker won't notice, because *their* is spelled correctly. If you're in a hurry and accidentally omit the *p* at the end of *top*, your spell checker will read *to* as correct. Or if you mistakenly type a semicolon instead of *p*, your spell checker will read *to;* as a correctly spelled word. Plus, some of the "errors" pointed out by spell checkers may actually be proper names, technical words, words that you misspelled on purpose, or simply words that weren't included in the spell checker's dictionary. It's up to you to decide whether each flagged word should be corrected or left alone, and it's up to you to find the errors that your spell checker has overlooked.

A computer *thesaurus* gives you alternative words, just as your printed thesaurus does. The electronic version of the *American Heritage Dictionary* provides not only a thesaurus but also a special WordHunter function that gives you a term when all you know is part of the definition. If you're racking your brain to remember the word that

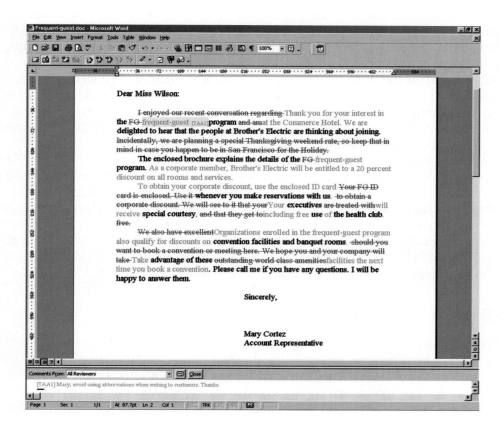

FIGURE 6–3
On-Screen Revision Marks

means a certain quantity of paper, you simply type *quantity AND paper* and then WordHunter searches for every definition in the dictionary that includes those two terms. In a few seconds, the word *ream* pops into view—just the word you were looking for.

Grammar checkers try to do for your grammar what a spell checker does for your spelling. The catch is that checking your grammar is much harder than checking your spelling. A grammar checker must determine whether you're using words correctly and constructing sentences according to the complex rules of composition. But the program doesn't have a clue about what you're trying to say, so it can't tell whether you've said it correctly. Even if you've used all the rules correctly, a grammar checker can't tell whether your document communicates clearly. However, grammar checkers can perform some helpful review tasks and point out things you should consider changing, such as passive voice, long sentences, and words that tend to be misused or overused. Some programs even run readability formulas for you.

Spell checkers, grammar checkers, and computerized thesauruses can all help with the revision process, but they can't take the place of good writing and editing skills.

By all means, use any software that you find helpful when revising your documents. Just remember that it's unwise to rely on grammar checkers or spell checkers to do all your revision work. What these programs can do is identify "mistakes" you may overlook on your own. It's up to you to decide what, if anything, needs to be done, and it's up to you to catch the mistakes that these computer programs can't.[11]

PRODUCING YOUR MESSAGE

Once you have revised and refined your message from start to finish, you're ready to produce it. You'll want to add elements such as graphics or hypertext and design a page layout that gives your message an attractive, contemporary appearance.

Adding Graphics, Sound, and Hypertext

You can use graphics software to add visual elements to your message.

With the recent advances in computer technology, it's becoming easier and easier to illustrate and enliven your text with full-color pictures, sound recordings, and hypertext links. The software for creating business visuals falls into two basic groups: *Presentation software* helps you create overhead transparencies and computerized slide shows (electronic presentations are discussed in Chapter 13). *Graphics software* ranges from products that can create simple diagrams and flowcharts (see Chapter 11) to comprehensive tools geared to artists and graphic designers. You can create your pictures from scratch, use *clip art* (collections of uncopyrighted images), or scan in drawings or photographs.

Adding sound bites to your electronic documents is an exciting new way to get your message across. Several systems now allow you to record a brief message or other sound and attach it to particular places in a document. You can also use hypertext markup language (HTML) to insert hyperlinks into your message. Readers can easily jump from one document to another by clicking on such a link. They can also go directly to a website (provided they have an active Internet hookup). Of course, you must make sure that the destination file (or the software program used to open that file) is either included with your electronic document or installed on the recipient's computer.

Designing Page Layout

Design affects the impression your message makes.

The way you package your ideas has a lot to do with how successful your communication will be. The first thing your readers will notice about your message is its appearance. If your document looks tired and out of date, it will give that impression to your readers—even if your ideas are innovative. Good looks can help you get your message across, especially to busy readers. Consider the memo in Figure 6–4. The

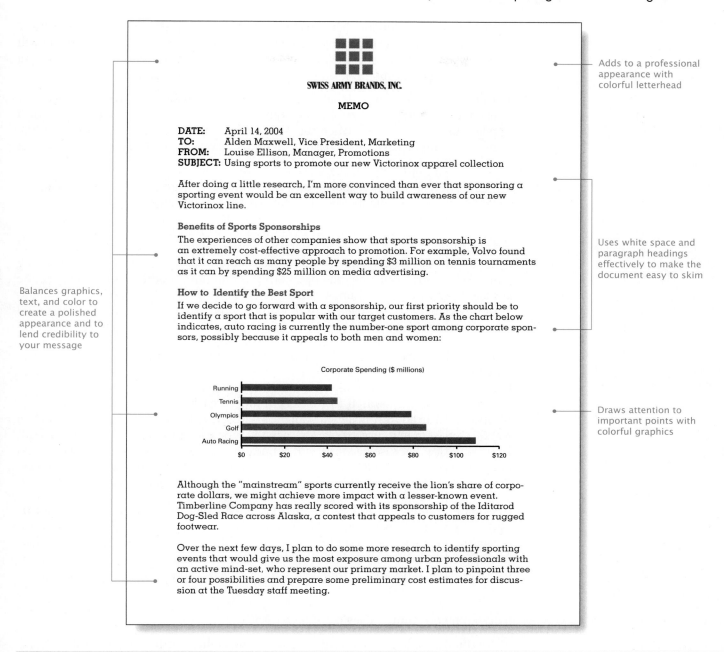

Balances graphics, text, and color to create a polished appearance and to lend credibility to your message

Adds to a professional appearance with colorful letterhead

Uses white space and paragraph headings effectively to make the document easy to skim

Draws attention to important points with colorful graphics

FIGURE 6–4
Effective Document Appearance

bar chart in this memo is centered to give a formal impression, and the color used in the graphic is balanced by the letterhead logo. Be sure your document's design has the following characteristics:

- **Consistency.** Throughout a message (and sometimes even from message to message), be consistent in your use of margins, typeface, type size, and spacing (for example, in paragraph indents, between columns, and around photographs). Also be consistent when using recurring design elements, such as vertical lines, columns, and borders.

- **Balance.** To create a pleasing design, balance the space devoted to text, artwork, and white space.

- **Restraint.** Strive for simplicity in design. Don't clutter your message with too many design elements, too much highlighting, or too many decorative touches. If you will be designing a lot of documents that contain a variety of elements, consider taking a course in page layout, or at least read more about effective design techniques.

- **Detail.** Pay attention to details that affect your design and thus your message. For instance, headings and subheadings that appear at the bottom of a column or a page can annoy readers when the promised information doesn't appear until the next column or page. Also, narrow columns with too much space between words can be distracting.

To make your message look professional, interesting, and up to date, you can use a variety of design elements, such as white space, margins and line justification, typefaces, and type styles.

White space is free of text and artwork.

White Space   **White space** is any space free of text or artwork. It provides visual contrast for your readers, and perhaps even more important, it gives them a resting point. White space includes the open area surrounding headings, margin areas, the vertical space between columns, the space created by ragged line endings, the paragraph indents or extra space between unindented paragraphs, and the horizontal space between lines of text.

Headings and captions should guide your readers without distracting them from your message.

Heading Placement   When placing headings and subheadings into your documents, remember that their purpose is to invite readers to become involved in your message. Centered heads should contain no more than two lines, since multiple lines will slow your readers as they search for the beginning of each line. To improve readability, position your headings "flush left" (aligned with the left-hand margin). You may even want to set them in a type size larger than the type used for text and perhaps in a different typeface. Because headings and subheadings clue readers in to the organization of your message's content, link them as closely as possible to the text they introduce. You can do so by putting more space above the heading than below it.

Caption Placement   Captions are the most widely read part of a document. They tie photographs and illustrations into the rest of your message. Although usually placed below the exhibits they describe, captions can also be placed beside or above their exhibits. Make sure that the width of your captions is pleasing in proportion to the width of the exhibit, the surrounding white space, and the text.

Margins frame your text with white space that changes according to how you align lines of type: justified, flush left, centered, or flush right.

Margins and Line Justification   Margins define the space around your text and between text columns. They're influenced by the way you place lines of type:

- **Justified (flush on the left and flush on the right).** Justified type "darkens" message appearance (because uniform line lengths lack the white space created by ragged margins). Justifying tends to make messages look less customized and more like form letters. Plus, it is often difficult to read because large gaps can appear between words and more words are hyphenated. Even so, many magazines and newspapers use it to accommodate more text.

- **Flush left with a ragged right margin.** Flush-left, ragged-right type "lightens" your message's appearance. It gives a document an informal, contemporary feeling of openness. Spacing between words is consistent, and only long words that fall at the ends of lines are hyphenated.

- **Centered.** Centered type lends a formal tone to your message. However, centering long blocks of type slows reading because your audience has to search for the beginning of each line. Avoid centering long passages of text.

- **Flush right with a ragged left margin.** Flush-right, ragged-left type has the same problems as centered type. Avoid flush-right type for long passages of text.

COMMON TYPEFACES		Table 6–4
Sample Serif Typeface	**Sample Sans Serif Typeface**	
Times Roman is often used for text.	Helvetica is often used for headings.	
TIMES ROMAN IS HARDER TO READ IN ALL CAPS.	HELVETICA IS A CLEANER FACE, EVEN IN ALL CAPS.	

Typefaces   **Typeface** refers to the physical design of letters, numbers, and other text characters. Most computers offer innumerable choices of typefaces, or fonts. Each typeface influences the tone of your message, making it look authoritative or friendly, businesslike or casual, classic or modern, and so on. So choose fonts that are appropriate for your message.

Serif typefaces have small crosslines (called serifs) at the ends of each letter stroke (see Table 6–4). Serif faces such as Times Roman (packaged with most laser printers) are commonly used for text; they can look busy and cluttered when set in large sizes for headings or other display treatments. Typefaces with rounded serifs can look friendly; those with squared serifs can look official.

Serif typefaces are commonly used for text.

Sans serif typefaces have no crosslines. Faces such as Helvetica and Arial are ideal for display treatments that use larger type. However, sans serif faces can be difficult to read in long blocks of text. They look best when surrounded by plenty of white space—as in headings or in widely spaced lines of text.

Sans serif typefaces are commonly used for headings.

Limit the number of typefaces in a single document.[12] In general, avoid using more than two typefaces on a page. Many great-looking documents are based on a single sans serif typeface for heads and subheads and a second, serif typeface for text and captions. Using too many typefaces clutters a document and reduces audience comprehension.

Type Styles   *Type style* refers to any modification that lends contrast or emphasis to type. Most computers offer boldface, italic, underlining, and other highlighting and decorative styles. Using boldface type for subheads breaks up long expanses of text. Just remember that too much boldfacing will darken the appearance of your message and make it look heavy. You can set isolated words in boldface type in the middle of a text block to draw more attention to them. If you boldface too many words, however, you might create a "checkerboard" appearance in a paragraph.

Use italic type for emphasis. Although italics are sometimes used when irony or humor is intended, quotation marks are usually best for that purpose. Italics can also be used to set off a quote and are often used in captions. Boldfaced type and italics are most effective when reserved for key words—those that help readers understand the main point of the text. A good example of using boldface type effectively is found in the document-revision tips listed under the heading "Editing for Clarity" on pages 170–172 of this chapter. Here the boldfaced type draws attention to the key tips, followed by a short, regular-typeface explanation of each tip.

Use italic type for emphasis.

As a general rule, avoid using any style that slows your audience's progress through your message. For instance, using underlining or all-uppercase letters can interfere with your reader's ability to recognize the shapes of words, improperly placed boldface or too much italicized type can slow down your reader, and shadowed or outlined type can seriously hinder legibility. So use these styles judiciously.

Generally avoid using any type styles that inhibit your audience's ability to read your messages.

Make sure the size of your type is proportionate to the importance of your message and the space allotted. For most business messages, use a type size of 10 to 12 points (a point is approximately 1/72 of an inch). Resist the temptation to reduce your type size so that you can squeeze in text. Likewise, avoid enlarging it to fill up space. Smaller type is hard to read, whereas larger type looks unprofessional and, if squeezed into a small area, is hard to read and visually claustrophobic.

Giving Your Message a Professional Look

The software most appropriate for assembling finished pages with graphics elements is desktop publishing (DTP), although word-processing software can handle graphics to a limited extent.

Most word-processing programs include several elements to help you assemble your finished pages, combine text and graphics, and create a professional and inviting appearance. But if you want a first-class report with photos and drawings, consider **desktop publishing (DTP)** software, which includes additional specialized tools for formatting, drawing, design, and layout. Desktop publishing software such as Quark XPress and Adobe Pagemaker can make it easy for anyone to produce great-looking documents in two ways:

- **Adding a first-class finish.** You can use DTP to select attractive typefaces, add color graphics, and turn a plain piece of text into a dazzling and persuasive document. However, the same technology can turn your document into garish, high-tech rubbish. Knowing how to use technological tools is critical for business communicators.

- **Managing document style.** To maintain consistent style in your document, most word processors and DTP packages use *styles,* formatting commands that you can save and apply as needed. High-end packages collect these commands into *style sheets* that save formatting effort, ensure consistency in each section you add to your report, and ensure a consistent look for all documents created in a department or even in an entire company.

PROOFREADING YOUR MESSAGE

Your attention to the details of mechanics and form affects your credibility.

Although spelling, punctuation, and typographical errors seem trivial to some people, most readers view your attention to detail as a sign of your professionalism. "When I get a college résumé and I see a typo on it, I instantly disregard that résumé," says Adrianne Proeller of Turner Broadcasting System. Whether you're writing a one-paragraph memo or a 500-page report, if you let mechanical errors slip through, your readers will wonder whether you're unreliable in more important ways.

What to Look for When Proofreading

The types of details to look for when proofreading include language errors, missing material, design errors, and typographical errors.

Proofread your message for correct grammar, usage, and punctuation (for a quick review, see the "Handbook of Grammar, Mechanics, and Usage" at the end of this textbook). You'll also want to be on the lookout for common spelling errors and typos. Check too for missing material: a missing source note, a missing exhibit, or even a missing paragraph. Look for design errors; for example, some headings and text might be in the wrong typeface (Helvetica rather than Times New Roman, or Arial Black rather than Arial Narrow). One or two special elements may be in the wrong type style (italic instead of boldface, or underlined instead of italic). Columns within tables and exhibits on a page might be misaligned. Graphic characters such as ampersands and percent signs may appear when they should be spelled out, and numerical symbols might be incorrect. Look for problems in columns of type, such as extra spacing between lines or between words, crowded type, a short line of type ending a paragraph at the top of a new page, a heading left hanging at the bottom of a page, or incorrect hyphenation. (See "Sharpening Your Career Skills: How to Proofread Like a Pro: Tips for Creating the Perfect Document.")

Also, give some attention to your overall format. Have you followed accepted conventions and company guidelines for laying out the document on the page (margin width, number of columns, running heads)? Have you included all the traditional elements that belong in documents of the type you're creating? Have you been consistent in handling page numbers, heading styles, exhibit titles, source notes, and other details? (To resolve questions about format and layout, see Appendix A.)

SHARPENING YOUR CAREER SKILLS

How to Proofread Like a Pro: Tips for Creating the Perfect Document

You've carefully revised and polished your document, and it's been sent off to the word-processing department or a designer to be put into final form. You can breathe a sigh of relief, but only for the moment: You'll still be proofreading what comes out of the printer. To ensure that any document is error-free, always proofread the final version. Following are some hints to help make your proofreading more effective.

- *Multiple passes.* Go through the document several times, focusing on a different aspect each time. The first pass might be to look for omissions and errors in content; the second pass could be for layout, spacing, and other aesthetic features; a final pass might be to check for typographical, grammatical, and spelling errors.

- *Perceptual tricks.* Your brain has been trained to ignore transposed letters, improper capitalization, and misplaced punctuation. Try (1) reading each page from the bottom to the top (starting at the last word in each line), (2) placing your finger under each word and reading it silently, (3) making a slit in a sheet of paper that reveals only one line of type at a time, and (4) reading the document aloud and pronouncing each word carefully.

- *Impartial reviews.* Have a friend or colleague proofread the document for you. Others are likely to catch mistakes that you continually fail to notice. (All of us have blind spots when it comes to reviewing our own work.)

- *Typos.* Look for the most common typographical errors (typos): transposition (such as *teh*), substitution (such as *ecomonic*), and omission (such as *productvity*).

- *Mechanics.* When looking for errors in spelling, grammar, punctuation, and capitalization, if you're unsure about something, look it up in a dictionary, a usage book, or another reference.

- *Accuracy.* Double-check the spelling of names and the accuracy of dates, addresses, and all numbers (quantities ordered, prices, and so on). It would not do to order 500 staplers when you want only 50.

- *Distance.* If you have time, set the document aside and proofread it the next day.

- *Vigilance.* Avoid reading large amounts of material in one sitting, and try not to proofread when you're tired.

- *Focus.* Concentrate on what you're doing. Try to block out distractions, and focus as completely as possible on your proofreading task.

- *Caution.* Take your time. Quick proofreading is not careful proofreading.

Proofreading may require patience, but it adds credibility to your document.

CAREER APPLICATIONS

1. What qualities does a person need to be a good proofreader? Are such qualities inborn, or can they be learned?

2. Proofread the following sentence:

   aplication of thse methods in stores in San Deigo nd Cinncinati have resultted in a 30 drop in roberies an a 50 precent decling in violnce there, acording ot thedevelpers if the securty sytem, Hanover brothrs, Inc.

How to Adapt the Proofreading Process

How many and what sorts of errors you catch when proofreading depends on the amount of time you have and the kind of document you are preparing. The more routine your document, the less time you'll need to spend. Routine documents have fewer elements to check. Moreover, the more often you prepare one type of document, the more you'll know about what sorts of errors to look for.

Longer, more complex documents can have many more components that need checking. For complicated documents, you may feel pressed for enough time to do a good proofreading job. But back in Step 1 of the writing process (look back at Figure 4–1 on page 95), you planned out how you would approach this message and you allotted a certain amount of

Document Makeover

IMPROVE THIS LETTER

To practice correcting drafts of actual documents, visit **www.prenhall.com/onekey** on the web. Click "Document Makeovers," then click Chapter 6. You will find a letter that contains problems and errors relating to what you've learned in this chapter about revising messages. Use the Final Draft decision tool to create an improved version of this letter. Check the message for organization, readability, clarity, and conciseness.

Even when you're pressed for time, try to maintain the schedule you laid out during the planning step of the writing process.

time for each task. Try to stick to your schedule. You want to do your best to create a perfect document, but you also want to meet your deadline and turn your work in promptly. As with every task in the writing process, practice helps—you not only become more familiar with what errors to look for but also become more skilled in identifying those errors. Look at the draft in Figure 6–5. The organization is basically sound, and the content is more or less satisfactory. However, the overall readability is poor. The message is filled with awkward language that is wordy and redundant. The revised letter is much improved.

DISTRIBUTING YOUR MESSAGE

Technology can also help you distribute your message in the most appropriate fashion.

Once you have revised, produced, and proofread your message, you are ready to distribute it. For multiple copies of your document, you can print as many as you like on an inkjet or laser printer, or you can print a single copy and reproduce it with a *photocopier*. For high-volume and complex reproduction (involving colors or photographs, for instance), you'll want to take your document to a *print shop,* a company that has the special equipment needed for such jobs.

When you need to send the same document (sales letter, invoice, or other customer communication) to a large number of people, *mail merge* automatically combines a standard version of the document with a list of names and addresses. It will produce one copy for each person on your mailing list, saving you the trouble of inserting the name and address each time. The names and addresses can come from your own customer databases or from mailing lists you rent from firms that specialize in collecting names and addresses.

Similarly, *broadcast faxing* allows you to enter mailing lists into your fax machine and transmit your document to the fax machines of all members on the list. Fax machines are indispensable for international business, particularly because they overcome the delay problems of regular mail and the time zone problems of trying to contact someone by telephone.[13]

Many companies now distribute information on CD-ROM or computer disk rather than on paper. For instance, several of Hewlett-Packard's product catalogs are available either on CD-ROM or in printed form. CD-ROMs hold a large amount of information, they're inexpensive, and their small size saves money in postage and shipping.

Of course, one of the most popular methods for distributing documents is the Internet. Most Internet browser software allows you to attach documents of all sizes and types to e-mail messages. If you are sending multiple documents or long documents over the Internet, you can use special software to encode or compress your message and reduce the file size so that it can be transmitted faster. Before doing so, however, make sure your recipients have similar software so that they can decode or uncompress the message and convert it back into its original file format.

Cushcity.com owners Gwen and Willie Richardson are e-tailers who sell Afrocentric books, videos, calendars, collectibles, toys, and educational items over the Internet. They also distribute business documents over the Internet, routinely sending e-mail messages and attachments of all sizes to employees and often to customers. This method of distribution is popular because of the speed. Mrs. Richardson says, "We have a very responsive e-mail system." Customers are especially impressed with the two-hour response time from Cushcity.

FIGURE 6–5
Poor and Improved Versions Showing Revision

Draft

In the time since I last wrote you, our new parking lot at the end of Oakcliff Avenue has been completely finished. I wanted to advise you that we're planning a little celebration on August 24, a sort of grand opening of our new parking lot. It would be appreciated if you or others from the commission could attend. This project seems to have solved the neighborhood parking problems we've all been experiencing.

So that the impact of the 80 cars parked in that lot will be minimized, we undertook the planting of more than 850 adult plants—all of them native to this area. This work has been performed exclusively by employee volunteers during their lunch hours. There was no cost to the taxpayers. While this work is not finished, the lot itself is working well and handling the overflow from our main lot. We've essentially moved all the cars associated with this company off neighborhood streets.

My dedication to good relations with our neighbors in this area is immense, so I am delighted with the opportunity to avoid any further problem with our cars filling neighborhood streets.

Annotations (draft): Unnecessary clause · Redundancy and unnecessary clause · Indefinite pronoun starter · Hedging sentence · Unnecessary clause · Wordy phrase · Camouflaged verb · Indefinite pronoun starter · Redundancy · Overly enthusiastic · Wordy phrase and negative word

Revision

Woodward Technical Labs
248 Oak Cliff Drive
San Juan Capistrano, CA 92675
(949) 696-8247
Fax: (949) 696-8249   www.woodwardlab.com

August 7, 2004

Ms. Jennifer Halter, Executive Director
San Juan Capistrano Planning Commission
8478 Ortega Hwy.
San Juan Capistrano, CA 92675

Dear Ms. Halter:

Our new parking lot at the end of Oakcliff Avenue has been completed. We're planning an opening celebration on August 24, and we invite you and others from the commission to attend. This project has solved the neighborhood parking situation.

Also, to minimize the impact of the 80 cars parked in our new lot, we have planted more than 850 adult native plants. This work has been performed exclusively by employee volunteers during their lunch hours at no cost to neighborhood taxpayers. Although the planting is not quite finished, the lot itself is effectively handling the overflow from our main lot. We've essentially moved all cars associated with Woodward off neighborhood streets.

Everyone at Woodward is dedicated to good relations with our neighbors, so we are pleased that our cars will no longer crowd neighborhood streets.

Sincerely,

Jeff Singleton
Vice President, Public Relations

Annotations (revision): Deletes all unnecessary clauses · Clarifies redundancy · Rewrites hedging sentence · Replaces wordy phrase with infinitive · Rewrites section to avoid indefinite pronoun starter · Moderates enthusiasm · Ends positively · Rewrites to avoid indefinite pronoun starter · Replaces camouflaged verb · Removes redundancy · Rewrites to avoid wordy phrase

On the Job:

SOLVING COMMUNICATION DILEMMAS AT MCDONALD'S

As a McDonald's quality control representative, David Giarla spends his day finding opportunities for improvement: A ceiling tile is stained and needs to be replaced; a cheeseburger bun is dented—probably because someone wrapped it too tightly; a storeroom is messy; a soft-serve cone is six inches high instead of the recommended three inches. Giarla calls attention to all these problems. You might expect the restaurant managers and employees to resent the criticism, but by and large they welcome his suggestions. Why? Because Giarla knows how to communicate.

You have recently joined McDonald's as a quality control representative. Like David Giarla, you cover seven or eight restaurants a day. Most of the managers are cooperative, and most of the restaurants maintain high standards. But over the past few months, you've pointed out a variety of problems to a particular McDonald's manager. You've been friendly, polite, and constructive in your suggestions, but nothing has been done to correct most of the problems. On your last visit, you warned the manager that you would have to file a negative report with headquarters if you didn't see some improvement immediately. You have decided to put your suggestions in writing and give the manager one week to take action. Here is the first draft of your letter. Using the questions that follow, analyze it according to the material in this chapter. Be prepared to explain your analysis.

Please correct the problems listed below. I will visit your facility within the next few days to monitor your progress. If nothing has been done toward rectifying these infractions of McDonald's principles of operation, you will be reported to headquarters for noncooperation and unsatisfactory levels of performance. As you know, I have mentioned these deviations from acceptable practice on previous visits. You have been given ample opportunity to comply with my suggestions. Your failure to comply suggests that you lack the necessary commitment to quality that has long been the hallmark of McDonald's restaurants.

On two occasions, I have ascertained that you are using expired ingredients in preparing hamburgers. On February 14, a package of buns with a freshness date of January 31 was used in your facility. Also, on March 2, you were using cheese that had expired by at least 10 days. McDonald's is committed to freshness. All our ingredients are freshness dated. Expired ingredients should be disposed of, not used in the preparation of products for sale to the public. For example, you might contact local charities and offer the expired items to them free of charge, provided, of course, that the ingredients do not pose a health hazard (e.g., sour milk should be thrown out). The Community Resource Center in your area can be reached by calling 555–0909. Although I have warned you before about using old ingredients, the last time I visited your facility, I found expired ingredients in the storeroom.

Your bathrooms should be refurbished and cleaned more frequently. The paper towel dispenser in the men's room was out of towels the last time I was there, and the faucet on the sink dripped. This not only runs up your water bill but also creates a bad impression for the customer. Additionally, your windows need washing. On all my visits, I have noticed fingerprints on the front door. I have never, in fact, seen your door anything but dirty. This, too, creates a negative impression. Similarly, the windows are not as clean as they might be. Also, please mop the floors more often. Nobody wants to eat in a dirty restaurant.

The most serious infraction pertains to the appearance of store personnel. Dirty uniforms are unforgivable. Also, employees, particularly those serving the public, must have clean fingernails and hands. Hair should be neatly combed, and uniforms should be carefully pressed. I realize that your restaurant is located in an economically depressed area, and I am aware that many of your employees are ethnic minorities from impoverished backgrounds and single-parent families. Perhaps you should hold a class in basic cleanliness for these people. It is likely that they have not been taught proper hygiene in their homes.

In addition, please instruct store personnel to empty the trash more frequently. The bins are constantly overflowing, making it difficult for customers to dispose of leftover food and rubbish. This is a problem both indoors and outdoors.

Also bear in mind that all patrons should be served within a few minutes of their arrival at your place of business. Waiting in line is annoying, particularly during the busy lunch hour when people are on tight schedules. Open new lines when you must in order to accommodate the flow of traffic. In addition, instruct the order takers and order fillers to work more rapidly during busy times. Employees should not be standing around chatting with each other while customers wait in line.

As I mentioned above, I will visit your facility within a few days to check on your progress toward meeting McDonald's criteria of operation. If no visible progress has been made, I will have no alternative other than to report you to top management at headquarters. If you have any questions or require clarification on any of these items, please feel free to contact me. I can be reached by calling 555–3549.

1. How would you rate this draft in terms of its content and organization?

a. Although the style of the letter needs work, the content and organization are basically okay.

b. The draft is seriously flawed in both content and organization. Extensive editing is required.

c. The content is fine, but the organization is poor.

d. The organization is fine, but the content is poor.

2. What should be done to eliminate the biased tone of the fourth paragraph?

a. Omit the last three sentences of the paragraph.

b. Omit the last three sentences and add something like the following: "Please have your employees review the videotape that deals with McDonald's standards of personal appearance."

c. Revise the last three sentences along the following lines: "Given the composition of your labor force, you may need to stress the basics of personal hygiene."

3. Which of the following is the best alternative to this sentence: "If nothing has been done toward rectifying these infractions of McDonald's principles of operation, you will be reported to headquarters for noncooperation and unsatisfactory levels of performance."

a. "If nothing has been done to correct these infractions, you will be reported to headquarters for noncompliance."

b. "If you don't shape up immediately, headquarters will hear about it."

c. "By correcting these problems promptly, you can avoid being reported to headquarters."

d. "You can preserve your unblemished reputation by acting immediately to bring your facility into compliance with McDonald's principles of operation."

4. Take a look at the third paragraph of the letter. What is its chief flaw?

a. There is no topic sentence.

b. The topic sentence is too narrow for the ideas encompassed in the paragraph.

c. The transition from the previous paragraph is poor.

d. The paragraph deals with more than one subject.

e. The topic sentence is not adequately developed with specific details in subsequent sentences.[14]

Learning Objectives Checkup

To assess your understanding of the principles in this chapter, read each learning objective and study the accompanying exercises. For fill-in items, write the missing text in the blank provided; for multiple choice items, circle the letter of the correct answer. You can check your responses against the answer key on page AK-1.

Objective 6.1: Discuss the main tasks involved in completing a business message.

1. Which of the following is *not* one of the main tasks involved in completing a business message?

a. Drafting the message

b. Revising the message

c. Producing the message

d. Proofreading the message

Objective 6.2: Explain how to evaluate the elements of your message, and indicate the order in which to evaluate them.

2. The first element of your message to evaluate is

a. The organization

b. The content

c. The style

d. The tone

3. Which sections of your message will have the greatest impact on your audience?

a. The beginning and the middle

b. The middle and the ending

c. The beginning and the ending

d. All of them

Objective 6.3: Describe four writing techniques you can use to improve the readability of your messages.

4. When it comes to sentence length, the best approach for business messages is to

a. Keep all sentences as short as possible

b. Make most of your sentences long, since you will usually have complex information to impart

c. Vary the length of your sentences

d. Aim for an average sentence length of 35 words

5. When it comes to paragraph length, the best approach for business messages is to

a. Keep paragraphs short

b. Make most of your paragraphs long, since that is the standard practice in business writing

c. Make most of your paragraphs one sentence in length

d. Aim for an average paragraph length of 200 words

6. When it comes to using lists, the best approach for business messages is to

a. Avoid using lists except where absolutely necessary

b. Make sure listed items are in parallel form

c. Use numbered lists rather than bulleted ones

d. Do all of the above

7. Which of the following is *not* an informative heading?

a. Why We Need a New Distributor

b. Five Challenges Facing Today's Distributors

c. Distributors Are Preferable to Wholesalers

d. Distributor Choices

Objective 6.4: List nine tips for making your writing clear.

8. Which of the following sentences contains hedging words?

a. It appears that we may have a problem completing the project by May 20.

b. There is a possibility that the project might be done by May 20.

c. It seems that the project could possibly miss its completion date of May 20.

d. All of the above contain hedging words.

9. Which of the following sentences lacks parallelism?
   a. Consumers can download stock research, electronically file their tax returns, create a portfolio, or choose from an array of recommended mutual funds.
   b. Consumers can download stock research, can electronically file their tax returns, create a portfolio, or they can choose from an array of recommended mutual funds.
   c. Consumers can download stock research, can electronically file their tax returns, can create a portfolio, or can choose from an array of recommended mutual funds.
   d. Consumers can download stock research, they can electronically file their tax returns, they can create a portfolio, or they can choose from an array of recommended mutual funds.

10. Which of the following sentences does *not* have a dangling modifier?
    a. Lacking brand recognition, consumers are wary of using Internet-only banks.
    b. Because Internet-only banks lack brand recognition, consumers are wary of using them.
    c. Because of a lack of brand recognition, consumers are wary of using Internet-only banks.
    d. All have dangling modifiers.

Objective 6.5: List four tips for making your messages more concise.

11. When editing for conciseness, you should look for
    a. Unnecessary words and phrases
    b. Dangling modifiers
    c. Lack of parallelism
    d. Awkward references

12. Which of the following is *not* an example of a redundancy?
    a. Visible to the eye
    b. Free gift

c. Very useful
d. Repeat again

Objective 6.6: Describe four characteristics of a successful design and explain how four specific design elements can change a document's appearance.

13. A well-designed document
    a. Includes a wide variety of typefaces
    b. Balances the space devoted to text, artwork, and white space
    c. Fills as much of the available space as possible with text and art
    d. Does all of the above

14. The best placement for headings longer than two lines is
    a. Flush left
    b. Centered
    c. Flush right
    d. Justified

15. Type that is "justified" is
    a. Flush on the left and ragged on the right
    b. Flush on the right and ragged on the left
    c. Flush on both the left and the right
    d. Centered

16. A sans serif typeface would be best for
    a. The headings in a report
    b. The text of a report
    c. Both the headings and the text of a report
    d. Things like footnotes and endnotes

Objective 6.7: Discuss the types of errors to look for when proofreading.

17. When proofreading, you look for errors in
    a. Spelling and punctuation
    b. Grammar and usage
    c. Typography and format
    d. All of the above

Apply Your Knowledge

1. Why is it important to let your draft "age" a day before you begin the editing process?
2. Given the choice of only one, would you prefer to use a grammar checker or a spell checker? Why?
3. When you are designing a formal business letter, which design elements do you have to consider and which are optional?
4. How does design contribute to a document's overall effectiveness?
5. **Ethical Choices** What are the ethical implications of using underlining, all capitals, and other hard-to-read type styles in a document explaining how customers can appeal the result of a decision made in the company's favor during a dispute?

Practice Your Knowledge

DOCUMENTS FOR ANALYSIS

Read the following documents; then (1) analyze the strengths and weaknesses of each sentence and (2) revise each document so that it follows the guidelines in Chapters 4 through 6.

DOCUMENT 6.A

The move to our new offices will take place over this coming weekend. For everything to run smooth, everyone will have to clean out their own desk and pack up the contents in boxes that will be provided. You will need to take everything off the walls too, and please pack it along with the boxes.

If you have a lot of personal belongings, you should bring them home with you. Likewise with anything valuable. I do not mean to infer that items will be stolen, irregardless it is better to be safe than sorry.

On Monday, we will be unpacking, putting things away, and then get back to work. The least amount of disruption is anticipated by us, if everyone does their part. Hopefully, there will be no negative affects on production schedules, and current deadlines will be met.

DOCUMENT 6.B

Dear Ms. Giraud:

Enclosed herewith please find the manuscript for your book, Careers in Woolgathering. After perusing the first two chapters of your 1,500-page manuscript, I was forced to conclude that the subject matter, handicrafts and artwork using wool fibers, is not coincident with the publishing program of Framingham Press, which to this date has issued only works on business endeavors, avoiding all other topics completely.

Although our firm is unable to consider your impressive work at the present time, I have taken the liberty of recording some comments on some of the pages. I am of the opinion that any feedback that a writer can obtain from those well versed in the publishing realm can only serve to improve the writer's authorial skills.

In view of the fact that your residence is in the Boston area, might I suggest that you secure an appointment with someone of high editorial stature at the Cambridge Heritage Press, which I believe might have something of an interest in works of the nature you have produced.

Wishing you the best of luck in your literary endeavors, I remain.

Arthur J. Cogswell
Editor

DOCUMENT 6.C

For delicious, air-popped popcorn, please read the following instructions: The popper is designed to pop 1/2 cup of popcorn kernels at one time. Never add more than 1/2 cup. A half cup of corn will produce three to four quarts of popcorn. More batches may be made separately after completion of the first batch. Popcorn is popped by hot air. Oil or shortening is not needed for popping corn. Add only popcorn kernels to the popping chamber. Standard grades of popcorn are recommended for use. Premium or gourmet type popping corns may be used. Ingredients such as oil, shortening, butter, margarine, or salt should never be added to the popping chamber. The popper, with popping chute in position, may be preheated for two minutes before adding the corn. Turn the popper off before adding the corn. Use electricity safely and wisely. Observe safety precautions when using the popper. Do not touch the popper when it is hot. The popper should not be left unattended when it is plugged into an outlet. Do not use the popper if it or its cord has been damaged. Do not use the popper if it is not working properly. Before using the first time, wash the chute and butter/measuring cup in hot soapy water. Use a dishcloth or sponge. Wipe the outside of the popper base. Use a damp cloth. Dry the base. Do not immerse the popper base in water or other liquid. Replace the chute and butter/measuring cup. The popper is ready to use.

Exercises

For live links to all websites discussed in this chapter, visit this text's website at www.prenhall.com/thill. Just log on, select Chapter 6, and click on "Student Resources." Locate the page or the URL related to the material in the text. For "Learning More on the Web" exercises, you'll also find navigational directions. Click on the live link to the site.

6.1 Message Readability: Writing Paragraphs Rewrite the following paragraph to vary the length of the sentences and to shorten the paragraph so that it looks more inviting to readers:

> *Although major league baseball remains popular, more people are attending minor league baseball games because they can spend less on admission, snacks, and parking and still enjoy the excitement of America's pastime. Connecticut, for example, has three AA minor league teams, including the New Haven Ravens, who are affiliated with the St. Louis Cardinals; the Norwich Navigators, who are affiliated with the New York Yankees; and the New Britain Rock Cats, who are affiliated with the Minnesota Twins. These teams play in relatively small stadiums, so fans are close enough to see and hear everything, from the swing of the bat connecting with the ball to the thud of the ball landing in the outfielder's glove. Best of all, the cost of a family outing to see rising stars play in a local minor league game is just a fraction of what the family would spend to attend a major league game in a much larger, more crowded stadium.*

6.2 Message Readability: Using Bullets Rewrite the following paragraph using a bulleted list:

> *With our alarm system, you'll have a 24-hour security guard who signals the police at the suggestion of an intruder. You'll also appreciate the computerized scanning device that determines exactly where and when the intrusion occurred. No need to worry about electrical failure, either, thanks to our backup response unit.[15]*

6.3 Revising Messages: Clarity Break these sentences into shorter ones by adding more periods:

a. The next time you write something, check your average sentence length in a 100-word passage, and if your sentences average more than 16 to 20 words, see whether you can break up some of the sentences.

b. Don't do what the village blacksmith did when he instructed his apprentice as follows: "When I take the shoe out of the fire, I'll lay it on the anvil, and when I nod my head, you hit it with the hammer." The apprentice did just as he was told, and now he's the village blacksmith.

c. Unfortunately, no gadget will produce excellent writing, but using a yardstick like the Fog Index gives us some guideposts to follow for making writing easier to read because its two factors remind us to use short sentences and simple words.

d. Know the flexibility of the written word and its power to convey an idea, and know how to make your words behave so that your readers will understand.

e. Words mean different things to different people, and a word such as *block* may mean city block, butcher block, engine block, auction block, or several other things.

6.4   **Revising Messages: Conciseness** Cross out unnecessary words in the following phrases:

a. Consensus of opinion.
b. New innovations.
c. Long period of time.
d. At a price of $50.
e. Still remains.

6.5   **Revising Messages: Conciseness** Revise the following sentences, using shorter, simpler words:

a. The antiquated calculator is ineffectual for solving sophisticated problems.
b. It is imperative that the pay increments be terminated before an inordinate deficit is accumulated.
c. There was unanimity among the executives that Ms. Jackson's idiosyncrasies were cause for a mandatory meeting with the company's personnel director.
d. The impending liquidation of the company's assets was cause for jubilation among the company's competitors.
e. The expectations of the president for a stock dividend were accentuated by the preponderance of evidence that the company was in good financial condition.

6.6   **Revising Messages: Conciseness** Use infinitives as substitutes for the overly long phrases in these sentences:

a. For living, I require money.
b. They did not find sufficient evidence for believing in the future.
c. Bringing about the destruction of a dream is tragic.

6.7   **Revising Messages: Conciseness** Rephrase the following in fewer words:

a. In the near future.
b. In the event that.
c. In order that.
d. For the purpose of.
e. With regard to.
f. It may be that.
g. In very few cases.
h. With reference to.
i. At the present time.
j. There is no doubt that.

6.8   **Revising Messages: Conciseness** Condense these sentences to as few words as possible:

a. We are of the conviction that writing is important.
b. In all probability, we're likely to have a price increase.
c. Our goals include making a determination about that in the near future.
d. When all is said and done at the conclusion of this experiment, I'd like to summarize the final windup.
e. After a trial period of three weeks, during which time she worked for a total of 15 full working days, we found her work was sufficiently satisfactory so that we offered her full-time work.

6.9   **Revising Messages: Modifiers** Remove all the unnecessary modifiers from these sentences:

a. Tremendously high pay increases were given to the extraordinarily skilled and extremely conscientious employees.
b. The union's proposals were highly inflationary, extremely demanding, and exceptionally bold.

6.10   **Revising Messages: Hedging** Rewrite these sentences so that they no longer contain any hedging:

a. It would appear that someone apparently entered illegally.
b. It may be possible that sometime in the near future the situation is likely to improve.
c. Your report seems to suggest that we might be losing money.
d. I believe Nancy apparently has somewhat greater influence over employees in the word-processing department.
e. It seems as if this letter of resignation means you might be leaving us.

6.11   **Revising Messages: Indefinite Starters** Rewrite these sentences to eliminate the indefinite starters:

a. There are several examples here to show that Elaine can't hold a position very long.
b. It would be greatly appreciated if every employee would make a generous contribution to Mildred Cook's retirement party.
c. It has been learned in Washington today from generally reliable sources that an important announcement will be made shortly by the White House.
d. There is a rule that states that we cannot work overtime without permission.
e. It would be great if you could work late for the next three Saturdays.

6.12   **Revising Messages: Parallelism** Present the ideas in these sentences in parallel form:

a. Mr. Hill is expected to lecture three days a week, to counsel two days a week, and must write for publication in his spare time.
b. She knows not only accounting, but she also reads Latin.
c. Both applicants had families, college degrees, and were in their thirties, with considerable accounting experience but few social connections.
d. This book was exciting, well written, and held my interest.
e. Don is both a hard worker and he knows bookkeeping.

6.13   **Revising Messages: Awkward Pointers** Revise the following sentences to delete the awkward pointers:

a. The vice president in charge of sales and the production manager are responsible for the keys to 34A and 35A, respectively.
b. The keys to 34A and 35A are in executive hands, with the former belonging to the vice president in charge of sales and the latter belonging to the production manager.
c. The keys to 34A and 35A have been given to the production manager, with the aforementioned keys being gold embossed.
d. A laser printer and a dot-matrix printer were delivered to John and Megan, respectively.
e. The walnut desk is more expensive than the oak desk, the former costing $300 more than the latter.

6.14 **Revising Messages: Dangling Modifiers** Rewrite these sentences to clarify the dangling modifiers:
  a. Running down the railroad tracks in a cloud of smoke, we watched the countryside glide by.
  b. Lying on the shelf, Ruby saw the seashell.
  c. Based on the information, I think we should buy the property.
  d. Being cluttered and filthy, Sandy took the whole afternoon to clean up her desk.
  e. After proofreading every word, the memo was ready to be signed.

6.15 **Revising Messages: Noun Sequences** Rewrite the following sentences to eliminate the long strings of nouns:
  a. The focus of the meeting was a discussion of the bank interest rate deregulation issue.
  b. Following the government task force report recommendations, we are revising our job applicant evaluation procedures.
  c. The production department quality assurance program components include employee training, supplier cooperation, and computerized detection equipment.
  d. The supermarket warehouse inventory reduction plan will be implemented next month.
  e. The State University business school graduate placement program is one of the best in the country.

6.16 **Revising Messages: Sentence Structure** Rearrange the following sentences to bring the subjects closer to their verbs:
  a. Trudy, when she first saw the bull pawing the ground, ran.
  b. It was Terri who, according to Ted, who is probably the worst gossip in the office (Tom excepted), mailed the wrong order.
  c. William Oberstreet, in his book *Investment Capital Reconsidered*, writes of the mistakes that bankers through the decades have made.
  d. Judy Schimmel, after passing up several sensible investment opportunities, despite the warnings of her friends and family, invested her inheritance in a jojoba plantation.
  e. The president of U-Stor-It, which was on the brink of bankruptcy after the warehouse fire, the worst tragedy in the history of the company, prepared a press announcement.

6.17 **Revising Messages: Camouflaged Verbs** Rewrite each sentence so that the verbs are no longer camouflaged:
  a. Adaptation to the new rules was performed easily by the employees.
  b. The assessor will make a determination of the tax due.
  c. Verification of the identity of the employees must be made daily.
  d. The board of directors made a recommendation that Mr. Ronson be assigned to a new division.
  e. The auditing procedure on the books was performed by the vice president.

6.18 **Producing Messages: Design Elements** Look back at your revised version of Document 6.C (see exercise under "Documents for Analysis"). Which design elements could you use to make this document more readable? Produce your revision of Document 6.C using your selected design elements. Then experiment by changing one of the design elements. How does the change affect readability? Exchange documents with another student and critique each other's work.

6.19 **Internet** Visit the stock market page of Bloomberg's website at www.bloomberg.com and evaluate the use of design in presenting the latest news. What design improvements can you suggest to enhance readability of the information posted on this page?

6.20 **Teamwork** Team up with another student and exchange your revised versions of Document 6.A, 6.B, or 6.C (see "Practice Your Knowledge, Documents for Analysis"). Review the assignment to be sure the instructions are clear. Then read and critique your teammate's revision to see whether it can be improved. After you have critiqued each other's work, take a moment to examine the way you expressed your comments and the way you felt listening to the other student's comments. Can you identify ways to improve the critiquing process in situations such as this?

6.21 **Proofreading Messages: E-Mail** Proofread the following e-mail message and revise it to correct any problems you find:

Our final company orrientation of the year will be held on Dec. 20. In preparation for this sesssion, please order 20 copies of the Policy handbook, the confindentiality agreenemt, the employee benefits Manual, please let me know if you anticipate any delays in obtaining these materials.

6.22 **Ethical Choices** Three of your company's five plants exceeded their expense budgets last month. You want all the plants to operate within their budgets from now on. You were thinking of using broadcast faxing to let all five plants see the memo you are sending to the managers of the three overbudget plants. Is this a good idea? Why or why not?

Expand Your Knowledge

LEARNING MORE ON THE WEB

Write It Right: Rethink and Revise www.powa.org
    Are you sure that readers perceive your written message as you intended? If you want help revising a message that you're completing, use the Paradigm Online Writing Assistant (POWA). With this interactive writer's guide, you can select topics to get tips on how to edit your work, reshape your thoughts, and rewrite for clarity. Read discussions about perfecting your

writing skills, and for practice, complete one of the many online activities provided to reinforce what you've learned. Or select the Forum to "talk" about writing. At POWA's website, you'll learn how to improve the final draft of your message.

ACTIVITIES

Go to www.powa.org for advice on organizing ideas, choosing the best word and appropriate style, and placing each paragraph effectively so that your message achieves its purpose:

1. Why is it better to write out ideas in a rough format and later reread your message to revise its content? When revising your message, what questions can you ask about your writing?
2. Name the four elements of the "writing context." Imagine that you're the reader of your message. What questions might you ask?

3. When you revise a written message, what is the purpose of "tightening"? What is one way to tighten your writing as you complete a message?

EXPLORING THE WEB ON YOUR OWN

Review these chapter-related websites on your own to learn more about writing business messages.

1. Take the fog out of your documents by visiting the Training Post, www.trainingpost.org/3–2-res.htm, and following the hotlinks to the Gunning Fog Index.
2. Produce flawless messages by reviewing the material at the Guide to Grammar and Writing, ccc.commnet.edu/grammar.
3. Need help with grammar? Visit the Grammar Slammer at englishplus.com/grammar and find out why it promotes itself as the complete English Grammar Resource.

Learn Interactively

INTERACTIVE STUDY GUIDE

Go to the Companion Website at www.prenhall.com/bovee. For Chapter 6, take advantage of the interactive "Study Guide" to test your knowledge of the chapter. Get instant feedback on whether you need additional studying. Also, visit this site's "Study Hall" where you'll find an abundance of valuable resources that will help you succeed in this course.

Conjunctions, and Articles." Take the Pretest to determine whether you have any weak areas. Review those areas in the Refresher Course, and take the Follow-Up Test to check your grasp of prepositions and conjunctions. For advanced practice, take the Advanced Test. Finally, for additional reinforcement, go to the "Improve Your Grammar, Mechanics, and Usage" section that follows, and complete those exercises.

PEAK PERFORMANCE GRAMMAR AND MECHANICS

To improve your skill with prepositions and conjunctions, visit this text's website at www.prenhall.com/onekey. Click "Peak Performance Grammar and Mechanics," then click "Prepositions,

Improve Your Grammar, Mechanics, and Usage

The following exercises help you improve your knowledge of and power over English grammar, mechanics, and usage. Turn to the "Handbook of Grammar, Mechanics, and Usage" at the end of this textbook and review all of Sections 1.6 (Other Parts of Speech). Then look at the following 10 items. Underline the preferred choice within each set of parentheses. (Answers to these exercises appear on page AK-3.)

1. Where was your argument (*leading to, leading*)?
2. I wish he would get (*off, off of*) the phone.
3. U.S. Mercantile must become (*aware, aware of*) and sensitive to its customers' concerns.
4. Dr. Namaguchi will be talking (*with, to*) the marketing class, but she has no time for questions.

5. Matters like this are decided after thorough discussion (*among, between*) all seven department managers.
6. We can't wait (*on, for*) their decision much longer.
7. Their computer is similar (*to, with*) ours.
8. This model is different (*than, from*) the one we ordered.
9. She is active (*in not only, not only in*) a civic group but also in an athletic organization.
10. She had neither the preferred educational background, nor (*did she have suitable experience, the suitable experience*).

For additional exercises focusing on prepositions, conjunctions, and articles go to www.prenhall.com/thill and select "Handbook of Grammar, Mechanics, and Usage Practice Sessions."

Part III

Writing Letters, Memos, E-Mail, and Other Brief Messages

Chapter 7

Writing Routine Messages

Learning Objectives

AFTER STUDYING THIS CHAPTER, YOU WILL BE ABLE TO

1 Apply the three-step writing process to routine messages

2 Illustrate the strategy for writing routine requests

3 Discuss the differences among three types of routine requests

4 Illustrate the strategy for writing routine replies and positive messages

5 Explain the main differences in messages granting a claim when the company, the customer, or a third party is at fault

6 Outline how best to protect yourself when referring to a candidate's shortcomings in a recommendation letter

7 Describe the importance of goodwill messages, and describe how to make them effective

On the Job:

COMMUNICATING AT CAMPBELL SOUP

KEEPING MILLIONS OF PEOPLE HAPPY, ONE SPOONFUL AT A TIME

You might say that Karen Donohue is in the business of solving problems. As supervisor of consumer response at Campbell Soup Company, she's in charge of answering consumer questions and responding to consumer complaints. She needs not only strong communication skills but also a special talent for working with people—a lot of people.

Campbell started selling high-quality condensed soups in 1869, soon after the Civil War, and ever since, the company has been evolving to fit the changing marketplace. Its line of condensed soups has expanded to include contemporary varieties, and Campbell's Healthy Request soups now combine great taste with less sodium, cholesterol, fat, and calories. Besides its well-known Campbell's Soup brands, the company markets Pace picante sauce, Pepperidge Farm cookies, Franco-American gravies and pastas, V8 vegetable juices, Swanson broths, and Godiva chocolate.

Many of the products familiar in the United States are offered internationally. In fact, the Campbell name is known in practically every country around the world. And to respond to cultural differences, Campbell has introduced regional varieties, such as Watercress and Duck-Gizzard soup (in China) and Cream of Chili Poblano soup (in Mexico). Every second of every hour, consumers around the world

The people at Campbell Soup Company do their best to communicate positive messages to consumers and strive to maintain good relationships with fellow employees and outside contacts. All their messages focus on clearly stating the main idea while showing a genuine understanding of the audience.

buy 100 packages (cans, envelopes, or boxes) of Campbell's products—more than 8.6 million purchases every day.

Working with customers can be a challenge in any business, but with such a huge customer base, Donohue and her team of specialists have their work cut out for them. They provide an important link between the public and the research kitchens, and they act as the company's eyes and ears. In her key position, Donohue not only relays important information to company managers but also makes sure that consumers are satisfied. Whenever people write, phone, or send e-mail, she's in charge of making sure their questions and complaints are answered satisfactorily.

Like so many companies these days, Campbell uses the Internet for two-way communication with its customers. Its homepage links to recipes, financial and investment news, educational support programs, an online store, and Donohue's consumer response center. Donohue's team answers frequently asked questions (for example: How many Os are in a 15-ounce can of Spaghetti-Os? Answer: 1,750) and invites consumers to e-mail other questions and comments. If anyone knows about the importance of routine messages, it is Karen Donohue.[1]

www.campbellsoup.com

USING THE THREE-STEP WRITING PROCESS FOR ROUTINE MESSAGES

Whether you're congratulating an employee on a job well done, requesting information from another firm, or responding to customers, like Campbell's Karen Donohue, you'll compose a lot of routine messages in the course of everyday business. That's because most business messages pertain to routine matters on any number of topics, including products, operations, company policy, claims, credit, employees, and so on.

This chapter discusses routine messages in two sections. First, you'll learn about routine requests. You'll study a helpful direct-approach strategy for organizing these messages, and then you'll examine various examples of typical business requests. Second, you'll look at routine replies and positive messages. You'll see how the direct-approach strategy is applied to these routine messages before taking a closer look at various examples. Figure 7–1 details the types of routine messages discussed in this chapter.

Routine messages are rarely long, nor are they very complex. Even so, to produce the best messages possible, you'll want to apply the three-step writing process.

Step 1: Planning Routine Messages

Even for routine situations, you need to analyze, investigate, and adapt your messages.

As with any business message, planning routine messages means analyzing your purpose and audience, gathering information, and adapting your message to your readers. However, this planning step may take only a few moments for routine messages. Start by analyzing your purpose to make sure that it's specific and worth pursuing at this time. Also, think a moment about your readers. Are you sure they'll receive your message positively (or at least neutrally)? Most routine messages are of interest to your readers because they contain information necessary to conduct day-to-day business. Even so, you may need to discover more about audience attitudes or needs in order to gauge your audience's probable reaction.

Next, gather information to learn exactly what your audience needs to know. Do you have all the relevant information? Do you need to take a little time to gather more?

Finally, adapt your routine messages to your readers. Consider whether your message should be written, rather than handled in a quick phone call or by walking down the hall for a brief chat. If so, select the most appropriate format (memo, letter, e-mail). Of course, you'll want to establish or maintain a good relationship with your audience, so be sure to use the "you" attitude and keep your language positive and polite.

FIGURE 7–1
Routine Messages

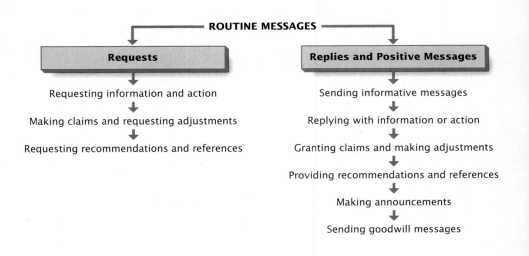

Step 2: Writing Routine Messages

Organizing and composing routine messages can go rather quickly. Your main idea may already be fairly well defined. Just be sure you stick to it by limiting the scope of your message. Cover only relevant points and group them in the most logical fashion. Since your readers will be interested or neutral, you can usually adopt the direct approach: Open with a clear statement of the main idea, include all necessary details in the body, and then close cordially. However, if you're not familiar with your audience's cultural differences, check to make sure your readers prefer direct organization. When you're addressing an audience with minimal cultural differences, keep your tone conversational and use plain English.

Organize your routine messages according to the direct approach.

Step 3: Completing Routine Messages

No matter how short or straightforward your message, make it professional by allowing plenty of time for revision, production, and proofreading. First, revise your routine message for overall effect. Evaluate your content and organization to make sure you've said what you want to say in the order you want to say it. Review your message's readability. Edit and rewrite routine messages for conciseness and clarity. Second, design your document to suit your audience. Choose effective design elements and appropriate delivery methods. Finally, proofread the final version of your routine message. Look for typos, errors in spelling and mechanics, alignment problems, poor print quality, and so on.

Just as you do for other messages, you need to revise, produce, and proofread routine messages.

DEVELOPING ROUTINE REQUESTS

Whenever you ask for something—information, action, products, adjustments, references—you are making a request. A request is routine if it's part of the normal course of business and you anticipate that your audience will want to comply. Be careful not to make unnecessary requests. If you can find information yourself, don't burden others and risk your credibility by asking someone else to find it for you. But when you must make a routine request, make sure it's efficient and effective.

Strategy for Routine Requests

Like all routine messages, routine requests may be thought of as having three parts: an opening, a body, and a close. Using the direct approach, you place your main idea (a clear statement of the request) in the opening. You use the middle to give details and justify your request. Then you close by requesting specific action and concluding cordially (see Figure 7–2). As you prepare your routine requests, keep in mind that despite their simple organization, they can still cause ill will if your wording is ambiguous or your tone is discourteous. In fact, even the briefest note can create confusion and hard feelings. As with any business message, keep your purpose in mind. Ask yourself what you want readers to do or to understand as a result of reading your message.

For routine requests and positive messages, you
- *State the request or main idea*
- *Give necessary details*
- *Close with a cordial request for specific action*

State Your Request Up Front   Begin routine requests by placing your request first—up front is where it stands out and gets the most attention. However, getting right to the point should not be interpreted as a license to be abrupt or tactless:

Keep your direct approach from being abrupt or tactless.

- **Pay attention to tone.** Even though you expect a favorable response, the tone of your initial request is important. Instead of demanding action ("Send me your catalog no. 33A"), soften your request with words such as *please* or *I would appreciate.*

- **Assume your audience will comply.** An impatient demand for rapid service isn't necessary. Generally, assume that your audience will go along with your request once they understand the reason for it.

FIGURE 7–2
The Parts of Routine Messages

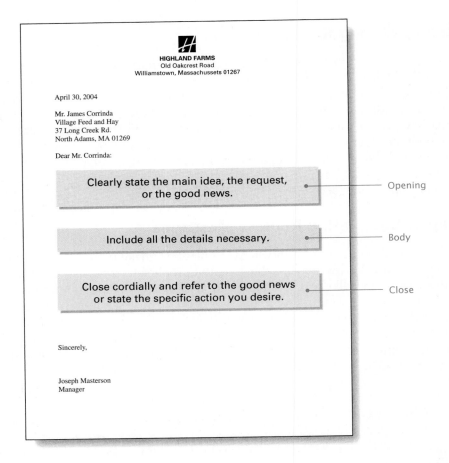

The figure shows a letter with the following content:

HIGHLAND FARMS
Old Oakcrest Road
Williamstown, Massachussets 01267

April 30, 2004

Mr. James Corrinda
Village Feed and Hay
37 Long Creek Rd.
North Adams, MA 01269

Dear Mr. Corrinda:

Clearly state the main idea, the request, or the good news. — Opening

Include all the details necessary. — Body

Close cordially and refer to the good news or state the specific action you desire. — Close

Sincerely,

Joseph Masterson
Manager

- **Avoid beginning with personal introductions.** Don't be tempted to begin your request with a personal introduction such as "I am the consumer response supervisor at Campbell Soup Company, and I am looking for information that . . ." Karen Donohue knows that this type of beginning buries the main idea, so the request may get lost.

- **Be specific.** State precisely what you want. For example, if you request the latest census figures from a government agency, be sure to say whether you want a page or two of summary figures or a detailed report running several thousand pages.

Although a direct question in your message requires a question mark, keep in mind that a polite request in question form requires no question mark: "Would you please help us determine whether Kate Kingsley is a suitable applicant for this position." (See section 2.2 in the "Handbook of Grammar, Mechanics, and Usage" at the end of this text.)

In the middle section of the request, give the details of your request.

Explain and Justify Your Request   Use the middle section of your message to explain your initial request. Make the explanation a smooth and logical outgrowth of your opening remarks. For example, you might show how your readers could benefit from complying. When Karen Donohue requests product information from unit managers she also tells them why she needs the information and explains how they might benefit from granting the request. For instance, Donohue might write, "By providing the customer response department with complete nutritional information on each of your products, you help us answer questions from your current and potential customers and you help them make informed choices."

Numbered lists help readers sort through multiple related items or multiple requests.

Whether you're writing a formal letter or a simple e-mail, you can use the middle section of your routine request to list a series of questions. This method is particularly useful if your inquiry concerns machinery or complex equipment. For instance, you might ask about technical specifications, exact dimensions, and the precise use of the equipment. Be sure to break down multiple requests, and when requesting several items or answers, number them and list them in logical order or in descending order of importance. When using a series of questions, just keep a few basics in mind:

- **Ask the most important questions first.** If cost is your main concern, you might begin with a question such as "What is the cost for shipping the merchandise by air versus shipping it by truck?" Then you may want to ask more specific but related questions about, say, the cost of shipping partial orders.

- **Ask only relevant questions.** So that your request can be handled quickly, ask only questions central to your main request. If your questions require simple yes-or-no answers, you might provide readers with a form or with boxes to check. If you need more elaborate answers, pose open-ended questions. "How fast can you ship the merchandise?" is more likely to elicit the information you want than "Can you ship the merchandise?"

- **Deal with only one topic per question.** If you have an unusual or complex request, list the request and provide supporting details in a separate, short paragraph. You may even use paragraph headings to make your reader's job easier.

Former fashion model B. Smith hosts *B. Smith with Style,* a nationally syndicated television series. She also has written two books on entertaining, has created her own line of bedding for Bed, Bath, and Beyond stores, has created four collections for Vogue Patterns, and owns three successful restaurants. Whether asking a celebrity to make a guest appearance on her television program or requesting information about restaurant locations, she knows that requests and questions are part of doing business.

Request Specific Action in a Courteous Close   Close your message with three important elements: (1) a specific request, (2) information about how you can be reached, and (3) an expression of appreciation or goodwill. Use the closing to request a specific action and to ask that readers respond by a specific and appropriate time ("Please send the figures by April 5 so that I can return first-quarter results to you before the May 20 conference"). Help your reader respond easily by including your phone number, office hours, and other contact information.

Conclude your message by sincerely expressing your goodwill and appreciation. However, don't thank the reader "in advance" for cooperating. If the reader's reply warrants a word of thanks, send it after you've received the reply.

Close with
- A request for some specific action
- Information about how you can be reached
- An expression of appreciation

Types of Routine Requests

The various types of routine requests are innumerable, from asking favors to requesting credit. However, many of the routine messages that you'll be writing will likely fall into major categories. The following sections discuss three of these categories: requesting information and action, making claims and requesting adjustments, and requesting recommendations and references.

Requesting Information and Action   When you need to know about something, to elicit an opinion from someone, or to suggest a simple action, you usually need only ask. In essence, simple requests say, "This is what I want to know or what I want you to do, why I'm making the request, and why it may be in your interest to help me." If your reader can do what you want, such a straightforward request gets the job done with a minimum of fuss.

Follow the direct approach: Start with a clear statement of your reason for writing. In the middle, provide whatever explanation is needed to justify your request. Then close with a specific account of what you expect, and include a deadline if appropriate. In more complex situations, readers might be unwilling to respond unless they understand how the request benefits them, so be sure to include this information in your explanation.

When making a routine request, say
- What you want to know
- Why you want to know
- Why it is in the reader's interest to help you

Asking Company Insiders   Requests to fellow employees are often oral and rather casual. However, as long as you avoid writing frequent, long, or unneeded messages, sending a clear, thoughtfully written memo or e-mail message can save time and questions by helping readers understand precisely what you want. Just be sure your message is simple and straightforward. Don't try to be fancy or to impress your colleagues with big words.

Keep internal requests plain and direct.

The memo in Figure 7–3 was sent to all employees of Ace Hardware. It seeks employee input about a new wellness and benefits program and about a new fee. The tone is matter-of-fact, and the memo assumes some shared background, which is appropriate when communicating about a routine matter to someone in the same company. As discussed in Chapter 4, both memos and e-mail messages have efficient headings that spell out who the message is for (*To:*), who wrote it (*From:*), when it was written (*Date:*), and what it's about (*Subject:*). For more information on formatting memos and other business messages, see Appendix A.

Asking Company Outsiders   Business writers often ask businesses, customers, or others outside their organization to provide information or to take some simple action: attend a meeting, return an information card, endorse a document, confirm an address, or supplement information on an order. Such requests are often in letter form, although some are sent via e-mail. These messages are usually short and simple, like this request for information:

Make sure your external requests are brief and straightforward.

Makes overall request in polite question form (no question mark)

Keeps reader's interest by hinting at possibility of future business

Avoids making an overly broad request by using a series of specific questions

Itemizes questions in a logical sequence

Avoids useless yes-or-no answers by including open-ended questions

Specifies a time limit in the courteous close.

> Would you please supply me with information about the lawn services you provide. Pralle Realty owns approximately 27 pieces of rental property in College Station, and we're looking for a lawn service to handle all of them. We are making a commitment to provide quality housing in this college town, and we are looking for an outstanding firm to work with us.
>
> **1. Lawn care:** What is your annual charge for each location for lawn maintenance, including mowing, fertilizing, and weed control?
>
> **2. Shrubbery:** What is your annual charge for each location for the care of deciduous and evergreen bushes, including pruning, fertilizing, and replacing as necessary?
>
> **3. Contract:** How does Agri-Lawn Service structure such large contracts? What additional information do you need from us?
>
> Please let us hear from you by February 15. We want to have a lawn-care firm in place by March 15.

A more complex request might require not only greater detail but information on how responding will benefit the reader.

The purpose of some routine requests to customers is to reestablish communication.

Sometimes businesses need to reestablish a relationship with former customers or suppliers. In many cases, when customers are unhappy about some purchase or about the way they were treated, they don't complain; they simply stay away from the offending business. Thus, a letter of inquiry might encourage customers to use idle credit accounts, offering them an opportunity to register their displeasure and then move on to a good relationship. In addition, a customer's response to such an inquiry may provide the company with insights into ways to improve its products and customer service. Even if they have no complaint, customers still welcome the personal attention. Such an inquiry to a customer might begin this way:

> When a good charge customer like you has not bought anything from us in six months, we wonder why. Is there something we can do to serve you better?

FIGURE 7–3
Effective Memo Requesting Action from Company Insiders

Planning

Writing

Completing

Analyze the Situation
Purpose is to request feedback from fellow employees.

Gather Information
Gather accurate, complete information on program benefits and local gym.

Adapt to the Audience
Office memo or e-mail is appropriate medium. Use "you" attitude, and make responding easy.

1

Organize the Information
Main idea is saving money while staying healthy. Save time and meet audience expectations using the direct approach.

Compose the Message
Keep style informal but businesslike. Using a "we" attitude includes readers in the decision-making process.

2

Revise the Message
Keep it brief—weed out overly long words and phrases. Avoid unnecessary details.

Produce the Message
No need for fancy design elements in this memo. Include a response form.

Proofread the Message
Review carefully for both content and typographical errors.

3

Ace Hardware Corporation

INTERNAL MEMORANDUM

TO: All Employees
FROM: Tony Ramirez, Human Resources
DATE: October 15, 2003
SUBJ: New Wellness Program Opportunity

The benefits package committee has asked me to contact everyone about an opportunity to save money and stay healthier in the bargain. As you know, we've been meeting to decide on changes in our benefits package. Last week, we sent you a memo detailing the Synergy Wellness Program.

In addition to the package as described in the memo (life, major medical, dental, hospitalization), Synergy has sweetened the pot by offering Ace a 10 percent discount. To meet the requirements for the discount, we have to show proof that at least 25 percent of our employees participate in aerobic exercise at least three times a week for at least 20 minutes. (Their actuarial tables show a resulting 10 percent reduction in claims.)

After looking around, we discovered a gymnasium just a few blocks south on Haley Boulevard. Sports Midwest will give our employees unlimited daytime access to their indoor track, gym, and pool for a group fee that comes to approximately $4.50 per month per employee if at least half of us sign up.

In addition to using the track and pools, we can play volleyball, take jazzercise, form our own intramural basketball teams, and much more. Our spouses and children can also participate at a deeply discounted monthly fee. If you have questions, please e-mail or call me (or any member of the committee). Let us know your wishes on the following form.

Sign and return the following no later than Friday, October 29.

===

_____ Yes, I will participate in the Synergy Wellness program and pay $4.50 a month.
_____ Yes, I am interested in a discounted family membership.
_____ No, I prefer not to participate.

Signature _____

Employee ID Number _____

Routes message efficiently, with all needed information

Presents the situation that makes the inquiry necessary

Provides an easy-to-use response form

States purpose in opening to avoid wasting busy readers' time

Lists reader benefits and requests action

Similar inquiry letters are sent from one business to another. For example, a sales representative of a housewares distributor might send the same type of letter to a retailer.

Making Claims and Requesting Adjustments   When you're dissatisfied with a company's product or service, you make a **claim** (a formal complaint) or request an **adjustment** (a claim settlement). Although a phone call or visit may solve the problem, a written claim letter is better because it documents your dissatisfaction. However, even though your first reaction to a clumsy mistake or a defective product is likely to be anger or frustration, the person reading your letter probably had nothing to do with the problem. So a courteous, clear, concise explanation will impress your reader much more favorably than an abusive, angry letter.

In most cases, and especially in your first letter, assume that a fair adjustment will be made, and follow the plan for direct requests. Begin with a straightforward statement of the problem. In the middle section, give a complete, specific explanation of the details. Provide any information an adjuster would need to verify your complaint about faulty merchandise or unsatisfactory service. In your closing, politely request specific action or convey a sincere desire to find a solution. And don't forget to suggest that the business relationship will continue if the problem is solved satisfactorily.

Companies usually accept the customer's explanation of what's wrong, so ethically it's important to be entirely honest when filing claims. Also, be prepared to back up your claim with invoices, sales receipts, canceled checks, dated correspondence, catalog descriptions, and any other relevant documents. Send copies and keep the originals for your files.

If the remedy is obvious, tell your reader exactly what will return the company to your good graces—for example, an exchange of merchandise for the right item or a refund if the item is out of stock. In some cases you might ask the reader to resolve the problem. However, if you're uncertain about the precise nature of the trouble, you could ask the company to make an assessment. But be sure to supply your contact information and the best time to call, so that the company can discuss the situation with you if necessary.

The letter in Figure 7–4 was written to a gas and electric company. As you read the draft, compare its tone with the tone of the revised letter. If you were the person receiving the complaint, which version would you respond to more favorably? Most people would react much more favorably to the revised version. A rational, clear, and courteous approach is best for any routine request.

Requesting Recommendations and References   The need to inquire about people arises often in business. For example, before awarding credit, contracts, jobs, promotions, scholarships, and so on, some companies ask applicants to supply references. If you're applying for a job and your potential employer asks for references, you may want to ask a close personal or professional associate to write a letter of recommendation. Or, if you're an employer considering whether to hire an applicant, you may want to write directly to the person the applicant named as a reference.

Companies ask applicants to supply references who can vouch for their ability, skills, integrity, character, and fitness for the job. Before you volunteer someone's name as a reference, ask that person's permission. Some people won't let you use their names, perhaps because they don't know enough about you to feel comfortable writing a letter or

Putting your claim in writing
- *Documents your dissatisfaction*
- *Requires courtesy, clarity, and conciseness*

In your claim letter, try to
- *Explain the problem and give details*
- *Provide backup information*
- *Request specific action*

Be prepared to document your claim. Send copies and keep the original documents.

Be as specific as possible about what you want to happen next.

Jyoti Gupta, owner of Jyoti Cuisine India, doesn't spend her entire day making specialty frozen meals for passengers of British Airways and US Airways. The company also supplies JYOTI foods nationwide to well-known distributors, supermarkets, specialty and ethnic food stores, natural food stores, and consumers (via mail order). Gupta routinely sends memos and letters requesting information and action. For claims, Gupta uses the direct approach and does her best to be cordial, logical, and clear.

FIGURE 7–4
Poor and Improved Versions of a Claim Letter

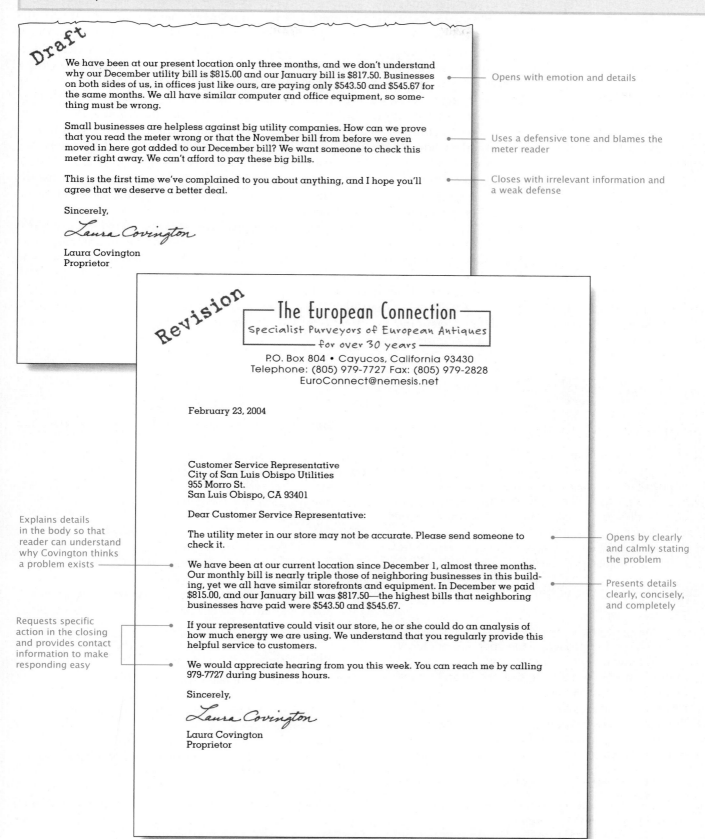

Draft

We have been at our present location only three months, and we don't understand why our December utility bill is $815.00 and our January bill is $817.50. Businesses on both sides of us, in offices just like ours, are paying only $543.50 and $545.67 for the same months. We all have similar computer and office equipment, so something must be wrong.

Small businesses are helpless against big utility companies. How can we prove that you read the meter wrong or that the November bill from before we even moved in here got added to our December bill? We want someone to check this meter right away. We can't afford to pay these big bills.

This is the first time we've complained to you about anything, and I hope you'll agree that we deserve a better deal.

Sincerely,

Laura Covington

Laura Covington
Proprietor

— Opens with emotion and details

— Uses a defensive tone and blames the meter reader

— Closes with irrelevant information and a weak defense

Revision

The European Connection
Specialist Purveyors of European Antiques
for over 30 years

P.O. Box 804 • Cayucos, California 93430
Telephone: (805) 979-7727 Fax: (805) 979-2828
EuroConnect@nemesis.net

February 23, 2004

Customer Service Representative
City of San Luis Obispo Utilities
955 Morro St.
San Luis Obispo, CA 93401

Dear Customer Service Representative:

The utility meter in our store may not be accurate. Please send someone to check it.

We have been at our current location since December 1, almost three months. Our monthly bill is nearly triple those of neighboring businesses in this building, yet we all have similar storefronts and equipment. In December we paid $815.00, and our January bill was $817.50—the highest bills that neighboring businesses have paid were $543.50 and $545.67.

If your representative could visit our store, he or she could do an analysis of how much energy we are using. We understand that you regularly provide this helpful service to customers.

We would appreciate hearing from you this week. You can reach me by calling 979-7727 during business hours.

Sincerely,

Laura Covington

Laura Covington
Proprietor

Explains details in the body so that reader can understand why Covington thinks a problem exists —

Requests specific action in the closing and provides contact information to make responding easy

— Opens by clearly and calmly stating the problem

— Presents details clearly, concisely, and completely

Always ask for permission before using someone's name as a reference.

because they have a policy of not providing recommendations. In any event, you are likely to receive the best recommendation from people who agree to write about you, so check first.

Because requests for recommendations and references are routine, you can assume your reader will honor your request, and you can organize your inquiry using the direct approach. See Joanne Tucker's letter in Figure 7–5. Begin your message by clearly stating that you're applying for a position and that you would like your reader to write a letter of recommendation. If you haven't had contact with the person for some time, use the opening to recall the nature of the relationship you had, the dates of association, and any special events that might bring a clear, favorable picture of you to mind.

Provide your reader with as much information as possible about your qualifications.

If you're applying for a job, a scholarship, or the like, include a copy of your résumé to give the reader an idea of the direction your life has taken. After reading the résumé, your reader will know what favorable qualities to emphasize and will be able to write the recommendation that best supports your application. If you don't have a résumé, use the middle of your letter to include any information about yourself that the reader might use to support a recommendation, such as a description of related jobs you've held.

Close your letter with an expression of appreciation and the full name and address of the person to whom the letter should be sent. When asking for an immediate recommendation, you should also mention the deadline. You'll make a response more likely if you enclose a stamped, preaddressed envelope. Look again at Figure 7–5. Joanne Tucker's letter covers all these points and adds important information about some qualifications that might be of special interest to her potential employer. To quickly review the major tasks involved in routine requests, see the "Checklist: Writing Routine Requests."

Refresh the memory of any potential reference you haven't been in touch with for a while.

✓ CHECKLIST: Writing Routine Requests

Effective Tone Through Audience Focus

- ✓ Maintain a tone that is confident, factual, fair, and unemotional.
- ✓ Present facts honestly, clearly, and politely.
- ✓ For claims, avoid all threats, sarcasm, exaggeration, and hostility; a nonargumentative tone shows your confidence in the reader's fairness.
- ✓ For claims, make no accusation against any person or company, unless you can back it up with hard facts.

Opening Statement of the Request

- ✓ For claims, write the document as soon as possible after the problem is identified.
- ✓ Use the direct approach, since your audience will respond favorably to your request.
- ✓ Phrase the opening clearly and simply so that the main idea cannot be misunderstood.
- ✓ Write in a polite, undemanding, personal tone.
- ✓ Preface complex requests with a sentence or two of explanation; for example, for claims, tell the specifics of the problem.

Middle Justification, Explanation, and Details

- ✓ Justify the request, or explain its importance.
- ✓ Explain the benefit(s) the reader will gain by responding.

- ✓ State desired actions in a positive and supportive (not negative or dictatorial) manner.
- ✓ For claims, gain reader understanding by praising some aspect of the good or service, or at least by explaining why the product was originally purchased.
- ✓ Itemize parts of a complex request in a logical or numbered series.
- ✓ List specific questions—but only those you can't answer through your own efforts.
- ✓ Ask only relevant questions, and cover only one topic per question.
- ✓ For claims, provide copies of necessary documents (invoices, canceled checks, confirmation letters, etc.); keep the originals.

Courteous Close with Request for Specific Action

- ✓ Courteously request a specific action.
- ✓ For claims, clearly state what you expect as a fair settlement, or ask the reader to propose a fair adjustment.
- ✓ Make it easy to comply by including your contact information: name, address, phone and fax numbers (with area code), and e-mail address.
- ✓ Indicate gratitude.
- ✓ Clearly state any important deadline or time frame for the request.

FIGURE 7-5
Effective Letter Requesting a Recommendation

Planning

Writing

Completing

Analyze the Situation
Purpose is to request a recommendation letter from your college professor.

Gather Information
Gather information to help the reader recall you and to clarify the position you want.

Adapt to the Audience
A letter format will give your message the formality you need. Be polite.

Organize the Information
Main idea is to convince your professor to send a glowing recommendation to a potential employer. Use the direct approach.

Compose the Message
Make message friendly but businesslike and slightly more formal than usual. Use plain English and an active voice.

Revise the Message
Be concise but thorough. Make sure that concrete detail flows logically.

Produce the Message
Use simple typeface with ample margins and spacing between text. Enclose a stamped, addressed envelope and perhaps your résumé.

Proofread the Message
Review letter and enclosures for errors.

1   **2**   **3**

1181 Ashport Dr.
Tate Springs, TN 38101
March 14, 2004

Professor Lyndon Kenton
School of Business
University of Tennessee, Knoxville
Knoxville, TN 37916

Dear Professor Kenton:

May I have a letter of recommendation from you? I recently interviewed with Strategic Investments and have been called for a second interview for their Analyst Training Program (ATP). They have requested at least one recommendation from a professor, and I immediately thought of you.

As you may recall, I took BUS 485, Financial Analysis, from you in the fall of 2003. I enjoyed the class and finished the term with an "A." Professor Kenton, your comments on assertiveness and cold-calling impressed me beyond the scope of the actual course material. In fact, taking your course helped me decide on a future as a financial analyst.

My enclosed résumé includes all my relevant work experience and volunteer activities, but I'd also like to add that I've handled the financial planning for our family since my father passed away several years ago. Although initially, I learned by trial and error, I have increasingly applied my business training in deciding what stocks or bonds to trade. This, I believe, has given me a practical edge over others who may be applying for the same job.

If possible, Ms. Blackmon in Human Resources needs to receive your letter by March 30. For your convenience, I've enclosed a preaddressed, stamped envelope.

I appreciate your time and effort in writing this letter of recommendation for me. It will be great to put my education to work, and I'll keep you informed of my progress.

Sincerely,

Joanne Tucker

Joanne Tucker

Enclosure

Includes information in the opening to refresh reader's memory about this former student

Gives a deadline for response in the closing and includes information about the person expecting the recommendation

Opens with the request, assumes the reader will honor the request, and names the potential employer

Refers to résumé in the body and mentions experience that could set applicant apart from other candidates

DEVELOPING ROUTINE REPLIES AND POSITIVE MESSAGES

When responding positively to a request or sending a positive message, you have several goals: to communicate the information or good news, answer all questions, provide all required details, and leave your reader with a good impression of you and your firm. Routine messages can be quite brief and to the point. And even though you may be doing someone a favor by responding to a request, you want to be courteous and upbeat and maintain a you-oriented tone.

Strategy for Routine Replies and Positive Messages

Use the direct organizational plan for positive messages.

Like requests, routine replies and positive messages have an opening, a body, and a close. Readers receiving these messages will generally be interested in what you have to say, so you'll usually use the direct approach. Place your main idea (the positive reply or the good news) in the opening. Use the middle to explain all the relevant details, and close cordially, perhaps highlighting a benefit to your reader.

Prepare your audience for the detail that follows by beginning your positive message with the main idea or good news.

Start with the Main Idea   By beginning your positive message with the main idea or good news, you're preparing your audience for the detail that follows. Try to make your opening clear and concise. Although the following introductory statements make the same point, one is cluttered with unnecessary information that buries the purpose, whereas the other is brief and to the point:

Instead of This	Write This
I am pleased to inform you that after deliberating the matter carefully, our human resources committee has recommended you for appointment as a staff accountant.	Congratulations. You've been selected to join our firm as a staff accountant, beginning March 20.

Before you begin, have a clear idea of what you want to say.

The best way to write a clear opening is to have a clear idea of what you want to say. Before you put one word on paper, ask yourself, "What is the single most important message I have for the audience?"

Provide Necessary Details and Explanation   The middle part of a positive message is typically the longest. You need the space to explain your point completely so that the audience won't experience any confusion or lingering doubt. In addition to providing details in the middle section, maintain the supportive tone established at the beginning. This tone is easy to continue when your message is purely good news, as in this example:

Your educational background and internship have impressed us, and we believe you would be a valuable addition to Green Valley Properties. As discussed during your interview, your salary will be $3,300 per month, plus benefits. In that regard, you will meet with our benefits manager, Paula Sanchez, at 8:00 A.M. on Monday, March 20. She will assist you with all the paperwork necessary to tailor our benefit package to your family situation. She will also arrange various orientation activities to help you acclimate to our company.

However, if your routine message is mixed and must convey mildly disappointing information, put the negative portion of your message into as favorable a context as possible:

Embed negative information in a positive context.

Instead of This	Write This
No, we no longer carry the Sportsgirl line of sweaters.	The new Olympic line has replaced the Sportsgirl sweaters that you asked about. Olympic features a wider range of colors and sizes and more contemporary styling.

The more complete description is less negative and emphasizes how the audience can benefit from the change. Be careful, though: You can use negative information in this type of message *only* if you're reasonably sure the audience will respond positively. Otherwise, use the indirect approach (discussed in Chapter 8).

If you are communicating to customers, you might also want to use the body of your message to assure the customer of the wisdom of his or her purchase selection. Talking favorably about something the customer has bought even though it may not have been delivered is a good way to build customer relationships. Such favorable comments are called **resale** and are most effective when they are relatively short and specific:

Use resale material to assure customers of the wisdom of their purchases.

The zipper on the carrying case you purchased is double-stitched and guaranteed for the life of the product.

The Kitchen Aid mixer you ordered is our best-selling model. It should service your cooking needs for many years.

Keep in mind that the purpose of resale is to increase the buyer's faith in goods or services already purchased or ordered. **Sales promotion** material is similar to resale, but it seeks to promote interest in goods or services in situations where a purchase commitment does not already exist.

End with a Courteous Close Your message is most likely to succeed if your readers are left feeling that you have their personal welfare in mind. You accomplish this task either by highlighting a benefit to the audience or by expressing appreciation or goodwill. If follow-up action is required, clearly state who will do what next.

Document Makeover

IMPROVE THIS E-MAIL

To practice correcting drafts of actual documents, visit **www.prenhall.com/onekey** on the web. Click "Document Makeovers," then click Chapter 7. You will find an e-mail message that contains problems and errors relating to what you've learned in this chapter about routine messages. Use the Final Draft decision tool to create an improved version of this routine e-mail. Check the message for skilled presentation of the main idea, clarity of detail, proper handling of negative information, appropriate use of resale, and the inclusion of a courteous close.

Types of Routine Replies and Positive Messages

Innumerable types of routine replies and positive messages are used in business every day. Most of these messages fall into six main categories: informative messages, grants of requests for information and action, grants of claims and requests for adjustments, recommendations and references, good-news announcements, and goodwill messages.

When writing informative messages, you
- State the purpose at the beginning and briefly mention the nature of the information you are providing
- Provide the necessary details
- End with a courtesy close

Sending Informative Messages All companies send routine informative messages such as reminder notices and policy statements. Employees must be informed

Paul Eichen and his team at Rokenbok Toys rely on a casual atmosphere in which a creative gang of workers come and go, focusing hard on work and life (rather than on politics and protocol). At Rokenbok people apply high-tech know-how to classic toys—LEGO-like construction sets with computerized, remote-controlled conveyors, lifts, monorails, and vehicles. Team members make suggestions, help solve problems, and commiserate— it all in routine messages.

of organizational changes, upcoming events, new procedures, and changing policies. Customers and suppliers must be informed of shipping and return policies, sales discount procedures, and company developments that might be helpful when doing business with the company or when using the company's products. When writing informative messages, use the beginning of the message to state the purpose (to inform) and briefly mention the nature of the information you are providing; use the body to provide the necessary details; and end with a courteous close.

Most informative communications are neutral, stimulating neither a positive nor a negative response from readers. However, some informative messages require additional care. In policy statements and procedural changes, for instance, benefits to employees may not be readily obvious. For example, even though a new procedure will help the company save money, some employees may not realize that such savings will provide additional resources for raises. In instances where the reader may not perceive the personal benefit right away, use the body to show exactly how the policy or procedure will enhance readers' work or personal life.

Granting Requests for Information and Action   If your answer to a request is 'yes' or is straightforward information, the direct plan is appropriate. Your prompt, gracious, and thorough response will positively influence how people think about your company, its products, your department, and you. Readers' perceptions are the reason that Campbell's Karen Donohue is so sensitive to the tone of her letters, memos, and e-mail messages. She makes it a point to adopt the "you" attitude in all her business correspondence.

> *An ungracious reply may increase customer dissatisfaction.*

Many requests are similar. For example, a human resources department gets numerous routine inquiries about job openings. To handle repetitive queries like these, companies usually develop form messages. Although such responses have often been criticized as being cold and impersonal, you can put a great deal of thought into wording them, and you can use computers to personalize and mix paragraphs. Thus, a computerized form letter prepared with care may actually be more personal and sincere than a quickly dictated, hastily typed "personal" reply. E-mail messages may be standardized as well. For example, Julian Zamakis sent an e-mail to Herman Miller asking for information about employment opportunities and received the encouraging e-mail reply in Figure 7–6.

> *Form messages can be personal and sincere when prepared carefully.*

When you're answering requests and a potential sale is involved, you have three main goals: (1) to respond to the inquiry and answer all questions, (2) to leave your reader with a good impression of you and your firm, and (3) to encourage future sales. The following letter succeeds in meeting all three objectives:

> *When a sale may result from a reply, you want to answer all reader questions, make a good impression, and encourage the future sale.*

> *Starts with a clear statement of the main point* →

Here is the brochure "Entertainment Unlimited" that you requested. This booklet describes the vast array of entertainment options available to you with an Ocean Satellite Device (OSD).

> *Presents key information immediately, along with resale and sales promotion* →

On page 12 of "Entertainment Unlimited" you'll find a list of the 338 channels that the OSD brings into your home. You'll have access to movie, sport,

Uses typical e-mail format

Refers to previous correspondence

Explains in the body how the company uses résumés that are kept on file

Closes on a warm, positive note

Includes plenty of contact information, in keeping with the friendly audience focus

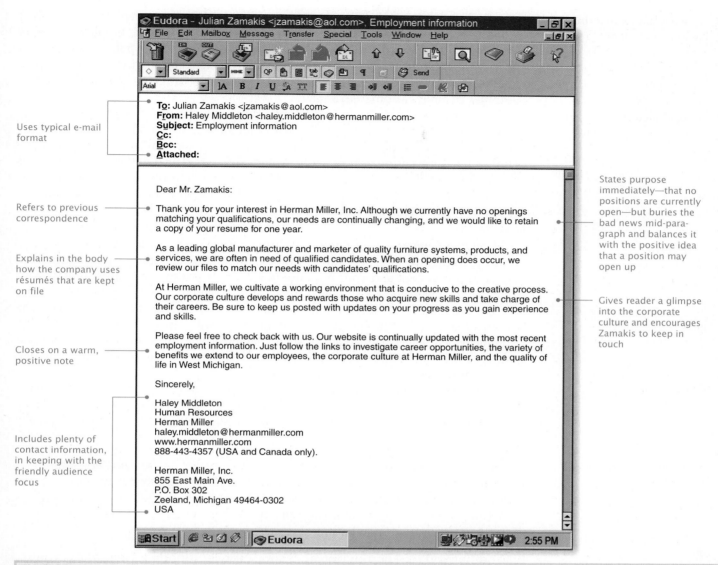

States purpose immediately—that no positions are currently open—but buries the bad news mid-paragraph and balances it with the positive idea that a position may open up

Gives reader a glimpse into the corporate culture and encourages Zamakis to keep in touch

To: Julian Zamakis <jzamakis@aol.com>
From: Haley Middleton <haley.middleton@hermanmiller.com>
Subject: Employment information
Cc:
Bcc:
Attached:

Dear Mr. Zamakis:

Thank you for your interest in Herman Miller, Inc. Although we currently have no openings matching your qualifications, our needs are continually changing, and we would like to retain a copy of your resume for one year.

As a leading global manufacturer and marketer of quality furniture systems, products, and services, we are often in need of qualified candidates. When an opening does occur, we review our files to match our needs with candidates' qualifications.

At Herman Miller, we cultivate a working environment that is conducive to the creative process. Our corporate culture develops and rewards those who acquire new skills and take charge of their careers. Be sure to keep us posted with updates on your progress as you gain experience and skills.

Please feel free to check back with us. Our website is continually updated with the most recent employment information. Just follow the links to investigate career opportunities, the variety of benefits we extend to our employees, the corporate culture at Herman Miller, and the quality of life in West Michigan.

Sincerely,

Haley Middleton
Human Resources
Herman Miller
haley.middleton@hermanmiller.com
www.hermanmiller.com
888-443-4357 (USA and Canada only).

Herman Miller, Inc.
855 East Main Ave.
P.O. Box 302
Zeeland, Michigan 49464-0302
USA

FIGURE 7–6
Effective E-mail Replying to a Request for Information

and music channels; 24-hour news channels; local channels; and all the major television networks. OSD gives you a clearer picture and more precise sound than those old-fashioned dishes that took up most of your yard—and OSD uses only a small dish that mounts easily on your roof.

More music, more cartoons, more experts, more news, and more sports are available to you with OSD than with any other cable or satellite connection in this region. Yes, it's all there, right at your fingertips.

Encourages readers to take one more step toward a purchase by highlighting product benefits

Just call us at 1-800-786-4331, and an OSD representative will come to your home to answer your questions. You'll love the programming and the low monthly cost. Call us today!

Points toward the sale confidently

Granting claims is your chance to build customer loyalty.

The best approach is to assume the claimant is being truthful.

Always refer to company errors with great care.

Granting Claims and Requests for Adjustment

Satisfied customers bring more business to a firm; angry or dissatisfied customers do not. In addition, angry customers complain to anyone who will listen, creating poor public relations. So even though claims and adjustments may seem unpleasant, progressive businesspeople such as Karen Donohue treat claims and requests for adjustment as golden opportunities to build customer loyalty.[2]

Few people go to the trouble of requesting an adjustment unless they actually have a problem. So the most sensible reaction to a routine claim is to assume that the claimant's account of the transaction is an honest statement of what happened—unless the same customer repeatedly submits dubious claims or the dollar amount is very large. When you receive a complaint, you'll want to investigate the problem first to determine what went wrong and why. You'll also want to determine whether your company, your customer, or a third party is at fault.

When Your Company Is at Fault

The usual human response to a bad situation is to say, "It wasn't my fault!" However, businesspeople can't take that stance. When your company is at fault and your response to a claim is positive, you must protect your company's image and try to regain the customer's goodwill by referring to company errors carefully. Don't blame an individual or a specific department. And avoid lame excuses such as "Nobody's perfect" or "Mistakes will happen." Don't promise that problems will never happen again; such guarantees are unrealistic and often beyond your control. Instead, explain your company's efforts to do a good job, implying that the error was an unusual incident.

For example, a large mail-order clothing company has created the following form letter to respond to customers who claim they haven't received exactly what was ordered. The form letter can be customized through word processing and then individually signed:

Starts with a "good attitude" statement (not the usual good-news statement) because it's going to people with various complaints

Puts customer at ease with "you" attitude

Avoids suggesting that customer was wrong to write to Klondike

Includes resale and sales promotion

Closes with statement of company's concern for all its customers

> Your letter concerning your recent Klondike order has arrived and has been forwarded to our director of order fulfillment. Your complete satisfaction is our goal; when you are satisfied, we are satisfied. Our customer service representative will contact you soon to assist with the issues raised in your letter.
>
> Whether you're skiing or driving a snowmobile, Klondike Gear offers you the best protection from wind, snow, and cold—and Klondike has been taking care of customers' outdoor needs for over 27 years! Because you're a loyal customer, enclosed is a $5 gift certificate. You may wish to consider our new line of quality snow goggles.
>
> Thank you for taking the time to write to us. Your input helps us better serve you and all our customers.

In contrast, a response letter written as a personal answer to a unique claim would start with a clear statement of the good news: the settling of the claim according to the customer's request. Here is a more personal response from Klondike Gear:

> Here is your heather-blue wool-and-mohair sweater (size large) to replace the one returned to us with a defect in the knitting on the left sleeve. Thanks for giving us the opportunity to correct this situation. Customers' needs have come first at Klondike Gear for 27 years. Our sweaters are handmade by the finest knitters in this area.

Our newest catalog is enclosed. Browse through it, and you'll see what wonderful new colors and patterns we have for you. Whether you are skiing or driving a snowmobile, Klondike Gear offers you the best protection available from wind, snow, and cold. Let us know how we may continue to serve you and your sporting needs.

When the Customer Is at Fault   When your customer is at fault (perhaps washing a dry-clean-only sweater in hot water), you can (1) refuse the claim and attempt to justify your refusal or (2) simply do what the customer asks. But remember, if you refuse the claim, you may lose your customer—as well as many of the customer's friends, who will hear only one side of the dispute. You must weigh the cost of making the adjustment against the cost of losing future business from one or more customers.

If you choose to grant the claim, you can start off with the good news: You're replacing the merchandise or refunding the purchase price. However, the middle section needs more attention. Your job is to make the customer realize that the merchandise was mistreated, but you want to avoid being condescending ("Perhaps you failed to read the instructions carefully") or preachy ("You should know that wool shrinks in hot water"). The dilemma is this: If the customer fails to realize what went wrong, you may commit your firm to an endless procession of returned merchandise; but if you insult the customer, your cash refund will have been wasted because you'll lose that customer's business anyway. Without being offensive, the letter in Figure 7–7 educates a customer about how to treat his in-line skates.

> When complying with an unjustified claim, let the customer know that the merchandise was mistreated, but maintain a respectful and positive tone.

When a Third Party Is at Fault   Sometimes neither you nor the claimant is at fault. Perhaps the carrier damaged merchandise in transit, or perhaps the original manufacturer is responsible for some product defect. When a third party is at fault, you have three options:

> You have three options when a third party is at fault.

- **Simply honor the claim.** This option is the most attractive. You can satisfy your customer with the standard good-news letter and no additional explanation. This way you maintain your reputation for fair dealing and bear no cost (because the carrier, manufacturer, or other third party will reimburse you for the damage).

- **Honor the claim, but explain you're not at fault.** This option corrects any impression that the damage was caused by your *negligence*. You can still write the standard good-news letter, but stress the explanation.

- **Refer the claimant to the third party.** This option is almost always a bad choice. When you suggest filing a claim with the firm that caused the defect or damage, you fail to satisfy the claimant's needs. The exception is when you're trying to dissociate yourself from any legal responsibility for the damaged merchandise, especially if it has caused a personal injury, in which case you would send a bad-news message (see Chapter 8).

Providing Recommendations and References   When writing a letter of recommendation, your goal is to convince readers that the person being recommended has the characteristics necessary for the job or benefit being sought. Your letter must contain all the relevant details:

> Be careful not to omit any necessary information from recommendation letters.

- Candidate's full name

- Job or benefit being sought

- Nature of your relationship with the candidate

- Whether you're answering a request or taking the initiative

FIGURE 7–7
Effective Response to a Claim When the Buyer Is at Fault

Planning

Writing

Completing

Analyze the Situation
Purpose is to grant a customer's claim, gently educate him, and encourage further business.

Gather Information
Gather information on product care, warranties, and resale information.

Adapt to the Audience
Use letter format to reinforce businesslike tone. Give customer relationship utmost attention.

Organize the Information
Main idea is that you're replacing the wheel assembly—even though you are not required to do so.

Compose the Message
Use an upbeat, conversational style, but remain businesslike. Choose words carefully, especially when educating the customer. Include resale information to reinforce future business.

Revise the Message
Revise for tone, focusing on conciseness, clarity, and the "you" attitude.

Produce the Message
Avoid confusing your positive message with fussy design elements. Keep it simple.

Proofread the Message
Review for the usual errors, and include all promised enclosures.

1   **2**   **3**

Skates Alive!
20901 El Dorado Hills
Laguna Niguel, CA 92677
(714) 332-7474 • Fax: (714) 336-5297
skates@speed.net

February 7, 2004

Mr. Steven Cox
1172 Amber Court
Jacksonville, FL 32073

Dear Mr. Cox:

Thank you for contacting us about your in-line skates. Even though your six-month warranty has expired, Skates Alive! is mailing you a complete wheel assembly replacement free of charge. The enclosed instructions make removing the damaged wheel line and installing the new one relatively easy.

The "Fastrax" (model NL 562) you purchased is our best-selling and most reliable skate. However, wheel jams may occur when fine particles of sand block the smooth rotating action of the wheels. These skates perform best when used on roadways and tracks that are relatively free of sand. We suggest that you remove and clean the wheel assemblies (see enclosed directions) once a month and have them checked by your dealer about every six months.

Because of your Florida location, you may want to consider our more advanced "Glisto" (model NL 988) when you decide to purchase new skates. Although more expensive than the Fastrax, the Glisto design helps shed sand and dirt quite efficiently and should provide years of carefree skating.

Enjoy the enclosed copy of "Rock & Roll," with our compliments. Inside, you'll read about new products, hear from other skaters, and have an opportunity to respond to our customer questionnaire.

We love hearing from our skaters, so keep in touch. All of us at Skates Alive! wish you good times and miles of healthy skating.

Sincerely,

Candace Parker

Candace Parker
Customer Service Representative

Enclosure

Acknowledges reader communication, keeps opening positive by avoiding words such as "problem," and conveys the good news right away

Explains the problem without blaming the customer by avoiding the pronoun "you" and by suggesting ways to avoid future problems

Adds value by enclosing a newsletter that invites future response from customer

Includes sales promotion in the body, encouraging the customer to "trade up"

Closes positively, ending on a "feel good" note that conveys an attitude of excellent customer service

- Facts relevant to the position or benefit sought

- Your overall evaluation of the candidate's suitability for the job or benefit

Oddly enough, the most difficult recommendation letters to write are those for truly outstanding candidates. Your audience will have trouble believing uninterrupted praise for someone's talents and accomplishments. So illustrate your general points with a specific example or two that point out the candidate's abilities. Be sure to discuss the candidate's abilities in relation to the "competition."

Most candidates aren't perfect, however. Omitting reference to a candidate's shortcomings may be tempting, especially if the shortcomings are irrelevant to the demands of the job in question. Even so, you have an obligation to refer to any shortcoming that is serious and related to job performance. You owe it to your audience, to your own conscience, and even to the better-qualified candidate who's relying on honest references.

Of course, the danger in writing a critical letter is that you might engage in libel (making a false and malicious written statement that injures the candidate's reputation). On the other hand, if negative information is truthful and relevant, it may be unethical and illegal to omit it from your recommendation. So if you must refer to a shortcoming, you can best protect yourself by sticking to the facts, avoiding value judgments, and placing your criticism in the context of a generally favorable recommendation, as in Figure 7–8. In this letter, the writer supports all statements with facts and steers clear of vague, critical judgments.

As Unocal's president and chief operating officer, Tim Ling encourages everyone in the company to embrace open information and communication. Likewise, in recommendation letters, he not only includes all the relevant facts but also relates specific examples of a candidate's accomplishments.

A serious shortcoming cannot be ignored, but beware of being libelous:
- Include only relevant, factual information
- Avoid value judgments
- Balance criticisms with favorable points

Recommendation letters are usually confidential; that is, they're sent directly to the person or committee who requested them and are not shown to the candidate. However, recent litigation has made it advisable in some situations to prepare a carefully worded letter that satisfies both parties. To explore the topic further, see "Promoting Workplace Ethics: Recommendation Letters: What's Right to Write?" on page 213. You can also avoid trouble by asking yourself the following questions before mailing a recommendation letter:

A recommendation letter presenting negatives can be carefully worded to satisfy both the candidate and the person or company requesting information.

- Does the person receiving this personal information have a legitimate right to it?

- Does all the information I've presented relate directly to the job or benefit being sought?

- Have I put the candidate's case as strongly and as honestly as I can?

- Have I avoided overstating the candidate's abilities or otherwise misleading the reader?

- Have I based all my statements on firsthand knowledge and provable facts?

Sending Goodwill Messages   You can enhance your relationships with customers, colleagues, and other businesspeople by sending friendly, unexpected notes with no direct business purpose. Jack Welch, former CEO of General Electric, is known for his handwritten notes to all employees, from managers to hourly workers. He once wrote a congratulatory note to one manager who had turned down a promotion because he didn't want to move his teenager to a different school: "Bill," wrote Welch, "we like you for a lot of reasons—one of them is that you are a very special person. You proved it again this morning. Good for you and your lucky family . . . ".[3]

Goodwill is the positive feeling that encourages people to maintain a business relationship.

Effective goodwill messages must be sincere and honest. Otherwise, the writer appears interested in personal gain rather than in benefiting customers or fellow

Make sure your compliments are grounded in reality.

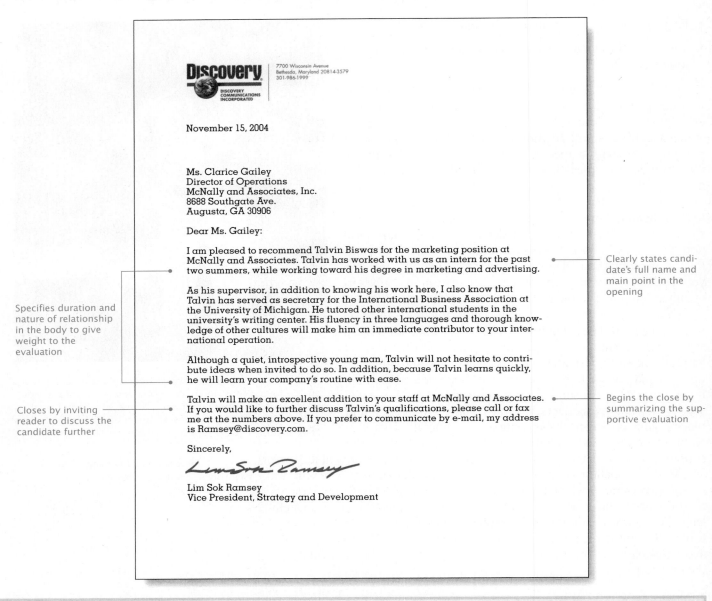

Clearly states candidate's full name and main point in the opening

Specifies duration and nature of relationship in the body to give weight to the evaluation

Begins the close by summarizing the supportive evaluation

Closes by inviting reader to discuss the candidate further

FIGURE 7–8
Effective Recommendation Letter

workers. To come across as sincere, avoid exaggeration and back up any compliments with specific points. In addition, readers often regard more restrained praise as being more sincere:

Instead of This	Write This
Words cannot express my appreciation for the great job you did. Thanks. No one could have done it better. You're terrific! You've made the whole firm sit up and take notice, and we are ecstatic to have you working here.	Thanks again for taking charge of the meeting in my absence. You did an excellent job. With just an hour's notice, you managed to pull the legal and public relations departments together so that we could present a united front in the negotiations. Your dedication and communication abilities have been noted and are truly appreciated.

PROMOTING WORKPLACE ETHICS

Recommendation Letters: What's Right to Write?

You were Frank Walker's supervisor for four years. When he left the company recently, he asked you to write a letter of recommendation for him. However, your company's legal experts said no.

WHY NOT GIVE RECOMMENDATIONS?

Thousands of lawsuits have been filed (and won) by employees, charging former employers with making slanderous (oral) and libelous (written) statements in job recommendations. During one seven-year period in California, employees won 72 percent of the libel and related suits they brought against employers, and their average award was $582,000. One employer lost for saying an employee had "suddenly resigned," which implied that the employee had resigned under "a veil of suspicion," said the court. Another employer lost for saying an employee was fired "for causes." Plus, when employees prove actual malice, damage awards skyrocket. To complicate matters, one court ruling held an employer liable for *omitting* information about a former employee.

So what sort of information should or should not be included in a recommendation? Even though some states have passed laws protecting companies against lawsuits when the employer acts in good faith, legal and human resources experts often advise companies to control what's being said by centralizing all recommendations. The cautious approach is to supply only dates of employment and titles of positions held—and to give that information only to people who have written authorization from former employees.

BUT WHAT IF YOU WANT TO GIVE A RECOMMENDATION?

Even so, Frank Walker was a terrific employee—a good friend—and you believe he really deserves a recommendation. You have two options. First, you can write the letter with Walker so that the contents satisfy you both and then discuss the letter with your human resources department before releasing it. The second option is to ask Walker to list you as a *personal* reference, which removes your company from any responsibility for statements you make. But be careful—you can still be held personally responsible for your comments.

Of course, if it had been Sharon Brown who asked for your recommendation, you'd be facing a different dilemma. Brown wasn't the greatest employee. So would you owe her potential employer the whole story? Including negative information could get you sued by Brown, and omitting negative information could get you sued by the hiring company for "failure to disclose" or "negligent referral."

Regardless of the circumstances, consult your human resources or legal department, and be sure to (1) comment only on your own experience working with a former employee, (2) make all comments in writing, and (3) limit your remarks to provable facts (don't exaggerate).

CAREER APPLICATIONS

1. A former employee was often late for work but was an excellent and fast worker who got along well with everyone. Do you think it's important to mention the tardiness to potential employers? If so, how will you handle it?

2. Step outside yourself for a moment and write a letter of recommendation about you from a former employer's perspective. Practice honesty, integrity, and prudence.

Congratulations   One prime opportunity for sending goodwill messages is to congratulate someone for a significant business achievement—perhaps for being promoted or for attaining an important civic position. The congratulatory note in Figure 7–9 moves swiftly to the subject: the good news. It gives reasons for expecting success and avoids extravagances such as "Only you can do the job!"

Other reasons for sending congratulations include the highlights in people's personal lives—weddings, births, graduations, success in nonbusiness competitions. You may congratulate business acquaintances on their own achievements or on the accomplishments of a spouse or child. You may also take note of personal events, even if you don't know the reader well. Of course, if you're already friendly with the reader, you can get away with a more personal tone.

Some companies even develop a mailing list of potential customers by assigning an employee to clip newspaper announcements of births, engagements, weddings, and graduations or to obtain information on real estate transactions in the local community. Then they introduce themselves by sending out a form letter that might read like this:

Taking note of significant events in someone's personal life helps cement the business relationship.

FIGURE 7-9
Effective Letter Congratulating a Business Acquaintance

Planning

Analyze the Situation
Purpose is to create goodwill with industry business associates.

Gather Information
Gather information on specific accomplishments of the reader's firm.

Adapt to the Audience
Letter format lets reader use your message (perhaps even reproduce it) as an industry testimonial.

Writing

Organize the Information
Main idea is to congratulate the reader. The direct approach is perfect for this welcome news.

Compose the Message
A conversational tone complements the slightly formal style, since this is your first contact with the reader. Avoid generalized praise by mentioning specific, concrete accomplishments.

Completing

Revise the Message
Review for consistency in tone, word choice, and sentence structure.

Produce the Message
A simple design avoids distracting your reader from the message.

Proofread the Message
Create a positive first impression by being especially careful to send an error-free message.

1 **2** **3**

Draft

We are so pleased when companies that we admire do well. When we attended our convention in Atlanta last month, we heard about your firm's recent selection to design and print media advertisements for the National Association of Business Suppliers (ABS).

We have long believed that the success of individual franchises is directly linked to the healthy growth of the industry at large. Lambert, Cutchen & Browt is the only firm for the job.

We wish you the best of luck with your new ad campaign. Congratulations on a job well done!

Sincerely,

Janice McCarthy

Janice McCarthy
Director, Media Relations

- Sounds condescending and self-centered—expressing the reason but failing to actually congratulate the reader

- Seems insincere because of the lack of supporting reasons and the exaggeration ("only you can do the job")

- Congratulating the reader in the close seems like an afterthought

---

Revision

Office DEPOT, Inc.
2200 Old Germantown Road, Delray Beach, FL 33445   407/278-4800
March 3, 2004

Mr. Ralph Lambert, President
Lambert, Cutchen & Browt, Inc.
14355 Pasadena Pky.
Pasadena, TX 74229

Dear Mr. Lambert:

Congratulations on your firm's recent selection to design print media advertisements for the National Association of Business Suppliers (ABS). Your appointment was announced at our convention in Atlanta last month, and we can think of no better firm to help our industry achieve wide recognition than Lambert, Cutchen & Browt.

Your success has been admirable in promoting associations of other industries such as soft drinks, snack foods, and recycling. Your "Dream Vision 2001" ads for the bottling industry were both inspirational and effective in raising consumer awareness. Your ABS campaign is sure to yield similar positive responses.

You can be sure we will follow your media campaign with great interest.

Sincerely,

Janice McCarthy

Janice McCarthy
Director, Media Relations

tw

- Immediately expresses the reason for congratulating the reader

- Uses body to make compliment more effective by showing knowledge of the reader's work, while avoiding exaggeration

- Closes by expressing interest in following the future success of the firm

> Congratulations on your new home! Our wish is that it brings you much happiness.
>
> To help you commemorate the occasion, we've enclosed a key chain with your new address engraved on the leather tab. Please accept it with our best wishes.

In this case, the company's letterhead and address are enough of a sales pitch. This simple message has a natural, friendly tone, even though the sender has never met the recipient.

Appreciation   An important business quality is the ability to recognize the contributions of employees, colleagues, suppliers, and other associates. Your praise does more than just make the person feel good; it encourages further excellence. Moreover, a message of appreciation may become an important part of someone's personnel file. So when you write a message of appreciation, try to specifically mention the person or people you want to praise. The brief message that follows expresses gratitude and reveals the happy result:

A message of appreciation documents a person's contributions.

> Thank you for sending the air-conditioning components by overnight delivery. You allowed us to satisfy the needs of two customers who were getting very impatient with the heat.
>
> Special thanks to Susan Brown, who took our initial call and never said, "It can't be done." Her initiative on our behalf is greatly appreciated.

Condolences   In times of serious trouble and deep sadness, written condolences and expressions of sympathy leave their mark. Granted, this type of message is difficult to write, but don't let the difficulty of the task keep you from responding promptly. Those who have experienced a health problem, the death of a loved one, or a business misfortune like to know that they're not alone.

  Begin condolences with a brief statement of sympathy, such as "I was deeply sorry to hear of your loss." In the middle, mention the good qualities or the positive contributions made by the deceased. State what the person or business meant to you. In closing, you can offer your condolences and your best wishes. One considerate way to end this type of message is to say something that will give the reader a little lift, such as a reference to a brighter future. Here are a few general suggestions for writing condolence messages:

In condolence messages, try to find a middle path between being superficial and causing additional distress.

- **Keep reminiscences brief.** Recount a memory or an anecdote (even a humorous one), but don't dwell on the details of the loss, lest you add to the reader's anguish.

- **Write in your own words.** Write as if you were speaking privately to the person. Don't quote "poetic" passages or use stilted or formal phrases. If the loss is a death, refer to it as such rather than as "passing away" or "departing."

- **Be tactful.** Mention your shock and dismay, but remember that bereaved and distressed loved ones take little comfort in lines such as "Richard was too young to die" or "Starting all over again will be so difficult." Try to strike a balance between superficial expressions of sympathy and heart-rending references to a happier past or the likelihood of a bleak future.

- **Take special care.** Be sure to spell names correctly and to be accurate in your review of facts. Try to be prompt.

- **Write about special qualities of the deceased.** You may have to rely on reputation to do this, but let the grieving person know you valued his or her loved one.

- **Write about special qualities of the bereaved person.** A pat on the back helps a bereaved family member feel more confident about handling things during such a traumatic time.[4]

Supervisor George Bigalow sent the following condolence letter to his administrative assistant, Janice Case, after learning of the death of Janice's husband:

> My sympathy to you and your children. All your friends at Carter Electric were so very sorry to learn of John's death. Although I never had the opportunity to meet him, I do know how very special he was to you. Your tales of your family's camping trips and his rafting expeditions were always memorable.

To review the primary tasks involved in routine replies and positive messages, see the "Checklist: Writing Routine Replies and Positive Messages."

✓ CHECKLIST: Writing Routine Replies and Positive Messages

Proper Format and Timing

✓ Send written goodwill messages whenever possible (so that they can be savored more than once), but a phone call is better than no message at all.

✓ Use letter format for all condolences and other goodwill messages sent to outsiders or mailed to an employee's home.

✓ Except for condolences, use a memo format for any routine messages sent through interoffice mail.

✓ Handwrite condolences and replies to handwritten invitations; use special stationery, if available.

✓ Be prompt: Reply to requests as soon as possible, and send goodwill messages before they lose their impact.

Opening Statement of the Good News or Main Idea

✓ Present the good news first, even if the message is mixed; for example, when granting only part of a claim, state your willingness to honor that part without negative comment.

✓ Be warm but concise.

✓ Avoid trite and obvious statements such as "I am pleased to," "We have received," "This is in response to," or "Enclosed please find."

✓ When granting a claim, thank the claimant for writing.

✓ Convey a courteous, you-oriented tone, and except for condolences, make it upbeat.

Middle, Informational Section

✓ Imply or express interest in the request, or provide details of the good news.

✓ Adapt replies to the reader's needs.

✓ When granting a claim, explain how you will remedy the problem, and make your explanation objective, nonvindictive, and impersonal.

✓ Use language that is sincere but neither emotional nor gushy.

✓ List all information in an orderly manner.

✓ If possible, answer all questions and requests in the order posed.

✓ Indicate what you have done and what you will do.

✓ When granting a claim, minimize or omit any disagreements with your reader's interpretation of events.

✓ Include any necessary details or interpretations that the reader may need in order to understand your answers.

✓ If you cannot comply with part of the request (perhaps because the information is unavailable or confidential), tell the reader why and then offer other assistance.

✓ Embed negative statements in positive contexts or balance them with positive alternatives; for example, when granting a claim, apologize only when appropriate, and then do so crisply and without an overly dramatic tone.

✓ Admit your firm's faults carefully: Don't shift blame, imply inefficiency, or make unrealistic promises.

✓ When granting a claim, be especially careful when discussing the claimant's role in creating the problem.

✓ Inform or remind the reader of the general benefits of doing business with your firm.

✓ Avoid exaggerations and flamboyant language.

✓ Maintain a supportive tone: "Thank you for," "May we ask," and "We are glad to work with you."

Warm, Courteous Close

✓ If further action is required, tell the reader how to proceed and encourage the reader to act promptly.

✓ Restate the important idea, when appropriate.

✓ Avoid clichés (such as "Please feel free to").

✓ Offer additional service but avoid implying that your answer is inadequate (by using doubtful statements such as "I trust that" or "I hope").

✓ When granting claims, remind the reader how you are honoring the claim.

✓ When granting claims, encourage the claimant to look favorably on your company or on the product in question.

✓ Close with a positive, forward-looking statement, when appropriate; express goodwill or take an optimistic look into the future.

On the Job:

SOLVING COMMUNICATION DILEMMAS AT CAMPBELL SOUP

Not surprisingly, Karen Donohue plays a major role in Campbell's efforts to better meet the needs of its millions of customers worldwide. Whether she's responding to dissatisfied customers or answering simple requests for information, Donohue is in a position to help satisfy consumers while gaining important insights into their needs and purchase behaviors.

You have joined Campbell's consumer marketing staff. As an assistant to Karen Donohue, you are responsible for handling correspondence with consumers and with Campbell employees. Your objective is to improve the flow of communication between the public and the company so that Campbell can respond quickly and knowledgeably to changing consumer needs. Choose the best alternatives for responding to the situations described below, and be prepared to explain why your choice is best.

1. Donohue has received a letter from a Mrs. Felton who is pleased that Campbell offers a line of Healthy Request reduced-sodium soups, but would like to see more flavors added. Which of the following is the best opening paragraph for your reply?

   a. The Campbell Soup Company was founded in 1869 in Camden, New Jersey. The Dorrance family took control from the founders in 1894. At the turn of the century, John Dorrance invented the soup condensation process, which enabled the company to sell a 10-ounce can for a dime. He was a conservative man and a stickler for quality. His only son, the late Jack Dorrance, followed his father into the business and had a similar management philosophy. As chairman of the company, he used to pinch the tomatoes and taste the carrots occasionally to be sure that the folks in the factory were maintaining high standards. Mr. Dorrance took personal interest in the development of the low-salt line and would be pleased to know that it appeals to you.

   b. Thank you for your enthusiastic letter about Campbell's Healthy Request soups. We are delighted that you enjoy the flavors currently available, and we are working hard to add new varieties to the line.

   c. Good news! Our world-renowned staff of food technologists is busy in the test kitchen at this very moment, experimenting with additional low-sodium recipes for Healthy Request soups. Hang on to your bowl, Mrs. Felton, more flavors are on the way!

2. Which of the following versions is preferable for the body of the letter to Mrs. Felton?

   a. You can expect to see several exciting new Healthy Request soups on your supermarket shelf within the next year. Before the new flavors make their debut, however, they must undergo further testing in our kitchens and in selected markets across the country. We want to be sure our soups satisfy consumer expectations.

   While you're waiting for the new flavors of Healthy Request, you might like to try some of Campbell's other products designed especially for people like you who are concerned about health and nutrition. I'm enclosing coupons that entitle you to sample both Pepperidge Farm Five-Star Fibre bread and Pace picante sauce "on the house." We hope you enjoy them.

   b. We are sorry that the number of Healthy Request flavors is limited at this time. Because of the complexities of testing flavors both in the Campbell kitchens and in test markets around the country, we are a bit behind schedule in releasing new varieties. But several new flavors should be available by the end of the year, if all goes according to plan. In the meantime, please accept these coupons; they can be redeemed for two other fine Campbell products designed for the health-conscious consumer.

   c. Additional flavors of Healthy Request reduced-sodium soups are currently in formulation. They will arrive on supermarket shelves soon. In the meantime, why not enjoy some of Campbell's other fine products designed for the health-conscious consumer? The enclosed coupons will allow you to sample Pace picante sauce and Pepperidge Farm Five-Star Fibre bread at our expense.

3. Campbell has received a letter from the American Heart Association asking for information on the fat and sodium content of Campbell's products. Your department has developed a brochure that provides the necessary data, and you plan to send it to the association. Which of the following cover letters should you send along with the brochure?

   a. Please consult the enclosed brochure for answers to your questions regarding the composition of Campbell's products. The brochure provides detailed information on sodium and fat content of all Campbell's products, which include well-known brands such as V-8, Pepperidge Farm, and Franco-American, as well as Campbell's Soups.

   b. Thanks for your interest in Campbell's products. We are concerned about nutrition and health issues and are trying to reduce the salts and fats in our products. At the same time, we are striving to retain the taste that consumers have come to expect from Campbell. In general, we feel very good about the nutritional value of our products and think that after you read the enclosed brochure, you will too.

   c. Thank you for your interest in Campbell's Soup. The enclosed brochure provides the information you requested about the fat and sodium content of our products. Over the past 10 years, we have introduced a number of reduced-sodium and low-fat products designed specifically for consumers on restricted diets. In addition, we've reformulated many of our regular products to reduce the salt and fat content. We have also revised our product labels so that information on sodium and fat content is readily apparent to health-conscious consumers. If you have any questions about our products, please contact our consumer information specialists at 1-800-227-9876.

4. Campbell has received a letter from a disgruntled consumer, Max Edwards, who was disappointed with his last can of Golden Classic beef soup with potatoes and mushrooms. It appears that the can contained an abundance of potatoes, little beef, and few mushrooms. You have been asked to reply to Mr. Edwards. Which of the following drafts is best?

a. We are extremely sorry that you did not like your last can of Golden Classic beef soup with potatoes and mushrooms. Although we do our very best to ensure that all our products are of the highest quality, occasionally our quality-control department slips up and a can of soup comes out a bit short on one ingredient or another. Apparently you happened to buy just such a can—one with relatively few mushrooms, not much beef, and too many potatoes. The odds against that ever happening to you again are probably a million to one. And to prove it, here's a coupon that entitles you to a free can of Golden Classic soup. You may pick any flavor you like, but why not give the beef with potatoes and mushrooms another try? We bet it will meet your standards this time around.

b. You are right, Mr. Edwards, to expect the highest quality from Campbell's Golden Classic soups. And you are right to complain when your expectations are not met. Our goal is to provide the best, and when we fall short of that goal, we want to know about it so that we can correct the problem.
And that is exactly what we have done. In response to your complaint, our quality-control department is reexamining its testing procedures to ensure that all future cans of Golden Classic soup have an even blend of ingredients. Why not see for yourself by taking the enclosed coupon to your supermarket and redeeming it for a free can of Golden Classic soup? If you choose beef with potatoes and mushrooms, you can count on getting plenty of beef and mushrooms this time.

c. Campbell's Golden Classic soups are a premium product at a premium price. Our quality-control procedures for this line have been carefully devised to ensure that every can of soup has a uniform distribution of ingredients. As you can imagine, your complaint came as quite a surprise to us, given the care that we take with our products. We suspect that the uneven distribution of ingredients was just a fluke, but our quality-control department is looking into the matter to ensure that the alleged problem does not recur.
We would like you to give our Golden Classic soup another try. We are confident that you will be satisfied, so we are enclosing a coupon that entitles you to a free can. If you are not completely happy with it, please call me at 1-800-227-9876.[5]

Learning Objectives Checkup

To assess your understanding of the principles in this chapter, read each learning objective and study the accompanying exercises. For fill-in items, write the missing text in the blank provided; for multiple choice items, circle the letter of the correct answer. You can check your responses against the answer key on page AK-1–AK-2.

Objective 7.1: Apply the three-step writing process to routine messages.

1. When it comes to routine messages, you can
   a. Skip the planning stage
   b. Keep the planning stage brief
   c. Begin by gathering all the information you'll need
   d. Begin by choosing the channel and medium
2. When writing routine messages, you
   a. Can assume that your readers will be interested or neutral
   b. Should open with an "attention getter"
   c. Should use the indirect approach with most audiences
   d. Need not allow much time for revision, production, or proofreading

Objective 7.2: Illustrate the strategy for writing routine requests.

3. When writing a routine request, you begin

a. With a personal introduction, such as "My name is Lee Marrs, and I am . . ."
b. With a vague reference to what you are writing about, such as "I have something to ask you"
c. With a strong demand for action
d. By politely stating your request

4. What should you do when asking questions in a routine request?
   a. Begin with the least important question and work your way up to the most important question.
   b. Include all possible questions about the topic, even if the list gets long.
   c. Deal with only one topic per question.
   d. Do all of the above.
5. Which of the following should you do when closing a routine request?
   a. Be sure to thank the reader "in advance" for complying with the request.
   b. Ask the reader to respond by a specific and appropriate time.
   c. Ask any remaining questions you may have.
   d. Do all of the above.

Objective 7.3: Discuss the differences among three types of routine requests.

6. Requests for information or action from an outsider
   a. Are most often in letter form
   b. Are usually full of complex details
   c. Should use the indirect approach
   d. Are never in e-mail form

7. When writing a claim letter requesting an adjustment, you should
   a. Assume that the recipient will be resistant to your claim
   b. Open with a buffer
   c. Be prepared to back up your claim with invoices, sales receipts, and other relevant documents
   d. Do all of the above

8. When making a request for a recommendation, you include
   a. A copy of your résumé if the recommendation is for a job
   b. Relevant information about yourself that the reader can use to support a recommendation
   c. A preaddressed, stamped envelope
   d. All of the above

Objective 7.4: Illustrate the strategy for writing routine replies and positive messages.

9. If you are making a routine reply to a customer, it's a good idea to
   a. Leave out any negative information
   b. Include resale information to assure the customer of the wisdom of his or her purchase
   c. Leave out sales promotion material, which would be tacky to include
   d. Do all of the above

Objective 7.5: Explain the main differences in messages granting a claim when the company, the customer, or a third party is at fault.

10. When your company is at fault, your letter granting a claim should
    a. Contain profuse apologies

    b. Promise that the problem will never occur again
    c. Explain that the company always attempts to do a good job, implying that the error was an unusual incident
    d. Lay the blame for the problem on a specific person or department

11. When a third party is at fault, your best response to a claim is to
    a. Simply honor the claim
    b. Honor the claim, but explain that your company is not at fault
    c. Refer the claimer to the third party
    d. Ignore the claim

Objective 7.6: Outline how best to protect yourself when referring to a candidate's shortcomings in a recommendation letter.

12. If you are writing a recommendation letter for a candidate who has shortcomings, your best bet is to
    a. Refrain from mentioning the shortcomings at all
    b. Mention just the facts about the shortcomings
    c. Offer your opinion on how those shortcomings could be drawbacks if the person is hired
    d. State in the letter that you do not recommend the person

Objective 7.7: Describe the importance of goodwill messages, and describe how to make them effective.

13. The purpose of goodwill messages is to
    a. Generate sales
    b. Impress others
    c. Make yourself feel better
    d. Enhance relationships with customers, colleagues, and other businesspeople

14. The most effective goodwill messages
    a. Include as much flattery and praise as possible
    b. Exaggerate where necessary
    c. Are sincere and honest
    d. Do all of the above

Apply Your Knowledge

1. When organizing request messages, why is it important to know whether any cultural differences exist between you and your audience? Explain.

2. Your company's error cost an important business customer a new client; you know it and your customer knows it. Do you apologize, or do you refer to the incident in a positive light without admitting any responsibility? Briefly explain.

3. You've been asked to write a letter of recommendation for an employee who is disabled and uses a wheelchair. The disability has no effect on the employee's ability to do the job, and you feel confident about writing the best recommendation possible. Nevertheless, you know the prospective company and its facilities aren't well suited to wheel-

chair access. Do you mention the employee's disability in your letter? Explain.

4. Every time you send a direct-request memo to Ted Jackson, he delays or refuses to comply. You're beginning to get impatient. Should you send Jackson a memo to ask what's wrong? Complain to your supervisor about Jackson's uncooperative attitude? Arrange a face-to-face meeting with Jackson? Bring up the problem at the next staff meeting? Explain.

5. **Ethical Choices** You have a complaint against one of your suppliers, but you have no documentation to back it up. Should you request an adjustment anyway? Why or why not?

Practice Your Knowledge

DOCUMENTS FOR ANALYSIS

Read the following documents; then (1) analyze the strengths and weaknesses of each sentence and (2) revise each document so that it follows this chapter's guidelines.

DOCUMENT 7.A: REQUESTING ROUTINE INFORMATION FROM A BUSINESS

Our college is closing its dining hall for financial reasons, so we want to do something to help the students prepare their own food in their dorm rooms if they so choose. Your colorful ad in Collegiate Magazine *caught our eye. We need the following information before we make our decision.*

- *Would you be able to ship the microwaves by August 15th? I realize this is short notice, but our board of trustees just made the decision to close the dining hall last week and we're scrambling around trying to figure out what to do.*
- *Do they have any kind of a warranty? College students can be pretty hard on things, as you know, so we will need a good warranty.*
- *How much does it cost? Do you give a discount for a big order?*
- *Do we have to provide a special outlet?*
- *Will students know how to use them, or will we need to provide instructions?*

As I said before, we're on a tight time frame and need good information from you as soon as possible to help us make our decision about ordering. You never know what the board might come up with next. I'm looking at several other companies, also so please let us know ASAP.

DOCUMENT 7.B: MAKING CLAIMS AND REQUESTS FOR ADJUSTMENT

At a local business-supply store, I recently purchased your "Negotiator Pro" for my computer. I bought the CD because I saw your ad for it in MacWorld *magazine, and it looked as if it might be an effective tool for use in my corporate seminar on negotiation.*

Unfortunately, when I inserted it in my office computer, it wouldn't work. I returned it to the store, but since I had already opened it, they refused to exchange it for a CD that would work or give me a refund. They told me to contact you and that you might be able to send me a version that would work with my computer.

You can send the information to me at the letterhead address. If you cannot send me the correct disk, please refund my $79.95. Thanks in advance for any help you can give me in this matter.

DOCUMENT 7.C: RESPONDING TO CLAIMS AND ADJUSTMENT REQUESTS WHEN THE CUSTOMER IS AT FAULT

We read your letter requesting your deposit refund. We couldn't figure out why you hadn't received it, so we talked to our maintenance engineer as you suggested. He said you had left one of the doors off the hinges in your apartment in order to get a large sofa through the door. He also confirmed that you had paid him $5.00 to replace the door since you had to turn in the U-Haul trailer and were in a big hurry.

This entire situation really was caused by a lack of communication between our housekeeping inspector and the maintenance engineer. All we knew was that the door was off the hinges when it was inspected by Sally Tarnley. You know that our policy states that if anything is wrong with the apartment, we keep the deposit. We had no way of knowing that George just hadn't gotten around to replacing the door.

But we have good news. We approved the deposit refund, which will be mailed to you from our home office in Teaneck, New Jersey. I'm not sure how long that will take, however. If you don't receive the check by the end of next month, give me a call.

Next time, it's really a good idea to stay with your apartment until it's inspected as stipulated in your lease agreement. That way, you'll be sure to receive your refund when you expect it. Hope you have a good summer.

DOCUMENT 7.D: LETTER OF RECOMMENDATION

Your letter to Tanaka Asata, President of SONY, was forwarded to me because I am the human resources director. In my job as head of HR, I have access to performance reviews for all of the SONY employees in the United States. This means, of course, that I would be the person best qualified to answer your request for information on Nick Oshinski.

In your letter of the 15th, you asked about Nick Oshinski's employment record with us because he has applied to work for your company. Mr. Oshinski was employed with us from January 5, 1995, until March 1, 2001. During that time, Mr. Oshinski received ratings ranging from 2.5 up to 9.6, with 10 being the top score. As you can see, he must have done better reporting to some managers than to others. In addition, he took all vacation days, which is a bit unusual. Although I did not know Mr. Oshinski personally, I know that our best workers seldom use all the vacation time they earn. I do not know if that applies in this case.

In summary, Nick Oshinski performed his tasks well depending on who managed him.

Exercises

For live links to all websites discussed in this chapter, visit this text's website at www.prenhall.com/thill. Just log on, select Chapter 7, and click on "Student Resources." Locate the page or the URL related to the material in the text. For the "Learning More on the Web" exercises, you'll also find navigational directions. Click on the live link to the site.

7.1 Revising Messages: Directness and Conciseness Revise the following short e-mail messages so that they are more direct and concise; develop a subject line for each revised message.

a. I'm contacting you about your recent order for a High Country backpack. You didn't tell us which backpack you wanted, and you know we make a lot of different ones. We have the canvas models with the plastic frames and vinyl trim and we have the canvas models with leather trim, and we have the ones that have more pockets than the other ones. Plus they come in lots of different colors. Also they make the ones that are large for a big-boned person and the smaller versions for little women or kids.

b. Thank you for contacting us about the difficulty you had collecting your luggage at the Denver airport. We are very sorry for the inconvenience this has caused you. As you know, traveling can create problems of this sort regardless of how careful the airline personnel might be. To receive compensation, please send us a detailed list of the items that you lost and complete the following questionnaire. You can e-mail it back to us.

c. Sorry it took us so long to get back to you. We were flooded with résumés. Anyway, your résumé made the final ten, and after meeting three hours yesterday, we've decided we'd like to meet with you. What is your schedule like for next week? Can you come in for an interview on June 15 at 3:00 P.M.? Please get back to us by the end of this work week and let us know if you will be able to attend. As you can imagine, this is our busy season.

d. We're letting you know that because we use over a ton of paper a year and because so much of that paper goes into the wastebasket to become so much more environmental waste, starting Monday, we're placing white plastic bins outside the elevators on every floor to recycle that paper and in the process, minimize pollution.

7.2 Revising Messages: Directness and Conciseness Rewrite the following sentences so that they are direct and concise.

a. We wanted to invite you to our special 40% off by-invitation-only sale. The sale is taking place on November 9.

b. We wanted to let you know that we are giving a tote bag and a free Phish CD with every $50 donation you make to our radio station.

c. The director planned to go to the meeting that will be held on Monday at a little before 11:00 A.M.

d. In today's meeting, we were happy to have the opportunity to welcome Paul Eccelson. He reviewed some of the newest types of order forms. If you have any questions about these new forms, feel free to call him at his office.

7.3 Internet Visit the business section of the Blue Mountain site at www.bluemountain.com/eng3/business and analyze one of the electronic greeting cards bearing a goodwill message of appreciation for good performance. Under what circumstances would you send this electronic message? How could you personalize it for the recipient and the occasion? What would be an appropriate close for this message?

7.4 Teamwork With another student, identify the purpose and select the most appropriate format for communicating these written messages. Next, consider how the audience is likely to respond to each message. Based on this audience analysis, determine whether the direct or indirect approach would be effective for each message, and explain your reasoning.

a. A notice to all employees about the placement of recycling bins by the elevator doors.

b. The first late-payment notice to a good customer who usually pays his bills on time.

7.5 Revising Messages: Conciseness, Courteousness, and Specificity Critique the following closing paragraphs. How would you rewrite each to be concise, courteous, and specific?

a. I need your response sometime soon so I can order the parts in time for your service appointment. Otherwise your air-conditioning system may not be in tip-top condition for the start of the summer season.

b. Thank you in advance for sending me as much information as you can about your products. I look forward to receiving your package in the very near future.

c. To schedule an appointment with one of our knowledgeable mortgage specialists in your area, you can always call our hotline at 1-800-555-8765. This is also the number to call if you have more questions about mortgage rates, closing procedures, or any other aspect of the mortgage process. Remember, we're here to make the home-buying experience as painless as possible.

7.6 Ethical Choices Your small supermarket chain has received dozens of complaints about the watery consistency of the ketchup sold under the chain's brand name. You don't want your customers to stop buying other store-brand foods, which are made and packaged for your chain by various suppliers, but you do want to address their concerns about the ketchup. In responding to these complaints, should you explain that the ketchup is actually manufactured by a local supplier and then name the supplier, who has already started bottling a thicker ketchup?

Expand Your Knowledge

LEARNING MORE ON THE WEB

The Medium and the Message www.about.com

Explore About.com's numerous links to sources of information on a variety of subjects. You can find tips on business writing with examples of letters, memos, and other business documents. You'll find web-design ideas and help from numerous guides on many business-related topics. You can even get online help with setting standards for a company's online communication.

ACTIVITIES

Choosing what to include in a message, deciding how to effectively express it, and selecting an appropriate format are all important considerations when you write. Go to About.com and add to what you've already learned in this chapter about writing requests and other messages.

1. Both the chapter and this site offer guidelines for writing effective messages. List the "Seven C's" that characterize good letters and memos. If you use clear language in a routine message, is it still important to restrict yourself to one topic? Why or why not?

2. Even the best-run businesses sometimes disappoint their customers. Imagine that you have been asked to write a response to an angrily worded e-mail message that charges your company with fraud because a product ordered through the web has not arrived. Which of the ten "secrets" of writing business letters do you think would be most useful in shaping your reply?

3. Describe some similarities and differences between a memo and a letter.

EXPLORING THE WEB ON YOUR OWN

1. Learn how to write effective thank-you notes by reviewing the steps at this Globaltowne webpage, www.globaltowne.com/aresume/thankyounotes.htm.

2. Polish your condolence letters by following the steps at www.abusinessresource.com/Business_Resources/Additional_Resources/Business_Letters_and_Forms/Condolence_Letter/.

3. Turn praise into prose when writing letters of recommendation by following the steps at this webpage, www.resumeedge.com/professionals/careercenter/recommendations.

Learn Interactively

INTERACTIVE STUDY GUIDE

Go to the Companion Website at www.prenhall.com/bovee. For Chapter 7, take advantage of the interactive "Study Guide" to test your knowledge of the chapter. Get instant feedback on whether you need additional studying. Also, visit this site's "Study Hall" where you'll find an abundance of valuable resources that will help you succeed in this course.

PEAK PERFORMANCE GRAMMAR AND MECHANICS

To improve your skill with sentences, visit this text's website at www.prenhall.com/onekey. Click "Peak Performance Grammar and Mechanics," then click "Sentences." Take the Pretest to determine whether you have any weak areas. Review those areas in the Refresher Course, and take the Follow-Up Test to check your grasp of sentences. For advanced practice, take the Advanced Test. Finally, for additional reinforcement, go to the "Improve Your Grammar, Mechanics, and Usage" section that follows, and complete those exercises.

Improve Your Grammar, Mechanics, and Usage

The following exercises help you improve your knowledge of and power over English grammar, mechanics, and usage. Turn to the "Handbook of Grammar, Mechanics, and Usage" at the end of this textbook and review all of Section 1.7 (Sentences). Then look at the following 10 items. Circle the letter of the preferred choice within each group of sentences. (Answers to these exercises appear on page AK-3.)

1. a. Joan Ellingsworth attends every stockholder meeting. Because she is one of the few board members eligible to vote.

   b. Joan Ellingsworth attends every stockholder meeting. She is one of the few board members eligible to vote.

2. a. The executive director, along with his team members, is working quickly to determine the cause of the problem.

   b. The executive director, along with his team members, are working quickly to determine the cause of the problem.

3. a. Listening on the extension, details of the embezzlement plot were overheard by the security chief.

   b. Listening on the extension, the chief overheard details of the embezzlement plot.

4. a. First the human resources department interviewed dozens of people. Then they hired a placement service.
    b. First the human resources department interviewed dozens of people then they hired a placement service.
5. a. Andrews won the sales contest, however he was able to sign up only two new accounts.
    b. Andrews won the sales contest; however, he was able to sign up only two new accounts.
6. a. To find the missing file, the whole office was turned inside out.
    b. The whole office was turned inside out to find the missing file.
7. a. Having finally gotten his transfer, he is taking his assistant right along with him.
    b. Having finally gotten his transfer, his assistant is going right along with him.

8. a. Irving was recruiting team members for her project, she promised supporters unprecedented bonuses.
    b. Because Irving was recruiting team members for her project, she promised supporters unprecedented bonuses.
9. a. He left the office unlocked overnight. This was an unconscionable act, considering the high crime rate in this area lately.
    b. He left the office unlocked overnight. An unconscionable act, considering the high crime rate in this area lately.
10. a. When it comes to safety issues, the abandoned mine, with its collapsing tunnels, are cause for great concern.
    b. When it comes to safety issues, the abandoned mine, with its collapsing tunnels, is cause for great concern.

For additional exercises focusing on sentences, go to www.prenhall.com/thill and select "Handbook of Grammar, Mechanics, and Usage Practice Sessions."

Cases

Applying the Three-Step Writing Process to Cases

Apply each step to the following cases as assigned by your instructor.

Planning

Analyze the Situation
What's your general purpose?
What's your specific purpose?
What do you want readers to do?
Who are your readers? (Who is the primary audience? What do readers have in common? What is their general background? How will they react?)

Gather Information
What information do readers need?

Adapt to the Audience
How will you establish credibility?

Writing

Organize the Information
What's your main idea?
Will you use the direct or indirect approach? Why?

Compose the Message
Will your tone be informal or more formal?
Draft the message as discussed in the "Your task" section of the case.

Completing

Revise the Message
Use the Checklist for Revising Business Messages on page 174 to edit and revise your message for clarity.

Produce the Message
What's the best way to distribute your message? By fax? By e-mail? By sealed envelope?

Proofread the Message
Proofread your message for errors in layout, spelling, and mechanics.

1   **2**   **3**

ROUTINE REQUESTS

1. Step on it: Letter to Floorgraphics requesting information about underfoot advertising You work for Mary Utanpitak, owner of Better Bike and Ski Shop. Yesterday, Mary met with the Schwinn sales representative, Tom Beeker, who urged her to sign a contract with Floorgraphics. That company leases floor space from retail stores, then creates and sells floor ads to manufacturers like Schwinn. Floorgraphics will pay Mary a fee for leasing the floor space, as well as a percentage for every ad it sells. Mary was definitely interested, and turned to you after Beeker left.

"Tom says that advertising decals on the floor in front of the product reach consumers right where they're standing when making a decision," explained Mary. "She says the ads increase sales from 25 to 75 percent."

You both look down at the dusty floor, and Mary laughs. "It seems funny that manufacturers will pay hard cash to put their names where customers are going to track dirt all over them! But if Tom's telling the truth, we could profit three ways: from the leasing fee, the increased sales, and the share in ad revenues. That's not so funny."

Your task: Mary Utanpitak wants you to write a letter to CEO Richard Rebh at Floorgraphics, Inc. (5 Vaughn Dr., Princeton,

NJ 08540) asking for financial details and practical information about the ads. For example, how will you clean your floors? Who installs and removes the ads? Can you terminate the lease if you don't like them? She'll sign the letter, but since you've been studying business communication, she thinks you'll do a better job writing the request.[6]

2. Fortune or folly: Letter requesting information from a Subway franchise operator Even before you heard Jared Fogle's story, you were thinking about buying into a franchise. Reading about the young man who lost 245 pounds while eating two Subway sandwiches a day has inspired your choice. If Jared can reach his goal by sheer determination, so can you. Maybe you should invest in a Subway franchise.

You do have some misgivings. From popular books such as Robert Kiyosaki's *Rich Dad, Poor Dad*, you know that franchises can be a smart first move for aspiring business owners. But you've also read that they demand long hours, steep investments, and rigid rule-following. What you'd like to know is exactly how long those hours will be, what unforeseen costs might suddenly arise, and whether it's hard for a would-be entrepreneur to fit into the franchise mold, where everything from the signage to the size of the ham slices is dictated by the company.

You decide to ask someone who's already taken the plunge, signed that 20-year agreement, and doled out the necessary $65,000 to $184,000 (depending on store size and location). That money covers franchise fees, leasehold improvements, equipment, outdoor signs, supplies, and inventory, but what isn't covered?

You also have questions you're embarrassed to ask Subway because you think maybe you should already know the answers. For instance, do you get any say-so in that range of 500 to 1,500 square feet, standard sizes for Subway outlets? Does Subway insist on choosing its own locations, or will you get to specify Bartlesville, Oklahoma, which you've determined to be an untapped market for the sandwich franchise? How long before you'll see any profit?

When you called Subway's headquarters and asked for references, you were told about Tharita Jones, who operates a Subway store in Tulsa, about 30 miles from Bartlesville. "She's been with us for about five years now," said the woman as she gave you Jones's name and number. Trouble is, you can't bring yourself to call her.

You have an image in your mind of a fast-food-franchise owner watching employees, doing paperwork, ordering supplies, talking to customers, and checking restrooms. She won't have the time to take a call from someone like you. You have so many questions: how to calculate the 8 percent royalties on gross sales and the 3.5 percent advertising fees charged weekly by the Subway franchise, whether franchise owners can switch suppliers if they find a better price, and what happens if royalty payments arrive late. You're also dying to find out whether Jones is happy with Subway's advertising programs and how much help she got from Subway in the beginning. You're even wondering whether you could drop by and observe Jones's operation for a day—sort of a behind-the-scenes look. How can you ask all this by phone?

You decide that a letter would be more considerate. You hate to impose, but you need to investigate before you sign a contract. With 14,700 stores worldwide, Subway *seems* like a good investment, but you need to be certain.

Your task: Write a letter to Tharita Jones (Owner, Subway Restaurant, 120 W. Greenfield St., Tulsa, OK 74133), requesting permission to visit her operation for a day (at her convenience) so that you can learn more about investing in a Subway franchise. Let her know how you got her name, and reassure her that you will need only about an hour of her time to address your specific questions. To make your meeting more productive, list your questions in the letter. You'll need to make your decision soon, so politely suggest a time limit for her reply.[7]

3. A juicy position: E-mail requesting information about careers at Jamba Juice You did not expect to find a job while working out at 24-Hour Fitness, but you're willing to explore an opportunity when it appears. As you were buying a smoothie at the Jamba Juice bar inside the gym, you overheard the manager talking about the company's incentives for employees, especially those interested in becoming managers. You ask her about it and she suggests you log on to the company's website (www.jambajuice.com) for more information.

You're still in business school, and you need a part-time job. Finding one at a company that offers a good future after graduation would be even better than simply earning some money to keep you going now. You check the Jamba Juice website.

You discover that the juice-bar chain has created a good reputation in the health, fitness, and nutrition industry. Also, you can submit your résumé online for an entry-level job. That sounds promising. If you could start now while finishing your degree, you'd be in a prime spot for promotion once you graduate.

But when you look at the careers page (www.jambacareers.com) you find the information a little confusing.

The "General Manager J.U.I.C.E. Plan" seems to be about profit-sharing, but the details are not fully explained. You'd like to know more.

Your task: You're going to write an e-mail message requesting additional information about careers and advancement at Jamba Juice. First, visit www.jambajuice.com and www.jambacareers.com to learn all that you can. Then compose your message. Ask for clarification on any points you don't understand, or ask for further instructions on submitting your application. You might want to mention that you're still in school, studying business.[8]

4. Air rage fiasco: Letter requesting refund from British Airways "There we were, cruising over the Atlantic, and the guy just went berserk! I couldn't believe it!" Samantha Alberts, vice president of sales at Richter Office Solutions, is standing over your desk, describing the scene for you. You notice that your boss is still pale and shaky, even though it's Monday and the "incident" happened last Friday.

She was flying back from a conference in London to make a presentation at your New York branch, before heading back home to San Francisco on Saturday. She admits it was a crushing schedule and probably foolish to plan to prepare her notes on the plane, but she never expected this.

"So how did it start?" you ask mildly, hoping your calm will help steady her nerves. She's got another meeting in two hours.

"Well, I didn't notice anything until this guy leaped up and lunged for the flight attendant with both fists flailing. But later I heard that he'd been viewing 'offensive images' on his laptop and that other passengers complained that they could see the screen. When the steward politely asked him to stop, the guy went nuts! He was a stocky, red-faced, bull-necked guy, and it took six crew members to handcuff him and strap him into a back-row seat. Maybe he was drunk or on drugs, I don't know, but he just kept screaming, 'I'm going to kill you!' and hitting people with his head, which was bleeding everywhere.

"Finally a passenger who was a pediatrician came forward and offered to inject the guy with a sedative for the rest of the flight. Thank goodness. Otherwise we would've been listening to his profanity for the next 10 hours . . ." she trails off. "You know, I thought he was a hijacker and I was going to die on that plane."

You pat her soothingly. "So did they arrest him?"

"As soon as we got on the ground. Police cars were everywhere. He just kept mumbling, 'I thought they were going to kill me.'" She shudders. "But the flight attendants and airline officials were wonderful. They told us to write to the airline, explain the details, and ask for a refund. Of course, I was late and unprepared for my meeting. Thank goodness it wasn't a client! When they heard about my 'air rage' encounter, the folks in our home office just handed me a cup of strong coffee and sat me down on a couch with a blanket."

Your task: You always handle Samantha's travel arrangements, and she's left you with her ticket stubs and other documents. Write the letter requesting a refund to British

Airways Ticket Refunds USA, 75-20 Astoria Blvd., Jackson Heights, NY 11370. (Make up any necessary times, dates, or flight numbers.)[9]

5. Blockbuster shake-up: Memo requesting information from retail managers Everyone knew there was trouble at Blockbuster's new headquarters in Dallas when CEO Bill Fields, a former Wal-Mart whiz, suddenly resigned. Then Sumner Redstone and Tom Dooley (chairman and deputy chairman of Blockbuster's parent company, Viacom) flew in to assess the damage wrought by Fields's departure. They started by giving orders—particularly to you, Fields's former executive assistant.

Before Fields resigned to take a position with Hudson's Bay Company in Canada, his strategy had been to boost Blockbuster's sagging DVD, game, and video rentals by establishing a new niche as a "neighborhood entertainment center." Using tricks he'd learned at Wal-Mart, he ordered the reconfiguration of more than 1,000 Blockbuster outlets, surrounding the cash registers with flashy displays of candy, potato chips, magazines, tie-in toys, and new and used DVDs and tapes for sale. His stated goal was to add $1 in retail purchases to every rental transaction. Meanwhile, he also relocated Blockbuster's headquarters from Florida to Dallas, losing 75 percent of the company's top staff when they declined to make the move. Then Fields initiated the construction of an 818,000-square-foot warehouse 25 miles outside of Dallas to centralize a new, highly sophisticated distribution operation (Fields's special expertise) for Blockbuster's 3,600 North American outlets. But revenues were still falling.

Redstone and Dooley's new plan is to get Blockbuster back into its core business—DVD, game, and video rentals. "This is still a healthy, growing business," Dooley insists. He believes that consumers coming in to rent movies and games were confused by the array of retail products that greeted them. "We want people to think of Blockbuster as the place to go to rent DVDs, games, and videotapes," he says.

Dooley and Redstone have been hiring new headquarters staff at the rate of about 50 people per week; they've been to the warehouse construction site; they've ordered outlets to rearrange merchandise to emphasize rentals; and now they've turned to you. "We've got a job you'll love," Dooley smiles. "We want to know what our store managers know, and we want you to ask them."

Your task: Briefly state the purpose of your message. Then draft a memo that will pick the brains of retail managers in the stores that Fields reconfigured. Dooley wants to know whether customers walk out when current hits aren't available, whether the emphasis on retail products affected cash flow, and whether sales and rental figures have changed now that the clutter has been removed. Ask them: Where's the cash coming from—movie and game rentals, movie and game sales, or candy bars? Dooley says, "I want a full report from every manager by the end of next week!" To get that kind of cooperation, you'd better organize your questions effectively.[10]

ROUTINE REPLIES

6. Lighten up: E-mail reply to a website designer at Organizers Unlimited When Kendra Williams, owner of Organizers Unlimited, wanted to create a website to sell her Superclean Organizer, she asked you, her assistant, to find a designer. After some research, you found three promising individuals. Williams chose Pete Womack, whose résumé impressed both of you. Now he's e-mailed his first design proposal and Williams is not happy.

"I detest cluttered websites!" she explodes. "This homepage has too many graphics and animations, too much 'dancing baloney.' He must have included at least 500 kilobytes of bouncing cotton balls and jogging soap bars! Clever, maybe, but we don't want it! If the homepage takes too long to load, our customers won't wait for it and we'll lose sales."

Williams's dislike of clutter is what inspired her to invent the Superclean Organizer in the first place, a neat device for organizing bathroom items.

Your task: "You found him," says Williams, "now you can answer and tell him what's wrong with this design." Before you write the e-mail reply to Womack explaining the need for a simpler homepage, read some of the articles offering tips at www.sitepoint.com. (select "Build" on the homepage, then "Planning Your Site"). Use these ideas to support your message.[11]

7. Dot-com trainee: Letter of recommendation for LifeSketch.com intern Mike Smith is founder, president, and CEO of LifeSketch.com (www.lifesketch.com), an online service offering photo archiving to members. As Smith's assistant, you've seen a lot of people come and go—but there's no one you'd rather see stay than your summer intern, Rolanda Winter. When you overheard her ask Smith for a letter of recommendation, you sat up and took notice. Is she leaving already?

"Don't worry," Smith assures you. "She'll be here until fall term starts. But she wants to be prepared with a recommendation letter because she's already lining up serious job interviews. I wish we could hire her full time."

"Maybe you'll find a place for her before September," you suggest hopefully. Winter has been such a patient learner, and a true help to you, that you hate to lose her. Interns usually move on, but in this case, you'd love it if Smith hired her.

For one thing, she learned your filing system overnight, whereas other interns left things in a hopeless mess. She asked lots of intelligent questions about the business. You've been teaching her website design principles, and she's picked them up rapidly, helping you redesign several pages on the LifeSketch site. Most impressive was the fact that she was always on time, neatly dressed, polite, and eager to assist. Also, she didn't mind doing mundane tasks.

On the down side, Winter is a popular student. Early on, you often found her busy on the phone planning her many social activities when you needed her help. After you had a little talk with her, this problem vanished.

"Since you know Rolanda's work better than anyone," says Smith, "I'd like you to draft the letter for me."

Your task: Working with a team of your classmates, discuss what should and should not be in the letter, which will be given to Rolanda Winter for general use. Then outline your ideas on paper. Finally, write the letter for Smith's signature.[12]

8. Satellite farming: Letter granting credit from Deere & Company This is the best part of your job with Deere & Co. in Moline, Illinois: saying yes to a farmer. In this case, it's Arlen Ruestman in Toluca, Illinois. Ruestman wants to take advantage of new farming technology. Your company's new GreenStar system uses satellite technology originally developed by the defense department: the Global Positioning System (GPS). By using a series of satellites orbiting Earth, the system can pinpoint (to the meter) exactly where a farmer is positioned at any given moment as he drives his GreenStar-equipped combine over a field. For farmers like Reustman, that means a new ability to micromanage even 10,000 acres of corn or soybeans.

For instance, using the GreenStar system, farmers can map and analyze characteristics such as acidity, soil type, or crop yields from a given area. Using this information, they know exactly how much herbicide or fertilizer to spread over precisely which spot—eliminating waste and achieving better results. With cross-referencing and accumulated data, farmers can analyze why crops are performing well in some areas and not so well in others. Then they can program farm equipment to treat only the problem area—for example, spraying a new insect infestation two meters wide, 300 yards down the row.

Some farms have already saved as much as $10 an acre on fertilizers alone. For 10,000 acres, that's $100,000 a year. Once Ruestman retrofits your GreenStar precision package on his old combine and learns all its applications, he should have no problem saving enough to pay off the $7,350 credit account you're about to grant him.

Your task: Write a letter to Mr. Ruestman (P.O. Box 4067, Toluca, IL 61369), informing him of the good news.[13]

9. Window shopping at Wal-Mart: Writing a positive reply via e-mail The Wal-Mart chain of discount stores is one of the most successful in the world: It designs, imports, and markets across national borders. In particular, Wal-Mart rarely fails to capitalize on a marketing scheme, and its online shopping page is no exception. To make sure the website remains effective and relevant, the webmaster asks various people to check out the site and give their feedback. As administrative assistant to Wal-Mart's director of marketing, you have just received a request from the webmaster to visit Wal-Mart's website and give feedback on the shopping page.

Your task: Visit Wal-Mart at www.wal-mart.com and do some online "window shopping." As you browse through the shopping page, consider the language, layout, graphics, ease of use, and background noise. Then compose a positive reply to the webmaster, and send your feedback to *cserve@wal-mart.com*. Print a copy of your e-mail message for submission to your instructor.

10. Red dirt to go: Positive e-mail reply from Paradise Sportswear Robert Hedin would agree with whoever said that it's possible to turn a failure into a success. But he'd probably add with a chuckle that it could take several failures before you finally hit "pay dirt." As the owner of Paradise Sportswear in Hawaii, Hedin was nearly done in by Hurricane Iniki in 1992, which wiped out his first silk-screened and airbrushed T-shirt business. He tried again, but then Hawaii's red dirt started seeping into his warehouse and ruining his inventory. Finally, a friend suggested that he stop trying to fight Mother Nature. Hedin took the hint: He mortgaged his condo and began producing Red Dirt Shirts, all made with dye created from the troublesome local dirt.

Bingo! So popular are Hedin's Red Dirt Sportswear designs, they're being snapped up by locals and tourists in Hedin's eight Paradise Sportswear retail outlets and in every Kmart on the islands. Last year Hedin added a new line: Lava Blues, made with real Hawaiian lava rock.

"You can make 500 shirts with a bucket of dirt," grins Hedin as he shows you around the operation on your first day. He's just a few years away from the usual retirement age, but he looks like a kid who's finally found the right playground.

Recently, Hedin decided to capitulate to all the requests he's received from retail outlets on the mainland. Buyers kept coming to the islands on vacation, discovering Hedin's "natural" sportswear, and plaguing him in person, by mail, and by e-mail, trying to set up a deal. For a long time his answer was no; he simply couldn't handle the extra work. But now he's hired you.

As special sales representative, you'll help Hedin expand slowly into this new territory, starting with one store. Wholesaling to the local Kmarts is easy enough, but handling all the arrangements for shipping to the mainland would be too much for the current staff. So you'll start with the company Hedin has chosen to become the first mainland retailer to sell Red Dirt and Lava Blues sportswear: Surf's Up in Chicago, Illinois—of all places. The boss figures that with less competi-

tion than he'd find on either coast, his island-influenced sportswear will be a big hit in Chicago, especially in the dead of winter.

Your task: Write a positive response to the e-mail received from Surf's Up buyer Ronald Draeger, who says he fell in love with the Paradise clothing concept while on a surfing trip to Maui. Let him know he'll have a temporary exclusive and that you'll be sending a credit application and other materials by snail mail. His e-mail address is *surfsup@insnet.com*.[14]

POSITIVE MESSAGES

11. Come back to us: Letter from EDS to dot-com deserters "Now's our chance to get them back," announces director Tom Templeton at a human resources staff meeting. You're his assistant, and for a moment you're confused.

"Get who back?"

"Everyone who left to join dot-com start-ups. You know how many people we lost when the Internet's promise of overnight fortunes lured away some of our best employees. But now it's our turn."

"You mean invite back the 550 employees we lost to dot-coms in recent years?" you ask.

"Exactly. I read that 12,000 dot-com jobs were cut in a nine-month period last year. That number is probably higher now."

You see his point and smile. He'll save EDS considerable money and trouble if some of these individuals return. Finding and keeping good employees is one of the greatest costs of operating any business.

"As dot-coms fail, some of our best people may be out there looking for jobs," Templeton adds. "Are we going to let our competitors have them?"

Your task: After the meeting, Templeton asks you to create a form letter he can send to ex-employees, telling them that EDS will welcome them back if their dot-com jobs haven't worked out as expected.[15]

12. Learn while you earn: Memo announcing Burger King's educational benefits Your boss, Herb Schervish, owner of a Burger King store in Detroit's downtown Renaissance Center, is worried about employee turnover. He needs to keep 50 people on his payroll to operate the outlet, but recruiting and retaining those people is tough. The average employee leaves after about seven months, so Schervish has to hire and train 90 people a year just to maintain a 50-person crew. At a cost of $1,500 per hire, the price tag for all that turnover is approximately $62,000 a year.

Schervish knows that a lot of his best employees quit because they think that flipping burgers is a dead-end job. But what if it weren't a dead end? What if a person could really get someplace flipping burgers? What if Schervish offered to pay his employees' way through college if they remained with the store? Would that keep them behind the counter?

He's decided to give educational incentives a try. Employees who choose to participate will continue to earn their usual salary, but they will also get free books and college

tuition, keyed to the number of hours they work each week. Those who work from 10 to 15 hours a week can take one free course at nearby Wayne County Community College; those who work 16 to 25 hours can take two courses; and those who work 26 to 40 hours can take three courses. The program is open to all employees, regardless of how long they have worked for Burger King, but no one is obligated to participate.

Your task: Draft a memo for Mr. Schervish to send out announcing the new educational incentives.[16]

13. Mind your own e-mail: Memo stating electronic privacy policy at the *Los Angeles Times* When you stepped into your office at the *Los Angeles Times* this morning, the place was buzzing with gossip about a reporter in the paper's Moscow bureau. Apparently he'd been snooping into his fellow reporters' e-mail. To catch him, supervisors there set up a sting operation, planting an exchange of phony e-mail messages with the Jerusalem bureau, which cooperated in catching the snoop. The bogus e-mail referred to "shrinking travel allowances." The suspect took the bait, apparently using a co-worker's password to view the e-mail. When he later mentioned the new travel rules, he was slapped with a reassignment back to Los Angeles, to an as-yet-undesignated job— probably writing obituaries, or so the rumormongers in your office have decided.

The *Los Angeles Times* has always observed strict discipline with regard to journalistic ethics. But because journalists traditionally hold "confidentiality" in high regard, management assumed that e-mail privacy needed no special rules or enforcement policies. Clearly, that assumption was wrong. In the past, the company casually conveyed a list of common-sense e-mail guidelines, such as not using the system for personal business; being aware that employee e-mail is not invisible to computer system administrators or even managers; not using derogatory language, obscenity, or copyrighted material; and so on. Now, a strict "privacy policy" will be added to the list, which will be sent out to bureau managers in an official memo.

As an employee of the newspaper's legal department, you've been handed the task of writing the memo to managers. Outline the company's policy for handling e-mail privacy violations. Management has already decided the penalties: reassignment, suspension without pay, or termination of employment. What you'll be communicating is how the new penalties are to be implemented. You will also suggest that managers immediately introduce these new rules to employees in a special meeting and that they routinely explain all the rules and guidelines to new hires.

For a first offense, the penalty will be a verbal warning in a personal meeting with a direct supervisor, which will also be entered in writing in the employee's human resources file. For a second offense, reassignment or suspension without pay, for a period to be determined by the employee's supervisor (who will know best the most appropriate length of time). A third offense will result in immediate termination without severance pay.

Your task: Address your memo to news bureau managers (who oversee editorial offices around the globe). Outline the company's policy for handling employees who violate e-mail privacy rules. Explain that a more detailed, company-issued memo covering all policy issues will be in their hands in a few weeks and must be posted at each bureau in an area visible to employees. For managerial reference in the meantime, list the penalties for privacy violations, and the appropriate sequence for applying them.[17]

14. Intercultural condolences: Letter conveying sympathy at IBM You've been working for two years as administrative assistant to J. T. "Ted" Childs, Jr., vice president of global workforce diversity at IBM's Learning Center in Armonk, New York. Chana Panichpapiboon has been with Childs even longer than you have, and, sadly, her husband, Surin, was killed (along with 19 others) in a bus accident yesterday. The bus skidded on icy pavement into a deep ravine, tipping over and crushing the occupants before rescue workers could get to them.

You met Surin last year at a company banquet. You can still picture his warm smile and the easy way he joked with you and others over chicken Florentine, even though you were complete strangers to him. He was only 32 years old, and he left Chana two children, a 12-year-old boy, Arsa, and 10-year-old girl, Veera. His death is a terrible tragedy.

Normally, you'd write a condolence letter immediately. But Chana is a native of Thailand, and so was Surin. In the past two years, you've listened many times to Childs's rousing, two-hour lecture to new managers on the benefits and demands of a multicultural workforce. You know you'd better do a little research first. Is Chana Buddhist or Catholic? Is there anything about the typical Western practice of expressing sympathy that might be inappropriate? Offensive?

After making some discreet inquiries among Chana's closest friends at work, you've learned that she is Theravada Buddhist, as are most people in Thailand. From a reference work in the company library about doing business around the world, you've gleaned only that in Thailand, "the person takes precedence over rule or law" and "people gain their social position as a result of karma, not personal achievement," which means Chana may believe in reincarnation. But the book also says that Theravada Buddhists are free to choose which precepts of their religion, if any, they will follow. So Chana's beliefs are still a mystery.

You do know that her husband was very important to her and much loved by all their family. That, at least, is universal. And you're toying with a phrase you once read, "The hand of time lightly lays, softly soothing sorrow's wound." Is it appropriate?

Your task: You've decided to handwrite the condolence note on a blank greeting card you've found that bears a peaceful, "Eastern-flavor" image. You know you're risking a cultural gaffe, but you won't commit the offense of not writing at all. Choose the most sincere wording you can, which should ring through any differences in custom or tradition.[18]

Chapter 8

Writing Bad-News Messages

Learning Objectives

AFTER STUDYING THIS CHAPTER, YOU WILL BE ABLE TO

1 Apply the three-step writing process to bad-news messages

2 Show how to achieve an audience-centered tone in bad-news messages and explain why it helps readers

3 Differentiate between the direct and indirect organizational approaches to bad-news messages and discuss when it's appropriate to use each one

4 Explain the purpose of buffers and list six things to avoid when writing them

5 Discuss the three techniques for saying no as clearly and as kindly as possible

6 Define defamation and explain how to avoid it in bad-news messages

7 List three guidelines for delivering bad news to job applicants and give a brief explanation of each one

8 Outline the main purpose of performance reviews, give three ways to accomplish that purpose, and list five guidelines to follow when giving negative reviews

On the Job:

COMMUNICATING AT AMERICAN AIRLINES

WHEN SAYING NO IS PART OF YOUR JOB

The past few years have challenged the airline industry from all sides: The trauma of September 11, 2001, and the ensuing security concerns, the economic downturn, the rapid emergence of low-cost-carrier competition, and the war in Iraq have cut the industry's revenue by 25 percent. To deal with this situation, American Airlines initiated hundreds of projects and changes to remove costs and to become leaner, smarter, more responsive, more efficient, and more successful.

Many of these changes have been in areas that customers don't value highly or don't see at all. The company is doing its best not to alienate the people whose business it depends on. In fact, American Airlines ensures that travel for passengers is as relaxing and hassle-free as possible. By focusing on the details, American is setting the standard for superior air travel—and that's where Donna Burnley comes in.

As a senior commodity manager, Burnley spends $23 million a year on in-flight food service supplies such as glasses, china, silverware, and napkins. In addition, she manages two warehouses and oversees the maintenance and repair of the in-flight food preparation and serving equipment. Naturally, many companies would like a part of that business, but few can meet Burnley's strict criteria. The biggest challenge these suppliers face is meeting the complex demands of the world's largest carrier, which serves more than 250 cities in 41 countries and territories with approximately 4,400 daily flights across the Americas, Europe, Asia, Africa, and Australia. As

One way American Airlines builds and retains strong relationships with its customers, employees, and investors is by focusing on audience feelings. By explaining the reasons for any bad news and by emphasizing the positive aspects of a negative situation, people at American Airlines communicate their understanding and demonstrate their goodwill.

Burnley puts it, "There are relatively few suppliers capable of manufacturing the volume of custom catering equipment required." She can't choose suppliers based solely on their price or quality; she needs partners who can also manufacture and distribute reliably on a global scale. Narrowing the field means having to say no—even to nice, ethical people who come to her with nothing but good intentions.

However, Burnley does have a choice about *how* she says no. She follows a thorough, objective decision-making process. She says that American's purchasing process "is designed to maximize total value by having me identify product specifications, assess supplier capabilities, research industry and raw material trends, understand the production process, and monitor the quality of end-products and services." When Burnley makes a decision, she knows what she's talking about.

Burnley uses her communication skills to convey negative messages in a professional and courteous manner. For example, because her decision process is so methodical and thorough, she has clear, objective reasons to present when she has to say no. She carefully explains to suppliers why they were rejected, not only to help these suppliers accept her messages but also to provide them with the concrete, factual information necessary to improve their products and perhaps be reconsidered in the future. Burnley says that communicating negative messages effectively is one of her primary responsibilities.[1]

www.aa.com

USING THE THREE-STEP WRITING PROCESS FOR BAD-NEWS MESSAGES

Saying no successfully depends on how you say it.

As Donna Burnley can attest, nobody likes bad news. The word *no* is so terse and abrupt, so negative, that a lot of people have difficulty saying it. And for most of us, it's the toughest word to hear or understand. Saying no to an idea from an employee, a proposal from a shareholder, a request from a customer, or even a suggestion from your boss can put knots in your stomach and cost you hours of sleep. How you deliver a negative answer can be far more damaging than the answer itself. But the most damaging *no* is usually the one you don't explain.[2] So be careful whenever you deliver bad news. Use the three-step process to help you write bad-news messages that are more effective and less damaging.

Step 1: Planning Bad-News Messages

When your message is a negative one, analysis becomes extremely important. Only when your purpose is specific are you able to word it in the best possible way. Also be sure that your bad-news message should indeed be sent and that it should be sent in writing (versus communicating it face-to-face or in a quick phone call). And more than ever, you need to know how your audience will receive your bad-news message. Do readers prefer to receive negative news up front, without delay? Or would they accept the news more readily if you explained your reasons first?

Any information gathering must yield reliable, unmistakable facts that will support your negative decision. Be sure that you have all the facts your audience will need. Once you send your bad news, you don't want to face a barrage of questions from confused readers.

Analysis, investigation, and adaptation help you avoid alienating your readers.

Finally, pay particular attention to maintaining a good relationship with your audience. Be sure to adapt your medium and tone to your audience. Careful attention to adaptation can help you avoid alienating your readers.

Step 2: Writing Bad-News Messages

When you must deliver bad news, you want to be careful to define your main idea as specifically as possible and to cover relevant points thoroughly and logically. You may need to reject an accounting firm's initial proposal because you can't afford both its tax and payroll services. However, you may be interested in discussing the cost of just one of those services, or you may want to inquire about the company's bookkeeping services. In such cases, your main idea encompasses more than just the rejection. Make sure you give your readers all the information.

The appropriate organization helps readers accept your negative news.

Choosing between the direct and indirect approaches takes on added importance in bad-news messages. You need to know whether it will be better to open with the bad news or to prepare your readers with a cogent explanation before giving them the negative bits. Also, pay special attention to word choice so that you can create sentences and paragraphs that are tactful and diplomatic.

Step 3: Completing Bad-News Messages

Revision is as important as the other steps in the writing process; it helps you make sure that your bad-news messages are organized properly, that they say what you want them to say, and that they do so concisely and clearly. Make sure that your design is appropriate for the bad news and contributes to your efforts to be sensitive. And as always, proofread your bad-news messages to guarantee that misunderstandings won't arise from typos, errors in spelling, or problems with mechanics.

DEVELOPING STRATEGIES FOR BAD-NEWS MESSAGES

Whether you refuse a claim, announce that quarter profits are down, or give an employee a negative performance review, you want your readers (1) to feel that they have been taken seriously and (2) to agree that your news is fair and reasonable. This section presents strategies you can use to help your readers understand your bad news and accept it with as little disappointment as possible. When delivering bad news, you have five main goals:

Bad-news messages must accomplish five goals.

- To convey the bad news
- To gain acceptance for it
- To maintain as much goodwill as possible with your audience
- To maintain a good image for your organization
- To reduce or eliminate the need for future correspondence on the matter

It is not easy to accomplish so many goals in a single message. But you can make your bad-news messages effective by creating an audience-centered tone, by using the direct or indirect approach to organize your message according to your audience's needs and expectations, and by modifying your approach for cultural differences.

Creating an Audience-Centered Tone

You've heard it before: It isn't *what* you say but *how* you say it that counts. That adage is certainly true for bad-news messages. Your tone alone goes a long way toward accomplishing all the goals that bad-news messages must achieve. An audience-centered tone helps your readers

Using an audience-centered tone helps readers understand and accept your bad news while continuing to respect your organization.

- Understand what your bad news is
- Accept your news as final
- View your news as fair and reasonable
- Remain well disposed toward your organization
- Preserve their own pride

When giving bad news orally, you can adopt an audience-centered tone by listening first instead of talking. Bad news involves emotions, so acknowledge the feelings of others. However, be careful not to let emotions interfere with your message; that is, if you must fire someone, you must do so even if that person is crying.[3]

When delivering bad news in writing, you won't be able to "listen" to your audience first, but you can certainly learn as much as possible about them beforehand. Then you'll be able to demonstrate in your document that you are aware of your readers' needs, concerns, and feelings. Several techniques will help you adopt an audience-centered tone:

- **Use the "you" attitude.** Although crucial to every message you write, using the "you" attitude is especially important in bad-news messages. For example, you could point out how your decision or information might actually further your audience's goals. Assume that your audience is interested in being fair, even when they are at fault. And convey your sincere concern by looking for the best in them.

The "you" attitude is especially important in bad-news messages.

- **Choose positive words.** As Donna Burnley can tell you, wording and tone work together to make a message either offensive or acceptable. Remember, you have an ethical obligation to convey your bad news clearly, not cover it up. Your readers must understand and accept what you're saying. Nevertheless, you can ease disappointment by using positive words rather than negative, counterproductive

Use positive rather than negative phrasing in bad-news messages.

Table 8–1 CHOOSING POSITIVE WORDS

Avoid a Negative Tone	*Use a Positive Tone*
I *cannot understand* what you mean.	Please clarify your request.
There will be a *delay* in your order.	We will ship your order as soon as possible.
Your account is in *error*.	Corrections have been made to your account.
The breakage was not our *fault*.	The merchandise was broken during shipping.
Sorry for your inconvenience.	The enclosed coupon will save you $5 next time.
I was *shocked* to learn that you're unhappy.	Your letter reached me yesterday.
The enclosed statement is *wrong*.	Please recheck the enclosed statement.

ones (see Table 8–1). Just be sure that you don't hide the bad news behind obscure language.[4]

Sometimes the "you" attitude is best observed by avoiding the word you.

- **Use respectful language.** To protect your audience's pride, use language that conveys respect and avoids an accusing tone. For instance, when refusing a claim, use impersonal, passive language to explain your audience's mistakes in an inoffensive way. Emphasize the action while downplaying the actor. Say, "The appliance won't work after being immersed in water" instead of "You shouldn't have immersed the appliance in water." When your audience is at fault, the "you" attitude is best observed by avoiding the word *you*.

Using the Direct Approach

Audience analysis is crucial for determining organization of bad-news messages.

As with most business messages, the key to choosing the best organizational approach for bad-news messages is to analyze audience members first. Try to put yourself in their shoes. What is their likely reaction to the news? How important is the message? How well do you know them? If you know that your audience is likely to prefer the bad news first, or if the situation is minor and the news will cause your audience little pain or disappointment, use the direct approach:

- Start with a clear statement of the bad news.
- Proceed to the reasons for the decision or information (perhaps offering alternatives).
- End with a positive statement aimed at maintaining a good relationship with the audience.

Stating the bad news at the beginning can have two advantages: (1) It makes a shorter message possible, and (2) it saves readers time by helping them reach the main idea more quickly.

Some organizations expect all internal correspondence to be brief and direct, regardless of whether the message is positive or negative. So memos and internal e-mail messages often use the direct approach, stating the bad news before the reasons.

When the city of New York (property owner) informed vendors of New York City's Mart 125 in Harlem that the property was being redeveloped for more "profitable" uses, the letter got right to the point. Omar Fall (vendor) received the eviction notice and immediately began packing up his merchandise for sale.

The direct approach is also standard for some external messages. Routine bad-news messages to other companies often start with the bad news, especially if they relay decisions that have little or no personal impact. The indirect approach can actually cause ill will in people who see bad news frequently (such as people searching for employment).[5] Thus, the direct approach might be best in messages rejecting employment applications.

You'll sometimes know from experience that your audience simply prefers reading the bad news first in any message. Also, the direct approach is appropriate when you want to present an image of firmness and strength; for example, the last message in a debt collection series (just before the matter is turned over to an attorney) usually gets right to the point.

You may choose to use the direct approach in a variety of circumstances, saving your positive comments for the close. Nevertheless, direct organization is no excuse for being abrupt, inconsiderate, or discourteous. To make your bad-news messages effective, remember to use a tactful tone and to focus on reasons.

> The direct approach in bad-news messages resembles the organization used for routine positive messages.

Using the Indirect Approach

In many cases, beginning a bad-news message with a blunt "no" could well prevent your audience from reading or listening to your reasons. To ease your readers into your message, you can explain your reasons before delivering the bad news; that is, use the indirect approach:

> Use the indirect approach when some preparation will help your audience accept your bad news.

- Open with a buffer.
- Continue with a logical, neutral explanation of the reasons for the bad news.
- Follow with a clear but diplomatic statement of the bad news.
- Close with a positive, forward-looking statement that is helpful and friendly.

Figure 8–1 highlights the differences between the direct and indirect approaches in bad-news messages. Presenting your reasons before stating your bad news increases your chances of gaining audience understanding and acceptance. Because this approach gradually prepares readers for the negative news to come, you don't want to undermine the attempt by carelessly stating the bad news in the subject line.

Make Subject Lines Neutral   When you need to use the indirect approach in a memo or an e-mail message, give plenty of thought to your subject line. If you state

> When sending negative memos or e-mail, don't blurt out the bad news in your subject line.

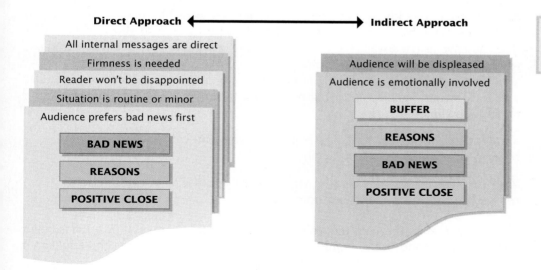

FIGURE 8–1
Indirect Approach Versus Direct Approach

Direct Approach ←——————→ Indirect Approach

All internal messages are direct
Firmness is needed
Reader won't be disappointed
Situation is routine or minor
Audience prefers bad news first

BAD NEWS

REASONS

POSITIVE CLOSE

Audience will be displeased
Audience is emotionally involved

BUFFER

REASONS

BAD NEWS

POSITIVE CLOSE

your bad news in the document heading, you defeat the purpose of using the indirect approach. It's easy enough to create an informative subject line without giving away the bad news. Simply make it neutral.

Instead of This	Say This
First-quarter sales figures plummet	First-quarter sales figures available
Delayed construction schedule	Revised construction schedule
Claim #A-14298 denied	Claim #A-14298
Budget cuts effective April 1	New budget effective April 1
Lost client	Client update

Be careful not to overcompensate. You don't want to raise expectations in your subject line only to dash hopes later on in your message.

Begin with a Buffer   Start your indirect bad-news messages with a neutral, non-controversial statement that is closely related to the point of the message; this statement is called a **buffer**. A good buffer is tricky to write. Its purpose is to establish common ground by broaching the topic of your message with a point that you and your readers can agree on. Buffers are not intended to "cushion" the bad news, insult readers with insincere flattery, or delay the bad news with self-promoting blather. Your goal in using a buffer is to set the stage for the bad news by giving yourself a chance to explain it.

> *A buffer is a neutral lead-in to bad news that both you and your reader can agree on.*

Good buffers are sincere and relevant so that readers don't feel they are being set up or "snowed." For example, if you use an unrelated buffer, you will seem to be avoiding the issue; that is, you'll appear manipulative and you'll lose your audience's respect. Some critics believe that using any buffer is manipulative, dishonest, and thus unethical. In fact, buffers are unethical only if they're insincere. Breaking bad news with kindness and courtesy is the humane way. Genuinely considering the feelings of others is never dishonest; your kind consideration helps your audience accept your message.

> *You can choose from among many on-topic beginnings.*

To create an effective buffer, you might express your appreciation for being thought of ("Thank you for inviting me to speak at your next meeting"). Or you might assure your reader of your attention to a request ("Our technicians have examined your hard drive closely"), compliment the reader ("The thoroughness and detail of this proposal illustrate how much work and thought you put into it"), or indicate your understanding of the reader's needs ("Our department shares your goal of processing orders quickly and efficiently"). Whenever possible, base your buffer on statements made by the person you're responding to. Doing so shows your reader that you have listened well. Table 8–2 displays several types of buffers you could use to open a bad-news message tactfully.

When composing a buffer, be honest, positive, and brief. A well-written buffer will draw readers logically into your reasons for the bad news. Imagine your reaction to the following:

Your résumé indicates that you would be well suited for a management trainee position with our company.

Your résumé shows very clearly why you are interested in becoming a management trainee with our company.

The first buffer misleads the reader into thinking that perhaps a position is being offered. The second buffer is much more effective. By emphasizing the applicant's

TYPES OF BUFFERS　　　　Table 8–2

Buffer	Strategy	Example
Agreement	Find a point on which you and the reader share similar views.	We both know how hard it is to make a profit in this industry.
Appreciation	Express sincere thanks for receiving something.	Your check for $127.17 arrived yesterday. Thank you.
Cooperation	Convey your willingness to help in any way you realistically can.	Employee Services is here to smooth the way for all of you who work to achieve company goals.
Fairness	Assure the reader that you've closely examined and carefully considered the problem, or mention an appropriate action that has already been taken.	For the past week, we have carefully monitored those using the photocopying machine to see whether we can detect any pattern of use that might explain its frequent breakdowns.
Good news	Start with the part of your message that is favorable.	A replacement knob for your range is on its way, shipped February 10 via UPS.
Praise	Find an attribute or an achievement to compliment.	Your résumé shows an admirable breadth of experience, which should serve you well as you progress in your career.
Resale	Favorably discuss the product or company related to the subject of the letter.	With their heavy-duty, full-suspension hardware and fine veneers, the desks and file cabinets in our Montclair line have become a hit with value-conscious professionals.
Understanding	Demonstrate that you understand the reader's goals and needs.	So that you can more easily find the printer with the features you need, we are enclosing a brochure that describes all the Panasonic printers currently available.

own interpretation of her qualifications rather than the company's evaluation, the buffer remains positive without misleading the audience. Here are some things to avoid when writing a buffer:

- **Never give the impression that good news will follow.** Building up your audience's expectations at the beginning only makes the actual bad news even more surprising, as illustrated in the example just discussed.

- **Never say no.** An audience encountering the blunt refusal right at the beginning usually reacts negatively to the rest of the message, no matter how reasonable and well phrased it is.

- **Don't use wordy and irrelevant phrases and sentences.** Sentences such as "We have received your letter," "This e-mail is in reply to your request," and "We are writing in response to your request" are irrelevant. Make better use of the space by referring directly to the subject of the message.

Use a buffer that
- Does not mislead the reader
- Is neutral
- Is relevant
- Maintains a respectful tone
- Is unapologetic
- Is succinct

- **Refrain from using a know-it-all tone.** When you use phrases such as "you should be aware that," readers expect your lecture to lead to a negative response, so they resist the rest of your message.

- **Avoid apologizing.** Unless warranted by extreme circumstances, an apology only weakens the explanation of the unfavorable news that follows.

- **Don't write a buffer that is too long.** Quickly identify something that both you and your audience are interested in and agree on before proceeding in a businesslike way.

After composing your buffer, evaluate it. Ask yourself four questions: Is it pleasant? Is it relevant? Is it neutral, saying neither yes nor no? Does it provide a smooth transition to the reasons that follow? If you can answer yes to every question, you can proceed confidently to the next section of your message.

Follow with Reasons   If you've done a good job of composing the buffer, the reasons will follow naturally. Cover the more positive points first, then move to the less positive ones. Provide enough detail for your audience to understand your reasons, but be concise; a long, roundabout explanation may make readers impatient. Your goal is to explain *why* you have reached your decision before you explain *what* that decision is. If you present your reasons effectively, they should convince your audience that your decision is justified, fair, and logical.

One way to be tactful when giving your reasons is to avoid focusing on why the decision is good for you or your company. When appropriate, highlight how your negative decision benefits your audience. For example, you might point out something simple. If your schedule is full and you need to turn down a client's project, you might say something like this:

> With two of our account representatives out on family leave, we are scrambling to cover current projects. Your campaign deserves the full-time attention of a dedicated representative.

When rejecting potential suppliers for American Airlines, Donna Burnley provides all the facts and figures necessary to work on improving their products.

Avoid apologizing when giving your reasons. Apologies are appropriate only when someone in your company has made a severe mistake or has done something terribly wrong. If no one in the company is at fault, an apology gives the wrong impression.

Similarly, avoid hiding behind company policy in bad-news messages. If you say, "Company policy forbids our hiring anyone who does not have two years' management experience," you seem to imply that you haven't considered the person on her or his own merits. You will do better to explain your company's policy without referring to it as "policy." That way, the audience can try to meet the requirements at a later time. A tactfully worded message might give these reasons for the decision not to hire:

> Because these management trainee positions are quite challenging, our human relations department has researched the qualifications needed to succeed in them. The findings show that the two most important qualifications are a bachelor's degree in business administration and two years' supervisory experience.

That paragraph does a good job of stating the reasons for the refusal:

- It provides enough detail to make the reason for the refusal logically acceptable.

- It implies that the applicant is better off avoiding a program in which he or she would probably fail, given the background of potential co-workers.

Present reasons to show that your decision is reasonable and fair.

Focus on how the audience might benefit from your negative message.

Well-written reasons are
- Detailed
- Tactful
- Individualized
- Unapologetic
- Positive

- It explains the company's policy as logical rather than rigid, without labeling the reason as "company policy."

- It offers no apology for the decision.

- It avoids negative personal expressions ("You do not meet our requirements").

Donna Burnley has learned that even though specific reasons help audiences accept bad news, reasons cannot always be given. Don't include reasons when they involve confidential, excessively complicated, or purely negative information or when they benefit only you or your firm (by enhancing the company's profits, for example). Instead, move directly to the next section.

Sometimes detailed reasons should not be provided.

State the Bad News   When the bad news is a logical outcome of the reasons that come before it, the audience is psychologically prepared to receive it. However, the audience may still reject your message if the bad news is handled carelessly. Even though you want to make your message as clear as possible, you don't want to be blunt, tactless, or harsh.

Three techniques are especially useful for saying no as clearly and as kindly as possible. First, do what you can to de-emphasize the bad news:

- **Minimize the space or time you devote to the bad news.** Don't dwell on the negative parts.

- **Subordinate your bad news in a complex or compound sentence.** This construction pushes the bad news into the middle of the sentence, the point of least emphasis ("My department is already shorthanded, so I'll need all my staff for at least the next two months").

- **Embed bad news mid-paragraph or use parenthetical expressions.** Again, the middle of a paragraph is the point of least emphasis ("Our profits, which are down, are only part of the picture").

To handle bad news carefully,
- *De-emphasize the bad news visually and grammatically*
- *Use a conditional statement*
- *Tell what you did do, not what you didn't do*

Don't let the bad news get lost by overemphasizing the positive.

Second, use a conditional (*if* or *when*) statement to imply that the audience could have received, or might someday receive, a favorable answer ("When you have more managerial experience, you are welcome to reapply"). Such a statement could motivate applicants to improve their qualifications.

Third, tell readers what you did do, can do, or will do rather than what you did not do, cannot do, or will not do. Instead of saying, "We are unable to serve you, so please call your nearest dealer," say, "We sell exclusively through retailers, and the one nearest you that carries our merchandise is . . ." By implying the bad news, you may not need to actually state it. Rather than blurting out, "You were not chosen for this position," say, "The five positions currently open have been filled with people whose qualifications match those uncovered in our research."

By focusing on the positive and implying the bad news, you soften the blow. However, be sure your audience understands the entire message—including the bad news. It would be unethical to overemphasize the positive; if an implied message might leave doubt, state your decision in direct terms. Just be sure to avoid overly blunt statements that are likely to cause pain and anger:

At Urban Terrain, a landscape design company, Hilberto Ortiz and his team try to play down negative messages. "When you have to say no, you want people to get the message," says Ortiz, "but you don't have to be harsh about it. Spend as little time as possible on the bad news and concentrate on the positive stuff."

Instead of This	Say This
I *must refuse* your request.	I will be out of town on the day you need me.
We *must deny* your application.	The position has been filled.
I am *unable* to grant your request.	Contact us again when you have established . . .
We *cannot* afford to continue the program.	The program will conclude on May 1.
Much as I would like to attend . . .	Our budget meeting ends too late for me to attend.
We *must reject* your proposal.	We've accepted the proposal from AAA Builders.
We *must turn down* your extension request.	Please send in your payment by June 14.

An upbeat, positive close
- Builds goodwill
- Offers a suggestion for action
- Provides a look toward the future

End with a Positive Close   After stating your bad news, end your message on an upbeat note. An effective close helps you build goodwill, offers a suggestion for action, and provides a look toward the future. You might propose an attainable solution to the audience's problem ("The human resources department has offered to bring in temporary workers when I need them, and they would probably consider doing the same for you"). In a message to a customer or potential customer, you might use an off-the-subject ending that includes resale information or sales promotion. If you've asked

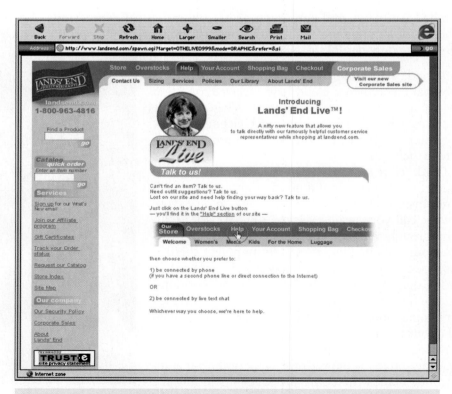

Problems are opportunities in disguise—at least that's how Lands' End sees it. Whether a customer is being notified about an out-of-stock item, a partial shipment, or a delivery delay, Lands' End strengthens the relationship by ending the message positively. The close is sincere, confident, and optimistic.

readers to decide between alternatives or to take some action, make sure that they know what to do, when to do it, and how to do it with ease. Whatever type of close you choose, follow these guidelines:

- **Be sincere.** Steer clear of clichés that are insincere in view of the bad news (avoid saying, "If we can be of any help, please contact us").

- **Be confident.** Don't show any doubt about keeping the person as a customer (avoid phrases such as "We hope you will continue to do business with us").

- **Keep it positive.** Don't refer to, repeat, or apologize for the bad news, and refrain from expressing any doubt that your reasons will be accepted (avoid statements such as "I trust our decision is satisfactory").

- **Limit future correspondence.** Encourage additional communication *only* if you're willing to discuss your decision further (avoid wording such as "If you have further questions, please write").

- **Be optimistic about the future.** Don't anticipate problems (avoid statements such as "Should you have further problems, please let us know").

If you are the one who has to reject the applicant for the management trainee position, you might observe these guidelines by writing a close like this:

> Many companies seek other qualifications in management trainees, so I urge you to continue your job search. You'll certainly find an opening in which your skills and aspirations match the job requirements exactly.

Keep in mind that the close is the last thing the audience has to remember you by. Try to make the memory a positive one.

Modifying Your Approach for Cultural Differences

Even though bad news is unwelcome in any language, the conventions for passing it on to business associates can vary considerably from country to country. For instance, all French business letters are very formal and writer-oriented (without reference to audience needs or benefits). Moreover, when the news is bad, French writers take a direct approach. They open with a reference to the problem or previous correspondence and then state the bad news clearly. While they don't refer to the audience's needs, they often do apologize and express regret for the problem.[6]

In contrast, Japanese letters traditionally open with remarks about the season, business prosperity, or health. When the news is bad, these opening formalities serve as a buffer. Explanations and apologies follow, and then comes the bad news or refusal. Japanese writers protect their readers' feelings by wording the bad news ambiguously. Western readers may even misinterpret this vague language as a condition of acceptance rather than as the refusal it truly is.[7]

In short, if you are communicating across cultures, you'll want to use the tone, organization, and other cultural conventions that your audience expects. Only then can you avoid the inappropriate or even offensive approaches that could jeopardize your business relationship.[8]

Be sure to choose an approach and style that matches your reader's cultural expectations.

Document Makeover

IMPROVE THIS MEMO

To practice correcting drafts of actual documents, visit **www.prenhall.com/onekey** on the web. Click "Document Makeovers," then click Chapter 8. You will find a memo that contains problems and errors relating to what you've learned in this chapter about handling bad-news messages. Use the Final Draft decision tool to create an improved version of this memo. Check the message for the use of buffers, apologies, explanations, subordination, embedding, positive action, conditional phrases, and upbeat perspectives.

EXAMINING TYPES OF BAD-NEWS MESSAGES

Now that you're familiar with the bad-news strategies at your disposal, you can look at various types of bad-news messages (from refusing invitations to giving negative performance reviews) and review examples of both effective and ineffective messages. Many of the messages that you'll be writing will likely fall into three major categories: negative answers to routine requests, negative organizational news, and negative employment messages.

Negative Answers to Routine Requests

The businessperson who tries to say yes to everyone probably won't win many promotions or stay in business for long. Occasionally, your response to routine requests must simply be no. It's a mark of your skill as a communicator to be able to say no clearly yet not cut yourself off from future dealings with other people.

Use either the direct or the indirect approach to tell someone you cannot provide what has been requested.

Refusing Requests for Information   When people ask you for information and you can't honor the request, you may answer with either the direct approach or the indirect approach. Say that you've asked a company to participate in your research project concerning sales promotion. However, that company has a policy against disseminating any information about projected sales figures.

The draft in Figure 8–2 uses the direct approach to refuse your request, even though you are outside the company and may be emotionally involved in the response. This message would offend most readers. Now look at the revised letter. It conveys the same negative message but without sounding offensive. As you think about the different impact those two versions might have on you, you can see why effective business writers take the time and the effort to give negative messages the attention they deserve.

When turning down an invitation or a request for a favor, consider your relationship with the reader.

Refusing Invitations and Requests for Favors   When you must say no to an invitation or a requested favor, your use of the direct or the indirect approach depends on your relationship with the reader. For example, suppose the president of the local community college asks your company to host graduation on your corporate grounds, but your sales meetings will be taking place at the same time. If you don't know the president well, you'll probably use the indirect approach. See Figure 8–3 on page 244, in which May Yee Kwan delivers this bad news in a helpful and supportive way. If you are friends with the president and work frequently on projects for the college, you might use the direct approach:

Sandra, thanks for asking us to host your graduation. You know we've always supported the college and would love to do this for you. During this same time, though, our annual company sales meeting will be taking place. Our special events staff will be devoting all of their time to logistics pertaining to the meeting.

Have you called Jerry Kane over at the Botanical Gardens? I can't think of a prettier site for graduation. Roberta in my office volunteers over there and knows Jerry. She can fill you in on the details, if you'd like to talk to her first.

Thanks again for considering us. Let's have lunch in mid-June to plan our involvement with the college for the next school year. You can think of all kinds of ways to make me sorry I had to say no! I'll look forward to seeing you and catching up on family news.

FIGURE 8–2
Effective Letter Refusing a Request for Information

Draft

Dear Mr. Phuoc:

Our company policy prohibits us from participating in research projects in which disclosure of discretionary information might be necessary. Therefore, we decline your invitation to our sales staff to fill out questionnaires for your study.

Thank you for trying to include Quality Information Services in your research. If we can be of further assistance, please let us know.

Sincerely,

Hides behind the blanket "company policy," a policy that the reader may find questionable

Makes tone unnecessarily negative and abrupt

Closes with an offer to help that is an unpleasant irony, given the writer's unwillingness to help in this instance

Revision

Quality
Information Services
1692 Pelham Avenue, New Rochelle, NY 10803
Voice: (914) 927-8219   Fax: (914) 927-8220

April 19, 2004

Mr. Tran Phuoc
774 Claremont Dr.
Wicker Park, Il 60622

Dear Mr. Phuoc:

We at Quality Information Services appreciate and benefit from the research of companies such as yours. Your study sounds interesting and useful.

Our board requires strict confidentiality of all sales information until quarterly reports are mailed to stockholders. We release press reports at the same time the quarterly reports go out, and we'll be sure to include you in all our future mailings.

Although we cannot release projected figures, we are more than willing to share information that is part of the public record. I've enclosed several of our past earnings reports for your inspection. We look forward to seeing the results of your study. Please let us know if there is any additional way we can help.

Sincerely,

Francis Newburgh

Francis Newburgh
Director, Human Resources

Makes buffer supportive and appreciative

Implies bad news

Explains reason for decision fully, without falling back on a blanket reference to company policy

Makes close friendly, positive, and helpful

FIGURE 8–3
Effective Letter Declining a Favor

Planning

Writing

Completing

1

2

3

Analyze the Situation
Gauge audience's reaction to refusal; gear level of formality to reader familiarity.

Gather Information
Collect information on possible alternatives.

Adapt to the Audience
For a more formal response, letterhead is best. Maintain the relationship with the "you" attitude, and focus on the reader's problem.

Organize the Information
Main idea is to refuse a request. Respect your reader by showing that the request received serious consideration. Use an indirect approach.

Compose the Message
Make your style conversational but keep it businesslike. Keep the letter brief, clear, and helpful.

Revise the Message
Maintain a friendly tone by eliminating overly formal words and phrases. Ensure that your tone is positive.

Produce the Message
Use letterhead with a straightforward format.

Proofread the Message
Be careful to review for accuracy, spelling, and mechanics.

InfoTech

927 Dawson Valley Road, Tulsa, Oklahoma 74151
Voice: (918) 669-4428   Fax: (918) 669-4429
www.infotech.com

March 5, 2004

Dr. Sandra Wofford, President
Whittier Community College
333 Whittier Ave.
Tulsa, OK 74150

Dear Dr. Wofford:

Buffers bad news by demonstrating respect and recapping request

Because we appreciate Whittier Community College and the many opportunities you have provided to deserving students over the years, we at Infotech have supported the college in many ways. Thank you for considering our grounds for your graduation ceremony.

Our companywide sales meetings will be held during the weeks of May 29 and June 5. We will host over 200 sales representatives and their families, and activities will take place at both our corporate campus and the Ramada Renaissance. As a result, our support staff will be devoting all of their time and effort to these events.

States reason for the bad news explicitly and in detail

Suggests an alternative—showing that Kwan cares about the college and has given the matter some thought

My assistant, Roberta Seagers, suggests you contact the Municipal Botanical Gardens as a possible graduation site. She recommends calling Jerry Kane, director of public relations. If we can help in any other way with graduation, please let us know.

Even though our annual meeting will most likely prevent us from ever hosting graduation, we remain firm in our commitment to you, President Wofford, and to the fine students you represent. We will continue to be a corporate partner to Whittier College and will support your efforts as you move forward.

Closes by renewing the corporation's future support

Sincerely,

May Yee Kwan

May Yee Kwan
Public Relations Director

lc

This letter gets right to the point but still uses some blow-softening techniques: It compliments the person and organization making the request, suggests an alternative, and looks toward future opportunities for cooperation.

Refusing Claims and Requests for Adjustment   Almost every customer who makes a claim is emotionally involved; therefore, the indirect method is usually the best approach for a refusal. Your job as a writer is twofold:

- Avoid accepting responsibility for the unfortunate situation.

- Avoid blaming or accusing the customer.

To steer clear of these pitfalls, pay special attention to the tone of your message. Demonstrate that you understand and have considered the complaint, but avoid any language that might have a negative impact on your reader. Even if the claim is unreasonable, rationally explain your refusal without apologizing or relying on company policy. End the message on a respectful and action-oriented note.

A tactful and courteous message can build goodwill even while denying the claim. For example, Village Electronics recently received a letter from Daniel Lindmeier, who purchased a digital video camera a year ago. He wrote to say that the unit doesn't work correctly and to inquire about the warranty. Lindmeier believes that the warranty covers one year, when it actually covers only three months (see Figure 8–4).

You may be tempted to respond to something particularly outrageous by calling the person responsible a crook, a swindler, or an incompetent. Resist! Otherwise, you could be sued for **defamation,** a false statement that tends to damage someone's character or reputation. Written defamation is called *libel*; spoken defamation is called *slander*.

Someone suing for defamation must prove (1) that the statement is false, (2) that the language is injurious to the person's reputation, and (3) that the statement has been "published." So beware of the irate message intended to let off steam. Avoid being accused of defamation by following these guidelines:

- Never let anger or malice motivate your messages.

- Communicate honestly, and make sure that what you're saying is what you believe to be true.

- Provide accurate information and stick to the facts.

- Avoid using any kind of abusive language or terms that could be considered defamatory.

- If you wish to express your own personal opinions about a sensitive matter, use your own stationery (not company letterhead), and don't include your job title or position. Take responsibility for your own actions without involving your company.

- Consult your company's legal department or an attorney whenever you think a message might have legal consequences.

Negative Organizational News

Refusing a request is only one type of bad news. At times, you may have to deliver bad news about your company's products or operations. Whether you're reporting to a supervisor or announcing your news to the media, the particular situation determines whether you use the direct or the indirect approach.

Providing Bad News About Products   Suppose you have to provide bad news about a product. If you were writing to tell your company's bookkeeping department that product prices are increasing, you'd use the direct approach. Your audience

Margin notes:

Use the indirect approach in most cases of refusing a claim.

When refusing a claim,
- Demonstrate your understanding of the complaint
- Explain your refusal
- Suggest alternative action

Avoid defamation by not responding emotionally.

Use either the direct or the indirect approach when providing bad news about a product.

FIGURE 8–4
Effective Letter Refusing a Claim

Planning

Writing

Completing

Analyze the Situation
Purpose is to explain that the warranty has expired and to offer repairs that the reader can pay for.

Gather Information
Briefly gather information on product warranties, terms for repair, and resale information.

Adapt to the Audience
Use letter format and focus on customer relationship.

1

Organize the Information
Main idea is that you're offering repairs, even though the warranty has expired. Use the indirect approach to help reader accept your message.

Compose the Message
Make the style conversational. Choose your words carefully, and enclose a catalog to encourage future business.

2

Revise the Message
Review for logical order and tone. Be clear but friendly.

Produce the Message
Use a clean letter format on letterhead.

Proofread the Message
Review for accuracy and correctness. Be sure to include promised enclosures.

3

NUMBER ONE IN ENTERTAINMENT

Village Electronics
68 Lake Itasca Boulevard • Hannover, MN 55341
Voice: (612) 878-1312 • Fax: (612) 878-1316

May 3, 2004

Mr. Daniel Lindmeier
849 Cedar St.
Lake Elmo, MN 55042

Dear Mr. Lindmeier:

Thank you for your letter about the battery release switch on your JVC digital camera. We believe, as you do, that electronic equipment should be built to last. That's why we stand behind our products with a 90-day warranty.

Even though your JVC camera is a year old and therefore out of warranty, we can still help. Please package your camera carefully and ship it to our store in Hannover. Include your complete name, address, phone number, and a brief description of the malfunction, along with a check for $35. After examining the unit, we will give you a written estimate of the needed parts and labor. Then just let us know whether you want us to make the repairs—either by phone or by filling out the prepaid card we'll send you with the estimate.

If you choose to repair the unit, the $35 will be applied toward your bill, the balance of which is payable by check or credit card. If you decide not to repair the unit, the $35 will pay for the technician's time examining the unit. JVC also has service centers available in your area. If you would prefer to take the unit to one of them, please see the enclosed list.

Thanks again for inquiring about our service. I've enclosed a catalog of our latest cameras and accessories. In June JVC is offering a "Trade-Up Special," at which time you can receive trade-in credit for your digital camera when you purchase a newer model. Come and visit Village Electronics soon.

Sincerely,

Walter Brodie

Walter Brodie
President

mk

Enclosures: List of service centers
            Catalog

Buffers the bad news by emphasizing a point that reader and writer both agree on

States bad news indirectly, tactfully leaving the repair decision to the customer

Closes by blending sales promotion with an acknowledgment of customer's interests

Puts company's policy in a favorable light

Helps soothe the reader with a positive alternative action

would have to make some arithmetical adjustments once the increases were put into effect, but readers would presumably be unemotional about the matter. On the other hand, if you were writing to convey the same information to customers or even to your own sales department, you would probably use the indirect approach. Customers never like to pay more, and your sales reps would see the change as weakening your product's competitive edge, thereby threatening their incomes and possibly even their jobs.

Delivering Bad News About Company Operations   In trying situations, apologies may be in order. Good writers usually make apologies brief and bury them somewhere in the middle of the message. Moreover, they try to leave readers with a favorable impression by closing on a positive note. At least three situations require bad-news messages about company operations or performance:

Whatever the situation, when conveying bad news about your company, focus on the reasons and possibly on reader benefits.

- **Problems with company performance.** If company performance declines, your customers and shareholders want to hear the news from you, not from newspaper accounts or rumors. Even if the news leaks out before you announce it, counter with your own explanation as soon as possible—using your common business sense and presenting the bad news in as favorable a light as possible. Business is based on mutual trust, and if stakeholders can't trust you to keep them informed, they may choose to work with someone they *can* trust.

- **Controversial or unpopular company operations.** Companies producing unpopular products or conducting controversial operations can find themselves in the thick of a political crossfire. Try to explain the reasons your company is manufacturing the controversial item or providing the unpopular service. You want to show why your operation is reasonable and necessary. So that no one interprets your actions as being motivated simply by villainy, carelessness, or greed.

- **Changes in company policy or future plans that affect readers negatively.** When a change in company policy negatively affects your audience, state the reasons for the change clearly and carefully. Your explanation section must convince readers that the change is necessary. If possible, explain how the change will benefit readers.

Examples of changes in future plans would be if you lost a major customer or if an important deal fell through. In such cases, you could present the bad news as an opportunity to focus on smaller, growing businesses or on new products (see Figure 8–5). Sybervantage pursued licensing agreements with Warner and expected to enter into a mutually profitable arrangement. But when Warner rejected the deal, Sybervantage had to notify its salesforce. Rather then dwelling on the bad news, the message focuses on possible options for the future and the upbeat close diminishes the effect of the bad news.

Negative Employment Messages

Most managers have to convey bad news about people from time to time. You can use the direct approach when communicating with other companies, sending a negative reference to a prospective employer, or writing to job applicants. But it's best to use the indirect approach when refusing requests for recommendation letters or giving negative performance reviews to employees. These readers will most certainly be emotionally involved in what you have to say. In addition, use great care when choosing the media for these messages (see "Promoting Workplace Ethics: Should Employers Use E-Mail to Deliver Negative Employment Messages?")

Use the direct approach when giving readers bad news about someone else's job; use the indirect approach when giving readers bad news about their own jobs.

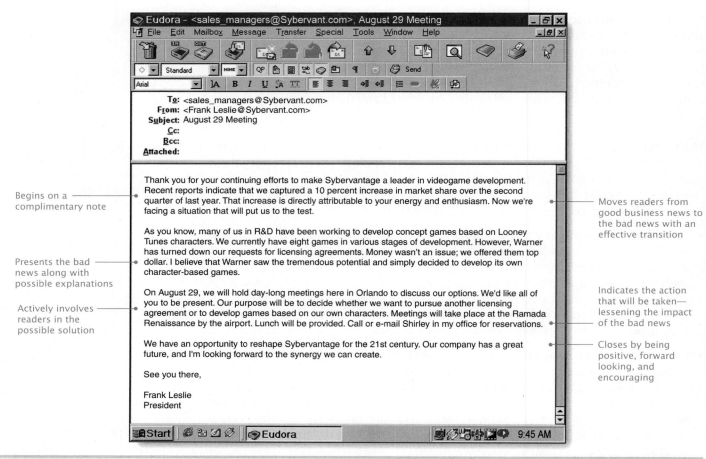

Begins on a complimentary note

Presents the bad news along with possible explanations

Actively involves readers in the possible solution

Moves readers from good business news to the bad news with an effective transition

Indicates the action that will be taken— lessening the impact of the bad news

Closes by being positive, forward looking, and encouraging

FIGURE 8–5
Effective E-Mail Providing Bad News About Operations

In letters informing prospective employers that you will not provide a recommendation, be direct, brief, and factual (to avoid legal pitfalls).

Refusing Requests for Recommendation Letters Even though many states have passed laws to protect employers who provide open and honest job references for former employees, legal hazards persist.[9] That's why many employers still refuse to write recommendation letters—especially for people whose job performance has been unsatisfactory. When sending refusals to prospective employers, your message may be brief and direct:

> According to guidelines from our human resources department, we are authorized to confirm only that Yolanda Johnson worked for Tandy, Inc., for three years, from June 1999 to July 2001. Best of luck as you interview the administrative applicants.

This message doesn't need to say, "We cannot comply with your request." It simply gets down to the business of giving readers the information that is allowable.

PROMOTING WORKPLACE ETHICS

Should Employers Use E-Mail to Deliver Negative Employment Messages?

Most people are more comfortable delivering bad news via e-mail than in person or on the phone. But is it appropriate to avoid the dreaded task of explaining layoffs and spending cuts in person by using e-mail to break such bad news? Some think it is.

Few executives advise using e-mail in extremely personal situations such as firing an employee, but some think using e-mail is perfectly fine for other uncomfortable scenarios such as job cuts, travel restrictions, hiring freezes, and significant spending changes. Consider these examples:

- Amazon.com called an in-person meeting to announce job cuts, but telecommuters who couldn't attend the meeting were informed via e-mail. "I want you to know that this was a very difficult decision for the company to make . . . we know this must be very painful to hear," the e-mail read.

- Discovery Communications used e-mail to alert Discover.com workers that staffing changes would take place before announcing layoffs of some of its dot-com full-time employees.

- Motorola sent e-mail to employees in its semiconductor sector explaining layoffs and other cost-cutting steps. Workers being let go were told in person, but word of what was happening went out electronically.

- Ameritrade online brokerage notified more than 2,000 call-center workers of layoffs via e-mail.

Employers who use e-mail to deliver bad news claim that it's a quick and effective way to get information to all employees—especially those in remote locations or home offices. With face-to-face or even voice-to-voice communication, people have a tendency to tune out the worst and sugarcoat the bad news. But delivering bad news via e-mail lets people be more honest. E-mail facilitates straight talk because senders don't see the discomfort of their recipients.

However, critics cry foul when companies break job-related bad news via e-mail. As they see it, e-mail is too impersonal. "The only advantage is that it gives management an opportunity to duck and dodge angry employees," says one communications expert. If you want to maintain good relationships with your employees, "these kinds of things should be done in person."

CAREER APPLICATIONS

1. Do you think employers should deliver negative employment messages via e-mail? Explain your answer.

2. Why does e-mail facilitate straight talk?

However, when you're communicating with the applicants themselves, any refusal to cooperate may seem a personal slight and a threat to the applicant's future. Diplomacy and careful preparation can help readers accept your refusal:

In letters telling job applicants that you will not write a recommendation, use the utmost tact.

> Thank you for letting me know about your job opportunity with Coca-Cola. Your internship there and the MBA you've worked so hard to earn should place you in an excellent position to land the marketing job.

> Although we send out no formal recommendations here at PepsiCo, I can certainly send Coke a confirmation of your employment dates. For more in-depth recommendations, be sure to ask the people you worked with during your internship to write evaluations of your work performance, and don't forget to ask several of your professors to write evaluations of your marketing skills. Best of luck to you in your career.

This letter deftly and tactfully avoids hurting the reader's feelings, because it makes positive comments about the reader's recent activities, implies the refusal, suggests an alternative, and uses a polite close.

In a letter turning down a job applicant, treat the reader with respect; by applying for a job, he or she has complimented your company.

Rejecting Job Applications It's also difficult to tactfully tell job applicants that you won't be offering them employment. But don't let the difficulty stop you from communicating the bad news. Rejecting an applicant with silence is unacceptable. At the same time, poorly written rejection letters do have negative consequences, ranging from the loss of qualified candidates for future openings to the loss of potential customers (not only the rejected applicants but also their friends and family).[10] When delivering bad news to job applicants, follow three guidelines:[11]

- **Open with the direct approach.** Employers fare better when they reject applicants up front.[12] Job applicants know that good news will most likely come by phone and that bad news will most likely come by letter. So if you try to buffer the bad news that your reader is expecting, you will seem manipulative and insincere.

- **Clearly state why the applicant was not selected.** Make your rejection less personal by stating that you hired someone with more experience or whose qualifications match the position requirements more closely.

- **Close by suggesting alternatives.** If you believe the applicant is qualified, mention other openings within your company. You might suggest professional organizations that could help the applicant find employment. Or you might simply mention that the applicant's résumé will be considered for future openings. Any of these positive suggestions may help the applicant be less disappointed and view your company more positively.

A rejection letter need not be long. Remember, sending a well-written form letter that follows these three guidelines is better than sending nothing. After all, the applicant wants to know only one thing: Did I land the job? Your brief message conveys the information clearly and with tactful consideration for the applicant's feelings. After Carol DeCicco interviewed with Bradley & Jackson, she was hopeful about receiving a job offer. Everything went well, and her résumé was in good shape. The e-mail draft in Figure 8–6 needed several changes to make the message effective. The revised e-mail helps DeCicco understand that (1) she would have been hired if she'd had more tax experience and (2) she shouldn't be discouraged.

In performance reviews, say what's right as well as what's wrong, and explain how the employee can improve performance.

Giving Negative Performance Reviews A performance review is a manager's evaluation of an employee. Few other communication tasks require such a broad range of skills and strategy as those needed for performance reviews, whether positive or negative. The main purpose of these reviews is to improve employee performance by

- Emphasizing and clarifying job requirements

- Giving employees feedback on their efforts toward fulfilling those requirements

- Guiding continued efforts by developing a plan of action, along with its rewards and opportunities

Another purpose of performance reviews is to help companies set organizational standards and communicate organizational values.[13]

Positive and negative performance reviews share several characteristics: The tone is objective and unbiased, the language is nonjudgmental, and the focus is problem resolution.[14] Also, to increase objectivity, more organizations are giving their employees feedback from multiple sources, with input from supervisors (upward), employees (downward), and colleagues (horizontal).[15]

Criticizing employees face-to-face is difficult, and it's just as hard to include criticism in written performance evaluations. Nevertheless, employee performance reviews can play an important role in lawsuits. If you fire an employee for incompetence and the performance evaluations are all positive, the employee can sue your company, maintaining you had no cause to terminate employment.[16] Also, if an injury is caused by an employee who received a negative evaluation but received no corrective action (such as retraining), your company could be sued for negligence.[17] So, as difficult as it may be, make sure your performance evaluations are well balanced and honest.

FIGURE 8–6

Poor and Improved Versions of E-Mail Rejecting a Job Application

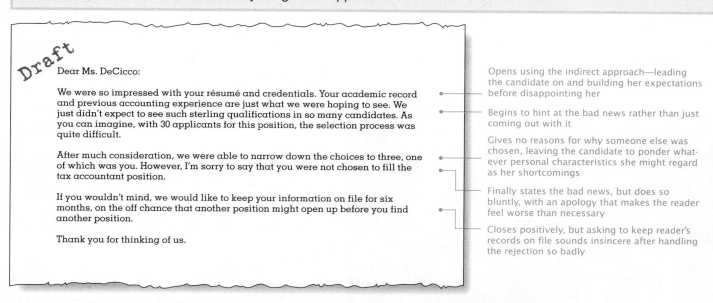

Dear Ms. DeCicco:

We were so impressed with your résumé and credentials. Your academic record and previous accounting experience are just what we were hoping to see. We just didn't expect to see such sterling qualifications in so many candidates. As you can imagine, with 30 applicants for this position, the selection process was quite difficult.

After much consideration, we were able to narrow down the choices to three, one of which was you. However, I'm sorry to say that you were not chosen to fill the tax accountant position.

If you wouldn't mind, we would like to keep your information on file for six months, on the off chance that another position might open up before you find another position.

Thank you for thinking of us.

Opens using the indirect approach—leading the candidate on and building her expectations before disappointing her

Begins to hint at the bad news rather than just coming out with it

Gives no reasons for why someone else was chosen, leaving the candidate to ponder whatever personal characteristics she might regard as her shortcomings

Finally states the bad news, but does so bluntly, with an apology that makes the reader feel worse than necessary

Closes positively, but asking to keep reader's records on file sounds insincere after handling the rejection so badly

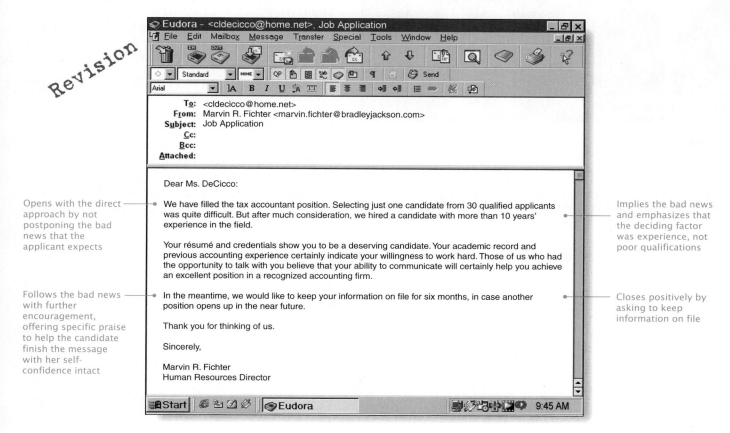

Opens with the direct approach by not postponing the bad news that the applicant expects

Follows the bad news with further encouragement, offering specific praise to help the candidate finish the message with her self-confidence intact

To: <cldecicco@home.net>
From: Marvin R. Fichter <marvin.fichter@bradleyjackson.com>
Subject: Job Application
Cc:
Bcc:
Attached:

Dear Ms. DeCicco:

We have filled the tax accountant position. Selecting just one candidate from 30 qualified applicants was quite difficult. But after much consideration, we hired a candidate with more than 10 years' experience in the field.

Your résumé and credentials show you to be a deserving candidate. Your academic record and previous accounting experience certainly indicate your willingness to work hard. Those of us who had the opportunity to talk with you believe that your ability to communicate will certainly help you achieve an excellent position in a recognized accounting firm.

In the meantime, we would like to keep your information on file for six months, in case another position opens up in the near future.

Thank you for thinking of us.

Sincerely,

Marvin R. Fichter
Human Resources Director

Implies the bad news and emphasizes that the deciding factor was experience, not poor qualifications

Closes positively by asking to keep information on file

Effective performance reviews require both promptness and consideration.

When you need to give a negative performance review, follow these guidelines:[18]

- **Confront the problem right away.** Avoiding performance problems only makes them worse. The one acceptable reason to wait is to allow yourself time to calm down and regain your objectivity.

- **Plan your message.** Be clear about your concerns, and include examples of the employee's specific actions. Think about any possible biases you may have, and get feedback from others. Collect and verify all relevant facts (both strengths and weaknesses).

- **Deliver the message in private.** Whether in writing or in person, be sure to address the performance problem privately. Don't send performance reviews by e-mail or fax. If you're reviewing an employee's performance face-to-face, conduct that review in a meeting arranged expressly for that purpose, and consider holding that meeting in a conference room, the employee's office, or some other neutral area.

- **Focus on the problem.** Discuss the problems caused by the employee's behavior (without attacking the employee). Compare the person's performance with what's expected, with company goals, or with job requirements (not with the performance of other employees). Identify the consequences of continuing poor performance, and show that you're committed to helping solve the problem.

- **Ask for a commitment from the employee.** Help the employee understand that planning for and making improvements are the employee's responsibility. However, finalize decisions jointly so that you can be sure that any action to be taken is achievable. Set a schedule for improvement and for following up with evaluations of that improvement.

Even if your employee's performance has been disappointing, you would do well to mention some good points in your performance review. Then, if your review is to be effective, clearly and tactfully state how the employee can improve to better meet the responsibilities of the job.[19] For example, instead of telling an employee only that he damaged some expensive machinery, suggest that he take a refresher course in the correct operation of that machinery. The goal is to help the employee succeed.

As director of sales and marketing at PruCare in Austin, Texas, Herman Wright knows that his sales and service staff need his support. Although he may set goals for his staff, he gives his team the responsibility for accomplishing them. "We stopped telling people what to do and started listening," says Wright. So even during negative performance reviews, Wright listens as much as he talks so that he and his employees can decide together what action to take.

Carefully word a termination letter to avoid creating undue ill will and grounds for legal action.

Terminating Employment   When writing a termination letter, you have three goals: (1) present the reasons for this difficult action, (2) avoid statements that might involve the company in legal action, and (3) leave the relationship between the terminated employee and the firm as favorable as possible. For both legal and personal reasons, present specific justification for asking the employee to leave.[20]

Make sure that all your reasons are accurate and verifiable. Avoid words that are open to interpretation, such as *untidy* and *difficult*. Make sure the employee leaves with feelings that are as positive as the circumstances allow. You can do so by telling the truth about the termination and by helping as much as you can to make the employee's transition as smooth as possible.[21] For a reminder of the strategies for delivering bad-news messages, see the "Checklist: Bad-News Messages."

✓ CHECKLIST Bad-News Messages

Overall Strategy

✓ Adopt an audience-centered tone (with sincerity, a "you" attitude, positive words, and a respectful attitude that uses impersonal and passive language).

✓ Avoid impersonal business clichés, terms with imprecise definitions, and a know-it-all tone.

✓ Use the direct approach when messages between fellow employees are routine, when readers are not emotionally involved, when a reader prefers the bad news first, or when firmness is necessary.

✓ Use the indirect approach in all other cases (neutral subject lines, buffer, reasons, bad news, and positive close).

✓ Modify your strategy when communicating with someone from a different culture.

Buffer

✓ Be brief and to the point.

✓ Express appreciation, cooperation, fairness, good news, praise, resale, or understanding.

✓ Introduce a topic that is relevant to the subject and that you and your reader can agree on.

✓ Don't mislead the reader.

✓ Avoid apologies, negative-sounding words (*won't, can't, unable to*), and all areas of disagreement.

✓ Maintain a confident, positive, supportive tone.

✓ When refusing a claim, indicate your full understanding of the nature of the complaint.

✓ In employment messages to a third party, identify the applicant or employee clearly.

Reasons

✓ Check the lead-in from the buffer for a smooth transition from the favorable to the unfavorable.

✓ Avoid apologies and expressions of sorrow or regret.

✓ Offer enough detail to show the logic of your position.

✓ Provide only accurate, factual information, without placing blame.

✓ Include only business reasons, not personal ones, and avoid relying on unexplained company policy.

✓ Carefully word the reasons so that readers can anticipate the bad news.

✓ Work from the general to the specific.

✓ Show how the decision benefits your audience.

✓ When refusing claims, emphasize the way things should have been handled, rather than dwelling on the reader's negligence.

✓ When rejecting applications, emphasize the positive qualities of the person hired rather than the shortcomings of the applicant being turned down.

✓ In performance reviews, describe the employee's limitations and suggest methods for improving performance.

Bad News

✓ De-emphasize bad news by minimizing the space devoted to it, subordinating it, or embedding it.

✓ State the bad news as clearly and as positively as possible, using tactful wording.

✓ Imply negative decisions whenever possible.

✓ Emphasize what the firm did do or is doing rather than what it can't or won't do.

✓ Avoid any hint that a negative decision is less than final.

✓ Emphasize a desire for a good relationship now and in the future.

✓ Avoid statements that might involve the company in legal action.

✓ When refusing a claim, make a counterproposal, offer a compromise, make a partial adjustment (if desirable), or suggest positive alternatives.

Positive, Friendly, Helpful Close

✓ Remind the reader of how his or her needs are being met.

✓ Make the close as positive as possible: Eliminate reference to the bad news, avoid apologies and words of regret, and eliminate words suggesting uncertainty.

✓ Suggest actions the reader might take and make compliance easy.

✓ Keep a positive outlook on the future.

✓ Refer to any enclosed sales materials.

✓ Be confident about keeping the person as a customer or other stakeholder.

✓ Extend good wishes.

✓ For performance reviews, express a willingness to help further.

✓ For termination letters, make suggestions for finding another job, if applicable.

On the Job:

SOLVING COMMUNICATION DILEMMAS AT AMERICAN AIRLINES

You're on the purchasing staff at American Airlines, working as Donna Burnley's assistant. Your job includes responding to requests and proposals from the airline's current suppliers and from companies that would like to become suppliers. Choose the best alternatives for responding to the situations described below, and be prepared to explain why your choice is best.

1. Your glassware supplier has announced a dramatic price increase that affects all the products that American buys from the company. The increase averages 12 percent, which is a lot of money in a tight-margin industry such as air travel. In all other respects, this supplier has been a stellar performer, offering great products with superb customer service. However, as much as everyone likes working with this company, if it doesn't cancel the price increase, American will be forced to find a new glassware supplier. You do have some room for compromise—an increase of not more than 3 or 4 percent would be workable. Which of the following paragraphs does the best job of presenting the bad news and the reasons?

   a. It's too bad that this is such a penny-pinching business, but that's the way things are. We can live with your current prices, but not the proposed increase. We'd love to go along with you, but I'm afraid we just can't.

   b. Because the airline industry competes primarily on price, we have no choice but to manage our costs carefully—it is our only hope of maintaining a minimal level of profitability. Your current prices fit our cost structure well. I'm sorry, but your proposed 12 percent increase does not, leaving us no choice but to find another supplier.

   c. As you are probably aware, the airline industry competes primarily on price, so managing our costs carefully is about the only option we have for maintaining a minimal level of profitability. Your current prices fit our cost structure, but the proposed 12 percent increase does not. If this increase goes into effect, we would be unable to continue purchasing from you.

2. Continuing with the case of the glassware price increase, which of the following closing paragraphs would you choose and why?

   a. We do appreciate quality and service, but we are not going to pay ridiculous prices to get it. I am confident that we can use American's vast buying power to find a more reasonable supplier somewhere in the world.

   b. Although the 12 percent increase is unacceptable, we do respect your need to be profitable

in a tough business environment. Consequently, we are open to some negotiation about a smaller price increase, if you would consider that.

   c. We are saddened by our decision, let me assure you. We'll not only miss the quality of your products, but the quality of the people we've dealt with at your firm as well. We've come to know many of them almost as personal friends. Please give my best wishes to everyone in your office.

3. The company that has supplied you with plastic drinking glasses for several years has suffered some quality and service problems in recent months. The problems include cracked glasses and late deliveries that leave some airplanes with too few glasses to serve all their passengers. The supplier has been dependable up to this point, and you're not sure whether your counterparts are even aware of the problems. The problems have caused no significant trouble yet, but you're afraid they might if the situation goes uncorrected. You and your colleagues have a good working relationship with your counterparts in the supplier organization, even socializing with them when you're in the same city. How should you start a letter to the supplier informing management of the need to address these problems?

   a. This is just a quick note to thank you for the great service you've provided us over the years. American Airlines always tries to offer the best to its customers, and your company's products have played a key role in that effort.

   b. I enjoyed that round of golf last time you were in town. I only wish your company was as good as your golf game. You guys used to be one of our star performers, but you've really been dropping the ball lately. I don't mean to sound too harsh, but you've got some problems that must be fixed immediately.

   c. You have always shared American's high standards for quality and service, so I know you'll be interested in some feedback that we've received from several of our field offices.

4. Personal contacts are an important source of new business opportunities in many industries. In some cases, businesspeople develop contacts through active participation in industry or professional groups, trade shows, alumni societies, and so on. You've recently received a request from a former college classmate (Marcia DeLancey) who is now a sales manager for a plastics manufacturer. She wants to visit your office to present her company's plastic containers. However, you are already famil-

iar with the company, and you know that it is too small to meet your needs for on-time global deliveries. You didn't know DeLancey all that well in school; in fact, you had to think for a minute to remember who she was (this is the first contact you've had with her since you both graduated five years ago). Which of the following openings would be most appropriate, keeping in mind that you know her company can't make the grade?

a. Congratulations on reaching such an impressive position at your new company. I hope you enjoy your work as much as I do. Thank you for your recent inquiry—evaluating such requests is one of my key responsibilities.

b. Great to hear from you; I'd love to catch up on old times with you and find out how you're doing in your new job. I bounced around a bit after college, but I really feel that I've found my niche here at American.

c. I'm sorry to say that American has already evaluated your company and found its resources were not a good match for our international delivery needs. However, I do appreciate your getting in touch, and I hope all is well with you.

5. Having a supplier falter on the job or even go out of business without warning would be a huge disruption for American. As a result, your department is concerned about every supplier's financial health. The company that provides American with napkins and paper towels has done a good job for years, but recent events have left the company in precarious financial shape. Your office has already told the company that American would be forced to find another paper source if the company's finances didn't improve. Unfortunately, its finances have grown even worse, and now you must act. You've already written the buffer, reasons, and bad news, and now you need a positive close for your message. Which of these would you choose?

a. Thank you very much for the service you've provided in the past. All of us here at American Airlines wish you the best in resolving your current situation. If you are able to meet these financial criteria in the future, by all means please get back in touch with us.

b. I understand that you're bound to be disappointed by our decisions. If you don't think our decision was valid or if there is more information that you believe we need to evaluate, please feel free to call me or my immediate supervisor to discuss the situation. We have to deal with quite a few suppliers, as you know, and I suppose there is a chance that we missed something in our initial evaluation.

c. I'm very sorry that we have to terminate our purchasing agreement with you. We have relied on your company's products for many years, and it's a shame that we won't be able to in the future. I hope this decision doesn't affect your workforce too negatively. If there's anything we can do to help, please don't hesitate to call.[22]

Learning Objectives Checkup

To assess your understanding of the principles in this chapter, read each learning objective and study the accompanying exercises. For fill-in items, write the missing text in the blank provided; for multiple choice items, circle the letter of the correct answer. You can check your responses against the answer key on page AK-2.

Objective 8.1: Apply the three-step writing process to bad-news messages.

1. When you are planning a negative message, _____ becomes extremely important.
   a. Analysis
   b. Taking a direct approach
   c. Using an emotional approach
   d. Message format

Objective 8.2: Show how to achieve an audience-centered tone in bad-news messages and explain why it helps readers.

2. Using an audience-centered tone
   a. Helps you avoid taking responsibility for the negative news
   b. Leaves readers well disposed toward your organization
   c. Means never having to say you're sorry
   d. Does all of the above

3. You can achieve an audience-centered tone by
   a. Using the "you" attitude
   b. Choosing positive words
   c. Using respectful language
   d. Doing all of the above

Objective 8.3: Differentiate between the direct and indirect organizational approaches to bad-news messages and discuss when it's appropriate to use each one.

4. When using the direct approach with bad-news messages, you begin with
   a. A buffer
   b. An attention-getter
   c. The bad news
   d. Any of the above

5. An advantage of using the direct approach with bad-news messages is that it
   a. Saves readers time by helping them reach the main idea more quickly
   b. Eases the reader into the message
   c. Is diplomatic
   d. Does all of the above

6. When using the indirect approach with bad-news messages, you begin with
   a. A buffer
   b. An attention-getter
   c. The bad news
   d. Any of the above

7. An advantage of using the indirect approach with bad-news messages is that
   a. Most readers prefer the direct approach for such messages
   b. It makes a shorter message possible
   c. It eases the reader into the message
   d. It does all of the above

Objective 8.4: Explain the purpose of buffers and list six things to avoid when writing them.

8. A buffer is
   a. A catchy opening that entices an audience to read further
   b. A neutral, noncontroversial statement that is closely related to the point of a message
   c. The sentence in which you embed your bad news
   d. The list of reasons for the bad news

9. When writing a buffer, you should
   a. Give the impression that good news will follow
   b. Apologize for the news that is about to come
   c. Be as wordy as possible to cushion what is to come
   d. Refrain from using a know-it-all tone

Objective 8.5: Discuss the three techniques for saying no as clearly and as kindly as possible.

10. To de-emphasize the bad news in your letter or memo, you
    a. Subordinate the bad news in a complex or compound sentence
    b. Put the bad news at the end of a paragraph
    c. Put the bad news at the beginning of a paragraph
    d. Don't state the bad news at all

11. When stating the bad news, it is best to
    a. Emphasize what you are unable to do
    b. Point out where the person has failed
    c. Emphasize the positive aspects of your decision
    d. Overemphasize the positive aspects

Objective 8.6: Define defamation and explain how to avoid it in bad-news messages.

12. Written defamation is called _____; spoken defamation is called _____.

13. To avoid being accused of defamation, you should
    a. Never let the possible defamatory statements get back to the person
    b. Make only oral comments about someone and never put them in writing
    c. Never let anger or malice motivate your messages
    d. Do all of the above

Objective 8.7: List three guidelines for delivering bad news to job applicants and give a brief explanation of each one.

14. The best way to begin a message rejecting a job applicant is with
    a. A buffer
    b. The bad news
    c. An attention-getting device
    d. An apology

15. When rejecting a job applicant, be sure to
    a. Enumerate the applicant's shortcomings
    b. Avoid using a form letter
    c. Clearly state why the applicant wasn't selected
    d. Do all of the above

Objective 8.8: Outline the main purpose of performance reviews, give three ways to accomplish that purpose, and list five guidelines to follow when giving negative reviews.

16. Which of the following is *not* a part of performance reviews?
    a. Emphasizing and clarifying job requirements
    b. Giving employees feedback on their efforts to fulfill job requirements
    c. Helping the company set organizational standards and communicate organizational values
    d. Discussing employee benefits programs and perks

17. Which of the following is *not* recommended when giving an employee a negative performance review?
    a. Pointing out the person's character flaws that are contributing to his or her poor performance
    b. Addressing the performance problem in private
    c. Identifying the consequences of continuing poor performance
    d. Arriving at a joint decision with the employee on what action he or she can take to improve performance

Apply Your Knowledge

1. Why is it important to end your bad-news message on a positive note? Explain.
2. If company policy changes, should you explain those changes to employees and customers at about the same time, or should you explain them to employees first? Why?
3. If the purpose of your message is to convey bad news, should you take the time to suggest alternatives to your reader? Why or why not?
4. When a company suffers a setback, should you soften the impact by letting out the bad news a little at a time? Why or why not?
5. **Ethical Choices** Is intentionally de-emphasizing bad news the same as distorting graphs and charts to de-emphasize unfavorable data? Why or why not?

Practice Your Knowledge

DOCUMENTS FOR ANALYSIS

Read the following documents; then (1) analyze the strengths and weaknesses of each sentence and (2) revise each document so that it follows this chapter's guidelines.

DOCUMENT 8.A: PROVIDING BAD NEWS ABOUT PRODUCTS

Your spring fraternity party sounds like fun. We're glad you've again chosen us as your caterer. Unfortunately, we have changed a few of our policies, and I wanted you to know about these changes in advance so that we won't have any misunderstandings on the day of the party.

We will arrange the delivery of tables and chairs as usual the evening before the party. However, if you want us to set up, there is now a $100 charge for that service. Of course, you might want to get some of the brothers and pledges to do it, which would save you money. We've also added a small charge for cleanup. This is only $3 per person (you can estimate because I know a lot of people come and go later in the evening).

Other than that, all the arrangements will be the same. We'll provide the skirt for the band stage, tablecloths, bar setup, and, of course, the barbecue. Will you have the tubs of ice with soft drinks again? We can do that for you as well, but there will be a fee.

Please let me know if you have any problems with these changes and we'll try to work them out. I know it's going to be a great party.

DOCUMENT 8.B: REFUSING REQUESTS FOR CLAIMS AND ADJUSTMENTS

I am responding to your letter of about six weeks ago asking for an adjustment on your fax/modem, model FM39Z. We test all our products before they leave the factory; therefore, it could not have been our fault that your fax/modem didn't work.

If you or someone in your office dropped the unit, it might have caused the damage. Or the damage could have been caused by the shipper if he dropped it. If so, you should file a claim with the shipper. At any rate, it wasn't our fault. The parts are already covered by warranty. However, we will provide labor for the repairs for $50, which is less than our cost, since you are a valued customer.

We will have a booth at the upcoming trade fair there and hope to see you or someone from your office. We have many new models of office machines that we're sure you'll want to see. I've enclosed our latest catalog. Hope to see you there.

DOCUMENT 8.C: REJECTING JOB APPLICATIONS

I regret to inform you that you were not selected for our summer intern program at Equifax. We had over a thousand résumés and cover letters to go through and simply could not get to them all. We have been asked to notify everyone that we have already selected students for the 25 positions based on those who applied early and were qualified.

We're sure you will be able to find a suitable position for summer work in your field and wish you the best of luck. We deeply regret any inconvenience associated with our reply.

Exercises

For live links to all websites discussed in this chapter, visit this text's website at www.prenhall.com/thill. Just log on, select Chapter 8, and click on "Student Resources." Locate the page or the URL related to the material in the text. For the "Learn More on the Web" exercises, you'll also find navigational directions. Click on the live link to the site.

8.1 **Selecting the Approach** Select the best approach (direct or indirect) to use for the following bad-news messages:

   a. A memo to your boss informing her that one of your key clients is taking its business to a different accounting firm
   b. An e-mail message to a customer informing her that one of the books she ordered over the Internet is temporarily out of stock
   c. A letter to a customer explaining that the tape backup unit he ordered for his new custom computer is on back order and that, as a consequence, the shipping of the entire order will be delayed
   d. A letter from the telephone company rejecting a customer's claim that the phone company should

reimburse the customer for the costs of a new high-speed modem (apparently, the phone lines will carry data at only half the modem's speed)
   e. A memo to all employees notifying them that the company parking lot will be repaved during the first week of June and that the company will provide a shuttle service from a remote parking lot during that period
   f. A letter from a travel agent to a customer stating that the airline will not refund her money for the flight she missed but that her tickets are valid for one year
   g. A form letter from a U.S. airline to a customer explaining that it cannot extend the expiration date of the customer's frequent flyer miles even though the customer has been living overseas for the past three years
   h. A letter from an insurance company to a policyholder denying a claim for reimbursement for a special medical procedure that is not covered under the terms of the customer's policy
   i. A letter from an electronics store stating that the customer will not be reimbursed for a malfunctioning cell phone still under warranty (the terms of

the warranty do not cover damages to phones that were accidentally placed in the freezer overnight)

j. An announcement to the repairs department listing parts that are on back order and will be three weeks late

8.2 **Teamwork** Working alone, revise the following statements to de-emphasize the bad news. (*Hint:* Minimize the space devoted to the bad news, subordinate it, embed it, or use the passive voice.) Then team up with a classmate and read each other's revisions. Did you both use the same approach in every case? Which approach seems to be most effective for each of the revised statements?

a. The airline can't refund your money. The "Conditions" segment on the back of your ticket states that there are no refunds for missed flights. Sometimes the airline makes exceptions, but only when life and death are involved. Of course, your ticket is still valid and can be used on a flight to the same destination.

b. I'm sorry to tell you, we can't supply the custom decorations you requested. We called every supplier and none of them can do what you want on such short notice. You can, however, get a standard decorative package on the same theme in time. I found a supplier that stocks these. Of course, it won't have quite the flair you originally requested.

c. We can't refund your money for the malfunctioning lamp. You shouldn't have placed a 250-watt bulb in the fixture socket; it's guaranteed for a maximum of 75 watts.

8.3 **Writing Buffers** Complete the following exercises pertaining to buffers:

a. You have to tell a local restaurant owner that your plans have changed and you have to cancel the 90-person banquet scheduled for next month. Do you need to use a buffer? Why or why not?

b. Write a buffer for a letter declining an invitation to speak at the association's annual fundraising event. Show your appreciation for being asked.

c. Write a buffer for a letter rejecting a job applicant who speaks three foreign languages fluently. Include praise for the applicant's accomplishments.

8.4 **Internet** Jennifer Sanderson has been seeking an executive position with your company and has been through several interviews in the process. She has all the education and experience necessary, but in all three interviews, she seemed uncomfortable and tense, no matter how you tried to put her at ease. The candidate you decided to hire was much more easygoing and able to discuss his qualifications and experience with grace and confidence. Now you need to write a rejection letter to Jennifer. Having spoken with her so many times, you feel obligated to say something more than simply, "We have hired someone else." Visit www.ppspublishers.com/articles/rejecting.htm, and read the article about rejecting applicants. Should you offer Jennifer more explanation in your letter? What can you tell her that might be helpful? Write the rejection letter.

8.5 **Ethical Choices** The insurance company where you work is planning to raise all premiums for healthcare coverage. Your boss has asked you to read a draft of her letter to customers announcing the new, higher rates. The first two paragraphs discuss some exciting medical advances and the expanded coverage offered by your company. Only in the final paragraph do customers learn that they will have to pay more for coverage starting next year. What are the ethical implications of this draft? What changes would you suggest?

Expand Your Knowledge

LEARNING MORE ON THE WEB

Protect Yourself When Sending Negative Employment Messages www.toolkit.cch.com/scripts/sohotoc.asp A visit to CCH's Business Owner's Toolkit can help you reduce your legal liability, whether you are laying off an employee, firing an employee, or contemplating a companywide reduction in your workforce. Find out the safest way to fire someone from a legal standpoint. Learn why it's important to document disciplinary actions. Discover why some bad news should be given face-to-face and never by a letter or over the phone.

ACTIVITIES

Log on to CCH Business Owner's Toolkit, and answer these questions.

1. What should a manager communicate to an employee during a termination meeting?

2. Why is it important to document employee disciplinary actions?

3. What steps should you take before firing an employee for misconduct or poor work?

EXPLORING THE WEB ON YOUR OWN

Review these chapter-related websites on your own to learn more about the bad-news issues human resources departments are facing today.

1. *Workforce* magazine online, www.workforce.com, has the basics and the latest on human resource issues such as recruiting, laws, managing the workforce, incentives, strategies, and more. Read the current edition online.

2. HR.com, www4.hr.com, is the place to go to read about workplace trends, legislation affecting employers, recruiting, compensation, benefits, staffing, and more. Log on and learn.

3. BusinessTown.com, www.businesstown.com/people/Reviews.asp, has the latest lowdown on how to conduct a performance review.

Learn Interactively

INTERACTIVE STUDY GUIDE

Go to the Companion Website at www.prenhall.com/bovee. For Chapter 8, take advantage of the interactive "Study Guide" to test your knowledge of the chapter. Get instant feedback on whether you need additional studying. Also, visit this site's "Study Hall" where you'll find an abundance of valuable resources that will help you succeed in this course.

PEAK PERFORMANCE GRAMMAR AND MECHANICS

To improve your skill with commas, visit this text's website at www.prenhall.com/onekey. Click "Peak Performance Grammar and Mechanics," then click "Commas." Take the Pretest to determine whether you have any weak areas. Review those areas in the Refresher Course, and take the Follow-Up Test to check your grasp of commas. For advanced practice, take the Advanced Test. Finally, for additional reinforcement, go to the "Improve Your Grammar, Mechanics, and Usage" section that follows, and complete those exercises.

Improve Your Grammar, Mechanics, and Usage

The following exercises help you improve your knowledge of and power over English grammar, mechanics, and usage. Turn to the "Handbook of Grammar, Mechanics, and Usage" at the end of this textbook and review all of Section 2.6 (Commas). Then look at the following 10 items. Circle the letter of the preferred choice in the following groups of sentences. (Answers to these exercises appear on page AK-3.)

1. a. Please send us four cases of filters two cases of wing nuts and a bale of rags.
   b. Please send us four cases of filters, two cases of wing nuts and a bale of rags.
   c. Please send us four cases of filters, two cases of wing nuts, and a bale of rags.
2. a. Your analysis, however, does not account for returns.
   b. Your analysis however does not account for returns.
   c. Your analysis, however does not account for returns.
3. a. As a matter of fact she has seen the figures.
   b. As a matter of fact, she has seen the figures.
4. a. Before May 7, 1999, they wouldn't have minded either.
   b. Before May 7, 1999 they wouldn't have minded either.
5. a. Stoneridge Inc. will go public on September 9, 2003.
   b. Stoneridge, Inc., will go public on September 9, 2003.
   c. Stoneridge Inc. will go public on September 9, 2003.

6. a. "Talk to me" Sandra said "before you change a thing."
   b. "Talk to me," Sandra said "before you change a thing."
   c. "Talk to me," Sandra said, "before you change a thing."
7. a. The firm was founded during the long hard recession of the mid-1970s.
   b. The firm was founded during the long, hard recession of the mid-1970s.
   c. The firm was founded during the long hard, recession of the mid-1970s.
8. a. You can reach me at this address: 717 Darby St., Scottsdale, AZ 85251.
   b. You can reach me at this address: 717 Darby St., Scottsdale AZ 85251.
   c. You can reach me at this address: 717 Darby St., Scottsdale, AZ, 85251.
9. a. Transfer the documents from Fargo, North Dakota to Boise, Idaho.
   b. Transfer the documents from Fargo North Dakota, to Boise Idaho.
   c. Transfer the documents from Fargo, North Dakota, to Boise, Idaho.
10. a. Sam O'Neill the designated representative is gone today.
    b. Sam O'Neill, the designated representative, is gone today.
    c. Sam O'Neill, the designated representative is gone today.

Cases

Applying the Three-Step Writing Process to Cases
Apply each step to the following cases as assigned by your instructor.

Planning

Writing

Completing

Analyze the Situation
What's your general purpose?
What's your specific purpose?
What do you want readers to do?
Who are your readers? (Who is the primary audience? What do readers have in common? What is their general background? How will they react?)

Gather Information
What information do readers need?
What facts must you gather?

Adapt to the Audience
How will you establish credibility?

Organize the Information
What's your main idea?
Will you use the direct or indirect approach? Why?

Compose the Message
Will your tone be informal or more formal?
Draft the message as discussed in the "Your task" section of the case.

Revise the Message
Use the Checklist for Revising Business Messages on page 174 to edit and revise your message for clarity.

Produce the Message
What's the best way to distribute your message? By fax? By e-mail? By sealed envelope?

Proofread the Message
Proofread your message for errors in layout, spelling, and mechanics.

1   **2**   **3**

NEGATIVE ANSWERS TO ROUTINE REQUESTS

1. No deal: Letter from Home Depot to faucet manufacturer As assistant to the vice president of sales for Atlanta-based Home Depot, you were present at Home Depot's biannual product-line review, held at Tropicana Field in St. Petersburg, Florida. Also present were hundreds of vendor hopefuls, eager to become one of the huge retail chain's 25,303 North American suppliers. These suppliers did their best to win, keep, or expand their spot in the Home Depot product lineup, in individual meetings with a panel of regional and national merchandisers for the chain.

Product suppliers know that Home Depot holds all the cards, so if they want to play, they have to follow Home Depot rules, offering low wholesale prices and swift delivery. Once chosen, they're constantly re-evaluated—and quickly dropped for infractions such as requesting a price increase or planning to sell directly to consumers via the Internet. They'll also hear sharp critiques of their past performance, which are not to be taken lightly.

A decade ago, General Electric failed to keep Home Depot stores supplied with lightbulbs, which caused shortages. Co-founder Bernard Marcus immediately stripped GE of its exclusive, 80-foot shelf space and flew off to negotiate with its Netherlands competitor, Philips. Two years later, after high-level negotiations, GE bulbs were back on Home Depot shelves—but in a position inferior to Philips's.

Such cautionary tales aren't lost on vendors. But they know that despite tough negotiating, Home Depot is always looking for variety to please its customers' changing tastes and demands. The sales potential is so enormous that the compromises and concessions are worthwhile. If selected, vendors get immediate distribution in more than 1,000 stores (a number that Home Depot plans to double in the next few years).

Still, you've seen the stress on reps' faces as they explain product enhancements and on-time delivery ideas in the review sessions. Their only consolation for this grueling process is that, although merchandisers won't say yes or no on the spot, they do let manufacturers know where they stand within a day or two. And the company is always willing to reconsider at the next product-line review—wherever it's held.

Your task: You're drafting some of the rejection letters, and the next one on your stack is to a faucet manufacturer, Brightway Manufacturing, 133 Industrial Ave., Gary, IN 46406. "Too expensive," "substandard plastic handles," and "a design not likely to appeal to Home Depot customers," say the panel's notes. (And knowing what its customers want has put Home Depot in the top 10 of the *Fortune* 500 list, with $40 billion in annual sales.) Find a way to soften the blow in your rejection letter to Brightway. After all, consumer tastes do change. Direct your letter to Pamela Wilson, operations manager.[23]

2. Too anomalous: E-mail declining Disclosure Project invitation As president of the Mid-State Flying Club, your job is to entice pilots to join your organization, which offers discounts on flying lessons and small plane rentals. Like most pilots, you're interested in anomalous aerial phenomena. But two Mid-State members who've become volunteers for the Disclosure Project are now pressuring you to sponsor the non-profit research organization's free public "Campaign for Disclosure" event in Phoenix next week. You're worried about the club's reputation. The last thing you want to hear is airport scuttlebutt about "those kooks over in Hangar 5."

The Disclosure Project is a high-profile endeavor founded by Dr. Steven Greer, an emergency room physician who gave up his doctor's salary to pursue a course he believes to be vital to our future. Greer and volunteers have documented more than 400 "top-secret military, government, and other witnesses to UFO and extraterrestrial events," from the United States, Britain, Russia, and other countries, and from the armed services, the CIA, NASA, and other agencies, according to the book of transcripts your two members showed you. They also sent the club's name to Greer's Virginia headquarters, so now you've received an e-mail from him, inviting Mid-State to sponsor next week's local event.

Your members, both retired military pilots, insisted that you watch the Disclosure Project videotape. You had to admit it was intriguing to see witnesses with impressive titles and affiliations discuss UFOs they've encountered, secret government "black projects" they know about, and amazing technologies they've witnessed. Their goal is to convince Congress to hold open hearings on the subject. They also want to encourage legislation banning space-based weapons in favor of peaceful cooperation with all cultures, since they say previous encounters prove that "ETs are not hostile." And they want a release of all information on "extraterrestrial technologies" allegedly captured and duplicated by the "black projects." They say these technologies could save the environment and provide new energy sources and therefore should belong to the public, not private interests.

You watched military and civilian pilots, astronauts, FAA investigation chiefs, air traffic controllers, Air Force intelligence officers, and even a space missile defense consultant and former spokesperson for Werhner von Braun on the tape. Some say they're speaking out despite death threats to remain silent. No wonder your two members sympathize! You've heard them telling their own tales of UFO encounters during airborne military maneuvers—events they were also advised to forget.

In private meetings, congressional representatives, presidential advisers, and military officials have all professed sympathy but concluded with the same statement: They cannot instigate disclosure hearings without an overwhelming public mandate. Considering that Greer's news conference at the National Press Club attracted 250,000 viewers to its simultaneous webcast (the NPC's largest ever), Greer might be closer to achieving that mandate than they suspect.

Your task: You're impressed by this businesslike effort to treat anomalous aerial phenomena seriously, but you know how people are. You don't want your business to become a laughingstock. Keeping your personal views private, write a courteous, appropriate e-mail to Dr. Steven Greer, *inquiries @disclosureproject.org*, refusing the sponsorship invitation.[24]

3. Not this time: Letter from Union Bank of California denying a request for ATM adjustment You work in operations in the ATM Error Resolution Department at Union Bank of California. Your department often adjusts customer accounts for multiple ATM debit errors. Mistakes are usually honest ones—such as a merchant swiping a customer's check debit card two or three times, thinking the first few times didn't "take" when they actually did.

Whenever customers call the bank about problems on their statements, they're instructed to write a claim letter to your department describing the situation and to enclose copies of receipts. Customers are notified of the outcome within 10 to 20 business days.

You usually credit their account. But this time, your supervisor is suspicious about a letter you've received from Margaret Caldwell, who maintains several hefty joint accounts with her husband at Union Bank of California.

Three debits to her checking account were processed on the same day, credited to the same market, Wilson's Gourmet. The debits carry the same transaction reference number, 1440022–22839837109, which is what caught Mrs. Caldwell's attention. But you know that number changes daily, not hourly, so multiple purchases made on the same day often carry the same number. Also, the debits are for different amounts ($23.02, $110.95, and $47.50), so these transactions weren't a result of repeated card swipes. No receipts are enclosed.

Mrs. Caldwell writes that the store was trying to steal from her, but your supervisor doubts that and asks you to contact Wilson's Gourmet. Manager Ronson Tibbits tells you that he's had no problems with his equipment and mentions that food shoppers commonly return at different times during the day to make additional purchases, particularly for beverages or to pick up merchandise they forgot the first time.

Your supervisor decides this was neither a bank error nor an error on the part of Wilson's Gourmet. It doesn't matter whether Mrs. Caldwell is merely confused or trying to commit an intentional fraud. Bank rules are clear for this situation: You must politely deny her request.

Your task: Write a letter to Margaret Caldwell, 2789 Aviara Pky., Carlsbad, CA 92008, explaining your refusal of her claim #7899. Remember, you don't want to lose this wealthy customer's business.[25]

4. A taxing matter: Letter from O&Y Tax Service refusing to pay for a customer's mistake During the mid-April rush at tax time last year, Hilda Black phoned to ask whether she could roll over funds from one retirement account into another without paying taxes on any gain. You answered that such a rollover was not considered a tax event, as long as the transaction was completed in 60 days. You also informed her that when she eventually draws out the funds to supplement her retirement income, she will pay taxes on the portion that represents interest earned on the account.

Today Ms. Black has phoned to say that she is being billed by the Internal Revenue Service for $1,309.72 in penalties and back interest because she failed to declare interest income earned when she cashed in "those bonds that I told you about last April." You explain that bonds are not the same thing as a retirement account. One difference, unfortunately, is that people are required to pay taxes the following April on any interest income or capital gains earned by cashing in bonds.

Your client is not satisfied. She demands "something in writing" to show to her lawyer. Her position is that you misled her, so you should pay the penalties and interest charges, which, of course, are getting larger every day. She is willing to pay the actual tax on the transaction.

Your task: Write a letter to Hilda Black (622 N. Bank Lane, Park Forest, IL 60045), explaining why you are unwilling to pay the penalties and interest charges requested by the IRS. Your position should be that you have done nothing to make yourself vulnerable in this transaction.

5. No nukes: Letter from SDG&E refusing adjustment request "I will not support nuclear power and I demand that you remove this 'nuclear decommissioning' charge from my bill," wrote Walter Wittgen to the president of San Diego Gas and Electric Company (SDG&E). The president has turned the letter over to you.

As a supervisor in customer service, your life has recently been filled with stress, overtime, and pressure from above. Between angry customers on overloaded phone lines and company directors under pressure from the news media, Mr. Wittgen is a minor problem. But he's part of your job. And his letter came to you all the way from president Edwin A. Guiles.

The larger crisis began when summer heat struck California. As the first former power monopoly in the country to fulfill deregulation requirements, SDG&E was required by law to pass on actual electricity costs to its customers. SDG&E no longer produces or prices electricity but purchases it from a new, open-market Power Exchange (PX). Prices fluctuate with supply and demand, and they had doubled with the heat wave. Customer bills doubled and just kept climbing. Even worse, SDG&E had failed to warn the public, so customers were stunned and angry.

The media descended, and politicians responded. With similar deregulation planned throughout the country, the governor and even the President of the United States have gotten involved, but no solution has emerged yet. Too late, SDG&E's marketing department tried to publicize that the utility's operations are still controlled by a government agency, the California Public Utilities Commission (CPUC). The new laws meant that SDG&E became only an "energy delivery service provider," selling off its generating plants. It passes on but does not set prices. Nevertheless, people saw SDG&E's name on huge bills, and a few started attacking employees and destroying property.

Then Mr. Wittgen called. Your phone operators pointed out the explanation for "nuclear decommissioning" charges on the back of his bill: "This charge pays for the retirement of nuclear power plants." The wording, like the fee itself, was ordered by the CPUC. When Wittgen called again, he was told that SDG&E bills more than a million customers every month, using a sophisticated software system. It would take a highly paid specialist more than an hour to hand-calculate Wittgen's bill every month, given all the complex line-items and formulas involved. For a 50-cent charge, that's unreasonable; plus, it could introduce errors that would cost him more. And the PUC requires that you charge him this fee.

How you handle the smallest customer problem in this volatile atmosphere could easily make tonight's news. It wouldn't be the first time.

Your task: Write a polite refusal letter to Mr. Walter Wittgen (732 La Cresta Blvd., El Cajon, CA 92021), explaining why his bill will not be adjusted. SDG&E asks employees to word and sign their letters personally. Your contact number is 1–800–411–SDG&E (7343).[26]

NEGATIVE ORGANIZATIONAL NEWS

6. The check's in the mail—almost: Letter from Sun Microsystems explaining late payments You'd think that a computer company could install a new management information system without a hitch, wouldn't you? The people at Sun Microsystems thought so too, but they were wrong. When they installed their own new computerized system for getting information to management, a few things, such as payments to vendors, fell through the cracks.

It was embarrassing when Sun's suppliers started clamoring for payment. Terence Lenaghan, the corporate controller, found himself in the unfortunate position of having to tell 6,000 vendors why Sun Microsystems had failed to pay its bills on time—and why it might be late with payments again. "Until we get these bugs ironed out," Lenaghan confessed, "we're going to have to finish some of the accounting work by hand. That means that some of our payments to vendors will probably be late next month too. We'd better write to our suppliers and let them know that there's nothing wrong with the company's financial performance. The last thing we want is for our vendors to think our business is going down the tubes."

Your task: Write a form letter to Sun Microsystems' 6,000 vendors explaining that bugs in their new management information system are responsible for the delays in payment.[27]

7. Safe selling: Memo from The Sports Authority headquarters about dangerous scooters You're not surprised that the Consumer Product Safety Commission (CPSC) has issued a consumer advisory on the dangers of motorized scooters. As a merchandising assistant at The Sports Authority, you've tried them and you've got the scars to prove it. Like too many riders, you skipped the elbow pads and learned to regret it.

The popular electric or gas-powered scooters, which feature two wheels similar to in-line skates, travel 9 to 14 miles per hour. As sales have grown, so have the reports of broken arms and legs, scraped faces, and bumped heads. The probem is that, unlike a motorcycle or bicycle, a scooter can be mastered by first-timers almost immediately. Both children and adults are hopping on and riding off—without helmets or other safety gear.

Over a six-month period, the CPSC says 2,250 motorized scooter injuries and three deaths were reported by emergency rooms around the country. The riders who were killed, ages 6, 11, and 46, might all have lived if they'd been wearing helmets. As a result, some states have already enacted laws restricting scooter operations.

Your stores sell a wide selection of both the foot-powered ($25 to $150) and motorized scooters ($350 to $1,000). The merchandising experts you work for are as concerned about the rise in injuries as they are about the CPSC advisory's potential negative effect on sales and legality. You've been assigned to a team that will brainstorm ideas for improving the situation.

For example, one team member has suggested developing a safety brochure to give to customers; another wants to train salespeople to discuss safety issues with customers before they buy. "We'd like to see increased sales of reflective gear ($6–15), helmets ($24), and elbow and knee pads ($19)," a store executive tells your team, "not to improve on The Sports Authority's $1.5 billion annual revenue, but to save lives."

Your task: Working as a team with classmates, discuss how The Sports Authority can use positive actions, including those mentioned in the case, to soften the effect of the CPSC advisory. Choose the best ideas and decide how to use them in a bad-news memo notifying the chain's 198 store managers about the consumer advisory. Then write the memo your team has outlined.[28]

8. Cell phone violations: E-mail message to associates at Wilkes Artis law firm "Company policy states that personnel are not to conduct business using cell phones while driving,"

David Finch reminds you. He's a partner at the law firm of Wilkes Artis in Washington, D.C., where you work as his administrative assistant.

You nod, waiting for him to explain. He already issued a memo about this rule last year, after that 15-year-old girl was hit and killed by an attorney from another firm. Driving back from a client meeting, the attorney was distracted while talking on her cell phone. The girl's family sued the firm and won $30 million, but that's not the point. The point is that cell phones can cause people to be hurt, even killed.

Finch explains, "Yesterday one of our associates called his secretary while driving his car. We can't allow this. According to the National Highway Transportation Safety Administration, 20 to 30 percent of all driving accidents are related to cell phone usage. From now on, any violation of our cell phone policy will result in suspension without pay, unless the call is a genuine health or traffic emergency."

Your task: Finch asks you to write an e-mail message to all employees, announcing the new penalty for violating company policy.[29]

9. Product recall: Letter from Perrigo to retailers about children's painkiller Discovering that a batch of its cherry-flavored children's painkiller contains more than the label-indicated amount of acetaminophen was not a happy occasion around Perrigo Company. But such errors do happen, and the best move is to be immediate, direct, and completely honest with retailers and the public—so say your superiors in the Customer Support and Service Department. Full and prompt disclosure is especially crucial when consumers' health is involved, as it always is in your line of business.

Perrigo is the leading manufacturer of more than 900 store-brand, over-the-counter (OTC) pharmaceuticals and nutritional products. These are the items found beside brand-name products such as Tylenol, Motrin, Aleve, Benadryl, NyQuil, Centrum, or Ex-Lax, but they're packaged under the name of the store that customers are shopping in. They're priced a bit lower and offer "comparable quality and effectiveness," as your sales literature proclaims.

For retailers, selling Perrigo products yields a higher profit margin than name brands. For consumers, buying the store brands can mean significant savings.

As of this morning, your marketing department calculates that 6,500 four-ounce bottles of the "children's nonaspirin elixir" (a Tylenol look-alike) are already in the hands of consumers. That leaves some 1,288 bottles still on store shelves. The problem is that the acetaminophen contained in the painkilling liquid is up to 29 percent more than labels state, enough to cause an overdose in the young children the product is designed for. Such overdoses can cause liver failure. No one is telling you how this error happened, and it's only been found in lot number 1AD0228, but frankly, finding a guilty party is not so important to your job. You're more concerned about getting the word out fast.

The painkiller has been sold under the Kroger label at stores in Alabama, Arkansas, Georgia, Illinois, Indiana, Kentucky, Louisiana, Michigan, Mississippi, Missouri, North Carolina, Ohio, South Carolina, Tennessee, Texas, Virginia, and West Virginia. It was sold under the Hy-Vee label in Illinois, Iowa, Kansas, Minnesota, Missouri, Nebraska, and South Dakota, and under the Good Sense label at independent retail chains throughout the United States. Perrigo needs to notify consumers throughout the United States that they should not give the product to children, but rather should check the lot number and return the bottle to the store they bought it from for a refund, if it's from the affected batch.

Your task: As Perrigo's customer service supervisor, you must notify retailers by letter. They've already been told verbally, but legal requirements mandate a written notification. That's good, because a form letter to your retail customers can also include follow-up instructions. Explain the circumstances behind the recall, and instruct stores to pull bottles from the shelves immediately for return to your company. Refunds they provide to

consumers will, of course, be reimbursed by Perrigo. Questions should be directed to Perrigo at 1-800-321-0105—and it's okay if they give that number to consumers. Be sure to mention all that your company is doing, and use resale information.[30]

NEGATIVE EMPLOYMENT MESSAGES

10. Survive this: Letter from Bank of America refusing a recommendation request Rogan Halliwell is highly intelligent, quick with his work, handsome, accurate, and one of the most conceited individuals you've ever met. As manager of a Bank of America branch office, you've never had an employee irritate you like Halliwell. But he charmed his way through the interview with agile diplomacy, and you made the mistake of hiring him.

You were dazzled at first, like his co-workers. But in the eight months he worked for you, you had to call him in three times and remind him of new harrassment laws, which prohibit any behavior that distracts or irritates others. Among the complaints about him was one from a woman who said he kept calling her "Babe."

"But a 60-year-old woman should be flattered!" he argued.

Most of his co-workers complained as well: His overbearing ego disgusted them and his steady chatter about his personal life ruined their days. He made jokes about customers behind their backs, and he amused himself by stirring up conflicts among employees. Morale was rapidly disintegrating.

The problem was that, despite his abysmal interpersonal skills, Halliwell was a good teller. His cash drawer almost always balanced perfectly. He was fast, he was charming to customers while they were present, and he learned quickly. You got so many compliments about that "nice young man" from older customers that you couldn't believe they were talking about the same Rogan Halliwell. How could you fire him?

One bright morning, Halliwell solved your problem. "I've decided to move to Hollywood," he announced, loudly enough for his co-workers to hear. "I think they're ready for me." You said a silent "thank-you" as you accepted his notice.

Today you received a letter from Halliwell. He writes that he expects to be hired by one of those *Survivor*-type reality TV shows. He wants a character reference.

You blanch. He may have the right qualities to make reality TV interesting, but listing them would sound slanderous coming from a bank manager. Moreover, you can't in good conscience recommend that anyone work with him. Yet his demonstrated skills make it risky for you to refuse.

Your task: Using techniques you've learned in this chapter, write a refusal letter that won't expose you or Bank of America to legal repercussions. Send it to Rogan Halliwell, 2388 Pitt Ave., Apt. 4, Hollywood, CA 90028.[31]

11. Reverse hiring: Form e-mail from Intel breaking bad news to campus recruits You know times are tough when a company stops hiring to fill vacancies, starts closing plants, defers payment of management raises for six months, and splits the rank-and-file raises into "half now, half in six months."

Intel's human resources department has done all of these things in an attempt to hit the numbers that management targeted for a large and immediate reduction in staff and salary expenses. But the company's scramble to survive will be small consolation to the talented college graduates that Intel recruited last winter. They're about to become the latest victims of a soft economy.

As a human resources manager at Intel, you truly despise certain aspects of your job. De-hiring college recruits is one of the worst. It's happening everywhere, particularly among your high-tech partners and competitors. A short time ago, recruiting new talent was so crucial to your success that companies were competing to hire the best college graduates in hot-and-heavy, on-campus recruiting sessions—and then figuring out later what jobs to place them in. Now you must gently rescind the job offers you made to campus recruits while they were in the last half of their last semester. It's too late for them to take other offers or to re-experience the job-fair atmosphere. They'll have to go out on the streets looking for something new on their own.

Worst of all, they'll be competing with hundreds of thousands of more experienced workers newly laid off from nearly every segment of industry during the economic slump. They'll also be up against the retirees trying to get back into the workplace after a sliding stock market devalued their retirement funds, the moms returning to work to help the family budget, and last year's college graduates who were let go under "last-in, first-out" layoff policies.

At least Intel plans to offer the grads a "reverse hiring bonus" of two months' salary if they agree not to come to work now. They can also retain any signing bonuses they were granted. By making this offer, Intel is trying avoid legal problems while straining to reach its job-reduction goals. Meanwhile, the company wants to preserve its reputation on campuses as an excellent employer, which will be as important as ever when the economy rebounds (it always does). Since company recruiters thought enough of these graduates to offer them jobs in the first place, you will do so again when you're able. You want them to maintain a good opinion of Intel.

If the recruits don't accept the offer to dismiss all claims against the company in exchange for the bonus, they can still come to work at Intel now, but you can't promise they'll have the jobs they were originally offered. The new job will likely be much lower on the employment ladder than what they were expecting, and that job could soon be "redeployed" as other Intel positions have been in recent weeks.

Then they'll wind up in a waiting pool with other workers whose jobs were eliminated, waiting their turn for another position.

Your task: Write a form e-mail to break the news to Intel's college recruits. Explain the options, give them an address for reply, and impose a time limit of two weeks.[32]

12. All in the family: E-mail message resigning a position at IBM Your brother, Ruben N. Rodriguez Jr., started the family-owned Los Amigos Tortilla Manufacturing, Inc., in 1969 with only $12,000. While Los Amigos developed, you were able to help support the family with your income as marketing director for the Latin American Division of IBM. Today, the Atlanta-based Los Amigos enjoys annual sales of about $4.5 million and its prospects look bright.

When Ruben asked you to resign from your position at IBM and work full-time for Los Amigos, you decided to do some research before answering. You found that Hispanic-owned businesses have outperformed U.S. business growth in general. You also learned that many Hispanic corporate executives are leaving big companies to start their own businesses. You want to be a part of this amazing trend, not only because of the profit potential but also because you love your family and want to help your brother develop the company. You hope your son will become a part of the organization some day. After considering all aspects, you made your decision: You submitted your letter of resignation to IBM. Today, you received e-mail from the division vice president urging you to stay and offering a lucrative incentive package, including an additional week's vacation, an upgrade on your company car, and an increase of $10,000 a year.

Your task: Write an e-mail message to George Packard, your division vice president, at *GPackard@lad.ibm.com*, thanking him for his offer. Explain the reasons behind your decision to resign and suggest that Consuela Vargas, who has worked with you for five years, would make an excellent marketing director. Vargas not only speaks Spanish and Portuguese but has played a key role in closing deals for IBM in several Latin American countries. Plus, she's a terrific strategic thinker.[33]

Chapter 9

Writing Persuasive Messages

Learning Objectives

1 Discuss the planning tasks that need extra attention when preparing persuasive messages

2 Describe the AIDA plan for persuasive messages

3 Distinguish between emotional and logical appeals, and discuss how to balance them

4 Explain the best way to overcome resistance to your persuasive message, and list four common mistakes to avoid when writing persuasive messages

5 Define *selling points* and *reader benefits* and discuss their differences

6 Briefly review the four areas of legal concern in sales letters

7 Discuss three techniques for keeping readers interested in your sales messages

8 Compare sales messages with fundraising messages

9 List eight guidelines that will help you strengthen your fundraising messages

On the Job:

COMMUNICATING AT PATAGONIA

GEARING UP TO SAVE THE ENVIRONMENT

Yvon Chouinard is committed to saving the earth's resources, and he believes that everyone—from consumers to corporations—should practice environmental protection. When he founded Patagonia, a leading outdoor gear and apparel company, Chouinard incorporated his personal passion for the environment into the operating values of his company. Under Chouinard's direction, Patagonia not only produces high-quality goods for extreme sports enthusiasts but also rigorously pursues a high standard of environmental responsibility while actively persuading consumers, communities, and other companies to follow its example.

Patagonia, leading designer and distributor of outdoor gear, does its best to persuade customers not only to buy its environmentally safe clothing but to actively protect and support the earth's environment. The company uses words and pictures in its persuasive messages to help people make an emotional connection with the environment.

The company makes every effort to reduce the environmental impact of its operations. For example, working with outside contractors, Patagonia developed Synchilla fleece, a fabric made from recycled plastic soda bottles—some 8 million bottles each year. It introduced a line of clothing made from organic cotton (which is grown without artificial pesticides or fertilizers), and it discovered ways to eliminate toxic dyes from its products.

But Patagonia's environmental commitment doesn't stop there. All those production goals were accomplished while attempting to persuade the world to support environmental protection in every area of life. Chouinard's mission is twofold: to create a desire for Patagonia's products and to educate consumers about practicing environmental responsibility. To convince his audience, he combines both emotional and logical appeals.

For example, Patagonia's catalogs capture attention and create an emotional desire for environmental responsibility by featuring lush, full-page scenic photos that resemble *National Geographic* layouts. These same catalogs feature logical appeals in essays that inform readers about the company's environmental values, explain Patagonia's rationale for developing environmentally sensitive production techniques, and delineate the long-term benefits of investing in organically grown products and recycled materials. The catalogs are printed on recycled paper that is 50 percent chlorine-free.

Patagonia also uses logical appeals in its environmental reports. The company's internal assessment group studies the environmental impact of Patagonia's operating procedures and then publishes these findings in public reports, welcoming suggestions from outside sources for refining procedures. Also for public consumption is Patagonia's own "earth tax," created to give environmental groups about $1 million each year—more money than it allocates for advertising. By inviting customers and others to apply for grants for local environmental projects, Patagonia demonstrates its support for environmental causes, thus establishing its credibility as an environmentally responsible company.

Even in-store customers are influenced by Patagonia's persuasive powers. To emphasize the value of environmental responsibility, stores use interactive displays of the earth's processes, and garment hangtags highlight merchandise that is made from organically grown cotton, Synchilla fleece, and natural dyes. Although aligning his company and his environmental philosophy has not been easy, Chouinard continues to get his persuasive message across.[1]

www.patagonia.com

USING THE THREE-STEP WRITING PROCESS FOR PERSUASIVE MESSAGES

Persuasion is the attempt to change someone's attitudes, beliefs, or actions.

Savvy businesspeople such as Yvon Chouinard understand that people today want to know not only *what* they should do but also *why* they should do it. To accomplish his business and environmental goals, Chouinard often uses techniques of **persuasion**— the attempt to change an audience's attitudes, beliefs, or actions.[2] To successfully persuade an audience, your message must present an argument that allows readers to decide that they agree with it and support it.[3]

The most successful business leaders know how to take the pulse of an audience and communicate with people in terms that they can both understand and embrace.[4] So whether you're selling real estate, asking people to support a cause, or trying to get your boss to okay your idea, writing effective persuasive messages is an important skill in today's competitive marketplace. Applying the three-step writing process to your persuasive messages will help you make them as effective as possible.

Step 1: Planning Persuasive Messages

For a persuasive message, some planning tasks require more effort.

Unlike routine positive messages (discussed in Chapter 7), persuasive messages aim to influence audiences who are inclined to resist. Therefore, persuasive messages are generally longer, are usually more detailed, and often depend heavily on strategic planning. Persuasive messages require that you pay particular attention to your purpose, your audience, your credibility, and your ethics.

Persuasive requests encounter two problems:
• Audiences are busy.
• Audiences receive many competing requests.

Analyze Your Purpose   In persuasive messages your purpose is to convince people to do something different or to try something new. But most people are busy, so they're reluctant to act, especially if doing so takes time and offers no guarantee of any reward in return. Plus, competing requests are plentiful. The public relations departments of many large corporations receive so many persuasive requests for donations that they must sometimes use lotteries to decide which worthy cause to support. Given the complexity and sensitivity of persuasive messages, you must be absolutely sure that your purpose is clear, necessary, and appropriate for written media.

Analyze Your Audience   Chapter 4 discusses the basics of audience analysis, but the process can become much more involved for persuasive messages. To write an effective persuasive argument, you need to search for common ground, establish points of agreement on which to build, and shape your argument to show that your proposal will satisfy their needs. The best persuasive messages are closely connected to your audience's existing desires and interests.[5]

The questions you ask before writing a persuasive message go beyond those you would ask for other types of messages.

Before starting your persuasive message, consider these important questions: Who is my audience? What are their needs? What do I want them to do? How might they resist? Are there alternative positions I need to examine? What does the decision maker consider to be the most important issue? How might the organization's culture influence my strategy?

You must appeal to the specific needs of your audience, especially in persuasive messages.

Finding the answers to these questions means learning about your audience's needs or concerns—and that can take weeks, even months. Why? Because everyone's needs differ, so everyone responds differently to any given message. For instance, not every reader is interested in economy or even in fair play; you may find that satisfying someone's need for status or appealing to someone's greed may at times be much more effective than focusing on human generosity or civic duty.

It may be necessary to satisfy some needs before others.

Gauging Audience Needs   Some theorists believe that certain needs have priority. Figure 9–1 represents psychologist Abraham Maslow's hierarchy of needs, with

FIGURE 9–1
Maslow's Hierarchy of Needs

the most basic needs appearing at the bottom of the figure. Maslow suggests that only after lower-level needs have been met will a person seek to fulfill needs on higher levels.[6]

For example, suppose you supervise someone who consistently arrives late for work. You must either persuade him to change or fire him. First, find out why he's coming in late. Is he oversleeping because he has a second job to support his family (a safety and security need)? Is he coming in late because of a misguided desire to have people notice his arrival (an esteem and status need)? Once you've analyzed the need motivating him to arrive late, you can appeal to that need so that he will be interested in your message about changing his behavior. If the need for safety and security is behind his tardiness, you might say, "Your job is very important to you, I know." If he craves esteem and status, you could say, "You've always seemed interested in being given more responsibility, perhaps even a promotion."

To assess various individual needs, you can refer to specific information such as **demographics** (the age, gender, occupation, income, education, and other quantifiable characteristics of the people you're trying to persuade) and **psychographics** (the personality, attitudes, lifestyle, and other psychological characteristics of an individual). Both types of information are strongly influenced by culture.

Considering Cultural Differences   When analyzing your audience, take into account their cultural expectations and practices. You don't want to undermine your persuasive message by using an inappropriate appeal or by organizing your message in a way that seems unfamiliar or uncomfortable to your audience. Your understanding and respect for cultural differences will help you satisfy your audience's needs and will help your audience respect you.

For example, in France, using an aggressive, hard-sell technique is no way to win respect. Such an approach would probably antagonize your audience. In Germany, where people tend to focus on technical matters, plan on verifying any figures you use for support, and make sure they are exact. In Sweden, audiences tend to focus on theoretical questions and strategic implications, whereas U.S. audiences are usually concerned with more practical matters.[7]

As with individuals, an organization's culture or subculture heavily influences your message's effectiveness. All the previous messages in an organization have established a tradition that defines persuasive writing preferred within that company's culture. When you accept and use these traditions, you establish one type of common ground with your audience. If you reject or never learn these traditions, you'll have difficulty achieving that common ground, which damages both your credibility and your persuasion attempts.

Demographics include characteristics such as age, gender, occupation, income, and education.

Psychographics include characteristics such as personality, attitudes, and lifestyle.

Cultural differences influence your persuasion attempts.

Every message written for a corporation adds to the corporate tradition.

Your credibility is defined by how reliable, believable, and trustworthy you are.

Establish Your Credibility As Yvon Chouinard will tell you, to persuade a skeptical or hostile audience, you must convince people that you know what you're talking about and that you're not trying to mislead them. Your *credibility* is your capability of being believed because you're reliable and worthy of confidence. Establishing your credibility takes time. The following tips will help you earn your audience's respect:

- **Support your message with facts.** Present testimonials, documents, guarantees, statistics, and research results that provide objective evidence for what you have to say. The more specific and relevant your proof, the better.

- **Name your sources.** Tell your audience where your information comes from and who agrees with you. If your audience already respects your sources, naming them is especially effective.

- **Be an expert.** Demonstrate your knowledge of your message's subject area (or even of some other area) as you give your audience the quality information necessary to make a decision.

- **Establish common ground.** Highlight those beliefs, attitudes, and background experiences you have in common with your audience so that people will identify with you.

Positive persuasion leaves your audience free to choose.

To maintain the highest ethics, try to persuade without manipulating.

- **Be enthusiastic.** Infect your audience with your excitement about your subject.

- **Be objective.** Understand and acknowledge all sides of an issue so that you present fair and logical arguments in your persuasive message.

- **Be sincere.** Exhibit your genuine concern and good faith by focusing on your audience's needs.

- **Be trustworthy.** Earn your audience's confidence with your honesty and dependability.

- **Have good intentions.** Keep your audience's best interests at heart.

To enhance your credibility even more, make sure that your motives, methods, and message are ethical. Maintaining high ethical standards is crucial for all business messages, but especially for persuasive ones.

Strive for High Ethical Standards Just the word *persuasion* is viewed by some as dishonest and unethical. They associate persuasion with coaxing, urging, and sometimes even tricking people into accepting an idea, buying a product, or taking an unwanted or unneeded action. However, the best businesspeople persuade honestly and ethically. They provide accurate information, promote full understanding, and allow audiences the freedom to choose.[8] Ethical businesspeople explain the benefits of an idea, an organization, a product, or an action so that their audiences can recognize just how well the idea, organization, product, or action will satisfy a need they truly have.

For anyone trying to influence the actions of others, it is crucial to know the law. However, merely avoiding what is illegal may not always be enough. To maintain the highest standards of business ethics, make every attempt to persuade without manipulating. Choose words that won't be misinterpreted, and be sure you don't distort the truth. Adopt the "you" attitude by truly being concerned about your audience's needs and interests. Your consideration of audience needs is more than ethical; it's the proper use of persuasion. That consideration is likely to achieve the response you want and to satisfy your audience's needs.

At R/C Country Hobbies, owners Chet and Terrie Van Scyoc have boosted sales by encouraging shoppers to handle the merchandise. It's a highly ethical and effective way to involve shoppers in the remote-control planes and cars, model kits, and other toys the store offers. Customers can test a display model, get firsthand advice from experienced employees, fly a model airplane on a computer simulator, test their yo-yo skills, or race their miniracers monthly on an 80-foot track in the store's parking lot. "We're developing lasting ties with many of our customers," says Terrie.

Step 2: Writing Persuasive Messages

As with all business messages, persuasive messages require that you define your main idea, limit the scope of your message, and group your points in a meaningful way. In addition, you must focus even more effort on choosing between the direct and indirect approach. Many situations call for the direct approach:

- When audience members are objective

- When you know your audience prefers the "bottom line" first (perhaps because it saves them time)

- When your corporate culture encourages directness

- When a message is long or complex (because your readers can become impatient if the main idea is buried seven pages in)

Your choice between the direct and indirect approach is also influenced by the extent of your authority, expertise, or power within an organization. As a first-line manager writing a persuasive message to top management, you may try to be diplomatic by using an indirect approach. However, your choice could backfire if some managers perceive your indirectness as manipulative and a waste of time. On the other hand, if you try to save your supervisors time by using a direct approach, you might be perceived as brash and presumptuous. Similarly, when writing a persuasive message to employees, you may use the indirect approach to ease into a major change, but your audience might see your message as weak, even wishy-washy.

Just as with the routine and bad-news messages discussed in Chapters 7 and 8, your choice of organizational approach for persuasive messages is based on your audience's likely reaction. However, because the purpose of persuasion is to convince your audience or to change their attitudes, beliefs, or actions, most persuasive messages use the indirect approach. That means you'll need to explain your reasons and build interest before revealing your purpose.

Use the direct approach in specific situations.

Choice of approach is also influenced by your position (or authority within the organization) relative to your audience's.

Most persuasive messages use the indirect approach.

Step 3: Completing Persuasive Messages

The length and complexity of persuasive messages make applying Step 3 even more crucial to your success. When you evaluate your content, try to judge your argument objectively and seriously appraise your credibility. When revising for clarity and conciseness, carefully match the purpose and organization to audience needs.

Your design elements must complement, not detract from, your argument. In addition, make sure your delivery methods fit your audience's expectations as well as your purpose. Finally, meticulous proofreading will identify any mechanical or spelling errors that would weaken your persuasive message.

As with other business messages, Step 3 of the writing process helps guarantee the success of your persuasive messages.

DEVELOPING STRATEGIES FOR PERSUASIVE MESSAGES

Your success as a businessperson is closely tied to your ability to convince others to accept or act on your recommendations. Minimally, you want them to pay close attention to your ideas and value your contributions. Of course, you have been using persuasion techniques for years. Perhaps you talked your coach into letting you play a position on a team or you convinced students to vote for you in a school election. You may even have persuaded your professor to change a grade. Regardless, being able to persuade others is vital in today's competitive workplace. Effective persuasion involves four distinct and essential strategies: framing your arguments, balancing emotional and logical appeals, reinforcing your position, and dealing with resistance.

Four essential persuasion strategies:
- *Framing your arguments*
- *Balancing your appeals*
- *Reinforcing your position*
- *Overcoming audience resistance*

The amount of detail you pursue in each of these strategies varies according to the complexity of your idea or request.

Framing Your Arguments with the AIDA Plan

Most persuasive messages follow an organizational plan that goes beyond the indirect approach used for negative messages. The opening does more than serve as a buffer; it grabs your audience's attention. The explanation section does more than present reasons, and it's expanded to two sections: The first advances your audience's interest, and the second changes your audience's attitude. Finally, your close does more than end on a positive note with a statement of what action is needed; it emphasizes reader benefits and motivates readers to take specific action. Although similar to the indirect approach of negative messages, this persuasive **AIDA plan** pushes the envelope in each of four phases: (1) attention, (2) interest, (3) desire, and (4) action (see Table 9–1).

- **Attention.** In the first phase, you spur audience members' curiosity so that they want to hear about your problem or idea. Open with a brief, engaging sentence that makes no extravagant claims or irrelevant points but that establishes some kind of common ground on which to build your case. Randy Thumwolt uses the AIDA plan in a persuasive memo about his program to reduce costs while curtailing consumer complaints about Host Marriott's recycling record (see Figure 9–2).

- **Interest.** In the first portion of the body, you explain the relevance of your message to your audience. Continuing the theme you started with, paint a more detailed word picture. Get your audience thinking. In Figure 9–2, Thumwolt's interest section introduces an additional, unforeseen problem with plastic product containers. (Note how he breaks out his suggestions into an easy-to-read list.)

- **Desire.** In the rest of the body, you explain how the change or new idea will benefit your audience. Reduce resistance by thinking up and answering in advance any questions the audience might have. If your idea is complex, explain how you would implement it. Back up all claims with hard evidence in order to increase audience willingness to take the action that you will suggest in the next section. Just be sure that all evidence is directly relevant to your point.

- **Action.** In the closing section, you suggest the action you want readers to take. Make it more than a statement such as "Please institute this program soon" or "Send me a refund." This is your opportunity to remind readers of the benefits of taking action. The secret of a successful action phase is making the action easy. You might ask readers to call a toll-free number for more information, use an enclosed order form, or use a prepaid envelope for donations. Include a deadline when applicable.

Organize persuasive messages using the AIDA plan:
- *Attention*
- *Interest*
- *Desire*
- *Action*

Begin every persuasive message with an attention-getting statement that is
- *Personalized*
- *You-oriented*
- *Straightforward*
- *Relevant*

In the interest section,
- *Continue the opening theme in greater detail*
- *Relate benefits specifically to the attention-getter*

In the desire section,
- *Provide evidence to prove your claim*
- *Draw attention to any enclosures*

End by
- *Suggesting a specific step the audience can take*
- *Restating how the audience will benefit by acting as you wish*
- *Making action easy*

Table 9–1   THE AIDA ORGANIZATIONAL PLAN

Phase	*Objective*
Attention	Get the reader's attention with a benefit that is of real interest or value.
Interest	Build the reader's interest by further explaining benefits and appealing to his or her logic or emotions.
Desire	Build desire by showing how your offer can really help the reader.
Action	Give a strong and simple call to action and provide a convenient means for the reader to take the next step.

FIGURE 9–2
Effective Persuasive Memo Using the AIDA Plan

Planning

Writing

Completing

Analyze the Situation
The purpose is to help solve an ongoing problem. The audience will be receptive.

Gather Information
Gather data on recycling problem areas.

Adapt to the Audience
Use a memo, and strengthen the point by reviewing the bulk-purchase idea, which has already been instituted.

Organize the Information
Follow the indirect approach by using background information to introduce the continuing problems. Then list the new recycling ideas.

Compose the Message
Make your style businesslike and your appeal logical. Use a conversational tone, and respect the reader's time by avoiding wordiness.

Revise the Message
Be sure the flow of this memo is logical. Edit and rewrite for conciseness and clarity.

Produce the Message
Minimal design is needed for an internal memo. Send the message either as a printed memo or via e-mail.

Proofread the Message
Review for accuracy and typos.

1　　　**2**　　　**3**

HOST MARRIOTT SERVICES

INTERNAL MEMORANDUM

TO: Eleanor Tran, Comptroller
FROM: Randy Thumwolt, Purchasing Director
DATE: May 7, 2004
SUBJECT: Cost Cutting in Plastics

In spite of our recent switch to purchasing plastic product containers in bulk, our costs for these containers are exorbitant. In my January 5 memo, I included all the figures showing that

- We purchase five tons of plastic product containers each year
- The price of the polyethylene terephthalate (PET) tends to rise and fall as petroleum costs fluctuate

In January I suggested that we purchase plastic containers in bulk during winter months, when petroleum prices tend to be lower. Because you approved that suggestion, we should realize a 10 percent savings this year. However, our costs are still out of line, around $2 million a year.

In addition to the cost in dollars of these plastic containers is the cost in image. We have recently been receiving an increasing number of consumer letters complaining about our lack of a recycling program for PET plastic containers, both on the airplanes and in the airport restaurants.

After conducting some preliminary research, I have come up with the following ideas:

- Provide recycling containers at all Host Marriott airport restaurants
- Offer financial incentives for the airlines to collect and separate PET containers
- Set up a specially designated dumpster at each airport for recycling plastics
- Contract with A-Batt Waste Management for collection

I've attached a detailed report of the costs involved. As you can see, our net savings the first year should run about $500,000. I've spoken to Ted Macy in marketing. If we adopt the recycling plan, he wants to build a PR campaign around it.

The PET recycling plan will help build our public image while improving our bottom line. If you agree, let's meet with Ted next week to get things started.

Grabs attention by clearly stating an ongoing problem and briefly providing background information that includes specific numbers

Makes suggestions in an easy-to-read list, providing detailed support in an attachment

Urges action within a specific time frame

Reminds reader of important facts that have already been established by breaking them out into a list

Builds interest by introducing an additional problem with the plastic product containers

Creates desire by providing another reader benefit

When using the indirect approach, make subject lines interesting without revealing your purpose.

When your AIDA message uses an indirect approach and is delivered by memo or e-mail, your challenge is to make the subject line interesting and relevant enough to capture reader attention without revealing your main idea. If you put your request in the subject line, you're likely to get a quick "no" before you've had a chance to present your arguments.

Instead of This	Try This
Proposal to Install New Phone Message System	Savings on Toll-Free Number

Using AIDA with the indirect approach allows you to save your idea for the action phase; using it with the direct approach allows you to use your main idea as your attention-getter.

The AIDA plan is tailor-made for using the indirect approach, allowing you to save your main idea for the action phase. However, it can also be used for the direct approach: Use your main idea as the attention-getter, build interest with your argument, create desire with your evidence, and emphasize your main idea in the action phase with the specific action you want your audience to take.

Bette McGiboney uses the AIDA plan with the direct approach in her e-mail to her boss (see Figure 9–3). She is administrative assistant to the athletic director of Auburn University. Each year, after season tickets have been mailed, the cost of the athletic department's toll-free phone number skyrockets as fans call with questions about their seats, complaints about their tickets, or orders for last-minute tickets. The August phone bill is usually over $3,000, in part because each customer is put on hold while operators serve others. McGiboney came up with an idea that could save the school money and save ticket holders time.

Include a brief justification or explanation even in direct persuasive messages.

When using the direct approach in persuasive messages, remember that even though your audience may be easy to convince, you'll still want to include at least a brief justification or explanation. Don't expect your reader to accept your idea on blind faith. For example, consider the following two openers:

Poor	Improved
I recommend building our new retail outlet on the West Main Street site.	After comparing the four possible sites for our new retail outlet, I recommend West Main Street as the only site that fulfills our criteria for visibility, proximity to mass transportation, and square footage.

To make the AIDA plan more successful, focus closely on one goal only.

Another thing to keep in mind when using the AIDA plan is to narrow your objectives. Focus on your primary goal when presenting your case, and concentrate your efforts on accomplishing that one goal. For example, if your main idea is to convince your company to install a new phone-messaging system, leave discussions about switching long-distance carriers until another day—unless it's relevant to your argument.

Balancing Emotional and Logical Appeals

Both emotional and logical appeals are needed to write successful persuasive messages.

How do you actually convince an audience that your position is the right one, that your plan will work, or that your company will do the most with readers' donations? One way is to appeal to the audience's minds and hearts. Most persuasive messages include both emotional and logical appeals. These two elements have a good chance of persuading your audience to act if they are balanced correctly. Finding just the right balance between the two types of appeals depends on four factors:[9]

- The actions you wish to motivate

- Your reader's expectations

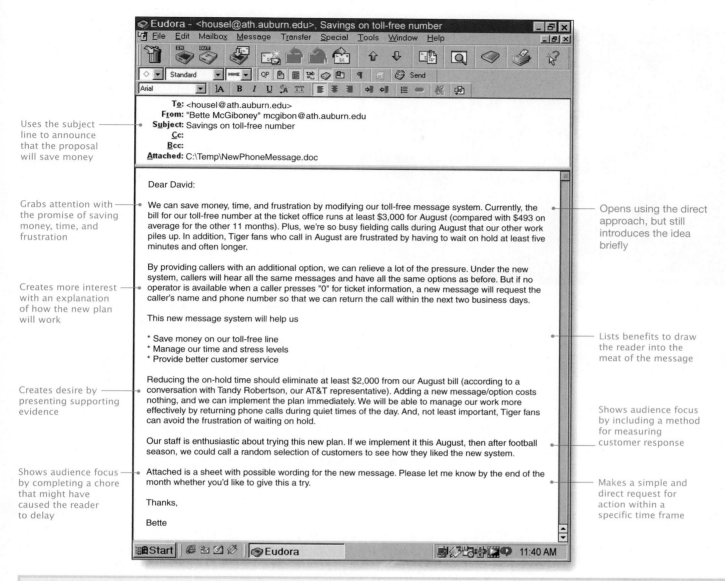

Uses the subject line to announce that the proposal will save money

Grabs attention with the promise of saving money, time, and frustration

Creates more interest with an explanation of how the new plan will work

Creates desire by presenting supporting evidence

Shows audience focus by completing a chore that might have caused the reader to delay

Opens using the direct approach, but still introduces the idea briefly

Lists benefits to draw the reader into the meat of the message

Shows audience focus by including a method for measuring customer response

Makes a simple and direct request for action within a specific time frame

FIGURE 9–3
Effective E-Mail Message Selling an Idea to a Boss

- The degree of resistance you must overcome

- How far you feel empowered to go in selling your point of view

When you're persuading someone to accept a complex idea, take a serious step, or make a large and important decision, lean toward logic and make your emotional appeal subtle. However, when you're persuading someone to purchase a product, join a cause, or make a donation, you can rely a bit more heavily on emotion.

Emotional Appeals   An **emotional appeal** calls on human feelings, basing the argument on audience needs or sympathies. But be careful; such an appeal must be subtle.[10] For instance, you can make use of the emotion surrounding certain words. The word *freedom* evokes strong feelings, as do words such as *success, prestige, credit record, savings, free, value,* and *comfort.* Such words put your audience in a certain frame of mind and help them accept your message. At Patagonia, Yvon Chouinard uses words and pictures

Emotional appeals are best if subtle.

Fily and Madeline Keita sell African art and clothing in their shop, Fara Fina Collection. Traveling several times a year and dealing with artists and craftspeople in Mali, Cameroon, Tanzania, and Zimbabwe, Fily finds persuasion useful. He knows that even if people can respond from the heart, decisions are made in the mind. Thus, both emotion and logic are necessary to persuade successfully.

to help people make an emotional connection with the environment. However, emotional appeals aren't necessarily effective by themselves. Emotion works with logic in a unique way: People apparently need rational support for attitudes they've already embraced emotionally.

Logical Appeals A **logical appeal** calls on human reason. In any argument you might use to persuade an audience, you make a claim and then support your claim with reasons or evidence. When appealing to your audience's logic, you might use three types of reasoning:

- **Analogy.** With analogy, you reason from specific evidence to specific evidence. For instance, to persuade employees to attend a planning session, you might use a town meeting analogy, comparing your company to a small community and your employees to valued members of that community.

- **Induction.** With induction, you reason from specific evidence to a general conclusion. To convince potential customers that your product is best, you might report the results of test marketing in which individuals preferred your product over others. After all, if some individuals prefer it, so will others.

Logical appeals can use analogy, induction, or deduction.

- **Deduction.** With deduction, you might reason from a generalization to a specific conclusion. To persuade your boss to hire additional employees, you might point to industrywide projections and explain that industry activity (and thus your company's business) will be increasing rapidly over the next three months, so you'll need more employees to handle increased business.

No matter what method you use to appeal to your audience's reason, do everything you can to strengthen your argument by basing it on points that your audience already accepts (common ground). Keep your arguments relevant, well grounded, and systematic. Any argument or statement can easily appear to be true when it's actually false. The following guidelines will help you avoid faulty logic:[11]

Faulty logic can appear in many guises.

- **Avoid hasty generalizations.** Make sure you have plenty of evidence before drawing conclusions.

- **Avoid begging the question.** Make sure you can support your claim without simply restating it in different words.

- **Avoid attacking your opponent.** Be careful to address the real question. Attack the argument your opponent is making, not your opponent's character.

- **Avoid oversimplifying a complex issue.** Make sure you present all the alternatives rather than rely on an "either/or" statement that makes it look as if only two choices are possible.

- **Avoid assuming a false cause.** Use cause-and-effect reasoning correctly; do not assume that one event caused another just because it happened first.

- **Avoid faulty analogies.** Be sure that the two objects or situations being compared are similar enough for the analogy to hold. Even if A resembles B in one respect, it may not hold true in other important respects.

- **Avoid illogical support.** Make sure the connection between your claim and your support is truly logical and not based on a leap of faith, a missing premise, or irrelevant evidence.

Reinforcing Your Position

Once you have framed your arguments and chosen your appeal, you can concentrate on strengthening your message with some important persuasive tools. Effective persuaders such as Yvon Chouinard know that the facts alone may not be enough to persuade an audience. So they supplement numerical data with examples, stories, metaphors, and analogies to make their position come alive. They use language to paint a vivid picture of the persuader's point of view.[12]

Your language helps reinforce your position.

Semantics   Suppose that you're trying to build your credibility. How do you let your audience know that you're trustworthy? Simply making an outright claim that people should believe you is sure to raise suspicion. However, you can use *semantics* (the meaning of words and other symbols) to do much of the job for you. The words you choose to state your message say much more than their dictionary definition.[13] For example, look at the following:

Semantics is the meaning of words and other symbols.

Instead of This	Say This
I think we should attempt to get approval on this before it's too late.	Let's get immediate approval.
It seems to me that . . .	I believe . . .
I've been thinking lately that maybe someone could . . .	After careful thought over the past two months, I've decided that . . .
This plan could work if we really push it.	With our support, this plan will work.

Another way that semantics can affect persuasive messages is in the variety of meanings that people attribute to certain words. As discussed in Chapter 5, abstract words are subject to interpretation because they refer to things that people cannot experience with their senses. Thus, you can use abstractions to enhance the emotional content of a persuasive message. For example, you may be able to sell more flags by appealing to your audience's patriotism than by describing the color and size of the flags. You may have better luck collecting an overdue bill by mentioning honesty and fair play than by repeating the sum owed and the date it was due. However, be sure to include the details along with the abstractions; the very fact that you're using abstract words leaves room for misinterpretation.

Two ways of using semantics are choosing your words carefully and using abstractions to enhance emotional content.

Other Tools   Using semantics skillfully isn't your only persuasive tool. Here are some additional techniques you can use to strengthen your persuasive messages:[14]

In addition to semantics, you have other persuasive tools at your disposal.

- **Be moderate.** Asking your audience to make major changes in attitudes or beliefs will most likely evoke a negative response. However, asking audience members to take one step toward that change may be a more reasonable goal.

- **Focus on your goal.** Your message will be clearest if you shift your focus away from changing minds and emphasize the action you want your audience to take.

- **Use simple language.** In most persuasive situations, your audience will be cautious, watching for fantastic claims, insupportable descriptions, and emotional manipulation. So speak plainly and simply.

- **Anticipate opposition.** Think of every possible objection in advance. In your message, you might raise and answer some of these counterarguments.

- **Provide sufficient support.** It is up to you to prove that the change you seek is necessary.

- **Be specific.** Back up your claims with evidence, and when necessary, cite actual facts and figures. Let your audience know that you've done your homework.

As owner of Long Island Lemonade Company, David Schwartz knows how to persuade with evidence. Being specific is an important way to convince people. To spur an audience to take action, give them all the relevant facts you can.

- **Create a win-win situation.** Make it possible for both you and your audience to gain something. Audience members will find it easier to deal with change if they stand to benefit.

- **Time your messages appropriately.** The time to sell roofs is right after the tornado. Timing is crucial in persuasive messages.

- **Speak metaphorically.** Metaphors create powerful pictures. One metaphor can convey a lifetime of experience or a head full of logic.

- **Use anecdotes and stories to make your points.** Anecdotes tie it all together—the logic and the emotions. Don't tell your audience what kinds of problems they can have if their system crashes. Tell them what happened to Jeff Porte when his hard drive crashed in the middle of his annual sales presentation.

All these tools will help your persuasive message be accepted, but none of them will actually overcome your audience's resistance. To accomplish that goal, your argument must be strong enough to persuade people to act.

Dealing with Resistance

You can overcome resistance by presenting the pros and cons of all sides of your argument.

The best way to deal with audience resistance is to eliminate it. If you expect a hostile audience, one biased against your plan from the beginning, present all sides—cover all options, explaining the pros and cons of each. You'll gain additional credibility if you present these options before presenting the decision.[15]

To uncover audience objections, try some "What if?" scenarios. Poke holes in your own theories and ideas before your audience does. Then find solutions to the problems you've uncovered. Recognize that people support what they help create, and ask your audience for their thoughts on the subject before you put your argument together. Let your audience recommend some solutions. With enough thought and effort, you may even be able to turn problems into opportunities; for example, you may show how your proposal will be more economical in the long run, even though it may cost more now. Just be thorough, open, and objective about all the facts and alternatives. When putting together persuasive arguments, avoid some common mistakes:[16]

Document Makeover

IMPROVE THIS E-MAIL

To practice correcting drafts of actual documents, visit **www.prenhall.com/onekey** on the web. Click "Document Makeovers," then click Chapter 9. You will find an e-mail message that contains problems and errors relating to what you've learned in this chapter about writing persuasive messages. Use the Final Draft decision tool to create an improved version of this persuasive e-mail request for action. Check the message for its effectiveness at gaining attention, building interest, stimulating desire, motivating action, focusing on the primary goal, and dealing with resistance.

Avoiding common mistakes helps you overcome resistance.

- **Using an up-front hard sell.** Setting out a strong position at the start of a persuasive message gives potential opponents something to grab onto—and fight against.

- **Resisting compromise.** Persuasion is a process of give and take. As one expert points out, a persuader rarely changes another person's behavior or viewpoint without altering his or her own behavior or viewpoint in the process.

- **Relying solely on great arguments.** Great arguments matter, but they are only one part of the persuasive equation. Your ability to create a mutually beneficial framework for your position, to connect with your audience on the right emotional level, and to communicate through vivid language are all just as important; they bring your argument to life.

- **Assuming persuasion is a one-shot effort.** Persuasion is a process, not a one-time event. More often than not, persuasion involves listening to people, testing a position, developing a new position that reflects new input, more testing, more compromise, and so on.

Successful persuasive messages depend on your ability to frame your argument, balance emotional and logical appeals, reinforce your position, and overcome resistance. To review the steps involved in developing persuasive messages, see the "Checklist: Developing Persuasive Messages."

✓ CHECKLIST: Developing Persuasive Messages

Increase the Effectiveness of Your AIDA Plan

✓ Use the AIDA plan for both direct and indirect approaches.
✓ Be careful not to give your message away in the subject line.
✓ Limit your objectives by focusing on your primary goal.

Get Your Reader's Attention

✓ Open with a reader benefit, a stimulating rhetorical question, an unexpected or agreeable statement, a sincere compliment, your statement of a problem, or a brief review of what has been done about the problem.
✓ Discuss something your audience can agree with (establishing common ground).
✓ Demonstrate that you understand the audience's concerns.

Build Your Reader's Interest

✓ Elaborate on the main benefit.
✓ Explain the relevance of your message to your audience.
✓ In persuasive claims, show readers that their firm is responsible for the problem.
✓ In persuasive claims, be especially careful to present your case in a calm, logical manner.

Increase Your Reader's Desire

✓ Make audience members want to change by explaining how the change will benefit them.
✓ Back up your claims with relevant evidence.
✓ In persuasive claims, appeal to readers' sense of fair play, desire for customer goodwill, need for a good reputation, or sense of legal or moral responsibility.
✓ In persuasive claims, emphasize your goal of having the requested adjustment granted.
✓ In persuasive claims, tell readers how you feel; your disappointment with the organization's products, policies, or services may well be the most important part of your argument.

Motivate Your Reader to Take Action

✓ Confidently ask for the audience's cooperation.
✓ Stress the positive results of the action.
✓ Include the due date (if any) for a response, and tie it in with audience benefits.
✓ Include one last reminder of the audience benefit.
✓ Make the desired action clear and easy.
✓ In persuasive claims, make your request factual and reasonable.
✓ In persuasive claims, be especially sure that the action request is a logical conclusion of your reasons, based solely on the problem and the stated facts.

Balance Emotional and Logical Appeals

✓ Use emotional appeals to help the audience accept your message.
✓ Use logical appeals when presenting facts and evidence for complex ideas or recommendations.
✓ Avoid faulty logic.

Reinforce Your Position

✓ Use semantics to build credibility and enhance the emotional content of your message.
✓ Use a variety of critical thinking and effective writing tools to strengthen your case.

Deal with Resistance

✓ Anticipate and answer possible objections. Turn them into opportunities when possible. Otherwise, give assurance that you will handle them as best you can.
✓ Try "What if?" scenarios to poke holes in your theories and then find solutions.
✓ Let others help you find solutions to problems that you uncover.
✓ Present the pros and cons of all options.
✓ Avoid common mistakes such as using a hard sell up front, resisting compromise, relying solely on great arguments, and assuming persuasion is a one-shot effort.

EXAMINING TYPES OF PERSUASIVE MESSAGES

Persuasive requests are used both inside and outside the organization.

You will have innumerable opportunities to write persuasive messages within an organization: selling a supervisor on an idea for more efficient operating procedures, eliciting cooperation from competing departments, winning employee support for a new benefits package, requesting money for new equipment or funding for a special project. Similarly, you may send a variety of persuasive messages to people outside the organization: requesting favors, demanding adjustments, asking for information, soliciting funds and cooperation, or collecting an overdue debt. In the rest of this chapter, we focus on three main categories of such persuasive messages: persuasive requests, sales messages, and fundraising messages.

Persuasive Requests

Make only reasonable requests.

The most important thing to remember when preparing a persuasive request is to keep your request within bounds. Avoid making any request so general, so all-encompassing, or so inconsiderate that it seems impossible to grant, no matter how worthy the cause. Take special care to highlight both the direct and the indirect benefits of fulfilling it.

Highlight the direct and indirect benefits of complying with your request.

For example, if you want to persuade your supervisor to institute flextime, a direct benefit for that person might be the reduced workload or the enhanced prestige. An indirect benefit might be better employee morale once flextime is instituted. If you are asking someone to respond to a survey, you might offer a premium as the direct benefit and a chance to make a meaningful contribution as the indirect benefit. Let's look at two examples of persuasive requests: (1) persuasive requests for action and (2) persuasive claims and requests for adjustments.

When making a persuasive request for action, be sure to use the AIDA plan to frame your argument.

Making Persuasive Requests for Action   Whether you're requesting a favor or a budget increase, use the AIDA plan to frame your message. Begin with an attention-getting device. Show readers that you know something about their concerns and that you have a reason for making such a request. In this type of persuasive message, more than in most others, a flattering comment about your reader is acceptable, as long as it's sincere.

Use the interest and desire sections of your message to cover what you know about the situation you're requesting action on: the facts and figures, the benefits of helping, and any history or experience that will enhance your appeal. Your goals are (1) to gain credibility for you and your request and (2) to make your readers believe that helping you will indeed help solve a significant problem. Be careful not to doom your request to failure by asking your reader to do all your work for you. For example, don't ask your readers to

- Provide information that you were too lazy to seek

- Take action that will save you from embarrassment or inconvenience

- Provide total financial support for a cause that nobody else is supporting

Once you've demonstrated that your message is relevant to your reader, you can close with a request for some specific action. Be aware, however, that a persuasive memo to a colleague would be somewhat more subdued than a persuasive letter to an outsider. Leslie Jorgensen wrote the memo in Figure 9–4. She's excited about the new Airbus A380 and thinks that purchasing this plane for appropriate markets could help Qantas meet its growth needs while lowering its operating costs. She now needs her boss's approval for a study of the plane's market potential. But whether you're writing to someone inside or outside the company, your choice of approach depends on the type of request you're making.

When requesting a favor that is routine (such as asking someone to attend a meeting in your absence), use the direct approach and the format for routine messages (see Chapter 7). However, when asking for a special favor (such as asking

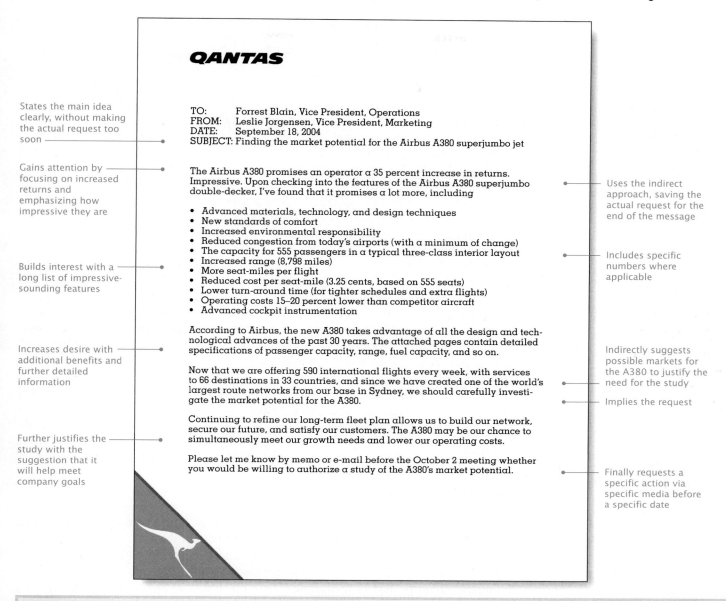

States the main idea clearly, without making the actual request too soon

Gains attention by focusing on increased returns and emphasizing how impressive they are

Builds interest with a long list of impressive-sounding features

Increases desire with additional benefits and further detailed information

Further justifies the study with the suggestion that it will help meet company goals

Uses the indirect approach, saving the actual request for the end of the message

Includes specific numbers where applicable

Indirectly suggests possible markets for the A380 to justify the need for the study

Implies the request

Finally requests a specific action via specific media before a specific date

FIGURE 9–4
Effective Persuasive Memo Requesting Action

someone to chair an event or to serve as the team leader because you can no longer fill that role), use persuasive techniques to convince your reader of the value of the project. Include all necessary information about the project and any facts and figures that will convince your reader that his or her contribution will be enjoyable, easy, important, and of personal benefit.

Making Persuasive Claims and Requests for Adjustments   When your goal is to persuade someone to make an adjustment in your favor, you're not merely trying to get a complaint off your chest. You want to demonstrate the difference between what you expected and what you actually received.

Most claim letters are routine messages that use the direct approach discussed in Chapter 7. However, suppose you purchase something and, after the warranty expires, you discover that the item was defective. You write the company a routine request asking for a replacement, but your request is denied. You're not satisfied, and

The goal of a persuasive claim or request for adjustment is to convince someone to make an adjustment in your favor.

you still believe you have a strong case. Perhaps you just didn't communicate it well enough the first time. Your next message must be a persuasive one. You must try to convey the essentially negative information in a way that will get positive results. Fortunately, most people in business are open to settling your claim fairly. It's to their advantage to maintain your goodwill and to resolve your problem quickly.

Make your persuasive claims
- Complete and specific when reviewing the facts
- Confident and positive in tone

To make a persuasive claim as effective as possible, review the facts completely and specifically, and make sure your tone is confident and positive. Base your message on two assumptions: that your reader is not trying to cheat you and that you have every right to be satisfied with the transaction. Discuss only the complaint at hand; don't bring up other issues involving similar products or other complaints about the company. Your goal is to solve a particular problem. Also, avoid focusing on the disadvantages of neglecting your complaint. Your audience is most likely to help if you focus on the audience benefits of doing so.

Begin a persuasive claim by stating the basic problem (or with a sincere compliment, rhetorical question, agreeable assertion, or brief review of what's been done about the problem). Include a statement that both you and your audience can agree with or that clarifies what you wish to convince your audience about. Be as specific as possible about what you want to happen.

Next, give your reader a good reason for granting your claim. Show how your audience is responsible for the problem, and appeal to your reader's sense of fair play, goodwill, or moral responsibility. Explain how you feel about the problem, but don't get carried away. Don't complain too much, and don't make threats. Keep your request calm and reasonable.

Finally, state your request specifically and confidently. Make sure your request proceeds logically from the problem and the facts you've explained. Remember to specify a deadline for action (when necessary or desirable). And don't forget to remind your audience of the main benefit of granting your claim. The best approach to resolving problems is to engage in a reasonable exchange rather than an adversarial struggle (see Figure 9–5).

Sales Messages

Since sales messages often come in special direct-mail packages, you'll need to decide what sort of campaign you'll conduct.

When planning a sales letter, you'll need to think about the type of sales campaign you'll conduct. Will you send a letter only, or will you send a direct-mail package that includes brochures, samples, response cards, and the like? If you send a brochure, how many pages will it run? Will you conduct a multistage campaign, with several mailings and some sort of telephone or in-person follow-up? Or will you rely on a single, hard-hitting mailing? Expensive items and hard-to-accept propositions call for a more elaborate campaign than low-cost products and simple actions.

All these decisions depend on the audience you're trying to reach—their characteristics and their likely acceptance of, or resistance to, your message. Analyze your audience and focus on their needs, interests, and emotional concerns—just as you would for any persuasive message. Try to form a mental image of the typical buyer for the product you wish to sell. But besides the usual questions, also ask: What might audience members want to know about this product? How can your product help them? Are readers driven by bottom-line pricing, or is quality more important to them?

When planning a sales message, know your product.

Determining Selling Points and Benefits   Your purpose in writing a sales message is to sell a product. One of the first things to do is gain a thorough understanding of that product. What does it look like? How does it work? How is it priced? Are there any discounts? How is it packaged? How is it delivered?

Sales letters require you to know your product's selling points and how each one benefits your particular audience. You'll need to highlight these points when you compose your persuasive message. For example, at Patagonia, sales letters emphasize the confidence that people can place not only in Patagonia's quality-made products but also in the company's environmentally safe production.

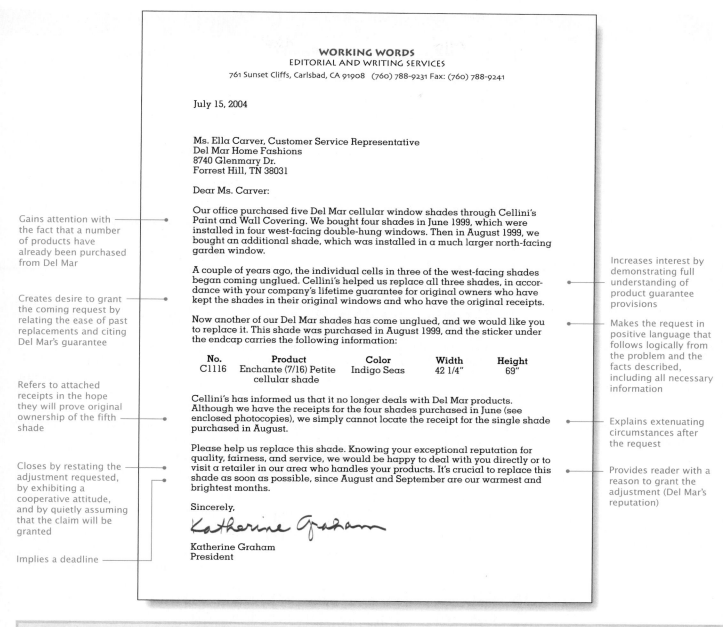

Gains attention with the fact that a number of products have already been purchased from Del Mar

Creates desire to grant the coming request by relating the ease of past replacements and citing Del Mar's guarantee

Refers to attached receipts in the hope they will prove original ownership of the fifth shade

Closes by restating the adjustment requested, by exhibiting a cooperative attitude, and by quietly assuming that the claim will be granted

Implies a deadline

Increases interest by demonstrating full understanding of product guarantee provisions

Makes the request in positive language that follows logically from the problem and the facts described, including all necessary information

Explains extenuating circumstances after the request

Provides reader with a reason to grant the adjustment (Del Mar's reputation)

WORKING WORDS
EDITORIAL AND WRITING SERVICES
761 Sunset Cliffs, Carlsbad, CA 91908 (760) 788-9231 Fax: (760) 788-9241

July 15, 2004

Ms. Ella Carver, Customer Service Representative
Del Mar Home Fashions
8740 Glenmary Dr.
Forrest Hill, TN 38031

Dear Ms. Carver:

Our office purchased five Del Mar cellular window shades through Cellini's Paint and Wall Covering. We bought four shades in June 1999, which were installed in four west-facing double-hung windows. Then in August 1999, we bought an additional shade, which was installed in a much larger north-facing garden window.

A couple of years ago, the individual cells in three of the west-facing shades began coming unglued. Cellini's helped us replace all three shades, in accordance with your company's lifetime guarantee for original owners who have kept the shades in their original windows and who have the original receipts.

Now another of our Del Mar shades has come unglued, and we would like you to replace it. This shade was purchased in August 1999, and the sticker under the endcap carries the following information:

No.	Product	Color	Width	Height
C1116	Enchante (7/16) Petite cellular shade	Indigo Seas	42 1/4"	69"

Cellini's has informed us that it no longer deals with Del Mar products. Although we have the receipts for the four shades purchased in June (see enclosed photocopies), we simply cannot locate the receipt for the single shade purchased in August.

Please help us replace this shade. Knowing your exceptional reputation for quality, fairness, and service, we would be happy to deal with you directly or to visit a retailer in our area who handles your products. It's crucial to replace this shade as soon as possible, since August and September are our warmest and brightest months.

Sincerely,

Katherine Graham

Katherine Graham
President

FIGURE 9–5
Effective Letter Making a Persuasive Claim

Selling points are the most attractive features of an idea or product; **benefits** are the particular advantages that readers will realize from those features (see Table 9–2). Selling points focus on the product. Benefits focus on the user. For example, if you say that your shovel has "an ergonomically designed handle," you've described a good feature. But to persuade someone to buy that shovel, say "the ergonomically designed handle will reduce your risk of back injury." That's a benefit. For a successful sales letter, your product's distinguishing benefit must correspond to your readers' primary needs or emotional concerns.

Take a look at Figure 9–6 on page 285. The sales letter for SecureAbel Alarms uses the AIDA plan to persuade students to buy its dorm-room alarm system. The features of the system are that it can be installed with a screwdriver, it has an activator that hooks to your key chain or belt loop, and it has a blinking red light to warn

Selling points focus on the product; benefits focus on the user.

For your sales letter to succeed, your product's benefits must match your audience's needs.

Table 9–2	**FEATURES VERSUS BENEFITS**	
	Product Feature (Selling Point)	***Consumer Benefit***
	No money down, no interest payments for 24 months.	You can buy what you want right now at no additional costs.
	This printer prints 17 pages a minute.	This printer can turn out one of your 100–page proposals in six minutes.
	Our shelter provides 100 adult beds and 50 children's beds for the needy.	Your donation will provide temporary housing for 100 women who don't want to return to abusive husbands.
	Your corporate sponsorship of the seminar will pay for the keynote speaker's travel and lodging.	Your corporate sponsorship of the seminar will allow your site manager a five-minute introduction at the beginning of the program to summarize your services.

intruders to stay away. The benefits are ease of installation, ease of activation, and a feeling of safety and security—all obtainable without investing in a full-blown, permanently installed alarm system. When composing sales messages, be sure to focus on relatively few product benefits. Ultimately, you'll single out one benefit, which will become the hallmark of your campaign. Safety seems to be the key benefit emphasized by SecureAbel Alarms.

To avoid both legal and ethical pitfalls, you must also know the law.

Staying Within the Law   Whether you're selling a good, a service, or your company's image, knowing the law can help you avoid serious legal problems (see "Promoting Workplace Ethics: What You May Legally Say in a Sales Letter" on page 286). The laws governing sales letters are quite specific:

- **Letters as contracts.** Sales letters are considered binding contracts in many states, so avoid even implying offers or promises that you can't deliver on.

- **Fraud.** Making a false statement in a sales letter is fraud if the recipient can prove that (1) you intended to deceive, (2) you made a statement regarding a fact rather than an opinion or a speculation, (3) the recipient was justified in relying on the statement, and (4) the recipient was damaged by it (in a legal sense). Misrepresenting the price, quality, or performance of a product in a sales letter is fraud. So is a testimonial by a person misrepresented to be an expert.

- **Permission.** Using a person's name, photograph, or other identity in a sales letter without permission is against the law—with some exceptions. Using a photo of a local softball team in your chamber of commerce mailer may be perfectly legal if team members are public figures in the community and if using the photo doesn't falsely imply their endorsement. However, using a photo of your governor, without consent, on a letter about the profits to be made in worm farming could be deemed an invasion of privacy.

- **Privacy.** Publicizing a person's private life in a sales letter can also result in legal problems. Stating that the president of a local bank (mentioned by name) served six months in prison for income tax evasion is a potentially damaging fact that may be considered an invasion of privacy. You would also risk a lawsuit by publicizing another person's past-due debts or by publishing without consent another person's medical records, x-rays, or photograph.

As with other persuasive messages, following the letter of the law isn't always enough. You'll also want to write sales letters of the highest ethical character. One

FIGURE 9–6
Effective Letter Selling a Product

Planning

Writing

Completing

Analyze the Situation
The purpose is to persuade readers to buy the portable alarm system. The audience will be neutral—or even resistant.

Gather Information
Gather data on product's features and benefits, as well as on audience needs.

Adapt to the Audience
Use a typical sales letter format.

Organize the Information
Make safety the central selling point. Follow the indirect AIDA approach. Get the reader's attention right away.

Compose the Message
Use both logical and emotional appeals. Use a friendly, conversational tone. Include a response card to make reader action easy.

Revise the Message
Don't emphasize emotional appeals. The point is to help readers, not threaten them. Edit for focus and clarity.

Produce the Message
Use a simple design for the letter and any brochures (in line with reasonable pricing).

Proofread the Message
Be accurate. Remove all typographical distractions.

1 **2** **3**

SecureAbel Alarms, Inc.

5654 Lakemont Drive • Altoona, PA 16602 • Voice: (814) 983-4424 • Fax: (814) 983-4422 • http://www.secure.com

October 14, 2004

Mr. Samuel Zolezzi
Penn State University, North Hall
104 Warnock Commons
State College, PA 16802

Dear Mr. Zolezzi:

Draws the reader into the letter with a provocative question

Did you know that one out of four college students becomes a victim of theft? How would you feel if you returned to your dorm and discovered that your hard-earned stereo, computer, or microwave had been stolen? Remember, locked doors won't stop a determined thief.

Raises reader's awareness of a need

Seeks to establish a common bond with the reader

My dorm room was burglarized when I was in college. That's why I've developed a portable security system for your dormitory room. This system works like an auto alarm and can be installed with an ordinary screwdriver. The small activator hooks to your key chain or belt loop. Just press the "lock" key. A "beep" tells you your room is secure, and a blinking red light warns intruders to stay away.

Explains how product works by comparing it to something familiar—a car alarm

Mentions an additional threat (to personal safety), implying another benefit of the security system

If a thief tries to break in, a loud alarm sounds. Your possessions will be safe. And, even more important, you can activate the system from your bedside, so you're safe while you sleep.

Uses both a logical appeal (protecting possessions) and an emotional appeal (personal safety)

You'd expect this peace of mind to cost a fortune—something most college students don't have. But we're offering the SecureAbel Dorm Alarm System for only $75. Here's what you'll receive by return mail:

Creates the sense of added value

- The patented alarm unit
- Two battery-operated programmable remote units
- A one-year warranty on all parts
- Complete and easy-to-follow installation instructions

Order additional alarm boxes to install on your window or bathroom door for only $50. Act now. Fill out the response card, and mail it along with your choice of payment method in the enclosed envelope. Don't give thieves and criminals a chance. Protect yourself and your belongings. Send in your card today.

Urges quick action

Sincerely,

Dan Abel

Dan Abel, President

Enclosures

PROMOTING WORKPLACE ETHICS

What You May Legally Say in a Sales Letter

As you prepare to write your sales letter, think carefully about your choice of words. False or misleading statements could land you in court, so make sure your language complies with legal and ethical standards. To keep your sales letters within the limits of the law, review the legal considerations of these typical sales phrases:

- *"Our product is the best on the market."* This statement is acceptable for a sales letter because the law permits you to express an opinion about your product. In the process of merchandising a product, statements of opinion are known as "puffery," which is perfectly legal as long as you make no deceptive or fraudulent claims.

- *"Our product will serve you well for many years to come."* This statement from a sales brochure triggered a lawsuit by a disgruntled customer who claimed the manufacturer's product lasted only a few years. The courts ruled that the statement was an acceptable form of puffery because the manufacturer did not promise that the product would last for a specific number of years.

- *"We're so confident you'll enjoy our products that we've enclosed a sample of our most popular line. This sample can be yours for only $5.00! Please send your payment in the enclosed, prepaid envelope."* If you include a product sample with your sales letter, your readers may keep the merchandise without paying for it. Under the law, consumers may consider unordered goods as gifts. They are not obligated to return the items to you or submit payments for unsolicited merchandise.

- *"Thousands of high school students—just like you—are already enjoying this fantastic CD collection! Order before March 1 and save!"* If your sales letter appeals to minors, you are legally obligated to honor their contracts. At the same time, however, the law permits minors to cancel their contracts and return the merchandise to you. Sellers are legally obligated to accept contracts voided by minors and any goods returned by them. Legal adult status is defined differently from state to state, ranging from age 18 to age 21.

- *"You'll find hundreds of bargains at our annual 'scratch and dent' sale! All sales are final on merchandise marked 'as is.'"* When you use the term *as is* in your sales letter, you are not misleading customers about the quality of your products. By warning consumers that the condition of sales items is less than perfect, you are not legally obligated to issue refunds to customers who complain about defects later on.

CAREER APPLICATIONS

1. Review two sales letters for content. List the "puffery" statements in each letter.

2. Note any statements in these sales letters that appear questionable to you. Rewrite one of the statements, carefully choosing words that won't be misleading to consumers.

To keep your sales letters ethical, be genuinely concerned about solving your reader's problem.

Most sales messages use the AIDA plan.

way to do so is to focus on solving your reader's problem rather than on selling your product. When you're genuinely concerned about your audience's needs and interests, you'll find it easier to avoid legal or ethical pitfalls.

Using the AIDA Plan in Sales Messages   Like other persuasive messages, most sales letters are prepared according to the AIDA plan. You begin with an attention-getting device, generate interest by describing some of the product's unique features, increase the desire for your product by highlighting the benefits that are most appealing to your audience, and close by suggesting the action you want the audience to take.

Certain tried-and-true attention-getting devices are used in sales letters for a wide variety of products.

Getting Attention   In sales letters the attention phase has a slightly different emphasis than it has in other persuasive messages. Sales-letter professionals use some common techniques to attract their audience's attention. One popular technique is opening with a provocative question. Look closely at the following three examples. Which seems most interesting to you?

How would you like straight A's this semester?

Get straight A's this semester!

Now you can get straight A's this semester, with . . .

If you're like most people, you'll find the first option the most enticing. The question invites your response—a positive response designed to encourage you to read on. The second option is fairly interesting too, but its commanding tone may make you wary of the claim. The third option is acceptable, but it certainly conveys no sense of excitement. Its quick introduction of the product may lead you to a snap decision against reading further.

Choose an attention-getter that encourages the reader to read more.

Other techniques can also help you open your sales letters with excitement. You can grab your audience's attention by emphasizing

- **A piece of genuine news.** "In the past 60 days, mortgage rates have fallen to a 30-year low."

- **A personal appeal to the reader's emotions and values.** "The only thing worse than paying taxes is paying taxes when you don't have to."

- **Your product's most attractive feature along with the associated benefit.** "New control device ends problems with employee pilferage!"

- **An intriguing number.** "Here are three great secrets of the world's most-loved entertainers."

- **A sample of the product.** "Here's your free sample of the new Romalite packing sheet."

- **A concrete illustration with story appeal.** "In 1985, Earl Colbert set out to find a better way to process credit applications. After 10 years of trial and error, he finally developed a procedure so simple and yet thorough that he was cited for service to the industry by the American Creditors Association."

- **A specific trait shared by the audience.** "Busy executives need another complicated 'time-saving' device like they need a hole in the head!"

- **A challenge.** "Don't waste another day wondering how you're going to become the success you've always wanted to be!"

- **A solution to a problem.** "Tired of arctic air rushing through the cracks around your windows? Stay warm and save energy with StormSeal Weather-stripping."

Analyze your own mail to see how many sales messages use these techniques. For a typical example, look back at Figure 9–6. Such attention-getting devices will give your sales letters added impact.

Sales-message professionals know that textual openings aren't the only way to get attention. In ads and catalogs, Patagonia's Chouinard captures attention and heightens emotional desire by featuring lush, vibrant photographs of nature. Other companies use a variety of formatting devices. You can grab your audience by using special sizes or styles of type, underlining, bullets, color, indentions, and so on. Even so, not all attention-getting devices are equally effective. Plus, using too many can alienate readers rather than draw them in. In short, the best attention-getter is the one that makes your audience read the rest of your message.

Other devices for grabbing attention include
- Photographs
- Formatting decisions
- Typographical devices

Building Interest   In the interest section of your message, highlight your product's key selling point. Say that your company's alarm device is relatively inexpensive, durable, and tamperproof. Although these are all attractive features, you want to focus on only one. Ask what the competition has to offer, what most distinguishes your product, and what most concerns potential buyers. The answers to these questions will help you select the **central selling point,** the single point around which to build your sales message. Build your audience's interest by highlighting this point, and make it stand out through typography, design, or high-impact writing.[17]

To determine your product's central selling point, ask:
- What does the competition offer?
- What is special about my product?
- What are potential buyers really looking for?

Determining the central selling point will also help you define the benefits to potential buyers. Perhaps your company built its new alarm to overcome competing products' susceptibility to tampering. Being tamperproof is the feature you choose as your central selling point, and its benefit to readers is that burglars won't be able to break in so easily.

Increasing Desire   In the desire section, mention your main benefit repeatedly, expanding and explaining as you go. Use both words and pictures, if possible. This main benefit is what will entice recipients to read on and take further action.

> To increase desire, expand your main benefit while adding others.

As you continue to stress your main benefit, weave in references to other benefits. ("You can get this worry-free protection for much less than you might think," and "The same technology that makes it difficult for burglars to crack your alarm system makes the device durable, even when it must be exposed to the elements.") Remember, in sales letters you reflect the "you" attitude by referring to reader benefits, so always phrase the selling points in terms of what your product's features can do for potential customers.

> To motivate action,
> - Ask for a small step toward the final decision
> - Convince readers to act quickly
> - Use a postscript to make a final impression
> - Select recipients carefully

Motivating Action   After you have raised enough interest and built the reader's desire for your product, you're ready to clearly explain how to take the next step. After all, the overriding purpose of a sales letter is to get your reader to do something. Many consumer products sold through the mail simply ask for a check—in other words, an immediate decision to buy. On the other hand, companies selling big-ticket and more complex items frequently ask for just a small step toward the final buying decision, such as sending for more information or authorizing a call by a sales representative.

Whatever you ask readers to do, try to persuade them to do it right away. Convince them that they must act now, perhaps to guarantee a specific delivery date.

If there's no particular reason to act quickly, many sales letters offer discounts for orders placed by a certain date, or they offer prizes or special offers to, say, the first 500 people to respond. Other letters suggest that purchases be charged to a credit card or be paid off over time. Still others offer a free trial, an unconditional guarantee, or a no-strings request card for information—all in an effort to overcome readers' natural inertia.

Adding a postscript (P.S.) is one of the most effective ways to boost audience response. This is the place to make your final impression, so be sure the information is noteworthy. Use the P.S. to reiterate your primary benefit, make an additional offer, or compel the reader to act quickly by emphasizing a deadline.[18]

Finally, use good judgment when distributing your messages to would-be customers. Do not send electronic junk mail (spam). Doing so only irritates consumers, and it can be illegal, depending on the state in which you reside. Federal laws against spam are pending.

With a $10,000 loan and a cargo of beachware ordered from a trade show in California, Joni Boldt Ridgway and Kyrle Boldt created "Splash"—five Splashes actually—in St. Louis. The owners know that producing effective sales messages is just as important to the stores' success as the creative merchandise they stock—some 70 kinds of snowboards, fluorescent bikinis, and lime-green nail polish. Both must get the customer's attention, build interest, increase desire, and motivate action.

Keeping Readers Interested   Because readers are usually pressed for time, they are interested only in what matters most to them.[19] Therefore, refrain from providing every last detail as you explain product benefits. The best letters are short (preferably one but no more than two pages) and use bullet points to highlight important benefits. They include enough detail to spur the reader's interest, but they don't try to be the sole source of information. To keep readers interested, effective sales letters use action terms, talk about price, and support any claims.

Using Action Terms   Action words give strength to any business message, but they are especially important in sales letters. Compare the following:

Instead of This	Write This
The NuForm desk chair is designed to support your lower back and relieve pressure on your legs.	The NuForm desk chair supports your lower back and relieves pressure on your legs.

The second version says the same thing in fewer words and emphasizes what the chair does for the user ("supports") rather than the intentions of the design team ("is designed to support").

Use colorful verbs and adjectives that convey a dynamic image to keep readers interested. Be careful, however, not to overdo it: "Your factory floors will sparkle like diamonds" is hard to believe and may prevent your audience from believing the rest of your message.

> To give force to a message,
> - Use action terms
> - Use colorful verbs and adjectives

Talking About Price   The price that people are willing to pay for a product depends on several factors: the prices of similar products, the general state of the economy, and the psychology of the buyer. Price is a complicated issue and often a sensitive one, so you need to be careful whenever you talk about price in your sales messages.

Whether you highlight or downplay the price of your product, prepare your readers for it. Words such as *luxurious* and *economical* provide unmistakable clues about how your price compares with that of competitors. Such words help your readers accept your price when you finally state it. Here's an example from a sales letter offering a product at a bargain price:

> You can prepare readers for your product's price with subtle word choice and arrangement.

> ***All the Features of Name-Brand Pantyhose at Half the Price!***
> Why pay for fancy packaging or for that little tag with a famous name on it when you can enjoy cotton lining, reinforced toes, and matchless durability for only $1.99?

In this excerpt the price falls right at the end of the paragraph, where it stands out. In addition, the price issue is featured in a bold headline. This technique may even be used as the opening of a letter, if (1) the price is the most important feature and (2) the audience for the letter is value-conscious.

> If the price is an attractive feature, emphasize it by displaying it prominently.

If price is not a major selling point, you can handle it in several ways. You could leave the price out altogether or mention it only in an accompanying brochure. You could de-emphasize the price by putting the actual figures in the middle of a paragraph that comes close to the end of your sales letter, well after you've presented the benefits and selling points.

> Only 100 prints of this exclusive, limited-edition lithograph will be created. On June 15, they will be made available to the general public, but you can reserve one now for only $350, the special advance reservation price. Simply rush the enclosed reservation card back today so that your order is in before the June 15 publication date.

> Emphasizes the rarity of the edition to signal value and thus prepare the reader for the big-ticket price that follows
>
> Buries the actual price in the middle of a sentence and ties it in with another reminder of the exclusivity of the offer

The pros also use two other techniques for minimizing price. One technique is to break a quantity price into units. Instead of saying that a case of wine costs $144, you might say that each bottle costs $12. The other technique is to compare your product's price with the cost of some other product or activity: "The cost of owning your own exercise equipment is less than you'd pay for a health-club membership." Your aim is to make the cost seem as small and affordable as possible, thereby eliminating price as a possible objection.

> To de-emphasize price,
> - Bury actual figures in the middle of a paragraph near the end
> - Mention benefits and favorable money matters before the actual price
> - Break a quantity price into units
> - Compare the price with the cost of some other product or activity

Supporting Your Claims   Because providing support for your claims boosts your credibility, it increases the audience's desire for your product. You can't assume that people will believe what you say about your product just because you've said it in writing. You'll have to prove your claims—especially if your product is complicated, costs a lot, or represents some unusual approach.

Types of support for product claims:
- Samples
- Brochures
- Examples
- Testimonials
- Statistics
- Guarantees

Support for your claims may take several forms. Samples and brochures, often with photographs, are enclosed in a sales package and are referred to in the letter. The letter also describes or typographically highlights examples of how the product has benefited others. It includes testimonials (quotations from satisfied customers) or cites statistics from scientific studies of the product's performance. Guarantees of exchange or return privileges may be woven into the letter or set off in a special way, indicating that you have faith in your product and are willing to back it up.

It's almost impossible to provide too much support. Try to anticipate every question your audience may want to ask. Put yourself in your audience's place so that you can discover, and solve, all the "what if" scenarios.[20]

Fundraising Messages

Fundraising messages and sales messages have important differences.

Motivating action is a challenge even for the best sales letters, but when you're trying to raise funds, motivating action is even more challenging. Whereas sales messages are usually sent by for-profit organizations to persuade readers to spend money on products for themselves, fundraising messages are usually sent by nonprofit organizations to persuade readers to donate money or time to help others.

Fundraising messages are really quite similar to sales messages.

Aside from these differences, sales and fundraising messages are quite similar. Both compete for their audience's attention, attempting to persuade readers to spend time or money on the value being offered—whether that value is the convenience of a more efficient vacuum cleaner or the satisfaction of helping save children's lives.[21] Like sales messages, fundraising messages are often sent in special direct-mail packages that can include brochures, reply forms, or other special inserts. Both types of messages are often written by professionals with specialized skills, both require a few more steps than other types of persuasive messages, and both generally use the AIDA plan.

Fundraising letters use many of the same techniques that are used in sales letters.

Most of the techniques used to write sales letters can also be used to write fundraising letters, as long as your techniques match your audience, your goals, and your cause or organization. Be careful to establish value in the minds of your donors. Above all, don't forget to include the "what's in it for me?" information—for example, telling your readers how good they'll feel by making a donation.[22]

Some special planning tasks help you write more successful fundraising messages.

To make sure that your fundraising letters outshine those of the competition, take some time to get ready before you actually begin writing.[23] You can start by reading the mail you receive from donors. Learn as much as you can about your audience by noting the tone of these letters, the language used, and the concerns raised. This exercise will help you write letters that donors will both understand and relate to.

You might also keep a file of competing fundraising letters. Study these samples to find out what other fundraisers are doing and what new approaches they're taking. Most important, find out what works and what doesn't. Then you can continue with your other research efforts, such as conducting interviews, holding focus groups, and reading trade journals to find out what people are concerned about, what they're interested in, and what gets their attention.

Be sure to focus on the concerns of your readers, not on the concerns of your organization.

Finally, before you begin writing, know whose benefits to emphasize. Make a two-column list: On one side, list what your organization does; on the other side, list what your donors want. You'll discover that the two columns are quite different. Make sure that the benefits you emphasize are related to what your donors want, not to what your organization does. Then you can work on stating those donor benefits in specific detail. For example: "Your donation of $100 will provide 15 people with a Christmas dinner."

Human interest stories are the best way to interest your readers in fundraising letters.

Personalizing Fundraising Messages Because fundraising letters depend so heavily on emotional appeals, keep your message personal. A natural, real-life lead-in is usually the best. People seem to respond best to slice-of-life stories. Storytelling is perfect when your narrative is unforced and goes straight to the heart of the matter.[24]

Professional fundraiser Conrad Squires advises you to "find and use relevant human-interest stories," to "show donors the faces of the people they are helping," and to "make the act of sending a contribution as real and memorable and personal" as you can.[25] Such techniques make people feel the warmth of other lives.[26]

So that your letters remain personal, immediate, and effective, steer clear of three common mistakes:[27]

- Don't let your letter sound like a business communication of any kind.

- Don't waste space on warm-up (the things you write while you're working up to your real argument).

- Don't assume that your organization's goals are more important than your readers' concerns (a deadly mistake).

The last caution is crucial when writing fundraising letters. Squires suggests that "the more space you spend writing about the reader, the better response you're likely to get."[28] Here are some examples:

> You've proven you are somebody who really cares about what happens to children, Mr. Jones.
>
> Ms. Smith, your company's kindness can change the world for Meta Singh and his family.

It's also up to you to help your donors identify with recipients. A busy company executive may not be able to identify with the homeless man she passes on the street every day. But every human being understands pain; we've all felt it. So do your best to portray that homeless man's pain using words that the busy executive can understand.[29]

Strengthening Fundraising Messages   The best fundraising letters do four things: They (1) thoroughly explain a specific need, (2) show how important it is for readers to help, (3) spell out exactly what amount of help is being requested, and (4) describe in detail the benefits of helping.[30] To help you accomplish these four major tasks, here are some fundraising guidelines:[31]

- **Interest your readers immediately.** If you don't catch your readers' interest with your first few words, you never will.

- **Use simple language.** Tell your story with simple, warm, and personal language. Nothing else is as effective for getting people to empathize.

- **Give readers an opportunity to accomplish something important.** Donors want to feel needed. They want the excitement of coming to your rescue.

- **Make it hard to say no.** Make the need so urgent and strong that your readers will find it difficult to turn you down. "Won't you send a gift now, knowing that children's lives are on the line?"

- **Make your needs clear.** Leave no doubt about the amount of money that you want. Be absolutely clear, and be sure the amount requested is appropriate for your audience. Explain why the money is needed as soon as possible. Also, make it extremely easy to respond by asking for a small gift.

- **Write no longer than you have to.** If you use a telegram-type format, keep your message short. However, longer messages are usually best for fundraising. Just keep sentences and paragraphs short, maximize content, and minimize wordiness.

- **Make your reply form complete and thorough.** Include all the basics: your name, address, and telephone number; a restatement of your request and the gift amount; your donor's name and address (or space enough for a label); information on how to make out the check; and information on tax deductibility.

Personalize fundraising letters by
- Writing about your readers
- Helping your readers identify with recipients

Strong fundraising letters accomplish four goals:
- Explain a specific need thoroughly
- Show how important it is for readers to help
- Spell out exactly what amount of help is being requested
- Describe in detail the benefits of helping

Effective fundraising messages use various techniques.

- **Use interesting enclosures.** Enclosures that simply give more information will decrease returns. Instead, use enclosures that are fun or that give the donor something to do, sign, return, or keep.

These guidelines should help you reach the humanity and compassion of your readers by focusing on specific reader benefits, detailing the unique need, emphasizing the urgency of the situation, and spelling out the exact help needed. As director of PETsMART Charities, Rita Gomez has the task of raising millions of dollars to help save the lives of and find families for thousands upon thousands of homeless pets. Her letter makes a compelling case for donations (see Figure 9–7).

Like sales letters, fundraising letters are simply particular types of persuasive messages. Both categories have their unique requirements, some of which only professional writers can master. (See the "Checklist: Composing Sales and Fundraising Letters" for a reminder of the tasks involved in writing these special messages.)

✓ CHECKLIST: Composing Sales and Fundraising Letters

Attention

✓ Design a positive opening that awakens a favorable association with the product, need, or cause.

✓ Write the opening so that it's appropriate, fresh, honest, interesting, specific, and relevant.

✓ Promise a benefit to the reader.

✓ Keep the first paragraph short, preferably two to five lines, and sometimes only one.

✓ For sales letters, get attention with a provocative question, a significant/startling fact, a solution to a problem, a special offer/gift, a testimonial, a current event, an illustration, a comparison, an event in the reader's life, a problem the reader may face, or a quotation.

✓ For fundraising letters, get attention with a human interest story.

Interest

✓ State information clearly, vividly, and persuasively by relating it to the reader's concerns.

✓ Develop the central selling point.

✓ Feature the product or charitable need in two ways: physical description and reader benefits.

✓ Place benefits first, or interweave them with a physical description.

✓ Describe objective details of the need or product (size, shape, color, scent, sound, texture, etc.).

✓ Use psychological appeals to present the sensation, satisfaction, or pleasure readers will gain.

✓ Blend cold facts with warm feelings.

Desire

✓ Use one or more appeals to support the central idea (selling point or fundraising goal).

✓ If the product is valued mainly because of its appearance, describe its physical details.

✓ If the product is machinery or technical equipment, describe its sturdy construction, fine crafting, and other technical details in terms that help readers visualize themselves using it.

✓ Include technical sketches and meaningful pictures, charts, and graphs, if necessary.

✓ For sales letters, provide test results from recognized experts, laboratories, or authoritative agencies.

✓ To raise funds, detail how donations are spent, using recognized accounting/auditing firms.

✓ To elicit donations, use strong visual details, good narrative, active verbs, and limited adjectives.

✓ Emphasize reader benefits.

✓ Anticipate and answer the reader's questions.

✓ Use an appropriate form of proof.

✓ Include verifiable reports/statistics about users' experience with the product or organization.

✓ Provide names (with permission only) of satisfied buyers, users, or donors.

✓ Present unexaggerated testimonials from persons or firms whose judgment readers respect.

✓ In sales letters, offer a free trial or a guarantee, and refer to samples if they are included.

✓ Note any enclosures in conjunction with a selling point or a reader benefit.

Action

✓ Clearly state the action you desire.

✓ Provide specific details on how to order the product, donate money, or reach your organization.

✓ Ease action with reply cards, preaddressed envelopes, phone numbers, and follow-up phone calls.

✓ Offer a special inducement to act now: time limit or situation urgency, special price for a limited time, premium for acting before a certain date, gift for acting, free trial, no obligation to buy with a request for more information or a demonstration, easy payments with no money down, credit card payments.

✓ Supply a final reader benefit.

✓ In a postscript, convey important donation information or an important sales point (if desired).

FIGURE 9–7
Effective Letter to Raise Funds

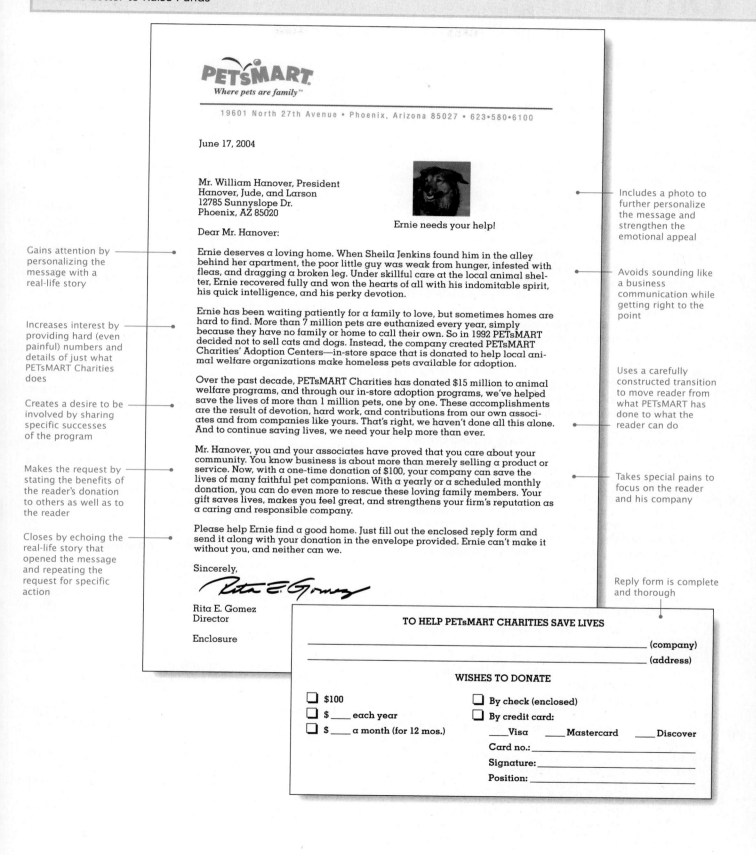

PETsMART.
Where pets are family™

19601 North 27th Avenue • Phoenix, Arizona 85027 • 623•580•6100

June 17, 2004

Mr. William Hanover, President
Hanover, Jude, and Larson
12785 Sunnyslope Dr.
Phoenix, AZ 85020

Ernie needs your help!

Dear Mr. Hanover:

Ernie deserves a loving home. When Sheila Jenkins found him in the alley behind her apartment, the poor little guy was weak from hunger, infested with fleas, and dragging a broken leg. Under skillful care at the local animal shelter, Ernie recovered fully and won the hearts of all with his indomitable spirit, his quick intelligence, and his perky devotion.

Ernie has been waiting patiently for a family to love, but sometimes homes are hard to find. More than 7 million pets are euthanized every year, simply because they have no family or home to call their own. So in 1992 PETsMART decided not to sell cats and dogs. Instead, the company created PETsMART Charities' Adoption Centers—in-store space that is donated to help local animal welfare organizations make homeless pets available for adoption.

Over the past decade, PETsMART Charities has donated $15 million to animal welfare programs, and through our in-store adoption programs, we've helped save the lives of more than 1 million pets, one by one. These accomplishments are the result of devotion, hard work, and contributions from our own associates and from companies like yours. That's right, we haven't done all this alone. And to continue saving lives, we need your help more than ever.

Mr. Hanover, you and your associates have proved that you care about your community. You know business is about more than merely selling a product or service. Now, with a one-time donation of $100, your company can save the lives of many faithful pet companions. With a yearly or a scheduled monthly donation, you can do even more to rescue these loving family members. Your gift saves lives, makes you feel great, and strengthens your firm's reputation as a caring and responsible company.

Please help Ernie find a good home. Just fill out the enclosed reply form and send it along with your donation in the envelope provided. Ernie can't make it without you, and neither can we.

Sincerely,

Rita E. Gomez

Rita E. Gomez
Director

Enclosure

TO HELP PETsMART CHARITIES SAVE LIVES

_____ (company)

_____ (address)

WISHES TO DONATE

☐ $100   ☐ By check (enclosed)
☐ $ ____ each year   ☐ By credit card:
☐ $ ____ a month (for 12 mos.)   ____ Visa   ____ Mastercard   ____ Discover

Card no.: _____

Signature: _____

Position: _____

Margin annotations:

Gains attention by personalizing the message with a real-life story

Increases interest by providing hard (even painful) numbers and details of just what PETsMART Charities does

Creates a desire to be involved by sharing specific successes of the program

Makes the request by stating the benefits of the reader's donation to others as well as to the reader

Closes by echoing the real-life story that opened the message and repeating the request for specific action

Includes a photo to further personalize the message and strengthen the emotional appeal

Avoids sounding like a business communication while getting right to the point

Uses a carefully constructed transition to move reader from what PETsMART has done to what the reader can do

Takes special pains to focus on the reader and his company

Reply form is complete and thorough

On the Job:

SOLVING COMMUNICATION DILEMMAS AT PATAGONIA

Yvon Chouinard knows that Patagonia's success depends on strong persuasive messages that educate consumers about environmental protection and that convince readers to think about long-term sustainability issues when choosing the products they will purchase. As vice president for corporate communications, you are responsible for handling a wide range of correspondence for Patagonia's managers and executives. Use your knowledge of persuasive messages to choose the best alternative in each of the following situations. Be prepared to explain why your choice is best.

1. Every year, Patagonia awards about 350 grants from its "Earth Tax" fund to support worthy environmental causes. However, several customers have complained that Patagonia's earth tax often supports radical environmental groups. In response to these complaints, you have been asked to draft a persuasive letter for Chouinard that explains Patagonia's position on supporting environmental causes. Which of the following appeals would be the most effective in such a letter?

   a. An entirely emotional appeal stressing Patagonia's commitment to support worthy environmental causes, regardless of a group's tactics for achieving environmental goals.
   b. An entirely logical appeal stressing the application process for grants, Patagonia's criteria for selecting earth tax recipients, and a brief history of Patagonia's contributions to environmental causes.
   c. A combination of emotional and logical appeals, stressing both the need to support worthy environmental causes and Patagonia's rationale for awarding grants based on the worthiness of the cause, not the tactics of the cause's supporters.
   d. A combination of emotional and logical appeals, stressing the need to save the earth's resources at any cost and stressing the importance of supporting any group that is attempting to save the environment for future generations.

2. An environmental activist is scheduled to speak at a Patagonia retail store about the importance of saving an ancient redwood forest in northern California. The store manager hopes the speaking venue will increase awareness and educate customers about the need for saving the forest and will raise money for the "Save the Redwood Forest" group. You have been asked to draft a letter for the store manager that will persuade customers to attend the store lecture. The manager plans to send the letter to a mailing list of customers who have supported environmental causes in the past, but you're not sure if all of those customers will support the "Save the Redwood Forest" cause. Brochures about the need for saving the forest are available

for distribution with the letter. Which of the following choices would be the most effective approach for the manager's letter?

   a. Use a direct approach, announcing the time, date, place, and purpose of the lecture and inviting customers to attend. Refer customers to the enclosed brochure for details about the cause and state that you've conveniently enclosed a self-addressed, stamped envelope for contributions to the "Save the Redwood Forest" group.
   b. Use an indirect approach, attracting readers' attention by naming the benefits of saving the ancient redwood forest. Encourage customers to learn more about the cause by attending the lecture at the Patagonia store. Don't include the brochure or a self-addressed envelope for contributions with your mailing; customers who are truly interested can pick up the brochure or make contributions while attending the seminar.
   c. Use a detailed, indirect approach, creating desire to save the forest by pointing out the direct and indirect benefits of supporting the cause. Include facts about the importance of saving the redwoods for future generations, and refer readers to the enclosed brochure for more information. Invite customers to take action by attending the lecture, but don't include a self-addressed envelope in your mailing. Instead, inform customers that their contributions will be welcomed at the store lecture.
   d. Follow the detailed, indirect approach outlined above, but include a self-addressed envelope for contributions. Make an appeal for contributions at the end of your letter and ask customers to send their donations in the enclosed envelope.

3. As human resource director, Jana Thomas wants to convince a promising job candidate to accept Patagonia's job offer. She wants (1) to emphasize the advantages of working for a company that practices environmental responsibility and (2) to show that many of Patagonia's employee benefits support the company's environmental values. Thomas has asked for your advice on writing a persuasive letter to the job candidate. Which of the following choices would you recommend?

   a. Recommend that Thomas send an employee handbook to the job candidate with a short cover letter. The job candidate can study the employee handbook and review all of Patagonia's employee benefits for himself.
   b. Offer to write a persuasive letter to the job candidate, based on your experiences at Patagonia. In your letter, describe how you've benefited from participating in a two-month internship at an envi-

ronmental nonprofit organization, fully paid for by Patagonia, and how much you enjoy taking off two days with pay each year to test expensive Patagonia products that you could not otherwise afford to buy. With your enthusiasm for Patagonia's environmental programs, your testimonial will present a more convincing case to the job candidate than an employee handbook.

c. You are not the right person to write the letter. As human resources director, Thomas is a more credible source. Suggest that Thomas write a persuasive letter outlining the personal benefits the job candidate will enjoy as a Patagonia employee, addressing his personal environmental concerns and creating desire on his part to become a member of the organization.

d. Advise Thomas to write a letter that emphasizes the company's selling points. Her letter should describe Patagonia's policies of offering two-month paid

internships at nonprofit organizations, paying employees to test new products, and making generous contributions to environmental groups.

4. The marketing department has asked you to review the copy for Patagonia's fall catalog. Which of the following sentences is the most effective for persuading customers to order Patagonia merchandise?

a. Patagonia sweaters are made from 100 percent organic cotton, meaning that the cotton is organically grown without fertilizers or pesticides.

b. By ordering Patagonia products with Synchilla fleece, you're helping to recycle more than eight million plastic soda bottles every year!

c. Editors of *Rod & Reel* insist that our fishing vest is "one of the best fishing accessories to come along in years."

d. Made from durable mesh, this Patagonia fishing vest features pockets that won't sag.[32]

Learning Objectives Checkup

To assess your understanding of the principles in this chapter, read each learning objective and study the accompanying exercises. For fill-in items, write the missing text in the blank provided; for multiple choice items, circle the letter of the correct answer. You can check your responses against the anwer key on page AK-2.

Objective 9.1: Discuss the planning tasks that need extra attention when preparing persuasive messages.

1. The audience for a persuasive message is likely to be
   a. Accepting of the message
   b. Neutral toward the message
   c. Resistant toward the message
   d. Enthusiastic about the message

2. When planning a persuasive message, analyzing your audience's needs
   a. Is a simple, easy process
   b. Involves determining your audience's position in Maslow's hierarchy of needs
   c. Is the same as the audience analysis process for routine messages
   d. Is all of the above

3. Which of the following is *not* a good way to establish credibility with your audience?
   a. Support your argument with plenty of facts.
   b. Name your sources.
   c. Be enthusiastic and sincere.
   d. Present only your side of the argument and avoid any mention of opposing ideas.

4. For a persuasive message to be ethical, it should
   a. Give the audience freedom to choose
   b. Avoid the "you" attitude
   c. Use manipulation as long as it doesn't violate any laws
   d. Do all of the above

Objective 9.2: Describe the AIDA plan for persuasive messages.

5. The first phase in the AIDA plan is to
   a. Do research
   b. Gain the audience's attention
   c. Analyze the audience
   d. Call for action

6. The body of a message that follows the AIDA plan
   a. Captures the audience's attention
   b. Contains the buffer
   c. Generates interest and instills desire
   d. Calls for action

7. The final phase of the AIDA plan
   a. Provides additional details to help generate interest
   b. Reduces resistance by increasing the audience's desire
   c. Calls for action
   d. Captures the audience's attention

8. The AIDA plan is tailor-made for
   a. The indirect approach
   b. The direct approach
   c. Bad-news messages
   d. Routine messages

Objective 9.3: Distinguish between emotional and logical appeals, and discuss how to balance them.

9. The best approach to using emotional appeals is to
   a. Use them by themselves
   b. Use them in conjunction with logical appeals
   c. Use them only when the audience is particularly hostile
   d. Avoid them in all business messages

10. Which of the following is *not* an example of a logical appeal?
    a. Analogy
    b. Induction

c. Deduction

d. Begging the question

Objective 9.4: Explain the best way to overcome resistance to your persuasive message, and list four common mistakes in writing persuasive messages.

11. The best way to overcome resistance to your message is to

a. Present all sides and involve your audience in problem solutions

b. Use a hard-sell approach

c. Rely on your logical arguing skills

d. Do all of the above

Objective 9.5: Define *selling points* and *reader benefits* and discuss their differences.

12. The particular advantages that the audience will realize from a product are referred to as its

a. Selling points

b. Features

c. Benefits

d. Highlights

13. The fact that a graphics program is "easy to install" would be an example of a

a. Main idea

b. Selling point

c. Benefit

d. Highlight

Objective 9.6: Briefly review the four areas of legal concern in sales letters.

14. Making a false statement in a sales letter is considered to be

a. Par for the course

b. Invasion of privacy

c. Fraud

d. Defamation

Objective 9.7: Discuss three techniques for keeping readers interested in your sales messages.

15. A good way to keep readers interested is to

a. Provide every possible detail about the product benefits

b. Use as many adjectives as possible

c. Provide as much support as possible for your claims

d. Do all of the above

Objective 9.8: Compare sales messages with fundraising messages.

16. Fundraising letters differ from sales letters in that fundraising letters

a. Are not accompanied by other materials, such as brochures or special inserts

b. Are not usually written by professionals with special skills

c. Do not follow the AIDA plan

d. Try to persuade people to spend money or time to help others rather than themselves

Objective 9.9: List eight guidelines that will help you strengthen your fundraising messages.

17. Which of the following is *not* a guideline for effective fundraising messages?

a. Begin with a buffer, to ease the reader into your fundraising pitch.

b. Make the need clear.

c. Make it difficult for readers to turn you down.

d. Make your reply form complete and thorough.

Apply Your Knowledge

1. Why is it important to present both sides of an argument when writing a persuasive message to a potentially hostile audience?

2. How are persuasive messages different from routine messages?

3. When is it appropriate to use the direct organizational approach in persuasive messages?

4. As an employee, how many of your daily tasks require persuasion? List as many as you can think of. Who are your audiences, and how do their needs and characteristics affect the way you develop your persuasive messages at work?

5. **Ethical Choices** Are emotional appeals ethical? Why or why not?

Practice Your Knowledge

DOCUMENTS FOR ANALYSIS

Read the following documents, then (1) analyze the strengths and weaknesses of each sentence and (2) revise each document so that it follows this chapter's guidelines.

DOCUMENT 9.A: WRITING PERSUASIVE REQUESTS FOR ACTION

At Tolson Auto Repair, we have been in business for over 25 years. We stay in business by always taking into account what the customer wants. That's why we are writing. We want to know your opinions to be able to better conduct our business.

Take a moment right now and fill out the enclosed questionnaire. We know everyone is busy, but this is just one way we have of making sure our people do their job correctly. Use the enclosed envelope to return the questionnaire.

And again, we're happy you chose Tolson Auto Repair. We want to take care of all your auto needs.

DOCUMENT 9.B: WRITING PERSUASIVE CLAIMS AND REQUESTS FOR ADJUSTMENT

Dear Gateway:

I'm writing to you because of my disappointment with my new TelePath x2 Faxmodem. The modem works all right, but the volume is set too high and the volume knob doesn't turn it down. It's driving us crazy. The volume knob doesn't seem to be connected to anything but simply spins around. I can't believe you would put out a product like this without testing it first.

I depend on the modem to run my small business and want to know what you are going to do about it. This reminds me of every time I buy electronic equipment from what seems like any company. Something is always wrong. I thought quality was supposed to be important, but I guess not.

Anyway, I need this fixed right away. Please tell me what you want me to do.

DOCUMENT 9.C: WRITING SALES AND FUNDRAISING LETTERS

We know how awful dining hall food can be, and that's why we've developed the "Mealaweek Club." Once a week, we'll deliver food to your dormitory or apartment. Our meals taste great. We have pizza, buffalo wings, hamburgers and curly fries, veggie roll-ups, and more!

When you sign up for just six months, we will ask what day you want your delivery. We'll ask you to fill out your selection of meals. And the rest is up to us. At "Mealaweek," we deliver! And payment is easy. We accept MasterCard and VISA or a personal check. It will save money especially when compared with eating out.

Just fill out the enclosed card and indicate your method of payment. As soon as we approve your credit or check, we'll begin delivery. Tell all your friends about Mealaweek. We're the best idea since sliced bread!

Exercises

For live links to all websites discussed in this chapter, visit this text's website at www.prenhall.com/bovee. Just log on, select Chapter 9, and click on "Student Resources." Locate the page or the URL related to the material in the text. For the "Learning More on the Web" exercises, you'll also find navigational directions. Click on the live link to the site.

9.1 Teamwork With another student, analyze the persuasive memo at Host Marriott (Figure 9.2 on page 273) by answering the following questions:
  a. What techniques are used to capture the reader's attention?
  b. Does the writer use the direct or the indirect organizational approach? Why?
  c. Is the subject line effective? Why or why not?
  d. Does the writer use an emotional or a logical appeal? Why?
  e. What reader benefits are included?
  f. How does the writer establish credibility?
  g. What tools does the writer use to reinforce his position?

9.2 Composing Subject Lines Compose effective subject lines for the following persuasive memos:
  a. A request to your supervisor to purchase a new high-speed laser printer for your office. You've been outsourcing quite a bit of your printing to AlphaGraphics, and you're certain this printer will pay for itself in six months.
  b. A direct mailing to area residents soliciting customers for your new business, "Meals à la Car," a carryout dining service that delivers from most of the local restaurants. All local restaurant menus are on the Internet. Mom and Dad can dine on egg rolls and chow mein while the kids munch on pepperoni pizza.
  c. A special request to the company president to allow managers to carry over their unused vacation days to the following year. Apparently, many managers canceled their fourth-quarter vacation plans to work on the installation of a new company computer system. Under their current contract, vacation days not used by December 31 aren't accruable.

9.3 Ethical Choices Your boss has asked you to draft a memo requesting that everyone in your department donate money to the company's favorite charity, an organization that operates a special summer camp for physically challenged children. You wind up writing a three-page memo packed with facts and heartwarming anecdotes about the camp and the children's experiences. When you must work that hard to persuade your audience to take an action such as donating money to a charity, aren't you being manipulative and unethical? Explain.

9.4 Focusing on Benefits Determine whether the following sentences focus on features or benefits; rewrite the sentences as necessary to focus them on benefits.
  a. All-Cook skillets are coated with a durable, patented nonstick surface.
  b. You can call anyone and talk as long as you like on Saturdays and Sundays with this new wireless telephone service.
  c. We need to raise $25 to provide each needy child with a backpack filled with school supplies.

9.5 Internet Visit the Federal Trade Commission website and read the "Catch the Bandit in Your Mailbox" consumer warning at www.ftc.gov/bcp/conline/pubs/tmarkg/bandit.htm. Select one or two sales or fundraising letters you've recently received and see whether they contain any of the suspicious content mentioned in the FTC warning. What does the FTC suggest you do with any materials that don't sound legitimate?

Expand Your Knowledge

LEARNING MORE ON THE WEB

Influence an Official and Promote Your Cause thomas.loc.gov
At the Thomas site compiled by the Library of Congress, you'll discover voluminous information about federal legislation, congressional members, and committee reports. You can also access committee homepages and numerous links to government agencies, current issues, and historical documents. You can review all kinds of regulatory information, including laws and relevant issues that might affect you in the business world. Maybe you'll want to convince a government official to support a business-related issue that affects you.

ACTIVITIES

Persuasion is necessary to convince someone to take action on your behalf. Explore the data at the Thomas site, and find an issue you can use to practice your skills at writing a persuasive message.
1. What key ideas would you include in an e-mail message to persuade your congressional representative to support an issue important to you?

2. In a letter to a senator or member of Congress, what information would you include to convince the reader to vote for an issue supporting small business?
3. When sending a message to someone who daily receives hundreds of written appeals, what attention-getting techniques can you use? How can you get support for a cause that concerns you as a businessperson?

EXPLORING THE WEB ON YOUR OWN

Review these chapter-related websites on your own to learn more about writing persuasive messages.
1. Visit the Federal Trade Commission website, www.ftc.gov, to find out how consumers can cut down on the number of unsolicited mailings, calls, and e-mails they receive.
2. Check out the how-to and reference articles at the Sales Marketing Network (SMN), www.info-now.com/SMN/home.asp, and learn what the FTC requirements are when using the word *free* in sales and marketing messages.
3. To learn some aggressive sales strategies that don't go overboard, visit Guerrilla Marketing at www.gmarketing.com.

Learn Interactively

INTERACTIVE STUDY GUIDE

Go to the Companion Website at www.prenhall.com/bovee. For Chapter 9, take advantage of the interactive "Study Guide" to test your knowledge of the chapter. Get instant feedback on whether you need additional studying. Also, visit this site's "Study Hall" where you'll find an abundance of valuable resources that will help you succeed in this course.

PEAK PERFORMANCE GRAMMAR AND MECHANICS

To improve your skill with semicolons and colons, visit this text's website at www.prenhall.com/onekey. Click "Peak Performance Grammar and Mechanics," then click "Punctuation I." Take the Pretest to determine whether you

have any weak areas. Review those areas in the Refresher Course, and take the Follow-Up Test to check your grasp of semicolons and colons. For advanced practice, take the Advanced Test. Finally, for additional reinforcement, go to the "Improve Your Grammar, Mechanics, and Usage" section that follows, and complete those exercises.

Improve Your Grammar, Mechanics, and Usage

The following exercises help you improve your knowledge of and power over English grammar, mechanics, and usage. Turn to the "Handbook of Grammar, Mechanics, and Usage" at the end of this textbook and review all of Sections 2.4 (Semicolons) and 2.5 (Colons). Then look at the following 10 items. Circle the letter of the preferred choice in the following groups of sentences. (Answers to these exercises appear on page AK-3.)

1. a. This letter looks good; that one doesn't.
   b. This letter looks good: that one doesn't.
2. a. I want to make one thing clear: none of you will be promoted without teamwork.
   b. I want to make one thing clear; none of you will be promoted without teamwork.
   c. I want to make one thing clear: none of you will be promoted; without teamwork.

3. a. The Zurich airport has been snowed in, therefore I can't attend the meeting.
   b. The Zurich airport has been snowed in, therefore, I can't attend the meeting.
   c. The Zurich airport has been snowed in; therefore, I can't attend the meeting.
4. a. His motivation was obvious: to get Meg fired.
   b. His motivation was obvious; to get Meg fired.
5. a. Only two firms have responded to our survey; J. J. Perkins and Tucker & Tucker.
   b. Only two firms have responded to our survey: J. J. Perkins and Tucker & Tucker.
6. a. Send a copy to: Nan Kent, CEO, Bob Bache, President, and Dan Brown, CFO.
   b. Send a copy to Nan Kent, CEO; Bob Bache, President; and Dan Brown, CFO.
   c. Send a copy to Nan Kent CEO; Bob Bache President; and Dan Brown CFO.
7. a. You shipped three items on June 7; however, we received only one of them.
   b. You shipped three items on June 7, however; we received only one of them.
   c. You shipped three items on June 7; however we received only one of them.
8. a. Workers wanted an immediate wage increase: they hadn't had a raise in ten years.
   b. Workers wanted an immediate wage increase; because they hadn't had a raise in ten years.
   c. Workers wanted an immediate wage increase; they hadn't had a raise in ten years.
9. a. His writing skills are excellent however; he needs to polish his management style.
   b. His writing skills are excellent; however, he needs to polish his management style.
   c. His writing skills are excellent: however he needs to polish his management style.
10. a. We want to address three issues; efficiency; profitability; and market penetration.
    b. We want to address three issues; efficiency, profitability, and market penetration.
    c. We want to address three issues: efficiency, profitability, and market penetration.

Cases

Applying the Three-Step Writing Process to Cases
Apply each step to the following cases as assigned by your instructor

Planning

Analyze the Situation
What's your general purpose? What's your specific purpose? What do you want readers to do? Who are your readers? (Who is the primary audience? What do readers have in common? What is their general background? How will they react?)

Gather Information
What information do readers need?

Adapt to the Audience
How will you establish credibility?

1

Writing

Organize the Information
What's your main idea? Will you use the direct or indirect approach? Why?

Compose the Message
Will your tone be informal or more formal? Draft the message as discussed in the "Your task" section of the case.

2

Completing

Revise the Message
Use the Checklist for Revising Business Messages on page 174 to edit and revise your message for clarity.

Produce the Message
What's the best way to distribute your message? By fax? By e-mail? By sealed envelope?

Proofread the Message
Proofread your message for errors in layout, spelling, and mechanics.

3

PERSUASIVE REQUESTS FOR ACTION

1. No choking matter: Persuasive letter from the Consumer Product Safety Commission about fast-food giveaways In 1999 two babies suffocated on plastic Pokémon balls that their parents had gotten from Burger King. The fast-food industry took notice, and some restaurants implemented safety tests on

the billions of free toys being distributed with kids' meals. But your boss isn't convinced that they're doing enough—Ann W. Brown, chairman of the Consumer Product Safety Commission, wants better quality control over fast-food give-aways, most of which are manufactured in China for about 30 to 50 cents apiece.

"Just because a toy is inexpensive and is given away doesn't mean it shouldn't be as safe as the safest toys," says Brown. She's afraid that toys designed for older children are being given to toddlers. She also believes that manufacturing defects are a problem, and the only way to catch those is to test large numbers of toys as they come off the assembly line. She thinks restaurants should be responsible for such tests.

Offering giveaways for young children is a major promotional method for fast-food restaurants because kids often influence a family's dining decision—not necessarily for the food, but for the toys. A popular giveaway can increase a restaurant's sales by about 4 percent; a big hit can boost sales by 15 percent.

As director of the safety commission's Office of Compliance, you applaud recent safety efforts by Burger King and McDonald's. Burger King has hired independent testers; strengthened safety standards; and conducted tests before, during, and after manufacturing. McDonald's has also developed a testing doll, "McBaby," with artificial lungs to check suffocation risks. (They've loaned McBaby to your department so that other restaurants can copy the design.)

Of course, no one wants children hurt. Moreover, both companies recognize that it's to their advantage to promote child safety. In addition to legal liabilities and damage to their reputations if children are injured from playing with their giveaway toys, restaurants can lose millions in promotional dollars. Restaurants may spend as much as $25 million advertising a tie-in with a popular film. They may also pay licensing fees of $250,000 to $1 million to movie studios for the right to produce a tie-in toy. The cost of recalling a toy is staggering.

The safety problem is growing. In one recent year, four fast-food companies voluntarily recalled five different toys. After receiving reports that "Hourglass Space Sprout" and "Look for Me Bumblebee" toys could release small beads on which toddlers might choke, Burger King recalled 2.6 million toys, urging parents to bring them back for replacement toys. Prior to that, Burger King recalled 400,000 "Rattling, Paddling Riverboat" toys after it received reports of metal pins coming loose from the paddle wheel. McDonald's recalled 234,000 "Scooter Bugs" after three children choked on the toys. Fortunately, none of the three was seriously injured.

Burger King gives away nearly 100 million toys annually. McDonald's distributes 1.5 billion toys worldwide. These companies are the most vigilant members in the huge fast-food industry, which accounts for one-third of all toys distributed in the United States.

Your task: Develop a letter to be sent to fast-food vendors in the United States, urging them to follow the lead of McDonald's and Burger King in pretesting giveaway toys. Use facts, anecdotes, and benefits to bolster your position.[33]

2. Customer crunch: Memo from Ed's food servers requesting relief To supplement your sparse financial resources as a business student at San Diego State University, you work as a food server at Ed's, a health-conscious eatery on famous Old Highway 101 in Cardiff, California. The view of the ocean from upstairs is amazing, and during big storms you can watch the waves breaking across the sea-level highway.

Last winter, when storms lashed the coastline relentlessly, nearly every high tide flooded and closed the highway. Before it could be re-opened, bulldozers had to clear away the wave-deposited cobbles, pushing them back along the shore into big mounds that were supposed to stave off the next stormy onslaught.

Now it's summer, and the state beach parking lots that the storms had washed away have all been restored. However, hardly any beach is left—just a narrow strip of mostly rocks with very little sand. Gone are the huge beach crowds that used to cross the highway in the late afternoons for Ed's $4 smoothies and gourmet organic dinners. Ed's owners are worried. As far as you can tell, the locals and some tourists still turn up in healthy numbers for the sunset dinner specials and to watch dolphins playing in the surf. Nevertheless, Ed's has instituted a new policy of short staffing and forced overtime, cutting back on the numbers of servers and kitchen staff in an effort to save money on overhead.

Unfortunately, customers must now wait longer for their food and even for a table (as much as 30 to 60 minutes during rush periods), so many of them leave in anger as orders back up in the kitchen. You're running twice as hard but getting smaller and smaller tips. No matter how nice you are, it's hard to smooth their ruffled feathers. You've even lost some faithful regulars who'd been coming to the restaurant for years, bringing all their out-of-town visitors, and leaving you healthy tips. This new policy can't possibly be good for Ed's in the long term. And it's certainly not good for you and your co-workers in the short term!

Your task: Since you're the business major, your fellow servers have nominated you to write a persuasive memo to Ed's owner, Mary Fenwick, explaining why the low-overhead policy should be abandoned. Make up any circumstantial details you need. Before you begin, however, jot down the main idea of your message. Then list the major points and supporting evidence you'll include to persuade Fenwick.[34]

3. Identity theft: Persuasive e-mail to eliminate social security numbers from Crossland Data ID cards As your employer insists, you've always carried your Crossland Data ID card in your wallet. You need the card to get into security doors at work and for other identification purposes outside the office. The problem is that the card prominently features your Social Security number. So when your wallet was stolen recently, you feared that your identity might be stolen too.

According to the Federal Trade Commission, identity theft is the fastest-rising crime in the United States, with as many as 1.1 million victims already. This new type of crime involves using a person's unique, identifying information to tap into bank and credit accounts to steal money. With a few key pieces of information, thieves can set up new accounts, apply for credit, make large purchases, even apply for a new driver's license in your name.

Meanwhile, you might not discover the theft until a suspicious merchant calls your home. Or you might find huge debts on your credit record. Even after the crooks are arrested, some victims have spent hundreds of dollars and hours of phone calls trying to clean up their credit records. To avoid this financial nightmare, law enforcement experts now warn against carrying Social Security numbers in your wallet.

Your task: Write a persuasive e-mail message to Crossland Data's human resources department, requesting that it eliminate Social Security numbers from employee ID cards.[35]

4. Not too late for others: Persuasive letter to the U.S. Department of Agriculture requesting a recall of Hillshire Farm products As administrative assistant to Veronica Sutfin, marketing manager at TriTech, Inc., you often purchase food for her lunch meetings. You've never had a problem before.

On the afternoon of January 22, you bought several lunchmeats from Bob and Jill's Market in Baltimore and refrigerated them. Yesterday, January 23, eight people attended Sutfin's lunch meeting, ate the sandwich meats you bought, and by 8:00 P.M. were all at Baltimore City Hospital's emergency room, undergoing treatment for food poisoning.

According to Dr. Samuel Jenkins, the culprit was salmonellosis, which can be fatal. He suggested that the Hillshire Farms cooked, sliced beef or ham might have been contaminated at the factory and should be investigated and recalled to protect others. He gave Sutfin the address of the agency to contact.

Your task: Sutfin asks you to write the letter urging a recall of these lunchmeats. Address the letter to Elijah Walker, Deputy Administrator, Office of Public Health and Science, Food Safety and Inspection Service, U.S. Department of Agriculture, Washington, D.C. 20250. Send a copy to Hillshire Farms.[36]

5. Point, click, recruit: Persuasive memo about e-cruiting at Boulder Construction More than 60 percent of computer-related companies are recruiting over the Internet, but only 2 percent of the companies in the building industry have tried it. You think Boulder Construction should join those "e-cruiting" pioneers. After all, you've got projects all over the state that need skilled workers, both in the field and behind the desk. As vice president, you're responsible for keeping costs down, and you're convinced that e-cruiting could save a bundle, while snatching talent from your competitors.

Display ads in the Sunday newspapers have always been the standby for your human resources director, Sheila Young. They typically cost $1,000 or more per job. On the other hand, major Internet career sites such as monster.com, hotjobs.com, or careermosaic.com may charge only $100 to $300 a month to list openings. Plus, since newspapers charge by the word, the amount of information you can put in an ad is limited, but online space is not. You can fully describe Boulder Construction's appeal to talented workers: its status as a major builder in the state of Colorado; its longevity; and its reputation for good benefits, safe working conditions, and upward mobility. *Air Conditioning, Heating, and Refrigeration News* says that in one survey, the average cost per hire via the web was $183, compared to $1,383 for traditional hiring.

Creating a website with a careers page is another good recruiting tactic, but you want to wait until you've tried the job boards. You've read that some 30,000 to 100,000 Internet sites are devoted to recruiting, with 148.8 million Internet users in the United States. Last year, 74 percent of those over the age of 18 used the Internet to look for a job. That means your pool of potential candidates could be huge, certainly much larger than the local newspaper can attract. And there are no geographical limitations online. If they're willing to relocate, you might land good employees you'd never have met otherwise.

Some companies claim they've started receiving résumés within moments of posting an opening. Hiring decisions that once took six weeks are now being made within the hour, these companies report. No more waiting for snail mail. Using available software, you can search through online résumés using keywords to prescreen candidates for certain qualifications or experience.

Of course, you won't totally abandon traditional hiring. E-cruiting can't do everything. For instance, you won't be able to see online applicants in person. Fulfilling diversity goals could be more difficult, which might lead to legal issues. And you could miss "passive" candidates, the type who are happily employed, highly qualified, and fought over by recruiters because they're often willing to take a good offer. But they rarely post résumés online. On the other hand, passive candidates might respond to an online job posting.

Overall, you think e-cruiting offers advantages that will make the effort worthwhile. Bank of Montreal claims to be saving more than $1 million by e-cruiting this year; other large companies say they've even hired executives using Internet tools.

Your task: Write a persuasive memo to Sheila Young, director of human resources, asking her to try e-cruiting for Boulder's next job openings. You don't want this message to be an order, so use the AIDA plan to convince her that the advantages outweigh the drawbacks.[37]

6. Life's little hassles: E-mail request for satisfaction It's hard to go through life without becoming annoyed at the way some things work. You have undoubtedly been dissatisfied with a product you've bought, a service you've received, or an action of some elected official or government agency.

Your task: Write a three- to five-paragraph persuasive e-mail message that expresses your dissatisfaction in a particular case and specifies the action you want the reader to take.

PERSUASIVE CLAIMS AND REQUESTS FOR ADJUSTMENTS

7. Endless trouble: Claim letter to Abe's Pool Installations As chief administrator, you worked hard to convince the board of directors of Westlake Therapy and Rehabilitation Center that a small, 8-by–15-foot Endless Pool would be a wonderful addition to the facility. Because the pool produces an adjustable current flow, a swimmer can swim "endlessly" against it, never reaching the pool's edge. With this new invention by a Philadelphia manufacturer, your patients could experience a complete range of water therapy in a year-round, indoor pool small enough to fit in a standard living room!

The board agreed, choosing the optional six-foot depth, which would allow for additional therapeutic uses but would require (1) a special platform and (2) installation in a room with a high ceiling. The old gymnasium would become your new Water Therapy Pavilion. Total cost with custom features: $20,080, plus $8,000 for installation.

According to the manufacturer, "The Endless Pool has been designed as a kit for bolt-together assembly. It can be assembled by two reasonably handy people with no prior installation experience following detailed procedural videos." You can do it yourself, they proclaim, or hire a local contractor.

You've hired Abe's Pool Installation, which will build the special access platform and install the pool. You passed along the instructional videos, along with the manufacturer's hotline numbers. The manufacturer offers a preinstallation engineering consultation for your customized pool, without additional charge, as you told Abe. And it will also help determine whether the planned site can handle the pool's 10-ton filled weight. Abe nodded and told you not to worry.

Finally, Abe's crew completed the platform and amid much excitement from your staff, assembled the galvanized steel pool. At the ribbon-cutting dedication ceremony, you personally flipped the switch.

Immediately the hydraulic motor began moving water through a grill at the front, which smoothes and straightens the current. Everyone's excitement grew as the first wave of water washed down the center of the pool. But instead of entering the turning vane arrays (which were supposed to recirculate the water through hidden channels back to the

front of the pool), the water kept going, splashing out the back of the pool, onto the platform, and over the gathered onlookers . . . at 5,000 gallons a minute. Panic and shouts erupted as you fumbled quickly to turn the thing off.

Final damages included a collapsed platform, a ruined floor, an incorrectly installed pool, and numerous dry-cleaning bills from onlookers. Fortunately, no one was hurt. Estimated cost with floor repair: $10,000. Abe is not returning your phone calls. But local reporters are coming to film the damage tomorrow, and it's your job to conduct their tour.

Your task: Write a claim letter to Abe Hanson, owner, Abe's Pool Installation, 2525 Rocket Lane, Manchester, MD 21088.[38]

8. Secondhand smoke: Letter requesting rent refund from Kuykendahl Joint, Inc. Last January, in Harris County, Texas, your branch of Contract Management Services, Inc. (CMSI) signed a lease with Kuykendahl Joint, Inc., for new office space at 3638 University Blvd., Suite 302, Houston, TX 77005–3396. No one anticipated the nightmare that would follow. You have been assistant manager since before the move. But after relocating, you've threatened to quit many times—and so has your manager, Kathleen Thomas.

The problem is secondhand smoke invading your offices from other tenants. The Environmental Protection Agency calls this ETS (environmental tobacco smoke) and classifies it as a Group A (known human) carcinogen. There is no safe level of exposure to Group A toxins. The Surgeon General says the 4,600 chemicals in ETS (including cyanide, arsenic, formaldehyde, carbon monoxide, and ammonia) are "a cause of disease, including lung cancer, in healthy nonsmokers."

The smoke wafts in the front door of your office and seeps through openings in hollow walls shared with tenants on either side of CMSI. You and others have suffered bronchitis, migraines, and respiratory infections since the move. One of your most valuable employees quit last week—a star performer responsible for landing many new contracts. "I can't risk this," she said. "I've had asthma since I was little, and it's getting worse."

Another employee is worried about his heart; he's in the high-risk category and there's evidence ETS can trigger heart attacks. Pneumonia, allergies, ear infections, and other forms of cancer (including breast, cervical, endocrine, etc.)—are problems "causally associated" with ETS, according to the EPA. In fact, secondhand smoke is more dangerous than what smokers inhale. That's because the heat of the draw burns off some of the toxins, which are also filtered by the cigarette or cigar.

Last month CMSI spent $3,000 hiring contractors to weather-strip around vents, electrical outlets, and other built-in fixtures—even to spray polyurethane foam around the pipes that are under sinks and behind toilets. But you're still choking and gagging on smelly carcinogens. By the end of the day, you've got red eyes, a runny nose, often a headache—and you smell like a poker game.

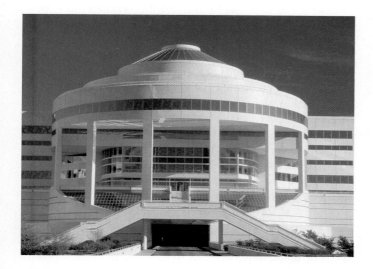

Thomas says it's no use talking to the offending smokers. She's collected a list (from Americans for Nonsmokers' Rights) that cites legal precedents around the country, in which courts have held landlords responsible both for eliminating ETS and for compensating tenants.

Your task: Thomas has asked you to write a persuasive claim letter for her signature to Robert Bechtold, Manager, Kukyendahl Joint, Inc. (88 North Park Rd., Houston, TX 77005). Insist that the landlord (1) improve the air quality immediately, (2) refund lease payments totaling $9,000 from January 1, and (3) reimburse CMSI for the improvements made in an attempt to solve the problem. "If this doesn't work, we're moving," she says grimly. "And then we'll sue."[39]

9. Cow-spotty text: Letter to Gateway requesting warranty extension Words Unlimited is a "microbusiness"—just two owners and you, the all-round office assistant. From a small office with two computers, you three provide editorial services to businesses.

When your employers, Tom and Miranda Goodman, decided to add a third computer, they ordered a Professional S1300 business system from Gateway, with a "flat screen" monitor that was supposed to offer superior visual display. They didn't realize that the monitor, recommended by salesman Chris Swanson, uses liquid crystal display (LCD) technology. That's great for graphics, but text is produced as disconnnected dots that are hard on the eyes. What they really need is an old-fashioned CRT monitor that displays text as a solid line.

They returned to the store and found one with a fast refresh rate, costing only $20 more, under Gateway's 30-day exchange program. But when they got to the register, they discovered that their 30-day exchange period had run out five days before. Gateway wouldn't take back the LCD monitor, and the Goodmans would have to pay full price for the CRT.

"How did the time run out?" you ask when they return.

"Remember how Swanson forgot to include a modem in our original order and we had to wait for it to be delivered from the factory?" Tom says. "Then UPS delivered the package to the wrong address. When we finally retrieved it, the installation technician was out sick and we had to wait for his return."

Miranda adds, "And then it took Tom forever to set up the new system, between phone calls and other jobs. By the time we saw the flat screen in action, our 30 days had already elapsed."

"At least Swanson apologized," Tom adds. "He thinks his manager will extend our 30-day exchange period if we write her a letter."

Your task: Since your bosses are busy, they've asked you to draft the persuasive letter to Ann Cameron, Manager, Gateway Country Store, 2900 Pine Lake Rd., Lincoln, NE 68516. So far Gateway employees have been courteous, quick, and eager to help, despite the mix-ups. You all have high hopes.[40]

10. Broadband blues: Persuasive claim letter to ZippieNet about cable modem failures When your cable company offered ZippieNet—high-speed, cable modem Internet access—you signed up. You figured $49.95 a month was a bargain for Internet speed.

Your career as a freelance journalist requires you to compete with staff writers at the various publications that buy your work. You need to deliver stories fast to meet short deadlines. Having access to Internet sources "five times faster" than your old dial-up modem should have made your work easier.

At first you were pleased. When the system worked, it worked beautifully. Then the problems began. Three days a week for four weeks, the system failed and you were stuck offline. When you called ZippieNet's support lines, you were put on hold for 30 minutes, and when someone finally answered, he seemed poorly trained and overworked. All you got were vague promises that the system was being repaired.

That was three months ago. Since then, you've experienced total shutdowns at least twice a month. During periods of high usage, the "zippy" speeds that ZippieNet promised slow down to a trickle—not much better than your old dial-up connection.

And now the unthinkable has happened. Last week you were working on an article that you had contracted to sell to *Arete* magazine for $1,000, and the system went down for more than 24 hours. You couldn't access critical information, your story was late, and you lost the sale. Moreover, the editor who'd hired you was so angry, he said he'll never work with you again.

Your task: Write a letter to ZippieNet, 1203 West Barber Ave., Nashville, TN 37214, demanding a refund for your four months of service, plus $1,000 for lost income on the lost article sale (include a copy of your contract), and $3,000 toward the loss of future sales to the same publication. If ZippieNet pays the $1,000, you'll be satisfied, but don't tell them that. Instead, suggest that you will remain a customer if they can deliver improved service within three weeks. When it works, you love broadband.[41]

SALES AND FUNDRAISING MESSAGES

11. Quotesmith.com: E-mail extolling a better way to buy insurance The great thing about Quotesmith.com is that no one is obligated to buy a thing. Consumers can log on to your website and ask for dozens of free insurance quotes, then go off and buy elsewhere. They can look at instant price-comparison quotes (from more than 300 insurers) for term life, dental, individual and family medical insurance, small group medical insurance, workers' compensation, short-term medical insurance, Medicare supplement insurance, "no-exam" whole life insurance, fixed annuity insurance, and (in a click-through arrangement with Progressive) private passenger automobile insurance. All rates are up-to-the-day accurate, and Quotesmith is the largest single source for comprehensive insurance price comparisons in the United States.

Once consumers see your price-comparison charts, many choose to fill out an easy insurance application request right on your site. Why deal with an insurance salesperson when you can see the price differences for yourself—especially over such a broad range of companies? Quotesmith backs up this application with toll-free customer-service lines operated by salaried representatives. They're not working on commission, but they know about insurance. And Quotesmith has based its new online service on a long history of serving the insurance industry.

The product pretty much sells itself, and that's what you love about your marketing job with Quotesmith. Consumers and computers do most of the work—and the results are at lightning speed, especially compared with what the insurance business was like just a few years ago. During peak periods, the site has been processing one quote request every four seconds, which leads, ultimately, to increased policy sales without an agent or intermediary.

Quotesmith advertises both in print and on TV, saying that it provides "the lowest term life rates in America or we'll overnight you $500." Your company also guarantees the accuracy of quotes against a $500 reward. Final rates depend on variables such as age, sex, state availability, hazardous activities, personal and family health history, driving records, and so on.

You're proud of the fact that Quotesmith has received positive press from *Nation's Business, Kiplinger's Personal Finance, Good Housekeeping,* the *Los Angeles Times, Money, U.S. News & World Report,* and *Forbes* ("Quotesmith.com provides rock-bottom quotes")—your favorite. For every term-life quote, you even provide consumers with a look at how each insurer's ability to pay claims is rated by A. M. Best, Duff & Phelps, Moody's, Standard & Poor's, and Weiss Ratings, Inc.

And all of this is free. Too bad more people don't know about your services.

Your task: It's your job to lure more insurance customers to Quotesmith. You've decided to use direct e-mail marketing (using a list of consumers who have inquired about rates in the past but never committed to purchase anything). Write an e-mail sales message extolling the benefits of Quotesmith's services.

Be sure your message is suited to an e-mail format, with an appropriate subject heading.[42]

12. A clean deal: Sales letter from ScrubaDub about its Car Care Club When Bob and Dan Paisner opened 11 ScrubaDub car washes in Massachusetts and Rhode Island, they applied high-tech solutions to the traditional business, and ScrubaDub emerged as the most innovative car wash in the industry. At ScrubaDub, computers track everything from customers' names to the date and type of their last wash. They even "sense" what kind of wheels a car has. These are just a few of the reasons your job in ScrubaDub's marketing department is so easy.

When customers arrive, a "touchless system" sizes up their cars—literally—then prescribes exactly how much of the chain's secret-formula "Superglo" detergent to dispense and how much water pressure to use. This process eliminates dull soap residues and handling marks or nicks from abrasive equipment. Special sensors automatically prescribe scrubbing for white walls, pressure spray for wire wheels, or buffing for chrome. Using softened, heated well water eliminates spots, and recycling that water for scrubbing wheels and undercarriages helps the environment. A soft cloth adds a final gloss.

A human "Satisfaction Supervisor" is present to handle special requests, such as towel drying or gas stain removal. Your Bumper to Bumper Guarantee lets dissatisfied customers go through the wash until they're happy, or they get a refund. With a driver's license for proof, people get a free wash on their birthdays.

Like thousands of others, you're surprised to find this *automated* car wash offering such *personalized* service. The Paisners say they're New England drivers' "best defense against a dirty world," offering relief from salt, snow, rain, mud, sleet, dust, and pigeons. Clean cars last longer and look newer. And now they have a new brainstorm for you to promote: the ScrubaDub Car Care Club.

By signing up for a $5.95 "lifetime membership" (good for as long as you own the car), drivers can combat whatever Mother Nature or nearby construction sites dish out. Whether members join in person at your locations or online at www.scrubadub.com/club.htm, members receive by mail a bar-coded sticker to place in the driver's-side window. When they drive in for a wash, the bar code is scanned and linked to a central database via the Internet. Customer information flashes on a screen, so a well-trained attendant can greet them by name and glance over their washing history, perhaps suggesting it's time for a wax.

This system improves customer relations while increasing sales, and club members get exclusive deals designed for northeastern drivers. The 48-Hour Express Guarantee lets members get the same exterior wash free within 48 hours if their car gets dirty—great for inclement weather. The 4-Day Clean Car Guarantee extends that to four days for purchasers of the premium Super Wash, Luxury Wash, Special Wash, or Works Wash. The Frequent Wash Bonus Program awards one free exterior Works Wash ("our best wash for our best customers") after every 10 washes purchased. Members don't have to collect stickers or hole punches—the computer tracks it. They also get an instant $5 rebate on any foam car wax. ScrubaDub offers three types: Turtle Wax (lasts 10 days), Simonize (20 days), or Blue Coral (30 days). And there will be additional members-only specials from time to time.

Your task: Write a sales letter promoting the Car Care Club. Since most customers are busy people, use techniques for quick-scan communications while following the AIDA plan.[43]

FUNDRAISING MESSAGES

13. Always urgent: Memo pleading case for hosting a Red Cross blood drive Not many people realize that donated blood lasts for only 72 hours. Some components are processed to last longer, but the mainstay of emergency blood supplies must be replenished in an ongoing effort. No one is more skilled, dedicated, or efficient about handling blood than the American Red Cross, which is responsible for half the nation's supply of blood and blood products. Its Jerome H. Holland Laboratory has helped pioneer the blood-collecting and blood-processing methods that make blood banks possible.

This morning before heading off to your job as food service manager at the Pechanga Casino Entertainment Center in Temecula, California, you were concerned to see on TV news that the Red Cross had put out a call for blood—national supplies have fallen dangerously low. When people are moved by a highly publicized disaster, they're emotionally eager to help out by donating blood. But in calm times, only 5 percent of eligible donors think of giving blood. You're one of those few. And today, you're going to do more than just roll up your own sleeve.

Donated blood helps victims of accidents and diseases such as cancer or heart disease, as well as surgery patients. You remember reading about Melissa, who was diagnosed with multiple congenital heart defects and underwent her first open-heart surgery at one week old. Now, at the age of five, she's used well over 50 units of donated blood, and she wouldn't be alive without them. In a thank-you letter, her mother lauded the many strangers who had "given a piece of themselves" to save her precious daughter—and countless others. A donor's pint of blood can benefit up to four people.

You know the local Red Cross chapter takes its Blood Mobile to corporations, restaurants—even beauty salons—willing to host public blood drives. Wouldn't it be wonderful if the board of directors agreed to support a blood drive at the casino? The slot machines and gaming tables are usually full, hundreds of employees are on hand, and people who've never visited might come down to donate blood. The positive publicity certainly couldn't hurt Pechanga's community image. With materials from the Red Cross, you're confident you can organize Pechanga's hosting effort and handle the promotion. (Last year you headed the casino's successful Toys for Tots drive.)

To give blood, one must be healthy, be at least 17 years old (with no upper age limit), and weigh at least 110 pounds. Donors can give every 56 days. You'll be urging Pechanga donors to eat well, drink water, and be rested before the Blood Mobile arrives.

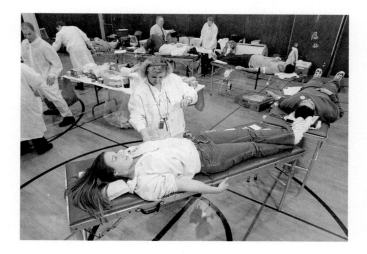

You like the local chapter's mission statement. It says, in part, that the Red Cross is "a humanitarian organization led by volunteers and guided by the Fundamental Principles of the International Red Cross Movement" which will "prevent and alleviate human suffering wherever it may be found." All assistance is given free of charge, made possible by "contributions of people's time, money, and skills."

And in the case of you and your co-workers, a piece of yourselves.

Your task: Write a memorandum persuading the Pechanga board of directors to host a public Red Cross blood drive. Ask the board to donate bottled water, orange juice, and snacks for donors. (You'll organize food service workers to handle the distribution.) To support your request, use a variety of appeals, mentioning both tangible and intangible benefits.[44]

14. Buses for seniors: Fundraising letter from Morris County Senior Center The Morris County Senior Center is one of New Jersey's oldest nonprofit institutions for the elderly. Over the past 50 years, it has relied on financial support from government, businesses, and individuals.

Unfortunately, recent state and federal cutbacks have dug into the organization's budget. In addition, in the last five years two of the county's largest companies, Hardwick Industries and McCarthy Electrical Motors, have moved offshore and shut down local operations. Both businesses were supporters of the center, as were many of the workers who lost their jobs when the companies left.

However, the needs of the center keep growing. For many of the county's roughly 1,000 seniors who live alone, it's the only place where they can meet their peers, use a special library, avoid extreme weather, or get a well-balanced meal. The center is not a nursing home and has no overnight facilities. Most individuals get to the facility on one of the three shuttle-type buses belonging to the center. The buses are also used for various day trips to museums, plays, and similar functions. Occasionally, they are used to help the temporarily disabled get to doctors' offices or pharmacists.

Each bus is more than eight years old. Although still safe, the buses are showing their age. The constant repairs are stop-gap measures at best, and most weeks at least one of the vehicles is inoperable. Monthly repairs are averaging a total of $300 for the three vehicles. In addition, when the vans aren't working, the clients, staff, and budget all suffer. Seniors can't get to the center, trips are canceled, and drivers are sometimes paid for coming to work even though they aren't able to drive.

Conservatively, it would cost about $28,000 to replace each van with a new one: $84,000 total. This cost includes estimates on how much the center could gain from selling the old vans. It's a fair amount of money, but in the opinion of your board of directors, buying new vans would be better than continuously repairing the old ones or risking the purchase of used ones.

Your task: As director of the center, draft a fundraising letter to send to all of the businesses in the county. Stress the good work the center does and the fact that this is a special fundraising effort. Mention that all the money collected will go directly toward the purchase of the vans.

Part IV

Preparing Reports and Oral Presentations

Chapter 10

Planning Business Reports and Proposals

Learning Objectives

1 Distinguish between informational and analytical business reports, and review the six common types

2 Differentiate between defining the problem and developing the purpose statement for an analytical report

3 Summarize the uses of a preliminary outline, and compare it with the final outline

4 Identify seven elements often included in a formal work plan

5 Discuss the differences between secondary and primary information, including where to find and how to gather each type

6 Describe what is involved in preparing an effective survey questionnaire

7 Define information interviews, and list four types of interview questions

8 Name nine criteria for evaluating the credibility of an information source

9 Explain the difference between drawing a conclusion and developing a recommendation

On the Job:

COMMUNICATING AT DELL COMPUTER

STAYING ON TOP OF THE COMPUTER WORLD

Since Michael Dell founded Dell Computer Corporation in 1984, his company has become the largest computer manufacturer in the United States and the fastest-growing computer systems company in the world. In selling computer systems and laptops directly to consumers over the web, the company faces two challenges: (1) attracting new customers to dell.com and (2) satisfying the needs of existing clients. To keep the company growing, Michael Dell and his management team need mountains of information. Dell knows the value of gathering and examining information, but as he points out, "information in its raw form doesn't present itself in neat and tidy packages." Thus, much of the information that he and his management team receive is in the form of reports.

Dell Computer Corporation founder Michael Dell relies on reports to keep up with current industry trends, statistics, and issues. As his company has grown, Michael Dell has learned the importance of preparing and reading reports for such widely diverse applications as establishing inventory controls and analyzing developments in the computer industry.

For reports to be useful, they must be well planned. They must clearly define each problem and present carefully researched data. Some reports at Dell Computer present organized information while leaving analysis and conclusions to the reader. However, most of the company's reports must analyze that information, identify and discuss pertinent issues, and offer well-thought-out recommendations.

Michael Dell uses reports to establish inventory procedures and maintain the right levels of stock. He relies on reports to track and analyze average discount rates and inventory turnover. Plus, with the help of his managers, Michael Dell sets up daily reports for suppliers so that they can provide timely communication about orders and delivery schedules. To limit the number of defective parts, Dell's managers also provide suppliers with regular progress reports on quality evaluations.

Reports play a key role in Dell Computer's competitiveness. Management gathers and analyzes information on the overall market, the trend of online purchases, and the potential for company products. Dell makes sure that his website is much more than an online ordering center for customers. Through dell.com, company managers can track customer satisfaction levels, measure customer responses, monitor complaint resolutions, and prepare performance reports.

Michael Dell uses reports to make decisions about entering new markets and offering new products. For example, before expanding into a new country, he examines his company's market share, country-by-country and product-by-product—evaluating the growth potential of the market under consideration. Such reports on customers and products from around the world allow Dell to forecast potential market penetration and salesforce productivity.

Dell also uses reports to analyze employee needs. He depends on his human resources staff to produce reports that measure turnover and productivity, identify key job openings, define training needs, and map out organizational charts. He even analyzes the key qualities of successful employees so that he can spot similar qualities in prospective job candidates.

Overall, Dell depends on more than 4,000 types of analyses to keep his operation running smoothly and to keep his company at the top of the computer industry. "To say that we have become a data-driven company is almost an understatement," Dell says. "Data is the engine that keeps us on track." And reports are the tools necessary to organize and analyze that data.[1]

www.dell.com

WORKING WITH BUSINESS REPORTS AND PROPOSALS

Business reports help companies make decisions and solve business problems.

Like Michael Dell, most managers rely on reports to provide information and analyses so that they can make decisions and solve problems. As a businessperson, you will be expected to prepare and read all kinds of **reports**, written factual accounts that objectively communicate information about some aspect of the business. Before you actually begin planning a report or proposal, you need to know about how reports are used in the workplace.

A variety of messages qualify as reports. The term covers everything, including fleeting images on a computer screen, preprinted forms, informal letters and memos, and formal three-volume bound manuscripts. In fact, report preparation varies according to the following factors:

Reports may be
- Voluntary or authorized
- Routine or special
- Internal or external
- Short or long
- Informational or analytical

- **Source (who initiates the report).** *Voluntary reports* are prepared on your own initiative, whereas *authorized reports* are prepared at the request of someone else. For a voluntary report, you need to provide more background on the subject and to explain your purpose more carefully than for an authorized report, which responds directly to the reader's request.

- **Frequency (how often the report is needed).** *Routine* (or *periodic*) *reports* are submitted on a recurring basis (daily, weekly, monthly, quarterly, annually), at times requiring little more than filling in a preprinted or computerized form or perhaps formatting information in a standard way. These routine reports need less introductory and transitional material than *special reports*, which are nonrecurring and present the results of specific, onetime studies or investigations.

- **Target audience (where the report is being sent).** Because they are used within an organization, *internal reports* are generally less formal than *external reports*, which are sent outside the organization. Many internal reports are written in memo format, especially those under 10 pages in length. External reports may be in letter format (if no longer than 5 pages) or in manuscript format (if they exceed 5 pages).

- **Length (how much detail the report contains).** *Short reports* (generally 1 to 9 pages) differ from *long reports* (10 pages or more) in scope, research, and timetable. A long report examines a problem in detail and generally requires more extensive research and preparation time. However, a short report may discuss just one part of the problem and may not require formal research.

- **Intent (whether the report is meant to educate or to draw conclusions).** *Informational reports* focus on facts and are intended mainly to explain something or to educate readers. *Analytical reports* are intended to solve problems by showing how the conclusions and recommendations are justified by the data, analysis, and interpretation. The information in analytical reports plays a supporting role; it is a means to an end, not an end in itself.

A single report may encompass all these factors. For instance, a monthly sales report is generally authorized, routine, internal, short, and informational, whereas a market analysis is generally authorized, special, internal, long, and analytical. Whatever factors are involved in a business report, most reports usually fall into one of six general categories (which are listed in Table 10–1). Being familiar with the various types of reports will help you plan your own reports more effectively, so let's take a closer look.

Informational Reports

The purpose of informational reports is to explain.

The goal of an informational report is to present data and facts with no analysis or recommendations. Common types of informational reports include those for moni-

INTENT, TYPE, AND PURPOSE OF BUSINESS REPORTS — Table 10–1

Intent	Purpose	Type
Informational	1. To oversee and manage company operations	Monitor/control reports
	2. To carry out company rules and ways of doing things	Policy/procedure reports
	3. To obey government and legal requirements	Compliance reports
	4. To inform others of what's been done on a project	Progress reports
Analytical	5. To guide decisions on particular issues	Problem-solving reports
	6. To get products, plans, or projects accepted by others	Proposals

toring and controlling operations, implementing policies and procedures, complying with government regulations, and documenting progress.

Reports for Monitoring and Controlling Operations   Managers rely on reports to find out what's happening to the operations under their control. These *monitor/control reports* focus on data, so they require special attention to accuracy, thoroughness, and honesty. They uncover problems to get them out in the open before it is too late, so they avoid covering up the bad news and emphasizing only accomplishments.

> Monitor/control reports help managers find out what's happening in the operations under their control.

Some monitor/control reports, such as strategic plans and annual budgets, establish guidelines for future action. Others, such as monthly sales reports, corporate annual reports, and scouting reports, provide detailed information about operations (see the example in Figure 10–1). Still other monitor/control reports describe what occurred during some personal activity, such as a conference, convention, or trip. A *summary report* is a special kind of short report that gives a concise overview of a situation, publication, or document. Summaries highlight important details but refrain from including background material, examples, or specific details.

Reports for Implementing Policies and Procedures   Managers provide *policy and procedure reports* to be read by anyone who wants a question answered. These reports present their information in a straightforward matter. The rules of an organization make up lasting guidelines (such as the process for standardizing quality-control procedures or directions for how to reserve the conference room for special meetings). Less permanent issues are treated as they arise in nonrecurring reports (such as a position paper on the need for extra security precautions after a rash of burglaries in the area).

> Policy/procedure reports help managers communicate the company's standards.

Reports for Complying with Government Regulations   All *compliance reports* are written in response to regulations of one sort or another, most of them imposed by government agencies. The regulatory agency issues instructions on how to write the necessary reports. The important thing is to be honest, thorough, and accurate. Annual compliance reports include income tax returns and annual shareholder reports. Interim compliance reports include reports from licensed institutions such as nursing homes and child-care facilities.

> Compliance reports explain what a company is doing to conform to government regulations.

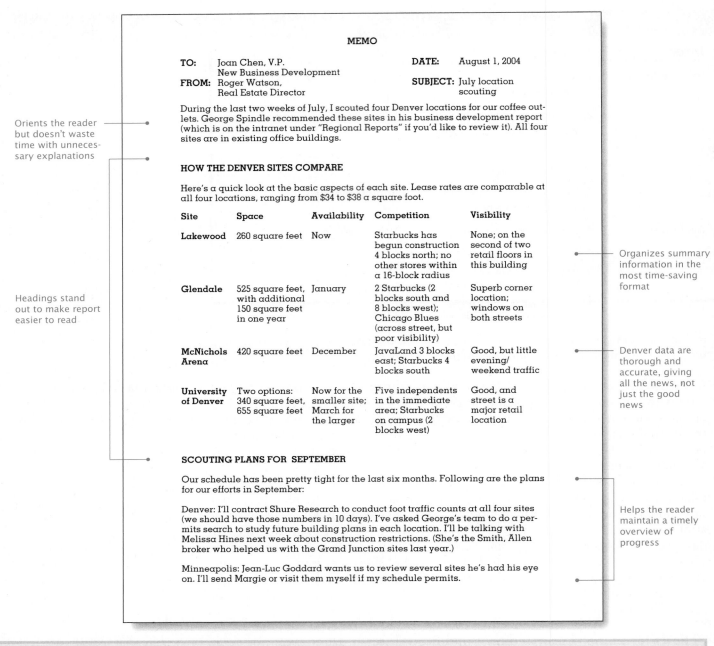

Orients the reader but doesn't waste time with unnecessary explanations

Headings stand out to make report easier to read

MEMO

TO: Joan Chen, V.P.
New Business Development
FROM: Roger Watson,
Real Estate Director

DATE: August 1, 2004

SUBJECT: July location
scouting

During the last two weeks of July, I scouted four Denver locations for our coffee outlets. George Spindle recommended these sites in his business development report (which is on the intranet under "Regional Reports" if you'd like to review it). All four sites are in existing office buildings.

HOW THE DENVER SITES COMPARE

Here's a quick look at the basic aspects of each site. Lease rates are comparable at all four locations, ranging from $34 to $38 a square foot.

Site	Space	Availability	Competition	Visibility
Lakewood	260 square feet	Now	Starbucks has begun construction 4 blocks north; no other stores within a 16-block radius	None; on the second of two retail floors in this building
Glendale	525 square feet, with additional 150 square feet in one year	January	2 Starbucks (2 blocks south and 8 blocks west); Chicago Blues (across street, but poor visibility)	Superb corner location; windows on both streets
McNichols Arena	420 square feet	December	JavaLand 3 blocks east; Starbucks 4 blocks south	Good, but little evening/weekend traffic
University of Denver	Two options: 340 square feet, 655 square feet	Now for the smaller site; March for the larger	Five independents in the immediate area; Starbucks on campus (2 blocks west)	Good, and street is a major retail location

SCOUTING PLANS FOR SEPTEMBER

Our schedule has been pretty tight for the last six months. Following are the plans for our efforts in September:

Denver: I'll contract Shure Research to conduct foot traffic counts at all four sites (we should have those numbers in 10 days). I've asked George's team to do a permits search to study future building plans in each location. I'll be talking with Melissa Hines next week about construction restrictions. (She's the Smith, Allen broker who helped us with the Grand Junction sites last year.)

Minneapolis: Jean-Luc Goddard wants us to review several sites he's had his eye on. I'll send Margie or visit them myself if my schedule permits.

Organizes summary information in the most time-saving format

Denver data are thorough and accurate, giving all the news, not just the good news

Helps the reader maintain a timely overview of progress

FIGURE 10–1
Effective Monitor/Control Report—Informational

Reports documenting progress on a contract provide all the information the client needs.

Reports for Documenting Progress Whether you're writing a progress report for a client or for your boss, you need to anticipate your reader's needs and provide the required information clearly and tactfully. Interim progress reports give an idea of the work that has been accomplished to date (see the example in Figure 10–2). In many cases these interim reports are followed by a final report at the conclusion of the contract or project. Final reports are generally more elaborate than interim reports and serve as a permanent record of what was accomplished. They focus on final results rather than on progress along the way.

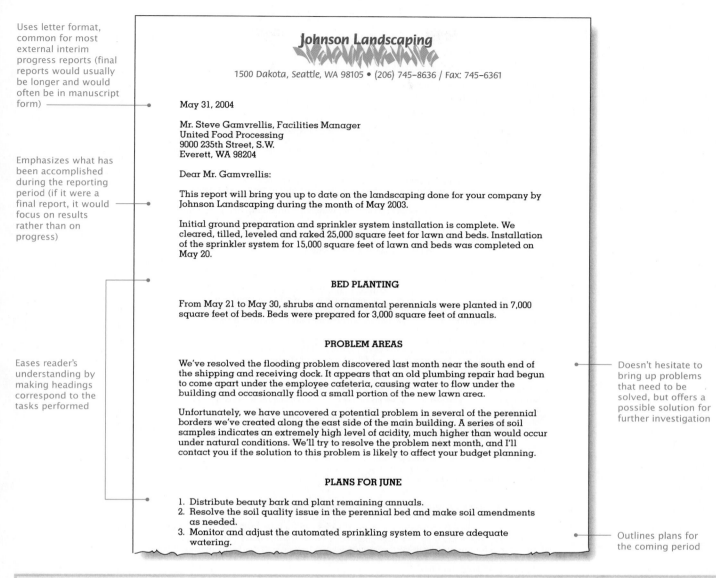

Uses letter format, common for most external interim progress reports (final reports would usually be longer and would often be in manuscript form)

Emphasizes what has been accomplished during the reporting period (if it were a final report, it would focus on results rather than on progress)

Eases reader's understanding by making headings correspond to the tasks performed

Johnson Landscaping

1500 Dakota, Seattle, WA 98105 • (206) 745–8636 / Fax: 745–6361

May 31, 2004

Mr. Steve Gamvrellis, Facilities Manager
United Food Processing
9000 235th Street, S.W.
Everett, WA 98204

Dear Mr. Gamvrellis:

This report will bring you up to date on the landscaping done for your company by Johnson Landscaping during the month of May 2003.

Initial ground preparation and sprinkler system installation is complete. We cleared, tilled, leveled and raked 25,000 square feet for lawn and beds. Installation of the sprinkler system for 15,000 square feet of lawn and beds was completed on May 20.

BED PLANTING

From May 21 to May 30, shrubs and ornamental perennials were planted in 7,000 square feet of beds. Beds were prepared for 3,000 square feet of annuals.

PROBLEM AREAS

We've resolved the flooding problem discovered last month near the south end of the shipping and receiving dock. It appears that an old plumbing repair had begun to come apart under the employee cafeteria, causing water to flow under the building and occasionally flood a small portion of the new lawn area.

Unfortunately, we have uncovered a potential problem in several of the perennial borders we've created along the east side of the main building. A series of soil samples indicates an extremely high level of acidity, much higher than would occur under natural conditions. We'll try to resolve the problem next month, and I'll contact you if the solution to this problem is likely to affect your budget planning.

PLANS FOR JUNE

1. Distribute beauty bark and plant remaining annuals.
2. Resolve the soil quality issue in the perennial bed and make soil amendments as needed.
3. Monitor and adjust the automated sprinkling system to ensure adequate watering.

Doesn't hesitate to bring up problems that need to be solved, but offers a possible solution for further investigation

Outlines plans for the coming period

FIGURE 10–2
Effective Progress Report—Informational (Excerpt)

Analytical Reports

To make informed decisions, managers such as Michael Dell rely on the supporting information, analyses, and recommendations presented in analytical reports. Typically, an analytical report presents a decision (or solution to a problem), often with recommendations for a number of actions. The body of the report presents all the facts (both good and bad) and persuades readers to accept the decision, solution, or recommendations that are detailed throughout the report. To persuade the reader, the writer carefully analyzes the facts and presents a compelling argument. Two of the more common examples of analytical reports are problem-solving reports and proposals.

An analytical report is intended to convince readers that its conclusions and recommendations are valid.

Reports for Solving Problems   When solving problems, managers need both basic information and detailed analysis. *Problem-solving reports* typically require research. They are used when a problem exists and someone must investigate and

Clarifies the purpose and origin of the report in the introduction

Presents logical and clear reasons for recommending that the firm establish a website

Includes not only the recommendation to establish a website but also one to hire a consultant to implement the website and integrate it with existing systems

Clarifies what's needed by wording recommendations simply and to the point

---

MEMO

TO: Board of Directors, Executive Committee members
FROM: Alycia Jenn, Business Development Manager
DATE: July 6, 2004
SUBJECT: World Wide Web retailing site

In response to your request, my staff and I investigated the potential for establishing a retailing site on the World Wide Web. After analyzing the behavior of our customers and major competitors and studying the overall development of electronic retailing, we have three recommendations:

1. Yes, we should establish an online presence within the next six months.
2. We should engage a firm that specializes in online retailing to design and develop the website.
3. We must take care to integrate online retailing with our store-based and mail-order operations.

WE SHOULD SET UP A WEBSITE

First, does a website make financial sense today? Studies suggest that our competitors are not currently generating significant revenue from their websites. Stallini's is the leader so far, but its sales haven't broken the $1 million mark. Moreover, at least half of our competitors' online sales are from current customers who would have purchased the same items in-store or by mail order. The cost of setting up a retailing site is around $120,000, so it isn't possible to justify a site solely on the basis of current financial return.

Second, do we need to establish a presence now in order to remain competitive in the future? The online situation is too fluid and unpredictable to answer this question in a quantitative profit-and-loss way, but a qualitative view of strategy indicates that we should set up a site:

- As younger consumers (more comfortable with online shopping) reach their peak earning years (ages 35–54), they'll be more likely to buy online than today's peak spenders.
- The web is erasing geographical shopping limits, presenting both a threat and an opportunity. Even though our customers can now shop websites anywhere in the world (so that we have thousands of competitors instead of a dozen), we can now target customers anywhere in the world.
- If the growth in online retailing continues, this will eventually be a viable market. Establishing a site now and working out any problems will prepare us for high-volume online business in the years ahead.

WE SHOULD ENGAGE A CONSULTANT TO IMPLEMENT THE SITE

Implementing a competitive retailing site can take anywhere from 1,000 to 1,500 hours of design and programming time. We have some of the expertise needed in-house, but the marketing and information systems departments have only 300 person-hours in the next six months. I recommend that we engage a web design consultant to help us with the design and to do all the programming.

(continued)

FIGURE 10–3
Effective Problem-Solving Report—Analytical

Problem-solving reports provide management with background information and analysis of options.

propose a solution. These troubleshooting reports usually start with some background information on the problem, then analyze alternative solutions, and finally recommend the best approach.

From time to time employees and managers write reports to evaluate the practicality and advisability of pursuing an optional course of action (such as buying equipment, changing a procedure, hiring a consultant). These feasibility reports study proposed options to assess whether any or all of them are sound (see Figure 10–3 for an example). Justification reports are written after a course of action has been taken to justify what was done.

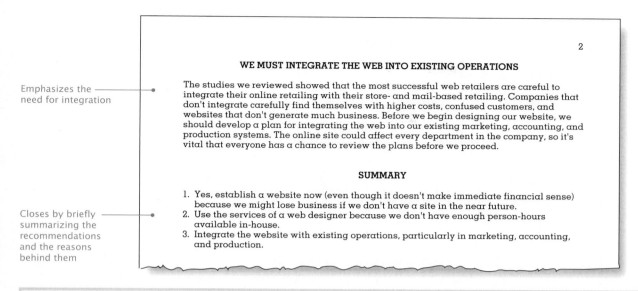

The studies we reviewed showed that the most successful web retailers are careful to integrate their online retailing with their store- and mail-based retailing. Companies that don't integrate carefully find themselves with higher costs, confused customers, and websites that don't generate much business. Before we begin designing our website, we should develop a plan for integrating the web into our existing marketing, accounting, and production systems. The online site could affect every department in the company, so it's vital that everyone has a chance to review the plans before we proceed.

Emphasizes the need for integration

WE MUST INTEGRATE THE WEB INTO EXISTING OPERATIONS

2

SUMMARY

1. Yes, establish a website now (even though it doesn't make immediate financial sense) because we might lose business if we don't have a site in the near future.
2. Use the services of a web designer because we don't have enough person-hours available in-house.
3. Integrate the website with existing operations, particularly in marketing, accounting, and production.

Closes by briefly summarizing the recommendations and the reasons behind them

FIGURE 10–3
(Continued)

Proposals   A **proposal** is a special type of analytical report designed to get products, plans, or projects accepted by others. Proposals can be one or two pages, or they can be hundreds of pages if they involve large, complex jobs. Regardless of the size and scope, these special types of reports analyze an audience's problem, present a solution, and persuade the audience that the solution presented is the best approach. Proposals are usually read by people in positions of authority.

> Proposals are reports written to get products, plans, or projects accepted by others.

Solicited proposals are generally prepared at the request of external parties who need something done; however, they may also be requested by such internal sources as management or the board of directors. Some external parties prepare an invitation to bid on their contract. Called a **request for proposal (RFP)**, such an invitation includes instructions that specify the exact type of work to be performed, along with guidelines on how and when the company wants the work completed.

> Effective solicited proposals address each item listed in the RFP while demonstrating that your organization is better qualified than competitors to handle a particular contract.

Unsolicited proposals are usually written to obtain business or funding without a specific invitation from management or a potential client. In other words, with an unsolicited proposal, the writer makes the first move. Because readers may not know about the problem, the writer must convince them that a problem exists and that he or she can solve it. Thus, unsolicited proposals generally devote considerable space to explaining why readers should take action and convincing them of the benefits of buying or funding something.

> An unsolicited proposal must first establish that a problem exists.

Internal Proposals   **Internal proposals** are submitted to decision makers in one's own organization. They have two primary purposes: (1) to seek approval for a course of action (such as changing recruiting procedures, revising the company's training programs, or reorganizing a department) or (2) to request additional resources (such as new equipment, more employees, or extra operating funds). Because most internal proposals advocate change, take extra care to understand whether your audience will feel threatened by your plan. A good internal proposal is completely unbiased and explains why a project or course of action is needed, what it will involve, how much it will cost, and how the company will benefit (see Figure 10–4).

> Internal proposals are directed to decision makers in the organization.

External Proposals   **External proposals** are submitted to current or potential clients and government agencies. Like internal proposals, they solicit approval for projects

> External proposals are directed to outsiders, and if accepted, they become legally binding documents.

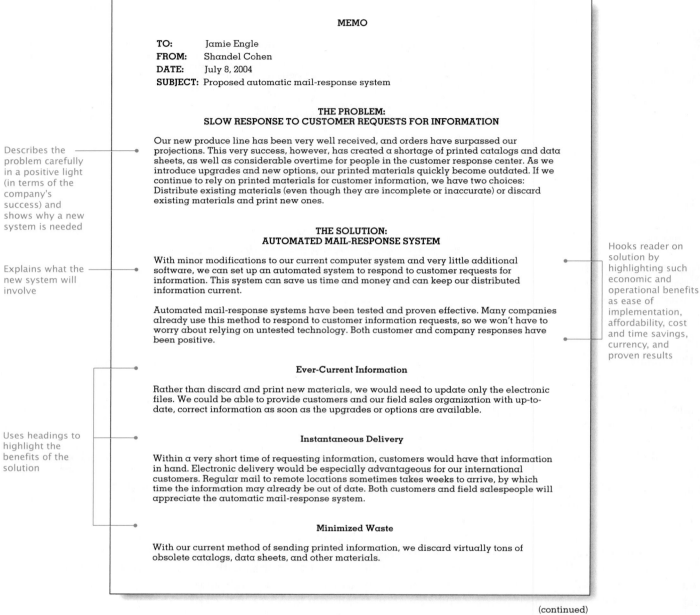

Describes the problem carefully in a positive light (in terms of the company's success) and shows why a new system is needed

Explains what the new system will involve

Uses headings to highlight the benefits of the solution

Hooks reader on solution by highlighting such economic and operational benefits as ease of implementation, affordability, cost and time savings, currency, and proven results

> **MEMO**
>
> **TO:** Jamie Engle
> **FROM:** Shandel Cohen
> **DATE:** July 8, 2004
> **SUBJECT:** Proposed automatic mail-response system
>
> **THE PROBLEM:**
> **SLOW RESPONSE TO CUSTOMER REQUESTS FOR INFORMATION**
>
> Our new produce line has been very well received, and orders have surpassed our projections. This very success, however, has created a shortage of printed catalogs and data sheets, as well as considerable overtime for people in the customer response center. As we introduce upgrades and new options, our printed materials quickly become outdated. If we continue to rely on printed materials for customer information, we have two choices: Distribute existing materials (even though they are incomplete or inaccurate) or discard existing materials and print new ones.
>
> **THE SOLUTION:**
> **AUTOMATED MAIL-RESPONSE SYSTEM**
>
> With minor modifications to our current computer system and very little additional software, we can set up an automated system to respond to customer requests for information. This system can save us time and money and can keep our distributed information current.
>
> Automated mail-response systems have been tested and proven effective. Many companies already use this method to respond to customer information requests, so we won't have to worry about relying on untested technology. Both customer and company responses have been positive.
>
> **Ever-Current Information**
>
> Rather than discard and print new materials, we would need to update only the electronic files. We could be able to provide customers and our field sales organization with up-to-date, correct information as soon as the upgrades or options are available.
>
> **Instantaneous Delivery**
>
> Within a very short time of requesting information, customers would have that information in hand. Electronic delivery would be especially advantageous for our international customers. Regular mail to remote locations sometimes takes weeks to arrive, by which time the information may already be out of date. Both customers and field salespeople will appreciate the automatic mail-response system.
>
> **Minimized Waste**
>
> With our current method of sending printed information, we discard virtually tons of obsolete catalogs, data sheets, and other materials.

(continued)

FIGURE 10–4
Effective Internal Proposal—Analytical (Unsolicited)

or funds, but they differ in several ways. First, because they're directed to outsiders, external proposals are more formal. Second, external proposals are legally binding. Once approved, they form the basis of a contract, so they are prepared with extreme care, spelling out precisely what your company will provide under specific terms and conditions.

Third, audience members may not know your company, so your proposal must convince them that your organization is the best source of a product or service. You can do so by devoting considerable space to explaining your experience, qualifications, facilities, and equipment. Also, show that you clearly understand your audience's problem or need (see Figure 10–5 on page 318).[2]

2

By maintaining and distributing the information electronically, we would eliminate this waste. We would also free up a considerable amount of floor space and shelving that is required for storing printed materials.

Of course, some of our customers may still prefer to receive printed materials, or they may not have access to electronic mail. For these customers, we could simply print copies of the files when we receive requests.

Lower Overtime Costs

Besides savings in paper and space, we would also realize considerable savings in wages. Because of the increased interest in our new products, we must continue to work overtime or hire new people to meet the demand. An automatic mail-response system would eliminate this need, allowing us to deal with fluctuating interest without a fluctuating work-force.

Setup and Operating Costs

The necessary equipment and software costs approximately $15,000. System maintenance and upgrades are estimated at $5,000 per year.

We expect the following annual savings from eliminating printed information:

$100,000	Printing costs
25,000	Storage costs
5,000	Postage
20,000	Wages
$150,000	Total savings

CONCLUSION

I will be happy to answer any questions you have about this system. I believe that such an automated mail-response system would greatly benefit our company, in terms of both cost and customer satisfaction. If you approve, we can have it installed and running in six weeks.

Carefully explains the costs of the proposal

Justifies the cost by detailing projected annual savings

Closes by offering to answer any questions management may have—rather than trying to anticipate management's questions and including unnecessary detail

FIGURE 10–4
(Continued)

APPLYING THE THREE-STEP WRITING PROCESS TO BUSINESS REPORTS AND PROPOSALS

As with other business messages, when writing reports and proposals, you benefit from following the three-step writing process: (1) planning, (2) writing, and (3) completing business messages. However, when preparing these longer messages, you may need to add some tasks to the familiar categories, and you may need to pay special attention to tasks you're already familiar with (see Figure 10–6 on page 320). For example, when planning a report, in addition to analyzing your purpose and your audience, you'll want to study the situation carefully to determine whether a report is necessary and for which purpose. Because much of the writing process is covered in Chapters 4, 5, and 6, the following sections discuss only those parts that differ for reports and proposals.

The three-step writing process applies to reports as well as to other business messages.

This chapter focuses on Step 1, planning business reports and proposals. Chapter 11 discusses Step 2, writing business reports and proposals, and Chapter 12 covers Step 3, completing business reports and proposals. The planning tasks for reports fall into the three familiar categories: analyzing the situation, gathering information, and adapting to the audience.

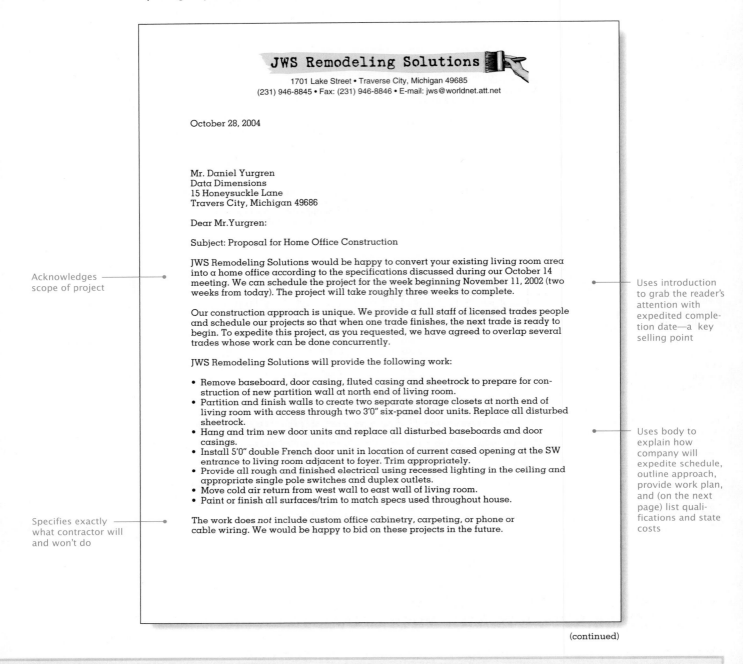

Acknowledges scope of project

Specifies exactly what contractor will and won't do

Uses introduction to grab the reader's attention with expedited completion date—a key selling point

Uses body to explain how company will expedite schedule, outline approach, provide work plan, and (on the next page) list qualifications and state costs

FIGURE 10–5
Effective External Proposal—Analytical (Solicited)

ANALYZING THE SITUATION

When writing analytical reports, pay special attention to analysis tasks such as defining the problem and developing the statement of purpose.

When planning a report, you will of course need to analyze your audience and purpose. But even before that, take a close look at your particular situation and decide whether it merits writing a report in the first place. You may decide that your situation would best be handled by making a phone call, sending an e-mail message, or holding a meeting. If you do decide that writing a report is your best approach, take a moment to determine whether to write an informational or an analytical report. For informational reports, simply define your specific purpose and select a type of report that is

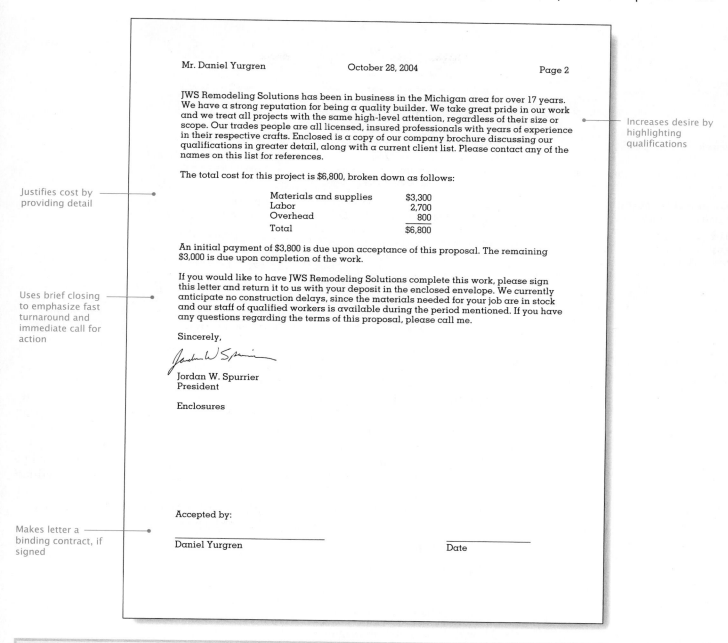

Mr. Daniel Yurgren   October 28, 2004   Page 2

JWS Remodeling Solutions has been in business in the Michigan area for over 17 years. We have a strong reputation for being a quality builder. We take great pride in our work and we treat all projects with the same high-level attention, regardless of their size or scope. Our trades people are all licensed, insured professionals with years of experience in their respective crafts. Enclosed is a copy of our company brochure discussing our qualifications in greater detail, along with a current client list. Please contact any of the names on this list for references.

Increases desire by highlighting qualifications

The total cost for this project is $6,800, broken down as follows:

Materials and supplies	$3,300
Labor	2,700
Overhead	800
Total	$6,800

Justifies cost by providing detail

An initial payment of $3,800 is due upon acceptance of this proposal. The remaining $3,000 is due upon completion of the work.

If you would like to have JWS Remodeling Solutions complete this work, please sign this letter and return it to us with your deposit in the enclosed envelope. We currently anticipate no construction delays, since the materials needed for your job are in stock and our staff of qualified workers is available during the period mentioned. If you have any questions regarding the terms of this proposal, please call me.

Uses brief closing to emphasize fast turnaround and immediate call for action

Sincerely,

Jordan W. Spurrier
President

Enclosures

Accepted by:

Makes letter a binding contract, if signed

_____   _____
Daniel Yurgren   Date

FIGURE 10–5
(Continued)

---

appropriate (monitor/control, policy/procedure, compliance, progress). For analytical reports, first define the problem your report will address; then state the purpose of your report and select an appropriate report type (problem-solving report or proposal).

Define the Problem for Analytical Reports

In some cases, the person who authorizes your report will define the problem for you. In other cases, you will have to define the problem you need to resolve. Be careful not to confuse a simple topic (campus parking) with a problem (the lack of

The problem you need to resolve may be defined by your superior.

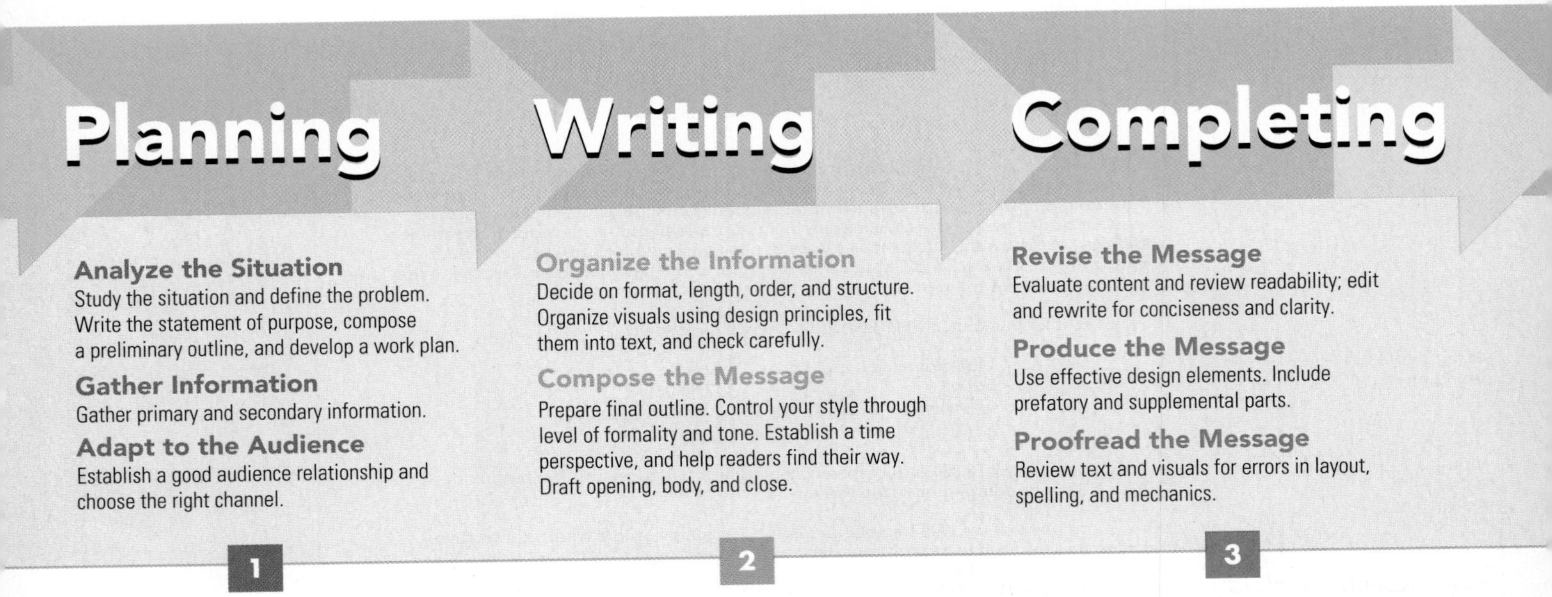

Planning

Writing

Completing

Analyze the Situation
Study the situation and define the problem. Write the statement of purpose, compose a preliminary outline, and develop a work plan.

Gather Information
Gather primary and secondary information.

Adapt to the Audience
Establish a good audience relationship and choose the right channel.

Organize the Information
Decide on format, length, order, and structure. Organize visuals using design principles, fit them into text, and check carefully.

Compose the Message
Prepare final outline. Control your style through level of formality and tone. Establish a time perspective, and help readers find their way. Draft opening, body, and close.

Revise the Message
Evaluate content and review readability; edit and rewrite for conciseness and clarity.

Produce the Message
Use effective design elements. Include prefatory and supplemental parts.

Proofread the Message
Review text and visuals for errors in layout, spelling, and mechanics.

1

2

3

FIGURE 10–6
The Three-Step Writing Process for Reports

enough campus parking). Moreover, if you're the only person who thinks a particular issue is a problem, your readers won't be interested in your solution unless your report first convinces them that a problem does exist. This need for persuasion is especially important in unsolicited proposals.

As the cost accounting manager for Electrovision, a high-tech company based in Los Gatos, California, Linda Moreno was recently asked to find ways to reduce employee travel and entertainment costs. Her task was to prepare an analytical report (the complete report appears in Chapter 12). To ensure that she understood exactly what was required, Moreno tried to answer several general questions:

- What needs to be determined?

- Why is this issue important?

- Who is involved in the situation?

- Where is the trouble located?

- How did the situation originate?

- When did it start?

Not all these questions apply in every situation, but asking them helps you define the problem, as well as limit the scope of your discussion.

You can define the problem by factoring it.

Next, try to identify cause and effect by breaking down the "defined" problem into a series of logical, connected questions—a process that is sometimes called **problem factoring.** You probably already approach most problems this way. When your car won't start, what do you do? You use the available evidence to start searching for cause-and-effect relationships. If the engine doesn't turn over at all, you might suspect a dead battery. If the engine does turn over but won't fire, you can conclude that the battery is okay but perhaps you're out of gas. When you speculate on the cause of a problem, you're forming a **hypothesis,** the potential explanation that needs to be tested. By subdividing a problem and forming hypotheses based on available evidence, you can tackle even the most complex situations.

Linda Moreno used problem factoring to structure her investigation into ways of reducing travel and entertainment costs at Electrovision. "I began with a two-part question," says Moreno. "Why have our travel costs grown so dramatically, and how can we reduce them? Then I factored that question into two subquestions: Do we have adequate procedures for tracking and controlling costs? Are these procedures being followed?" Once she determined what was wrong with her company's cost-control system, she could make recommendations for improvement. Breaking the problem into a series of subproblems allowed Moreno and her colleagues to approach the task methodically.

Develop the Statement of Purpose

Developing a statement of purpose will help you keep your report-writing on task. In contrast to the problem statement, which defines *what* you are going to investigate, the statement of purpose defines *why* you are preparing the report (see Table 10–2).

The statement of purpose defines the objective of your report.

The most useful way to phrase your purpose statement is to begin with an infinitive phrase. For instance, in an informational report, your statement of purpose can be as simple as these:

- To identify customers and explain how the company will service them (monitor/control report)

- To explain the building access procedures (policy/procedure report)

- To submit required information to the SEC (compliance report)

- To update clients on the progress of the research project (progress report)

Using an infinitive phrase (*to* plus a verb) encourages you to take control and decide where you're going before you begin. When you choose an infinitive phrase (*to inform, to confirm, to analyze, to persuade, to recommend*), you pin down your general goal in preparing the report.

The statement of purpose for analytical reports is often more comprehensive than for informational reports. In her report at Electrovision, Linda Moreno was supposed to suggest specific ways of reducing travel costs, so she phrased her statement of purpose accordingly:

Statements of purpose for analytical reports are often more complex than are those for informational reports.

> To analyze the T&E [travel and entertainment] budget, evaluate the impact of recent changes in airfares and hotel costs, and suggest ways to tighten management's control over T&E expenses.

PROBLEM STATEMENTS VERSUS PURPOSE STATEMENTS — Table 10–2

Problem Statement	Statement of Purpose
Our company's market share is steadily declining.	To explore different ways of selling our products and to recommend the ones that will most likely increase our market share.
Our current computer network system is inefficient and cannot be upgraded to meet our future needs.	To analyze various computer network systems and to recommend the system that will best meet our company's current and future needs.
We need $2 million to launch our new product.	To convince investors that our new business would be a sound investment so that we can obtain desired financing.
Our current operations are too decentralized and expensive.	To justify the closing of the Newark plant and the transfer of East Coast operations to a single Midwest location in order to save the company money.

If Moreno had been assigned an informational report instead, she might have stated her purpose differently:

> To summarize Electrovision's spending on travel and entertainment.

The purpose statement helps shape the scope of your report.

You can see from these two examples how much influence the purpose statement has on the scope of your report. If Moreno had collected only cost data when her manager had expected her to suggest ways to reduce costs, her report would have failed to meet expectations. Because her assignment was to prepare an analytical report rather than an informational report, Moreno had to go beyond merely collecting data to drawing conclusions and making recommendations.

Review your statement of purpose with the person who authorized the study.

The more specific your purpose statement, the more useful it will be as a guide to planning your report. Furthermore, always double-check your statement of purpose with the person who authorized the report. Given the opportunity to see the purpose written down in black and white, the authorizer may decide that the report needs to go in a different direction. Once your statement is confirmed, you can use it as the basis for your preliminary outline.

Develop a Preliminary Outline

Preliminary outlines establish the framework for planning and researching your report.

Developing a preliminary outline gives you a visual diagram of your report, its important points, the order in which they will be discussed, and the detail to be included. Since you'll be using the preliminary outline to guide your research and organization efforts, it will look different from the final outline that you develop to write your report. Your preliminary outline is a working draft that you will revise and modify as you go along. You will rework it to account for things you learn during your investigation and to balance your discussion so that coverage is neither too light in one area nor too heavy in another. For example, say that your preliminary outline lists five possible causes of a problem. Then during your investigation, you discover that only two of the five are relevant. You wouldn't introduce the three unrelated causes in your report at all. Your final outline must include only those items that you plan to discuss in your report (regardless of any additional topics that were once included in your preliminary outline).

Chapter 5 presents two common outline formats: alphanumeric and decimal. Regardless of which format you use, make sure that items of the same level are grammatically parallel. Parallel construction shows that the ideas are related, of similar importance, and on the same level of generality, as the following example demonstrates:

Why We Are Having Trouble Hiring Secretaries

I. Are salaries too low?

   a. What we pay our secretaries

   b. What comparable companies pay their secretaries

   c. The importance of pay in influencing secretaries' job choices

II. Is our location poor?

   a. Are we accessible by public transportation and major roads?

   b. Is the area physically attractive?

   c. Are housing costs affordable?

   d. Is crime a problem?

III. Is the supply of secretaries diminishing?

   a. The number of secretaries available five years ago (as opposed to today)

   b. The demand for secretaries five years ago (as opposed to today)

In some cases you may use these same headings for your final report. When wording your outlines, choose between descriptive (topical) and informative (talking) headings. As Chapter 6 points out, descriptive headings label the subject that will be discussed, whereas informative headings suggest more about the meaning of the issues. If team members are going to use or comment on your outline, they may not have a clear idea of what you mean by the descriptive heading "Advertising." However, they will get the main idea if you use the informative heading "Did Ad Budget Cuts Cause Sales to Decline?" Although outlines with informative headings take a little longer to write, they're generally more useful in guiding your work and easier for others to review.

> Use parallel construction to show that your ideas are related, of similar importance, and on the same level of generality.

> Informative outline headings are useful in guiding your work.

Writing a report can be a lengthy and encompassing task that involves primary and secondary research, preparation of visuals, scheduling, and a number of other tasks. Preparing a work plan is one way to coordinate and monitor your efforts.

Prepare the Work Plan

In business, most reports have a firm deadline and finite resources. You not only have to produce quality reports, you have to do so quickly and efficiently. A carefully thought-out work plan is the best way to ensure that you produce quality work on schedule. By identifying all the tasks that must be performed, you overlook nothing.

If you are preparing the work plan for yourself, it can be relatively informal: a simple list of the steps you plan to take and an estimate of their sequence and timing. If you're conducting a lengthy, formal study, however, your work plan must be detailed enough to guide the performance of many tasks over a span of time. Most proposals require a detailed work plan, which becomes the basis for a contract if the proposal is accepted. A formal work plan might do any of the following (but especially the first two items):

> Whether you prepare an informal work plan for yourself or a detailed work plan for your team, be sure it identifies all the tasks that must be performed.

- **State the problem.** Clarify the challenge you face. Doing so helps you (and anyone working with you) stay focused on the core problem and avoid the distractions that arise during report preparation.

- **State the purpose and scope.** Describe what you plan to accomplish with this report, stating which issues you will and will not cover. This effort is especially important with complex, lengthy investigations.

- **Discuss the tasks to be accomplished.** Indicate your sources of information, the research necessary, and any constraints on time, money, personnel, or data. For simple reports, the list of tasks will be short and probably obvious. However, longer reports and complex investigations require an exhaustive list so that you can schedule time with customers, executives, or outside services such as pollsters or print shops.

- **Describe resulting products.** In many cases, the only product of your efforts will be the report itself. In other cases, you may produce something beyond a report, perhaps a new marketing plan or even a tangible product. Clarify these expectations at the outset, and schedule enough time and resources to get the job done.

- **Review project assignments, schedules, and costs.** Indicate who is responsible for what, when tasks will be completed, and how much the study will cost. If more than one person will be involved, you might include a brief section to coordinate report writing and production. (Chapter 2 discusses collaborative writing in detail.)

- **State plans for following up.** Follow-up may be as simple as checking that people have received your report and that it provided what they needed. However,

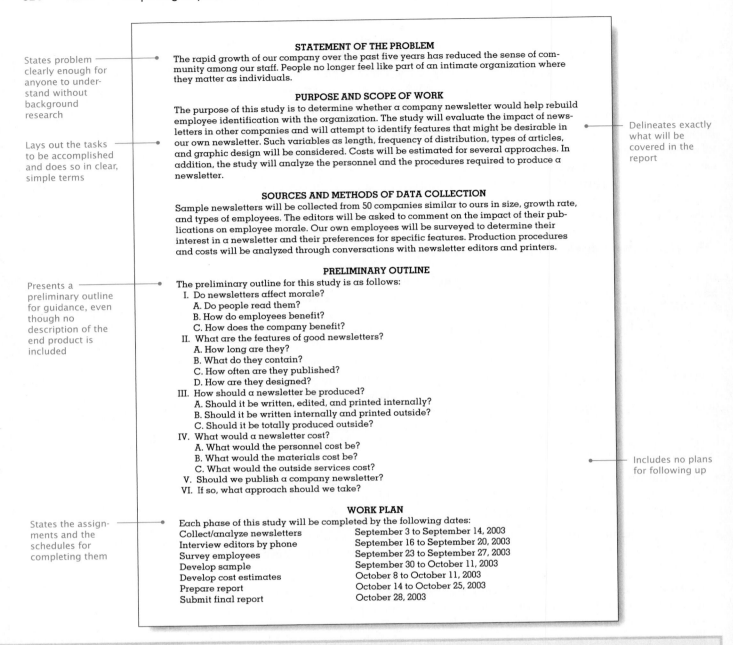

States problem clearly enough for anyone to understand without background research

Lays out the tasks to be accomplished and does so in clear, simple terms

Presents a preliminary outline for guidance, even though no description of the end product is included

States the assignments and the schedules for completing them

Delineates exactly what will be covered in the report

Includes no plans for following up

STATEMENT OF THE PROBLEM

The rapid growth of our company over the past five years has reduced the sense of community among our staff. People no longer feel like part of an intimate organization where they matter as individuals.

PURPOSE AND SCOPE OF WORK

The purpose of this study is to determine whether a company newsletter would help rebuild employee identification with the organization. The study will evaluate the impact of newsletters in other companies and will attempt to identify features that might be desirable in our own newsletter. Such variables as length, frequency of distribution, types of articles, and graphic design will be considered. Costs will be estimated for several approaches. In addition, the study will analyze the personnel and the procedures required to produce a newsletter.

SOURCES AND METHODS OF DATA COLLECTION

Sample newsletters will be collected from 50 companies similar to ours in size, growth rate, and types of employees. The editors will be asked to comment on the impact of their publications on employee morale. Our own employees will be surveyed to determine their interest in a newsletter and their preferences for specific features. Production procedures and costs will be analyzed through conversations with newsletter editors and printers.

PRELIMINARY OUTLINE

The preliminary outline for this study is as follows:
I. Do newsletters affect morale?
  A. Do people read them?
  B. How do employees benefit?
  C. How does the company benefit?
II. What are the features of good newsletters?
  A. How long are they?
  B. What do they contain?
  C. How often are they published?
  D. How are they designed?
III. How should a newsletter be produced?
  A. Should it be written, edited, and printed internally?
  B. Should it be written internally and printed outside?
  C. Should it be totally produced outside?
IV. What would a newsletter cost?
  A. What would the personnel cost be?
  B. What would the materials cost be?
  C. What would the outside services cost?
V. Should we publish a company newsletter?
VI. If so, what approach should we take?

WORK PLAN

Each phase of this study will be completed by the following dates:

Collect/analyze newsletters	September 3 to September 14, 2003
Interview editors by phone	September 16 to September 20, 2003
Survey employees	September 23 to September 27, 2003
Develop sample	September 30 to October 11, 2003
Develop cost estimates	October 8 to October 11, 2003
Prepare report	October 14 to October 25, 2003
Submit final report	October 28, 2003

FIGURE 10–7
Effective Work Plan for a Formal Study

follow-up may be as complex as conducting additional research to evaluate the outcome of recommendations you made. Even informal follow-up can help you improve future reports. It certainly signals that you care about your work's effectiveness and its impact on the organization.

- **Include a preliminary outline.** Some work plans include a preliminary outline of the report, like the plan in Figure 10–7. This plan was developed for a report on whether to launch a company newsletter.

Once your work plan is set, with a purpose and a preliminary outline in place, you are ready to begin your research.

GATHERING INFORMATION

When it comes to finding information, many people make the mistake of rushing into their research without developing a plan. They go to the library, log on to a database or the Internet, type in some key words, produce almost endless resources, and immediately begin taking notes on whatever comes up under their topic. Resist the temptation.

The best way to learn about something new is to browse through materials on your topic. Leaf through some books and periodicals, conduct some loosely structured interviews, or log on to a database (either at the library or on the Internet) and see what comes up. You may even want to visit your favorite bookstore (whether physical or online), find some business books on your topic, and then scan their table of contents. As you browse, keep a written bibliographical list of those resources that you find to be helpful. But instead of taking copious notes at this point, start a list of phrases, terms, and key words that recur. This list is what you'll use later to locate and access relevant information.

Once you have gathered some preliminary information, use what you have learned to clarify your assignment. If you're conducting research at the request of someone else, make sure you both agree on what needs to be done. If you're conducting research for reasons of your own, use your preliminary information to make your purpose as clear and specific as possible.

Once you have a better understanding of your topic and assignment, you're ready to begin your research in earnest: identifying the *best* sources of information and gathering the details you'll need to answer your questions. In most cases you'll begin your research by looking for sources of secondary information—information on your subject that already exists and has already been collected, usually in the form of books, periodicals, newspapers, and websites. If secondary information doesn't exist or isn't helpful, then you'll collect firsthand, primary information for your specific needs.

Finding business information on the Internet is relatively easy, but separating the good from the bad takes patience, skill, and practice.

Become familiar with your topic by browsing and gathering preliminary information.

Verify and clarify your assignment.

Locate Sources of Secondary Information

Many sources of secondary information are easily accessible in print and online.[3] Your challenge as a business researcher is to identify and prioritize the best sources for your needs. To get started, know what to look for first. Find out where to begin when you need information about the following:

- **A specific company.** Find out whether the company is public (sells shares of stock to the general public) or private. Public companies generally have more information available than private companies. Public companies are listed in the *Directory of Companies Required to File Annual Reports with the Securities and Exchange Commission*, which is available in most public libraries.

- **An entire industry.** Find out the North American Industry Classification System (NAICS) code of that particular industry. The U.S. government requires all companies, from sole proprietorships to corporations, to assign themselves a six-digit industry number that classifies their business by the type of product or service

Search: 🔍 Web 📖 Dictionary ▾ 🛍 Shopping ▾ 💡 Travel 🌐 Games 🛡 AdZapper

COMPANY, INDUSTRY, AND PRODUCT RESOURCES (PRINT)

- *Brands and Their Companies/Companies and Their Brands.* Data on over 281,000 consumer products and 51,000 manufacturers, importers, marketers, and distributors.
- *Corporate and Industry Research Reports (CIRR).* Collection of industry reports produced by industry analysts for investment purposes. Unique coverage includes industry profitability, comparative company sales, market share, profits, and forecasts.
- *Directory of Companies Required to File Annual Reports with the Securities and Exchange Commission.* Listing of U.S. publicly held firms.
- *Dun's Directory of Service Companies.* Information on 205,000 U.S. service companies.
- *Forbes.* Annual Report on American Industry published in first January issue of each year.
- *Hoover's Handbook of American Business.* Profiles of over 500 public and private corporations.
- *Manufacturing USA.* Data series listing nearly 25,000 companies, including detailed information on over 450 manufacturing industries.
- *Market Share Report.* Data covering products and service categories originating from trade journals, newsletters, and magazines.
- *Moody's Industry Review.* Data on 4,000 companies in about 150 industries. Ranks companies within industry by five financial statistics (revenue, net income, total assets, cash and marketable securities, and long-term debt) and includes key performance ratios.
- *Moody's Manuals.* Weekly manual of financial data in each of six business areas: industrials, transportation, public utilities, banks, finance, and over-the-counter (OTC) industrials.
- *Service Industries USA.* Comprehensive data on 2,100 services grouped into over 150 industries.
- *Standard & Poor's Industry Surveys.* Concise investment profiles for a broad range of industries. Coverage is extensive, with a focus on current situation and outlook. Includes some summary data on major companies in each industry.
- *Standard & Poor's Register of Corporations, Directors, and Executives.* Index of major U.S. and international corporations. Lists officers, products, sales volume, and number of employees.
- *Thomas's Register of American Manufacturers.* Information on thousands of U.S. manufacturers indexed by company name and product.
- *U.S. Industrial Outlook.* Annual profiles of several hundred key U.S. industries. Each industry report covers several pages and includes tables, graphs, and charts that visually demonstrate how an industry compares with similar industries, including important component growth factors and other economic measures.

COMPANY, INDUSTRY, AND PRODUCT RESOURCES (ONLINE)

- *Hoover's Online* **www.hoovers.com.** Profiles of publicly listed U.S. companies traded on major stock exchanges and more than 1,200 large private companies. Search by ticker symbol, company name, location, industry, or sales.
- *NAICS Codes* **www.census.gov/epcd/naics/naicstb2.txt.** North American Industry Classification System.
- *SEC filings* **www.sec.gov/edgarhp.shtml.** SEC filings including 10Ks, 10Qs, annual reports, and prospectuses for 35,000 U.S. public firms.
- *Fortune.com* **www.fortune.com.** Brief profiles of the 500 leading companies in the U.S.
- *Yahoo!* **dir.yahoo.com/business.** More than 50 categories of information with dozens of links.

🌐 Internet

(continued)

FIGURE 10–8
Major Business Resources

they provide. This six-digit NAICS replaced the four-digit Standard Industrial Classification (SIC) in 1997.

- **Statistics, trends, or business issues.** You may be seeking data on company or industry statistics, economic forecasts, business concerns, legal issues, competition, or industry performance ratios and averages, among other things. Figure 10–8 lists some of the more popular resources for company and industry information (many of which are available both in print and in electronic database formats).

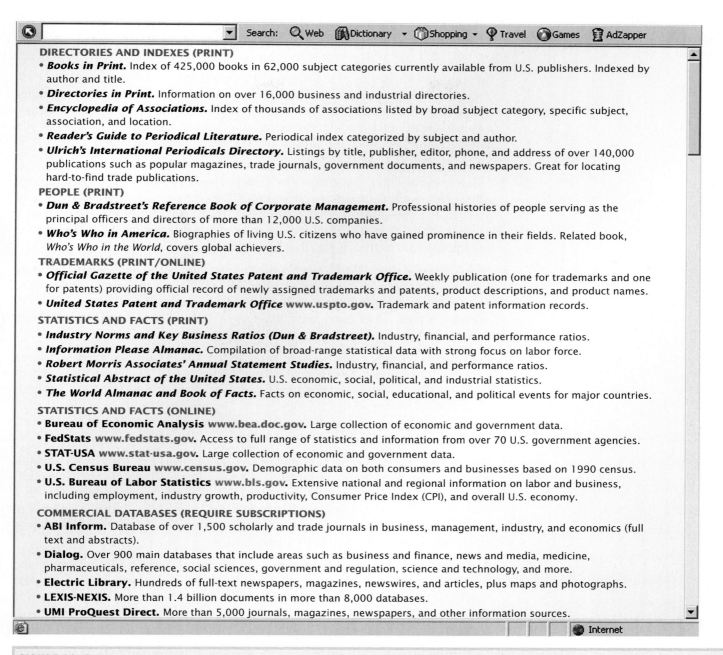

FIGURE 10–8
(Continued)

Once you know what you're looking for, locate and access the information you need. One of the best places to begin your search for secondary information is the nearest public or university library.

Finding Information at the Library   Libraries are where you'll find business books, electronic databases, newspapers, periodicals, directories, almanacs, and government publications. In addition, you'll find your most important resource: librarians. Reference librarians are trained in research techniques and spend their days managing information and helping people find materials. They can show you how to

Reference librarians are there to assist you with your research efforts.

Libraries offer many types of business resources, whether in print, online, or on microfilm.

use the library's many databases, and they can help you find obscure information. Whether you're trying to locate information in printed materials, on databases, or on microfilm, each type of resource serves a special function.

- **Business books.** Although less timely than journal articles, business books provide in-depth coverage of a variety of business topics. Because of budgetary constraints, public libraries must be selective about the books they put on their shelves, so you may have better luck finding specialized information at company libraries or at a college library (assuming the college offers courses in those subjects).

- **Electronic databases.** An **electronic database** is a computer-searchable collection of information, often categorized by subject (business, law, science, technology, education). Such databases are stored on CD-ROM or online (stored on a computer that is accessible to other computers). Try to get a list of the publications a database includes, plus the time period it covers, so that you can fill in the gaps for any important resources not in the database.

- **Newspapers.** Libraries subscribe to only a select number of newspapers and store a limited number of back issues in print. However, they frequently subscribe to databases containing newspaper articles in full text (available online, on CD-ROM, or on microfilm). In addition, most newspapers today offer full-text or limited editions of their papers on the Internet.

- **Periodicals.** Most periodicals are categorized as (1) popular magazines (not intended for business, professional, or academic use), (2) trade journals (providing news and other facts about specific professions and industries), (3) business magazines (covering all major industries and professions), and (4) academic journals (providing data from professional researchers and educators). To locate a certain periodical, check your library's database.

- **Directories.** More than 14,000 directories are published in the United States—covering everything from accountants to zoos. Many include membership information for various special-interest groups. For instance, business directories provide entries for companies, products, and individuals, including the names of contact persons. Directories are considered invaluable for marketers, job seekers, and others who need to establish a prospect list.

- **Almanacs and statistical resources.** Almanacs are handy guides to factual and statistical information about countries, politics, the labor force, and so on. Also check out the *Statistical Abstract of the United States* (published annually by the U.S. Department of Commerce). This resource contains statistics about life, work, government, population patterns, health issues, business, crime, and the environment.

- **Government publications.** For information on a law, a court decision, current population patterns, or business trends, consult government documents. A librarian can direct you to the information you want. You'll need the name of the government agency you're interested in (U.S. Congress, Ninth Circuit Court of Appeals, Department of Labor) and some description for the information you need (Safe Drinking Water Act of 1974, Price v. Shell Oil, the latest census). If you know the date and name of a publication, the search will be easier.

When doing research on the Internet, you need to be selective because anyone can publish anything.

Finding Business Information on the Internet   Today's most popular source of company and industry information is the Internet, which contains material ranging from current news and industry trends to company-related data on financial performance, products, goals, and employment. Remember that anyone (including you) can post anything on a website. In many cases information on the web has not been validated by an independent party, which means that it may be biased, inaccurate, or exaggerated. Thus, it's best to refrain from seriously surfing the web for business information until you've had a chance to learn a bit about your topic from journals, books, and commercial databases. You'll be able to detect skewed or erroneous information, and you can be more selective about which websites and documents you choose to use as resources.

One good place to start on the web is the Internet Public Library at www.ipl.org. Modeled after a real library, this site provides a carefully selected collection of links to high-quality business resources that offer information such as company profiles, trade data, business news, corporate tax and legal advice, small-business information, prepared forms and documents, biographies of executives, financial reports, job postings, online publications, and so on.

If you're looking for specific company information, your best source may be the company's website (if it maintains one). These websites generally include detailed information about the firm's products, services, history, mission, strategy, financial performance, and employment needs. Many sites provide links to related company information, such as SEC filings, news releases, and more.

> You can find all kinds of information about a company on its website.

You can obtain news releases and general company news from news-release sites such as PRNewswire (www.prnewswire.com) and Business Wire (www.businesswire. com). These two sites offer free databases of news releases from companies subscribing to their services. News-release sites also offer announcements of new products, management changes, earnings, dividends, mergers, acquisitions, and other company information. If you subscribe to a commercial online database system (such as those listed in Figure 10–8 on pp. 326–327), you can also use the Internet to access information from the provider's database.

> News releases and general news about companies are also available at news-release sites and through online databases.

Keep in mind that the web doesn't have everything. You may find nothing about small organizations, or perhaps just their address and phone number. And even if the information exists on the web, you may not be able to locate it. The Internet holds more than 800 million webpages, with hundreds of pages being added every day, and even the best Internet search engines manage to index only about one-third of the pages on the web.[4]

Fine-Tuning Your Search Techniques   You can get the most dependable search results from well-known, commercially backed search engines, which are likely to be well maintained and upgraded. Most have simple or advanced search features, plus extras such as interactive maps, weather information, travel information, phone and e-mail directories, and company financial information. Table 10–3 lists some of the more popular search engines.

Although search engines will often turn up what you're looking for, they're also likely to turn up a mountain of stuff you don't need. Suppose you're looking for information about available jobs for writers. The search engine may turn up information on being an accountant at an insurance company. Why? Because the insurance company described itself on the web as one of the largest *writers* of insurance policies. Whether you are using a library database or an Internet search engine, the search strategies listed in "Checklist: Improving Search Results" on page 331 will improve your effectiveness.

> Fine-tune your search techniques until you get the results you want.

As you find and review source materials, take some brief notes to keep track of your progress. These are not the detailed notes you'll be taking later, but you'll need enough to locate and evaluate your sources.

Collect Primary Information

As Michael Dell can tell you, sometimes the information you need is not available from sources of secondary information, or you may need something beyond what is covered in secondary information. In that case, plan on gathering the data yourself.

> Conduct primary research by collecting basic information yourself.

Table 10–3   BEST OF INTERNET SEARCHING

Major Search Engines

AllTheWeb	www.alltheweb.com Remains one of the largest indexes of the web
Alta Vista	www.altavista.com Indexes data from millions of webpages and articles from thousands of Usenet newsgroups
Ask Jeeves	www.ask.com Finds answers to natural-language questions such as "Who won Super Bowl XXV?"
Excite	www.excite.com Is an all-purpose site loaded with options
Fedstats	www.fedstats.gov/search.html Simultaneously queries 14 federal agencies for specified statistics and numerical data
Google	www.google.com Is a simple directory that is especially useful for finding homepages of companies and organizations
LookSmart	www.looksmart.com Remains the closest rival to Yahoo! in terms of being a human-compiled directory (Choose "Your Town" for local directories)
Open Directory	http://dmoz.org Is the largest, most comprehensive human-edited directory of the web (maintained by a vast, global community of volunteer editors)
Teoma	www.teoma.com Offers a "refine" feature, which gives suggested topics to explore after you do a search
WebBrain	www.webbrain.com Lets you search the web visually, so you can explore a dynamic picture of related information
WebCrawler	www.webcrawler.com Allows you to either search the entire site or browse any of the preselected categories
WiseNut	www.wisenut.com Automatically generates WiseGuide categories that are semantically related to the words in your query
Yahoo!	www.yahoo.com Is the oldest major website directory, listing over 500,000 sites

Multiple Search Engine Sites—Metacrawlers

Dogpile	www.dogpile.com Lets you enter one query and then sniffs through FTP files, Usenet message boards, and websites (despite the silly name)
IXQuick	www.ixquick.com Searches up to 14 search engines at the same time, ranking results by relevancy
Kartoo	www.kartoo.com Gathers the results, compiles them, and presents them graphically in a series of interactive maps
Mamma	www.mamma.com Claims to be the "Mother of All Search Engines" (this multilegged spider queries the major search engines for fast results)
ProFusion	www.profusion.com Retrieves only the "best" results from selected search engines (The University of Kansas Spider)
Vivisimo	www.vivisimo.com Organizes results with document-clustering technology, which provides users with lists of documents in meaningful groups
Zworks	www.zworks.com Ranks results based on the cumulative score of all the engines used in the search

✓ CHECKLIST: Improving Search Results

Select the Right Tools

✓ Select a good business database, but remember that journals on your topic may also be found in databases that include journals on psychology, computers, or medicine.

✓ Use **metacrawlers**, special engines that explore several search engines at once.

✓ Evaluate results to refine your search, especially if you get more than 60 to 100 links or if your first page of results has nothing of interest.

✓ Searching in the title, subject, or document field of a database will return different results.

Choose Search Words Carefully

✓ Translate concepts into keywords and phrases; to find the "effect of TQM on company profits," select keywords *TQM, total quality management, profits, sales, companies,* and *corporations.*

✓ Whenever possible, use synonyms or word equivalents.

✓ When looking for an entire phrase (instead of separate words), enclose it in quotation marks.

✓ Use a short phrase or single term, rather than a long phrase.

✓ Make sure search words are in the correct order—if words occur in a document, but not in the same order, you may miss relevant hits.

✓ Leave out stopwords—those words that computers disregard and will not search for (database documentation will identify any stopwords in addition to the common ones: *a, an, the, of, by, with, for,* and *to*).

✓ Leave out words contained in the name of a database; for example, the words *business* or *finance* appear so often in the ABI Inform database (see Figure 10–8 on pp. 326–327) that searching for them slows the processing time and adds no precision to your results.

✓ Use variations of your terms: abbreviations (*CEO, CPA*), synonyms (*man, male*), related terms (*child, adolescent, youth*), different spellings (*dialog, dialogue*), singular and plural forms (*woman, women*), nouns and adjectives (*manager, management, managerial*), and various forms of compounds (*online, on line, on-line*).

Understand Search Logic

✓ Specify a logical relationship between the keywords; for example, must the document contain both *companies,* and *corporations,* or is either fine? Must it contain both *profits* and *companies,* or should it contain *profits* or *sales*?

✓ Use Boolean operators: including AND, OR, and NOT to narrow or broaden your search.

✓ Use proximity operators to specify how close one of your keywords should be to another; for example, "marketing NEAR/2 organizations" means that *marketing* must be within two words of *organizations.*

✓ Use wildcard characters to help you find plurals and alternate spellings of your keywords; for example, *organi?ations,* will find documents with both *organisations* (British spelling) and *organizations.* Similarly, *chair** will find *chairman, chairperson, chairs,* and *chairlift.*

Five methods of collecting primary information are examining documents, making observations, conducting experiments, surveying people, and conducting interviews.

Documents, Observation, and Experiments Often the most useful method of collecting primary information is to examine internal documents, such as company sales reports, memos, balance sheets, income statements, policy statements, brochures, newsletters, annual reports, correspondence with customers or suppliers, and contracts. You can often find a great deal of information in company databases, and by scouring a company's files, you can often piece together an accurate, factual, historical record from the tidbits of evidence revealed in various letters, memos, and reports.

Depending on how you use a document, it may be considered either a secondary or a primary source of information. If you simply cite financial figures from an annual report, you are using that document as a secondary source of information—because someone has already summarized the data for you. However, if you analyze that same report's design features, compare it with annual reports from other years, or compare

Documents and records can be good sources of primary data.

it with reports from other companies, you are using that document as a primary source of information.

Observation applies your five senses and your judgment to the investigation.

Another common method of collecting primary business information is to make formal observations. For instance, you can observe people performing their jobs or customers interacting with a product. Observation is a useful technique when you're studying objects, physical activities, processes, the environment, or human behavior. However, it can be expensive and time-consuming, and the value of the observation depends on the reliability of the observer.

Experiments can be effective, but they are expensive.

Some companies collect primary information by conducting experiments, but this method is far more common in technical fields than in general business. An experiment requires extensive, accurate, and measurable manipulation of the factors involved—not only tweaking the variables being tested but also controlling the variables that aren't being tested. This sort of experiment management is usually very expensive.

Marketing surveys are a common way of gathering data directly from customers.

Surveys One of the best methods of collecting primary information is to ask people with relevant experience and opinions. Surveys include everything from conducting a one-time, one-on-one interview to distributing thousands of questionnaires. When prepared and conducted properly, surveys can tell you what a cross section of people think about a given topic.

Surveys are useful only when they are both reliable and valid. A survey is *reliable* if it produces identical results when repeated. A survey is *valid* if it measures what it's intended to measure.

Developing a Survey Questionnaire One of the most crucial elements of a survey is the questionnaire. Essential to a successful questionnaire is providing clear instructions. Your respondents need to know exactly how to fill out your questionnaire. Also, keep your questionnaire short and easy to answer by asking only those questions that are relevant to your research. People are most likely to respond if they can complete your questionnaire within 10 to 15 minutes.

Developing an effective survey questionnaire requires care and skill.

To develop effective questions, begin by making a list of the points you need to determine. Then break these points into specific questions. Various types of questions can be used (see Figure 10–9); you must choose the type that will give you the information you need. The following guidelines will help you design questions that produce valid and reliable results:[5]

- **Design questions whose answers are easily tabulated or analyzed.** Numbers and facts are easier to summarize than opinions.

- **Avoid leading questions.** Questions that lead to a particular answer bias your survey. If you ask, "Do you prefer that we stay open in the evenings for customer convenience?" you'll no doubt get a "yes." Instead, ask, "What time of day do you normally do your shopping?"

- **Ask only one thing at a time.** A compound question such as "Do you read books and magazines regularly?" doesn't allow for the respondent who reads one but not the other.

- **Pretest your questions.** Have a sample group identify questions that are subject to misinterpretation.

FIGURE 10–9
Types of Survey Questions

QUESTION TYPE	EXAMPLE
Open-ended	How would you describe the flavor of this ice cream?
Either-or	Do you think this ice cream is too rich? _____ Yes _____ No
Multiple choice	Which description best fits the taste of this ice cream? (Choose only one.) a. Delicious b. Too fruity c. Too sweet d. Too intensely flavored e. Bland f. Stale
Scale	Please mark an X on the scale to indicate how you perceive the texture of this ice cream. Too light Light Creamy Too creamy
Checklist	Which flavors of ice cream have you had in the past 12 months? (Check all that apply.) _____ Vanilla _____ Chocolate _____ Strawberry _____ Chocolate chip _____ Coffee
Ranking	Rank these flavors in order of your preference, from 1 (most preferred) to 5 (least preferred): _____ Vanilla _____ Cherry _____ Maple nut _____ Chocolate ripple _____ Coconut
Short-answer	In the past month how many times did you buy ice cream in the supermarket? _____ In the past month how many times did you buy ice cream in ice cream shops? _____

If you're mailing your questionnaire rather than administering it in person, include a return postage-paid envelope along with a persuasive cover letter that explains why you're conducting the research. Your letter must convince your readers that a response is important. Remember that even under the best of circumstances, you may get no more than a 10 to 20 percent response.

Conducting Surveys on the Internet   An increasingly popular vehicle for conducting surveys or polling customers is the Internet. Online surveys offer distinct benefits: They cost less to conduct than traditional surveys, they reach large numbers of people quickly and economically, and their response rates are higher. For example, Harris Interactive recently conducted an e-commerce online survey of 100,000 people concerning their online shopping habits. The survey took only

Internet surveys
- Cost less
- Reach large numbers of people quickly
- Improve response rates

17 days to complete and cost $150,000. Harris estimates that the same survey by phone could have taken one year and cost about $5 million.[6]

Interviews Getting information straight from an expert can be an effective method for collecting primary information. *Interviews* are planned conversations that have a predetermined purpose and involve asking and answering questions. Before you decide to conduct an interview, ask yourself whether doing so is really the best way to get the information you need. Although interviews are relatively easy to conduct, they require careful planning and a lot of time.

In a typical information interview, the interviewer seeks facts that bear on a decision or that contribute to basic understanding. The interviewer controls the action by asking a list of questions to elicit information from the interviewee. When you conduct an interview, you must decide in advance what kind of information you want and how you will use it. Such planning saves you time and builds goodwill with the people you interview.

An interview is any planned conversation that has a specific purpose and involves two or more people.

Planning Interviews Planning an interview is similar to planning any other form of communication. Begin by analyzing your purpose, learning about the other person, and formulating your main idea. Then decide on the length, style, and organization of the interview.

Organize an interview much as you would organize a written message.

Good interviews have an opening, a body, and a close. The opening establishes rapport and orients the interviewee to the remainder of the session. You might begin by introducing yourself, asking a few polite questions, and then explaining the purpose and ground rules of the interview. The body of the interview is used for asking questions. The close summarizes the outcome, previews what will come next, and underscores the rapport that you have established with the other person.

Preparing Interview Questions The answers you receive during interviews are influenced by the types of questions you ask, by the way you ask them, and by your subject's cultural and language background. Race, gender, age, educational level, and social status are all influential factors, so know your subject before you start writing questions.[7] In addition, be aware of ethical implications. For example, asking someone to divulge personal information about a co-worker may be asking that person to make an unethical choice. Always be careful about confidentiality, politics, and other sensitive issues.

Consider providing a list of questions a day or two before the interview, especially if you'd like to quote your subject in writing or if your questions might require your subject to conduct research or think extensively about the answers. Receiving your questions early gives your subject time to prepare more complete (and therefore more helpful) answers. Consider tape-recording the interview if the topic is complex or if you plan to quote or paraphrase the interviewee in a written document.

Most questions fall along a continuum of openness. The more open-ended questions explore the depth of potential information and require the interviewer to be skilled. The more closed-ended questions save time and allow the interviewer more control over the session.

A successful interview requires careful planning and organization to ensure that you get the information you really need.

Sometimes you'll want to provide a list of questions days before the interview.

- **Open-ended questions** invite the interviewee to reveal feelings, provide information, and offer an opinion: "What do you think your company wants most from suppliers?" Such questions help you learn the reasons behind a decision rather than just the facts. However, they diminish your control of the interview.

- **Direct open-ended questions** suggest a response: "What have you done about smoothing out intercultural clashes in your department?" These questions give you more control while still giving the interviewee some freedom in framing a response.

- **Restatement questions** mirror a respondent's previous answer and invite the respondent to expand on that answer: "You said you dislike sales quotas. Is that correct?" They also signal the interviewee that you're paying attention.

- **Closed-ended questions** require yes-or-no answers or call for short responses: "Did you meet your sales quota?" Such questions produce specific information, yielding data that are precise, reproducible, and reliable. Closed-ended questions require less effort from the interviewee and eliminate bias and prejudice in answers. On the other hand, they also limit the respondent's initiative and may prevent important information from being revealed.

Try to design questions that won't waste anyone's time. Make them concise, relevant, and easily understood. The following guidelines will help you come up with a great set of interview questions:[8]

- **Think about sequence.** Arrange your questions in a way that helps uncover layers of information or that helps the subject tell you a complete story.

- **Rate your questions and highlight the ones you really need answers to.** If you start to run out of time during the interview, you may have to skip less important questions.

- **Ask smart questions.** If you ask a question that your subject perceives to be less than intelligent, the interview could go downhill in a hurry.

- **Use a mix of question types.** Vary the pacing of your interview by using open-ended, direct open-ended, closed-ended, and restatement questions.

- **Limit the number of questions.** Don't try to cover more questions than you have time for. Because people speak at a rate of about 125 to 150 words (or about one paragraph) per minute, you can probably handle about 20 questions in a half-hour, using a mix of question types. Keep in mind that open-ended questions take longer to answer than other types do.

- **Edit your questions.** Try to make your questions as neutral and as easy to understand as possible. Then practice them several times to make sure you're ready for the interview.

Interviews don't necessarily have to take place in person. As more and more people come online, e-mail interviews are becoming more common. Perhaps one of the biggest advantages of an e-mail interview is that it gives subjects a chance to think through their responses thoroughly, rather than rushing to fit the time constraints of an in-person interview.[9]

Processing Interview Information   When you've concluded the interview, take a few moments to write down your thoughts, go over your notes, and organize your material. Look for important themes, helpful facts or statistics, and direct quotes. Fill in any blanks while the interview is fresh in your mind. If you made a tape recording, *transcribe* it (take down word for word what the person said) or take notes from the tape just as you would while listening to someone in person. (As a reminder of the tasks involved in interviews, see the "Checklist: Conducting Effective Information Interviews.")

Four basic types of interview questions range from open-ended to closed-ended.

Six tips help you design effective interview questions.

Carefully review your interview notes immediately after the interview and fill in the gaps before you forget.

✓ CHECKLIST: Conducting Effective Information Interviews

Preparing for the Interview

- ✓ Analyze your purpose, goals, and audience.
- ✓ Determine the needs of your interviewee, and gather background information.
- ✓ Outline your interview on the basis of your goals, audience, and interview category.
- ✓ Set the level of formality.
- ✓ Choose a structured or an unstructured approach.
- ✓ Formulate questions as clearly and concisely as possible.
- ✓ Ask questions in an order that helps your subject tell you a complete story.
- ✓ Ask intelligent questions that show you've done your homework.
- ✓ Use a mix of question types.
- ✓ Select a time and a site.
- ✓ Inform the interviewee of the nature of the interview and the agenda to be covered.
- ✓ Provide a list of questions in advance if the interviewee will need time to research and formulate quality answers.

Conducting the Interview

- ✓ Be on time for the interview appointment.
- ✓ Remind the interviewee of the purpose and format.
- ✓ Clear the taking of notes or the use of a tape recorder with the interviewee.
- ✓ Use your ears and eyes to pick up verbal and nonverbal cues.
- ✓ Follow the stated agenda but be willing to explore relevant subtopics.
- ✓ Close the interview by restating the interviewee's key ideas and by reviewing the actions, goals, and tasks that each of you has agreed to.

Following Up

- ✓ Write a thank-you memo or letter that provides the interviewee with a record of the meeting.
- ✓ Review notes and revise them while the interview is fresh in your mind.
- ✓ Transcribe tape recordings.
- ✓ Monitor progress by keeping in touch with your interviewee.

Finalize Your Sources

Once you've gathered your sources of primary and secondary information, review them carefully to select the best ones for your information needs. Also, be sure you know when to quote an author directly and when to paraphrase the original material. And not least, carefully document your information.

Evaluating Your Sources   Common sense will help you judge the credibility of the sources you plan to use. Ask yourself the following questions about each piece of material:

- **Does the source have a reputation for honesty and reliability?** Naturally, you'll feel more comfortable using information from a publication that has a reputation for accuracy. But don't let your guard down completely; even the finest reporters and editors make mistakes. Find out how the publication accepts articles and whether it has an editorial board.

- **Is the source potentially biased?** Depending on what an organization stands for, its messages may be written with a certain bias—which is neither bad nor unethical. The Tobacco Institute and the American Association of Retired Persons have different points of view. In order to interpret an organization's information, you need to know its point of view. An organization's source of funding may also influence its information output.

- **What is the purpose of the material?** Was the material designed to inform others of new research, summarize existing research, advocate for a position, or stimulate discussion? Was it designed to promote or sell a product? Be sure to distinguish between advertising and informing.

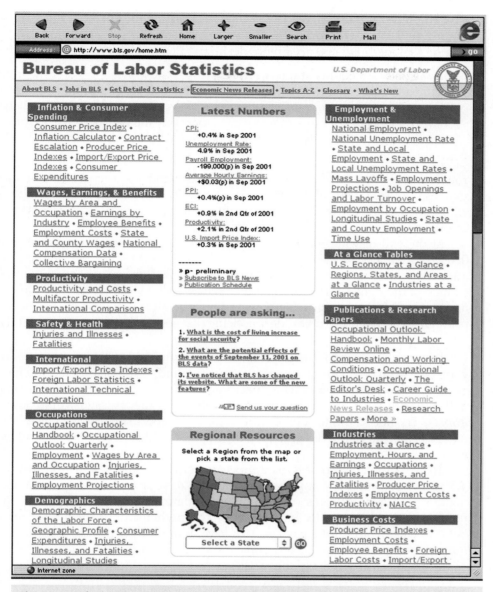

The Bureau of Labor Statistics is a reliable resource for current economic and job-related data.

- **Is the author credible?** Find out whether the person or publisher is well known in the field. Is the author an amateur? Merely someone with an opinion to air?

- **Where did the source get its information?** Many sources of secondary information get their material from other sources, removing you even further from the original data. If a newspaper article says that pollutants in a local river dropped by 50 percent since last year, that information was obtained from someone else. If possible, check on who collected the data, the methods they used, their qualifications, and their professional reputation.

- **Can you verify the material independently?** A good way to uncover bias or a mistake is to search for the same information from another source. Verification can be particularly important when the information goes beyond simple facts to include projections, interpretations, and estimates.

- **Is the material current?** Make sure you are using the most current information available by checking the publication date of a source. Timeliness is especially important if you are using statistics or citing law.

Ask questions about the reference works you use.

- **Is the material complete?** Determine whether the information you have is the entire text or a selection from another document. If it's a selection, which parts were excluded? Do you need more detail?

- **Do the source's claims stand up to scrutiny?** Ask yourself whether the information makes sense. If a researcher claims that the market for a product will triple in the next five years, ask yourself what would have to happen for that prediction to come true. Will three times as many customers buy the product? Will existing customers buy three times more than they do now? Why? Is this information relevant to your needs?

You probably won't have time to conduct a thorough background check on all your sources, so focus your efforts on the most important or most suspicious pieces of information. If the material is from a website, take extra care to verify its accuracy and credibility.

Stop when you reach the point at which additional effort provides little new information.

At the end of your evaluation, you should have narrowed everything down so that you have a complete list of the sources you intend to use. Ask yourself several questions: Do I need more? What type of information am I missing? Do I have enough of the right kind of information to answer all my questions? You'll know you have enough information when you can answer all the questions that began the research project and when you start noticing that sources are becoming redundant.[10]

Quoting and Paraphrasing   To incorporate your research into your report, use your own words to summarize what you've found, and occasionally include the exact words of your sources. Use direct quotations only when the original language will enhance your argument or when rewording the passage would lessen its impact. Try not to quote sources at great length. Too many quotes create a rough patchwork of varying styles and gives the impression that you've lost control of your material.

Express material in your own words unless quoting the original language will have a greater impact.

To avoid such choppiness, **paraphrase** material, or express it in your own words. When you paraphrase, you present information to your reader in a fresh, condensed manner that demonstrates your complete understanding of the material. In fact, paraphrasing may actually increase your comprehension of the source material, because when you recast a passage, you have to think carefully about its meaning—more carefully than if you merely copied it word for word.[11]

To paraphrase effectively, follow these tips:[12]

- Reread the original passage until you fully understand its meaning.

- Save your paraphrase in written or electronic form.

- Use business language and jargon that your audience is familiar with.

- Check your version with the original source to verify that you have not altered the meaning.

- Identify any unique terms or phrases you have borrowed exactly from the source by enclosing them in quotation marks.

- Record the source (including the page number) so that you can give proper credit if you use this material in your report.

In short, a good paraphrase accomplishes three goals: (1) It's shorter than the original text, (2) it's presented in your own words, and (3) it does not alter or distort the meaning of the original text.[13]

Documenting Sources and Giving Credit   Whether you paraphrase or use direct quotes, you're using someone else's ideas. Doing so without proper credit is

plagiarism, so to maintain your credibility and ethics, give proper credit to the original source. Document source material by using one of the systems explained in Appendix B, "Documentation of Report Sources." Whether you use footnotes, endnotes, or some similar system, you must document sources for books, articles, tables, charts, diagrams, song lyrics, scripted dialogue, letters, speeches—anything that you take from someone else. Even if you paraphrase material, give credit to the person you obtained the original information from.

Always give proper credit when you use someone else's material or ideas.

At times, merely crediting the source is not enough. According to the *fair use doctrine,* you can use other people's work only as long as you don't unfairly prevent them from benefiting as a result. For example, if you reproduce someone else's copyrighted questionnaire in a report you're writing, even if you identify the source thoroughly, you may be preventing the author from selling a copy of that questionnaire to your readers. In general, avoid relying so heavily on someone else's work; however, when you can't avoid it, request permission to reprint by contacting the copyright holder (usually the author or publisher). You'll usually be asked to pay a fee.

The fair use doctrine offers guidelines for determining how copyrighted material may be used.

A work is considered copyrighted as soon as it's put into fixed form, even if it hasn't been registered.[14] Copyright law covers printed materials, audiovisual material, many forms of artistic expression, computer programs, maps, mailing lists, and even answering-machine messages. However, copyright law does not protect

- Titles, names, short phrases, and slogans

- Familiar symbols or designs

- Lists of ingredients or contents

- Ideas, procedures, methods, systems, processes, concepts, principles, discoveries, or devices (although it does cover their description, explanation, or illustration)

Also, you do not have to cite a source for general knowledge or for specialized knowledge that's generally known among your readers. For example, everyone knows that Franklin D. Roosevelt was elected to the presidency of the United States four times. You can say so on your own authority, even if you've read an article in which the author says the same thing.

It's not necessary to give source credit for material that is general knowledge.

Analyze Your Data and Interpret Your Findings

Much of the information you compile during the research phase will be in numerical form. However, Michael Dell can tell you that such statistical information in its raw state is of little practical value. By themselves, the data you've collected won't offer much meaning or insight. You'll need to search for relationships among the facts and the bits of evidence you've compiled. Your data must be manipulated so that you and your readers can interpret their significance. Such analysis allows you to draw conclusions about the problem that instigated your report and perhaps make recommendations to solve it.

Analyze your results by calculating statistics, drawing reasonable and logical conclusions, and, if appropriate, developing a set of recommendations.

Look at your data from various angles and try to detect patterns by fitting pieces together to form tentative conclusions. This process enables you to answer the questions you generated when defining the problem. As you proceed with your analysis, either verify or reject your conclusions.

One useful way of looking at numerical data is to find three key numbers. The **mean** is the sum of all the items in the group divided by the number of items in that group. The **median** is the midpoint of a series (with an equal number of items above and below). The **mode** is the number that occurs more often than any other in your sample. It's the best number for answering a question such as "What is the usual amount?" (See Table 10–4.)

The same set of data can be used to produce three key numbers: mean, median, and mode.

Table 10–4	THREE KEY NUMBERS: MEAN, MEDIAN, AND MODE	
Salesperson	**Sales**	
Wilson	$3,000	
Green	5,000	
Carrick	6,000	
Wimper	7,000	——— Mean
Keeble	7,500	——— Median
Kemble	8,500	┐
O'Toole	8,500	│ Mode
Mannix	8,500	┘
Caruso	9,000	
Total	$63,000	

Trend analysis involves examining data over time in order to detect patterns and relationships.

It's also helpful to look for a **trend,** a steady upward or downward movement in a pattern of events taking place over time. Trend analysis is common in business. By looking at data over a period of time, you can detect patterns and relationships that will help you answer important questions.

A correlation is a statistical relationship between two or more variables.

Once you have identified a trend, you'll want to look for a cause. To do so, you could look for a **correlation,** a statistical relationship between two or more variables. But be careful. Correlations are useful evidence, but they do not necessarily prove a cause-and-effect relationship. For example, if the salespeople with the largest accounts consistently produced higher sales, you might assume that those two factors were related in a predictable way. However, your conclusion might be wrong. To be certain that factors are correlated, you might have to collect more evidence.

Once your data are in a form that both you and your readers can understand, your next step is to draw conclusions and, if requested, develop recommendations.

Drawing Conclusions   A **conclusion** is a logical interpretation of the facts in your report. Reaching good conclusions based on the evidence at hand is one of the most important skills you can develop in your business career. A sound conclusion must

- **Fulfill the original statement of purpose.** After all, drawing a conclusion is why you took on the project in the first place.

- **Be based strictly on the information included in the rest of the report.** Consider all the information in your report. Don't ignore anything—even if it doesn't support your conclusion. Moreover, don't introduce any new information in your conclusion. (After all, if something is that important, it should be in the body of your report.)

- **Be logical.** A logical conclusion is one that follows accepted patterns of reasoning.

Conclusions are interpretations of the facts.

Even though conclusions need to be logical, they may not automatically flow from the evidence. Most business decisions require assumptions and judgment; relatively few are based strictly on the facts. Your personal values or your organization's values may also influence your conclusions; just be sure that you're aware of how these biases affect your judgment. Also, don't expect all team members to examine the evidence and arrive at the same conclusion. One of the reasons for bringing additional people into a decision is to gain their unique perspectives and experiences.

Developing Recommendations   Whereas a conclusion interprets the facts, a **recommendation** suggests what to do about the facts. The difference between a conclusion and a recommendation can be seen in the following example:

Recommendations are suggestions for action.

Conclusion	**Recommendation**
On the basis of its track record and current price, I conclude that this company is an attractive buy.	I recommend that we write a letter to the president offering to buy the company at a 10 percent premium over the market value of its stock.

Recommendations are inappropriate in a report when you're not expected to supply them. But when asked to take the final step and develop recommendations, try not to let your assumptions and personal values influence them. Be sure to clarify the relationship between your conclusions and your recommendations.

To be credible, recommendations must be based on logical analysis and sound conclusions. They must also be practical and acceptable to your readers, the people who have to make the recommendations work. Finally, when making a recommendation, be certain that you have adequately described the steps that come next. Don't leave your readers scratching their heads and saying, "This all sounds good, but what do I do on Monday morning?"

Good recommendations are
- *Practical*
- *Acceptable to readers*
- *Explained in enough detail for readers to take action*

ADAPTING YOUR REPORT TO YOUR AUDIENCE

As with any business communication, you'll want to make sure that your report is audience-centered. To do that, you need to select a channel and medium that are appropriate to your readers and your purpose. And as always, you must do what you can to establish a good relationship with your readers.

Establishing a good relationship with an audience is just as important for reports as for other business messages.

Select the Appropriate Channel and Medium

Be sure to select the best format for conveying your report. In some cases a simple letter, memo, or e-mail message will do. At other times you'll need to write a formal report or discuss your findings in an oral presentation. You may even decide to prepare your report in an electronic format and post it on the company intranet.

- **Oral reports.** Use oral reports when you want immediate feedback, when there's an emotional component to your report, or when nonverbal communication is an important element of your message. Oral presentations can take the place of a written report, or they may accompany a written report. Chapter 13 discusses how to plan, write, and complete oral presentations.

Report formats may be oral, written, or electronic.

- **Written reports.** Most reports are produced in writing for one of two reasons: (1) They contain complex information that must be presented in a logical and structured format, or (2) they are needed for future reference. Chapter 4 discusses all the benefits of a written format.

USING THE POWER OF TECHNOLOGY

Minding Your Business with Online Reporting

Mrs. Fields uses them. Mrs. Paul's uses them. However, you don't have to be in the cookie or fish business to work with electronic reports. More and more companies are adopting electronic reports over hard-copy reports to keep employees, managers, investors, and other stakeholders informed.

Computerized cash registers in Mrs. Fields cookie outlets are the heart of a sophisticated reporting system for monitoring and controlling operations. Rather than taking the time to write reports by hand, store managers enter data into the computer system by following report formats on their screen. Then they electronically transmit these reports to corporate headquarters in Park City, Utah. The computer system also serves as a two-way communication device, allowing store and corporate personnel to send messages back and forth in seconds. So corporate managers at Mrs. Fields can quickly receive the information they need in order to track sales and productivity trends—and to spot potential problems—in more than 700 outlets around the world.

At Mrs. Paul's, a computerized reporting system allows production managers to continuously monitor and control the yield from the company's fish-processing operation. The system calculates the production yield using the weight of the fish before it's processed, the weight of any scraps, and the weight of the finished fish meals. If the reports show that the actual yield drops below the expected yield, the managers

can immediately adjust the equipment to improve the yield. The production managers have instant access to electronic reports at each stage of the operation, so they can find and fix problems more quickly than if they had to wait for printed reports.

FedEx, the well-known package-shipping firm, uses extensive satellite and computer technologies to track the location of every package in the company's system. Customers can then access electronic reports to monitor the status of their shipments at any time. This tracking system not only helps the company serve its customers better, but it puts valuable information in the hands of customers with a click of the mouse. Like many companies, FedEx posts an electronic copy of its annual report and other corporate informational reports at its website.

As Mrs. Fields, Mrs. Paul's, FedEx, and other companies know, keeping customers, employees, investors, and other stakeholders informed with electronic reports is the only way to do business in the global workplace.

CAREER APPLICATIONS

1. What advantages and disadvantages do you see in asking store managers at Mrs. Fields to file electronic troubleshooting reports immediately on the company's intranet?

2. What kinds of electronic reports might a company want to post on its website?

- **Electronic reports.** Electronic reports are an increasingly popular option. They are stored on electronic media and may be distributed on disk, attached to an e-mail, or posted on a website. They can include video, sound, and other multimedia effects. Thousands of companies use electronic reports to communicate with employees, customers, and suppliers (see "Using the Power of Technology: Minding Your Business with Online Reporting").[15]

Establish a Good Relationship with Your Audience

Six tips will help you establish a good relationship with your audience.

Even though reports are meant to be factual, objective, and logical, they will succeed only if they focus on the audience. To help your audience accept what you're saying, remember the following advice:

- **Use the "you" attitude.** Show readers how your report answers *their* questions and solves *their* problems.

- **Emphasize the positive.** Even if your report recommends a negative action, remember to state the facts and make your recommendations positively. Instead of using a negative tone ("The only way we'll ever strengthen our cash position is to reduce employee spending"), use a positive, forthright one ("Reducing employee spending will strengthen our cash position").

- **Establish your credibility.** One of the best ways to gain your audience's trust is to be thorough, research all sides of your topic, and document your findings with credible sources.

- **Be polite.** Earn your audience's respect by being courteous, kind, and tactful.

- **Use bias-free language.** Avoid unethical and embarrassing blunders in language related to gender, race, ethnicity, age, and disability.

- **Project the company's image.** Whether your report is intended for people inside or outside the company, be sure to plan how you will adapt your style and your language to reflect the image of your organization.

   The "Checklist: Planning Business Reports" reviews the tasks and concepts involved in planning business reports and proposals. Chapter 11 discusses the next step of the report writing process: how to organize and compose reports and proposals. And Chapter 12 concludes the three-step report writing process by explaining how to assemble and format formal reports and proposals.

Document Makeover

IMPROVE THIS REPORT

To practice correcting drafts of actual documents, visit **www.prenhall.com/onekey** on the web. Click "Document Makeovers," then click Chapter 10. You will find an informational report that contains problems and errors relating to what you've learned in this chapter about planning business reports and proposals. Use the Final Draft decision tool to create an improved version of this personal activity report. Check the report for parallel construction, appropriate headings, suitable content, positiive and bias-free language, and use of the "you" attitude.

✓ CHECKLIST: Planning Business Reports

Analyzing the Situation

- ✓ Determine whether the situation merits writing a report.
- ✓ Define the problem (for analytical reports) by answering questions, factoring the problem, and forming a hypothesis.
- ✓ Develop a statement of purpose that specifically defines why you're preparing the report.
- ✓ Develop a preliminary outline, using informative headings in parallel construction.
- ✓ Prepare a work plan to clarify the tasks to be accomplished; describe any products that result from the investigation; review all project assignments, schedules, and resource requirements; and plan for following up after the report has been delivered.

Gathering Information

- ✓ Understand your topic, track key terms and phrases, and clarify your assignment.

- ✓ Locate sources of secondary information.
- ✓ Collect primary information if necessary.
- ✓ Finalize your sources by evaluating your list, quoting or paraphrasing the original material, and documenting the ideas of others.
- ✓ Analyze data to draw conclusions and develop recommendations, if requested to do so.

Adapting to the Audience

- ✓ Select the appropriate channel and medium for your report: written, oral, or electronic.
- ✓ Establish a good relationship with your audience, using the "you" attitude, emphasizing the positive, establishing your credibility, being polite, using bias-free language, and projecting the company image.

On the Job:

SOLVING COMMUNICATION DILEMMAS AT DELL COMPUTER

Michael Dell realizes that to stay on top, his company must continue to improve customer service at dell.com. You are vice president of customer relations, and Dell has asked you to plan a report that will outline ways to increase customer service and satisfaction. You'll need to conduct the necessary research, analyze the findings, and present your recommendations. From the following, choose the best responses, and be prepared to explain why your choices are best.

1. Which of the following represents the most appropriate statement of purpose for this study?

   a. The purpose of this study is to identify any customer service problems at dell.com.
   b. This study answers the following question: "What improvements in customer service can dell.com make in order to increase overall customer satisfaction?"
   c. This study identifies the dell.com customer service representatives who are most responsible for poor customer satisfaction.
   d. This study identifies steps that Dell's customer service representatives should take to change customer service practices at dell.com.

2. You have tentatively identified the following factors for analysis:

   I. To improve customer service, we need to hire more customer service representatives.
      A. Compute competitors' employee-to-sales ratio
      B. Compute our employee-to-sales ratio
   II. To improve customer service, we need to hire better customer service representatives.
      A. Assess skill level of competitors' customer service representatives
      B. Assess skill level of our customer service representatives
   III. To improve customer service, we need to retrain our customer service representatives.
      A. Review competitors' training programs
      B. Review our training programs
   IV. To improve customer service, we need to compensate and motivate our people differently.
      A. Assess competitors' compensation levels and motivational techniques
      B. Assess our compensation levels and motivational techniques

   Should you proceed with the investigation on the basis of this preliminary outline, or should you consider other approaches to factoring the problem?

   a. Proceed with this outline.
   b. Do not proceed. Factor the problem by asking customers how they perceive current customer service efforts at dell.com. In addition, ask customer service representatives what they think should be done differently.
   c. Do not proceed. Factor the problem by surveying nonbuyers to find out if current customer service efforts influenced their decision not to buy at dell.com. In addition, ask nonbuyers what they think should be done differently.
   d. Do not proceed. Factor the problem by asking customer service representatives for suggestions on how to improve customer service. In addition, ask nonbuyers and current customers what they think should be done differently.

3. Which of the following work plans is the best option for guiding your study of ways to improve customer service?

   a. Version One
      - **Statement of Problem:** As part of Dell's continuing efforts to offer the most attractive computers in the world, Michael Dell wants to improve customer service at dell.com. The challenge here is to identify service improvements that are meaningful and valuable to the customer without being too expensive or time-consuming.
      - **Purpose and Scope of Work:** The purpose of this study is to identify ways to increase customer satisfaction by improving customer service at dell.com. A four-member study team, composed of the vice president of customer relations and three customer service representatives, has been appointed to prepare a written service-improvement plan. To accomplish this objective, this study will survey customers to learn what changes they'd like to see in terms of customer service at dell.com. The team will analyze these potential improvements in terms of cost and time requirements and then will design new service procedures that customer service representatives can use to better satisfy customers.
      - **Sources and Methods of Data Collection and Analysis:** The study team will assess current customer service efforts by (1) querying customer service representatives regarding their customer service, (2) observing representatives in action dealing with customers through e-mail responses and telephone calls, (3) surveying current Dell owners regarding their purchase experiences, and (4) surveying visitors to dell.com who decide not to purchase from Dell (by intercepting a sample of these people as they leave the website). The team will also visit competitive websites to determine firsthand how they treat

customers, and the team will submit online questionnaires to a sample of computer owners and classify the results by brand name. Once all these data have been collected, the team will analyze them to determine where buyers and potential buyers consider customer service to be lacking. Finally, the team will design procedures to meet their expectations.

> **Schedule:**
>
> | | |
> |---|---|
> | Jan. 10–Jan. 30: | Query customer service representatives |
> | | Observe representatives in action |
> | | Survey current Dell owners |
> | | Survey nonbuyers at dell.com |
> | Jan. 31–Feb. 15: | Visit competitive websites |
> | | Conduct online survey of computer owners |
> | Feb. 16–Mar. 15: | Analyze data |
> | | Draft new procedures |
> | Mar. 16–Mar. 25: | Prepare final report |
> | Mar. 28: | Present to management/customer service committee |

b. Version Two

- **Statement of Problem:** Dell's customer service representatives need to get on the ball in terms of customer service, and we need to tell them what to do in order to fix their customer service shortcomings.
- **Purpose and Scope of Work:** This report will address how we plan to solve the problem. We'll design new customer service procedures and prepare a written report that customer service representatives can learn from.
- **Sources and Methods of Data Collection:** We plan to employ the usual methods of collecting data, including direct observation and surveys.

> **Schedule:**
>
> | | |
> |---|---|
> | Jan. 10–Feb 15: | Collect data |
> | Feb. 16–Mar. 1: | Analyze data |
> | Mar. 2–Mar. 15: | Draft new procedures |
> | Mar. 16–Mar 25: | Prepare final report |
> | Mar. 28: | Present to management/Customer service committee |

c. Version Three

- **Task 1—Query customer service representatives:** We will interview a sampling of customer service representatives to find out what steps they take to ensure customer satisfaction. Dates: Jan. 10–Jan. 20.
- **Task 2—Observe representatives in action:** We will observe a sampling of customer service representatives as they work with potential buyers and current owners, in order to learn firsthand what steps employees typically take. Dates: Jan. 21–Jan. 30.
- **Task 3—Survey current Dell owners:** Using a sample of names from Dell's database of current owners, we'll ask owners how they felt about the purchase process when they bought their computers and how they feel they've been treated since then. We'll also ask them to suggest steps we could take to improve service. Dates: Jan. 15–Feb. 15.
- **Task 4—Survey nonbuyers at dell.com:** While we are observing customer service representatives, we will also approach visitors at dell.com who leave the site without making a purchase. As visitors exit the site, we'll present a quick online survey, asking them what they think about Dell's customer service policies and practices and whether these had any bearing on their decisions not to a buy a Dell product. Dates: Jan. 21–Jan. 30.
- **Task 5—Visit competitive websites:** Under the guise of shoppers looking for new computers, we will visit a selection of competitive websites to discover how they treat customers and whether they offer any special service that Dell doesn't. Dates: Jan. 31–Feb. 15.
- **Task 6—Conduct online survey of computer owners:** Using Internet-based technology, we will survey a sampling of computer owners (of all brands). We will then sort the answers by brand of computer owned to see which dealers are offering which services. Dates: Jan. 15–Feb. 15.
- **Task 7—Analyze data:** Once we've collected all these data, we'll analyze them to identify (1) services that customers would like to see Dell offer, (2) services offered by competitors that aren't offered by Dell, and (3) services currently offered by Dell that may not be all that important to customers. Dates: Feb. 16–Mar. 1.
- **Task 8—Draft new procedures:** From the data we've analyzed, we'll select new services that should be considered by dell.com. We'll also assess the time and money burdens that these services are likely to present, so that management can see whether each new service will yield a positive return on investment. Dates: Mar. 2–Mar. 15.
- **Task 9—Prepare final report:** This is essentially a documentation task, during which we'll describe our work, make our recommendations, and prepare a formal report. Dates: Mar. 16–Mar. 25.
- **Task 10—Present to management/customer relations committee:** We'll summarize our findings and recommendations and will make the full report available to dealers at the quarterly meeting. Date: Mar. 28.

d. Version Four

- **Problem:** To identify meaningful customer service improvements that can be implemented by Dell Computer at dell.com.

- **Data Collection:** Use direct observation and online surveys to gather details about customer service at dell.com and at competing websites. Have the study team survey current Dell owners and people who visited dell.com but did not buy, and send an online questionnaire to computer owners.
  Schedule:
  Step 1:   Data collection. Work will begin on January 10 and end on February 15.

Step 2:   Data analysis. Work will start on February 16 and end on March 1.

Step 3:   Drafting new procedures. Work will start on March 2 and end on March 15.

Step 4:   Preparation of the final report. Work will start on March 16 and end on March 25.

Step 5:   Presentation of the final report. The report will be presented to management and the customer service committee on March 28.[16]

Learning Objectives Checkup

To assess your understanding of the principles in this chapter, read each learning objective and study the accompanying exercises. For fill-in items, write the missing text in the blank provided; for multiple choice items, circle the letter of the correct answer. You can check your responses against the answer key on page AK-2.

Objective 10.1: Distinguish between informational and analytical business reports, and review the six common types.

1. Which of the following is *not* an example of an informational report?
   a. Monitor/control report
   b. Progress report
   c. Compliance report
   d. Problem-solving report
2. An example of an analytical report would be
   a. A corporation's annual report
   b. A proposal to provide services to a corporation
   c. A corporation's monthly sales report
   d. A report to a client, documenting progress on a project

Objective 10.2: Differentiate between defining the problem and developing the purpose statement for an analytical report.

3. Which of the following is *not* part of defining the problem when planning an analytical report?
   a. Factoring the problem
   b. Forming a hypothesis
   c. Stating it as an infinitive phrase
   d. Determining how and when the problem started
4. Which of the following is a good example of a statement of purpose for an analytical report?
   a. To compare potential sites for a new bank branch in Los Angeles County and recommend the best location
   b. To update the clients on the status of renovations on their law offices
   c. To summarize information obtained at the book industry trade show last weekend
   d. A proposal to eliminate costly shipping charges

Objective 10.3: Summarize the uses of a preliminary outline, and compare it with the final outline.

5. Your preliminary outline
   a. Guides your research effort
   b. Is a working draft that you will modify as you go along
   c. Gives you a visual diagram of your report
   d. Does all of the above
6. Your final outline should
   a. Be identical to your preliminary outline
   b. Consist of descriptive, not informative, headings
   c. Be set up so that items of the same level are grammatically parallel
   d. Do all of the above

Objective 10.4: Identify seven elements often included in a formal work plan.

7. Which of the following is *not* an element usually included in a formal work plan?
   a. Statement of the problem
   b. A copy of the RFP
   c. A preliminary outline of the report
   d. A list of tasks to be accomplished

Objective 10.5: Discuss the differences between secondary and primary information, including where to find and how to gather each type.

8. Which of the following is *not* a source of secondary information?
   a. Experiments
   b. Government publications
   c. Websites
   d. Magazines and journals
9. When searching for business information on the Internet, the best approach is to
   a. Start your Internet search first, before checking other sources of information about your topic
   b. Try to be as general as possible in your search wording so that you will turn up the maximum number of hits
   c. Use well-known, commercially backed search engines
   d. Do all of the above

10. Which of the following is *not* a main method for collecting primary information?
    a. Conducting surveys
    b. Making formal observations
    c. Conducting interviews
    d. Searching electronic databases

Objective 10.6: Describe what is involved in preparing an effective survey questionnaire.

11. Surveys are useful only when they are both
    a. Well-documented and well-researched
    b. Reliable and valid
    c. Open-ended and closed-ended
    d. Thorough and exhaustive

12. Which of the following is *not* a guideline for designing effective survey questions?
    a. Design questions whose answers are easily tabulated or analyzed.
    b. Ask only one thing at a time.
    c. Fulfill the original statement of purpose.
    d. Pretest your questions.

Objective 10.7: Define information interviews, and list four types of interview questions.

13. An information interview is
    a. A type of secondary research
    b. A planned conversation with a predetermined purpose that involves asking and answering questions
    c. An interview designed by human resources professionals to gain information from employees about the inner workings of an organization
    d. All of the above

14. Which of the following is an example of an open-ended question?
    a. "Are you pleased with the results of your latest ad campaign?"
    b. "Did you see an increase in first-quarter sales as a result of your latest ad campaign?"
    c. "What were the goals of your latest ad campaign?"
    d. All of the above are open-ended questions.

15. During an interview, you ask the following: "So you're saying that you expect your online sales to increase significantly this year, is that right?" This question is an example of
    a. A restatement question
    b. A closed-ended question
    c. A direct open-ended question
    d. An open-ended question

Objective 10.8: Name nine criteria for evaluating the credibility of an information source.

16. Which of the following is *not* one of the criteria for the credibility of a source?
    a. Does the source have a reputation for honesty and reliability?
    b. Can the material be verified independently?
    c. Where did the source get its information?
    d. Does the source reinforce my hypothesis or approach?

Objective 10.9: Explain the difference between drawing a conclusion and developing a recommendation.

17. A sound conclusion should
    a. Fulfill the original statement of purpose
    b. Be based strictly on the information in the rest of the report
    c. Be logical
    d. Do all of the above

18. Which of the following is an example of a recommendation as opposed to a conclusion?
    a. Attending trade shows costs our company too much money.
    b. We should reduce the number of trade shows we attend to just the Chicago and San Diego events.
    c. The San Diego and Chicago trade shows are the key events in our industry.
    d. It is important to attend at least some of the large trade shows in our industry.

Apply Your Knowledge

1. Why are unsolicited proposals more challenging to write than solicited proposals?
2. Why must you be careful when citing information from a webpage?
3. Why do you need to evaluate your sources?
4. After an exhaustive study of an important problem, you have reached a conclusion that you believe your company's management will reject. What will you do? Explain your answer.
5. **Ethical Choices** If you want to make a specific recommendation following your research, should you include information that might support a different recommendation? Explain your answer.

Practice Your Knowledge

DOCUMENT FOR ANALYSIS

The Securities and Exchange Commission (SEC) requires all public companies to file a comprehensive annual report (form 10-K) electronically. Many companies post links to these reports on their websites along with links to other company reports. Visit the website of Dell at dell.com and view the company's most recent annual reports: 10-K and Year in Review. (To view the reports, follow the links at the homepage to About Dell, Investor Relations, and Annual Reports.) Compare the style and format of the two reports. For which audience(s) is the Year in Review targeted? Who besides the SEC might be interested in the Annual Report 10-K? Which report do you find easier to read? More interesting? More detailed?

Exercises

For live links to all websites discussed in this chapter, visit this text's website at www.prenhall.com/thill. Just log on, select Chapter 10, and click on "Student Resources." Locate the page or the URL related to the material in the text. For the "Learning More on the Web" exercises, you'll also find navigational directions. Click on the live link to the site.

10.1 **Understanding Business Reports and Proposals: How Companies Use Reports** Interview several people working in a career you might like to enter, and ask them about the written reports they receive and prepare. How do these reports tie in to the decision-making process? Who reads the reports they prepare? Summarize your findings in writing, give them to your instructor, and be prepared to discuss them with the class.

10.2 **Understanding Business Reports and Proposals: Report Classification** Using the information presented in this chapter, identify the purpose of the following reports. In addition, write a brief paragraph about each, explaining who the audience is likely to be, what type of data would be used, and whether conclusions and recommendations would be appropriate.
   a. A statistical study of the pattern of violent crime in a large city during the last five years
   b. A report prepared by a seed company demonstrating the benefits of its seed corn for farmers
   c. A report prepared by an independent testing agency evaluating various types of cold remedies sold without prescription
   d. A trip report submitted at the end of a week by a traveling salesperson
   e. A report indicating how 45 acres of undeveloped land could be converted into an industrial park
   f. An annual report to be sent to the shareholders of a large corporation
   g. A report from a U.S. National Park wildlife officer to Washington, D.C., headquarters showing the status of the California condor (an endangered species)
   h. A written report by a police officer who has just completed an arrest

10.3 **Internet** Government reports vary in purpose and structure. Read through the Department of Education's report on how population growth is affecting school enrollment, posted online at www.ed.gov/pubs/bbecho00/index.html. What is the purpose of this document? Does the title communicate this purpose? What type of report is this?

10.4 **Informational Reports: Monitor/Control Report** Imagine you're the manager of campus recruiting for Nortel, a Canadian telecommunications firm. Each of your four recruiters interviews up to 11 college seniors every day. What kind of personal activity report can you design to track the results of these interviews? List the areas you would want each recruiter to report on, and explain how each would help you manage the recruiting process (and the recruiters) more effectively.

10.5 **Informational Reports: Policy/Procedure Report** You're the vice president of operations for a Florida fast-food chain. In the aftermath of a major hurricane, you're drafting a report on the emergency procedures to be followed by personnel in each restaurant when storm warnings are in effect. Answer who, what, when, where, why, and how, and then prepare a one-page draft of your report.

10.6 **Analytical Reports: Unsolicited Proposal** You're getting ready to launch a new lawn-care business that offers mowing, fertilizing, weeding, and other services. The lawn surrounding a nearby shopping center looks as if it could use better care, so you target that business for your first unsolicited proposal. To help prepare this proposal, write your answers to these questions:
   a. What questions will you need to answer before you can write a proposal to solve the reader's problem? Be as specific as possible.
   b. What customer benefits will you include in your proposal?
   c. Will you use a letter or memo format for your proposal? Explain your answer.

10.7 **Teamwork: Unsolicited Proposal** Break into small groups and identify an operational problem occurring at your campus involving either registration, university housing, food services, parking, or library services. Then develop a workable solution to that problem. Finally, develop a list of pertinent facts that your team will need to gather to convince the reader that the problem exists and that your solution will work.

10.8 **Analyzing the Situation: Statement of Purpose** Sales at The Style Shop, a clothing store for men, have declined for the third month in a row. Your boss is not sure whether this decline is due to a weak economy or to another unknown reason. She has asked you to investigate the situation and to submit a report to her highlighting some possible reasons for the decline. Develop a statement of purpose for your report.

10.9 **Preparing the Work Plan** Using the situation described in Exercise 10.6, assume that you're the shopping center's facilities manager. You report to the general manager, who must approve any new contracts for lawn service. Before you contract for lawn care, you want to prepare a formal study of the current state of your lawn's health. The report will include conclusions and recommendations for your boss's consideration. Draft a work plan, including the problem statement, the statement of purpose and scope, a description of what will result from your investigation, the sources and methods of data collection, and a preliminary outline.

10.10 Understanding Your Topic: Subquestions Your boss has asked you to do some research on franchising. Actually, he's thinking about purchasing a few Subway franchises, and he needs some information. Visit www.amazon.com and review the site. On the homepage, perform a keyword search on "franchise." Explore some of the books by clicking on "read more about this title."

a. Use the information to develop a list of subquestions to help you narrow your focus.

b. Write down the names of three books you might purchase for your boss.

c. How can this website assist you with your research efforts?

10.11 Finding Secondary Information Using online, database, or printed sources, find the following information. Be sure to properly cite your source using the formats discussed in Appendix B. (*Hint:* Start with Figure 10.8, Major Business Resources.)

a. Contact information for the American Management Association

b. Median weekly earnings of men and women by occupation

c. Current market share for Perrier water

d. Performance ratios for office supply retailers

e. Annual stock performance for Hewlett-Packard

f. Number of franchise outlets in the United States

g. Composition of the U.S. workforce by profession

10.12 Finding Secondary Information Businesspeople have to know where to look for secondary information when they conduct research. Prepare a list of the most important magazines and professional journals in the following fields of study:

a. Marketing/advertising

b. Insurance

c. Communications

d. Accounting

10.13 Finding Information: Industry Information Locate the NAICS codes for the following industries:

a. Hotels and motels

b. Breakfast cereals

c. Bottled water

d. Automatic vending machines

10.14 Finding Information: Company Information Select any public company and find the following information:

a. Names of the company's current officers

b. List of the company's products or services

c. Current issues in the company's industry

d. Outlook for the company's industry as a whole

10.15 Finding Information: Primary Information Deciding how to collect primary data is an important part of the research process. Which one or more of the five methods of data collection (examining documents, making observations, surveying people, conducting experiments, and performing interviews) would you use if you were researching these questions?

a. Has the litter problem on campus been reduced since the cafeteria began offering fewer take-out choices this year than in past years?

b. Has the school attracted more transfer students since it waived the formal application process and allowed students at other colleges simply to send their transcripts and a one-page letter of application?

c. Have the number of traffic accidents at the school's main entrance been reduced since a traffic light was installed?

d. Has student satisfaction with the campus bookstore improved now that students can order their books over the Internet and pick them up at several campus locations?

10.16 Finding Information: Interviews Plan to conduct an informational interview with a professional working in your chosen field of study. Plan the structure of the interview and create a set of interview questions. Conduct the interview. Using the information you gathered, write a memo to another student describing the tasks, advantages, and disadvantages of jobs in this field of study. (Your reader is a person who also plans to pursue a career in this field of study.)

10.17 Teamwork: Evaluating Sources Break into small groups and surf the Internet to find websites that provide business information such as company or industry news, trends, analyses, facts, or performance data. Using the criteria discussed under "Evaluating Your Sources" (see pp. 336–338), evaluate the credibility of the information presented at these websites.

10.18 Quoting and Paraphrasing Select an article from a business journal such as *BusinessWeek, Fortune*, or *Forbes*. Read the article and highlight the article's key points. Summarize the main idea of the article, paraphrasing the key points.

10.19 Documenting Sources Select five business articles from sources such as journals, books, newspapers, or websites. Develop a resource list using Appendix B as a guideline.

10.20 Adapting Reports to the Audience Review the progress report in Figure 10.2. Give concrete examples of how this report establishes a good relationship with its audience. Consider such things as using the "you" attitude, emphasizing the positive, establishing credibility, being polite, using bias-free language, and projecting a good company image.

Expand Your Knowledge

LEARNING MORE ON THE WEB

Pointers for Business Plans www.bizplanit.com
What's involved in a business plan? Bizplanit.com offers tips and advice, consulting services, a free e-mail newsletter, and a sample virtual business plan. You'll find suggestions on what details and how much information to include in each section of a business plan. You can explore the site's numerous links to business-plan books and software, online magazines, educational programs, government resources, and women's and minority resources, and even find answers to your business-plan questions.

ACTIVITIES

What are the components of a business plan? What do readers of a plan look for? What common mistakes should you avoid? For answers to these questions and to learn more about the function and content of business plans, log on to bizplanit.com.

1. Why is the executive summary such an important section of a business plan? What kind of information is contained in the executive summary?

2. What is the product/services section? What information should it contain? List some of the common errors to avoid when planning this part.

3. What type of business planning should you describe in the exit strategy section? Why?

EXPLORING THE WEB ON YOUR OWN

Review these chapter-related websites on your own to learn more about planning business reports.

1. If your report writing involves researching other companies, Wall Street Research network, www.wsrn.com, is one of the most comprehensive company information sites on the Internet.

2. Searching for information on a company or industry? Corporate Information, at www.corporateinformation.com, is a good place to begin your online research.

3. Visit Microsoft's Complete Internet Guide at www.microsoft.com/insider/internet/default.htm, and take the web tutorial to improve your online researching skills.

Learn Interactively

INTERACTIVE STUDY GUIDE

Go to the Companion Website at www.prenhall.com/bovee. For Chapter 10, take advantage of the interactive "Study Guide" to test your knowledge of the chapter. Get instant feedback on whether you need additional studying. Also, visit this site's "Study Hall" where you'll find an abundance of valuable resources that will help you succeed in this course.

PEAK PERFORMANCE GRAMMAR AND MECHANICS

To improve your skill with periods, question marks, and exclamation points, visit this text's website at www.prenhall.com/onekey. Click "Peak Performance Grammar and Mechanics," then click "Punctuation II." Take the Pretest to deter-

mine whether you have any weak areas. Review those areas in the Refresher Course, and take the Follow-Up Test to check your grasp of periods, question marks, and exclamation points. For advanced practice, take the Advanced Test. Finally, for additional reinforcement, go to the "Improve Your Grammar, Mechanics, and Usage" section that follows, and complete those exercises.

Improve Your Grammar, Mechanics, and Usage

The following exercises help you improve your knowledge of and power over English grammar, mechanics, and usage. Turn to the "Handbook of Grammar, Mechanics, and Usage" at the end of this textbook and review all of Sections 2.1 (Periods), 2.2 (Question Marks), and 2.3 (Exclamation Points). Then look at the following 10 items. Circle the letter of the preferred choice in the following groups of sentences. (Answers to these exercises appear on page AK-3–AK-4.)

1. a. Dr. Eleanor H Hutton has requested information on TaskMasters, Inc.?
   b. Dr. Eleanor H. Hutton has requested information on TaskMasters, Inc.

2. a. That qualifies us as a rapidly growing new company, don't you think?
   b. That qualifies us as a rapidly growing new company, don't you think.

3. a. Our president is a C.P.A. On your behalf, I asked him why he started the firm.
   b. Our president is a CPA. On your behalf, I asked him why he started the firm.
4. a. Contact me at 1358 N. Parsons Ave., Tulsa, OK 74204.
   b. Contact me at 1358 N. Parsons Ave, Tulsa, OK. 74204.
5. a. Jeb asked, "Why does he want to know! Maybe he plans to become a competitor."
   b. Jeb asked, "Why does he want to know? Maybe he plans to become a competitor!"
6. a. The debt load fluctuates with the movement of the U.S. prime rate.
   b. The debt load fluctuates with the movement of the US prime rate.

7. a. Is consumer loyalty extinct? Yes and No!
   b. Is consumer loyalty extinct? Yes and No.
8. a. Will you please send us a check today so that we can settle your account.
   b. Will you please send us a check today so that we can settle your account?
9. a. Will you be able to speak at the conference, or should we find someone else.
   b. Will you be able to speak at the conference, or should we find someone else?
10. a. So I ask you, "When will we admit defeat?" Never!
    b. So I ask you, "When will we admit defeat"? Never!

Chapter 11

Writing Business Reports and Proposals

Learning Objectives

AFTER STUDYING THIS CHAPTER, YOU WILL BE ABLE TO

1 Name four decisions you must make before drafting your business report or proposal

2 Compare and contrast the structures of informational and analytical reports

3 List five of the most popular types of visuals and indicate when to use them

4 Discuss five design principles to keep in mind when preparing visuals

5 Describe three ways to tie visuals to your text

6 List four questions to ask yourself when checking visuals

7 Review four tasks to keep in mind while composing your report or proposal

8 Identify the goals to accomplish in the opening of your reports, solicited proposals, and unsolicited proposals

9 Summarize the various goals to accomplish in the close of your reports and proposals

On the Job:

COMMUNICATING AT FEDEX

DELIVERING ON TIME, EVERY TIME

Imagine collecting, transporting, and delivering 5.3 million letters and packages each day. Now imagine that every one of these parcels absolutely, positively has to arrive at its destination when expected. Living up to this exacting standard day in and day out presents founder and CEO Frederick W. Smith and his entire management team with a variety of communication challenges, not the least of which is distributing information inside and outside this huge organization.

In the beginning, Fred Smith used business reports to raise the money to start his company, and since then reports have remained important as he and his managers have built FedEx into a global business with $22 billion in annual revenues. FedEx delivers throughout the United States and to more than 210 countries around the world. To make those deliveries on time, every time, the company operates more than 650 airplanes, maintains a fleet of 98,950 trucks and vans, and supports a workforce of more than 218,000 employees and contractors around the world. Making sure that all these people have the information they need in the form they need it is a tough assignment.

For example, because of FedEx's heavy orientation toward customer satisfaction, the company strongly emphasizes training. So the human resources department must prepare analytical reports to justify expenditures such as the computer-networking equipment it needs to support its interactive training program. The internal auditors at FedEx must prepare both informational and analyti-

At FedEx, reports of all kinds are used to track both system and employee performance, as well as to assemble information needed for making managerial decisions. Not only does Frederick Smith read innumerable reports, he wrote a very famous one, which detailed the idea of his air express delivery service and persuaded investors to fund him.

cal reports to study how the company controls its finances, daily operations, and legal compliance.

But the challenge doesn't stop there. FedEx also battles a host of rivals, including United Parcel Service (UPS), the U.S. Postal Service, Airborne Express, DHL, and other delivery companies. Competition is fierce, so FedEx is constantly on the lookout for information on competitors and innovative ways to serve its own customers better.

In addition to gathering information, Smith and his team are also responsible for reporting information to customers. For example, FedEx helps commercial and industrial customers by taking over their warehouse and inventory chores. Instead of just acting as a shipping service, FedEx operates as part of the customer's organization, so it must generate reports that give its customers the information they need.

Smith and his management team have their work cut out for them—monitoring and controlling company operations, training new employees, tracking competitor service and performance, making a host of decisions about how to serve customers better. All these activities require the communication of timely, accurate information, and much of that information comes in the form of reports. To keep the business running smoothly, maintain satisfied customers, and hold competitors at bay, the people at FedEx organize and compose reports of all kinds.[1]

www.fedex.com

ORGANIZING BUSINESS REPORTS AND PROPOSALS

The second step of the report writing process involves organizing and composing your message. Before you can compose a business report or proposal, you must organize the material you've collected and arrange it in a logical order that meets your audience's needs. Fred Smith advises that before you draft the first word, you make four important decisions about your report or proposal: Determine its format, length, order, and structure.

Deciding on Format and Length

You may present a report in one of four formats.

At times, the person requesting the report makes the decision about format and length. Such guidance is often the case with monitor/control reports, procedural reports, proposals, progress reports, and compliance reports. When selecting a format for your report, you have four options:

- **Preprinted form.** Used for fill-in-the-blank reports. Most are relatively short (five or fewer pages) and deal with routine information, often mainly numerical. Use this format when it's requested by the person authorizing the report.

- **Letter.** Commonly used for reports of five or fewer pages that are directed to outsiders. These reports include all the normal parts of a letter, but they may also have headings, footnotes, tables, and figures.

- **Memo.** Commonly used for short (fewer than 10 pages), informal reports distributed within an organization. Like longer reports, they often have internal headings and sometimes include visual aids. Memos exceeding 10 pages are sometimes referred to as *memo reports* to distinguish them from their shorter cousins.

- **Manuscript.** Commonly used for reports that require a formal approach, whether a few pages or several hundred. As length increases, reports in manuscript format require more elements before the text (prefatory parts) and after (supplementary parts). Chapter 12 explains these elements in detail.

As mentioned earlier, the option you choose depends on your subject, your purpose, and your relationship with your audience. Tell your readers what they need to know in a format that is easy for them to use.

Don't judge the quality or content of a report by its size. Like Smart Cars, smart, compact reports get you where you need to be—easily and conveniently.

Choosing the Direct or Indirect Approach

The direct approach saves time and makes the report easier to understand by giving readers the main idea first.

The direct approach is by far the most popular and convenient for business reports; it saves time and makes the rest of the report easier to follow. It also produces a more forceful report, because stating your conclusions confidently in the beginning makes you sound sure of yourself. However, confidence may be misconstrued as arrogance, especially if you're a junior member of a status-conscious organization. Although the indirect approach gives you a chance to prove your points and gradually overcome

Global companies often post business reports on the web. Microsoft's annual report is prepared for investors and posted on the company's website in 11 languages (including French for Canadian readers and Portuguese for Brazilian readers). Readers simply click on the link for the language they want—and then read on (see www.microsoft.com).

your audience's reservations, the longer the message, the less effective an indirect approach is likely to be. Therefore, carefully consider report length before deciding on the direct or indirect approach.

The indirect approach helps you overcome resistance by withholding the main idea until later in the report; however, carefully consider length before choosing it.

Both approaches have merit, so businesspeople often combine them, revealing their conclusions and recommendations as they go along, rather than putting them first or last. Figure 11–1 presents the introductions from two reports with the same general outline. In the direct version, a series of statements summarize the conclusion reached about each main topic in the outline. In the indirect version, the same topics are introduced in the same order but without drawing any conclusions about them. Instead, the conclusions appear in the body of the report.

Businesspeople often combine the direct and indirect approaches.

Regardless of the format, length, or order you use, you must still decide how your ideas will be subdivided and developed. You must choose the most appropriate structure—the one that suits your topic and goals and that makes the most sense to your audience.

Structuring Informational Reports

Informational reports provide nothing more than facts. Most readers will respond unemotionally, so you can use the direct approach. However, you need to present the facts logically and accurately so that readers will understand exactly what you mean and be able to use your information easily. For example, when describing a machine, make report headings correspond to each component. Or when describing an event, discuss it chronologically. Let the nature of your subject dictate the structure of your

Reader reaction is rarely an issue in informational reports.

FIGURE 11–1
Direct Approach Versus
Indirect Approach in an
Introduction

THE DIRECT APPROACH

Since the company's founding 25 years ago, we have provided regular repair service for all our electric appliances. This service has been an important selling point as well as a source of pride for our employees. However, we are paying a high price for our image. Last year, we lost $500,000 on our repair business.

Because of your concern over these losses, you have asked me to study the pros and cons of discontinuing our repair service. With the help of John Hudson and Susan Lefkowitz, I have studied the issue for the past two weeks and have come to the conclusion that we have been embracing an expensive, impractical tradition.

By withdrawing from the electric appliance repair business, we can substantially improve our financial performance without damaging our reputation with customers. This conclusion is based on three basic points that are covered in the following pages:
- It is highly unlikely that we will ever be able to make a profit in the repair business.
- Service is no longer an important selling point with customers.
- Closing down the service operation will create few internal problems.

THE INDIRECT APPROACH

Since the company's founding 25 years ago, we have provided repair service for all our electric appliances. This service has been an important selling point as well as a source of pride for our employees. However, the repair business itself has consistently lost money.

Because of your concern over these losses, you have asked me to study the pros and cons of discontinuing our repair service. With the help of John Hudson and Susan Lefkowitz, I have studied the issue for the past two weeks. The following pages present my findings for your review. Three basic questions are addressed:
- What is the extent of our losses, and what can we do to turn the business around?
- Would withdrawal hurt our sales of electrical appliances?
- What would be the internal repercussions of closing down the repair business?

informational reports. Use a **topical organization**, and arrange material according to one of the following:

- **Importance.** If you're reviewing five products, you might organize your report according to product sales, from highest to lowest.

- **Sequence.** If you're studying a process, discuss it step by step—1, 2, 3, and so on.

- **Chronology.** When investigating a chain of events, organize the study according to what happened in January, what happened in February, and so on.

- **Spatial orientation.** If you're explaining how a physical object works, describe it from left to right (or right to left in some cultures), top to bottom, outside to inside.

- **Geography.** If location is important, organize your study according to geography, perhaps by region of a country or by area of a city.

- **Category.** If you're asked to review several distinct aspects of a subject, look at one category at a time, such as sales, profit, cost, or investment.

Arrange informational reports according to topic.

Some informational reports (especially compliance reports and internal reports) are prepared on preprinted forms; they are organized according to the instructions supplied by the person requesting the information.

Structuring Analytical Reports

The structure of analytical reports depends on audience reaction.

For analytical reports, your choice of structural approach depends on the reaction you anticipate. When you expect your audience to agree with you, use a structure that focuses attention on conclusions and recommendations. When you expect your audience to disagree with you or to be hostile, use a structure that focuses attention on the reasons behind your conclusions and recommendations. Thus, the three most common approaches to structuring analytical reports are (1) focusing on conclusions, (2) focusing on recommendations, and (3) focusing on logical arguments.

Focusing on Conclusions When writing an analytical report for people from your own organization who are likely to accept your conclusions, you can structure your report around conclusions, using a direct approach. However, the direct approach does have some drawbacks. Not only can strong statements at the beginning intensify reader resistance, but focusing on conclusions may make everything seem too simple. Your readers could criticize your report as being superficial: "Why didn't you consider this option?" or "Where did you get this number?"

> When readers are receptive and concerned with conclusions, focus on conclusions as your main points—but only when your credibility is high.

You're generally better off taking the direct approach in a report only when your readers know from experience that you'll do a thorough job, when they trust your judgment and are likely to accept your conclusions. When you focus on conclusions, those readers mainly interested in your conclusions can grasp them quickly, and those readers who want to know more about your analysis can look further to examine the data you provide.

Cynthia Zolonka works on the human resources staff of a bank in Houston, Texas. Her company decided to have an outside firm handle its employee training, and a year after the outsourcing arrangement was established, Zolonka was asked to evaluate the results. She explains: "Moving our training programs to an outside supplier was a tough—and controversial—decision for the entire company. Some people were convinced that outsourcing would never work; others thought it might save money but would hurt training quality. I took special care to thoroughly analyze the data, and I supported my conclusion with objective answers, not personal opinions." Figure 11–2 is the outline of Zolonka's report, which uses the direct approach to focus on conclusions.

Focusing on Recommendations A slightly different approach is useful when your readers want to know what they ought to do (as opposed to what they ought to

> When readers are receptive and concerned about what action to take, focus on your recommendations as your main points.

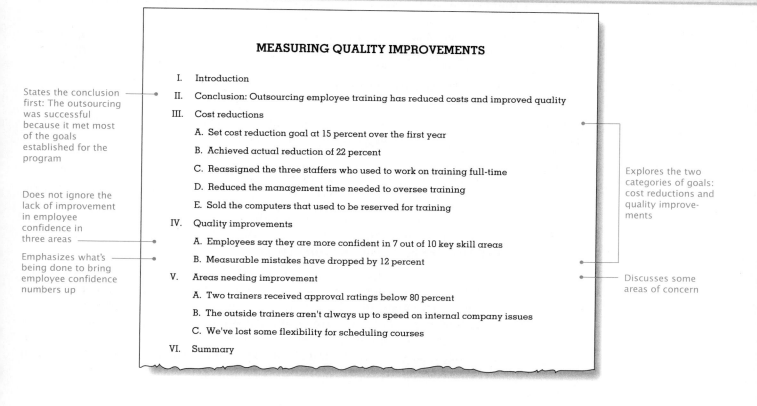

FIGURE 11–2
Effective Outline of an Analytical Report Focusing on Conclusions

MEASURING QUALITY IMPROVEMENTS

I. Introduction

II. Conclusion: Outsourcing employee training has reduced costs and improved quality

III. Cost reductions
    A. Set cost reduction goal at 15 percent over the first year
    B. Achieved actual reduction of 22 percent
    C. Reassigned the three staffers who used to work on training full-time
    D. Reduced the management time needed to oversee training
    E. Sold the computers that used to be reserved for training

IV. Quality improvements
    A. Employees say they are more confident in 7 out of 10 key skill areas
    B. Measurable mistakes have dropped by 12 percent

V. Areas needing improvement
    A. Two trainers received approval ratings below 80 percent
    B. The outside trainers aren't always up to speed on internal company issues
    C. We've lost some flexibility for scheduling courses

VI. Summary

States the conclusion first: The outsourcing was successful because it met most of the goals established for the program

Does not ignore the lack of improvement in employee confidence in three areas

Emphasizes what's being done to bring employee confidence numbers up

Explores the two categories of goals: cost reductions and quality improvements

Discusses some areas of concern

conclude). You'll often be asked to solve a problem rather than just study it. So the actions you want your readers to take become the main divisions of your report.

When structuring a report around recommendations, use the direct approach as you would for a report that focuses on conclusions. Then unfold your recommendations using a series of five steps:

Unfold recommendations in steps.

1. Establish the need for action in the opening, generally by briefly describing the problem or opportunity.

2. Introduce the benefit that can be achieved, without providing any details.

3. List the steps (recommendations) required to achieve the benefit, using action verbs for emphasis.

4. Explain each step more fully, giving details on procedures, costs, and benefits.

5. Summarize the recommendations.

After losing market share to competing retailers with websites, the board of directors of a Chicago-based retail chain asked Alycia Jenn, the business development manager, to make a recommendation about whether the company should set up a retailing site on the web and, if so, how the site could be implemented. As Jenn noted, "Setting up shop on the Internet is a big decision for our company. We don't have the computer staff that our larger competitors have, and our business development team is stretched rather thin already. On the other hand, more and more people are shopping online, and we don't want to be left out of this mode of retailing. After studying the issue for several weeks, I concluded that we should go ahead with a site but that we should be careful about how we implement it."

Look back at Jenn's memo in Figure 10–3 (on pp. 314–315). She uses her recommendations to structure her thoughts. Because the directors wouldn't be interested in a lot of technical detail, she keeps her discussion at a pretty high level. She also maintains a formal and respectful tone for this audience.

When readers are unreceptive, analytical reports may be organized around logical arguments (indirect approach).

Focusing on Logical Arguments   When your purpose is to collaborate with your audience and solve a problem or to persuade them to take a definite action, your structural approach must highlight logical arguments that focus the audience's attention on what needs to be done. Use the indirect approach and a logical organization to encourage your readers to weigh all the facts before you present your conclusions or recommendations. Arrange your ideas around the reasoning behind your report's conclusions and recommendations. Three basic structural approaches may be used to argue your case:

Three organizational approaches are useful for convincing skeptical readers that your conclusions and recommendations are well founded.

- **The 2 + 2 = 4 approach.** This versatile approach convinces readers by demonstrating that everything adds up. Your arguments often fall naturally into this pattern. Your main points are the main reasons behind your conclusions and recommendations, and you support each reason with evidence. For example, Binh Phan was asked to analyze his company's ability to sell to its largest customers: "We sell sporting goods to retail chains across the country . . . but we've had less success with large national customers than with smaller local or regional companies." Because his plan would be controversial, Phan's thinking had to be clear and easy to follow (see his outline in Figure 11–3).

- **The scientific method.** To discover whether an explanation is true or which option will solve a problem, this method shows the strengths and weaknesses of all ideas. The main drawback is that you must discuss all alternatives, even though many may end up being irrelevant—and the more ideas your cover, the greater your risk of confusing readers. In the opening, you state the problem and briefly describe the hypothetical solutions. In the body, you discuss each alternative and offer evidence that either confirms it or rules it out. In the close,

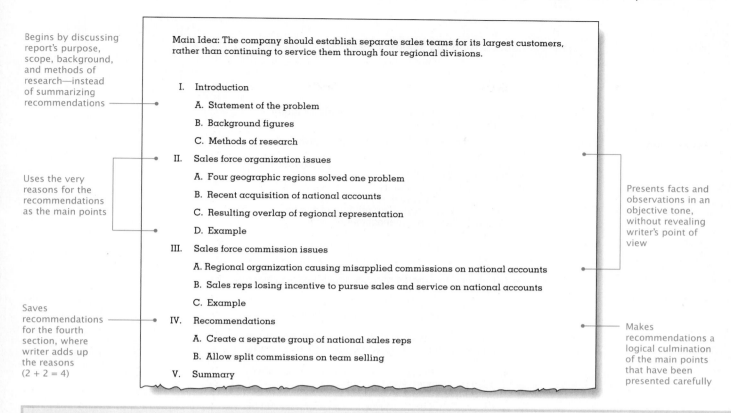

Begins by discussing report's purpose, scope, background, and methods of research—instead of summarizing recommendations

Uses the very reasons for the recommendations as the main points

Saves recommendations for the fourth section, where writer adds up the reasons (2 + 2 = 4)

Presents facts and observations in an objective tone, without revealing writer's point of view

Makes recommendations a logical culmination of the main points that have been presented carefully

Main Idea: The company should establish separate sales teams for its largest customers, rather than continuing to service them through four regional divisions.

I. Introduction

    A. Statement of the problem

    B. Background figures

    C. Methods of research

II. Sales force organization issues

    A. Four geographic regions solved one problem

    B. Recent acquisition of national accounts

    C. Resulting overlap of regional representation

    D. Example

III. Sales force commission issues

    A. Regional organization causing misapplied commissions on national accounts

    B. Sales reps losing incentive to pursue sales and service on national accounts

    C. Example

IV. Recommendations

    A. Create a separate group of national sales reps

    B. Allow split commissions on team selling

V. Summary

FIGURE 11–3
Effective Outline of Analytical Report Using the 2 + 2 = 4 Approach

you summarize your findings, indicate the valid solutions, and state your recommendations. Fredrik Swensen was asked to help his firm decide which franchise operations to invest in: "We wanted to buy 45 or 50 additional outlets, and we had a good idea of how to evaluate them." By analyzing each alternative, Swensen hoped to bring about a consensus (see his outline in Figure 11–4).

- **The yardstick approach.** Similar to the scientific method, this approach reviews all alternatives against the same standard (or yardstick). After stating the problem and briefly describing hypothetical solutions, you set up the criteria that must be met to solve the problem. In the body you evaluate each alternative in relation to these criteria, and the main points are either the criteria themselves or the alternatives. One drawback is that this approach can be boring, so try to minimize repetition by discussing only the most significant differences. Another drawback is that all readers must agree on which criteria to use. When J. C. Hartley was asked to analyze the feasibility of expanding into new markets, the criteria had been agreed on before she began her investigation: "Our irrigation equipment had been so successful in the agricultural market that we needed to investigate markets such as commercial buildings and residences." (See Figure 11–5 on page 361.)

These three approaches are not mutually exclusive. Essentially, you choose an approach that matches the reasoning process you used to arrive at your conclusions. That way you can lead readers along the same mental pathways you used, in hopes that they will follow you to the same conclusions.

Particularly in a long report, you may find it convenient to use differing organizational approaches for various sections. In general, however, simplicity of organization is a virtue. You need a clear, comprehensible argument in order to

The three indirect approaches can be used in different sections of the same report.

Main Idea: We should purchase the 45 franchises currently for sale in the Burger World chain.

I. Statement of problem and purpose of this proposal
II. Scope of the investigation
III. Method used to compare the business opportunities
   A. Establish decision criteria
   B. Get input from consultants
   C. Gather secondary research
   D. Conduct market surveys for primary research
   E. Meet with franchisor management teams
   F. Analyze quantitative and qualitative data
   G. Prioritize and select the best opportunity
IV. Analysis of the four franchise operations
   A. Wacky Taco
      1. Description: Low-fat Mexican food; most locations in malls
      2. Pros: 58 units available within a year; consultants believe the concept has significant growth potential; operations easy to manage
      3. Cons: Company recently hit with employment discrimination lawsuit; franchise fees are 30 percent above average
      4. Conclusion: Priority = 3; lawsuit may be indicative of mismanagement; fees too high
   B. Thai in the Sky
      1. Description: Thai food served in New Age settings
      2. Pros: Healthy and interesting food; unusual theme concept; no franchised competition
      3. Cons: Complexity of food preparation; only 40 franchises available; franchisor's top management team replaced only six months ago
      4. Conclusion: Priority = 4; too risky and not enough units available
   C. Dog Tower
      1. Description: Gourmet hot dogs
      2. Pros: No nationwide competition; more than 60 franchises available within a year; easy to manage; fees lower than average
      3. Cons: Limited market appeal; many stores need updating
      4. Conclusion: Priority = 2; needs too much investment
   D. Burger World
      1. Description: Mainstream competitor to McDonald's and Burger King

Covers two major steps: (1) establishing the decision criteria and (2) testing each of four alternatives against those criteria

Assigns each of the four alternatives to an appropriate subdivision: description, pros, cons, and conclusion (priority)

      2. Pros: Aggressive franchisor willing to invest in national marketing; start-up costs are low; unique demographic target (teenagers and young adults; not a little kids' place)
      3. Cons: Fierce competition in burgers overall; some units in unproved locations
      4. Conclusion: Priority = 1; finances look good; research shows that teenagers will support a chain that doesn't cater to small children
V. Summary
VI. Appendixes
   A. Financial data
   B. Research results

Presents each alternative objectively—Swensen's task, even though the decision can never be black and white

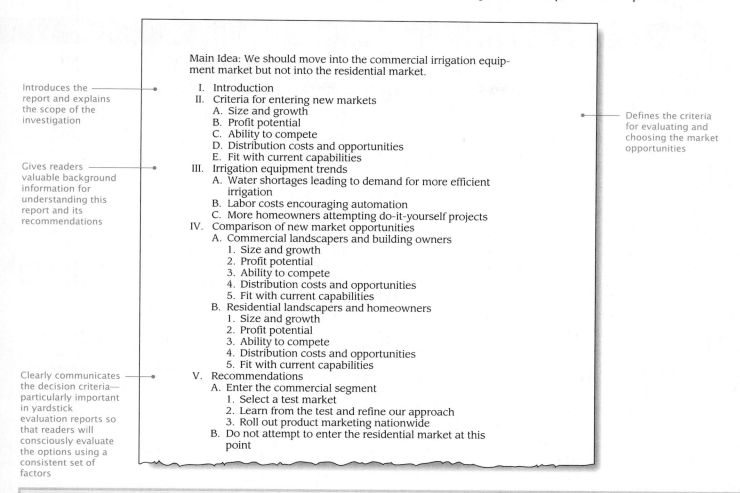

Introduces the report and explains the scope of the investigation

Gives readers valuable background information for understanding this report and its recommendations

Clearly communicates the decision criteria—particularly important in yardstick evaluation reports so that readers will consciously evaluate the options using a consistent set of factors

Defines the criteria for evaluating and choosing the market opportunities

Main Idea: We should move into the commercial irrigation equipment market but not into the residential market.

I.   Introduction
II. Criteria for entering new markets
     A. Size and growth
     B. Profit potential
     C. Ability to compete
     D. Distribution costs and opportunities
     E. Fit with current capabilities
III. Irrigation equipment trends
     A. Water shortages leading to demand for more efficient irrigation
     B. Labor costs encouraging automation
     C. More homeowners attempting do-it-yourself projects
IV. Comparison of new market opportunities
     A. Commercial landscapers and building owners
        1. Size and growth
        2. Profit potential
        3. Ability to compete
        4. Distribution costs and opportunities
        5. Fit with current capabilities
     B. Residential landscapers and homeowners
        1. Size and growth
        2. Profit potential
        3. Ability to compete
        4. Distribution costs and opportunities
        5. Fit with current capabilities
V.   Recommendations
     A. Enter the commercial segment
        1. Select a test market
        2. Learn from the test and refine our approach
        3. Roll out product marketing nationwide
     B. Do not attempt to enter the residential market at this point

FIGURE 11–5
Effective Outline of an Analytical Report Using the Yardstick Approach

convince skeptical readers to accept your conclusions or recommendations (see Table 11–1).

Structuring Business Proposals

As with reports, how you structure proposals depends on whether you expect your audience to be receptive. In general, your audience may be more receptive with solicited proposals, since the problem and the solution have already been identified. Your solicited proposal would use the direct approach, and you would focus on your recommendations, which respond to the work specified in the RFP.

The direct approach is common for solicited proposals; the indirect approach is more common for unsolicited proposals.

Because your audience may be less receptive to unsolicited proposals, you may do better to use the indirect approach. When writing unsolicited proposals, you must first convince the audience that a problem exists, and, if you're unknown to the reader, you need to establish your credibility. To convince the reader that your recommendations are solid and logical, you unfold your solution to the problem using one of the logical arguments just discussed (2 + 2 = 4 approach, scientific method, or yardstick approach). As you unfold your solution, you have two goals: (1) to persuade readers to accept your idea and award you a contract, and (2) to spell out the terms of your proposal in the report's content.

A proposal is both a selling tool and a contractual commitment.

For a review of the tasks involved in organizing business reports and proposals, see "Checklist: Organizing Business Reports and Proposals."

Table 11–1   STRUCTURING ANALYTICAL REPORTS

Structure to Use:	Focus on Conclusions	Focus on Recommendations	Focus on Logical Argument		
			2 + 2 = 4	**Scientific**	**Yardstick**
When readers are . . .	Likely to accept	Likely to accept	Skeptical and need to be convinced of logic	Skeptical and need to be convinced of the best solution	Skeptical and need to be convinced with criteria
When the order is . . .	Direct	Direct	Indirect	Indirect	Indirect
When your credibility is . . .	High	High	Low	Low	Low
ADVANTAGES: Structure allows readers to . . .	Quickly grasp recommendations	Quickly grasp conclusions	Follow writer's thinking process	Draw their own conclusions	Measure alternatives against the same standards (criteria)
DRAWBACKS: Structure can make the report . . .	Seem too simple	Seem too simple	Longer	Very long, by discussing each alternative	Very long (often boring) by measuring each item against each criterion (also requires readers to agree on criteria)

✓ CHECKLIST: Organizing Business Reports and Proposals

Decide on Format and Length

✓ Use preprinted forms only when requested to do so.
✓ Use letter format for brief external reports.
✓ Use memo or manuscript format for brief internal reports.
✓ Follow company guidelines.
✓ Choose a report length that matches your subject, your purpose, and your audience's expectations.

Choose an Organizational Approach

✓ Use direct order only when your credibility is high.
✓ Use direct order for informational reports to receptive readers.
✓ Use direct order for analytical reports to receptive readers.
✓ Use indirect order for analytical reports to skeptical or hostile readers.

Choose a Structure that Matches the Situation and Reader Needs

✓ For informational reports, use one of six topical arrangements: importance, sequence, chronology, spatial orientations, geography, and category.
✓ For analytical reports to receptive audiences, focus on conclusions or recommendations.
✓ For analytical reports to skeptical audiences, focus on one of three logical arguments: 2 + 2 = 4 (to determine that everything adds up), the scientific method (to reveal the most effective solution), or the yardstick approach (to weigh possible solutions against criteria).
✓ For solicited proposals, use the direct approach, and focus on recommendations.
✓ For unsolicited proposals, use the indirect approach and unfold recommendations by focusing on logical argument.

ORGANIZING VISUALS

Businesspeople such as FedEx's Fred Smith include charts and other visuals in their reports to convey important ideas. Carefully prepared visuals can help your audience understand your message and make your report more interesting. But don't overdo it. Use visuals selectively to enhance your words, not replace them. Table 11–2 will help you figure out when to include visuals. To organize visual aids effectively, you need to be selective, balanced, and economical:

- **Decide which points require visual support.** Some information is clearest when presented in words; other information may be clearest in visual form. Or you may simply want to draw attention to a particular fact or detail by reinforcing the message visually.

- **Maintain a balance between illustrations and words.** The ideal blend depends on the nature of your subject. However, illustrating every point dilutes the effectiveness of your visuals. Plus, readers usually assume that the amount of space allocated to a topic indicates its relative importance. So by using visuals to illustrate a minor point, you may be sending a misleading message about its significance.

- **Consider your production schedule.** If you're producing your report or presentation without appropriate computer-graphics tools or the help of an art department, you may want to restrict the number of visuals in your report. Creating charts, tables, and diagrams takes time, particularly if you're inexperienced. In addition, constructing visuals requires imagination and attention to detail.

Organize visual aids effectively by
- *Picking out the points that can best be made visually*
- *Balancing your words and visuals*
- *Limiting the number of visuals to the time available*

WHEN TO USE VISUALS	Table 11–2

Purpose	*Application*
To clarify	Support text descriptions of "graphic" topics: quantitative or numerical information, explanations of trends, descriptions.
To simplify	Break complicated descriptions into components that can be depicted with conceptual models, flowcharts, organization charts, or diagrams.
To emphasize	Call attention to particularly important points by illustrating them with line, bar, and pie charts.
To summarize	Review major points in the narrative by providing a chart or table that sums up the data.
To reinforce	Present information in visual and written form to increase reader's retention.
To attract	Make material seem more interesting by decorating the cover or title page and by breaking up the text with visual aids.
To impress	Build credibility by putting ideas into visual form to convey the impression of authenticity and precision.
To unify	Depict the relationship among points—for example, with a flowchart.

Selecting the Right Visual for the Job

Choose a type of graphic that best presents your message.

Once you've selected which points to illustrate visually, your next step is to select the types of visuals that will present those data clearly and effectively to your audience. Some types of visuals depict certain kinds of data better than others:

- To present detailed, exact values, use tables.
- To illustrate trends over time, use a line chart or a bar chart.
- To show frequency or distribution, use a pie chart, segmented bar chart, or surface chart.
- To compare one item with another, use a bar chart.
- To compare one part with the whole, use a pie chart.
- To show correlations, use a line chart or a bar chart.
- To show geographic relationships, use a map.
- To illustrate a process or a procedure, use a flowchart or a diagram.

Use tables to help your audience understand detailed information.

Tables   To present detailed, specific information, choose a **table**, a systematic arrangement of data in columns and rows (for the parts of a table, see Table 11–3). Tables are ideal when the audience needs the information that would be either difficult or tedious to handle in the main text. If the table has too many columns to fit comfortably between the margins of the page, position the table horizontally on the page with the top toward the binding. When preparing tables, be sure to

- Use common, understandable units, and clearly identify the units you're using: dollars, percentages, price per ton, and so on.
- Express all items in a column in the same unit, and round off for simplicity.
- Label column headings clearly, and use a subhead if necessary.
- Separate columns or rows with lines or extra space to make the table easy to follow.
- Provide column or row totals or averages when relevant.
- Document the source of the data using the same format as a text footnote (see Appendix B).

Line and Surface Charts   A **line chart** illustrates trends over time or plots the relationship of two variables. In line charts showing trends, the vertical, or *y*, axis

---

Table 11–3   **PARTS OF A TABLE**

	Multicolumn Head*		Single-column head	Single-column head
Stub Head	**Subhead**	**Subhead**		
Row head	xxx	xxx	xx	xx
Row head				
Subhead	xx	xxx	xx	x
Subhead	xx	xxx	xx	xx
Total	xxx	xxx	xx	xx

Source: (In the same format as a text footnote; see Appendix B.)

*Footnote (for explanation of elements in the table; a superscript number or small letter may be used instead of a asterisk or other symbol.)

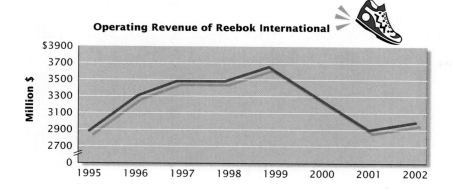

Operating Revenue of Reebok International

FIGURE 11–6
Line Chart with Broken Axis

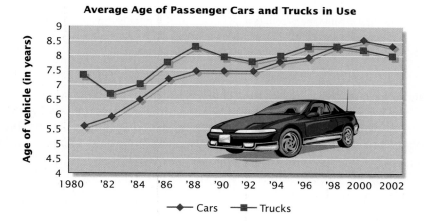

Average Age of Passenger Cars and Trucks in Use

◆ Cars   ■ Trucks

FIGURE 11–7
Line Chart with Multiple Lines

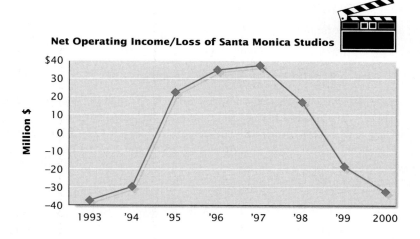

Net Operating Income/Loss of Santa Monica Studios

FIGURE 11–8
Line Chart with Positive and Negative Values on Vertical Axis

shows the amount, and the horizontal, or *x*, axis shows the time or the quantity being measured. Ordinarily, both scales begin at zero and proceed in equal increments; however, in Figure 11–6 the vertical axis is broken to show that some of the increments have been left out. A broken axis is appropriate when the data are plotted far above zero, but be sure to clearly indicate the omission of data points.

A simple line chart may be arranged in many ways. One of the most common is to plot several lines on the same chart for comparative purposes, as shown in Figure 11–7. Try to use no more than three lines on any given chart, particularly if the lines cross. Another variation of the simple line chart has a vertical axis with both positive and negative numbers (see Figure 11–8). This arrangement is handy when you have to illustrate losses.

Use line charts
- To indicate changes over time
- To plot the relationship of two variables

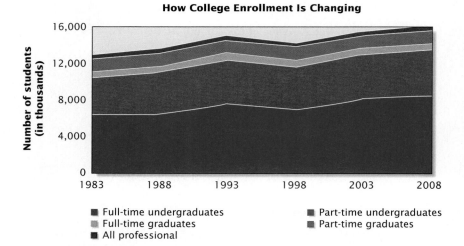

FIGURE 11–9
Surface Chart

A surface chart (area chart) is a kind of line chart showing a cumulative effect.

A **surface chart**, also called an **area chart**, is a form of line chart with a cumulative effect; all the lines add up to the top line, which represents the total (see Figure 11–9). This form of chart helps you illustrate changes in the composition of something over time. When preparing a surface chart, put the most important segment against the baseline, and restrict the number of strata to four or five.

Bar charts, in which numbers are visually portrayed by rectangular bars, can take a variety of forms.

Bar Charts   A **bar chart** portrays numbers by the height or length of its rectangular bars, making a series of numbers easy to read or understand. Bar charts are particularly valuable when you want to

• Compare the size of several items at one time

• Show changes in one item over time

• Indicate the composition of several items over time

• Show the relative size of components of a whole

As Figure 11–10 shows, bar charts can be singular (Where the College Students Are) or grouped (Eating Occasions), comparing more than one set of data by using a different color or pattern for each set. Segmented bar charts (Targeted Newscast) show how individual components contribute to a total number, using a different color or pattern for each component. Combination bar and line charts (Commercial Superhighway) compare quantities that require different intervals.

You can be creative with bar charts in many ways (Conference Attendance by Gender). You can align the bars either vertically or horizontally, but be careful to keep all the bars in the chart the same width; otherwise, you seem to mislead viewers by implying a relative importance for various bars. Also, space the bars evenly and place them in a logical order, such as chronological or alphabetical. Keep in mind that most computer software (such as Microsoft Excel) will generate charts from data tables.

Use pie charts to show the relative sizes of the parts of a whole.

Pie Charts   Like segmented bar charts and area charts, a **pie chart** shows how parts of a whole are distributed. Each segment represents a slice of a complete circle, or *pie*. As you can see in Figure 11–11 on page 368, pie charts are an effective way to show percentages or to compare one segment with another. You can combine pie charts with tables to expand the usefulness of such visuals.

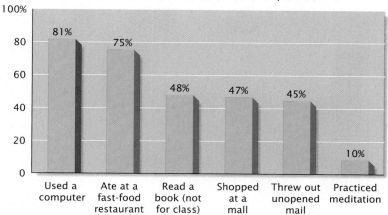

Where the College Students Are

Percentage of undergraduates enrolled full-time in four-year colleges and universities who did selected activities in the past week

FIGURE 11–10
The Versatile Bar Chart

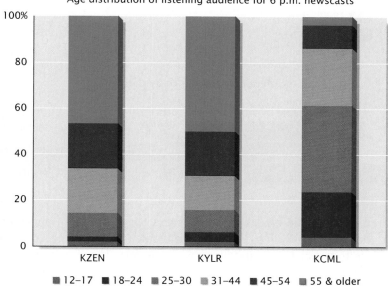

Targeted Newscast

Age distribution of listening audience for 6 p.m. newscasts

■ 12–17 ■ 18–24 ■ 25–30 ■ 31–44 ■ 45–54 ■ 55 & older

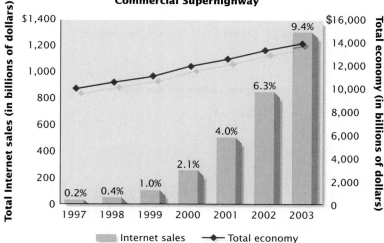

Commercial Superhighway

(continued)

FIGURE 11–10
(Continued)

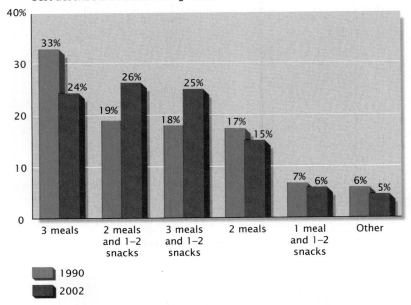

Eating Occasions

Percentage of adults aged 18 and older who say that selected patterns best describe their usual eating habits

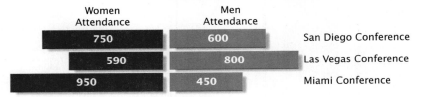

Conference Attendance by Gender

When composing pie charts, try to restrict the number of slices in the pie. Otherwise, the chart looks cluttered and is difficult to label. If necessary, lump the smallest pieces together in a "miscellaneous" category. Ideally, the largest or most important slice of the pie is placed at the twelve o'clock position; the rest are arranged clockwise either in order of size or in some other logical progression. Use different colors or patterns to distinguish the various pieces. To emphasize one piece, you can explode it, or pull it away from the rest of the pie. Label all segments and indicate their value either in percentages or in units of measure. Keep in mind that the segments must add up to 100 percent if percentages are used, or to the total number if units are used.

FIGURE 11–11
Pie Chart

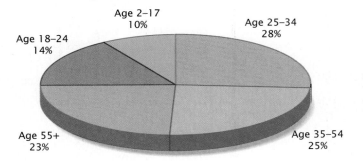

Time Spent Online by Age Group

Flowcharts and Organization Charts   If you need to show physical or conceptual relationships rather than numerical ones, you might want to use a flowchart or an organization chart. A **flowchart** illustrates a sequence of events from start to finish. Flowcharts are indispensable when illustrating processes, procedures, and sequential relationships. The various elements in the process you want to portray may be represented by pictorial symbols or geometric shapes, as shown in Figure 11–12.

As the name implies, an **organization chart** illustrates the positions, units, or functions of an organization and the way they interrelate. An organization's normal communication channels are almost impossible to describe without the benefit of a chart like the one in Figure 11–13.

Use flowcharts
- To show a series of steps from beginning to end
- To show sequential relationships

Use organization charts to depict the interrelationships among the parts of an organization.

Drawings, Diagrams, and Photographs   Although less commonly used than other visual aids, drawings, diagrams, and photographs can also be valuable elements in business reports and presentations. Drawings and diagrams are most often used to show how something looks or operates, since they can be much clearer than words alone. Photographs have always been popular in certain types of business documents, such as annual reports, where their visual appeal is used to capture reader interest. Nothing can demonstrate the exact appearance of a new facility, a piece of property or equipment, or a new product the way a photograph can.

Technology makes it easier to use photographs in reports and presentations, but it also presents an important ethical concern. Software tools such as Photoshop and CorelDraw! allow users to make dramatic changes to photos—without leaving a clue that the visuals have been altered. You can remove people from photographs, put Person A's head on Person B's body, and make products look more attractive than they really are. As you do when using other technological tools, stop and ask yourself where the truth lies before you alter photographs.[2]

Use drawings, diagrams, and photos
- To show how something looks or works
- To show how something is made or used
- For visual appeal

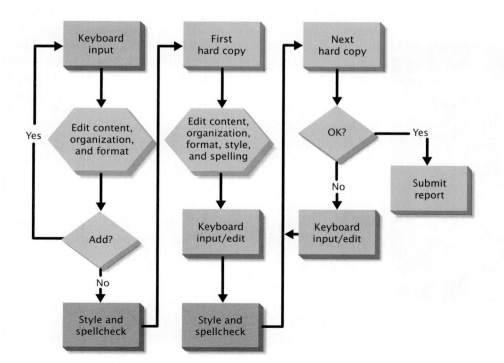

FIGURE 11–12
Flowchart

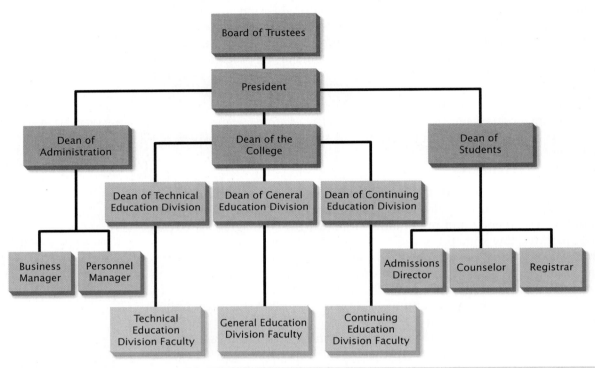

Administration and Faculty of Atlantic College

FIGURE 11–13
Organization Chart

Creating Visuals

Computer-graphics systems cut the time and cost involved in producing visuals.

Professional-looking visuals used to be extremely expensive and time-consuming to produce, but personal computer technology has changed all that. Visuals that used to cost hundreds of dollars and take several days to complete can now be done in minutes for little cost. Instead of relying on graphic designers, businesspeople are turning out their own professional-looking visual aids by turning to **computer graphics:** visuals created and produced using a computer program, such as CorelDraw!, PowerPoint, Photoshop, Painter, Excel, Lotus 1-2-3, and Visio—to name just a few.

Computer graphics offer several advantages, including speed, accuracy, and ease of use. They also offer the ability to save your results and reuse the visuals in various reports. But before using any computer-graphics tools, think about the kind of image you want to project. The style of your visuals communicates a subtle message about your relationship with the audience, whether you choose simple, hand-drawn diagrams for a working meeting or full-color visuals for a formal presentation or report.

Whatever style of visual you choose to create, each design element has a meaning of its own. A thick line implies more power than a thin one, a deep-shaded color suggests strength, a solid mass seems substantial. To create effective visuals, be aware of a few design principles:

The use of color in visuals accelerates learning, retention, and recall by 55 percent to 78 percent, and it increases motivation and audience participation up to 80 percent.

- **Continuity.** Readers assume that design elements will be consistent from one visual to the next. So if your first chart shows data for Division A in blue, the audience will expect Division A to be shown in blue throughout the report. You'll confuse people if you make arbitrary changes in color, shape, size, texture, position, scale, or typeface.

- **Contrast.** Readers expect visual distinctions to match verbal ones. Emphasize differences with contrasting colors (red and blue, black and white), but depict similarities with more subtle color differences. A pie chart might depict two similar items in two shades of blue and a dissimilar item in yellow. Remember that contrast loses its effect if you overdo it.

- **Emphasis.** Readers assume that the most important point will receive the greatest visual emphasis. So present the key item on the chart in the most prominent way—through color, position, size, or similar means. Visually downplay less important items.

- **Simplicity.** Limit the number of colors and design elements you use. Avoid *chartjunk*, decorative elements that clutter documents (and confuse readers) without adding relevant information.[3] The two charts in Figure 11–14 show the same information, but the second one is cluttered with useless decoration.

The principles of design help you create effective visuals.

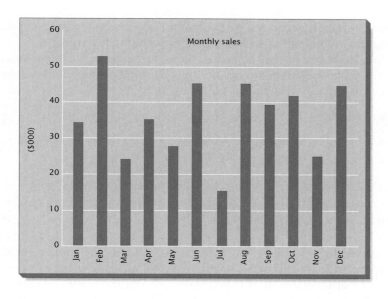

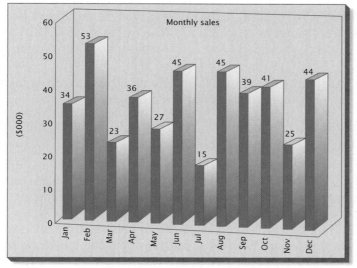

FIGURE 11–14
Simplify Graphics to Avoid Clutter and Confusion

- **Experience.** People expect visuals to look a certain way, depending on their culture and education. Green may be associated with money in the United States, but not in countries whose currency is red, blue, or yellow. A red cross on a white background signifies emergency medical care in many countries, but the International Red Cross uses a red crescent in Islamic countries.[4]

The best time to think about the principles of good design is before preparing your visuals; making changes after the fact increases the amount of time required to produce them.

Fitting Visuals into the Text

Because visuals clarify your text, tie them closely to the relevant discussion. Fit visuals into your text in a manner that is convenient for your audience and practical from a production standpoint.

To tie visuals to the text, refer to them by number before they appear.

Introduce Visuals in the Text   Every visual you use should be clearly referred to by number in the text of your report. Some report writers refer to all visuals as "exhibits" and number them consecutively throughout the report; many others number tables and figures separately (everything that isn't a table is regarded as a figure). In a very long report with numbered chapters (as in this book), illustrations may have a double number (separated by a period or a hyphen) representing the chapter number and the individual illustration number within that chapter.

Refer to visuals before they appear. The textual reference helps readers understand why the table or chart is important. The following examples show how you can make this connection in the text:

Figure 1 summarizes motorcycle sales over the past five years.

Total sales were steady over this period, but the mix of sales by category changed dramatically (see Figure 2).

The underlying reason for the remarkable growth in our sales of low-end fax machines is suggested in Table 4, which provides data on fax machine sales in the United States by region and model.

An in-text reference tells readers why a visual is important, without repeating the specific data that the visual presents.

When describing the data shown in your visual aids, be sure to emphasize the main point you are trying to make. Don't make the mistake of simply repeating the data shown. Paragraphs like this are guaranteed to put the reader to sleep:

Among women who replied to the survey, 17.4 percent earn less than $5 per hour; 26.4 percent earn $5–$7; 25.7 percent, $8–$12; 18.0 percent, $13–$24; 9.6 percent, $25–$49; and 2.9 percent, $50 and over.

The visual will provide these details; there is no need to repeat them in the text. Instead, use round numbers that sum up the message:

Over two-thirds of the women who replied to the survey earn less than $12 per hour.

Place a visual as close as possible to its in-text reference to help readers understand the illustration's relevance.

Place Visuals Near the Points They Illustrate   Try to place each visual right beside or right after the paragraph it illustrates so that your audience won't have to flip back and forth between them too much. Most word-processing programs and desktop publishing systems let you create layouts with artwork and text on the same page. However, if you don't have these programs, put the visuals on separate pages. Most writers insert these pages throughout the manuscript, as close as possible to their textual references; however, some writers prefer to cluster visuals at the end of the report (sometimes in an appendix) or even at the end of each chapter.

If you have four or more visuals, prepare a separate list to be placed with the table of contents at the front of the report. Some writers itemize tables separately from figures. If both lists won't fit on the same page, then start each one on a separate page.

Write Titles and Legends with a Message   One of the best ways to tie your visuals to your text is to create titles (or captions) and descriptions (or legends) that reinforce the point you want to make. This practice is especially necessary when the visuals are widely separated from the text. When combined with the labels and legends on the piece itself, the title of a visual should be complete enough to tell the reader what the content is. The title "Petroleum Tanks in the United States" is sufficient if it's the title of a line chart labeled "Year" along the horizontal axis and "Number (in thousands)" along the vertical axis. However, if the visual is a map overlaid with dots of different sizes, the title needs to explain a bit more: "Concentrations of Petroleum Tanks in the United States in 2002." A legend might then explain how many petroleum tanks each size of dot represents.

When you place a visual next to the text discussion that pertains to it, clear labeling and a good title are usually enough; the text can explain the visual's significance and details. However, when you place a visual elsewhere or when the illustration requires considerable explanation that would disrupt the flow of the text, you may need to add a legend to the visual. Legends are generally written as one or more complete sentences, and they do more than merely repeat what's already clear from the title and figure labels. It's better to be too specific than too general when identifying the content of an illustration. As a check, ask yourself whether you've covered the who, what, when, where, why, and how of the illustration.

If you're using informative headings in your report, reflect this style in exhibit titles and legends. Instead of using a **descriptive title,** which identifies the topic of the illustration, call attention to the conclusion that ought to be drawn from the data by using an **informative title.** Here's the difference:

Descriptive Title	Informative Title
Relationship Between Petroleum Demand and Refinery Capacity in the United States	Shrinking Refinery Capacity Results from Stagnant Petroleum Demand

Regardless of whether your titles and legends are informative or descriptive, phrase them consistently throughout the report. At the same time, be consistent in your format. If the title of the first visual is typed entirely in capital letters, type all the remaining titles that way as well. Although your employer may specify the placement of titles, generally place all table titles at the top. Figure titles may be placed at the top or the bottom. When using legends, make them all roughly the same length.

Checking Visuals

Your visuals exist to help readers absorb, understand, and accept your message. Their appearance is crucial to the success of your message, so be sure to check them for mistakes such as typographical errors, inconsistent color treatment, and misaligned elements. Also take a few extra minutes to ask yourself four important questions:

- **Is the visual necessary?** A few well-placed visuals can clarify and dramatize your message, but an avalanche of illustrations may bury it. Avoid the temptation to overload your reports with unnecessary tables, graphs, and charts. Remember that

Titles and legends should
- *Reinforce the point you want to make*
- *Be specific*

Use a legend if an explanation of the illustration would disrupt the flow of the text.

Whether you use descriptive or informative titles and legends, phrase these elements consistently throughout the report.

Proof visuals as carefully as you proof text.

With today's software you can digitally alter photos. In the photo on the right, the bakery has been given a complete name, the man's shirt has been changed to green, and a dog has been added. Is it ethical to change a photo without revealing the changes that were made to the original?

your audience is busy. Don't give people information they don't need simply because you want to impress them or because you've fallen in love with your computer's graphics capabilities.

- **Is the visual accurate?** Make sure that every number is correct. Verify that every line is plotted accurately and that every piece of information included in a visual is consistent with what is said in the text. When you're proofreading, be sure to check each visual's source notes and content notes for accuracy.

- **Is the visual honest?** With visuals, you can get all the numbers right and still give your audience a false impression. True, charts tend to oversimplify some numerical relationships. But deliberately leaving out important information is highly unethical. Don't omit data points that don't fit your needs. And don't distort a visual with the wrong scale. As Figure 11–15 illustrates, you can transform modest results into dramatic ones by compressing the horizontal scale or by expanding the vertical scale. But when you do so, you mislead your audience and abandon good business ethics. Choose a scale that conveys a realistic picture of what's happening, and maintain the same scale in all charts that compare the same factors.

- **Is the visual properly documented?** If you use someone else's data to create a visual, you need to give credit on the visual itself. Identify the actual source of data (such as the name of the journal the information came from) or refer simply to the nature of the information (for example, "interviews with 50 soybean farmers"). If you gathered the data yourself (through observation, survey, interview, or other method), say so. To avoid cluttering your visual, you could use a shortened citation on the visual itself and include a complete citation elsewhere in the report.

For a brief review of the points covered in this section, see "Checklist: Organizing Visual Aids."

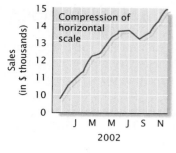

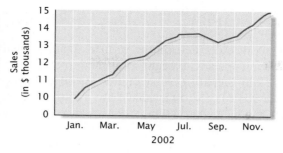

FIGURE 11–15
The Impact of Scale on the Slope of a Curve

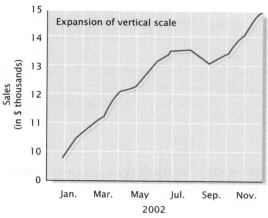

✓ CHECKLIST: Organizing Visual Aids

Prepare Carefully

✓ Use visuals to enhance, not replace, your words.
✓ Select the points that need to be supported by visuals.
✓ Balance your words with your visuals.
✓ Keep your production schedule in mind.

Select the Proper Types of Visuals

✓ Use tables to display detailed, specific information.
✓ Use line charts to illustrate trends over time or the relationship of two variables.
✓ Use surface charts to show cumulative effects.
✓ Use bar charts to compare the size of several items at once, show changes in one item over time, indicate the composition of several items over time, and show the relative size of components of a whole.
✓ Use pie charts to show how parts of a whole are distributed.
✓ Use flowcharts and organization charts to show physical or conceptual relationships.
✓ Use drawings, diagrams, and photographs to illustrate how something looks or operates.

Create Effective Visuals

✓ Gain speed, accuracy, ease of use, and reusability from computer graphics.

✓ Think about the style of the visuals you use and what that says about your image.
✓ Make design elements consistent.
✓ Use contrasting colors to emphasize differences and similar colors to emphasize similarities.
✓ Emphasize only the most important points with visuals.
✓ Make visuals simple and easy to understand, and avoid excessive clip art and all unnecessary details.
✓ Make sure that design elements meet audience expectations.

Tie Visuals to Your Text

✓ Clearly reference illustrations in text.
✓ Assign each illustration a number or letter.
✓ Place visuals close to the points they illustrate.
✓ Make headings, labels, titles, and legends clear, whether descriptive or informative.

Check Over Your Visuals

✓ Proof visuals for typos, color treatment, and alignment.
✓ Make sure each visual is necessary.
✓ Ensure the accuracy of each visual.
✓ Properly document each visual.
✓ Create honest, ethical visuals.

COMPOSING BUSINESS REPORTS AND PROPOSALS

Preparing a final outline offers distinct advantages.

Once you've decided on the proper organizational structure for your report or proposal, you're ready to begin composing your first draft. Effective writers begin the writing task by preparing a final outline. Aside from guiding you in the writing effort, a final outline forces you to reevaluate the information you have selected to include and the order in which you present it. For instance, you may decide to use an indirect approach instead of a direct one because now that you see your conclusions up front, you think this approach might be too forceful for your audience. Preparing a final outline also gives you a chance to rephrase your outline points and set the tone of your report's headings. Use informative phrasing for a hard-hitting, direct tone, or use descriptive phrasing for an objective, indirect tone. Also, be sure to use parallel construction.

To draft successful reports, begin with Step 2 of the writing process (discussed in Chapter 5).

Once you have fine-tuned your final outline, your new tasks are to control your style and tone, select the best words, and create effective sentences and paragraphs—as discussed in Chapter 5. As you compose your first draft, also keep in mind how you achieve the proper degree of formality, establish an appropriate time perspective, help readers find their way, and develop content for the text of your report (its opening, body, and close).

Choosing the Proper Degree of Formality

If you know your readers reasonably well and if your report is likely to meet with their approval, you can generally adopt a fairly informal tone. You can speak to readers in the first person, referring to yourself as *I* and to your readers as *you*. This personal approach is often used in brief memo or letter reports, although there are many exceptions.

Certain audiences and situations require a more formal style.

Use a more formal approach for longer reports, especially those dealing with controversial or complex information, and for reports that will be sent to other parts of the organization or to customers or suppliers. Also, communicating with people in other cultures often calls for more formality. Use an impersonal style, and eliminate all references to *you* and *I* (including *we, us,* and *our*). However, make sure that avoiding personal pronouns doesn't lead you to overuse phrases such as *there are* and *it is*, which are both dull and wordy. Also, be careful not to slip into the passive voice more than necessary.

You can often tell what tone is appropriate for your readers by looking at other reports of a similar type in your company. If all the other reports on file are impersonal, you should probably adopt the same tone yourself, unless you're confident that your readers prefer a more personal style. Most organizations expect an unobtrusive, impersonal writing style for business reports (see "Sharpening Your Career skills: Top Tips for Writing Reports That Mean Business").

Establishing a Consistent Time Perspective

Decide what time frame your report will use: past or present. The person who wrote this paragraph never decided:

Of those interviewed, 25 percent <u>report</u> that they <u>are</u> dissatisfied with their present brand. The wealthiest participants <u>complained</u> most frequently, but all income categories <u>are</u> interested in trying a new brand. Only 5 percent of the interviewees <u>said</u> they <u>have</u> no interest in alternative products.

Be consistent in the verb tense you use.

By switching from tense to tense throughout your report, you only confuse your readers. They wonder whether the shift is significant or whether you are just being sloppy. Eliminate such confusion by using tense consistently.

Follow a proper chronological sequence in your report.

Also be careful to observe the chronological sequence of events in your report. If you're describing the history or development of something, start at the beginning and

SHARPENING YOUR CAREER SKILLS

Top Tips for Writing Reports That Mean Business

Put nothing in writing that you're unwilling to say in public, and write nothing that may embarrass or jeopardize your employer. Does this directive mean you should cover up problems? Of course not. However, when you're dealing with sensitive information, be discreet. Present the information in such a way that it will help readers solve a problem. Avoid personal gripes, criticisms, alibis, attempts to blame other people, sugar-coated data, and unsolicited opinions.

To be useful, the information must be accurate, complete, and honest. Of course, being honest is not always a simple matter. Everyone sees reality a little differently, and individuals describe what they see in their own way. To restrict the distortions introduced by differences in perception, follow these guidelines:

- Describe facts or events in concrete terms. Indicate quantities whenever you can. Say, "Sales have increased 17 percent," or "Sales have increased from $40,000 to $43,000 in the past two months." Don't say, "Sales have skyrocketed."

- Report all relevant facts. Regardless of whether all pertinent facts support your theories or please your readers, they must be included. Omitting the details that undermine your position may be convenient, but it is misleading and inaccurate.

- Put the facts in perspective. Taken out of context, the most concrete facts are misleading. If you say, "Stock values have doubled in three weeks," you offer an incomplete picture. Instead, say, "Stock values have doubled in three weeks, rising from $2 to $4 per share."

- Give plenty of evidence for your conclusions. Statements such as "We have to reorganize the sales force or we'll lose market share" may or may not be true. Readers have no way of knowing unless you provide enough data to support your claim.

- Present only verifiable conclusions. Check facts, and use reliable sources. Don't draw conclusions too quickly (one rep may say that customers are unhappy, but that doesn't mean they all are). And don't assume that one event caused another (sales may have dipped right after you switched ad agencies, but that doesn't mean the new agency is at fault—the general state of the economy may be responsible).

- Keep your personal biases in check. Even if you feel strongly about your topic, keep those feelings from influencing your choice of words. If you say, "Locating a plant in Kraymore is a terrible idea because the people there are mostly students who would rather play than work and who don't have the ability to operate our machines," you will not only offend some readers but also obscure the facts and provoke emotional responses.

CAREER APPLICATIONS

1. When would you use vague language instead of concrete detail? Would this action be unethical or merely one form of emphasizing the positive?

2. Recent budget cuts have endangered the day-care program at your local branch of a national company. You're writing a report for headquarters about the grave impact on employees. Describe the situation in a single sentence that reveals nothing about your personal feelings but that clearly shows your position.

---

cover each event in the order of its occurrence. If you're explaining the steps in a process, take each step in proper sequence.

Helping Readers Find Their Way

Readers have no concept of how the various pieces of your report relate to one another. Although you can see how each page fits into the overall structure, readers see your report one page at a time. So give them a road map of your report's structure, and clarify how the various parts are related. You can give them a sense of the overall structure of your document by using three tools:

Help readers navigate your report by using three techniques.

- **Headings.** These brief titles cue readers about the content of a section. They improve readability (see Chapter 6) and clarify a report's framework. *Subheadings* (lower-level headings) help show which ideas are more important. Many companies specify a format for headings; if yours does, use it. Otherwise, you can use the scheme shown in Figure 11–16.

- **Transitions.** These words or phrases tie ideas together and show how one thought is related to another. Whether words, sentences, or complete paragraphs, use transitions

FIGURE 11–16
Heading Format for Reports

TITLE

The title is centered at the top of the page in all-capital letters, usually bold-faced (or underlined if typewritten), often in a large font (type size), and often using a sans serif typeface. When the title runs to more than one line, the lines are usually double-spaced and arranged as an inverted pyramid (longer line on the top).

FIRST-LEVEL HEADING

A first-level heading indicates what the following section is about, perhaps by describing the subdivisions. All first-level headings are grammatically parallel, with the possible exception of such headings as "Introduction," "Conclusions," and "Recommendations." Some text appears between every two headings, regardless of their levels. Still boldfaced and sans serif, the font may be smaller than that used in the title but still larger than the typeface used in the text and still in all-capital letters.

Second-Level Heading

Like first-level headings, second-level headings indicate what the following material is about. All second-level headings within a section are grammatically parallel. Still boldfaced and sans serif, the font may either remain the same or shrink to the size used in the text, and the style is now initial capitals with lower case. Never use only one second-level heading under a first-level heading. (The same is true for every other level of heading.)

Third-Level Heading

A third-level heading is worded to reflect the content of the material that follows. All third-level headings beneath a second-level heading should be grammatically parallel.

Fourth-Level Heading. Like all the other levels of headings, fourth-level headings reflect the subject that will be developed. All fourth-level headings within a subsection are parallel.

Fifth-level headings are generally the lowest level of heading used. However, you can indicate further breakdowns in your ideas by using a list:

1. *The first item in a list.* You may indent the entire item in block format to set it off visually. Numbers are optional.
2. *The second item in a list.* All lists have at least two items. An introductory phrase or sentence may be italicized for emphasis, as shown here.

to help readers move from one section of a report to the next. When writing transitions, be sure to list upcoming topics in the order they will be discussed.

- **Previews and reviews.** *Preview sections* introduce an important topic and help readers get ready for new information. *Review sections* come after a body of material and summarize the information for your readers, which helps them absorb details while keeping track of the big picture.

Developing the Text

Reports and proposals have an opening, body, and close, much like other forms of written communication.

As with other written business communications, the text of a report or proposal has three main sections: an opening, a body, and a closing. The content and length of each section varies with the type and purpose of the document, the document's organizational structure, the length and depth of the material, the document's degree of formality, and the writer's relationship with the audience. A proposal's content and length are governed primarily by its source. Unsolicited proposals are allowed some latitude in the scope and organization of content; however, solicited proposals must conform to the request for proposal. Most RFPs spell out precisely what you should cover and in what order so that the client can evaluate competing proposals in a systematic way.

The quality of your report's content will likely influence your professional success. After all, it shows how well you think, gather and analyze data, draw conclusions, and develop and support your recommendations. You'll create more successful reports if your content is

- **Accurate.** In addition to checking for typos, double-check your facts and references.

- **Complete.** Include all the necessary information—no more, no less.

- **Balanced.** Present all sides of the issue fairly and equitably.

- **Well structured.** Write uncluttered sentences and paragraphs that organize your ideas clearly and proceed logically with helpful transitions.[5]

- **Well documented.** Properly give credit to your sources, using one of the schemes discussed in Appendix B.

Effective reports share certain characteristics.

Proposals are a special kind of report whose general purpose is to persuade readers to do something (purchase goods or services, fund a project, implement a program). Therefore, writing a proposal is similar to writing a persuasive sales message (see Chapter 9). Use the AIDA plan to gain attention, build interest, create desire, and motivate action. In addition, be sure to do the following:[6]

Six strategies improve proposal content.

- **Demonstrate your knowledge.** Show your reader that you have the knowledge and experience to solve the problem. Disclose enough information to win the job without giving away your ideas so that your services aren't needed.

- **Provide concrete examples.** Avoid vague, unsupported generalizations such as "We are losing money on this program." Instead, provide quantifiable details such as the amount of money being lost, how, why, and so on. Explain how much money your proposed solution will save. Spell out your plan and give details on how the job will be done.

- **Research the competition.** Use trade publications and the Internet to become familiar with your competitors' product lines, services, and prices. This strategy is especially important if you are competing against others for a job.

- **Prove that your proposal is workable.** Your proposal must be feasible for the audience. For instance, it would be foolish to recommend a solution that doubles the budget or requires three times the number of current employees.

- **Adopt a "you" attitude.** Relate your product, service, or personnel to the reader's exact needs, either as stated in the RFP for a solicited proposal or as discovered through your own investigation for an unsolicited proposal.

- **Package your proposal attractively.** Make sure your proposal is letter perfect, inviting, and readable. Readers will judge the type of work you perform by your submitted proposal. If it contains errors, omissions, or inconsistencies, they will likely withhold approval.

Keeping these points in mind will help you draft the most effective opening, body, and closing for your reports and proposals.

Drafting the Opening In the *opening*, prepare your readers for the information that follows. Invite them to continue reading by telling

Document Makeover

IMPROVE THIS REPORT

To practice correcting drafts of actual documents, visit **www.prenhall.com/onekey** on the web. Click "Document Makeovers," then click Chapter 11. You will find an excerpt from a policy report that contains problems and errors relating to what you've learned in this chapter about writing business reports and proposals. Use the Final Draft decision tool to create an improved version of this informational report. Check the message for an effective opening, consistent levels of formality or informality, consistent time perspective, and the use of headings, lists, transitions, and previews, and reviews to help orient readers.

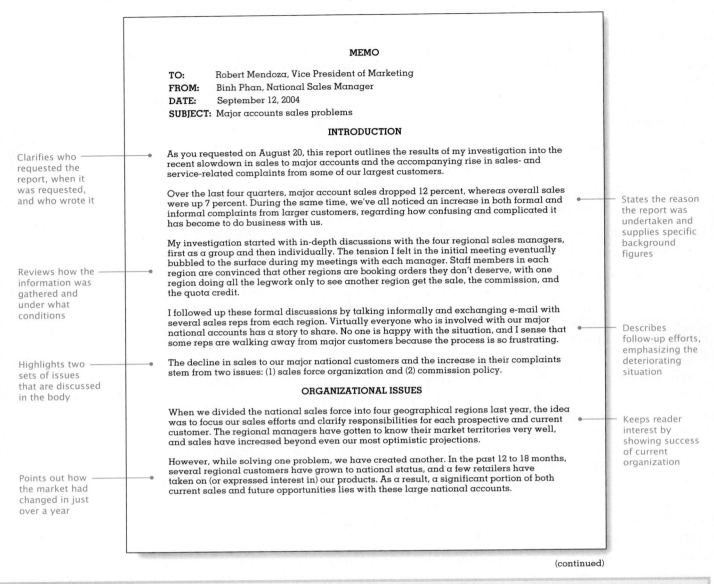

Clarifies who requested the report, when it was requested, and who wrote it

Reviews how the information was gathered and under what conditions

Highlights two sets of issues that are discussed in the body

Points out how the market had changed in just over a year

States the reason the report was undertaken and supplies specific background figures

Describes follow-up efforts, emphasizing the deteriorating situation

Keeps reader interest by showing success of current organization

MEMO

TO: Robert Mendoza, Vice President of Marketing
FROM: Binh Phan, National Sales Manager
DATE: September 12, 2004
SUBJECT: Major accounts sales problems

INTRODUCTION

As you requested on August 20, this report outlines the results of my investigation into the recent slowdown in sales to major accounts and the accompanying rise in sales- and service-related complaints from some of our largest customers.

Over the last four quarters, major account sales dropped 12 percent, whereas overall sales were up 7 percent. During the same time, we've all noticed an increase in both formal and informal complaints from larger customers, regarding how confusing and complicated it has become to do business with us.

My investigation started with in-depth discussions with the four regional sales managers, first as a group and then individually. The tension I felt in the initial meeting eventually bubbled to the surface during my meetings with each manager. Staff members in each region are convinced that other regions are booking orders they don't deserve, with one region doing all the legwork only to see another region get the sale, the commission, and the quota credit.

I followed up these formal discussions by talking informally and exchanging e-mail with several sales reps from each region. Virtually everyone who is involved with our major national accounts has a story to share. No one is happy with the situation, and I sense that some reps are walking away from major customers because the process is so frustrating.

The decline in sales to our major national customers and the increase in their complaints stem from two issues: (1) sales force organization and (2) commission policy.

ORGANIZATIONAL ISSUES

When we divided the national sales force into four geographical regions last year, the idea was to focus our sales efforts and clarify responsibilities for each prospective and current customer. The regional managers have gotten to know their market territories very well, and sales have increased beyond even our most optimistic projections.

However, while solving one problem, we have created another. In the past 12 to 18 months, several regional customers have grown to national status, and a few retailers have taken on (or expressed interest in) our products. As a result, a significant portion of both current sales and future opportunities lies with these large national accounts.

(continued)

FIGURE 11–17
Effective Analytical Report

In the opening of your report, tell readers what to expect, explain why your subject is important, describe how your report is organized, and set the tone.

them what your report is about, why the audience should be concerned, and how the report is organized. Your opening should accomplish four goals:

- Tie the report or proposal to a problem or an assignment.
- Introduce the report's subject (purpose) and indicate why the subject is important.
- Preview the main ideas and the order in which they'll be covered.
- Establish the tone of the document and your relationship with the audience.

Take a look at the report in Figure 11–17. This report was written by Binh Phan from the outline presented in Figure 11–3 on page 359. Phan's opening (introduction) accomplishes all four of these important tasks.

In proposals, your opening not only presents the problem you want to solve but also summarizes your solution. In a solicited proposal, the opening should refer to the RFP; in an unsolicited proposal, the opening should mention any factors that led

Openings for solicited proposals also mention the RFP, and those for unsolicited proposals mention the reasons you're submitting your document.

FIGURE 11–17
Continued

2

Explains organizational problems without going into unneeded detail

I uncovered more than a dozen cases in which sales reps from two or more regions found themselves competing with each other by pursuing the same customers from different locations. Moreover, the complaints from our major accounts about overlapping or nonexistent account coverage are a direct result of the regional organization. In some cases, customers aren't sure which of our reps they're supposed to call with problems and orders. In others, no one has been in contact with them for several months.

For example, having retail outlets across the lower tier of the country, AmeriSport received pitches from reps out of our West, South, and East regions. Because our regional offices have a lot of negotiating freedom, the three were offering different prices. But all AmeriSport buying decisions were made at the Tampa headquarters, so all we did was confuse the customer. The irony of the current organization is that we're often giving our weakest selling and support efforts to the largest customers in the country.

Supports the first main idea with evidence

COMMISSION ISSUES

Explains commission problems concisely

The regional organization issues are compounded by the way we assign commissions and quota credit. Salespeople in one region can invest a lot of time in pursuing a sale, only to have the customer place the order in another region. So some sales rep in the second region ends up with the commission on a sale that was partly or even entirely earned by someone in the first region. Therefore, sales reps sometimes don't pursue leads in their regions, thinking that a rep in another region will get the commission.

For example, Athletic Express, with outlets in 35 states spread across all four regions, finally got so frustrated with us that the company president called our headquarters. Athletic Express has been trying to place a large order for tennis and gold accessories, but none of our local reps seem interested in paying attention. I spoke with the rep responsible for Nashville, where the company is headquartered, and asked her why she wasn't working the account more actively. Her explanation was that last time she got involved with Athletic Express, the order was actually placed from their L.A. regional office, and she didn't get any commission after more than two weeks of selling time.

Supports the second main idea with evidence

RECOMMENDATIONS

Presents recommended action

Our sales organization should reflect the nature of our customer base. To accomplish that goal, we need a group of reps who are free to pursue accounts across regional borders— and who are compensated fairly for their work. The most sensible answer is to establish a national account group. Any customers whose operations place them in more than one region would automatically be assigned to the national group.

Further, we need to modify our commission policy to reward people for team selling. I'll talk with the sales managers to work out the details, but in general, we'll need to split

3

commissions whenever two or more reps help close a sale. This policy will also involve a "finder's fee" for a regional rep who pulls in national leads and passes them on to the national account team.

SUMMARY

The regional sales organization is effective at the regional and local levels but not at the national level. We should establish a national accounts group to handle sales that cross regional boundaries. Then we'll have one set of reps who are focused on the local and regional levels and another set who are pursuing national accounts.

To make sure that the sales reps (at both the regional and national levels) are adequately motivated and fairly compensated, we need to devise a system of commission splitting and finder's fees. Rather than working against each other, as they are now, the two groups will have incentive to work together.

Clearly and succinctly recaps recommendations and how the company will benefit from following them

Table 11–4	**TOPICS COMMONLY ADDRESSED IN REPORTS AND PROPOSALS**
Report Contents	**Proposal Contents**
Introduction	**Introduction**

Report Contents	Proposal Contents
• **Authorization.** Review who authorized the report (when, how), who wrote it, when it was submitted.	• **Background or statement of the problem.** Briefly review the reader's situation, establish a need for action, and explain how things could be better. In unsolicited proposals, convince readers that a problem or opportunity exists.
• **Problem/purpose.** Explain the reason for the report's existence and what the report will achieve.	
• **Scope.** Describe what will and won't be covered in the report—indicating size and complexity.	• **Solution.** Briefly describe the change you propose, highlighting your key selling points and their benefits to show how your proposal will solve the reader's problem.
• **Background.** Review historical conditions or factors that led up to the report.	
• **Sources and methods.** Discuss the primary and secondary sources consulted and the methods used.	• **Scope.** State the boundaries of your proposal—what you will and will not do.
• **Definitions.** List terms and their definitions—may also be defined in the body, explanatory notes, or glossary.	• **Report organization.** Orient the reader to the remainder of the proposal and call attention to the major divisions of thought.
• **Limitations.** Discuss factors beyond your control that affect report quality—not an excuse for a poor study or bad report.	
• **Report organization.** Tell what topics are covered in what order.	

Body	**Body**
• **Explanations.** Give complete details of the problem, project, or idea.	• **Facts and evidence to support your conclusions.** Give full details of the proposed solution and the anticipated results.
• **Facts, statistical evidence, and trends.** Lay out the results of studies or investigations.	• **Proposed approach.** Describe your concept, product, or service. Stress reader benefits and emphasize any advantages you have over your competitors.
• **Analysis of action.** Discuss potential courses of action.	

you to submit your proposal. You might mention mutual acquaintances, or you might refer to previous conversations you've had with readers. For examples of solicited and unsolicited proposals, look back at Figures 10–4 (on p. 360) and 10–5 (on p. 361).

The opening in reports and proposals commonly addresses certain topics, ranging from background information and scope to limitations and definitions (see Table 11–4). Some of these items may be combined, and some may not be discussed at all. You need only include those elements that will help your readers understand and accept your report. In a relatively brief report, these topics may be discussed in only a paragraph or two. Here's an example of a brief, indirect opening, taken from a memo on why a new line of luggage has failed to sell well. The writer's ultimate goal is to recommend a shift in marketing strategy.

> The performance of the Venturer line can be improved. In the two years since its introduction, this product line has achieved a sales volume lower than we expected, resulting in a drain on the company's overall earnings. The purpose of this report is to review the luggage-buying habits of consumers in all markets where the Venturer line is sold, so that we can determine where to put our marketing emphasis.

- **Pros and cons.** Explain advantages, disadvantages, costs, and benefits of a particular course of action.

- **Procedures.** Outline steps for a process.

- **Methods and approaches.** Discuss how you've studied a problem (or gathered evidence) and arrived at your solution.

- **Criteria.** Describe the benchmarks for evaluating options and alternatives.

- **Conclusions and recommendations.** Discuss what you think the evidence reveals and what you propose to do about it.

- **Support.** Give the reasons behind your conclusions or recommendations.

- **Work plan.** Describe how you'll accomplish what must be done (unless you're providing a standard, off-the-shelf item). Explain the steps you'll take, their timing, the methods or resources you'll use, and the person(s) responsible. State when work will begin, how it will be divided into stages, when you'll finish, and whether follow-up will be needed.

- **Statement of qualifications.** Describe your organization's experience, personnel, and facilities—relating it all to readers' needs. Include a list of client references.

- **Costs.** Prove that your costs are realistic—break them down so that readers can see the cost of labor, materials, transportation, travel, training, and other categories.

Close

- **For direct order.** Summarize key points (except in short memos), listing them in the order they appear in the body. Briefly restate your conclusions or recommendations, if appropriate.

- **For indirect order.** You may present your conclusions or recommendations for the first time—just don't present any new facts.

- **For motivating action.** Spell out exactly what should happen next and provide a schedule with specific task assignments.

Close

- **Review of argument.** Briefly summarize the key points.

- **Review of reader benefits.** Briefly summarize how your proposal will help the reader.

- **Review of the merits of your approach.** Briefly summarize why your approach will be more effective than that of competitors.

- **Restatement of qualifications.** Briefly reemphasize why you and your firm should do the work.

This paragraph quickly introduces the subject (disappointing sales), tells why the problem is important (drain on earnings), and indicates the main points to be addressed in the body of the report (review of markets where the Venturer line is sold), without revealing what the conclusions and recommendations will be. In a major formal report, the discussion of these topics may span several pages.

Drafting the Body   The *body* of your report or proposal includes the major divisions or chapters that present, analyze, and interpret the information you gathered during your investigation. Give complete details of your proposed solution and specify what results you anticipate. The body contains the "proof," the detailed information necessary to support your conclusions and recommendations. Look again at Figure 11–17 on pp. 379–380. The body of Binh Phan's report supports his recommendations about reorganizing the salesforce and revising the company's commission policy.

One of the decisions you need to make when writing the body of your report is how much detail to include. Here again, your decision depends on many variables, including the needs of your audience. Some audiences and situations require detailed coverage; others lend themselves to shorter treatment. Provide only enough detail in the body to support your conclusions and recommendations; put additional detail in tables, charts, and appendixes.

The body contains the substance of your report or proposal.

Restrict the body to those details necessary to prove your conclusions and recommendations.

Refer again to Table 11–4 on pp. 382–383 for some of the topics commonly covered in the body of reports and proposals. For analytical reports using the direct organizational approach, you'll generally state your conclusions or recommendations up front and use the body of your report to provide your evidence and support. If you're using the indirect organizational approach, you'll likely use the body to discuss your logic and reserve your conclusions or recommendations until the very end. You may even refrain from stating them until the closing of your report.

Drafting the Close   The *close* is the final section of text in your report or proposal, and it must leave a strong, lasting impression. This is your last chance to make sure that your report says what you intended or that your proposal persuades readers to accept your suggestions.[7] Your report close should accomplish four goals:

- Emphasize the main points of the message.

- Summarize reader benefits (if some sort of change or other course of action is suggested).

- Refer back to all the pieces and remind readers how those pieces fit together.

- Bring all the action items together in one place and give details about who should do what, when, where, and how.

Your choice of a direct or indirect order can determine the content and length of your closing. If your report is organized in the direct order, end with a summary of key points (except in short memos), and list them in order, as they appear in the report body. If appropriate, briefly restate your conclusions or recommendations, as Alycia Jenn does in her closing summary (see Figure 10–3 on page 315). If your report is organized in the indirect order, your conclusions or recommendations may be presented for the first time at the end, as in Bin Phan's report (see Figure 11–17 on page 380). Just remember that new facts are never presented in a report's conclusion or recommendation.

If your report is intended to lead to action, use the ending to spell out exactly what should happen next. Readers may agree with everything you say in your report but still fail to take any action if you're vague about what should happen next. Providing a schedule and specific task assignments is helpful because concrete plans have a way of commanding action.

In a short report, the ending may be only a paragraph or two. However, a long report may have separate sections for conclusions, recommendations, and actions. Using separate sections helps your reader locate this material. It also gives you a final opportunity to emphasize this important content. Keep in mind that it's fine to combine the conclusions and recommendations under one heading, because it is often difficult to present a conclusion without implying a recommendation.

If you have multiple conclusions, recommendations, or actions, you may want to number and list them. An appropriate lead-in to such a list might be, "The findings of this study lead to the following conclusions." A statement that could be used for a list of recommendations might be, "Based on the conclusions of this study, the following recommendations are made." A statement that could be used for actions might be, "In order to accomplish our goals on time, the following actions must be completed before the end of the year."

In the final section of a proposal, you should accomplish five goals:

- Summarize the key points of the proposal.

- Emphasize the benefits that the readers will realize from your solution.

- Summarize the merits of your approach.

- Re-emphasize why you and your firm are the ones to do the work.

- Ask for a decision from the client.

The close of your report has four specific goals.

The length and depth of your closing will depend on your organizational approach.

Use the closing to tell your readers what's expected of them.

You may present your conclusions and recommendations under separate headings or together under one heading.

Number or list multiple recommendations or actions.

The close of your proposal has five goals.

In both formal and informal proposals, make this section relatively brief, assertive, and confident.

To review the tasks discussed in this section, see "Checklist: Composing Business Reports and Proposals."

✓ CHECKLIST: Composing Business Reports and Proposals

Prepare a Final Outline

✓ Use the outline to revise the order and content of information as needed.
✓ Use informative headings for a hard-hitting, direct tone.
✓ Use descriptive headings for an objective, indirect tone.
✓ Use parallel construction.

Develop the Text

✓ Reports and proposals have an opening, body, and close.
✓ Content and length of each section varies.
✓ Be sure report content is accurate, complete, balanced, well-structured, and well-documented.
✓ In proposals, be sure to demonstrate your knowledge, provide concrete examples, research the competition, prove that your proposal is workable, adopt a "you" attitude, and package your proposal attractively.

Draft the Opening

✓ Tie the message to a problem or assignment.
✓ Introduce your subject and explain why it's important.
✓ Preview the main ideas and the order in which they are discussed.
✓ Establish the tone of the message and your relationship with the audience.
✓ In proposals, be sure to also summarize the solution to the problem, and mention the RFP in unsolicited proposals or the factors that led you to submit an unsolicited proposal.

Drafting the Body

✓ Present, analyze, and interpret the information you gathered during your investigation.
✓ Include the "proof" that supports your conclusions and recommendations.
✓ Provide only as much detail as you need to support your conclusions and recommendations.
✓ In direct analytical reports, provide the evidence to support your conclusions and recommendations.
✓ In indirect analytical reports, explain and discuss your logic, reserving your conclusions and recommendations until the very end.

Draft the Close

✓ Leave a strong and lasting impression.
✓ Emphasize the main points.
✓ Summarize the reader benefits of the recommended action.
✓ Remind readers of how all the pieces of your report fit together.
✓ Review all action items and delineate who should do what, when, where, and how.
✓ In direct reports, summarize key points and briefly restate your conclusions and recommendations.
✓ In indirect reports, you may state your conclusions and recommendations for the first time.
✓ You may cover your conclusions and recommendations in separate sections or under one heading.
✓ In a proposal, in addition to summarizing key points and emphasizing reader benefits, review the merits of your approach, restate why your firm or group should do the work, and ask for a decision from the client.

Choose the Proper Degree of Formality

✓ Use an informal style (*I* and *you*) for letter and memo reports (unless your company prefers impersonal third person).
✓ Use an impersonal style for more formal, short reports in manuscript format.

Maintain a Consistent Time Frame

✓ Write in either the present or the past tense, using other tenses only to indicate prior or future events.
✓ Don't flip from tense to tense.
✓ Observe the chronological sequence of events.

Help Readers Find Their Way

✓ Provide headings to improve readability, clarify framework, and indicate shifts in discussion.
✓ Use transitions to tie ideas together and help readers move from one topic to the next.
✓ Provide previews to prepare readers for new information.
✓ Provide reviews to summarize information and help readers see the big picture.

On the Job:

SOLVING COMMUNICATION DILEMMAS AT FEDEX

As Frederick Smith and his managers vie with the competition, work toward customer satisfaction, and keep the business running smoothly, business reports continue to play a key role at FedEx. You have recently been hired as Frederick Smith's administrative assistant to help him with a variety of special projects. In each of the following situations, choose the best communication alternative from among those listed, and be prepared to explain why your choice is best.

1. To keep tabs on the industry, Smith has asked you to research two online services offered by FedEx's top competitors: online pickup requests and online package tracking. How should you introduce your report? Choose the best opening from the four shown below.

   a. Begin by introducing the purpose of the study (to review what online services competitors are offering) and making recommendations about how FedEx can better compete with these offerings.

   b. Begin by introducing the purpose of the study (to review what online services competitors are offering) and outlining how you will present your data.

   c. Begin by giving a brief history of the rivalry between FedEx and its top three competitors.

   d. Begin by summarizing FedEx efforts to stay on top of the technology wave and how important such technology will be to the future of the company.

2. As you work on your report about competitors' online services, you want to include a visual that compares FedEx's online statistics with those of its major competitors. For example, you know that fedex.com receives 3 million visitors each month and gets 1.1 million tracking requests per day. Once you have located the same information for all major competitors, what is the best way to present it?

   a. Use a table to present the numbers for each company.

   b. Use a line chart to present the numbers for each company.

   c. Use a bar chart to present the numbers for each company.

   d. Use a pie chart to present the numbers for each company.

3. Smith wants to celebrate the company's thirty-fifth anniversary by creating a special advertising insert on FedEx history. He wants to distribute this insert inside the April issue of a national business magazine. The magazine's publisher is excited about the concept and has asked Smith to send her "something in writing." Smith asks you to draft the proposal, which should be no more than ten pages long. Which of the following outlines should you use?

   a. First Version
      I. An overview of FedEx's history
         A. How company was founded
         B. Overview of company services
         C. Overview of markets served
         D. Overview of transportation operations
      II. The FedEx magazine insert
         A. Historic events to be included
         B. Employees to be interviewed
         C. Customers to be discussed
         D. Production schedule
      III. Pros and cons of FedEx magazine insert
         A. Pros: Make money for magazine, draw new customers for FedEx
         B. Cons: Costs, questionable audience interest

   b. Second Version
      I. Introduction: Overview of the FedEx special insert
         A. Purpose
         B. Content
         C. Timing
      II. Description of the insert
         A. Text
            1. Message from CEO
            2. History of FedEx
            3. Interviews with employees
            4. Customer testimonials
         B. Advertising
            1. Inside front and back covers
            2. Color spreads
            3. Congratulatory ads placed by customers
      III. Next steps
      IV. Summary

   c. Third Version
      Who: FedEx
      What: Special magazine insert
      When: Inserted in April issue
      Where: Coordinated by magazine's editors
      Why: To celebrate FedEx's anniversary
      How: Overview of content, production responsibilities, and schedule

   d. Fourth Version
      I. Introduction: The rationale for producing a magazine insert promoting FedEx
         A. Insert would make money for magazine
         B. Insert would boost morale of FedEx employees
         C. Insert would attract new customers
      II. Insert description
         A. Interview with founder Frederick Smith
         B. Interviews with employees
         C. Description of historic moments
         D. Interviews with customers
         E. Advertisements

III. Production plan
    A. Project organization
    B. Timing and sequence of steps
    C. FedEx's responsibilities
    D. Magazine's responsibilities
IV. Detailed schedule
V. Summary of benefits and responsibilities

4. Smith has asked you to think about ways of attracting new customers that need FedEx's expertise in managing international parts and parcel distribution. You have talked with executives at Laura Ashley and National Semiconductor, two current customers, and discovered that they care most about the time needed to process orders and deliver parts to stores or factories. FedEx can cut the delivery time from as much as 21 days to as little as 4 days after ordering.

You believe that an advertising campaign featuring testimonials from these two satisfied customers will give FedEx a tremendous advantage over competitors. As a relatively junior person at FedEx, you are a little apprehensive about suggesting your idea. You don't want to seem presumptuous, but on the other hand, you think your idea is good. You have decided to raise the issue with Smith. Which of the following approaches is preferable?

a. Instead of writing a report, arrange a meeting to discuss your ideas with Smith, the advertising manager, and an executive from the company's advertising agency. This allows you to address the issues and ideas firsthand in an informal setting.

b. You write the following short report:
You recently asked me to give some thought to how FedEx might attract new customers for its international parts distribution business. I decided to sound out two of our largest customers to get a feel for why they hired us to handle this operation. Interestingly, they didn't choose FedEx because they wanted to reduce their shipping costs. Rather, they were interested in reducing the time needed to process and ship orders to stores and factories.

Many companies are in the same situation as Laura Ashley and National Semiconductor. They're not just looking for the carrier with the lowest prices, they're looking for the carrier with the proven ability to process orders and get shipments to their destinations as quickly as possible. Instead of waiting as long as 21 days for shipments to reach their destination, these companies can promise delivery in 4 days.

Clearly, our track record with Laura Ashley and National Semiconductor is the key to capturing the attention of other global companies. After all, how many competitors can show they have the ability to cut as much as 17 days off the time needed to process and deliver an order? Of course, companies might be skeptical if we made this claim on our own, but they would be more likely to accept it if our customers told their own stories. That's why FedEx should ask executives from Laura Ashley and National Semiconductor to offer testimonials in an advertising campaign.

c. You write the following short report:
In response to your request, I have investigated ways in which FedEx might attract new customers for its international parts distribution business. In conducting this investigation, I have talked with executives at two of our largest customers, Laura Ashley and National Semiconductor, and discussed the situation with our advertising manager and our advertising agency. All agreed that companies are interested in more than merely saving money on international shipments.

Typically, a global company has to keep a lot of parts or materials on hand and be ready to ship these whenever a store or factory places an order. As soon as an order arrives, the company packages the parts and ships it out. The store or factory doesn't want to wait a long time because it, in turn, has to keep a lot of money tied up in parts to be sure it doesn't run out before the new shipment arrives. Thus, if the company can cut the time between ordering and delivery, it will save its stores or factories a lot of money and, at the same time, build a lot of customer loyalty.

As a result, shipping costs are less important than the need to process orders and get shipments to their destinations as quickly as possible. Instead of delivery in 21 days, these companies can promise deliveries in 4 days. If we can show global companies how to do this, we will attract many more customers.

d. You write the following short report:
This report was authorized by Frederick W. Smith on May 7. Its purpose is to analyze ways of attracting more customers to FedEx's international parts distribution business.

Laura Ashley and National Semiconductor are two large, global companies that use our international parts distribution service. Both companies are pleased with our ability to cut the time between ordering and parts delivery. Both are willing to give testimonials to that effect.

These testimonials will help attract new customers if they are used in newspaper, magazine, and television advertising. A company is more likely to believe a satisfied customer than someone who works for FedEx. If the advertising department and the advertising agency start working on this idea today, it could be implemented within two months.[8]

Learning Objectives Checkup

To assess your understanding of the principles in this chapter, read each learning objective and study the accompanying exercises. For fill-in items, write the missing text in the blank provided; for multiple choice items, circle the letter of the correct answer. You can check your responses against the answer key on page AK-2.

Objective 11.1: Name four decisions you must make before drafting your business report or proposal.

1. Which of the following is *not* one of the major decisions you need to make before drafting your business report or proposal?
   a. Decide on format and length.
   b. Decide on the number and type of visuals.
   c. Choose the direct or the indirect approach.
   d. Choose the most appropriate structure.

2. Your report is likely to be longer if
   a. Your material is controversial
   b. Your readers are relative strangers
   c. Your readers are likely to be hostile or skeptical
   d. All of the above are the case

3. The _____ approach is by far the most popular and convenient for business reports.
   a. Direct
   b. Indirect
   c. Spatial
   d. Democratic

Objective 11.2: Compare and contrast the structures of informational and analytical reports.

4. Informational reports usually use a _____ organization.
   a. Scientific
   b. Yardstick
   c. Topical
   d. Logical

5. An analytical report that focuses on _____ uses the direct approach and establishes the need for action in the opening.
   a. Conclusions
   b. Recommendations
   c. Logical arguments
   d. The scientific method

6. When you use the _____, you show the strengths and weaknesses of all possible solutions.
   a. 2 + 2 approach
   b. Yardstick approach
   c. Scientific method
   d. Topical approach

Objective 11.3: List five of the most popular types of visuals and indicate when to use them.

7. If you want to present a lot of precise, detailed information, the best visual to use is
   a. A table
   b. A line chart
   c. A bar chart
   d. A pie chart

8. If you want to show trends over time, the best visual to use is
   a. A table
   b. A line chart
   c. A pie chart
   d. A diagram

9. If you want to compare one part with the whole, the best visual to use is
   a. A table
   b. A line chart
   c. A pie chart
   d. A diagram

10. If you want to illustrate a process or procedure, the best visual to use is
    a. A table
    b. A line chart
    c. A pie chart
    d. A diagram

Objective 11.4: Discuss five design principles to keep in mind when preparing visuals.

11. For an effective design, it is important to
    a. Include as much decoration as possible to keep the material lively and interesting
    b. Use as many colors as possible
    c. Keep design elements consistent from one visual to the next
    d. Do all of the above

Objective 11.5: Describe three ways to tie visuals to your text.

12. When introducing visuals in the text, you
    a. Give each visual a number that can be referred to in the text
    b. Refer to the visuals after they appear
    c. Include the same details in the text as you do in the visual
    d. Do all of the above

13. To draw attention to the conclusion that ought to be drawn from the data, give your visual
    a. A descriptive title
    b. An informative title
    c. An analytical title
    d. A conclusive title

Objective 11.6: List four questions to ask yourself when checking visuals.

14. Which of the following is *not* one of the main questions to ask yourself when checking visuals?
    a. Is the visual necessary?
    b. Is the visual accurate?
    c. Is the visual properly documented?
    d. Is the visual pretty?

Objective 11.7: Review four tasks to keep in mind while composing your report or proposal.

15. To determine the appropriate tone for your report, you should consider
    a. Other reports of similar type in your company
    b. How well you know your readers
    c. Whether the audience is multicultural
    d. All of the above

16. Which of the following is *not* a major tool for helping readers find their way through your document?
    a. Headings
    b. Captions and legends
    c. Transitions
    d. Previews and reviews
17. When preparing the content for your report, it is important to make sure that it is
    a. Accurate
    b. Complete
    c. Balanced
    d. All of the above

Objective 11.8: Identify the goals to accomplish in the opening of your reports, solicited proposals, and unsolicited proposals.

18. Which of the following is *not* a goal to be accomplished in your report's opening?
    a. Tie the report to a problem or assignment.
    b. Preview the main ideas.
    c. Capture the reader's attention with an anecdote or provocative question.
    d. Introduce the report's subject and indicate why it is important.

Objective 11.9: Summarize the various goals to accomplish in the close of your reports and proposals.

19. Which of the following is *not* a goal to be accomplished in your report's closing?
    a. Emphasize the main points of the message.
    b. Introduce new facts to help support your conclusion or recommendations.
    c. Summarize reader benefits.
    d. Refer back to all the pieces and remind readers of how those pieces fit together.

Apply Your Knowledge

1. Would you use the direct or the indirect approach to document inventory shortages at your manufacturing plant? To propose an employee stock-option plan? Why?
2. Which tense is better for most business reports, past or present? Explain.
3. What similarities do you see between visuals and nonverbal communication? Explain your answer.
4. When you read a graph, how can you be sure that the visual impression you are receiving is an accurate reflection of reality? Please explain.
5. **Ethical Choices** If a company receives a solicited formal proposal, is it ethical for the company to adopt the recommendations discussed in the proposal even though the company does not want to hire the submitting firm?

Practice Your Knowledge

DOCUMENTS FOR ANALYSIS
DOCUMENT 11.A

Read Figure 11–18, a solicited proposal; then (1) analyze the strengths and weaknesses of this document and (2) revise the document so that it follows this chapter's guidelines.

DOCUMENT 11.B

Examine the pie charts in Figure 11–19 and point out any problems or errors you notice.

Exercises

For live links to all websites discussed in this chapter, visit this text's website at www.prenhall.com/thill. Just log on, select Chapter 11, and click on "Student Resources." Locate the page or the URL related to the material in the text. For the "Learning More on the Web" exercises, you'll also find navigational directions. Click on the live link to the site.

11.1 **Organizing Reports: Choosing the Direct or Indirect Approach** Of the organizational approaches introduced in this chapter, which is best suited for reports answering each of the following questions? Briefly explain why. (Note, you will write one report for each question item.)
    a. In which market segment—root beer, cola, or lemon-lime—should Fizz Drinks, Inc., introduce a new soft drink to take advantage of its enlarged research and development budget?
    b. Should Major Manufacturing, Inc., close down operations of its antiquated Bellville, Arkansas, plant despite the adverse economic impact on the town that has grown up around the plant?
    c. Should you and your partner adopt a new accounting method to make your financial statements look better to potential investors?
    d. Should Grand Canyon Chemicals buy disposable test tubes to reduce labor costs associated with cleaning and sterilizing reusable test tubes?
    e. What are some reasons for the recent data loss at the college computer center, and how can we avoid similar problems in the future?

FIGURE 11–18
Solicited Proposal for Analysis

FAX

TO: Ken Estes, Northern Illinois Concrete
FROM: Kris Beiersdorf, Memco Construction
DATE: April 19, 2004
PROJECT: IDOT Letting Item #83 Contract No. 79371 DuPage County

Memco Construction proposes to furnish all labor, material, equipment, and supervision to provide Engineered Fill—Class II and IV for the following unit prices.

Engineered Fill – Class II and IV

Description	Unit	Quantity	Unit Price	Total
Mobilization*	Lump Sum	1	$4,500.00	$4,500.00
Engineered Fill Class II	Cubic Yards	1,267	$33.00	$41,811.00
Engineered Fill Class IV	Cubic Yards	1,394	$38.00	$52,972.00

* Mobilization includes one move-in. Additional move-ins to be billed at $1,100.00 each.

The following items clarify and qualify the scope of our subcontracting work:
1. All forms, earthwork, clearing, etc. to be provided and maintained by others at no cost to Memco Construction.
2. General Contractor shall provide location for staging, stockpiling material, equipment, and storage at the job site.
3. Memco Construction shall be paid strictly based upon the amount of material actually used on the job.
4. All prep work, including geotechnical fabrics, geomembrane liners, etc. to be done by others at no cost to Memco Construction.
5. Water is to be available at project site at no charge to Memco Construction.
6. Dewatering to be done by others at no cost to Memco Construction.
7. Traffic control setup, devices, maintenance, and flagmen are to be provided by others at no cost to Memco Construction.
8. Memco Construction LLC may withdraw this bid if we do not receive a written confirmation that we are the apparent low sub-bidder within 10 days of your receipt of this proposal.
9. Our F.E.I.N. is 36-4478095.
10. Bond is not included in above prices. Bond is available for an additional 1 percent.

If you have any questions, please contact me at the phone number listed below.

Kris Beiersdorf
Memco Construction
187 W. Euclid Avenue, Glenview, IL 60025
Office: (847) 352-9742, ext. 30
Fax: (847) 352-6595
E-mail: Kbeiersdorf@memco.com
www.memco.com

FIGURE 11–19
Pie Charts for Analysis

What types of life insurance policies are in effect?

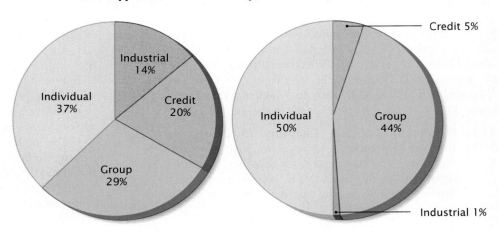

2000   2002

11.2 Organizing Reports: Deciding on Format Go to the library or visit the Internet site www.annualreportservice.com, and review the annual reports recently released by two corporations in the same industry. Analyze each report and be prepared to discuss the following questions in class:

a. What organizational differences, if any, do you see in the way each corporation discusses its annual performance? Are the data presented clearly so that shareholders can draw conclusions about how well the company performed?

b. What goals, challenges, and plans do top managers emphasize in their discussion of results?

c. How do the format and organization of each report enhance or detract from the information being presented?

11.3 Organizing Reports: Structuring Informational Reports Assume that your college president has received many student complaints about campus parking problems. You are appointed to chair a student committee organized to investigate the problems and recommend solutions. The president gives you the file labeled "Parking: Complaints from Students," and you jot down the essence of the complaints as you inspect the contents. Your notes look like this:

- Inadequate student spaces at critical hours
- Poor night lighting near the computer center
- Inadequate attempts to keep resident neighbors from occupying spaces
- Dim marking lines
- Motorcycles taking up full spaces
- Discourteous security officers
- Spaces (usually empty) reserved for college officials
- Relatively high parking fees
- Full fees charged to night students even though they use the lots only during low-demand periods
- Vandalism to cars and a sense of personal danger
- Inadequate total space
- Resident harassment of students parking on the street in front of neighboring houses

Prepare an outline for an informational report to be submitted to committee members. Use a topical organization that categorizes this information.

11.4 Organizing Reports: Structuring Analytical Reports Three years ago, your company (a carpet manufacturer) modernized its Georgia plant in anticipation of increasing demand for carpets. Because of the stuttering economy, the predicted increase in demand for new carpets has been slow to materialize. As a result, the company has excess capacity at both its Georgia and California plants. On the basis of your research, you have recommended that the company close the California plant. The company president, J. P. Lawrence, has asked you to prepare a justification report to support your recommendation. Here are the facts you gathered by interviewing the respective plant managers:

OPERATIONAL STATISTICS

- Georgia plant: Plant has newer equipment, productivity is higher, employs 100 nonunion production workers, and ships $12 million in carpets a year. Hourly base wage is $16.
- California plant: California plant employs 80 union production workers and ships $8 million in carpets a year. Hourly base wage is $20.

FINANCIAL IMPLICATIONS

- Savings by closing California plant: (1) Increase productivity by 17%; (2) reduce labor costs by 20% (total labor savings would be $1 million per year; see assumptions); (3) annual local tax savings of $120,000 (Georgia has a more favorable tax climate).
- Sale of Pomona, California, land: Purchased in 1952 for $200,000. Current market value $6.5 million. Net profit (after capital gains tax) over $4.5 million.
- Sale of plant and equipment: Fully depreciated. Any proceeds a windfall.
- Costs of closing California plant: One-time deductible charge of $750,000 (relocation costs of $350,000 and severance payments totaling $280,000).

ASSUMPTIONS

- Transfer 5 workers from California to Georgia.
- Hire 45 new workers in Georgia.
- Lay off 75 workers in California.
- Georgia plant would require a total of 150 workers to produce the combined volume of both plants.

a. Which approach (focus on conclusions, recommendations, or logical arguments) will you use to structure your report to the president? Why?

b. Suppose this report were to be circulated to plant managers and supervisors instead. What changes, if any, might you make in your approach?

c. List some conclusions that you might draw from the above information to use in your report.

d. Using the structure you selected for your report to the president, draft a final report outline with first- and second-level informative headings.

11.5 Visual Aids: Preparing Pie Charts As a market researcher for a statewide chain of car dealerships, you're examining car and truck ownership and lease patterns among single drivers in various age groups. By discovering which age groups have the highest percentages of owners, you will be better able to target advertising that promotes the leasing option. Using the following information, prepare a bar chart comparing the number of owners with the number of leasers in each age category. Be sure to label your chart, and include combined totals for owners and leasers ("total drivers"). Then prepare a pie chart showing the proportion of owners and leasers in the one age group that you think holds the most promise for leasing a new vehicle. Write a sentence that prepares your company's management for the information shown in the pie chart.

Age group	Number of owners (in 000s)	Number of leasers (in 000s)
18–24	1,830	795
25–29	1,812	1,483
30–34	1,683	1,413
35–44	1,303	1,932
45–54	1,211	1,894
55–64	1,784	1,435
65–74	3,200	1,142
75+	3,431	854

11.6 **Visual Aids: Preparing Line Charts** The pet food manufacturer you work for is interested in the results of a recent poll of U.S. pet-owning households. Look at the statistics that follow and decide on the most appropriate scale for a chart; then create a line chart of the trends in cat ownership. What conclusions do you draw from the trend you've charted? Draft a paragraph or two discussing the results of this poll and the potential consequences for the pet food business. Support your conclusions by referring readers to your chart.

In 1985, 22 million U.S. households owned a cat. In 1990, 24 million households owned a cat. In 1995, 28 million households owned a cat. In 2000, 32 million households owned a cat.

11.7 **Visual Aids: Selection** You're preparing the annual report for FretCo Guitar Corporation. For each of the following types of information, select the right chart or visual to illustrate the text. Explain your choices.
a. Data on annual sales for the past 20 years.
b. Comparison of FretCo sales, product by product (electric guitars, bass guitars, amplifiers, acoustic guitars), for this year and last year.
c. Explanation of how a FretCo acoustic guitar is manufactured.
d. Explanation of how the FretCo Guitar Corporation markets its guitars.
e. Data on sales of FretCo products in each of 12 countries.
f. Comparison of FretCo sales figures with sales figures for three competing guitar makers over the past 10 years.

11.8 **Visual Aids: Preparing Bar Charts** Team up with a classmate to design charts based on a comparison of the total tax burden of the U.S. taxpayer with that of people in other nations. One teammate should sketch a horizontal or vertical bar chart and the other should sketch a pictogram from the estimates that follow. Then exchange charts and analyze how well each conveys the situation of the U.S. taxpayer. Would the bar chart look best with vertical or horizontal bars? Why? What scale is best? How does the symbol used in the pictogram enhance or obscure the meaning or impact of the data? What suggestions can each student make for improving the other's visual aid?

Estimates show that Swedish taxpayers spend 51 percent of their incomes on taxes, British taxpayers spend 48 percent, French taxpayers spend 37 percent, Japanese taxpayers spend 28 percent, and U.S. taxpayers spend 27 percent.

11.9 **Visual Aids: Creating Organization Charts** Create an organization chart for your school. You will probably need to consult your school library or administration office for documents listing the various offices and departments. Figure 11–13 can serve as a model for how to structure your chart.

11.10 **Internet** One of the best places to see how data can be presented visually is in government statistical publications, which are often available on the Internet. For example, the International Trade Administration (ITA), a branch of the U.S. Department of Commerce, publishes monthly reports about U.S. trade with other countries. Visit the report page of its website at www.ita.doc.gov and follow the link to the latest monthly trade update. Using what you learned in this chapter, evaluate the charts in the report. Do they present the data clearly? Are they missing any elements? What would you do to improve the charts? Print out a copy of the report to turn in with your answers, and indicate which charts you are evaluating.

11.11 **Ethical Choices** Create a bar or line chart using data you find online or in a business publication. Make a copy of your chart and alter the chart's scale. How does the altered chart distort the information? How might you detect whether a chart's scale has been altered?

11.12 **Composing Reports: Report Content** You are writing an analytical report on the U.S. sales of your newest product. Of the following topics, identify those that should be covered in the report's opening, body, and closing. Briefly explain your decisions:
a. Regional breakdowns of sales across the country
b. Date the product was released in the marketplace
c. Sales figures from competitors selling similar products worldwide
d. Predictions of how the struggling U.S. economy will affect sales over the next six months
e. Method used for obtaining the above predictions
f. The impact of similar products being sold in the United States by Japanese competitors
g. Your recommendation as to whether the company should sell this product internationally
h. Actions that must be completed by year-end if the company decides to sell this product internationally

11.13 **Composing Business Reports** Your boss, Len Chow (vice president of corporate planning), has asked you to research opportunities in the cosmetics industry and to prepare a report that presents your findings and your recommendation for where you think the company should focus its marketing efforts. Here's a copy of your note cards (data were created for this exercise):

Sub: Demand Industry grew through 1970s, 1980s, and early 1990s fueled by per capita consumption	ref:1.1
Sub: Competition 700 companies currently in cosmetics industry	ref:1.2
Sub: Niches Focusing on special niches avoids head-on competition with industry leaders	ref:1.3
Sub: Competition Industry dominated by market leaders: Revlon, Procter & Gamble, Avon, Gillette	ref: 1.4
Sub: Demand Industry no longer recession-proof: Past year, sales sluggish; consumer spending is down; most affected were mid- to high-priced brands; consumers traded down to less expensive lines	ref: 1.5
Sub: Competition Smaller companies (Neutrogena, Mary Kay, Soft Soap, and Noxell) survive by specializing in niches, differentiating product line, focusing on market segment	ref: 1.6
Sub: Demand Consumption of cosmetics relatively flat for past five years	ref: 1.7
Sub: Competition Prices are constant while promotion budgets are increasing	ref: 1.8
Sub: Niches Men: 50% of adult population; account for one-fifth of cosmetic sales; market leaders have attempted this market but failed	ref: 1.9
Sub: Demand Cosmetic industry is near maturity but some segments may vary. Total market currently produces annual retail sales of $14.5 billion: Cosmetics/lotions/fragrances—$5.635 billion; Personal hygiene products—$4.375 billion; Hair-care products—$3.435 billion; Shaving products—$1.055 billion	ref: 1.10
Sub: Niches Ethnic groups: Some firms specialize in products for African Americans; few firms oriented toward Hispanic, Asian, or Native Americans, which tend to be concentrated geographically	ref: 1.11
Sub: Demand Average annual expenditure per person for cosmetics is $58	ref: 1.12
Sub: Competition Competition is intensifying and dominant companies are putting pressure on smaller ones	ref: 1.13
Sub: Demand First quarter of current year, demand is beginning to revive; trend expected to continue well into next year	ref: 1.14
Sub: Niches Senior citizens: large growing segment of population; account for 6% of cosmetic sales; specialized needs for hair and skin not being met; interested in appearance	ref: 1.15
Sub: Demand Demographic trends: (1) Gradual maturing of baby-boomer generation will fuel growth by consuming greater quantities of shaving cream, hair-coloring agents, and skin creams; (2) population is increasing in the South and Southwest, where some brands have strong distribution	ref: 1.16

List the main idea of your message (your recommendation), the major points (your conclusions), and supporting evidence. Then construct a final report outline with first- and second-level informative headings focusing on your conclusions. Because Chow requested this report, you can feel free to use the direct approach. Finish by writing a draft of your memo report to Chow.

11.14 Composing Reports: Navigational Clues Review a long business article in a journal or newspaper. Highlight examples of how the article uses headings, transitions, and previews and reviews to help the readers find their way.

Expand Your Knowledge

LEARNING MORE ON THE WEB

Research Before You Report www.corporateinformation.com Research your competition at Corporate Information and find out what you need to know before you write your next report or proposal. This website has links to over 350,000 company profiles, data on 30 industries in 65 countries, and current economic information for over 100 countries. You'll also find research reports analyzing sales, dividends, earnings, and profit ratios on some 15,000 companies, current foreign exchange rates, and the definitions of commonly used global company extensions such as GmbH, SA, de CV, and more.

ACTIVITIES

Visit Corporate Information to find information on numerous companies, industries, and countries.

1. Select an industry of your choice from one of the listed countries and follow the links to reports, analyses, and data on that industry. What specific types of information did you find on the industry? How might you use this information when writing a report or proposal?

2. Read the online research reports for a company of your choice. What types of specific information are available in these reports? How might you use this information when writing a report or proposal?

3. What do the company extensions GmbH, KK, LLC, OHG, SA, and SNC mean?

EXPLORING THE WEB ON YOUR OWN

Review these chapter-related websites to learn more about writing reports and proposals.

1. Become an Excel pro by reading the Tips and Tricks and How-to Articles at the Microsoft Excel homepage, www.microsoft.com/office/excel/default.htm. Click on Using Excel to get started.

2. Learn how to find specific information on the web and validate what you find at Internet Search FAQ, www.purefiction.com/pages/res1/htm. Click on links, then click on Using the Internet for Research FAQ.

3. Learn how to create effective diagrams at the Microsoft Visio website, www.microsoft.com/office/visio. Click on Using Visio to get started.

Learn Interactively

INTERACTIVE STUDY GUIDE

Go to the Companion Website at www.prenhall.com/bovee. For Chapter 11, take advantage of the interactive "Study Guide" to test your knowledge of the chapter. Get instant feedback on whether you need additional studying. Also, visit this site's "Study Hall" where you'll find an abundance of valuable resources that will help you succeed in this course.

PEAK PERFORMANCE GRAMMAR AND MECHANICS

To improve your skill with dashes and hyphens, visit this text's website at www.prenhall.com/onekey. Click "Peak Performance

Grammar and Mechanics," then click "Punctuation II." Take the Pretest to determine whether you have any weak areas. Review those areas in the Refresher Course, and take the Follow-Up Test to check your grasp of dashes and hyphens. For advanced practice, take the Advanced Test. Finally, for additional reinforcement, go to the "Improve Your Grammar, Mechanics, and Usage" section that follows, and complete those exercises.

Improve Your Grammar, Mechanics, and Usage

The following exercises help you improve your knowledge of and power over English grammar, mechanics, and usage. Turn to the "Handbook of Grammar, Mechanics, and Usage" at the end of this textbook and review all of Sections 2.7 (Dashes) and 2.8 (Hyphens). Then look at the following 10 items. Circle the letter of the preferred choice in the following groups of sentences. (Answers to these exercises appear on page AK-4.)

1. a. Three qualities—speed, accuracy, and reliability are desirable in any applicant.
   b. Three qualities—speed, accuracy, and reliability—are desirable in any applicant.

2. a. A highly placed source explained the top-secret negotiations.
   b. A highly-placed source explained the top-secret negotiations.

c. A highly placed source explained the top secret negotiations.

3. a. The file on Mary Gaily—yes—we finally found it reveals a history of tardiness.
   b. The file on Mary Gaily, yes—we finally found it—reveals a history of tardiness.
   c. The file on Mary Gaily—yes, we finally found it—reveals a history of tardiness.

4. a. They're selling a well designed machine.
   b. They're selling a well-designed machine.

5. a. Argentina, Brazil, Mexico—these are the countries we hope to concentrate on.
   b. Argentina, Brazil, Mexico—these are the countries—we hope to concentrate on.

6. a. Only two sites maybe three—offer the things we need.
   b. Only two sites—maybe three—offer the things we need.

7. a. How many owner operators are in the industry?
   b. How many owner—operators are in the industry?
   c. How many owner-operators are in the industry?

8. a. Your ever-faithful assistant deserves—without a doubt—a substantial raise.
   b. Your ever faithful assistant deserves—without a doubt—a substantial raise.

9. a. The charts are well placed—on each page—unlike the running heads and footers.
   b. The charts are well-placed on each page—unlike the running heads and footers.
   c. The charts are well placed on each page—unlike the running heads and footers.

10. a. Your devil-may-care attitude affects everyone in the decision-making process.
    b. Your devil may care attitude affects everyone in the decision-making process.
    c. Your devil-may-care attitude affects everyone in the decision making process.

Cases

INFORMAL INFORMATIONAL REPORTS

1. My progress to date: Interim progress report on your academic career As you know, the bureaucratic process involved in getting a degree or certificate is nearly as challenging as any course you could take.

Your task: Prepare an interim progress report detailing the steps you've taken toward completing your graduation or certification requirements. After examining the requirements listed in your college catalog, indicate a realistic schedule for completing those that remain. In addition to course requirements, include steps such as completing the residency requirement, filing necessary papers, and paying necessary fees. Use memo format for your report, and address it to anyone who is helping or encouraging you through school.

2. Gavel to gavel: Personal activity report of a meeting Meetings, conferences, and conventions abound in the academic world, and you have probably attended your share.

Your task: Prepare a personal activity report on a meeting, convention, or conference that you recently attended. Use memo format, and direct the report to other students in your field who were not able to attend.

3. Check that price tag: Informational report on trends in college costs Your college's administration has asked you to compare your college's tuition costs with those of a nearby college and determine which has risen more quickly. Research the trend by checking your college's annual tuition costs for each of the most recent four years. Then research the four-year tuition trends for a neighboring college. For both colleges, calculate the percentage change in tuition costs from year to year and between the first and fourth year.

Your task: Prepare an informal report (using the letter format) presenting your findings and conclusions to the president of your college. Include graphics to explain and support your conclusions.

4. Get a move on it: Lasting guidelines for moving into college dormitories Moving into a college dormitory is one experience you weren't quite prepared for. In addition to lugging your earthly belongings up four flights of stairs in 90-degree heat, channeling electrical cords to the one room outlet tucked in the corner of the room, lofting your beds, and negotiating with your roommate over who gets the bigger closet, you had to hug your parents goodbye in the parking lot in front of the entire freshman class—or so it seemed. Now that you are a pro, you've offered to write some lasting guidelines for future freshmen so they know what is expected of them on moving day.

Your task: Prepare an informational report for future freshmen classes outlining the rules and procedures to follow when moving into a college dorm. Lay out the rules such as starting time, handling trash and empty boxes, items permitted and not permitted in dorm rooms, common courtesies, and so on. Be sure to mention what the policy is for removing furniture from the room, lofting beds, and overloading electrical circuits. Of course, any recommendations on how to handle disputes with roommates would be helpful. So would some brief advice on how to cope with anxious parents. Direct your memo report to the college dean.

INFORMAL ANALYTICAL REPORTS

5. My next career move: Feasibility report organized around recommendations If you've ever given yourself a really good talking-to, you'll be quite comfortable with this project.

Your task: Write a memo report directed to yourself and signed with a fictitious name. Indicate a possible job that your college education will qualify you for, mention the advantages of the position in terms of your long-range goals, and then outline the actions you must take to get the job.

6. Staying the course: Unsolicited proposal using the 2 + 2 = 4 approach Think of a course you would love to see added to the core curriculum at your school. Conversely, if you would like to see a course offered as an elective rather than being required, write your e-mail report accordingly.

Your task: Write a short e-mail proposal using the 2 + 2 = 4 approach. Prepare your proposal to be submitted to the academic dean by e-mail. Be sure to include all the reasons supporting your idea.

7. Planning my program: Problem-solving report using the scientific method Assume that you will have time for only one course next term.

Your task: List the pros and cons of four or five courses that interest you, and use the scientific method to settle on the course that is best for you to take at this time. Write your report in memo format, addressing it to your academic adviser.

8. "Would you carry it?" Unsolicited sales proposal recommending a product to a retail outlet Select a product you are familiar with, and imagine that you are the manufacturer trying to get a local retail outlet to carry it. Use the Internet and other resources to gather information about the product.

Your task: Write an unsolicited sales proposal in letter format to the owner (or manager) of the store, proposing that the item be stocked. Use the information you gathered to describe some of the product's features and benefits to the store. Then make up some reasonable figures, highlighting what the item costs, what it can be sold for, and what services your company provides (return of unsold items, free replacement of unsatisfactory items, necessary repairs, and so on).

9. Restaurant review: Troubleshooting report on a restaurant's food and operations Visit any restaurant, possibly your school cafeteria. The workers and fellow customers will assume that you are an ordinary customer, but you are really a spy for the owner.

Your task: After your visit, write a short memo to the owner, explaining (a) what you did and what you observed, (b) any violations of policy that you observed, and (c) your recommendations for improvement. The first part of your report (what you did and what you observed) will be the longest. Include a description of the premises, inside and out. Tell how long it took for each step of ordering and receiving your meal. Describe the service and food thoroughly. You are interested in both the good and bad aspects of the establishment's décor, service, and food. For the second section (violations of policy), use some common sense. If all the servers but one have their hair covered, you may assume that policy requires hair to be covered; a dirty window or restroom obviously violates policy. The last section (recommendations for improvement) involves professional judgment. What management actions will improve the restaurant?

10. On the books: Troubleshooting report on improving the campus bookstore Imagine that you are a consultant hired to improve the profits of your campus bookstore.

Your task: Visit the bookstore and look critically at its operations. Then draft a memo to the bookstore manager, offering recommendations that would make the store more profitable;

perhaps suggesting products it should carry, hours that it should remain open, or added services that it should make available to students. Be sure to support your recommendations.

11. Press 1 for efficiency: Unsolicited proposal on a telephone interviewing system How can a firm be thorough yet efficient when considering dozens of applicants for each position? One tool that just may help is IntelliView, a 10-minute programmed interview conducted by touch-tone telephone. The company recruiter dials up the IntelliView computer and then leaves the room. The candidate punches in answers to roughly 100 questions about work attitudes and other issues. In a few minutes, the recruiter can call Pinkerton, which offers the service, and find out the results. On the basis of what the IntelliView interview reveals, the recruiter can delve more deeply into certain areas and, ultimately, have more information on which to base the hiring decision.

Your task: As a recruiter for Curtis Box and Crate, you think that IntelliView might help your firm. Write a brief memo to Wallace Jefferson, the director of human resources, in which

you suggest a test of the IntelliView system. Your memo should tell your boss why you believe your firm should test the system before making a long-term commitment.[9]

12. Day and night: Problem-solving report on stocking a 24-hour convenience store When a store is open all day, every day, when's the best time to restock the shelves? That's the challenge at Store 24, a retail chain that never closes. Imagine you're the assistant manager of a Store 24 branch that just opened near your campus. You want to set up a restocking schedule that won't conflict with prime shopping hours. Think about the number of customers you're likely to serve in the morning, afternoon, evening, and overnight hours. Consider, too, how many employees you might have during these four periods.

Your task: Using the scientific approach, write a problem-solving report in letter form to the store manager (Isabel Chu) and the regional manager (Eric Angstrom), who must agree on a solution to this problem. Discuss the pros and cons of each of the four periods, and include your recommendation for restocking the shelves.

Chapter 12

Completing Formal Business Reports and Proposals

Learning Objectives

AFTER STUDYING THIS CHAPTER, YOU WILL BE ABLE TO

1 Identify the three tasks involved in completing business reports and proposals, and briefly explain what's involved in each one

2 Describe the 10 prefatory parts of a formal report

3 Explain the difference between a synopsis and an executive summary

4 List the three supplementary parts of a formal report and briefly describe each one

5 Identify the three prefatory parts of a formal proposal that differ from those of a formal report

6 Explain how the prefatory parts of a proposal differ depending on whether the proposal is solicited or unsolicited

On the Job:

COMMUNICATING AT LEVI STRAUSS

PLACING A HIGH VALUE ON REPORTS

Bob Haas takes business ethics seriously. As chairman of the board at Levi Strauss and Company (and as great-great-grandnephew of founder Levi Strauss), Haas defines his company's goal as "responsible commercial success." He envisions Levi Strauss being run according to principles such as teamwork, trust, ethical management, environmental care, diversity, and individual respect. One way to communicate such a complex vision to employees, customers, and members of the community is through reports. So in addition to ethics, Haas takes business communication seriously too, especially reports, even to the point of editing his staff's documents for grammar.

Robert Haas isn't the only one in his company who places value on reports. Employees at Levi Strauss and Company know how important it is to produce reports that are easily understood, logical, attractive, persuasive, and thorough. So they include all the necessary components to accomplish these goals.

Like most executives, Haas relies on reports to make decisions and set company policy. For example, to support his claim that employee empowerment leads to greater business success, he used a report from the California Public Employees' Retirement System (CalPERS). That is, he concluded from this report that stock prices actually rise when people on the front lines are given greater authority to act and to make decisions that are in the best interests of both the customer and the company.

Besides relying on reports for information, Haas strives to know everything he can about the best ways to develop reports. He has made effective reports one of his company's fundamental values.

Reports at Levi Strauss must be not only clear and well organized but also complete—containing all the elements necessary to promote easy understanding. One key report at Levi Strauss, based on Haas's vision of an ethically driven business, helps guide the decisions and actions of all 37,500 employees. Called the "Aspiration Statement," this report clearly outlines the types of values and behaviors that the company expects from its employees. It covers issues ranging from trust to empowerment and even to good business communication skills—all of which help the company become the organization that it aspires to be. By laying out these complex issues clearly and presenting them in a way that all employees can understand, Haas's report helps ensure that everyone is "reading from the same page." It helps him lead the company forward.

Although most business reports are not accessible to the general public, anyone visiting the Levi Strauss corporate website (www.levistrauss.com) can see how much the company values the written word. The site allows access to a number of reports, from the Aspirations Statement to a complete history of the company. All of these reports are clear and concise, and all have the components necessary to make the material easily understandable.[1]

www.levistrauss.com

REVISING REPORTS AND PROPOSALS

After finishing your first draft, complete your report:
- Revise
- Produce
- Proofread

Experienced business communicators such as Bob Haas realize that the process of writing a report doesn't end with the first draft. As Chapter 5 points out, when you compose a first draft, you simply try to get your ideas on paper with some semblance of organization, and you save strengthening, tightening, and polishing for later. Once you have finished your first draft, you perform three tasks to complete your report: revise, produce, and proofread.

The revision process is basically the same for reports as for any business message, but it may take longer, depending on the length of your report or proposal. In this process you evaluate your report's organization, style, and tone, making sure that you've said what you want to say and that you've said it in the most logical order and in a way that responds to your audience's needs. You then work on improving your report's readability by varying sentence length, keeping paragraphs short, using lists and bullets, and adding headings and subheadings. As you go along, you also edit the content of your report to make it as clear and concise as possible.

PRODUCING FORMAL REPORTS AND PROPOSALS

Once you are satisfied with your revision, the next step is to format and produce your report by incorporating the design elements discussed in Chapter 6. Typographical devices (such as capital letters, italics, and boldface type), margins, line justifications, and white space are just some of the techniques and tools you can use to present your material effectively. Also useful are visual aids to illustrate and emphasize major points, as well as preview and review statements to frame sections of your text. Many organizations have format guidelines that make your design decisions easier, but your goal is always to focus reader attention on major points and the flow of ideas.

Be sure to schedule enough time to turn out a document that looks professional.

Make sure that you schedule enough time for formatting and production. When working on reports (or any other business document), remember Murphy's law: If anything can go wrong, it will. Corrupted disk files, printing problems, and other glitches can consume hours. If you are preparing a long, formal report, you will need extra time to prepare and assemble all the various prefatory and supplementary parts.

A formal report's format and impersonal tone convey an impression of professionalism. A formal report can be either short (fewer than 10 pages) or long (10 pages or more). It can be informational or analytical, direct or indirect. It may be targeted to readers inside or outside the organization. What sets it apart from other reports is its polish. The more formal your report, the more components you'll include.

Components of a Formal Report

The three basic divisions of a formal report:
- Prefatory parts
- Text
- Supplementary parts

When deciding what components to include in reports at Levi Strauss, Bob Haas pays close attention to the needs of his readers, whether they are employees, customers, or members of the community. As listed in Figure 12–1, report components fall into three categories, depending on where they are found in a report:

- Prefatory parts

- Text parts

- Supplementary parts

For an illustration of how these various parts fit together, see Linda Moreno's Electrovision report in the "Report Writer's Notebook: Analyzing a Formal Report."

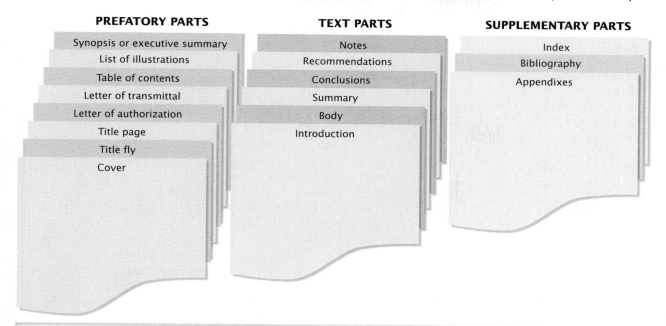

PREFATORY PARTS	TEXT PARTS	SUPPLEMENTARY PARTS
Synopsis or executive summary	Notes	Index
List of illustrations	Recommendations	Bibliography
Table of contents	Conclusions	Appendixes
Letter of transmittal	Summary	
Letter of authorization	Body	
Title page	Introduction	
Title fly		
Cover		

FIGURE 12-1
Parts of Formal Report

Many of the components in a formal report start on a new page, but not always. Inserting page breaks consumes more paper and adds to the bulk of your report (which may be a significant financial concern if you plan to distribute many copies). On the other hand, starting a section on a new page helps your readers navigate the report and recognize transitions between major sections or features.

Most prefatory parts (such as the table of contents) should be placed on their own pages, whereas the various parts in the text are often run together and seldom stand alone. For example, in this textbook, each chapter starts on a new page to provide a clear break between major topics. However, the opening vignettes flow right into the chapter without a page break. If your opening (or introduction) is only a paragraph long, don't bother with a page break before moving into the body of your report. But if your introduction runs longer than one page, a page break can signal the reader that a major shift is about to occur in the flow of the report.

The following sections discuss the three categories of report components: the prefatory parts, the text of the report, and the supplementary parts.

Prefatory Parts Prefatory parts are front-end materials that provide key preliminary information so that readers can decide whether to (and how to) read the report.[2] Although these parts are placed before the text of the report, you may not want to prepare them until after you've written the text. Many of these parts—such as the table of contents, list of illustrations, and executive summary—are easier to do after the text has been completed, because they directly reflect the contents. Other parts can be prepared at almost any time.

Cover Many companies have standard covers for reports, made of heavy paper and imprinted with the company's name and logo. Report titles are either printed on these covers or attached with gummed labels. If your company has no standard covers, you can usually find something suitable in a good stationery store. Look

Steve Jobs is CEO of Apple, which he co-founded in 1976, and CEO of Pixar, the Academy Award-winning computer animation studio, which he co-founded in 1986. Jobs revolutionized the computer hardware and software industry. Among other innovative ideas for software applications, Jobs developed the user-friendly interface with picture-like icons, giving any businessperson (even those lacking computer skills) the ability to produce professional-looking reports.

(continued on page 417)

REPORT WRITER'S NOTEBOOK
Analyzing an Effective Formal Report

The report presented in the following pages was prepared by Linda Moreno, manager of the cost accounting department at Electrovision, a high-tech company based in Los Gatos, California. Electrovision's main product is optical character recognition equipment, which is used by the U.S. Postal Service for sorting mail. Moreno's job is to help analyze the company's costs. She has this to say about the background of the report:

> For the past three or four years, Electrovision has been on a roll. Our A-12 optical character reader was a real breakthrough, and the post office grabbed up as many as we could make. Our sales and profits kept climbing, and morale was fantastic. Everybody seemed to think that the good times would last forever. Unfortunately, everybody was wrong. When the Postal Service announced that it was postponing all new equipment purchases because of cuts in its budget, we woke up to the fact that we are essentially a one-product company with one customer. At that point, management started scrambling around looking for ways to cut costs until we could diversify our business a bit.
>
> The vice president of operations, Dennis McWilliams, asked me to help identify cost-cutting opportunities in travel and entertainment. On the basis of his personal observations, he felt that Electrovision was overly generous in its travel policies and that we might be able to save a significant amount by controlling these costs more carefully. My investigation confirmed his suspicion.
>
> I was reasonably confident that my report would be well received. I've worked with Dennis for several years and know what he likes: plenty of facts, clearly stated conclu-

sions, and specific recommendations for what should be done next. I also knew that my report would be passed on to other Electrovision executives, so I wanted to create a good impression. I wanted the report to be accurate and thorough, visually appealing, readable, and appropriate in tone.

When writing the analytical report that follows, Moreno used an organization based on conclusions and recommendations, presented in direct order. The first two sections of the report correspond to Moreno's two main conclusions: that Electrovision's travel and entertainment costs are too high and that cuts are essential. The third section presents recommendations for achieving better control over travel and entertainment expenses. As you review the report, analyze both the mechanical aspects and the way Moreno presents her ideas. Be prepared to discuss the way the various components convey and reinforce the main message.

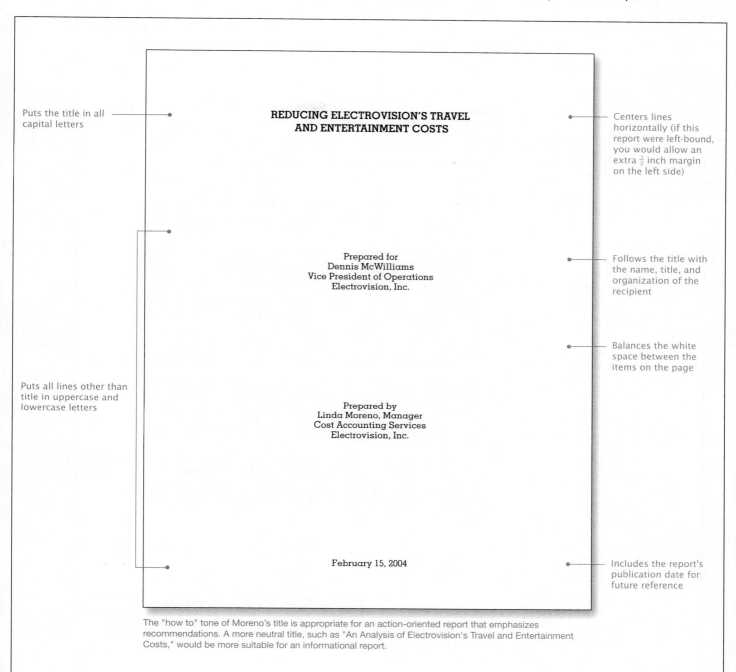

Puts the title in all capital letters

Puts all lines other than title in uppercase and lowercase letters

Centers lines horizontally (if this report were left-bound, you would allow an extra $\frac{1}{2}$ inch margin on the left side)

Follows the title with the name, title, and organization of the recipient

Balances the white space between the items on the page

Includes the report's publication date for future reference

REDUCING ELECTROVISION'S TRAVEL AND ENTERTAINMENT COSTS

Prepared for
Dennis McWilliams
Vice President of Operations
Electrovision, Inc.

Prepared by
Linda Moreno, Manager
Cost Accounting Services
Electrovision, Inc.

February 15, 2004

The "how to" tone of Moreno's title is appropriate for an action-oriented report that emphasizes recommendations. A more neutral title, such as "An Analysis of Electrovision's Travel and Entertainment Costs," would be more suitable for an informational report.

Uses memo format
for transmitting this
internal report;
otherwise, letter
format would be
used for transmitting
external reports

Presents the main
conclusion right away
(because Moreno
expects a positive
response)

Uses an informal,
conversational style

Acknowledges help
that has been
received

Closes with thanks
and an offer to
discuss results (when
appropriate, you
could also include an
offer to help with
future projects)

MEMORANDUM

TO: Dennis McWilliams, Vice President of Operations

FROM: Linda Moreno, Manager of Cost Accounting Services

DATE: February 15, 2004

SUBJECT: Reducing Electrovision's Travel and Entertainment Costs

Here is the report you requested January 30 on Electrovision's travel and entertainment costs.

Your suspicion was right. We are spending far too much on business travel. Our unwritten policy has been "anything goes," leaving us with no real control over T&E expenses. Although this hands-off approach may have been understandable when Electrovision's profits were high, we can no longer afford the luxury.

The solutions to the problem seem rather clear. We need to have someone with centralized responsibility for travel and entertainment costs, a clear statement of policy, an effective control system, and a business-oriented travel service that can optimize our travel arrangements. We should also investigate alternatives to travel, such as videoconferencing. Perhaps more important, we need to change our attitude. Instead of viewing travel funds as a bottomless supply of money, all traveling employees need to act as though they were paying the bills themselves.

Getting people to economize is not going to be easy. In the course of researching this issue, I've found that our employees are deeply attached to their first-class travel privileges. I think they would almost prefer a cut in pay to a loss in travel status. We'll need a lot of top-management involvement to sell people on the need for moderation. One thing is clear: People will be very bitter if we create a two-class system in which top executives get special privileges while the rest of the employees make the sacrifices.

I'm grateful to Mary Lehman and Connie McIlvain for their help in collecting and sorting five years' worth of expense reports. Their efforts were huge.

Thanks for giving me the opportunity to work on this assignment. It's been a real education. If you have any questions about the report, please give me a call.

In this report, Moreno decided to write a brief memo of transmittal and include a separate executive summary. Short reports (fewer than 10 pages) often combine the synopsis or executive summary with the memo or letter of transmittal.

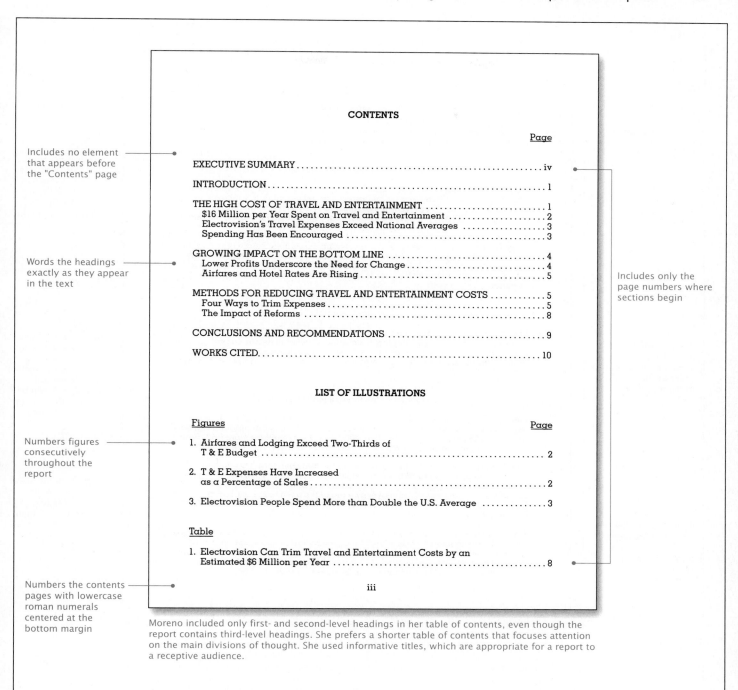

CONTENTS

LIST OF ILLUSTRATIONS

iii

Callout annotations (left margin):

Includes no element that appears before the "Contents" page

Words the headings exactly as they appear in the text

Numbers figures consecutively throughout the report

Numbers the contents pages with lowercase roman numerals centered at the bottom margin

Callout annotations (right margin):

Includes only the page numbers where sections begin

Moreno included only first- and second-level headings in her table of contents, even though the report contains third-level headings. She prefers a shorter table of contents that focuses attention on the main divisions of thought. She used informative titles, which are appropriate for a report to a receptive audience.

Begins by stating the purpose of the report

EXECUTIVE SUMMARY

This report analyzes Electrovision's travel and entertainment (T&E) costs and presents recommendations for reducing those costs.

Travel and Entertainment Costs Are Too High

T&E is a large and growing expense category for Electrovision. The company spends over $16 million per year on business travel, a cost that is increasing 12 percent annually. Employees make some 3,500 trips a year, each trip averaging $4,720. Airfares are the largest expense, followed by hotels and meals.

The nature of Electrovision's business requires extensive travel, but the company's costs seem excessive. Electrovision employees spend more than double what the average business traveler spends. Although the location of company facilities may partly explain this discrepancy, the firm's philosophy and managerial style invite employees to go first class and pay relatively little attention to travel costs.

Presents the points in the executive summary in the same order as they appear in the report

Cuts Are Essential

Electrovision management now recognizes the need to gain more control over this element of costs. The company is entering a period of declining profits, prompting management to look for every opportunity to reduce spending. Also, rising airfares and hotel rates are making T&E expenses more important to the bottom line.

Electrovision Can Save $6 Million per Year

Electrovision should be able to save up to $6 million per year, based on the experience of other companies. A sensible travel-management program can save firms up to 35 percent a year (Gilligan 2003). Since we purchase more first-class tickets than the average, we should be able to achieve even greater savings.

The first priority should be hiring a director for T&E spending. This director should develop a written T&E policy, establish a cost-control system, retain a national travel agency, and investigate electronic alternatives to travel. Electrovision should make employees aware of the need to reduce T&E spending by forgoing unnecessary travel and by economizing on tickets, hotels, meals, and rental cars.

Continues numbering the executive summary pages with lowercase roman numerals centered about 1 inch from the bottom of the page

We should also negotiate preferential rates with travel providers. These changes are likely to hurt short-term morale. Management will need to explain the rationale for reduced spending and set an example by economizing on their own travel arrangements. On the plus side, cutting travel will reduce the burden on employees and help them balance their business and personal lives.

iv

Uses subheadings that summarize the content of the main sections of the report without repeating what appears in the text

Targets a receptive audience with a hard-hitting tone in the executive summary (a more neutral approach would be better for hostile or skeptical readers)

Appears in the same typeface and type style as the text of the report. Uses single-spacing because the report is single-spaced, and follows the text's format for margins, paragraph indentions, and headings

Moreno included an executive summary because her audience was mixed—some readers would be interested in the details of her report and some would prefer to focus on the big picture.

Moreno's impersonal style adds to the formality of her report. She chose an impersonal style for several reasons: (1) several members of her audience were considerably higher up in the organization and she did not want to sound too familiar, (2) she wanted the executive summary to be compatible with the text, and (3) her company prefers the impersonal style for formal reports.

Some writers prefer a more personal approach. Generally, you should gear your choice of style to your relationship with the readers.

Centers the title of the report on the first page of the text, 2 inches from the top of the page ($2\frac{1}{2}$ inches if top-bound)

REDUCING ELECTROVISION'S TRAVEL AND ENTERTAINMENT COSTS

INTRODUCTION

Electrovision has always encouraged a significant amount of business travel. To compensate employees for the inconvenience and stress of frequent trips, management has authorized generous travel and entertainment (T&E) allowances. This philosophy has been good for morale, but last year Electrovision spent $16 million on T&E—$7 million more than it spent on research and development.

Begins the introduction by establishing the need for action

This year's T&E costs will affect profits even more, due to changes in airfares and hotel rates. Also, the company anticipates that profits will be relatively weak for a variety of other reasons. Therefore, Dennis McWilliams, Vice President of Operations, asked the accounting department to look into the T&E budget.

The purpose of this report is to analyze the T&E budget, evaluate the effect of changes in airfares and hotel costs, and suggest ways to tighten management's control over T&E expenses. The report outlines several steps to reduce our expenses, but the precise financial impact of these measures is difficult to project. Estimates are a "best guess" view of what Electrovision can expect to save.

For this report, the accounting department analyzed internal expense reports for the past five years to determine how much Electrovision spends on T&E. These figures were compared with average statistics compiled by Dow Jones (publisher of *The Wall Street Journal*) and presented as the Dow Jones Travel Index. We also analyzed trends and suggestions published in a variety of business journal articles to see how other companies are coping with the high cost of business travel.

This report reviews the size and composition of Electrovision's T&E expenses, analyzes trends in travel costs, and recommends ways to reduce the T&E budget.

THE HIGH COST OF TRAVEL AND ENTERTAINMENT

Many companies view T&E as an "incidental" cost of business, but the dollars add up. Electrovision's bill for airfares, hotels, rental cars, meals, and entertainment totaled $16 million last year and has increased by 12 percent per year for the past five years. Compared to the average U.S. business, Electrovision's expenditures are high, largely because of management's generous policy on travel benefits.

Mentions sources and methods to increase credibility and to give readers a complete picture of the study's background

Uses the arabic numeral 1 for the first page, centering the number about 1 inch from the bottom of the page

In her brief introduction, Moreno omitted the subheadings within the introduction and relied on topic sentences and on transitional words and phrases to indicate that she is discussing the purpose, scope, and limitations of the study. To conserve space, Moreno used single-spacing and 1-inch side margins.

2

Uses arabic numerals to number the second and succeeding pages of the text in the upper right-hand corner where the top and right-hand margins meet

$16 Million per Year Spent on Travel and Entertainment

Electrovision's annual T&E budget is 8 percent of sales. Because this is a relatively small expense category, compared with salaries and commissions, it is tempting to dismiss T&E costs as insignificant. But T&E is Electrovision's third-largest controllable expense, directly behind salaries and information systems.

Last year Electrovision personnel made 3,390 trips. The average trip cost $4,720 and involved a round-trip flight of 3,000 miles, meals, two to three days of hotel accommodations, and a rental car. About 80 percent of trips were made by 20 percent of the staff—top managers and sales personnel averaged 18 trips per year.

Figure 1 shows how the T&E budget is spent. Airfares and lodging account for $7 out of every $10 employees spend on T&E. This breakdown has been steady for the past five years and is consistent with other companies' distribution.

Introduces visual aids before they appear and indicates what readers should notice about the data

Places the visual aid as close as possible to the point it illustrates

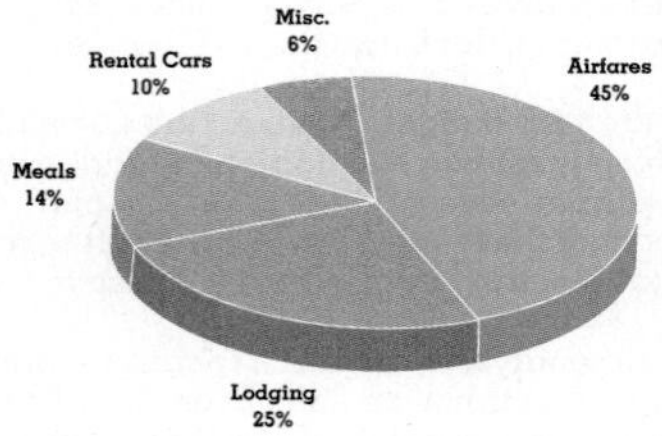

Misc. 6%
Rental Cars 10%
Airfares 45%
Meals 14%
Lodging 25%

Figure 1
Airfares and Lodging Exceed Two-Thirds of T&E Budget

Makes placement of visual aid titles consistent throughout a report (options for placement include above, below, or beside the visual)

Although the composition of the T&E budget has been consistent, its size has not. With T&E costs increasing 12 percent per year for five years, roughly twice the rate of the company's sales growth (see Figure 2), T&E is Electrovision's fastest-growing expense item.

Numbers the visual aids consecutively and refers to them in the text by their numbers (if your report is a book-length document, you may number the visual aids by chapter; for example, Figure 4-2 would be the second figure in the fourth chapter)

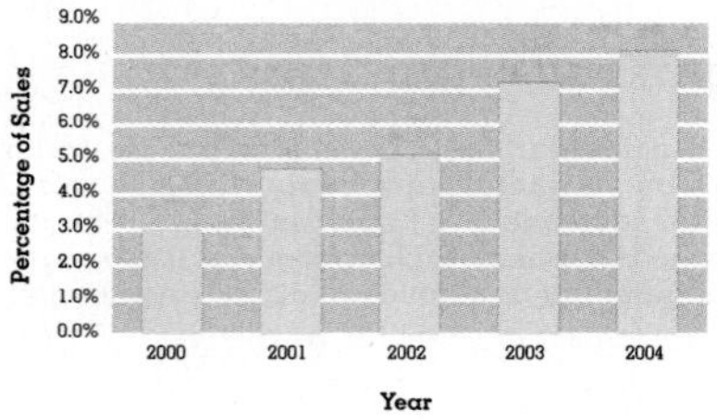

Percentage of Sales
9.0%
8.0%
7.0%
6.0%
5.0%
4.0%
3.0%
2.0%
1.0%
0.0%
2000 2001 2002 2003 2004
Year

Figure 2
T&E Expenses Have Increased as a Percentage of Sales

Gives each visual aid a title that clearly indicates what it's about

Moreno opened the first main section of the body with a topic sentence that introduces an important fact about the subject of the section. Then she oriented the reader to the three major points developed in the section.

Moreno decided to use a bar chart in Figure 2 to express the main idea in terms of percentage and make the main idea easy to grasp.

3

Electrovision's Travel Expenses Exceed National Averages

Much of our travel budget is justified. Two major contributing factors are

- Our headquarters are on the West Coast and our major customer is on the East Coast, so we naturally spend a lot on cross-country flights.

- Corporate managers and division personnel make frequent trips between our headquarters here on the West Coast and the manufacturing operations in Detroit, Boston, and Dallas to coordinate these disparate operations.

However, even with such justifiable expenses, Electrovision spends considerably more on T&E than the average business traveler spends (see Figure 3).

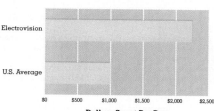

Electrovision

U.S. Average

$0 $500 $1,000 $1,500 $2,000 $2,500

Dollars Spent Per Day

Figure 3
Electrovision People Spend More
than Double the U.S. Average

Source: Wall Street Journal and
company records

The Dow Jones Travel Index calculates the average cost per day of business travel in the United States, based on average rates for airfare, hotel, and rental car. This average fluctuates weekly as travel companies change their rates, but it has been running about $1,000 per day for the last year or so. In contrast, Electrovision's average daily expense over the past year has been $2,250—125 percent higher than average. This figure is based on the average trip cost of $4,720 and an average trip length of 2.1 days.

Spending Has Been Encouraged

Although a variety of factors may contribute to this differential, Electrovision's relatively high T&E costs are at least partially due to the company's philosophy and management style. Since many employees do not enjoy business travel, management has tried to make the trips more pleasant by authorizing first-class airfare, luxury hotel accommodations, and full-size rental cars. The sales staff is encouraged to entertain clients at top restaurants and to invite them to cultural and sporting events.

Leaves a bit more white space above a heading than below to help readers associate that heading with the text it describes

The chart in Figure 3 is very simple, but it creates an effective visual comparison. Moreno included just enough data to make her point. She was as careful about the appearance of her report as she was about its content.

4

The cost of these privileges is easy to overlook, given the weakness of Electrovision's system for keeping track of T&E expenses:

Uses bulleted list to make it easy for readers to identify and distinguish related points

- Monthly financial reports have no separate T&E category; this information is buried in Cost of Goods Sold and in Selling and General Expenses.

- Department heads can approve expense reports, no matter how large.

- Receipts are not required for expenditures of less than $100.

- Individuals are allowed to make their own travel arrangements.

- No one has responsibility for controlling the company's total T&E spending.

GROWING IMPACT ON THE BOTTOM LINE

Uses informative headings to focus reader attention on the main points (such headings are appropriate when a report is in direct order and intended for a receptive audience; however, descriptive headings are more effective when a report is in indirect order and readers are less receptive)

During the past three years, the company's healthy profits have disguised the need for tighter controls over all aspects of the business. However, as we all know, the projection is for flat to declining profits over the next two years, which has prompted all of us to search for ways to cut costs. Also, rising airfares and hotel rates have increased the impact of T&E expenses on the company's finances.

Lower Profits Underscore the Need for Change

The next two years promise to be difficult for Electrovision. After several years of steady spending increases, the Postal Service is tightening procurement policies for automated mail-handling equipment. Funding for our A-12 optical character reader has been canceled. As a result, our marketing people expect sales to drop 15 percent. Even though Electrovision is negotiating several R&D contracts with nongovernment clients, the marketing department foresees no major procurements for two to three years.

At the same time, Electrovision is facing cost increases on several fronts. As we have known for several months, the new production facility now under construction in Salt Lake City, Utah, is behind schedule and over budget. Labor contracts in Boston and Dallas will expire within the next six months, and plant managers there anticipate that significant salary and benefits concessions may be necessary to avoid strikes.

Moreover, marketing and advertising costs are expected to increase as we attempt to strengthen these activities to better cope with competitive pressures. Given the expected decline in revenues and increase in costs, the Executive Committee's prediction that profits will fall by 12 percent in the coming fiscal year does not seem overly pessimistic.

Moreno designed her report to include plenty of white space so that pages having no graphics would appear inviting and easy to read.

5

Airfares and Hotel Rates Are Rising

Business travelers got used to frequent fare wars and discounting in the travel industry. Excess capacity and aggressive price competition made travel a relative bargain. However, that situation has changed as weaker competitors have been forced out and the remaining players have grown stronger and smarter. Airlines and hotels are better at managing inventory and keeping occupancy rates high, which translates into higher prices since suppliers have less reason to compete on price. Last year we saw some of the steepest rate hikes in years. Business airfares jumped 40 percent in many markets. The trend is expected to continue, with rates increasing another 5 to 10 percent overall (Phillips 2003; Dahl 2002).

Since air and hotel costs account for 70 percent of Electrovision's T&E budget, the trend toward higher prices in these two categories will have serious effects on the company's expenses, unless management takes action to control these costs.

METHODS FOR REDUCING TRAVEL AND ENTERTAINMENT COSTS

By implementing a number of reforms, management can expect to reduce Electrovision's T&E budget by as much as 40 percent. This estimate is based on the general assessment made by American Express (Gilligan 2003) and our chance to reduce or eliminate first-class travel. However, these measures are likely to be unpopular with employees. To gain acceptance for such changes, management will need to sell employees on the need for moderation in T&E allowances.

Four Ways to Trim Expenses

By researching what other companies are doing to curb T&E expenses, the accounting department has identified four prominent opportunities that should enable Electrovision to save about $6 million annually in travel-related costs.

Institute Tighter Spending Controls

One person should be appointed director of travel and entertainment to lead the T&E budget-control effort. More than a third of all U.S. companies now employ travel managers to keep costs in line ("Businesses Use Savvy Managers" 2002). Reporting to the vice president of operations, the director should be familiar with the travel industry and well versed in both accounting and information technology. The director should establish a written T&E policy and implement a system for controlling T&E costs. Electrovision currently has no written policy on travel and entertainment, a step widely recommended by air travel experts (Smith 2002). Creating a policy would clarify management's position and serve as a vehicle for

---

[Margin annotations:]

Documents the facts to add weight to Moreno's argument

Gives recommendations an objective flavor by pointing out both the benefits and the risks of taking action

---

Because airfares represent Electrovision's biggest T&E expense, Moreno included a subsection that deals with the possible impact of trends in the airline industry. Airfares are rising, so it is especially important to gain more control over employees' air travel arrangements.

Moreno created a forceful tone by using action verbs in the third-level subheadings of this section. This approach is appropriate to the nature of the study and the attitude of the audience. However, in a status-conscious organization, the imperative verbs might sound a bit too presumptuous coming from a junior member of the staff.

6

communicating the need for moderation. At a minimum, the policy should include provisions such as the following:

- Limiting all T&E to business purposes and getting approval in advance

- Ensuring that all employees travel by coach and stay in mid-range business hotels (with rare exceptions to be approved on a case-by-case basis)

- Applying policy equally to employees at all levels

To implement the new policy, Electrovision must create a system for controlling T&E expenses. Each department should prepare an annual T&E budget. These budgets should be presented in detail so that management can evaluate how T&E dollars will be spent and can recommend appropriate cuts. To help management monitor performance relative to these budgets, the T&E director should prepare monthly financial statements showing actual T&E expenditures by department.

The director of travel should also be responsible for retaining a business-oriented travel service that will schedule all employee business trips and look for the best travel deals, especially in airfares. In addition to centralizing Electrovision's reservation and ticketing activities, the agency will negotiate reduced group rates with hotels and rental car agencies. The agency should have offices nationwide so that all Electrovision facilities can channel their reservations through the same company. This step is particularly important in light of the differing airfares available from city to city. It's common to find dozens of fares along commonly traveled routes (Rowe 2002). Plus, the director can help coordinate travel across the company to secure group discounts when possible (Barker 2003; Miller 2002).

Reduce Unnecessary Travel and Entertainment

One of the easiest ways to reduce expenses is to reduce the amount of traveling and entertaining that occurs. An analysis of last year's expenditures suggests that as much as 30 percent of Electrovision's T&E is discretionary. The professional staff spent $2.8 million attending seminars and conferences last year. Some of these gatherings are undoubtedly beneficial, but the company could save money by sending fewer people and eliminating the less valuable functions.

Electrovision could also economize on trips between headquarters and divisions by reducing these visits and sending fewer people each time. Although face-to-face meetings are often necessary, management could try to resolve more internal issues through telephone, electronic, and written communication.

Electrovision can urge employees to economize by flying tourist instead of first class or by taking advantage of discount fares. Instead of taking clients to dinner, Electrovision personnel can hold breakfast meetings, which tend to be less costly.

Breaks up text with bulleted lists, which not only call attention to important points but also add visual interest (you can also use visual aids, headings, and direct quotations to break up large, solid blocks of print)

Specifies the steps required to implement recommendations

Moreno decided to single-space her report to create a formal, finished look; however, double-spacing can make the text of a long report somewhat easier to read and provide more space for readers to write comments.

7

Rather than ordering a $50 bottle of wine, employees can select a less expensive bottle or dispense with alcohol entirely. People can book rooms at moderately priced hotels and drive smaller rental cars.

Obtain Lowest Rates from Travel Providers

Apart from urging individual employees to economize, Electrovision can also save money by searching for the lowest available rates for airfares, hotels, and rental cars. Few Electrovision employees have the time or specialized knowledge to seek out travel bargains, making the most convenient and comfortable arrangements. However, by contracting with a professional travel service, the company will have access to professionals who can more efficiently obtain lower rates.

Judging by the experience of other companies, Electrovision may be able to trim 30 to 40 percent from the travel budget by looking for bargains in airfares and negotiating group rates with hotels and rental car companies. The company should be able to achieve these economies by analyzing travel patterns, identifying frequently visited locations, and selecting a few hotels that are willing to reduce rates in exchange for guaranteed business. Also, the company should be able to save up to 40 percent on rental car charges by negotiating a corporate rate.

The possibilities for economizing are promising; however, making the best arrangements is a complicated undertaking, requiring trade-offs such as the following:

- The best fares may not always be the lowest (e.g., indirect flights often cost less than direct ones, but they take longer, costing more in lost work time).

- The cheapest tickets may need to be booked far in advance, often impossible.

- Nonrefundable discount tickets are a drawback if the trip must be canceled.

Replace Travel with Technological Alternatives

We might be able to replace a major portion of our interdivisional travel with electronic meetings, such as videoconferencing or real-time on-screen document sharing. Many companies use these tools to cut costs and reduce employee stress.

Rather than make specific recommendations in this report, I suggest that the new T&E director conduct an in-depth study of the company's travel patterns. An analysis of why employees travel and what they accomplish will highlight any opportunities for replacing face-to-face meetings. Part of this study should include limited testing of various electronic systems as a way of measuring their effect on both workplace effectiveness and overall costs.

Points out possible difficulties to show that all angles have been considered and to build reader confidence in the writer's judgment

Note how Moreno made the transition from section to section. The first sentence under the first heading on this page refers to the subject of the previous paragraph and signals a shift in thought.

8

The Impact of Reforms

By implementing tighter controls, reducing unnecessary expenses, negotiating more favorable rates, and exploring "electronic travel," Electrovision should be able to reduce its travel and entertainment budget significantly. As Table 1 illustrates, the combined savings should be in the neighborhood of $6 million, although precise figures are somewhat difficult to project.

Table 1
Electrovision Can Trim Travel and Entertainment Costs
by an Estimated $6 Million per Year

Source of Savings	Amount Saved
Switching from first-class to coach airfare	$2,300,000
Negotiating preferred hotel rates	940,000
Negotiating preferred rental car rates	460,000
Systematically searching for lower airfares	375,000
Reducing interdivisional travel	675,000
Reducing seminar and conference attendance	1,250,000
TOTAL POTENTIAL SAVINGS	**$6,000,000**

To achieve the economies outlined in the table, Electrovision will incur expenses for hiring a director of travel and for implementing a T&E cost-control system. These costs are projected at $95,000: $85,000 per year in salary and benefits for the new employee and a one-time expense of $10,000 for the cost-control system. The cost of retaining a full-service travel agency is negligible because agencies receive a commission from travel providers rather than a fee from clients.

The measures required to achieve these savings are likely to be unpopular with employees. Electrovision personnel are accustomed to generous travel and entertainment allowances, and they are likely to resent having these privileges curtailed. To alleviate their disappointment

- Management should make a determined effort to explain why the changes are necessary.

- The director of corporate communication should develop a multifaceted campaign to communicate the importance of curtailing T&E costs.

- Management should set an example by adhering strictly to the new policies.

- The limitations should apply equally to employees at all levels in the organization.

Uses informative title in the table, which is consistent with the way headings are handled and is appropriate for a report to a receptive audience

Words title to help readers focus immediately on the point of the illustrations

Includes dollar figures to help management envision the impact of the suggestions, even though estimated savings are difficult to project

Note how Moreno calls attention in the first paragraph to items in the following table, without repeating the information in the table.

The table puts Moreno's recommendations in perspective. She calls attention to the most important sources of savings and also spells out the costs required to achieve those results.

9

Uses a descriptive heading for the last section of the text (in informational reports, this section is often called "Summary"; in analytical reports, it is called "Conclusions" or "Conclusions and Recommendations")

Emphasizes the recommendations by presenting them in list format

CONCLUSIONS AND RECOMMENDATIONS

Electrovision is currently spending $16 million per year on travel and entertainment. Although much of this spending is justified, the company's costs are high relative to competitors', mainly because Electrovision has been generous with its travel benefits.

Electrovision's liberal approach to T&E expenses made sense during years of high profitability; however, the company is facing the prospect of declining profits for the next several years. Thus management is motivated to cut costs in all areas of the business. Reducing T&E spending is particularly important because the impact of these costs will increase as airfares and hotel accommodations increase.

Electrovision should be able to reduce T&E costs by as much as 40 percent by taking four important steps:

1. *Institute tighter spending controls.* Management should hire a T&E director to assume overall responsibility for relevant activities. Within the next six months, this director should develop a written travel policy, institute a T&E budget and a cost-control system, and retain a professional, business-oriented travel agency.

2. *Reduce unnecessary travel and entertainment.* Electrovision should encourage employees to economize on T&E spending. Management can authorize fewer trips and urge employees to be more conservative in their spending.

3. *Obtain lowest rates from travel providers.* Electrovision should focus on obtaining the best rates on airline tickets, hotel rooms, and rental cars. By channeling all arrangements through a professional travel agency, the company can optimize its choices and gain clout in negotiating preferred rates.

4. *Replace travel with technological alternatives.* With the number of computers already installed in our facilities, it seems likely that we could take advantage of desktop videoconferencing and other distance-meeting tools. This won't be quite as feasible with customer sites, since these systems require compatible equipment at both ends of a connection, but it is certainly a possibility for communication with Electrovision's own sites.

Because these measures may be unpopular with employees, management should make a concerted effort to explain the importance of reducing travel costs. The director of corporate communication should be given responsibility for developing a plan to communicate the need for employee cooperation.

Summarizes conclusions in the first two paragraphs—a good approach because Moreno organized her report around conclusions and recommendations, so readers have already been introduced to them

Uses a simple list to remind readers of the four main recommendations

Moreno introduces no new facts in this entire section. In a longer report, she might have divided this section into subsections, labeled "Conclusions" and "Recommendations," to distinguish between the two.

10

WORKS CITED

Barker, Julie. "How to Rein in Group Travel Costs." *Successful Meetings* Feb. 2003: 31.

"Businesses Use Savvy Managers to Keep Travel Costs Down." *Christian Science Monitor* 17 July 2002: 4.

Dahl, Jonathan. "2001: The Year Travel Costs Took Off." *Wall Street Journal* 29 Dec. 2002: B6.

Gilligan, Edward P. "Trimming Your T&E Is Easier than You Think." *Managing Office Technology* Nov. 2003: 39–40.

Miller, Lisa. "Attention, Airline Ticket Shoppers." *Wall Street Journal* 7 July 2002: B6.

Phillips, Edward H. "Airlines Post Record Traffic." *Aviation Week & Space Technology* 8 Jan. 2003: 331.

Rowe, Irene Vlitos. "Global Solution for Cutting Travel Costs." *European* 12 Oct. 2002: 30.

Smith, Carol. "Rising, Erratic Airfares Make Company Policy Vital." *Los Angeles Times* 2 Nov. 2002: D4.

Lists references alphabetically by the author's last name, and when the author is unknown, by the title of the reference (see Appendix B for additional details on preparing reference lists)

Moreno's list of references follows the style recommended in *The MLA Style Manual.*

for a cover that is attractive, convenient, and appropriate to the subject matter. Also, make sure it can be labeled with the report title, the writer's name (optional), and the submission date (also optional).

Think carefully about the title you put on the cover. A business report is not a mystery novel, so give your readers all the information they need: the who, what, when, where, why, and how of the subject. At the same time, try to be reasonably concise. You don't want to intimidate your audience with a title that's too long or awkward. You can reduce the length of your title by eliminating phrases such as *A Report of, A Study of,* or *A Survey of.*

Choose a report title that is informative but not too long.

Title Fly and Title Page

Title Fly and Title Page   The **title fly** is a plain sheet of paper with only the title of the report on it. You don't really need one, but it adds a touch of formality.

The **title page** includes four blocks of information, as shown in Moreno's Electrovision report: (1) the title of the report; (2) the name, title, and address of the person, group, or organization that authorized the report (usually the intended audience); (3) the name, title, and address of the person, group, or organization that prepared the report; and (4) the date on which the report was submitted. On some title pages the second block of information is preceded by the words *Prepared for* or *Submitted to,* and the third block of information is preceded by *Prepared by* or *Submitted by.* In some cases the title page serves as the cover of the report, especially if the report is relatively short and is intended solely for internal use.

The title page usually includes four blocks of information.

Letter of Authorization and Letter of Acceptance   The **letter of authorization** (or *memo of authorization*) is a document requesting that a report be prepared. You may want to include that document in your report. Following the direct-request plan described in Chapter 5, it typically specifies the problem, scope, time and money restrictions, special instructions, and due date.

A letter of authorization usually follows the direct-request plan.

You may sometimes want to include the **letter of acceptance** (or *memo of acceptance*), which acknowledges the assignment to conduct the study and to prepare the report. Following the good-news plan, the letter of acceptance confirms time and money restrictions and other pertinent details. However, this document is rarely included in reports.

Use the good-news plan for a letter of acceptance.

Letter of Transmittal   The **letter of transmittal** (or *memo of transmittal*) conveys your report to your audience. (In a book, this section is called the preface.) The letter of transmittal says what you'd say if you were handing the report directly to the person who authorized it, so the style is less formal than the rest of the report. For example, the letter would use personal pronouns (*you, I, we*) and conversational language. Moreno's Electrovision report includes a one-page transmittal memo from Moreno to her boss (the person who requested the report).

Use a less formal style for the letter of transmittal than for the report itself.

The transmittal letter usually appears right before the table of contents. If your report will be widely distributed, however, you may decide to include the letter of transmittal only in selected copies so that you can make certain comments to a specific audience. If your report discusses layoffs or other issues that affect people in the organization, you might want to discuss your recommendations privately in a letter of transmittal to top management. If your audience is likely to be skeptical of or even hostile to something in your report, the transmittal letter is a good opportunity to acknowledge their concerns and explain how the report addresses the issues they care about.

The letter of transmittal follows the routine and good-news plans described in Chapter 7. Begin with the main idea, officially conveying the report to the readers

Use the good-news plan for a letter of transmittal.

and summarizing its purpose. Such a letter typically begins with a statement such as "Here is the report you asked me to prepare on . . ." The rest includes information about the scope of the report, the methods used to complete the study, and the limitations that became apparent. In the middle section of the letter, you may also highlight important points or sections of the report, make comments on side issues, give suggestions for follow-up studies, and offer any details that will help readers understand and use the report. You may also wish to acknowledge help given by others. The concluding paragraph is a note of thanks for having been given the report assignment, an expression of willingness to discuss the report, and an offer to assist with future projects.

The synopsis of short reports is often included in the letter of transmittal.

If the report does not have a synopsis, the letter of transmittal may summarize the major findings, conclusions, and recommendations. This material would be placed after the opening of the letter.

Table of Contents   The table of contents (which should be titled simply "Contents") indicates in outline form the coverage, sequence, and relative importance of the information in the report. The headings used in the text of the report are the basis for the table of contents. Depending on the length and complexity of the report, your contents page may show only the top two or three levels of headings or only first-level headings. The exclusion of some levels of headings may frustrate readers who want to know where to find every subject you cover. On the other hand, a simpler table of contents helps readers focus on the major points. No matter how many levels you include, make sure readers can easily distinguish between them (see Figure 11–16 for examples of various levels of headings).

The table of contents outlines the text and lists prefatory and supplementary parts.

The table of contents is prepared after the other parts of the report have been typed, so that the beginning page numbers for each heading can be shown. The headings should be worded exactly as they are in the text of the report. Also listed on the contents page are the prefatory parts (only those that follow the contents page) and the supplementary parts. If you have fewer than four visual aids, you may wish to list them in the table of contents, too; but if you have four or more visual aids, create a separate list of illustrations.

Be sure the headings in the table of contents match up perfectly with the headings in the text.

List of Illustrations   For simplicity's sake, some reports refer to all visual aids as illustrations or exhibits. In other reports, such as Moreno's Electrovision report, tables are labeled separately from other types of visual aids, which are called figures. Regardless of the system used to label visual aids, the list of illustrations gives their titles and page numbers.

Put the lists of figures and tables on separate pages if they won't fit on one page with the table of contents.

If you have enough space on a single page, include the list of illustrations directly beneath the table of contents. Otherwise, put the list on the page after the contents page. When tables and figures are numbered separately, they should also be listed separately. The two lists can appear on the same page if they fit; otherwise, start each list on a separate page.

A synopsis briefly overviews a report's most important points.

Synopsis or Executive Summary   A **synopsis** is a brief overview (one page or less) of a report's most important points, designed to give readers a quick preview of the contents. It's often included in long informational reports dealing with technical, professional, or academic subjects and can also be called an *abstract*. Because it's a concise representation of the whole report, it may be distributed separately to a wide audience; then interested readers can request a copy of the entire report.

The phrasing of a synopsis can be either informative or descriptive, depending on whether the report is in direct or indirect order. In an informative synopsis, you present the main points of the report in the order in which they appear in the text. A descriptive synopsis, on the other hand, simply tells what the report is about, using only moderately greater detail than the table of contents; the actual findings of the report are omitted. Here are examples of statements from each type:

Informative Synopsis	**Descriptive Synopsis**
Sales of super-premium ice cream make up 11 percent of the total ice cream market.	This report contains information about super-premium ice cream and its share of the market.

The way you handle a synopsis reflects the approach you use in the text. If you're using an indirect approach in your report, you're better off with a descriptive synopsis. An informative synopsis, with its focus on conclusions and key points, may be too confrontational if you have a skeptical audience. You don't want to spoil the effect by providing a controversial beginning. No matter which type of synopsis you use, be sure to present an accurate picture of the report's contents.[3]

Many business report writers prefer to include an **executive summary** instead of a synopsis or an abstract. Whereas a synopsis is a prose table of contents that outlines the main points of the report, an executive summary is a fully developed "mini" version of the report itself. An executive summary is more comprehensive than a synopsis; it may contain headings, well-developed transitions, and even visual aids. A good executive summary opens a window into the body of the report and allows the reader to quickly see how well you have managed your message. It is often organized in the same way as the report, using a direct or an indirect approach, depending on the audience's receptivity. However, executive summaries can also deviate from the sequence of material in the remainder of the report.

Executive summaries are intended for readers who lack the time or motivation to study the complete text. As a general rule, keep the length of an executive summary proportionate to the length of the report. A brief business report may have only a one-page or shorter executive summary. Longer business reports may have a two- or three-page summary. Anything longer, however, might cease to be a summary.[4]

Linda Moreno's Electrovision report provides one example of an executive summary. After reading the summary, audience members know the essentials of the report and are in a position to make a decision. Later, when time permits, they may read certain parts of the report to obtain additional detail. However, from daily newspapers to websites, businesspeople are getting swamped with more and more data and information. They are looking for ways to cut through all the clutter, and reading executive summaries is a popular shortcut. Because you can usually assume that many of your readers will not read the main text of your report, make sure you cover all your important points (along with significant supporting information) in the executive summary.

Many reports require neither a synopsis nor an executive summary. Length is usually the determining factor. Most reports of fewer than 10 pages either omit such a preview or combine it with the letter of transmittal. However, if your report is over 30 pages long, you'll probably include either a synopsis or an executive summary as a convenience for readers. Which one you'll provide depends on the traditions of your organization.

Text of the Report   Although reports can contain a variety of components, the text is always composed of three main parts: an opening (or introduction), a body, and a close. Chapter 11 discusses composing these three parts and emphasizes that the content of each one varies with the length and type of report, the organizational structure, and the reader's familiarity with the topic:

- **Opening.** A good introduction helps readers follow and comprehend the information in a report. It invites readers to continue by telling them what your report is about, why they should be concerned, and how the report is organized. If your report has a synopsis or an executive summary, avoid redundancy by balancing the material in your introduction with that in your summary. For example, the executive

Use a descriptive synopsis (abstract) for a skeptical or hostile audience, an informative synopsis for most other situations.

Put enough information in an executive summary so that an executive can make a decision without reading the entire report.

Three main text parts of a report are:
- *Opening*
- *Body*
- *Close*

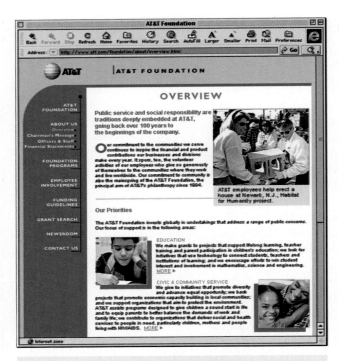

A report's introduction gives readers just a brief overview of the main points covered. Readers who want more information must then flip back to the table of contents to locate the right page within the body. On the web, however, your introduction can include links to bring readers directly to the report sections covering main points. For example, when the AT&T Foundation (www.att.com/foundation) posted an executive summary of its philanthropic activities on the web, it added links labeled "more" to encourage readers to click for more details on each activity.

summary in Moreno's Electrovision report is fairly detailed, so she makes her introduction relatively brief. If you must repeat information in your introduction that has already been covered in a prefatory part, try to use different wording.

- **Body.** This section presents the information that supports your conclusions and recommendations, as well as your analysis, logic, and interpretation of the information. The body of Moreno's Electrovision report exemplifies the types of supporting detail commonly included in this section. Note her effective use of visuals. Most inexperienced writers tend to include too much information in their reports or to place too much data in paragraph format, rather than use tables and charts. Include only the essential supporting data in the body, use visuals, and place any additional information in an appendix.

- **Close.** You want the close to summarize the main idea of your report, highlight your conclusions or recommendations, and list any courses of action you expect the reader to take. In a long report, this section may be labeled "Summary," or "Conclusions and Recommendations." As Chapter 11 points out, if you have organized your report in a direct pattern, your closing should be relatively brief, like Linda Moreno's. If you have organized your report indirectly, you may be using this section to present your recommendations and conclusions for the first time, in which case this section could be relatively long.

Supplementary Parts   Supplementary parts follow the text of the report and provide information for readers who seek more detailed discussion. Supplements are more common in long reports than in short ones and typically include the appendixes, bibliography, and index.

Put into an appendix materials that are
- Bulky or lengthy
- Not directly relevant to the text

Appendixes   An **appendix** contains materials related to the report but not included in the text because they're too lengthy or bulky or because they lack direct relevance. However, as Bob Haas warns, be sure not to include too much ancillary material. Keep your reports straightforward and concise. Well-designed appendixes provide enough but not too much additional information for those readers who want it.

Frequently included in appendixes are sample questionnaires and cover letters, sample forms, computer printouts, statistical formulas, financial statements and spreadsheets, copies of important documents, and complex illustrations; a glossary may be put in an appendix or may stand as a separate supplementary part. The best

Put visuals in the body of the report nearest the point of discussion.

place to include visual aids is in the text body nearest the point of discussion, but if any visuals are too large to fit on one page or are only indirectly relevant to your report, they too may be put in an appendix. In fact, some organizations specify that all visual aids be placed in an appendix.

Each type of material deserves a separate appendix. Identify the appendixes by labeling them—for example, "Appendix A: Questionnaire," "Appendix B: Computer Printout of Raw Data," and so on. All appendixes should be mentioned in the text and listed in the table of contents.

List your secondary sources in the bibliography.

Bibliography   You have an ethical and a legal obligation to give other people credit for their work. A **bibliography** is a list of secondary sources consulted when preparing your report. In her Electrovision report, Moreno labeled her bibliography "Works

Cited" because she listed only the works that were mentioned in the report. You might call this section "Sources" or "References" if it includes works consulted but not mentioned in your report. The Electrovision report uses the author-date system. An alternative is to use numbered footnotes (bottom of the page) or endnotes (end of the report). For more information on citing sources, see Appendix B, "Documentation of Report Sources."

In addition to providing a bibliography, some authors prefer to cite references in the report text. Acknowledging your sources in the body of your report demonstrates that you have thoroughly researched your topic. Furthermore, mentioning the names of well-known or important authorities on the subject helps build credibility for your message. It's often a good idea to mention a credible source's name several times if you need to persuade your audience. On the other hand, you don't want to make your report read like an academic treatise, dragging along from citation to citation. The source references should be handled as conveniently and inconspicuously as possible. One approach, especially for internal reports, is simply to mention a source in the text:

Give credit where credit is due.

According to Dr. Lewis Morgan of Northwestern Hospital, hip replacement operations account for 7 percent of all surgery performed on women age 65 and over.

However, if your report will be distributed to outsiders, include additional information on where you obtained the data. Most college students are familiar with citation methods suggested by the Modern Language Association (MLA) or the American Psychological Association (APA). *The Chicago Manual of Style* is a reference often used by typesetters and publishers. All of these sources encourage the use of in-text citations (inserting the author's last name and a year of publication or a page number directly into the text).

Index   An **index** is an alphabetical list of names, places, and subjects mentioned in the report, along with the pages on which they occur (see the indexes for this book). An index is rarely included in unpublished reports.

Components of a Formal Proposal

As discussed in Chapter 11, proposals are analytical reports that include bids to perform work under a contract or pleas for financial support from outsiders. Such bids and pleas are almost always formal. As Bob Haas knows only too well, the goal of a proposal is to impress readers with your professionalism and to make your service and your company stand out. This goal is best achieved through a structured and deliberate approach.

Formal proposals contain many of the same components as other formal reports (see Figure 12–2). The difference lies mostly in the text, although a few of the prefatory parts are also different. With the exception of an occasional appendix, most proposals have few supplementary parts.

Formal proposals contain most of the same prefatory parts as other formal reports.

Prefatory Parts   The cover, title fly, title page, table of contents, and list of illustrations are handled the same as in other formal reports. However, other prefatory parts are handled quite differently, such as the copy of the RFP, the synopsis or executive summary, and the letter of transmittal.

Copy of the RFP   Instead of having a letter of authorization, a formal proposal may have a copy of the request for proposal (RFP), which is a letter or memo soliciting a proposal or a bid for a particular project. If the RFP includes detailed specifications, it may be too long to bind into the proposal; in that case, you may want to include only the introductory portion of the RFP. Another option is to omit the RFP and simply refer to it in your letter of transmittal.

Use a copy of the request for proposal (RFP) in place of the letter of authorization.

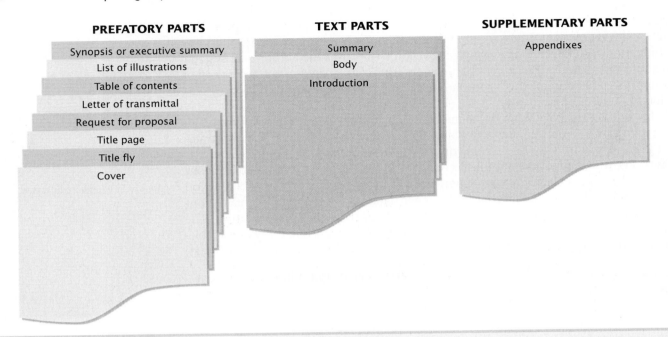

FIGURE 12-2
Parts of a Formal Proposal

Senior Vice President June Yee Felix solicited proposals from consultants and research firms when she needed to start a service for online bill payment at Chase Manhattan Bank. The RFP stated her criteria and detailed requirements for selecting a service provider.

Synopsis or Executive Summary   Although you may include a synopsis or an executive summary for your reader's convenience when your proposal is quite long, these components are often less useful in a formal proposal than they are in a formal report. If your proposal is unsolicited, your transmittal letter will already have caught the reader's interest, making a synopsis or an executive summary pointless. It may also be unnecessary if your proposal is solicited, because the reader is already committed to studying your proposal to find out how you intend to satisfy the terms of a contract. The introduction to a solicited proposal would provide an adequate preview of the contents.

Letter of Transmittal   The way you handle the letter of transmittal depends on whether the proposal is solicited or unsolicited. If the proposal is solicited, the transmittal letter follows the pattern for good-news messages, highlighting those aspects of your proposal that may give you a competitive advantage. If the proposal is unsolicited, the transmittal letter follows the pattern for persuasive messages (see Chapter 9). The letter must persuade the reader that you have something worthwhile to offer, something that justifies the time required to read the entire proposal. Because the transmittal letter may be all that the client reads, it must be especially convincing.

Text of the Proposal   As with reports, the text of a proposal is composed of three main parts: the opening, body, and close. The content and depth of each part depend on whether the proposal is solicited or unsolicited, formal or informal. See Chapter 11 for a more detailed discussion of the topics covered in each part:[5]

Use the good-news pattern for the letter of transmittal if the proposal is solicited; use the persuasive plan if the proposal is unsolicited.

- **Opening.** The introduction presents and summarizes the problem you intend to solve and your solution to that problem, including any benefits the reader will receive from the solution.

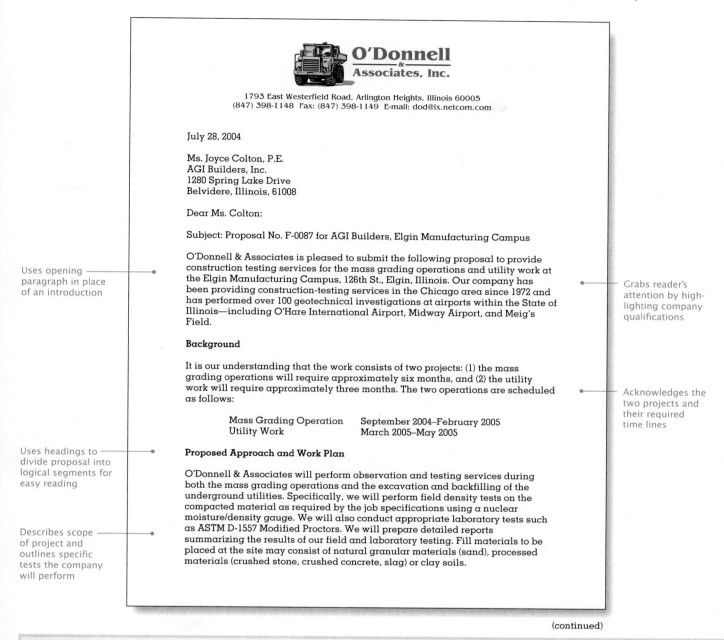

O'Donnell & Associates, Inc.

1793 East Westerfield Road, Arlington Heights, Illinois 60005
(847) 398-1148 Fax: (847) 398-1149 E-mail: dod@ix.netcom.com

July 28, 2004

Ms. Joyce Colton, P.E.
AGI Builders, Inc.
1280 Spring Lake Drive
Belvidere, Illinois, 61008

Dear Ms. Colton:

Subject: Proposal No. F-0087 for AGI Builders, Elgin Manufacturing Campus

O'Donnell & Associates is pleased to submit the following proposal to provide construction testing services for the mass grading operations and utility work at the Elgin Manufacturing Campus, 126th St., Elgin, Illinois. Our company has been providing construction-testing services in the Chicago area since 1972 and has performed over 100 geotechnical investigations at airports within the State of Illinois—including O'Hare International Airport, Midway Airport, and Meig's Field.

Uses opening paragraph in place of an introduction

Grabs reader's attention by highlighting company qualifications

Background

It is our understanding that the work consists of two projects: (1) the mass grading operations will require approximately six months, and (2) the utility work will require approximately three months. The two operations are scheduled as follows:

Mass Grading Operation	September 2004–February 2005
Utility Work	March 2005–May 2005

Acknowledges the two projects and their required time lines

Proposed Approach and Work Plan

Uses headings to divide proposal into logical segments for easy reading

O'Donnell & Associates will perform observation and testing services during both the mass grading operations and the excavation and backfilling of the underground utilities. Specifically, we will perform field density tests on the compacted material as required by the job specifications using a nuclear moisture/density gauge. We will also conduct appropriate laboratory tests such as ASTM D-1557 Modified Proctors. We will prepare detailed reports summarizing the results of our field and laboratory testing. Fill materials to be placed at the site may consist of natural granular materials (sand), processed materials (crushed stone, crushed concrete, slag) or clay soils.

Describes scope of project and outlines specific tests the company will perform

(continued)

FIGURE 12–3
Effective Solicited Proposal—Informal

- **Body.** This section explains the complete details of the solution: how the job will be done, how it will be broken into tasks, what method will be used to do it (including the required equipment, material, and personnel), when the work will begin and end, how much the entire job will cost (including a detailed breakdown), and why your company is qualified.
- **Closing.** This section emphasizes the benefits that readers will realize from your solution, and it urges readers to act.

Content may be different for solicited and unsolicited proposals.

Figure 12–3 is an informal proposal submitted by Dixon O'Donnell, vice president of O'Donnell & Associates, a geotechnical engineering firm that conducts a variety of environmental testing services. The company is bidding on the mass

O'Donnell & Associates, Inc.   July 28, 2003   Page 2

O'Donnell & Associates will provide qualified personnel to perform the necessary testing. Mr. Kevin Patel will be the lead field technician responsible for the project. A copy of Mr. Patel's résumé is included with this proposal for your review. Kevin will coordinate field activities with your job site super-intendent and make sure that appropriate personnel are assigned to the job site. Overall project management will be the responsibility of Mr. Joseph Proesel. Project engineering services will be performed under the direction of Mr. Dixon O'Donnell, P.E. All field personnel assigned to the site will be familiar with and abide by the Project Site Health and Safety Plan prepared by Carlson Environmental, Inc., dated April 2003.

Qualifications

O'Donnell & Associates has been providing quality professional services since 1972 in the areas of

- Geotechnical engineering
- Materials testing and inspection
- Pavement evaluation
- Environmental services
- Engineering and technical support (CADD) services

The company provides Phase I and Phase II environmental site assessments, preparation of LUST site closure reports, installation of groundwater monitoring wells, and testing of soil/groundwater samples of environmental contaminants. Geotechnical services include all phases of soil mechanics and foundation engineering, including foundation and lateral load analysis, slope stability analysis, site preparation recommendations, seepage analysis, pavement design, and settlement analysis.

O'Donnell & Associates' materials testing laboratory is certified by AASHTO Accreditation Program for the testing of Soils, Aggregate, Hot Mix Asphalt and Portland Cement Concrete. A copy of our laboratory certification is included with this proposal. In addition to in-house training, field and laboratory technicians participate in a variety of certification programs, including those sponsored by American Concrete Institute (ACI) and Illinois Department of Transportation (IDOT).

Costs

On the basis of our understanding of the scope of the work, we estimate the total cost of the two projects to be $100,260.00, as follows:

(continued)

Explains who will be responsible for the various tasks

Encloses résumé rather than listing qualifications in the document

Grabs attention by mentioning distinguishing qualifications

Gains credibility by describing certifications

FIGURE 12–3
Continued

grading and utility work specified by AGI Builders. As you review this document, pay close attention to the specific items addressed in the proposal's opening, body, and close.

PROOFREADING FORMAL REPORTS AND PROPOSALS

Once you have assembled all the components of your report or proposal, revised the document's content for clarity and conciseness, and designed the document to please

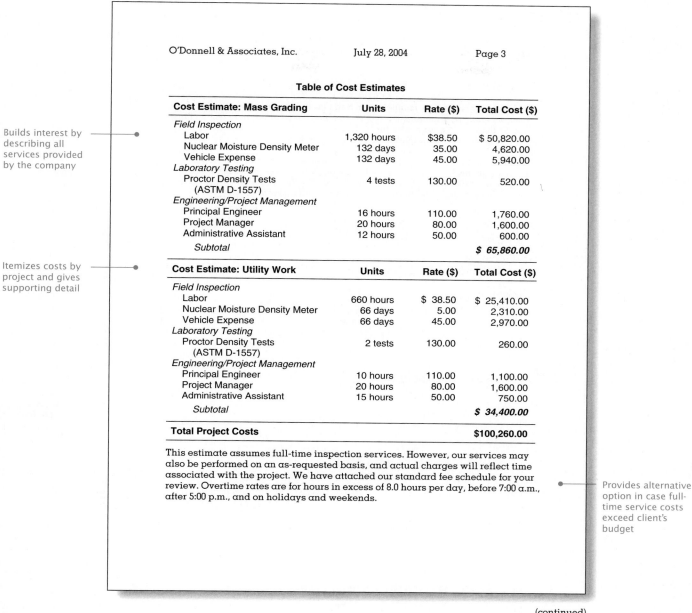

Builds interest by describing all services provided by the company

Itemizes costs by project and gives supporting detail

O'Donnell & Associates, Inc.   July 28, 2004   Page 3

Table of Cost Estimates

Cost Estimate: Mass Grading	Units	Rate ($)	Total Cost ($)
Field Inspection			
Labor	1,320 hours	$38.50	$ 50,820.00
Nuclear Moisture Density Meter	132 days	35.00	4,620.00
Vehicle Expense	132 days	45.00	5,940.00
Laboratory Testing			
Proctor Density Tests (ASTM D-1557)	4 tests	130.00	520.00
Engineering/Project Management			
Principal Engineer	16 hours	110.00	1,760.00
Project Manager	20 hours	80.00	1,600.00
Administrative Assistant	12 hours	50.00	600.00
Subtotal			**$ 65,860.00**

Cost Estimate: Utility Work	Units	Rate ($)	Total Cost ($)
Field Inspection			
Labor	660 hours	$ 38.50	$ 25,410.00
Nuclear Moisture Density Meter	66 days	5.00	2,310.00
Vehicle Expense	66 days	45.00	2,970.00
Laboratory Testing			
Proctor Density Tests (ASTM D-1557)	2 tests	130.00	260.00
Engineering/Project Management			
Principal Engineer	10 hours	110.00	1,100.00
Project Manager	20 hours	80.00	1,600.00
Administrative Assistant	15 hours	50.00	750.00
Subtotal			**$ 34,400.00**

Total Project Costs			**$100,260.00**

This estimate assumes full-time inspection services. However, our services may also be performed on an as-requested basis, and actual charges will reflect time associated with the project. We have attached our standard fee schedule for your review. Overtime rates are for hours in excess of 8.0 hours per day, before 7:00 a.m., after 5:00 p.m., and on holidays and weekends.

Provides alternative option in case full-time service costs exceed client's budget

(continued)

FIGURE 12–3
Continued

---

readers, you have essentially produced your document in its final form. Now you need to review it thoroughly one last time, looking for inconsistencies, errors, and missing components. For instance, if you changed a heading in the report's text part, make sure that you also changed the corresponding heading in the table of contents and in all references to that heading in your report.

Proofreading the textual part of your report is pretty much the same as proofreading any business message—you check for typos, spelling errors, and mistakes in punctuation. However, reports often have elements that may not be included in other messages, so don't forget to proof your visual aids thoroughly, as Chapter 11 points out, and make sure they are positioned correctly. If you need specific tips on proofreading

Don't forget to proofread everything one last time.

O'Donnell & Associates, Inc.   July 28, 2004   Page 4

Authorization

With a staff of over 30 personnel, including registered professional engineers, resident engineers, geologists, construction inspectors, laboratory technicians, and drillers, we are convinced that O'Donnell & Associates is capable of providing the services required for a project of this magnitude.

If you would like our firm to provide the services as outlined in this proposal, please sign this letter and return it to us along with a certified check in the amount of $10,000 (our retainer) by August 15, 2004. Please call me if you have any questions regarding the terms of this proposal or our approach.

Sincerely,

Dixon O'Donnell

Dixon O'Donnell
Vice President

Enclosures

Accepted for AGI BUILDERS, INC.

By _____   Date _____

[Margin note left: Uses brief closing to emphasize qualifications and ask for client decision]

[Margin note right: Provides deadline and makes response easy]

[Margin note right: Makes letter a binding contract, if signed]

FIGURE 12–3
Continued

documents, look back at Chapter 6 for some tips on how to proofread like a pro. For instance, you'll want to make sure that nothing has been left out or overlooked and that every word contributes to your report's purpose.

GETTING FEEDBACK FROM FORMAL REPORTS AND PROPOSALS

[Margin note: Ask for feedback, and learn from your mistakes.]

Once you've completed your formal report and sent it off to your audience, you'll naturally expect a positive response, and quite often you'll get one—but not always. You may get half-hearted praise or no action on your conclusions and recommendations. Even worse, you may get some serious criticism. Try to learn from these experiences. Sometimes you won't get any response at all. If you don't hear from your readers within a week or two, you might want to ask politely whether the report arrived. In hopes of stimulating a response, you might also offer to answer any questions or provide additional information.

To review the ideas presented in this chapter, consult the "Checklist: Producing Formal Reports and Proposals."

Document Makeover

IMPROVE THIS DOCUMENT

To practice correcting drafts of actual documents, visit **www.prenhall.com/onekey** on the web. Click "Document Makeovers," then click Chapter 12. You will find an excerpt from an executive summary that contains problems and errors relating to what you've learned in this chapter about completing formal reports and proposals. Use the Final Draft decision tool to create an improved version of this document. Check the executive summary for an appropriate degree of formality, parallel structures, the skillful inclusion or exclusion of detail, and a consistent time perspective.

✓ CHECKLIST: Producing Formal Reports and Proposals

Prepare the Text of the Report

- ✓ Leave a two-inch margin at the top of the first page, and center the title of the document.
- ✓ In a long document, type the first-level heading "Introduction" three lines below title.
- ✓ In a short document, omit "Introduction" heading and begin typing three lines below title.
- ✓ For left-bound documents, number all pages with arabic numerals in the upper right-hand corner (except for the first page, where the number is centered one inch from the bottom).
- ✓ For top-bound documents, number all pages with arabic numerals centered one inch from the bottom.

Prepare the Appendixes, If Necessary

- ✓ Begin each appendix on a separate page.
- ✓ Give each appendix a title.
- ✓ For multiple appendixes, number or letter them consecutively in the order the text refers to them.

Prepare the Reference List (Bibliography), If Necessary

- ✓ Begin on a separate page.
- ✓ Use a consistent format.

Develop a Synopsis or Executive Summary (for Long, Formal Documents)

- ✓ Tailor the synopsis or executive summary to the document's length and tone.
- ✓ Condense the document's main points, using either the informative or the descriptive approach.
- ✓ In a synopsis, present the major points in the same order as they appear in the document. In an executive summary, you may deviate from the order of points appearing in the report.
- ✓ Include a Copy of Letter of Authorization or Request for Proposal, If Appropriate

Prepare a Letter or Memo of Transmittal

- ✓ Include only in some copies if it contains sensitive information suitable for some but not all readers.
- ✓ Convey the document officially to the readers.
- ✓ Refer to authorization and discuss purpose, scope, background, source and methods, and limitations.
- ✓ Acknowledge everyone who was especially helpful in preparing the document.
- ✓ Close with thanks, offer to be of further assistance, and suggest future projects, if appropriate.

Prepare the Table of Contents

- ✓ List the synopsis or executive summary (if there is one), with beginning page number.
- ✓ List all first- and second-level headings (and perhaps all third-level headings), with a page number for each.
- ✓ Word all headings exactly as they appear in the text.
- ✓ List all supplementary parts, with page numbers.
- ✓ Number table of contents and all prefatory pages with lowercase roman numerals (bottom center).

Prepare the List of Illustrations (If You Have Four or More Visual Aids)

- ✓ Format the list the same as the table of contents.
- ✓ List visuals either directly under table of contents or on a separate page with its own heading.

Prepare the Title Page

- ✓ List title; recipient's name, title, affiliation; author's name, title, affiliation; date of submission.
- ✓ Balance the information in blocks on the page.

Prepare a Sturdy, Attractive Cover

- ✓ Label the cover clearly with the title of the document.
- ✓ Use a title that tells the audience exactly what the document is about.

On the Job:

SOLVING COMMUNICATION DILEMMAS AT LEVI STRAUSS

Levi Strauss chairman Robert Haas uses reports not only to communicate his vision to employees, customers, and the community but also to make decisions and set company policy. You are manager of internal communication at Levi Strauss and responsible for maintaining the communication channels up, down, and across the organization. One of your most important tasks is updating 37,500 employees on the company's progress toward reaching the goals of the Aspirations Statement. Each year, you prepare a long report that is distributed both online and in printed form. Study the following questions, select the best answer in each case, and be prepared to explain why your choice is best.

1. Because people have too much information to digest and too little time to read, the executive summary has become a particularly important part of corporate reports. Which of the following approaches would you take with the executive summary in this year's Aspiration Statement?

   a. Use the executive summary to provide a quick score card for the company's performance in each of the areas addressed by the Aspirations Statement. Readers may be tempted to skip the detail contained in the body of the report, but at least they'll get the highlights in the executive summary.
   b. Use the executive summary to highlight changes in the report from previous years. You believe that the report is widely read within the company every year, so people will need guidance to understand how this year's content and organization differ from that of past reports.
   c. Do not use an executive summary at all. This report is made available to everyone in the company, not just a handful of executives, so an executive summary is not appropriate.

2. One of your responsibilities in preparing this report is to recommend specific solutions for any problems uncovered in your investigation. This year, several customer service reps have complained that the Customer Service Center's manager places too much emphasis on community service. Employees volunteering for AIDS awareness rallies or environmental cleanup projects are allowed to do so on company time as often as they want—which frequently leaves the center shorthanded. Employees who choose not to participate in these outside events are overloaded with work and beginning to resent both the community service program and certain employees who frequently volunteer. Remember that this report is distributed worldwide, so even though it's intended only for internal use, you must assume that people outside the company (including competitors and the news media) may gain access to it. Which of the following best states your recommendation on this issue?

   a. At one of our customer service centers, we uncovered a conflict between the company's desire to support the local community and the need to maintain a productive work environment. Specifically, too many employees were taking too much volunteer time off from work, leaving their co-workers overloaded. We have discussed our concerns with the manager involved, who is working with us to balance these conflicting needs. However, we recommend that all regional managers discuss the issue with their employees to see whether specific situations need to be resolved or whether the company's overall volunteer policy needs to be reviewed.
   b. Our investigation raised some concerns about the management style of Sarah Blackstone, head of the Denver customer service center. Her commendable interest in supporting the local community through employee volunteerism is unfortunately in conflict with her responsibilities as a business manager. Too many employees are taking too much time off from work to participate in community activities, leaving other employees behind to take up the slack. The result is both a decline in customer service and a growing resentment among the employees who stay in the office and have to work harder and longer to cover for their absent co-workers.
   c. Our investigation raised some concerns about the management style of Sarah Blackstone, manager of the Denver customer service center. Her commendable interest in supporting the local community through employee volunteerism is unfortunately in conflict with her responsibilities as a business manager. Too many employees are taking too much time off from work to participate in community activities, leaving other employees behind to take up the slack. The result is both a decline in customer service and a growing resentment among the employees who stay in the office and have to work harder and longer to cover for their absent co-workers. We strongly recommend that Ms. Blackstone retake the standard LS&Co. management-training program to help realign her priorities with the company's business priorities.

3. Much of the information you've collected from your interviews around the world is difficult or impossible to represent numerically. However, you believe that readers would appreciate a brief summary of the interview results. For one issue, you posed the following open-ended question to 153 employees and managers: "How would you describe our progress toward empowering frontline employees with the authority to make decisions and take actions that satisfy our customers

quickly and completely?" The responses range from simple, one-sentence answers to long, involved essays complete with examples. All together, the responses fill 13 pages. What's the best way of summarizing your findings?

a. Pick a half dozen responses that in your opinion represent the range of responses. For example, you might include one that says "we've made no progress at all," one that says "I believe we've been very successful at our empowerment efforts," and four more that fall between these two extremes.

b. Create a five-step measurement scale that ranges from "little or no progress" to "completely successful." Together with a few experienced members of your staff, review each response and decide in which of the five categories it belongs. Then create a chart that shows how the 153 responses are distributed among the five categories. Explain how you developed the chart, and offer to provide a complete listing of the responses to any reader who requests one.

c. Since the information is not quantitative, it's impossible to summarize and boil down to a few facts and figures. It would therefore be inappropriate to summarize the information at all. Simply include all 13 pages of responses as an appendix in your report.

4. One of the questions you asked 153 employees was to rate their feelings about the company's response to employee complaints. You provided a scale that included five choices: 1 (very satisfied), 2 (satisfied), 3 (no opinion), 4 (unsatisfied), and 5 (very unsatisfied). A staff member illustrated these data in a line chart, but during the revision process, you've realized that a line chart is not a good choice. (It attempts to show trends in the relationship between two variables, but you have five data points, and you need to show how many employees chose each one.) What would be the best visual to replace the original?

a. A bar chart with five bars that indicate the number of responses in each category.

b. A surface chart with one line for each choice, which shows the sum of all five lines.

c. A pie chart with five slices that indicate the number of responses in each category.[6]

Learning Objectives Checkup

To assess your understanding of the principles in this chapter, read each learning objective and study the accompanying exercises. For fill-in items, write the missing text in the blank provided; for multiple choice items, circle the letter of the correct answer. You can check your responses against the answer key on page AK-2.

Objective 12.1: Identify the three tasks involved in completing business reports and proposals, and briefly explain what's involved in each one.

1. Which of the following is *not* one of three major tasks involved in completing business reports and proposals?
   a. Revising the report's organization, style, tone, and readibility
   b. Formatting the report
   c. Deciding on the report's visuals
   d. Proofreading the report

2. What sets a formal report apart from less-formal reports is
   a. Its audience
   b. Its length
   c. That it is usually analytical rather than informative
   d. Its polish

Objective 12.2: Describe the 10 prefatory parts of a formal report.

3. Which of the following may be omitted from the prefatory parts of a formal report?
   a. Letter of transmittal
   b. Introduction

c. Synopsis
d. List of illustrations

4. The title fly
   a. Is a plain sheet of paper with only the title of the report on it
   b. Is a page that includes the report's title, writer, date, and authorizer
   c. Is the page that contains the letter of authorization
   d. Takes the place of the title page in most formal reports

5. The letter of transmittal
   a. Conveys your report to the audience
   b. Usually appears right before the table of contents
   c. Follows the direct approach
   d. Does all of the above

6. The table of contents should
   a. Be titled "Table of Contents"
   b. List only the first-level headings from the report
   c. Be prepared after the other parts of the report have been typed
   d. Do all of the above

Objective 12.3: Explain the difference between a synopsis and an executive summary.

7. A synopsis
   a. Is a an overview of a report's most important points
   b. Runs four to five pages in most reports
   c. Can contain headings and even visual aids
   d. Does all of the above

8. How does an executive summary differ from a synopsis? An executive summary
   a. Is shorter
   b. Is a fully developed "mini" version of the report itself
   c. Is informative rather than descriptive
   d. Does all of the above

Objective 12.4: List the three supplementary parts of a formal report and briefly describe each one.

9. Which of the following is *not* a typical supplementary part of a formal report?
   a. Appendixes
   b. Bibliography
   c. Letter of authorization
   d. Index

Objective 12.5: Identify the three prefatory parts of a formal proposal that differ from those in a formal report.

10. How does a formal proposal differ from a formal report?

   a. Instead of a letter of authorization, the proposal has a copy of the RFP.
   b. The proposal doesn't include a table of contents.
   c. The proposal has a "disclaimer" page.
   d. All of the above are true.

Objective 12.6: Explain how the prefatory parts of a proposal differ depending on whether a proposal is solicited or unsolicited.

11. If a proposal is unsolicited, the transmittal letter
   a. Uses the direct approach
   b. Follows the pattern for good-news messages
   c. Follows the pattern for persuasive messages
   d. Is unnecessary

Apply Your Knowledge

1. When is the best time to proofread your report? As soon as you finish revising your first draft, when everything is fresh in your mind? After preparing your supplementary parts, when your report has had time to sit a bit? After producing your entire report, when everything is in place? At some other point during the completion of your report? Explain your answer.

2. Under what circumstances would you include more than one index in a lengthy report?

3. If you were submitting a solicited proposal to build an indoor pool, would you include as references the names and addresses of other clients for whom you recently built

similar pools? Would you include these references in an unsolicited proposal? Where in either proposal would you include these references? Why?

4. If you included a bibliography in your report, would you also need to include in-text citations? Please explain.

5. **Ethical Choices** How would you report on a confidential survey in which employees rated their managers' capabilities? Both employees and managers expect to see the results. Would you give the same report to employees and managers? What components would you include or exclude for each audience? Explain your choices.

Practice Your Knowledge

DOCUMENT FOR ANALYSIS

Visit the U.S. Department of Justice reports page at www. ins.usdoj.gov/graphics/aboutins/repsstudies/addition.html. Read the brief description of the department's "Triennial

Comprehensive Report on Immigration" and follow the link to the executive summary. Using the information in this chapter, analyze the executive summary and offer specific suggestions for revising it.

Exercises

For live links to all websites discussed in this chapter, visit this text's website at www.prenhall.com/thill. Just log on, select Chapter 12, and click on "Student Resources." Locate the page or the URL related to the material in the text. For the "Learning More on the Web" exercises, you'll also find navigational directions. Click on the live link to the site.

12.1 Teamwork You and a classmate are helping Linda Moreno prepare her report on Electrovision's travel and entertainment costs (see "Report Writer's Notebook," on pp. 402–416). This time, however, the report is to be informational rather than analytical, so it will not include recommendations. Review the existing report

and determine what changes would be needed to make it an informational report. Be as specific as possible. For example, if your team decides the report needs a new title, what title would you use? Now draft a transmittal memo for Moreno to use in conveying this informational report to Dennis McWilliams, Electrovision's vice president of operations.

12.2 Producing Reports: Letter of Transmittal You are president of the Friends of the Library, a nonprofit group that raises funds and provides volunteers to support your local library. Every February, you send a report of the previous year's activities and accomplishments to the County Arts Council, which provides an annual grant of $1,000 toward your group's summer reading festival. Now it's February 6, and you've completed your formal report. Here are the highlights:

- Back-to-school book sale raised $2,000.
- Holiday craft fair raised $1,100.
- Promotion and prizes for summer reading festival cost $1,450.
- Materials for children's program featuring local author cost $125.
- New reference databases for library's career center cost $850.
- Bookmarks promoting library's website cost $200.

Write a letter of transmittal to Erica Maki, the council's director. Because she is expecting this report, you can use the direct approach. Be sure to express gratitude for the council's ongoing financial support.

12.3   Internet Follow the step-by-step hints and examples for writing a funding proposal at www.learnerassociates. net/proposal. Review the writing hints and the entire sample proposal online. What details did the author decide to include in appendixes? Why was this material placed in the appendixes and not the main body of the report?

12.4   Ethical Choices: Team Challenge You submitted what you thought was a masterful report to your boss over three weeks ago. The report analyzes current department productivity and recommends several steps that you think will improve employee output without increasing individual workloads. Brilliant, you thought. But you haven't heard a word from your boss. Did you overstep your boundaries by making recommendations that might imply that she has not been doing a good job? Did you overwhelm her with your ideas? You'd like some feedback. In your last e-mail to her, you asked if she had read your report. So far you've received no reply. Then yesterday, you overhead the company vice president talk about some productivity changes in your department. The changes were ones that you had recommended in your report. Now you're worried that your boss submitted your report to senior management and will take full credit for your terrific ideas. What, if anything, should you do? Should you confront your boss about this? Should you ask to meet with the company vice president? Discuss this situation among your teammates and develop a solution to this sticky situation. Present your solution to the class, explaining the rationale behind your decision.

Expand Your Knowledge

LEARNING MORE ON THE WEB

Preview Before You Produce www.profusion.com; www.zworks.com A good way to get ideas for the best style, organization, and format of a report is by looking at copies of professional business reports. To find samples of various types of reports, you can use a metasearch engine such as www.profusion.com or www.zworks.com. Such sites search many engines simultaneously. See what Profusion and Zworks produce when you enter the phrase *analytical reports* or *informational reports*. Choose from various titles or descriptions to compare different kinds of reports. This research could result in your preparing better reports and proposals.

ACTIVITIES

One way to learn how to write more skillfully and effectively is by reading other writers' work. Look at examples of professional business reports, and skim their contents to reinforce what you've learned in this chapter about structure, style, and organization. Let www.ixquick.com work for you. Log on and enter the phrase *business reports* in the search window, then choose a report and review it.

1. What is the purpose of the report you read? Who is its target audience? Explain why the structure and style of the report make it easy or difficult to follow the main idea.
2. What type of report did you read? Briefly describe the main message. Is the information well organized? If you answer "yes," explain how you can use the report as a guide for a report you might write. If you answer "no," explain why the report is not helpful.
3. Drawing on what you know about the qualities of a good business report, review a report and describe what features contribute to its readability.

EXPLORING THE WEB ON YOUR OWN

Review these chapter-related websites to learn more about writing reports and proposals.

1. Plan your way to profit by learning how to write effective business plans at The Business Plan: Road Map to Success, www.sba.gov/starting/indexbusplans.html.
2. Looking for the perfect transitional word? Cues and Transitions for the Reader, at www.mapnp.org/library/ writing/cuestran.html, has some recommendations to help you.
3. Visit agcomwww.tamu.edu/ed_med/training/T2C.proofread. htm for more tips on proofreading.

Learn Interactively

INTERACTIVE STUDY GUIDE

Go to the Companion Website at www.prenhall.com/bovee. For Chapter 12, take advantage of the interactive "Study Guide" to test your knowledge of the chapter. Get instant feedback on whether you need additional studying. Also, visit this site's "Study Hall" where you'll find an abundance of valuable resources that will help you succeed in this course.

PEAK PERFORMANCE GRAMMAR AND MECHANICS

To improve your skill with quotation marks, parentheses, and ellipses, visit this text's website at www.prenhall.com/onekey. Click "Peak Performance Grammar and Mechanics," then click "Punctuation II." Take the Pretest to determine

whether you have any weak areas. Review those areas in the Refresher Course, and take the Follow-Up Test to check your grasp of quotation marks, parentheses, and ellipses. For advanced practice, take the Advanced Test. Finally, for additional reinforcement, go to the "Improve Your Grammar, Mechanics, and Usage" section that follows, and complete those exercises.

Improve Your Grammar, Mechanics, and Usage

The following exercises help you improve your knowledge of and power over English grammar, mechanics, and usage. Turn to the "Handbook of Grammar, Mechanics, and Usage" at the end of this textbook and review all of Sections 2.10 (Quotation Marks), 2.11 (Parentheses), and 2.12 (Ellipses). Then look at the following 10 items. Circle the letter of the preferred choice in the following groups of sentences. (Answers to these exercises appear on page AK-4.)

1. a. Be sure to read (How to Sell by Listening) in this month's issue of *Fortune*.
    b. Be sure to read "How to Sell by Listening" in this month's issue of *Fortune*.
    c. Be sure to read "How to Sell by Listening . . ." in this month's issue of *Fortune*.
2. a. Her response . . . see the attached memo . . . is disturbing.
    b. Her response (see the attached memo) is disturbing.
    c. Her response "see the attached memo" is disturbing.
3. a. We operate with a skeleton staff during the holidays (December 21 through January 2).
    b. We operate with a skeleton staff during the holidays "December 21 through January 2".
    c. We operate with a skeleton staff during the holidays (December 21 through January 2.)
4. a. "The SBP's next conference . . ." the bulletin noted, ". . . will be held in Minneapolis."
    b. "The SBP's next conference," the bulletin noted, "will be held in Minneapolis."
    c. "The SBP's next conference," the bulletin noted, "will be held in Minneapolis".

5. a. The term "up in the air" means "undecided."
    b. The term "up in the air" means *undecided.*
    c. The term *up in the air* means "undecided."
6. a. Her assistant (the one who just had the baby) won't be back for four weeks.
    b. Her assistant (the one who just had the baby), won't be back for four weeks.
    c. Her assistant . . . the one who just had the baby . . . won't be back for four weeks.
7. a. "Ask not what your country can do for you," begins a famous John Kennedy quotation.
    b. ". . . Ask not what your country can do for you" begins a famous John Kennedy quotation.
    c. "Ask not what your country can do for you . . ." begins a famous John Kennedy quotation.
8. a. Do you remember who said "And away we go?"
    b. Do you remember who said "And away we go"?
9. a. Refinements may prove profitable. (More detail about this technology appears in Appendix A).
    b. Refinements may prove profitable. (More detail about this technology appears in Appendix A.)
10. a. The resignation letter begins, "Since I'll never regain your respect . . . ," and goes on to explain why that's true.
    b. The resignation letter begins, "Since I'll never regain your respect, . . ." and goes on to explain why that's true.
    c. The resignation letter begins, "Since I'll never regain your respect . . ." and goes on to explain why that's true.

For additional exercises focusing on punctuation, go to www.prenhall.com/thill and select "Handbook of Grammar, Mechanics, and Usage Practice Sessions."

Cases

SHORT FORMAL REPORTS REQUIRING NO ADDITIONAL RESEARCH

1. Giving it the online try: Report analyzing the advantages and disadvantages of corporate online learning As the newest member of the corporate training division of Paper Products, Inc., you have been asked to investigate and analyze the merits of establishing Internet courses (e-learning) for the company's employees. The president of your company thinks e-learning might be a good employee benefit as well as a terrific way for employees to learn new skills that they can use on the job. You've already done your research and here's a copy of your notes:

Online courses open up new horizons for working adults, who often find it difficult to juggle conventional classes with jobs and families.

Adults over 25 now represent nearly half of higher-ed students; most are employed and want more education to advance their careers.

Some experts believe that online learning will never be as good as face-to-face instruction.

Online learning requires no commute and is appealing for employees who travel regularly.

Enrollment in courses offered online by postsecondary institutions is expected to increase from 2 million students in 2001 to 5 million students in 2006.

E-learning is a cost-effective way to get better-educated employees.

Corporate spending on e-learning is expected to more than quadruple by 2005, to $18 billion.

At IBM, some 200,000 employees received education or training online last year, and 75 percent of the company's Basic Blue course for new managers is online. E-learning cut IBM's training bill by $350 million last year—mostly because online courses don't require travel.

There are no national statistics, but a recent report from the *Chronicle of Higher Education* found that institutions are seeing dropout rates that range from 20 to 50 percent for online learners. The research does not adequately explain why the dropout rates for e-learners are higher.

A recent study of corporate online learners reported that employees want the following things from their online courses: college credit or a certificate; active correspondence with an online facilitator who has frequent virtual office hours; access to 24-hour, seven-day-a-week technical support; and the ability to start a course anytime.

Corporate e-learners said that their top reason for dropping a course was lack of time. Many had trouble completing courses from their desktops because of frequent distractions caused by co-workers. Some said they could only access courses through the company's intranet, so they couldn't finish their assignments from home.

Besides lack of time, corporate e-learners cited the following as e-learning disadvantages: lack of management oversight; lack of motivation; problems with technology; lack of student support; individual learning preferences; poorly designed courses; substandard/inexperienced instructors.

A recent study by GE Capital found that finishing a corporate online course was dependent on whether managers gave reinforcement on attendance, how important employees were made to feel, and whether employee progress in the course was tracked.

Sun Microsystems found that interactivity can be a critical success factor for online courses. Company studies showed that only 25 percent of employees finish classes that are strictly self-paced. But 75 percent finish when given similar assignments and access to tutors through e-mail, phone, or threaded discussion.

Too often companies dump courses on their employees and wonder why they don't finish them.

Company managers must supervise e-learning just as they would any other important initiative.

For online learning to work, companies must develop a culture that takes online learning just as seriously as classroom training.

For many e-learners, studying at home is optimal. Whenever possible, companies should offer courses through the Internet or provide intranet access at home. Having employees studying on their own time will more than cover any added costs.

Corporate e-learning has flared into a $2.3 billion market, making it one of the fastest-growing segments of the education industry.

Rather than fly trainers to 7,000 dealerships, General Motors University now uses interactive satellite broadcasts to teach salespeople the best way to highlight features on the new Buick.

Fast and cheap, e-training can shave companies' training costs while it saves employees travel time.

Pharmaceutical companies such as Merck are conducting live, interactive classes over the web, allowing sales reps to learn about the latest product information at home rather than fly them to a conference center.

McDonald's trainers can log onto Hamburger University to learn such skills as how to assemble a made-to-order burger or properly place the drink on a tray.

One obstacle to the spread of online corporate training is the mismatch between what employees really need—customized courses that are tailored to a firm's products and its unique corporate culture—and what employers can afford.

80 percent of companies prefer developing their own online training courses in-house. But creating even one customized e-course can take months, involve armies of experts, and cost anywhere from $25,000 to $50,000. Thus, most companies either stick with classroom training or buy generic courses on such topics as how to give performance appraisals, understanding basic business ethics, and so on. Employers can choose from a wide selection of noncustomized electronic courses.

For online learning to be effective, content must be broken into short "chunks" with lots of pop quizzes, online discussion groups, and other interactive features that let students demonstrate what they've learned. For instance, Circuit City's tutorial on digital camcorders consists of three 20-minute segments. Each contains audio demonstrations of how to handle customer product queries, tests on terminology, and "try-its" that propel trainees back onto the floor to practice what they've learned.

Your task: Write a short (3–5 pages) memo report to the director of human resources, Kerry Simmons, presenting the advantages and disadvantages of e-learning and making a recommendation as to whether Paper Products, Inc., should invest time and money in training its employees this way. Be sure to organize your information so that it is clear, concise, and logically presented. Simmons likes to read the "bottom line" first, so be direct: Present your recommendation up front and support your recommendation with your findings.[7]

2. Climbing the ladder: Report summarizing data about corporate opportunities for women As the assistant director of human resources for a large financial services firm, you hear the concerns of many different employees. Lately, increasing numbers of female employees have been complaining about being passed up for promotions and management positions. They feel that male employees receive preferential treatment, even though many females are more highly qualified.

Table 12–1 indicates the results of a research study conducted by your staff. The study displays several key statistics pertaining to the male and female employees working for your company. Table 12–2 depicts how executives in *Fortune* 1000 companies perceive the barriers to female advancement, and Table 12–3 shows why female executives feel that women should be given more opportunities in the corporate world. These studies may help shed light on what could be viewed as a pattern of sex discrimination by your company. Because your company believes in equitable treatment for all employees,

Table 12–1	STATISTICS FOR MALE AND FEMALE MANAGERS	
Employee Statistics	**Female Managers**	**Male Managers**
Average number of years with the company	12.3	9.5
Average number of years of management experience	7.2	6.9
Percentage who have an MBA or other advanced degree	74%	63%
Average annual salary	$76,000	$84,000
Average number of times promoted	4.2	4.4

Table 12–2	WHY FEMALE EXECUTIVES DON'T ADVANCE INTO CORPORATE LEADERSHIP POSITIONS	
Reason Cited	**According to Female Executives**	**According to Male CEOs**
Male stereotyping preconceptions	52%	25%
Exclusion from informal networks	49	15
Lack of general management/line experience	47	82
Inhospitable corporate culture	35	18
Women not in pipeline long enough	29	64

WHY FEMALE EXECUTIVES THINK COMPANIES SHOULD INCREASE THE NUMBER OF FEMALE SENIOR MANAGERS	Table 12–3	
Reason	**Agree**	**Strongly Agree**
Women are large part of management talent pool	29%	69%
Women contribute unique perspective	32	61
Women are large part of consumer base	45	36
Companies have social responsibility	41	10
Shareholders want more executive women	41	7
Customers want more executive women	34	7
Lawsuits are increasing	40	5

regardless of their gender, you believe your boss will be interested in this information.

Your task: Write a short report to the director of human resources, interpreting and summarizing the information in these tables. Suggest a possible course of action to remedy the situation at your company.[8]

SHORT FORMAL REPORTS REQUIRING ADDITIONAL RESEARCH

3. Picking the better path: Research report assisting a client in a career choice You are employed by Open Options, a career-counseling firm, where your main function is to help clients make career choices. Today a client with the same name as yours (a truly curious coincidence!) came to your office and asked for help in deciding between two careers—careers that you yourself had been interested in (an even greater coincidence!).

Your task: Do some research on the two careers and then prepare a short report that your client can study. Your report should compare at least five major areas, such as salary, working conditions, and education required. Interview the client to understand her or his personal preferences regarding each of the five areas. For example, what is the minimum salary the client will accept? By comparing the client's preferences with the research material you collect, such as salary data, you will have a basis for concluding which of the two careers is best. The report should end with a career recommendation. (Note: One good place for career-related information is the *Occupational Outlook Handbook,* published by the U.S. Bureau of Labor Statistics, available in print and online at www.stats.bls.gov/oco/ocoiab.htm.)

4. Selling overseas: Research report on the prospects for marketing a product in another country Select (a) a product and (b) a country. The product might be a novelty item that you own (an inexpensive but accurate watch or clock, a desk organizer, or a coin bank). The country should be one that you are not currently familiar with. Imagine that you are with the

international sales department of the company that manufactures and sells the novelty item and that you are proposing to make it available in the country you have selected.

The first step is to learn as much as possible about the country where you plan to market the product. Check almanacs, encyclopedias, the Internet, and library databases for the most recent information, paying particular attention to descriptions of the social life of the inhabitants, their economic conditions, and cultural traditions that would encourage or discourage use of the product.

Your task: Write a short report that describes the product you plan to market abroad, briefly describes the country you have selected, indicates the types of people in this country who would find the product attractive, explains how the product would be transported into the country (or possibly manufactured there if materials and labor are available), recommends a location for a regional sales center, and suggests how the product should be sold. Your report is to be submitted to the chief operating officer of the company, whose name you can either make up or find in a corporate directory. The report should include your conclusions (how the product will do in this new environment) and your recommendations for marketing (steps the company should take immediately and those it should develop later).

LONG FORMAL REPORTS REQUIRING NO ADDITIONAL RESEARCH

5. Selling to Online America: Report analyzing the who, what, when, where, and why of U.S. online shoppers You are the administrative manager to Jerry Ordonez, the vice president of new business at First Horizon Bank. Recently, Ordonez has been flooded with requests to finance electronic commerce initiatives from both start-up e-tailers (those who will operate an online business for the first time) and existing retail stores that want to expand their physical-store sales by selling goods online. All loan applicants are claiming that the potential for online sales is very attractive. All claim to understand the online consumer quite well. Trouble is, Ordonez has

Table 12–4	ONLINE BEHAVIOR BY ETHNIC GROUP FOR 10 KEY ACTIVITIES		
Activity	**Whites**	**African-Americans**	**Hispanics**
E-mail	93%	88%	87%
Get product information	73	71	73
Get travel information	65	64	63
Get weather information	63	53	55
Surf just for fun	61	73	69
Get news	59	62	58
Do research for school	54	65	59
Do research for work	49	48	51
Buy a product	48	35	42
Buy a travel product	29	28	29

received marketing reports with conflicting data: online sales projections, profiles of the online consumer, what the online consumer wants—none of it adds up. "Where did they get these data from?" he wonders. "I can't take their word for this. There's too much money at stake, so I did my own research—using reliable sources," he adds as he hands you a file. When you glance inside the file, you find Ordonez's research notes and statistics:

- Typical Internet users frequent an average of 10 websites per month, down from 15 websites one year ago, but they're visiting more pages per site, digging deeper rather than wider.
- Typical Internet users spend only 50 seconds at each webpage.
- 56 percent of the U.S. population (about 154 million people) accessed the Internet in November of this year—a 30 percent increase over the same month of the previous year. Newer research shows that 64 million U.S. adults go online *every* month.
- 56 percent of U.S. companies sell their products online, and this number is expected to rise.
- More than 60 percent of U.S. online consumers made at least one purchase on the web within a 90-day period this year.
- Average Internet user age is 39 years and rising.
- Small businesses that use the Internet to sell goods have grown 46 percent faster than those that do not.
- Many online shoppers behave like they do at the local mall: buying from the same merchants.
- Almost half of all U.S. adults with Internet access now purchase goods and services online.
- Offline, Americans tend to shop lightly during the week and then invade stores on the weekends. The opposite occurs online: Shoppers buy throughout the week, peaking on Wednesday, before fading on the weekend.

- Seasonal shopping patterns are different online. Traditional brick-and-mortar stores record the lion's share of their sales during the Christmas season, but most e-tailers operate at a steady pace throughout the year: less of a high in December, less of a low in January.
- Despite studies showing that the Internet gap is shrinking between ethnic groups, differences remain, as suggested by Table 12–4.
- Women continue to purchase online at a slightly higher rate than men (73 percent versus 71 percent).
- American teenagers actually spend about 30 percent less time on the web than adults.
- Airline tickets is the largest category of goods purchased online. Other top categories of items purchased online are listed in Table 12–5.
- Consumers spent $101 billion online in 2001, $59.7 billion online in 2000, and $30.1 billion in 1999. Consumer online spending was $167 billion in 2002, $250 billion in 2003, and $428 billion by 2004.
- Online consumers want satisfactory fulfillments: They want to receive the correct ordered items in a timely way, and they want an efficient and simple way to make returns, if necessary. A recent survey of online buyers found that 83 percent would like to be able to return purchases at offline stores, 59 percent would like to buy products online and pick them up at an offline store; one survey found that 71 percent of online consumers value convenience when making a purchase online, compared with 29 percent who value price savings.
- As an alternative to crowded shopping malls, buying online provides speed, simplicity, and comparison-shopping capabilities.
- A survey of online purchasers reports that the following percentage of respondents said these factors influenced their online buying decision: shipping fees (92 percent),

TOP 15 ITEMS PURCHASED ONLINE MONTHLY			Table 12–5
Item	**Dollars (in thousands)**	**Percent**	
Airline tickets	$746,170	21.60	
Hotel reservations	445,186	12.89	
Other	365,567	10.58	
Computer hardware	335,784	9.72	
Apparel	224,743	6.50	
Consumer electronics	191,878	5.55	
Car rental	188,620	5.46	
Toys/videogames	162,449	4.70	
Books	151,561	4.39	
Health and beauty	121,444	3.52	
Music	118,318	3.42	
Software	112,759	3.26	
Videos	109,814	3.18	
Sporting goods	92,005	2.66	
Food/beverages	88,680	2.57	
Total	$3,454,978	100.00%	

prices (92 percent), product availability (86 percent), special promotions or incentives (76 percent), product selection (69 percent), order tracking (66 percent), clearly identified delivery time (65 percent), return policy (63 percent), ease of using website (62 percent), website performance/speed (51 percent).

- More than 60 percent of online shoppers abandon their shopping carts before reaching the credit card transaction.
- A report cited these reasons that online consumers abandon their shopping carts: high shipping prices (72 percent), comparison shopping or browsing (61 percent), changed mind (56 percent), saving items for later purchase (51 percent), total cost of items is too high (43 percent), checkout process is too long (41 percent), checkout requires too much personal information (35 percent), site requires registration before purchase (34 percent), site is unstable or unreliable (31 percent), checkout process is confusing (27 percent).
- A survey showed that 47 percent of online consumers said that having a physical store makes a difference in where they shop, and 53 percent said it doesn't matter.
- A survey showed that online shoppers prefer the following promotions: savings/discount (67 percent), free shipping (25 percent), free gift with purchase (8 percent).

Your task: Use Jerry Ordonez's research to write a formal informational report profiling today's online consumer. Organize and present your information using three to four categories and use headings so that Ordonez can easily compare your profile to those submitted by loan applicants. Don't worry about citing the information sources; Ordonez did the research and he is confident that he selected only reliable sources. Ordonez complimented you on your use of tables and charts in the last report you submitted to him, so he's probably expecting more of the same.[9]

LONG FORMAL REPORTS REQUIRING ADDITIONAL RESEARCH

6. Is there any justice? Report critiquing legislation Plenty of people complain about their state legislators, but few are specific about their complaints. Here's your chance.

Your task: Write a long formal report about a law that you believe should not have been enacted or should be enacted. Be objective. Write the report using specific facts to support your beliefs. Reach conclusions and offer your recommendation at the end of the report. As a final step, send a copy of the report to an appropriate state official or legislator.

7. Travel opportunities: Report comparing two destinations You are planning to take a two-week trip abroad sometime within the next year. Because there are a couple of destinations that appeal to you, you are going to have to do some research before you can make a decision.

Your task: Prepare a lengthy comparative study of two countries that you would like to visit. Begin by making a list of important questions you will need to answer. Do you want a relaxing vacation or an educational experience? What types of services will you require? What will your transportation needs be? Where will you have the least difficulty with the language? Using resources in your library, the Internet, and perhaps travel agencies, analyze the suitability of these two destinations with respect to your own travel criteria. At the end of the report, recommend the better country to visit this year.

8. Secondary sources: Report based on library research Perhaps one of the following questions has been on your mind.

a. Which is the best college at which to pursue a graduate degree in business?

b. How can you organize a student group to make your campus safer at night?

c. Which of three companies that you would like to work for has the most responsible environmental policies?

d. What market factors led to the development of a product that you use frequently, and how are those factors different today?

e. Which three U.S. companies have had the best stock price performance over the past 30 years and why?

f. What are the best small-business opportunities available today?

Your task: Answer one of those questions, using secondary sources for information. Be sure to document your sources in the correct form. Give conclusions and recommendations in your report.

FORMAL PROPOSALS

9. Creative marketing: Proposal to sell educational/advertising materials to schools Reaching children poses significant challenges to marketers because children typically don't listen to the radio or read magazines or newspapers. They do watch television, but television ads can be expensive. However, marketers have a new opportunity to get their messages out to children, thanks to Jeff Lederman. His company, Planet Report, targets youngsters by placing ads where they are most likely to be

noticed—in the classroom. The ads are part of teaching materials that Planet Report distributes free to schools. These materials usually take the form of posters displaying information about current events. Each month, the company sends teachers a new poster containing tidbits of current news items and facts about science, politics, and culture. Along with this information are attractive ads for Disney movies, ABC television programs, Vans sneakers, and other products that appeal to young consumers. Lederman and an employee create two versions of each poster, one aimed at high school students and the other at elementary or middle school students. Teachers who use the posters also receive prepared questions they can use to test the students on the information in the posters. Besides questions about the factual information on the posters, the tests contain questions about the ads. Planet Report also distributes bookmarks with ads printed on them that teachers can give out as prizes or awards.

At a time when schools are facing tough financial constraints, Planet Report's strategy can be a real win-win situation. "Teachers get something they can use and a marketing purpose is served," says Lederman. Many teachers like the posters because they encourage students to read and learn. As one teacher who uses the posters says, "Whatever we can get that encourages voluntary reading is a plus."

However, not everyone supports the idea. Critics say that ads don't belong in the classroom. They complain that the posters distract students from their studies and encourage a commercial culture. Moreover, including test questions on the commercial content of the posters may cause confusion about what is most important for students to learn. One fourth-grade teacher points out that his students rarely miss questions about the ads, but they are likely to forget some of the other information.

Your task: You are communications director for Planet Report. Write a proposal that Jeff Lederman can use to convince school administrators to adopt Planet Report's posters in their schools. Provide details such as how the posters will benefit students. Keep in mind that not everyone supports the idea of advertising in schools, even if it is linked to effective learning materials. How will you address the concerns of your critics and convince your audience that your product is good for both students and schools?[10]

10. Put me in, Coach: Proposal to provide executive coaching services In today's fast-paced business world, companies are spending increasing sums of money on employee training and development. As part of this trend, many companies are turning to executive coaches to help make their managers more effective and productive. Coaches work with employees both one-on-one and in groups. They may provide guidance on how to communicate more effectively, build stronger leadership abilities, work with teams, develop career goals that mesh with company goals, embrace change, and develop the additional skills they need to move up the corporate ladder. Many companies offer coaching as a perk to managers. Some, such as financial services giant Chase Manhattan, even tie coaching to employee performance reviews. What's more, companies are willing to pay anywhere between $75 and $400 an hour for a coach's services.

Jean Isberg is an executive coach who has been increasing her clientele steadily for almost a decade. Isberg, a former sales executive in the information technology field, made a career change in the early 1990s by opening her own sales training business. After a while, she noticed that she was most effective at helping her clients understand themselves and their role in their organization. Following her talents, Isberg began to coach executives about how to be more effective both in their life and in their work. Soon she began to focus exclusively on coaching female executives, and she named her company Executive Coaching for Women.

Isberg meets with her clients over a nine-week period in sessions lasting 60 to 90 minutes. She also gives reading, writing, and thinking exercises to be completed between sessions. And once each quarter, clients are invited to participate in group review sessions. Isberg tells her clients that to reach their career goals, they must know what they really want, make sure they have the training necessary to make their goals realistic, let others know they are capable, and let others help them achieve success.

Isberg operates her business from her home, renting office and conference space for meetings as needed. But low over-head doesn't necessarily mean a low price; Isberg's services start at $3,000.

Until now, Isberg has counseled clients on a one-on-one basis, with the client paying the cost herself. However, one of Isberg's clients, the vice president of marketing and sales at international telecommunications company Cable & Wireless USA, is so pleased with the coaching she received that she has asked Isberg to submit a proposal to provide coaching services to the company's top female managers. The client believes that many of these managers have yet to realize their full potential in their work and that with Isberg's help, they will become far more effective managers. However, Isberg will need a top-notch proposal in order to get the rest of the company's top brass to buy in and foot the bill. Isberg has delegated the task of drafting the proposal to you, her business development coordinator.

Your task: Jean Isberg has given you the important information about her skills and about the clients she is seeking. Now she needs you to draft a proposal that will land her the Cable & Wireless contract. Give special consideration to how you can help Isberg distinguish herself from other executive coaches the company has dealt with. Use your imagination to fill in the details.[11]

Chapter 13

Planning, Writing, and Completing Oral Presentations

Learning Objectives

On the Job:

COMMUNICATING AT HEWLETT-PACKARD

SPEAKING OF TECHNOLOGY

"Let your fear motivate you, not inhibit you." So said Hewlett-Packard CEO Carleton "Carly" Fiorina in a commencement speech at Stanford University. Fiorina is widely regarded as the most powerful woman in business; she is at the helm of a company that boasts $50 billion in revenues. Clearly, she has not allowed herself to be inhibited by fear—not in her career, and certainly not in her public speaking. She has all the qualities of a great speaker. She is considered customer-centric, articulate, and charismatic. And Fiorina does give speeches—a lot of them.

She speaks inside HP, across the country, and around the world. Her audiences include customers, business partners, employees, financial analysts, world leaders, industry representatives, government officials, academics, and many others. She is noted for speaking purposefully. She scans her audience slowly, often departing from her prepared script. Fiorina has mastered the art of delivery, and she knows the importance of a well-written speech.

During her recent battle to gain support for HP's merger with Compaq, Fiorina had to crisscross the country again and again. She needed to keep her board behind her, score major points with institutional shareholders, and charm TV interviewers—not just with her style but with the logic of her arguments. And she had to accomplish most of this by giving speeches. In one address to institutional investors in Palm Springs, California, Fiorina bravely began her speech with just a touch of humor:

It's great to be here this morning—I haven't had the opportunity to address a room full of institutional investors since, well, Friday. I was having withdrawal.

As CEO of Hewlett-Packard, Carly Fiorina is responsible for addressing many different kinds of audiences. Whether she is explaining policy to the press, motivating employees, or persuading investors, her speeches and presentations are successful because she focuses on her audience and on making her ideas clear, interesting, and easy to follow.

Next, she grabbed their attention with a fact that interested them:

You may already know that we will substantially exceed current consensus estimates for our first fiscal quarter, which ended January 31. I'll touch on this a little more at the end of my remarks today.

Now that everyone was listening, she stated her purpose clearly and concisely:

My purpose this morning is to answer a question that I've been asked many times in recent weeks, which is this: In light of all the adversity we've faced since announcing our plans to merge with Compaq last September, why do we remain so steadfast in our commitment to pursuing this merger? Why do we still think this merger is a good deal that deserves a second look?

At the end of her opening, she carefully previewed what she would say in the rest of her speech so that her listeners would know what to expect:

To answer that question, I want to step back in time for a moment—to show you what we saw; to take you through why we decided what we did—and to share with you our board's collective view of the industry and HP's place in it.

Note how smoothly she moved from purpose to preview, ending one paragraph with a question and beginning the next with the answer. Fiorina is a successful speaker because she relies on more than charisma and a smooth delivery. She develops well-written speeches that convey her message clearly and powerfully.[1]

www.hp.com

THE THREE-STEP ORAL PRESENTATION PROCESS

Like HP's Carly Fiorina, chances are you'll have the opportunity to deliver a number of oral presentations throughout your career. You may not speak before large audiences of employees or the media, but you'll certainly be expected to present ideas to your colleagues, make sales presentations to potential customers, or engage in other kinds of spoken communication. For instance, if you're in the human resources department, you may give orientation briefings to new employees or explain company policies, procedures, or benefits at assemblies. If you're a department supervisor, you may conduct training programs. Or, if you're a problem solver or consultant, you may give analytical presentations on the merits of various proposals.

The three-step oral presentation process is quite similar to the three-step writing process.

Regardless of your job or the purpose of your presentation, you will be more effective if you adopt an oral presentation process that follows these three steps (see Figure 13–1):

1. Plan your presentation.
2. Write your presentation.
3. Complete your presentation.

STEP 1: PLANNING ORAL PRESENTATIONS

Planning presentations requires some special adjustments for the oral communication channel.

Planning oral presentations is much like planning any other business message: It requires analyzing your purpose and your audience, gathering necessary information, and adapting your message to the occasion and audience so that you can establish a good relationship. However, adjusting your technique to an oral communication channel presents both opportunities and challenges.

The major opportunity lies in the interaction that is possible between you and your audience. When you speak before a group, you can receive information as well as transmit it. Instead of simply expressing your ideas, you can draw ideas from your

FIGURE 13–1
The Three-Step Oral Presentation Process

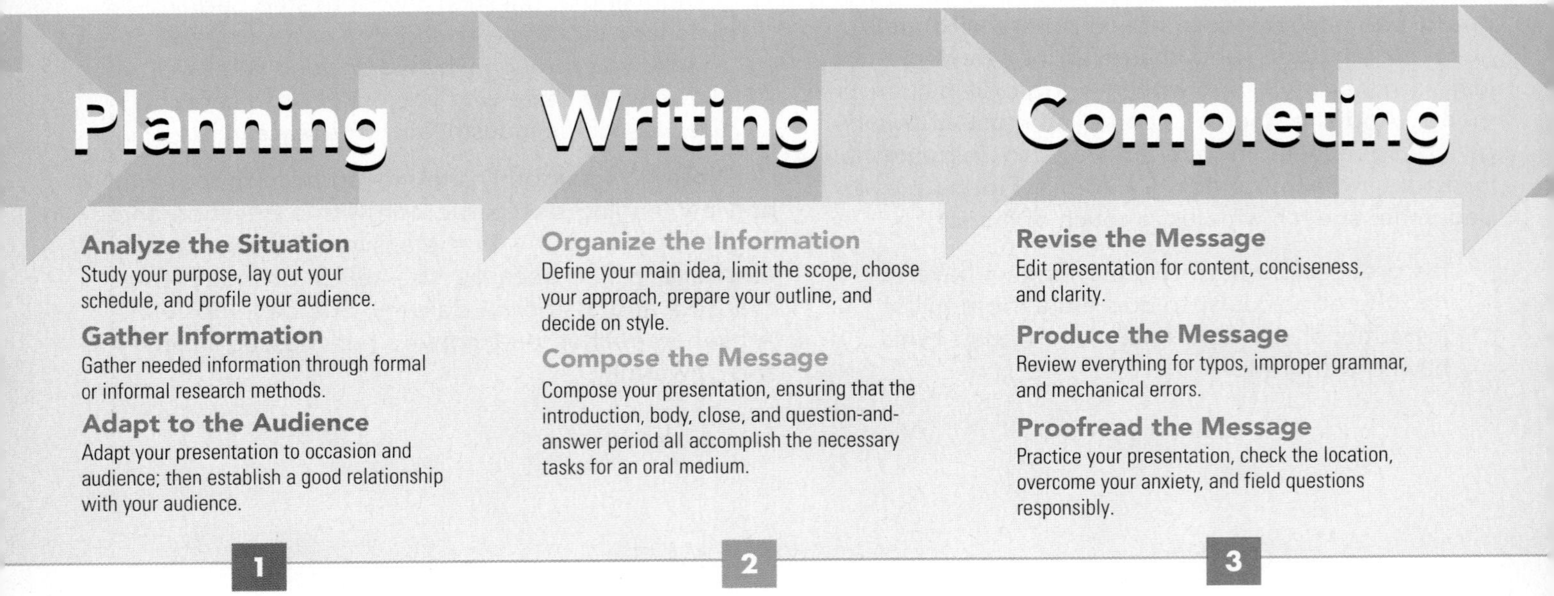
Planning
Analyze the Situation
Study your purpose, lay out your schedule, and profile your audience.
Gather Information
Gather needed information through formal or informal research methods.
Adapt to the Audience
Adapt your presentation to occasion and audience; then establish a good relationship with your audience.
1
Writing
Organize the Information
Define your main idea, limit the scope, choose your approach, prepare your outline, and decide on style.
Compose the Message
Compose your presentation, ensuring that the introduction, body, close, and question-and-answer period all accomplish the necessary tasks for an oral medium.
2
Completing
Revise the Message
Edit presentation for content, conciseness, and clarity.
Produce the Message
Review everything for typos, improper grammar, and mechanical errors.
Proofread the Message
Practice your presentation, check the location, overcome your anxiety, and field questions responsibly.
3

audience and then reach a mutually acceptable conclusion. You also have the opportunity to reinforce your message with nonverbal cues. Audiences receive much richer stimuli during a speech than while reading a written report.

The major challenge of using an oral communication channel is being able to control what happens. The more you expect to interact with your audience, the less control you'll have. As you plan each part of your presentation, think about how you will deliver the information. Halfway through your presentation, a comment from someone in the audience might force you to shift topics, organization, or even style of delivery. Try to anticipate such shifts, so that you don't lose control by being caught off guard.

Because your presentation is a onetime event, your audience cannot leaf back through printed pages to review something you said earlier. To make sure that your audience will hear what you say and remember it, pay special attention to defining your purpose clearly and learning about your audience's needs.

Defining Your Purpose

The four basic purposes for giving a presentation are to inform, to persuade, to motivate, and to entertain. Many of your presentations or speeches will be informative, a straightforward statement of the facts. However, you can convey straightforward information in a memo or a report. Speaking in front of an audience is an interactive process, affording you tremendous opportunity to persuade your listeners.[2] Quite a few of your presentations will probably be persuasive, based on the organizational and

You usually give an oral presentation for one of four purposes.

Companies such as Sears, Avon, Nike, and America Online use webcast speeches to make live announcements of financial news, new products, and management changes, as shown on the Yahoo! Broadcast site. Unlike ordinary speeches that address a particular audience at a particular time and place, webcast speeches can be viewed and listened to long after the speaker has left the podium.

writing techniques discussed in Chapter 9. Motivational speeches tend to be more specialized, so many companies bring in outside professional speakers to handle this type of presentation. Entertainment speeches are perhaps the rarest in the business world; they are usually limited to after-dinner speeches and to speeches at conventions or retreats. Here are sample statements of purpose for business presentations:

- To inform the accounting department of the new remote data-access policy

- To explain to the executive committee the financial ramifications of OmniGroup's takeover offer

- To persuade potential customers that our bank offers the best commercial banking services for their needs

Regardless of your purpose, you will be more effective if you keep your audience interested in your message. To do so, try to understand who your audience members are and what they need.

Getting to Know Your Audience

Gear the content, organization, and style of your message to your audience's size, background, attitudes, needs, and interests.

If you're involved in selecting the audience or speaking to a group of peers at work, you'll certainly have information about their characteristics. But in many cases, you'll be speaking to a group of people you know little about, so you'll want to investigate their needs and characteristics before showing up to speak. Carly Fiorina knows that analyzing your audience is particularly important when addressing people from other cultures.

You can ask your host or some other contact person for help with audience analysis, and you can supplement that information with some educated estimates of your own. For a reminder of how to analyze an audience, review Chapter 4's "Develop an Audience Profile." Also take a look at this chapter's "Checklist: Audience Analysis." For even more insight into audience evaluation (including emotional and cultural issues), consult a good textbook on public speaking.

✓ CHECKLIST: Audience Analysis

Determine Audience Size and Composition

✓ Estimate how many people will attend.
✓ Consider whether they have some political, religious, professional, or other affiliation in common.
✓ Analyze the mix of men and women, age ranges, socioeconomic and ethnic groups, occupations, and geographic regions represented.

Predict the Audience's Probable Reaction

✓ Analyze why audience members are attending the presentation.
✓ Determine the audience's general attitude toward the topic: interested, moderately interested, unconcerned, open-minded, or hostile.
✓ Analyze the mood that people will be in when you speak to them.
✓ Find out what kind of backup information will most impress the audience: technical data, historical information, financial data, demonstrations, samples, and so on.
✓ Consider whether the audience has any biases that might work against you.
✓ Anticipate possible objections or questions.

Gauge the Audience's Level of Understanding

✓ Analyze whether everybody has the same background and experience.
✓ Determine what the audience already knows about the subject.
✓ Decide what background information the audience will need to better understand the subject.
✓ Consider whether the audience is familiar with your vocabulary.
✓ Analyze what the audience expects from you.
✓ Think about the mix of general concepts and specific details you will need to present.

STEP 2: WRITING ORAL PRESENTATIONS

You may never actually write out a presentation word for word. But that doesn't mean that developing its content will be any easier or quicker than preparing a written document. Speaking intelligently about a topic may actually involve more work and more time than preparing a written document about the same topic.

Organizing Your Presentation

Every facet of organizing your oral presentation is driven by what you know about your audience. For example, if you're organizing a sales presentation, focus on how much your product will benefit the people in your audience, not on how great the product is. If you're explaining a change in medical benefits for company employees, address the concerns your audience is likely to have, such as cost and quality of care. You should organize an oral message just as you would a written message, by focusing on your audience as you define your main idea, limit your scope, choose your approach, prepare your outline, and decide on the most effective style for your presentation.

> What you know about your audience affects your main idea, scope, approach, outline, and style.

Defining the Main Idea   What is the one message you want audience members to walk away with? What do you want them to do after listening to you? Look for a one-sentence generalization that links your subject and purpose to your audience's frame of reference, much as an advertising slogan points out how a product can benefit consumers. Here are some examples:

> The main idea points out how the audience can benefit from your message.

- Convince department members that reorganizing the data-processing unit will improve customer service and reduce employee turnover.

- Convince board members that we should build a new plant in Texas to eliminate manufacturing bottlenecks and improve production quality.

- Address employee concerns about a new health-care plan by showing how the plan will reduce their costs and improve the quality of their care.

Each of these statements puts a particular slant on the subject, one that directly relates to the audience's interests. This sort of "you" attitude helps you keep your audience's attention and convince people that your points are relevant. For example, a group of new employees will be much more responsive to your discussion of plant safety procedures if you focus on how the procedures can save lives rather than on how the rules conform to Occupational Safety and Health Administration guidelines.

> Using the "you" attitude makes your material relevant to your audience and helps keep their attention.

Limiting Your Scope   Effective presentations not only focus on the audience's needs but also tailor the material to the time allowed, which is often strictly regulated. You can use your outline to estimate how much time your presentation will take. The average speaker can deliver about 125 to 150 words per minute (or roughly 7,500 to 9,000 words per hour), which corresponds to between 20 and 25 double-spaced, typed pages of text per hour. The average paragraph is about 125 to 150 words, so most of us can speak at a rate of about one paragraph per minute.

> Fit your oral presentation to the time allotted.

> In one minute, the average speaker can deliver about one paragraph, or 125 to 150 words.

Say you want to make three basic points. In a 10-minute presentation, you could take about 2 minutes to explain each point, using roughly two paragraphs for each. If you devoted a minute each to the opening and the close, you would have 2 minutes left to interact with the audience. If you had an hour, however, you could spend the first 5 minutes on your opening: introducing the presentation, establishing rapport with the audience, providing background information, and giving an overview of your topic. In the next 30 to 40 minutes, you could explain each of the three points, spending about 10 to 13 minutes on each (the equivalent of 5 or 6 typewritten pages). Your close might take another 3 to 5 minutes. The remaining 10 to 20 minutes would then be available for responding to questions and comments from the audience.

Which is better, the 10-minute speech or the hour-long presentation? If your speech doesn't have to fit into a specified time slot, the answer depends on your subject, your audience's attitude and knowledge, and the relationship you have with your audience. For a simple, easily accepted message, 10 minutes may be enough. On the other hand, if your subject is complex or your audience is skeptical, you'll probably need more time. Don't squeeze a complex presentation into a period that is too brief, and don't spend any more time than necessary on a simple talk.

Choosing Your Approach   With a well-defined main idea to guide you and a clear idea about the scope of your presentation, you can begin to arrange your message. If you have 10 minutes or less to deliver your message, organize your presentation much as you would a letter or a brief memo: Use the direct approach if the subject involves routine information or good news, and use the indirect approach if the subject involves bad news or persuasion.

Longer presentations are organized like reports. If the purpose is to entertain, motivate, or inform, use direct order and a structure imposed naturally by the subject: importance, sequence, chronology, spatial orientation, geography, or category (as discussed in Chapter 11). If your purpose is to analyze, persuade, or collaborate, organize your material around conclusions and recommendations or around a logical argument. Use direct order if the audience is receptive and indirect if you expect resistance.

You may have to adjust the organization of your presentation in response to feedback from your audience, especially if your purpose is to collaborate. You can plan ahead by thinking of several organizational possibilities (based on "what if" assumptions about your audience's reactions). Then, if someone says something that undercuts your planned approach, you can switch smoothly to another one.

Oral communication demands simplicity of organization. If listeners lose the thread of your comments, they'll have a hard time catching up and following the remainder of your message. They can't review a paragraph or flip pages back and forth as they can when reading. So look for the most obvious and natural way to organize your ideas, and use a direct order of presentation whenever possible.

Explain at the beginning how you've organized your material, and try to limit the number of main points to three or four—even when the speech or presentation is rather long. Include only the most useful, interesting, and relevant supporting evidence. And at the end of each section, reorient the audience by summarizing the point you've just made and explaining how it fits into your overall framework.

Preparing Your Outline   A carefully prepared outline can be more than just the starting point for composing a speech or presentation—it will help you stay on task. You can use your outline to make sure your message accomplishes its purpose, which is to help you keep your presentation both audience-centered and within the allotted time. Prepare your outline in several stages:[3]

- **State your purpose and main idea.** As you develop your outline, check frequently to be sure that the points, organization, connections, and title relate to your purpose and main idea.

- **Organize your major points and subpoints.** Express each major point as a single, complete sentence to help you keep track of the one specific idea you want to convey in that point. Then look at the order of points to make sure their arrangement is logical and effective.

Marginal notes:

Structure a short oral presentation like a letter or a memo.

Organize longer speeches and presentations like formal reports.

Use a clear, direct organization to accommodate your listeners' limitations.

Outlines can help you compose your presentation and stay on task.

- **Identify your opening, body, and close.** Start with the body, numbering each major point and subpoint according to its level in your outline. Then lay out the points for your opening (or introduction) and close (or conclusion). Be sure you begin your numbering system anew for each section—opening, body, and close.

- **Show your connections.** Write out in sentence form the transitions you plan to use to move from one part to the next. Remember to include additional transitions between major points in the body of your speech. Don't number transitions; position each one on a separate line between the two sections and enclose it in parentheses.

- **Show your sources.** Prepare your bibliography, making sure that it is easy to read, follows a consistent format, and includes all the details to identify your various sources.

- **Choose a title.** Not all speeches need or have a title. However, a title can be useful if your speech will be publicized ahead of time or introduced by someone else.

Figure 13–2 is an outline for a 30-minute analytical presentation. It is organized around conclusions and presented in direct order. This outline is based on the Electrovision report, written by Linda Moreno. (See Chapter 12's "Report Writer's Notebook" on page 402.)

To sound as natural as possible, plan to deliver your presentation from notes rather than from written text, and use your outline as your final "script." When your outline will serve as your speaking notes, its purpose is merely to prompt your memory about what you plan to say and in what order. Therefore, you put much less detail into your speaking outline than you have in your planning outline.[4] To prepare an effective speaking outline, follow these steps:[5]

> When you use your outline as speaking notes, you'll make some special alterations.

- **Follow the planning outline.** Follow the same format as you used for your planning outline (so that you can see at a glance where you are in your speech and how each part and point relates to the one before and after). However, strip away anything you don't plan to say to your audience (statements of general purpose, specific purpose, main idea, bibliography, etc.).

- **Condense points and transitions to keywords.** Choose words that will prompt you to remember what each point is about so that you can speak fluently. However, write out statistics, quotations, and other specifics so that you don't stumble over them. You may also want to write complete sentences for transitions that connect main points or for critical points in your opening or your close. Aim for the shortest outline you can comfortably use.

- **Add delivery cues.** During rehearsals, note the places in your outline where you plan to enhance your meaning by pausing, speaking more slowly, using visual aids, and so on. You might use colored ink to highlight your cues. But avoid cluttering your outline; just show the most important cues.

- **Arrange your notes.** Whether you hand-print or type your speaking outline on paper or note cards, make sure your final version is legible and accessible so that you can refer to it as you speak. Number your cards (or sheets of paper) so that you can keep them in order.

Deciding on an Appropriate Style Another important element in your preparation is style. Will you give a formal presentation in an impressive setting, with professionally produced visual aids? Or will you lead a casual, roll-up-your-sleeves working session? Choose your style to fit the occasion. Your audience's size, your subject, your purpose, your budget, and the time available for preparation all influence your style.

If you're speaking to a relatively small group, you can use a casual style that encourages audience participation. A small conference room, with your audience seated around a table, may be appropriate. Use simple visual aids, and invite your

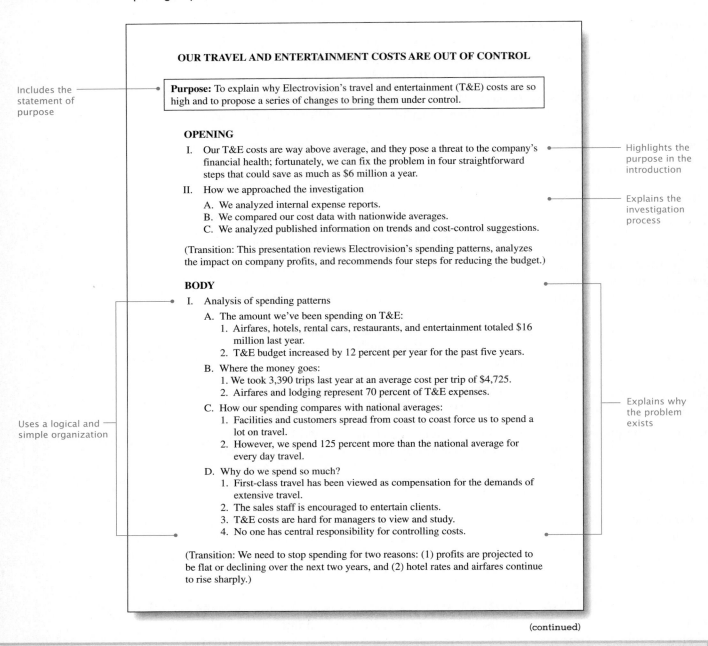

Includes the statement of purpose

OUR TRAVEL AND ENTERTAINMENT COSTS ARE OUT OF CONTROL

Purpose: To explain why Electrovision's travel and entertainment (T&E) costs are so high and to propose a series of changes to bring them under control.

OPENING

I. Our T&E costs are way above average, and they pose a threat to the company's financial health; fortunately, we can fix the problem in four straightforward steps that could save as much as $6 million a year.

Highlights the purpose in the introduction

II. How we approached the investigation

A. We analyzed internal expense reports.
B. We compared our cost data with nationwide averages.
C. We analyzed published information on trends and cost-control suggestions.

Explains the investigation process

(Transition: This presentation reviews Electrovision's spending patterns, analyzes the impact on company profits, and recommends four steps for reducing the budget.)

BODY

I. Analysis of spending patterns

A. The amount we've been spending on T&E:
1. Airfares, hotels, rental cars, restaurants, and entertainment totaled $16 million last year.
2. T&E budget increased by 12 percent per year for the past five years.

B. Where the money goes:
1. We took 3,390 trips last year at an average cost per trip of $4,725.
2. Airfares and lodging represent 70 percent of T&E expenses.

C. How our spending compares with national averages:
1. Facilities and customers spread from coast to coast force us to spend a lot on travel.
2. However, we spend 125 percent more than the national average for every day travel.

Explains why the problem exists

D. Why do we spend so much?
1. First-class travel has been viewed as compensation for the demands of extensive travel.
2. The sales staff is encouraged to entertain clients.
3. T&E costs are hard for managers to view and study.
4. No one has central responsibility for controlling costs.

Uses a logical and simple organization

(Transition: We need to stop spending for two reasons: (1) profits are projected to be flat or declining over the next two years, and (2) hotel rates and airfares continue to rise sharply.)

(continued)

FIGURE 13–2
Effective Outline for a 30-Minute Presentation

audience to interject comments. Deliver your remarks in a conversational tone, using notes to jog your memory if necessary.

Use a casual style for small groups; use a formal style for large groups and important events.

If you're addressing a large audience and the event is an important one, you'll want to establish a more formal atmosphere. A formal style is well suited to announcements about mergers or acquisitions, new products, financial results, and other business milestones. During formal presentations, speakers are often located on a stage or platform, standing behind a lectern and using a microphone so that their remarks can be heard throughout the room. These presentations are often accompanied by slides and other visual aids showcasing major products, technological breakthroughs, and other information that the speakers want audience members to remember.

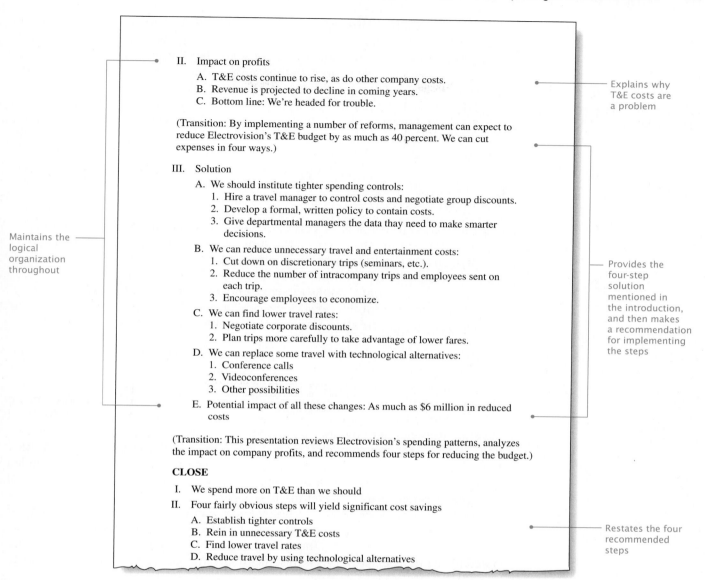

II. Impact on profits

    A. T&E costs continue to rise, as do other company costs.

    B. Revenue is projected to decline in coming years.

    C. Bottom line: We're headed for trouble.

Explains why T&E costs are a problem

(Transition: By implementing a number of reforms, management can expect to reduce Electrovision's T&E budget by as much as 40 percent. We can cut expenses in four ways.)

III. Solution

    A. We should institute tighter spending controls:

        1. Hire a travel manager to control costs and negotiate group discounts.

        2. Develop a formal, written policy to contain costs.

        3. Give departmental managers the data thay need to make smarter decisions.

    B. We can reduce unnecessary travel and entertainment costs:

        1. Cut down on discretionary trips (seminars, etc.).

        2. Reduce the number of intracompany trips and employees sent on each trip.

        3. Encourage employees to economize.

    C. We can find lower travel rates:

        1. Negotiate corporate discounts.

        2. Plan trips more carefully to take advantage of lower fares.

    D. We can replace some travel with technological alternatives:

        1. Conference calls

        2. Videoconferences

        3. Other possibilities

    E. Potential impact of all these changes: As much as $6 million in reduced costs

Maintains the logical organization throughout

Provides the four-step solution mentioned in the introduction, and then makes a recommendation for implementing the steps

(Transition: This presentation reviews Electrovision's spending patterns, analyzes the impact on company profits, and recommends four steps for reducing the budget.)

CLOSE

I. We spend more on T&E than we should

II. Four fairly obvious steps will yield significant cost savings

    A. Establish tighter controls

    B. Rein in unnecessary T&E costs

    C. Find lower travel rates

    D. Reduce travel by using technological alternatives

Restates the four recommended steps

FIGURE 13–2
Continued

Whether you're delivering a formal or an informal presentation, never try to impress your audience with obscure or unfamiliar vocabulary. Make sure you can define all the words you use. And keep things simple. If you repeatedly stumble over a word as you rehearse, use a different one.[6]

In both formal and informal presentations, keep things simple.

Developing the Opening of Your Presentation

A good opening arouses the audience's interest in your topic, establishes your credibility, and prepares the audience by previewing what will follow. That's a lot to pack into the first few minutes of your presentation. So, of the total time you allocate to writing your oral presentation, plan on spending a disproportionate amount on developing your opening.

The opening must capture attention, inspire confidence, and preview the contents.

Arousing Audience Interest   Some subjects are naturally more interesting than others. If you will be discussing a matter of profound significance that will personally affect the members of your audience, chances are they'll listen regardless of how you begin. All you really have to do is announce your topic ("Today I'll be explaining the reorganization of our company").

To capture attention, connect your topic to your listeners' needs and interests.

Other subjects call for more imagination. How do you get people to listen when you're explaining your pension program to a group of new clerical employees, none of whom will be full participants for another five years and most of whom will probably leave the company within two? The best approach to dealing with an uninterested audience is to appeal to human nature and encourage people to take the subject personally. Show them how they'll be affected as individuals. For example, you might begin addressing the new clerical employees like this:

> If somebody offered to give you $200,000 in exchange for $5 per week, would you be interested? That's the amount you can expect to collect during your retirement years if you choose to contribute to the voluntary pension plan. During the next two weeks, you will have to decide whether you want to participate. Although retirement is many years away for most of you, it is an important financial decision. During the next 20 minutes, I hope to give you the information you need to make that decision intelligently.

Some speakers grab attention by drawing comments from audience members.

Another way to arouse audience interest is to draw out ideas and encourage comments from listeners throughout your presentation. Of course, this technique works better with a small group of co-workers than it does when you're addressing a large audience—particularly if the members of that large audience are hostile or unknown to you. During a presentation to a large group or a speech that covers controversial material, responding to questions and comments can interrupt the flow of information, weaken your argument, and reduce your control of the situation. In such situations, it's best to ask people to hold their questions until after you have concluded your remarks. Just be sure to allow ample time for audience questions at the end of your presentation, as this chapter discusses later.

Table 13–1 suggests several techniques you can use to arouse audience interest and keep listeners involved. Regardless of which technique you choose, always make sure that the opening matches the tone of your presentation. If the occasion is supposed to be fun, you may begin with something light; but if you're talking business to

Table 13–1	FIVE WAYS TO GET ATTENTION AND KEEP IT
Use humor	Even though the subject of most business presentations is serious, including a light comment now and then can perk up the audience. Just be sure the humor is relevant to the presentation and not offensive to the audience.
Tell a story	Slice-of-life stories are naturally interesting and can be compelling. Be sure your story illustrates an important point.
Pass around a sample	Psychologists say that you can get people to remember your points by appealing to their senses. The best way to do so is to pass around a sample. If your company is in the textile business, let the audience handle some of your fabrics. If you sell chocolates, give everybody a taste.
Ask a question	Asking questions will get the audience actively involved in your presentation and, at the same time, will give you information about them and their needs.
State a startling statistic	People love details. If you can interject an interesting statistic, you can often wake up your audience.

a group of executives, don't waste their time with cute openings. Avoid jokes and personal anecdotes when you're discussing a serious problem. If you're giving a routine oral report, don't be overly dramatic. Most of all, be natural. Nothing turns off the average audience faster than a trite, staged beginning.

Building Your Credibility   You want your audience to like you as a person and to respect your opinion. Use your opening to establish your credentials—and quickly; people will decide within a few minutes whether you're worth listening to.[7] But to establish this sort of credibility, you need to lay the groundwork while you're developing your speech. Achieving credibility with a familiar, open-minded audience is relatively easy. The difficulty comes when you're trying to earn the confidence of strangers, especially those predisposed to be skeptical or antagonistic.

One way to build credibility is to let someone else introduce you. That person can present your credentials so that you won't appear boastful. Just make sure that the person introducing you doesn't exaggerate your qualifications. If you're introducing yourself, plan simple comments, but don't be afraid to mention your accomplishments. Briefly tell listeners who you are and why you're there. You need mention only a few aspects of your background: your position in an organization, your profession, and the name of your company. You might plan to say something like this:

> I'm Karen Whitney, a market research analyst with Information Resources Corporation. For the past five years, I've specialized in studying high-technology markets. Your director of engineering, John LaBarre, has asked me to talk to you about recent trends in computer-aided design so that you'll have a better idea of how to direct your research efforts.

This speaker establishes credibility by tying her credentials to the purpose of her presentation. By mentioning her company's name, her specialization and position, and the name of the audience's boss, she lets her listeners know immediately that she is qualified to tell them something they need to know. She connects her background to their concerns.

Previewing Your Presentation   A reader can get an idea of the structure and content of a report by looking at the table of contents and scanning the headings. In an oral presentation, however, the speaker provides that framework with a preview. Without cues from the speaker, the audience may be unable to figure out how the main points of the message fit together.

Your preview should summarize the main idea of your presentation, identify the supporting points, and indicate the order in which you'll develop those points. Tell your listeners in so many words, "This is the subject, and these are the points I will cover." Once you've established the framework, you can be confident that the audience will understand how the individual facts and figures are related to your main idea as you move into the body of your presentation.

Developing the Body of Your Presentation

The bulk of your speech or presentation is devoted to a discussion of the three or four main points in your outline—the who, what, when, where, why, and how of your subject. Use the same organizational patterns you'd use in a letter, memo, or report, but keep things simple. As Carly Fiorina can tell you, your goals are to make sure that (1) the organization of your presentation is clear and (2) your presentation holds the audience's attention.

Connecting Your Ideas   To show how ideas are related, a written report uses typographical and formatting clues, such as headings, paragraph indentions, white

---

Margin notes:

Although many techniques will arouse audience interest, avoid staged beginnings.

You have only a few minutes to establish your credibility.

To build credibility, you can let someone else introduce you or you can introduce yourself—explaining (without boasting) why you are qualified to speak on the subject.

Let the audience know what lies ahead.

Limit the body of your message to three or four main points.

space, and lists. However, an oral presentation must rely on words to link various parts and ideas.

Help your audience follow your presentation by using clear transitions between sentences and paragraphs, as well as between major sections.

For the small links between sentences and paragraphs, use one or two transitional words: *therefore, because, in addition, in contrast, moreover, for example, consequently, nevertheless,* or *finally.* To link major sections of a presentation, use complete sentences or paragraphs, such as "Now that we've reviewed the problem, let's take a look at some solutions." Every time you shift topics, be sure to stress the connection between ideas. Summarize what's been said, and preview what's to come.

Emphasize your transitions by repeating key ideas, using gestures, changing your tone of voice, or introducing a visual aid.

The longer your presentation, the more important your transitions become. If you will be presenting many ideas, audience members may have trouble absorbing them and seeing the relationships among them. Your listeners need clear transitions to guide them to the most important points. Furthermore, they need transitions to pick up any ideas they may have missed. So by repeating key ideas in your transitions, you can compensate for lapses in your audience's attention. When you actually give your presentation, you might also want to call attention to the transitions by using gestures, changing your tone of voice, or introducing a visual aid.

Make a special effort to capture wandering attention.

Holding Your Audience's Attention Communicating your points effectively requires that you do more than simply connect your ideas with clear transitions. Here are a few helpful tips for holding your audience's attention:

- **Relate your subject to your audience's needs.** People are interested in things that affect them personally. Plan to present every point in light of your audience's needs and values.

- **Anticipate your audience's questions.** Prepare for as many questions as you can think of, and address them in the body of your presentation. Also prepare and reserve additional material to use during the question-and-answer period, should the audience ask for greater detail.

- **Use clear, vivid language.** People become bored quickly when they don't understand the speaker. If your presentation will involve abstract ideas, plan to show how those abstractions connect with everyday life. Use familiar words, short sentences, and concrete examples.

- **Explain the relationship between your subject and familiar ideas.** Plan how you'll relate your subject to ideas that audience members already understand. Doing so gives people a way to categorize and remember your points.[8]

When attempting to hold an audience's attention, public speakers sometimes must compete with distractions in the background. It takes focus to overcome such physical interruptions and get one's message across.

Carly Fiorina involves audience members by asking for opinions or pausing occasionally for questions or comments. Audience feedback helps you determine whether your listeners understand a key point before you launch into another section. Feedback also gives your audience a chance to switch for a time from listening to participating. Plan your pauses, even going so far as to note them in your outline so that you won't forget to pause once you're on stage.

Developing the Close of Your Presentation

The close of a speech or presentation is almost as important as the beginning, because audience attention peaks at this point. Plan about 10 percent of your total time for the ending. Tell listeners that you're about to finish, so that they'll make one final effort to listen intently. Don't be afraid to sound obvious; consider saying something such as "In conclusion" or "To sum it all up." You want people to know that this is the home stretch. In your close, you need to accomplish three important tasks: review the points you've made, make sure everyone knows what to do next, and leave listeners with a statement that will help them remember the subject of your talk.

The close should leave a strong and lasting impression.

Restating Your Main Points Once you've decided how to indicate that your close is imminent, plan on repeating your main idea. Be sure to emphasize what you want your audience to do or think, and state the key motivating factor. Then reinforce your theme by repeating your three or four main supporting points. A few sentences are generally enough to refresh people's memories.

Summarize the main idea, and restate the main points.

Describing the Next Steps Some presentations require the audience to reach a decision or agree to take specific action. In such cases the close provides a clear wrap-up. If the audience agrees on an issue covered in the presentation, plan to review the consensus in a sentence or two. If they don't agree, make the lack of consensus clear by saying something like "We seem to have some fundamental disagreement on this question." Then be ready to suggest a method of resolving the differences.

Be certain that everyone agrees on the outcome and understands what should happen next.

If you expect any action to occur as a result of your speech, you must explain who is responsible for doing what. One effective technique is to list the action items, with an estimated completion date and the name of the person responsible. You can present this list in a visual aid and ask each person on the list to agree to accomplish his or her assigned task by the target date. This public commitment to action is the best insurance that something will happen. If the required action is likely to be difficult, make sure that everyone understands the potential problems or pitfalls. You want everyone to have a realistic attitude and to be prepared to handle whatever arises.

Ending on a Strong Note Make sure that your final remarks are encouraging and memorable. After summarizing the key points of your presentation, conclude with a quote, a call to action, or some encouraging words. For instance, you might stress the benefits of action or express confidence in the listeners' ability to accomplish the work ahead. An alternative is to end with a question or a statement that will leave your audience thinking.

One speaker ended a presentation on the company's executive compensation program by repeating his four specific recommendations and then concluding with a memorable statement that would motivate his audience to take action:

Make your final words memorable.

We can all be proud of the way our company has grown. If we want to continue that growth, however, we will have to adjust our executive compensation program to reflect competitive practices. If we don't, our best people will look for opportunities elsewhere.

In summary, our survey has shown that we need to do four things to improve executive compensation:

- Increase the overall level of compensation
- Install a cash bonus program
- Offer a variety of stock-based incentives
- Improve our health insurance and pension benefits

By making these improvements, we can help our company cross the threshold of growth into the major leagues.

Document Makeover

IMPROVE THIS SPEECH

To practice correcting drafts of actual documents, visit **www.prenhall.com/onekey** on the web. Click "Document Makeovers," then click Chapter 13. You will find a speech that contains problems and errors relating to what you've learned in this chapter about preparing effective speeches and oral presentations. Use the Final Draft decision tool to create an improved version of this speech. Check the message for effective choices in scope, style, opening, use of transitions, and closing.

At the completion of your presentation, your audience should feel satisfied. The close is not the place to introduce new ideas or to alter the mood of the presentation. Even if parts of your presentation are downbeat, you want to close on a positive note. Avoid using a staged finale—keep it natural. As with everything else in your oral presentation, plan your closing remarks carefully. You don't want to wind up on stage with nothing to say but "Well, I guess that's it."

Using Visual Aids in Oral Presentations

The ability to create and deliver an effective presentation is a vital skill in today's workplace. As HP's Carly Fiorina knows, good content and a smooth delivery are not enough. Audiences will also expect you to use visual aids in your oral presentations.

Visual aids help the audience remember important points.

Visual aids can improve the quality and impact of your oral presentation by creating interest, illustrating points that are difficult to explain in words alone, adding variety, and increasing the audience's ability to absorb and remember information. Studies of behavioral research have shown that visual aids can improve learning by up to 400 percent because humans can process visuals 60,000 times faster than text.[9]

Effective speakers can choose from a variety of visual aids.

As a speaker, you'll find that visual aids can help you remember the details of your message (no small feat in a lengthy presentation). They can also improve your professional image, since speakers who use visuals generally appear to be better prepared and more knowledgeable than speakers who do not. To enhance oral presentations, today's speakers can select from a variety of visual aids:

- **Overhead transparencies.** For decades, transparencies have been the standard visual aid. An **overhead transparency** is a piece of clear plastic with text or some other image on it. You show a transparency by placing it on an overhead projector that reflects the image or text onto a screen. You can create transparencies by using word-processing, page-layout, or electronic-slide-presentation software, and you can even prepare them by hand. Because their content and design elements are similar to electronic slides, we sometimes refer to transparencies as slides, for purposes of this chapter.

- **Electronic presentations.** In most business situations today, the visual aid of choice is the **electronic presentation** or *slide show*. It consists of **electronic slides** that you can create using software such as Microsoft PowerPoint, Lotus Freelance Graphics, or Corel Draw. These slides can incorporate photos, sound, video, graphics, and animation to capture and engage your audience like no other visual. Special projection equipment grabs images from your computer monitor and displays them on the same screen used for viewing transparencies. You can create, display, and modify your electronic slides as your speech unfolds.[10]

- **35-millimeter slides.** The content of 35-millimeter slides may be text, graphics, or pictures. If you're trying to create a polished, professional atmosphere, you might find this approach worthwhile, particularly if you'll be addressing a crowd and don't mind speaking in a darkened room. If you choose this visual aid, you will need to coordinate your slides with your speech and appoint someone to operate the projector.

- **Chalkboards and whiteboards.** Because content for chalkboards and whiteboards is produced on the spot, they offer flexibility. They are effective tools for recording points made during small-group brainstorming sessions; however, they're too informal for some situations.

- **Flip charts.** Large sheets of paper attached at the top like a tablet can be propped on an easel so that you can flip the pages as you speak, with each chart illustrating or clarifying a point. You might have a few lines from your outline on one, a graph or diagram on another, and so on. By using felt-tip markers of various colors, you can also record ideas generated during a discussion.

- **Other visual aids.** A sample of a product or material allows an audience to experience your subject directly. Models built to scale conveniently represent an object. Audiotapes may be used to supplement a slide show or to present a precisely worded and timed message. Movies and filmstrips can capture audience attention with color and movement. Television and videotapes are good for showing demonstrations, interviews, and other events. Plus, filmstrips, movies, television, and videos can be used as stand-alone vehicles (independent of a speaker) to communicate with dispersed audiences at various times.

Because the two most popular types of visual aids are overhead transparencies and electronic presentations, we will focus on them in the remainder of this section. Even though these two visual aids differ in the features they offer and in the way they are delivered, both consist of a collection of slides that must be well written and well designed to be effective. Once the slides are created, they are either printed on clear plastic sheets for overhead transparencies or stored electronically and further embellished with multimedia effects for electronic presentations.

Overhead transparencies and electronic presentations are the most popular types of visual aids.

Choosing Overhead Transparencies or Electronic Presentations   Both overhead transparencies and electronic slides have advantages and disadvantages. Many businesspeople prefer to use overhead transparencies, because they are inexpensive, easy to create, and simple to use. You can prepare high-quality overheads using a computer and a high-resolution color inkjet or laser printer. Moreover, they require little extra equipment to show: Most conference rooms or classrooms have overhead projectors and a table large enough to stack transparencies. And, because transparency images can be projected in full daylight, speakers can maintain eye contact with the audience. They can also use special markers to write on transparencies as they present information.

Simplicity, availability, and affordability are key advantages of overhead transparencies.

Despite these advantages, transparencies have a number of drawbacks. First, because they are in a permanent printed format, they must be replaced if their content changes. You cannot erase or change a word, color, or graph on a transparency as you can on an electronic slide. Second, each time you add or remove a transparency from a sequence, you must manually renumber the batch. Third, transparencies are fragile: They chip, flake, scratch, and tear easily. You can protect transparencies with cardboard or plastic frames or with transparent sleeves, but these protectors are costly and are bulky to store or transport. Fourth, overhead projectors can be noisy and a challenge to talk over. Finally, transparencies must be aligned carefully on the overhead projector (one at a time). This requirement limits the presenter's ability to move freely about the room.

Overhead transparencies are fragile, difficult to modify, and clumsy to use.

Electronic presentations are another story. Their biggest advantage is their computerized format, which makes real-time manipulation of data easy. You can change a graphic, add a bulleted phrase, and even alter the sequence of your slides with a simple click of the mouse. You can add animation, video clips, sound, hypertext, and other multimedia effects to slides—turning them into dazzling professional presentations. You can even preprogram and automate the release of text

Electronic slides offer more features and benefits than overhead transparencies.

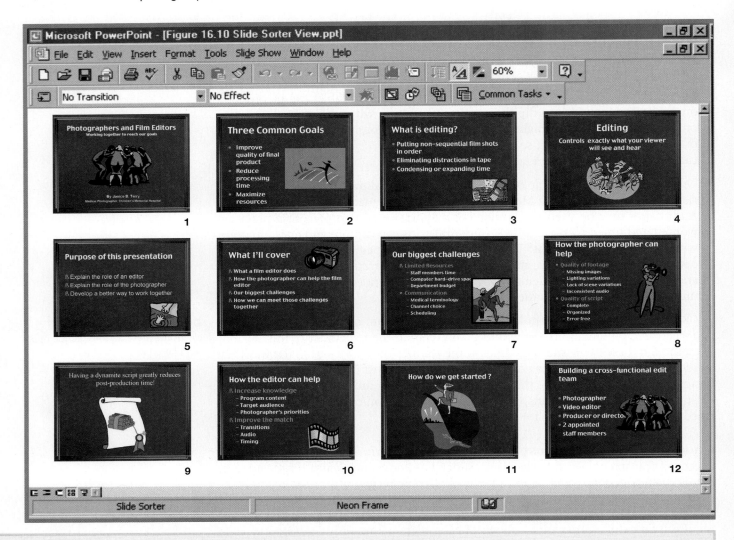

FIGURE 13–3
Slide Sorter View

and graphical elements. Furthermore, electronic presentations are easy to store, transport, and customize for different audiences.

Another advantage of electronic presentations is the slide sorter view, which lets you see a file's entire batch of slides at once (see Figure13–3). This view makes it relatively easy to add and delete slides, reposition them, and check them for design consistency. You can also use this view to preview animation and transition effects and experiment with design elements.

However, electronic presentations have disadvantages, too. First, electronic slides require more expensive display equipment than overhead transparencies—especially if you are presenting to large audiences. This equipment can be complicated to use and may not be available in all situations. Second, most people spend too much time focusing on the technical components of an electronic presentation—they pay more attention to the animation and special effects of their slide shows than they do to the content of their message. Third, inexperienced presenters tend to pack too many special effects into their electronic slides, creating a visual feast of pictures and graphics that dazzle the audience but blur the key message.

Electronic presentations require expensive, complicated equipment, which can tempt presenters to pay too much attention to technical components and special effects.

Electronic presentations can and often do go awry. When planning an electronic presentation, ensure success even in the face of equipment failure by following these tips:[11]

- **Set up in advance.** Schedule plenty of time to set up and test your equipment before your speech. You don't want to troubleshoot hardware glitches in front of your audience.

- **Bring two of everything.** Borrow backup laptop computers, display panels or projectors, modems, or any other hardware you plan to use.

- **Back up your programs.** Save a copy of your show on a floppy disk, Zip drive, CD, or other storage medium so that you'll have it if you need it.

- **Have backup technical support available.** Line up an expert you can call if something doesn't work.

- **Avoid real-time use of the Internet.** When using the Internet during a speech, you may encounter slow phone connections, downed websites, and general frustration. You can save the sites you want on your hard drive and then access them offline. (Consult your browser's help menu.)

- **Have a contingency plan.** Take along copies of key exhibits prepared as handouts or overhead transparencies. These backups may be less glamorous, but if your electronic equipment fails, they are certainly better than nothing.

Creating Effective Slides for Oral Presentations   Too many people design their slides before preparing the slides' content. Although design is an important element, it is secondary to a well-organized, well-developed, audience-centered message. So plan what each slide is going to say and organize the content, as you would for any written message. Then write and polish the written content before focusing on the slide's design elements. Your primary focus when putting together text or graphic slides is to create content that is simple and readable, select design elements that enhance your message without overshadowing it, keep your design selections consistent, and use special effects selectively.

Creating Simple, Readable Content   Text visuals help the audience follow the flow of ideas. They are simplified outlines of your presentation that summarize and preview your message or that signal major shifts in thought. Don't overload them with too much information. Keep your messages short and simple. When writing text slides, do the following:

- Limit each slide to one thought, concept, or idea.

- Limit the content to about 40 words—with no more than six lines of text containing about six or seven words per line.

- Write short, bulleted phrases rather than long sentences or paragraph-length blocks of text.

- Phrase list items in grammatical form and use telegraphic wording ("Profits Soar," for example) without being cryptic ("Profits").

- Make your slides easy to read by using the active voice.

- Include short, informative titles.

Figure 13–4 is a good example of text slides that have been revised according to these principles to make their content more readable.

Graphic visuals can be an effective way to clarify a concept, show a process, or highlight important information (see Figure 13–5 on page 459). In addition to increasing audience interest and retention, they can help the audience absorb information in a short time. Chapter 11 discusses how to create effective graphics such as

Electronic equipment can fail, so be sure to have a backup plan.

Plan slide content before making design decisions.

Text slides are most effective when they are simple.

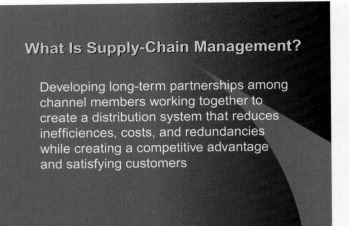

Figure 13.4a—Inappropriate paragraph style

Figure 13.4b—Appropriate bulleted phrases

Figure 13.4c—Wordy bullets

Figure 13.4d—Concise bullets

FIGURE 13–4
Writing Readable Content

Graphics used in oral presentations should be simplified versions of those used in written reports.

charts, diagrams, maps, drawings, and tables for written documents. When using such graphics in oral presentations, your first task is to simplify them. Create effective graphic visuals by following these guidelines:

- **Reduce the detail.** Eliminate anything that is not absolutely essential to the message. Show only key numbers on a chart. If people need to see only trends, then show only the trend line and not the numbers. If necessary, break information into more than one graphic illustration.

- **Avoid repeating text.** Don't repeat the same word five times. Minimize repetition by including the word in a title, subtitle, label, or legend.

- **Shorten numbers.** On graphs, use 02 for the year 2002; round off numbers such as $12,500.72 to $12 or $12.5, and then label the axis to indicate thousands.

- **Limit data.** Don't put more than five lines or five sets of bars on one chart.

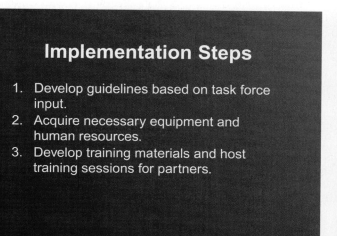

Figure 13.5a—Steps in written format

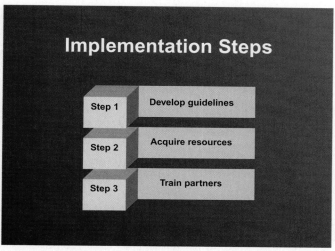

Figure 13.5b—Steps in graphic format

FIGURE 13–5
Converting Text into Graphics

- **Highlight key points.** Use arrows, boldface type, and color to direct your audience's eyes to the main point of a visual. Summarize the intent of the graphic in one clear phrase or sentence, such as "Earnings have increased by 15 percent."

- **Adjust the size and design.** Modify the size of the graphic to accommodate the size of a slide. Leave plenty of white space (area with no text or graphics) so that the audience members can view and interpret content from a distance. Use colors that stand out from the slide's background, and choose a font that's clear and easy to read.

Selecting Design Elements   Once you've composed the text and graphic elements of your slides, you're ready to focus on their design. Chapter 11 highlights five principles of effective design: continuity, contrast, emphasis, simplicity, and experience (see pp. 371–372). Pay close attention to these principles as you select the color, background design, artwork, fonts, and typestyles for your slides. To make your slides as effective as possible, handle the following design elements carefully:

- **Color.** Limit color choices to a few complementary ones. Some colors work better together than others; for example, contrasting colors increase readability. So when selecting color for backgrounds, titles, and text, avoid colors that are close in hue (yellow text on a white background, brown on green, blue on black).[12] Because electronic presentations are usually shown in a dark room, use darker colors (such as blue) for the background, midrange brightness for illustrations, and light colors for text. To show overhead transparencies in a well-lit room, reverse the scheme: use light colors for background and dark colors for text (see Figure 13–6).[13]

  > Color can increase the appeal and impact of your slides.

- **Background designs and clip art.** If you are not using a custom company background design, choose one that is simple, is appropriate for the subject, and will appeal to the audience—nothing too busy or too colorful. You don't want to use a blue-jean background when the audience is wearing pin-striped suits. Similarly, clip art that is inappropriate, improperly sized, or overpowering can detract from a slide's message. Use art to help explain the main idea of your message and draw attention to key parts of your slide. Make sure it fits the slide's overall design, and place it carefully so that it doesn't compete with text or other design elements.

  > Your choice of background design and clip art sends a message to the audience.

Figure 13.6a—Electronic slide

Figure 13.6b—Overhead transparency

FIGURE 13–6
Adjusting Color for Lighting Differences

Test your font and typeface selections by viewing slides from the back of a room.

- **Fonts and type styles.** When selecting fonts and type styles for slides, avoid script or decorative fonts. Limit your fonts to one or two per slide (if two fonts are used, reserve one for headings and the other for bulleted items). Using boldface type for electronic slides will keep letters from looking washed out. Be sure to avoid italicized type; it is difficult to read when projected. Use both uppercase and lowercase letters, with extra white space between lines of text. For electronic presentations, use type that is between 24 and 36 points, reserving the larger size for titles and the smaller for bullet items. Use the same font, type size, and color for headings of the same level of importance.

Be consistent in designing slides.

- **Consistency.** Graphic elements such as borders, backgrounds, and company logos should repeat on every visual. Consistency of design makes your slides easier to read and gives your presentation a clean, professional look. You can also achieve design consistency by using the layout templates that are included with most presentation software packages. As Figure 13–7 shows, each layout contains placeholders for specific slide elements such as a title, a piece of graphic art, or bulleted text. The templates use a landscape orientation, which minimizes the amount of text wrapping to the next line. When possible, place bulleted text toward the top of the slide, where it is easier to read from a distance.

FIGURE 13–7
PowerPoint's Predefined Layouts

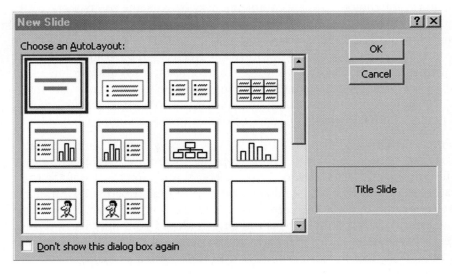

Adding Animation and Special Effects   Electronic slide shows can utilize a number of special effects, including sound, animation, and video. You can even automate your program to move from one slide to the next without the speaker's intervention. Automation is especially useful for running electronic presentations on television monitors in large places such as conventions and trade shows, where the slide show is, in effect, the only information present. Some common special effects include the following:

- **Transitions.** By controlling how one electronic slide replaces another on screen, transitions can make your presentation flow smoothly from slide to slide. Most electronic software packages include a number of effective transition effects.

- **Builds.** Builds control the release of text, graphics, and other elements on slides. You can make your bullet points appear one at a time rather than having all of them appear on a slide at once. This special effect helps draw the audience's attention to the point being discussed and prevents them from reading ahead.

- **Hyperlinks.** Hyperlinks make your electronic slides interactive. When you click on a slide's hyperlink, you are transported to a different slide in your presentation, to other files on a computer, or even to a webpage. Hyperlinks are a great tool for illustrating fine details without having to incorporate each detail into a slide.

As with design elements, use the same transitions and builds throughout your presentation. Don't introduce text that builds left to right on one slide and from top to bottom on the next.

A major challenge to those new to creating presentations is overcoming the tendency to use too many of these features. Excessive special effects overwhelm and distract audiences. Used sparingly, however, special effects can add punch to an oral presentation. So before you add animation or special effects to your presentation, ask yourself, Will the special effect support and enhance the message? If not, don't use it. For online resources offering PowerPoint tips, visit the following sites:

- Microsoft: www.microsoft.com/education/default.asp?ID = PPTTutorial

- Indiana University—Purdue University, Indianapolis: www.iupui.edu/~webtrain/ tutorials/powerpoint2000_basics.html

- University of Maryland: www.education.umd.edu/blt/tcp/resetpp.html

Creating Effective Handouts

Handouts are a terrific way to offer your audience additional material without overloading your slides with information. Candidates for good handout material include complex charts and diagrams, company reports, magazine articles, case studies, websites, and copies of presentation slides.[14] Other good handout materials include brochures, pictures, outlines, and a copy of the presentation agenda.

A well-prepared handout is the best way to jog someone's memory and make sure the hard work you put into your presentation is not wasted. Plan handouts together with your presentation. Think of handouts as a place to store information overflow. Include "need to know" information in your presentation and save "nice to know" information for your handouts. But be selective. Once you've assembled material for your handouts, sort through it to eliminate duplicate material and to minimize information overkill. Make sure handout information directly supports the goal of your presentation.[15]

Deciding when to distribute handouts is difficult. Base your decision on the content of your handouts, the nature of your presentation, and your personal preference. Some speakers distribute handout materials—perhaps copies of slides, with space for taking notes—before the presentation begins. The drawback of doing so is that it allows your audience to read ahead instead of listening to you. Other speakers simply advise the audience of the types of information they are including in handouts but delay distributing anything until they have finished speaking.

Margin notes:

You can add sound, animation, and video to electronic slides.

Don't overdo special effects.

Good handouts keep the audience informed without overwhelming them with information.

Handouts can be both useful and distracting.

STEP 3: COMPLETING ORAL PRESENTATIONS

To complete your oral presentation, you will need to evaluate the content of your message and edit your remarks for clarity and conciseness as you would for any business message. Besides these tasks, three additional areas require your special attention: mastering the art of delivery, overcoming anxiety, and handling questions responsively.

Mastering the Art of Delivery

Not all methods of delivery are ideal.

Once you've planned, written, and developed visuals for your presentation, you're ready to begin practicing your delivery. You may choose from a variety of delivery methods (some of which are more effective than others):

- **Memorizing.** Avoid memorizing your speech, especially a long one. You're likely to forget your lines, you'll speak in a monotone, and your speech will sound stilted. Besides, you'll often need to address audience questions during your speech, so you must be flexible enough to adjust your speech as you go. However, memorizing a quotation, an opening paragraph, or a few concluding remarks can bolster your confidence and strengthen your delivery.

- **Reading.** If you're delivering a technical or complex presentation, you may want to read it. Policy statements by government officials are sometimes read because the wording may be critical. If you choose to read your speech, practice enough so that you can still maintain eye contact with your audience. Triple-spaced copy, wide margins, and large type will help. You might even want to include stage cues, such as *pause, raise hands, lower voice.*

- **Speaking from notes.** Making a presentation with the help of an outline, note cards, or visual aids is probably the most effective and easiest delivery mode. This approach gives you something to refer to and still allows for eye contact and interaction with the audience. If your listeners look puzzled, you can expand on a point or rephrase it. (Generally, note cards are preferable to sheets of paper, because nervousness is easier to see in shaking sheets of paper.)

- **Impromptu speaking.** Unrehearsed speaking is what you do during a job interview, when you are called on to speak unexpectedly, or when you have agreed to speak but neglected to prepare your remarks. Avoid speaking unprepared unless you've spoken countless times on the same topic or are an extremely good public speaker. When you're asked to speak "off the cuff," take a moment to think through what you'll say. Then avoid the temptation to ramble.

Practicing your oral presentation with a co-worker or a friend is a terrific way to polish your public speaking skills in a relaxed setting.

Regardless of which delivery mode you use, be sure that you're thoroughly familiar with your subject. Knowing what you're talking about is the best way to build your self-confidence.

Don't read your slides to the audience.

The most common mistake people make when delivering a presentation is reading their slides. When speakers read bulleted points to the audience word for word, they lose contact with the audience and lose voice inflection. As a result, the listeners become bored and eventually stop paying attention. Moreover, people who read slides insult the audience's intelligence. Audiences expect speakers to add valuable information that is not included on slides. To do so, however, speakers

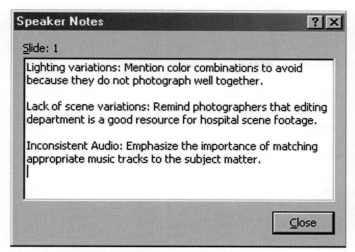

Figure 13.8a—Speaker's notes

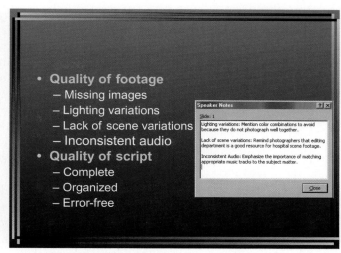

Figure 13.8b—Corresponding slide

FIGURE 13–8
Speaker's Notes

must know enough about the subject of their presentation to elaborate on each bullet point. Conducting thorough research will give you the knowledge; the rest comes with practice.

Practicing Your Delivery   When practicing your presentation, run through it about five times using your electronic slides or overhead transparencies. Your credibility is dramatically enhanced when you move seamlessly through your presentation. Practicing helps keep you on track, helps you maintain a conversational tone with your audience, and boosts your confidence and composure.

As you practice, try not to be so dependent on your slides that you're unable to function without them. Some people are quite capable of delivering a perfect presentation without notes. But for those who require notes, electronic software gives you an added advantage. Speaker's notes (as shown in Figure 13–8) are a helpful tool included with most popular electronic presentation software packages. You can display these notes along with a scaled-down version of your slide on a computer screen so that only you can see the notes. Use speaker's notes to list important facts or to remind yourself of supporting comments you should make as you present the slide. For instance, you might input such notes as "Don't forget to explain the impact of last year's bad weather on sales."

Use speaker's notes to jog your memory.

Practicing in front of a mirror is always a good idea, especially if your primary concern is the mechanics of the presentation. But if you're concerned about the content of your presentation and the effectiveness of your slides, nothing beats practicing in front of people who are willing to stop you when they don't understand your message or when they need you to clarify a point on your slide.

Practicing in front of a live audience is the best way to perfect your presentation.

Introducing Slides   All visual aids must be properly introduced. Effective speakers verbally introduce the next visual aid before they show it. They don't say, "The next slide illustrates . . ." Instead, they match their words to the slide and let the audience make the proper connection:

Introduce your slides before you show them.

"We can get started with this new program by introducing these policies . . ."

"The next segment of my presentation discusses . . ."

"The three most significant issues facing our company are . . ."

Practice placing overhead transparencies on a projector so that it becomes second nature.

If you are using overhead transparencies, the best approach is to introduce the next overhead as you remove the old one and position the new one on the projector. Immediately cover all but the first bulleted phrase with a sheet of paper to prevent the audience from reading ahead. Then step aside to give the audience about five seconds to look it over before you start discussing it. As you advance through your discussion, you can move the paper down the transparency to uncover the next bullet item, waiting a few seconds for the audience to find your point of reference. When you are finished using the transparency, it's often a good idea to cover it until you're ready to introduce a new slide.

If you are using electronic slides, the best approach is to introduce the slide before you show it and then give the audience a few seconds to view the title and design elements. With electronic slides, you can release bulleted points or sections of a graph as you discuss them. This control gives you more flexibility to move about the room—something you don't have with overheads.

If you're using a pointer, keep in mind that it's a tool meant to guide the audience to a specific part of a visual. It is not a riding crop, conductor's baton, leg scratcher, or walking stick. Use the pointer only at the time you need it, then fold it and remove it from sight. If you are using a laser pointer that puts a focused dot of light on the desired part of your visual, don't overdo it. A laser pointer is an excellent tool if used judiciously, but in the hands of the overzealous presenter, it can become a distraction.[16]

Limiting the Number of Slides   Even if you produce an outstanding set of slides, they'll do you no good if you can't complete your presentation in the allotted time. Having too many visuals can detract from your message. It forces you to either rush through a presentation or skip slides—some of which may be critical to your message.

Limit the number of slides to a few good ones.

Gauging the correct number of slides to include depends on the length of your presentation and the complexity of the subject matter. If you are using electronic slides, also factor in the time it takes for the special effects. As a general guideline, try to average one slide for every 90 seconds you speak. For a 30-minute presentation, you would create about 20 slides.[17] Of course, you may spend more time discussing some slides than others, so the best way to find the "right" number is to time your presentation as you practice.

Delete slides that take too long to discuss, either because they are too complex or because they cover too much information. Similarly, if you discover that you're taking only a few seconds to discuss a slide, it may be a clue that the slide is too elementary.[18]

Audiences like speakers who run on time, smile, and let them out early.

As you time your presentation, keep in mind that it is much better to cover less information in a relaxed style than to cover too much information in a hurried and disorganized state. No one likes to listen to someone who keeps saying, "I just don't have enough time."[19] Build enough time in your presentation for a smile, an anecdote, or further illustration of a point. Remember, audiences won't be angry if you let them out early, but they might be upset if you keep them late.

Preparing to Speak   In addition to knowing your material and practicing your delivery, you can build confidence in other ways. First, know that your location is ready and that you will have everything you'll need. Second, make sure you're prepared to address audiences from other cultures.

Before you speak, prepare the location.

Whenever you can, check the location for your presentation in advance. Check the seating arrangements to make sure they're appropriate for your needs. If you want audience members to sit at tables, be sure tables are available. Check the room for any outlets you'll need for a projector or microphone. Locate light switches and dimmers. If you need a flipchart easel or a chalkboard, be sure it's on hand. Check for chalk, an eraser, a pointer, extension cords, and any other small but crucial items you might need. If at all possible, practice giving your presentation in the room where you will be speaking.

ACHIEVING INTERCULTURAL COMMUNICATION

Five Tips for Making Presentations Around the World

In any successful oral presentation, getting your message across to an audience requires clear communication. But how can you communicate successfully with members of an international audience—especially if their fluency in your language ranges from expert to novice?

1. *Speak slowly and distinctly.* The most common complaint of international audiences is that English-speakers talk too fast. If you speak too rapidly, your less fluent listeners will be lost. Articulate every word carefully. Emphasize consonants for clarity, and pause frequently so that the audience will have time to absorb each key point.

2. *Repeat key words and phrases.* When audiences are less familiar with your language, they need to hear important information more than once. In addition, they may not be familiar with synonyms, so refer to key points in the same way throughout your presentation. If you introduce the concept of *benefits*, for example, continue to use the same word. Don't refer to *advantages* later on.

3. *Aim for clarity.* Keep your message simple. Eliminate complex sentence structure, abbreviations, and acronyms. Avoid two-word verbs such as *look over* and *check out.* Such verbs are confusing because the definition of each separate word differs from the meaning of the two words combined. For clearer communication, use one specific term (substitute *review* for *look over; examine* for *check out; write* for *jot down; visit* for *drop by*). Stay away from cultural idioms, such as *once in a blue moon,* which may be unfamiliar to an international audience.

4. *Communicate with body language.* Establish a relationship with your audience through strong eye contact. And don't forget to smile! Smiles are universally recognized facial expressions. Moreover, multilingual audiences pay close attention to a speaker's body language to get clues about the meanings of unfamiliar words. For example, prepositions can often be confusing to multilingual listeners, so use gestures to illustrate the meaning of words such as *up, down,* or *under.*

5. *Support your oral message with visual aids.* For most audiences, visual messages support and clarify spoken words. As this chapter discusses in detail, handouts, flip charts, overheads, and electronic slides can help you describe your key points. To eliminate problems with rapid speech, unclear pronunciations, or strange accents, prepare captions both in English and in your audience's native language. Avoid confusion about quantities by presenting numbers in graphs or pie charts and by converting financial figures into local currency.

CAREER APPLICATIONS

1. As marketing director for an international corporation, you will be making a presentation to the company's marketing representatives in Germany. How will you communicate company goals and sales projections clearly?

2. Make a list of 10 two-word verbs. How does the meaning of each separate word differ from the definition of the combined words? Replace each two-word verb with a single, specific word that will be clearer to an international audience.

If you're addressing an audience that doesn't speak your language, consider using an interpreter. Working with an interpreter does constrain your presentation somewhat—make sure you speak slowly enough for the interpreter to keep up with you but not so slowly that the rest of your audience loses interest. Send your interpreter a copy of your speech and any visual aids as far in advance as possible.

Any time you deliver an oral presentation to people from other cultures, you may need to adapt the content of your presentation (see "Achieving Intercultural Communication: Five Tips for Making Presentations Around the World"). It is also important to take into account any cultural differences in appearance, mannerisms, and other customs. Your interpreter will be able to suggest appropriate changes for a specific audience or particular occasion.

Consider cultural differences and whether you need to use an interpreter.

Overcoming Anxiety

If you're nervous about facing an audience and experience stage fright, you're not alone. Even speakers with years of experience feel some anxiety about getting up in front of an audience. Although you might not be able to make your nervous feelings disappear, you can learn to cope with your anxiety.

Several techniques can help you feel more confident as a speaker.

Feeling More Confident   Nervousness shows that you care about your audience, your topic, and the occasion. If your palms get wet or your mouth goes dry, don't think of nerves, think of excitement. Such stimulation can give you the extra energy you need to make your presentation sparkle. Here are some ways to harness your nervous energy to become a more confident speaker:[20]

- **Prepare more material than necessary.** Combined with a genuine interest in your topic, extra knowledge will reduce your anxiety.

- **Rehearse.** The more familiar you are with your material, the less panic you'll feel.

- **Think positively.** See yourself as polished and professional, and your audience will too.

- **Visualize your success.** Use the few minutes before you actually begin speaking to tell yourself you're on and you're ready.

- **Take a few deep breaths.** Before you begin to speak, remember that your audience is silently wishing you success.

- **Be ready.** Have your first sentence memorized and on the tip of your tongue.

- **Be comfortable.** If your throat is dry, drink some water.

- **Don't panic.** If you feel that you're losing your audience during your speech, try to pull them back by involving them in the action; ask for their opinions or pause for questions.

- **Keep going.** Things usually get better as you go.

Perhaps the best way to overcome stage fright and feel more confident is to concentrate on your message and on your audience, not on yourself. When you're busy thinking about your subject and observing your audience's response, you tend to forget your fears.

The best technique for overcoming your anxiety is to concentrate on your listeners and on their needs, rather than focusing on yourself.

You will appear more confident if you follow a few tips.

Appearing More Confident   As you deliver your presentation, try to be aware of the nonverbal signals you're transmitting. Regardless of how you feel inside, your effectiveness greatly depends on how you look and sound. To appear confident, try the following tips:

- **Don't rush.** Well-delivered presentations start with your first minute at the podium. As you approach the speaker's lectern, walk slowly, breathe deeply, and stand up straight. Face your audience, adjust the microphone, count to three slowly, then survey the room. When you find a friendly face, make eye contact and smile. Count to three again, and then begin your presentation.[21] This slow, controlled beginning will help you establish rapport.

- **Maintain eye contact.** Once your presentation is under way, pick out several people positioned around the room and shift your gaze from one to another. Looking directly at your listeners will make you appear sincere, confident, and trustworthy. It also helps you get an idea of the impression you're creating.

- **Stand tall.** Your posture is important in projecting more confidence. Stand with your weight on both feet and your shoulders back. Avoid gripping the lectern. In fact, you might step out from behind the lectern to help your audience feel more comfortable with you and to express your own comfort and confidence in what you're saying. Vary your facial expressions to make your message more dynamic.

- **Don't overdo hand gestures.** Use your hands to emphasize your remarks with appropriate gestures, but keep them still at other times. Don't distract your audience with nervous hand movements. Keep your hands out of your pockets; in fact, empty your pockets before you speak.

- **Use your voice.** People who speak with lower vocal tones at a slightly faster-than-average rate are perceived as being more credible.[22] Speak in a normal, conversational tone but with enough volume for everyone to hear you. Try to sound poised and confident, varying your pitch and speaking rate to add emphasis. Don't ramble. Speak clearly and crisply, articulating all the syllables, and sound enthusiastic about what you're saying. Use silence instead of meaningless filler words such as *um, you know, okay,* and *like.*

Handling Questions Responsively

The question-and-answer period is one of the most important parts of an oral presentation. Questions give you a chance to obtain important information and to emphasize your main idea and supporting points. This period also gives you a chance to build enthusiasm for your point of view, work in material that didn't fit into the formal presentation, and identify and try to overcome audience resistance. Without questions, you might just as well write a report.

Since you've already spent time anticipating these questions, you will be ready with your answers. Some experts recommend that you hold back some dramatic statistics as ammunition for the question-and-answer session.[23] If your message is unpopular, you should also be prepared for hostile questions. Treat them as legitimate requests for information. Maintaining your professionalism will improve your credibility. The following tips will help you handle audience questions responsively:

- **Focus on the questioner.** Pay attention to the questioner's body language and facial expression to help determine what the person really means. Nod your head to acknowledge the question; then repeat it aloud to confirm your understanding and to ensure that the entire audience has heard it. If the question is vague or confusing, ask for clarification; then give a simple, direct answer. If you're asked to choose between two alternatives, don't feel you must do so. Offer your own choice instead, if that makes more sense.[24]

- **Respond appropriately.** Answer the question you're asked. Don't sidestep it, ignore it, or laugh it off. Also avoid saying more than you need to (you want to have enough time to cover all the questions). If giving an adequate answer would take too long, simply say, "I'm sorry, we don't have time to get into that issue right now, but if you'll see me after the presentation, I'll be happy to discuss it with you." If you don't know the answer, don't pretend that you do. Instead, say something like "I don't have those figures. I'll get them for you as quickly as possible."

- **Maintain control.** Before you begin, try suggesting a time limit, announcing a question limit per person, or asking people to identify themselves before asking a question. Such ground rules will protect you from questioners who try to engage you in a heated exchange, monopolize the floor, or mount their own soapbox. Encourage participation from as many audience members as possible. To move on, you might admit that you and the questioner have differing opinions, offer to get back to someone once you've done more research, or simply respond with a brief answer that avoids lengthy debate or more questions.[25]

- **Survive the hot seat.** If a question ever puts you on the hot seat, remember to be honest, but keep your cool. Look the person in the eye, answer the question as well as you can, and try not to show your feelings. Don't get into an argument. Defuse

Be ready with answers so that you can
- Emphasize your most important points
- Refer to material that didn't fit in the formal presentation
- Overcome audience resistance

You can do several things to maintain control of the question-and-answer period.

During meetings at Tellme.com, polished speakers use question-and-answer sessions to reinforce their ideas and credibility.

hostility by paraphrasing the question and asking the questioner to confirm that you've understood it correctly. Break long, complicated questions into parts that you can answer simply. Once you've answered, move on to the next question. Maintain a businesslike tone of voice and a pleasant expression.[26]

- **Motivate questions.** In case your audience is too timid or hostile to ask questions, you might plant some of your own. If a friend or the meeting organizer gets the ball rolling, other people will probably join in. You might ask a question yourself: "Would you like to know more about . . ." If someone in the audience answers, act as if the question came from that person in the first place. When all else fails, say something like "I know from experience that most questions are asked after the question period. So I'll be around afterward to talk."[27]

Concluding Your Presentation

Finish up on time—even if people are eager to continue.

When the time allotted for your presentation is up, call a halt to the question-and-answer session, even if more people want to talk. Prepare the audience for the end by saying, "Our time is almost up. Let's have one more question." After you've made your reply, summarize the main idea of the presentation and thank people for their attention. Conclude the way you opened: by looking around the room and making eye contact. Then gather your notes and leave the podium, shoulders straight, head up. (The "Checklist: Oral Presentations" is a reminder of the tasks involved in oral communication.)

✓ CHECKLIST: Oral Presentations

Planning your Oral Presentation

✓ Define your purpose.
✓ Analyze your audience.

Writing the Oral Presentation

✓ Organize your presentation: Define your main idea, limit your scope, choose an appropriate approach, prepare your outline, and decide on an appropriate style.
✓ Develop the opening: Arouse audience interest, build credibility, and preview the main points.
✓ Develop the body: Connect your ideas and hold the audience's interest.
✓ Develop the close: Restate the main points, describe the next steps, and end on a strong note.
✓ Prepare for the question-and-answer period: Figure out how to control the situation, and anticipate questions and objections.
✓ Prepare visual aids.
✓ Create effective slides: Create simple, readable content; select design elements; and add animation and special effects.
✓ Create effective handouts.
✓ Have a backup plan in case of equipment failure.

Completing the Oral Presentation

✓ Decide which delivery method to use: memorizing, reading, speaking from notes, or speaking impromptu.

✓ Practice delivery elements: Try not to read slides, use speaker's notes, practice in front of someone willing to stop you for clarification, introduce each slide before showing it, use pointers judiciously, and don't include too many slides.
✓ Check out the room ahead of time, and make sure the equipment works.
✓ Consider using an interpreter for audiences who don't speak your language.
✓ Control your anxiety by using your nervousness as a tool.
✓ Try to feel more confident: Prepare more material than necessary, rehearse, think positively, visualize your success, take a few deep breaths, be ready, be comfortable, don't panic, and keep going.
✓ Try to appear more confident: Pace yourself (don't rush), maintain eye contact, stand tall, use hand gestures without overdoing them, and use your voice.
✓ Handle questions responsively: Focus on the questioner, respond appropriately, maintain control, survive the hot seat, and motivate questions.
✓ Conclude your presentation gracefully: Announce that your presentation is ending, summarize your main idea, thank people for listening, look around the room (making eye contact), gather your notes, and leave the podium.

On the Job:

SOLVING COMMUNICATION DILEMMAS AT HEWLETT-PACKARD

Now that the merger has taken place, Fiorina and Compaq CEO Michael Capellas face a tough challenge trying to integrate Compaq with HP. Fiorina's straight talk is exactly what she'll need to win the support and allegiance of colleagues and employees. You are a member of HP's corporate communications team, and Fiorina sometimes asks you to help her write the speeches that she delivers to business partners, employees, professional organizations, and civic groups. For the following assignments, choose the best solution and be prepared to explain your choice.[28]

1. Fiorina has agreed to give a 20-minute talk in Atlanta, Georgia, to a group of approximately 35 business leaders who meet for lunch and networking on a monthly basis. The president of the group has suggested that Fiorina address the topic of e-commerce, conducting business over the Internet. The purpose of her speech is to briefly summarize the impact of e-commerce on major businesses around the world, while maintaining a tone that is appropriate for a luncheon gathering. How should Fiorina accomplish her purpose?

   a. She should focus her speech on entertaining the audience with stories about her previous experiences in the telecommunication industry.
   b. She should focus on a detailed history of e-commerce in the United States.
   c. She should concentrate on presenting serious statistics that show current trends in e-commerce.
   d. She should balance her speech between choices (a) and (c).

2. Fiorina has asked you to help plan a 10-minute speech that she can give to HP managers during the upcoming "Town Meeting" being held at headquarters in Palo Alto, California. She expects up to 600 managers to attend. Her topic is "the state of the company." Her purpose is to inspire these managers to keep up the good work. Her main idea is that the company is doing an excellent job integrating with Compaq, thanks to the efforts of these managers. How should she handle audience questions?

   a. To maintain an upbeat atmosphere, Fiorina should state early in her speech that she will be happy to accept questions at any time during her speech.
   b. Since these managers have done such a great job, Fiorina should be prepared to answer every single question, even if she ends up running over her allotted time.

   c. To make sure she understands a questioner's meaning, she should focus on the questioner, paying attention to body language and facial expression.
   d. She should prepare enough material beforehand to be able to answer all questions immediately, without needing extra time or further research.

3. You are helping Fiorina write a speech on "Life Lived in Motion" and the need for mobile technology. She will deliver this speech at a technology trade show in Hannover, Germany. Fiorina wants to talk about delivering a truly valuable experience for consumers who live life in motion. The audience includes inventors of mobile technology, influential business and professional people with fairly technical backgrounds. Which visual aid should she use to emphasize the importance of technology for today's consumers?

   a. An electronic slide showing a person in a mall talking on a cell phone, another person on a train using a palmtop, and perhaps another person in a café using a laptop
   b. An overhead transparency showing a line graph of increased demand for mobile communications
   c. A short video clip showing a consumer in motion—working during a commute to work, picking up children from school and escorting them to some activity, jumping on a plane with a briefcase, etc.
   d. A professionally prepared booklet of handouts that include copies of slides used in (a) and (b), along with other relevant information

4. In her speech to the trade show in Germany, Fiorina wants to present some statistics to suggest what's truly important to people while they're on the move. How should she handle the quantitative details for this high-tech audience?

   a. Fiorina should prepare handouts that summarize the financial data in tabular and graphic form. Everyone in the audience should receive a copy of the handout to refer to during the speech.
   b. Fiorina should write the information on a blackboard while she delivers the speech.
   c. She should prepare simple overhead transparencies to use during the speech. As she concludes her remarks, she should tell the audience that detailed financial statements are available at the door for those who are interested.
   d. Given the technical knowledge of the audience, she should show full-color 35-mm slides that summarize the financial information in tabular and graphic format. The slides should be professionally prepared to ensure their quality.

Learning Objectives Checkup

To assess your understanding of the principles in this chapter, read each learning objective and study the accompanying exercises. For fill-in items, write the missing text in the blank provided; for multiple choice items, circle the letter of the correct answer. You can check your responses against the answer key on page AK-2.

Objective 13.1: Explain how planning oral presentations differs from planning written documents.

1. When planning oral presentations (as opposed to written documents), the major factor that you need to account for is
   a. The increased opportunity for interaction with your audience
   b. The greater importance of visuals
   c. Overcoming anxiety
   d. The setting for the presentation

Objective 13.2: Describe the five tasks that go into organizing oral presentations.

2. When defining the main idea for your oral presentation, you need to
   a. Figure out three or four angles for approaching your main idea
   b. Make sure that it is descriptive rather than informative
   c. Relate it to the audience's interests
   d. Do all of the above

3. Most people speak at a rate of about
   a. 50–60 words per minute
   b. 125–150 words per minute
   c. 200 words per minute
   d. 250 words per minute

4. Longer oral presentations are organized like
   a. Good-news messages
   b. Routine messages
   c. Bad-news messages
   d. Reports

5. When preparing your outline for an oral presentation, you need to begin by
   a. Choosing a title
   b. Stating your purpose and main idea
   c. Identifying your opening, body, and close
   d. Arranging your main points in order

6. Your speaking outline
   a. Should be identical to your planning outline
   b. Is more detailed than your planning outline
   c. Should be in narrative form
   d. Should include delivery cues regarding pauses, emphasis, and so on

7. You should use a more formal style for your presentation when
   a. Speaking to a relatively small group
   b. Making announcements about mergers, new products, and other business milestones
   c. You have few visual aids
   d. Conducting work sessions

Objective 13.3: Delineate the tasks involved in developing the opening, body, and close of your oral presentation.

8. Which of the following is *not* a goal to be achieved in the opening of a formal oral presentation?
   a. Arouse audience interest.
   b. Establish your credibility.
   c. Encourage audience participation.
   d. Preview your presentation.

9. A good way to hold your audience's attention during your speech is to
   a. Relate your subject to your audience's needs
   b. Explain the relationship between your subject and familiar ideas
   c. Use clear, vivid language
   d. Do all of the above

10. You should devote about _____ percent of your total time to the close of your presentation.
    a. 1
    b. 5
    c. 10
    d. 15

11. In the close of your presentation, you need to
    a. End on a positive note
    b. Introduce new ideas to add to the points you've made earlier
    c. Use a gimmick to bring the talk to a rousing conclusion
    d. Do all of the above

Objective 13.4: Discuss the pros and cons of using overhead transparencies versus electronic presentations in your speeches.

12. Which of the following is *not* an advantage of overhead transparencies?
    a. They are inexpensive to create.
    b. They are easy to make corrections on.
    c. They can be used in daylight.
    d. They require little equipment to show.

13. Which of the following is a disadvantage of electronic presentations?
    a. They require more expensive display equipment than overhead transparencies.
    b. The slides cannot be easily rearranged.
    c. The presenter is not free to move about the room.
    d. All of the above are disadvantages.

Objective 13.5: Identify six ways to make your text slides more effective and six ways to make your graphic slides more effective.

14. An effective text slide
    a. Is in bulleted list form rather than long sentences
    b. Contains no more than 40 words
    c. Covers only one thought or idea
    d. Does all of the above

15. Graphic slides can be made more effective by
    a. Including more detail than a comparable report graphic
    b. Having minimal white space
    c. Using arrows, boldface, and color to direct the audience's eyes to the main point
    d. Doing all of the above

16. Which of the following would be the best color combination for slides being shown in a darkened room?
    a. Dark blue on a yellow background
    b. Yellow on a dark blue background
    c. Yellow on a white background
    d. Yellow on a green background

17. When choosing type styles for slides, avoid
    a. Boldface
    b. Uppercase and lowercase letters
    c. Italics
    d. All of the above

Objective 13.6: Explain how to master the art of delivery through practice and preparation.

18. Which of the following is the most effective method for delivering a presentation?
    a. Memorizing
    b. Reading
    c. Speaking from notes
    d. Impromptu speaking

19. When practicing your delivery, you should
    a. Run through your speech about five times using your visuals
    b. Learn to give your speech without ever relying on speaker's notes
    c. Run through your speech by yourself to avoid interruptions and distractions
    d. Do all of the above

20. When introducing slides during your presentation, you should
    a. Make sure the visual aid is in full view before you introduce it
    b. Remove the previous overhead transparency completely before introducing the next one
    c. Be as clear as possible by saying, "The next slide illustrates . . ."
    d. Verbally introduce the visual aid before you show it

21. When gauging the correct number of electronic slides to include in your speech, you must
    a. Try to average one slide for every five minutes you speak
    b. Time your presentation when you practice

c. Consider the length of your presentation, regardless of the complexity of your subject matter
    d. Plan on spending exactly the same amount of time discussing each slide

22. When preparing to speak, you need to
    a. Check the location in advance for appropriate seating, location of light switches and electrical outlets, the presence of necessary equipment and extension cords, and so on
    b. Consider using an interpreter when addressing an audience that doesn't speak your language
    c. Practice your speech in the room where you'll be speaking (if possible)
    d. Do all of the above

Objective 13.7: List nine ways to feel more confident and five ways to appear more confident.

23. Which of the following is *not* a way to feel more confident as a speaker?
    a. Prepare more material than necessary.
    b. Visualize being successful.
    c. Take a few deep breaths.
    d. Avoid drinking water before you begin speaking.

24. To appear more confident as a speaker, you should
    a. Speak more quickly than you normally would
    b. Maintain eye contact with members of the audience
    c. Keep your hands gripped on the lectern
    d. Keep your hands in your pockets

Objective 13.8: Describe six ways that effective speakers handle questions responsively.

25. When handling questions from the audience, it is best to
    a. Pay attention to the questioner's body language and facial expression to help determine what the person really means
    b. Sidestep or ignore any embarrassing questions
    c. Engage in lively arguments with questioners who disagree with you
    d. Do all of the above

Apply Your Knowledge

1. Would you rather (a) deliver an oral presentation to an outside audience, (b) be interviewed for a news story, or (c) make a presentation to a departmental meeting? Why? How do the communication skills differ among those situations? Explain.

2. How might the audience's attitude affect the amount of audience interaction during or after a presentation? Explain your answer.

3. If you were giving an oral presentation on the performance of a company product, what three attention-getters might you use to enliven your talk?

4. Why do most people include too much information on their slides?

5. **Ethical Choices** How can you use design elements and special effects to persuade an audience? Is it ethical to do so?

Practice Your Knowledge

DOCUMENTS FOR ANALYSIS

DOCUMENT 13.A

Pick a speech from *Vital Speeches of the Day*, a publication containing recent speeches on timely and topical subjects. As an alternative, select a speech from an online source such as

the speech archives of NASA (www.nasa.gov) or AT&T (www.att.com/speeches). Examine both the opening and the close; then analyze how these two sections work together to emphasize the main idea. What action does the speaker want the audience to take?

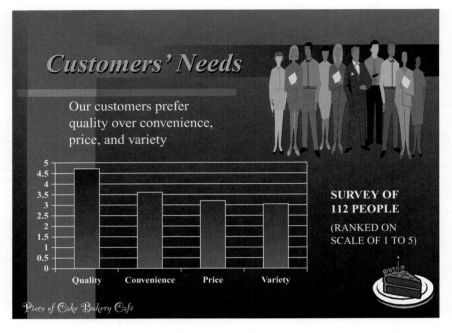

Next, identify the transitional sentences or phrases that clarify the speech's structure for the listener, especially those that help the speaker shift between supporting points. Using these transitions as clues, list the main message and supporting points; then indicate how each transitional phrase links the current supporting point to the succeeding one. Finally, prepare a brief (two- to three-minute) oral presentation summarizing your analysis for your class.

DOCUMENT 13.B

Examine the slide in Figure 13–9 and point out any problems you notice. How would you correct these problems?

Exercises

For live links to all websites discussed in this chapter, visit this text's website at www.prenhall.com/bovee. Just log on, select Chapter 13, and click on "Student Resources." Locate the page or the URL related to the material in the text. For the "Learning More on the Web" exercises, you'll also find navigational directions. Click on the live link to the site.

13.1 Internet For many years, Toastmasters has been dedicated to helping its members give speeches. Instruction, good speakers as models, and practice sessions aim to teach members to convey information in lively and informative ways. Visit the Toastmasters website at www.toastmasters.org and carefully review the linked pages about listening, speaking, voice, and body. Evaluate the information and outline a three-minute presentation to your class, telling why Toastmasters and its website would or would not help you and your classmates write and deliver an effective speech.

13.2 Mastering Delivery: Analysis Attend a presentation at your school or in your town, or watch a speech on television. Categorize the speech as one that motivates or entertains, one that informs or analyzes, or one that persuades or urges collaboration. Then compare the speaker's delivery with this chapter's "Checklist: Oral Presentations" on page 468. Write a two-page report analyzing the speaker's performance and suggesting improvements.

13.3 Mastering Delivery: Nonverbal Signals Observe and analyze the delivery of a speaker in a school, work, or other setting. What type of delivery did the speaker use? Was this delivery appropriate for the occasion? What nonverbal signals did the speaker use to emphasize key points? Were these signals effective? Which nonverbal signals would you suggest to further enhance the delivery of this oral presentation—and why?

13.4 Ethical Choices Think again about the oral presentation you observed and analyzed in Exercise 13.3. How could the speaker have used nonverbal signals to unethically manipulate the audience's attitudes or actions?

13.5 Teamwork You've been asked to give an informative 10-minute talk on vacation opportunities in your home state. Draft your opening, which should last no more than 2 minutes. Then pair off with a classmate and analyze each other's openings. How well do these two openings arouse the audience's interest, build credibility, and preview the presentation? Suggest ways that these openings might be improved.

13.6 Completing Oral Presentations: Self-Assessment How good are you at planning, writing, and delivering oral presentations? Rate yourself on each of the following

Element of Presentation Process	Always	Frequently	Occasionally	Never
Do you				
1. Start by defining your purpose?	_____	_____	_____	_____
2. Analyze your audience before writing your speech?	_____	_____	_____	_____
3. Match your presentation length to the allotted time?	_____	_____	_____	_____
4. Begin your speeches with an attention-getting opening?	_____	_____	_____	_____
5. Look for ways to build credibility as a speaker?	_____	_____	_____	_____
6. Cover only a few main points in the body of your speech?	_____	_____	_____	_____
7. Use transitions to help listeners follow your ideas?	_____	_____	_____	_____
8. Review main points and describe the next steps in your close?	_____	_____	_____	_____
9. Practice your presentation beforehand?	_____	_____	_____	_____
10. Prepare in advance for questions and objections?	_____	_____	_____	_____
11. Conclude speeches by summarizing your main idea?	_____	_____	_____	_____

elements of the oral presentation process. Then examine your ratings to identify where you are strongest and where you can improve, using the tips in this chapter.

13.7 Creating Effective Slides: Content and Design You've been asked to give an informative 10-minute talk to a group of conventioneers on great things to see and do while visiting your hometown. To keep them interested, you've decided to whip up a couple of slides for your oral presentation. Write the content for two or three slides. Then think about the design elements for your slides. Which colors, clip art, and other design elements will you use to enhance your slides?

13.8 Creating Effective Slides: Design Elements Most word-processing software packages include a large selection of fonts. Review the fonts available to you and select three to five fonts suitable for electronic slides or overhead transparencies. Explain the criteria you use for your selections.

Expand Your Knowledge

LEARNING MORE ON THE WEB

Virtual Presentation Assistant www.ukans.edu/cwis/units/coms2/vpa/vpa.htm. This website offers abundant resources with related links to other websites that contain useful articles, reviews, or supplemental materials for planning presentations. You can also connect to popular media and library pages with worldwide research information. You'll find examples of presentation types, suggestions for selecting and focusing your topic, tips on audience analysis, delivery, use of visual aids, and various other guidelines to help you prepare and deliver an effective oral presentation. If you need inspiration, check out this site.

ACTIVITIES

Log on to the Virtual Presentation Assistant (VPA), and check out the sample presentations, delivery advice, and plentiful resources.

1. Suppose you have been asked to prepare an oral presentation on a business issue currently in the news. How could you use what you've discovered at the VPA site to help you select a topic? How could you use this site to find additional information or supplementary materials related to your topic?
2. According to this website, what factors should you consider when analyzing your audience?
3. What topics or information will entice you to return to this site or its links? (If you don't find the Virtual Presentation Assistant useful, explain why.)

EXPLORING THE WEB ON YOUR OWN

Review these chapter-related websites on your own to enhance your oral presentation skills and knowledge.

1. Take the free Public Speaker's Online Tutorials and read some online articles about public speaking at the Gove-Siebold website, www.govesiebold.com.
2. Visit the Advanced Public Speaking Institute, at www.public-speaking.org, and learn how to be the best public speaker you can be.
3. Take the online tutorial at the KU Medical Center, www.kumc.edu/SAH/OTEd/jradel/effective.html, and learn how to design effective visual aids.

Learn Interactively

INTERACTIVE STUDY GUIDE

Go to the Companion Website at www.prenhall.com/bovee. For Chapter 13, take advantage of the interactive "Study Guide" to test your knowledge of the chapter. Get instant feedback on whether you need additional studying. Also, visit this site's "Study Hall" where you'll find an abundance of valuable resources that will help you succeed in this course.

PEAK PERFORMANCE GRAMMAR AND MECHANICS

To improve your skill with mechanics, visit this text's website at www.prenhall.com/onekey. Click "Peak Performance Grammar and Mechanics," then click "Mechanics." Take the

Pretest to determine whether you have any weak areas. Review those areas in the Refresher Course, and take the Follow-Up Test to check your grasp of mechanics. For advanced practice, take the Advanced Test. Finally, for additional reinforcement, go to the "Improve Your Grammar, Mechanics, and Usage" section that follows, and complete those exercises.

Improve Your Grammar, Mechanics, and Usage

The following exercises help you improve your knowledge of and power over English grammar, mechanics, and usage. Turn to the "Handbook of Grammar, Mechanics, and Usage" at the end of this textbook and review all of Section 3.1 (Capitals), 3.2 (Underscores and Italics), and 3.3 (Abbreviations). Then look at the following 10 items. Circle the letter of the preferred choice in the following groups of sentences. (Answers to these exercises appear on page AK-4.)

1. a. Send this report to Mister H. K. Danforth, RR 1, Albany, NY 12885.
   b. Send this report to Mister H. K. Danforth, Rural Route 1, Albany, New York 12885.
   c. Send this report to Mr. H. K. Danforth, RR 1, Albany, NY 12885.
2. a. She received her MBA degree from the University of Michigan.
   b. She received her Master of Business Administration degree from the university of Michigan.
3. a. Sara O'Rourke (a reporter from The <u>Wall Street Journal</u>) will be here Thursday.
   b. Sara O'Rourke (a reporter from <u>The Wall Street Journal</u>) will be here Thursday.
   c. Sara O'Rourke (a reporter from The *Wall Street Journal*) will be here Thursday.
4. a. The building is located on the corner of Madison and Center streets.
   b. The building is located on the corner of Madison and Center Streets.
5. a. Call me at 8 a.m. tomorrow morning, PST, and I'll have the information you need.
   b. Call me at 8 tomorrow morning, PST, and I'll have the information you need.

   c. Call me tomorrow at 8 a.m. PST, and I'll have the information you need.
6. a. Whom do you think *Time* magazine will select as its Person of the Year?
   b. Whom do you think *Time magazine* will select as its *Person of the Year*?
   c. Whom do you think *Time magazine* will select as its Person of the Year?
7. a. The art department will begin work on Feb. 2, just one wk. from today.
   b. The art department will begin work on February 2, just one week from today.
   c. The art department will begin work on Feb. 2, just one week from today.
8. a. You are to meet him on friday at the UN building in NYC.
   b. You are to meet him on Friday at the UN building in NYC.
   c. You are to meet him on Friday at the un building in New York city.
9. a. You must help her distinguish between <u>i.e.</u> (which means "that is") and <u>e.g.</u> (which means "for example").
   b. You must help her distinguish between <u>i.e.</u> (which means "that is") and *e.g.* (which means "for example").
   c. You must help her distinguish between *i.e.* (which means <u>that is</u>) and *e.g.* (which means <u>for example</u>).
10. a. We plan to establish a sales office on the West coast.
    b. We plan to establish a sales office on the west coast.
    c. We plan to establish a sales office on the West Coast.

Part V

Writing Employment Messages and Interviewing for Jobs

Chapter 14

Writing Résumés and Application Letters

Learning Objectives

1 Discuss three ways that you can adapt to today's changing workplace

2 Describe six ways to prepare for and successfully complete your search for employment

3 List three ways of organizing your résumé, and discuss the pros and cons of each one

4 Identify the major elements of a traditional résumé

5 Explain seven ways you can avoid deception in your résumé

6 Describe how to produce a traditional résumé and what you can do to adapt it to a scannable format

7 Define the purpose of an application letter, and explain how to apply the AIDA organizational approach to it

On the Job:

COMMUNICATING AT FORD MOTOR COMPANY

LOOKING FOR PEOPLE WHO NEVER STOP LEARNING

"If you're an active learner, you'll find you fit in at Ford Motor Company," says Chairman and CEO Bill Ford (great-grandson of founder Henry Ford). Ford Motor Company makes vehicles with such brand names as Aston Martin, Ford, Jaguar, Lincoln, Mercury, and Volvo. The company owns a controlling 33 percent stake in Mazda, has purchased BMW's Land Rover SUV operations, and owns Hertz rental cars. Ford Motor Credit is the number-one auto finance company in the United States. Ford offers numerous, challenging assignments, not only in design and manufacturing but also in marketing, sales and service, purchasing, finance, information technology, and other areas.

CEO Bill Ford will tell you that Ford Motor Company is about lifelong learning, both on the job and in the classroom. The company wants applicants who are well educated, well trained, and well spoken. Finding them usually begins with a résumé and culminates in an interview.

Ford's hiring process involves two steps. The first is initial recruiting. Through the company's website, on campus, or at a career fair, you can find out about career programs, see whether Ford's environment fits your style, read about Ford people, and find out what it's like to work at Ford. To apply for a position, you answer an online questionnaire and paste in your résumé. If your online assessment and résumé are what Ford is looking for, the company may invite you to a leadership conference. Don't be discouraged if you aren't invited right away. You are given a personal webpage on Ford's career website, and the company continues to consider you for openings, unless it notifies you otherwise.

The second step is the leadership conference, an expenses-paid event at a Ford facility. You and other guests meet and interact with Ford people. Through activities such as workshops, interviews, problem-solving teams, and tours, both you and the company have ample opportunity to learn about and evaluate each other. As you interact with Ford people, they give you meaningful feedback on how you're doing, where you would best fit in at Ford, and where you are in the process. Finally, you can choose whether to receive your assessment results in person at the conference, or later on by letter.

Ford looks for particular qualities in employment candidates. The company hopes to find well-rounded individuals who have high academic standing, leadership potential, the ability to work well with others, and achievements in extracurricular activities. Successful candidates exhibit characteristics showing that they behave with honor and dignity, have a passion for excellence, and can sustain relationships (fostering teamwork, connecting with customers, committing to community). To help you gain experience and knowledge, Ford offers a range of student programs, including a Summer Intern Program, a Co-op Program that lets you alternate semesters between school and work, and Full-Time Programs for college graduates and experienced professionals.[1]

www.ford.com

BUILDING TOWARD A CAREER

As Bill Ford will tell you, getting the job that's right for you takes more than sending out a few résumés and application letters. Before entering the workplace, you need to learn as much as you can about your own capabilities and about the job marketplace.

Understanding Today's Changing Workplace

Numerous forces are changing today's workplace.

The workplace today is changing constantly.[2] The attitudes and expectations of both employers and employees are being affected not only by globalization, technology, diversity, and teams but also by deregulation, shareholder activism, corporate downsizing, mergers and acquisitions, outsourcing, and entrepreneurism (people starting their own business or buying a franchise).[3] This constant change is affecting the job search in several ways:

Today, employment is viewed as more flexible, with much less focus on lifelong employment.

- **How often people look for work.** Rather than look for lifelong employees, many employers now hire temporary workers and consultants on a project-by-project basis. Likewise, rather than staying with one employer for their entire career, growing numbers of employees are moving from company to company.

- **Where people find work.** Fewer jobs are being created by large companies. One expert predicts that soon 80 percent of the labor force will be working for firms employing fewer than 200 people. Moreover, self-employment seems to be an increasingly attractive option for many former employees.[4]

- **The type of people who find work.** Employers today are looking for people who are able and willing to adapt to diverse situations and who continue to learn throughout their careers. Companies want team players with strong work records, leaders who are versatile, and employees with diversified skills and varied job experience.[5] Plus, most employers expect employees to be sensitive to intercultural differences.[6]

Adapting to the Changing Workplace

Before you limit your employment search to a particular industry or job, do some preparation. Analyze what you have to offer, what you hope to get from your work, and how you can make yourself more valuable to potential employers. This preliminary analysis will help you identify employers who are likely to want you and vice versa.

What you have to offer:
- *Functional skills*
- *Education and experience*
- *Personality traits*

Analyze What You Have to Offer   When seeking employment, you'll be asked to tell people about yourself, about who you are. So knowing what talents and skills you have is essential. And to be most effective, be sure you can explain how these skills will benefit potential employers. Here are some suggestions to help your self-analysis:

- **Jot down 10 achievements you're proud of.** Did you learn to ski, take a prize-winning photo, tutor a child, edit your school paper? Think about what skills these achievements demanded (leadership skills, speaking ability, and artistic talent may have helped you coordinate a winning presentation to your school's administration). You'll begin to recognize a pattern of skills, many of which might be valuable to potential employers.

- **Look at your educational preparation, work experience, and extracurricular activities.** What do your knowledge and experience qualify you to do? What have you learned from volunteer work or class projects that could benefit you on the job? Have you held any offices, won any awards or scholarships, mastered a second language?

- **Take stock of your personal characteristics.** Are you aggressive, a born leader? Or would you rather follow? Are you outgoing, articulate, great with people? Or do you prefer working alone? Make a list of what you believe are your four or five most important qualities. Ask a relative or friend to rate your traits as well.

Your college placement office may be able to administer a variety of tests to help you identify interests, aptitudes, and personality traits. These tests won't reveal your "perfect" job, but they'll help you focus on the types of work best suited to your personality.

Decide What You Want to Do   Knowing what you *can* do is one thing. Knowing what you *want* to do is another. Don't lose sight of your own values. Discover the things that will bring you satisfaction and happiness on the job. Ask yourself some questions:

> What you want from your career is as important as what you have to offer employers.

- **What would you like to do every day?** Talk to people in various occupations about their typical workday. You might consult relatives, local businesses, or former graduates (through your school's alumni relations office). Read about various occupations. Start with your college library or placement office.

- **How would you like to work?** Consider how much independence you want on the job, how much variety you like, and whether you prefer to work with products, machines, people, ideas, figures, or some combination thereof. Do you like physical work, mental work, or a mix? Constant change or a predictable role?

- **What specific compensation do you expect?** What do you hope to earn in your first year? What kind of pay increase do you expect each year? What's your ultimate earnings goal? Would you be comfortable getting paid on commission, or do you prefer a steady paycheck? Are you willing to settle for less money in order to do something you really love?

- **Can you establish some general career goals?** Consider where you'd like to start, where you'd like to go from there, and the ultimate position you'd like to attain. How soon after joining the company would you like to receive your first promotion? Your next one? What additional training or preparation will you need to achieve them?

- **What size company would you prefer?** Do you like the idea of working for a small, entrepreneurial operation? Or would you prefer a large corporation?

- **What type of operation is appealing to you?** Would you prefer to work for a profit-making company or a nonprofit organization? Are you attracted to service businesses or manufacturing operations? Do you want regular, predictable hours, or do you thrive on flexible, varied hours? Would you enjoy a seasonally varied job such as education (which may give you summers off) or retailing (with its selling cycles)?

- **What location would you like?** Would you like to work in a city, a suburb, a small town, an industrial area, or an uptown setting? Do you favor a particular part of the country? A country abroad? Do you like working indoors or outdoors?

- **What facilities do you envision?** Is it important to you to work in an attractive place, or will simple, functional quarters suffice? Do you need a quiet office to work effectively, or can you concentrate in a noisy, open setting? Is access to public transportation or freeways important?

- **What sort of corporate culture are you most comfortable with?** Would you be happy in a formal hierarchy with clear reporting relationships? Or do you prefer less structure? Are you looking for a paternalistic firm or one that fosters individualism? Do you like a competitive environment? One that rewards teamwork? What qualities do you want in a boss?

Make Yourself More Valuable to Employers   Take positive steps toward building your career. Before you graduate from college or while you are seeking

> Your chances of getting a job are increased by career-building efforts.

employment, you can do a lot. The following suggestions will help potential employers recognize the value of hiring you:

- **Keep an employment portfolio.** Get a three-ring notebook and a package of plastic sleeves that open at the top. Collect anything that shows your ability to perform (classroom or work evaluations, certificates, awards, papers you've written). Your portfolio is a great resource for writing your résumé, and it gives employers tangible evidence of your professionalism.

- **Consider an e-portfolio.** You can think of an e-portfolio as a multimedia presentation about your skills and experiences. It's an extensive résumé that links to an electronic collection of your student papers, problem-solving situations, pictures from study-abroad stints, internship projects, and anything else that demonstrates your accomplishments and activities. Although such portfolios are usually stored on college websites, students can make copies on CD-ROMs and send them out instead of résumés.[7]

- **Take interim assignments.** As you search for a permanent job, consider temporary or freelance work. Also gain a competitive edge by participating in an internship program. These temporary assignments not only help you gain valuable experience and relevant contacts but also provide you with important references and with items for your portfolio.[8]

- **Work on polishing and updating your skills.** Whenever possible, join networks of professional colleagues and friends who can help you keep up with your occupation and industry. While waiting for responses to your résumé, take a computer course or seek out other educational or life experiences that would be hard to get while working full-time.

Even after you're hired, you can increase your value to employers by continuing to improve your skills. Lifelong learning will distinguish you from your peers, help you advance within a company, and help you follow opportunities with other employers. To reach your personal goals in the workplace, become a lifelong learner by doing the following:[9]

- Obtain as much technical knowledge as you can.

- Learn to accept and adapt to change.

- Regularly read publications such as the *Wall Street Journal, BusinessWeek,* and *U.S. News & World Report.*

- View each job as an opportunity to learn more and to expand your knowledge, experience, and social skills.

- Take on as much responsibility as you can (listening to and learning from others while actively pursuing new or better skills).

- Stay abreast of what's going on in your organization and industry.

- Share what you know with others.

- Understand the big picture.

Seeking Employment in the Changing Workplace

Look at Figure 14–1 for an idea of what an employment search entails. The first two tasks are discussed in this chapter; the rest are discussed in Chapter 15. Gather as much information as you can, narrowing it as you go until you know precisely the companies you want to approach.

Your career-building efforts don't stop after you are hired.

The search for employment is a process.

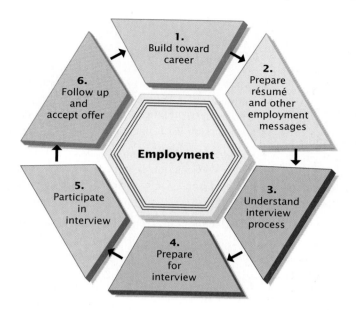

FIGURE 14–1
The Employment Search

Begin by finding out where the job opportunities are, which industries are strong, which parts of the country are booming, and which specific job categories offer the best prospects for the future. From there you can investigate individual organizations, doing your best to learn as much about them as possible. To prepare for and successfully complete your search for employment, do the following:

Find out where the job opportunities are.

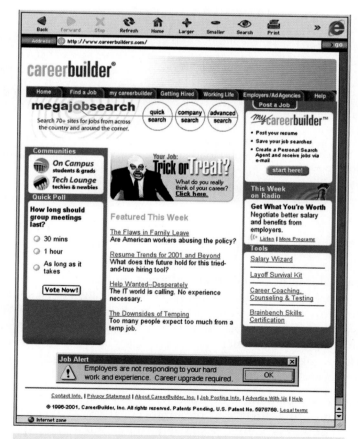

CareerBuilder is just one of the many websites that job seekers turn to for career advice, as well as for employer information and company job postings.

USING THE POWER OF TECHNOLOGY

Netting a Job on the Web

Can the web provide the answer to all your employment dreams? Perhaps . . . or perhaps not. As the web grows, the employment information it provides is constantly expanding. And you're fortunate, because you don't have to start from scratch like some intrepid adventurer. For helpful hints and useful web addresses, you can turn to books such as *What Color Is Your Parachute?* by Richard Nelson Bolles. Other places to check out online include the following:*

- *America's Career InfoNet* (www.acinet.org). Good place to begin. Offers information on typical wages and employment trends. Gives education, knowledge, and skills requirements for most occupations. Includes links to multiple career resources on the Internet.

- *The Monster Board* (www.monster.com). Posts more than 25,000 openings and 300,000 résumés. Heavily marketed, it brings a flood of employers (many with under 500 employees).

- *America's Job Bank* (www.ajb.dni.us). State agencies post an average of 5,000 new openings each day on this government site. Companies contribute another 3,000.

- *HotJobs.Com* (www.hotjobs.com). A member-based site that charges companies a hefty fee to post openings or search through résumés. Job seekers can create a personal page to manage their search and collect statistics on how many companies have retrieved their résumé.

- *NationJob Network* (www.nationjob.com). Posts more than 15,000 jobs nationwide, with an emphasis on those in the Midwest.

- *4Work* (www.4work.com). One of the few sites that includes listings of internships and volunteer opportunities.

- *Net-Temps* (www.net-temps.com). Maintained by career consultants; offers several thousand updated listings and real-time seminars. Network forums help you develop new contacts and job leads. Includes chat room for online interviews.

- *CareerBuilder* (www.careerbuilder.com). Offers a network of career services, job-search information, and tips on how to succeed once you're hired. Includes a database of 20,000 openings.

- *MonsterTrak* (www.monstertrak.com). Has formed partnerships with 750 campuses nationwide and serves as a virtual career center for students and alumni. Many entry-level postings.

- *Yahoo! Classifieds* (www.classifieds.yahoo.com). Offers extensive listing of companies by city, in addition to a wealth of job-related information at the parent website, www.yahoo.com. Click on Business & Economy/Jobs/Company Job Listings.

*Direct links to many of these websites and other valuable information can be found at *The Riley Guide* (www.dbm.com/jobguide).

CAREER APPLICATIONS

1. Surfing the web can chew up a disproportionate amount of your job-seeking time. Explain how you can limit the amount of time you spend on the web and still make it work for you.

2. When posting your résumé on the web, you're revealing a lot of information about yourself that could be used by people other than employers (salespeople, people competing for similar positions, con artists). What sort of information might you leave off your web résumé that would certainly appear on a traditional résumé?

- **Stay abreast of business and financial news.** Subscribe to a major newspaper (print or online) and scan the business pages every day. Watch some of the television programs that focus on business, such as *Wall Street Week*. Consult the *Dictionary of Occupational Titles* (U.S. Employment Service), the employment publications of Science Research Associates, and the *Occupational Outlook Handbook* (U.S. Bureau of Labor Statistics—in print and online at www.bls.gov/oco).

- **Research specific companies.** Compile a list of specific organizations that appeal to you (by consulting directories of employers at your college library, at your career center, or on the web). Consult company profiles, press releases, financial information, and information on employment opportunities. Find out about a company's mission, products, annual reports, and employee benefits. Send an e-mail request for annual reports, brochures, or newsletters.

- **Look for job openings.** Check company websites for job openings, or find sites that list openings from multiple companies—many of which allow you to search by region, industry, job title, company, skills, or requirements (see "Using the Power of Technology: Netting a Job on the Web"). And don't forget to look in newspapers and sign up for campus interviews.

- **Respond to job openings.** You can respond directly to job listings by posting tailor-made résumés (that match required qualifications) and by sending e-mail résumés and focused cover letters directly to the people doing the hiring. Since companies receive thousands of electronic résumés a day, also consider a printed letter or a phone call.[10]

- **Network.** Find people in your field by participating in student business organizations (such as the American Marketing Association or the American Management Association). Visit organizations, contact their personnel departments, and talk with key employees. On the web, locate and communicate with potential employers using discussion groups, Usenet groups (where you can post messages on electronic bulletin boards) and listservs (where e-mail messages are sent to every member). Once you locate a potential contact, send an e-mail requesting information about the company or about job openings.

- **Find career counseling.** College placement offices offer counseling, credential services, job fairs, on-campus interviews, and job listings. They provide workshops in job-search techniques, résumé preparation, interview techniques, and more.[11] College- and university-run online career centers are excellent. Commercial career centers (online and off) range from award winning to depressing, so find those with advice that is both useful and sensible.

While looking for employment, you'll need to send out messages such as résumés and application letters. Whenever you send out such employment messages, you have an opportunity to showcase your communication skills—skills valued highly by the majority of employers, such as CEO Bill Ford. So write these messages carefully by following the three-step writing process (see Figure 14–2).

FIGURE 14–2
Three-Step Writing Process for Employment Messages

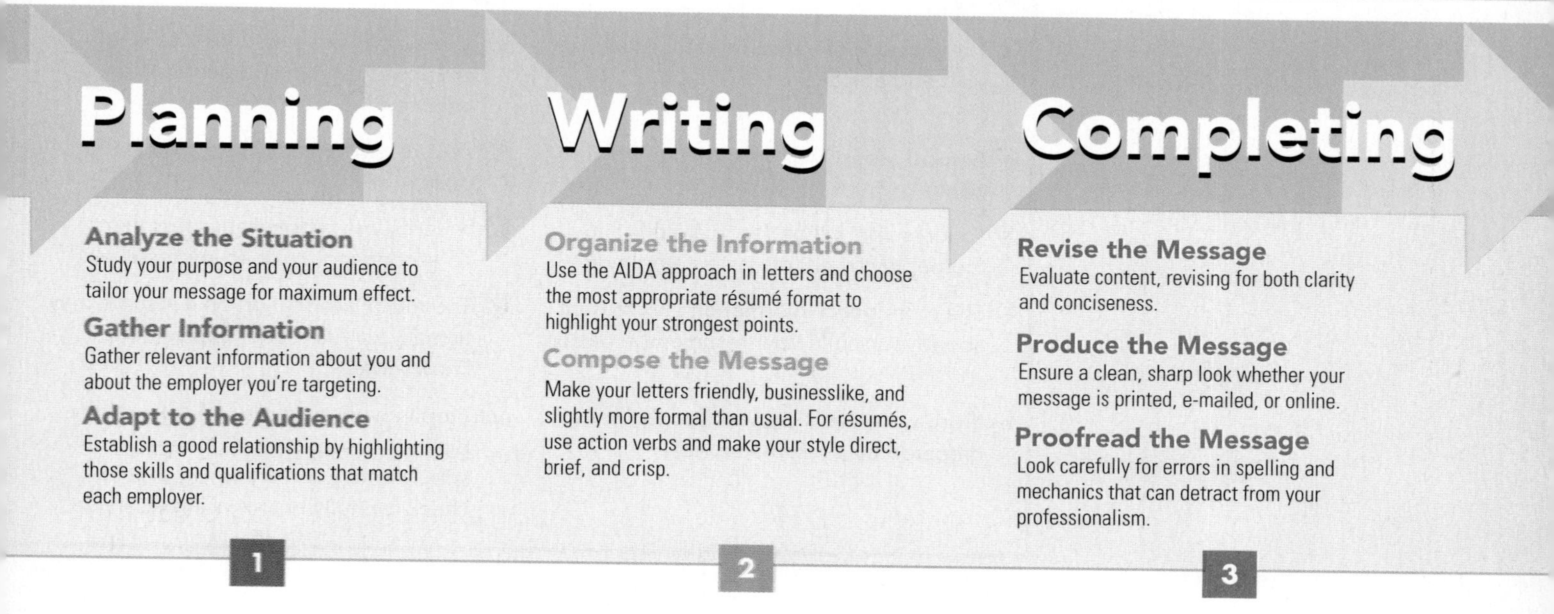

Planning

Analyze the Situation
Study your purpose and your audience to tailor your message for maximum effect.

Gather Information
Gather relevant information about you and about the employer you're targeting.

Adapt to the Audience
Establish a good relationship by highlighting those skills and qualifications that match each employer.

Writing

Organize the Information
Use the AIDA approach in letters and choose the most appropriate résumé format to highlight your strongest points.

Compose the Message
Make your letters friendly, businesslike, and slightly more formal than usual. For résumés, use action verbs and make your style direct, brief, and crisp.

Completing

Revise the Message
Evaluate content, revising for both clarity and conciseness.

Produce the Message
Ensure a clean, sharp look whether your message is printed, e-mailed, or online.

Proofread the Message
Look carefully for errors in spelling and mechanics that can detract from your professionalism.

PLANNING YOUR RÉSUMÉ

Your résumé is a structured, written summary of your educational and employment background and shows your qualifications for a job.

Begin preparing your résumé by planning carefully.

A **résumé** is a structured, written summary of a person's education, employment experience, and job qualifications. Many people have misconceptions about the value and function of résumés (see Table 14–1). As with other business messages, planning a résumé means analyzing your purpose and audience, gathering information, and adapting the document to your purpose and audience:

- **Analyze your purpose and audience.** Your résumé must be more than a simple list of jobs you've held. It is a form of advertising intended to stimulate an employer's interest in you—in meeting you and learning more about you. With this purpose in mind, put yourself in your audience's position and tailor your résumé to satisfy audience needs.

- **Gather pertinent information.** Gather every scrap of pertinent personal history you can and have it at your fingertips: all details of previous jobs (dates, duties, accomplishments), all relevant educational experience (formal degrees, skill certificates, academic or civic awards), all relevant information about personal endeavors (dates of membership in an association, offices you held in a club or organization, presentations you made to a community group).

- **Adapt your résumé to your audience.** Your résumé must make an impression quickly. Focus on your audience. Ask yourself what key qualifications this employer will be looking for. Decide which qualifications are your greatest strengths. Choose three or four of your most relevant accomplishments and what resulted from these accomplishments. A good résumé is flexible and can be customized for various situations and employers.

Cisco Systems participates in college job fairs as one way to recruit new employees.

Table 14–1	FALLACIES AND FACTS ABOUT RÉSUMÉS	
Fallacy	*Fact*	
⊗ The purpose of a résumé is to list all your skills and abilities.	☑ The purpose of a résumé is to kindle employer interest and generate an interview.	
⊗ A good résumé will get you the job you want.	☑ All a résumé can do is get you in the door.	
⊗ Your résumé will be read carefully and thoroughly by an interested employer.	☑ Your résumé probably has less than 45 seconds to make an impression.	
⊗ The more good information you present about yourself in your résumé, the better.	☑ Too much information on a résumé may actually kill the reader's appetite to know more.	
⊗ If you want a really good résumé, have it prepared by a résumé service.	☑ Prepare your own résumé—unless the position is especially high-level or specialized. Even then, you should check carefully before using a service.	

Think in terms of an image or "theme" you'd like to project. Are you academically gifted? A campus leader? A well-rounded person? A creative genius? A technical wizard? Avoid exaggerating, altering the past, or claiming skills you don't have. However, don't dwell on negatives. By knowing yourself and your audience, you'll focus successfully on the strengths needed by potential employers.

WRITING YOUR RÉSUMÉ

To write a successful résumé, you need to convey seven qualities that employers seek. You want to show that you (1) think in terms of results, (2) know how to get things done, (3) are well rounded, (4) show signs of progress, (5) have personal standards of excellence, (6) are flexible and willing to try new things, and (7) possess strong communication skills. As you organize and compose your résumé, try to convey those seven qualities.

> Employers look for seven qualities in a job candidate.

Organize Your Résumé Around Your Strengths

Although you may want to include a little information in all categories, emphasize the information that has a bearing on your career objective, and minimize or exclude any that is irrelevant or counterproductive. Call attention to your best features and downplay your weaknesses—but be sure you do so without distorting or misrepresenting the facts.[12] To focus attention on your strongest points, adopt the appropriate organizational approach—make your résumé chronological, functional, or a combination of the two. The "right" choice depends on your background and your goals.

> Select an organizational pattern that focuses attention on your strengths.

The Chronological Résumé   In a **chronological résumé,** the work-experience section dominates and is placed in the most prominent slot, immediately after your name, your contact information, and the objective (if one is included). List your jobs sequentially in reverse order, beginning with the most recent position and working backward toward earlier jobs. Under each listing, describe your responsibilities and accomplishments, giving the most space to the most recent positions. Within this format, try to make the chronology clear, use bulleted lists effectively, and emphasize important points. The résumé in Figure 14–3 fails to use the chronological format effectively.

The chronological approach is the most common way to organize a résumé, and many employers prefer it. This approach has three key advantages: (1) employers are familiar with it and can easily find information, (2) it highlights growth and career progression, and (3) it highlights employment continuity and stability.[13] If you're just starting your career, you can vary this approach by putting your educational qualifications before your experience, thereby focusing attention on your academic credentials. The chronological approach is especially appropriate if you have a strong employment history and are aiming for a job that builds on your current career path. This is the case for Roberto Cortez. Compare the ineffective version of his résumé (Figure 14–3) with the effective version in Figure 14–4 on page 487.

> Most recruiters prefer the chronological plan: a historical summary of your education and work experience.

The Functional Résumé   A **functional résumé** emphasizes a list of skills and accomplishments, and identifies employers and academic experience in subordinate sections. This pattern stresses areas of competence, so it's useful for people who are just entering the job market, who want to redirect their careers, or who have little continuous career-related experience. The functional approach also has three advantages: (1) Without having to read through job descriptions, employers can see what

> A functional résumé focuses attention on your areas of competence.

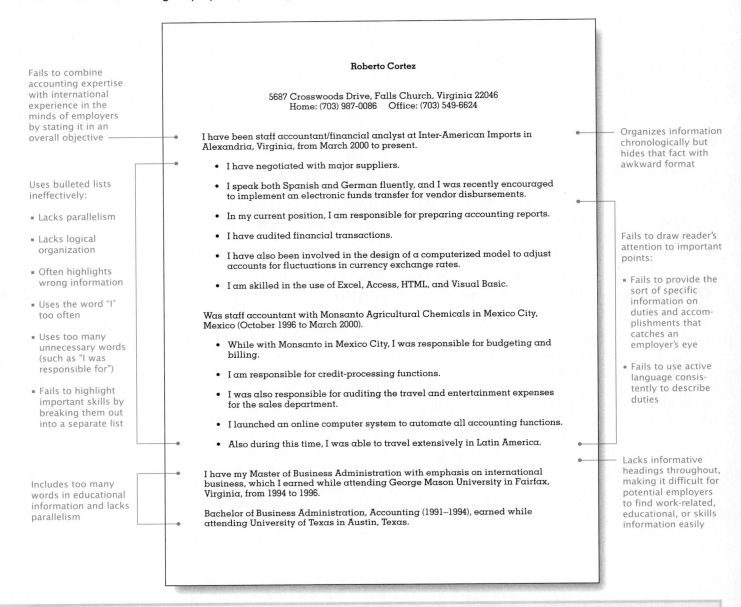

Roberto Cortez

5687 Crosswoods Drive, Falls Church, Virginia 22046
Home: (703) 987-0086   Office: (703) 549-6624

I have been staff accountant/financial analyst at Inter-American Imports in Alexandria, Virginia, from March 2000 to present.

- I have negotiated with major suppliers.
- I speak both Spanish and German fluently, and I was recently encouraged to implement an electronic funds transfer for vendor disbursements.
- In my current position, I am responsible for preparing accounting reports.
- I have audited financial transactions.
- I have also been involved in the design of a computerized model to adjust accounts for fluctuations in currency exchange rates.
- I am skilled in the use of Excel, Access, HTML, and Visual Basic.

Was staff accountant with Monsanto Agricultural Chemicals in Mexico City, Mexico (October 1996 to March 2000).

- While with Monsanto in Mexico City, I was responsible for budgeting and billing.
- I am responsible for credit-processing functions.
- I was also responsible for auditing the travel and entertainment expenses for the sales department.
- I launched an online computer system to automate all accounting functions.
- Also during this time, I was able to travel extensively in Latin America.

I have my Master of Business Administration with emphasis on international business, which I earned while attending George Mason University in Fairfax, Virginia, from 1994 to 1996.

Bachelor of Business Administration, Accounting (1991–1994), earned while attending University of Texas in Austin, Texas.

Callout annotations (left):
Fails to combine accounting expertise with international experience in the minds of employers by stating it in an overall objective

Uses bulleted lists ineffectively:
- Lacks parallelism
- Lacks logical organization
- Often highlights wrong information
- Uses the word "I" too often
- Uses too many unnecessary words (such as "I was responsible for")
- Fails to highlight important skills by breaking them out into a separate list

Includes too many words in educational information and lacks parallelism

Callout annotations (right):
Organizes information chronologically but hides that fact with awkward format

Fails to draw reader's attention to important points:
- Fails to provide the sort of specific information on duties and accomplishments that catches an employer's eye
- Fails to use active language consistently to describe duties

Lacks informative headings throughout, making it difficult for potential employers to find work-related, educational, or skills information easily

FIGURE 14–3
Ineffective Chronological Résumé

you can do for them; (2) you can emphasize earlier job experience; and (3) you can de-emphasize any lack of career progress or lengthy unemployment.

Figure 14–5 on page 488 illustrates how Glenda Johns uses the functional approach to showcase her qualifications for a career in retail. Although she has not held any paid, full-time positions in retail sales, Johns has participated in work-experience programs, and she knows a good deal about the profession from research and from talking with people in the industry. She organized her résumé in a way that demonstrates her ability to handle such a position. Bear in mind, however, that many seasoned employment professionals are suspicious of this résumé style. They assume that candidates who use it are trying to hide something.[14]

FIGURE 14–4
Effective Chronological Résumé

Planning

Writing

Completing

Analyze the Situation
Decide how best to combine accounting expertise with international experience.

Gather Information
Gather data from contacts and research.

Adapt to the Audience
Point out specific achievements to interest potential employers.

Organize the Information
A chronological résumé will best emphasize years of work experience.

Compose the Message
The style is direct, brief, and crisp, using action verbs to focus on employment history, professional achievements, and international abilities.

Revise the Message
Make content clear and concise.

Produce the Message
Give traditional résumé a clean, sharp look with dates set off in margin.

Proofread the Message
Review for spelling and mechanical errors.

1

2

3

Combines accounting expertise with international experience in the minds of employers by stating it in an overall objective

Organizes information chronologically and emphasizes that organization with format

Makes each description concise, easy to read, and informative:

- Avoids the word "I" throughout

- Uses no unnecessary words

Highlights important skills by breaking them out into a list in a separate section

---

ROBERTO CORTEZ
5687 Crosswoods Drive
Falls Church, Virginia 22046
Home: (703) 987-0086 Office: (703) 549-6624 RCortez@silvernet.com

OBJECTIVE

Accounting management position requiring a knowledge
of international finance

EXPERIENCE

March 2000
to present

Staff Accountant/Financial Analyst, Inter-American Imports
(Alexandria, Virginia)
- Prepare accounting reports for wholesale giftware importer ($15 million annual sales)
- Audit financial transactions with suppliers in 12 Latin American countries
- Created a computerized model to adjust accounts for fluctuations in currency exchange rates
- Negotiated joint-venture agreements with major suppliers in Mexico and Colombia
- Implemented electronic funds transfer for vendor disbursements, improving cash flow and eliminating payables clerk position

October 1996
to March 2000

Staff Accountant, Monsanto Agricultural Chemicals
(Mexico City, Mexico)
- Handled budgeting, billing, and credit-processing functions for the Mexico City branch
- Audited travel/entertainment expenses for Monsanto's 30-member Latin American sales force
- Assisted in launching an online computer system to automate all accounting functions

EDUCATION

1994 to 1996

Master of Business Administration with emphasis in international business
George Mason University (Fairfax, Virginia)

1991 to 1994

Bachelor of Business Administration, Accounting,
University of Texas, Austin

INTERCULTURAL AND TECHNICAL SKILLS

- Fluent in Spanish and German
- Traveled extensively in Latin America
- Excel • Access • HTML • Visual Basic

Draws reader's attention to important points:

- Provides the sort of specific information on duties and accomplishments that catches an employer's eye

- Highlights duties and work achievements in bulleted lists

- Uses active language to describe duties

Includes informative headings throughout, making it easy for potential employers to find work-related, educational, or skills information

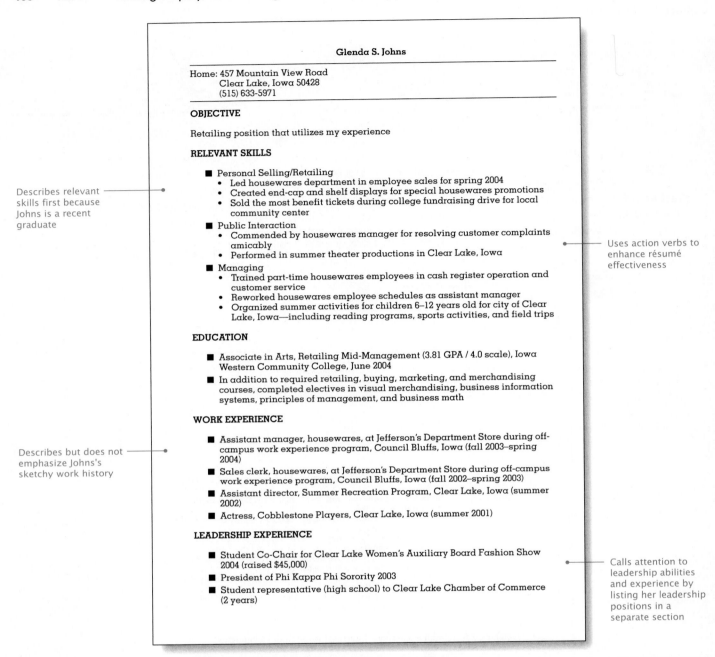

Glenda S. Johns

Home: 457 Mountain View Road
Clear Lake, Iowa 50428
(515) 633-5971

OBJECTIVE

Retailing position that utilizes my experience

RELEVANT SKILLS

- ■ Personal Selling/Retailing
  - • Led housewares department in employee sales for spring 2004
  - • Created end-cap and shelf displays for special housewares promotions
  - • Sold the most benefit tickets during college fundraising drive for local community center
- ■ Public Interaction
  - • Commended by housewares manager for resolving customer complaints amicably
  - • Performed in summer theater productions in Clear Lake, Iowa
- ■ Managing
  - • Trained part-time housewares employees in cash register operation and customer service
  - • Reworked housewares employee schedules as assistant manager
  - • Organized summer activities for children 6–12 years old for city of Clear Lake, Iowa—including reading programs, sports activities, and field trips

EDUCATION

- ■ Associate in Arts, Retailing Mid-Management (3.81 GPA / 4.0 scale), Iowa Western Community College, June 2004
- ■ In addition to required retailing, buying, marketing, and merchandising courses, completed electives in visual merchandising, business information systems, principles of management, and business math

WORK EXPERIENCE

- ■ Assistant manager, housewares, at Jefferson's Department Store during off-campus work experience program, Council Bluffs, Iowa (fall 2003–spring 2004)
- ■ Sales clerk, housewares, at Jefferson's Department Store during off-campus work experience program, Council Bluffs, Iowa (fall 2002–spring 2003)
- ■ Assistant director, Summer Recreation Program, Clear Lake, Iowa (summer 2002)
- ■ Actress, Cobblestone Players, Clear Lake, Iowa (summer 2001)

LEADERSHIP EXPERIENCE

- ■ Student Co-Chair for Clear Lake Women's Auxiliary Board Fashion Show 2004 (raised $45,000)
- ■ President of Phi Kappa Phi Sorority 2003
- ■ Student representative (high school) to Clear Lake Chamber of Commerce (2 years)

Callouts (left):
Describes relevant skills first because Johns is a recent graduate

Describes but does not emphasize Johns's sketchy work history

Callouts (right):
Uses action verbs to enhance résumé effectiveness

Calls attention to leadership abilities and experience by listing her leadership positions in a separate section

FIGURE 14–5
Effective Functional Résumé

A combination résumé is a hybrid of the chronological and functional résumés.

The Combination Résumé   A **combination résumé** includes the best features of the chronological and functional approaches. Nevertheless, it is not commonly used, even though it has two major disadvantages: (1) It tends to be longer, and (2) it can be repetitious if you have to list your accomplishments and skills in both the functional section and the chronological job descriptions.[15] When Erica Vorkamp developed her résumé, she chose not to use a chronological pattern, which would focus attention on her lack of recent work experience. As Figure 14–6 shows, she used a combination approach to emphasize her abilities, skills, and accomplishments while also including a complete job history.

Erica Vorkamp

993 Church Street, Barrington, Illinois 60010
(847) 884-2153

OBJECTIVE

To obtain a position as a special event coordinator that will utilize my skills and experience

SKILLS AND CAPABILITIES

- Plan and coordinate large-scale public events
- Develop community support for concerts, festivals, and the arts
- Manage publicity for major events
- Coordinate activities of diverse community groups
- Establish and maintain financial controls for public events
- Negotiate contracts with performers, carpenters, electricians, and suppliers

SPECIAL EVENT EXPERIENCE

- Arranged 2003's week-long Arts and Entertainment Festival for the Barrington Public Library, involving performances by 25 musicians, dancers, actors, magicians, and artists
- Supervised the 2002 PTA Halloween Carnival, an all-day festival with game booths, live bands, contests, and food service that raised $7,600 for the PTA
- Organized the 2001 Midwestern convention for 800 members of the League of Women Voters, which extended over a three-day period and required arrangements for hotels, meals, speakers, and special tours
- Served as chairperson for the 2000 to 2002 Children's Home Society Fashion Show, a luncheon for 400–500 that raised $5,000–$6,700 for orphans and abused children

EDUCATION

- Associate of Applied Science, Administrative Assistant program with specialization in General Business, Lincoln School of Commerce (Lincoln, Nebraska), 1989

EMPLOYMENT HISTORY

- First National Bank of Chicago, 1989 to 1991, operations processor; processed checks with a lost/stolen status, contacted customers by phone, inspected checks to determine risk characteristics, processed payment amounts, verified receipt reports, researched check authenticity, managed orientation program for entry-level trainees
- Lincoln School of Commerce, 1987 to 1989, part-time administrative assistant for admissions (Business Department)

Relates all capabilities and experience to the specific job objective, giving a selective picture of the candidate's abilities

Includes event attendance statistics and fundraising results to quantify accomplishments

Includes work history (even though it has little bearing on job target) because Vorkamp believes recruiters want to see evidence that she's held a paying position

FIGURE 14–6
Effective Combination Résumé

Compose Your Résumé to Impress

To save your readers time and to state your information as forcefully as possible, write your résumé using a simple and direct style. Use short, crisp phrases instead of whole sentences, and focus on what your reader needs to know. Avoid using the word *I*. Instead, start your phrases with impressive action verbs such as the ones listed in Table 14–2. For instance, you might say, "Coached a Little League team to the regional playoffs" or "Managed a fast-food restaurant and four employees." Here are some additional examples of how to phrase your accomplishments using active statements that show results:

To capture attention quickly, leave out the word I, and begin your phrases with strong action verbs.

Table 14–2	ACTION VERBS TO USE IN RÉSUMÉS			
accomplished	coordinated	initiated	participated	set up
achieved	created	installed	performed	simplified
administered	demonstrated	introduced	planned	sparked
approved	developed	investigated	presented	streamlined
arranged	directed	joined	proposed	strengthened
assisted	established	launched	raised	succeeded
assumed	explored	maintained	recommended	supervised
budgeted	forecasted	managed	reduced	systematized
chaired	generated	motivated	reorganized	targeted
changed	identified	operated	resolved	trained
compiled	implemented	organized	saved	transformed
completed	improved	oversaw	served	upgraded

Avoid Weak Statements	Use Active Statements That Show Results
Responsible for developing a new filing system	Developed a new filing system that reduced paperwork by 50 percent
I was in charge of customer complaints and all ordering problems	Handled all customer complaints and resolved all product order discrepancies
Won a trip to Europe for opening the most new customer accounts in my department	Generated the highest number of new customer accounts in my department
Member of special campus task force to resolve student problems with existing cafeteria assignments	Assisted in implementing new campus dining program that allows students to eat at any college dorm

Make sure you include all necessary elements in your résumé: your name and address, academic credentials, employment history, activities and achievements, and relevant personal data.

The opening section shows at a glance
• Who you are
• How to reach you

Name and Address   The first thing an employer needs to know is who you are and where you can be reached: your name, address, and phone number (plus your e-mail address or URL, if you have one). If you have contact information at school and at home, you can include both. Similarly, if you have a work phone and a home phone, list both and indicate which is which. Many résumé headings are nothing more than the name and address centered at the top of the page. You don't really need to include the word *résumé*. Just make sure the reader can tell in an instant who you are and how to communicate with you.

Stating your objective or summarizing your qualifications helps the recruiter categorize you.

Career Objective or Summary of Qualifications   Experts disagree about the need to state a career objective on your résumé. Some argue that your objective is obvious from your qualifications. Some also maintain that such a statement only limits you as a candidate (especially if you want to be considered for a variety of openings) because it labels you as being interested in only one thing. Other experts argue that employers will try to categorize you anyway, so you might as well make sure they attach the right label. Remember that your goal is to generate interest immediately. If you decide to state your objective, make it effective by being as specific as possible about what you want:

A software sales position in a growing company requiring international experience. Advertising assistant, with print media emphasis and strong customer-contact skills

If you have different types of qualifications (such as a certificate in secretarial science and two years' experience in retail sales), prepare separate résumés, each with a different objective. If your immediate objective differs from your ultimate one, combine the two in a single statement:

A marketing position with an opportunity for eventual managerial status. Proposal writer, with the ultimate goal of becoming a contracts administrator

Instead of stating your objective, you might summarize your qualifications in a brief statement that highlights your strongest points, particularly if you have had a good deal of varied experience. Use a short, simple phrase:

Summary of qualifications: Ten years of experience in commission sales, generating new customer leads through creative advertising and community leadership positions

The career objective or summary may be the only section read fully by the employer, so if you include either one, make it strong, concise, and convincing.

Education   If you're still in school, education is probably your strongest selling point. Present your educational background in depth, choosing facts that support your "theme." Give this section a heading such as "Education," "Professional College Training," or "Academic Preparation." Then, starting with the school you most recently attended, list the name and location of each one, the term of your enrollment (in years), your major and minor fields of study, significant skills and abilities you've developed in your course work, and the degrees or certificates you've earned. If you're working on an uncompleted degree, include in parentheses the expected date of completion. Showcase your qualifications by listing courses that have directly equipped you for the job you are seeking, and indicate any scholarships, awards, or academic honors you've received.

> If education is your strongest selling point, discuss it thoroughly and highlight it visually.

The education section also includes off-campus training sponsored by business or government. Include any relevant seminars or workshops you've attended, as well as the certificates or other documents you've received. Mention high school training only if the associated achievements are pertinent to your career goals. Whether you list your grades depends on the job you want and the quality of your grades. If you choose to show a grade-point average, be sure to mention the scale, especially if a five-point scale is used instead of a four-point scale.

Education is usually given less emphasis in a résumé after you've worked in your chosen field for a year or more. If work experience is your strongest qualification, save the section on education for later in the résumé and provide less detail.

Work Experience, Skills, and Accomplishments   Like the education section, the work-experience section focuses on your overall theme. Tailor your description to highlight the relationship between your previous responsibilities and your target field. Call attention to skills you've developed and your progression from jobs of lesser to greater responsibility.

The work-experience section lists all the related jobs you've had:
- Name and location of employer
- What the organization does (if not clear from its name)
- Your functional title
- How long you worked there
- Your duties and responsibilities
- Your significant achievements or contributions

When describing your work experience, list your jobs in chronological order, with the current or last one first. Include any part-time, summer, or intern positions, even if unrelated to your current career objective. Employers will see that you have the ability to get and hold a job—an important qualification in itself. If you have worked your way through school, say so. Employers interpret such an endeavor as a sign of character.

Each listing includes the name and location of the employer. If readers are unlikely to recognize the organization, briefly describe what it does. When you want to keep the name of your current employer confidential, identify the firm by industry only ("a large film-processing laboratory") or use the name but request confidentiality in the application letter or in an underlined note ("Résumé submitted in confidence") at the top or bottom of the résumé. If an organization's name or location has since changed, state the current name and location and then "formerly . . . "

Before or after each job listing, state your functional title, such as "clerk typist" or "salesperson." If you were a dishwasher, say so. Don't try to make your role seem more important by glamorizing your job title, functions, or achievements. Also state how long you worked on each job, from month/year to month/year. Use the phrase "to present" to denote current employment. If a job was part-time, say so.

Quantify your accomplishments whenever possible.

Devote the most space to the jobs that are related to your target position. If you were personally responsible for something significant, be sure to mention it ("Devised a new collection system that accelerated payment of overdue receivables"). Facts about your skills and accomplishments are the most important information you can give a prospective employer, so quantify them whenever possible:

Designed a new ad that increased sales by 9 percent

Raised $2,500 in 15 days for cancer research

Include miscellaneous facts that are related to your career objective:
- Command of other languages
- Computer expertise
- Date you can start working

You may also include a section describing other aspects of your background that pertain to your career objective. If you were applying for a position with a multinational organization, you would mention your command of another language or your travel experience. Other skills you might mention include the ability to operate a computer, word processor, or other specialized equipment. You might title a special section "Computer Skills" or "Language Skills" and place it near your education or work-experience section.

If samples of your work might increase your chances of getting the job, insert a line at the end of your résumé offering to supply them on request. You may put "References available upon request" at the end of your résumé, but doing so is not necessary; the availability of references is usually assumed. Don't include actual names of references. List your references on a separate sheet and take them to your interview.

Nonpaid activities may provide evidence of work-related skills.

Activities and Achievements   Your résumé should also describe any volunteer activities that demonstrate your abilities. List projects that require leadership, organization, teamwork, and cooperation. Emphasize career-related activities such as "member of the Student Marketing Association." List skills you learned in these activities, and explain how these skills are related to the job you're applying for. Include speaking, writing, or tutoring experience; participation in athletics or creative projects; fundraising or community service activities; and offices held in academic or professional organizations. (However, mention of political or religious organizations may be a red flag to someone with differing views, so use your judgment.)

Note any awards you've received. Again, quantify your achievements whenever possible. Instead of saying that you addressed various student groups, state how many and the approximate audience sizes. If your activities have been extensive, you may want to group them into divisions such as "College Activities," "Community Service," "Professional Associations," "Seminars and Workshops," and "Speaking Activities." An alternative is to divide them into two categories: "Service Activities" and "Achievements, Awards, and Honors."

Personal Data   Experts advise you to leave personal interests off your résumé—unless including them enhances the employer's understanding of why you would be the best candidate for the job.[16] For instance, candidates applying for a bodyguard position with Pinkerton's security division may want to list martial arts achievements among their personal interests. Or if you were applying for a sales position with Recreational Equipment Incorporated (REI), you might list outdoor activities to show how you would fit in with the organization's culture.

Provide only the personal data that will help you get the job.

Some information is best excluded from your résumé. Civil rights laws prohibit employers from discriminating on the basis of gender, marital or family status, age (although only persons aged 40 to 70 are protected), race, religion, national origin, and physical or mental disability. So be sure to exclude any items that could encourage discrimination. Experts also recommend excluding salary information, reasons for leaving jobs, names of previous supervisors, your Social Security number, and other identification codes. Save these items for the interview, and offer them only if the employer specifically requests them.

You may list military service in this section (or under "Education" or "Work Experience"). List the date of induction, the branch of service, where you served, the highest rank you achieved, any accomplishments related to your career goals, and the date you were discharged.

Avoid Résumé Deception

In an effort to put your best foot forward, you may be tempted to waltz around a few points that could raise questions about your résumé. Although statistics on the prevalence of résumé inflation are difficult to gather, the majority of recruiters agree that distortion is common. Avoid the most frequent forms of deception:[17]

Do not misrepresent your background or qualifications.

- **Do not claim educational credits you don't have.** Candidates may state (or imply) that they earned a degree when, in fact, they never attended the school or they attended but never completed the regular program. A typical claim might read, "Majored in business administration at Wayne State University."

- **Do not inflate your grade-point average.** Students who feel pressured to impress employers with their academic performance may claim a higher GPA than they actually achieved.

- **Do not stretch dates of employment to cover gaps.** Many candidates try to camouflage gaps in their work history by giving vague dates of employment. For example, a candidate who left a company in January 1992 and joined another in December 1993 might cover up by showing that the first job ended in 1992 and the next began in 1993.

- **Do not falsely claim to be self-employed.** Another common way people cover a period of unemployment is by saying that they were "self-employed" or a "consultant." The candidate claims to have operated an independent business during the period in question.

- **Do not claim to have worked for companies that are out of business.** Candidates who need to fill a gap in their work record sometimes say they worked for a firm that has gone out of business. Checking such claims is difficult because the people who were involved in the disbanded business are hard to track down.

- **Do not omit jobs that might cause embarrassment.** Being fired from one or two jobs is understandable when corporate mergers and downsizing are commonplace. However, a candidate who has lost several jobs in quick succession may seem a poor employee to recruiters. To cover a string of job losses, candidates may decide to leave out a few positions and stretch the dates of employment for the jobs held before and after.

• **Do not exaggerate expertise or experience.** Candidates often inflate their accomplishments by using verbs somewhat loosely. Words such as *supervised, managed, increased, improved,* and *created* imply that the candidate was personally responsible for results that, in reality, were the outcome of a group effort.

Think twice before trying one of these ploys yourself. If you misrepresent your background and your résumé raises suspicion, you will probably get caught, and your reputation will be damaged. A deceptive résumé can seriously affect your ability to get hired and pursue your career.

Experienced recruiters are familiar with the games that candidates play to enhance their image. Many employers fire people who lied on their résumés, and companies today are hiring highly skilled investigators who can access much-improved databases to seek the truth. Sure, it's fine to present your strongest, most impressive qualifications and to minimize your weaknesses. But don't exaggerate, alter the past, or claim to have skills you don't have (see Table 14–3).

COMPLETING YOUR RÉSUMÉ

The last step in the three-step writing process is no less important than the other two. As with any other business message, you need to revise your résumé, produce it in an appropriate form, and proofread it for any errors. For résumés, you'll also be concerned with submitting electronic versions and building online versions.

Revising Your Résumé

The "perfect" résumé responds to the reader's needs and preferences and avoids some common faults.

The key to writing a successful résumé is to adopt the "you" attitude and focus on your audience. Think about what the prospective employer needs, and then tailor your résumé accordingly. Recruiters at organizations such as Ford Motor Company read thousands of résumés every year, and they complain about résumés that are:

• **Too long.** The résumé is not concise, relevant, and to the point.

• **Too short or sketchy.** The résumé does not give enough information for a proper evaluation of the applicant.

Table 14–3	HOW FAR CAN YOU GO TO MAKE YOUR RÉSUMÉ STRONG AND POSITIVE?
Do	*Don't*
☑ **Tell the truth.** If you lie, you will almost certainly get caught, and the damage to your career could be significant.	⊗ **Fabricate.** Fake academic degrees and nonexistent jobs are checked first and will cost you the job, before or after you're hired.
☑ **Make your story positive.** Most blemishes on your record can be framed in a positive way.	⊗ **Make blatant omissions.** Failing to disclose a job that didn't work out is almost as bad as making one up.
☑ **Sanitize your record.** Clear up unresolved issues such as tax liens and lawsuits.	⊗ **Exaggerate successes.** Be ready to prove any claim about your accomplishments.
☑ **Think small.** Candidates with criminal histories or other career impediments should focus on smaller companies, which are less likely to conduct background checks.	⊗ **Go overboard.** There's usually no need to disclose career or personal history that's more than 15 years old. If asked directly, answer truthfully—but with a minimum of elaboration.

- **Hard to read.** A lack of "white space" and of devices such as indentions and bold-facing makes the reader's job more difficult.

- **Wordy.** Descriptions are verbose, with numerous words used for what could be said more simply.

- **Too slick.** The résumé appears to have been written by someone other than the applicant, which raises the question of whether the qualifications have been exaggerated.

- **Amateurish.** The applicant appears to have little understanding of the business world or of a particular industry, as revealed by including the wrong information or presenting it awkwardly.

- **Poorly reproduced.** The print is faint and difficult to read.

- **Misspelled and ungrammatical throughout.** Recruiters conclude that candidates who make spelling and grammar mistakes lack good verbal skills, which are important on the job.

- **Boastful.** The overconfident tone makes the reader wonder whether the applicant's self-evaluation is realistic.

- **Dishonest.** The applicant claims to have expertise or work experience that he or she does not possess.

- **Gimmicky.** The words, structure, decoration, or material used in the résumé depart so far from the usual as to make the résumé ineffective.

Compare the final version of your résumé with the suggestions in the "Checklist: Writing Résumés."

Producing Your Traditional Résumé

With less than a minute to make a good impression, your résumé needs to look sharp and grab a recruiter's interest in the first few lines. A typical recruiter devotes 45 seconds to each résumé before tossing it into either the "maybe" or the "reject" pile.[18] Most recruiters skim a résumé rather than read it from top to bottom. If yours doesn't stand out, chances are the recruiter won't look at it long enough to judge your qualifications.

To give your printed résumé the best appearance possible, use a clean typeface on high-grade, letter-size bond paper (in white or some light earth tone). Your stationery and envelope should match. Leave ample margins all around, and make sure that any corrections are unnoticeable. Avoid italic typefaces, which are difficult to read, and use a quality printer.

The length of your résumé depends on how much space you need in order to show what you can do. For entry-level positions, a one-page résumé may be just the ticket. If you have a great deal of experience and are applying for a higher-level position, you may need to prepare a somewhat longer résumé (and don't forget to head succeeding pages with your name and the page number). The important thing is to allow enough space to clearly portray your skills and accomplishments persuasively, accurately, and concisely.

Lay out your résumé to make information easy to grasp.[19] Break up the text with headings that call attention to various aspects of your background, such as work experience and education. Underline or capitalize key points, or set them off in the left margin. Use lists to itemize your most important qualifications, and leave plenty of white space, even if doing so forces you to use an extra page.

Under Jeff Taylor's guidance, Monster.com now lists more than 10 million résumés on its recruitment website.

✓ CHECKLIST: Writing Résumés

Planning Your Résumé

✓ Analyze your purpose and audience (both the organization and the individuals there).

✓ Gather all pertinent information, including work history (specific dates, duties, and accomplishments), educational experience, and personal endeavors.

✓ Adapt your résumé to your audience, combining your experiences into a straightforward message that communicates what you can do for your potential employer.

Organizing Your Résumé

✓ Use the chronological approach unless you have a weak employment history.

✓ Use the functional approach if you are new to the job market, want to redirect your career, or have gaps in your employment history.

✓ Use the combined approach to maximize the advantages of both chronological and functional résumés, but only when neither of the other two formats will work.

Composing Your Résumé in a Simple, Direct Style

✓ Use short noun phrases and action verbs, not whole sentences.

✓ Use facts, not opinions.

✓ Adopt a "you" attitude.

✓ Omit personal pronouns (especially *I*).

✓ Omit the date of preparation, desired salary, and work schedule.

✓ Use parallelism when listing multiple items.

✓ Use positive language and simple words.

✓ Use white space, quality paper, and quality printing.

Opening Your Résumé

✓ Include contact information (name, address).

✓ Include a career objective or a skills summary, if desired.

✓ Make your career objective specific and interesting.

✓ Prepare two separate résumés if you can perform two unrelated types of work.

✓ In a skills summary, present your strongest qualifications first.

Presenting Your Educational Background

✓ List the name and location of every postsecondary school you've attended (with dates, and with degrees/certificates obtained).

✓ Indicate your college major (and minor).

✓ Indicate numerical scale (4.0 or 5.0) if you include your grade-point average.

✓ List other experiences (seminars, workshops), with dates and certificates obtained.

Presenting Your Work Experience, Skills, and Accomplishments

✓ List all relevant work experience (paid employment, volunteer work, internships).

✓ List full-time and part-time jobs.

✓ Provide name and location of each employer (with dates of employment).

✓ List job title and describe responsibilities.

✓ Note on-the-job accomplishments and skills; quantify them whenever possible.

Describing Activities and Achievements

✓ List all relevant offices and leadership positions.

✓ List projects you have undertaken.

✓ Show abilities such as writing or speaking, and list publications and community service.

✓ List other information, such as your proficiency in languages other than English.

✓ Mention ability to operate special equipment, including technical, computer, and software skills.

Including Personal Data

✓ Omit personal details that might be seen as negative or used to discriminate against you.

✓ Leave personal interests off unless they enhance your value to potential employers.

✓ List a reference only with permission to do so.

Converting Your Traditional Résumé to an Electronic One

✓ Eliminate graphics, boldface, underlines, italics, small print, tabs, and all format codes.

✓ Save the file in plain-text (ASCII) format.

✓ Add blank spaces, align text, and use asterisks for bullets.

✓ Add a "Keyword Summary," listing nouns to define skills, experience, education, and professional attributes.

✓ Mirror the job description when possible.

✓ Add job-related jargon, but don't overdo it.

Building Your Online Résumé

✓ Provide your URL and e-mail address.

✓ Use a keyword hyperlink to an ASCII version so that employers can download it.

✓ Use a keyword hyperlink to a fully formatted résumé that can be read online and printed.

Converting Your Traditional Résumé to a Scannable Format

You need to format your résumé in at least two and maybe three ways: (1) as a traditional printed document (such as the one just discussed), (2) as a plain-text (or ASCII) document that can be scanned from a hard copy or submitted electronically, and (3) as an HTML-coded document that can be uploaded to the Internet to post on a webpage (should you choose to).

> Reformatting your traditional résumé is helpful if it will be scanned or if you will be posting it on the Internet or submitting it via e-mail.

Overwhelmed by the number of résumés they receive, most *Fortune* 1000 companies encourage applicants to submit electronic (scannable) résumés. Scannable résumés convey the same information as traditional résumés, but the format must be changed to one that is computer friendly, because scannable résumés are not intended to be read by humans. During the scanning process, special hardware and software are used to convert a paper résumé into an image on the employer's computer, which can be searched and sorted by keywords, criteria, or almost anything the employer wants (see Figure 14–7).

> A system with special software and hardware reads your scannable résumé and stores it in a database that can be searched by employers.

To make your traditional résumé a scannable one, format it as a plain-text (ASCII) document, improve its look, and modify its content slightly by providing a list of keywords and by balancing common language with current jargon.[20]

Prepare Your Résumé in ASCII Format   ASCII is a common plain-text language that allows your résumé to be read by any scanner and accessed by any computer, regardless of the word-processing software you used to prepare the document. All word-processing programs allow you to save files as plain text. To convert your résumé to an ASCII plain-text file, do the following:

> ASCII is a plain-text language that can be read by any computer, regardless of the word-processing software.

- Remove all formatting (boldfacing, underlining, italics, centering, bullets, graphic lines, etc.) and all formatting codes such as tab settings or tables.

FIGURE 14–7
Understanding the Scanning Process

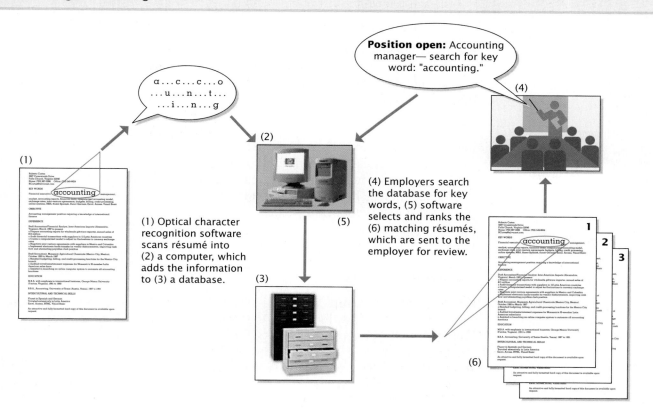

To make your scanable résumé computer friendly,
- Eliminate graphics
- Eliminate formatting codes
- Use a scannable typeface between 10 and 14 points

- Remove shadows and reverse print (white letters on black background).

- Remove graphics and boxes.

- Use scannable typefaces (such as Helvetica, Futura, Optima, Univers, Times New Roman, Palatino, New Century Schoolbook, and Courier).

- Use a font size of 10 to 14 points.

- Remove multicolumn formats that resemble newspapers or newsletters.

- Save your document under a different name by using your word processor's "save as" option and selecting "text only with line breaks."

Simple formatting improves the appearance of ASCII documents.

Improve the Look of Your Scannable Résumé   Résumés in ASCII format (without special formatting) look ugly in comparison to traditional résumés. Use the following formatting techniques (which are acceptable for scannable résumés) to enhance the résumé's overall look and effectiveness:[21]

- Align text by adding some blank spaces (rather than tabs).

- Create headings and separate paragraphs by adding a few blank lines.

- Indicate bullets with an asterisk or the lowercase letter *o.*

- Use white space so that scanners and computers can tell when one topic ends and another begins.

- Do not condense the spacing between letters.

- Use all capital letters for section headings (as long as the letters do not touch each other).

- Put your name at the top of each page on its own line (with no text appearing above or beside your name).

- Use the standard address format below your name.

- List each phone number on its own line.

- Use white or light-colored 8½-by-11-inch paper, printing on one side only.

Because scannable résumés are designed to be read by computers, it's fine to submit multiple pages—but don't get carried away. To increase your chances of a quality scan, do not fold or staple the résumé and do not send a photocopy. Provide a printed original, if possible.

Keywords help potential employers sort through an entire database of résumés.

Provide a List of Keywords   When converting your résumé to a scannable format, emphasize certain keywords to help potential employers select your résumé from the thousands they scan. Employers generally search for nouns (since verbs tend to be generic rather than specific to a particular position or skill). To maximize the number of matches (or hits), include a keyword summary of 20 to 30 words and phrases that define your skills, experience, education, professional affiliations, and so on. Place this list right after your name and address. Here's an example of a possible keyword summary for an accountant:

> ### Keyword Summary
>
> Accountant, Corporate Controller, *Fortune* 1000, Receivables, Payables, Inventory, Cash Flow, Financial Analysis, Payroll Experience, Corporate Taxes, Activity-Based Accounting, Problem Solving, Computer Skills, Excel, Access, Networks, HTML, Peachtree, Quick Books, BA Indiana University— Accounting, CPA, Dean's List, Articulate, Team Player, Flexible, Willing to Travel, Fluent Spanish

INTERPERSONAL KEYWORDS				Table 14–4
ability to delegate	communication skills	follow instructions	open-minded	self-accountable
ability to implement	competitive	follow through	oral communication	self-managing
ability to plan	conceptual ability	follow up	organizational skills	sensitive
ability to train	creative	high energy	persuasive	setting priorities
accurate	customer oriented	industrious	problem solving	supportive
adaptable	detail-minded	innovative	public speaking	takes initiative
aggressive work	empowering others	leadership	results oriented	team player
analytical ability	ethic	multitasking	risk taking	tenacious
assertive	flexible	open communication	safety conscious	willing to travel

One way to determine which keywords to include in your electronic summary is to underline all the skills listed in ads for the types of jobs you're interested in. Make sure these ads match your qualifications and experience. Although most employers search for keywords that tell whether you *can* do the job, some employers also look for keywords that tell whether you *will* do the job. These *interpersonal keywords* tell what kind of person you are (see Table 14–4).

Some job candidates try to beat the system by listing every conceivable skill and by guessing which words the computer is likely to be looking for. But that strategy seldom works. The computer may be looking for a Harvard Business School graduate who once worked at Netscape and now lives in Arizona. If you went to Yale, worked at Yahoo!, and live in Maine, you're out of luck.[22]

Balance Common Language with Current Jargon   Another way to maximize hits on your résumé is to use words that potential employers will understand (for example, use *keyboard*, not *input device*). Also, use abbreviations sparingly (except for common ones such as BA or MBA). At the same time, learn and use the important buzzwords in your field. Look for current jargon in the want ads of major newspapers such as the *Wall Street Journal* and in other résumés in your field that are posted online. Be careful to check and recheck the spelling, capitalization, and punctuation of any jargon you include, and use only those words you see most often.

Use words your employer will understand by including some jargon specific to your field.

Roberto Cortez created an electronic résumé by changing his formatting and adding a list of keywords. However, the information remains essentially the same and appears in the same order, as you can see in Figure 14–8. Now his target employers can scan his résumé into a database, and Cortez can submit his résumé via e-mail or post it on the Internet.

Proofreading Your Résumé

Bill Ford knows that a résumé is a concrete example of how someone will prepare material on the job. So in every format, remember to pay close attention to mechanics and details. Check all headings and lists for parallelism, and be sure that your grammar, spelling, and punctuation are correct.

Once your résumé is complete, update it continuously. As already mentioned, employment is becoming much more flexible these days, so it's likely you'll want to change employers at some point. Besides, you'll also need your résumé to apply for membership in professional organizations and to work toward a promotion, so keeping it updated is a good idea.

Keep your résumé up to date.

Removes all boldfacing, rules, bullets, and two-column formatting

Includes carefully selected keywords that describe Cortez's skills and accomplishments

Uses a lowercase letter o in bulleted lists

Singles Cortez out from the crowd by including in the keyword section specific attributes such as "team player" and "willing to travel"

Uses ample white space to make his plain-text résumé easier to scan

```
Roberto Cortez
5687 Crosswoods Drive
Falls Church, Virginia 22046
Home: (703) 987-0086    Office: (703) 549-6624
RCortez@silvernet.com

KEYWORDS

Financial executive, accounting management, international finance, financial
analyst, accounting reports, financial audit, computerized accounting model,
exchange rates, joint-venture agreements, budgets, billing, credit processing,
online systems, MBA, fluent Spanish, fluent German, Excel, Access, Visual Basic,
team player, willing to travel

OBJECTIVE

Accounting management position requiring a knowledge of international
finance

EXPERIENCE

Staff Accountant/Financial Analyst, Inter-American Imports (Alexandria,
Virginia), March 2000 to present
o Prepare accounting reports for wholesale giftware importer, annual sales of
$15 million
o Audit financial transactions with suppliers in 12 Latin American countries
o Created a computerized model to adjust for fluctuations in currency exchange
rates
o Negotiated joint-venture agreements with suppliers in Mexico and Colombia
o Implemented electronic funds transfer for vendor disbursements, improving
cash flow and eliminating payables clerk position

Staff Accountant, Monsanto Agricultural Chemicals (Mexico City, Mexico),
October 1996 to March 2000
o Handled budgeting, billing, and credit-processing functions for the Mexico
City branch
o Audited travel/entertainment expenses for Monsanto's 30-member Latin
American sales force
o Assisted in launching an online computer system to automate accounting

EDUCATION

Master of Business Administration with emphasis in international business,
George Mason University (Fairfax, Virginia), 1994 to 1996

Bachelor of Business Administration, Accounting, University of Texas (Austin,
Texas), 1991 to 1994

INTERCULTURAL AND TECHNICAL SKILLS

Fluent in Spanish and German
Traveled extensively in Latin America
Excel, Access, HTML, Visual Basic

An attractive and fully formatted hard copy of this document is available upon
request.
```

FIGURE 14–8
Effective Electronic Résumé

Submitting Scannable Résumés

E-mail is the best way to transmit your plain-text résumé.

If an employer gives you an option of submitting a scannable résumé by mail, by fax, or by e-mail, choose e-mail. E-mail puts your résumé directly into the employer's database, bypassing the scanning process. If you send your résumé in a paper format by regular mail or by fax, you run the risk that an OCR scanning program will create an error when reading it. In fact, increasing numbers of job applicants are submitting both a traditional and a scannable résumé, explaining in their cover letter that the scannable résumé is for downloading into a database if the company desires.[23]

When submitting your résumé by e-mail, find out how the company wants to receive it. Many human resources departments won't accept attached files; they're concerned about computer viruses. If preferred, you can paste your résumé into the body of your e-mail message. Whenever you know a reference number or a job ad number, include it in your e-mail subject line.

If you're posting your scannable résumé to an employer's online résumé builder, copy and paste the appropriate sections from your electronic file directly into the employer's form. This method avoids rekeying and eliminates errors.

If you fax your scannable résumé, set your machine to "fine" mode (to ensure a high-quality printout on the receiving end). If you're mailing your résumé, you may want to send both a well-designed traditional résumé and a scannable one. Simply attach Post-it notes, labeling one "visual résumé" and the other "scannable résumé."

Document Makeover

IMPROVE THIS RÉSUMÉ

To practice correcting drafts of actual documents, visit **www.prenhall.com/onekey** on the web. Click "Document Makeovers," then click Chapter 14. You will find a résumé that contains problems and errors relating to what you've learned in this chapter about writing effective résumés and application letters. Use the Final Draft decision tool to create an improved version of this document. Check the résumé for spelling and grammatical errors, effective use of verbs and pronouns, inclusion of unnecessary information, or omission of important facts.

Building an Online Résumé

If you wish to post your résumé on your webpage, provide employers with your URL; most recruiters won't take the time to use search engines to find your site.[24] As you design your website résumé, think of important keywords to use as hyperlinks—words that will grab an employer's attention and make the recruiter want to click on that hyperlink to learn more about you. You can make links to papers you've written, recommendations, and sound or video clips. Don't distract potential employers from your credentials by using hyperlinks to organizations or other websites.

To post your résumé with an index service, you must convert it to an electronic format (see page 497) and transmit it by mail, fax, modem, or e-mail. Once your résumé is in the service's database, it is sent to employers who match the keywords you've listed.

Do not use photos, and avoid providing information that reveals your age, gender, race, marital status, or religion. Because a website is a public access area, you should also leave out the names of references and previous employers. Either mention that references are available on request, or say nothing. Finally, include an ASCII version of your résumé on your webpage so that prospective employers can download it into their company's database.

One advantage of posting your résumé on your website is the opportunity to use hyperlinks.

JobDirect.com is a leading job-search site for college and entry-level professional positions, with résumé matching and daily e-mails to students.

PREPARING OTHER TYPES OF EMPLOYMENT MESSAGES

Although your résumé will take the greatest amount of time and effort, you'll need to prepare other employment messages as well, including application letters, job-inquiry letters, and application follow-ups.

Application Letters

Whenever you submit your résumé, accompany it with a cover, or application, letter to let readers know what you're sending, why you're sending it, and how they can benefit from reading it. Because your application letter is in your own style (rather than the choppy, shorthand style of your résumé), it gives you a chance to show your communication skills and some personality.

Always send your résumé and application letter together, because each has a unique job to perform. The purpose of your résumé is to get employers interested enough to contact you for an interview. The purpose of your application letter is to get employers interested enough to read your résumé.

Before drafting a letter, learn something about the organization you're applying to; then focus on your audience so that you can show you've done your homework. Imagine yourself in the recruiter's situation, and show how your background and talents will solve a particular problem or fill a specific need the company has. The more you can learn about the organization, the better you'll be able to capture the reader's attention and convey your interest in the company.[25] During your research, find out the name, title, and department of the person you're writing to. Reaching and addressing the right person is the most effective way to gain attention. Avoid phrases such as "To Whom It May Concern" and "Dear Sir."

When putting yourself in your reader's shoes, remember that this person's in-box is probably overflowing with résumés and cover letters. So respect your reader's time. Steer clear of gimmicks, which almost never work, and include nothing in your cover letter that already appears in your résumé. Keep your letter straightforward, fact based, short, upbeat, and professional. Some quick tips for cover letters include the following:[26]

- **Be specific.** Avoid general objectives. Be as clear as possible about the kind of opportunity and industry you're looking for.

- **Include salary.** If you've been working in your field, include your current salary, but make sure your reader understands that this information is not a demand but intended to inform and assist.

- **Make e-mail covers even shorter.** When sending a cover letter by e-mail, make it a bit shorter than traditional application letters. Remember, e-mail readers want the gist very quickly.

- **Aim for high quality.** Meticulously check your spelling, mechanics, and grammar. Recruiters are complaining about the declining quality of written communication, including cover letters.

Bill Ford will tell you that a good application letter is no longer than three paragraphs. Maintain a friendly yet conversational tone, and highlight the specific points the company is looking for. To sell the employer on you, show that you know the job.

If you're sending a **solicited application letter**—in response to an announced job opening—you'll usually know what qualifications the organization is seeking. You'll also have more competition because hundreds of other job seekers will have seen the listing and may be sending applications too. The letter in Figure 14–9 was written in response to a help-wanted ad. Kenneth Sawyer highlights his chief qualifications and mirrors the requirements specified in the ad. He actually grabs attention by focusing on the phrase "proven skills" used in the ad: He elaborates on his own proven skills throughout the letter and even mentions the term in the closing paragraph.

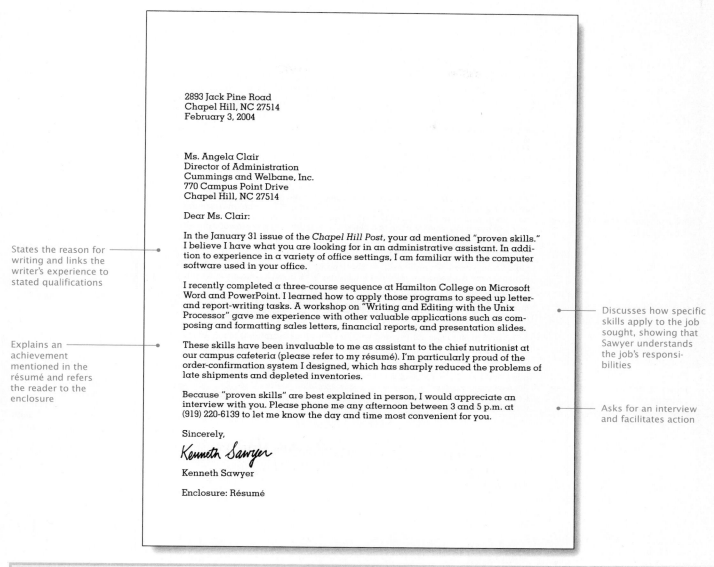

States the reason for writing and links the writer's experience to stated qualifications

Explains an achievement mentioned in the résumé and refers the reader to the enclosure

2893 Jack Pine Road
Chapel Hill, NC 27514
February 3, 2004

Ms. Angela Clair
Director of Administration
Cummings and Welbane, Inc.
770 Campus Point Drive
Chapel Hill, NC 27514

Dear Ms. Clair:

In the January 31 issue of the *Chapel Hill Post*, your ad mentioned "proven skills." I believe I have what you are looking for in an administrative assistant. In addition to experience in a variety of office settings, I am familiar with the computer software used in your office.

I recently completed a three-course sequence at Hamilton College on Microsoft Word and PowerPoint. I learned how to apply those programs to speed up letter- and report-writing tasks. A workshop on "Writing and Editing with the Unix Processor" gave me experience with other valuable applications such as composing and formatting sales letters, financial reports, and presentation slides.

These skills have been invaluable to me as assistant to the chief nutritionist at our campus cafeteria (please refer to my résumé). I'm particularly proud of the order-confirmation system I designed, which has sharply reduced the problems of late shipments and depleted inventories.

Because "proven skills" are best explained in person, I would appreciate an interview with you. Please phone me any afternoon between 3 and 5 p.m. at (919) 220-6139 to let me know the day and time most convenient for you.

Sincerely,

Kenneth Sawyer

Kenneth Sawyer

Enclosure: Résumé

Discusses how specific skills apply to the job sought, showing that Sawyer understands the job's responsibilities

Asks for an interview and facilitates action

FIGURE 14–9
Effective Solicited Application Letter

In some respects, an **unsolicited letter**—sent to an organization that has not announced an opening—stands a better chance of being read and receiving individualized attention. Glenda Johns wrote the unsolicited application letter in Figure 14–10. She manages to give a snapshot of her qualifications and skills without repeating what is said in her résumé (which appears in Figure 14–5). She gains attention by focusing on the needs of the employer.

Like your résumé, your application letter is a form of advertising, so organize it as you would a sales letter: Use the AIDA approach, focus on your audience, and emphasize reader benefits (as discussed in Chapter 9). Make sure your style projects confidence. To sell a potential employer on your merits, you must believe in them and sound as though you do.

Both solicited and unsolicited letters present your qualifications similarly. The main difference is in the opening paragraph. In a solicited letter, you need no special

You write an unsolicited application letter to an organization that has not announced a job opening.

Follow the AIDA approach when writing your application letter: attention, interest, desire, action.

457 Mountain View Rd.
Clear Lake, IA 50428
June 16, 2004

Ms. Patricia Downings, Store Manager
Wal-Mart
840 South Oak
Iowa Falls, IA 50126

Dear Ms. Downings:

Gains attention in the first paragraph → You want retail clerks and managers who are accurate, enthusiastic, and experienced. You want someone who cares about customer service, who understands merchandising, and who can work with others to get the job done. When you're ready to hire a manager trainee or a clerk who is willing to work toward promotion, please consider me for the job.

Working as a clerk and then as an assistant department manager in a large department store has taught me how challenging a career in retailing can be. Moreover, my AA degree in retailing (including work in such courses as retailing, marketing, and business information systems) will provide your store with a well-rounded associate. Most important, I can offer Wal-Mart's Iowa Falls store more than my two years of study and field experience, which taught me how to anticipate customer problems and deliver the type of service that keeps customers coming back. You'll find that I'm interested in every facet of retailing, eager to take on responsibility, and willing to continue learning throughout my career. Please look over my résumé to see how my skills can benefit your store. ← *Points out personal qualities that aren't specifically stated in her résumé*

Interests reader with knowledge of the company's policy toward promotion → I understand that Wal-Mart prefers to promote its managers from within the company, and I would be pleased to start out with an entry-level position until I gain the necessary experience. Do you have any associate positions opening up soon? Could we discuss my qualifications? I will phone you early next Wednesday to arrange a meeting at your convenience. ← *Focuses on the audience and displays the "you" attitude, even though the last paragraph uses the word "I"*

Sincerely,

Glenda Johns
Glenda Johns

Enclosure

FIGURE 14–10
Effective Unsolicited Application Letter

attention-getter because you have been invited to apply. In an unsolicited letter, you need to start by capturing the reader's attention and interest.

Getting Attention Table 14–5 highlights some important ways to spark interest and grab attention in your opening paragraph. All these examples demonstrate the "you" attitude, and many indicate how the applicant can serve the employer. The opening paragraph of your application letter must also state your reason for writing and the position you are applying for. You can give your reason in one of these ways:

The opening of an application letter captures attention, gives the reason you're writing, and states which job you're applying for.

> **Please** consider my application for an entry-level position in technical writing.

> Your firm advertised a fleet sales position (on September 23, 2002, in the *Baltimore Sun*). With my 16 months of new-car sales experience, won't you consider me for that position?

TIPS FOR GETTING ATTENTION IN APPLICATION LETTERS   Table 14–5

Tip	Example
Unsolicited Application Letters	
• Show how your strongest skills will benefit the organization. A 20-year-old in her third year of college might begin like this:	When you need a secretary in your export division who can take shorthand at 125 words a minute and transcribe notes at 70—in English, Spanish, or Portuguese—call me.
• Describe your understanding of the job's requirements and then show how well your qualifications fit them.	Your annual report states that Mobil Corporation runs employee-training programs about workforce diversity. The difficulties involved in running such programs can be significant, as I learned while tutoring inner-city high school students last summer. My 12 pupils were enrolled in vocational training programs and came from diverse ethnic and racial backgrounds. The one thing they had in common was a lack of familiarity with the typical employer's expectations. To help them learn the "rules of the game," I developed exercises that cast them in various roles: boss, customer, new recruit, and co-worker. Of the 12 students, 10 subsequently found full-time jobs and have called or written to tell me how much they gained from the workshop.
• Mention the name of a person known to and highly regarded by the reader.	When Janice McHugh of your franchise sales division spoke to our business communication class last week, she said you often need promising new marketing graduates at this time of year.
• Refer to publicized company activities, achievements, changes, or new procedures.	Today's issue of the *Detroit News* reports that you may need the expertise of computer programmers versed in robotics when your Lansing tire plant automates this spring.
• Use a question to demonstrate your understanding of the organization's needs.	Can your fast-growing market research division use an interviewer with 1½ years of field survey experience, a B.A. in public relations, and a real desire to succeed? If so, please consider me for the position.
• Use a catchphrase opening if the job requires ingenuity and imagination.	*Haut monde*—whether said in French, Italian, or Arabic, it still means "high society." As an interior designer for your Beverly Hills showroom, not only could I serve and sell to your distinguished clientele, but I could do it in all these languages. I speak, read, and write them fluently.
Solicited Application Letters	
• Identify the publication in which the ad ran; then describe what you have to offer.	Your ad in the April issue of *Travel & Leisure* for a cruise-line social director caught my eye. My eight years of experience as a social director in the travel industry would allow me to serve your new Caribbean cruise division well.

Another way to state your reason for writing is to use a title at the opening of your letter:

Subject: Application for bookkeeper position

Building Interest and Increasing Desire   The middle section of your application letter presents your strongest selling points in terms of their potential benefit to the organization, thereby building interest in you and creating a desire to interview you. If you already mentioned your selling points in the opening, don't repeat them. Simply give supporting evidence. Be careful not to repeat the facts presented in your résumé; simply interpret those facts for the reader. Otherwise, spell out a few of your key qualifications, and back up your assertions with some convincing evidence of your ability to perform:

The middle section of an application letter:
• Summarizes your relevant qualifications
• Emphasizes your accomplishments
• Suggests desirable personal qualities
• Justifies salary requirements
• Refers to your résumé

- **Poor:** I completed three college courses in business communication, earning an A in each course, and have worked for the past year at Imperial Construction.

- **Improved:** Using the skills gained from three semesters of college training in business communication, I developed a system of collection letters for Imperial Construction. Instead of using timeworn terminology, the new letters offered discount incentives for speedy payment. The collections system reduced the company's 2001 bad-debt losses by 3.7 percent, or $9,902, over those of 2000.

- **Improved:** Experience in customer relations and college courses in public relations have taught me how to handle the problem-solving tasks that arise in a leading retail clothing firm like yours. Such important tasks include identifying and resolving customer complaints, writing letters that build good customer relations, and above all, promoting the organization's positive image.

When writing a solicited letter responding to an advertisement, be sure to discuss each requirement specified in the ad. If you are deficient in any of these requirements, stress other solid selling points to help strengthen your overall presentation.

The middle of your application letter also demonstrates a few significant job-related qualities, such as your diligence or your ability to work hard, learn quickly, handle responsibility, or get along with people:

While attending college full-time, I trained 3 hours a day with the varsity track team. In addition, I worked part-time during the school year and up to 60 hours a week each summer in order to be totally self-supporting while in college. I can offer your organization the same level of effort and perseverance.

You might also bring up your salary requirements in this section —but *only* if the organization has asked you to state them. Unless you know approximately what the job pays, suggest a salary range, or indicate that the salary is negotiable or open. You might consult the latest government "Area Wage Survey" at the library to get an idea of the salary range for various job classifications and geographic areas. If you do state a target salary, tie it to the benefits you would bring to the organization (much as you would handle price in a sales letter):

For the past two years, I have been helping a company similar to yours organize its database. I would therefore like to receive a salary in the same range (the mid-20s) for helping your company set up a more efficient customer database.

Toward the end of this section, refer the reader to your résumé by citing a specific fact or general point covered there:

You will find my people skills an asset. As you can see in the attached résumé, I've been working part-time with a local publisher since my sophomore year, and during that time, I have successfully resolved more than a few "client crises."

Close by asking for an interview and making the interview easy to arrange.

Motivating Action   The final paragraph of your application letter has two important functions: to ask the reader for a specific action and to make a reply easy. In almost all cases, the action you request is an interview. However, don't demand it; try to sound natural and appreciative. Offer to come to the employer's office at a convenient time or, if the firm is some distance away, to meet with its nearest representative. Make the request easy to fulfill by stating your phone number and the best time to reach you—or, if you wish to be in control, by mentioning that you will follow up with a phone call in a few days. Refer again to your strongest selling point and, if desired, your date of availability:

After you have reviewed my qualifications, could we discuss the possibility of putting my marketing skills to work for your company? Because I will be on spring break the week of March 8, I would like to arrange a time to talk then. I will call in late February to schedule a convenient time when we could discuss employment opportunities at your company.

Once you have edited and proofread your application letter, mail it and your résumé promptly, especially if they have been solicited.

Adapting Style and Approach to Culture   The AIDA approach isn't appropriate for job seekers in every culture. If you're applying for a job abroad or want to work with a subsidiary of an organization based in another country, you may need to adjust your tone. Blatant self-promotion is considered bad form in some cultures. Other cultures stress group performance over individual contributions. As for format, recruiters in some countries (including France) prefer handwritten letters to printed or typed ones—another good reason to research a company carefully before drafting your application letter. For U.S. and Canadian companies, let your letter reflect your personal style. Be yourself, but be businesslike too; avoid sounding cute. Don't use slang or a gimmicky layout. Compare your own letters with the tasks in "Checklist: Writing Application Letters."

You may need to vary your approach according to your reader's culture.

Job-Inquiry Letters

Before considering you for a position, some organizations require you to fill out and submit an **application form**, a standardized data sheet that simplifies the comparison

✓ CHECKLIST: Writing Application Letters

Attention (Opening Paragraph)

- ✓ Open the letter by capturing the reader's attention in a businesslike way.
- ✓ Use your strongest skills, the job's requirements, an employee's name, company activities, a question that demonstrates your understanding of the company's needs, and so on.
- ✓ State that you are applying for a job, and identify the position or the type of work you seek.

Interest and Desire (Middle Paragraph)

- ✓ Present your key qualifications for the job, highlighting what is on your résumé: job-related education and training; relevant work experience; and related activities, interests, and qualities.
- ✓ Adopt a mature, businesslike tone.
- ✓ Eliminate boasting and exaggeration.
- ✓ Back up your claims by citing specific achievements in educational, work, and outside settings.
- ✓ Demonstrate your knowledge of the organization by citing its operations or trends in the industry.
- ✓ Link your education, experience, and personal qualities to the job requirements.

- ✓ Relate aspects of your training or work experience to those of the target position.
- ✓ Outline your educational preparation for the job.
- ✓ Provide evidence that you can learn quickly, work hard, handle responsibility, and get along with others.
- ✓ Show that you possess personal qualities and work attitudes that are desirable for job performance.
- ✓ If asked to state salary requirements in your letter, state current salary or a desired salary range, and link it to the benefits of hiring you.
- ✓ Refer the reader to the enclosed résumé.

Action (Closing Paragraph)

- ✓ Request an interview at the reader's convenience.
- ✓ Request a screening interview with the nearest regional representative, if company headquarters is some distance away.
- ✓ Make it easy to comply with your request by providing your phone number (with area code) and stating the best time to reach you, or mention a time when you will be calling to set up an interview.
- ✓ Express your appreciation for an opportunity to have an interview.
- ✓ Repeat your strongest qualification, to reinforce your claim that you can contribute to the organization.

Use a job-inquiry letter to request an application form, which is a standardized data sheet that simplifies comparison of applicants' credentials.

of applicants' qualifications. To request such a form, send a job-inquiry letter and include enough information about yourself in the letter to show that you have at least some of the requirements for the position you are seeking:

> Please send me an application form for work as an interior designer in your home furnishings department. For my certificate in design, I took courses in retail merchandising and customer relations. I have also had part-time sales experience at Capwell's department store.

Instead of writing a letter of this kind, you may want to drop in at the office you're applying to. You probably won't be able to talk to anyone other than the receptionist or a human resources assistant, but you can pick up the form, get an impression of the organization, and demonstrate your initiative and energy.

Your care in filling out application forms suggests to the employer that you will be thorough and careful in your work.

Organizations will use your application form as a convenient one-page source for information about your qualifications, so try to be thorough and accurate when filling it out. Have your résumé with you to remind yourself of important information, and if you can't remember something and have no record of it, provide the closest estimate possible. If you cannot provide some information because you have no such background (military experience, for example), write "Not applicable." When filling out applications, use a pen (unless specifically requested to use a pencil) and print legibly.

Application forms rarely give you enough space or ask you the right questions to reflect your skills and abilities accurately. Nevertheless, show your cooperation by doing your best to fill out the form completely. If you get an interview, you'll have an opportunity to fill in the gaps. You can also ask whether you might submit a résumé and an application letter along with the application.

Application Follow-Ups

Use a follow-up letter to let the employer know you're still interested in the job.

If your application letter and résumé fail to bring a response within a month or so, follow up with a second letter to keep your file active. This follow-up letter also gives you a chance to update your original application with any recent job-related information:

> Since applying to you on May 3 for an executive secretary position, I have completed a course in office management at South River Community College. I received straight A's in the course. I now am a proficient user of MS Word, including macros and other complex functions.
>
> Please keep my application in your active file, and let me know when you need a skilled executive secretary.

Even if you've received a letter acknowledging your application and saying that it will be kept on file, don't hesitate to send a follow-up letter three months later to show that you are still interested:

> Three months have elapsed since I applied to you for an underwriting position, and I am still very interested in joining your company.
>
> I recently completed a four-week temporary work assignment at a large local insurance agency. I learned several new verification techniques and gained experience in using the online computer system. This experience could increase my value to your underwriting department.
>
> Please keep my application in your active file, and let me know when a position opens for a capable underwriter.

Unless you state otherwise, the human resources office is likely to assume that you've already found a job and are no longer interested in the organization. Moreover, requirements change. A follow-up letter can demonstrate that you're sincerely interested in working for the organization, that you're persistent in pursuing your goals, and that you're upgrading your skills to make yourself a better employee. It might just get you an interview.

On the Job:

SOLVING COMMUNICATION DILEMMAS AT FORD MOTOR COMPANY

CEO Bill Ford says, "Employees are the only sustainable competitive advantage that any company has. I want the company to succeed, and to do that, we need to get the best people." As a member of Ford's human resources department, you regularly review résumés that are attached to the web-based personal assessments. You have received assessments and résumés from four people. Give your team leader your best advice about the following applicants, and be prepared to explain your recommendations.

1. Of the career objectives that were listed on these résumés, which of the following is the most effective?

   a. An entry-level management position in a large company.

   b. To invest my management talent and business savvy in shepherding Ford Motor Company toward explosive growth.

   c. A management position in which my degree in business administration and my experience in managing personnel will be useful.

   d. To learn all I can about personnel management in an exciting environment with a company whose reputation is as outstanding as Ford's.

2. Of the education sections included in the résumés, which of the following is the most effective?

   a. **Morehouse College, Atlanta, GA, 1994–1998.** Received BA degree with a major in Business Administration and a minor in Finance. Graduated with a 3.65 grade-point average. Played varsity football and basketball. Worked 15 hours per week in the library. Coordinated the local student chapter of the American Management Association. Member of Alpha Phi Alpha social fraternity.

   b. I attended Wayne State University in Detroit, Michigan, for two years and then transferred to the University of Michigan at Ann Arbor, where I completed my studies. My major was economics, but I also took many business management courses, including employee motivation, small business administration, history of business start-ups, and organizational behavior. I selected courses based on the professors' reputation for excellence, and I received mostly A's and B's. Unlike many college students, I viewed the acquisition of knowledge—rather than career preparation—as my primary goal. I believe I have received a well-rounded education that has prepared me to approach management situations as problem-solving exercises.

   c. **University of Connecticut, Storrs, Connecticut.** Graduated with a BA degree in 1997. Majored in Physical Education. Minored in Business Administration. Graduated with a 2.85 average.

   d. **North Texas State University and University of Texas at Tyler.** Received BA and MBA degrees. I majored in business as an undergraduate and concentrated in manufacturing management during my MBA program. Received a special $2,500 scholarship offered by Rotary International recognizing academic achievement in business courses. I also won the MEGA award in 1995. Dean's list.

3. Based only on their experience, which of the following four candidates would you recommend to your team leader?

   a. **McDonald's, Peoria, IL, 1992–1993.** Part-time cook. Worked 15 hours per week while attending high school. Prepared hamburgers, chicken bits, and french fries. Received employee-of-the-month award for outstanding work habits.

   University Grill, Ames, IA, 1993–1996. Part-time cook. Worked 20 hours per week while attending college. Prepared hot and cold sandwiches. Helped manager purchase ingredients. Trained new kitchen workers. Prepared work schedules for kitchen staff.

   b. Although I have never held a full-time job, I have worked part-time and during summer vacations throughout my high school and college years. During my freshman and sophomore years in high school, I bagged groceries at the A&P store three afternoons a week. The work was not terribly challenging, but I liked the customers and the other employees. During my junior and senior years, I worked at the YMCA as an after-school counselor for elementary school children. The kids were really sweet, and I still get letters from some of them. During summer vacations while I was in college, I did construction work for a local homebuilder. The job paid well, and I also learned a lot about carpentry. The guys I worked with were a mixed bag who expanded my vocabulary and knowledge of the world. I also worked part-time in college in the student cafeteria, where I scooped food onto plates. This did not require much talent, but it taught me a lot about how people behave when standing in line. I also learned quite a bit about life from my boss, Sam "the man" Benson, who has been managing the student cafeteria for 25 years.

c. **The Broadway Department Store, Sherman Oaks, CA, Summers, 1997–2000.** Sales Consultant, Furniture Department. I interacted with a diverse group of customers, including suburban matrons, teenagers, career women, and professional couples. I endeavored to satisfy their individual needs and make their shopping experience memorable, efficient, and enjoyable. Under the direction of the sales manager, I helped prepare employee schedules and fill out departmental reports. I also helped manage the inventory, worked the cash register, and handled a variety of special orders and customer complaints with courtesy and aplomb. During the 1997 annual storewide sale, I sold more merchandise than any other salesperson in the entire furniture department.

d. **Belle Fleure, GA, Civilian Member of Public Safety Committee, January–December 2001.**
- Organized and promoted a lecture series on vacation safety and home security for the residents of Belle Fleure, GA; recruited and trained seven committee members to help plan and produce the lectures; persuaded local businesses to finance the program; designed, printed, and distributed flyers; wrote and distributed press releases; attracted an average of 120 people to each of three lectures
- Developed a questionnaire to determine local residents' home security needs; directed the efforts of 10 volunteers working on the survey; prepared written report for city council and delivered oral summary of findings at town meeting; helped persuade city to fund new home security program
- Initiated the Business Security Forum as an annual meeting at which local business leaders could meet to discuss safety and security issues; created promotional flyers for the first forum; convinced 19 business owners to fund a business security survey; arranged press coverage of the first forum

4. You've received the following résumé. What action will you take?

Maria Martin
1124 2nd S.W., Rhinelander, WI 54501
(715) 369–0098

Career Objective: To build a management career in a growing U.S. company

Summary of Qualifications: As a student at the University of Wisconsin in Madison, carried out various assignments that have required skills related to a career in management. For example:

Planning Skills. As president of the university's foreign affairs forum, organized six lectures and workshops featuring 36 speakers from 16 foreign countries within a nine-month period. Identified and recruited the speakers, handled their travel arrangements, and scheduled the facilities.

Interpersonal Skills. As chairman of the parade committee for homecoming weekend, worked with the city of Madison to obtain approval, permits, and traffic control for the parade. Also encouraged local organizations such as the Lion's Club, the Kiwanis Club, and the Boy Scouts to participate in the parade. Coordinated the efforts of the 15 fraternities and 18 sororities that entered floats in the parade. Recruited 12 marching bands from surrounding communities and coordinated their efforts with the university's marching band. Also arranged for local auto dealers to provide cars for the 10 homecoming queen candidates.

Communication Skills. Wrote over 25 essays and term papers dealing with academic topics. Received an A on all but two of these papers. As a senior, wrote a 20-page analysis of the paper products industry, interviewing the five top executives at the Rhinelander paper company. Received an A+ on this paper.

a. Definitely recommend that Ford take a look at this outstanding candidate.
b. Turn down the candidate. She doesn't give enough information about when she attended college, what she majored in, or where she has worked.
c. Review the candidate's web-based personal assessment. If the assessment contains the missing information and the candidate sounds promising, recommend her to your team leader. If vital information is still missing, send the candidate an e-mail (or place a message on her personal page at Ford), requesting additional information. Make the decision once you receive all necessary information.
d. Consider the candidate's qualifications relative to those of other applicants. Recommend her to your team leader if you do not have three or four other applicants with more directly relevant qualifications.[27]

Learning Objectives Checkup

To assess your understanding of the principles in this chapter, read each learning objective and study the accompanying exercises. For fill-in items, write the missing text in the blank provided; for multiple choice items, circle the letter of the correct answer. You can check your responses against the answer key on page AK-2–AK-3.

Objective 14.1: Discuss three ways that you can adapt to today's changing workplace.

1. Which of the following is *not* a good way to adapt to today's changing workplace?
   a. Analyze your talents and skills and how they will benefit potential employers.
   b. Determine the sorts of jobs that will bring you satisfaction and happiness.
   c. Pick the place you'd most like to work and stop at nothing until you get a job there.
   d. Take steps that will make you more valuable to potential employers.

Objective 14.2: Describe six ways to prepare for and successfully complete your search for employment.

2. To prepare for and successfully complete your job search, you should
   a. Keep on top of business and financial news
   b. Research specific companies that appeal to you
   c. Network both in person and online with potential job contacts
   d. Do all of the above

Objective 14.3: List three ways of organizing your résumé, and discuss the pros and cons of each one.

3. In a chronological résumé, you place _____ in the most prominent spot.
   a. The work-experience section
   b. The education section
   c. A list of skills and accomplishments
   d. Your career objective

4. In a functional résumé, you place _____ in the most prominent spot.
   a. The work-experience section
   b. The education section
   c. A list of skills and accomplishments
   d. Your career objective

5. The _____ résumé is the least commonly used, because it tends to be long and repetitive.
   a. Chronological
   b. Functional
   c. Combination
   d. Electronic

Objective 14.4: Identify the major elements of a traditional résumé.

6. The first element of your résumé should be
   a. The title "Résumé"
   b. Your name
   c. Your career objective
   d. Keywords

7. Listing a career objective
   a. Is mandatory
   b. Can limit you as a candidate because it labels you as being interested in only one thing
   c. Is preferable to including a "summary of qualifications"
   d. Does all of the above

8. The education section
   a. Begins with the school you most recently attended
   b. Should not list any off-campus seminars or workshops you've attended
   c. Is emphasized in a chronologically organized résumé
   d. Encompasses all of the above

9. Which of the following does *not* use effective wording for résumé content?
   a. Supervised and trained staff of four sales clerks
   b. Created new method for processing deliveries that saved 10 man-hours per week
   c. Ran audio-visual department at my school
   d. Taught two-day seminar on Photoshop for six other employees

10. Which of the following is the preferred way to handle references?
    a. You should include a section headed "References" and list the names and contact information of your references.
    b. You should include a list of names and then add "Complete references available on request."
    c. You should simply state "References available on request."
    d. You do not need to mention references, since the availability of references is generally assumed.

11. In the "Personal Data" section of your résumé, you should list
    a. Your age
    b. Any military service, if you haven't listed it elsewhere on the résumé
    c. Any disabilities you may have
    d. Your marital status
    e. All of the above

Objective 14.5: Explain seven ways you can avoid deception in your résumé.

12. Most job recruiters agree that it is okay for job applicants to
    a. State that they received a degree when they didn't complete their college program
    b. Stretch dates of employment to cover gaps
    c. Omit jobs that might cause embarrassment
    d. Do all of the above

Objective 14.6: Describe how to produce a traditional résumé and what you can do to adapt it to a scannable format.

13. When producing a traditional résumé, do *not*
    a. Use high-grade, letter-size bond paper with matching envelope
    b. Include itemized lists and plenty of white space
    c. Use italic typefaces to make the document more readable
    d. Use headings, underlining, or boldfacing to set off key points

14. How long should your résumé be?
    a. No longer than one page
    b. No longer than two pages
    c. As long as three pages
    d. As long as it needs to be

15. To make your traditional résumé a scannable one, you need to format it as _____ document.
    a. An ASCII
    b. A Word
    c. An HTML
    d. A Quark or Pagemaker

16. When converting your résumé to a scannable format, you should provide _____ summary to help employers when they conduct a search.
    a. An ASCII
    b. A keyword
    c. A qualifications
    d. An education

17. When building an online résumé, you need to
    a. Link to helpful professional organizations and other websites
    b. Think of important keywords to use as hyperlinks
    c. Include plenty of photos
    d. Include your age, marital status, and religion

Objective 14.7: Define the purpose of an application letter, and explain how to apply the AIDA organizational approach to it.

18. The purpose of an application letter is to
    a. Include the information from your résumé, in case the employer doesn't read the résumé
    b. Take the place of a résumé
    c. Get the employer interested enough to read your résumé
    d. Get the employer interested enough to contact you for an interview

19. In an unsolicited application letter, you begin
    a. By stating your name
    b. With a buffer
    c. With an attention-getter
    d. By stating that you've enclosed your résumé

20. In the middle section of your application letter, you
    a. Present your strongest selling points
    b. State the salary you expect to receive
    c. List all the key education and work-experience items from your résumé
    d. Do all of the above

Apply Your Knowledge

1. According to experts in the job placement field, the average job seeker relies too heavily on the résumé and not enough on other elements of the job search. Which elements do you think are most important? Please explain.

2. One of the disadvantages of résumé scanning is that some qualified applicants will be missed because the technology isn't perfect. However, more companies are using this approach. Do you think that résumé scanning is a good idea? Please explain.

3. Stating your career objective on a résumé or application might limit your opportunities by labeling you too narrowly. Not stating your objective, however, might lead an employer to categorize you incorrectly. Which outcome is riskier? Do summaries of qualifications overcome such drawbacks? If so, how? Explain briefly.

4. When writing a solicited application letter and describing the skills requested in the employer's ad, how can you avoid using *I* too often? Explain and give examples.

5. **Ethical Choices** Between your sophomore and junior years, you quit school for a year to earn the money to finish college. You worked as a clerk in a finance company, checking references on loan applications, typing, and filing. Your manager made a lot of the fact that he had never attended college. He seemed to resent you for pursuing your education, but he never criticized your work, so you thought you were doing okay. After you'd been working there for six months, he fired you, saying that you failed to be thorough enough in your credit checks. You were actually glad to leave, and you found another job right away at a bank doing similar duties. Now that you've graduated from college, you're writing your résumé. Will you include the finance company job in your work history? Please explain.

Practice Your Knowledge

DOCUMENTS FOR ANALYSIS

Read the following documents; then (1) analyze the strengths or weaknesses of each document and (2) revise each document so that it follows the guidelines presented in this chapter.

DOCUMENT 14.A: WRITING A RÉSUMÉ

Sylvia Manchester
765 Belle Fleur Blvd.
New Orleans, LA 70113
(504) 312–9504
smanchester@rcnmail.com

PERSONAL: Single, excellent health, 5'8", 116 lbs.; hobbies include cooking, dancing, and reading.

JOB OBJECTIVE: To obtain a responsible position in marketing or sales with a good company.

EDUCATION: BA degree in biology, University of Louisiana. Graduated with a 3.0 average. Member of the varsity cheerleading squad. President of Panhellenic League. Homecoming queen.

WORK EXPERIENCE   *Fisher Scientific Instruments, 2000 to present, field sales representative.* Responsible for calling on customers and explaining the features of Fisher's line of laboratory instruments. Also responsible for writing sales letters, attending trade shows, and preparing weekly sales reports.

Fisher Scientific Instruments, 1997–99, customer service representative. Was responsible for handling incoming phone calls from customers who had questions about delivery, quality, or operation of Fisher's line of laboratory instruments. Also handled miscellaneous correspondence with customers.

Medical Electronics, Inc., 1994–97, administrative assistant to the vice president of marketing. In addition to handling typical secretarial chores for the vice president of marketing, I was in charge of compiling the monthly sales reports, using figures provided by members of the field sales force. I also was given responsibility for doing various market research activities.

New Orleans Convention and Visitors Bureau, 1991–94, summers, tour guide. During the summers of my college years, I led tours of New Orleans for tourists visiting the city. My duties included greeting conventioneers and their spouses at hotels, explaining the history and features of the city during an all-day sight-seeing tour, and answering questions about New Orleans and its attractions. During my fourth summer with the bureau, I was asked to help train the new tour guides. I prepared a handbook that provided interesting facts about the various tourist attractions, as well as answers to the most commonly asked tourist questions. The Bureau was so impressed with the handbook they had it printed up so that it could be given as a gift to visitors.

University of Louisiana, 1991–94, part-time clerk in admissions office. While I was a student in college, I worked 15 hours a week in the admissions office. My duties included filing, processing applications, and handling correspondence with high school students and administrators.

DOCUMENT 14.B: WRITING AN APPLICATION LETTER

I'm writing to let you know about my availability for the brand manager job you advertised. As you can see from my enclosed résumé, my background is perfect for the position. Even though I don't have any real job experience, my grades have been outstanding considering that I went to a top-ranked business school.

I did many things during my undergraduate years to prepare me for this job:

- *Earned a 3.4 out of a 4.0 with a 3.8 in my business courses*
- *Elected representative to the student governing association*
- *Selected to receive the Lamar Franklin Award*
- *Worked to earn a portion of my tuition*

I am sending my résumé to all the top firms, but I like yours better than any of the rest. Your reputation is tops in the industry, and I want to be associated with a business that can pridefully say it's the best.

If you wish for me to come in for an interview, I can come on a Friday afternoon or anytime on weekends when I don't have classes. Again, thanks for considering me for your brand manager position.

DOCUMENT 14.C: WRITING APPLICATION FOLLOW-UP MESSAGES

Did you receive my résumé? I sent it to you at least two months ago and haven't heard anything. I know you keep résumés on file, but I just want to be sure that you keep me in mind. I heard you are hiring health-care managers and certainly would like to be considered for one of those positions.

Since I last wrote you, I've worked in a variety of positions that have helped prepare me for management. To wit, I've become lunch manager at the restaurant where I work, which involved a raise in pay. I now manage a waitstaff of 12 girls and take the lunch receipts to the bank every day.

Of course, I'd much rather be working at a real job, and that's why I'm writing again. Is there anything else you would like to know about me or my background? I would really like to know more about your company. Is there any literature you could send me? If so, I would really appreciate it.

I think one reason I haven't been hired yet is that I don't want to leave Atlanta. So I hope when you think of me, it's for a position that wouldn't require moving. Thanks again for considering my application.

Exercises

For live links to all websites discussed in this chapter, visit this text's website at www.prenhall.com/thill. Just log on and select Chapter 14, and click on "Student Resources." Locate the page or the URL related to the material in the text. For "Learning More on the Web" exercises, you'll also find navigational directions. Click on the live link to the site.

14.1   Work-Related Preferences: Self-Assessment What work-related activities and situations do you prefer? Evaluate your preferences in each of the following areas. Use the results as a good start for guiding your job search.

Activity or Situation	Strongly Agree	Agree	Disagree	No Preference
1. I want to work independently.	_____	_____	_____	_____
2. I want variety in my work.	_____	_____	_____	_____
3. I want to work with people.	_____	_____	_____	_____
4. I want to work with products or machines.	_____	_____	_____	_____
5. I want physical work.	_____	_____	_____	_____
6. I want mental work.	_____	_____	_____	_____
7. I want to work for a large organization.	_____	_____	_____	_____
8. I want to work for a nonprofit organization.	_____	_____	_____	_____
9. I want to work for a small family business.	_____	_____	_____	_____
10. I want to work for a service business.	_____	_____	_____	_____
11. I want regular, predictable work hours.	_____	_____	_____	_____
12. I want to work in a city location.	_____	_____	_____	_____
13. I want to work in a small town or suburb.	_____	_____	_____	_____
14. I want to work in another country.	_____	_____	_____	_____
15. I want to work outdoors.	_____	_____	_____	_____
16. I want to work in a structured environment.	_____	_____	_____	_____

14.2   Internet Based on the preferences you identified in the self-assessment (Exercise 14.1) and the academic, professional, and personal qualities you have to offer, perform an Internet search for an appropriate career, using any of the websites listed in "Using the Power of Technology: Netting a Job on the Web" on page 482. Draft a brief report indicating how the careers you select and job openings you find match your strengths and preferences.

14.3 **Teamwork** Working with another student, change the following statements to make them more effective for a traditional résumé by using action verbs.

   a. Have some experience with database design.

   b. Assigned to a project to analyze the cost-accounting methods for a large manufacturer.

   c. I was part of a team that developed a new inventory control system.

   d. Am responsible for preparing the quarterly department budget.

   e. Was a manager of a department with seven employees working for me.

   f. Was responsible for developing a spreadsheet to analyze monthly sales by department.

   g. Put in place a new program for ordering supplies.

14.4 **Résumé Preparation: Work Accomplishments** Using your team's answers to Exercise 14.3, make the statements stronger by quantifying them (make up any numbers you need).

14.5 **Ethical Choices** Assume that you achieved all the tasks shown in Exercise 14.3, not as an individual employee, but as part of a work team. In your résumé, should you mention other team members? Explain your answer.

14.6 **Résumé Preparation: Electronic Version** Using your revised version of Document for Analysis 14.A (on page 513), prepare a fully formatted print résumé. What formatting changes would Sylvia Manchester need to make if she were sending her résumé electronically? Develop a keyword summary and make all the changes needed to complete this electronic résumé.

Expand Your Knowledge

LEARNING MORE ON THE WEB

Post an Online Résumé www.careerbuilder.com

At CareerBuilder, you'll find sample résumés, tips on preparing different types of résumés (including scannable ones), links to additional articles, and expert advice on creating résumés that bring positive results. After you've polished your résumé-writing skills, you can search for jobs online using the site's numerous links to national and international industry-specific websites. You can access the information at CareerBuilder to develop your résumé and then post it with prospective employers—all free of charge. Take advantage of what this site offers, and get ideas for writing or improving a new résumé.

ACTIVITIES

Your résumé is like a letter of introduction: It should make a good first impression. It must be organized, error-free, and in an appropriate format. In today's electronic business world, you should know how to prepare a résumé to post on the Internet or to send by e-mail. Learn more by logging on to CareerBuilder.

1. Before writing a new résumé, make a list of action verbs that describe your skills and experience.
2. Describe the advantages and disadvantages of chronological and functional résumé formats. Do you think a combination résumé would be an appropriate format for your new résumé? Explain why or why not.
3. List some of the tips you learned for preparing an electronic résumé.

EXPLORING THE WEB ON YOUR OWN

Review these chapter-related websites on your own to learn more about writing résumés and cover letters.

1. To find out what happens when résumés are scanned, log on to Proven Résumés (www.provenresumes.com/ reswkshps/electronic/scnres.html).
2. Learn how to produce cover letters with brilliance, flair, and speed at So You Wanna Write a Cover Letter? (www. soyouwanna.com/site/syws/coverletter/coverletter.html).
3. Take measures to ensure that your e-mail résumé arrives intact by following the helpful advice from *BusinessWeek* online (www.businessweek.com/careers/content/nov2001/ ca20011113_7790.html).

Learn Interactively

INTERACTIVE STUDY GUIDE

Go to the Companion Website at www.prenhall.com/bovee. For Chapter 14, take advantage of the interactive "Study Guide" to test your knowledge of the chapter. Get instant feedback on whether you need additional studying. Also, visit this site's "Study Hall" where you'll find an abundance of valuable resources that will help you succeed in this course.

PEAK PERFORMANCE GRAMMAR AND MECHANICS

To improve your skill with numbers, visit this text's website at www.prenhall.com/onekey. Click "Peak Performance Grammar and Mechanics," then click "Mechanics." Take the Pretest to determine whether you have any weak areas. Review those areas in the Refresher Course, and take the Follow-Up Test to check your grasp of mechanics. For advanced practice, take the Advanced Test. Finally, for additional reinforcement, go to the "Improve Your Grammar, Mechanics, and Usage" section that follows, and complete those exercises.

Improve Your Grammar, Mechanics, and Usage

The following exercises help you improve your knowledge of and power over English grammar, mechanics, and usage. Turn to the "Handbook of Grammar, Mechanics, and Usage" at the end of this textbook and review all of Section 3.4 (Numbers). Then look at the following 10 items. Circle the letter of the preferred choice in the following groups of sentences. (Answers to these exercises appear on page AK-4.)

1. a. We need to hire one office manager, four bookkeepers, and 12 clerk-typists.
    b. We need to hire one office manager, four bookkeepers, and twelve clerk-typists.
    c. We need to hire 1 office manager, 4 bookkeepers, and 12 clerk-typists.

2. a. The market for this product is nearly 6 million people in our region alone.
    b. The market for this product is nearly six million people in our region alone.
    c. The market for this product is nearly 6,000,000 million people in our region alone.

3. a. Make sure that all 1,835 pages are on my desk no later than 9:00 a.m.
    b. Make sure that all 1835 pages are on my desk no later than nine o'clock in the morning.
    c. Make sure that all 1,835 pages are on my desk no later than nine o'clock a.m.

4. a. Our deadline is 4/7, but we won't be ready before 4/11.
    b. Our deadline is April 7, but we won't be ready before April 11.
    c. Our deadline is 4/7, but we won't be ready before April 11.

5. a. 95 percent of our customers are men.
    b. Ninety-five percent of our customers are men.
    c. Of our customers, ninety-five percent are men.

6. a. More than half the U.S. population is female.
    b. More than 1/2 the U.S. population is female.
    c. More than one-half the U.S. population is female.

7. a. Last year, I wrote 20 15-page reports, and Michelle wrote 24 three-page reports.
    b. Last year, I wrote 20 fifteen-page reports, and Michelle wrote 24 three-page reports.
    c. Last year, I wrote twenty 15-page reports, and Michelle wrote 24 three-page reports.

8. a. Our blinds should measure 38 inches wide by 64 and one-half inches long by 7/16 inches deep.
    b. Our blinds should measure 38 inches wide by 64–1/2 inches long by 7/16 inches deep.
    c. Our blinds should measure 38 inches wide by 64–8/16 inches long by 7/16 inches deep.

9. a. Deliver the couch to 783 Fountain Rd., Suite 3, Procter Valley, CA 92074.
    b. Deliver the couch to 783 Fountain Rd., Suite three, Procter Valley, CA 92074.
    c. Deliver the couch to seven eighty-three Fountain Rd., Suite three, Procter Valley, CA 92074.

10. a. Here are the corrected figures: 42.7% agree, 23.25% disagree, 34% are undecided, and the error is 0.05%.
    b. Here are the corrected figures: 42.7% agree, 23.25% disagree, 34.0% are undecided, and the error is .05%.
    c. Here are the corrected figures: 42.70% agree, 23.25% disagree, 34.00% are undecided, and the error is 0.05%.

For additional exercises focusing on mechanics, go to www.prenhall.com/thill and select "Handbook of Grammar, Mechanics, and Usage Practice Sessions."

Cases

BUILDING TOWARD A BETTER CAREER

1. **Taking stock and taking aim: Application package for the right job** Think about yourself. What are some things that come easily to you? What do you enjoy doing? In what part of the country would you like to live? Do you like to work indoors? Outdoors? A combination of the two? How much do you like to travel? Would you like to spend considerable time on the road? Do you like to work closely with others or more independently? What conditions make a job unpleasant? Do you delegate responsibility easily, or do you like to do things yourself? Are you better with words or numbers? Better at speaking or writing? Do you like to work under fixed deadlines? How important is job security to you? Do you want your supervisor to state clearly what is expected of you, or do you like the freedom to make many of your own decisions?

Your task: After answering these questions, gather information about possible jobs that suit your profile by consulting reference materials (from your college library or placement center) and by searching the Internet (using some of the search strategies discussed in Chapter 10). Next, choose a location, a company, and a job that interests you. With guidance from your instructor, decide whether to apply for a job you're qualified for now or one you'll be qualified for with additional education. Then, as directed by your instructor, write one or more of the following: (a) a job-inquiry letter, (b) a résumé, (c) a letter of application, (d) a follow-up letter to your application letter.

2. Scanning the possibilities: Résumé for the Internet In your search for a position, you discover Career Magazine, a website that lists hundreds of companies advertising on the Internet. Your chances of getting an interview with a leading company will be enhanced if you submit your résumé and cover letter electronically. On the web, explore www.careermag.com.

Your task: Prepare a scannable résumé that could be submitted to one of the companies advertising at the Career Magazine website. Print out the résumé for your instructor.

3. Online application: Electronic cover letter introducing a résumé *Motley Fool* (www.fool.com) is a "Generation X" online magazine accessed via the web. Although its founders and writers are extremely creative and motivated, they lack business experience and need a fellow "X'er" to help them manage the business. Among articles in a recent edition was one titled "The Soul of the Dead," about the influence of the Grateful Dead on more than one generation of concert-goers. Other articles deal with lifestyle issues, pop movies, music, and "trends for an old-young generation."

Your task: Write an e-mail message that will serve as your job application letter and address your message to Louis Corrigan, Managing Editor. Try to limit your message to one screen (about 23 lines). You'll need a creative "hook" and a reassuring approach that identifies you as the right person to help *Motley Fool* become financially viable.

WRITING A RÉSUMÉ AND AN APPLICATION LETTER

4. Help wanted": Application for a job listed in the classified section Among the jobs listed in today's *Chicago Tribune* (435 N. Michigan Avenue, Chicago, IL 60641) are the following:

- ***Accounting Assistant.*** Established leader in the vacation ownership industry has immediate opening in its Northbrook Corp. accounting dept. for an Accounting Assistant. Responsibilities include: bank reconciliation, preparation of deposits, AP, and cash receipt posting. Join our fast-growing company and enjoy our great benefits package. Flex work hours, medical, dental insurance. Fax résumé to Lisa: 847-564-3876.

- ***Administrative Assistant.*** Fast-paced Wood Dale office seeks professional with strong computer skills. Proficient in MS Word & Excel, PowerPoint a plus. Must be detail oriented, able to handle multiple tasks, and possess strong communication skills. Excellent benefits, salary, and work environment. Fax résumé to 630-350-8649.

- ***Customer Service.*** A nationally known computer software developer has an exciting opportunity in customer service and inside sales support in its fast-paced downtown Chicago office. You'll help resolve customer problems over the phone, provide information, assist in account management, and administer orders. If you're friendly, self-motivated, energetic, and have 2 years of experience, excellent problem-solving skills, organizational, communication, and PC skills, and communicate well over the phone, send résumé to J. Haber, 233 North Lake Shore Drive, Chicago, IL 60641.

- ***Sales-Account Manager.*** MidCity Baking Company is seeking an Account Manager to sell and coordinate our programs to major accounts in the Chicago market. The candidate should possess strong analytical and selling skills and demonstrate computer proficiency. Previous sales experience with major account-level assignment desired. A degree in business or equivalent experience preferred. For confidential consideration please mail résumé to Steven Crane, Director of Sales, MidCity Baking Company, 133 N. Railroad Avenue, Northlake IL 60614.

Your task: Send a résumé and an application letter to one of these potential employers.

WRITING OTHER TYPES OF EMPLOYMENT MESSAGES

5. Crashing the last frontier: Letter of inquiry about jobs in Alaska Your friend can't understand why you would want to move to Alaska. So you explain: "What really decided it for me was that I'd never seen the northern lights."

"But what about the bears? The 60-degree-below winters? The permafrost?" asks your friend.

"No problem. Anchorage doesn't get much colder than Buffalo does. It is just windier and wetter. Anyhow, I want to live near Fairbanks, which is near the gold-mining area—and the university is there. Fairbanks has lots of small businesses, like a frontier town in the West about 150 years ago. I think it still has homesteading tracts for people who want to do their own building and are willing to stay for a certain number of years."

"Your plans seem a little hasty," your friend warns. "Maybe you should write for information before you just take off. How do you know you could get a job?"

Your task: Take your friend's advice and write to the Chamber of Commerce, Fairbanks, AK 99701. Ask what types of employment are available to someone with your education and experience, and ask who specifically is hiring year-round employees.

Chapter 15

Interviewing for Employment and Following Up

Learning Objectives

AFTER STUDYING THIS CHAPTER, YOU WILL BE ABLE TO

1 Explain the typical sequence of interviews

2 Identify and briefly describe the most common types of job interviews

3 Discuss six tasks you need to complete to prepare for a successful job interview

4 Describe the three stages of a successful employment interview

5 Name six common employment messages that follow an interview, and state briefly when you would use each one

On the Job:

COMMUNICATING AT HERMAN MILLER, INC.

HOW TO TELL A GOOD DANCER BEFORE THE WALTZ BEGINS

Looking for a company that cares about people? You might try Herman Miller, a highly successful establishment that manufactures office furniture in Zeeland, Michigan. Founded in 1923 by D. J. DePree, Herman Miller is justifiably famous for its corporate culture. DePree wanted people inside and outside the company to look at Herman Miller and say, "Those folks have a gift of the spirit." Today, under the guidance of chairman and CEO Mike Volkema, the company still pursues an environment in which people can unleash their creativity.

Herman Miller may be the only company on the *Fortune* 500 list that actually has a "vice president for people." Participation is the name of the game in this organization. Employees at all levels are consulted about important decisions and reap the rewards if the business does well. The most important quality in a Herman Miller employee is the capacity for teamwork. "To be successful here," says one Herman Miller executive, "you have to know how to dance."

So how do you know whether someone is a good dancer before you actually begin the waltz? To identify people who have the right mix of attitudes, Herman Miller uses what it calls "value-based" interviewing. During an initial job interview, the staffing department probes the candidate's work style, likes, and dislikes by posing "what if" questions. By evalu-

Herman Miller's recruiters look at a candidate's education and experience, but even more important is the candidate's personality. Finding people who can operate successfully in the company's participative environment can be challenging.

ating how the candidate would handle a variety of scenarios, the recruiter gets a good idea of how well the individual would fit into the company. If the fit seems good, the candidate is invited back for follow-up interviews with members of the department where he or she would be working. During these follow-up interviews, the candidate's functional expertise is evaluated along with his or her psychological makeup.

During the interview process, Herman Miller's recruiters look at a candidate's education and experience, but they also look for the ability to get along with others. If the candidate's personality is outstanding, the company may even be willing to overlook a lack of relevant experience. A senior vice president of research was once a high school football coach. The senior vice president of marketing and sales used to be the dean of agriculture at Michigan State. And the vice president for people had been planning to become a prison warden but joined Herman Miller instead. On the surface, these people didn't seem to be good candidates for management jobs in the office furniture business, but Herman Miller looked beyond the superficial to see their true potential. By the end of the interview process, Herman Miller staffers had a good idea that these candidates "knew how to dance."[1]

www.hermanmiller.com

UNDERSTANDING THE INTERVIEWING PROCESS

An employment interview is a formal meeting in which both employer and applicant ask questions and exchange information to learn more about each other.

Herman Miller's Mike Volkema can tell you that most recruiters have a list of qualities and accomplishments they are looking for in job candidates. Good interviewers aren't attempting to intimidate or scare anyone; they're simply trying to learn as much as they can about each candidate. An **employment interview** is a formal meeting during which both employer and applicant ask questions and exchange information. These meetings have a dual purpose: (1) The organization wants to find the applicant best suited to the job and the organization, and (2) the applicant wants to find the job best suited to his or her goals and capabilities. While recruiters are trying to decide whether you are right for them, you must decide whether the company is right for you.

In a typical job search, you can expect to have many interviews before you accept a job offer.

Because interviewing takes time, begin seeking jobs well in advance of the date you want to start work. Some students begin their job search as early as nine months before graduation. During downturns in the economy, early planning is even more crucial. Since many employers have become more selective and many corporations have reduced their campus visits and campus hiring programs, more of the job-search burden now falls on you. It can take an average of 10 interviews to get one job offer, so if you hope to have several offers to choose from, expect to go through 20 or 30 interviews during your job search.[2] Also plan on facing a series of interviews, each with a different purpose.

The Typical Sequence of Interviews

Most organizations interview an applicant several times before extending a job offer:
• Screening stage
• Selection stage
• Final stage

Not all organizations interview potential candidates the same way. However, most employers interview an applicant two or three times before deciding to make a job offer.

The Screening Stage

During the screening stage of interviews, try to differentiate yourself from other candidates by presenting a memorable headline.

The Screening Stage   The preliminary *screening stage* may be held on campus or on company premises to help employers screen out unqualified applicants. These interviews are fairly structured: Applicants are often asked roughly the same questions so that all candidates will be measured against the same criteria. In some cases, technology has transformed the initial, get-to-know-you interview, allowing employers to screen candidates by phone, video interview, or computer.[3]

Your best approach to the screening stage is to follow the interviewer's lead. Keep your responses short and to the point. Time is limited, so talking too much can be a big mistake. However, your goal is to differentiate yourself from other candidates. Without resorting to gimmicks, call attention to one key aspect of your background. Then the recruiter can say, "Oh yes, I remember Jones—the one who sold used Toyotas in Detroit." Just be sure the trait you accentuate is relevant to the job in question. Also be ready to demonstrate a particular skill (perhaps problem solving), if asked to do so. Candidates who meet the company's requirements are invited to participate in additional interviews.

During the selection stage of interviews, cover all your strengths by going into more detail about your experiences and qualifications.

The Selection Stage   The next stage of interviews helps the organization narrow the field a little further. Typically, if you're invited for additional interviews, you will talk with several people: a member of the human resources department, one or two potential colleagues, and your potential supervisor. By noting how you listen, think, and express yourself, interviewers can decide how likely you are to get along with colleagues.

Your best approach during this *selection stage* of interviews is to show interest in the job and relate your skills and experience to the organization's needs. Broaden your sales pitch. Instead of telegraphing the headline, give the interviewer the whole story. Touch briefly on all your strengths, but explain three or four of your best qualifications.

At the same time, probe for information that will help you evaluate the position objectively. As important as it is to get an offer, it's also important to learn whether the job is right for you. Be sure to listen attentively, ask insightful questions, and display enthusiasm. If the interviewer believes that you're a good candidate, you may receive a job offer, either on the spot or a few days later by phone or mail.

Final Stage   You may be invited back for a final evaluation by a higher-ranking executive with the authority to make an offer and negotiate terms. This person may already have concluded that your background is right and may be more concerned with sizing up your personality. You both need to see whether there is a good psychological fit, so be honest about your motivations and values. If the interview goes well, your goal is to clinch the deal on the best possible terms. An underlying objective of the *final stage* is often to sell you on the advantages of joining the organization.

> During the final stage, the interviewer may try to sell you on working for the firm.

Types of Interviews

Organizations use various types of interviews to discover as much as possible about applicants.

- **Structured interviews.** Generally used in the screening stage, structured interviews are controlled by the employer, who asks a series of prepared questions in a set order. All answers are noted. Although useful in gathering facts, the structured interview is generally a poor measure of an applicant's personal qualities. Nevertheless, some companies use structured interviews to create uniformity in their hiring process.[4]

  > A structured interview is controlled by the interviewer to gather facts.

- **Open-ended interviews.** Less formal, and unstructured, these interviews can have a relaxed format. To bring out a candidate's personality and test professional judgment, the interviewer asks broad, open-ended questions, encouraging the applicant to talk freely. However, some candidates reveal too much, rambling on about personal details or family problems, so try to strike a balance between being friendly and remembering that you're in a business situation.

  > In an open-ended interview, the recruiter encourages the candidate to speak freely.

- **Panel interviews.** These interviews allow multiple members of the staff to meet and question each candidate. Panels usually consist of three to six members, perhaps including a supervisor, a person from human resources, a co-worker, and maybe someone from a division or department that you would often be required to interact with. Each panel member may ask you a prepared list of questions and may take copious notes on your response.

  > Panel interviews let you meet more members of the staff.

- **Group interviews.** To judge interpersonal skills, some employers meet with several candidates simultaneously to see how they interact. The Walt Disney Company uses group interviews when hiring people for its theme parks. During a 45-minute session, the Disney recruiter watches how three candidates relate to one another. Do they smile? Are they supportive of one another's comments? Do they try to score points at each other's expense?[5]

  > Group interviews help recruiters see how candidates interact with one another.

- **Stress interviews.** Some employers set up stress interviews to see how a candidate handles pressure (an important qualification for some jobs, such as consulting, investment banking, or any job that subjects you to stressful situations). To irk or unsettle you, the interviewer might ask you pointed questions, subject you to long periods of silence, criticize your appearance, deliberately interrupt you, and react abruptly or even with hostility.

  > Stress interviews help recruiters see how you handle yourself under pressure.

- **Video interviews.** To cut travel costs, many large companies use videoconferencing systems. You need to prepare a bit differently for a video interview: (1) request a preliminary phone conversation to establish rapport with the interviewer, (2) arrive early enough to get used to the equipment and setting, (3) speak clearly but no more slowly than normal, (4) sit straight (looking up but not down), and (5) show some animation (but not so much that you blur your appearance to the interviewer).[6]

  > Video interviews require some special preparation.

In situational interviews, candidates must explain how they would handle a specific set of circumstances.

- **Situational interviews.** Many companies claim that interviewing is about the job, not about a candidate's five-year goals, weaknesses or strengths, challenging experiences, or greatest accomplishments. An interviewer describes a situation and asks, "How would you handle this?" So the situational interview is a hands-on, at-work meeting between an employer who needs a job done and a worker who must be fully prepared to do the work.[7]

  Regardless of the types of interviews you may face, a personal interview is vital because your résumé can't show whether you're lively and outgoing or subdued and low key, able to take direction or able to take charge. Each job requires a different mix of personality traits, and the interviewer's task is to find out whether you will be effective on the job.

PREPARING FOR A JOB INTERVIEW

Just as written messages need planning, employment interviews need preparation.

For a successful interview, preparation is mandatory. Herman Miller's recruiters can tell you that it's perfectly normal to feel a little anxious before an interview. But good preparation will help you perform well. Be sure to consider any cultural differences when preparing for interviews, and base your approach on what your audience expects. The advice in this chapter is most appropriate for companies and employers in the United States and Canada. Before an interview, know what employers look for in applicants, do some follow-up research, think ahead about questions, bolster your confidence, polish your interview style, plan to look good, and be ready when you arrive.

Know What Employers Look For

Compatibility with the organization is judged on the basis of personal background, attitudes, and style.

Suitability for the specific job is judged on the basis of
- Academic preparation
- Work experience
- Job-related personality traits

When it comes down to it, every job has basic qualifications. Employers want candidates who will fit in with the organization, who can handle a specific job, and who perform well during preemployment testing. As you prepare for job interviews, you'll be more successful if you understand what employers are looking for:

- **A good fit.** Some interviewers view personal background as a clue to a candidate's fit, so they ask about your interests, hobbies, awareness of world events, and so on. To anticipate such questions, read widely, try to meet new people, and participate in discussion groups (seminars and workshops). Some interviewers also take into account a candidate's personal style, so try to be open, enthusiastic, interested, courteous, and sincere. Try to show that you're positive, self-confident, and willing to learn. (See Chapter 2 for how to emphasize your personal style nonverbally.)

- **Qualifications for the job.** Although your résumé highlights your qualifications, you'll be asked to describe your education and previous jobs in more depth during interviews. In many cases, the interviewer will be seeking someone with the flexibility to apply diverse skills in several areas.[8] When describing your skills, be honest. If you don't know how to do something, say so.

- **Preemployment testing.** To defray the costs of hiring, some employers require tests. The most common tests measure competency or specific abilities needed to do a job. Psychological tests (usually questionnaires) assess overall intellectual ability, work attitudes, interests, managerial potential, and

In his efforts to find work, Mark Calimlim gets help from the Career Center at Syracuse University. (Source: Syracuse University, School of Management, Career Center)

so on. If an employee harms an innocent party on the job, employers can be held liable for negligent hiring practices, so about 45 percent of companies now require drug and alcohol testing.[9] To protect candidates' interests, such tests must meet strict fairness criteria set forth by the Equal Employment Opportunity Commission (EEOC).

> Preemployment tests attempt to provide objective, quantitative information about a candidate's skills, attitudes, and habits.

Do Some Follow-Up Research

You will probably already have researched the companies you sent your résumé to. But now that you've been invited for an interview, you'll want to fine-tune your research and brush up on the facts you've collected (see Table 15–1). You can review Chapter 10 for ideas on where to look for information.

FINDING OUT ABOUT THE ORGANIZATION AND THE JOB	Table 15–1

Where to Look for Information

• Annual report	Summarizes operations; describes products, lists events, names key personnel
• In-house magazine or newspaper	Reveals information about company operations, events, personnel
• Product brochure or publicity release	Gives insight into firm's operations and values (obtain from public relations office)
• Stock research report	Helps assess stability and growth prospects (obtain online or from stockbroker)
• Newspaper's business or financial pages	Contain news items about organizations, current performance figures
• Periodicals indexes	Contain descriptive listings of magazine/newspaper articles about firms (obtain from library)
• Better Business Bureau and Chamber of Commerce	Distribute information about some local organizations
• Former and current employees	Have insight into job and work environment
• College placement office	Collects information on organizations that recruit and on job qualifications and salaries

What to Find Out About the Organization

• Full name	How the firm is officially known (e.g., 3M is Minnesota Mining & Manufacturing Company)
• Location	Where the organization's headquarters, branch offices, and plants are
• Age	How long the organization has been in business
• Products	What goods and services the organization produces and sells
• Industry position	What the organization's current market share, financial position, and profit picture are
• Earnings	What the trends in the firm's stock prices and dividends are (if firm is publicly held)
• Growth	How the firm's earnings/holdings have changed in recent years and prospects for expansion
• Organization	What subsidiaries, divisions, and departments make up the whole

What to Find Out About the Job

• Job title	What you will be called
• Job functions	What the main tasks of the job are
• Job qualifications	What knowledge and skills the job requires
• Career path	What chances for ready advancement exist
• Salary range	What the firm typically offers and what is reasonable in this industry and geographic area
• Travel opportunities	How often, long, and far you'll be allowed (or required) to travel
• Relocation opportunities	Where you might be allowed (or required) to move and how often

Be prepared to relate your qualifications to the organization's needs.

Today's companies expect serious candidates to demonstrate an understanding of the company's operations, its market, and its strategic and tactical problems.[10] Learning about the organization and the job enables you to show the interviewer just how you will meet the organization's particular needs. With a little research, for instance, you would discover that Microsoft plans on investing heavily in the technical and marketing support of software developers as well as making things simpler for all users and system administrators.[11] Knowing these facts might help you pinpoint aspects of your background (such as the ability to simplify processes) that would appeal to Microsoft's recruiters.

Think Ahead About Questions

Planning ahead for the interviewer's questions will help you handle them more confidently and intelligently. (See "Sharpening Your Career Skills: Interview Strategies: Answering the 16 Toughest Questions.") Moreover, you will want to prepare intelligent questions of your own.

Planning for the Employer's Questions   Employers usually gear their interview questions to specific organizational needs. You can expect to be asked about your skills, achievements, and goals, as well as about your attitude toward work and school, your relationships with others (work supervisors, colleagues, and fellow students), and occasionally your hobbies and interests. Candidates might be asked to collaborate on a decision or to develop a group presentation. Trained observers evaluate the candidates' performance using predetermined criteria and then advise management on how well each person is likely to handle the challenges normally faced on the job.[12]

Practice answering interview questions.

For a look at the types of questions often asked, see Table 15–2 on page 526. Jot down a brief answer to each one. Then read over the answers until you feel comfortable with each of them. Although practicing your answers will help you feel prepared and confident, you don't want to memorize responses or sound overrehearsed. You might also give a list of interview questions to a friend or relative and have that person ask you various questions at random. This method helps you learn to articulate answers and to look at the person as you answer.

Planning Questions of Your Own   The questions you ask in an interview are just as important as the answers you provide. By asking intelligent questions, you demonstrate your understanding of the organization, and you can steer the discussion into those areas that allow you to present your qualifications to best advantage. Before the interview, prepare a list of about a dozen questions you need answered in order to evaluate the organization and the job.

You are responsible for deciding whether the work and the organization are compatible with your goals and values.

Don't limit your questions to those you think will impress the interviewer, or you won't get the information you'll need to make a wise decision if and when you're offered the job. Here's a list of some things you might want to find out:

- **Are these my kind of people?** Observe the interviewer, and if you can, arrange to talk with other employees.

- **Can I do this work?** Compare your qualifications with the requirements described by the interviewer.

- **Will I enjoy the work?** Know yourself and what's important to you. Will you find the work challenging? Will it give you feelings of accomplishment, of satisfaction, and of making a real contribution?

- **Is the job what I want?** You may never find a job that fulfills all your wants, but the position you accept should satisfy at least your primary ones. Will it make use of your best capabilities? Does it offer a career path to the long-term goals you've set?

SHARPENING YOUR CAREER SKILLS

Interview Strategies: Answering the 16 Toughest Questions

The answers to challenging interview questions can reveal a lot about a candidate. You can expect to face several such questions during every interview. If you're prepared with thoughtful answers that are related to your specific situation, you're bound to make a good impression. Here are 16 tough questions and guidelines for planning answers that put your qualities in the best light.

1. *What was the toughest decision you ever had to make?* Be prepared with a good example, explaining why the decision was difficult and how you decided.

2. *Why do you want to work for this organization?* Show that you've done your homework, and cite some things going on in the company that appeal to you.

3. *Why should we employ you?* Emphasize your academic strengths, job skills, and enthusiasm for the firm. Tie specific skills to the employer's needs, and give examples of how you can learn and become productive quickly. Cite past activities to prove you can work with others as part of a team.

4. *If we hire you, what changes would you make?* No one can know what to change in a position before settling in and learning about the job and company operations. State that you would take a good hard look at everything the company is doing before making recommendations.

5. *Can we offer you a career path?* Reply that you believe so, but you need to know more about the normal progression within the organization.

6. *What are your greatest strengths?* Answer sincerely by summarizing your strong points: "I can see what must be done and then do it" or "I'm willing to make decisions" or "I work well with others."

7. *What are your greatest weaknesses?* Describe a weakness so that it sounds like a virtue—honestly revealing something about yourself while showing how it works to an employer's advantage. If you sometimes drive yourself too hard, explain that it has helped when you've had to meet deadlines.

8. *What didn't you like about previous jobs you've held?* Rather than talking about what you didn't like, state that you liked some tasks better than others. Discuss what the experience taught you, and avoid making slighting references to former employers.

9. *How do you spend your leisure time?* Rather than focusing on just one, mention a cross section of interests—active and quiet, social and solitary. But be careful not to give out any of the sort of personal information that interviewers are not allowed to ask about.

10. *Are there any weaknesses in your education or experience?* Take stock of your weaknesses before the interview, and practice discussing them in a positive light. You'll see they're minor when discussed along with the positive qualities you have to offer.

11. *Where do you want to be five years from now?* This question tests (1) whether you're merely using this job as a stopover until something better comes along and (2) whether you've given thought to your long-term goals. Saying that you'd like to be company president is unrealistic, and yet few employers want people who are content to sit still. Your answer should reflect your long-term goals and the organization's advancement opportunities.

12. *What are your salary expectations?* If you're asked this at the outset, say, "Why don't we discuss salary after you decide whether I'm right for the job?" If the interviewer asks this after showing real interest in you, speak up. Do your homework, but if you need a clue about salary levels, say, "Can you discuss the salary range with me?"

13. *What would you do if . . .* This question tests your resourcefulness. For example: "What would you do if your computer broke down during an audit?" Your answer is less important than your approach to the problem—and a calm approach is best.

14. *What type of position are you interested in?* Job titles and responsibilities vary from firm to firm. So state your skills ("I'm good with numbers") and the positions that require those skills ("accounts payable").

15. *Tell me something about yourself.* Answer that you'll be happy to talk about yourself, and ask what the interviewer wants to know. If this point is clarified, respond. If it isn't, explain how your skills can contribute to the job and the organization. This is a great chance to sell yourself.

16. *Do you have any questions about the organization or the job?* Employers like candidates who are interested in the organization. Convey your interest and enthusiasm.

Be sure that your answers are sincere, truthful, and positive. Take a moment to compose your thoughts before responding, so that your answers are to the point.

CAREER APPLICATION

1. What makes an effective answer to an interviewer's question? Consider some of the ways answers can vary: specific versus general, assertive versus passive, informal versus formal.

2. Think of four additional questions that pertain specifically to your résumé. Practice your answers.

Table 15–2	**TWENTY-FIVE COMMON INTERVIEW QUESTIONS**

Questions About College

1. What courses in college did you like most? Least? Why?

2. Do you think your extracurricular activities in college were worth the time you spent on them? Why or why not?

3. When did you choose your college major? Did you ever change your major? If so, why?

4. Do you feel you did the best scholastic work you are capable of?

5. Which of your college years was the toughest? Why?

Questions About Employers and Jobs

6. What jobs have you held? Why did you leave?

7. What percentage of your college expenses did you earn? How?

8. Why did you choose your particular field of work?

9. What are the disadvantages of your chosen field?

10. Have you served in the milltary? What rank did you achieve? What jobs did you perform?

11. What do you think about how this industry operates today?

12. Why do you think you would like this particular type of job?

Questions About Personal Attitudes and Preferences

13. Do you prefer to work in any specific geographic location? If so, why?

14. How much money do you hope to be earning in 5 years? In 10 years?

15. What do you think determines a person's progress in a good organization?

16. What personal characteristics do you feel are necessary for success in your chosen field?

17. Tell me a story.

18. Do you like to travel?

19. Do you think grades should be considered by employers? Why or why not?

Questions About Work Habits

20. Do you prefer working with others or by yourself?

21. What type of boss do you prefer?

22. Have you ever had any difficulty getting along with colleagues or supervisors? With instructors? With other students?

23. Would you prefer to work in a large or a small organization? Why?

24. How do you feel about overtime work?

25. What have you done that shows initiative and willingness to work?

- **Does the job pay what I'm worth?** By comparing jobs and salaries before you're interviewed, you'll know what's reasonable for someone with your skills in your industry.

- **What kind of person would I be working for?** If the interviewer is your prospective boss, watch how others interact with that person, tactfully query other employees, or pose a careful question or two during the interview. If your prospective boss is someone else, ask for that person's name, job title, and responsibilities. Try to learn all you can.

TWENTY QUESTIONS TO ASK THE INTERVIEWER   Table 15–3

Questions About the Job	Questions About the Organization
What are the job's major responsibilities?	What are your organization's major strengths?
What qualities do you want in the person who fills this position?	What are your organization's major markets?
How often has this position been filled during the past 5 years?	Who are your organization's main competitors, and what are their strengths and weaknesses?
For what reasons have people left this position in the past?	What makes your organization different from others in the industry?
What would you like the next person in this job to do differently?	Does your organization have any plans for new products? New acquisitions?
What is the first issue facing the person you hire?	What do you see as the future of this organization?
What support does this position have (people, budget, equipment, etc.)?	How would you define your organization's managerial philosophy?
What are the criteria for success in this position?	What additional training does your organization provide?
What might be the next career steps for a person who does well in this position?	Do employees have an opportunity to continue their education with help from the organization?
Would relocation be required now or in the future?	
What can you tell me about the person I would report to?	

- **What sort of future can I expect with this organization?** How healthy is the organization? Can you look forward to advancement? Does the organization offer insurance, pension, vacation, or other benefits?

Rather than bombarding the interviewer with these questions the minute you walk in the room, use a mix of formats to elicit this information. Start with a warm-up question to help break the ice. You might ask a Herman Miller recruiter, "Which departments usually hire new graduates?" After that, you might build rapport by asking an open-ended question that draws out the interviewer's opinion ("How do you think Internet sales will affect Herman Miller's continued growth?"). Indirect questions can elicit useful information and show that you've prepared for the interview ("I'd really like to know more about Herman Miller's plans for expanding its corporate presence on the web" or "That recent *Fortune* article about the company was very interesting"). Any questions you ask should be in your own words so that you don't sound like every other candidate. For a list of other good questions you might use as a starting point, see Table 15–3.

Write your list of questions on a notepad and take it to the interview. If you need to, jot down brief notes during the meeting, and be sure to record answers in more detail afterward. Having a list of questions should impress the interviewer with your organization and thoroughness. It will also show that you're there to evaluate the organization and the job as well as to sell yourself.

Types of questions to ask during an interview:
- *Warm-up*
- *Open-ended*
- *Indirect*

Impress the interviewer with your ability to organize and be thorough by bringing a list of questions to the job interview.

Bolster Your Confidence

By building your confidence, you'll make a better impression. The best way to counteract any apprehension is to remove its source. You may feel shy or self-conscious because you think you have some flaw that will prompt others to reject you.

If some aspect of your appearance or background makes you uneasy, correct it or offset it by exercising positive traits such as warmth, wit, intelligence, or charm. Instead of dwelling on your weaknesses, focus on your strengths so that you can emphasize them to an interviewer. Make a list of your good points and compare them with what you see as your shortcomings. And bear in mind that you're much more conscious of your limitations than other people are.

If you feel shy or self-conscious, remember that recruiters are human too.

Remember that you're not alone. All the other candidates for the job are just as nervous as you are. Even the interviewer may be nervous.

Polish Your Interview Style

Confidence helps you walk into an interview, but once you're there, you want to give the interviewer an impression of poise, good manners, and good judgment. Some job seekers hire professional coaches and image consultants to create just the right impression. Charging anywhere from $125 to $500 an hour, these professionals spend most of their time teaching clients how to assess communication styles by using role playing, videotaping, and audiotaping.[13] You can use these techniques too.

Staging mock interviews with a friend is a good way to hone your style.

You can develop an accomplished style by staging mock interviews with a friend. After each practice session, try to identify opportunities for improvement. Have your friend critique your performance, using the list of interview faults shown in Figure 15–1. You can tape-record or videotape these mock interviews and then evaluate them yourself. The taping process can be intimidating, but it helps you work out any problems before you begin actual job interviews.

Nonverbal behavior has a significant effect on the interviewer's opinion of you.

As you stage your mock interviews, pay particular attention to your nonverbal behavior. You are more likely to have a successful interview if you maintain eye contact, smile frequently, sit in an attentive position, and use frequent hand gestures. These nonverbal signals convince the interviewer that you're alert, assertive, dependable, confident, responsible, and energetic.[14] Some companies based in the United States are owned and managed by people from other cultures, so during your research, find out about the company's cultural background and preferences regarding nonverbal behavior.

The way you speak is almost as important as what you say.

The sound of your voice can also have a major impact on your success in a job interview.[15] You can work with a tape recorder to overcome voice problems. If you

FIGURE 15–1
Marks Against Applicants (in General Order of Importance)

WHAT EMPLOYERS DO NOT LIKE TO SEE IN CANDIDATES

- ☑ Poor personal appearance
- ☑ Overbearing, overaggressive, conceited demeanor; a "superiority complex"; know-it-all attitude
- ☑ Inability to express ideas clearly; poor voice, diction, grammar
- ☑ Lack of knowledge or experience
- ☑ Poor preparation for the interview
- ☑ Lack of interest in the job
- ☑ Lack of planning for career; lack of purpose, goals
- ☑ Lack of enthusiasm; passive and indifferent demeanor
- ☑ Lack of confidence and poise; appearance of being nervous and ill at ease
- ☑ Insufficient evidence of achievement
- ☑ Failure to participate in extracurricular activities
- ☑ Overemphasis on money; interest only in the best dollar offer
- ☑ Poor scholastic record; just got by
- ☑ Unwillingness to start at the bottom; expecting too much too soon
- ☑ Tendency to make excuses
- ☑ Evasive answers; hedges on unfavorable factors in record
- ☑ Lack of tact
- ☑ Lack of maturity
- ☑ Lack of courtesy; ill-mannered
- ☑ Condemnation of past employers
- ☑ Lack of social skills
- ☑ Marked dislike for schoolwork
- ☑ Lack of vitality
- ☑ Failure to look interviewer in the eye
- ☑ Limp, weak handshake

tend to speak too rapidly, practice speaking more slowly. If your voice sounds too loud or too soft, practice adjusting it. Work on eliminating speech mannerisms such as *you know, like,* and *um,* which might make you sound inarticulate.

Plan to Look Good

Physical appearance is important because clothing and grooming reveal something about a candidate's personality and professionalism. When it comes to clothing, the best policy is to dress conservatively. Wear the best-quality businesslike clothing you can, preferably in a dark, solid color. Select an outfit you have worn before and are comfortable wearing.[16] Avoid flamboyant styles, colors, and prints. Even in companies where interviewers may dress casually, it's important to show good judgment by dressing (and acting) in a professional manner.

Company websites may give you information on what to wear to interviews. Some candidates ask interviewers ahead of time what they should wear. For example, one human resources executive tells job seekers that dressing in a suit looks awkward at his company, and he advises them to dress business casual (for men, perhaps a sport shirt and tie or a polo shirt and sport jacket; for women, a sweater suit or a sport jacket and pants).[17] You might try checking things out for yourself: A few days before your interview, wear something you believe to be appropriate and visit the company to pick up its annual report or company newsletter. While you're there, take a good look at what people are wearing and dress that way on the day of the interview.[18] In the absence of other information about what to wear for your interview, follow the guidelines in Table 15–4.

Good grooming makes any style of clothing look better. Make sure your clothes are clean and unwrinkled, your shoes unscuffed and well shined, your hair neatly styled and combed, your fingernails clean, and your breath fresh. If possible, check your appearance in a mirror before entering the room for the interview. Finally, remember that one of the best ways to look good is to smile at appropriate moments (see Chapter 2).

To look like a winner:
• Dress conservatively
• Be well groomed
• Smile when appropriate

Be Ready When You Arrive

When preparing for a job interview, plan to take a small notebook, a pen, a list of the questions you want to ask, and at least two copies of your résumé (protected in a folder). You may want to take five or more résumés, just in case your interview turns out to be a panel interview or you're asked to participate in multiple interviews that day with different people. Also take along an outline of what you have learned about the organization and any past correspondence about the position. You may want to take a small calendar, a transcript of your college grades, a list of references, and a portfolio containing samples of your work, performance reviews, and certificates of achievement. In an era when many people exaggerate their qualifications, visible proof of your abilities carries a lot of weight.[19]

Be sure you know when and where the interview will be held. The worst way to start any interview is to be late. Check the route you will take, even if it means phoning the interviewer's secretary to ask. Find out how much time it takes to get there; then plan to arrive early. Allow a little extra time in case you run into a problem on the way.

Once you arrive, relax. You may have to wait a little while, so bring along something to read (the less frivolous or controversial, the better). If company literature is available, read it while you wait. In any case, be polite to the interviewer's assistant. If the opportunity presents itself, ask a few questions about the organization or express enthusiasm for the job. Refrain from smoking before the interview (nonsmokers can smell smoke on the clothing of interviewees), and avoid chewing

When Emily Chang interviews potential employees, she looks for people who communicate well. She expects them to be prepared with résumés and work samples. She also expects them to have a professional appearance.

Table 15–4	WHAT TO WEAR FOR A JOB INTERVIEW	
Category	*Dress Guidelines*	
Men and women	Conservative dark business suit (navy or gray)	
	White, long-sleeved shirt or blouse (pastel is second best)	
	Clothing freshly dry-cleaned and in good repair (no bulging pockets or sagging lining)	
	Polished, conservative shoes (comfortable)	
	Clean, well-groomed hair and nails	
	Little or no scent (interviewers may be allergic to cologne or perfume)	
	Empty pockets (no gum, candy, cigarettes, or jingling coins)	
	Light briefcase or portfolio case (cleaned and polished)	
	Umbrella—if necessary (solid black, tan, navy, gray—in good working order)	
	Little or no jewelry (no rhinestone cufflinks, cloth watchbands, novelty tie tacks)	
	No visible body piercing (nose rings, eyebrow rings, etc.)	
Women	Suit with jacket—no dresses (blue, gray, beige, black)	
	No high heels	
	No purse (carry a briefcase or portfolio case instead)	
	Sparing make-up	
	Nail polish—if you wear it (clear or conservative color)	
	No more than one ring per hand	
	One set of earrings only	
Men	Conservative necktie (silk)	
	Dark shoes (black lace-ups are best)	
	Over-the-calf dark socks (black is best)	
	Short hair	
	No beards (mustache if you must, but neat and trimmed)	
	No rings other than wedding ring or college ring	
	No earrings	

gum in the waiting room. Anything you do or say while you wait may well get back to the interviewer, so make sure your best qualities show from the moment you enter the premises. That way you'll be ready for the interview itself once it actually begins.

INTERVIEWING FOR SUCCESS

As discussed at the beginning of this chapter, how you handle a particular interview depends on where you stand in the interview process. Is this your first interview in the screening process? Have you made it to the selection interview or even the final interview? Regardless of where you are in the interview process, every interview will proceed through three stages: the warm-up, the question-and-answer session, and the close.

The Warm-Up

Of the three stages, the warm-up is the most important, even though it may account for only a small fraction of the time you spend in the interview. Psychologists say that 50 percent of an interviewer's decision is made within the first 30 to 60 seconds, and another 25 percent is made within 15 minutes. If you get off to a bad start, it's extremely difficult to turn the interview around.[20]

Body language is important at this point. Because you won't have time to say much in the first minute or two, you must sell yourself nonverbally. Begin by using the interviewer's name if you're sure you can pronounce it correctly. If the interviewer extends a hand, respond with a firm but gentle handshake, and wait until you're asked to be seated. Let the interviewer start the discussion, and listen for cues that tell you what he or she is interested in knowing about you as a potential employee.

The first minute of the interview is crucial.

The Question-and-Answer Stage

Questions and answers will consume the greatest part of the interview. The interviewer will ask you about your qualifications and discuss many of the points mentioned in your résumé. You'll also be asking questions of your own.

Dealing with Questions   Let the interviewer lead the conversation, and never answer a question before he or she has finished asking it. Surprisingly, the last few words of the question might alter how you respond. As questions are asked, tailor your answers to make a favorable impression. Don't limit yourself to yes-or-no answers. If you're asked a difficult question, be sure you pause to think before responding.

Tailor your answers to emphasize your strengths.

If you periodically ask a question or two from the list you've prepared, you'll not only learn something but also demonstrate your interest. Probe for what the company is looking for in its new employees so that you can show how you meet the firm's needs. Also try to zero in on any reservations the interviewer might have about you so that you can dispel them.

Listening to the Interviewer   Paying attention when the interviewer speaks can be as important as giving good answers or asking good questions. The recruiters at Herman Miller agree that listening should make up about half the time you spend in an interview. For tips on becoming a better listener, see Chapter 2.

Paying attention to both verbal and nonverbal messages can help you turn the question-and-answer stage to your advantage.

The interviewer's facial expressions, eye movements, gestures, and posture may tell you the real meaning of what is being said. Be especially aware of how your comments are received. Does the interviewer nod in agreement or smile to show approval? If so, you're making progress. If not, you might want to introduce another topic or modify your approach.

Fielding Discriminatory Questions   Employers cannot legally discriminate against a job candidate on the basis of race, color, gender, age (from 40 to 70), marital status, religion, national origin, or disability. In general, the following topics should not be directly or indirectly introduced by an interviewer:[21]

Some topics should not be introduced by interviewers.

- Your religious affiliation or organizations and lodges you belong to

- Your national origin, age, marital status, or former name

- Your spouse, spouse's employment or salary, dependents, children, or child-care arrangements

- Your height, weight, gender, pregnancy, or any health conditions or disabilities that are not reasonably related to job performance

- Arrests or criminal convictions that are not related to job performance

Table 15–5   INTERVIEW QUESTIONS THAT MAY AND MAY NOT BE ASKED

You may ask this . . .	But not this . . .
What is your name?	What was your maiden name?
Are you over 18?	When were you born?
Did you graduate from high school?	When did you graduate from high school?
[No questions about race are allowed.]	What is your race?
Can you perform [specific tasks]?	Do you have physical or mental disabilities?
	Do you have a drug or alcohol problem?
	Are you taking any prescription drugs?
Would you be able to meet the job's requirement to frequently work weekends?	Would working on weekends conflict with your religion?
Do you have the legal right to work in the United States?	What country are you a citizen of?
Have you ever been convicted of a felony?	Have you ever been arrested?
This job requires that you speak Spanish. Do you?	What language did you speak in your home when you were growing up?
What is your place of residence?	Do you own or rent your home?
Do you have any physical condition or handicap that may limit your ability to perform the job applied for? If yes, what can be done to accommodate this limitation?	Do you have any physical disabilities or handicaps?

Although federal law does not specifically prohibit questions that touch on these areas, the Equal Employment Opportunity Commission (EEOC) considers such questions with "extreme disfavor." Table 15–5 compares specific questions that may and may not be asked during an employment interview.

Think about how you might respond if you are asked to answer unlawful interview questions.

How to Respond   If your interviewer asks these personal questions, how you respond depends on how badly you want the job, how you feel about revealing the information asked for, what you think the interviewer will do with the information, and whether you want to work for a company that asks such questions. If you don't want the job, you can tell the interviewer that you think a particular question is unethical or simply refuse to answer—responses that will leave an unfavorable impression.[22] If you do want the job, you might (1) ask how the question is related to your qualifications, (2) explain that the information is personal, (3) respond to what you think is the interviewer's real concern, or (4) answer both the question and the concern. If you choose to answer an unethical or discriminatory question, you run the risk that what you say may hurt your chances, so think carefully before answering.[23]

Where to File a Complaint   When a business can show that the safety of its employees or customers is at stake, it may be allowed to ask questions that would seem discriminatory in another context. Despite this exception, if you believe an interviewer's questions are unreasonable, unrelated to the job, or an attempt to discriminate, you may complain to the EEOC or to the state agency that regulates fair employment practices. To report discrimination on the basis of age or physical disability, contact the employer's equal opportunity officer or the U.S. Department of Labor. If you file a complaint, be prepared to spend a lot of time and effort on it—and keep in mind that you may not win.[24]

The Close

Like the opening, the end of the interview is more important than its duration would indicate. In the last few minutes, you need to evaluate how well you've done. You also need to correct any misconceptions the interviewer might have.

Concluding Gracefully   You can generally tell when the interviewer is trying to conclude the session. He or she may ask whether you have any more questions, sum up the discussion, change position, or indicate with a gesture that the interview is over. When you get the signal, respond promptly, but don't rush. Be sure to thank the interviewer for the opportunity and express an interest in the organization. If you can do so comfortably, try to pin down what will happen next, but don't press for an immediate decision.

> Conclude the interview with courtesy and enthusiasm.

    If this is your second or third visit to the organization, the interview may culminate with an offer of employment. You have two options: Accept it or request time to think it over. The best course is usually to wait. If no job offer is made, the interviewer may not have reached a decision yet, but you may tactfully ask when you can expect to know the decision.

Discussing Salary   If you do receive an offer during the interview, you'll naturally want to discuss salary. However, let the interviewer raise the subject. If asked your salary requirements, say that you would expect to receive the standard salary for the job in question. If you have added qualifications, point them out: "With my 18 months of experience in the field, I would expect to start in the middle of the normal salary range." Some applicants find the Internet a terrific resource for salary information.

> Be realistic in your salary expectations and diplomatic in your negotiations.

When to Negotiate   If you don't like the offer, you might try to negotiate, provided you're in a good bargaining position and the organization has the flexibility to accommodate you. You'll be in a fairly strong position if your skills are in short supply and you have several other offers. It also helps if you're the favorite candidate and the organization is booming. However, many organizations are relatively rigid in their salary practices, particularly at the entry level. In the United States and some European countries, it is perfectly acceptable to ask, "Is there any room for negotiation?"

> Negotiating salary can be tricky.

What to Negotiate   Even if you can't bargain for more money, you may be able to win some concessions on benefits and perquisites. The value of negotiating can be significant because benefits often cost the employer 25 to 45 percent of your salary. In other words, if you're offered an annual salary of $20,000, you'll ordinarily get an additional $5,000 to $9,000 in benefits: life, health, and disability insurance; pension and savings plans; vacation time; or even tuition reimbursement.[25]

    If you can trade one benefit for another, you may be able to enhance the value of the total package. For example, life insurance may be relatively unimportant to you if you're single, whereas extra vacation time might be very valuable indeed. Don't inquire about benefits, however, until you know you have a job offer.

> Negotiating benefits may be one way to get more value from an employment package.

Interview Notes

If yours is a typical job search, you'll have many interviews before you accept an offer. For that reason, keeping a notebook or binder of interview notes can help you refresh your memory of each conversation. As soon as the interview ends, jot down the names and titles of the people you met. Briefly summarize the interviewer's answers

> Keep a written record of your job interviews.

✓ CHECKLIST: Succeeding with Job Interviews

Preparation

✓ Fine-tune the research you already conducted before sending your résumé to the company (determine the requirements and general salary range of the job; review the organization's products, structure, financial standing, and prospects for growth; determine the interviewer's name, title, and status in the firm).

✓ Prepare (but don't overrehearse) answers for the questions you are likely to be asked.

✓ Develop relevant questions to ask.

✓ Work on increasing your confidence levels.

✓ Dress in a businesslike manner, regardless of the mode of dress preferred within the organization.

✓ Take a briefcase or portfolio—with pen, paper, list of questions, résumés, and work samples.

✓ Double-check the location and time of the interview, mapping out the route beforehand.

✓ Plan to arrive 10 to 15 minutes early; allow 10 to 15 minutes for possible problems en route.

The Warm-Up Stage of the Interview

✓ Greet the interviewer by name, with a smile and direct eye contact.

✓ Offer a firm (not crushing) handshake if the interviewer extends a hand.

✓ Take a seat only after the interviewer invites you to be seated or has taken his or her own seat.

✓ Listen for cues about what the questions are trying to reveal about you and your qualifications.

✓ Assume a calm and poised attitude (avoiding gum chewing, smoking, and other signs of nervousness).

The Question-and-Answer Stage of the Interview

✓ Display a genuine (not artificial) smile, when appropriate.

✓ Convey interest and enthusiasm.

✓ Listen attentively so that you can give intelligent responses (taking few notes).

✓ Relate your knowledge and skills to the position and stress your positive qualities.

✓ Keep responses brief, clear, and to the point.

✓ Avoid exaggeration, and convey honesty and sincerity.

✓ Avoid slighting references to former employers.

The Close of the Interview

✓ Watch for signs that the interview is about to end.

✓ Tactfully ask when you will be advised of the decision on your application.

✓ If you're offered the job, either accept or ask for time to consider the offer.

✓ Let the interviewer initiate the discussion of salary, but put it off until late in the interview if possible.

✓ If asked, state that you would like to receive the standard salary for the position.

✓ With a warm smile and a handshake, thank the interviewer for meeting with you.

---

to your questions. Then quickly evaluate your performance during the interview, listing what you handled well and what you didn't. Going over these notes can help you improve your performance in the future.[26] In addition to improving your performance during interviews, your notes will help you keep track of any follow-up messages you'll need to send. Whenever you need to review important tips, consult the "Checklist: Succeeding with Job Interviews."

FOLLOWING UP AFTER THE INTERVIEW

Touching base with the prospective employer after the interview, either by phone or in writing, shows that you really want the job and are determined to get it. Herman Miller's Mike Volkema can tell you that follow-up messages bring your name to the interviewer's attention once again and remind him or her that you're waiting for the decision.

Six types of follow-up messages:
- Thank-you message
- Inquiry
- Request for a time extension
- Letter of acceptance
- Letter declining a job offer
- Letter of resignation

The two most common forms of follow-up are the thank-you message and the inquiry. These messages are often handled by letter, but an e-mail or a phone call can be just as effective, particularly if the employer seems to favor a casual, personal style. Other types of follow-up messages are sent only in certain cases—letters requesting a time extension, letters of acceptance, letters declining a job offer, and letters of resignation. These four types of employment messages are best handled in writing to document any official actions relating to your employment.

Evelyn Gilardi followed up her job interview by sending a thank-you letter within 48 hours. Then a week later, she followed up with a phone call, in which she was careful to build rapport and sell her strengths. If the employer's timetable for filling the position had been shorter, Gilardi would have telephoned even sooner.

Thank-You Message

Express your thanks within two days after the interview, even if you feel you have little chance for the job. Acknowledge the interviewer's time and courtesy, and be sure to restate the specific job you're applying for. Convey your continued interest, then ask politely for a decision.

Keep your thank-you message brief (less than five minutes for a phone call or only one page for a letter), and organize it like a routine message. Demonstrate the "you" attitude, and sound positive without sounding overconfident. The following sample thank-you message shows how to achieve all this in three brief paragraphs:

A note or phone call thanking the interviewer
- Is organized like a routine message
- Closes with a request for a decision or future consideration

After talking with you yesterday, touring your sets, and watching the television commercials being filmed, I remain enthusiastic about the possibility of joining your staff as a television/film production assistant. Thanks for taking so much time to show me around.

Reminds the interviewer of the reasons for meeting and graciously acknowledges the consideration shown to the applicant

During our meeting, I said that I would prefer not to relocate, but I've reconsidered the matter. I would be pleased to relocate wherever you need my skills in set decoration and prop design.

Indicates the writer's flexibility and commitment to the job if hired

Now that you've explained the details of your operation, I feel quite strongly that I can make a contribution to the sorts of productions you're lining up. You can also count on me to be an energetic employee and a positive addition to your crew. Please let me know your decision as soon as possible.

Reminds the recruiter of special qualifications

Closes on a confident you-oriented note

Ends with a request for decision

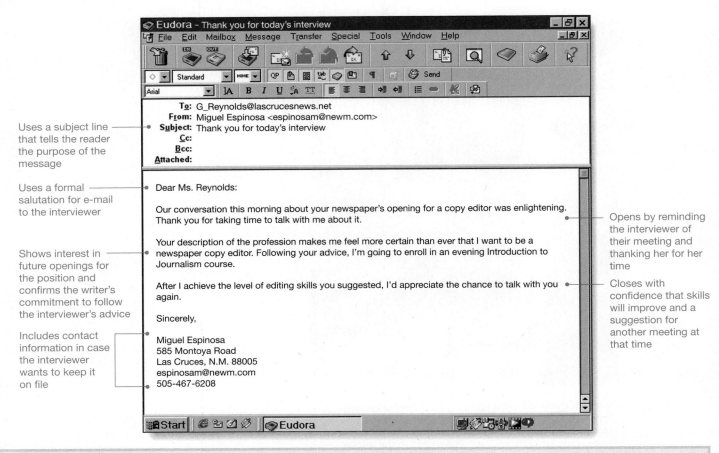

Uses a subject line that tells the reader the purpose of the message

Uses a formal salutation for e-mail to the interviewer

Shows interest in future openings for the position and confirms the writer's commitment to follow the interviewer's advice

Includes contact information in case the interviewer wants to keep it on file

Opens by reminding the interviewer of their meeting and thanking her for her time

Closes with confidence that skills will improve and a suggestion for another meeting at that time

FIGURE 15–2
Effective Thank-You Message

Even if the interviewer has said that you are unqualified for the job, a thank-you message may keep the door open. Miguel Espinosa followed up a recent job interview with a thank-you message sent by e-mail the same day (see Figure 15–2).

Letter of Inquiry

An inquiry about a hiring decision follows the plan for a direct request.

If you're not advised of the interviewer's decision by the promised date or within two weeks, you might make an inquiry. A letter of inquiry is particularly appropriate if you've received a job offer from a second firm and don't want to accept it before you have an answer from the first. The following letter illustrates the general plan for a direct request; the writer assumes that a simple oversight, and not outright rejection, is the reason for the delay:

Identifies the position and introduces the main idea

> When we talked on April 7 about the fashion coordinator position in your Park Avenue showroom, you said you would let me know your decision before May 1. I would still like the position, so I'm eager to know what conclusion you've reached.

Places the reason for the request second

> To complicate matters, another firm has now offered me a position and has asked that I reply within the next two weeks.

Makes a courteous request for specific action last, while clearly stating a preference for this organization

> Because your company seems to offer a greater challenge, I would appreciate knowing about your decision by Thursday, May 12. If you need more information before then, please let me know.

Javier Favares understands that inquiring about interview results electronically can be faster than sending a letter. But he is careful to make sure that the potential employer is open to electronic communication.

Request for a Time Extension

If you receive a job offer while other interviews are still pending, you'll probably want more time to decide, so write to the offering organization and ask for a time extension. Employers understand that candidates often interview with several companies. They want you to be sure you're making the right decision, so most are happy to accommodate you with a reasonable extension. The letter in Figure 15–3 is a good example of such a request.

Requesting more time requires extra tact.

Preface your request with a friendly opening. Ask for more time, stressing your enthusiasm for the organization. Conclude by allowing for a quick decision if your request for additional time is denied. Ask for a prompt reply confirming the time extension if the organization grants it. This type of letter is, in essence, a direct request. However, because the recipient may be disappointed, be sure to temper your request for an extension with statements indicating your continued interest.

Document Makeover

IMPROVE THIS LETTER

To practice correcting drafts of actual documents, visit **www.prenhall.com/onekey** on the web. Click "Document Make-overs," then click Chapter 15. You will find a letter that contains problems and errors relating to what you've learned in this chapter about interviewing for employment and following up. Use the Final Draft decision tool to create an improved version of this request for a time extension. Check the letter for all the elements necessary to reassure the potential employer, ask for the extension, explain the reasons for the request, offer to compromise, and facilitate a quick reply.

Letter of Acceptance

When you receive a job offer that you want to accept, reply within five days. Begin by accepting the position and expressing thanks. Identify the job that you're accepting. In the next paragraph, cover any necessary details. Conclude by saying that you look forward to reporting for work. As always, a good-news letter should convey your enthusiasm and eagerness to cooperate:

A letter of acceptance follows the good-news plan.

1448 Solsbury Avenue
Thunderhawk, SD 57655
January 5, 2004

Mr. Frank Lapuzo, Vice President
Customer Relations
Lone Star Foods
7499 Hackberry Parkway
San Antonio, TX 78210

Dear Mr. Lapuzo:

Begins with a strong statement of interest in the job →
The customer relations position in your snack foods division seems like an exciting challenge and a great opportunity. I'm very pleased that you offered it to me.

Emphasizes specific reasons for preferring the first job offer to help reassure the reader of sincerity →
Because of another commitment, I would appreciate your giving me until February 16 to make a decision. Before our interview, I scheduled a follow-up interview with another company. I'm interested in your organization because of its impressive quality-control procedures and friendly, attractive work environment, but I do feel obligated to keep my appointment.

← Stresses professional obligations, not the desire to learn what the other company may offer

If you need my decision immediately, I'll gladly let you know. However, if you can allow me the added time to fulfill the earlier commitment, I'd be grateful. Please let me know right away by telephoning me at (605) 234-6897.

← Closes with expression of willingness to yield or compromise, conveying continued interest in the position

Sincerely,

Chang Li

Chang Li

FIGURE 15–3
Effective Request for a Time Extension

Confirms the specific terms of the offer with a good-news statement at the beginning →
I'm delighted to accept the graphic design position in your advertising department at the salary of $1,575 a month.

Covers miscellaneous details in the middle →
Enclosed are the health insurance forms you asked me to complete and sign. I've already given notice to my current employer and will be able to start work on Monday, January 18.

Closes with another reference to the good news and a look toward the future →
The prospect of joining your firm is exciting. Thank you for giving me this opportunity for what I'm sure will be a challenging future.

Written acceptance of a job offer is legally binding.

Be aware that a job offer and a written acceptance of that offer constitute a legally binding contract, for both you and the employer. Before you write an acceptance letter, be sure you want the job.

Letter Declining a Job Offer   After all your interviews, you may find that you need to write a letter declining a job offer. The bad-news plan is ideally suited to this type of letter. Open warmly, state the reasons for refusing the offer, decline the offer explicitly, and close on a pleasant note, expressing gratitude. By taking the time to write a sincere, tactful letter, you leave the door open for future contact:

A letter declining a job offer follows the bad-news plan.

One of the most interesting interviews I have had was the one last month at your Durham textile plant. I'm flattered that you would offer me the computer analyst position that we talked about.

— Makes the opening paragraph a buffer

During my job search, I applied to five highly rated firms like your own, each one a leader in its field. Both your company and another offered me a position. Because my desire to work abroad can more readily be satisfied by the other company, I have accepted that job offer.

— Precedes the bad news with tactfully phrased reasons for the applicant's unfavorable decision, and leaves the door open

I deeply appreciate the hour you spent talking with me. Thank you again for your consideration and kindness.

— Lets the reader down gently with a sincere and cordial ending

Letter of Resignation

If you get a job offer and are currently employed, you can maintain good relations with your current employer by writing a letter of resignation to your immediate supervisor. Follow the bad-news plan, and make the letter sound positive, regardless of how you feel. Say something favorable about the organization, the people you work with, or what you've learned on the job. Then state your intention to leave and give the date of your last day on the job. Be sure you give your current employer at least two weeks' notice:

A letter of resignation also follows the bad-news plan.

My sincere thanks to you and to all the other Emblem Corporation employees for helping me learn so much about serving the public these past 11 months. You have given me untold help and encouragement.

— Uses an appreciative opening to serve as a buffer

You may recall that when you first interviewed me, my goal was to become a customer relations supervisor. Because that opportunity has been offered to me by another organization, I am submitting my resignation. I will miss all of you, but I want to take advantage of this opportunity.

— States reasons before the bad news itself, using tactful phrasing to help keep the relationship friendly, should the writer later want letters of recommendation

I would like to terminate my work here two weeks from today but can arrange to work an additional week if you want me to train a replacement.

— Discusses necessary details in an extra paragraph

My sincere thanks and best wishes to all of you.

— Tempers any disappointment with a cordial close

Compare your messages with the suggestions in the "Checklist: Writing Follow-Up Messages."

✓ CHECKLIST: Writing Follow-Up Messages

Thank-You Message

✓ Write a thank-you letter within two days of the interview (keeping it to one page).
✓ If you have no alternative, thank the interviewer by phone (taking less than five minutes).
✓ In the opening, express thanks and identify the job and the time and place of the interview.
✓ Use the middle section for supporting details.
✓ Express your enthusiasm about the organization and the job.
✓ Add any new facts that may help your chances.
✓ Try to repair any negative impressions you may have left during the interview.
✓ Use an action ending.

Letter of Inquiry

✓ Make an inquiry—by letter, phone, or e-mail—if you aren't informed of the decision by the promised date.
✓ Follow the plan for direct requests: main idea, necessary details, specific request.

Request for a Time Extension

✓ Request an extension if you have pending interviews and need time to decide about an offer.
✓ Open with an expression of warmth.
✓ In the middle, explain why you need more time and express continued interest in the company.

✓ In the close, promise a quick decision if your request is denied, and ask for a confirmation if your request is granted.

Letter of Acceptance

✓ Send this message within five days of receiving the offer.
✓ State clearly that you accept the offer, identify the job you're accepting, and include vital details.
✓ Conclude with a statement that you look forward to reporting for work.

Letter Declining a Job Offer

✓ Open a letter of rejection warmly.
✓ Explain why you are refusing the offer, and express your appreciation.
✓ End on a sincere, positive note.

Letter of Resignation

✓ Send a letter of resignation to your current employer as soon as possible.
✓ Begin with an appreciative buffer.
✓ In the middle section, state your reasons for leaving, and actually state that you are resigning.
✓ Close cordially.

On the Job:
SOLVING COMMUNICATION DILEMMAS AT HERMAN MILLER, INC.

As a member of Herman Miller's staffing department, you are responsible for screening job candidates and arranging for candidates to interview with members of Herman Miller's professional staff. Your responsibilities include the development of interview questions and evaluation forms for use by company employees involved in the interview process. You also handle all routine correspondence with job candidates. In each of the following situations, choose the best alternative, and be prepared to explain why your choice is best.

1. Herman Miller has decided to establish a management-training program for recent college gradu-

ates. The program will groom people for careers in finance, strategic planning, marketing, administration, and general management. To recruit people for the program, the firm will conduct on-campus interviews at several colleges—something it has not generally done. You and the other Herman Miller interviewers will be talking with 30 or 40 applicants on campus. You will have 20 minutes for each interview. Your goal is to identify the candidates who will be invited to come to the office for evaluation interviews. You want the preliminary screening process to be as fair and objective as possible, so how will you approach the task?

a. Meet with all the Herman Miller interviewers to discuss the characteristics that successful candidates will exhibit. Allow each interviewer to use his or her individual approach to identify these characteristics in applicants. Encourage the interviewers to ask whatever questions seem most useful in light of the individual characteristics of each candidate.

b. Develop a list of 10 to 15 questions that will be posed to all candidates. Instruct the Herman Miller interviewers to adhere strictly to the list so that all applicants will respond to the same questions and be evaluated on the same basis.

c. Develop a written evaluation form for measuring all candidates against criteria such as academic performance, relevant experience, capacity for teamwork, and communication skills. For each criterion, suggest four or five questions that interviewers might use to evaluate the candidate. Instruct the interviewers to cover all the criteria and to fill out the written evaluation form for each applicant immediately after the interview.

d. Design a questionnaire for candidates to complete prior to their interviews. Then ask the interviewers to outline the ideal answers they would like to see a candidate offer for each item on this questionnaire. These ideal answers give you a standard against which to measure actual candidate answers.

2. During the on-campus screening interviews, you ask several candidates, "Why do you want to work for this organization?" Of the following responses, which would you rank the highest?

a. "I'd like to work here because I'm interested in the office furniture business. I've always been fascinated by industrial design and the interaction between people and their environment. In addition to studying business, I have taken courses in industrial design and industrial psychology. I also have some personal experience in building furniture. My grandfather is a cabinet maker and an antique restorer, and I have been his apprentice since I was 12 years old. I've paid for college by working as a carpenter during summer vacations."

b. "I'm an independent person with a lot of internal drive. I do my best work when I'm given a fairly free reign to use my creativity. From what I've read about your corporate culture, I think my working style would fit very well with your management philosophy. I'm also the sort of person who identifies very strongly with my job. For better or worse, I define myself through my affiliation with my employer. I get a great sense of pride from being part of a first-rate operation, and I think Herman Miller is first-rate. I've read

about the design awards you've won and about your selection as one of America's most admired companies. The articles say that Herman Miller is a well-managed company. I think I would learn a lot working here, and I think my drive and creativity would be appreciated."

c. "There are several reasons why I'd like to work for Herman Miller. For one thing, I have family and friends in Zeeland, and I'd like to stay in the area. Also, I have friends who work for Herman Miller, and they both say it's terrific. I've also heard good things about your compensation and benefits."

d. "My ultimate goal is to start my own company, but first I need to learn more about managing a business. I read in *Fortune* that Herman Miller is one of America's most admired corporations. I think I could learn a lot by joining your management-training program and observing your operations."

3. You are preparing questions for the professional staff to use when conducting follow-up interviews at Herman Miller's headquarters. You want a question that will reveal something about the candidates' probable loyalty to the organization. Which of the following questions is the best choice?

a. If you knew you could be one of the world's most successful people in a single occupation, such as music, politics, medicine, or business, what occupation would you choose? If you knew you had only a 10 percent chance of being so successful, would you still choose the same occupation?

b. We value loyalty among our employees. Tell me something about yourself that demonstrates your loyalty as a member of an organization.

c. What would you do if you discovered that a co-worker routinely made personal, unauthorized long-distance phone calls from work?

d. What other companies are you interviewing with?

4. In concluding an evaluation interview, you ask the candidate, "Do you have any questions?" Which of the following answers would you respond most favorably to?

a. "No. I can't think of anything. You've been very thorough in describing the job and the company. Thank you for taking the time to talk with me."

b. "Yes. I have an interview with one of your competitors, Steelcase, next week. How would you sum up the differences between your two firms?"

c. "Yes. If I were offered a position here, what would my chances be of getting promoted within the next 12 months?"

d. "Yes. Do you think Herman Miller will be a better or worse company 15 years from now?"[27]

Learning Objectives Checkup

To assess your understanding of the principles in this chapter, read each learning objective and study the accompanying exercises. For fill-in items, write the missing text in the blank provided; for multiple choice items, circle the letter of the correct answer. You can check your responses against the answer key on page AK-3.

Objective 15.1: Explain the typical sequence of interviews.

1. During the _____ stage of the interview process, you and other candidates are likely to be interviewed by several representatives from the employer, including a member of the human resources department and your potential supervisor.
   a. Screening
   b. Selection
   c. Final
   d. Group

2. In the final stage of the interview sequence, your goal is to
   a. Differentiate yourself from other candidates
   b. Showcase your best qualifications for the job
   c. Learn as much as you can about the organization
   d. Clinch the job on the best possible terms

Objective 15.2: Identify and briefly describe the most common types of job interviews.

3. When an employer asks a series of prepared questions in a set order, the interview is
   a. A structured interview
   b. An open-ended interview
   c. A situational interview
   d. A stress interview

4. When an employer uses questions that encourage the applicant to talk freely, the interview is
   a. A structured interview
   b. An open-ended interview
   c. A situational interview
   d. A stress interview

5. When an employer asks questions designed to irk or unsettle you, the interview is
   a. A structured interview
   b. An open-ended interview
   c. A panel interview
   d. A stress interview

6. In a group interview,
   a. Multiple members of the staff meet and question each candidate
   b. The employer meets with several candidates simultaneously to see how they interact
   c. A human resources staff member briefs all candidates on the company's policies
   d. Candidates are given hands-on tasks to see how they will handle on-the-job situations

Objective 15.3: Discuss six tasks you need to complete to prepare for a successful job interview.

7. Employers are looking for job candidates who
   a. Are a good fit with the organization
   b. Have high grade-point averages
   c. Have glowing recommendation letters
   d. Have a "flashy" appearance

8. When preparing for an interview, it is a good idea to
   a. Do additional research on the company where you are applying
   b. Practice answering the most commonly asked questions
   c. Think of some questions of your own to ask the interviewer
   d. Do all of the above

9. To make a good impression on a job interviewer, you
   a. Refrain from using any hand gestures during the interview
   b. Work on your speaking voice, including eliminating speech mannerisms that may make you sound inarticulate
   c. Wear colorful clothing so that you will stand out from other candidates
   d. Do all of the above

Objective 15.4: Describe the three stages of a successful employment interview.

10. Half of the interviewer's decision about a candidate is made
   a. In the first 30 to 60 seconds of the interview
   b. In the final 30 to 60 seconds of the interview
   c. On the basis of the résumé
   d. On the basis of the cover letter

11. What do you do if a job interviewer asks you about your marital status, how many children you have, and what their ages are?
   a. Answer them—it is perfectly within the interviewer's right to ask you such personal questions, even if they are not directly related to the job you are applying for.
   b. Tell the interviewer that such questions are illegal and threaten to sue for invasion of privacy.
   c. If you want the job, respond to what you think is the interviewer's real concern.
   d. If you want the job, refuse to answer the questions but say that you won't report the employer to the EEOC.

12. What should you do if the interviewer tells you the salary for the job being offered?
   a. Always take whatever the company offers.
   b. Respond with a figure higher than what is offered.
   c. Respond with a figure lower than what is offered.
   d. Ask the interviewer, "Is there any room to negotiate?"

Objective 15.5: Name six common employment messages that follow an interview, and state briefly when you would use each one.

13. Following a job interview, you should send a thank-you message
   a. Within two days after the interview
   b. Only if you think you got the job
   c. That follows the AIDA organizational plan
   d. That does all of the above

14. A letter declining a job offer should follow
   a. The direct plan
   b. The AIDA plan
   c. The bad-news plan
   d. The polite plan

Apply Your Knowledge

1. How can you distinguish yourself from other candidates in a screening interview and still keep your responses short and to the point? Explain.
2. What can you do to make a favorable impression when you discover that an open-ended interview has turned into a stress interview? Briefly explain your answer.
3. If you want to switch jobs because you can't work with your supervisor, how can you explain this situation to a prospective employer? Give an example.
4. During a group interview you notice that one of the other candidates is trying to monopolize the conversation. He's always the first to answer, his answer is the longest, and he even interrupts the other candidates while they are talking. The interviewer doesn't seem to be concerned about his behavior, but you are. You would like to have more time to speak so that the interviewer could get to know you better. What should you do?
5. **Ethical Choices** Why is it important to distinguish unethical or illegal interview questions from acceptable questions? Explain.

Practice Your Knowledge

DOCUMENTS FOR ANALYSIS

Read the following documents; then (1) analyze the strengths or weaknesses of each document and (2) revise each document so that it follows this chapter's guidelines.

DOCUMENT 15.A: THANK-YOU MESSAGE

Thank you for the really marvelous opportunity to meet you and your colleagues at Starret Engine Company. I really enjoyed touring your facilities and talking with all the people there. You have quite a crew! Some of the other companies I have visited have been so rigid and uptight that I can't imagine how I would fit in. It's a relief to run into a group of people who seem to enjoy their work as much as all of you do.

I know that you must be looking at many other candidates for this job, and I know that some of them will probably be more experienced than I am. But I do want to emphasize that my two-year hitch in the Navy involved a good deal of engineering work. I don't think I mentioned all my shipboard responsibilities during the interview.

Please give me a call within the next week to let me know your decision. You can usually find me at my dormitory in the evening after dinner (phone: 877-9080).

DOCUMENT 15.B: LETTER OF INQUIRY

I have recently received a very attractive job offer from the Warrington Company. But before I let them know one way or another, I would like to consider any offer that your firm may extend. I was quite impressed with your company during my recent interview, and I am still very interested in a career there.

I don't mean to pressure you, but Warrington has asked for my decision within 10 days. Could you let me know by Tuesday whether you plan to offer me a position? That would give me enough time to compare the two offers.

DOCUMENT 15.C: LETTER DECLINING A JOB OFFER

I'm writing to say that I must decline your job offer. Another company has made me a more generous offer, and I have decided to accept. However, if things don't work out for me there, I will let you know. I sincerely appreciate your interest in me.

Exercises

For live links to all websites discussed in this chapter, visit this text's website at www.prenhall.com/thill. Just log on and select Chapter 15, and click on "Student Resources." Locate the page or the URL related to the material in the text. For "Learning More on the Web" exercises, you'll also find navigational directions. Click on the live link to the site.

15.1 **Internet** Select a large company (one that you can easily find information on) where you might like to work. Use Internet sources to gather some preliminary research on the company.
  a. What did you learn about this organization that would help you during an interview there?
  b. What Internet sources did you use to obtain this information?
  c. Armed with this information, what aspects of your background do you think might appeal to this company's recruiters?
  d. If you choose to apply for a job with this company, what keywords would you include on your electronic résumé, and why?

15.2 **Teamwork** Divide the class into two groups. Half the class will be recruiters for a large chain of national department stores looking to fill manager trainee positions (there are 15 openings). The other half of the class will be candidates for the job. The company is specifically looking for candidates who demonstrate these three qualities: initiative, dependability, and willingness to assume responsibility.

    a. Have each recruiter select and interview an applicant for 10 minutes.

    b. Have all the recruiters discuss how they assessed the applicant in each of the three desired qualities. What questions did they ask or what did they use as an indicator to determine whether the candidate possessed the quality?

    c. Have all the applicants discuss what they said to convince the recruiters that they possessed each of these qualities.

15.3 **Interviews: Understanding Qualifications** Write a short memo to your instructor, discussing what you believe are your greatest strengths and weaknesses from an employment perspective. Next, explain how these strengths and weaknesses would be viewed by interviewers evaluating your qualifications.

15.4 **Interviews: Being Prepared** Prepare written answers to 10 of the questions listed in Table 15–2, "Twenty-Five Common Interview Questions" (see page 526).

15.5 **Ethical Choices** You have decided to accept a new position with one of your current company's competitors. Write a letter of resignation to your supervisor, announcing your decision.

    a. Will you notify your employer that you are joining a competing firm? Please explain.

    b. Will you use the direct or the indirect approach? Please explain.

    c. Will you send your letter by e-mail, send it by regular mail, or place it on your supervisor's desk?

Expand Your Knowledge

LEARNING MORE ON THE WEB

Planning for a Successful Interview www.job-interview.net

How can you practice for a job interview? What are some questions that you might be asked, and how should you respond? What questions are you not obligated to answer? Job-interview.net provides mock interviews based on actual job openings. It provides job descriptions, questions and answers for specific careers and jobs, and links to company guides and annual reports. You'll find a step-by-step plan that outlines key job requirements, lists practice interview questions, and helps you put together practice interviews. The site offers tips on the keywords to look for in a job description, which will help you narrow your search and anticipate the questions you might be asked on your first or next job interview.

ACTIVITIES

If you have not interviewed recently (or ever) for a job, do you have an idea of the kind of questions you might be asked? How can you prepare for an interview so that you'll appear knowledgeable about the job and confident in your skills? At Job-interview.net you'll get advice and ideas to make your next interview successful.

1. What are some problem questions you might be asked during a job interview? How would you handle these questions?

2. Choose a job title from the list, and read more about it. What did you learn that could help during an actual interview for the job you selected?

3. Developing an "interview game plan" ahead of time helps you make a strong, positive impression during an interview. What are some of the things you can practice to help make everything you do during an interview seem to come naturally?

EXPLORING THE WEB ON YOUR OWN

Review these chapter-related websites on your own to learn more about interviewing for jobs.

1. Get over 2,000 pages of career advice at Monster.com, www.monster.com, and talk to career experts in your choice of industry or profession.

2. Learn how to prepare for and handle yourself with care during a job interview at So You Wanna Ace A Job Interview, www.soyouwanna.com/site/syws/aceinterview/aceinterview.html.

3. To be better prepared for your next interview, visit CampusProgram.com's Job Interview Tips and Guidelines at www.campusprogram.com/employment/interview.html.

Learn Interactively

INTERACTIVE STUDY GUIDE

Go to the Companion Website at www.prenhall.com/bovee. For Chapter 15, take advantage of the interactive "Study Guide" to test your knowledge of the chapter. Get instant feedback on whether you need additional studying. Also, visit this site's "Study Hall" where you'll find an abundance of valuable resources that will help you succeed in this course.

PEAK PERFORMANCE GRAMMAR AND MECHANICS

To improve your skill with vocabulary, visit this text's website at www.prenhall.com/onekey. Click "Peak Performance Grammar and Mechanics," then click first on "Vocabulary I" and second on "Vocabulary II." In both sections, take the Pretest to determine whether you have any weak areas. Review those areas in the Refresher Course, and take the Follow-Up Test to check your grasp of vocabulary. For advanced practice, take the Advanced Test. Finally, for additional reinforcement, go to the "Improve Your Grammar, Mechanics, and Usage" section that follows, and complete those exercises.

Improve Your Grammar, Mechanics, and Usage

The following exercises help you improve your knowledge of and power over English grammar, mechanics, and usage. Turn to the "Handbook of Grammar, Mechanics, and Usage" at the end of this textbook and review all of Sections 4.1 (Frequently Confused Words), 4.2 (Frequently Misused Words), and 4.3 (Frequently Misspelled Words). Then look at the following 10 items. Underline the preferred choice within each set of parentheses. (Answers to these exercises appear on page AK-4.)

1. Everyone (*accept/except*) Barbara King has registered for the company competition.
2. We need to find a new security (*device/devise*).
3. The Jennings are (*loath/loathe*) to admit that they are wrong.
4. That decision lies with the director, (*who's/whose*) in charge of this department.
5. In this department, we see (*a lot, alot*) of mistakes like that.
6. In my (*judgement, judgment*), you'll need to redo the cover.
7. He decided to reveal the information, (*irregardless, regardless*) of the consequences.
8. Why not go along when it is so easy to (*accomodate, accommodate*) his demands?
9. When you say that, do you mean to (*infer, imply*) that I'm being unfair?
10. All we have to do is try (*and, to*) get along with him for a few more days.

For additional exercises focusing on misused and misspelled words, go to www.prenhall.com/thill and select "Handbook of Grammar, Mechanics, and Usage Practice Sessions."

Cases

INTERVIEWING WITH POTENTIAL EMPLOYERS

1. Interviewers and interviewees: Classroom exercise in interviewing Interviewing is clearly an interactive process involving at least two people. The best way to practice for interviews is to work with others.

Your task: You and all other members of your class are to write letters of application for an entry-level or management-trainee position requiring a pleasant personality and intelligence but a minimum of specialized education or experience. Sign your letter with a fictitious name that conceals your identity. Next, polish (or prepare) a résumé that accurately identifies you and your educational and professional accomplishments.

Now, three members of the class who volunteer as interviewers divide up all the anonymously written application letters. Then each interviewer selects a candidate who seems the most pleasant and convincing in his or her letter. At this time the selected candidates identify themselves and give the interviewers their résumés.

Each interviewer then interviews his or her chosen candidate in front of the class, seeking to understand how the items on the résumé qualify the candidate for the job. At the end of the interviews, the class may decide who gets the job and discuss why this candidate was successful. Afterward, retrieve your letter, sign it with the right name, and submit it to the instructor for credit.

2. Internet interview: Exercise in interviewing Using the Web 100 site at www.web100.com, locate the homepage of a company you would like to work for. Then identify a position within the company for which you would like to apply. Study the company, using any of the online business resources discussed in Chapter 10, and prepare for an interview with that company.

Your task: Working with a classmate, take turns interviewing each other for your chosen positions. Interviewers should take notes during the interview. Once the interview is complete, critique each other's performance (interviewers should critique how well candidates prepared for the interview and answered the questions; interviewees should critique the quality of the questions asked). Write a follow-up letter thanking your interviewer and submit the letter to your instructor.

FOLLOWING UP AFTER THE INTERVIEW

3. A slight error in timing: Letter asking for delay of an employment decision You botched your timing and applied for your third-choice job before going after what you really wanted. What you want to do is work in retail marketing with Neiman Marcus in Dallas; what you have been offered is a similar job with Longhorn Leather and Lumber, 55 dry and dusty miles away in Commerce, just south of the Oklahoma panhandle.

You review your notes. Your Longhorn interview was three weeks ago with the human resources manager, R. P. Bronson, a congenial person who has just written to offer you the position. The store's address is 27 Sam Rayburn Dr., Commerce, TX 75428. Mr. Bronson notes that he can hold the position open for 10 days. You have an interview scheduled with Neiman Marcus next week, but it is unlikely that you will know the store's decision within this 10-day period.

Your task: Write to R. P. Bronson, requesting a reasonable delay in your consideration of his job offer.

4. Job hunt: Set of employment-related letters to a single company Where would you like to work? Pick a real or an imagined company, and assume that a month ago you sent your résumé and application letter. Not long afterward, you were invited to come for an interview, which seemed to go very well.

Your task: Use your imagination to write the following: (a) a thank-you letter for the interview, (b) a note of inquiry, (c) a request for more time to decide, (d) a letter of acceptance, and (e) a letter declining the job offer.

FORMAT AND LAYOUT OF BUSINESS DOCUMENTS

The format and layout of business documents vary from country to country; they even vary within regions of the United States. In addition, many organizations develop their own variations of standard styles, adapting documents to the types of messages they send and the kinds of audiences they communicate with. The formats described here are more common than others.

FIRST IMPRESSIONS

Your documents tell readers a lot about you and about your company's professionalism. So all your documents must look neat, present a professional image, and be easy to read. Your audience's first impression of a document comes from the quality of its paper, the way it is customized, and its general appearance.

Paper

To give a quality impression, businesspeople consider carefully the paper they use. Several aspects of paper contribute to the overall impression:

- **Weight.** Paper quality is judged by the weight of four reams (each a 500-sheet package) of letter-size paper. The weight most commonly used by U.S. business organizations is 20-pound paper, but 16- and 24-pound versions are also used.

- **Cotton content.** Paper quality is also judged by the percentage of cotton in the paper. Cotton doesn't yellow over time the way wood pulp does, plus it's both strong and soft. For letters and outside reports, use paper with a 25 percent cotton content. For memos and other internal documents, you can use a lighter-weight paper with lower cotton content. Airmail-weight paper may save money for international correspondence, but make sure it isn't too flimsy.[1]

- **Size.** In the United States, the standard paper size for business documents is 8½ by 11 inches. Standard legal documents are 8½ by 14 inches. Executives sometimes have heavier 7-by-10-inch paper on hand (with matching envelopes) for personal messages such as congratulations and recommendations.[2] They may also have a box of note cards imprinted with their initials and a box of plain folded notes for condolences or for acknowledging formal invitations.

- **Color.** White is the standard color for business purposes, although neutral colors such as gray and ivory are sometimes used. Memos can be produced on pastel-colored paper to distinguish them from external correspondence. In addition, memos are sometimes produced on various colors of paper for routing to separate departments. Light-colored papers are appropriate, but bright or dark colors make reading difficult and may appear too frivolous.

Customization

For letters to outsiders, U.S. businesses commonly use letterhead stationery, which may be either professionally printed or designed in-house using word-processing templates and graphics. The letterhead includes the company's name and address, usually at the top of the page but sometimes along the left side or even at the bottom. Other information may be included in the letterhead as well: the company's telephone number, fax number, cable address, website address, product lines, date of establishment, officers and directors, slogan, and symbol (logo). Well-designed letterhead gives readers[3]

- Pertinent reference data

- A favorable image of the company

- A good idea of what the company does

For as much as it's meant to accomplish, the letterhead should be as simple as possible. Too much information makes the page look cluttered, occupies space needed for the message, and might become outdated before all the stationery can be used. If you correspond frequently with people abroad, your letterhead must be intelligible to foreigners. It must include the name of your country in addition to your cable, telex, e-mail, or fax information.

In the United States, businesses always use letterhead for the first page of a letter. Successive pages are usually plain sheets of paper that match the letterhead in color and quality. Some companies use a specially printed second-page letterhead that bears only the company's name. Other countries have other conventions.

Many companies also design and print standardized forms for memos and frequently written reports that always require the same sort of information (such as sales reports and expense reports). These forms may be printed in sets for use with carbon paper or in carbonless-copy sets that produce multiple copies automatically. More and more organizations use computers to generate their standardized forms, which can save them both money and time.[4]

Appearance

Produce almost all of your business documents using either a printer (letter-quality, not a dot matrix) or a typewriter. Certain documents, however, should be handwritten (such as a short informal memo or a note of condolence). Be sure to handwrite, print, or type the envelope to match the document. However, even a letter on the best-quality paper with the best-designed letterhead may look unprofessional if it's poorly produced. So pay close attention to all the factors affecting appearance, including the following:

- **Margins.** Companies in the United States make sure that documents (especially external ones) are centered on the page, with margins of at least an inch all around. Using word-processing software, you can achieve this balance simply by defining the format parameters. When using a typewriter, either establish a standard line length (usually about 6 inches) or establish a "picture frame."

- **Line length.** Lines are rarely justified, because the resulting text looks too much like a form letter and can be hard to read (even with proportional spacing). Varying line length makes the document look more personal and interesting. Pica type (12 points) gives you 60 characters in a line; elite type (10 points) gives you 72 characters in a line.

- **Line spacing.** You can adjust the number of blank lines between elements (such as between the date and the inside address) to ensure that a short document fills the page vertically or that a longer document extends at least two lines of the body onto the last page.

- **Character spacing.** Use proper spacing between characters and after punctuation. For example, U.S. conventions include leaving one space after commas, semicolons, colons, and sentence-ending periods. Each letter in a person's initials is followed by a period and a single space. However, abbreviations such as U.S.A. or MBA may or may not have periods, but they never have internal spaces.

- **Special symbols.** When using a computer, use appropriate symbols to give your document a professional look (see Table A–1 for examples). When using a typewriter, use a hyphen for the en dash, and use two hyphens (with no space before, between, or after) for the em dash. Find other details of this sort in your company's style book or in most secretarial handbooks.

- **Corrections.** Messy corrections are obvious and unacceptable in business documents. Reprint or retype any letter, report, or memo requiring a lot of corrections. Word-processing software and self-correcting typewriters can produce correction-free documents at the push of a button.

LETTERS

All business letters have certain elements in common. Several of these elements appear in every letter; others appear only when desirable or appropriate. In addition, these letter parts are usually arranged in one of three basic formats.

Standard Letter Parts

The letter in Figure A–1 shows the placement of standard letter parts. The writer of this business letter had no letterhead available but correctly included a heading. All business letters typically include these seven elements.

Heading

Letterhead (the usual heading) shows the organization's name, full address, telephone number (almost always), and e-mail address (often). Executive letterhead also bears the name of an individual within the organization. Computers allow you to design your own letterhead (either one to use for all correspondence or a new one for each piece of correspondence). If letterhead stationery is not available, the heading includes a return address (but no name) and starts 13 lines from the top of the page, which leaves a two-inch top margin.

Date

If you're using letterhead, place the date at least one blank line beneath the lowest part of the letterhead. Without letterhead, place the date immediately below the return address. The standard method of writing the date in the United States uses the full name of the month (no abbreviations), followed by the day (in numerals, without *st, nd, rd,* or *th*), a comma, and then the year: July 14, 2003 (7/14/03). Some organizations follow other conventions (see Table A–2). To maintain the utmost clarity in international correspondence, always spell out the name of the month in dates.[5]

When communicating internationally, you may also experience some confusion over time. Some companies in the United States refer to morning (A.M.) and afternoon (P.M.), dividing a 24-hour day into 12-hour blocks so that they refer to four o'clock in the morning (4:00 A.M.) or four o'clock in the afternoon (4:00 P.M.). The U.S. military and European companies refer to one 24-hour period so that 0400 hours (4:00 A.M.) is always in the morning and 1600 hours (4:00 P.M.) is always in the afternoon.[6] Make sure your references to time are as clear as possible, and be sure you clearly understand your audience's time references.

Inside Address

The inside address identifies the recipient of the letter. For U.S. correspondence, begin the inside address at least one line below the date. Precede the addressee's name with a courtesy title, such as *Dr., Mr.,* or *Ms.* The accepted courtesy title for women in business is *Ms.,* although a woman known to prefer the title *Miss* or *Mrs.* is always accommodated. If you don't know whether a person is a man or a woman (and you have no way of finding out), omit the courtesy title. For example, *Terry Smith* could be either a man or a woman. The first line of the inside address would be just *Terry Smith,* and the salutation would be *Dear Terry Smith.* The same is true if you know only a person's initials, as in *S. J. Adams.*

Spell out and capitalize titles that precede a person's name, such as *Professor* or *General* (see Table A–3 on page A-4 for the proper forms of address). The person's organizational title, such as *Director,* may be included on this first line (if it is short) or on the line below; the name of a department may follow. In addresses and signature lines, don't forget to capitalize any professional title that follows a person's name:

Mr. Ray Johnson, Dean

Ms. Patricia T. Higgins

Assistant Vice President

However, professional titles not appearing in an address or signature line are capitalized only when they directly precede the name.

President Kenneth Johanson will deliver the speech.

Maria Morales, president of ABC Enterprises, will deliver the speech.

The Honorable Helen Masters, senator from Arizona, will deliver the speech.

Table A–1	**SPECIAL SYMBOLS ON COMPUTER**	
	Computer Symbol	*Typed Symbol*
Case fractions	½	1/2
Copyright	©	(c)
Registered trademark	®	(R)
Cents	¢	None
British pound	£	None
Paragraph	¶	None
Bullets	●,◆,■,□,✓,☑,⊗	*, #, 0
Em dash	—	-- (two hyphens)
En dash	–	- (one hyphen)

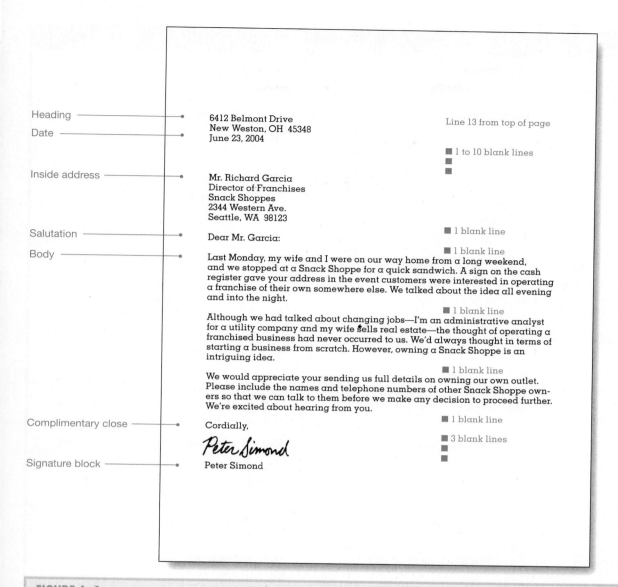

Heading — 6412 Belmont Drive
Date — New Weston, OH 45348
June 23, 2004

Line 13 from top of page

■ 1 to 10 blank lines
■
■

Inside address — Mr. Richard Garcia
Director of Franchises
Snack Shoppes
2344 Western Ave.
Seattle, WA 98123

Salutation — Dear Mr. Garcia: ■ 1 blank line

Body —   ■ 1 blank line
Last Monday, my wife and I were on our way home from a long weekend, and we stopped at a Snack Shoppe for a quick sandwich. A sign on the cash register gave your address in the event customers were interested in operating a franchise of their own somewhere else. We talked about the idea all evening and into the night.

■ 1 blank line
Although we had talked about changing jobs—I'm an administrative analyst for a utility company and my wife sells real estate—the thought of operating a franchised business had never occurred to us. We'd always thought in terms of starting a business from scratch. However, owning a Snack Shoppe is an intriguing idea.

■ 1 blank line
We would appreciate your sending us full details on owning our own outlet. Please include the names and telephone numbers of other Snack Shoppe owners so that we can talk to them before we make any decision to proceed further. We're excited about hearing from you.

■ 1 blank line
Complimentary close — Cordially,

■ 3 blank lines
■
Peter Simond   ■

Signature block — Peter Simond

FIGURE A–1
Standard Letter Parts

Table A–2	COMMON DATE FORMS		
Convention	**Description**	**Date—Mixed**	**Date—All Numerals**
U.S. standard	Month (spelled out) day, year	July 14, 2003	7/14/03
U.S. government and some U.S. industries	Day (in numerals) month (spelled out) year	14 July 2003	14/7/03
European	Replace U.S. solidus (diagonal line) with periods	14 July 2003	14.7.2003
International standard	Year month day	2003 July 14	2003,7,14

Table A–3   FORMS OF ADDRESS

Person	In Address	In Salutation
Personal Titles		
Man	Mr. [first & last name]	Dear Mr. [last name]:
Woman (marital status unknown)	Ms. [first & last name]	Dear Ms. [last name]:
Woman (single)	Ms. *or* Miss [first & last name]	Dear Ms. *or* Miss [last name]:
Woman (married)	Ms. *or* Mrs. [wife's first & last name] *or* Mrs. [husband's first & last name]	Dear Ms. *or* Mrs. [last name]:
Woman (widowed)	Ms. *or* Mrs. [wife's first name & last name]	Dear Ms. *or* Mrs. [last name]:
Woman (separated or divorced)	Ms. *or* Mrs. [first & last name]	Dear Ms. *or* Mrs. [last name]:
Two men (or more)	Mr. [first & last name] and Mr. [first & last name]	Dear Mr. [last name] and Mr. [last name] *or* Messrs. [last name] and [last name]:
Two women (or more)	Ms. [first & last name] and Ms. [first & last name] *or*	Dear Ms. [last name] and Ms. [last name] *or* Mses. [last name] and [last name]:
	Mrs. [first & last name] and Mrs. [first & last name]	Dear Mrs. [last name] and Mrs. [last name]: *or* Dear Mesdames [last name] and [last name] *or* Mesdames:
	Miss [first & last name] Mrs. [first & last name]	Dear Miss [last name] and Mrs. [last name]:
One woman and one man	Ms. [first & last name] and Mr. [first & last name]	Dear Ms. [last name] and Mr. [last name]:
Couple (married)	Mr. and Mrs. [husband's first & last name]	Dear Mr. and Mrs. [last name]:
Couple (married with different last names)	[title] [first & last name of husband] [title] [first & last name of wife]	Dear [title] [husband's last name] and [title] [wife's first & last name]:
Couple (married professionals with same title and same last name)	[title in plural form] [husband's first name] and [wife's first & last name]	Dear [title in plural form] [last name]:
Couple (married professionals with different titles and same last name)	[title] [first & last name of husband] and [title] [first & last name of wife]	Dear [title] and [title] [last name]:

(continued)

If the name of a specific person is unavailable, you may address the letter to the department or to a specific position within the department. Also, be sure to spell out company names in full, unless the company itself uses abbreviations in its official name.

Other address information includes the treatment of buildings, house numbers, and compass directions (see Table A-4 on page A-8). The following example shows all the information that may be included in the inside address and its proper order for U.S. correspondence:

Ms. Linda Coolidge, Vice President
Corporate Planning Department
Midwest Airlines
Kowalski Building, Suite 21-A
7279 Bristol Ave.
Toledo, OH 43617

Table A–3   CONTINUED

Person	In Address	In Salutation
Professional Titles		
President of a college or university (doctor)	Dr. [first & last name], President	Dear Dr. [last name]:
Dean of a school of college	Dean [first & last name] *or* Dr., Mr., Mrs., *or* Miss [first & last name] Dean of (title)	Dear Dean [last name]: Dear Dr., Mr., Ms., Mrs., *or* Miss [last name]:
Professor	Professor [first & last name]	Dear Professor [last name]:
Physician	[first & last name], M.D.	Dear Dr. [last name]:
Lawyer	Mr., Ms., Mrs., *or* Miss [first & last name]	Dear Mr., Ms., Mrs., *or* Miss [last name]:
Service personnel	[full rank, first & last name, abbreviation of service designation] (add *Retired* if applicable)	Dear [rank] [last name]:
Company or corporation	[name of organization]	Ladies and Gentlemen *or* Gentlemen and Ladies
Governmental Titles		
President of the United States	The President	Dear Mr. *or* Madam President:
Senator of the United States	Honorable [first & last name]	Dear Senator [last name]:
Cabinet member Postmaster General Attorney General	Honorable [first & last name]	Dear Mr. *or* Madam Secretary: Dear Mr. *or* Madam Postmaster General: Dear Mr. *or* Madam Attorney General:
Mayor	Honorable [first & last name] Mayor of [name of city]	Dear Mayor [last name]:
Judge	The Honorable	Dear Judge [last name]:
Religious Titles		
Priest	The Reverend [first & last name], [initials of order, if any]	Reverend Sir: (formal) *or* Dear Father [last name]: (informal)
Rabbi	Rabbi & [first & last name]	Dear Rabbi [last name]:
Minister	The Reverend [first & last name] [title, if any]	Dear Reverend [last name]:

Canadian addresses are similar, except that the name of the province is usually spelled out:

Dr. H. C. Armstrong
Research and Development
Commonwealth Mining Consortium
The Chelton Building, Suite 301
585 Second St. SW
Calgary, Alberta T2P 2P5

The order and layout of address information vary from country to country. So when addressing correspondence for other countries, carefully follow the format and information that appear in the company's letterhead. However, when you're sending mail from the United States, be sure that the name of the destination country appears on the last line of the address in capital letters. Use the English version of the country name so that your mail is routed from the United States to the right country. Then, to be sure your mail is routed correctly within the destination country, use the foreign spelling of the city name (using the characters and

Table A–4	INSIDE ADDRESS INFORMATION
Description	**Example**
Capitalize building names.	Empire State Building
Capitalize locations within buildings (apartments, suites, rooms).	Suite 1073
Use numerals for all house or building numbers, except the number *one*.	One Trinity Lane 637 Adams Ave., Apt. 7
Spell out compass directions that fall within a street address	1074 West Connover St.
Abbreviate compass directions that follow the street address	783 Main St. N.E., Apt. 27

diacritical marks that would be commonly used in the region). For example, the following address uses *Köln* instead of *Cologne*:

H. R. Veith, Director	Addressee
Eisfieren Glaswerk	Company Name
Blaubachstrasse 13	Street address
Postfach 10 80 07	Post office box
D-5000 Köln I	District, city
GERMANY	Country

For additional examples of international addresses, see Table A–5.

Be sure to use organizational titles correctly when addressing international correspondence. Job designations vary around the world. In England, for example, a managing director is often what a U.S. company would call its chief executive officer or president, and a British deputy is the equivalent of a vice president. In France, responsibilities are assigned to individuals without regard to title or organizational structure, and in China the title *project manager* has meaning, but the title *sales manager* may not.

To make matters worse, businesspeople in some countries sign correspondence without their names typed below. In Germany, for example, the belief is that employees represent the company, so it's inappropriate to emphasize personal names.[7] Use the examples in Table A–5 as guidelines when addressing correspondence to countries outside the United States.

Salutation

In the salutation of your letter, follow the style of the first line of the inside address. If the first line is a person's name, the salutation is *Dear Mr.* or *Ms. Name.* The formality of the salutation depends on your relationship with the addressee. If in conversation you would say "Mary," your letter's salutation should be *Dear Mary,* followed by a colon. Otherwise, include the courtesy title and last name, followed by a colon. Presuming to write *Dear Lewis* instead of *Dear Professor Chang* demonstrates a disrespectful familiarity that the recipient will probably resent.

If the first line of the inside address is a position title such as *Director of Personnel*, then use *Dear Director.* If the addressee is unknown, use a polite description, such as *Dear Alumnus, Dear SPCA Supporter,* or *Dear Voter.* If the first line is plural (a department or company), then use *Ladies and Gentlemen* (look again at Table A–3). When you do not know whether you're writing to an individual or a group (for example, when writing a reference or a letter of recommendation), use *To whom it may concern.*

In the United States some letter writers use a "salutopening" on the salutation line. A salutopening omits *Dear* but includes the first few words of the opening paragraph along with the recipient's name.

After this line, the sentence continues a double space below as part of the body of the letter, as in these examples:

Thank you, Mr. Brown,	Salutopening
for your prompt payment of your bill.	Body
Congratulations, Ms. Lake!	Salutopening
Your promotion is well deserved.	Body

Whether your salutation is informal or formal, be especially careful that names are spelled right. A misspelled name is glaring evidence of carelessness, and it belies the personal interest you're trying to express.

Body

The body of the letter is your message. Almost all letters are single-spaced, with one blank line before and after the salutation or salutopening, between paragraphs, and before the complimentary close. The body may include indented lists, entire paragraphs indented for emphasis, and even subheadings. If it does, all similar elements should be treated in the same way. Your department or company may select a format to use for all letters.

Complimentary Close

The complimentary close begins on the second line below the body of the letter. Alternatives for wording are available, but currently the trend seems to be toward using one-word closes, such as *Sincerely* and *Cordially.* In any case, the complimentary close reflects the relationship between you and the person you're writing to. Avoid cute closes, such as *Yours for bigger profits.* If your audience doesn't know you well, your sense of humor may be misunderstood.

Signature Block

Leave three blank lines for a written signature below the complimentary close, and then include the sender's name (unless it appears in the letterhead). The person's title may appear on the same line as the name or on the line below:

Cordially,

Raymond Dunnigan
Director of Personnel

Your letterhead indicates that you're representing your company. However, if your letter is on plain paper or runs to a second page, you may want to emphasize that you're speaking legally for the company. The accepted way of doing that is to place the company's

Table A–5 INTERNATIONAL ADDRESSES AND SALUTATIONS

Country	Postal Address	Address Elements	Salutations
Argentina	Sr. Juan Pérez Editorial Internacional S.A. Av. Sarmiento 1337, 8° P. C. C1035AAB BUENOS AIRES – CF ARGENTINA	S.A. = Sociedad Anónima (corporation) Av. Sarmiento (name of street) 1337 (building number) 8°= 8th. P = Piso (floor) C (room or suite) C1035AAB (postcode + city) CF = Capital Federal (federal capital)	Sr. = Señor (Mr.) Sra. = Señora (Mrs.) Srta. = Señorita (Miss) Don't use given names except with people you know well.
Australia	Mr. Roger Lewis International Publishing Pty. Ltd. 166 Kent Street, Level 9 GPO Box 3542 SYDNEY NSW 2001 AUSTRALIA	Pty. Ltd. = Proprietory Limited (corp.) 166 (building number) Kent Street (name of street) Level (floor) GPO Box (post office box) city + state (abbrev.) + postcode	Mr. and Mrs. used on first contact. Ms. not common (avoid use). Business is informal—use given name freely.
Austria	Herrn Dipl.-Ing. J. Gerdenitsch International Verlag Ges.m.b.H. Glockengasse 159 1010 WIEN AUSTRIA	Herrn = To Mr. (separate line) Dipl.-Ing. (engineering degree) Ges.m.b.H. (a corporation) Glockengasse (street name) 159 (building number) 1010 (postcode + city) WIEN (Vienna)	Herr (Mr.) Frau (Mrs.) Fräulein (Miss) obsolete in business, so do not use. Given names are almost never used in business.
Brazil	Ilmo. Sr. Gilberto Rabello Ribeiro Editores Internacionais S.A. Rua da Ajuda, 228–6° Andar Caixa Postal 2574 20040–000 RIO DE JANEIRO – RJ BRAZIL	Ilmo. = Ilustrissimo (honorific) Ilma. = Ilustrissima (hon. female) S.A. = Sociedade Anônima (corporation) Rua = street, da Ajuda (street name) 228 (building number) 6° = 6th. Andar (floor) Caixa Postal (P.O. box) 20040–000 (postcode + city) - RJ (state abbrev.)	Sr. = Senhor (Mr.) Sra. = Senhora (Mrs.) Srta. = Senhorita (Miss) Family name at end, e.g., Senhor Ribeiro (Rabello is mother's family—as in Portugal) Given names readily used in business.
China	Xia Zhiyi International Publishing Ltd. 14 Jianguolu Chaoyangqu BEIJING 100025 CHINA	Ltd. (limited liability corporation) 14 (building number) Jianguolu (street name), lu (street) Chaoyangqu (district name) (city + postcode)	Family name (single syllable) first. Given name (2 syllables) second, sometimes reversed. Use Mr. or Ms. at all times (Mr. Xia).
France	Monsieur LEFÈVRE Alain Éditions Internationales S.A. Siège Social Immeuble Le Bonaparte 64–68, av. Galliéni B.P. 154 75942 PARIS CEDEX 19 FRANCE	S.A. = Société Anonyme Siège Social (head office) Immeuble (building + name) 64–68 (building occupies 64, 66, 68) av. = avenue (no initial capital) B.P. = Boîte Postale (P.O. box) 75942 (postcode) CEDEX (postcode for P.O. box)	Monsieur (Mr.) Madame (Mrs.) Mademoiselle (Miss) Best not to abbreviate. Family name is sometimes in all caps with given name following.
Germany	Herrn Gerhardt Schneider International Verlag GmbH Schillerstraße 159 44147 DORTMUND GERMANY	Herrn = To Herr (on a separate line) GmbH (inc.—incorporated) -straße (street—'ß' often written 'ss') 159 (building number) 44147 (postcode + city)	Herr (Mr.) Frau (Mrs.) Fräulein (Miss) obsolete in business. Business is formal: (1) do not use given names unless invited, and (2) use academic titles precisely.

(continued)

Table A–5   CONTINUED

Country	Postal Address	Address Elements	Salutations
India	Sr. Shyam Lal Gupta International Publishing (Pvt.) Ltd. 1820 Rehaja Centre 214, Darussalam Road Andheri East BOMBAY – 400049 INDIA	(Pvt.) (privately owned) Ltd. (limited liability corporation) 1820 (possibly office #20 on 18th floor) Rehaja Centre (building name) 214 (building number) Andheri East (suburb name) (city + hyphen + postcode)	Shri (Mr.), Shrimati (Mrs.) but English is common business language, so use Mr., Mrs., Miss. Given names are used only by family and close friends.
Italy	Egr. Sig. Giacomo Mariotti Edizioni Internazionali S.p.A. Via Terenzio, 21 20138 MILANO ITALY	Egr. = Egregio (honorific) Sig. = Signor (not nec. a separate line) S.p.A. = Società per Azioni (corp.) Via (street) 21 (building number) 20138 (postcode + city)	Sig. = Signore (Mr.) Sig.ra = Signora (Mrs.) Sig.a (Ms.) Women in business are addressed as Signora. Use given name only when invited.
Japan	Mr. Taro Tanaka Kokusai Shuppan K.K. 10–23, 5-chome, Minamiazabu Minato-ku TOKYO 106 JAPAN	K.K. = Kabushiki Kaisha (corporation) 10 (lot number) 23 (building number) 5-chome (area #5) Minamiazabu (neighborhood name) Minato-ku (city district) (city + postcode)	Given names not used in business. Use family name + job title. Or use family name + "-san" (Tanaka-san) or more respectfully, add "-sama" or "-dono."
Korea	Mr. Kim Chang-ik International Publishers Ltd. Room 206, Korea Building 33–4 Nonhyon-dong Kangnam-ku SEOUL 135–010 KOREA	English company names common Ltd. (a corporation) 206 (office number inside the building) 33–4 (area 4 of subdivision 33) -dong (city neighborhood name) -ku (subdivision of city) (city + postcode)	Family name is normally first but sometimes placed after given name. A two-part name is the given name. Use Mr. or Mrs. in letters, but use job title in speech.
Mexico	Sr. Francisco Pérez Martínez Editores Internacionales S.A. Independencia No.322 Col. Juárez 06050 MEXICO D.F.	S.A. = Sociedad Anónima (corporation) Independencia (street name) No. = Número (number) 322 (building number) Col. = Colonia (city district) Juárez (locality name) 06050 (postcode + city) D.F. = Distrito Federal (federal capital)	Sr. = Señor (Mr.) Sra. = Señora (Mrs.) Srta. = Señorita (Miss) Family name in middle: e.g., Sr. Pérez (Martínez is mother's family). Given names are used in business.
South Africa	Mr. Mandla Ntuli International Publishing (Pty.) Ltd. Private Bag X2581 JOHANNESBURG 2000 SOUTH AFRICA	Pty. = Proprietory (privately owned) Ltd. (a corporation) Private Bag (P.O. Box) (city + postcode) or (postcode + city)	Mnr. = Meneer (Mr.) Mev. = Mevrou (Mrs.) Mejuffrou (Miss) is not used in business. Business is becoming less formal, so the use of given names is possible.
United Kingdom	Mr. N. J. Lancaster International Publishing Ltd. Kingsbury House 12 Kingsbury Road EDGEWARE Middlesex HA8 9XG ENGLAND	N. J. (initials of given names) Ltd. (limited liability corporation) Kingsbury House (building name) 12 (building number) Kingsbury Road (name of street/road) EDGEWARE (city—all caps) Middlesex (county—not all caps) HA8 9XG	Mr. and Ms. used mostly. Mrs. and Miss sometimes used in North and by older women. Given names—called Christian names—are used in business after some time. Wait to be invited.

name in capital letters a double space below the complimentary close and then include the sender's name and title four lines below that:

Sincerely,

WENTWORTH INDUSTRIES

(Mrs.) Helen B. Taylor
President

If your name could be taken for either a man's or a woman's, a courtesy title indicating gender should be included, with or without parentheses. Also, women who prefer a particular courtesy title should include it:

Mrs. Nancy Winters

(Miss) Juana Flores

Ms. Pat Li

(Mr.) Jamie Saunders

Additional Letter Parts

Letters vary greatly in subject matter and thus in the identifying information they need and the format they adopt. The letter in Figure A–2 shows how these additional parts should be arranged. The following elements may be used in any combination, depending on the requirements of the particular letter:

- **Addressee notation.** Letters that have a restricted readership or that must be handled in a special way should include such addressee notations as *Personal, Confidential,* or *Please Forward.* This sort of notation appears a double space above the inside address, in all-capital letters.

- **Attention line.** Although not commonly used today, an attention line can be used if you know only the last name of the person you're writing to. It can also direct a letter to a position title or department. Place the attention line on the first line of the inside address and put the company name on the second.[8] Match the address on the envelope with the style of the inside address. An attention line may take any of the following forms or variants of them:

  Attention: Dr. McHenry

  Attention Director of Marketing

  Attention Marketing Department

- **Subject line.** The subject line tells recipients at a glance what the letter is about (and indicates where to file the letter for future reference). It usually appears below the salutation, either against the left margin, indented (as a paragraph in the body), or centered. It can be placed above the salutation or at the very top of the page, and it can be underscored. Some businesses omit the word *Subject,* and some organizations replace it with *Re:* or *In re:* (meaning "concerning" or "in the matter of"). The subject line may take a variety of forms, including the following:

  Subject: RainMaster Sprinklers

  About your February 2, 2003, order

  FALL 1998 SALES MEETING

  Reference Order No. 27920

- **Second-page heading.** Use a second-page heading whenever an additional page is required. Some companies have second-page letterhead (with the company name and address on one line and in a smaller typeface). The heading bears the name

---

FIGURE A–2
Additional Letter Parts

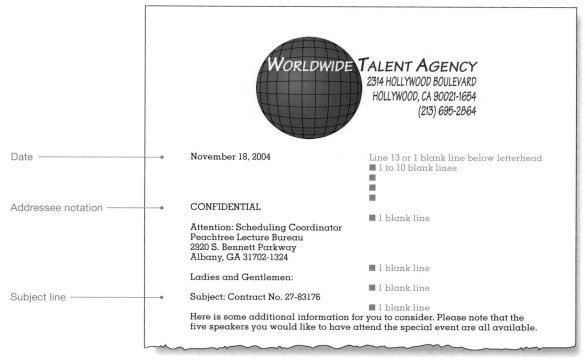

(continued)

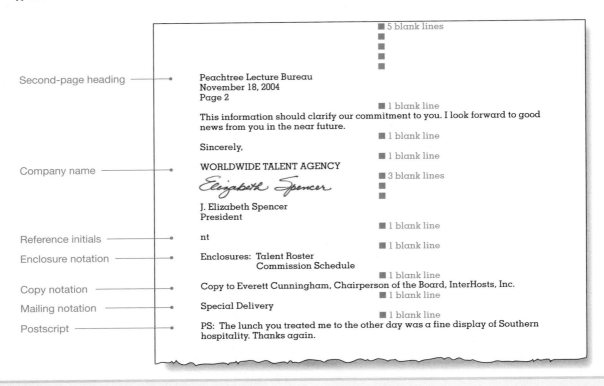

The following labels appear to the left of the figure with leader lines:

- Second-page heading
- Company name
- Reference initials
- Enclosure notation
- Copy notation
- Mailing notation
- Postscript

Figure content (right side annotations): 5 blank lines, 1 blank line, 1 blank line, 1 blank line, 3 blank lines, 1 blank line, 1 blank line, 1 blank line, 1 blank line, 1 blank line

> Peachtree Lecture Bureau
> November 18, 2004
> Page 2
>
> This information should clarify our commitment to you. I look forward to good news from you in the near future.
>
> Sincerely,
>
> WORLDWIDE TALENT AGENCY
>
> *Elizabeth Spencer*
>
> J. Elizabeth Spencer
> President
>
> nt
>
> Enclosures: Talent Roster
>   Commission Schedule
>
> Copy to Everett Cunningham, Chairperson of the Board, InterHosts, Inc.
>
> Special Delivery
>
> PS: The lunch you treated me to the other day was a fine display of Southern hospitality. Thanks again.

FIGURE A–2
(Continued)

(person or organization) from the first line of the inside address, the page number, the date, and perhaps a reference number. Leave two blank lines before the body. Make sure that at least two lines of a continued paragraph appear on the first and second pages. Never allow the closing lines to appear alone on a continued page. Precede the complimentary close or signature lines with at least two lines of the body. Also, don't hyphenate the last word on a page. All the following are acceptable forms for second-page headings:

Ms. Melissa Baker

May 10, 2003

Page 2

Ms. Melissa Baker, May 10, 2003, Page 2

Ms. Melissa Baker   -2-   May 10, 2003

- **Company name.** If you include the company's name in the signature block, put it all in capital letters a double space below the complimentary close. You usually include the company's name in the signature block only when the writer is serving as the company's official spokesperson or when letterhead has not been used.

- **Reference initials.** When businesspeople keyboard their own letters, reference initials are unnecessary, so they are becoming rare. When one person dictates a letter and another person produces it, reference initials show who helped prepare it. Place initials at the left margin, a double space below the signature block. When the signature block includes the writer's name, use only the preparer's initials. If the signature block includes only the department, use both sets of initials, usually in one of the

following forms: *RSR/sm, RSR:sm,* or *RSR:SM* (writer/preparer). When the writer and the signer are different people, at least the file copy should bear both their initials as well as the typist's: *JFS/RSR/sm* (signer/writer/preparer).

- **Enclosure notation.** Enclosure notations appear at the bottom of a letter, one or two lines below the reference initials. Some common forms include the following:

Enclosure

Enclosures (2)

Enclosures: Résumé
                      Photograph
                      Attachment

- **Copy notation.** Copy notations may follow reference initials or enclosure notations. They indicate who's receiving a *courtesy copy (cc)*. Some companies indicate copies made on a photocopier *(pc)*, or they simply use *copy (c)*. Recipients are listed in order of rank or (rank being equal) in alphabetical order. Among the forms used are the following:

cc: David Wentworth, Vice President

pc: Dr. Martha Littlefield

Copy to Hans Vogel
                748 Chesterton Rd.
                Snowhomish, WA 98290

c: Joseph Martinez with brochure and technical sheet

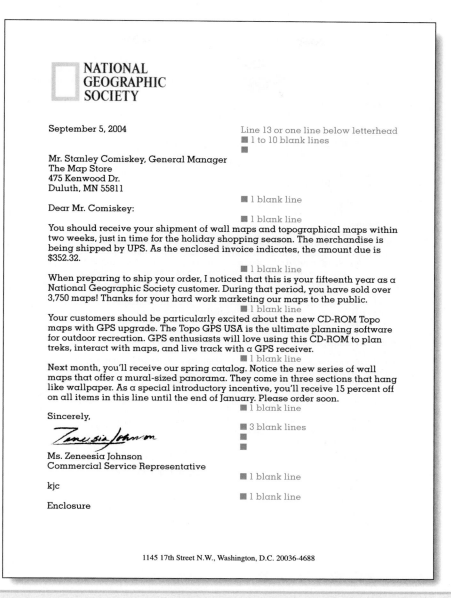

NATIONAL
GEOGRAPHIC
SOCIETY

September 5, 2004   *Line 13 or one line below letterhead*
                     ■ *1 to 10 blank lines*
                     ■

Mr. Stanley Comiskey, General Manager
The Map Store
475 Kenwood Dr.
Duluth, MN 55811
                     ■ *1 blank line*
Dear Mr. Comiskey:
                     ■ *1 blank line*
You should receive your shipment of wall maps and topographical maps within two weeks, just in time for the holiday shopping season. The merchandise is being shipped by UPS. As the enclosed invoice indicates, the amount due is $352.32.
                     ■ *1 blank line*
When preparing to ship your order, I noticed that this is your fifteenth year as a National Geographic Society customer. During that period, you have sold over 3,750 maps! Thanks for your hard work marketing our maps to the public.
                     ■ *1 blank line*
Your customers should be particularly excited about the new CD-ROM Topo maps with GPS upgrade. The Topo GPS USA is the ultimate planning software for outdoor recreation. GPS enthusiasts will love using this CD-ROM to plan treks, interact with maps, and live track with a GPS receiver.
                     ■ *1 blank line*
Next month, you'll receive our spring catalog. Notice the new series of wall maps that offer a mural-sized panorama. They come in three sections that hang like wallpaper. As a special introductory incentive, you'll receive 15 percent off on all items in this line until the end of January. Please order soon.
                     ■ *1 blank line*
Sincerely,
                     ■ *3 blank lines*
                     ■
                     ■
Ms. Zeneesia Johnson
Commercial Service Representative
                     ■ *1 blank line*
kjc
                     ■ *1 blank line*
Enclosure

1145 17th Street N.W., Washington, D.C. 20036-4688

FIGURE A–3
Block Letter Format

When sending copies to readers without other recipients knowing place *bc, bcc,* or *bpc* ("blind copy," "blind courtesy copy," or "blind photocopy") along with the name and any other information only on the copy, not on the original.

- **Mailing notation.** You may place a mailing notation (such as *Special Delivery* or *Registered Mail*) at the bottom of the letter, after reference initials or enclosure notations (whichever is last) and before copy notations. Or you may place it at the top of the letter, either above the inside address on the left side or just below the date on the right side. For greater visibility, mailing notations may appear in capital letters.

- **Postscript.** A postscript is an afterthought to the letter, a message that requires emphasis, or a personal note. It is usually the last thing on any letter and may be preceded by *P.S., PS., PS:,* or nothing at all. A second afterthought would be designated *P.P.S.* (post postscript). Since postscripts usually indicate poor planning, generally avoid them. However, they're common in sales letters as a punch line to remind readers of a benefit for taking advantage of the offer.

Letter Formats

A letter format is the way of arranging all the basic letter parts. Sometimes a company adopts a certain format as its policy; sometimes the individual letter writer or preparer is allowed to choose the most appropriate format. In the United States, three major letter formats are commonly used:

- **Block format.** Each letter part begins at the left margin. The main advantage is quick and efficient preparation (see Figure A–3).

- **Modified block format.** Same as block format, except that the date, complimentary close, and signature block start near

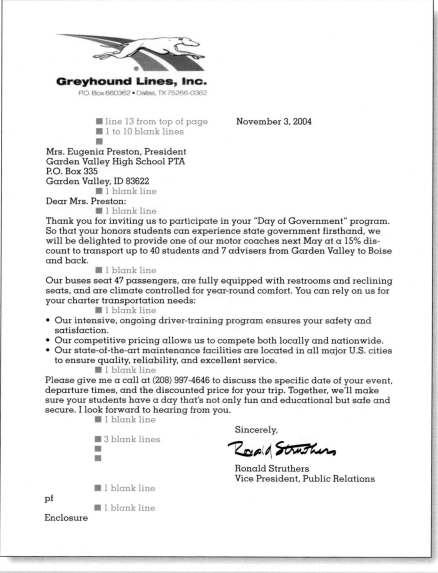

FIGURE A–4
Modified Block Letter Format

the center of the page (see Figure A–4). The modified block format does permit indentions as an option. This format mixes preparation speed with traditional placement of some letter parts. It also looks more balanced on the page than the block format does.

- **Simplified format.** Instead of using a salutation, this format often weaves the reader's name into the first line or two of the body and often includes a subject line in capital letters (see Figure A–5). With no complimentary close, your signature appears after the body, followed by your printed (or typewritten) name (usually in all capital letters). This format is convenient when you don't know the reader's name; however, some people object to it as mechanical and impersonal (a drawback you can overcome with a warm writing style). Because certain letter parts are eliminated, some line spacing is changed.

These three formats differ in the way paragraphs are indented, in the way letter parts are placed, and in some punctuation. However, the elements are always separated by at least one blank line, and the printed (or typewritten) name is always separated from the line above by at least three blank lines to allow space for a signature. If paragraphs are indented, the indention is normally five spaces. The most common formats for intercultural business letters are the block style and the modified block style.

In addition to these three letter formats, letters may also be classified according to their style of punctuation. *Standard,* or *mixed, punctuation* uses a colon after the salutation (a comma if the letter is social or personal) and a comma after the complimentary close. *Open punctuation* uses no colon or comma after the salutation or the complimentary close. Although the most popular style in business communication is mixed punctuation, either style of punctuation may be used with block or modified block letter formats. Because the simpli-

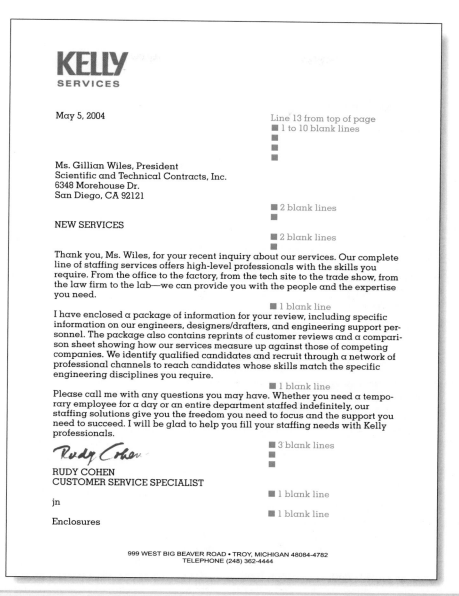

KELLY
SERVICES

May 5, 2004

Ms. Gillian Wiles, President
Scientific and Technical Contracts, Inc.
6348 Morehouse Dr.
San Diego, CA 92121

NEW SERVICES

Thank you, Ms. Wiles, for your recent inquiry about our services. Our complete line of staffing services offers high-level professionals with the skills you require. From the office to the factory, from the tech site to the trade show, from the law firm to the lab—we can provide you with the people and the expertise you need.

I have enclosed a package of information for your review, including specific information on our engineers, designers/drafters, and engineering support personnel. The package also contains reprints of customer reviews and a comparison sheet showing how our services measure up against those of competing companies. We identify qualified candidates and recruit through a network of professional channels to reach candidates whose skills match the specific engineering disciplines you require.

Please call me with any questions you may have. Whether you need a temporary employee for a day or an entire department staffed indefinitely, our staffing solutions give you the freedom you need to focus and the support you need to succeed. I will be glad to help you fill your staffing needs with Kelly professionals.

RUDY COHEN
CUSTOMER SERVICE SPECIALIST

jn

Enclosures

999 WEST BIG BEAVER ROAD • TROY, MICHIGAN 48084-4782
TELEPHONE (248) 362-4444

FIGURE A–5
Simplified Letter Format

fied letter format has no salutation or complimentary close, the style of punctuation is irrelevant.

ENVELOPES

For a first impression, the quality of the envelope is just as important as the quality of the stationery. Letterhead and envelopes should be of the same paper stock, have the same color ink, and be imprinted with the same address and logo. Most envelopes used by U.S. businesses are No. 10 envelopes (9½ inches long), which are sized for an 8½-by-11-inch piece of paper folded in thirds. Some occasions call for a smaller, No. 6¾, envelope or for envelopes proportioned to fit special stationery. Figure A–6 shows the two most common sizes.

Addressing the Envelope

No matter what size the envelope, the address is always single-spaced with all lines aligned on the left. The address on the envelope is in the same style as the inside address and presents the same information. The order to follow is from the smallest division to the largest:

1. Name and title of recipient
2. Name of department or subgroup
3. Name of organization
4. Name of building
5. Street address and suite number, or post office box number
6. City, state or province, and ZIP code or postal code
7. Name of country (if the letter is being sent abroad)

Because the U.S. Postal Service uses optical scanners to sort mail, envelopes for quantity mailings, in particular, should be addressed in the prescribed format. Everything is in capital letters, no punctuation is included, and all mailing instructions of interest to the post office are placed above the address area (see Figure A–6). Canada Post

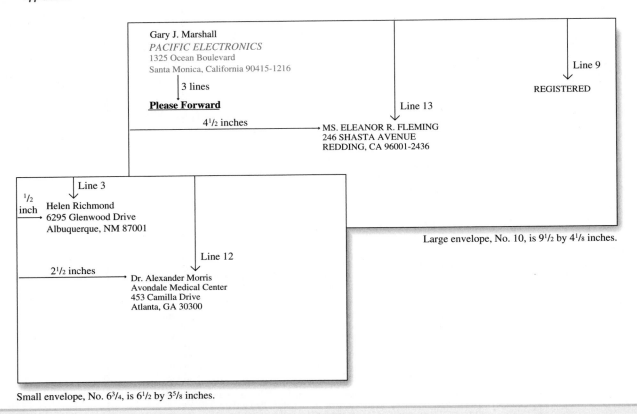

Small envelope, No. 6³/4, is 6¹/2 by 3⁵/8 inches.

FIGURE A–6
Prescribed Envelope Format

requires a similar format, except that only the city is all in capitals, and the postal code is placed on the line below the name of the city. The post office scanners read addresses from the bottom up, so if a letter is to be sent to a post office box rather than to a street address, the street address should appear on the line above the box number. Figure A–6 also shows the proper spacing for addresses and return addresses.

The U.S. Postal Service and the Canada Post Corporation have published lists of two-letter mailing abbreviations for states, provinces, and territories (see Table A–6). Postal authorities prefer no punctuation with these abbreviations, but some executives prefer to have state and province names spelled out in full and set off from city names by a comma. The issue is unresolved, although the comma is most often included. Quantity mailings follow post office requirements. For other letters, a reasonable compromise is to use traditional punctuation, uppercase and lowercase letters for names and street addresses, but two-letter state or province abbreviations, as shown here:

Mr. Kevin Kennedy

2107 E. Packer Dr.

Amarillo, TX 79108

For all out-of-office correspondence, use ZIP and postal codes that have been assigned to speed mail delivery. The U.S. Postal Service has divided the United States and its territories into 10 zones (0 to 9); this digit comes first in the ZIP code. The second and third digits represent smaller geographical areas within a state, and the last two digits identify a "local delivery area." Canadian postal codes are alphanumeric, with a three-character "area code" and a three-character "local code" separated by a single space (K2P 5A5). ZIP

codes should be separated from state and province names by one space. Canadian postal codes may be treated the same or may be put in the bottom line of the address all by itself.

The U.S. Postal Service has added ZIP + 4 codes, which add a hyphen and four more numbers to the standard ZIP codes. The first two of the new numbers may identify an area as small as a single large building, and the last two digits may identify one floor in a large building or even a specific department of an organization. The ZIP + 4 codes are especially useful for business correspondence. The Canada Post Corporation achieves the same result with special postal codes assigned to buildings and organizations that receive a large volume of mail.

Folding to Fit

The way a letter is folded also contributes to the recipient's overall impression of your organization's professionalism. When sending a standard-size piece of paper in a No. 10 envelope, fold it in thirds, with the bottom folded up first and the top folded down over it (see Figure A–7 on page A-16); the open end should be at the top of the envelope and facing out. Fit smaller stationery neatly into the appropriate envelope simply by folding it in half or in thirds. When sending a standard-size letterhead in a No. 6³/4 envelope, fold it in half from top to bottom and then in thirds from side to side.

International Mail

Postal service differs from country to country. For example, street addresses are uncommon in India, and the mail there is unreliable.[9] It's usually a good idea to send international correspondence by airmail and to ask that responses be sent that way as well. Also, remember to check the postage; rates for sending mail to most other countries differ from the rates for sending mail within your own country.

Table A–6	TWO-LETTER MAILING ABBREVIATIONS FOR THE UNITED STATES AND CANADA

State/ Territory/ Province	Abbreviation	State/ Territory/ Province	Abbreviation	State/ Territory/ Province	Abbreviation
United States		Massachusetts	MA	Texas	TX
Alabama	AL	Michigan	MI	Utah	UT
Alaska	AK	Minnesota	MN	Vermont	VT
American Samoa	AS	Mississippi	MS	Virginia	VA
Arizona	AZ	Missouri	MO	Virgin Islands	VI
Arkansas	AR	Montana	MT	Washington	WA
California	CA	Nebraska	NE	West Virginia	WV
Canal Zone	CZ	Nevada	NV	Wisconsin	WI
Colorado	CO	New Hampshire	NH	Wyoming	WY
Connecticut	CT	New Jersey	NJ	**Canada**	
Delaware	DE	New Mexico	NM	Alberta	AB
District of Columbia	DC	New York	NY	British Columbia	BC
Florida	FL	North Carolina	NC	Labrador	NL
Georgia	GA	North Dakota	ND	Manitoba	MB
Guam	GU	Northern Mariana	MP	New Brunswick	NB
Hawaii	HI	Ohio	OH	Newfoundland	NL
Idaho	ID	Oklahoma	OK	Northwest Territories	NT
Illinois	IL	Oregon	OR	Nova Scotia	NS
Indiana	IN	Pennsylvania	PA	Nunavut	NU
Iowa	IA	Puerto Rico	PR	Ontario	ON
Kansas	KS	Rhode Island	RI	Prince Edward Island	PE
Kentucky	KY	South Carolina	SC	Quebec	QC
Louisiana	LA	South Dakota	SD	Saskatchewan	SK
Maine	ME	Tennessee	TN	Yukon Territory	YT
Maryland	MD	Trust Territories	TT		

International mail falls into three main categories:

- **LC mail.** An abbreviation of the French *Lettres et Cartes* ("letters and cards"), this category consists of letters, letter packages, aerograms, and postcards.

- **AO mail.** An abbreviation of the French *Autres Objets* ("other articles"), this category includes regular printed matter, books and sheet music, matter for the blind, small packets, and publishers' periodicals (second class).

- **CP mail.** An abbreviation of the French *Colis Postaux* ("parcel post"), this category resembles fourth-class mail, including packages of merchandise or any other articles not required to be mailed at letter rates.

Along with several optional special services, the U.S. Postal Service also offers the following:

- **Express Mail International Service (EMS).** A high-speed mail service to many countries

- **International Priority Airmail (IPA).** An international service that's as fast as or faster than regular airmail service

- **International Surface Air Lift (ISAL).** A service providing quicker delivery and lower cost for all kinds of printed matter

- **Bulk Letter Service to Canada.** An economical airmail service for letters weighing 1 ounce or less

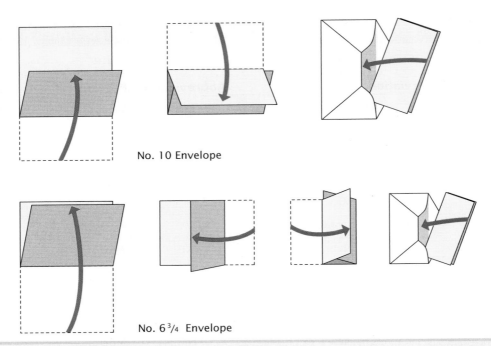

No. 10 Envelope

No. 6³/₄ Envelope

FIGURE A–7
Folding Standard-Size Letterhead

- **VALUEPOST/CANADA.** A reduced postage rate for bulk mailings

- **International Electronic Post (INTELPOST).** A service offering same- or next-day delivery of fax documents

- **International Postal Money Orders.** A service for transferring funds to other countries

To prepare your mail for international delivery, follow the instructions in the U.S. Postal Service Publication 51, *International Postal Rates and Fees.* Be sure to note instructions for the address, return address, and size limits. Envelopes and wrappers must be clearly marked to show their classification (letter, small packet, printed matter, airmail). All registered letters, letter packages, and parcel post packages must be securely sealed. Printed matter may be sealed only if postage is paid by permit imprint, postage meter, precanceled stamps, or second-class imprint. Otherwise, prepare contents so that they're protected without

hindering inspection. Finally, because international mail is subject to customs examination in the country of destination, the contents and value must be declared on special forms.

MEMOS

Many organizations have memo forms preprinted, with labeled spaces for the recipient's name (or sometimes a checklist of all departments in an organization or all persons in a department), the sender's name, the date, and the subject (see Figure A–8). If such forms don't exist, you can use a memo template (which comes with word-processing software and provides margin settings, headings, and special formats), or you can use plain paper.

On your document, include a title such as *MEMO* or *INTEROFFICE CORRESPONDENCE* (all in capitals) centered at the top of the page or aligned with the left margin. Also at the top, include the words *To, From, Date,* and *Subject*—followed

FIGURE A–8
Preprinted Memo Form

MEMO

TO: _____

DEPT: _____   FROM: _____

DATE: _____   TELEPHONE: _____

SUBJECT: _____   *For your*
☐ APPROVAL ☐ INFORMATION ☐ COMMENT

by the appropriate information—with a blank line between, as shown here:

MEMO

TO:

FROM:

DATE:

SUBJECT:

Sometimes the heading is organized like this:

MEMO

TO: DATE:

FROM: SUBJECT:

You can arrange these four pieces of information in almost any order. The date sometimes appears without the heading *Date*. The subject may be presented with the letters *Re:* (in place of *SUBJECT:*) or may even be presented without any heading (but in capital letters so that it stands out clearly). You may want to include a file or reference number, introduced by the word *File*.

The following guidelines will help you effectively format specific memo elements:

- **Addressees.** When sending a memo to a long list of people, include the notation *See distribution list* or *See below* in the *To* position at the top; then list the names at the end of the memo. Arrange this list alphabetically, except when high-ranking officials deserve more prominent placement. You can also address memos to groups of people—*All Sales Representatives, Production Group, New Product Team*.

- **Courtesy titles.** You need not use courtesy titles anywhere in a memo; first initials and last names, first names, or even initials alone are often sufficient. However, use a courtesy title if you would use one in a face-to-face encounter with the person.

- **Subject line.** The subject line of a memo helps busy colleagues quickly find out what your memo is about. Although the subject "line" may overflow onto a second line, it's most helpful when it's short (but still informative).

- **Body.** Start the body of the memo on the second or third line below the heading. Like the body of a letter, it's usually single-spaced with blank lines between paragraphs. Indenting paragraphs is optional. Handle lists, important passages, and subheadings as you do in letters. If the memo is very short, you may double-space it.

- **Second page.** If the memo carries over to a second page, head the second page just as you head the second page of a letter.

- **Writer's initials.** Unlike a letter, a memo doesn't require a complimentary close or a signature, because your name is already prominent at the top. However, you may initial the memo—either beside the name appearing at the top of the memo or at the bottom of the memo—or you may even sign your name at the bottom, particularly if the memo deals with money or confidential matters.

- **Other elements.** Treat elements such as reference initials, enclosure notations, and copy notations just as you would in a letter.

Memos may be delivered by hand, by the post office (when the recipient works at a different location), or through interoffice mail.

Interoffice mail may require the use of special reusable envelopes that have spaces for the recipient's name and department or room number; the name of the previous recipient is simply crossed out. If a regular envelope is used, the words *Interoffice Mail* appear where the stamp normally goes, so that it won't accidentally be stamped and mailed with the rest of the office correspondence.

Informal, routine, or brief reports for distribution within a company are often presented in memo form (see Chapter 10). Don't include report parts such as a table of contents and appendixes, but write the body of the memo report just as carefully as you'd write a formal report.

E-MAIL

Because e-mail messages can act both as memos (carrying information within your company) and as letters (carrying information outside your company and around the world), their format depends on your audience and purpose. You may choose to have your e-mail resemble a formal letter or a detailed report, or you may decide to keep things as simple as an interoffice memo. A modified memo format is appropriate for most e-mail messages.[10] All e-mail programs include two major elements: the header and the body (see Figure A–9 on the following page).

Header

The e-mail header depends on the particular program you use. Some programs even allow you to choose between a shorter and a longer version. However, most headers contain similar information.

- **To:** Contains the audience's e-mail address (see Figure A–10 on page A-19). Most e-mail programs also allow you to send mail to an entire group of people all at once. First, you create a distribution list. Then you type the name of the list in the *To:* line instead of typing the addresses of every person in the group.[11] The most common e-mail addresses are addresses such as

  nmaa.betsy@c.si.edu (Smithsonian Institute's National Museum of American Art)

  webwsj@dowjones.com (*Wall Street Journal*'s home page)

  relpubli@mairie-toulouse.mipnet.fr (Municipal Services, Toulouse, France)

- **From:** Contains your e-mail address.

- **Date:** Contains the day of the week, date (day, month, year), time, and time zone.

- **Subject:** Describes the content of the message and presents an opportunity for you to build interest in your message.

- **Cc:** Allows you to send copies of a message to more than one person at a time. It also allows everyone on the list to see who else received the same message.

- **Bcc:** Lets you send copies to people without the other recipients knowing—a practice considered unethical by some.[12]

- **Attachments:** Contains the name(s) of the file(s) you attach to your e-mail message. The file can be a word-processing document, a digital image, an audio or video message, a spreadsheet, or a software program.[13]

Most e-mail programs now allow you the choice of hiding or revealing other lines that contain more detailed information, including

- **Message-Id:** The exact location of this e-mail message on the sender's system

- **X-mailer:** The version of the e-mail program being used

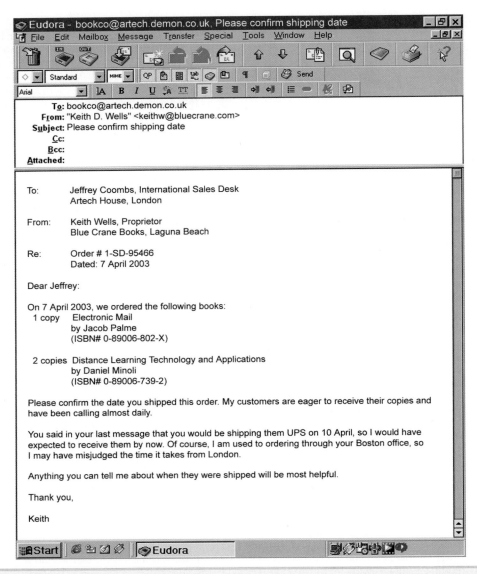

FIGURE A–9
A Typical E-Mail Message

- **Content type:** A description of the text and character set that is contained in the message

- **Received:** Information about each of the systems your e-mail passed through en route to your mailbox.[14]

Body

The rest of the space below the header is for the body of your message. In the *To:* and *From:* lines, some headers actually print out the names of the sender and receiver (in addition to their e-mail addresses). Other headers do not. If your mail program includes only the e-mail addresses, you might consider including your own memo-type header in the body of your message, as in Figure A–9. The writer even included a second, more specific subject line in his memo-type header. Some recipients may applaud the clarity of such second headers; however, others will criticize the space it takes. Your decision depends on how formal you want to be.

Do include a greeting in your e-mail. As pointed out in Chapter 6, greetings personalize your message. Leave one line space

above and below your greeting to set it off from the rest of your message. You may end your greeting with a colon (formal), a comma (conversational), or even two hyphens (informal)—depending on the level of formality you want.

Your message begins one blank line space below your greeting. Just as in memos and letters, skip one line space between paragraphs and include headings, numbered lists, bulleted lists, and embedded lists when appropriate. Limit your line lengths to a maximum of 80 characters by inserting a hard return at the end of each line.

One blank line space below your message, include a simple closing, often just one word. A blank line space below that, include your signature. Whether you type your name or use a signature file, including your signature personalizes your message.

REPORTS

Enhance your report's effectiveness by paying careful attention to its appearance and layout. Follow whatever guidelines your organization prefers, always being neat and consistent throughout. If it's up to you to decide formatting questions, the following conventions may

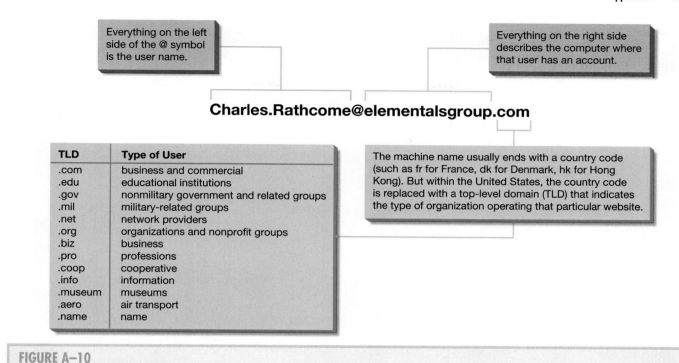

Everything on the left side of the @ symbol is the user name.

Everything on the right side describes the computer where that user has an account.

Charles.Rathcome@elementalsgroup.com

TLD	Type of User
.com	business and commercial
.edu	educational institutions
.gov	nonmilitary government and related groups
.mil	military-related groups
.net	network providers
.org	organizations and nonprofit groups
.biz	business
.pro	professions
.coop	cooperative
.info	information
.museum	museums
.aero	air transport
.name	name

The machine name usually ends with a country code (such as fr for France, dk for Denmark, hk for Hong Kong). But within the United States, the country code is replaced with a top-level domain (TLD) that indicates the type of organization operating that particular website.

FIGURE A–10
Anatomy of an E-Mail Address

help you decide how to handle margins, headings, spacing and indention, and page numbers.

Margins

All margins on a report page are at least 1 inch wide. For double-spaced pages, use 1-inch margins; for single-spaced pages, set margins between $1\frac{1}{4}$ and $1\frac{1}{2}$ inches. The top, left, and right margins are usually the same, but the bottom margins can be $1\frac{1}{2}$ times deeper. Some special pages also have deeper top margins. Set top margins as deep as 2 inches for pages that contain major titles: prefatory parts (such as the table of contents or the executive summary), supplementary parts (such as the reference notes or bibliography), and textual parts (such as the first page of the text or the first page of each chapter).

If you're going to bind your report at the left or at the top, add half an inch to the margin on the bound edge (see Figure A–11). The space taken by the binding on left-bound reports makes the center point of the text a quarter inch to the right of the center of the paper. Be sure to center headings between the margins, not between the edges of the paper. Computers can do this for you automatically. Other guidelines for report formats are in the Chapter 12 samples.

Headings

Headings of various levels provide visual clues to a report's organization. Figure 11–16, on page 378, illustrates one good system for showing these levels, but many variations exist. No matter which system you use, be sure to be consistent.

Spacing and Indentions

If your report is double-spaced (perhaps to ease comprehension of technical material), indent all paragraphs five character spaces (or about $\frac{1}{2}$ inch). In single-spaced reports, block the paragraphs (no indentions) and leave one blank line between them.

Make sure the material on the title page is centered and well balanced, as on the title page of the sample report in Chapter 12.

When using a typewriter, proper spacing takes some calculation. To center text in left-bound reports, start a quarter inch to the right of the paper's center. From that point, backspace once for each two letters in the line. The line will appear centered once the report is bound.

To place lines of type vertically on the title page, follow these steps:

1. Count the number of lines in each block of copy, including blank lines.

2. Subtract that total from 66 (the number of lines on an 11-inch page); the result is the number of unused lines.

3. Divide the number of unused lines by the number of blank areas (always one more than the number of blocks of copy). The result is the number of blank lines to allocate above, between, and below the blocks of copy.

A computer with a good word-processing program will do these calculations for you at the click of a mouse.

Page Numbers

Remember that every page in the report is counted; however, not all pages show numbers. The first page of the report, normally the title page, is unnumbered. All other pages in the prefatory section are numbered with a lowercase roman numeral, beginning with *ii* and continuing with *iii, iv, v,* and so on. The unadorned (no dashes, no period) page number is centered at the bottom margin.

Number the first page of the text of the report with the unadorned arabic numeral 1, centered at the bottom margin (double- or triple-spaced below the text). In left-bound reports, number the following pages (including the supplementary parts) consecutively with unadorned arabic numerals (2, 3, and so on), placed at the top right-hand margin (double- or triple-spaced above the text). For top-bound reports and for special pages having 2-inch top margins, center the page numbers at the bottom margin.

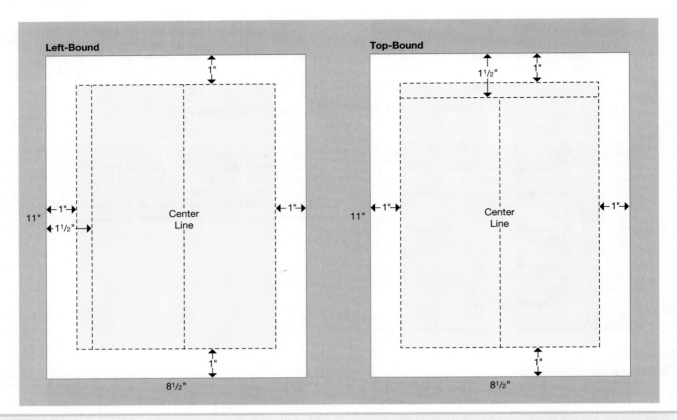

FIGURE A–11
Margins for Formal Reports

Documenting a report is too important a task to undertake haphazardly. By providing information about your sources, you improve your own credibility as well as the credibility of the facts and opinions you present. Documentation gives readers the means for checking your findings and pursuing the subject further. Also, documenting your report is the accepted way to give credit to the people whose work you have drawn from.

What style should you use to document your report? Experts recommend various forms, depending on your field or discipline. Moreover, your employer or client may use a form different from those the experts suggest. Don't let this discrepancy confuse you. If your employer specifies a form, use it; the standardized form is easier for colleagues to understand. However, if the choice of form is left to you, adopt one of the styles described here. Whatever style you choose, be consistent within any given report, using the same order, punctuation, and format from one reference citation or bibliography entry to the next.

A wide variety of style manuals provide detailed information on documentation. Here is a brief annotated list:

- American Psychological Association, *Publication Manual of the American Psychological Association,* 5th ed. (Washington, DC: American Psychological Association, 2001). Details the author-date system, which is preferred in the social sciences and often in the natural sciences as well.

- *The Chicago Manual of Style,* 14th ed. (Chicago: University of Chicago Press, 1993). Often referred to only as *Chicago* and widely used in the publishing industry; provides detailed treatment of documentation in Chapters 15 and 16.

- Joseph Gibaldi, *MLA Style Manual and Guide to Scholarly Publishing,* 2d ed. (New York: Modern Language Association, 1998). Serves as the basis for the note and bibliography style used in much academic writing and is recommended in many college textbooks on writing term papers; provides a lot of examples in the humanities.

- Andrew Harnack and Eugene Kleppinger, *Online! A Reference Guide to Using Internet Sources—2000* (New York: St. Martin's Press, 2000). Offers an approach to style for citing online references.

Although many schemes have been proposed for organizing the information in source notes, all of them break the information into parts: (1) information about the author (name), (2) information about the work (title, edition, volume number), (3) information about the publication (place, publisher), (4) information about the date, and (5) information on relevant page ranges.

In the following sections, we summarize the major conventions for documenting sources in three styles: *The Chicago Manual of Style* (Chicago), the *Publication Manual of the American Psychological Association* (APA), and the *MLA Style Manual* (MLA).

CHICAGO HUMANITIES STYLE

The Chicago Manual of Style recommends two types of documentation systems. The *documentary-note,* or *humanities,* style gives bibliographic citations in notes—either footnotes (when printed at the bottom of a page) or endnotes (when printed at the end of the report). The humanities system is often used in literature, history, and the arts. The other system strongly recommended by Chicago is the *author-date* system, which cites the author's last name and the date of publication in the text, usually in parentheses, reserving full documentation for the reference list (or bibliography). For the purpose of comparing styles, we will concentrate on the humanities system, which is described in detail in Chicago.

In-Text Citation—Chicago Humanities Style

To document report sources in text, the humanities system relies on superscripts—arabic numerals placed just above the line of type at the end of the reference:

> Toward the end of his speech, Myers sounded a note of caution, saying that even though the economy is expected to grow, it could easily slow a bit.[10]

The superscript lets the reader know how to look for source information in either a footnote or an endnote (see Figure B–1 on the following page). Some readers prefer footnotes so that they can simply glance at the bottom of the page for information. Others prefer endnotes so that they can read the text without a clutter of notes on the page. Also, endnotes relieve the writer from worrying about how long each note will be and how much space it will take away from the page. Both footnotes and endnotes are handled automatically by today's word-processing software.

For the reader's convenience, you can use footnotes for **content notes** (which may supplement your main text with asides about a particular issue or event, provide a cross-reference to another section of your report, or direct the reader to a related source). Then you can use endnotes for **source notes** (which document direct quotations, paraphrased passages, and visual aids). Consider which type of note is most common in your report, and then choose whether to present these notes all as endnotes or all as footnotes. Regardless of the method you choose for referencing textual information in your report, notes for visual aids (both content notes and source notes) are placed on the same page as the visual.

Bibliography—Chicago Humanities Style

The humanities system may or may not be accompanied by a bibliography (because the notes give all the necessary bibliographic information). However, endnotes are arranged in order of appearance in the text, so an alphabetical bibliography can be valuable to your readers. The bibliography may be titled *Bibliography, Reference List, Sources, Works Cited* (if you include only those sources you actually cited in your report), or *Works Consulted* (if you include uncited sources as well). This list of sources may also serve as a reading list for those who want to pursue the subject of your report further, so you may want to annotate each entry—that is, comment on the subject matter and viewpoint of the source, as well as on its usefulness to readers. Annotations may be written in either complete or incomplete sentences. (See the annotated list of style manuals early in this appendix.) A bibliography may also be

NOTES

1. James Assira, "Are They Speaking English in Japan?" *Journal of Business Communication* 36, no. 4 (Fall 2002): 72.

2. BestTemp Staffing Services, *An Employer's Guide to Staffing Services,* 2d ed. (Denver: BestTemp Information Center, 2000), 31.

3. "Buying Asian Supplies on the Net," *Los Angeles Times,* 12 February 2000, sec. D, p. 3.

4. Eurotec, *2001 Annual Report* (New York: Eurotec, Inc., 2001), 48.

5. Holly Graves, "Prospecting Online," *Business Week,* 17 November 2002, 43–5.

6. Daniel Han, "Trade Wars Heating Up Around the Globe," *CNN Headline News* (Atlanta: CNN, 5 March 2002).

7. "Intel—Company Capsule," Hoover's Online [cited 8 March 2003], 3 screens; available from www.hoovers.com/capsules/13787.html.

8. Sonja Kuntz, "Moving Beyond Benefits," in *Our Changing Workforce,* ed. Randolf Jacobson (New York: Citadel Press, 2001), 213–27.

9. George H. Morales, "The Economic Pressures on Industrialized Nations in a Global Economy" (Ph.D. diss., University of San Diego, 2001), 32–47.

10. Charles Myers, "HMOs in Today's Environment" (paper presented at the Conference on Medical Insurance Solution, Chicago, Ill., August 2001), 16–17.

11. Preston Norwalk, "Training Managers to Help Employees Accept Change," in *Business Line* [online] (San Francisco, 2002 [updated 17 September 2002; cited 3 October 2002]); available from www.busline.com/news.

12. Robert Parkings, "George Eastman," *The Concise Columbia Encyclopedia* (New York: Columbia University Press, 1998) [CD-ROM].

13. Georgia Stainer, general manager, Day Cable and Communications, interview by author, Topeka, Kan., 2 March 2000.

14. Evelyn Standish, "Global Market Crushes OPEC's Delicate Balance of Interests," *Wall Street Journal,* 19 January 2002, sec. A, p. 1.

15. Miriam Toller and Jay Fielding, *Global Business for Smaller Companies* (Rocklin, Calif.: Prima Publishing, 2001), 102–3.

16. U.S. Department of Defense, *Stretching Research Dollars: Survival Advice for Universities and Government Labs* (Washington, D.C.: GPO, 2002), 126.

FIGURE B–1
Sample Endnotes—Chicago Humanities Style

more manageable if you subdivide it into categories (a classified bibliography), either by type of reference (such as books, articles, and unpublished material) or by subject matter (such as government regulation, market forces, and so on). Following are the major conventions for developing a bibliography according to Chicago style (see Figure B–2):

- Exclude any page numbers that may be cited in source notes, except for journals, periodicals, and newspapers.

- Alphabetize entries by the last name of the lead author (listing last name first). The names of second and succeeding authors are listed in normal order. Entries without an author name are alphabetized by the first important word in the title.

- Format entries as hanging indents (indent second and succeeding lines three to five spaces).

- Arrange entries in the following general order: (1) author name, (2) title information, (3) publication information, (4) date, (5) periodical page range.

- Use quotation marks around the titles of articles from magazines, newspapers, and journals—capitalizing the first and last words, as well as all other important words (except prepositions, articles, and coordinating conjunctions).

- Use italics to set off the names of books, newspapers, journals, and other complete publications—capitalizing the first and last words, as well as all other important words.

BIBLIOGRAPHY

Journal article with volume and issue numbers
Assira, James. "Are They Speaking English in Japan?" *Journal of Business Communication* 36, no. 4 (Fall 2002): 72.

Brochure
BestTemp Staffing Services. *An Employer's Guide to Staffing Services.* 2d ed. Denver: BestTemp Information Center, 2000.

Newspaper article, no author
"Buying Asian Supplies on the Net." *Los Angeles Times,* 12 February 2000, sec. D, p. 3.

Annual report
Eurotec. 2001 *Annual Report.* New York: Eurotec, Inc., 2001.

Magazine article
Graves, Holly. "Prospecting Online." *Business Week,* 17 November 2002, 43–5.

Television broadcast
Han, Daniel. "Trade Wars Heating Up Around the Globe." *CNN Headline News.* Atlanta: CNN, 5 March 2002.

Internet, World Wide Web
"Intel—Company Capsule." *Hoover's Online* [cited 8 March 2003]. 3 screens; Available from www.hoovers.com/capsules/13787.html.

Book, component parts
Kuntz, Sonja. "Moving Beyond Benefits." In *Our Changing Workforce*, edited by Randolf Jacobson. New York: Citadel Press, 2001.

Unpublished dissertation or thesis
Morales, George H. "The Economic Pressures on Industrialized Nations in a Global Economy." Ph.D. diss., University of San Diego, 2001.

Paper presented at a meeting
Myers, Charles. "HMOs in Today's Environment." Paper presented at the Conference on Medical Insurance Solutions, Chicago, Ill., August 2001.

Online magazine article
Norwalk, Preston. "Training Managers to Help Employees Accept Change." In *Business Line* [online]. San Francisco, 2002 [updated 17 September 2002; cited 3 October 2002]. Available from www.busline.com/news.

CD-ROM encyclopedia article, one author
Parkings, Robert. "George Eastman." *The Concise Columbia Encyclopedia.* New York: Columbia University Press, 1998. [CD-ROM].

Interview
Stainer, Georgia, general manager, Day Cable and Communications. Interview by author. Topeka, Kan., 2 March 2000.

Newspaper article, one author
Standish, Evelyn. "Global Market Crushes OPEC's Delicate Balance of Interests." *Wall Street Journal,* 19 January 2002, sec. A, p. 1.

Book, two authors
Toller, Miriam, and Jay Fielding. *Global Business for Smaller Companies.* Rocklin, Calif.: Prima Publishing, 2001.

Government publication
U.S. Department of Defense. *Stretching Research Dollars: Survival Advice for Universities and Government Labs.* Washington, D.C.: GPO, 2002.

FIGURE B–2
Sample Bibliography—Chicago Humanities Style

• For journal articles, include the volume number and the issue number (if necessary). Include the year of publication inside parentheses and follow with a colon and the page range of the article: *Journal of Business Communication* 36, no. 4 (2001): 72. (In this source, the volume is 36, the number is 4, and the page is 72.)

• Use brackets to identify all electronic references: [Online database] or [CD-ROM].

• Explain how electronic references can be reached: Available from www.spaceless.com/WWWVL.

• Give the citation date for online references: Cited 23 August 2002.

APA STYLE

The American Psychological Association (APA) recommends the author-date system of documentation, which is popular in the physical, natural, and social sciences. When using this system, you simply insert the author's last name and the year of publication within parentheses following the text discussion of the material cited. Include a page number if you use a direct quote. This approach briefly identifies the source so that readers can locate complete information in the alphabetical reference list at the end of the report. The author-date system is both brief and clear, saving readers time and effort.

In-Text Citation—APA Style

To document report sources in text using APA style, insert the author's surname and the date of publication at the end of a statement. Enclose this information in parentheses. If the author's name is referred to in the text itself, then the number can be omitted from parenthetical material.

> Some experts recommend both translation and back-translation when dealing with any non-English-speaking culture (Assira, 2001).

> Toller and Fielding (2000) make a strong case for small companies succeeding in global business.

Personal communications and interviews conducted by the author would not be listed in the reference list at all. Such citations would appear in the text only.

> Increasing the role of cable companies is high on the list of Georgia Stainer, general manager at Day Cable and Communications (personal communication, March 2, 2001).

List of References—APA Style

For APA style, list only those works actually cited in the text (so you would not include works for background or for further reading). Report writers must choose their references judiciously. Following are the major conventions for developing a reference list according to APA style (see Figure B–3):

- Format entries as hanging indents.

- List all author names in reversed order (last name first), and use only initials for the first and middle names.

- Arrange entries in the following general order: (1) author name, (2) date, (3) title information, (4) publication information, (5) periodical page range.

FIGURE B–3
Sample References—APA Style

REFERENCES

Journal article with volume and issue numbers
: Assira, J. (2002). Are they speaking English in Japan? *Journal of Business Communication, 36*(4), 72.

Brochure
: BestTemp Staffing Services. (2000). *An employer's guide to staffing services* (2d ed.) [Brochure]. Denver: BestTemp Information Center.

Newspaper article, no author
: Buying Asian supplies on the net. (2000, February 12). *Los Angeles Times*, p. D3.

Annual report
: Eurotec. (2001). 2001 *annual report*. New York: Eurotec.

Magazine article
: Graves, H. (2002, November 17). Prospecting online. *Business Week*, 43–45.

Television broadcast
: Han, D. (2002, March 5). Trade wars heating up around the globe. *CNN Headline News*. [Television broadcast]. Atlanta, GA: CNN.

Internet, World Wide Web
: Hoover's Online. (2003). *Intel—Company Capsule*. Retrieved March 8, 2002, from http://www.hoovers.com/capsules/13787.html

Book, component parts
: Kuntz, S. (2001). Moving beyond benefits. In Randolph Jacobson (Ed.), *Our changing workforce* (pp. 213–227). New York: Citadel Press.

Unpublished dissertation or thesis
: Morales, G. H. (2001). *The economic pressures on industrialized nations in a global economy*. Unpublished doctoral dissertation, University of San Diego.

Paper presented at a meeting
: Myers, C. (2001, August). *HMOs in today's environment*. Paper presented at the Conference on Medical Insurance Solutions, Chicago, IL.

Online magazine article
: Norwalk, P. (2002, July 17). Training managers to help employees accept change. *Business Line*. Retrieved March 8, 2002, from http://www.busline.com/news

CD-ROM encyclopedia article, one author
: Parkings, R. (1998). George Eastman. On *The concise Columbia encyclopedia*. [CD-ROM]. New York: Columbia University Press.

Interview
: *Cited in text only, not in the list of references.*

Newspaper article, one author
: Standish, E. (2002, January 19). Global market crushes OPEC's delicate balance of interests. *Wall Street Journal*, p. A1.

Book, two authors
: Toller, M., & Fielding, J. (2001). *Global business for smaller companies*. Rocklin, CA: Prima Publishing.

Government publication
: U.S. Department of Defense. (2002). *Stretching research dollars: Survival advice for universities and government labs*. Washington, DC: U.S. Government Printing Office.

- Follow the author name with the date of publication in parentheses.

- List titles of articles from magazines, newspapers, and journals without underlines or quotation marks. Capitalize only the first word of the title, any proper nouns, and the first word to follow an internal colon.

- Italicize titles of books, capitalizing only the first word, any proper nouns, and the first word to follow a colon.

- Italicize names of magazines, newspapers, journals, and other complete publications—capitalizing all the important words.

- For journal articles, include the volume number (in italics) and, if necessary, the issue number (in parentheses). Finally, include the page range of the article: *Journal of Business Communication, 36*(4), 72. (In this example, the volume is 36, the number is 4, and the page number is 72.)

- Include personal communications (such as letters, memos, e-mail, and conversations) only in text, not in reference lists.

- Electronic references include author, date of publication, title of article, name of publication (if one), volume, date of retrieval (month, day, year), and the source.

- For electronic references, indicate the actual year of publication, and the exact date of retrieval.

- For electronic references, specify the URL, leave periods off the ends of URLs.

MLA STYLE

The style recommended by the Modern Language Association of America is used widely in the humanities, especially in the study of language and literature. Like APA style, MLA style uses brief parenthetical citations in the text. However, instead of including author name and year, MLA citations include author name and page reference.

In-Text Citation—MLA Style

To document report sources in text using MLA style, insert the author's last name and a page reference inside parentheses following the cited material: (Matthews 63). If the author's name is mentioned in the text reference, the name can be omitted from the parenthetical citation: (63). The citation indicates that the reference came from page 63 of a work by Matthews. With the author's name, readers can find complete publication information in the alphabetically arranged list of works cited that comes at the end of the report.

> Some experts recommend both translation and back-translation when dealing with any non-English-speaking culture (Assira 72).

> Toller and Fielding make a strong case for small companies succeeding in global business (102–03).

List of Works Cited—MLA Style

The *MLA Style Manual* recommends preparing the list of works cited first so that you will know what information to give in the parenthetical citation (for example, whether to add a short title if you're citing more than one work by the same author, or whether to give an initial or first name if you're citing two authors who have the same last name). The list of works cited appears at the end of your report, contains all the works that you cite in your text, and lists them in alphabetical order. Following are the major conventions for developing a reference list according to MLA style (see Figure B–4):

- Format entries as hanging indents.

- Arrange entries in the following general order: (1) author name, (2) title information, (3) publication information, (4) date, (5) periodical page range.

- List the lead author's name in reverse order (last name first), using either full first names or initials. List second and succeeding author names in normal order.

- Use quotation marks around the titles of articles from magazines, newspapers, and journals—capitalize all important words.

- Italicize the names of books, newspapers, journals and other complete publications, capitalizing all main words in the title.

- For journal articles, include the volume number and the issue number (if necessary). Include the year of publication inside parentheses and follow with a colon and the page range of the article: *Journal of Business Communication* 36.4 (2001): 72. (In this source, the volume is 36, the number is 4, and the page is 72.)

- Electronic sources are less fixed than print sources, and they may not be readily accessible to readers. So citations for electronic sources must provide more information. Always try to be as comprehensive as possible, citing whatever information is available.

- The date for electronic sources should contain both the date assigned in the source and the date accessed by the researcher.

- The URL for electronic sources must be as accurate and complete as possible, from access-mode indentifier (http, ftp, gopher, telnet) to all relevant directory and file names. Be sure to enclose this path inside angle brackets: <http://www.hoovers.com/capsules/13787.html>.

WORKS CITED

Journal article with volume and issue numbers	Assira, James. "Are They Speaking English in Japan?" *Journal of Business Communication* 36.4 (2002): 72.
Brochure	BestTemp Staffing Services. *An Employer's Guide to Staffing Services.* 2d ed. Denver: BestTemp Information Center, 2000.
Newspaper article, no author	"Buying Asian Supplies on the Net." *Los Angeles Times* 12 Feb. 2000: D3.
Annual report	Eurotec. *2000 Annual Report.* New York: Eurotec, Inc., 2001.
Magazine article	Graves, Holly. "Prospecting Online." *Business Week* 17 Nov. 2002: 43–45.
Television broadcast	Han, Daniel. "Trade Wars Heating Up Around the Globe." *CNN Headline News.* CNN, Atlanta. 5 Mar. 2002.
Internet, World Wide Web	"Intel—Company Capsule." *Hoover's Online.* 2003. Hoover's Company Information. 8 Mar. 2002 <http://www.hoovers.com/capsules/13787.html>.
Book, component parts	Kuntz, Sonja. "Moving Beyond Benefits." *Our Changing Workforce.* Ed. Randolf Jacobson. New York: Citadel Press, 2001. 213–27.
Unpublished dissertation or thesis	Morales, George H. "The Economic Pressures on Industrialized Nations in a Global Economy." Diss. U of San Diego, 2001.
Paper presented at a meeting	Myers, Charles. "HMOs in Today's Environment." Conference on Medical Insurance Solutions. Chicago. 13 Aug. 2001.
Online magazine article	Norwalk, Preston. "Training Managers to Help Employees Accept Change." *Business Line* 17 July 2002. 8 Mar. 2002 <http://www.busline.com/news>.
CD-ROM encyclopedia article, one author	Parkings, Robert. "George Eastman." *The Concise Columbia Encyclopedia.* CD-ROM. New York: Columbia UP, 1998.
Interview	Stainer, Georgia, general manager, Day Cable and Communications. Telephone interview. 2 Mar. 2000.
Newspaper article, one author	Standish, Evelyn. "Global Market Crushes OPEC's Delicate Balance of Interests." *Wall Street Journal* 19 Jan. 2002: A1.
Book, two authors	Toller, Miriam, and Jay Fielding. *Global Business for Smaller Companies.* Rocklin, CA: Prima Publishing, 2001.
Government publication	United States. Department of Defense. *Stretching Research Dollars: Survival Advice for Universities and Government Labs.* Washington: GPO, 2002.

FIGURE B-4
Sample Works Cited—MLA Style

Instructors often use these short, easy-to-remember correction symbols and abbreviations when evaluating students' writing. You can use them too, to understand your instructor's suggestions and to revise and proofread your own letters, memos, and reports. Refer to the Handbook of Grammar, Mechanics, and Usage (pp. H-1–H-20) for further information.

CONTENT AND STYLE

Acc	Accuracy. Check to be sure information is correct.
ACE	Avoid copying examples.
ACP	Avoid copying problems.
Adp	Adapt. Tailor message to reader.
App	Follow proper organization approach. (Refer to Chapter 4.)
Assign	Assignment. Review instructions for assignment.
AV	Active verb. Substitute active for passive.
Awk	Awkward phrasing. Rewrite.
BC	Be consistent.
BMS	Be more sincere.
Chop	Choppy sentences. Use longer sentences and more transitional phrases.
Con	Condense. Use fewer words.
CT	Conversational tone. Avoid using overly formal language.
Depers	Depersonalize. Avoid attributing credit or blame to any individual or group.
Dev	Develop. Provide greater detail.
Dir	Direct. Use direct approach; get to the point.
Emph	Emphasize. Develop this point more fully.
EW	Explanation weak. Check logic; provide more proof.
Fl	Flattery. Avoid compliments that are insincere.
FS	Figure of speech. Find a more accurate expression.
GNF	Good news first. Use direct order.
GRF	Give reasons first. Use indirect order.
GW	Goodwill. Put more emphasis on expressions of goodwill.
H/E	Honesty/ethics. Revise statement to reflect good business practices.
Imp	Imply. Avoid being direct.
Inc	Incomplete. Develop further.
Jar	Jargon. Use less specialized language.
Log	Logic. Check development of argument.
Neg	Negative. Use more positive approach or expression.
Obv	Obvious. Do not state point in such detail.
OC	Overconfident. Adopt humbler language.
OM	Omission.
Org	Organization. Strengthen outline.
OS	Off the subject. Close with point on main subject.
Par	Parallel. Use same structure.
Pom	Pompous. Rephrase in down-to-earth terms.
PV	Point of view. Make statement from reader's perspective rather than your own.
RB	Reader benefit. Explain what reader stands to gain.
Red	Redundant. Reduce number of times this point is made.
Ref	Reference. Cite source of information.
Rep	Repetitive. Provide different expression.
RS	Resale. Reassure reader that he or she has made a good choice.
SA	Service attitude. Put more emphasis on helping reader.
Sin	Sincerity. Avoid sounding glib or uncaring.
SL	Stereotyped language. Focus on individual's characteristics instead of on false generalizations.
Spec	Specific. Provide more specific statement.
SPM	Sales promotion material. Tell reader about related goods or services.
Stet	Let stand in original form.
Sub	Subordinate. Make this point less important.
SX	Sexist. Avoid language that contributes to gender stereotypes.
Tone	Tone needs improvement.
Trans	Transition. Show connection between points.
UAE	Use action ending. Close by stating what reader should do next.
UAS	Use appropriate salutation.
UAV	Use active voice.
Unc	Unclear. Rewrite to clarify meaning.
UPV	Use passive voice.
USS	Use shorter sentences.
V	Variety. Use different expression or sentence pattern.
W	Wordy. Eliminate unnecessary words.
WC	Word choice. Find a more appropriate word.
YA	"You" attitude. Rewrite to emphasize reader's needs.

GRAMMAR, MECHANICS, AND USAGE

Ab	Abbreviation. Avoid abbreviations in most cases; use correct abbreviation.
Adj	Adjective. Use adjective instead.
Adv	Adverb. Use adverb instead.
Agr	Agreement. Make subject and verb or noun and pronoun agree.
Ap	Appearance. Improve appearance.
Apos	Apostrophe. Check use of apostrophe.
Art	Article. Use correct article.
BC	Be consistent.
Cap	Capitalize.
Case	Use cases correctly.
CoAdj	Coordinate adjective. Insert comma between coordinate adjectives; delete comma between adjective and compound noun.
CS	Comma splice. Use period or semicolon to separate clauses.
DM	Dangling modifier. Rewrite so that modifier clearly relates to subject of sentence.
Exp	Expletive. Avoid expletive beginnings, such as it is, there are, there is, this is, and these are.

F	Format. Improve layout of document.
Frag	Fragment. Rewrite as complete sentence.
Gram	Grammar. Correct grammatical error.
HCA	Hyphenate compound adjective.
lc	Lowercase. Do not use capital letter.
M	Margins. Improve frame around document.
MM	Misplaced modifier. Place modifier close to word it modifies.
NRC	Nonrestrictive clause (or phrase). Separate from rest of sentence with commas.
P	Punctuation. Use correct punctuation.
Par	Parallel. Use same structure.
PH	Place higher. Move document up on page.
PL	Place lower. Move document down on page.
Prep	Preposition. Use correct preposition.
RC	Restrictive clause (or phrase). Remove commas that separate clause from rest of sentence.
RO	Run-on sentence. Separate two sentences with comma and coordinating conjunction or with semicolon.
SC	Series comma. Add comma before *and*.
SI	Split infinitive. Do not separate *to* from rest of verb.
Sp	Spelling error. Consult dictionary.
S-V	Subject-verb pair. Do not separate with comma.
Syl	Syllabification. Divide word between syllables.
WD	Word division. Check dictionary for proper end-of-line hyphenation.
WW	Wrong word. Replace with another word.

PROOFREADING MARKS

Symbol	Meaning	Symbol Used in Context	Corrected Copy
═══	Align horizontally	meaningful result	meaningful result
‖	Align vertically	1. Power cable 2. Keyboard	1. Power cable 2. Keyboard
≡	Capitalize	Pepsico, Inc.	PepsiCo, Inc.
⊐⊏	Center	⌐Awards Banquet⌐	Awards Banquet
◡	Close up space	self- confidence	self-confidence
ℓ	Delete	harrassment and abuse	harassment
(ds)	Double-space	text in first line text in second line (ds)	text in first line text in second line
∧	Insert	tirquoise shirts (u, and white)	turquoise and white shirts
ⱽ	Insert apostrophe	our teams goals	our team's goals
∧	Insert comma	a, b and c	a, b, and c
=	Insert hyphen	third quarter sales	third-quarter sales
⊙	Insert period	Harrigan et al	Harrigan et al.
ᵛᵛ ᵛᵛ	Insert quotation marks	This team isn't cooperating.	This "team" isn't cooperating.
#	Insert space	real estate testcase	real estate test case
/	Lowercase	TULSA, South of here	Tulsa, south of here
⌞ ⌟	Move down	Sincerely,	Sincerely,
⊏	Move left	Attention: ⌐ Security	Attention: Security
⊐	Move right	February 2, 2003 ⌐⌐	February 2, 2003
⌐⌐	Move up	THIRD-QUARTER SALES	THIRD-QUARTER SALES
(STET)	Restore	staff talked openly and frankly (STET)	staff talked openly
⌇	Run lines together	Manager,⌐ Distribution	Manager, Distribution
(ss)	Single space	text in first line text in second line (ss)	text in first line text in second line
⬭	Spell out	(COD)	cash on delivery
(sp)	Spell out	(sp) Assn. of Biochem. Engrs.	Association of Biochemical Engineers
⌐⌐	Start new line	Marla Fenton, Manager, Distri-bution	Marla Fenton, Manager, Distribution
¶	Start new paragraph	¶The solution is easy to determine but difficult to implement in a competitive environment like the one we now face.	The solution is easy to determine but difficult to implement in a competitive environment like the one we now face.
∼	Transpose	airy, light, casual tone	light, airy, casual tone
(bf)	Use boldface	Recommendations (bf)	**Recommendations**
(ital)	Use italics	Quarterly Report (ital)	*Quarterly Report*

Video Guide and Exercises

TECHNOLOGY AND THE TOOLS OF COMMUNICATION

LEARNING OBJECTIVES
After viewing this video, you will be able to

1. Identify issues to consider when developing communication strategies

2. Identify advantages of using technology as a tool for effective communication

3. Differentiate between "push" and "pull" communication

BACKGROUND INFORMATION
Achieving success in today's workplace depends on effective communication between employees and their managers as well as with people outside the organization, such as customers and suppliers. Communication is effective only when the message is understood and when it stimulates action or encourages the receiver to think in new ways. Effective communication will help you use and benefit from advances in technological tools.

THE VIDEO
This video discusses how the Internet, e-mail, voice mail, faxes, pagers, and other wireless devices have revolutionized the way people communicate. These technological tools increase the speed, frequency, and range of our communication. The video also discusses factors to consider when choosing the most appropriate vehicle for your communication. The challenge is to get your audience's attention so that they will read and respond in some way to your message. The advantages of using technology as a communication tool are presented throughout the video.

Discussion Questions

1. You must consider many issues when developing a communication strategy. Identify the six issues presented in the video.

2. List the advantages of communicating via e-mail in an organization.

3. What role does technology play in ensuring effective communication within an organization?

4. What challenge might a company encounter if it chooses to use technology for communication purposes?

5. Technology enhances both "push" and "pull" communications. What is the difference between "push" and "pull" communications? Give at least one example of each.

Follow-up Assignment

VolResource, a company that provides practical informative resources for various organizations, presents ideas for developing online communication strategies. The VolResource website (www.volresource. org.uk/samples/olcomms.htm) offers additional questions that need to be addressed in the process of developing an effective communication strategy for any organization. What issues do you think are the most important to consider? Why?

For Further Exploration

Visit the Yellow Freight website (www.yellowfreight.com) and explore the various e-commerce tools this company uses to communicate effectively with its customers. Examine these tools and consider their effectiveness. What are some of the advantages of these online communication tools? How do they benefit the client? How do they benefit the company (Yellow Freight)?

COMMUNICATING EFFECTIVELY IN THE GLOBAL WORKPLACE

LEARNING OBJECTIVES

After viewing this video, you will be able to

1. Discuss the challenges of communicating in the global workplace

2. Identify barriers to effective communication across borders

3. Explain the critical role of time in global communication efforts

BACKGROUND INFORMATION

Many companies are crossing national boundaries to engage in international business. Operating in a global environment can be challenging, so it is important for companies to avoid negative business consequences by understanding and appreciating cultural differences. Executives must learn about the specific cultures and countries that their organization intends to do business with.

THE VIDEO

This video identifies the barriers to effective communication in the global marketplace, including language, culture, time, and technology. A significant amount of research must be conducted before a company can engage in successful global business ventures. Business people must thoroughly examine differences in gesture, expression, and dialect. Differences in time zones also affect an organization's efforts to develop, translate, and deliver information in a timely manner.

Discussion Questions

1. Language can be a barrier to effective communication. What steps can a company take to minimize language barriers?

2. What characteristics of a country's culture need to be researched to ensure business success across borders?

3. How does a company ensure that communication is properly translated into the language and dialect of the people it conducts business with?

4. What challenges does a company face when trying to hold conference calls or video meetings with affiliates and employees around the world?

5. The video mentions that some companies rely on trusted contacts within a country to brief them on relevant cultural issues, while other companies rely on a significant amount of research to learn more about such issues. What method do you think is more effective for gathering useful, accurate, and up-to-date information on cultural issues?

Follow-up Assignment

The Coca-Cola Company has local operations in almost 20 countries throughout the world. Visit the Coca-Cola Company website (www2.coca-cola.com) to learn about the company's local strategy. What steps does this company take to communicate with customers around the world through its website? Does the company strive to develop products that meet local tastes and needs? If so, how and why?

For Further Research

Research a country other than the United States to identify important cultural characteristics specific to that country. For example, you may want to gather information about gestures and other nonverbal communication that would be considered offensive, the local work ethic, and the laws related to conducting business in that country. The characteristics you identify should be useful and accurate.

Do you think you might be prejudiced or ethnocentric if you were to do business with this country? Why or why not?

ETHICAL COMMUNICATION

LEARNING OBJECTIVES

After viewing this video, you will be able to

1. Describe a process for deciding what is ethical or unethical

2. Explain the importance of meeting your personal and professional responsibilities in an ethical manner

3. Discuss the possible consequences of both ethical and unethical choices and the impact of these choices on direct and related audiences

BACKGROUND INFORMATION

Ethical communication includes all relevant information, is true in every sense, and is not deceptive in any way. In contrast, unethical communication can include falsehoods and misleading information (or exclude important information). When making personal and professional decisions, it is always important to consider both the law and the needs of your audience (at the very least). Companies that make ethical choices gain credibility in the eyes of their consumers and employees. They benefit from this credibility because employees may be willing to work harder for an honest organization, and consumers have more confidence in their products.

THE VIDEO

This video identifies two important tools in a communicator's toolbox: honesty and objectivity. The communicator's job is to meet personal and professional responsibilities in an ethical manner. Individuals face many ethical decisions in business, both inside and outside the company. Unfortunately, negative consequences can result from unethical conduct. This video discusses the importance of maintaining credibility in order to be an effective business communicator.

Discussion Questions

1. Would you ever consider compromising your ethics for self-gain? If so, under what circumstances? If not, why?

2. The video mentions the collapse of Enron due to a series of misrepresentations. If you had been the head of communications at Enron and had even some knowledge of the true situation, what would you have done?

3. Identify the risks involved when you choose to act in an unethical manner.

4. How can you be an effective business communicator without credibility?

5. Is it ethical to call in sick to work even though you are not ill? What happens to your credibility when someone finds out you were just taking a day off to relax? To take your kids on a school field trip? To meet an old friend for lunch?

Follow-up Assignment

Many businesses, from small companies to large corporations, design a code of ethics to outline ethical standards for employees. International Business Machines (IBM) has "conduct guidelines" posted on its website (www-1.ibm.com/partnerworld/pwhome.nsf/weblook/guide_index.html). Review these guidelines and answer the following questions:

- What does IBM want employees to do if they are aware of unethical instances within the organization?

- How does IBM view misleading statements or innuendos about competitors?

- What are IBM's views on bribes, gifts, and entertainment?

For Further Research

The National Council on Alcoholism and Drug Dependence (www.ncadd.org/links/index.html) reports statistics related to advertising alcohol and tobacco products and the negative effect these advertisements can have on children. To what extent is it ethical for Anheuser Busch to use the Budweiser frog or Philip Morris to use Joe Camel in its advertisements, even though these characters are well known to children? What steps is Anheuser Busch taking to improve its image and communicate better to consumers, young and old?

Handbook of Grammar, Mechanics, and Usage

Grammar and mechanics are nothing more than the way words are combined into sentences. Usage is the way words are used by a network of people—in this case, the community of businesspeople who use English. You'll find it easier to get along in this community if you know the accepted standards of grammar, mechanics, and usage. This handbook offers you valuable opportunities in two sections:

- **Diagnostic Test of English Skills.** Testing your current knowledge of grammar, mechanics, and usage helps you find out where your strengths and weaknesses lie. This test offers 60 items taken from the topics included in this Handbook.

- **Assessment of English Skills.** After completing the diagnostic test, use the assessment form to highlight those areas you most need to review.

To quickly review the basics, you can visit www.prenhall.com/thill and select "Handbook of Grammar, Mechanics, and Usage Practice Sessions." Test yourself and reinforce what you learn. Use this essential review not only to study and improve your English skills but also as a reference for any questions you may have during this course.

Without a firm grasp of the basics of grammar, punctuation, mechanics, and vocabulary, you risk being misunderstood, damaging your company's image, losing money for your company, and possibly even losing your job. However, once you develop strong English skills, you will create clear and concise messages, you will enhance your company's image as well as your own, and you will not only increase your company's profits but expand your own chances of success.

DIAGNOSTIC TEST OF ENGLISH SKILLS

Use this test to help you determine whether you need more practice with grammar, punctuation, mechanics, or vocabulary. When you've answered all the questions, ask your instructor for an answer sheet so that you can score the test. On the Assessment of English Skills form (page H-2), record the number of questions you answered correctly in each section.

The following choices apply to items 1–10. In each blank, write the letter of the choice that best describes the problem with each sentence.

A. sentence incomplete
B. too many phrases/clauses strung together
C. modifying elements misplaced (dangling)
D. structure not parallel
E. nothing wrong

_____ 1. Stop here.

_____ 2. Your duties are interviewing, hiring, and also to fire employees.

_____ 3. After their presentation, I was still undecided.

_____ 4. Speaking freely, the stock was considered a bargain.

_____ 5. Margaret, pressed for time, turned in unusually sloppy work.

_____ 6. Typing and filing, routine office chores.

_____ 7. With care, edit the report.

_____ 8. When Paul came to work here, he brought some outmoded ideas, now he has accepted our modern methods.

_____ 9. To plan is better than improvising.

_____ 10. Hoping to improve performance, practice is advisable.

The following choices apply to items 11–20. In each blank, write the letter of the choice that identifies the underlined word(s) in each sentence.

A. subject
B. predicate (verb)
C. object
D. modifier
E. conjunction/preposition

_____ 11. Take his <u>memo</u> upstairs.

_____ 12. Before leaving, he <u>repaired</u> the photocopier.

_____ 13. <u>Velnor, Inc.</u>, will soon introduce a new product line.

_____ 14. We must hire only <u>qualified</u>, ambitious graduates.

_____ 15. They <u>are having</u> trouble with their quality control systems.

_____ 16. <u>After</u> she wrote the report, Jill waited eagerly for a response.

_____ 17. The route to the plant isn't paved <u>yet</u>.

_____ 18. See <u>me</u> after the meeting.

_____ 19. Your new <u>home</u> is ready and waiting.

_____ 20. BFL is large <u>but</u> caring.

In the blanks for items 21–30, write the letter of the word that best completes each sentence.

_____ 21. Starbucks (A. is, B. are) opening five new stores in San Diego in the next year.

_____ 22. There (A. is, B. are) 50 applicants for the job opening.

_____ 23. Anyone who wants to be (A. their, B. his or her) own boss should think about owning a franchise.

_____ 24. Neither of us (A. was, B. were) prepared for the meeting.

_____ 25. Another characteristic of a small business is that (A. they tend, B. it tends) to be more innovative than larger firms.

_____ 26. After he had (A. saw, B. seen) the revised budget, Raymond knew he wouldn't be getting a new desk.

_____ 27. The number of women-owned small businesses (A. has, B. have) increased sharply in the past two decades.

_____ 28. If I (A. was, B. were) you, I'd stop sending personal e-mails at work.

_____ 29. Eugene (A. lay, B. laid) the files on the desk.

_____ 30. Either FedEx or UPS (A. has, B. have) been chosen as our preferred shipping service.

The following choices apply to items 31–40. In each blank, write the letter of the choice that best describes each sentence.

A. all punctuation used correctly

B. some punctuation used incorrectly or incorrectly omitted

_____ 31. The president who rarely gave interviews, agreed to write an article for the company newsletter.

_____ 32. Give the assignment to Karen Schiff, the new technical writer.

_____ 33. Could you please send a replacement for Item No. 3–303.

_____ 34. Debbie said that, "technicians must have technical degrees."

_____ 35. We'll have branches in Bakersfield, California, Reno, Nevada, and Medford, Oregon.

_____ 36. Before leaving her secretary finished typing the memo.

_____ 37. How many of you consider yourselves "computer literate?"

_____ 38. This, then, is our goal: to increase market share by 50 percent.

_____ 39. They plan to move soon, however, they still should be invited.

_____ 40. Health, wealth, and happiness—those are my personal goals.

The following choices apply to items 41–50. In each blank, write the letter of the choice that best describes the problem with each sentence.

A. error in punctuation

B. error in use of abbreviations or symbols

C. error in use of numbers

D. error in capitalization

E. no errors

_____ 41. Most of last year's sales came from the midwest.

_____ 42. We can provide the items you are looking for @ $2 each.

_____ 43. Alex noted: "few of our competitors have tried this approach."

_____ 44. Address the letter to professor Elliott Barker, Psychology Department, North Dakota State University.

_____ 45. They've recorded 22 complaints since yesterday, all of them from long-time employees.

_____ 46. Leslie's presentation—"New Markets for the Nineties"—was well organized.

_____ 47. We're having a sale in the childrens' department, beginning Wednesday, August 15.

_____ 48. About 50 of the newly inducted members will be present.

_____ 49. Mister Spencer has asked me to find ten volunteers.

_____ 50. Let's meet in Beth and Larry's office at one o'clock.

In the blanks for items 51–60, write the letter of the word that best completes each sentence.

_____ 51. Will having a degree (A. affect, B. effect) my chances for promotion?

_____ 52. Place the latest drawings (A. beside, B. besides) the others.

_____ 53. Try not to (A. loose, B. lose) this key; we will charge you a fee to replace it.

_____ 54. Let us help you choose the right tie to (A. complement, B. compliment) your look.

_____ 55. The five interviewers should discuss the candidates' qualifications (A. among, B. between) themselves.

_____ 56. New employees spend their time looking for (A. perspective, B. prospective) clients.

_____ 57. Are the goods you received different (A. from, B. than) the goods you ordered?

_____ 58. He took those courses to (A. farther, B. further) his career.

_____ 59. We are (A. anxious, B. eager) to see you next Thursday.

_____ 60. All commissions will be (A. disbursed, B. dispensed, C. dispersed) on the second Friday of every month.

ASSESSMENT OF ENGLISH SKILLS

In the space provided below, record the number of questions you answered correctly.

Question	Number You Got Correct	Skill Area
1–10	_____	Sentence structure
11–20	_____	Grammar: Parts of speech
21–30	_____	Grammar: Verbs and agreement
31–40	_____	Punctuation
41–50	_____	Punctuation and mechanics
51–60	_____	Vocabulary

If you scored 8 or lower in any of the skills areas, focus on those areas in the appropriate sections of this Handbook.

ESSENTIALS OF GRAMMAR, MECHANICS, AND USAGE

The sentence below looks innocent, but is it really?

We sell tuxedos as well as rent.

You might sell rent, but it's highly unlikely. Whatever you're selling, some people will ignore your message because of a blunder like this. The following sentence has a similar problem:

> Vice President Eldon Neale told his chief engineer that he would no longer be with Avix, Inc., as of June 30.

Is Eldon or the engineer leaving? No matter which side the facts are on, the sentence can be read the other way. Now look at this sentence:

> The year before we budgeted more for advertising sales were up.

Confused? Perhaps this is what you meant:

> The year before, we budgeted more for advertising. Sales were up.

Maybe you meant this:

> The year before we budgeted more for advertising, sales were up.

The meaning of language falls into bundles called sentences. A listener or reader can take only so much meaning before filing a sentence away and getting ready for the next one. So, as a business writer, you have to know what a sentence is. You need to know where one ends and the next one begins.

If you want to know what a sentence is, you have to find out what goes into it, what its ingredients are. Luckily, the basic ingredients of an English sentence are simple: The parts of speech combine with punctuation, mechanics, and vocabulary to convey meaning.

1.0 Grammar

Grammar is the study of how words come together to form sentences. Categorized by meaning, form, and function, English words fall into various parts of speech: nouns, pronouns, verbs, adjectives, adverbs, prepositions, conjunctions, articles, and interjections. You will communicate more clearly if you understand how each of these parts of speech operates in a sentence.

1.1 Nouns

A noun names a person, place, or thing. Anything you can see or detect with one of your other senses has a noun to name it. Some things you can't see or sense are also nouns—ions, for example, or space. So are things that exist as ideas, such as accuracy and height. (You can see that something is accurate or that a building is tall, but you can't see the idea of accuracy or the idea of height.) These names for ideas are known as abstract nouns. The simplest nouns are the names of things you can see or touch: car, building, cloud, brick.

1.1.1 Proper Nouns and Common Nouns

So far, all the examples of nouns have been common nouns, referring to general classes of things. The word *building* refers to a whole class of structures. Common nouns such as *building* are not capitalized.

If you want to talk about one particular building, however, you might refer to the Glazier Building. The name is capitalized, indicating that *Glazier Building* is a proper noun.

Here are three sets of common and proper nouns for comparison:

Common	Proper
city	Kansas City
company	Blaisden Company
store	Books Galore

1.1.2 Nouns as Subject and Object

Nouns may be used in sentences as subjects or objects. That is, the person, place, idea, or thing that is being or doing (subject) is represented by a noun. So is the person, place, idea, or thing that is being acted on (object). In the following sentence, the nouns are underlined.

> The <u>secretary</u> keyboarded the <u>report</u>.

The secretary (subject) is acting in a way that affects the report (object). The following sentence is more complicated:

> The <u>installer</u> delivered the <u>carpeting</u> to the <u>customer</u>.

Installer is the subject. *Carpeting* is the object of the main part of the sentence (acted on by the installer), whereas *customer* is the object of the phrase *to the customer*. Nevertheless, both *carpeting* and *customer* are objects.

1.1.3 Plural Nouns

Nouns can be either singular or plural. The usual way to make a plural noun is to add *s* to the singular form of the word:

Singular	Plural
rock	rocks
picture	pictures
song	songs

Many nouns have other ways of forming the plural. Letters, numbers, and words used as words are sometimes made plural by adding an apostrophe and an *s*. Very often, 's is used with abbreviations that have periods, lowercase letters that stand alone, and capital letters that might be confused with words when made into plurals:

> Spell out all *St.*'s and *Ave.*'s.

> He divided the page with a row of *x*'s.

> Sarah will register the *A*'s through the *G*'s at the convention.

In other cases, however, the apostrophe may be left out:

> They'll review their ABCs.

> The stock market climbed through most of the 1980s.

> Circle all *the*s in the paragraph.

In some of these examples, the letters used as letters and words used as words are *italicized* (a mechanics issue that is discussed later).

Other nouns, such as those below, are so-called irregular nouns; they form the plural in some way other than by simply adding *s*:

Singular	Plural
tax	taxes
specialty	specialties
cargo	cargoes
shelf	shelves
child	children
woman	women
tooth	teeth
mouse	mice
parenthesis	parentheses
son-in-law	sons-in-law
editor-in-chief	editors-in-chief

Rather than memorize a lot of rules about forming plurals, use a dictionary. If the dictionary says nothing about the plural of a word, it's formed the usual way: by adding *s*. If the plural is formed in some irregular way, the dictionary often shows the plural spelling.

1.1.4 Possessive Nouns

A noun becomes possessive when it's used to show the ownership of something. Then you add 's to the word:

> the man's car   the woman's apartment

However, ownership does not need to be legal:

> the secretary's desk   the company's assets

Also, ownership may be nothing more than an automatic association:

> a day's work   the job's prestige

An exception to the rule about adding 's to make a noun possessive occurs when the word is singular and already has two "s" sounds at the end. In cases like the following, an apostrophe is all that's needed:

> crisis' dimensions   Mr. Moses' application

When the noun has only one "s" sound at the end, however, retain the 's:

> Chris's book   Carolyn Nuss's office

With hyphenated nouns (compound nouns), add 's to the last word:

Hyphenated Noun	Possessive Noun
mother-in-law	mother-in-law's
mayor-elect	mayor-elect's

To form the possessive of plural nouns, just begin by following the same rule as with singular nouns: add 's. However, if the plural noun already ends in an s (as most do), drop the one you've added, leaving only the apostrophe:

> the clients' complaints   employees' benefits

1.2 Pronouns

A pronoun is a word that stands for a noun; it saves repeating the noun:

> Drivers have some choice of weeks for vacation, but *they* must notify this office of *their* preference by March 1.

The pronouns *they* and *their* stand in for the noun *drivers*. The noun that a pronoun stands for is called the antecedent of the pronoun; *drivers* is the antecedent of *they* and *their*.

When the antecedent is plural, the pronoun that stands in for it has to be plural; *they* and *their* are plural pronouns because *drivers* is plural. Likewise, when the antecedent is singular, the pronoun has to be singular:

> We thought the *contract* had expired, but we soon learned that *it* had not.

1.2.1 Multiple Antecedents

Sometimes a pronoun has a double (or even a triple) antecedent:

> *Kathryn Boettcher* and *Luis Gutierrez* went beyond *their* sales quotas for January.

If taken alone, *Kathryn Boettcher* is a singular antecedent. So is *Luis Gutierrez*. However, when together they are the plural antecedent of a pronoun, so the pronoun has to be plural. Thus the pronoun is *their* instead of *her* or *his*.

1.2.2 Unclear Antecedents

In some sentences the pronoun's antecedent is unclear:

> Sandy Wright sent Jane Brougham *her* production figures for the previous year. *She* thought they were too low.

To which person does the pronoun *her* refer? Someone who knew Sandy and Jane and knew their business relationship might be able to figure out the antecedent for *her*. Even with such an advantage, however, a reader might receive the wrong meaning. Also, it would be nearly impossible for any reader to know which name is the antecedent of *she*.

The best way to clarify an ambiguous pronoun is usually to rewrite the sentence, repeating nouns when needed for clarity:

> Sandy Wright sent her production figures for the previous year to Jane Brougham. *Jane* thought they were too low.

The noun needs to be repeated only when the antecedent is unclear.

1.2.3 Gender-Neutral Pronouns

The pronouns that stand for males are *he, his,* and *him.* The pronouns that stand for females are *she, hers,* and *her.* However, you'll often be faced with the problem of choosing a pronoun for a noun that refers to both females and males:

> Each manager must make up (his, her, his or her, its, their) own mind about stocking this item and about the quantity that (he, she, he or she, it, they) can sell.

This sentence calls for a pronoun that's neither masculine nor feminine. The issue of gender-neutral pronouns responds to efforts to treat females and males evenhandedly. Here are some possible ways to deal with this issue:

> Each manager must make up *his* . . .

> (Not all managers are men.)

> Each manager must make up *her* . . .

> (Not all managers are women.)

> Each manager must make up *his* or *her* . . .

> (This solution is acceptable but becomes awkward when repeated more than once or twice in a document.)

> Each manager must make up *her* . . . Every manager will receive *his* . . . A manager may send *her* . . .

> (A manager's gender does not alternate like a windshield wiper!)

> Each manager must make up *their* . . .

> (The pronoun can't be plural when the antecedent is singular.)

> Each manager must make up *its* . . .

> (*It* never refers to people.)

The best solution is to make the noun plural or to revise the passage altogether:

> Managers must make up *their* minds . . .

> Each manager must decide whether . . .

Be careful not to change the original meaning.

1.2.4 Case of Pronouns

The case of a pronoun tells whether it's acting or acted upon:

> *She sells* an average of five packages each week.

In this sentence, *she* is doing the selling. Because *she* is acting, *she* is said to be in the nominative case. Now consider what happens when the pronoun is acted upon:

> After six months, Ms. Browning promoted *her.*

In this sentence, the pronoun *her* is acted upon. The pronoun *her* is thus said to be in the objective case.

Contrast the nominative and objective pronouns in this list:

Nominative	Objective
I	me
we	us
he	him
she	her
they	them
who	whom
whoever	whomever

Objective pronouns may be used as either the object of a verb (such as *promoted*) or the object of a preposition (such as *with*):

> Rob worked with *them* until the order was filled.

In this example, *them* is the object of the preposition *with* because Rob acted upon—worked with—them. Here's a sentence with three pronouns, the first one nominative, the second the object of a verb, and the third the object of a preposition:

> *He* paid *us* as soon as the check came from *them.*

He is nominative; *us* is objective because it's the object of the verb *paid; them* is objective because it's the object of the preposition *from.*

Every writer sometimes wonders whether to use *who* or *whom:*

> (Who, Whom) will you hire?

Because this sentence is a question, it's difficult to see that *whom* is the object of the verb *hire.* You can figure out which pronoun to use if you rearrange the question and temporarily try *she* and *her* in place of *who* and *whom:* "Will you hire *she?*" or "Will you hire *her?*" *Her* and *whom* are both objective, so the correct choice is "*Whom* will you hire?" Here's a different example:

> (Who, Whom) logged so much travel time?

Turning the question into a statement, you get:

> *He* logged so much travel time.

Therefore, the correct statement is:

> *Who* logged so much travel time?

1.2.5 Possessive Pronouns

Possessive pronouns work like possessive nouns: They show ownership or automatic association.

> her job   their preferences
>
> his account   its equipment

However, possessive pronouns are different from possessive nouns in the way they are written. That is, possessive pronouns never have an apostrophe.

Possessive Noun	Possessive Pronoun
the woman's estate	her estate
Roger Franklin's plans	his plans
the shareholders' feelings	their feelings
the vacuum cleaner's attachments	its attachments

The word *its* is the possessive of *it.* Like all other possessive pronouns, its has no apostrophe. Some people confuse *its* with *it's,* the contraction of *it is.* Contractions are discussed later.

1.3 Verbs

A verb describes an action:

> They all *quit* in disgust.

It may also describe a state of being:

> Working conditions *were* substandard.

The English language is full of action verbs. Here are a few you'll often run across in the business world:

verify	perform	fulfill
hire	succeed	send
leave	improve	receive
accept	develop	pay

You could undoubtedly list many more.

The most common verb describing a state of being instead of an action is *to be* and all its forms:

> I *am, was,* or *will be;* you *are, were,* or *will be*

Other verbs also describe a state of being:

> It *seemed* a good plan at the time.

> She *sounds* impressive at a meeting.

These verbs link what comes before them in the sentence with what comes after; no action is involved. (See Section 1.7.5 for a fuller discussion of linking verbs.)

1.3.1 Verb Tenses

English has three simple verb tenses: present, past, and future.

Present:	Our branches in Hawaii *stock* other items.
Past:	We *stocked* Purquil pens for a short time.
Future:	Rotex Tire Stores *will stock* your line of tires when you begin a program of effective national advertising.

With most verbs (the regular ones), the past tense ends in *ed,* and the future tense always has *will* or *shall* in front of it. But the present tense is more complex, depending on the subject:

	First Person	Second Person	Third Person
Singular	I stock	you stock	he/she/it stocks
Plural	we stock	you stock	they stock

The basic form, *stock,* takes an additional *s* when *he, she,* or *it* precedes it. (See section 1.3.4 for more on subject-verb agreement.)

In addition to the three simple tenses, there are three perfect tenses using forms of the helping verb *have.* The present perfect tense uses the past participle (regularly the past tense) of the main verb, *stocked,* and adds the present-tense *have* or *has* to the front of it:

> (I, we, you, they) *have stocked.*

> (He, she, it) *has stocked.*

The past perfect tense uses the past participle of the main verb, *stocked,* and adds the past-tense *had* to the front of it:

> (I, you, he, she, it, we, they) *had stocked.*

The future perfect tense also uses the past participle of the main verb, *stocked*, but adds the future-tense *will have*:

> (I, you, he, she, it, we, they) *will have stocked*.

Keep verbs in the same tense when the actions occur at the same time:

> When the payroll checks *came* in, everyone *showed* up for work.

> We *have found* that everyone *has pitched* in to help.

When the actions occur at different times, you may change tense accordingly:

> The shipment *came* last Wednesday, so if another one *comes* in today, please *return* it.

> The new employee *had been* ill at ease, but now she *has become* a full-fledged member of the team.

1.3.2 Irregular Verbs

Many verbs don't follow in every detail the patterns already described. The most irregular of these verbs is *to be*:

Tense	Singular	Plural
Present:	I *am*	we *are*
	you *are*	you *are*
	he, she, it *is*	they *are*
Past:	I *was*	we *were*
	you *were*	you *were*
	he, she, it *was*	they *were*

The future tense of *to be* is formed in the same way that the future tense of a regular verb is formed.

The perfect tenses of *to be* are also formed as they would be for a regular verb, except that the past participle is a special form, *been*, instead of just the past tense:

Present perfect:	you have been
Past perfect:	you had been
Future perfect:	you will have been

Here's a sampling of other irregular verbs:

Present	Past	Past Participle
begin	began	begun
shrink	shrank	shrunk
know	knew	known
rise	rose	risen
become	became	become
go	went	gone
do	did	done

Dictionaries list the various forms of other irregular verbs.

1.3.3 Transitive and Intransitive Verbs

Many people are confused by three particular sets of verbs:

lie/lay	sit/set	rise/raise

Using these verbs correctly is much easier when you learn the difference between transitive and intransitive verbs.

Transitive verbs convey their action to an object; they "transfer" their action to an object. Intransitive verbs do not. Here are some sample uses of transitive and intransitive verbs:

Intransitive	Transitive
We should include in our new offices a place to *lie* down for a nap.	The workers will be here on Monday to *lay* new carpeting.
Even the way an interviewee *sits* is important.	That crate is full of stemware, so *set* it down carefully.
Salaries at Compu-Link, Inc., *rise* swiftly.	They *raise* their level of production every year.

The workers *lay* carpeting, you *set* down the crate, they *raise* production; each action is transferred to something. In the intransitive sentences, one *lies* down, an interviewee *sits*, and salaries *rise* without (at least grammatically) affecting anything else. Intransitive sentences are complete with only a subject and a verb; transitive sentences are not complete unless they also include an object, or something to transfer the action to.

Tenses are a confusing element of the *lie/lay* problem:

Present	Past	Past Participle
I lie	I lay	I have lain
I lay (something down)	I laid (something down)	I have laid (something down)

The past tense of *lie* and the present tense of *lay* look and sound alike, even though they're different verbs.

1.3.4 Subject-Verb Agreement

Whether regular or irregular, every verb must agree with its subject, both in person (first, second, or third) and in number (singular or plural).

	First Person	**Second Person**	**Third Person**
Singular	I *am*; I *write*	you *are*; you *write*	he/she/it *is*; he/she/it *writes*
Plural	we *are*; we *write*	you *are*; you *write*	they *are*; they *write*

In a simple sentence, making a verb agree with its subject is a straightforward task:

> Hector Ruiz *is* a strong competitor. (third-person singular)

> We *write* to you every month. (first-person plural)

Confusion sometimes arises when sentences are a bit more complicated. For example, be sure to avoid agreement problems when words come between the subject and verb. In the following examples, the verb appears in italics, and its subject is underlined:

> The <u>analysis</u> of existing documents *takes* a full week.

Even though *documents* is a plural, the verb is in the singular form. That's because the subject of the sentence is *analysis*, a singular noun. The phrase *of existing documents* can be disregarded. Here is another example:

> The <u>answers</u> for this exercise *are* in the study guide.

Take away the phrase *for this exercise* and you are left with the plural subject *answers*. Therefore, the verb takes the plural form.

Verb agreement is also complicated when the subject is not a specific noun or pronoun and when the subject may be considered either singular or plural. In such cases, you have to analyze the surrounding sentence to determine which verb form to use.

> The <u>staff</u> *is* quartered in the warehouse.

The <u>staff</u> *are* at their desks in the warehouse.

The <u>computers</u> and the <u>staff</u> *are* in the warehouse.

Neither the staff nor the <u>computers</u> *are* in the warehouse.

<u>Every</u> computer *is* in the warehouse.

Many a <u>computer</u> *is* in the warehouse.

Did you notice that words such as *every* use the singular verb form? In addition, when an *either/or* or a *neither/nor* phrase combines singular and plural nouns, the verb takes the form that matches the noun closest to it.

In the business world, some subjects require extra attention. Company names, for example, are considered singular and therefore take a singular verb in most cases—even if they contain plural words:

<u>Stater Brothers</u> *offers* convenient grocery shopping.

In addition, quantities are sometimes considered singular and sometimes plural. If a quantity refers to a total amount, it takes a singular verb; if a quantity refers to individual, countable units, it takes a plural verb:

Three <u>hours</u> *is* a long time.

The eight <u>dollars</u> we collected for the fund *are* tacked on the bulletin board.

Fractions may also be singular or plural, depending on the noun that accompanies them:

One-third of the <u>warehouse</u> *is* devoted to this product line.

One-third of the <u>products</u> *are* defective.

For a related discussion, see Section 1.7.2, "Longer Sentences," later in this Handbook.

1.3.5 Voice of Verbs

Verbs have two voices, active and passive. When the subject comes first, the voice is active. When the object comes first, the voice is passive:

Active: The buyer paid a large amount.

Passive: A large amount was paid by the buyer.

The passive voice uses a form of the verb *to be,* which adds words to a sentence. In the example, the passive-voice sentence uses eight words, whereas the active-voice sentence uses only six to say the same thing. The words *was* and *by* are unnecessary to convey the meaning of the sentence. In fact, extra words usually clog meaning. So be sure to opt for the active voice when you have a choice.

At times, however, you have no choice:

Several items *have been taken,* but so far we don't know who took them.

The passive voice becomes necessary when you don't know (or don't want to say) who performed the action; the active voice is bolder and more direct.

1.3.6 Mood of Verbs

You have three moods to choose from, depending on your intentions. Most of the time you use the indicative mood to make a statement or to ask a question:

The secretary *mailed* a letter to each supplier.

Did the secretary *mail* a letter to each supplier?

When you wish to command or request, use the imperative mood:

Please *mail* a letter to each supplier.

Sometimes, especially in business, a courteous request is stated like a question; in that case, however, no question mark is required:

Would you *mail* a letter to each supplier.

The subjunctive mood, most often used in formal writing or in presenting bad news, expresses a possibility or a recommendation. The subjunctive is usually signaled by a word such as *if* or *that.* In these examples, the subjunctive mood uses special verb forms:

If the secretary *were to mail* a letter to each supplier, we might save some money.

I suggested that the secretary *mail* a letter to each supplier.

Although the subjunctive mood is not used as often as it once was, it's still found in such expressions as *Come what may* and *If I were you.* In general, it is used to convey an idea that is contrary to fact: If iron *were* lighter than air.

1.4 Adjectives

An adjective modifies (tells something about) a noun or pronoun. Each of the following phrases says more about the noun or pronoun than the noun or pronoun would say alone.

an *efficient* staff   a *heavy* price

brisk trade   *poor* you

Adjectives always tell us something that we wouldn't know without them. So you don't need to use adjectives when the noun alone, or a different noun, will give the meaning:

a *company* employee
(An employee ordinarily works for a company.)

a *crate-type* container
(*Crate* gives the entire meaning.)

Verbs in the *ing* (present participle) form can be used as adjectives:

A *boring* job can sometimes turn into a *fascinating* career.

So can the past participle of verbs:

A freshly *painted* house is a *sold* house.

Adjectives modify nouns more often than they modify pronouns. When adjectives do modify pronouns, however, the sentence usually has a linking verb:

They were *attentive.*   It looked *appropriate.*

He seems *interested.*   You are *skillful.*

At times, a series of adjectives precedes a noun:

It was a *long* and *active* workday.

Such strings of adjectives are acceptable as long as they all convey a different part of the phrase's meaning. However, adjectives often pile up in front of a noun, like this:

The *superficial, obvious* answer was the one she gave.

The most valuable animal on the ranch is a *small black* horse.

The question is whether a comma should be used to separate the adjectives. The answer is to use a comma when the two adjectives independently modify the noun; do not use a comma when one of the adjectives is closely identified with the noun. In the first example above, the answer was both superficial and obvious. But in the second example, the black horse is small.

Another way to think about this is to use the word *and* as a replacement for the comma. Study the following example:

We recommend a diet of leafy green vegetables.

We recommend a diet of green, leafy vegetables.

Because some green vegetables are not leafy (cucumbers and zucchini, for example), it is correct to leave out the comma in the first example so that you know which kind of green vegetables are being discussed. But because all leafy vegetables are also green (green and leafy), the comma must be included in the second example.

You might also try switching the adjectives. If the order of the adjectives can be reversed without changing the meaning of the phrase, you should use a comma. If the order cannot be reversed, you should not use a comma. Consider these examples:

Here's our *simplified credit* application.

Here's our *simplified, easy-to-complete* application.

Here's our *easy-to-complete, simplified* application.

A credit application may be simple or complex; however, you cannot talk about a credit, simplified application; therefore, leave the comma out of the first example. The application in the second and third examples is both simplified and easy to complete, no matter how you arrange the words, so include the comma in these examples.

1.4.1 Comparative Degree

Most adjectives can take three forms: simple, comparative, and superlative. The simple form modifies a single noun or pronoun. Use the comparative form when comparing two items. When comparing three or more items, use the superlative form.

Simple	Comparative	Superlative
hard	harder	hardest
safe	safer	safest
dry	drier	driest

The comparative form adds *er* to the simple form, and the superlative form adds *est*. (The *y* at the end of a word changes to *i* before the *er* or *est* is added.)

A small number of adjectives are irregular, including these:

Simple	Comparative	Superlative
good	better	best
bad	worse	worst
little	less	least

When the simple form of an adjective is two or more syllables, you usually add *more* to form the comparative and *most* to form the superlative:

Simple	Comparative	Superlative
useful	more useful	most useful
exhausting	more exhausting	most exhausting
expensive	more expensive	most expensive

The most common exceptions are two-syllable adjectives that end in *y*:

Simple	Comparative	Superlative
happy	happier	happiest
costly	costlier	costliest

If you choose this option, change the *y* to *i,* and tack *er* or *est* onto the end.

Some adjectives cannot be used to make comparisons because they themselves indicate the extreme. For example, if something is perfect, nothing can be more perfect. If something is unique or ultimate, nothing can be more unique or more ultimate.

1.4.2 Hyphenated Adjectives

Many adjectives used in the business world are actually combinations of words: *up-to-date* report, *last-minute* effort, *fifth-floor* suite, *well-built* engine. As you can see, they are hyphenated when they come before the noun they modify. However, when they come after the noun they modify, they are not hyphenated. In the following example, the adjectives appear in italics, and the nouns they modify are underlined:

The <u>report</u> is *up to date* because of our team's *last-minute* <u>efforts</u>.

Hyphens are not used when part of the combination is a word ending in *ly* (because that word is usually not an adjective). Hyphens are also omitted from word combinations that are used frequently.

We live in a *rapidly shrinking* world.

Our *highly motivated* employees will be well paid.

Please consider renewing your *credit card* account.

Send those figures to our *data processing* department.

Our new intern is a *high school* student.

1.5 Adverbs

An adverb modifies a verb, an adjective, or another adverb:

Modifying a verb:	Our marketing department works *efficiently*.
Modifying an adjective:	She was not dependable, although she was *highly* intelligent.
Modifying another adverb:	His territory was *too* broadly diversified, so he moved *extremely* cautiously.

Most of the adverbs mentioned are adjectives turned into adverbs by adding *ly*, which is how many adverbs are formed:

Adjective	Adverb
efficient	efficiently
extreme	extremely
high	highly
official	officially
separate	separately
special	specially

Some adverbs are made by dropping or changing the final letter of the adjective and then adding *ly*:

Adjective	Adverb
due	duly
busy	busily

Other adverbs don't end in *ly* at all. Here are a few examples of this type:

often	fast	too
soon	very	so

Some adverbs are difficult to distinguish from adjectives. For example, in the following sentences, is the underlined word an adverb or an adjective?

They worked <u>well</u>.

The baby is <u>well</u>.

In the first sentence, *well* is an adverb modifying the verb worked. In the second sentence, *well* is an adjective modifying the noun *baby*. To choose correctly between adverbs and adjectives, remember that verbs of being link a noun to an adjective describing the noun. In contrast, you would use an adverb to describe an action verb.

Adjective	Adverb
He is a *good* worker. (What kind of worker is he?)	He works *well*. (How does he work?)
It is a *real* computer. (What kind of computer is it?)	It *really* is a computer. (To what extent is it a computer?)
The traffic is *slow*. (What quality does the traffic have?)	The traffic moves *slowly*. (How does the traffic move?)

1.5.1 Negative Adverbs

Negative adverbs (such as *neither, no, not, scarcely,* and *seldom*) are powerful words and therefore do not need any help in conveying a negative thought. In fact, using double negatives gives a strong impression of illiteracy, so avoid sentences like these:

I don't want no mistakes.
(Correct: "I don't want any mistakes," or "I want no mistakes.")

They couldn't hardly read the report.
(Correct: "They could hardly read the report," or "They couldn't read the report.")

They scarcely noticed neither one.
(Correct: "They scarcely noticed either one," or "They noticed neither one.")

1.5.2 Comparative Degree

Like adjectives, adverbs can be used to compare items. Generally, the basic adverb is combined with *more* or *most,* just as long adjectives are. However, some adverbs have one-word comparative forms:

One Item	Two Items	Three Items
quickly	more quickly	most quickly
sincerely	less sincerely	least sincerely
fast	faster	fastest
well	better	best

1.6 Other Parts of Speech

Nouns, pronouns, verbs, adjectives, and adverbs carry most of the meaning in a sentence. Four other parts of speech link them together in sentences: prepositions, conjunctions, articles, and interjections.

1.6.1 Prepositions

Prepositions are words like these:

of	to	for	with
at	by	from	about

Some prepositions consist of more than one word—like these:

because of	in addition to	out of	except for

And some prepositions are closely linked with a verb. When using phrases such as *look up* and *wipe out,* keep the phrase intact and do not insert anything between the verb and the preposition.

Prepositions most often begin prepositional phrases, which function like adjectives and adverbs by telling more about a pronoun, noun, or verb:

of a type	*by* Friday
to the point	*with* characteristic flair

To prevent misreading, prepositional phrases should be placed near the element they modify:

Of all our technicians, <u>she</u> is the best trained.

They couldn't see the <u>merit</u> *in my proposal.*

Someone left a <u>folder</u> *on my desk.*

It was once considered totally unacceptable to put a preposition at the end of a sentence. Now you may:

I couldn't tell what they were interested in.

What did she attribute it to?

However, be careful not to place prepositions at the end of sentences when doing so is unnecessary. In fact, avoid using any unnecessary preposition. In the following examples, the prepositions in parentheses should be omitted:

All (of) the staff members were present.

I almost fell off (of) my chair with surprise.

Where was Mr. Steuben going (to)?

They couldn't help (from) wondering.

The opposite problem is failing to include a preposition when you should. Consider the two sentences that follow:

Sales were over $100,000 for Linda and Bill.

Sales were over $100,000 for Linda and for Bill.

The first sentence indicates that Linda and Bill had combined sales over $100,000; the second, that Linda and Bill each had sales over $100,000, for a combined total in excess of $200,000. The preposition *for* is critical here.

Prepositions are also required in sentences like this one:

Which type of personal computer do you prefer?

Certain prepositions are used with certain words. When the same preposition can be used for two or more words in a sentence without affecting the meaning, only the last preposition is required:

We are familiar (*with*) and satisfied *with* your company's products.

But when different prepositions are normally used with the words, all the prepositions must be included:

We are familiar *with* and interested *in* your company's products.

Here is a partial list of prepositions that are used in a particular way with particular words:

among/between: *Among* is used to refer to three or more (*Circulate the memo among the staff*); *between* is used to refer to two (*Put the copy machine between Judy and Dan*).

as if/like: *As if* is used before a clause (*It seems as if we should be doing something*); *like* is used before a noun or pronoun (*He seems like a nice guy*).

have/of: *Have* is a verb used in verb phrases (*They should have checked first*); *of* is a preposition and is never used in such cases.

in/into: *In* is used to refer to a static position (*The file is in the cabinet*); *into* is used to refer to movement toward a position (*Put the file into the cabinet*).

And here is a partial list of some prepositions that have come to be used with certain words:

according to	independent of
agree to (a proposal)	inferior to
agree with (a person)	plan to
buy from	prefer to
capable of	prior to
comply with	reason with
conform to	responsible for
differ from (things)	similar to
differ with (person)	talk to (without
different from	interaction)
get from (receive)	talk with (with interaction)
get off (dismount)	wait for (person or thing)
in accordance with	wait on (like a waiter)
in search of	

1.6.2 Conjunctions

Conjunctions connect the parts of a sentence: words, phrases, and clauses. You are probably most familiar with coordinating conjunctions such as the following:

and	for	or	yet
but	nor	so	

Conjunctions may be used to connect clauses (which have both a subject and a predicate) with other clauses, to connect clauses with phrases (which do not have both a subject and a predicate), and to connect words with words:

We sell designer clothing *and* linens.
(Words with words)

Their products are expensive *but* still appeal to value-conscious consumers.
(Clauses with phrases)

I will call her on the phone today, *or* I will visit her office tomorrow.
(Clauses with clauses)

Some conjunctions are used in pairs:

both . . . and	neither . . . nor	whether . . . or
either . . . or	not only . . . but also	

With paired conjunctions, you must be careful to construct each phrase in the same way.

They *not only* <u>are out of</u> racquets *but also* <u>are out of</u> balls.

They are *not only* <u>out of</u> racquets *but also* <u>out of</u> balls.

They <u>are out of</u> *not only* racquets *but also* balls.

In other words, the construction that follows each part of the pair must be parallel, containing the same verbs, prepositions, and so on. The same need for parallelism exists when using conjunctions to join the other parts of speech:

He is listed in *either* <u>your</u> roster *or* <u>my</u> roster.

He is listed *neither* <u>in</u> your roster *nor* <u>on</u> the master list.

They *both* <u>gave</u> *and* <u>received</u> notice.

A certain type of conjunction is used to join clauses that are unequal—that is, to join a main clause to one that is subordinate or dependent. Here is a partial list of conjunctions used to introduce dependent clauses:

although	before	once	unless
as soon as	even though	so that	until
because	if	that	when

Using conjunctions is also discussed in sections 1.7.3 and 1.7.4.

1.6.3 Articles and Interjections

Only three articles exist in English: *the, a,* and *an*. These words are used, like adjectives, to specify which item you are talking about.

Interjections are words that express no solid information, only emotion:

Wow!	Well, well!
Oh, no!	Good!

Such purely emotional language has its place in private life and advertising copy, but it only weakens the effect of most business writing.

1.7 Sentences

Sentences are constructed with the major building blocks, the parts of speech.

Money talks.

This two-word sentence consists of a noun (*money*) and a verb (*talks*). When used in this way, the noun works as the first requirement for a sentence, the subject, and the verb works as the second requirement, the predicate. Now look at this sentence:

They merged.

The subject in this case is a pronoun (*they*), and the predicate is a verb (*merged*). This is a sentence because it has a subject and a predicate. Here is yet another kind of sentence:

The plans are ready.

This sentence has a more complicated subject, the noun *plans* and the article *the*; the complete predicate is a state-of-being verb (*are*) and an adjective (*ready*).

Without a subject (who or what does something) and a predicate (the doing of it), you have merely a collection of words, not a sentence.

1.7.1 Commands

In commands, the subject (always *you*) is only understood, not stated:

(You) Move your desk to the better office.

(You) Please try to finish by six o'clock.

1.7.2 Longer Sentences

More complicated sentences have more complicated subjects and predicates, but they still have a simple subject and a predicate verb. In the following examples, the subject is underlined once, the predicate verb twice:

<u>Marex</u> and <u>Contron</u> <u>enjoy</u> higher earnings each quarter.

(*Marex* [and] *Contron* do something; *enjoy* is what they do.)

My <u>interview</u>, coming minutes after my freeway accident, <u>did</u> not <u>impress</u> or <u>move</u> anyone.

(*Interview* is what did something. What did it do? It *did* [not] *impress* [or] *move*.)

In terms of usable space, a steel <u>warehouse</u>, with its extremely long span of roof unsupported by pillars, <u>makes</u> more sense.

(*Warehouse* is what *makes*.)

These three sentences demonstrate several things. First, in all three sentences, the simple subject and predicate verb are the "bare bones" of the sentence, the parts that carry the core idea of the sentence. When trying to find the subject and predicate verb, disregard all prepositional phrases, modifiers, conjunctions, and articles.

Second, in the third sentence the verb is singular (*makes*) because the subject is singular (*warehouse*). Even though the plural noun *pillars* is closer to the verb, *warehouse* is the subject. So *warehouse* determines whether the verb is singular or plural. Subject and predicate must agree.

Third, the subject in the first sentence is compound (*Marex* [and] *Contron*). A compound subject, when connected by *and*, requires a plural verb (*enjoy*). Also in the second sentence, compound predicates are possible (*did* [not] *impress* [or] *move*).

Fourth, the second sentence incorporates a group of words—*coming minutes after my freeway accident*—containing a form of a verb (*coming*) and a noun (*accident*). Yet this group of words is not a complete sentence for two reasons:

- Not all nouns are subjects: *Accident* is not the subject of *coming*.

- Not all verbs are predicates: A verb that ends in *ing* can never be the predicate of a sentence (unless preceded by a form of *to be*, as in *was coming*).

Because they don't contain a subject and a predicate, the words *coming minutes after my freeway accident* (called a phrase) can't be written as a sentence. That is, the phrase cannot stand alone; it cannot begin with a capital letter and end with a period. So a phrase must always be just one part of a sentence.

Sometimes a sentence incorporates two or more groups of words that do contain a subject and a predicate; these word groups are called clauses:

My *interview*, because it <u>came</u> minutes after my freeway accident, <u>did</u> not <u>impress</u> or <u>move</u> anyone.

The independent clause is the portion of the sentence that could stand alone without revision:

My <u>interview</u> <u>did</u> not <u>impress</u> or <u>move</u> anyone.

The other part of the sentence could stand alone only by removing *because*:

(because) <u>It</u> <u>came</u> minutes after my freeway accident.

This part of the sentence is known as a dependent clause; although it has a subject and a predicate (just as an independent clause does), it's linked to the main part of the sentence by a word (*because*) showing its dependence.

In summary, the two types of clauses—dependent and independent—both have a subject and a predicate. Dependent clauses, however, do not bear the main meaning of the sentence and are therefore linked to an independent clause. Nor can

phrases stand alone, because they lack both a subject and a predicate. Only independent clauses can be written as sentences without revision.

1.7.3 Sentence Fragments

An incomplete sentence (a phrase or a dependent clause) that is written as though it were a complete sentence is called a fragment. Consider the following sentence fragments:

Marilyn Sanders, having had pilferage problems in her store for the past year. Refuses to accept the results of our investigation.

This serious error can easily be corrected by putting the two fragments together:

Marilyn Sanders, having had pilferage problems in her store for the past year, refuses to accept the results of our investigation.

Not all fragments can be corrected so easily. Here's more information on Sanders's pilferage problem.

Employees a part of it. No authority or discipline.

Only the writer knows the intended meaning of those two phrases. Perhaps the employees are taking part in the pilferage. If so, the sentence should read:

Some employees are part of the pilferage problem.

On the other hand, it's possible that some employees are helping with the investigation. Then the sentence would read:

Some employees are taking part in our investigation.

It's just as likely, however, that the employees are not only taking part in the pilferage but are also being analyzed:

Those employees who are part of the pilferage problem will accept no authority or discipline.

Even more meanings could be read into these fragments. Because fragments can mean so many things, they mean nothing. No well-written memo, letter, or report ever demands the reader to be an imaginative genius.

One more type of fragment exists, the kind represented by a dependent clause. Note what *because* does to change what was once a unified sentence:

Our stock of sprinklers is depleted.

Because our stock of sprinklers is depleted.

Although the second version contains a subject and a predicate, adding *because* makes it a fragment. Words such as *because* form a special group of words called subordinating conjunctions. Here's a partial list:

after	if	unless
although	since	whenever
even if	though	while

When a word of this type begins a clause, the clause is dependent and cannot stand alone as a sentence. However, if a dependent clause is combined with an independent clause, it can convey a complete meaning. The independent clause may come before or after the dependent clause:

We are unable to fill your order because our stock of sprinklers is depleted.

Because our stock of sprinklers is depleted, we are unable to fill your order.

Also, to fix a fragment that is a dependent clause, remove the subordinating conjunction. Doing so leaves a simple but complete sentence:

> Our stock of sprinklers is depleted.

The actual details of a situation will determine the best way for you to remedy a fragment problem.

The ban on fragments has one exception. Some advertising copy contains sentence fragments, written knowingly to convey a certain rhythm. However, advertising is the only area of business in which fragments are acceptable.

1.7.4 Fused Sentences and Comma Splices

Just as there can be too little in a group of words to make it a sentence, there can also be too much:

> All our mail is run through a postage meter every afternoon someone picks it up.

This example contains two sentences, not one, but the two have been blended so that it's hard to tell where one ends and the next begins. Is the mail run through a meter every afternoon? If so, the sentences should read:

> All our mail is run through a postage meter every afternoon. Someone picks it up.

Perhaps the mail is run through a meter at some other time (morning, for example) and is picked up every afternoon:

> All our mail is run through a postage meter. Every afternoon someone picks it up.

The order of words is the same in all three cases; sentence division makes all the difference. Either of the last two cases is grammatically correct. The choice depends on the facts of the situation.

Sometimes these so-called fused sentences have a more obvious point of separation:

> Several large orders arrived within a few days of one another, too many came in for us to process by the end of the month.

Here the comma has been put between two independent clauses in an attempt to link them. When a lowly comma separates two complete sentences, the result is called a comma splice. A comma splice can be remedied in one of three ways:

- Replace the comma with a period and capitalize the next word: ". . . one another. Too many . . . "

- Replace the comma with a semicolon and do not capitalize the next word: ". . . one another; too many . . . " This remedy works only when the two sentences have closely related meanings.

- Change one of the sentences so that it becomes a phrase or a dependent clause. This remedy often produces the best writing, but it takes more work.

The third alternative can be carried out in several ways. One is to begin the blended sentence with a subordinating conjunction:

> Whenever several large orders arrived within a few days of one another, too many came in for us to process by the end of the month.

Another way is to remove part of the subject or the predicate verb from one of the independent clauses, thereby creating a phrase:

> Several large orders arrived within a few days of one another, too many for us to process by the end of the month.

Finally, you can change one of the predicate verbs to its *ing* form:

> Several large orders arrived within a few days of one another, too many coming in for us to process by the end of the month.

At other times a simple coordinating conjunction (such as *or, and,* or *but*) can separate fused sentences:

> You can fire them, or you can make better use of their abilities.

> Margaret drew up the designs, and Matt carried them out.

> We will have three strong months, but after that sales will taper off.

Be careful using coordinating conjunctions: Use them only to join simple sentences that express similar ideas.

Also, because they say relatively little about the relationship between the two clauses they join, avoid using coordinating conjunctions too often: *and* is merely an addition sign; *but* is just a turn signal; *or* only points to an alternative. Subordinating conjunctions such as *because* and *whenever* tell the reader a lot more.

1.7.5 Sentences with Linking Verbs

Linking verbs were discussed briefly in the section on verbs (Section 1.3). Here you can see more fully the way they function in a sentence. The following is a model of any sentence with a linking verb:

> A (*verb*) B.

Although words such as *seems* and *feels* can also be linking verbs, let's assume that the verb is a form of *to be*:

> A *is* B.

In such a sentence, A and B are always nouns, pronouns, or adjectives. When one is a noun and the other is a pronoun, or when both are nouns, the sentence says that one is the same as the other:

> She is president.

> Rachel is president.

When one is an adjective, it modifies or describes the other:

> She is forceful.

Remember that when one is an adjective, it modifies the other as any adjective modifies a noun or pronoun, except that a linking verb stands between the adjective and the word it modifies.

1.7.6 Misplaced Modifiers

The position of a modifier in a sentence is important. The movement of *only* changes the meaning in the following sentences:

> Only we are obliged to supply those items specified in your contract.

> We are obliged only to supply those items specified in your contract.

> We are obliged to supply only those items specified in your contract.

> We are obliged to supply those items specified only in your contract.

In any particular set of circumstances, only one of those sentences would be accurate. The others would very likely cause problems. To prevent misunderstanding, place such modifiers as close as possible to the noun or verb they modify.

For similar reasons, whole phrases that are modifiers must be placed near the right noun or verb. Mistakes in placement create ludicrous meanings.

> Antia Information Systems has bought new computer chairs for the programmers *with more comfortable seats*.

The anatomy of programmers is not normally a concern of business writers. Obviously, the comfort of the chairs was the issue:

> Antia Information Systems has bought new computer chairs *with more comfortable seats* for the programmers.

Here is another example:

> I asked him to file all the letters in the cabinet that had been answered.

In this ridiculous sentence the cabinet has been answered, even though no cabinet in history is known to have asked a question.

That had been answered is too far from *letters* and too close to *cabinet*. Here's an improvement:

> I asked him to file in the cabinet all the letters that had been answered.

In some cases, instead of moving the modifying phrase closer to the word it modifies, the best solution is to move the word closer to the modifying phrase.

2.0 Punctuation

On the highway, signs tell you when to slow down or stop, where to turn, when to merge. In similar fashion, punctuation helps readers negotiate your prose. The proper use of punctuation keeps readers from losing track of your meaning.

2.1 Periods

Use a period (1) to end any sentence that is not a question, (2) with certain abbreviations, and (3) between dollars and cents in an amount of money.

2.2 Question Marks

Use a question mark after any direct question that requests an answer:

> Are you planning to enclose a check, or shall we bill you?

Don't use a question mark with commands phrased as questions for the sake of politeness:

> Will you send us a check today.

2.3 Exclamation Points

Use exclamation points after highly emotional language. Because business writing almost never calls for emotional language, you will seldom use exclamation points.

2.4 Semicolons

Semicolons have three main uses. One is to separate two closely related independent clauses:

> The outline for the report is due within a week; the report itself is due at the end of the month.

A semicolon should also be used instead of a comma when the items in a series have commas within them:

> Our previous meetings were on November 11, 1998; February 20, 1999; and April 28, 2000.

Finally, a semicolon should be used to separate independent clauses when the second one begins with a word such as *however, therefore,* or *nevertheless* or a phrase such as *for example* or *in that case:*

> Our supplier has been out of part D712 for 10 weeks; however, we have found another source that can ship the part right away.

> His test scores were quite low; on the other hand, he has a lot of relevant experience.

Section 4.4 has more information on using transitional words and phrases.

2.5 Colons

Use a colon after the salutation in a business letter. You also use a colon at the end of a sentence or phrase introducing a list or (sometimes) a quotation:

> Our study included the three most critical problems: insufficient capital, incompetent management, and inappropriate location.

In some introductory sentences, phrases such as *the following* or *that is* are implied by using a colon.

A colon should not be used when the list, quotation, or idea is a direct object or part of the introductory sentence:

> We are able to supply
> staples
> wood screws
> nails
> toggle bolts

> This shipment includes 9 videotapes, 12 CDs, and 14 cassette tapes.

Another way you can use a colon is to separate the main clause and another sentence element when the second explains, illustrates, or amplifies the first:

> Management was unprepared for the union representatives' demands: this fact alone accounts for their arguing well into the night.

However, in contemporary usage, such clauses are frequently separated by a semicolon.

2.6 Commas

Commas have many uses; the most common is to separate items in a series:

> He took the job, learned it well, worked hard, and succeeded.

> Put paper, pencils, and paper clips on the requisition list.

Company style often dictates omitting the final comma in a series. However, if you have a choice, use the final comma; it's often necessary to prevent misunderstanding.

A second place to use a comma is between independent clauses that are joined by a coordinating conjunction (*and, but,* or *or*) unless one or both are very short:

> She spoke to the sales staff, and he spoke to the production staff.

> I was advised to proceed and I did.

A third use for the comma is to separate a dependent clause at the beginning of a sentence from an independent clause:

> Because of our lead in the market, we may be able to risk introducing a new product.

However, a dependent clause at the end of a sentence is separated from the independent clause by a comma only when the dependent clause is unnecessary to the main meaning of the sentence:

> We may be able to introduce a new product, although it may involve some risk.

A fourth use for the comma is after an introductory phrase or word:

> Starting with this amount of capital, we can survive in the red for one year.

> Through more careful planning, we may be able to serve more people.

> Yes, you may proceed as originally planned.

However, with short introductory prepositional phrases and some one-syllable words (such as *hence* and *thus*), the comma is often omitted:

> Before January 1 we must complete the inventory.

> Thus we may not need to hire anyone.

> In short the move to Tulsa was a good idea.

Fifth, commas are used to surround nonrestrictive phrases or words (expressions that can be removed from the sentence without changing the meaning):

> The new owners, the Kowacks, are pleased with their purchase.

Sixth, commas are used between adjectives modifying the same noun (coordinate adjectives):

> She left Monday for a long, difficult recruiting trip.

To test the appropriateness of such a comma, try reversing the order of the adjectives: *a difficult, long recruiting trip.* If the order cannot be reversed, leave out the comma (*a good old friend* isn't the same as *an old good friend*). A comma is also not used when one of the adjectives is part of the noun. Compare these two phrases:

> a distinguished, well-known figure

> a distinguished public figure

The adjective-noun combination of *public* and *figure* has been used together so often that it has come to be considered a single thing: *public figure.* So no comma is required.

Seventh, commas are used both before and after the year in sentences that include month, day, and year:

> It will be sent by December 15, 1999, from our Cincinnati plant.

Some companies write dates in another form: 15 December 2000. No commas should be used in that case. Nor is a comma needed when only the month and year are present (December 2000).

Eighth, commas are used to set off a variety of parenthetical words and phrases within sentences, including state names, dates, abbreviations, transitional expressions, and contrasted elements:

> They were, in fact, prepared to submit a bid.

> Our best programmer is Ken, who joined the company just a month ago.

> Habermacher, Inc., went public in 1999.

> Our goal was increased profits, not increased market share.

> Service, then, is our main concern.

> The factory was completed in Chattanooga, Tennessee, just three weeks ago.

> Joanne Dubiik, M.D., has applied for a loan from First Savings.

> I started work here on March 1, 2001, and soon received my first promotion.

Ninth, a comma is used to separate a quotation from the rest of the sentence:

> Your warranty reads, "These conditions remain in effect for one year from date of purchase."

However, the comma is left out when the quotation as a whole is built into the structure of the sentence:

> He hurried off with an angry "Look where you're going."

Finally, a comma should be used whenever it's needed to avoid confusion or an unintended meaning. Compare the following:

> Ever since they have planned new ventures more carefully.

> Ever since, they have planned new ventures more carefully.

2.7 Dashes

Use a dash to surround a comment that is a sudden turn in thought:

> Membership in the IBSA—it's expensive but worth it—may be obtained by applying to our New York office.

A dash can also be used to emphasize a parenthetical word or phrase:

> Third-quarter profits—in excess of $2 million—are up sharply.

Finally, use dashes to set off a phrase that contains commas:

> All our offices—Milwaukee, New Orleans, and Phoenix—have sent representatives.

Don't confuse a dash with a hyphen. A dash separates and emphasizes words, phrases, and clauses more strongly than a comma or parentheses can; a hyphen ties two words so tightly that they almost become one word.

On computer, use the em dash symbol. When typing a dash in e-mail or on a typewriter, type two hyphens with no space before, between, or after.

2.8 Hyphens

Hyphens are mainly used in three ways. The first is to separate the parts of compound words beginning with such prefixes as *self-*, *ex-*, *quasi-*, and *all-*:

self-assured	quasi-official
ex-wife	all-important

However, omit hyphens from and close up those words that have prefixes such as *pro, anti, non, re, pre, un, inter,* and *extra*:

prolabor	nonunion
antifascist	interdepartmental

Exceptions occur when (1) the prefix occurs before a proper noun or (2) the vowel at the end of the prefix is the same as the first letter of the root word:

pro-Republican anti-American
anti-inflammatory extra-atmospheric

When in doubt, consult your dictionary.

Hyphens are also used in some compound adjectives, which are adjectives made up of two or more words. Specifically, you should use hyphens in compound adjectives that come before the noun:

an interest-bearing account well-informed executives

However, you need not hyphenate when the adjective follows a linking verb:

This account is interest bearing.

Their executives are well informed.

You can shorten sentences that list similar hyphenated words by dropping the common part from all but the last word:

Check the costs of first-, second-, and third-class postage.

Finally, hyphens may be used to divide words at the end of a typed line. Such hyphenation is best avoided, but when you have to divide words at the end of a line, do so correctly (see Section 3.5). A dictionary will show how words are divided into syllables.

2.9 Apostrophes

Use an apostrophe in the possessive form of a noun (but not in a pronoun):

On *his* desk was a reply to Bette *Ainsley's* application for the *manager's* position.

Apostrophes are also used in place of the missing letter(s) of a contraction:

Whole Words	Contraction
we will	we'll
do not	don't
they are	they're

2.10 Quotation Marks

Use quotation marks to surround words that are repeated exactly as they were said or written:

The collection letter ended by saying, "This is your third and final notice."

Remember: (1) When the quoted material is a complete sentence, the first word is capitalized. (2) The final comma or period goes inside the closing quotation marks.

Quotation marks are also used to set off the title of a newspaper story, magazine article, or book chapter:

You should read "Legal Aspects of the Collection Letter" in *Today's Credit.*

The book title is shown here in italics. When typewritten, the title is underlined. The same treatment is proper for newspaper and magazine titles. (Appendix B explains documentation style in more detail.)

Quotation marks may also be used to indicate special treatment for words or phrases, such as terms that you're using in an unusual or ironic way:

Our management "team" spends more time squabbling than working to solve company problems.

When you are defining a word, put the definition in quotation marks:

The abbreviation *etc.* means "and so forth."

When using quotation marks, take care to insert the closing marks as well as the opening ones.

Although periods and commas go inside any quotation marks, colons and semicolons go outside them. A question mark goes inside the quotation marks only if the quotation is a question:

All that day we wondered, "Is he with us?"

If the quotation is not a question but the entire sentence is, the question mark goes outside:

What did she mean by "You will hear from me"?

2.11 Parentheses

Use parentheses to surround comments that are entirely incidental:

Our figures do not match yours, although (if my calculations are correct) they are closer than we thought.

Parentheses are also used in legal documents to surround figures in arabic numerals that follow the same amount in words:

Remittance will be One Thousand Two Hundred Dollars ($1,200).

Be careful to put punctuation (period, comma, and so on) outside the parentheses unless it is part of the statement in parentheses.

2.12 Ellipses

Use ellipsis points, or dots, to indicate that material has been left out of a direct quotation. Use them only in direct quotations and only at the point where material was left out. In the following example, the first sentence is quoted in the second:

The Dow Jones Industrial Average, which skidded 38.17 points in the previous five sessions, gained 4.61 to end at 2213.84.

According to the Honolulu *Star Bulletin,* "The Dow Jones Industrial Average . . . gained 4.61" on June 10.

The number of dots in ellipses is not optional; always use three. Occasionally, the points of ellipsis come at the end of a sentence, where they seem to grow a fourth dot. Don't be fooled: One of the dots is a period.

3.0 Mechanics

The most obvious and least tolerable mistakes that a business writer makes are probably those related to grammar and punctuation. However, a number of small details, known as writing mechanics, demonstrate the writer's polish and reflect on the company's professionalism.

3.1 Capitals

Capitals are used at the beginning of certain word groups:

- **Complete sentence:** *Before* hanging up, he said, "*We'll* meet here on Wednesday at noon."

- **Formal statement following a colon:** She has a favorite motto: Where there's a will, there's a way. (Otherwise, the first word after a colon should not be capitalized—see Section 2.5.)

- **Phrase used as sentence:** Absolutely not!

- **Quoted sentence embedded in another sentence:** Scot said, "Nobody was here during lunch hour except me."

- **List of items set off from text:** Three preliminary steps are involved:
  Design review
  Budgeting
  Scheduling

Capitalize proper adjectives and proper nouns (the names of particular persons, places, and things):

> Darrell Greene lived in a Victorian mansion.

> We sent Ms. Larson an application form, informing her that not all applicants are interviewed.

> Let's consider opening a branch in the West, perhaps at the west end of Tucson, Arizona.

> As office buildings go, the Kinney Building is a pleasant setting for TDG Office Equipment.

Ms. Larson's name is capitalized because she is a particular applicant, whereas the general term *applicant* is left uncapitalized. Likewise, *West* is capitalized when it refers to a particular place but not when it means a direction. In the same way, *office* and *building* are not capitalized when they are general terms (common nouns), but they are capitalized when they are part of the title of a particular office or building (proper nouns).

Titles within families, governments, or companies may also be capitalized:

> I turned down Uncle David when he offered me a job, since I wouldn't be comfortable working for one of my relatives.

> We've never had a president quite like President Sweeney.

People's titles are capitalized when they are used in addressing a person, especially in a formal context. They are not usually capitalized, however, when they are used merely to identify the person:

> Address the letter to Chairperson Anna Palmer.

> I wish to thank Chairperson Anna Palmer for her assistance.

> Please deliver these documents to board chairperson Anna Palmer.

> Anna Palmer, chairperson of the board, took the podium.

Also capitalize titles if they are used by themselves in addressing a person:

> Thank you, Doctor, for your donation.

Titles that are used to identify a person of very high rank are capitalized regardless of where they fall or how much of the name is included:

> the President of the United States

> the Prime Minister of Canada

> the Pope

In addresses, salutations, signature blocks, and some formal writing (such acknowledgments), all titles are capitalized whether they come before or after the name. In addition, always capitalize the first word of the salutation and complimentary close of a letter:

> *Dear* Mr. Andrews: *Yours* very truly,

The names of organizations are capitalized, of course; so are the official names of their departments and divisions. However, do not use capitals when referring in general terms to a department or division, especially one in another organization:

> Route this memo to Personnel.

> Larry Tien was transferred to the Microchip Division

> Will you be enrolled in the Psychology Department?

> Someone from the engineering department at EnerTech stopped by the booth.

> Our production department has reorganized for efficiency.

> Send a copy to their school of business administration.

Capitalization is unnecessary when using a word like *company, corporation,* or *university* alone:

> The corporation plans to issue 50,000 shares of common stock.

Likewise, the names of specific products are capitalized, although the names of general product types are not:

> Compaq computer   Tide laundry detergent

One problem that often arises in writing about places is the treatment of two or more proper nouns of the same type. When the common word comes before the specific names, it is capitalized; when it comes after the specific names, it is not:

> Lakes Ontario and Huron

> Allegheny and Monongahela rivers

The names of languages, races, and ethnic groups are capitalized: *Japanese, Caucasian, Hispanic.* But racial terms that denote only skin color are not capitalized: *black, white.*

When referring to the titles of books, articles, magazines, newspapers, reports, movies, and so on, you should capitalize the first and last words and all nouns, pronouns, adjectives, verbs, adverbs, and prepositions and conjunctions with five letters or more. Except for the first and last words, do not capitalize articles:

> *Economics During the Great War*

> "An Investigation into the Market for Long-Distance Services"

> "What Successes Are Made Of"

When *the* is part of the official name of a newspaper or magazine, it should be treated this way too: *The Wall Street Journal.*

References to specific pages, paragraphs, lines, and the like are not capitalized: *page 73, line 3.* However, in most other numbered or lettered references, the identifying term is capitalized: *Chapter 4, Serial No. 382–2203, Item B-11.*

Finally, the names of academic degrees are capitalized when they follow a person's name but are not capitalized when used in a general sense:

> I received a bachelor of science degree.

> Thomas Whitelaw, Doctor of Philosophy, will attend.

Similarly, general courses of study are not capitalized, but the names of specific classes are:

> She studied accounting as an undergraduate.

> She is enrolled in Accounting 201.

3.2 Underscores and Italics

Usually a line typed underneath a word or phrase either provides emphasis or indicates the title of a book, magazine, or newspaper. If possible, use italics instead of an underscore. Italics (or underlining) should also be used for defining terms and for discussing words as words:

> In this report *net sales* refers to after-tax sales dollars.

> The word *building* is a common noun and should not be capitalized.

3.3 Abbreviations

Abbreviations are used heavily in tables, charts, lists, and forms. They're used sparingly in prose paragraphs, however. Here are some abbreviations often used in business writing:

Abbreviation	Full Term
b/l	bill of lading
ca.	circa (about)
dol., dols.	dollar, dollars
etc.	et cetera (and so on)
FDIC	Federal Deposit Insurance Corporation
Inc.	Incorporated
L.f.	Ledger folio
Ltd.	Limited
mgr.	manager
NSF or N/S	not sufficient funds
P&L or P/L	profit and loss
reg.	regular
whsle.	wholesale

One way to handle an abbreviation that you want to use throughout a document is to spell it out the first time you use it, follow it with the abbreviation in parentheses, and then use the abbreviation in the remainder of the document.

Because *etc.* contains a word meaning "and," never write *and etc.* In fact, try to limit your use of such abbreviations to tables and parenthetical material.

3.4 Numbers

Numbers may be correctly handled many ways in business writing, so follow company style. In the absence of a set style, however, generally spell out all numbers from one to nine and use arabic numerals for the rest.

There are some exceptions to this general rule. For example, never begin a sentence with a numeral:

> *Twenty* of us produced *641* units per week in the first *12* weeks of the year.

Use numerals for the numbers one through ten if they're in the same list as larger numbers:

> Our weekly quota rose from *9* to *15* to *27*.

Use numerals for percentages, time of day (except with *o'clock*), dates, and (in general) dollar amounts.

> Our division is responsible for *7* percent of total sales.

> The meeting is scheduled for *8:30* A.M. on August *2*.

> Add *$3* for postage and handling.

Use a comma in numbers expressing thousands (*1,257*), unless your company specifies another style. When dealing with numbers in the millions and billions, combine words and figures: *7.3 million, 2 billion.*

When writing dollar amounts, use a decimal point only if cents are included. In lists of two or more dollar amounts, use the decimal point either for all or for none:

> He sent two checks, one for *$67.92* and one for *$90.00*.

When two numbers fall next to each other in a sentence, use figures for the number that is largest, most difficult to spell, or part of a physical measurement; use words for the other:

> I have learned to manage a classroom of 30 twelve-year-olds.

> She's won a bonus for selling 24 thirty-volume sets.

> You'll need twenty 3-inch bolts.

In addresses, all street numbers except *One* are in figures. So are suite and room numbers and ZIP codes. For street names that are numbered, practice varies so widely that you should use the form specified on an organization's letterhead or in a reliable directory. All of the following examples are correct:

> One Fifth Avenue   297 Ninth Street
>
> 1839 44th Street   11026 West 78 Place

Telephone numbers are always expressed in figures. Parentheses may separate the area code from the rest of the number, but a slash or a dash may be used instead, especially if the entire phone number is enclosed in parentheses:

> 382–8329   (602/382–8329)   602–382–8329

Percentages are always expressed in figures. The word *percent* is used in most cases, but % may be used in tables, forms, and statistical writing.

Physical measurements such as distance, weight, and volume are also often expressed in figures: *9 kilometers, 5 feet 3 inches, 7 pounds 10 ounces.*

Ages are usually expressed in words—except when a parenthetical reference to age follows someone's name:

> Mrs. Margaret Sanderson is seventy-two.

> Mrs. Margaret Sanderson, 72, swims daily.

Also, ages expressed in years and months are treated like physical measurements that combine two units of measure: *5 years 6 months.*

Decimal numbers are always written in figures. In most cases, add a zero to the left of the decimal point if the number is less than one and does not already start with a zero:

> 1.38   .07   0.2

In a series of related decimal numbers with at least one number greater than one, make sure that all numbers smaller than one have a zero to the left of the decimal point: *1.20, 0.21, 0.09*. Also, express all decimal numbers in a series to the same number of places by adding zeroes at the end:

> The responses were Yes, 37.2 percent; No, 51.0; Not Sure, 11.8.

Simple fractions are written in words, but more complicated fractions are expressed in figures or, if easier to read, in figures and words:

> two-thirds   9/32   2 hundredths

A combination of whole numbers and a fraction should always be written in figures. Note that a hyphen is used to separate the fraction from the whole number when a slash is used for the fraction: *2–11/16*.

3.5 Word Division

In general, avoid dividing words at the ends of lines. When you must do so, follow these rules:

- Don't divide one-syllable words (such as *since, walked,* and *thought*); abbreviations (*mgr.*); contractions (*isn't*); or numbers expressed in numerals (*117,500*).

- Divide words between syllables, as specified in a dictionary or word-division manual.

- Make sure that at least three letters of the divided word are moved to the second line: *sin-cerely* instead of *sincere-ly.*

- Do not end a page or more than three consecutive lines with hyphens.

- Leave syllables consisting of a single vowel at the end of the first line (*impedi-ment* instead of *imped-iment*), except when the single vowel is part of a suffix such as *-able, -ible, -ical,* or *-ity* (*re-spons-ible* instead of *re-sponsi-ble*).

- Divide between double letters (*tomor-row*), except when the root word ends in double letters (*call-ing* instead of *cal-ling*).

- Wherever possible, divide hyphenated words at the hyphen only: instead of *anti-inde-pendence,* use *anti-independence.*

4.0 Vocabulary

Using the right word in the right place is a crucial skill in business communication. However, many pitfalls await the unwary.

4.1 Frequently Confused Words

Because the following sets of words sound similar, be careful not to use one when you mean to use the other:

Word	Meaning
accede	to comply with
exceed	to go beyond
accept	to take
except	to exclude
access	admittance
excess	too much
advice	suggestion
advise	to suggest
affect	to influence
effect	the result
allot	to distribute
a lot	much or many
all ready	completely prepared
already	completed earlier
born	given birth to
borne	carried
capital	money; chief city
capitol	a government building
cite	to quote
sight	a view
site	a location
complement	complete amount; to go well with
compliment	expression of esteem; to flatter
corespondent	party in a divorce suit
correspondent	letter writer

council	a panel of people
counsel	advice; a lawyer
defer	to put off until later
differ	to be different
device	a mechanism
devise	to plan
die	to stop living; a tool
dye	to color
discreet	careful
discrete	separate
envelop	to surround
envelope	a covering for a letter
forth	forward
fourth	number four
holey	full of holes
holy	sacred
wholly	completely
human	of people
humane	kindly
incidence	frequency
incidents	events
instance	example
instants	moments
interstate	between states
intrastate	within a state
later	afterward
latter	the second of two
lead	a metal; to guide
led	guided
lean	to rest at an angle
lien	a claim
levee	embankment
levy	tax
loath	reluctant
loathe	to hate
loose	free; not tight
lose	to mislay
material	substance
materiel	equipment
miner	mineworker
minor	underage person
moral	virtuous; a lesson
morale	sense of well-being
ordinance	law
ordnance	weapons
overdo	to do in excess
overdue	past due
peace	lack of conflict
piece	a fragment
pedal	a foot lever
peddle	to sell
persecute	to torment
prosecute	to sue
personal	private
personnel	employees

precedence	priority
precedents	previous events
principal	sum of money; chief; main
principle	general rule
rap	to knock
wrap	to cover
residence	home
residents	inhabitants
right	correct
rite	ceremony
write	to form words on a surface
role	a part to play
roll	to tumble; a list
root	part of a plant
rout	to defeat
route	a traveler's way
shear	to cut
sheer	thin, steep
stationary	immovable
stationery	paper
than	as compared with
then	at that time
their	belonging to them
there	in that place
they're	they are
to	a preposition
too	excessively; also
two	the number
waive	to set aside
wave	a swell of water; a gesture
weather	atmospheric conditions
whether	if
who's	contraction of "who is" or "who has"
whose	possessive form of who

In the preceding list, only enough of each word's meaning is given to help you distinguish between the words in each group. Several meanings are left out entirely. For more complete definitions, consult a dictionary.

4.2 Frequently Misused Words

The following words tend to be misused for reasons other than their sound. Reference books (including the *Random House College Dictionary,* revised edition; Follett's *Modern American Usage;* and Fowler's *Modern English Usage*) can help you with similar questions of usage.

a lot: When the writer means "many," *a lot* is always two separate words, never one.

correspond with: Use this phrase when you are talking about exchanging letters. Use *correspond to* when you mean "similar to." Use either *correspond with* or *correspond to* when you mean "relate to."

disinterested: This word means "fair, unbiased, having no favorites, impartial." If you mean "bored" or "not interested," use *uninterested.*

etc.: This abbreviated form of the Latin phrase *et cetera* means "and so on" or "and so forth." The current tendency among business writers is to use English rather than Latin.

imply/infer: Both refer to hints. Their great difference lies in who is acting. The writer implies; the reader infers, sees between the lines.

lay: This word is a transitive verb. Never use it for the intransitive *lie.* (See Section 1.3.3.)

less: Use *less* for uncountable quantities (such as amounts of water, air, sugar, and oil). Use *fewer* for countable quantities (such as numbers of jars, saws, words, pages, and humans). The same distinction applies to *much* and *little* (uncountable) versus *many* and *few* (countable).

like: Use *like* only when the word that follows is just a noun or a pronoun. Use *as* or *as if* when a phrase or clause follows:

> She looks like him.

> She did just as he had expected.

> It seems as if she had plenty of time.

many/much: See *less.*

regardless: The *less* ending is the negative part. No word needs two negative parts, so don't add *ir* (a negative prefix) to the beginning. There is no such word as *irregardless.*

to me/personally: Use these phrases only when personal reactions, apart from company policy, are being stated (not often the case in business writing).

try: Always follow with *to,* never *and.*

verbal: People in the business community who are careful with language frown on those who use *verbal* to mean "spoken" or "oral." Many others do say "verbal agreement." Strictly speaking, *verbal* means "of words" and therefore includes both spoken and written words. Follow company usage in this matter.

4.3 Frequently Misspelled Words

All of us, even the world's best spellers, sometimes have to check a dictionary for the spelling of some words. People who have never memorized the spelling of commonly used words must look up so many that they grow exasperated and give up on spelling words correctly.

Don't expect perfection, and don't surrender. If you can memorize the spelling of just the words listed here, you'll need the dictionary far less often, and you'll write with more confidence.

absence	asterisk
absorption	auditor
accessible	
accommodate	bankruptcy
accumulate	believable
achieve	brilliant
advantageous	bulletin
affiliated	
aggressive	calendar
alignment	campaign
aluminum	category
ambience	ceiling
analyze	changeable
apparent	clientele
appropriate	collateral
argument	committee
asphalt	comparative
assistant	competitor
	concede

congratulations
connoisseur
consensus
convenient
convertible
corroborate
criticism

definitely
description
desirable
dilemma
disappear
disappoint
disbursement
discrepancy
dissatisfied
dissipate

eligible
embarrassing
endorsement
exaggerate
exceed
exhaust
existence
extraordinary

fallacy
familiar
flexible
fluctuation
forty

gesture
grievous

haphazard
harassment
holiday

illegible
immigrant
incidentally
indelible
independent
indispensable
insistent
intermediary
irresistible

jewelry
judgment
judicial

labeling
legitimate
leisure
license
litigation

maintenance
mathematics
mediocre
minimum

necessary
negligence
negotiable
newsstand
noticeable

occurrence
omission

parallel
pastime
peaceable
permanent
perseverance
persistent
personnel
persuade
possesses
precede
predictable
preferred
privilege
procedure
proceed
pronunciation
psychology
pursue

questionnaire

receive
recommend
repetition
rescind
rhythmical
ridiculous

salable
secretary
seize
separate

sincerely
succeed
suddenness
superintendent
supersede
surprise

tangible
tariff
technique

tenant
truly

unanimous
until

vacillate
vacuum
vicious

4.4 Transitional Words and Phrases

The following sentences don't communicate as well as they might because they lack a transitional word or phrase:

> Production delays are inevitable. Our current lag time in filling orders is one month.

A semicolon between the two sentences would signal a close relationship between their meanings, but it wouldn't even hint at what that relationship is. Here are the sentences again, now linked by means of a semicolon, with a space for a transitional word or phrase:

> Production delays are inevitable; _____ , our current lag time in filling orders is one month.

Now read the sentence with *nevertheless* in the blank space. Now try *therefore, incidentally, in fact,* and *at any rate* in the blank. Each substitution changes the meaning of the sentence.

Here are some transitional words (called conjunctive adverbs) that will help you write more clearly:

accordingly	furthermore	moreover
anyway	however	otherwise
besides	incidentally	still
consequently	likewise	therefore
finally	meanwhile	

The following transitional phrases are used in the same way:

as a result	in other words
at any rate	in the second place
for example	on the other hand
in fact	to the contrary

When one of these words or phrases joins two independent clauses, it should be preceded by a semicolon and followed by a comma, as shown here:

> The consultant recommended a complete reorganization; moreover, she suggested that we drop several products.

Answer Keys

ANSWER KEY FOR "LEARNING OBJECTIVES CHECKUP"

Chapter 1:

1. d
2. a
3. technology
4. intercultural
5. teams
6. b
7. c
8. b
9. b
10. c
11. c
12. c
13. c
14. b
15. a
16. c
17. b
18. d
19. d
20. dilemma, lapse

Chapter 2:

1. c
2. b
3. d
4. c
5. a
6. b
7. d
8. c
9. b
10. a
11. eyes
12. appearance
13. dominance
14. b
15. a
16. d
17. d
18. c

Chapter 3:

1. c
2. c
3. a
4. b
5. c
6. d
7. a
8. c
9. d
10. b
11. a
12. c
13. c
14. d
15. a
16. c
17. b
18. d

Chapter 4:

1. c
2. a
3. b
4. d
5. a
6. c
7. b
8. c
9. d
10. a
11. c
12. b
13. d
14. b
15. a
16. c

Chapter 5:

1. a
2. d
3. c
4. b
5. c
6. d
7. a
8. d
9. b
10. c
11. c
12. d
13. b
14. b
15. a
16. c
17. c
18. d
19. b
20. a

Chapter 6:

1. a
2. b
3. c
4. c
5. a
6. b
7. d
8. d
9. b
10. b
11. a
12. c
13. b
14. a
15. c
16. a
17. d

Chapter 7:

1. b
2. a

3. d
4. c
5. b
6. a
7. c
8. d
9. b
10. c
11. a
12. b
13. d
14. c

Chapter 8:

1. a
2. b
3. d
4. c
5. a
6. a
7. c
8. b
9. d
10. a
11. c
12. libel, slander
13. c
14. b
15. c
16. d
17. a

Chapter 9:

1. c
2. b
3. d
4. a
5. b
6. c
7. c
8. a
9. b
10. d
11. a
12. c
13. b
14. c
15. c
16. d
17. a

Chapter 10:

1. d
2. b
3. c
4. a
5. d
6. c
7. b
8. a
9. c
10. d
11. b
12. c
13. b
14. c
15. a
16. d
17. d
18. b

Chapter 11:

1. b
2. d
3. a
4. c
5. b
6. c
7. a
8. b
9. c
10. d
11. c
12. a
13. b
14. d
15. d
16. b
17. d
18. c
19. b

Chapter 12:

1. c
2. d
3. b
4. a
5. d
6. c
7. a
8. b

9. c
10. a
11. c

Chapter 13:

1. a
2. c
3. b
4. d
5. b
6. d
7. b
8. b
9. d
10. c
11. a
12. b
13. a
14. d
15. c
16. b
17. c
18. c
19. a
20. d
21. b
22. d
23. d
24. b
25. a

Chapter 14:

1. c
2. d
3. a
4. c
5. c
6. b
7. b
8. a
9. c
10. d
11. b
12. d
13. c
14. d
15. a
16. b
17. b
18. c

19. c
20. a

Chapter 15:

1. c
2. d

3. a
4. b
5. d
6. b
7. a
8. d

9. b
10. a
11. c
12. d
13. a
14. c

ANSWER KEY FOR "IMPROVE YOUR GRAMMAR, MECHANICS, AND USAGE" EXERCISES

Chapter 1:

1. boss's (1.1.4)
2. sheep (1.1.3)
3. 1990s (1.1.3)
4. Joneses, stopwatches (1.1.3)
5. attorneys (1.1.3)
6. copies (1.1.3)
7. employees' (1.1.4)
8. sons-in-law, businesses (1.1.3, 1.1.4)
9. parentheses (1.1.3)
10. Ness's, week's (1.1.4)

Chapter 2:

1. its (1.2.5)
2. their (1.2.5)
3. its (1.2.5)
4. their (1.2.1)
5. his or her (1.2.3)
6. his or her (1.2.3)
7. a / them (1.2.3, 1.2.4)
8. who (1.2.4)
9. whom (1.2.4)
10. its (1.2.5)

Chapter 3:

1. b (1.3.1)
2. b (1.3.1)
3. a (1.3.1)
4. b (1.3.5)
5. a (1.3.5)
6. a (1.3.4)
7. b (1.3.4)
8. b (1.3.4)
9. a (1.3.4)
10. b (1.3.4)

Chapter 4:

1. greater (1.4.1)
2. perfect (1.4.1)

3. most interesting (1.4.1)
4. hardest (1.4.1)
5. highly placed, last-ditch (1.4.2)
6. top-secret (1.4.2)
7. 30-year-old (1.4.2)
8. all-out, no-holds-barred struggle (1.4)
9. tiny metal (1.4)
10. usual cheerful, prompt service (1.4)

Chapter 5:

1. good (1.5)
2. surely (1.5)
3. sick (1.5)
4. well (1.5)
5. good (1.5)
6. faster (1.5.2)
7. better (1.5.2)
8. any (1.5.1)
9. ever (1.5.1)
10. can, any (1.5.1)

Chapter 6:

1. leading (1.6.1)
2. off (1.6.1)
3. aware of (1.6.1)
4. to (1.6.1)
5. among (1.6.1)
6. for (1.6.1)
7. to (1.6.1)
8. from (1.6.1)
9. not only in
10. the suitable experience (1.6.2)

Chapter 7:

1. b (1.7.3)
2. a (1.7.2)
3. b (1.7.6)
4. a (1.7.4)
5. b (1.7.4)

6. b (1.7.6)
7. a (1.7.6)
8. b (1.7.4)
9. a (1.7.3)
10. b (1.7.2)

Chapter 8:

1. c (2.6)
2. a (2.6)
3. b (2.6)
4. a (2.6)
5. b (2.6)
6. c (2.6)
7. b (2.6)
8. a (2.6)
9. c (2.6)
10. b (2.6)

Chapter 9:

1. a (2.4)
2. a (2.5)
3. c (2.4)
4. a (2.5)
5. b (2.5)
6. b (2.4)
7. a (2.4)
8. c (2.4)
9. b (2.4)
10. c (2.5)

Chapter 10:

1. b (2.1)
2. a (2.2)
3. b (2.1)
4. a (2.1)
5. b (2.2, 2.3)
6. b (2.1)
7. b (2.2, 2.1)
8. a (2.2)

9. b (2.2)

10. a (2.2, 2.3)

Chapter 11:

1. b (2.7)
2. a (2.8)
3. c (2.7)
4. b (2.8)
5. a (2.7)
6. b (2.7)
7. c (2.8)
8. a (2.8, 2.7)
9. c (2.8, 2.7)
10. a (2.8)

Chapter 12:

1. b (2.10)
2. b (2.11)
3. a (2.11)
4. b (2.10)
5. c (2.10)

6. a (2.11)
7. c (2.10, 2.12)
8. b (2.10)
9. b (2.11)
10. c (2.10, 2.12)

Chapter 13:

1. c (3.1, 3.3)
2. a (3.1, 3.3)
3. b (3.2)
4. a (3.1)
5. c (3.3)
6. a (3.1, 3.2)
7. b (3.1, 3.3)
8. b (3.1, 3.3)
9. a (3.2)
10. c (3.1)

Chapter 14:

1. c (3.4)
2. a (3.4)

3. a (3.4)
4. b (3.4)
5. b (3.4)
6. a (3.4)
7. b (3.4)
8. c (3.4)
9. a (3.4)
10. c (3.4)

Chapter 15:

1. except (4.1)
2. device (4.1)
3. loath (4.1)
4. who's (4.1)
5. a lot (4.2)
6. judgment (4.3)
7. regardless (4.2)
8. accommodate (4.3)
9. imply (4.2)
10. to (4.2)

References

CHAPTER 1

1. Adapted from GE website [accessed 28 August 2002], www.ge.com; David Drucker, "Virtual Teams Light Up GE," *InternetWeek*, 10 April 2000, 1+; Monica C. Higgins, Lloyd Trotter, Steven Luria Ablon, Stuart Pearson, Mohan Mohan, Yoram "Jerry" Wind, "What Should C. J. Do?," *Harvard Business Review*, November–December 2000, 43 +; Matt Murray, "General Electric Mentoring Program Turns Underlings into Web Teachers," *Wall Street Journal*, 15 February 2000 [accessed 30 August 2002], www.db.com/wows/career/publish/950720551.html; Carol Hymowitz, "In the Lead: What Happens When Your Valued Employee Makes a Bad Manager?," *Wall Street Journal,* 23 January 2001, B1; Alex Poole, "Six Sigma: Communication's Perfect Role," *Strategic Communication Management* 4, no. 2 (February–March 2000): 34+; David A. Thomas and Suzy Wetlaufer, "A Question of Color: A Debate on Race in the U.S. Workplace," *Harvard Business Review,* September–October 1997, 118; William Keenan Jr., "How GE Stays on Top of Its Markets," *Sales and Marketing Management* 146, no. 8 (August 1994): 61; D. Keith Denton, "Open Communication," *Business Horizons,* September– October 1993, 64+; Shelly Branch and Alfred Edmond Jr., "Lloyd G. Trotter," *Black Enterprise,* February 1993, 130.

2. Raymond M. Olderman, *10 Minute Guide to Business Communication* (New York: Simon & Schuster, 1997), 1–2.

3. Ieva M. Augstums, "Experts Call Communication Key to Effective Leadership," *Knight Ridder Tribune Business News,* 4 June 2002 [accessed 6 June 2002], http://proquest.umi.com.

4. Philip C. Kolin, *Successful Writing at Work,* 6th ed. (Boston: Houghton Mifflin, 2001), 17–23.

5. "Interpersonal Skills Are Key in Office of the Future," *TMA Journal,* July–August 1999, 53.

6. Lillian H. Chaney and Jeanette S. Martin, *Intercultural Business Communications* (Upper Saddle River, N.J.: Prentice Hall, 2000), 1–2.

7. Timothy Aeppel, "A 3Com Factory Hires a Lot of Immigrants, Gets Mix of Languages," *Wall Street Journal,* 30 March 1999, A1, A12.

8. James M. Citrin and Thomas J. Neff, "Digital Leadership," *Strategy and Business,* First Quarter 2000, 42–50; Gary L. Neilson, Bruce A. Pasternack, and Albert J. Viscio, "Up the E-Organization," *Strategy and Business,* First Quarter 2000, 52–61.

9. Donald O. Wilson, "Diagonal Communication Links with Organizations," *Journal of Business Communication* 29, no. 2 (Spring 1992): 129–143.

10. Carol Hymowitz, "Spread the Word: Gossip Is Good," *Wall Street Journal,* 4 November 1988, B1; Donald B. Simmons, "The Nature of the Organizational Grapevine," *Supervisory Management,* November 1985, 40.

11. J. David Johnson, William A. Donohoe, Charles K. Atkin, and Sally Johnson, "Differences Between Formal and Informal Communication Channels," *Journal of Business Communication* 31, no. 2 (1994): 111–122.

12. "Presumed Guilty: Managing When Your Company's Name Is Mud," *Working Woman,* November 1991, 31; Judy A. Smith, "Crisis Communications: The War on Two Fronts," *Industry Week,* 20 May 1996, 136.

13. Timothy Aeppel, Clare Ansberry, Milo Geyelin, and Robert L. Simison, "Road Signs: How Ford, Firestone Let the Warnings Slide by as Debacle Developed," *Wall Street Journal,* 6 September 2000, A1; Joann Muller, David Welch, Jeff Green, Lorraine Woellert, and Nicole St. Pierre, "A Crisis of Confidence," *Business Week,* 18 September 2000, 40–42.

14. Paul Franson, *High Tech, High Hope* (New York: Wiley, 1998), 252.

15. Maria Godoy, "Instant Messaging Goes to Work," *ABCNews.com* [accessed 20 August 2001], www.abcnews.go.com.

16. Anne Zieger, "Enterprise Computing: IP Telephony Gets Real," *InfoWorld,* 5 January 1998, 20; Laura Kujubu, "Telcos Answer Wake-Up Call from Internet," *InfoWorld,* 15 December 1997, 19.

17. David Morse, ed., *CyberDictionary: Your Guide to the Wired World* (Santa Monica, Calif.: Knowledge Exchange, 1996), 113.

18. Morse, *CyberDictionary,* 233.

19. Some material adapted from Courtland L. Bovée, John V. Thill, Marian Burk Wood, and George P. Dovel, *Management* (New York: McGraw-Hill, 1993), 537–538.

20. Gillian Flynn, "Pillsbury's Recipe Is Candid Talk," *Workforce,* February 1998, 56–57+.

21. Bruce W. Speck, "Writing Professional Codes of Ethics to Introduce Ethics in Business Writing," *Bulletin of the Association for Business Communication* 53, no. 3 (September 1990): 21–26; H. W. Love, "Communication, Accountability and Professional Discourse: The Interaction of Language Values and Ethical Values," *Journal of Business Ethics* 11 (1992): 883–892; Kathryn C. Rentz and Mary Beth Debs, "Language and Corporate Values: Teaching Ethics in Business Writing Courses," *Journal of Business Communication* 24, no. 3 (Summer 1987): 37–48.

22. Gerry McGovern, "Less Is More," *Publish,* March–April 2001, 24.

23. Don Clark, "Managing the Mountain," *Wall Street Journal,* 21 June 1999, R4.

24. Samuel Greengard, "Surviving Internet Speed," *Workforce,* April 2001, 28–43.

25. Jay Stuller, "Overload," *Across the Board,* April 1996, 16–22.

26. Carol Hymowitz, "If the Walls Had Ears You Wouldn't Have Any Less Privacy," *Wall Street Journal,* 19 May 1998, B1.

27. Kenneth Hein, "Hungry for Feedback," *Incentive,* September 1997, 9+.

28. A. Thomas Young, "Ethics in Business: Business of Ethics," *Vital Speeches,* 15 September 1992, 725–730.

29. Philip C. Kolin, *Successful Writing at Work,* 6th ed. (Boston: Houghton Mifflin, 2001), 24–30.

30. David Grier, "Confronting Ethical Dilemmas: The View from Inside—A Practitioner's Perspective," *Vital Speeches,* 1 December 1989, 100–104.

31. Kenneth Blanchard and Norman Vincent Peale, *The Power of Ethical Management* (New York: Ballentine Books, 1996), 7–17; Joseph L. Badaracco, Jr., "Business Ethics: Four Spheres of Executive Responsibility," *California Management Review,* Spring 1992, 64–79.

32. Jules Harcourt, "Developing Ethical Messages: A Unit of Instruction for the Basic Business Communication Course," *Bulletin of the Association for Business Communication* 53, no. 3 (September 1990): 17–20; John D. Pettit, Bobby Vaught, and Kathy J. Pulley, "The Role of Communication in Organizations," *Journal of Business Communication* 27, no. 3 (Summer 1990): 233–249; Kenneth R. Andrews, "Ethics in Practice," *Harvard Business Review,* September–October 1989, 99–104; Priscilla S. Rogers and John M. Swales, "We the People? An Analysis of the Dana Corporation Policies Document," *Journal of Business Communication* 27, no. 3 (Summer 1990): 293–313; Larry Reynolds, "The Ethics Audit," *Business Ethics,* July–August 1991, 120–122.

33. See note 1.

34. "When Rumors Disrupt Your Staff," *Working Woman,* October 1992, 36.

CHAPTER 2

1. Adapted from the American Express website [accessed 29 February 2001], www.americanexpress.com; Mahlon Apgar IV, "The Alternative Workplace: Changing Where and How People Work," *Harvard Business Review*, May–June 1998, 121–130; "How Senior Executives at American Express View the Alternative Workplace," *Harvard Business Review*, May–June 1998, 132–133; Michelle Marchetti, "Master Motivators," *Sales and Marketing Management*, April 1998, 38–44; Sally Richards, "Make the Most of Your First Job," *Informationweek*, 21 June 1999, 183–186; Carrie Shook, "Leader, Not Boss," *Forbes*, 1 December 1997, 52–54.

2. Michael H. Mescon, Courtland L. Bovée, and John V. Thill, *Business Today* (Upper Saddle River, N.J.: Prentice Hall, 1999), 203.

3. "Teamwork Translates into High Performance," *HR Focus*, July 1998, 7.

4. Ellen Neuborne, "Companies Save, But Workers Pay," *USA Today*, 25 February 1997, B1; Richard L. Daft, *Management*, 4th ed. (Fort Worth: Dryden, 1997), 594–595; Stephen P. Robbins and David A. De Cenzo, *Fundamentals of Management*, 2d ed. (Upper Saddle River, N.J.: Prentice Hall, 1998), 336–338.

5. Stephen P. Robbins, *Essentials of Organizational Behavior*, 6th ed. (Upper Saddle River, N.J.: Prentice Hall, 2000), 109.

6. Daft, *Management*, 612–615.

7. Robbins, *Essentials of Organizational Behavior*, 98.

8. B. Aubrey Fisher, *Small Group Decision Making: Communication and the Group Process*, 2d ed. (New York: McGraw-Hill, 1980), 145–149; Robbins and De Cenzo, *Fundamentals of Management*, 334–335; Daft, *Management*, 602–603.

9. Daft, *Management*, 609–612.

10. Thomas K. Capozzoli, "Conflict Resolution—A Key Ingredient in Successful Teams," *Supervision*, November 1999, 14–16.

11. Janis Graham, "Sharpen Your Negotiating Skills," *Sylvia Porter's Personal Finance*, December 1985, 54–58.

12. Jesse S. Nirenberg, *Getting Through to People* (Paramus, N.J.: Prentice Hall, 1973), 134–142.

13. Nirenberg, *Getting Through to People*.

14. Nirenberg, *Getting Through to People*.

15. Lynda McDermott, Bill Waite, and Nolan Brawley, "Executive Teamwork," *Executive Excellence*, May 1999, 15.

16. Larry Cole and Michael Cole, "Why Is the Teamwork Buzz Word Not Working?," *Communication World*, February–March 1999, 29; Patricia Buhler, "Managing in the 90s: Creating Flexibility in Today's Workplace," *Supervision*, January 1997, 24+ ; Allison W. Amason, Allen C. Hochwarter, Wayne A. Thompson, and Kenneth R. Harrison, "Conflict: An Important Dimension in Successful Management Teams," *Organizational Dynamics*, Autumn 1995, 20+.

17. Jon Hanke, "Presenting as a Team," *Presentations*, January 1998, 74–82.

18. William P. Galle, Jr., Beverly H. Nelson, Donna W. Luse, and Maurice F. Villere, *Business Communication: A Technology-Based Approach* (Chicago: Irwin, 1996), 260.

19. Ruth G. Newman, "Communication: Collaborative Writing with Purpose and Style," *Personnel Journal*, April 1988, 37–38; Galle, Nelson, Luse, and Villere, *Business Communication*, 256.

20. Joel Haness, "How to Critique a Document," *IEEE Transactions on Professional Communication* PC-26, no. 1 (March 1983): 15–17.

21. Charles E. Risch, "Critiquing Written Material," *Manage* 35, no. 4 (1983): 4–6.

22. Risch, "Critiquing Written Material."

23. Brenda Park Sundo, "Are You Noticing Too Many Yawns?," *Workforce*, April 1998, 16–17.

24. William C. Waddell and Thomas A. Rosko, "Conducting an Effective Off-Site Meeting," *Management Review*, February 1993, 40–44.

25. "Better Meetings Benefit Everyone: How to Make Yours More Productive," *Working Communicator Bonus Report,* July 1998, 1.

26. Kathy E. Gill, "Board Primer: Parliamentary Procedure," *Association Management*, 1993, L-39.

27. Judi Brownell, *Listening: Attitudes, Principles, and Skills* (Boston: Allyn and Bacon, 2002), 330.

28. Sherwyn P. Morreale and Courtland L. Bovée, *Excellence in Public Speaking* (Orlando, Fla.: Harcourt Brace, 1998), 72–76; Lyman K. Steil, Larry L. Barker, and Kittie W. Watson, *Effective Listening: Key to Your Success* (Reading, Mass.: Addison-Wesley, 1983), 21–22.

29. Bob Lamons, "Good Listeners Are Better Communicators," *Marketing News*, 11 September 1995, 13 + ; Phillip Morgan and H. Kent Baker, "Building a Professional Image: Improving Listening Behavior," *Supervisory Management*, November 1985, 35–36.

30. Robyn D. Clarke, "Do You Hear What I Hear?," *Black Enterprise*, May 1998, 129; Dot Yandle, "Listening to Understand," *Pryor Report Management Newsletter Supplement* 15, no. 8 (August 1998): 13.

31. Larry Barker and Kittie Watson, *Listen Up* (New York: St. Martin's Press, 2000), 8.

32. Patrick J. Collins, *Say It with Power and Confidence* (Upper Saddle River, N.J.: Prentice Hall, 1997), 40–45.

33. Collins, *Say It with Power and Confidence*, 40–45.

34. Augusta M. Simon, "Effective Listening: Barriers to Listening in a Diverse Business Environment," *Bulletin of the Association for Business Communication* 54, no. 3 (September 1991): 73–74.

35. "An Added Joy of E-Mail: Fewer Face-to-Face Meetings," *Wall Street Journal*, 14 July 1998, A1.

36. Madelyn Burley-Allen, *Listening: The Forgotten Skill* (New York: Wiley, 1995), 120–123.

37. "Listening: Hearing Better at Meetings," *Communication Briefings* 18, no. 11 (September 1999): 2.

38. J. Michael Sproule, *Communication Today* (Glenview, Ill.: Scott, Foresman, 1981), 69.

39. Sproule, *Communication Today*.

40. Sproule, *Communication Today*.

41. Barker and Watson, *Listen Up*, 75–83.

42. Judi Brownell, *Listening: Attitudes, Principles, and Skills* (Boston: Allyn and Bacon, 2002), 85; Burley-Allen, *Listening: The Forgotten Skill*, 120–123.

43. Burley-Allen, *Listening: The Forgotten Skill*, 120–123.

44. Barker and Watson, *Listen Up*, 109–122; Burley-Allen, *Listening: The Forgotten Skill*, 120–123.

45. Burley-Allen, *Listening: The Forgotten Skill*, 120–123.

46. Brownell, *Listening: Attitudes, Principles, and Skills*, 85–90; Burley-Allen, *Listening: The Forgotten Skill*, 120–123.

47. Brownell, *Listening: Attitudes, Principles, and Skills*, 85–90; Burley-Allen, *Listening: The Forgotten Skill*, 120–123.

48. Marilyn Pincus, *Everyday Business Etiquette* (Hauppauge, N.Y.: Barron's Educational Series, 1996), 106; Barker and Watson, *Listen Up*, 109–122; Brownell, *Listening: Attitudes, Principles, and Skills*, 85–90.

49. Teri Kwal Gamble and Michael Gamble, *Communication Works* (Burr Ridge, Ill.: McGraw-Hill/Irwin, 2002), 146.

50. Gamble and Gamble, *Communication Works*, 146.

51. Nido Qubein, *Communicate Like a Pro* (New York: Berkeley Books, 1986), 97.

52. Dale G. Leathers, *Successful Nonverbal Communication: Principles and Applications* (New York: Macmillan, 1986), 19.

53. Gerald H. Graham, Jeanne Unrue, and Paul Jennings, "The Impact of Nonverbal Communication in Organizations: A Survey of Perceptions," *Journal of Business Communication* 28, no. 1 (Winter 1991): 45–62.

54. Gamble and Gamble, *Communication Works*, 147–148.

55. David Lewis, *The Secret Language of Success* (New York: Carroll & Graf, 1989), 67, 170.

56. H. L. Goodall Jr., and Sandra Goodall, *Communicating in Professional Contexts* (Belmont, Calif.: Wadsworth/Thompson Learning, 2002), 128, 136.

57. Dale G. Leathers, *Successful Nonverbal Communication: Principles and Applications* (Boston: Allyn & Bacon, 1997), 246; Dana May Casperson, *Power Etiquette: What You Don't Know Can Kill Your Career* (New York: AMACOM, 1999), 22.

58. Casperson, *Power Etiquette: What You Don't Know Can Kill Your Career*, 9.

59. Pincus, *Everyday Business Etiquette*, 7, 133.

60. Pincus, *Everyday Business Etiquette*, 7.

61. Casperson, *Power Etiquette: What You Don't Know Can Kill Your Career*, 31.

62. Pincus, *Everyday Business Etiquette*, 136, 138–139.

63. Pincus, *Everyday Business Etiquette*, 136.

64. Casperson, *Power Etiquette: What You Don't Know Can Kill Your Career*, 23.

65. Casperson, *Power Etiquette: What You Don't Know Can Kill Your Career*, 24.

66. Graham, Unrue, and Jennings, "The Impact of Nonverbal Communication in Organizations: A Survey of Perceptions," 45–62.

67. Pincus, *Everyday Business Etiquette*, 100–101.

68. Pincus, *Everyday Business Etiquette*, 101.

69. Casperson, *Power Etiquette: What You Don't Know Can Kill Your Career*, 11.

70. Casperson, *Power Etiquette: What You Don't Know Can Kill Your Career*, 10–14; Ellyn Spragins, "Introducing Politeness," *Fortune Small Business*, November 2001, 30.

71. Casperson, *Power Etiquette: What You Don't Know Can Kill Your Career*, 14.

72. Casperson, *Power Etiquette: What You Don't Know Can Kill Your Career*, 19; Pincus, *Everyday Business Etiquette*, 7–8.

73. Casperson, *Power Etiquette: What You Don't Know Can Kill Your Career*, 44–46.

74. Casperson, *Power Etiquette: What You Don't Know Can Kill Your Career*, 44–46, 56–57.

75. Jo Ind, "Hanging on the Telephone," *Birmingham Post*, 28 July 1999, PS10.

76. Barker and Watson, *Listen Up*, 64–65.

77. Lin Walker, *Telephone Techniques* (New York: AMACOM, 1998), 46–47.

78. Ind, "Hanging on the Telephone"; Dorothy Neal, *Telephone Techniques*, 2d ed. (New York: Glencoe McGraw-Hill, 1998), 31; Walker, *Telephone Techniques*, 46–47.

79. Casperson, *Power Etiquette: What You Don't Know Can Kill Your Career*, 109–110.

80. Ind, "Hanging on the Telephone"; Neal, *Telephone Techniques*; Walker, *Telephone Techniques*; Jeannie Davis, *Beyond "Hello"* (Aurora, Col.: Now Hear This, Inc., 2000), 2–3.

81. Mike Bransby, "Voice Mail Makes a Difference," *Journal of Business Strategy* (January–February 1990): 7–10.

82. "Ten Steps to Caller-Friendly Voice Mail," *Managing Office Technology*, January 1995, 25; Rhonda Finniss, "Voice Mail: Tips for a Positive Impression," *Administrative Assistant's Update*, August 2001, 5; "How to Get the Most Out of Voice Mail," *The CPA Journal*, February 2000, 11.

83. Ruth Davidhizar and Ruth Shearer, "The Effective Voice Mail Message," *Hospital Material Management Quarterly*, 45–49; "How to Get the Most Out of Voice Mail," 11.

84. Davidhizar and Shearer, "The Effective Voice Mail Message."

85. See note 1.

CHAPTER 3

1. Adapted from Target Stores website [accessed 21 March 2001], www.target.com; D. R. Barnes, "Company Plans to Establish Community Partnerships," *Washington Informer*, 13 December 1995, 5; Susan Moffat, "Work Force Diversity; The Young and the Diverse; The Next Generation May Be Better Equipped to Deal with Cultural Complexities at Work," Home Edition, *Los Angeles Times*, 16 May 1994, 2–15.

2. N. Hed Seelye and Alan Seelye-James, *Culture Clash* (Chicago: NTC Business Books, 1995), xv, xviii.

3. Sari Kalin, "The Importance of Being Multiculturally Correct," *Computerworld*, 6 October 1997, G16–G17; Lawrence M. Fisher, "REI Climbs Online," *Strategy and Business*, First Quarter 2000, 116–129.

4. Teri Kwal Gamble and Michael Gamble, *Communication Works* (Burr Ridge, Ill.: McGraw-Hill/Irwin, 2002), 39.

5. Rona Gindin, "Dealing with a Multicultural Workforce," *Nation's Restaurant News*, September–October 1998, 31, 83; Howard Gleckman, "A Rich Stew in the Melting Pot," *Business Week*, 31 August 1998, 76+; Toby B. Gooley, "A World of Difference," *Logistics Management and Distribution Report*, June 2000, 51–55; William H. Miller, "Beneath the Surface," *Industry Week*, 20 September 1999, 13–16.

6. Lillian H. Chaney and Jeanette S. Martin, *Intercultural Business Communication* (Upper Saddle River, N.J.: Prentice Hall, 2000), 6.

7. Gary P. Ferraro, *The Cultural Dimensions of International Business*, 4th ed. (Upper Saddle River, N.J.: Prentice Hall, 2002), 98.

8. Chaney and Martin, *Intercultural Business Communication*, 9.

9. Larry A. Samovar and Richard E. Porter, "Basic Principles of Intercultural Communication," in *Intercultural Communication: A Reader*, 6th ed., edited by Larry A. Samovar and Richard E. Porter (Belmont, Calif.: Wadsworth, 1991), 12.

10. Chaney and Martin, *Intercultural Business Communication*, 159.

11. Otto Kreisher, "Annapolis Has a New Attitude Toward Sexual Harassment," *San Diego Union*, 30 July 1990, A–6.

12. Linda Beamer, "Teaching English Business Writing to Chinese-Speaking Business Students," *Bulletin of the Association for Business Communication* 57, no. 1 (1994): 12–18.

13. Edward T. Hall, "Context and Meaning," in *Intercultural Communication*, edited by Samovar and Porter, 46–55.

14. Beamer, "Teaching English Business Writing to Chinese-Speaking Business Students."

15. Charley H. Dodd, *Dynamics of Intercultural Communication*, 3d ed. (Dubuque, Ia.: Brown, 1991), 69–70.

16. Chaney and Martin, *Intercultural Business Communication*, 206–211.

17. James Wilfong and Toni Seger, *Taking Your Business Global* (Franklin Lakes, N.J.: Career Press, 1997), 277–278.

18. Phillip R. Harris and Robert T. Moran, *Managing Cultural Differences*, 3d ed. (Houston: Gulf, 1991), 260.

19. Skip Kaltenheuser, "Bribery Is Being Outlawed Virtually Worldwide," *Business Ethics*, May–June 1998, 11; Thomas Omestad, "Bye-bye to Bribes," *U.S. News & World Report*, 22 December 1997, 39, 42–44.

20. Guo-Ming Chen and William J. Starosta, *Foundations of Intercultural Communication* (Boston: Allyn & Bacon, 1998), 288–289.

21. Sharon Ruhly, *Intercultural Communication*, 2d ed. MODCOM (Modules in Speech Communication) (Chicago: Science Research Associates, 1982), 14.

22. Mary A. DeVries, *Internationally Yours* (New York: Houghton Mifflin, 1994), 194.

23. Robert O. Joy, "Cultural and Procedural Differences That Influence Business Strategies and Operations in the People's Republic of China," *SAM Advanced Management Journal*, Summer 1989, 29–33.

24. Chaney and Martin, *Intercultural Business Communication*, 122–123.

25. Laray M. Barna, "Stumbling Blocks in Intercultural Communication," in *Intercultural Communication*, edited by Samovar and Porter, 345–352; Jean A. Mausehund, Susan A. Timm, and Albert S. King, "Diversity Training: Effects of an Intervention Treatment on Nonverbal Awareness," *Business Communication Quarterly* 38, no. 1 (1995): 27–30.

26. Chen and Starosta, *Foundations of Intercultural Communication*, 39–40.

27. Richard W. Brislin, "Prejudice in Intercultural Communication," in *Intercultural Communication*, edited by Samovar and Porter, 366–370.

28. James S. O'Rourke IV, "International Business Communication: Building a Course from the Ground Up," *Bulletin of the Association for Business Communication* 56, no. 4 (1993): 22–27.

29. Jensen J. Zhao and Calvin Parks, "Self-Assessment of Communication Behavior: An Experiential Learning Exercise for Intercultural Business Success," *Business Communication Quarterly* 58, no. 1 (1995): 20–26; Dodd, *Dynamics of Intercultural Communication*, 142–143, 297–299; Stephen P. Robbins, *Organizational Behavior*, 6th ed. (Paramus, N.J.: Prentice Hall, 1993), 345.

30. Daren Fonda, "Selling in Tongues," *Time Global Business,* November 2001, B12; "Less Yiddish, More Tagalog," *U.S. News & World Report,* 10 May 1993, 16; Gary Levin, "Marketers Learning New Languages for Ads," *Advertising Age,* 10 May 1993, 33.

31. Chaney and Martin, *Intercultural Business Communication,* 130.

32. Sondra Thiederman, "Improving Communication in a Diverse Health-care Environment," *Healthcare Financial Management,* November 1996, 72–74.

33. Myron W. Lustig and Jolene Koester, *Intercultural Competence: Interpersonal Communication Across Culture,* 4th ed. (Boston: Allyn and Bacon, 2003), 196, 253.

34. Bob Nelson, "Motivating Workers Worldwide," *Global Workforce,* November 1998, 25–27.

35. Stephen Dolainski, "Are Expats Getting Lost in the Translation?," *Workforce,* February 1997, 32–39.

36. Wilfong and Seger, *Taking Your Business Global,* 232.

37. Vern Terpstra, *The Cultural Environment of International Business* (Cincinnati: South-Western, 1979), 19.

38. Mona Casady and Lynn Wasson, "Written Communication Skills of International Business Persons," *Bulletin of the Association for Business Communication* 57, no. 4 (1994): 36–40.

39. See note 1.

40. Michael Copeland, specialist, international training, personal communication, January 1990.

CHAPTER 4

1. Adapted from Jim Kvicala, "Home Depot CEO Bob Nardelli Reaffirms Goal of Becoming $100 Billion Company," *News & Announcements,* 16 August 2002 [accessed 19 February 2003], www.terry.uga.edu/news/releases/2002/ttt_nardelli.html; Home Depot's Web site [accessed 8 March 2000], www.homedepot.com; Bernie Marcus and Arthur Blank with Bob Andelman, *Built from Scratch* (New York: Random House, 1999), 105, 110, 125, 135–137, 142, 149, 155–161, 178, 205, 216, 240–241, 255–258, 280, 287–289, 313; Carlton P. McNamara, "Making Human Capital More Productive," *Business and Economic Review,* October–December 1999, 10–13; Sarah Rose, "Building a Powerhouse," *Money,* December 1999, 62–64; Chris Roush, *Inside Home Depot* (New York: McGraw-Hill, 1999), 5–6, 12, 29, 31–35, 89, 101–108, 115, 141, 213–215, 221; Robert S. Salomon, Jr., "Reinventing Retail," *Forbes,* 19 October 1998, 171; Bruce Upin, "Profit in a Big Orange Box," *Forbes,* 24 January 2000, 122–127.

2. Kevin J. Harty and John Keenan, *Writing for Business and Industry: Process and Product* (New York: Macmillan Publishing Company, 1987), 3–4; Richard Hatch, *Business Writing* (Chicago: Science Research Associates, 1983), 88–89; Richard Hatch, *Business Communication Theory and Technique* (Chicago: Science Research Associates, 1983), 74–75; Center for Humanities, *Writing as a Process: A Step-by-Step Guide.* Four Filmstrips and Cassettes (Mount Kiscko, N.Y.: Center for Humanities, 1987); Michael L. Keene, *Effective Professional Writing* (New York: D. C. Heath, 1987), 28–34.

3. Sanford Kaye, "Writing Under Pressure," *Soundview Executive Book Summaries* 10, no. 12, part 2 (December 1988): 1–8.

4. Peter Bracher, "Process, Pedagogy, and Business Writing," *Journal of Business Communication* 24, no. 1 (Winter 1987): 43–50.

5. Mahalingam Subbiah, "Adding a New Dimension to the Teaching of Audience Analysis: Cultural Awareness," *IEEE Transactions on Professional Communication* 35, no. 1 (March 1992): 14–19; Ronald E. Dulek, John S. Fielden, and John S. Hill, "International Communication: An Executive Primer," *Business Horizons,* January–February 1991, 20–25; Dwight W. Stevenson, "Audience Analysis Across Cultures," *Journal of Technical Writing and Communication* 13, no. 4 (1983): 319–330.

6. Iris I. Varner, "Internationalizing Business Communication Courses," *Bulletin of the Association for Business Communication* 50, no. 4 (December 1987): 7–11.

7. Laurey Berk and Phillip G. Clampitt, "Finding the Right Path in the Communication Maze," *IABC Communication World,* October 1991, 28–32.

8. Berk and Clampitt, "Finding the Right Path in the Communication Maze."

9. Berk and Clampitt, "Finding the Right Path in the Communication Maze."

10. Raymond M. Olderman, *10 Minute Guide to Business Communication* (New York: Alpha Books, 1997), 19–20.

11. Mohan R. Limaye and David A. Victor, "Cross-Cultural Business Communication Research: State of the Art and Hypotheses for the 1990s," *Journal of Business Communication* 28, no. 3 (Summer 1991): 277–299.

12. Berk and Clampitt, "Finding the Right Path in the Communication Maze."

13. Berk and Clampitt, "Finding the Right Path in the Communication Maze."

14. Mike Bransby, "Voice Mail Makes a Difference," *Journal of Business Strategy,* January–February 1990, 7–10.

15. J. D. Biersdorfer, "To Nail the Sale, E-Mail's Too Slow," *New York Times,* 13 June 2001, 3; Heather Newman, "Instant Messaging a Communications Revolution," *San Diego Union-Tribune,* 12 June 2001, 4.

16. Tim McCollum, "The Net Result of Computer Links," *Nation's Business,* March 1998, 55–58.

17. Elizabeth Blackburn and Kelly Belanger, "You-Attitude and Positive Emphasis: Testing Received Wisdom in Business Communication," *Bulletin of the Association for Business Communication* 56, no. 2 (June 1993): 1–9.

18. Annette N. Shelby and N. Lamar Reinsch, Jr., "Positive Emphasis and You Attitude: An Empirical Study," *Journal of Business Communication* 32, no. 4 (1995): 303–322.

19. Judy E. Pickens, "Terms of Equality: A Guide to Bias-Free Language," *Personnel Journal,* August 1985, 24.

20. Lisa Taylor, "Communicating About People with Disabilities: Does the Language We Use Make a Difference?," *Bulletin of the Association for Business Communication* 53, no. 3 (September 1990): 65–67.

21. See note 1.

CHAPTER 5

1. Adapted from Barnes & Noble website [accessed 12 September 2002], www.barnesandnobleinc.com; "Company Information—Barnes & Noble," *Hoover's Online* [accessed 12 September 2002], www.hoovers.com; John Mutter, "Barnes & Noble Ready for More Expansion," *Publishers Weekly,* 10 June 2002 [accessed 12 September 2002], www.publishersweekly.reviewsnews.com; Judith Rosen, "Buying Customer Loyalty," *Publishers Weekly,* 15 October 2001 [accessed 12 September 2002], www.publishersweekly.reviewsnews.com; John L. Mariotti, "Mass Customization Revisited," *IndustryWeek.com,* 8 December 1998 [accessed 12 September 2002], www.industryweekcom/columns/asp/columns.asp?ColumnId5396.

2. Carol S. Mull, "Orchestrate Your Ideas," *The Toastmaster,* February 1987, 19.

3. Mull, "Orchestrate Your Ideas," 19.

4. Bruce B. MacMillan, "How to Write to Top Management," *Business Marketing,* March 1985, 138.

5. Ernest Thompson, "Some Effects of Message Structure on Listener's Comprehension," *Speech Monographs* 34 (March 1967): 51–57.

6. Based on the Pyramid Model developed by Barbara Minto of McKinsey & Company, management consultants.

7. Philip Subanks, "Messages, Models, and the Messy World of Memos," *Bulletin of the Association for Business Communication* 57, no. 1 (1994): 33–34.

8. Mary A. DeVries, *Internationally Yours* (Boston: Houghton Mifflin, 1994), 61.

9. Randolph H. Hudson, Gertrude M. McGuire, and Bernard J. Selzler, *Business Writing: Concepts and Applications* (Los Angeles: Roxbury, 1983), 79–82.

10. William M. Bulkeley, "Software Writers Try to Speak a Language Users Understand," *Wall Street Journal,* 30 June 1992, B6.

11. Peter Crow, "Plain English: What Counts Besides Readability?," *Journal of Business Communication* 25, no. 1 (Winter 1988): 87–95.

12. Alinda Drury, "Evaluating Readability," *IEEE Transactions on Professional Communication* PC-28 (December 1985): 12.

13. Portions of this section are adapted from Courtland L. Bovée, *Techniques of Writing Business Letters, Memos, and Reports* (Sherman Oaks, Calif.: Banner Books International, 1978), 13–90.

14. Iris I. Varner, "Internationalizing Business Communication Courses," *Bulletin of the Association for Business Communication* 50, no. 4 (December 1987): 7–11.

15. Renee B. Horowitz and Marian G. Barchilon, "Stylistic Guidelines for E-Mail," *IEEE Transactions on Professional Communication* 37, no. 4 (December 1994): 207–212; David Angell and Brent Heslop, *The Elements of E-Mail Style* (Reading, Mass.: Addison-Wesley, 1994), 22.

16. Jill H. Ellsworth and Matthew V. Ellsworth, *The Internet Business Book* (New York: Wiley, 1994), 91.

17. Angell and Heslop, *The Elements of E-Mail Style*, 20.

18. Lance Cohen, "How to Improve Your E-Mail Messages," galaxy.einet/galaxy/Business-and-Commerce/Management/Communications/How_to_Improve_YourEmail.html.

19. Angell and Heslop, *The Elements of E-Mail Style*, 18–19.

20. Horowitz and Barchilon, "Stylistic Guidelines for E-Mail"; Cohen, "How to Improve Your E-Mail Messages."

21. Reid Goldsborough, "Words for the Wise," *Link-Up*, September–October 1999, 25–26.

22. Jakob Nielsen, "Reading on the Web" [accessed 23 April 2000], www.useit.com/alertbox/9710a.html.

23. Goldsborough, "Words for the Wise."

24. Jakob Nielsen, "Failure of Corporate Websites" [accessed online 23 April 2000], www.useit.com/alertbox/981018.html.

25. Shel Holtz, "Writing for the Wired World," *International Association of Business Communicators*, 1999, 72–73.

26. Holtz, "Writing for the Wired World," 95.

27. "Web Writing: How to Avoid Pitfalls," *Investor Relations Business*, 1 November 1999, 15.

28. Michael Lerner, "Building Worldwide Websites," IBM website [accessed 23 April 2000], www.4.ibm.com/software/developer/library/web-localization.html.

29. John Morkes and Jakob Nielsen, "How to Write for the Web" [accessed 23 April 2000], www.useit.com/papers/webwriting/writing.html.

30. Carol Holstead, "Three Steps to Web-Smart Editing," *Folio Supplement*, 2000, 195–196.

31. See note 1.

32. Milton Moskowitz, Michael Katz, and Robert Levering, eds., *Everybody's Business: An Almanac* (San Francisco: Harper & Row, 1980), 131.

33. Hudson, McGuire, and Selzler, *Business Writing: Concepts and Applications*, 27.

CHAPTER 6

1. Adapted from Brian Bremner, "The Burger Wars Were Just a Warmup for McDonald's," *Business Week*, 8 May 1989, 67, 70; Richard Gibson and Robert Johnson, "Big Mac Plots Strategy to Regain Sizzle; Besides Pizza, It Ponders Music and Low Lights," *Wall Street Journal*, 29 September 1989, B1; Dyan Machan, "Great Hash Browns, but Watch Those Biscuits," *Forbes*, 19 September 1988, 192–196; Penny Moser, "The McDonald's Mystique," *Fortune*, 4 July 1988, 112–116; Thomas N. Cochran, "McDonald's Corporation," *Barron's*, 16 November 1987, 53–55; Lenore Skenazy, "McDonald's Colors Its World," *Advertising Age*, 9 February 1987, 37.

2. Susan Benjamin, *Words at Work* (Reading, Mass.: Addison-Wesley, 1997), 71.

3. Cynthia Crossen, "If You Can Read This, You Most Likely Are a High School Grad," *Wall Street Journal*, 1 December 2000, A1, A11; Kevin T.

Stevens, Kathleen C. Stevens, and William P. Stevens, "Measuring the Readability of Business Writing: The Cloze Procedure Versus Readability Formulas," *Journal of Business Communication* 29, no. 4 (1992): 367–382; Alinda Drury, "Evaluating Readability," *IEEE Transactions on Professional Communication* PC-28 (December 1985): 11.

4. Iris I. Varner, "Internationalizing Business Communication Courses," *Bulletin of the Association for Business Communication* 50, no. 4 (December 1987): 7–11.

5. Mary A. DeVries, *Internationally Yours* (Boston: Houghton Mifflin, 1994), 168; Benjamin, *Words at Work*, 61, 140–141.

6. William Zinsser, *On Writing Well*, 5th ed. (New York: HarperCollins, 1994), 9.

7. Gary Blake, "Hedging Your Bets: How Weasel Words Weaken Your Writing," *Claims Communication*, 1 April 2002 [accessed 11 June 2002], www.claimsmag.com/Issues/Apr02/claims_communication.asp.

8. Zinsser, *On Writing Well*, 7, 17.

9. Paula LaRocque, "A Very Dangerous Crutch: Unnecessary Qualifiers Weaken Writing," *The Quill*, May 2002 [accessed 11 June 2002], Society of Professional Journalists, www.spj.org/quill_archives.asp.

10. DeVries, *Internationally Yours*, 160.

11. William Wresch, Donald Pattow, and James Gifford, *Writing for the Twenty-First Century: Computers and Research Writing* (New York: McGraw-Hill, 1988), 192–211; Melissa E. Barth, *Strategies for Writing with the Computer* (New York: McGraw-Hill, 1988), 108–109, 140, 172–177.

12. Patsy Nichols, "Desktop Packaging," *Bulletin of the Association for Business Communication* 54, no. 1 (March 1991): 43–45; Raymond W. Beswick, "Designing Documents for Legibility," *Bulletin of the Association for Business Communication* 50, no. 4 (December 1987): 34–35.

13. Eric J. Adams, "The Fax of Global Business," *World Trade*, August–September 1991, 34–39.

14. See note 1.

15. Benjamin, *Words at Work*, 121.

CHAPTER 7

1. Adapted from Campbell Soup website [accessed 13 October 1997], www.campbellsoup.com; "Campbell Soup Company," *Hoover's Online* [accessed 23 January 1997], www.hoovers.com; 1993 Campbell Soup *Annual Report*; Joseph Weber, "Campbell: Now It's M-M-Global," *Business Week*, 15 March 1993, 52–54; Pete Engardio, "Hmm. Could Use a Little More Snake," *Business Week*, 15 March 1993, 53; Joseph Weber, "Campbell Is Bubbling, but for How Long?," *Business Week*, 17 June 1991, 56–57; Joseph Weber, "From Soup to Nuts and Back to Soup," *Business Week*, 5 November 1990, 114, 116; Alix Freedman and Frank Allen, "John Dorrance's Death Leaves Campbell Soup with Cloudy Future," *Wall Street Journal*, 19 April 1989, A1, A14; Claudia H. Deutsch, "Stirring up Profits at Campbell," *New York Times*, 20 November 1988, sec. 3, 1, 22; Bill Saporito, "The Fly in Campbell's Soup," *Fortune*, 9 May 1988, 67–70.

2. Daniel P. Finkelman and Anthony R. Goland, "Customers Once Can Be Customers for Life," *Information Strategy: The Executive's Journal*, Summer 1990, 5–9.

3. John A. Byrne, "Jack," *Business Week*, 8 June 1998, 91–112.

4. Donna Larcen, "Authors Share the Words of Condolence," *Los Angeles Times*, 20 December 1991, E11.

5. See note 1.

6. Adapted from Floorgraphics website [accessed 18 June 2001], www.floorgraphics.com; John Grossman, "It's an Ad, Ad, Ad, Ad World," *Inc.*, March 2000, 23–26; David Wellman, "Floor Toons," *Supermarket Business*, 15 November 1999, 47; "Floorshow," *Dallas Morning News*, 4 September 1998, 11D.

7. Adapted from Subway website, www.subway.com; Robert Maynard, "Choosing a Franchise," *Nation's Business*, October 1996, 54–55.

8. Adapted from Jamba Juice website [accessed 19 July 2001], jambacareers.com/benefits.html; Brenda Paik Sunoo, "Blending a Successful Workforce," *Workforce*, March 2000, 44–48; Michael Adams, "Kirk Perron:

Jamba Juice," *Restaurant Business*, 15 March 1999, 38; "Live in a Blender," *Restaurant Business*, 1 December 2000, 48–50; David Goll, "Jamba Juices Up 24-Hour Fitness Clubs," *East Bay Business Times*, 30 June 2000, 6.

9. Adapted from Bruce Frankel and Alex Tresniowski, "Stormy Skies," *People Weekly*, 31 July 2000, 112–115.

10. Eben Shapiro, "Blockbuster Rescue Bid Stars Viacom Top Guns," *Wall Street Journal*, 7 May 1997, B1, B10.

11. Adapted from Dylan Tweney, "The Defogger: Slim Down that Homepage," *Business 2.0*, 13 July 2001 [accessed 1 August 2001], www.business2.com/articles/web/0,1653,16483,FF.html.

12. Adapted from LifeSketch.com website [accessed 24 July 2000], www.lifesketch.com.

13. Adapted from Barbara Carton, "Farmers Begin Harvesting Satellite Data to Boost Yields," *Wall Street Journal*, 11 July 1996, B4.

14. "Entrepreneurs across America," *Entrepreneur Magazine Online* [accessed 12 June 1997], www.entrepreneurmag.com/entmag/50states5.hts.

15. Adapted from Carol Vinzant, "They Want You Back," *Fortune*, 2 October 2000, 271–272; Stephanie Armour, "Companies Recruiting Former Employees," *USA Today*, 2 February 2000, B1.

16. Sal D. Rinalla and Robert J. Kopecky, "Recruitment: Burger King Hooks Employees with Educational Incentives," *Personnel Journal*, October 1989, 90–99.

17. Adapted from Calvin Sims, "Reporter Disciplined for Reading His Co-workers' Electronic Mail," *New York Times*, 6 December 1993, A8.

18. Adapted from Keith H. Hammonds, "Difference Is Power," *Fast Company*, 36, 258 [accessed 11 July 2000], www.fastcompany.com/online/36/power.html; Terri Morrison, Wayne A. Conaway, and George A. Borden, *Kiss, Bow, or Shake Hands* (Holbrook, Mass.: Adams Media Corporation, 1995).

CHAPTER 8

1. "Purchasing: Professional Profile, American Airlines," *Purchasing*, 17 October 1996, 32; "AMR Corporation," *Hoover's Online* [accessed 22 January 1997], www.hoovers.com; Carole A. Shifrin, "American Commits to All-Boeing Jet Fleet," *Aviation Week & Space Technology*, 25 November 1996, 34.

2. Mark H. McCormack, *On Communicating* (Los Angeles: Dove Books, 1998), 87.

3. Curtis Sittenfeld, "Good Ways to Deliver Bad News," *Fast Company*, April 1999, 58–60.

4. Ram Subramanian, Robert G. Insley, and Rodney D. Blackwell, "Performance and Readability: A Comparison of Annual Reports of Profitable and Unprofitable Corporations," *Journal of Business Communication* 30, no. 2 (1993): 49–61.

5. *Techniques for Communicators* (Chicago: Lawrence Ragan Communication, 1995), 18.

6. Iris I. Varner, "A Comparison of American and French Business Correspondence," *Journal of Business Communication* 24, no. 4 (Fall 1988): 55–65.

7. Susan Jenkins and John Hinds, "Business Letter Writing: English, French, and Japanese," *TESOL Quarterly* 21, no. 2 (June 1987): 327–349; Saburo Haneda and Hiosuke Shima, "Japanese Communication Behavior as Reflected in Letter Writing," *Journal of Business Communication* 19, no. 1 (1982): 19–32.

8. James Calvert Scott and Diana J. Green, "British Perspectives on Organizing Bad-News Letters: Organizational Patterns Used by Major U.K. Companies," *Bulletin of the Association for Business Communication* 55, no. 1 (March 1992): 17–19.

9. Maura Dolan and Stuart Silverstein, "Court Broadens Liability for Job References," *Los Angeles Times*, 28 January 1997, A1, A11; Frances A. McMorris, "Ex-Bosses Face Less Peril Giving Honest Job References," *Wall Street Journal*, 8 July 1996, B1, B8.

10. Thomas S. Brice and Marie Waung, "Applicant Rejection Letters: Are Businesses Sending the Wrong Message?," *Business Horizons*, March–April 1995, 59–62.

11. Gwendolyn N. Smith, Rebecca F. Nolan, and Yong Dai, "Job-Refusal Letters: Readers' Affective Responses to Direct and Indirect Organizational Plans," *Business Communication Quarterly* 59, no. 1 (1996): 67–73; Brice and Waung, "Applicant Rejection Letters."

12. Korey A. Wilson, "Put Rejection Up-Front," *Black Enterprise*, November 1999, 69.

13. Judi Brownell, "The Performance Appraisal Interviews: A Multipurpose Communication Assignment," *Bulletin of the Association for Business Communication* 57, no. 2 (1994): 11–21.

14. Brownell, "The Performance Appraisal Interviews."

15. Stephanie Gruner, "Feedback from Everyone," *Inc.*, February 1997, 102–103.

16. Howard M. Bloom, "Performance Evaluations," *New England Business*, December 1991, 14.

17. David I. Rosen, "Appraisals Can Make—or Break—Your Court Case," *Personnel Journal*, November 1992, 113.

18. Patricia A. McLagan, "Advice for Bad-News Bearers: How to Tell Employees They're Not Hacking It and Get Results," *Industry Week*, 15 February 1993, 42; Michael Lee Smith, "Give Feedback, Not Criticism," *Supervisory Management*, 1993, 4; "A Checklist for Conducting Problem Performer Appraisals," *Supervisory Management*, December 1993, 7–9.

19. Jane R. Goodson, Gail W. McGee, and Anson Seers, "Giving Appropriate Performance Feedback to Managers: An Empirical Test of Content and Outcomes," *Journal of Business Communication* 29, no. 4 (1992): 329–342.

20. Craig Cox, "On the Firing Line," *Business Ethics*, May–June 1992, 33–34.

21. Cox, "On the Firing Line."

22. See note 1.

23. Adapted from Michal H. Mescon, Courtland L. Bovée, and John V. Thill, *Business Today*, 10th ed. (Upper Saddle River, N.J.: Prentice Hall, 2002), 369; Bruce Upbin, "Profit in a Big Orange Box," *Forbes*, 24 January 2000 [accessed 2 August 2001], www.forbes.com/forbes/2000/0124/6502122a.html.

24. Adapted from the Disclosure Project website [accessed 20 August 2001], www.disclosureproject.org; Katelynn Raymer and David Ruppe, "UFOs, Aliens and Secrets," ABCNews.com, 10 May 2001 [accessed 20 August 2001], http://more.abcnews.go.com/sections/scitech/DailyNews/ufo010509.html; Rachael Myer, "UFO Probe Sought," *Las Vegas Review-Journal*, 11 May 2001 [accessed 20 August 2001], www.lvrj.com/cgi-bin/printable.cgi?/lvrj_home/2001/May-11-Fri-2001/news/16064080.html.

25. Adapted from Union Bank of California teleservices, personal communication, 16 August 2001.

26. Adapted from Dan McSwain, "Consumers Could Owe $1.4B for Cuts," *North County Times*, 20 August 2000, A1; R. J. Ignelzi, "Now, Bill Can Be Clearer than Mud/But that Won't Ease Baseline Frustration," *San Diego Union-Tribune*, 15 August 2000, E-1 [accessed 29 August 2000], www.uniontrib.com/news/utarchives/cgi/idoc.cgi?589762+unix++www.uniontrib.com..80+Union-Tribune+Union-Tribune+Library+Library++%28sdge%29; Craig D. Rose, "Power Industry Politics: Ominous Signs Point to Higher Electricity Bills," *San Diego Union-Tribune*, 22 July 2000, A-1 [accessed 29 August 2000], www.uniontrib.com/news/utarchives/cgi/idoc.cgi?585891+unix++www.uniontrib.com..80+Union-Tribune+Union-Tribune+Library+Library++%28sdge%29.

27. Pascal Zachary, "Sun Microsystems Apologizes in Letter for Late Payments," *Wall Street Journal*, 11 October 1989, B4.

28. Adapted from Julie Vallese, "Motorized Scooter Injuries on the Rise," *CNN.com/U.S.*, 22 August 2001 [accessed 22 August 2001], www.cnn.com/2001/US/08/22/scooter.advisory/index.html; The Sports Authority website [accessed 28 August 2001], www.thesportauthority.com.

29. Adapted from Associated Press, "Employers Restricting Use of Cell Phones in Cars," CNN.com/Sci-Tech, 27 August 2001 [accessed 27 August 2001], www.cnn.com/2001/TECH/27/cellphones.cars.ap/index.html; Julie Vallese, "Study: All Cell Phones Distract Drivers," *CNN.com/U.S.*, 16 August 2001 [accessed 7 September 2001], www.cnn.com/2001/US/08/16/cell.phone.driving/index.html.

30. Adapted from Associated Press, "Children's Painkiller Recalled," CNN.com/Health website, 16 August 2001 [accessed 22 August 2001], www.cnn.com/2001/HEALTH/parenting/08/16/kids.drug.recalled.ap/index.html; Perrigo Company website [accessed 29 August 2001], www.perrigo.com.

31. Adapted from Ty Holland, "Vision Quest," *TV Guide,* 22 July 2000, 3.

32. Adapted from Dan Goodin, "Graduating Students Weigh New Job Incentive: Money to Stay Away," *Wall Street Journal,* 4 May 2001, B1; Mark Larson, "Intel Offering Buy-outs to Workers, College Recruits," *Sacramento Business Journal,* 4 May 2001, 1; Barbara Clements, "The Workplace: This Year's College Grads Will Face a More Challenging Job Hunt," *Tacoma* (Wash.) *News Tribune,* 7 May 2001, D1.

33. Patti Bond, "Hispanics Display Growing Muscle in Entrepreneurship," *Atlanta Journal-Constitution,* 11 July 1996, B1.

CHAPTER 9

1. Adapted from Andrea Adelson, "Wedded to Its Moral Imperatives: Patagonia Weaves Sales and Advocacy," *New York Times,* 17 May 1999, 9; Jim Collins, "The Foundation for Doing Good," *Inc.,* December 1997, 41–42; Stan Friedman, "Apparel with Conscience: The Givers," *Apparel Industry Magazine,* June 1999, 78–79; Paul C. Judge, "It's Not Easy Being Green," *Business Week,* 24 November 1997, 180; Jacquelyn Ottman, "Proven Environmental Commitment Helps Create Committed Customers," *Marketing News,* 2 February 1998, 5–6; Roger Rosenblatt, "The Root of All Good: Reaching the Top by Doing the Right Thing," *Time,* 18 October 1999, 88–91; John Steinbreder, "Yvon Chouinard, Founder and Owner of the Patagonia Outdoor . . .", *Sports Illustrated,* 11 February 1991, 200.

2. Jay A. Conger, "The Necessary Art of Persuasion," *Harvard Business Review,* May–June 1998, 84–95; Jeanette W. Gilsdorf, "Write Me Your Best Case for . . .", *Bulletin of the Association for Business Communication* 54, no. 1 (March 1991): 7–12.

3. "Vital Skill for Today's Managers: Persuading, Not Ordering Others," *Soundview Executive Book Summaries,* September 1998, 1.

4. Anne Fisher, "Success Secret: A High Emotional IQ," *Fortune,* 16 October 1998, 293–298.

5. Mary Cross, "Aristotle and Business Writing: Why We Need to Teach Persuasion," *Bulletin of the Association for Business Communication* 54, no. 1 (March 1991): 3–6.

6. Abraham H. Maslow, *Motivation and Personality* (New York: Harper & Row, 1954), 12, 19.

7. Robert T. Moran, "Tips on Making Speeches to International Audiences," *International Management,* April 1980, 58–59.

8. Gilsdorf, "Write Me Your Best Case for . . ."

9. Raymond M. Olderman, *10-Minute Guide to Business Communication* (New York: Macmillan Spectrum/Alpha Books, 1997), 57–61.

10. Gilsdorf, "Write Me Your Best Case for . . ."

11. John D. Ramage and John C. Bean, *Writing Arguments: A Rhetoric with Readings,* 3d ed. (Boston: Allyn & Bacon, 1995), 430–442.

12. Conger, "The Necessary Art of Persuasion."

13. Dianna Booher, *Communicate with Confidence* (New York: McGraw-Hill, 1994), 110.

14. Tamra B. Orr, "Persuasion Without Pressure," *Toastmaster,* January 1994, 19–22; William Friend, "Winning Techniques of Great Persuaders," *Association Management,* February 1985, 82–86; Patricia Buhler, "How to Ask for—and Get—What You Want!" *Supervision,* February 1990, 11–13.

15. Booher, *Communicate with Confidence,* 102.

16. Conger, "The Necessary Art of Persuasion."

17. Teri Lammers, "The Elements of Perfect Pitch," *Inc.,* March 1992, 53–55.

18. Kimberly Paterson, "The Writing Process—Sales Letters That Work," *Rough Notes,* April 1998, 59–60.

19. Paterson, "The Writing Process."

20. William North Jayme, quoted in Albert Haas Jr., "How to Sell Almost Anything by Direct Mail," *Across the Board,* November 1986, 50.

21. Robert L. Hemmings, "Think Before You Write," *Fund Raising Management,* February 1990, 23–24.

22. Hemmings, "Think Before You Write."

23. Hemmings, "Think Before You Write."

24. Conrad Squires, "How to Write a Strong Letter, Part Two: Choosing a Theme," *Fund Raising Management,* November 1991, 65–66.

25. Conrad Squires, "Getting the Compassion Out of the Box," *Fund Raising Management,* September 1992, 55, 60.

26. Squires, "Getting the Compassion Out of the Box."

27. Constance L. Clark, "25 Steps to Better Direct-Mail Fundraising," *Nonprofit World,* July–August 1989, 11–13; Squires, "How to Write a Strong Letter."

28. Squires, "How to Write a Strong Letter."

29. Clark, "25 Steps to Better Direct-Mail Fundraising."

30. Conrad Squires, "Why Some Letters Outpull Others," *Fund Raising Management,* January 1991, 67, 72.

31. Squires, "Why Some Letters Outpull Others"; Clark, "25 Steps to Better Direct-Mail Fundraising"; Jerry Huntsinger, "My First 29 1/2 Years in Direct-Mail Fundraising: What I've Learned," *Fund Raising Management,* January 1992, 40–43.

32. See note 1.

33. Adapted from Julian E. Barnes, "Fast-Food Giveaway Toys Face Rising Recalls," *New York Times,* 16 August 2001, A1; Shirley Leung, "Burger King Recalls 2.6 Million Kids Meal Toys," *Wall Street Journal,* 1 August 2001, B2.

34. "US West Labor Strike Ends," CNNfn, CNN Interactive [accessed 31 August 1998], cnnfn.com:80/hotsotreis/companies/9808/31/uswest.

35. Adapted from Annelena Lobb, "Identity Theft Survival Guide," CNN.com [accessed 4 April 2002], money.cnn.com/2002/04/03/pf/q_identity/index.htm.

36. Adapted from Michael S. James, "No Expiration on Recall Risk," ABCNews.com, 31 August 2001 [accessed on 31 August 2001], http://abcnews.go.com/sections/living/DailyNews/meat_recall010830.html; James F. Balch, M.D., and Phyllis A. Balch, C.N.C, *Prescription for Nutritional Healing,* 2d ed. (Garden City, N.Y.: Avery Publishing Group, 1997), 277–282.

37. Adapted from Michael Mescon, Courtland Bovée, and John Thill, *Business Today,* 10th ed. (Upper Saddle River, N.J.: Prentice Hall, 2002), 306–307; John R. Hall, "Recruiting via the Internet," *Air Conditioning, Heating & Refrigeration News,* 9 April 2001, 26; Kim Peters, "Five Keys to Effective E-cruiting," *Ivey Business Journal* (London), January–February 2001, 8–10; C. Glenn Pearce and Tracy L. Tuten, "Internet Recruiting in the Banking Industry," *Business Communication Quarterly,* March 2001, 9–18; Christopher Caggiano, "The Truth About Internet Recruiting," *Inc.,* December 1999, 156.

38. Adapted from advertisement, *Atlantic Monthly,* January 2000, 119; Endless Pools, Inc., website [accessed 31 August 2000], www.endlesspools.com/.

39. Adapted from "Tobacco Smoke and the Nonsmoker," Americans for Nonsmokers' Rights, 1988, revised 1994; "Nuisance/Real Property" case citation and abstract, *Contract Management Services, Inc., et al. v. Kuykendahl Joint, Inc., and Kamen Management, Inc.,* Dist. Ct. Harris County (TX), 61st Jud. Dist., No. 93-006228 (1993), Tobacco Control Resource Center, 1998, 39.

40. Adapted from Gateway website [accessed 2 October 2001], www.gateway.com; Gateway customer service sales representative, 1-800-GATEWAY, personal interview, 10 October 2001.

41. Adapted from Bruce Haring, "Trouble Getting up to Speed," *USA Today,* 27 December 1999, D3, D2; Mike Rogoway, "AT&T Seeks to Improve Internet Connections," *Columbian,* Vancouver, WA, 9 March 2001, E1.

42. Adapted from Quotesmith.com website, Investor Overview and FAQ [accessed 31 August 2000], investor.quotesmith.com/ireye/ir_site.zhtml?ticker=QUOT&script=2100.

43. Mescon, Bovée, and Thill, *Business Today,* 211; ScrubaDub website [accessed 2 October 2001], www. scrubadub.com.

44. Adapted from the American Red Cross website [accessed 3 October 2001], www.redcross.org; American Red Cross San Diego Chapter website [accessed 3 October 2001], www.sdarc.org/blood.htm.

CHAPTER 10

1. Adapted from Dell Computer Corporation's website [accessed 22 March 2000], www.dell.com; Neel Chowdhury, "Dell Cracks China," *Fortune,* 21 June 1999, 120–124; Michael Dell with Catherine Fredman, *Direct from Dell* (New York: HarperCollins Publishers, 1999), 8–15, 36–38, 66–80, 92–101, 133, 144, 175–182, 186, 196–197, 208; Louise Fickel, "Know Your Customer," *CIO,* 15 August 1999, 62–72; "Interview: E-Commerce Drives Dell Computer's Success," *IT Cost Management Strategies,* June 1999, 4–6; Carla Joinson, "Moving at the Speed of Dell," *HRMagazine,* April 1999, 50–56; Daniel Roth, "Dell's Big New Act," *Fortune,* 6 December 1999, 152–156.

2. Tom Sant, *Persuasive Business Proposals* (New York: American Management Association, 1992), summarized in *Soundview Executive Book Summaries* 14, no. 10, pt. 2 (October 1992): 3.

3. Information for this section was obtained from "Finding Industry Information" [accessed 3 November 1998], www.pitt.edu/~buslibry/industries.htm; Thomas P. Bergman, Stephen M. Garrison, and Gregory M. Scott, *The Business Student Writer's Manual and Guide to the Internet* (Upper Saddle River, N.J.: Prentice Hall, 1998), 67–80; Ernest L. Maier, Anthony J. Faria, Peter Kaatrude, and Elizabeth Wood, *The Business Library and How to Use It* (Detroit: Omnigraphics, 1996), 53–76; Sherwyn P. Morreale and Courtland L. Bovée, *Excellence in Public Speaking* (Fort Worth, Tex.: Harcourt Brace College Publishers, 1998), 166–171.

4. Jason Zien, "Measuring the Internet," *About.com,* 13 July 1999 [accessed 17 July 1999], internet.about.com/library/weekly/1999/aa071399a.htm; "FAST Aims for Largest Index," *Search Engine Watch,* 4 May 1999 [accessed 17 July 1999], searchenginewatch.internet.com/sereport/99/05-fast.htm.

5. "How to Design and Conduct a Study," *Credit Union Magazine,* October 1983, 36–46.

6. Erin White, "Market Research on the Internet Has Its Drawbacks," *Wall Street Journal,* 2 March 2000, B4.

7. Morreale and Bovée, *Excellence in Public Speaking,* 177.

8. Morreale and Bovée, *Excellence in Public Speaking,* 178–180.

9. Morreale and Bovée, *Excellence in Public Speaking,* 182.

10. Robert E. Cason, *Writing for the Business World* (Upper Saddle River, N.J.: Prentice Hall, 1997), 102.

11. Bergman, Garrison, and Scott, *The Business Student Writer's Manual and Guide to the Internet,* 65.

12. "How to Paraphrase Effectively: 6 Steps to Follow," Researchpaper.com [accessed 26 October 1998], www.researchpaper.com/writing-center/30.html.

13. Cason, *Writing for the Business World,* 71–72.

14. Dorothy Geisler, "How to Avoid Copyright Lawsuits," *IABC Communication World,* June 1984, 34–37.

15. Susan L. Leach, "SEC Takes Next Leap into Computer Age," *Christian Science Monitor,* 7 June 1994, 8.

16. See note 1.

CHAPTER 11

1. Adapted from FedEx website [accessed 25 April 2003], www.fedex.com; UPS website [accessed 27 October 1997], www.ups.com; DHL website [accessed 27 October 1997], www.dhl.com; Airborne Express website [accessed 27 October 1997], www.airborne.com; Hoover's Online [accessed 27 October 1997], www.hoovers.com; "All Strung Up," *The Economist,* 17 April 1993, 70; Gary M. Stern, "Improving Verbal Communications," *Internal Auditor,* August 1993, 49–54; Gary Hoover, Alta Campbell, and Patrick J. Spain, *Hoover's Handbook of American Business 1994* (Austin, Tex.: Reference Press, 1993), 488–489; "Pass the Parcel," *The Economist,* 21 March 1992, 73–74; "Federal Express," *Personnel Journal,* January 1992, 52.

2. Sheri Rosen, "What Is Truth?," *IABC Communication World,* March 1995, 40.

3. Edward R. Tufte, *The Visual Display of Quantitative Information* (Cheshire, Conn.: Graphic Press, 1983), 113.

4. Courtland L. Bovée, Michael J. Houston, and John V. Thill, *Marketing,* 2d ed. (New York: McGraw-Hill, 1995), 250.

5. David A. Hayes, "Helping Students GRASP the Knack of Writing Summaries," *Journal of Reading* (November 1989): 96–101.

6. Philip C. Kolin, *Successful Writing at Work,* 6th ed. (Boston: Houghton Mifflin, 2001), 552–555.

7. A. S. C. Ehrenberg, "Report Writing—Six Simple Rules for Better Business Documents," *Admap,* June 1992, 39–42.

8. See note 1.

9. Adapted from Bob Smith, "The Evolution of Pinkerton," *Management Review,* September 1993, 54–58.

CHAPTER 12

1. "Responsible Commercial Success," "A Unique Company Culture at Levi Strauss & Co.," "Levi Strauss & Co. Global Sourcing & Operating Guidelines," and "Levi Strauss & Co. General Information," Levi Strauss and Company website [accessed 29 September 1997], www.levistraus.com; Charlene Marmer Solomon, "Put Your Ethics to the Test," *Personnel Journal* 75, no. 1 (January 1996): 66–74; Russell Mitchell and Michael O'Neal, "Managing by Values," *BusinessWeek,* 1 August 1994, 46–52.

2. Michael Netzley and Craig Snow, *Guide to Report Writing* (Upper Saddle River, N.J.: Prentice Hall, 2001), 57.

3. Oswald M. T. Ratteray, "Hit the Mark with Better Summaries," *Supervisory Management,* September 1989, 43–45.

4. Netzley and Snow, *Guide to Report Writing,* 43.

5. Alice Reid, "A Practical Guide for Writing Proposals" [accessed 31 May 2001], www.members.dca.net/areid/proposal.htm.

6. See note 1.

7. Adapted from William C. Symonds, "Giving It the Old Online Try," *Business Week,* 3 December 2001, 76–80; Karen Frankola, "Why Online Learners Drop Out," *Workforce,* October 2001, 52–60; Mary Lord, "They're Online and on the Job; Managers and Hamburger Flippers Are Being E-Trained at Work," *U.S. News & World Report,* 15 October 2001, 72–77.

8. Bickley Townsend, "Room at the Top," *American Demographics,* July 1996, 28–37.

9. Adapted from Michael J. Weiss, "Online America," *American Demographics,* March 2001, 53–60; "E-Commerce Shows Signs of Waking from Summer Slumber," *CyberAtlas,* 23 August 2001 [accessed 14 December 2001], http://cyberatlas.internet.com/markets/retailing/artcle/0,6061_871621,00.html; "E-Commerce Survives an Enigmatic September," *CyberAtlas,* 16 October 2001 [accessed 14 December, 2001], http://cyberatlas.internet.com/markets/retailing/article/0,6061_904451,00.html; "Despite Customer Service Woes, Online Retailing Keeps Growing," *CyberAtlas,* 21 March 2001 [accessed 14 December, 2001], http://cyberatlas.internet.com/markets/retailing/article/0,6061_719771,00.html; "E-Commerce Should Hold Its Own This Holiday Season," *CyberAtlas,* 15 October 2001 [accessed 14 December 2001], http://cyberatlas.internet.com/markets/retailing/article/0,6061_903401,00.html; "Lump of Coal for E-Commerce Predictions," *CyberAtlas,* 5 November 2001 [accessed 14 December 2001], http://cyberatlas.internet.com/markets/retailing/article/0,6061_916681,00.html; "Online Shoppers Want a Real Store, Too," USA Today Snapshot, *USA Today,* 18 July 2001, B1; "Online Shoppers Prefer Discounts," USA Today Snapshot, *USA Today,* 16 January 2001, B1.

10. Denis Gellene, "Marketers Target Schools by Offering Facts and Features," *Los Angeles Times,* 4 June 1998, D1.

11. Sandra Evans, "First Come Goals, Then Guts and Glory," *Washington Post,* 5 October 1998, F10; Lisa Lee Freeman, "Getting Ahead May Mean Getting a Coach," *Investor's Business Daily,* 2 December 1997, A1; Anita Bruzzese, "Considering Taking a New Job?," *Gannett News Service,* 14 August 1997, S12.

CHAPTER 13

1. Adapted from Hewlett-Packard website [accessed 24 August 2002], www.hp.com; Amy Tsao, "Fiorina's Stereotype-Smashing Performance," *BusinessWeek Online,* 3 April 2002 [accessed 24 August 2002], www.businessweek.com/bwdaily/dnflash/apr2002/nf2002043_3881.htm; Cliff Edwards and Andrew Park, "HP and Compaq: It's Showtime," *BusinessWeek Online,* 17 June 2002 [accessed 24 August 2002], www.businessweek.com/@@@kIfe4cQNraOhA0A/magazine/content/02_24/b3787090.htm; Eric Nee, "Open Season on Carly Fiorina," *Fortune,* 23 July 2001, 114+; Heather Clancy and Sean Keating, "Carly Fiorino," *Computer Reseller News,* 12 November 2001, 90+; Craig Zarley, "Carly Fiorina," *Computer Reseller News,* 13 November 2000, 102+.

2. Jim Barlow, "PowerPoint Talks Can Be Sparkling," *Houston Chronicle,* 28 November 2000, C1+.

3. Sherwyn P. Morreale and Courtland L. Bovée, *Excellence in Public Speaking* (Fort Worth, Tex.: Harcourt Brace, 1998), 234–237.

4. Morreale and Bovée, *Excellence in Public Speaking,* 230.

5. Morreale and Bovée, *Excellence in Public Speaking,* 241–243.

6. "Choose and Use Your Words Deliberately," *Soundview Executive Book Summaries* 20, no. 6, pt. 2 (June 1998): 3.

7. Walter Kiechel III, "How to Give a Speech," *Fortune,* 8 June 1987, 180.

8. *Communication and Leadership Program* (Santa Ana, Calif.: Toastmasters International, 1980), 44, 45.

9. "Polishing Your Presentation," 3M Meeting Network [accessed 8 June 2001], www.mmm.com/meetingnetwork/readingroom/meetingguide_pres.html.

10. Kathleen K. Weigner, "Visual Persuasion," *Forbes,* 16 September 1991, 176; Kathleen K. Weigner, "Showtime!" *Forbes,* 13 May 1991, 118.

11. Ronald B. Adler and Jeanne Marquardt Elmhorst, *Communicating at Work* (Boston: McGraw-Hill, 2002), 379.

12. Jon Hanke, "Five Tips for Better Visuals," 3M Meeting Network [accessed 8 June 2001], www.mmm.com/meetingnetwork/presentations/pmag_better_visuals.html.

13. Hanke, "Five Tips for Better Visuals."

14. Ted Simons, "Handouts That Won't Get Trashed," *Presentations,* February 1999, 47–50.

15. Simons, "Handouts That Won't Get Trashed," 47–50; David Green, personal communication, 13 July 2001; "Help 'Em Remember with Handouts," Idea Café: Handouts for Your Business Presentations [accessed 4 October 2001], www.ideacafe.com/fridge/spotlight/spothandouts.html; Bob Lamons, "Good Listeners Are Better Communicators," *Marketing News,* 11 September 1995, 13+; Phillip Morgan and H. Kent Baker, "Building a Professional Image: Improving Listening Behavior," *Supervisory Management,* November 1985, 35–36.

16. Patrick J. Collins, *Say It with Power and Confidence* (Upper Saddle River, N.J.: Prentice Hall, 1997), 122–124.

17. Allbee, personal communication, 13 July 2001.

18. Ed Bott and Woody Leonard, *Special Edition—Using Microsoft Office 2000* (Indianapolis: Que Corporation, 1999), 907.

19. Mary Munter, *Guide to Managerial Communication,* 5th ed. (Upper Saddle River, N.J.: Prentice Hall, 2000), 59.

20. Morreale and Bovée, *Excellence in Public Speaking,* 24–25.

21. Judy Linscott, "Getting On and Off the Podium," *Savvy,* October 1985, 44.

22. Iris R. Johnson, "Before You Approach the Podium," *MW,* January–February 1989, 7.

23. Sandra Moyer, "Braving No Woman's Land," *The Toastmaster,* August 1986, 13.

24. "Control the Question-and-Answer Session," *Soundview Executive Book Summaries* 20, no. 6, pt. 2 (June 1998): 4.

25. "Control the Question-and-Answer Session"; Teresa Brady, "Fielding Abrasive Questions During Presentations," *Supervisory Management,* February 1993, 6.

26. Robert L. Montgomery, "Listening on Your Feet," *The Toastmaster,* July 1987, 14–15.

27. Adapted from Ronald L. Applebaum and Karl W. E. Anatol, *Effective Oral Communication: For Business and the Professions* (Chicago: Science Research Associates, 1982), 240–244.

28. See note 1.

CHAPTER 14

1. James Cox and David Kiley, "Ford Jr. Takes on Role He Was Born to Plan," *USA Today,* 31 October 2001 [accessed 10 September 2002], www.usatoday.com; "Ford Motor Company Capsule," *Hoover's Online* [accessed 10 September 2002], www.hoovers.com; Betsy Morris, Noshua Watson, and Patricia Neerings, "Idealist on Board: This Ford Is Different," *Fortune,* 3 April 2000 [accessed 11 September 2002], www.fortune.com/indexw.jhtml?channel = artcol.jhtml&doc_id = 00001487; 2001 *Annual Report,* Ford Motor Company website [accessed 10 September 2002], www.ford.com.

2. Camille DeBell, "Ninety Years in the World of Work in America," *Career Development Quarterly* 50, no. 1 (September 2001): 77–88.

3. John A. Challenger, "The Changing Workforce: Workplace Rules in the New Millennium," *Vital Speeches of the Day* 67, no. 23 (15 September 2001): 721–728.

4. Marvin J. Cetron and Owen Davies, "Trends Now Changing the World: Technology, the Workplace, Management, and Institutions," *Futurist* 35, no. 1 (March–April 2001): 27–42.

5. Amanda Bennett, "GE Redesigns Rungs of Career Ladder," *Wall Street Journal,* 15 March 1993, B1, B3.

6. Robin White Goode, "International and Foreign Language Skills Have an Edge," *Black Enterprise,* May 1995, 53.

7. Jeffrey R. Young, "'E-Portfolios' Could Give Students a New Sense of Their Accomplishments," *Chronicle of Higher Education,* 8 March 2002, A31.

8. Nancy M. Somerick, "Managing a Communication Internship Program," *Bulletin of the Association for Business Communication* 56, no. 3 (1993): 10–20.

9. Joan Lloyd, "Changing Workplace Requires You to Alter Your Career Outlook," *Milwaukee Journal Sentinel,* 4 July 1999, 1; DeBell, "Ninety Years in the World of Work in America."

10. Stephanie Armour, "Employers: Enough Already with the E-Résumés," *USA Today,* 15 July 1999, 1B.

11. Cheryl L. Noll, "Collaborating with the Career Planning and Placement Center in the Job-Search Project," *Business Communication Quarterly* 58, no. 3 (1995): 53–55.

12. Pam Stanley-Weigand, "Organizing the Writing of Your Resume," *Bulletin of the Association for Business Communication* 54, no. 3 (September 1991): 11–12.

13. Richard H. Beatty and Nicholas C. Burkholder, *The Executive Career Guide for MBAs* (New York: Wiley, 1996), 133.

14. Beatty and Burkholder, *The Executive Career Guide for MBAs,* 151.

15. Rockport Institute, "How to Write a Masterpiece of a Résumé" [accessed 16 October 1998], www.rockportinstitute.com/résumés.html:

16. Rockport Institute, "How to Write a Masterpiece of a Résumé."

17. Anne Field, "Coach, Help Me Out with This Interview," *Business Week,* 22 October 2001, 134E4, 134E6; Joan E. Rigdon, "Deceptive Résumés Can Be Door-Openers but Can Become an Employee's Undoing," *Wall Street Journal,* 17 June 1992, B1; Diane Cole, "Ethics: Companies Crack Down on Dishonesty," *Managing Your Career,* Spring 1991, 8–11; Nancy Marx Better, "Résumé Liars," *Savvy,* December 1990–January 1991, 26–29.

18. Beverly Culwell-Block and Jean Anna Sellers, "Résumé Content and Format—Do the Authorities Agree?," *Bulletin of the Association for Business Communication* 57, no. 4 (1994): 27–30.

19. Janice Tovey, "Using Visual Theory in the Creation of Résumés: A Bibliography," *Bulletin of the Association for Business Communication* 54, no. 3 (September 1991): 97–99.

20. Bronwyn Fryer, "Job Hunting the Electronic Way," *Working Woman,* March 1995, 59–60, 78; Joyce Lane Kennedy and Thomas J. Morrow, *Electronic Resume Revolution,* 2d ed. (New York: Wiley, 1995), 30–33;

Mary Goodwin, Deborah Cohn, and Donna Spivey, *Netjobs: Use the Internet to Land Your Dream Job* (New York: Michael Wolff, 1996), 149–150; Zane K. Quible, "Electronic Résumés: Their Time Is Coming," *Business Communication Quarterly* 58, no. 3 (1995): 5–9; Alfred Glossbrenner and Emily Glossbrenner, *Finding a Job on the Internet* (New York: McGraw-Hill, 1995), 194–197; Pam Dixon and Silvia Tiersten, *Be Your Own Headhunter Online* (New York: Random House, 1995), 80–83.

21. Zane K. Quible, "The Electronic Resume: An Important New Job-Search Tool," *Journal of Education for Business* 74, no. 2 (1998): 79–82.

22. Ellen Joe Pollock, "Sir: Your Application for a Job Is Rejected; Sincerely, Hal 9000," *Wall Street Journal,* 30 July 1998, A1, A12.

23. Quible, "The Electronic Resume: An Important New Job-Search Tool."

24. Regina Pontow, "Electronic Résumé Writing Tips" [accessed 18 October 1998], www.provenresumes.com/reswkshops/electronic/senres.html.

25. William J. Banis, "The Art of Writing Job-Search Letters," *CPC Annual,* 36th ed., no. 2 (1992): 42–50.

26. Toni Logan, "The Perfect Cover Story," *Kinko's Impress* 2 (2000): 32, 34.

27. See note 1.

CHAPTER 15

1. Adapted from On Call Plus Company News, *PRNewswire* [accessed 9 November 1997], www.prnewswire.com/cgi-bin/liststory?4063251; Herman Miller website [accessed 9 November 1997], www.hermanmiller.com; *Hoover's Online* [accessed 23 January 1997], www.hoovers.com; A. J. Vogl, "Risky Work," *Across the Board,* July–August 1993, 27–31; Kenneth Labich, "Hot Company, Warm Culture," *Fortune,* 27 February 1989, 74–78; George Melloan, "Herman Miller's Secrets of Corporate Creativity," *Wall Street Journal,* 3 May 1988, A31; Beverly Geber, "Herman Miller: Where Profits and Participation Meet," *Training,* November 1987, 62–66; Robert J. McClory, "The Creative Process at Herman Miller," *Across the Board,* May 1985, 8–22; Tom Peters and Nancy Austin, *A Passion for Excellence* (New York: Random House, 1985), 204–205.

2. Sylvia Porter, "Your Money: How to Prepare for Job Interviews," *San Francisco Chronicle,* 3 November 1981, 54.

3. Stephanie Armour, "The New Interview Etiquette," *USA Today,* 23 November 1999, B1, B2.

4. Samuel Greengard, "Are You Well Armed to Screen Applicants?," *Personnel Journal,* December 1995, 84–95.

5. Charlene Marmer Solomon, "How Does Disney Do It?," *Personnel Journal,* December 1989, 53.

6. Marcia Vickers, "Don't Touch That Dial: Why Should I Hire You?," *New York Times,* 13 April 1997, F11.

7. Nancy K. Austin, "Goodbye Gimmicks," *Incentive,* May 1996, 241.

8. Joel Russell, "Finding Solid Ground," *Hispanic Business,* February 1992, 42–44, 46.

9. Tyler D. Hartwell, Paul D. Steele, and Nathaniel F. Rodman, "Workplace Alcohol-Testing Programs: Prevalence and Trends," *Monthly Labor Review,* June 1998, 27–34.

10. Austin, "Goodbye Gimmicks."

11. *Microsoft 1997 Annual Report* [accessed 23 October 1998], www.microsoft.com.

12. Peter Rea, Julie Rea, and Charles Moonmaw, "Training: Use Assessment Centers in Skill Development," *Personnel Journal,* April 1990, 126–131; Greengard, "Are You Well Armed to Screen Applicants?"

13. Anne Field, "Coach, Help Me Out with This Interview," *Business Week,* 22 October 2001, 134E2, 134E4.

14. Robert Gifford, Cheuk Fan Ng, and Margaret Wilkinson, "Nonverbal Cues in the Employment Interview: Links Between Applicant Qualities and Interviewer Judgments," *Journal of Applied Psychology* 70, no. 4 (1985): 729.

15. Dale G. Leathers, *Successful Nonverbal Communication* (New York: Macmillan, 1986), 225.

16. Leslie Plotkin, "Dress for Success," worktree.com [accessed 29 May 2003], www.worktree.com/tb/IN_dress.cfm.

17. Armour, "The New Interview Etiquette."

18. Lynne Waymon, "Don't Stress over Interview Dress," *The Industrial Physicist,* September 1998 [accessed 29 May 2003], www.aip.org/tip/0998.html.

19. Shirley J. Shepherd, "How to Get That Job in 60 Minutes or Less," *Working Woman,* March 1986, 119.

20. Shepherd, "How to Get That Job in 60 Minutes or Less," 118.

21. H. Anthony Medley, *Sweaty Palms: The Neglected Art of Being Interviewed* (Berkeley, Calif.: Ten Speed Press, 1993), 179.

22. Gerald L. Wilson, "Preparing Students for Responding to Illegal Selection Interview Questions," *Bulletin of the Association for Business Communication* 54, no. 2 (1991): 44–49.

23. Jeff Springston and Joann Keyton, "Interview Response Training," *Bulletin of the Association for Business Communication* 54, no. 3 (1991): 28–30; Gerald L. Wilson, "An Analysis of Instructional Strategies for Responding to Illegal Selection Interview Questions," *Bulletin of the Association for Business Communication* 54, no. 3 (1991): 31–35.

24. Stephen J. Pullum, "Illegal Questions in the Selection Process: Going Beyond Contemporary Business and Professional Communication Textbooks," *Bulletin of the Association for Business Communication* 54, no. 3 (1991): 36–43; Alicia Kitsuse, "Have You Ever Been Arrested?," *Across the Board,* November 1992, 46–49; Christina L. Greathouse, "Ten Common Hiring Mistakes," *Industry Week,* 20 January 1992, 22–23, 26.

25. Marilyn Moats Kennedy, "Are You Getting Paid What You're Worth?," *New Woman,* November 1984, 110.

26. Harold H. Hellwig, "Job Interviewing: Process and Practice," *Bulletin of the Association for Business Communication* 55, no. 2 (1992): 8–14.

27. See note 1.

APPENDIX A

1. Mary A. De Vries, *Internationally Yours* (Boston: Houghton Mifflin, 1994), 9.

2. Patricia A. Dreyfus, "Paper That's Letter Perfect," *Money,* May 1985, 184.

3. "When Image Counts, Letterhead Says It All," *Stamford (Conn.) Advocate and Greenwich Times,* 10 January 1993, F4.

4. Mel Mandell, "Electronic Forms Are Cheap and Speedy," *D&B Reports,* July–August 1993, 44–45.

5. Linda Driskill, *Business and Managerial Communication: New Perspectives* (Orlando, Fla.: Harcourt Brace Jovanovich, 1992), 470.

6. Driskill, *Business and Managerial Communication,* 470.

7. Lennie Copeland and Lewis Griggs, *Going International: How to Make Friends and Deal Effectively in the Global Marketplace,* 2d ed. (New York: Random House, 1985), 24–27.

8. De Vries, *Internationally Yours,* 8.

9. Copeland and Griggs, *Going International,* 24–27.

10. U.S. Postal Service, *Postal Addressing Standards* (Washington, D.C.: GPO, 1992).

11. Copeland and Griggs, *Going International,* 24–27.

12. Renee B. Horowitz and Marian G. Barchilon, "Stylistic Guidelines for E-Mail," *IEEE Transactions on Professional Communications,* 37, no. 4 (1994): 207–212.

13. Jill H. Ellsworth and Matthew V. Ellsworth, *The Internet Business Book* (New York: Wiley, 1994), 93.

14. William Eager, *Using the Internet* (Indianapolis: Que Corporation, 1994), 11.

15. Eager, *Using the Internet,* 10.

16. William Eager, Larry Donahue, David Forsyth, Kenneth Mitton, and Martin Waterhouse, *Net.Search* (Indianapolis: Que Corporation, 1995), 221.

17. Rosalind Resnick and Dave Taylor, *Internet Business Guide* (Indianapolis: Sams.net Publishing, 1995), 117.

18. James L. Clark and Lyn R. Clark, *How 7: A Handbook for Office Workers,* 7th ed. (Cincinnati: South-Western, 1995), 431–432.

Acknowledgments

TEXT

41 (Mastering the Art of Constructive Criticism) Adapted from Les Giblin, *How to Have Confidence and Power in Dealing with People* (New York: Prentice Hall, 1956), 132–133. **50 (Checklist: Improving Your Listening Skills)** Adapted from Robert A. Luke, Jr., "Improving Your Listening Ability," *Supervisory Management,* June 1992, 7; Madelyn Burley-Allen, "Listening for Excellence in Communication," *The Dynamics of Behavior Newsletter* 2, no. 2 (Summer 1992): 1; Bob Lamons, "Good Listeners Are Better Communicators," *Marketing News,* 11 September 1995, 13+. **54 (Checklist: Improving Nonverbal Communication Skills)** Gerald H. Graham, Jeanne Unrue, and Paul Jennings, "The Impact of Nonverbal Communication in Organizations: A Survey of Perceptions," *Journal of Business Communication* 28, no. 1 (Winter 1991): 45–62; Dianna Booher, *Communicate with Confidence* (New York: McGraw-Hill, 1994), 363–370. **81 (Communicating with a Global Audience on the Web)** Adapted from Laura Morelli, "Writing for a Global Audience on the Web," *Marketing News,* 17 August 1998, 16; Yuri and Anna Radzievsky, "Successful Global Web Sites Look Through Eyes of the Audience," *Advertising Age's Business Marketing,* January 1998, 17; Sari Kalin, "The Importance of Being Multiculturally Correct," *Computerworld,* 6 October 1997, G16–G17; B. G. Yovovich "Making Sense of All the Web's Numbers," *Editor & Publisher,* November 1998, 30–31; David Wilford, "Are We All Speaking the Same Language?," *The Times* (London), 20 April 2000, 4. **107 (Caution! E-Mail Can Bite)** Adapted from "E-mail As Evidence: Threat or Opportunity?," *Africa News Service,* 10 January 2001 [accessed 11 June 2002], premium.search.yahoo.com/search/premium; John J. DeGilio, "Electronic Mail: From Computer to Courtroom," *Information Management Journal,* April 2000, 32–44; Mary Beth Currie and Daniel Black, "E-mergin Issues in the Electronic Workplace," *Ivey Business Journal,* January–February 2001, 18–29; Mike Elgan, "The Trouble with E-Mail," *Windows Magazine,* November 1998, 31; Jerry Adler, "When E-Mail Bites Back," *Newsweek,* 23 November 1998, 45–46; Amy Harmon, "Corporate Delete Keys Busy as E-Mail Turns Up in Court," *New York Times,* 12 November 1998, A1, C2, 95. **108 (Observing E-mail Etiquette)** Adapted from Dianna Booher, *E-Writing* (New York: Pocket Books, 2001), 6; Eve Milrod and Arthur VanDam, *Mastering Communication Through Technology* (Woodmere, N.Y.: Career Advance Center, Inc., 2001), 13–14, 20–22, 24–29, 30–32, 37, 39, 40, 43; Nancy Flynn and Tom Flynn, *Writing Effective E-Mail* (Menlo Park, Calif.: Crisp Publications, 1998), 3, 5–6, 10, 14–15, 17, 29, 47, 55, 61, 62, 71; Diana Booher, *E-Writing* (New York: Pocket Books, 2001), ix, 2, 6–7, 16, 19, 23, 25–27, 30, 33, 36, 39, 41–42, 49; Morey Stettner, "The Right Way to Write: Composing Clear, Crisp Memos and E-Mail," *The Edward Lowe Report,* June 2000, 2; Karen Kalis, "Make Your E-Mail More Effective," *Supervision* 62, no. 9 (September 2001): 23–25; T. L. Aardsma, "Improve Your E-Mail Etiquette," *Inside the Internet* 8, no. 7 (July 2001): 6–9; Andrea C. Poe, "Don't Touch that 'Send' Button!," *HRMagazine* 46, no. 7 (July 2001): 74–80. **151 (Developing E-Mail Style)** Adapted from Dianna Booher, *E-Writing,* (New York: Pocket Books, 2001), 6; Eve Milrod and Arthur VanDam, *Mastering Communication Through Technology* (Woodmere, N.Y.: Career Advance Center, Inc., 2001), 13–14, 20–22, 24–29, 31–32, 37, 39, 40, 43; Nancy Flynn and Tom Flynn, *Writing Effective E-Mail* (Menlo Park, Calif.: Crisp Publications, 1998), 3, 5–6, 10, 14–15, 17, 20, 47, 55, 61, 62, 71; Booher, *E-Writing,* ix, 2, 6–7, 16, 19, 23, 25–27, 30, 33, 36, 39, 41–42, 49; Morey Stettner, "The Right Way to Write: Composing Clear, Crisp Memos and E-Mail," *The Edward Lowe Report,* June 2002, 2; Karen Kalis, "Make Your E-Mail More Effective," *Supervision* 62, no. 9 (September 2001): 23–25; T. L. Aardsma, "Improve Your E-Mail Etiquette," *Inside the Internet* 8, no. 7 (July 2001): 6–9; Andrea C. Poe, "Don't Touch that 'Send' Button!," *HRMagazine* 46, no. 7 (July 2001): 74–80. **181 (How to Proofread Like a Pro)** Adapted from Philip C. Kolin, *Successful Writing at Work,* 2d ed., 102. Used with permission of D. C. Heath & Company; Dennis Hensley, "A Way with Words: Proofreading Can Save Cash and Careers," *Dallas Magazine,* May 1986, 57–58. Reprinted with permission. **213 (Recommendation Letters: What's Right to Write?)** Adapted from Maura Dolan and Stuart Silverstein, "Court Broadens Liability for Job References," *Los Angeles Times,* 28 January 1997, A1, A11; David A. Price, "Good References Pave Road to Court," *USA Today,* 13 February 1997, 11A; Frances A. McMorris, "Ex-Bosses Face Less Peril Giving Honest Job References," *Wall Street Journal,* 8 July 1996, B1, B8; Dawn Gunsch, "Gray Matters: Centralize Control of Giving References," *Personnel Journal,* September 1992, 114, 116–117; Betty Southard Murphy, Wayne E. Barlow, and D. Diane Hatch, "Manager's Newsfront: Job Reference Liability of Employees," *Personnel Journal,* September 1991, 22, 26; Ross H. Fishman, "When Silence Is Golden," *Nation's Business,* July 1991, 48–49. **249 (Should Employers Use E-Mail to Deliver Negative Employment Messages?)** Adapted from Stephanie Armour, "E-Mail Lets Companies Deliver Bad News from Afar," *USA Today,* 20 February 2001, B1; Cheryl Maday, "How to Break Bad News," *Psychology Today,* November–December 1999, 18; Nancy Flynn and Tom Flynn, *Writing Effective E-Mail* (Menlo Park, Calif: Crisp Learning, 1998), 4. **286 (What You May Legally Say in a Sales Letter)** Ronald A. Anderson, Ivan Fox, David P. Twomey, and Marianne M. Jennings, *Business Law and the Legal Environment* (Cincinnati: West Educational Publishing, 1999), 229–230, 237–240, 247, 524–526, 567; Sales Letter Tips [accessed 26 June 2000], www.smartbiz.com/sbs/arts/sbs47.htm; Instant Sales Letters [accessed 26 June 2000], instantsalesletters.com. **331 (Checklist: Improving Search Results)** Ernest L. Maier, Anthony J. Faria, Peter Kaatrude, and Elizabeth Wood, *The Business Library and How to Use It* (Detroit: Omnigraphics, 1996), 84–97; Matt Lake, "Desperately Seeking Susan OR Suzie NOT Sushi," New York Times, 3 September 1998, D1, D7. **342 (Minding Your Business with Online Reporting)** Adapted from Scott Steinacher, "Putting the Power Back in Reports," *InfoWorld,* 24 January 2000, 69–70; Federal Express website "accessed 25 November 2001", www.fedex.com; Jack Schember, "Mrs. Fields' Secret Weapon, " *Personnel Journal,* September 1991, 56–58; Paul Kondstadt, "Ship 54—Where Are You?," *CIO,* May 1990, 80–81, 84, 86; Bruce G. Posner and Bo Burlingham, "The Hottest Entrepreneur in America," *Inc.,* January 1988, 44–48. **377 (Top Tips for Writing Reports That Mean Business)** Adapted from Joan Minninger, *The Perfect Memo* (New York: Doubleday, 1990), 169–170. Copyright © 1990 by Joan Minninger. Used by permission of Doubleday, a division of Bantam Doubleday Dell Publishing Group, Inc. **465 (Five Tips for Making Presentations Around the World)** Adapted from Patricia L. Kurtz, *The Global Speaker* (New York: AMACOM, 1995), 35–47, 56–68, 75–82, 87–100; David A. Victor, *International Business Communication* (New York: HarperCollins Publishers, 1992), 39–45; Lalita Khosla, "You Say Tomato," *Forbes,* 21 May 2001, 36; Stephen Dolainski, "Are Expats Getting Lost in the Translation?," *Workforce,* February 1997, 32–39. **482 (Netting a Job on the Web)** Adapted from Richard N. Bolles, "Career Strategizing or, What Color Is Your Web Parachute?," *Yahoo! Internet Life,* May 1998, 116, 121; Tara Weingarten, "The All-Day, All-Night, Global, No-Trouble Job Search," *Newsweek,* 6 April 1998, 17; Michele Himmelberg, "Internet An Important Tool in Employment Search," *San Diego Union-Tribune,* 7 September 1998, D2; Gina Imperato, "35 Ways to Land a Job Online," *Fast Company,* August 1998, 192–197; Roberta Maynard, "Casting the Net for Job Seekers," *Nation's Business,* March 1997, 28–29. **525 (Interview Strategies: Answering the 16 Toughest Questions)** Adapted from "Career Strategies," *Black Enterprise,* February 1986, 122. Copyright © 1986, *Black Enterprise* Magazine, The Earl Graves Publishing Company, Inc., New York, N.Y. All rights reserved.

FIGURES AND TABLES

7 (Figure 1–3): Racial and Ethnic Makeup of U.S. Workforce Projected to 2020, based on U.S. Department of Labor Statistics, compiled by Richard W. Judy and Carol D'Amico, *Workforce 2000: Work and Workers in the 21st Century* (Indianapolis, Ind.: Hudson Institute, 1997). **46** (Figure 2–2): Adapted from Phillip Smorgan and H. Ken Baker, "Building a Professional Image: Improving Listening Behavior." Reprinted by permission of the publisher, from *Supervisory Management,* November 1985, 34. © 1985 American Management Association, New York. All rights reserved. **55** (Table 2–2): Marilyn Pincus, *Everyday Business*

Etiquette (Hauppauge, N.Y.: Barron's Educational Series, 1996), 134–135. **71** (Table 3–1): Gary P. Ferraro, *The Cultural Dimension of International Business,* 4th ed. (Upper Saddle River, N.J.: Prentice Hall, 2002), 58; Mary O'Hara-Devereaux and Robert Johansen, *Global Work: Bridging Distance, Culture, and Time* (San Francisco: Jossey-Bass, 1994), 55, 59. **73** (Figure 3–1): Lillian H. Chaney and Jeanette S. Martin, *Intercultural Business Communication,* 2d ed. (Upper Saddle River, N.J.: Prentice Hall, 2000), 50. **145** Courtesy Ace Hardware. **207** (Figure 7.6): Courtesy Herman Miller. **212** (Figure 7.8): Courtesy Discover Communications. **269** (Figure 9–1): Adapted from Abraham H. Maslow, *Motivation and Personality* (New York: Harper & Row, 1954), 12, 19. Copyright © 1970 by Abraham H. Maslow. Reprinted by permission of HarperCollins Publishers. **365** (Figure 11–6): Standard & Poor's Industry Surveys—Footware, 1 December 1998, 26; Hoover's Capsules online [accessed 11 November 2001], www. hoovers.com/co/capsule. **369** (Figure 11–12): Iris I. Varner, *Contemporary Business Report Writing,* 2d ed. (Chicago: Dryden Press, 1991), 75. **436** (Table 12–4): Adapted from multiple sources listed for Case #5, ("Selling to Online America"). **437** (Table 12–5): Adapted from multiple sources listed for Case #5, ("Selling to Online America") **442** (Figure 13–1): Adapted from Eric J. Adams, "Management Focus: User-Friendly Presentation Software," *World Trade,* March 1995, 92. **450** (Table 13–1): Adapted from Eric J. Adams, "Management Focus: User-Friendly Presentation Software," *World Trade,* March 1995, 92. **460** (Figure 13–7): Microsoft PowerPoint2000 software. **490** (Table 14–2): Rockport Institute, "How to Write a Masterpiece of a Résumé [accessed 16 October 1998], www.rockportinstitute.com/résumés.html. **494** (Table 14–3): Anne Field, "Coach, Help Me Out with This Interview," *Business Week,* 22 October 2001, 134E4, 134E6; Joan E. Rigdon, "Deceptive Résumés Can Be Door-Openers but Can Become an Employee's Undoing," *Wall Street Journal,* 17 June 1992, B1; Diane Cole, "Ethics: Companies Crack Down on Dishonesty," *Managing Your Career,* Spring 1991, 8–11; Nancy Marx Better, "Résumé Liars," *Savvy,* December 1990–January 1991, 26–29. **499** (Table 14–4): Joyce Lain Kennedy and Thomas J. Morrow, *Electronic Resume Revolution* (New York: Wiley, 1994). **526** (Table 15–2): Adapted from *The Northwestern Endicott Report* (Evanston, Ill.: Northwestern University Placement Center). **527** (Table 15–3): Adapted from Ronald B. Adler and Jeanne Marquardt Elmhorst, *Communicating at Work,* 7th ed. (New York: McGraw-Hill, 2002), 213; H. Lee Rust, *Job Search: The Completion Manual for Jobseekers* (New York: American Management Association, 1979), 56. **528** (Figure 15–1): Adapted from *The Northwestern Endicott Report* (Evanston: Ill.: Northwestern University Placement Center). **530** (Table 15–4): Adapted from Leslie Plotkin, "Dress for Success," worktree.com [accessed 29 May 2003], www.worktree.com/ tb/IN_dress.cfm: "Guidelines for Successful Interview Dress," CollegeGrad.com [accessed 29 May 2003], www.collegegrad.com/book/app-a.shtml. **532** (Table 15–5): Ronald B. Adler and Jeanne Marquardt Elmhorst, *Communicating at Work,* 7th ed. (New York: McGraw-Hill, 2002), 218–219; "Dangerous Questions," *Nation's Business,* May 1999, 22.

PHOTO CREDITS

3 Kistone Photography/Ki Ho Park **5** PhotoEdit/Spencer Grant **7** Black Cat Studio/Jay Daniel **8** Dell, Inc. **8** Ethan Hill **8** Belkin Corporation **8** Digital Vision Ltd. **8** PhotoEdit/Spencer Grant **9** 3M Corporation **9** Ethan Hill **9** AGE Fotostock America, Inc. © Stuart Pearce/AGE fotostock **9** Copyright © 1998–2003 Ezonics Corp. All Rights Reserved. **10** United Parcel Service **10** Masterfile Corporation © Peter Christopher/ Masterfile **00** Jim Whitmer Photography Photo by Jim and Mary Whitmer **10** AGE Fotostock America, Inc. © J. D. Dallet/AGE Fotostock **10** FEDEX Corporation FedEx Corporation **10** Corbis/SABA Press Photos, Inc./Keith Dannemiller **11** PhotoLibrary.com **11** Masterfile Corporation © Raoul Minsart/Masterfile **11** Staples, Inc. **11** Corbis/Bettmann © Ed Bock/CORBIS **22** Danny Turner Photography **25** Industrial Light & Magic, A Lucasfilm Ltd. Company**34** AP/Wide World Photos **38** Andy Freeberg Photography **48** AP/Wide World Photos **58** PhotoEdit/Bill Aron **67** AP/Wide World Photos **69** Brian Coats Photography **74** John Abbott Photography/John Abbott **79** PhotoEdit/ Myrleen Ferguson Cate **93** PhotoEdit/Michael Newman **97** Jamaican Hut Foods, Inc **98** Mark Richards **109** Evan Kafka **112** Ward-Williams Inc. © 2000 Chip Williams **125** Bloomberg News /Landov **135** Churchill & Klehr Photography **142** Getty Images, Inc.—Taxi/Michael Krasowitz **145** PetFoodDirect.com Courtesy of PetFoodDirect.com **163** The Image Works/Francis Dean **168** Corbis/Stock Market/Ariel Skelley **170** Sam Holden Photography © Sam Holden Photography **172** Starbucks Coffee Company **182** Caldwell Photography **193** AP/Wide World Photos **197** B. Smith With Style Courtesy of B. Smith With Style **200** Jyoti Cuisine India Jyoti Cuisine India **206** Michael Grecco Photography, Inc. © Michael Grecco Photography, Inc./Icon **211** Corbis/SABA Press Photos, Inc. © Gail Albert Halaban/CORBIS SABA **224** PhotoEdit/Amy C. Etra **226** Deere & Company **228** Corbis/Bettmann © AFP/CORBIS **231** AP/Wide World Photos **234** New York Times Pictures/ Ozier Muhammad **239** Corbis/Bettmann © Paul Barton/CORBIS **252** Francisco J. Rangel **261** Masterfile Corporation © Nora Good / Masterfile **263** Corbis/Bettmann © Tom Stewart/CORBIS **264** David R. Frazier Photolibrary, Inc. **267** Pictor/ImageState/International Stock Photography Ltd. **270** Marc Longwood Photography **276** Richard Howard Photography **278** Douglas Levere Photo © 2003 Douglas Levere **288** Ferguson and Katzman Photography, Inc./Mark Katzman **301** Corbis Digital Stock © PictureArts/ CORBIS **303** The Image Works © Daniel Wray/The Image Works **305** The Image Works © Syracuse Newspapers / Dick Blume / The Image Works **309** Getty Images Inc. – Hulton Archive Photos **325** Corbis/ Bettmann © David Raymer/CORBIS **332** The Image Works © Jeff Greenberg / The Image Works **334** Corbis/Bettmann © Bill Varie/CORBIS **353** Corbis/ Sygma/Allan Tannenbaum **354** Getty Images, Inc – Liaison/Reuters/ Michael Dalder/ Archive Photos **370** Getty Images Inc. – Stone Allstock/Tim Brown/ Stone **374** Getty Images, Inc.– Photodisc/John A. Rizzo **395** The Image Works © Syracuse Newspapers / Frank Ordoéz / The Image Works **396** The Image Works © Bob Mahoney/The Image Works **399** Landov LLC Bloomberg News/Landov **401** Getty Images Inc. – Hulton Archive Photos Getty Images, Inc. **402** Stockbyte © Stockbyte Royalty Free Photos **422** Peter Gregoire/Peter Gregoire **434** GettyImages, Inc. – Liaison Getty Images, Inc. **438** Getty Images, Inc. – Liaison **441** Getty Images, Inc. – Liaison Getty Images, Inc. **452** Baerbel Schmidt Photography **462** Getty Images, Inc. – Liaison Getty Images, Inc. **467** Mark Richards **477** AP/Wide World Photos **484** PhotoEdit/Mark Richards **495** Mark Wilson Photographer **501** Bo Parker **519** Michael L. Abramson Photography **522** Syracuse University Syracuse University, School of Management, Career Center **529** The Image Works/Bob Daemmirich **535** Ian Shaw/Getty Images Inc. – Stone Allstock **537** Getty Images Inc. – Stone Allstock/Dan Bosler

Organization/ Brand/Company Index

Subject Index